2011
PowerBoat Guide

Ed McKnew • Mark Parker

American Marine Publishing, Inc.

PUBLISHED BY
American Marine Publishing, Inc.
www.powerboatguide.com
info@powerboatguide.com

ISBN 978-0-9773539-6-5

For information on advertising in the PowerBoat Guide, contact
Shari at 231-360-0827

Printed and bound in the United States of America.

Table of Contents

Introduction

Welcome to the 2011 PowerBoat Guide, the latest edition of what has become one of the best-selling publications in the marine industry. First published in 1989, the PowerBoat Guide was originally conceived as a reference handbook for yacht brokers and dealers. Within a few short years, however, the book found it's way into the public domain, and its been an invaluable resource for hundreds — perhaps thousands — of boat buyers ever since. Produced by experienced yacht brokers, the PowerBoat Guide has stood the test of time with marine industry professionals across the country.

In making the selections for this year's edition, the editors have endeavoured to include those boats of the greatest potential interest to our readers. No effort has been made to include *all* models from *any* manufacturer, and there are many builders whose products we have not featured at all. Because we don't charge manufacturers to include their products in the PowerBoat Guide, we are able to make our selections without any outside pressure.

For ease of use, the book is divided into three sections: Motoryachts & Trawlers; Sportfishermen; and Cruisers & Sportboats. Models featured in each section are sorted by manufacturer name first, and then by size. Note that there are occassions where the same boat appears in two different sections — some models simply resist catagorization. In general, however, the sections are tightly drawn and easy to navigate.

About The Prices

Retail high-low values are provided for models built only after 1995. In the case of new or limited production models, we may choose not offer price estimates due to lack of resale activity. The prices quoted in this book reflect the market conditions projected by our staff for the 2011 model year, a difficult task indeed considering the uncertainty of today's boating market.

Just as it is with cars, RVs, and homes, you get what you pay for. High-end yachts are nearly always the leaders when it comes to resale value. Trawlers and motoryachts — especially those from quality manufacturers — typically retain roughly 50% of their original purchase price after five years of ownership. Very high-end trawlers may retain 60–70% of their original value after five years if they're well equipped and maintained.

It is especially important to review the section "About These Prices" on page 529 before referencing the assigned values. And remember, no matter what the various price guides (including ours) might say, the fact remains that the only real value of a boat is what someone is willing to pay for it on a given day. *The prices in this book are provided as rough estimates only.* They are meant to be used as a starting point in determining a boat's actual value in a given market. Do not take them too literally.

Finding A Specific Model

If you don't find what you're looking for in a given section, be sure to check the index to make sure it isn't featured elsewhere in the book. Keep in mind that the PowerBoat Guide covers boats between 27' and 65' in length built after 1980.

Companion CD Volume

Note that the 2011 PowerBoat Guide is available on CD or may be downloaded directly to your desktop. For details, please visit our website at www.powerboatguide.com.

* * * * * *

We sincerely hope you will find the information in the PowerBoat Guide to be useful, and we welcome any comments you might care to offer regarding the content or the character of this publication.

About the Authors

Ed McKnew

Mark Parker

Ed McKnew began his career in the boating industry in 1979 when he purchased a small brokerage operation in Traverse City, MI. Moving to Texas in 1980, Ed continued to sell boats in Clear Lake until 1987 when he and partner Mark Parker published the first edition of the PowerBoat Guide. Ed has spent the past two decades serving as editor of the PowerBoat Guide while living in both Florida and northern Michigan. He has a bachelors degree in Business from Oakland University in Rochester, MI. He and his wife Shari are currently traveling the U.S. full time in their motorhome.

Mark Parker has been a yacht broker since 1982, first in Texas and, starting in 1990, in South Florida. Mark started his boating career as a mate, then a captain and managed to complete an education along the way with a BA in Marketing. Mark and Ed started writing the first PowerBoat Guide in 1987 and have worked together ever since to keep the publication up to date. Now closing in on three decades of full time yacht brokerage service, Mark spends his spare time in the Bahamas and touring on his motorcycle.

How to Use This Book

For the most part, the contents of this book are straightforward and easily understood. Before launching into the pages, however, we strongly suggest that you take a few moments and review the following points. Failure to do so is likely to result in some confusion and misunderstanding.

Pricing Information
Used boat prices have been compiled from 1995, the base year for our calculations. Boats whose production runs were previous to that year are noted in the Price Schedule with four asterisks (****).

In the Price Schedule, six asterisks (******) indicate that we have insufficient data to render a value for a particular model or model year.

The *Retail High* is the average selling price of a clean, well-equipped and well-maintained boat with low-to-moderate engine hours. Boats with an exceptional equipment list, outstanding maintenance, or those with unusually low hours will usually sell at a figure higher than the published Retail High.

The *Retail Low* is the average selling price of a boat with below-average maintenance, poor equipment, high-time engines, or excessive wear. High-time boats in poor condition will generally sell for less than the published Retail Low.

Used boats located in the following markets are generally valued at 10–15 percent higher than published prices:

Great Lakes	+10–15%
Pacific Northwest	+10–15%
Inland Rivers & Lakes	+5–10%
California	+10–15%

The prices presented in this book reflect our best estimates of used boat prices for the model year 2011. They are intended for general use only and are not meant to represent exact market values.

Factory Specifications
The specifications listed for each model are self-explanatory although the following factors are noted:

Clearance refers to bridge clearance, or the height above the waterline to the highest point on the boat. Note that this is often a highly ambiguous piece of information since the manufacturer may or may not include such things as an arch, hardtop, or mast. Use this figure with caution.

Weight is a factory-provided specification that may or may not be accurate. Manufacturers differ in the way they compute this figure. For the most part, it refers to a dry boat with no gear.

NA means that information (or data) is not available.

Performance Data
Whenever possible, performance figures have been obtained from the manufacturer or a reliable dealer or broker. When such information was unavailable, the authors have relied upon their own research together with actual hands-on experience. The speeds are estimates and (in most cases) based on boats with average loads of fuel, water, options and gear.

All speeds are reported in knots. Readers in the Great Lakes or inland waterways may convert knots to miles-per-hour by multiplying a given figure by 1.14.

Cruising Speeds, Gas Engines
Unless otherwise noted, the cruising speed for gas-powered inboard (or stern drive) boats is calculated at 3,000–3,200 rpm.

Cruising Speeds, Diesel Engines
The cruising speeds for diesel-powered boats are calculated as follows:

Detroit (2-stroke) Diesels: about 200–250 rpm off the top rpm rating.

Other (4-stroke) Diesels: about 350–400 rpm off the manufacturer's maximum rpm rating.

Cruising Speeds, Outboard Engines
The cruising speeds for outboard-powered boats is generally figured at 4,000 rpm.

Useful Terms

Abaft—behind

Athwartships—at a right angle to the boat's length

Bulkhead—an upright partition separating compartments in a boat

Bulwark—a raised portion of the deck designed to serve as a barrier

Chine—the point at which the hullsides and the bottom of the boat come together

Coaming—vertical surface surrounding the cockpit

Cuddy—generally refers to the cabin of a small boat

Deadrise—the angle from the bottom of the hull (not the keel) to the chine

Deep-V Hull—a planing hull form with at least 18 degrees of deadrise at the transom and a fairly constant "V" bottom shape from stem to stern.

Displacement Hull—a hull designed to go through the water and not capable of planing speed

Forefoot—the underwater shape of the hull at the bow

Freeboard—the height of the sides of the hull above the waterline

gph—gallons per hour (of fuel consumption)

Gunwale (also gunnel)— the upper edge of the sheerline

Hull Speed—the maximum practical speed of a displacement hull. To calculate, take the square root of the LWL (waterline hull length) and multiply by 1.34.

Knot—one nautical mile per hour. To convert knots to statute mph, multiply by 1.14.

Modified-V Hull—a planing hull form with (generally) less than 18 degrees of transom deadrise

Nautical Mile—measurement used in salt water. A nautical mile is 6,076 feet.

Planing Speed—the point at which an accelerating hull rises onto the top of the water. To calculate a hull's planing speed, multiply the square root of the waterline length by 2.

Semi-Displacement Hull—a hull designed to operate economically at low speeds while still able to attain planing speed performance

Sheerline—the fore-and-aft line along the top edge of the hull

Sole—a nautical term for floor

Statute Mile—measurement used in fresh water. A statute mile equals 5,280 feet.

Tender—may refer to either (a) a dinghy, or (b) lack of hull stability.

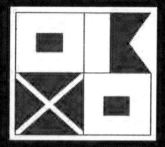

Marine Surveyor Directory

ABYC ....American Boat & Yacht Council
NAMI ....National Association of Marine Investigators
NAMS ....National Association of Marine Surveyors
NFPA.....................................National Fire Prevention Association
SAMS ....Society of Accredited Marine Surveyors
SNAME ....Society of Naval Architects & Marine Engineers

Alaska

Paul Fleenor
Edgewater Marine
PO Box 3505
Homer, AK 99603
907-235-1063
edwater@xyz.net

Rick Martin
Marine Surveyors of SE Alaska
PO Box 2124
Wrangell, AK 99929
907-874-4548
rick@marinesurveyorsofsoutheastalaska.com

James Steffen
Norcoast Marine Surveyors, Inc.
PO Box 936
Sitka, AK 99835-0936
907-747-5394
Cell: 907-738-6394
www.marinesurveyor.com/norcoast/
1norcoast@gmail.com
ABYC, SAMS

Matthew Jones
Resurrection Technologies
14550 Rainforest Cr.
Seward, AK 99664-9619
907-362-2927
mattj@selltech.com
SAMS

Ronald Long
Ronald E. Long Marine Surveys
PO Box 2464
Seward, AK 99664
907-224-7068
Cell: 907-362-1107
rlms@ptialaska.net
ABYC, SNAME

Alabama

James Dinges
AYS Marine
2610 Gawain Rd SE
Huntsville, AL 35803-1878
256-603-1076
jdinges@hiwaay.net
SAMS

Gary Swearengin
GDS Services
1001 Riverchase Rd. SE
Huntsville, AL 35803-2327
256-881-2589; Cell: 256-682-1745
www.gdssco.com
survey@gdssco.com
ABYS, SAMS

Richard Leasure
Leasure Marine Survey
103710 Crepe Myrtle Rd.
Grand Bay, AL 36541
251-377-8369
www.leasuremarinesurvey.vpweb.com
rleasure@centurytel.net
ABYC, SAMS

Richard Schiehl
M.J. Schiehl & Associates, Inc.
6650 River Pl
Gulf Shores, AL 36542-2518
251-979-5912
Cell: 251-979-5912
www.thermalndt.com
rschiehl@gulftel.com
ABYC, NAMS

Dennis Heine
Nautical Services, Inc
767 Wedgewood Dr.
Gulf Shores, AL 36542
251-979-2024
nsi@mchsi.com

Hugh Pardue
Orange Beach Marine Surveying
6706 County Rd 95
Elberta, AL 36530
251-752-2125
hpardue@gulftel.com

Donald Jack Smith
Port City Marine Surveyors
PO Box 190321
Mobile, AL 36619
251-661-5426
masurveyor@aol.com
ABYC, SAMS, SNAME

Arkansas

John Linck
Linck Marine Surveying
600 Pine Forest Dr. 4-D
Maumelle, AR 72113
501-231-9350
Cell: 501-231-9350
jelmarine@aol.com
ABYC, SAMS

California

Gene Hillger
Arnold & Arnold, Inc.
2329 India St
San Diego, CA 92101-1219
619-233-1096
www.arnoldoffice.com
gene@arnoldoffice.com
SAMS

R.Clark Barthol
Clark Barthol Marine Surveyors
27 Buccaneer St
Marina del Rey, CA 90292-5103
310-823-3350
Cell: 310-612-1955
cbarms@aol.com
ABYC, NAMS

Marine Surveyor Directory

George Castagnola
George Castagnola, Marine Surveyor
802 Wine Ct.
Petaluma, CA 94954
707-778-0282
mizsea@aol.com
NAVTECH, USSA

Ron Grant
Grant Marine Surveys
31091 Paseo Valencia
San Juan Capistrano, CA 92675-2950
949-240-8353
vaimalu@cox.net
ABYC, SAMS

Odus Hayes
Marine Services
PO Box 1122
Sausalito, CA 94966-1122
415-461-8425; Cell: 415-860-0295
ohayesurvey@comcast.net
SAMS

William C. Young
Marine Survey
1272 Scott St.
San Diego, CA 92106-2736
619-224-2944; Cell: 619-854-3748
captainwcyoung@yahoo.com
NAMS, SAMS

John Bradshaw
Marine Surveyor
1621 W 25th St # 313
San Pedro, CA 90732-4300
310-547-5400
john.bradshaw@cox.net
NAMS

Alan Ross Hugenot
Marine Surveyor
425 Burnett Ave
San Francisco, CA 94131
415-531-6172
ahugenot@comcast.net

F.Lee Frain Jr.
Maritime Consultant, Inc.
PO Box 3457
Newport Beach, CA 92659
949-675-2881
maritimeconsultant@att.net
ABYC, NAMS

John Marples
Marples Marine

17240 Hillcrest Ave
Sonoma, CA 95476-3422
707-343-1378; Cell: 707-548-4734
www.searunner.com
marplesmarine@comcast.net
ABYC, NAMS

Marvin Henderson
Marvin Henderson Marine Surveyors
2726 Shelter Island Dr PMB -1
San Diego, CA 92106-2731
619-588-4702
www.nams-cms.org
mhms@cox.net
ABYC, CMS-NAMS, NFPA

Peggy Feakes
R.J. Whitfield & Associates
835 Yerba Buena Ave
Stockton, CA 95210
209-956-8488; Cell: 209-406-9679
www.rjwsurvey.com
peggy@rjwsurvey.com
ABYC, SAMS, IAMI

Randell B. Sharpe
Sharpe Surveying & Consulting
242 Inverness Ct
Alameda, CA 94502-6421
877-337-0706
www.sharpesurveying.com
rsharpe@sharpesurveying.com
ABYC, SAMS, SNAME

Peter Minkwitz
Worldwide Marine Surveys, Ltd.
351 Embarcadero
Oakland, CA 94606-5115
510-465-2527; Cell: 510-821-5652
peter@sanfranciscomarinesursveyors.com
ABYC, NAMS, SNAME

Gary Beck
Yachtsman Marine
5318 E. 2nd St. #415
Long Beach, CA 90803
562-234-3585
Cell: 562-234-3585
www.vesselsurveyor.com
yachtsmanmarine@aol.com
ABYC, SAMS

Colorado

James Beck
Columbine Marine Service
PO Box 3545

Breckenridge, CO 80424-3545
970-453-0350
Cell: 970-393-2425
yachtsurveyor@hotmail.com
ABYC, SAMS

Connecticut

Chris Nebel
Advanced Marine Surveyors
38B State St.
Guilford, CT 06437
203-623-0301
captainchris@thatboatguy.com

Phillip Gaudreau
Allpoint Marine Services, LLC
11 Pettipaug Rd.
Haddam Neck, CT 06424
860-467-6956
pgaudreau41@comcast.net
ABYC, SAMS

Barnaby Blatch
Atlantic Marine Survey
5 Elizabeth Court
Mystic, CT 06355-3111
860-536-4354; Cell: 860-460-0060
www.marinesurveyor.com/atlantic
bblatch1@gmail.com
AYBC, SAMS

Steve Hayes
Hayes Marine Surveying
10 Bluff Ave
Clinton, CT 06413
860-664-9808
stevehayes3@yahoo.com

Adrian Johnson
Johnson Marine Services
PO Box 271
West Mystic, CT 06388-0271
860-572-8866; Cell: 860-235-2990
www.johnsonmarineservices.com
aj@johnsonmarineservices.com
ABYC, SAMS

James Curry
Marine Surveyor
5 Pleasant Hill Lane
Clinton, CT 06413-2535
860-669-3119; Cell: 860-834-1600
jcurry01@snet.net
ABYC, SAMS

Marine Surveyor Directory

William Robbins
New England Marine Surveyors
302 Plains Rd.
Haddam, CT 06438
860-227-4071
www.newenglandmarinesurvey.com
billrobbins@newenglandmarinesurvey.com
SAMS

Joseph Stoltz
North Cove Associates LLC
45 Lynde St.
Old Saybrook, CT 06475
northcoveassociates@yahoo.com

Glen Carpenter
Ocean Air Marine Services LLC
PO Box 818
Watertown, CT 06795
203-565-2000
www.marinesurvey.pro
glen@oceanairservices.com
ABYC, SAMS

Dist. Of Columbia

Guy Nolan
Cascade Corporation
1000 Water St SW
Washington, DC 20024-2425
571-344-1239; Cell: 571-344-1239
cascadegrn@starpower.net
ABYC, SAMS, SNAME

Florida

Michael Pickthorne
A1 Marine Surveyors
US Link 2265, 3537 NW 82nd Ave
Doral, FL 33122
345-949-9210; Cell: 345-916-1765
www.a1marinecayman.com
lloyds@candw.ky
ABYC, NAMS

Ronald Morgan
Accredited Marine Consultants
313 Lake Cr. Apt 113
West Palm Beach, FL 33408-5227
800-884-9689
www.accmarcon.com
info@accmarcon.com
ABYC, SAMS, SNAME

Ted Crosby
ACE Marine Advisory Services
1844 N. Nob Hill Rd, PMB #612

Plantation, FL 33322
954-583-9969
ted.crosby@acegroup.com
NAMS

Dewey Acker
Acker Marine Survey Co.
801 73rd St.
Marathon, FL 33050
305-743-2397
info@ackermarinesurvey.com
ABYC, SAMS

John Allinson II
Allinson Associates, Inc.
222 University Blvd N. #2
Jacksonville, FL 32211-7534
904-721-2177
www.allinson.com
jna2@allinson.com

Rolando Santos
Alpha Marine Surveyors, Inc.
1330 NW 7th St.
Miami, FL 33125-3704
305-624-1555
www.alphamarine.com
roland_santos@alphamarine.com

Johnny Smith
Anchor Marine Services, LLC
2720 Semoran Dr.
Pensacola, FL 32503
850-982-5079
www.anchormarineonline.com
surveys@anchormarineonline.com
ABYC, SAMS

Glenn Reagan
Aqua Marine Surveying & Services
5818 SW 88th Pl.
Ocala, FL 34476-6103
352-598-6750
aquamarinesurveying@embarqmail.com
ABYC, SAMS

James Purvis
Aqua Marine Surveyors LLC
1619 Myrtlewood Ln
Niceville, FL 32578
850-225-4659; Cell: 850-225-4659
amsurveyors@embarqmail.com
SAMS

Patrick Guckian
Aquarius Marine Systems
160 SE Duxbury Ave

Port St Lucie, FL 34983-2604
772-871-0364
www.aquariusmarinesytems.com
aquariusmarinesy@bellsouth.net
ABYC, SAMS, SNAME

Frank Bailey
Bailey's Boat Surveying & Consulting
6105 Anvil Rd.
Jacksonville, FL 32277
904-403-1151
frankabout@aol.com
ABYC, SAMS,

William Potter
Bill Potter's Marine Service
15810 SW 88th Ave
Miami, FL 33157
305-235-5760
billpotter@ymail.com
SAMS

Kevin Behen
Boat Whisperer, Inc.
6371 Cocoa Lane
Apollo Beach, FL 33572
813-334-3274
behenk@hotmail.com
ABYC, SAMS

John Campbell
Campbell Yacht Survey
1836 Dogwood Drive
Marco Island, FL 34145
239-389-9769
doc@southwestfloridamarinesurvey.com
SAMS

Stanley Konz
Captain Stanley G. Konz
348 Pearl Ave
Sarasota, FL 34243-1522
941-351-6311
Cell: 941-737-3495
www.boatquotes.com
skonz1@tampabay.rr.com
ABYC, SAMS, SNAME

Capt. Ric Corley
Captain Tom Corley & Son Surveyors
1701 Grant Ave
Panama City, FL 32401-1140
888-784-9939
Cell: 850-527-5287
www.captcorleyandson.com
ABYC, NAMS, SAMS, IAMI

Marine Surveyor Directory

Bruce Evangelista
CMI Custom Maintenance
210 SE 7th St.
Pompano Beach, FL 33060
954-650-3838
cmibruce@aol.com
SAMS

Michael Schneider
Custom Offshore Systems
15719 121st Ter N.
Jupiter, FL 33478
561-313-5593
customoffshoresystems@gmail.com
SAMS

Keith Douglass
Douglass Marine Co.
113 Willow Lane
Islamorada, FL 33036-0157
305-664-9702;; Cell: 305-393-2438
www.douglassmarine.com
comish1@aol.com
ABYC, SAMS

Vivian Rowe
Ed Rowe & Associates
9116 86th Pl.
Vero Beach, FL 32967
772-589-7463
Cell: 954-328-5780
eroweassoc@comcast.net
ABYC, SAMS

Tony Blanton
Edgewater Marine
4417 Bellwood Cr.
Pace, FL 32571
850-380-1996
edgewatermarine@bellsouth.net
ABYC, SAMS,

James Avery
Emerald Coast Marine Services
981Highway 98 E. Ste 3 Unit #224
Destin, FL 32541
850-582-9880; Cell: 850-582-9880
averyjamesr@gmail.com
ABYC, SAMS

James Filosa
Filosa Marine Marketing
17706 Maplewood Dr
Boca Raton, FL 33487-2171
561-997-8769
filosamarine@yahoo.com

Jeff Hahn
Florida Boat & Yacht Surveyors
4267 NW Federal Hwy #196
Jensen Beach, FL 34957
866-352-2628
jeff@jeffhahn.com
SAMS

Malcom Elliott
Florida Nautical Surveyors
2727 NE 32nd St
Ft. Lauderdale, FL 33306-1507
954-630-2141; Cell: 954-801-2140
fnsurveys@aol.com

Kerry Nikula
Florida Nautical Surveyors
2727 NE 32nd St.
Ft. Lauderdale, FL 33306
954-630-2141
Cell: 954-232-3416
www.floridanauticalsurveyors.com
kerrynikula@yahoo.com
ABYC, ACMS

William Gladding
Gladding Marine Survey
1738 Pickwick Pl
Orange Park, FL 32003-7286
904-945-0511
bill@gladdingmarinesurvey.com
SAMS

Lou Gonzalez
Global International Marine Surveyors
10773 NW 58th St. #530
Miami, FL 33178
305-718-9742; Cell: 305-986-2563
globalmarsurvey@aol.com
SAMS

Robert Garay
Global Yacht & Ship Surveyors
6805 SW 89th Ct
Miami, FL 33173-2429
305-858-4175
marinesurveys@gmail.com
ABYC, SAMS

Van D. Kline
Gulf Coast Marine Survey
12635 115th St North
Largo, FL 33778-1809
727-588-0546; Cell: 727-278-8162
www.gulfcoastmarinesurveyinc.com
vankline@yahoo.com
ABYC, SAMS

Arthur Whiting
Harden Marine Associates, Inc.
202 S. 22nd St. Ste 203
Tampa, FL 33605-6396
813-248-3505; Cell: 813-361-8126
awhiting3@aol.com
ABYC, SAMS

David Huffman
Huffman Marine Surveyors
2015 SW 25th Terrace
Ft. Lauderdale, FL 33312
954-205-3153
dwhuffman@earthlink.net
ABYC, NAMS

Steven Berlin
Independent Marine Surveyors
17080 Safety St Unit 105
Ft. Myers, FL 33908
239-466-4544
indmarine@cs.com
SAMS

Adam Johnson
Johnson Marine Survey
6533 SE Federal Hwy #102
Stuart, FL 34997
760-550-3171
surveyoradam@gmail.com

Matthew Jones
Jones Marine Surveyors & Consultants
6131 SW 20th St.
Plantation, FL 33317-5226
954-791-6224
www.JonesMarineSurveyors.com.
sylvia@jonesmarinesurveyors.com
ABYC,ACMS, NSPA

William (Bill) King
Kingsway Marine Surveyors
222A 99th St. Ocean
Marathon, FL 33050
305-965-3600; Cell: 305-965-3600
www.kingswaymarineent.com
bking@kingswaymarineent.com

Thomas Nolan
Latitude Marine
PO Box 249
Deerfield Beach, FL 33443-0249
954-421-0502
www.boatinspect.com
latitudemarine@mindspring.com
ABYC, SAMS

Marine Surveyor Directory

Richard Learned
Learned Associates, Marine Surveyor
702 NW Sunset Dr
Stuart, FL 33994-7613
772-692-7740
www.learnedmarinesurvey.com
rflearned@bellsouth.net
NAMS

Marc Slakoff
Marc Slakoff & Associates
757 SE 17th St. #432
Ft. Lauderdale, FL 33316
954-525-7930
www.yachtsurveyors.com
marc.slakoff@yachtsurveyors.com
ABYC, SAMS, SNAME

David Foley
March Hare Marine Services
383 Lime Ave
Marathon, FL 33050
305-743-3368
www.mhms.biz
mhms@juno.com
ABYC, ACMS, NFPA, USSA

Daniel Mattos
Marine Engine Surveyor, Inc.
3450 Metro Pkwy Unit 5
Ft. Myers, FL 33916-7504
239-461-0366
drmamse@earthlink.net
SAMS

Richard Whittington
Marine Surveyor
2641 SW 5th St.
Boynton Beach, FL 33435
954-553-5690
whittingtonr@bellsouth.net
SAMS

Jesse Marsano
Marine Surveyor
425 10th Ave NE
St. Petersburg, FL 33701
jmarsano@tmsnational.com
SAMS

James McCrory
McCrory & Assoc.
5224 SW 89th Ave
Miami, FL 33165
305-358-4775
mccrsurv@earthlink.net

Kurt Merolla
Merolla Yacht & Boat Surveyors, Inc.
925 Intracoastal Dr. #5
Ft. Lauderdale, FL 33304
954-782-8484
Cell: 954-401-5399
www.YachtSurveyor.org
YotSurveyR@aol.com
ABYC, SAMS, NAMS, SNAME

Noel Miley
Miley Marine Surveying
1021 Twin Lakes Rd
Longwood, FL 32750-4537
877-897-4180
www.floridamarinesurveyors.us
boatpkr@aol.com
ABYC, SAMS

Jonathan Howe
Nautical Services Group
2442 Marathon Lane
Ft. Lauderdale, FL 33312
954-584-5819
Cell: 772-557-7563
www.marinesurveyor.com/nsg
nautserv@aol.com
ABYC, SAMS, NFPA

Navtech US Surveyors Assoc.
13430 McGregor Blvd
Ft. Myers, FL 33919
800-245-4425
Virginia Harper wants ad info 11/3/09 v
ABYC, US Surveyors Assoc

Scott Grabner
Power & Sail Marine Surveyors
PO Box 10685
Daytona Beach, FL 32120
Cell: 386-631-2528
www.powerandsailmarinesurveyors.com
pwrsail@msn.com
ABYC, SAMS

Thomas Price
Price Marine Services, Inc.
9418 SE Sharon St
Hobe Sound, FL 33455-6833
772-546-0928
Cell: 772-285-0433
tprice45@gmail.com
ABYC, SAMS

Mark Rhodes
Rhodes Marine Surveyors
10302 S. Federal Hwy Ste 285

Port St. Lucie, FL 34952-5605
772-398-0860; Cell: 954-646-3760
marmarklhp@aol.com
ABYC, SAMS

Gerard Schmitt
Schmitt Marine
801 S Ocean Dr Apt 406
Ft. Pierce, FL 34949-3380
561-971-6562
gschm4287@aol.com
SAMS

Scott Carlson
Scott Carlson Marine Surveyor
PO Box 531128
Miami Shores, FL 33153-1128
305-891-0445; Cell: 786-295-0573
scsail4@aol.com
ABYC, SAMS

Steve Snider
Snider Marine Surveyors
328 N. Ocean Blvd Ste 502
Pompano Beach, FL 33062-5142
954-942-4803
Cell: 954-444-9136
www.florida-boatsurvey.com
powerboatsurvey@msn.com
ABYC, SAMS

Stephen J. Klaity
South Florida Marine Surveyors
2000 NW 37th Ave
Coconut Creek, FL 33066-3010
954-975-5149
Cell: 954-270-8005
www.southfloridamarinesurveyors.net
soflmarinesurveyors@msn.com
ABYC, SAMS

Stephen J. Klaity
South Florida Marine Surveyors
701 Spanish Main Dr.
Kudjoe Key, FL 33042
305-745-2348
www.southfloridamarinesurveyors.net
soflmarinesurveyors@msn.com
ABYC, SAMS

T.J. Day
Southeast Fire & Marine Assoc.
1749 SW 4th St.
Ft. Lauderdale, FL 33312-7539
954-527-1981; Cell: 954-536-1981
sefmarine@aol.com
ABYC, SAMS

Marine Surveyor Directory

Robert Mooney
West Atlantic Marine
1837 SE Federal Hwy
Stuart, FL 34994
772-834-6585
rmaseasafe@earthlink.net
SAMS

Gordon Wright
Wright Way Marine Surveys
1017 Lewis Cove Road
Delray Beach, FL 33483-6512
561-274-0166
Cell: 561-702-1027
gordonwright1@comcast.net
ABYC, SAMS

David C. Robertson
Yacht Surveying & Consulting
3415 North A1A
Ft. Pierce, FL 34949
772-342-5833
couragelll@msn.com
ABYC, SAMS

Georgia

Larry Credle
Coastal Marine Surveyors & Consultants
1699 Blythe Island Dr
Brunswick, GA 31523-6040
912-230-4014
Cell: 912-230-4014
www.watercraftcrash.com
capt.larry@watercraftcrash.com

Gerald Sisco
Select Marine Surveying
155 Runner Rd.
Savannah, GA 31410
vagabondxx@bellsouth.net

Illinois

Rick Lenschow
Certified Marine Surveyors
716 Edward St
Sycamore, IL 60178-2011
866-627-7878
www.cmsurveyors.com
rick@cmsurveyors.com
ABYC, SAMS

Scott Hollister
Hollister Marine
PO Box 472
Lemont, IL 60439

888-836-3483
Cell: 630-878-6362
www.hollistermarine.com
scott@hollistermarine.com
SAMS

John Walsh
Marine Services Corp
14001 S. Cottage Grove Ave
Dolton, IL 60419
708-841-5660
lc@marineservicescorp.com

John Russell
Marine Specialists
PO Box 322
Winthrop Harbor, IL 60096
847-731-1400
expertinboats@aol.com
ABYC, SAMS, IAMI

Indiana

Lloyd Kittredge
Lake Effect Surveying
801 Ivy St.
Chesterton, IN 46304-3227
219-926-5186
Cell: 219-877-7982
kittsurvey@verizon.net
ABYC, SAMS

Kentucky

Tom Munsterman
Aboveboard Marine Surveyors
11650 US Highway 62
Calvert City, KY 42029
270-898-3679
amstrm@gmail.com

Greg Weeter
Riverlands Marine Surveyors & Consultants
935 Riverside Dr
Louisville, KY 40207-1036
502-897-9900
www.riverlandsmarine.com
riverlandsmarine@insightbb.com
ABYC, SAMS, NAMS

Louisiana

J. Kevin Martin
Arthur H. Terry & Co.
700 Mariners Plaza Ste 704
Mandeville, LA 70448-4799
985-727-4495; Cell: 985-707-3776

www.yachtsurveying.com
kevin@yachtsurveying.com
SAMS

Hjalmar Breit
Breit Marine Surveying
23747 Hwy 40
Bush, LA 70431-2905
504-283-2929
Cell: 504-559-3075
hbreitiii@aol.com
ABYC, NAMS

Kenneth Helmrich
K.P. Helmrich & Assoc. Corp.
11964 River Highlands Dr.
St. Amant, LA 70774
225-698-0883
atthehelmkph@eatel.net
ABYC, NAMS

Curt Boudreaux
Southeast LA Marine Surveying
127 Napoleon St.
Lockport, LA 70374-0321
504-532-6703
boud6057@bellsouth.net
SAMS, SNAME, IAMA

Maine

Robert Lynch
Atlantic Maritime Services
139 Oakledge Rd.
Harpswell, ME 04079
207-650-2714
Cell: 207-650-2714
bob2dboat@yahoo.com
NAMS

Geordie King
King Marine LLC
26 Thunder Rock Rd.
Eliot, ME 03903
207-439-9314
kinggeordie@comcast.net
ABYC, SAMS

Maryland

Raymond Bracken
About The Boat Marine Surveys
2501 Boston St. Ste 301
Baltimore, MD 21224
410-340-3208
ray@abouttheboat.com
ABYC, SAMS

Marine Surveyor Directory

Reno Panico
Atlantic Seaboard Marine Surveyors
2839 Cox Neck Rd.
Chester, MD 21619-2874
Cell: 301-807-7593
www.atlanticseaboardmarine.com
asmsrp@verizon.net
ABYC, SAMS

Richard Warren
Chesapeake Marine Surveyors
2412 Eugene St
Wheaton, MD 20902-4706
240-472-5128
captrichard@verizon.net
SAMS

William Weyant
East Coast Marine Consulting
321 Tidwater Dr.
Havre de Grace, MD 21078
410-322-6701
Cell: 410-322-6701
www.eastcoastmarineconsulting.com
weyantb@comcast.net
ABYC, SAMS, BCMTA, VBMTA

Bill Woodside
G-B Marine Services Inc.
117 Congressional Dr.
Stevensville, MD 21666-3325
410-643-0951
gbmarineservices@yahoo.com
SAMS, ABYC

Richard Levy
Independent Marine Survey, LLC
5715 Ross Neck Road
Cambridge, MD 21613
410-221-1108
labradog@dmv.com
ABYC, SAMS

F. Michael Kaufman
Kaufman Design, Inc.
40 Boone Trail
Severna Park, MD 21146-4533
410-263-8900
www.kaufmandesign.com
kaufman99@aol.com
ABYC, NAMS, SNAME

Kirk Hall
Latitude 39 Marine Services
302 Rosin Dr.
Chestertown, MD 21620-2822
305-395-1352

kirk.hall.marine@gmail.com
SAMS

William Love
Love Machine Marine LLC
8096 Ventnor Rd.
Pasadena, MD 21122
410-330-8564
Cell: 410-330-8564
www.lovemachinemarine.com
lovemachinemarine@comcast.net
ABYC, SAMS

Michael McCook
M.J. McCook Associates, Inc.
PO Box 1059
La Plata, MD 20646-1059
301-934-5800
mike@mccookassoc.com

Jack Hornor
Marine Survey & Design Co.
1291 B Lavall Dr
Davidsonville, MD 21035-1135
410-451-8133
www.msdco.com
jack@msdco.com
ABYC, NAMS, SNAME

Frank Pettolina
Pettolina Marine Surveying
9800 Morringview Lane Unit 14
Ocean City, MD 21842-9387
410-251-0575
surveyfp@yahoo.com
ABYC, SAMS

Harry Seemans
Quaker Neck Marine Surveying
PO Box 69
Bozman, MD 21612-0069
410-745-5452
Cell: 410-829-3007
seemans@atlanticbb.net
ABYC, SAMS

Steven Uhthoff
Steven Uhthoff Marine Surveys
PO Box 3438
Annapolis, MD 21403
410-263-8980; Cell: 443-336-3560
www.annapolismarinesurveys.com
steve@annapolismarinesurveys.com
ABYC, SAMS

Lon Acheson
SurvTech Inc.

PO Box 372
Davidsonville, MD 21035-0372
Cell: 301-318-1089
www.survtech.us
survtech@comcast.net
ABYC, SAMS, SNAME

Massachusetts

Donald Walwer
D&G Marine
PO Box 629
North Eastham, MA 02651-0629
774-487-0275
ddwsurvey@aol.com
SAMS

Kevin Duchak
Duchak Maritime Services LLC
3 Bradford Rd
Danvers, MA 01923-2317
978-777-9700
Cell: 508-641-0749
duchakmaritime@msn.com
ABYC

Bob Gallagher
Gallagher Marine Surveyors
6 Fosters Point
Beverly, MA 01915
978-807-2163
Cell: 978-807-2163
www.gallaghermarinesurveyors.com
captbgallagher@comcast.net
ABYC, SAMS

Gerald P. Connors
GPC Enterprises
15 Thomas St.
Quincy, MA 02169
617-471-4503
gpcent@comcast.net
SAMS

Patrick Goodrow
High Tech Marine Surveys
85 Humphrey St.
Marblehead, MA 01945
781-290-6782
pggoodrow@gmail.com
ABYC, SAMS

Joseph Lombardi
Ocean Technical Services
10 Dalton Ave Unit #1
Gloucester, MA 01930
978-526-1894; Cell: 508-958-1299

Marine Surveyor Directory

www.oceantechserv.com
joe@oceantechserv.com
ABYC, SAMS, SNAME, HNSA

Timothy Pitts
Ocean Way Technology, Inc.
PO Box 158
East Falmouth, MA 02536-4619
Cell: 508-564-8680
www.oceanwaytech.com
tpitts@capecod.net
ABYC, SAMS

Michigan

Les Salliotte
Downriver Marine Surveyors
2304 18th St
Wyandotte, MI 48192-4140
734-283-1886; Cell: 734-516-1176
www.downrivermarinesurveyors.com
lessalliotte@aol.com
ABYC, SAMS

Bob Ptak
Lakeshore Professional Marine Surveys
3098 Viewpoint St SW
Jenison, MI 49428-9160
616-340-1931; Cell: 616-340-1931
www.promarinesurveys.com
bobptak@promarinesurveys.com
ABYC, SAMS

Raymond Dezenski
Quality Marine Surveyors
41571 Gloca Mora
Harrison Twp, MI 48045-1450
586-468-3324
qualmar49@yahoo.com
ABYC, SAMS

Mississippi

Todd Hansen
Hansen & Assoc., LLC
PO Box 7116
D'iberville, MS 39532
228-396-3133; Cell: 228-697-3133
www.hansenclaims.net
Teh237@yahoo.com
ABYC, SAMS, IAMI

Capt. Jim Twiggs
Marine Surveyor
2071 Carolwood Dr.
Biloxi, MS 39532
228-388-4070

captjim42@gmail.com
ABYC, SAMS

Missouri

Nick Koprivica
Apex Marine
2042 Victor St.
St. Louis, MO 63104
314-265-5636
apexmarinellc@gmail.com

David Davis
Cutting Edge Marine Services
3251 Bahnell Dam Blvd PMB 252
Lake Ozark, MO 65049
573-216-0742
cuttingedgemarine@charter.net

Michael Hunter
Hunter Consulting & Survey
PO Box 14761
Springfield, MO 65814
417-929-0005; Cell: 417-929-0005
www.huntersurveying.com
michael@huntersurveying.com
ABYC, SAMS, AMS

John T. Stockmann
Merrill Marine Services
7909 Big Bend Blvd
St. Louis, MO 63119-2703
314-968-0001
jts11050@sbcglobal.net

Todd Hansen
Hansen & Assoc., LLC
PO Box 7116
D'iberville, MS 39532
228-396-3133; Cell: 228-697-3133
www.hansenclaims.net
Teh237@yahoo.com
ABYC, SAMS, IAMI

Capt. Jim Twiggs
Marine Surveyor
2071 Carolwood Dr.
Biloxi, MS 39532
228-388-4070
captjim42@gmail.com
ABYC, SAMS

New Jersey

John Klose
Bayview Assoc.

PO Box 368
Barnegat Light, NJ 08006
609-494-4924
jkboats@gmail.com
ABYC, SAMS, SNAME

Robert Duane
Bob Duane Marine Service, Inc
819 Donna Dr
Pt Pleasant, NJ 08742-4503
732-295-5951; Cell: 732-300-5705
bobduane@comcast.net
ABYC, SAMS

Robert Moro
Capt. Bob Moro, LLC
74 Skytop Rd.
Cedar Grove, NJ 07009
973-239-5821
captbmoro@hotmail.com
ABYC, SAMS, SNAME

Rob Cozen
Captain Rob Cozen, Marine Surveyor
PO Box 220
Somer's Point, NJ 08244-0220
609-926-4949
rcozen1418@comcast.net

Case-McCaniel Marine Group
17 Ave D
Atlantic Highlands, NJ 07716
732-291-7400; Cell: 732-768-0990
jeff@case-mcdaniel.com
ABYC, SAMS, IAMI

Peter Downham
Downham Marine Services
300 Monmouth Ave
Marmora, NJ 08223-1324
609-390-2036
downhammarine@gmail.com
SAMS

A.William Gross
Midatlantic Marine Consulting
39 Waterford Rd
Blue Anchor, NJ 08037-2327
888-321-5254
b-gross@comcast.net
ABYC, NAMS, SAMS

Scott O'Donnell
O'Donnell Marine Surveying
36 Woodroe Pl.
W. Caldwell, NJ 07006-7711
973-226-3053; Cell: 609-312-8606

Marine Surveyor Directory

surveyorscott@aol.com
ABYC, SAMS

Robert Gibble
Robert Gibble, Inc.
69 Golf View Dr.
Little Egg Harbor, NJ 08087
609-294-6177
RGGINC@comcast.net
SAMS, NAMS

Reinier Van Der Herp
RV Marine Surveying & Consulting
126 Station Dr.
Forked River, NJ 08731
609-618-8511
rvmarinesurveying@gmail.com

William Hymans
The Boat Doc Marine Surveys, LLC
260 Pennington Rocky Hill Rd
Pennington, NJ 08534-1817
609-730-1200
billhymans@aol.com

New York

Ronald Alcus
Alcus Marine Technical Services, Inc.
PO Box 700
Moriches, NY 11955-0700
631-874-1000
alcusmt@aol.com
ABYC, SAMS

Shawn Bartnett
Bartnett Marine Services, Inc.
52 Ontario St.
Honeoye Falls, NY 14472-1120
585-624-1380
bartmarser@aol.com
ABYC, NAMS, SNAME

James R. Smith
Captains Boating Services LLC
1941 Fix Rd.
Grand Island, NY 14072
716-773-7374
jrs1202@yahoo.com
SAMS

Brian Crowley
Crowley Marine Consultants
PO Box 53
Brewerton, NY 13029
315-708-7447
CrowleyConsult@aol.com

Eric Green
Eric Green Marine Surveyor & Consultant
2976 Hillcrest Rd.
Schenectady, NY 12309
518-785-4299; Cell: 518-495-0837
egreenmarine@gmail.com
SAMS

Joseph Oldak
Farragut Marine Service Co.
192 Farragut Cir
New Rochelle, NY 10801-5739
914-589-0104; Cell: 914-589-0104
www.farragutmarine.com
marinesurveyor@farragutmarine.com
ABYC, SAMS

Paul Pellegrino
Island-Wide Maritime Services
PO Box 937
Nesconset, NY 11767-0937
Cell: 516-729-6832
pmp409@optonline.net
ABYC, SAMS

John Lowe
Lowe's Marine Survey
5 Elton Dr.
East Northport, NY 11731
631-462-2624
www.marinesurveyor.com/lowe/
captursa@aol.com
ABYC, SAMS

Daniel J. Sheehan
Marine Surveyor
56 Lake Rd.
Valley Cottage, NY 10989-2360
914-268-9340
captdans@aol.com
SAMS

Anthony Fazio
Marine Surveyor
PO Box 81
East Northport, NY 11731-0081
516-429-7365; Cell: 516-429-7365
fazioams@optonline.net
ABYC, SAMS

Alan Ross Hugenot
Marine Surveyor
425 Davenport Ave
New Rochelle, NY 10805
914-325-2525
Alan@captainhugenot.com
SAMS

Frederick Rose
Marine Surveyor
PO Box 22
Alexandria Bay, NY 13607
315-783-7155
captainric@verizon.net
SAMS

Charles Avalos
Marinetech Inc.
101 Rider Ave
Patchogue, NY 11772
631-289-5161
info@marinetechnology.info

Jan Muntz
Muntz Marine Surveyors
87 Cross Pond Rd.
Pound Ridge, NY 10576-1303
914-763-6359; Cell: 914-525-5939
www.muntzmarinesurveyors.com
muntzmarine@optonline.net
ABYC, SAMS

Charles Gruetzner
Oceanis Marine Services
1124 Main St.
Peekskill, NY 10566
845-225-6111
www.oceanismarine.com
charlie@oceanismarine.com
ABYC, SAMS, SNAME

Allen J. Dannewitz
Professional Marine Services, LLC
2 Oak Lane
Long Island, NY 11946
631-728-1754; Cell: 631-258-6177
www.apromarine.com
apromarine@optonline.net
ABYC, SAMS

Wayne Robinson
Robinson Marine Services
838 Dumar Dr
Elbridge, NY 13060-9749
315-689-6854; Cell: 315-246-3253
wer1441@aol.com
ABYC, SAMS

Gary Friend
Seaside Marine Surveyors
PO Box 25
Port Jefferson Station, NY 11776
631-838-7450
gary@seasidemarinesurveyors.com

Marine Surveyor Directory

Anthony Peel
Shipshape Surveying
30 Manor Lane
Copiague, NY 11726-5204
631-608-3127; Cell: 631-926-2993
makopeel@yahoo.com
SAMS

Al Prisco
Small Craft & Yacht Surveys
67 Palmer Trail
Carmel, NY 10512
845-228-1071; Cell: 914-645-3525
www.marinesurveyorny.com
boatsurvey@yahoo.com

Anthony Somma
Somma Marine Surveying
81 Belfast Ave
Staten Island, NY 10306-2103
718-351-7497; Cell: 347-210-0379
www.tonysomma.com
asomma@aol.com
ABYC, SAMS

Peter Luciano
Stay New Yacht Service
50 Davenport Ave #2F
New Rochelle, NY 10805-3660
914-260-6092
sloopquest@aol.com
ABYC, SAMS, SNAME

New Jersey

Patrick Dender
Accredited Marine Technologies, LLC
35 Belle Pl
Neptune City, NJ 07753-6701
888-835-9985; Cell: 732-988-5483
www.amtmarine.com
pdender@amtmarine.com
ABYC, SAMS, APBA

John Klose
Bayview Assoc.
PO Box 368
Barnegat Light, NJ 08006
609-494-4924
jkboats@gmail.com
ABYC, SAMS, SNAME

Robert Duane
Bob Duane Marine Service, Inc
819 Donna Dr
Pt Pleasant, NJ 08742-4503
732-295-5951; Cell: 732-300-5705

bobduane@comcast.net
ABYC, SAMS

Robert Moro
Capt. Bob Moro, LLC
74 Skytop Rd.
Cedar Grove, NJ 07009
973-239-5821
captbmoro@hotmail.com
ABYC, SAMS, SNAME

Rob Cozen
Captain Rob Cozen, Marine Surveyor
PO Box 220
Somer's Point, NJ 08244-0220
609-926-4949
rcozen1418@comcast.net

Case-McCaniel Marine Group
17 Ave D
Atlantic Highlands, NJ 07716
732-291-7400; Cell: 732-768-0990
jeff@case-mcdaniel.com
ABYC, SAMS, IAMI

Peter Downham
Downham Marine Services
300 Monmouth Ave
Marmora, NJ 08223-1324
609-390-2036
downhammarine@gmail.com
SAMS

A.William Gross
Midatlantic Marine Consulting
39 Waterford Rd
Blue Anchor, NJ 08037-2327
888-321-5254
b-gross@comcast.net
ABYC, NAMS, SAMS

Scott O'Donnell
O'Donnell Marine Surveying
36 Woodroe Pl.
W. Caldwell, NJ 07006-7711
973-226-3053
Cell: 609-312-8606
surveyorscott@aol.com
ABYC, SAMS

Robert Gibble
Robert Gibble, Inc.
69 Golf View Dr.
Little Egg Harbor, NJ 08087
609-294-6177
RGGINC@comcast.net
SAMS, NAMS

Reinier Van Der Herp
RV Marine Surveying & Consulting
126 Station Dr.
Forkcd River, NJ 08731
609-618-8511
rvmarinesurveying@gmail.com

William Hymans
The Boat Doc Marine Surveys, LLC
260 Pennington Rocky Hill Rd
Pennington, NJ 08534-1817
609-730-1200
billhymans@aol.com

North Carolina

Albert G. Vandermeer
AGV Marine Survey
126 Mellen Rd.
New Bern, NC 28562
252-288-6610; Cell: 603-320-2619
surveyor@agvmarinesurvey.com

T. Fred Wright
Carolina/Atlantic Marine Services
PO Box 77053
Charlotte, NC 28271-7000
704-708-570; Cell: 704-953-9486
tfredwright@aol.com
ABYC, SAMS, NAMS

John Day
Day Yacht Services
2707 Homes Dr.
Morehead City, NC 28557
252-241-7287
sday@ec.rr.com
SAMS

Lloyd Griffin
Frigate Marine Services
751 Riverside Ave
Elizabeth City, NC 27909
252-333-6105
www.frigatemarinesurveyors.com
lgriffin111@yahoo.com
ABYC, SAMS, IAMI, AIMU

Jon Roop
Marine Surveyor
180 Lewistown Rd.
Beaufort, NC 28516-7812
252-725-0209
www.marinesurveyor.com/jonroop
jonroop@earthlink.net
ABYC, NAMS, SAMS

Marine Surveyor Directory

Donald Davis
Maritime Services
3312 Mandy Lane
Morehead City, NC 28557
252-240-3928
msi@ec.rr.com

Patrick Dender
Accredited Marine Technologies, LLC
35 Belle Pl
Neptune City, NJ 07753-6701
888-835-9985; Cell: 732-988-5483
www.amtmarine.com
pdender@amtmarine.com
ABYC, SAMS, APBA

Ohio

Kevin Ropes
River City Marine Services
PO Box 16484
Rocky River, OH 44116
440-364-2776
survey@rivercitymarineservice.com

John Roesch
Waters Edge Marine Survey
2012 W. Water St.
Sandusky, OH 44870
419-609-0852
msurveyor@sbcglobal.net
SAMS

Oklahoma

Thomas Benton
Marine Damage Consultants, LLC
PO Box 627
Ketchum, OK 74349-0627
918-782-1001
Cell: 918-519-1972
www.marinesurveyor.com/benton
tom.benton@marinesurveyor.com
ABYC, SAMS, NAMS

James McDougal
Marine Specialty Inspections LLC
PO Box 407925
Tulsa, OK 74147
918-836-3263; Cell: 918-836-3263
msisurveyor@cox.net
ABYC, SAMS

Ben Harmon
Marine Surveyor
2135 E 18th St
Tulsa, OK 74104

marinesurvey@sbcglobal.net
ABYC, ACMS

Oregon

Alison Mazon
A. Mazon & Associates
1425 N. Marine Dr. Ste B
Portland, OR 97217
503-286-4252; Cell: 503-358-6983
www.alisonmazon.com
inthebilge@gmail.com
ABYC, SAMS

Pennsylvania

Stephen Montemuro
Marine Surveyor
619 S. Mt. Vernon Cr.
Bensalem, PA 19020
Cell: 215-512-7003
fbpdplt@comcast.net
ABYC, USSA

Charles Miller
North Coast Marine Services
1903 W 8th St
Erie, PA 16505-4936
814-835-8233; Cell: 814-833-9098
nrthcost@velocity.net
SAMS

Robert Stefanowicz
Susquehanna Marine Surveys
1404 Montfort Dr.
Harrisburg, PA 17110-3015
717-233-4989; Cell: 717-497-8974
www.americanyachtsurveyors.com
smsurveys@msn.com
SAMS, ABYC

Charles Ulrick
Ulrick Marine
528 Sugartree Rd.
Holland, PA 18966-1835
215-416-9349
www.yachtexam.com
info@yachtexam.com
ABYC, SAMS

Puerto Rico

Joseph Barlia
Azimuth Maritime Corp
PO Box 193308
San Juan, PR 00919-3308
787-397-8028

www.azimuthmaritime.com
marinesurveyor@prtc.net
ABYC, SAMS, SNAME

Carlos Suarez
Carlos Suarez & Associates
PO Box 141737
Arecibo, PR 00614-1737
787-879-1048
Cell: 787-635-7030
suarez.307@hotmail.com
ABYC, SAMS Myrna

Ciro Malatrasi
Marine Surveyor
PO Box 85
Puerto Real, PR 00740
787-504-4066
ciromsurveys@yahoo.com
ABYC, SAMS

Jorge Mosquera
Marine Surveyor
PMB 402 El Senorial Mail Station
San Juan, PR 00926
787-529-4718
jorgemosquera1@hotmail.com

Rhode Island

James Hilton
EBCS Marine
128 Church Pond Dr.
Tiverton, RI 02878
401-864-7161
ebcs@cox.net

South Carolina

Robert Webber
Admiralty Marine Surveyors
887 Portabella Lane
Charleston, SC 29412-8410
843-762-7176
Cell: 843-991-4796
www.admiraltysurveyors.com
rmwebber@ix.netcom.com
ABYC, SAMS

Neil Haynes
Blue Water Surveys, Inc.
1739 Maybank Hwy #T
Charleston, SC 29412-2103
843-559-2857
www.boatsurveyor.com
nhaynes@boatsurveyor.com
ABYC, NAMS, SAMS, IAMI

Marine Surveyor Directory

David Hill
Carolina Yacht Services, Inc.
24 Nuffield Rd.
Charleston, SC 29407
843-571-5808; Cell: 843-607-3834
uphilldph@knology.net
ABYC, SAMS

Richard Newsome
Dana C. McLendon
PO Box 481
Isle of Palms, SC 29451-0481
843-886-3852; Cell: 843-813-5210
dcmsurvey@bellsouth.net
ABYC, SAMS

Hershel Lantz
Dana C. McLendon Co.
3331 Londonderry Rd.
Charleston, SC 29420-8711
843-552-2931
redsmarine@bellsouth.net

Louis Harrison
Harrison Marine Services
3520 Johan Blvd
Johns Island, SC 29455-8917
843-559-3383
harrisonimc@aol.com
ABYC, SAMS

Ted Yates Lemmond
Lemmond's Marine, LLC
460 Silver Cypress Lane
Fort Mill, SC 29709-8060
800-671-4440; Cell: 803-57-5837
lemmondsmarine@yahoo.com
ABYC, SAMS

Robert Dolce
Marine Surveyors & Appraisers Assoc.
PO Box 21066
Hilton Head, SC 29925
843-681-2674; Cell: 843-384-9945
marinesurveyor1@yahoo.com
ABYC, SNAME, NFPA

Tennessee

Gary Wright
American Marine Specialists
2425 N. Shore Acres Rd
Soddy Daisy, TN 37379-7949
423-451-0128
www.marinesurveyor-sams.com
gr.wright@comcast.net

Edward Fry
Fry Associates, Inc.
5420 Waddell Hollow Rd
Franklin, TN 37064-9422
615-591-8455
Cell: 954-494-1557
www.frycoyachts.com
ed.fry@frycoyachts.com

Gale Chapman
Gale C Marine, Inc.
PO Box 110664
Nashville, TN 37222-0664
615-943-4789; Cell: 615-430-6902
www.galecmarine.com
gcmarine@comcast.net
ABYC, NAMS

Pete Hosemann
Hosemann Marine Services
396 Pleasant View Cr.
Jasper, TN 37347
423-653-3558
captpete@hosemannmarine.com
ABYC, USSA

C. Stanley Johnson
Riverport Marine Surveying
286 Stonewall St
Memphis, TN 38112-5143
901-278-2161
Cell: 901-485-2072
www.riverportms.com
riverportms@aol.com
ABYC, SAMS, IAMI, CMI, AMS

Texas

Dale Vandermolen
Aloha Marine Surveyors
3336 Floyd St
Corpus Christi, TX 78411-1461
361-960-4674
alohasurv@msn.com

Kurtis Samples, AMS
Anchor Marine Consultants
1920 Abrams Pkwy #169
Dallas, TX 75214
Cell: 214-796-4305
kkboat@airmail.net
ABYC, SAMS, IAMI

Jason Shane Dunham
Anchor Marine Surveying
4008 Louetta Rd. #543
Spring, TX 77388

281-905-7424
anchormarinesurveying@yahoo.com
ABYC, SAMS, IAMI

Paul Post
Aqua-Marine Surveyors, LLC
2332 Amhearst Lane
Flower Mound, TX 75028
972-355-0252; Cell: 214-457-0918
www.a-msllc.biz
boatchecker@a-msllc.biz

Bobby Brown
Blue Water Surveyors
9434 Zyle Rd.
Austin, TX 78737
214-522-3505; Cell: 214-704-7750
www.bluewatersurveyors.com
bluwater@airmail.net
ABYC, SAMS

Joseph Curry
Capt. Curry Marine Surveyor
13231 Visa Del Mundo
San Antonio, TX 78216-2245
210-492-7143
www.curryboatpoking.com
captcurry@yahoo.com
ABYC, SAMS

Louis Stahlberg
LHS Marine
PO Box 1587
League City, TX 77574-1587
281-332-7306; Cell: 281-639-3014
lou@lhsmarine.com
ABYC, SAMS

Steve Boudreaux
Nova Marine Surveyors
6409 Meadowcrest Lane
Flower Mound, TX 75022
817-937-1130
www.novamarinesurveyors.com
steve@surveyaboat.com
SAMS

James G. Merritt
Tangent Development Co.
1715 Harliquin Run
Austin, TX 78758-6121
512-837-9170
Cell: 512-731-5708
www.marinesurvey.org
survrjim@austin.rr.com
ABYC, SAMS, SNAME

Marine Surveyor Directory

Utah

Billie Streelman
Desert Marine Surveys
PO Box 410203
Big Water, UT 84741
866-675-5866
Cell: 435-675-5866
www.desertmarinesurveysusa.com
tom@desertmarineclaims.com
SAMS

Karl Axelgard
Marine Survey Associates
PO Box 251
Leeds, UT 84723-0251
435-275-7163; Cell: 435-632-6442
www.mymarinesurvey.com
mymarinesurvey@yahoo.com
ABYC, SAMS, IAMI

Virginia

Brian McCauley
BMI Marine
921 Holladay Point
Virginia Beach, VA 23451-3912
757-646-5695
bmimarine@cox.net
ABYC, SAMS

G. Emory Shover
Eastern Marine Services LLC
6505 Palisades Dr
Centreville, VA 20121-3811
703-830-0791
www.easternmarine.us
easternmarine@msn.com

Thomas Kimball
Kimball Marine Services
4316 Charity Neck Rd.
Virginia Beach, VA 23457
757-721-3163
tommykimball@yahoo.com
SAMS

George Lambert
Lambert Marine Surveyors
4229 Raleigh Rd.
Chesapeake, VA 23321
757-488-1473
lambert.marine@verizon.net
SAMS

R. Earl Joyner, CMI
Lighthouse Marine Surveying
1722 Back Creek Rd.

Seaford, VA 23696
866-860-5672; Cell: 757-870-1111
www.marinesurveying.com
earl@marinesurveying.com
ABYC, IAMI, NFPA

John Schnoering
Traditional Yacht Surveyors
16467 General Puller Hwy
Deltavilla, VA 23043
804-776-0433
ipyacht@crosslink.net
SAMS

Donald McCann
Tranquil Waters Marine Services
5570 Windmill Point Rd
White Stone, VA 22578-3200
804-435-6942
www.tranquilwaters.com
tranqwlw@crosslink.net
SAMS

Washington

Ralph Stanley
American Marine Surveys
8105 101st St. NW
Gig Harbor, WA 98332
253-853-9500
www.americanmarinesurveys.com
rlistanley@comcast.net
ABYC, SAMS

Donald Bell
Bell Assoc. Marine Survey
2219 Fairview Ave E HB#11
Seattle, WA 98102-6523
206-325-0848
bellupaway@msn.com

Stephen Berg
Berg Marine Surveys
1004 Commercial Ave #354
Anacortes, WA 98221-4117
360-301-6879
Cell: 360-301-6879
www.bergmarinesurveys.com
bergmarinesurveys@verizon.net
ABYC, SAMS

Chisolm T. (Sam) Colt
Colt Marine Surveying
718 Onamac Way
Camano Island, WA 98282
360-387-4030
Cell: 360-708-6463

www.coltmarsurv.com
comarsrv@wavecable.com
ABYC, SAMS

David MacKay
David B. MacKay Inc.
2420 E. 36th Ter
Bellingham, WA 98226-1701
360-588-2265
Cell: 360-739-3861
dbmackay@msn.com
ABYC, NAMS

Jane Christen
Michel & Christen Marine Damage
Surveyors
501 E Bayview Dr
Shelton, WA 98584-7300
800-794-0089
mcms@marinelosssurveyors.com
ABYC, SAMS, SNAME

Terry Larson
Northwest Marine Surveyors
4234 Soundview Dr. West
Tacoma, WA 98466
Cell: 253-229-9653
nwms@harbornet.com

Leif Pedersen
Pedersen Marine LLC
18908 8th Ave NW #320
Shoreline, WA 98177
360-730-2430
Cell: 206-799-6728
pedersenmarine@yahoo.com
ABYC, SAMS

Christopher Mathers
Mathers Marine Inc
806 Sundown Lane
Camano Island, WA 98282
360-770-0921; Cell: 360-202-7700
www.mathersmarineinc.com
chris@mathersmarineinc.com
ABYC, SAMS

Washington D.C.

Guy Nolan
Cascade Corporation
1000 Water St SW
Washington, DC 20024-2425
571-344-1239; Cell: 571-344-1239
cascadegrn@starpower.net
ABYC, SAMS, SNAME

Marine Surveyor Directory

Wisconsin

Scott Schoeler
C3 Marine Services
PO Box 908
Superior, WI 54880
218-343-6794
www.c3marine.com
sdschoeler@c3marine.com
ABYC, SAMS

Chris Kelly
Chris Kelly & Associates, LLC
7528 Pershing Blvd B-135
Kenosha, WI 53142
800-299-3197
www.chriskellyassociates.com
ckelly@chriskellyassociates.com
AYBC, SAMS

David Hense
D.W.H. Marine
282 Cove Rd
Hudson, WI 54016-8181
715-386-6250
dwmdhense@att.net

Richard Lawrence
Lawrence Marine Service
9746 Sheridan Rd
Pleasant Prairie, WI 53158-5403
262-694-5609
lawrencemarine@wi.rr.com
ABYC

Jim Ledenbach
Superior Marine Survey
PO Box 805
Bayfield, WI 54814
715-292-1311
superiorsurveyor@yahoo.com
SAMS

Tim Graul
Timothy Graul Marine Surveys
PO Box 290
Sturgeon Bay, WI 54235-0290
920-743-5092
www.timgraul.com
tag@tgmd.net
ABYC, SNAME

Canada

Edward Greene
Green Turtle Services
264 Queens Quay West Ste 208
Toronto, ON M5J1B5
ted@greeneturtleservices.com

Timothy McGivney
Aegis Marine Surveyors
4051 Prospect Rd.
N. Vancouver, BC V7N3L6
604-983-2050
Cell: 604-250-5601
tjmcgivney@shaw.ca
ABYC, NAMS

Gerry Montpellier
G.R. Montpellier Appraisals
18 Suave St. RR #3
Chelmsford, ON P0M1L0
705-855-9363
motorsport.north@sympatico.ca
ASA

Barry Goodyear
Ra Kon Marine Surveyors & Appraisers
1826 St. John's Rd.
Innisfil, ON L9S1T4
705-431-9485; Cell: 905-853-8100
www.rakon.ca
bgoodyear@rakon.ca
ABYC

Sylvain Dupont
Marine Surveyor
807 Napoleon St.
St. Colomban, QC J5K1P9
sylvaindupont@videotron.ca

Mexico

Sheldon Caughey
Baja Marine Service
Marina Cabo Plaza 107 Blvd De Marina 39
Cabo San Lucas, BCS 23410
Cell: 011-521-624-110-2673
www.bajamarineservice.com
drsheldoncaughey@prodigy.net.mx
NAMS

Broker/Dealer Directory

Alaska

A&M Yacht Sales
5004 Dauphin Island Pkwy
Mobile, AL 36605-9644
800-548-9193
www.amyachts.com
boats@amyachts.com

Alabama

Gulf Coast Hatteras
PO Box 1280
Orange Beach, AL 36561
251-980-2220
rebecca@gulfcoasthatteras.com

Marine Group Emerald Coast LLC
PO Box 650
Orange Beach, AL 36561
251-981-9200
Cell: 850-496-1172
www.marinegroupec.com
jodi@marinegroupec.com
Brokerage

California

Adair Yachts
PO Box 1418
Sunset Beach, CA 90742
562-592-6220; Cell: 562-252-2167
www.adairyachts.com
Adairyachts@gmail.com
Brokerage

Altair Yacht Group
3424 Via Oporto, #208
Newport Beach, CA 92663
949-673-0014
terie@altairyachtgroup.com

Ardell Yacht & Ship Brokers
2101 W. Coast Hwy
Newport Beach, CA 92663-4712
949-642-5735
www.ardell.com
kay@ardell.com
Brokerage

Cardel Yachts
4625 Admiralty Way
Marina del Rey, CA 90292
0310-578-6100
Tony@Cardelyachts.com

Cays Yacht Sales, Inc.
550 Marina Pkwy # D3
Chula Vista, CA 91910-4054
619-422-7376
Cell: 619-572-8245
www.caysyachtsaleinc.com
drcatcays@hotmail.com
Brokerage

Chuck Hovey Yachts
717 Lido Park Dr Ste A
Newport Beach, CA 92663-4461
949-675-8092
www.chuckhoveyyachts.com
brian@chuckhoveyyachts.com

Craig Belden Yachts
2738 Dollar St.
Lakewood, CA 90712
beldenyachts@gmail.com

Cruisers West
2353 Shelter Island Dr.
San Diego, CA 92106-3109
949-723-1098
Cell: 949-274-1826
www.cruiserswestyachts.com
nbsales@cruiserswest.com
New Boat Sales, Brokerage, Service Yard

Delano Int'l Yacht Sales
1356 Muirlands Vista Way
La Jolla, CA 92037-6213
858-454-9789

Discovery Bay Yacht Sales
5901 Marina Rd #6
Discovery Bay, CA 94514-9144
925-634-1107
www.discoverybayyachts.com
discoyachts@cs.com

Franklin Yachts
3419 Via Lido #643

Newport Beach, CA 92663
562-449-6054

Heritage Yacht Sales
231 N. Marina Dr.
Long Beach, CA 90803-4623
866-569-2248; Cell: 310-995-9989
www.heritageyachts.com
info@heritageyachts.com
New Boat Sales, Brokerage, Marina

Long Beach Yacht Sales
6400 Marina Dr., #8
Long Beach, CA 90803
ed4boats@yahoo.com

Mariners Group
19521 Pompano Lane Unit 108
Huntington Beach, CA 92648-2840
866-364-0677
www.marineryachtsales.com
art@marineryachtsales.com
Brokerage

My Boat Company
701 Shore Rd. #201
Wilmington, CA 90744
310-923-8414
myboatcompany@yahoo.com

National Liquidators
25802 Victoria Blvd
Capistrano Beach, CA 92624
949-631-6715
www.yachtauctions.com

Newport Coast Yachts
2751 West Coast Hwy Ste 205
Newport Beach, CA 92663
949-295-9654
cme4yachts@aol.com

Oceanic Yacht Sales
308 Harbor Dr
Sausalito, CA 94965-1416
415-331-0533
www.oceanicyachts.com
info@oceanicyachts.com

Broker/Dealer Directory

Offshore West
2436 W. Coast Hwy Ste 101
Newport Beach, CA 92663
949-673-5401
www.offshorewest.com
diane@offshorewest.com

Orange Coast Yachts
342 Dolphin Isle
Novato, CA 94949
501-523-2628
yachtcowboy@yahoo.com

Purcell Yachts
14000 Palawan Way Ste A
Marina del Rey, CA 90292-6285
877-298-4519
www.purcellyachts.com
gerry@purcellyachts.com

Seacoast Yacht Sales
125 Harbor Way Ste 11
Santa Barbara, CA 93109-2352
805-962-8195
greg@seacoastyachts.com

South Mountain Yachts
10 Corniche Dr. #H
Monarch Beach, CA 92629
949-240-8198; Cell: 949-842-2344
www.southmountainyachts.com
lou@smyyachts.com
Brokerage

Stan Miller Yachts
2540 Shelter Island Dr. Ste A
San Diego, CA 92106
619-224-1510
www.stanmiller.com
nikki@stanmiller.com

Tower Park Boat Sales
14900 W Highway 12 Ste D
Lodi, CA 95242-9325
209-339-4418
tpbs@jps.net

Vaught's Yacht Sales
5866 E Naples Plaza
Long Beach, CA 90803-5008
562-438-8669
www.vysyachts.com
info@vysyachts.com

Yorath Yachts
16400 Pacific Coast Hwy #107
Huntington Beach, CA 92649-1852

714-840-2373
Cell: 714-264-3443
www.yorathyachts.com
tomjr@yorathyachts.com

Connecticut

Cedar Island Marina
PO Box 181
Clinton, CT 06413-0181
860-669-8681
brokercim@aol.com

Hank Aldrich Yacht Sales
PO Box 72
Essex, CT 06426-0072
860-767-4988
Cell: 860-391-4303
www.hankaldrichyachtsales.com

Marine Sales & Service
PO Box 318
East Hampton, CT 06424
860-267-6914
marinesales@aol.com

Northeast Marine Liquidation
PO Box 144
Stonington, CT 06378-0144
860-599-0123
Neml@aol.com

Port Niantic Inc.
17 Smith Ave
Niantic, CT 06357-3229
860-739-2155
port.niantic.inc@snet.net

Total Marine
160 Water St
Norwalk, CT 06854-3739
203-838-3210
www.totalmarine.com
vantolini@totalmarine.com

Florida

Admiralty Yacht Sales
911 SE 6th Ave Ste 109
Delray Beach, FL 33483-5190
561-330-9095
www.admiraltyyacht.com
dlash@admiraltyyacht.com

Adventure Yachts, Inc.
1845 Cordova Rd. Ste 207
Ft. Lauderdale, FL 33316

954-580-0550
www.adventureyachtsinc.com
info@adventureyachts.net

Alliance Marine, Inc.
2608 N Ocean Blvd #9
Pompano Beach, FL 33062-2955
954-941-5000
www.ayacht.net
debi@ayacht.net

Anthony Cataldo Yacht Sale
127 Whippoorwill Dr.
Palm Coast, FL 32164-7263
386-446-6673
tcfl2005@bellsouth.net

AT Yacht
10418 Big Tree Cr E
Jacksonville, FL 32257
954-257-9221; Cell: 904-262-7609
atyachts@aol.com

Atlantic Yacht & Ship
850 NE 3rd St #213
Dania Beach, FL 33004
954-921-1500
www.atlanticyachtandship.com
colleen@atlanticyachtandship.com

Bay Pines Marina
5000 92nd St N
St. Petersburg, FL 33708-3900
727-392-4922
http://baypinesmarina.com/
royal@baypinesmarina.com

Blue Marlin Yachts LLC
101 N. Riverside Dr. Ste 119W
Pompano Beach, FL 33302
954-552-0464
bentley@bluemy.com

Bob Seeger Yacht Sales
600 Cedar St
LongBoat Key, FL 34228
seegeryachtsales@comcast.net

Camper & Nicholsons
450 Royal Palm Way
Palm Beach, FL 33480-4139
561-655-2121
info@pal.cnyachts.com

Cape Regal Yachts
1507 SE 47th Terrace
Cape Coral, FL 33904

Broker/Dealer Directory

239-699-3981; Cell: 239-699-3981
www.caperegal.com
bob@caperegal.com

Complete Marine
2637 E. Atlantic Blvd
Pompano Beach, FL 33062-4939
954-415-3151
www.completeboat.com
completeboat@aol.com

Crown International Yacht Sales
1751 Mound St. Ste 204
Sarasota, FL 34236
941-552-6713
www.crownyachtsales.com
barry@crownyachtsales.com
Brokerage

Dick Boger Yacht Sales
2305 Beach Blvd Ste 106
Jacksonville Beach, FL 32250-4031
904-247-7966
rboger6979@aol.com

Distinction Yachts
12864 Biscayne Blvd #153
N. Miami, FL 33181
305-494-8081
lrubio@distinctionyachts.com

Dolphin Int'l Yacht Sales
985 Riverside Dr.
Palmetto, FL 34221
941-722-0436
Cell: 941-587-4229
www.dolphinyachtsales.com

Dwight Tracy & Friends
1515 SE 17th St. Ste A131
Ft. Lauderdale, FL 33316-1736
954-767-0007; Cell: 954-325-3461
www.dtfyachts.com
info@dtfyachts.com
New Boat Sales, Brokerage

DYB Charter & Yacht Sales
1514 Royal Palm Dr
Edgewater, FL 32132-2520
386-409-0854
www.dybyachts.com
howard-dybyachts@cfl.rr.com

FCM Yacht Sales/Florida Coast Marine
Palm Beach/Ft. Pierce/Amelia Island
Palm Beach, FL 33412
561-756-2628

www.fcmyachts.com
dkennedy@fcmyachts.com
Brokerage

Fillingham Yacht Sales
105 - 15th Ave SE
St. Petersburg, FL 33701-5605
727-403-0520
Cell: 727-460-5687
www.fillinghamyachts.com
sales@fillinghamyachts.com
Brokerage, Service Yard

Florida Coast Marine Yacht Sales
2010 Harbortown Dr Ste O
Ft. Pierce, FL 34946-1451
772-489-0110
www.fcmyachts.com
info@fcmyachts.com
Brokerage, Marina, Service Yard

Fresh Water Boats, Inc.
1017 34th Dr. West
Palmetto, FL 34221
brent@freshwaterboats.ca

Galati Yacht Sales
126 Harbor Blvd
Destin, FL 32541-7344
850-654-1575
www.galatiyachts.com
jcovington@galatiyachts.com
New Boat Sales, Brokerage, Service Yard

Gilman Yachts
1510 SE 17th St #300
Ft. Lauderdale, FL 33316-1737
954-525-8112
www.gilmanyachts.com
jeff@gilmanyachts.com

HMY Yacht Sales
817 NE 3rd Street
Dania Beach, FL 33004 USA
954-926-0400
www.hmy.com
New Boats, Brokerage, Service Facilities

HMY Yacht Sales
2401 PGA Blvd. Suite 182
Palm Beach Gardens, FL 33410 USA
561- 775-6000
www.hmy.com
New Boats, Brokerage, Service Facilities

Island Trader Yacht Sales
415 NW Flagler Ave #202

Stuart, FL 34994
772-201-1100
mickey@ityachts.com

Kniffin Marine Group
13711 Roanoke St.
Ft. Lauderdale, FL 33325
954-889-7330
kniffinmarinegroup.com
andy@akyachts.com

Latin Yachts
1048 NW 123 Ct
Miami, FL 33182
305-389-0953
latinyachts@gmail.com

Lowe's Marine Sales
298 Capri Blvd
Naples, FL 34113
239-642-3439
Cell: 239-571-0045
Henry_LMSFL@comcast.net
Brokerage

Luke Brown Yachts
1500 Cordova Rd. #200
Ft. Lauderdale, FL 33316-2190
954-525-6617
www.lukebrown.com
marc@lukebrown.com
New Boat Sales, Brokerage

Luxury Yachts International
2495 Cat Cay Lane
Ft. Lauderdale, FL 33312-4751
954-584-1888; Cell: 954-465-9775
www.luxuryyachtsinternational.com
linda@luxuryyachtsinternational.com
Brokerage

Manasota Yacht Brokers
1736 Larson St.
Englewood, FL 34223
941-473-4018
myb@verizonmail.com

Manatee Pocket Yacht Sales
2906 SW Brighton Way
Palm City, FL 34997
tom.whittington@comcast.net

Marcali Yachts
1342 Colonial Blvd #B10
Ft. Meyers, FL 33907-1001
239-275-3600
Cell: 239-777-7824

Broker/Dealer Directory

www.marcaliyacht.com
marc@teammarcali.com
Brokerage

MarineMax
1485 S. Tamiami Trail S.
Venice, FL 34285
941-313-2212

MarineMax
2370 SW Palm City Rd
Stuart, FL 34994-4681
772-287-4495
steve.gale@marinemax.com

Marlow Marine Sales, Inc.
4204 13th Street Ct West
Palmetto, FL 34221-5705
941-729-3370
www.marlowmarine.com
sales@marlowmarine.com
New Boat Sales, Brokerage, Service Yard

Charles Winter
Massey Yacht Sales
1015 Riverside Dr.
Palmetto, FL 34221
941-723-1610
Cell: 941-757-1255
www.masseyyacht.com
dougj@masseyyacht.com

Melbourne Harbor Marina
2210 Front St #101
Melbourne, FL 32901-7360
321-725-9054
www.melbourneharbor.com
melbourneharbor@aol.com

Merritt Yacht Brokers
2890 State Rd. 84 #105
Ft. Lauderdale, FL 33312
954-761-1300
sales@merrittyachts.com

Naples Yacht Brokerage
PO Box 882
Naples, FL 34106
239-434-8338
Cell: 239-777-4489
www.naplesyachtbrokerage.com
naplesyb@earthlink.net
Brokerage

National Liquidators
1915 SW 21st Ave
Ft. Lauderdale, FL 33312-3113

954-791-9601
www.yachtauctions.com
rbrozic@natliq.com
Palm Beach Power Boats
105 S. Narcissus Ave
W. Palm Beach, FL 33401
561-514-0855
rob@pbpbi.com

Portside Yacht Sales
527 Anclote Rd.
Tarpon Springs, FL 34689
727-942-4004
www.portsideyacht.net
sales@portsideyachts.com

Robert J. Cury Yacht Sales
399 SE 18th Ct.
Ft. Lauderdale, FL 33316-2809
954-525-7484
www.rjcyachts.com
rjcyachts@aol.com
Brokerage

Ross Yacht Sales
500 Main St.
Dunedin, FL 34698
727-210-1800
www.rossyachtsales.com
rick@rossyachtsales.com
New Boat Sales, Brokerage

Sanlorenzo of the Americas/Yachtblue
190 SE 10th Ave
Ft. Lauderdale, FL 33301
954-376-4794
angela@sanlorenzoamericas.com

Sarasota Yacht & Ship
1306 Main St.
Sarasota, FL 34236-5614
941-365-9095
www.sarasotayacht.com
info@sarasotayacht.com
New Boat Sales, Brokerage

Sarasota Yacht & Ship
990 Blvd of the Arts
Sarasota, FL 34236
roykap@aol.com

Scorpions Newport Marine
960 Mullet Rd.
Pt Canaveral , FL 32920
321-784-5788x16
ptcanaveral@gmail.com
Scott B. Jones Yacht Brokers

1323 SE 17th St. #427
Ft. Lauderdale, FL 33316-1632
954-763-6937
www.scottbjones.com
info@scottbjones.com

Sparkman & Stephens
1845 Cordova Rd. #205
Ft. Lauderdale, FL 33316
954-524-4616
www.sparkmanstephens.com
brokerfl@sparkmanstephens.com

Starboard Yacht Brokerage
PO Box 512522
Punta Gorda, FL 33951-2522
941-637-7788; Cell: 941-628-5404
www.starboardyachtinc.com
starboardyacht@earthlink.net

Suncoast Marine Management
8290 Bay Pines Blvd N
St. Petersburg, FL 33709-4002
727-384-2628
www.suncoast-marine.com
mark@suncoast-marine.com
Brokerage

Sundance Marine
1335 SE 16th St
Ft. Lauderdale, FL 33316-1780
954-522-2800
kbeattie@sundancemarineusa.com

Tierra Verde Yacht Brokerage
18 Madonna Blvd
Tierra Verde, FL 33715-1731
727-867-3191
www.tierraverdeyachts.com
boating@tierraverdeyachts.com

Treasure Coast Boating Center
420 SW Federal Hwy
Stuart, FL 34994-2802
772-287-9800
tony@tcboating.com

US Liquidators
2605 43rd St. N.
Tampa, FL 33605
813-627-0172
www.usliquidatorsonline.com
johna@usliquidatorsonline.com
Brokerage

West Florida Yachts
4880 37th St S

Broker/Dealer Directory

St. Petersburg, FL 33711-4530
727-864-0310
www.westfloridayachts.com
sales@westfloridayachts.com

Westport Yacht Sales
2957 State Rd. 84
Ft. Lauderdale, FL 33312-7702
954-316-6364
www.westportyachts.com
info@westportyachtsales.com
New Boat Sales, Brokerage

Wilson Yacht Sales
7181 College Pkwy Ste 6
Ft. Myers, FL 33907
877-258-0282
www.wilsonyacht.com
srw777@aol.com

World Class Yacht Sales
1673 Oak Park Ct.
Tarpon Springs, FL 34689
727-945-7500
www.world-yachts.com
worldyachts@wcyachtsales.com
New Boat Sales, Brokerage

Worldwide Yacht Sales, Inc.
3501 Del Prado Blvd
Cape Coral, FL 33904
239-549-8683
www.worldwideyachts.net
info@worldwideyachts.net

Yacht Sales Consultants
4561 SW Long Bay Dr.
Palm City, FL 34990-8810
772-463-2645
matt@yachtsalesconsultants.com
Brokerage

Yachting Experts
2550 S Bayshore Dr. Ste 205
Coconut Grove, FL 33133
305-812-2854
frank.devarona@yachtingexperts.com

Georgia

MarineMax
1850 Bald Ridge Marina Rd.
Cumming, GA 30041-8643
877-240-7671
New Boat Sales, Brokerage

Park Marine Boating Center
1989 Cobb Parkway N.
Kennesaw, GA 30152
770-919-2628
www.parkmarine.com
cbell@parkmarine.com
New Boat Sales, Brokerage, Service Yard

Illinois

Boating-A-Dream
445 Mill Ridge Dr.
Byron, IL 61010
815-222-2097
www.boatingadream.com
d.boats@boatingadream.com

Pier 11 Marina
826 E. 138th St.
Chicago, IL 60827
773-468-9605
Cell: 773-468-1965
www.pier11marina.com
pier11marina@hotmail.com
New Boat Sales, Brokerage, Marina

Spring Brook Marina
PO Box 379
Seneca, IL 61360
815-357-8666
www.springbrookmarina.com
sales@springbrookmarina.com
New Boat Sales, Brokerage, Service Yard

Starved Rock Marina
PO Box 2460
Ottawa, IL 61350-7060
815-433-4218; Cell: 815-228-1988
www.starvedrockmarina.com
tom@starvedrockmarina.com
New Boat Sales, Brokerage, Service Yard

Windy City Yacht Brokerage
934 N. Branch St.
Chicago, IL 60642-4230
312-440-9500
Cell: 630-240-0409
www.windycityyachts.com
jeff@windycityyachts.com
Brokerage

Indiana

Kentuckiana Yacht Sales
700 E Market St
Jeffersonville, IN 47130-3975
812-282-7579

www.kys.com
info@kys.com
New Boat Sales, Brokerage, Service Yard

Stevens Marine
3213 E. US Hwy 12
Michigan City, IN 46360
stevensmarine@sbcglobal.net

Kentucky

Green Turtle Bay Yacht Sales
PO Box 102
Grand Rivers, KY 42045
800-498-0428; Cell: 270-362-8364
www.greenturtlebay.com
bhuffman@greenturtlebay.com
Brokerage, Marina

Paradigm Yacht Sales
PO Box 1043
Prospect, KY 40059
502-419-6649
george@paradigmyachts.com
Charles Cyr

Louisiana

CYR Boat Works
3501 N. Causeway Blvd Ste 319
Metarie, LA 70002
504-338-3738
pic@gulfcoasthatteras.com

MG Mayer Yacht Services, Inc.
406 S. Roadway
New Orleans, LA 70124
504-282-1700; Cell: 504-251-6565
www.mayeryacht.com
mmayer@mayeryacht.com
Brokerage, Service Yard

Maryland

Bohemia Vista/Covenant Cove Marine
140 Vista Marina Rd.
Chesapeake City, MD 21915
410-885-5402
bovista@bohemiavista.com

Burr Yacht Sales
1106 Turkey Point Rd
Edgewater, MD 21037-4101
410-798-5900
www.burryachtsales.com
mick@burryachtsales.com
New Boat Sales, Brokerage, Service Yard

Broker/Dealer Directory

CFL Marine
114 Carroll Island Rd.
Baltimore, MD 21220-2208
410-335-1544
www.yachtworld.com/cfl
cbboats@msn.com
Brokerage, Marina

Coastline Yacht Sales
2501 Boston St.
Baltimore, MD 21224
410-207-4400
www.coastlineyachtsales.com/
usaboatexporters@aol.com

Interyacht
7076 Bembe Beach Rd
Annapolis, MD 21403-3623
410-280-6100
www.interyacht.com
alanh@interyacht.com

Island Yacht Brokers
206 Piney Narrows Rd
Chester, MD 21619-2400
410-643-3131
Cell: 410-708-0470
www.islandyachtbrokers.com
brycen@islandyachtbrokers.com

McDaniel Yacht Basin, Inc.
PO Box E
North East, MD 21901-0286
410-287-8121
www.mcdanielyacht.com
t.trainer@mcdanielyacht.com

Mears Point Yacht Sales
428 Kent Narrows Way North
Grasonville, MD 21638-1022
410-827-8888
Cell: 410-382-6346
www.mearspointyachtsales.com
mike@mearspoint.com
Brokerage

North Star Marine Group
6233 Ironwood Way
Columbia, MD 21045
410-381-3121
beverly@northstarmarinegroup.net

Yachtfinders Annapolis
98 Shipwright St.
Annapolis, MD 21401
nickc@yachtfindersannapolis.com

Massachusetts

American Marine & Boat Sales
58ñ Merrimac St.
Newburyport, MA 01950-3065
978-462-2323
www.usedpowerboats,com
rvorias@usedpowerboats.com
Brokerage

Boston Yacht Sales
275 River St.
North Weymouth, MA 02191-2238
781-331-2400; Cell: 617-227-3397
www.bostonyacht.com
keeponfishin@aol.com

Captain O'Connell Inc.
180 River St.
Fall River, MA 02720-1616
508-672-6303
www.captoconnell.com
captainoconnell@comcast.net
Brokerage, Service Yard

Niemiec Marine Inc.
173 Popes Island
New Bedford, MA 02740-7252
508-997-7390
www.niemiecmarine.com
bniemic@niemiecmarine.com
New Boat Sales, Brokerage, Service Yard

Russo Marine
291 Mystic Ave
Medford, MA 02155-6312
781-395-0050
www.russomarine.com
info@russomarine.com
New Boat Sales, Brokerage, Service Yard

Slip's Capeway Marine
1619 New State Hwy
Raynham, MA 02767-1020
508-822-6948
www.slipscapewaymarine.com
jackpills@aol.com

Tern Harbor Marina
275 River St.
N. Weymouth, MA 02191-2239
781-337-1964
Cell: 781-760-4157
www.ternharbormarina.com/
knoonan@ternharbormarina.com
New Boat Sales, Brokerage, Service Yard

Michigan

Coral Gables Yachts LLC
PO Box 103
Macatawa, MI 49434
josh@cgyacht.com

Gregory Boat Co
9666 E Jefferson Ave
Detroit, MI 48214-2993
313-823-1900
Cell: 586-915-4341
www.gregoryboat.com
gary@gregoryboat.com
Brokerage, Marina, Service Yard

Harborview Yacht Sales
12935 W Bayshore Dr #105
Traverse City, MI 49684-6214
231-933-5414
www.harborviewyachtsales.com
info@harborviewyachtsales.com
New Boat Sales, Brokerage

Harrison Marine
32575 S. River Rd.
Harrison Twp, MI 48045
586-465-3054
jeff@harrisonmarine.com

John B. Slaven, Inc.
31300 N. River Rd.
Harrison Town, MI 48045
586-463-0000
www.jbslaven.com
yachts@jbslaven.com

Onekama Marine
PO Box 210
Onekama, MI 49675-0210
231-889-5000
www.onekamamarine.com
steveb@onekamamarine.com

Pier 1000 Marina
1000 Riverview Dr
Benton Harbor, MI 49022-5028
616-927-4471
www.pier1000.com
chillout@pier1000.com

South River Marine
30137 S. River Rd.
Harrison Township, MI 48045
586-783-6600x10; Cell: 586-530-3430
www.cashforyourboatnow.com
andy@southrivermarine.com

Broker/Dealer Directory

Starboard Yachts, Inc.
1111 Ottawa Beach Rd.
Holland, MI 49424
616-796-0505
www.starboardyachts.com
erob@starboardyachts.com
New Boat Sales, Brokerage

Minnesota

Watergate Marina Boat Sales
2500 Crosby Farm Rd.
St. Paul, MN 55116-2691
651-695-3780; Cell: 612-916-1171
www.watergatemarina.net
jason@watergatemarina.net
New Boat Sales, Brokerage, Service Yard

Yacht Brokers Inc.
PO Box 732
Stillwater, MN 55082-0732
612-430-9703
www.yachtbrokersinc.com
yachtbrokers@yahoo.com
Brokerage

Missouri

Lake Services Boat Brokerage
51 Anemone Ct.
Lake Ozark, MO 65049
lakeservices@charter.net

MarineMax
3070 Bagnell Dam Blvd
Lake Ozark, MO 65049-9741
573-365-5382

Ozark Yacht Brokers, Inc.
PO Box 40
Lake Ozark, MO 65049-0040
573-365-8100
www.ozarkyachts.com
sales@ozarkyachts.com
Brokerage

Safe Harbor Yacht Sales
6171 Highway V
St. Charles, MO 63301-5937
636-250-3500
www.safeharboryachts.com
jim@safeharboryachts.com

North Carolina

Bluewater Yacht Sales
10 Marina St, Pierhouse A5

Wrightsville Beach, NC 28480-1727
910-256-6643
JRiggs@BluewaterYachtSales.com

Cape Fear Docking Pilots, Inc.
23 Moore St.
Ocean Isle Beach, NC 28469
radar5@ec.rr.com

Dyson Yachts
4629 Terry Ln
Wilmington, NC 28405-2425
910-397-0267
jdyson@ec.rr.com

Magnum Marine
335 S. Belvedere Dr.
Hampstead, NC 28443
910-250-6087
Cell: 910-250-6087
gp163@aol.com
New Boat Sales, Brokerage

Morehead Yacht Sales
208 Arendell St.
Morehead City, NC 28557
252-726-6862
www.moreheadcityyachtbasin.com
littman@moreheadcityyachtbasin.com
Brokerage, Marina Facility

New Hampshire

Northeast Yachts
2456 Lafayette Rd
Portsmouth, NH 03801-5624
877-811-0205; Cell: 617-573-5345
www.neyachts.com
skipper@neyachts.com
New Boat Sales, Brokerage

New Jersey

Brightwater Yacht Brokers
311 Channel Dr.
Pt. Pleasant Beach, NJ 08742-2623
732-714-0500; Cell: 732-599-7646
www.brightwateryachts.com
brightwateryachts@comcast.net

Holiday Harbor Yacht Sales
115 Admiral Way
Waretown, NJ 08758-1902
609-693-7188
www.holidayharboryachtsales.com
hhys@verizon.net
Brokerage

Shore Point Yacht Sales
PO Box 440
Pine Beach, NJ 08741
732-920-9700
www.shorepointyachts.com
spys@comcast.net

Southwinds Harbour Yacht Sales
362 E. Lacey Rd.
Forked River, NJ 08731
609-693-9898
www.southwindsharbouryachtsales.com
jimp628@aim.com

New York

Babylon Marine
122 Wagstaff Lane
West Islip, NY 11795
631-587-0333
csbabylonmarina@optonline.net

Bay Watch Yachts
86 Orchard Beach Blvd
Port Washington, NY 11050-1427
516-767-6970
Cell: 516-946-0182
www.baywatchyachts.com
baywatchys@aol.com
Brokerage

Blue Water Boat Brokers
3 East Moriches Blvd
E. Moriches, NY 11940
631-567-0545
Cell: 631-495-0811
www.bluewaterboatbrokers.com
oak@bluewaterboatbrokers.com

Blue Water Yacht Club
1944 Bayberry Ave
Merrick, NY 11566-5502
516-623-5757
bluewaterandgary@cs.com

Brick Cove Marina & YS
PO Box 1172
Southold, NY 11971
866-354-7676
www.brickcove.com
bill@brickcove.com

Bruce Tait & Associates
PO Box 1928
Sag Harbor, NY 11963-0067
631-725-4222
info@taityachts.com

Broker/Dealer Directory

Long Island Marine Group
81 Fort Salonga Rd
Northport, NY 11768-2889
631-261-5464
www.yachtworld.com/limg
longislandmarine@aol.com

MarineMax
846 S. Wellwood Ave
Lindenhurst, NY 11757
chrissy.tackett@marinemax.com

Northeast Marine Group
PO Box 769
Coeymans, NY 12045
518-756-6111
captnc7@aol.com

RCR Yachts
PO Box 399
Youngstown, NY 14174-0399
716-745-3862; Cell: 716-695-4328
dbfinkle@aol.com
New Boat Sales, Brokerage, Service Yard

Ron Haege Yacht Sales
322 Lakeside Dr.
Mayfield, NY 12117
877-571-4885
rhaege@nycap.rr.com

Smith Boys Marine
280 Michigan St
North Tonawanda, NY 14120-6845
716-695-3472
smithboy@smithboys.com

Staten Island Yacht Sales
222 Mansion Ave
Staten Island, NY 10308-3409
718-984-7676
www.siyachts.com
bongiorno@siyachts.com

Westchester Yacht Sales
500 Rushmore Ave
Mamaroneck, NY 10543
914-844-4492
tom.schaub@westchesteryachtsales.com

World Maritime Exchange
24 Otter St.
Alexandria Bay, NY 13607-1803
315-482-6415; Cell: 315-303-5052
www.wmeyachts.com
berny@wmeyachts.com

Ohio

Catawba Moorings
2313 NE Catawba Rd
Port Clinton, OH 43452-3548
419-797-4775
www.catawbamoorings.com
cmi@cros.net

Marine Tech Concepts
145 SE Catawba Rd Ste A
Port Clinton, OH 43452
419-732-3355
Cell: 419-552-0080
www.marinetechconcepts.com
jeff@marinetechconcepts.com
New Boat Sales, Brokerage, Service Yard

National Liquidators
5401 N. Marginal Rd.
Cleveland, OH 44114
216-391-1900
www.yachtauctions.com
leonettid@natliq.com
Brokerage, Service Yard

South Shore Marine
PO Box 25
Huron, OH 44839-2247
419-433-5798
www.southshoremarine.com
ted@southshoremarine.com
New Boat Sales, Brokerage, Service Yard

Oregon

Hayden Island Yacht Center
50 NE Tomahawk Island Dr
Portland, OR 97217-7934
503-289-4007; Cell: 503-519-4234
rlaird6905@aol.com
New Boat Sales, Brokerage

Seaward Yacht Sales
303 NE Tomahawk Island Dr. Ste 2
Portland, OR 97217
503-224-2628
www.seawardyachtsales.com
info@seawardyachtsales.com

Puerto Rico

CFR Yacht Sales, Inc.
PO Box 16816
San Juan, PR 00908-0816
787-722-7088; Cell: 787-360-3370
www.cfryachts.com

carlosluis@cfryachtsales.com
New Boat Sales, Brokerage

South Carolina

Ashley Yachts
3 Lockwood Dr # 302B
Charleston, SC 29401-1100
843-577-7222
www.ashleyyachts.com
info@ashleyyachts.com
Brokerage

Berry-Boger Yacht Sales
PO Box 36
N. Myrtle Beach, SC 29597-0036
843-249-6167
www.bbyacht.com
jeff@bbyacht.com
Brokerage

Coastal Carolina Yacht Sales
145 Lockwood Dr.
Charleston, SC 29403
843-723-7557
Cell: 843-290-3939
maria@ccyachtsales.com

Low Country Yacht Sales
1144 Wyndham Rd
Charleston, SC 29412
843-452-1335
cptkk@aol.com

United Yacht Sales
830 Toler Dr.
Mt. Pleasant, SC 29464
843-814-1443
keithcallery@unitedyacht.com

Texas

Eisenhower Yacht Club
2141 Park Rd. # 20
Denison, TX 75020-7107
903-463-3999
eyc@eisenhoweryachtclub.com

Fox Yacht Sales
203 W Cotter Ave
Port Aransas, TX 78373-4035
361-749-4870
www.foxyachtsales.com
foxyachtsales@centurytel.net
New Boat Sales, Brokerage

Broker/Dealer Directory

Grandpappy Point Marina
132 Grandpappy Dr
Denison, TX 75020-2638
903-465-6330
www.grandpappy.com
gpmsales@grandpappy.com

Lone Star Yacht Sales
1500 Marina Bay Dr. Bldg 125 #3380
Clear Lake Shores, TX 77565
281-334-3500
www.lsyachts.com
jhedges@lsyachts.com
New Boat Sales, Brokerage

Texas Sportfishing Yacht Sales
2951 Marina Dr. Ste 130-463
League City, TX 77573
281-535-2628
www.texassportfishingyachts.com
txboats@quik.com

Washington

Anacortes Yacht Brokers/Charters
PO Box 69
Anacortes, WA 98221
360-293-4555
www.ayc.com
mike@ayc.com

Anchor Yacht Brokers
PO Box 480
LaConner, WA 98257
360-202-1648
captaingalen@yahoo.com

Breakwater Marina Yacht Sales
5603 N Waterfront Dr
Tacoma, WA 98407-6536
253-752-6663
www.breakwatermarina.com
yachtsales@breakwatermarina.com
Brokerage, Marina, Service Yard

Classic Yachts Inc.
PO Box 98964
Des Moines, WA 98198-0964
206-824-1200; Cell: 206-255-3469
www.classicyachtsinc.com
sdwilkes@yahoo.com
Brokerage

Wisconsin

Cal-Marine, Inc.
10884 N. Bay Shore Dr.
Sister Bay, WI 54234
920-854-4521
www.cal-marine.com
sales@cal-marinecom

Emerald Yacht-Ship Group
4930 Chester Lane #6
Racine, WI 53402
262-681-0600; Cell: 414-350-8505
www.emeraldyachtship.com
sales@emeraldyachtship.com
Brokerage

Harvey Yacht Sales
6018 Trillium Ln
Sturgeon Bay, WI 54235-9753
920-743-0980
tad@harveyyachtsales.com

Trawlers Midwest
425 Maritime Dr.
Manitowoc, WI 54220
920-894-2632
www.trawlersmidwest.com
trawlers@trawlersmidwest.com

Canada

Pacific Boat Brokers
#6 1025 Lee Rd.
Parksville, BC V9P2E1
360-332-9526
carl@pacificboatbrokers.com

Advance Yachts
12335 Rocky Point Rd.
Ladysmith, BC V9G 1K4
250-924-2628
www.advanceyachts.com
Brokerage, Marina

Crates Marine Sales
35 Front St. S. Ste 202
Mississauga, ON L5H2C6
905-990-3434
petsol@msn.com

Harris & Ellis Yachts
491 1000 Island Parkway
Lansdowne, ON K0E1L0
CANADA
grantandpat@harrisellis.com

McGregor on the Water
3331 MCClelland Rd. Box 60
Washago, ON L0K2B0
www.ontarioboats.com
mcgregoronthewater@rogers.com

Fraser Campbell
North South Nautical Group
28 Leverton Rd.
Ottawa, ON K2K3P7
613-270-8151
jfcampbell@rogers.com

Greg Heffering
Simcoe Yacht Sales
Unit 26 1111 Wilson Rd. North
Oshawa, ON L1G8C2
905-576-8288
pghsimcoe@rogers.com

Westwind Yacht Sales
Box 117
Port Severn, ON L0K1S0
705-528-9979; Cell: 705-528-9979
www.westwindyachtscanada.com
westwind@csolve.net
Brokerage

Section I:
Motoryachts & Trawlers

See index for complete list of models.

Motoryachts & Trawlers

www.powerboatguide.com   231-360-0827

Alaskan 53 Pilothouse
2000–05

Quality-built motoryacht with classic pilothouse styling appeals to owner/operators seeking versatility, comfort, security. Highlights include full teak interior with two roomy staterooms (most 53-footers have three), U-shaped galley with serving counter, covered walkways, dual pilothouse doors, Portuguese bridge, covered aft deck, roomy flybridge with dinghy storage, large cockpit lazarette. Bow thruster, granite counters were standard. Very well-organized engineroom. Cruise at 12 knots with 450hp Cats (around 16 knots top).

Length	53'0"	Fuel, Std.	800 gals.
Beam	15'3"	Fuel, Opt.	1,000 gals.
Draft	4'7"	Water	250 gals.
Weight	53,000#	Waste	100 gals.
Clearance	NA	Hull Type	Semi-Disp.

Insuficient Resale Data To Assign Values

Alaskan Yachts
Ft. Lauderdale, FL
www.alaskanyachts.com

---

www.powerboatguide.com   231-360-0827

Alaskan 60/64 Pilothouse
1998–Current

Popular pilothouse yacht with classic DeFever styling is designed for extended cruising in maximum comfort, security. Expansive three-stateroom teak interior includes midships master with private salon entry, VIP guest stateroom forward, home-size galley with breakfast bar, day head forward in salon. Stabilizers, granite counters, bow thruster are standard. Note Portuguese bridge, prop-protected keel. Alaskan 64 has slightly enlarged main salon, engineroom and cockpit. About 30 built to date. Cruise at 12–14 knots with 660hp Cats.

Length	64'0"	Fuel, Std.	1,300 gals.
Beam	17'2"	Fuel, Opt.	2,000 gals.
Draft	4'9"	Water	400 gals.
Weight	80,000#	Waste	100 gals.
Clearance	NA	Hull Type	Semi-Disp.

Insuficient Resale Data To Assign Values

Alaskan Yachts
Ft. Lauderdale, FL
www.alaskanyachts.com

---

www.powerboatguide.com   231-360-0827

Alaskan 65 Flushdeck
2000–Current

Handsome long-range motoryacht couples traditional pilothouse profile with elegant teak interior, seaworthy semi-displacement hull. Four-stateroom, three-head layout includes large pilothouse with dinette, gourmet galley with serving counter, spacious full-beam master, two VIP guest staterooms, ondeck day head, stand-up engine room, covered side decks, fishing cockpit, large swim platform. Stabilizers, granite counters, bow thruster are standard. Note Portuguese bridge, expansive foredeck. Cruise at 12–14 knots with 600hp Cats.

Length Overall	65'0"	Headroom	6'5"
Beam	17'2"	Fuel	1,300 gals.
Draft	4'9"	Water	400 gals.
Weight	80,000#	Waste	100 gals.
Clearance	NA	Hull Type	Semi-Disp.

Insuficient Resale Data To Assign Values

Alaskan Yachts
Ft. Lauderdale, FL
www.alaskanyachts.com

231-360-0827

Albin 34 Aft Cabin
1987–92

Small aft-cabin trawler/cruiser with standard diesel power combines versatility, economy, simplicity. Generous 11'6" beam allows for roomy cabin layout with teak trim, lower helm, fore and aft heads, L-shaped galley, wraparound dinette. Large cabin windows provide panoramic views. Note twin deck doors, integral swim platform, extended flybridge with ample seating. Tiny aft deck is useful mostly for line-handling. Single 250hp Cummins diesel (or twin 157hp Isuzus) cruise at 12 knots with top speed of 15–16 knots.

Length Overall	34'3"	Fuel	200 gals.
Length WL	30'6"	Water	70 gals.
Beam	11'6"	Waste	30 gals.
Draft	3'0"	Hull Type	Modified-V
Weight	16,500#	Deadrise Aft	NA

Prices Not Provided for Pre-1995 Models

Albin is no longer in business.

231-360-0827

Albin 36 Express Trawler
1999–2004

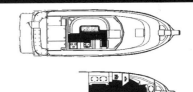

Handsome performance cruiser with trawler profile targets boaters looking for an affordable blend of speed, comfort, versatility. Space-efficient interior has guest stateroom to port with athwartships double berth extending under salon floor. U-shaped dinette can seat six. Good visibility from lower helm. Hardtop shades entire cockpit. Wide side decks are a plus. Reverse-slanted windshield reduces glare. Aft engineroom uses V-drives to deliver the power. Cruise at 12 knots with single 450hp Cat diesel; 16-18 knots with twin 330hp Cummins.

Length w/Pulpit	37 5"	Clearance	11'10"
Hull Length	36'0"	Fuel	380 gals.
Beam	12'9"	Water	120 gals.
Draft	3'3"	Hull Type	Modified-V
Weight	18,000#	Deadrise Aft	12°

See Page 530 For Resale Values

Albin is no longer in business.

231-360-0827

Albin 36 Trawler
1978–93

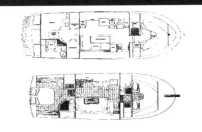

Classic Taiwan trawler with single-diesel power, traditional teak interior pairs sturdy construction with economical operation. Practical galley-up interior includes port and starboard deck doors, generous storage, teak parquet flooring, tub/shower in aft head. Flared bow keeps decks dry; full-length keel protects running gear from grounding. Lots of exterior bright work means lots of maintenance. Very popular boat—over were 500 built. Cruise at 7–8 knots with 120hp Lehman diesel; 9–10 knots with single 210hp Cummins.

Length Overall	35'9"	Clearance	12'4"
Length WL	31'3"	Fuel	350 gals.
Beam	13'2"	Water	220 gals.
Draft	3'6"	Waste	40 gals.
Weight	18,500#	Hull Type	Semi-Disp.

Prices Not Provided for Pre-1995 Models

Albin is no longer in business.

Motoryachts & Trawlers

www.powerboatguide.com | 231-360-0827

Albin 40 North Sea Cutter
2005–07

High-performance trawler combines unusual interior layout with traditional styling, good build quality. Open floorplan is arranged with owner's stateroom forward rather than aft. Versatile aft cabin with direct cockpit access, convertible U-shaped dinette can be used as a den/office or second stateroom. Generous galley storage is a plus. Note twin salon deck doors, planked cabin sole, wide side decks, large cockpit. Well-constructed boat is built to last. Yanmar 370hp diesels cruise at 20 knots (24–26 knots top).

Length	39'6"	Fuel	500 gals.
Beam	13'0"	Water	200 gals.
Draft	4'0"	Waste	40 gals.
Weight	25,000#	Hull Type	Modified-V
Clearance	NA	Deadrise Aft	NA

See Page 530 For Resale Values

Albin is no longer in business.

---

www.powerboatguide.com | 231-360-0827

Albin 40 Sundeck
1987–93

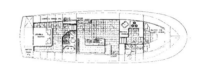

Conventional Taiwan-built trawler with full-beam aft cabin is sturdy, comfortable, economical to operate. Two-stateroom, galley-down interior includes lower helm, fold-down serving counter, parquet flooring, port/starboard deck doors, excellent storage. Teak interior woodwork is finished to high Asian standards. Flybridge seats six. Wide side decks, roomy aft deck are a plus. Good range. Full-length keel protects props, rudders from grounding. Cruise at 10 knots with twin 135hp Lehman diesels; 12 knots with 210hp Cummins diesels.

Length Overall	40'3"	Clearance	NA
Length WL	34'2"	Fuel	400 gals.
Beam	13'8"	Water	180 gals.
Draft	3'6"	Waste	50 gals.
Weight	26,000#	Hull Type	Semi-Disp.

Prices Not Provided for Pre-1995 Models

Albin is no longer in business.

---

www.powerboatguide.com | 231-360-0827

Albin 40 Trawler
1987–93

Traditional double-cabin trawler with walkaround decks gets high marks for interior volume, resale value. Two-stateroom, galley-down layout includes lower helm, fold-down serving counter, parquet flooring, twin deck doors. Teak woodwork is finished to high Asian standards. Aft stateroom has queen-size bed, head with tub/shower. Flybridge with facing settees seats six. Note simulated lapstrake hull lines. Keel protects props, rudders from grounding. Cruise at 10 knots with 135hp Lehmans; 12 knots 210hp Cummins diesels.

Length Overall	40'3"	Headroom	6'4"
Length WL	34'2"	Fuel	400 gals.
Beam	13'8"	Water	180 gals.
Draft	3'6"	Waste	50 gals.
Weight	26,000#	Hull Type	Semi-Disp.

Prices Not Provided for Pre-1995 Models

Albin is no longer in business.

231-360-0827

Albin 43 Sundeck
1981–94

Two-stateroom Interior

Optional three-stateroom Layout

Sturdy Taiwan trawler with full-beam aft stateroom makes the cut with cruising couples. Standard two-stateroom teak interior boasts lower helm, parquet flooring, twin salon deck doors, tub/shower in aft head. Note wide side decks, teak handrails, teak window frames, simulated lapstrake hull lines. Keel protects prop, running gear. Three-stateroom interior was optional. Salon lacks access door to sundeck—unusual in a trawler this size. Lehman 135hp diesels cruise at 8–9 knots; 210hp Cummins cruise at 12–14 knots.

Length Overall	42'6"	Headroom	6'5"
Length WL	37'11"	Fuel	500 gals.
Beam	14'6"	Water	300 gals.
Draft	4'1"	Waste	60 gals.
Weight	30,000#	Hull Type	Semi-Disp.

Prices Not Provided for Pre-1995 Models

Albin is no longer in business.

231-360-0827

Albin 43 Trawler
1979–94

Two-stateroom Interior

Optional three-stateroom layout

Traditional trunk-cabin trawler with walkaround decks targets buyers looking for interior comfort, cruising economy. Two-stateroom teak interior includes full lower helm, parquet flooring, twin salon deck doors, tub/shower in aft head. Note wide side decks, teak handrails, teak window frames, simulated lapstrake hull lines. Keel protects prop, running gear. Three-stateroom interior was optional. No rear salon door to aft deck—unusual in a trawler this size. Lehman 135hp diesels cruise at 8–9 knots; 210hp Cummins cruise at 12–14 knots.

Length Overall	42'6"	Headroom	6'5"
Length WL	37'11"	Fuel	500 gals.
Beam	14'6"	Water	300 gals.
Draft	4'1"	Waste	60 gals.
Weight	30,000#	Hull Type	Semi-Disp.

Prices Not Provided for Pre-1995 Models

Albin is no longer in business.

231-360-0827

American Tug 34
2001–Current

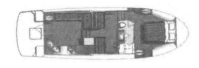

Fuel-efficient coastal cruiser with tug-like profile is built tough, loaded with practical features. Single-stateroom layout with ensuite head, full-beam salon with teak-planked flooring is well suited for cruising couples. Visibility from raised pilothouse is excellent. Side decks are wide with raised bulwarks for added security. Bow thruster is standard. Reversed windshield reduces glare. False stack creates unique raised area in forward salon overhead. Single Cummins 330hp diesel will cruise at 12-14 knots (about 16 knots top).

Length Overall	34 5"	Clearance	NA
Length WL	32'9"	Fuel	400 gals.
Beam	13'3"	Water	150 gals.
Draft	3 5"	Waste	45 gals.
Weight	20,000#	Hull Type	Semi-Disp.

See Page 530 For Resale Values

**American Tugs
LaConner, WA
www.americantugs.com**

Motoryachts & Trawlers

www.powerboatguide.com   231-360-0827

American Tug 41
2005–Current

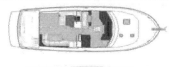

Stout pilothouse trawler with semi-displacement hull combines classic styling with solid construction, luxury-class accommodations. Wide beam results in roomy interior with two double staterooms, two full heads, full-beam salon with Ultraleather seating, U-shaped galley. Good visibility from raised pilothouse. Bow thruster is standard, flybridge is optional. Note underwater exhaust, deep cockpit. False stack creates unique raised area in forward salon overhead. Cruise at 12–14 knots with single 540hp Cummins diesel (about 16 knots top).

Length Overall	45'6"	Clearance	16'0"
Hull Length	37'9"	Fuel	640 gals.
Beam	15'10"	Water	210 gals.
Draft	4'10"	Waste	60 gals.
Weight	30,000#	Hull Type	Semi-Disp.

See Page 530 For Resale Values

American Tugs
LaConner, WA
www.americantugs.com

---

www.powerboatguide.com   231-360-0827

Atlantic 37 Double Cabin
1982–92

Prairie 36 Floorplan

Atlantic 37 Layout

Re-branded version of popular Prairie 36 Trawler (1979-81) earned an enviable reputation for quality construction, strong resale values. Compact two-stateroom interior boasts stall showers in both heads—a real plus in a boat this size. Teak woodwork is finished to high standards. Port and starboard deck doors provide good deck access. Spacious engineroom makes service easy. Keel protects prop and rudder. Cruise at 10 knots with twin 135hp diesels; 12 knots with twin 250hp diesels.

Length	36'7"	Headroom	6'5"
Beam	13'9"	Fuel	250 gals.
Draft	3'3"	Water	200 gals.
Weight	22,000#	Waste	Semi-Disp.30 gals.
Clearance, Mast	19'9"	Hull Type	Semi-Disp.

Prices Not Provided for Pre-1995 Models

No longer in business.

---

www.powerboatguide.com   231-360-0827

Atlantic 44 Motor Yacht
1977–92

Heavily built, Hargrave-designed cruising yacht with classic lines enjoys continued popularity of today's used-boat market. Several two-stateroom floorplans were offered. Highlights include wide side decks, full teak interior, spacious engineroom. Very fuel efficient with small diesels. Early models came with mast and boom assembly. Most were sold with optional hardtop. Above-average fit and finish throughout. Planing speeds of 18-19 knots are possible with Caterpillar 300 diesels.

Length Overall	43'8"	Clearance	13'8"
Length WL	38'6"	Water	240 gals.
Beam	14'0"	Fuel, Std.	320 gals.
Draft	3'5"	Fuel, Opt.	620 gals.
Weight	30,000#	Hull Type	Modified-V

Prices Not Provided for Pre-1995 Models

No longer in business.

Atlantic 47 Motor Yacht
1982–92

2-Stateroom Floorplan

3-Stateroom Floorplan

Premium Hargrave-designed motoryacht delivers time-tested mix of feature-rich accommodations, proven heavy-weather performance. Available with two- or three-stateroom floorplans—original three-cabin layout proved most popular. Lower helm position was standard. Note spacious aft deck dimensions, roomy master suite. Optional hard aft enclosure turned aft deck into fully enclosed second salon. Cat 375hp diesels cruise at 14–15 knots; 435hp GM diesels cruise at 16 knots. Originally marketed as the Prairie 46 LRC (1979–81).

Length	46'9"	Headroom	6 5"
Beam	16'0"	Fuel, Std.	400 gals.
Draft	3'9"	Fuel, Opt.	800 gals.
Weight	41,000#	Water	400 gals.
Clearance, Arch	18'0"	Hull Type	Modified-V

Prices Not Provided for Pre-1995 Models

No longer in business.

Azimut 39
1999–2005

Polished Italian cruising yacht with striking profile offers impressive display of stylish design, interior craftsmanship. Luxurious two-stateroom interior with cherry accents, wraparound salon windows is finished to very high standards. Corner posts obstruct visibility from lower helm. Teak decks, teak cockpit sole, low-profile radar arch, foredeck sun pad are standard. Tight engineroom is typical of Mediterranean yachts. Note modest fuel capacity. Cat—or Cummins—355hp diesels cruise at 26–28 knots (30+ knots top).

Length	39'10"	Water	132 gals.
Beam	13'3"	Clearance	12'0"
Draft	3 7"	Headroom	6'4"
Weight	22,000#	Hull Type	Modified-V
Fuel	264 gals.	Deadrise Aft	14.6°

See Page 530 For Resale Values

Azimut Yachts
Avigliana, Italy
www.azimutyachts.com

Azimut 42
1999–2005

Sleek flybridge cruiser is Italian styling at its best in midsize performance yacht. Interior highlights include spacious salon, two full heads, sunken galley, large master stateroom. Lower helm lacks chart space; helm seat is not adjustable. Engineroom, accessed from cockpit lazarette, is very tight. Note roomy cockpit with twin transom doors, well-placed handrails. Well-arranged bridge seats several guests in comfort. Excellent fit and finish. Agile and quick, 390hp Cat diesels cruise at 28 knots (32–33 knots top).

Length	43'4"	Fuel	317 gals.
Beam	13'6"	Water	132 gals.
Draft	3 5"	Headroom	6'4"
Weight	24,000#	Hull Type	Deep-V
Clearance	14'6"	Deadrise Aft	17°

See Page 530 For Resale Values

Azimut Yachts
Avigliana, Italy
www.azimutyachts.com

Azimut 43
1993–98

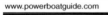

2-Stateroom Layout

3-Stateroom Layout

Early Azimut import seems conservative compared with recent high-style Azimut designs. Well-appointed galley-down interior with choice of two or three staterooms is an impressive display of Italian design and craftsmanship. Portside lower helm position is unusual—most lower helms are to starboard. Note bidet in master head. Additional features include huge flybridge sun pad, power side windows at lower helm, built-in cockpit seating, hull pockets. Tight engineroom, so-so lower helm visibility. Cat 435hp engines cruise at 23–24 knots (high 20s top).

Length	43'0"	Water	132 gals.
Beam	14'6"	Clearance	NA
Draft	3'4"	Headroom	6'5"
Weight	27,500#	Hull Type	Deep-V
Fuel	396 gals.	Deadrise Aft	19°

See Page 530 For Resale Values

Azimut Yachts
Avigliana, Italy
www.azimutyachts.com

Azimut 46
1997–2004

2-Stateroom Interior

3-Stateroom Interior

Elegant styling, impeccable workmanship make this Med cruiser a modern classic. Choice of two- or three-stateroom interiors. Ultra-stylish salon is surrounded by vast amounts of window space, beautiful high-gloss cherry woodwork. Galley is set below salon level where it's hidden from view. Uncomfortable lower helm position. Engineroom, accessed from cockpit lazarette, is a tight fit. Cat 435hp diesels cruise in low 20s (27–28 knots top); newer models with 505hp Cats top out at 30 knots. Very popular model—over 350 were sold.

Length	49'0"	Fuel	449 gals.
Beam	14'4"	Water	132 gals.
Draft	3'4"	Headroom	6'5"
Weight	27,000#	Hull Type	Deep-V
Clearance	NA	Deadrise Aft	18°

See Page 530 For Resale Values

Azimut Yachts
Avigliana, Italy
www.azimutyachts.com

Azimut 50
2004–08

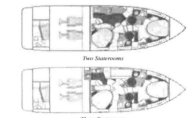

Two Staterooms

Three Staterooms

Leading-edge sportyacht with sweeping lines, distinctive shark-fin windows turns heads in every marina. Lavish two-stateroom interior (most 50-foot flybridge yachts have three) boasts exceptionally spacious salon. Lower helm is a work of art, but seating ergonomics are poor. Galley is big in the two-stateroom layout, small when optional third stateroom is added. Note large cockpit lazarette, extended swim platform, roomy engine compartment. MAN 660hp—or Cat 700hp—diesels cruise at 28 knots (30+ knots top).

Length	52'6"	Headroom	6'6"
Beam	14'11"	Fuel	581 gals.
Draft	3'11"	Water	132 gals.
Weight	40,344#	Hull Type	Modified-V
Clearance	18.5"	Deadrise Aft	13°

Insufficient Resale Data To Assign Values

Azimut Yachts
Avigliana, Italy
www.azimutyachts.com

Azimut 50/52
1996–2002

3 Staterooms, 2 Heads

3 Staterooms, 3 Heads

Powerful sportyacht with elliptical windows, sharply raked profile combines speed, luxury, performance. Posh three-stateroom interior with two or three heads includes small crew cabin beneath cockpit. Unlike many Azimuts, galley is open to salon rather than sunken. Ultra-low railings surrounding flybridge provide very little security. Note underwater exhausts, power vent windows. Engineroom is tight fit. Called Azimut 50 until 1998 when swim platform was extended. Cruise at 28 knots (low 30s top) with 660hp Cats.

Length	51'11"	Fuel	475 gals.
Beam	14'8"	Water	158 gals.
Draft	4'1"	Headroom	6 5"
Weight	38,000#	Hull Type	Deep-V
Clearance	NA	Deadrise Aft	18°

See Page 530 For Resale Values

Azimut Yachts
Avigliana, Italy
www.azimutyachts.com

Azimut 54/58
1993–2001

54 Layout

58 Layout

Distinctive flybridge yacht (called Azimut 54 until swim platform was extended in 1998) boasts timeless Italian styling, exceptional handling, lavish interior. Highlights include large cockpit with teak sole, aft crew quarters, twin transom walk-throughs to bathing platform. Spacious flybridge has two sun pads, wet bar, seating for a small crowd. Good engine access. Cruise at 23 knots with 600hp V-drive Cats (27–28 knots top); optional 765hp MTUs will cruise at a fast 28 knots (32–33 knots top). Over 150 were sold.

Length, 54	54 7"	Weight, 58	48,500#
Length, 58	57'8"	Fuel	688 gals.
Beam	15'1"	Water	238 gals.
Draft	4'1"	Hull Type	Deep-V
Weight, 54	44,092#	Deadrise Aft	18°

See Page 531 For Resale Values

Azimut Yachts
Avigliana, Italy
www.azimutyachts.com

Azimut 55
2001–05

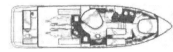

Italian masterwork is a sophisticated blend of yachting style, substance. Huge salon with swivel tables, circular seating, central bar unit is far more spacious than other yachts in her class. (Few other aft-cockpit 55-footers have a full-beam owner's cabin.) Highlights include distinctive shark-fin styling, ergonomic lower helm, good engineroom access. Aft crew quarters sleep a single adult. Extended swim platform can stow small tender. Note stylish flybridge with posh lounge seating. Cat 710hp engines cruise in the mid 20s (about 28 knots top).

Length	57 5"	Fuel	665 gals.
Beam	15 7"	Water	169 gals.
Draft	4'0"	Headroom	6 5"
Weight	44,600#	Hull Type	Deep-V
Clearance	16'2"	Deadrise Aft	16.6°

See Page 531 For Resale Values

Azimut Yachts
Avigliana, Italy
www.azimutyachts.com

Motoryachts & Trawlers

231-360-0827

Azimut 62 Flybridge
2003–06

Beautifully styled luxury yacht introduced in 2003 raised the bar for sex appeal, big-boat performance. Expansive salon/dinette/helm area with posh furnishings, high-gloss cherry cabinetry dominates spacious three-stateroom interior. Highlights include opulent master suite with elliptical hull ports, well-executed lower helm, large flybridge with dinghy stowage. Note foredeck, flybridge sun pads. Large engineroom—rare in a European yacht—is a plus. Cat 1,150hp diesels cruise at 28–30 knots (about 32 knots wide open).

Length	65'1"	Fuel	898 gals.
Beam	16.5'	Water	265 gals.
Draft	4'6"	Max Headroom	6'10"
Weight	60,400#	Hull Type	Deep-V
Clearance	19'9"	Deadrise Aft	17°

Insufficient Resale Data To Assign Values

Azimut Yachts
Avigliana, Italy
www.azimutyachts.com

231-360-0827

Bayliner 3587 Motor Yacht
1995–99

Contemporary aft-cabin motoryacht broke new ground for midsize cruisers with innovative three-stateroom interior. In addition to standard fore, aft staterooms, small midcabin sleeping area is located under salon dinette. Compact salon is arranged with galley aft, standard lower helm. Awkward three-door configuration provides access to forward head and staterooms. Engineroom is a tight fit. Hardtop was a popular option. MerCruiser 310hp gas inboards cruise at 18 knots and deliver 26–27 knots top.

Length Overall	37'3"	Fuel	220 gals.
Hull Length	34'8"	Water	77 gals.
Beam	13'1"	Waste	68 gals.
Draft	3'9"	Hull Type	Modified-V
Weight	22,000#	Deadrise Aft	10°

See Page 531 For Resale Values

Bayliner Boats
Arlington, WA
www.bayliner.com

231-360-0827

Bayliner 3688 Motor Yacht
1992–94

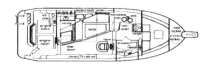

Rakish styling, low price, innovative interior set this early-1990s cruiser apart from the pack. Narrow staircase just inside salon door descends to private cabin with partial standing headroom, cabinet, and sink. Salon—with raised dinette, standard lower helm—is small for a 36-foot boat. Forward stateroom privacy is limited to just a curtain; absence of stall shower in head is notable. Bow pulpit, radar arch, transom door, fender rack were standard. Twin 200hp V-drive diesels cruise at 15 knots, top out at 17–18 knots.

Length	36'1"	Fuel	250 gals.
Beam	12'2"	Water	96 gals.
Draft	2'11"	Waste	23 gals.
Weight	13,700#	Hull Type	Modified-V
Clearance	13'10"	Deadrise Aft	14°

Prices Not Provided for Pre-1995 Models

Bayliner Boats
Arlington, WA
www.bayliner.com

Bayliner 3788 Motor Yacht
1996–99

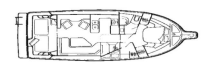

Popular 1990s flybridge cruiser offered crisp styling, family-friendly accommodations at affordable price. Spacious interior is arranged with salon-level galley, midcabin berth with hanging locker, bow stateroom with privacy door, head with tub/shower. Additional features include cockpit sink, roomy engineroom, transom door, swim platform, radar arch, bow pulpit. MerCruiser 310hp gas inboards cruise at 18 knots (27–28 knots top); 250hp Cummins diesels cruise at 20 knots and top out at 23–24 knots. Updated 3788 model came out in 2001.

Length	38'6"	Water	100 gals.
Beam	13'4"	Waste	30 gals.
Draft	2'11"	Headroom	6'5"
Weight	20,000#	Hull Type	Modified-V
Fuel	250 gals.	Deadrise Aft	10°

See Page 531 For Resale Values

Bayliner Boats
Arlington, WA
www.bayliner.com

Bayliner 3788 Motor Yacht
2001–02

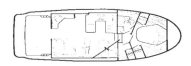

Updated version of the original Bayliner 3788 MY (above) with refined styling, updated interior made a good boat even better. Wide-open salon with dinette and galley forward offers lots of usable space, good overall finish. Both staterooms have double berths. Tub/shower is fitted in head compartment. Molded steps make bridge access easy and safe. Swim platform, transom door, radar arch were standard. MerCruiser 310hp gas inboards cruise at 17–18 knots; 330hp Cummins diesels cruise at 20 knots.

Length	39'4"	Water	125 gals.
Beam	13'7"	Waste	36 gals.
Draft	3'4"	Headroom	6'5"
Weight	22,274#	Hull Type	Modified-V
Fuel	300 gals.	Deadrise Aft	7.5°

See Page 531 For Resale Values

Bayliner Boats
Arlington, WA
www.bayliner.com

Bayliner 3870/3888 Motor Yacht
1983–94

Super-popular diesel cruiser (called Bayliner 3870 MY in 1983-89) offered buyers remarkable comfort, economy at surprisingly affordable price. Boxy profile conceals expansive interior with innovative midcabin floorplan. Master stateroom is very spacious. Lower helm was standard. Fuel economy at cruise is an impressive 1 mpg. Engine room is tight. Over 1,000 built. Early models with twin 135hp diesels cruise at 10 knots; later models with 210hp Hino diesels cruise at16 knots.

Length	38'2"	Fuel	304 gals.
Beam	13'5"	Water	80 gals.
Draft	3'2"	Waste	40 gals.
Weight	17,500#	Hull Type	Modified-V
Clearance	14'10"	Deadrise Aft	6°

Prices Not Provided for Pre-1995 Models

Bayliner Boats
Arlington, WA
www.bayliner.com

Motoryachts & Trawlers

231-360-0827

Bayliner 3988 Motor Yacht
1995–2002

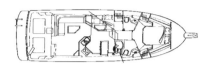

Feature-rich motoryacht enjoys continued popularity thanks to spacious interior, affordable price. Two-stateroom, two-head floorplan includes standard lower helm station, spacious U-shaped galley, comfortable L-shaped settee. Large cabin windows provide excellent natural lighting. Note teak-and-holly galley floor, bathtub in starboard head, foredeck sun lounge. Cummins 250hp diesels cruise at 20 knots (23–24 knots top); Cummins 330hp Cummins engines cruise at 24 knots (high 20s top).

Length w/Pulpit	46'3"	Fuel	298 gals.
Hull Length	39'0"	Water	100 gals.
Beam	14'1"	Waste	36 gals.
Draft	3'3"	Hull Type	Modified-V
Weight	21,000#	Deadrise Aft	10°

See Page 531 For Resale Values

Bayliner Boats
Arlington, WA
www.bayliner.com

231-360-0827

Bayliner 4087 Cockpit MY
1997–2001

Cockpit version of Bayliner 3587 MY boasts sporty lines, innovative three-stateroom interior. In addition to roomy fore and aft staterooms, small midcabin is located under salon dinette. Compact salon is arranged with galley aft, standard lower helm. Note spacious aft deck with hardtop, wet bar. Flybridge seats four aft of helm. Bow pulpit, swim platform were standard; hardtop, radar arch were popular options. MerCruiser 310hp gas inboards cruise at 18 knots (26–27 knots top); Cummins 270hp diesels cruise at 20 knots.

Length Overall	41 5"	Water	77 gals.
Beam	13'1"	Waste	68 gals.
Draft	3'9"	Clearance	15 5"
Weight	24,000#	Hull Type	Modified-V
Fuel	220 gals.	Deadrise Aft	10°

See Page 532 For Resale Values

Bayliner Boats
Arlington, WA
www.bayliner.com

231-360-0827

Bayliner 4387 Aft Cabin MY
1990–93

Affordable double-cabin motoryacht with roomy interior, large aft deck was considered a lot of boat for the money in her day. Two-stateroom floorplan is arranged with galley and dinette down, standard lower helm, salon entertainment center. Both staterooms have diagonal double berths to save space. Cheap interior furnishings, so-so fit and finish. Lightweight hull is a hard ride in a chop. Standard 330hp gas engines cruise at 16 knots (mid 20s top); 250hp Hino diesels cruise at 18–19 knots (about 24 knots top).

Length	43'1"	Fuel	300 gals.
Beam	14'3"	Water	100 gals.
Draft	3'0"	Waste	74 gals.
Weight	20,000#	Hull Type	Modified-V
Clearance	13'6"	Deadrise Aft	14°

Prices Not Provided for Pre-1995 Models

Bayliner Boats
Arlington, WA
www.bayliner.com

231-360-0827

Bayliner 4388 Motor Yacht
1991–94

Low-priced 1990s flybridge yacht with spacious mid-cabin interior is well-suited to coastal cruising, dockside entertaining. Large salon offers full 360-degree visibility, extensive lounge seating, wet bar, lower helm station. Mid stateroom with partial standing headroom extends under galley. Note common shower stall between both heads. Transom door, shower, bench seat were standard in cockpit. Small fuel capacity limits cruising range. Twin Hino 250hp V-drive diesels cruise at 19 knots and (24–25 knots top).

Length	43'1"	Fuel	300 gals.
Beam	14'3"	Water	100 gals.
Draft	3'0"	Waste	46 gals.
Weight	19,000#	Hull Type	Modified-V
Clearance	13'6"	Deadrise Aft	14°

Prices Not Provided for Pre-1995 Models

Bayliner Boats
Arlington, WA
www.bayliner.com

231-360-0827

Bayliner 4550/4588 Pilothouse MY
1984–93

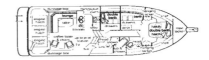

Popular all-weather pilothouse yacht introduced in 1984 remains the best-selling 45-foot yacht ever produced. Spacious layout includes two VIP staterooms, third stateroom/office adjacent to master suite, roomy salon/galley area, raised pilothouse with excellent helm visibility. Both heads share common tub/shower. Extended hardtop shelters cockpit where hatches provide access to compact engineroom. Efficient Hino 220hp (or 250hp) diesels cruise at 15 knots burning 1 mile per gallon. Nearly 400 were built.

Length	45'4"	Fuel	444 gals.
Beam	14'11"	Water	200 gals.
Draft	3'0"	Waste	48 gals.
Weight	28,000#	Hull Type	Modified-V
Clearance	15'6"	Deadrise Aft	6°

Prices Not Provided for Pre-1995 Models

Bayliner Boats
Arlington, WA
www.bayliner.com

231-360-0827

Bayliner 4587 Cockpit MY
1994–95

Cockpit version of Bayliner's 4387 Aft Cabin MY combined versatile deck plan with comfortable layout, economical operation. Prop pockets used on 4387 were eliminated and a spray rail was added for a drier ride, but in most other respects the two boats are very similar. Two-stateroom floorplan is arranged with the galley and dinette down. No shower stall in forward guest head. Large salon windows provide excellent lower helm visibility. Small engineroom, modest fuel capacity. Hino 250hp diesels cruise at 18–19 knots (about 25 knots top).

Length	45'1"	Cockpit	NA
Beam	14'3"	Water	100 gals.
Draft	3'0"	Fuel	300 gals.
Weight	22,000#	Hull Type	Modified-V
Clearance	14'0"	Deadrise Aft	14°

See Page 532 For Resale Values

Bayliner Boats
Arlington, WA
www.bayliner.com

Motoryachts & Trawlers

231-360-0827

Bayliner 4788 Pilothouse MY
1994–2002

Slightly restyled, lengthened version of Bayliner 4550/4588 Pilothouse remains one of the most in-demand used models her size on the market. Efficient two-stateroom floorplan with third stateroom/dressing area is tough to beat. Increased hull length is seen in larger galley and salon dimensions. Excellent lower helm visibility; both heads share common tub/shower. Extended hardtop shelters cockpit. Early models with 315hp Hino diesels cruise at 18 knots; later models with 370hp Cummins diesels cruise at 20–21 knots.

Length w/Pulpit	54'0"	Fuel	444 gals.
Hull Length	47'4"	Water	200 gals.
Beam	15'1"	Waste	48 gals.
Draft	3'4"	Hull Type	Modified-V
Weight	29,990#	Deadrise Aft	6°

See Page 532 For Resale Values

Bayliner Boats
Arlington, WA
www.bayliner.com

231-360-0827

Bayliner 5288 Pilothouse MY
1999–2002

Handsome pilothouse yacht for all-weather cruising offered solid value at reasonable price. Highlights include fully cored hull, spacious three-stateroom layout with full-beam master, large cockpit, generous side decks. Open salon/galley is ideal for entertaining. Spacious flybridge can seat a small crowd. Additional highlights include washer/dryer in third stateroom, large engineroom, underwater exhausts, dinghy davit, tub/shower in owner's head. Cruise at 20 knots with 600hp MANs (24–25 knots top).

Length w/Platform	56'0"	Fuel	700 gals.
Beam	16'3"	Water	200 gals.
Draft	4'10"	Waste	73 gals.
Weight	47,560#	Hull Type	Modified-V
Clearance	19'3"	Deadrise Aft	12°

See Page 532 For Resale Values

Bayliner Boats
Arlington, WA
www.bayliner.com

231-360-0827

Bayliner 5788 Motor Yacht
1997–2002

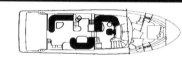

Feature-packed pilothouse yacht gets high marks for comfort, value. Spacious three-stateroom interior includes two big sleeping cabins, superb galley with plenty of workspace, full-beam salon. Owner's stateroom has walk-in wardrobe, home-size bath with tub/shower. Excellent visibility from both helm stations. Surprisingly good fit and finish considering the low price. Note huge salon windows, narrow side decks, pilothouse deck doors, spacious engineroom. MAN 610hp diesels cruise at 20 knots (23–24 knots top).

Length	59'4"	Fuel	800 gals.
Beam	17'2"	Water	222 gals.
Draft	4'11"	Waste	76 gals.
Weight	49,000#	Hull Type	Modified-V
Clearance, Arch	19'7"	Deadrise Aft	10°

See Page 532 For Resale Values

Bayliner Boats
Arlington, WA
www.bayliner.com

Beneteau 42 Swift Trawler
2004–Current

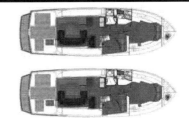

French-built cruiser with high-performance hull, sporty Europa styling is fast, priced right, easy on the eye. Well-appointed interior with varnished woodwork includes two double staterooms, two heads, two deck doors, convertible salon settee. Not much storage in master cabin. Excellent helm visibility. Teak decks, transom door, bow pulpit are standard. Note protected sidedecks, good engine access, hullside boarding gate. Early models had a single head. Yanmar 370hp diesels cruise at 18–20 knots (mid 20s top).

Length Overall	44'3"	Fuel	395 gals.
Length WL	37 5"	Water	169 gals.
Beam	13'11"	Waste	24 gals.
Draft	3 5"	Hull Type	Modified-V
Weight	22,000#	Deadrise Aft	12°

See Page 532 For Resale Values

Beneteau USA
Marion, SC
www.beneteauusa.com

Bertram 42 Motor Yacht
1973–87

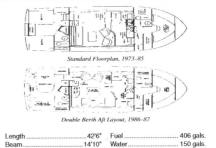

Standard Floorplan, 1973–85

Double Berth Aft Layout, 1986–87

Traditional flush-deck motoryacht introduced in 1973 gets high marks for build quality, ride comfort, lasting popularity. Unusual floorplan layout has mid-level galley forward, companionway to starboard. Teak interior replaced original mica woodwork in 1983; queen berth replaced the single beds in master stateroom in 1986. Excellent visibility from semi-enclosed lower helm. Note small, old-style flybridge. GM 335hp 6-71 diesels cruise at 16 knots (18–19 knots top); GM 435hp 6V71 diesels cruise at 20 knots (24 knots top).

Length	42'6"	Fuel	406 gals.
Beam	14'10"	Water	150 gals.
Draft	4'0"	Waste	60 gals.
Weight	39,000#	Hull Type	Deep-V
Clearance	17'11"	Deadrise Aft	17°

Prices Not Provided for Pre-1995 Models

Bertram Yacht
Miami, FL
www.bertram.com

Bertram 46 Motor Yacht
1973–87

Twin Berths Aft, 1973–85

Double Berth Aft, 1986–87

Traditional flush-deck motoryacht introduced in 1973 appealed to buyers with an eye for solid construction, roomy accommodations, exceptional seakeeping qualities. Built on proven deep-V hull used in production of original Bertram 46 Convertible. Two-stateroom interior features spacious salon with galley and dinette down, tub/shower in aft head. Good visibility from both helm positions. Note large aft deck, small flybridge. Cruise at 19–20 knots with 435hp 8V71 diesels; 22 knots with 570hp 8V92s offered after 1982.

Length	46'6"	Fuel	615 gals.
Beam	16'0"	Water	230 gals.
Draft	4'8"	Waste	50 gals.
Weight	45,600#	Hull Type	Deep-V
Clearance	18'8"	Deadrise Aft	19°

Prices Not Provided for Pre-1995 Models

Bertram Yacht
Miami, FL
www.bertram.com

Motoryachts & Trawlers

Bertram 58 Motor Yacht
1976–86

Heavily built flushdeck cruiser introduced 30 years ago set high standards for motoryacht design, construction. Original three-stateroom floorplan with home-size galley, huge master suite remained unchanged during her decade in production. Highlights include spacious aft deck platform, tub/shower in aft head, molded foredeck seating, wide side decks, good range. Bridge is tiny compared with modern motoryachts. Good lower-helm visibility. Standard GM 12V71 diesels (650hp/675hp) cruise at 18 knots (21–22 knots top).

Length	58'3"	Fuel	1,250 gals.
Beam	17'11"	Water	275 gals.
Draft	5'4"	Headroom	6'6"
Weight	87,500#	Hull Type	Modified-V
Clearance	18'0"	Deadrise Aft	15°

Prices Not Provided for Pre-1995 Models

Bertram Yacht
Miami, FL
www.bertram.com

Bristol 42 Trawler
1969–81

Classic (and still popular) Eldridge-McInnis design with full-displacement hull combines rich teak interior with timeless trawler styling. Several two-stateroom layouts were offered, all with deckhouse galley, teak-planked flooring, twin salon deck access doors. Salon seems large for a boat this size. Teak-over-fiberglass decks were standard. Note functional mast and boom. Soft-chined hull offers secure open-water ride. Deep keel protects running gear. Built for Bristol Yachts in India. Twin Perkins 130hp diesels cruise efficiently at 8–9 knots.

Length Overall	41'6"	Clearance	NA
Length WL	38'6"	Fuel	500 gals.
Beam	13'6"	Water	250 gals.
Draft	4'0"	Waste	40 gals
Weight	29,000#	Hull Type	Displacement

Prices Not Provided for Pre-1995 Models

No longer in production

Californian 34 LRC
1977–84

Two-stateroom Floorplan

Single-Stateroom Floorplan

Popular sedan cruiser with trawler styling combined planing-speed performance with versatile deck layout, low-cost operation. Well-finished interior was available with single- or twin-stateroom floorplans, both with standard lower helm. Highlights include mahogany interior cabinetry, head with stall shower, wide side decks, roomy cockpit. Note that two-stateroom layouts are rare on a 34-footer. Perkins 85hp diesels cruise at 7 knots; optional 210hp Cat (or 200hp Perkins) diesels cruise at 16-18 knots (20+ knots wide open).

Length	34'6"	Fuel	250 gals.
Beam	12'4"	Water	75 gals.
Draft	3'2"	Waste	30 gals.
Weight	18,000#	Hull Type	Modified-V
Clearance	10'8"	Deadrise Aft	NA

Prices Not Provided for Pre-1995 Models

No longer in business.

Californian 35 Motor Yacht
1985–87

Small aft-cabin motoryacht from 1980s was comfortable, stylish, built to last. Compact two-stateroom interior includes comfortable salon, galley and dinette down, stall shower in each head. Note twin double beds in aft stateroom. Additional features include integral bow pulpit, wide side decks, radar arch, swim platform. Lower helm, hardtop were optional. Above-average fit and finish. Standard gas engines cruise at 17–18 knots; optional 210hp Cat diesels cruise at 16 knots and reach 20 knots wide open.

Length	34'11"	Water	75 gals.
Beam	12'4"	Fuel	270 gals.
Draft	3'2"	Waste	40 gals.
Weight	19,000#	Hull Type	Modified-V
Clearance	NA	Deadrise Aft	15°

Prices Not Provided for Pre-1995 Models

No longer in business.

Californian 38 LRC Sedan
1980–84

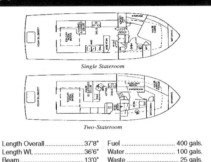

Single Stateroom

Two-Stateroom

This well-built sedan may look like a trawler on the outside, but her modified-V hull provides true planing-speed performance. Single- and twin-stateroom mahogany floorplans were offered, both galley-up layouts with a convertible settee in the salon, lower helm with deck access door, large head with separate stall shower. Cockpit is big enough for fishing. Note wide side decks, teak bow pulpit. Small engineroom. Good lower helm visibility. Cruise at 12 knots with twin 210hp Cat diesels; 1–20 knots with 300hp Cats.

Length Overall	37'8"	Fuel	400 gals.
Length WL	36'6"	Water	100 gals.
Beam	13'0"	Waste	25 gals.
Draft	3'6"	Hull Type	Modified-V
Weight	28,000#	Deadrise Aft	NA

Prices Not Provided for Pre-1995 Models

No longer in business.

Californian 38 Motor Yacht
1983–87

Galley Up

Galley Down

Handsome aft-cabin motoryacht with many appealing features has held her value well over the years. Highlights include dark mahogany interior paneling, lower helm station with deck door, upright refrigerator, stall showers in both heads. Large master stateroom for a 38-footer with vanity, generous stowage. Note spacious aft deck. Bow pulpit, radar arch, teak handrails, swim platform were standard. Hardtop was a popular option. Twin 210hp Cat diesels will cruise at 12 knots; 300hp turbo-Cats cruise at 18–20 knots.

Length Overall	37'8"	Clearance	14'6"
Length WL	36'6"	Fuel	365 gals.
Beam	13'0"	Water	100 gals.
Draft	3'6"	Hull Type	Modified-V
Weight	28,000#	Deadrise Aft	NA

Prices Not Provided for Pre-1995 Models

No longer in business.

231-360-0827

Californian 39 SL
1999–2003

Sturdy west coast cruiser (built by Navigator Yachts) is notable for conservative styling, comfortable ride, affordable price. Innovative interior plan has dinette centered on pilothouse level, next to the helm. Bi-level galley extends into the pilothouse making it somewhat awkward to use. Both staterooms are fitted with double berths, both heads have enclosed showers. Lower helm visibility is excellent. Note flybridge dinghy stowage. Radar arch, transom door were standard. Volvo 318hp diesels cruise at 20 knots (23–24 knots wide open).

Length	39'0"	Headroom	6 5"
Beam	15'0"	Fuel	250 gals.
Draft	4'4"	Water	100 gals.
Weight	27,500#	Cockpit	60 sq. ft.
Clearance	NA	Hull Type	Modified-V

See Page 534 For Resale Values

Navigator Yachts
Parris, CA
www.navigatoryachts.com

231-360-0827

Californian 42 LRC
1975–84

Good-selling performance trawler (over 200 were built) combines solid construction with traditional styling, comfortable accommodations. Standard two-stateroom, galley-up mahogany interior with two full heads includes roomy aft cabin with two double beds and cockpit access door. Forward stateroom was offered with doubleberth or over/under bunks. Large cockpit is a plus. Note tub/shower in aft head. Slender hull is very fuel-efficient. Cruise at 10 knots with 185hp Perkins diesels; 12 knots with 210hp Cats.

Length	41'8"	Fuel	500 gals.
Beam	13'8"	Water	175 gals.
Draft	3'4"	Waste	50 gals.
Weight	31,000#	Hull Type	Modified-V
Clearance	NA	Deadrise Aft	NA

Prices Not Provided for Pre-1995 Models

No longer in business.

231-360-0827

Californian 42 Motor Yacht
1986–87

Well-built flybridge yacht from mid 1980s still appeals to knowledgeable boaters with an eye for quality. Comfortable two-stateroom teak (or mahogany) interior features large salon with entertainment center, fully equipped galley, well-appointed master with dresser. Space for washer/dryer in forward stateroom. Lower helm was a popular option; big U-shaped dinette seats six. Wet bar, wing doors, hardtop, bow pulpit, swim platform were standard. Cruise at 16–18 knots with 375hp Cat diesels (around 20 knots top).

Length w/Pulpit	45'8"	Fuel	400 gals.
Beam	15'2"	Water	190 gals.
Draft	4'3"	Waste	60 gals.
Weight	38,000#	Hull Type	Modified-V
Clearance	13'6"	Deadrise Aft	15°

Prices Not Provided for Pre-1995 Models

No longer in business.

Californian 43 Cockpit MY
1983—87

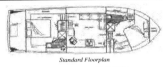

Standard Floorplan

Optional Floorplan

Popular cockpit motoryacht received high marks in her day for quality construction, practical accommodations, good handling qualities. Standard layout had galley up with huge forward stateroom; optional galley-down floorplan opens up salon at expense of smaller bow stateroom. Features include lower station with deck door, large master stateroom, spacious aft deck, full-beam bridge. Hardtop was a popular option. Cat 210 diesels cruise at 10 knots; 300hp Cats cruise at 14 knots (16–17 knots top).

Length Overall	43'8"	Clearance	14'6"
Length WL	NA	Fuel	400 gals.
Beam	13'3"	Water	140 gals.
Draft	3'6"	Hull Type	Modified-V
Weight	32,000#	Deadrise Aft	NA

Prices Not Provided for Pre-1995 Models

No longer in business.

Californian 45 Motor Yacht
1988—91

Over/Under Bunks Forward

Island Berth Forward

Late-model motoryacht came with full array of features, amenities at a reasonable price. Available with two floorplan configurations: one with over/under berths in forward stateroom, the other with island double berth forward. Lower helm was optional; both heads have separate stall showers. Hardtop, aft-deck enclosure panels, bow pulpit were standard. Above-average fit and finish. Slender modified-V hull is easily driven, dry in a chop. Cruise at 16–18 knots with 375hp Cat diesels (about 20 knots top).

Length	45'0"	Fuel	400 gals.
Beam	15'2"	Water	190 gals.
Draft	4'0"	Waste	70 gals.
Weight	40,000#	Hull Type	Modified-V
Clearance, Arch	17'3"	Deadrise Aft	15°

Prices Not Provided for Pre-1995 Models

No longer in business.

Californian 48 Cockpit MY
1986—89

Over/Under Bunks Forward

Island Berth Forward

Quality construction, well-appointed accommodations, comfortable ride have kept this 1980s cockpit yacht popular on the used markets. Galley-down floorplan came with choice of forward stateroom configurations. Interior woodwork updated from walnut to teak in 1988. Cockpit has a transom door as well as door to aft stateroom—a convenience many cockpit yachts fail to provide. Hardtop, radar arch, swim platform, bow pulpit were standard. Twin 375hp Cat diesels will cruise at 16–17 knots (about 20 knots top).

Length	48'5"	Fuel	500 gals.
Beam	15'2"	Water	190 gals.
Draft	4'8"	Waste	70 gals.
Weight	41,000#	Hull Type	Modified-V
Clearance, Arch	16'3"	Deadrise Aft	15°

Prices Not Provided for Pre-1995 Models

No longer in business.

Motoryachts & Trawlers

Californian 48 Motor Yacht
1985–91

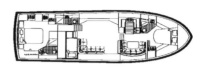

Quality flush-deck yacht was one of Californian's most popular models in late 1980s. Big interior for a 48-footer—slide-out settee in small guest stateroom aft of salon converts into double berth; all three heads have separate stall showers. Relatively narrow beam results in modest salon dimensions. Huge afterdeck is a great entertainment center. Excellent ride; above-average fit and finish. Cruise at 15–16 knots with 375hp Cat diesels; 18 knots with 485hp GM 6-71s. Clean used models are always in demand.

Length	48'5"	Fuel	560 gals.
Beam	15'2"	Water	210 gals.
Draft	4'8"	Waste	165 gals.
Weight	43,000#	Hull Type	Modified-V
Clearance, Arch	17'3"	Deadrise Aft	15°

Prices Not Provided for Pre-1995 Models

No longer in business.

Californian 52 Cockpit MY
89–91

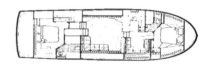

Handsome cockpit motoryacht came with full array of cruising amenities at a reasonable price. Interior highlights include handsome teak cabinetry, two large staterooms, full dinette, built-in washer/dryer, salon entertainment center, generous storage. Lower helm station was optional. Cockpit has transom door, access door to master stateroom. Note standard hardtop and radar arch. Modified-V hull delivers a comfortable rough-water ride. Cruise at 15–16 knots with 375hp Cat diesels (about 18 knots top).

Length Overall	51'11"	Fuel	747 gals.
Beam	15'2"	Water	185 gals.
Draft	4'5"	Waste	60 gals.
Weight	44,200#	Hull Type	Modified-V
Clearance, Arch	17'3"	Deadrise Aft	15°

Prices Not Provided for Pre-1995 Models

No longer in business.

Californian 55 Cockpit MY
1986–91

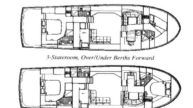

3-Stateroom, Over/Under Berths Forward

3-Stateroom, Island Berth Forward

Quality-built cockpit yacht is highly regarded by knowledgeable boaters for her classic profile, elegant accommodations, comfortable ride. Big interior for 55-footer—slide-out settee in small guest stateroom aft of salon converts into double berth; all three heads have separate stall showers. Relatively narrow beam results in modest salon dimensions. Large aft deck can seat a small crowd. Cruise at 18 knots with 485hp GM 6-71 diesels; 20+ knots with 550hp GM 6V92s. Popular boat—about 40 were built.

Length Overall	54'6"	Fuel	650 gals.
Beam	15'2"	Water	210 gals.
Draft	4'3"	Waste	80 gals.
Weight	46,200#	Hull Type	Modified-V
Clearance, Arch	17'3"	Deadrise Aft	15°

Prices Not Provided for Pre-1995 Models

No longer in business.

Camano 28/31
1990–Current

Popular Canadian cruiser (called Camano 28 in 1990–2002) is salty, efficient, surprisingly spacious. Highlights include large flybridge, well-crafted interior, wide side decks, roomy cockpit with transom door, good storage. Distinctive trolley-style windows provide panoramic outside views. Fuel capacity was increased in 2003. Bow thruster is standard. Full keel protects running gear against grounding. Bridge ladder is very steep. Single 150hp Volvo diesel will cruise at 12 knots (16–17 knots top); 200hp Volvo runs a little faster. Not inexpensive.

Length w/Pulpit	31'0"	Clearance	NA
Hull Length	28'0"	Fuel	100/133 gals.
Beam	10'6"	Water	77 gals.
Draft	3'3"	Waste	12 gals.
Weight	10,000#	Hull Type	Semi-Disp.

See Page 534 For Resale Values

Camano Marine
Delta, BC (Canada)
www.camanomarine.com

Camano 41
2006–Current

High-quality sedan with trawler-style profile combines comfortable accommodations with economical operation, good turn of speed. Spacious salon with big windows boasts leather seating, hardwood flooring, meticulous workmanship. Excellent lower-helm visibility. Note overhead salon grabrail. Topside features include very wide side decks, large cockpit, integral swim platform. Easily driven hull with prop-protecting keel is fuel efficient, stable. Bow thruster is standard. Cruise at 12 knots (15–16 top) with 440hp Yanmar diesel.

Length Overall	41'0"	Clearance	NA
Length WL	38'7"	Fuel	385 gals.
Beam	14'0"	Water	170 gals.
Draft	3'9"	Waste	42 gals.
Weight	28,000#	Hull Type	Semi-Disp.

Insufficient Resale Data To Assign Values

Camano Marine
Delta, BC (Canada)
www.camanomarine.com

Carver 28 Aft Cabin; 300 Aft Cabin
1991–94

Maxi-volume family cruiser with wide beam (called the Carver 28 Aft Cabin in 1991–92; 300 Aft Cabin in 1993–94) offered big-boat comfort in modest 28-foot hull. Highlights include small aft stateroom with double and single berth, roomy salon with convertible settee, full galley, roomy head compartment. Lower helm was optional. Molded bow pulpit, swim platform, swim ladder were standard. Aft deck is small, side decks are narrow. Modified-V hull delivers stable ride. Cruise at 16 knots with twin 210hp gas engines (low 20s top).

Length Overall	32'9"	Fuel	168 gals.
Beam	11'10"	Water	51 gals.
Draft	2'11"	Waste	20 gals.
Weight	12,600#	Hull Type	Modified-V
Clearance	NA	Deadrise Aft	16°

Prices Not Provided for Pre-1995 Models

Carver Yachts
Pulaski, WI
www.carveryachts.com

Motoryachts & Trawlers

---

www.powerboatguide.com   231-360-0827

Carver 3007 Aft Cabin
1981–82

Portly aft-cabin cruiser with three distinct cabins packs a lot of usable space in a 30-foot hull. Roomy layout with standard lower helm features convertible salon sofa, head with stall shower, slide-out double berth in aft cabin. (To save space, fuel tanks are under berths in aft cabin.) Lower helm was a popular option. Storage space is at a premium in this boat. Flybridge can seat four, but aft deck is tiny. Low-deadrise hull is a stiff ride in a chop. Twin 270hp gas engines cruise at 18–20 knots. Single-engine models have full-length keel.

Length	29'10"	Fuel	172 gals.
Beam	11'4"	Water	92 gals.
Draft	2'10"	Waste	25 gals.
Weight	10,500#	Hull Type	Modified-V
Clearance	NA	Deadrise Aft	12°

Prices Not Provided for Pre-1995 Models

Carver Yachts
Pulaski, WI
www.carveryachts.com

---

www.powerboatguide.com   231-360-0827

Carver 32 Aft Cabin
1983–90

1983–89

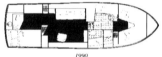

1990

Spacious double-cabin cruiser with boxy profile makes up in comfort whatever she lacks in sex appeal. Accommodations include two private staterooms, two heads, full-size galley, compact salon with convertible sofa, lower helm. Note limited stowage space. Small aft deck can accommodate a couple of folding chairs; flybridge offers seating for four. Aft stateroom was redesigned in 1990. Definitely a stiff ride when the waves pick up. Cruise at 16–18 knots with standard 270hp gas engines (mid 20s top).

Length Overall	32'0"	Clearance	11'6"
Length WL	28'1"	Fuel	182 gals.
Beam	11'7"	Water	84 gals.
Draft	2'10"	Hull Type	Modified-V
Weight	12,000#	Deadrise Aft	10°

Prices Not Provided for Pre-1995 Models

Carver Yachts
Pulaski, WI
www.carveryachts.com

---

www.powerboatguide.com   231-360-0827

Carver 325/326 Aft Cabin
1995–2001

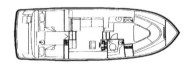

Popular aft-cabin cruiser (called 325 Aft Cabin in 1995–98; 326 Aft Cabin in 1999–2001) set class standards in her day for space-efficient floorplan. Galley-down interior includes roomy salon with standard lower helm, full galley, convertible dinette forward, small stateroom aft with vanity/sink. Note that double berth in aft cabin extends slightly below salon sole. Single head lacks stall shower. Integrated swim platform has handy storage locker. Cruise at 18 knots with twin 300hp inboard gas engines (25–26 knots top).

Length w/Pulpit	35'0"	Fuel	162 gals.
Hull Length	32'2"	Water	51 gals.
Beam	11'11"	Waste	20 gals.
Draft	2'11"	Hull Type	Modified-V
Weight	15,100#	Deadrise Aft	16°

See Page 534 For Resale Values

Carver Yachts
Pulaski, WI
www.carveryachts.com

Carver 33 Aft Cabin; 350 Aft Cabin
1991–94

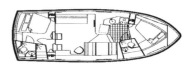

Full-bodied mini-motoryacht (called the Carver 33 Aft Cabin in 1991–92; 350 Aft Cabin in 1993–94) targeted 1990s boaters with an eye for value. Few other 33-footers can match her for interior volume. Highlights include double staterooms fore and aft, roomy salon with large windows, well-equipped galley with upright refrigerator, convertible booth dinette. Good engineroom access, wide sidedecks are a plus. Hardtop, swim platform were standard. Twin 300hp gas inboards cruise at 16–18 knots (mid 20s top).

Length	39'0"	Fuel	220 gals.
Beam	13'3"	Water	81 gals.
Draft	2'7"	Waste	36 gals.
Weight	16,600#	Hull Type	Modified-V
Clearance	NA	Deadrise Aft	11°

Prices Not Provided for Pre-1995 Models

Carver Yachts
Pulaski, WI
www.carveryachts.com

Carver 355/356 Motor Yacht
1995–2003

Updated version of Carver 33/350 MY (1991–94) with integrated transom, revised interior gets high marks for solid construction, common-sense accommodations. Expansive interior offers the amenities of a much larger boat. Highlights include two double staterooms, full dinette, well-appointed salon with built-in entertainment center. Note molded steps leading down to extended swim platform. Hardtop, radar arch, bow pulpit were standard; lower helm station was optional. Cruise at 16–18 knots with twin 320hp gas inboards (about 25 knots top).

Length w/Pulpit	41'2"	Fuel	318 gals.
Beam	13'3"	Water	70 gals.
Draft	3'3"	Waste	36 gals.
Weight	23,400#	Hull Type	Modified-V
Clearance, Arch	17'6"	Deadrise Aft	11°

See Page 535 For Resale Values

Carver Yachts
Pulaski, WI
www.carveryachts.com

Carver 36 Aft Cabin
1982–89

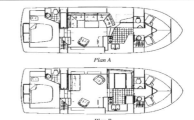

Plan A

Plan B

Popular 1980s double-cabin cruiser offered impressive blend of solid construction, roomy accommodations, proven owner satisfaction. Interior is spacious for a 36-footer with good headroom, generous stowage. Plan A with extended salon sleeps eight; Plan B with booth-style dinette sleeps six. Lower helm, tub/shower in aft head were standard in both floorplans. Numerous opening ports permit good cabin ventilation. Wide side decks are a plus. Twin 350hp gas engines cruise at 16 knots (25–26 knots top).

Length Overall	35'7"	Clearance	11'9"
Length WL	31'4"	Fuel	240 gals.
Beam	12'6"	Water	109 gals.
Draft	3'2"	Hull Type	Modified-V
Weight	18,500#	Deadrise Aft	8°

Prices Not Provided for Pre-1995 Models

Carver Yachts
Pulaski, WI
www.carveryachts.com

Motoryachts & Trawlers

Section I: Motoryachts & Trawlers

231-360-0827

Carver 36 Motor Yacht
2002–07

346 Interior (2002 Only)

Standard Layout

Opulent condo-yacht (called Carver 346 MY in 2002; 366 MY in 2003–06; 37 MY in 2007) gives owners the space, amenities required for cruising or entertaining. Vast two-stateroom interior with full-width salon is enhanced by tiered cabin windows. Original floorplan was redesigned in 2003 to include dinette—a major improvement. Features include integrated transom with molded steps, wide side decks, spacious bridge with L-shaped lounge. Cruise at 18 knots with 385hp gas inboards; 20 knots with 310hp Volvo diesels.

Length	36'11"	Fuel	250 gals.
Beam	13'2"	Water	70 gals.
Draft	2'4"	Waste	36 gals.
Weight	21,800#	Hull Type	Modified-V
Headroom	6'6"	Deadrise Aft	16°

See Page 535 For Resale Values

Carver Yachts
Pulaski, WI
www.carveryachts.com

231-360-0827

Carver 36 Aft Cabin; 370 Aft Cabin
1990–96

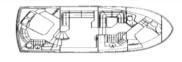

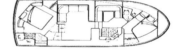

Compact motoryacht (called Carver 36 MY in 1990–92) offered buyers an impressive mix of comfort, amenities at a reasonable price. Space-efficient interior features two double staterooms, stall showers in both heads, full dinette, well-equipped galley. Flybridge seats up to six in comfort. Additional features include wide side decks, bow pulpit, radar arch, swim platform. Lower helm station, hardtop were popular options. Modified-V hull can handle a chop. Twin 300hp gas inboards cruise at 15–16 knots (mid 20s top).

Length w/Pulpit	41'3"	Clearance	15'0"
Hull Length	38'2"	Fuel	240 gals.
Beam	13'10"	Water	80 gals.
Draft	3'1"	Hull Type	Modified-V
Weight	18,500#	Deadrise Aft	19°

See Page 535 For Resale Values

Carver Yachts
Pulaski, WI
www.carveryachts.com

231-360-0827

Carver 370/374 Voyager
1993–2002

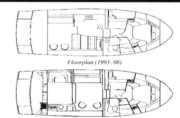

Floorplan (1993–98)

Floorplan (1999–2002)

Good-selling 1990s pilothouse yacht struck the right mix of price, comfort, performance. Original two-stateroom floorplan has galley and dinette forward in salon; revised layout in 1999 moved galley and dinette aft. Principal features include large owner's stateroom, double-entry head, spacious flybridge, wide side decks. Note small cockpit, side-dumping exhausts, standard radar arch. Twin 310hp inboard gas engines cruise at 16 knots (25 knots top); 330hp Cummins diesels cruise at 24 knots (high 20s top).

Length w/Pulpit	40'1"	Fuel	297 gals.
Hull Length	37'1"	Water	83 gals.
Beam	13'3"	Waste	35 gals.
Draft	3'8"	Hull Type	Modified-V
Weight	21,350#	Deadrise Aft	11°

See Page 535 For Resale Values

Carver Yachts
Pulaski, WI
www.carveryachts.com

Carver 38 Aft Cabin; 390 Aft Cabin
1987–95

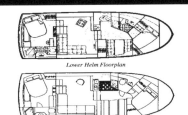

Lower Helm Floorplan

Without Lower Helm

Durable double-cabin cruiser mixed conservative styling with space-efficient layout, rugged construction. Offered with several floorplans during her production years, all with two double staterooms, full dinette, stall showers in both heads. Lower helm station was optional. Large interior results in small aft-deck platform. Relatively heavy boat is a handful for gas engines to push. Crusader 340hp gas engines cruise at 14–15 knots (low 20s top). Optional 375hp Cat—or 370hp Cummins—diesels cruise at 21 knots (25 knots top).

Length	42'6"	Fuel	280 gals.
Beam	14'0"	Water	91 gals.
Draft	3'4"	Waste	75 gals.
Weight	22,750#	Hull Type	Modified-V
Clearance	NA	Deadrise Aft	12°

See Page 535 For Resale Values

Carver Yachts
Pulaski, WI
www.carveryachts.com

Carver 396/39 Motor Yacht
2000–07

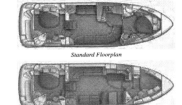

Standard Floorplan

Dinette Floorplan

Popular aft-cabin yacht (called the 396 MY in 2000–04; 39 MY in 2005–6; 40 MY in 2007) gets high marks for dramatic styling, cavernous interior. Full-beam salon—focal point of the entire boat—boasts nearly seven feet of headroom. Updated dinette floorplan introduced in 2003. Wing doors, hardtop were standard. Note small swim platform. Huge bridge features centerline helm, wraparound seating, wet bar. Twin 370hp gas engines cruise at a modest 14–15 knots; optional 370hp Cummins diesels cruise at 20 knots.

Length	40'7"	Fuel	330 gals.
Beam	13'11"	Water	90 gals.
Draft	3'6"	Waste	72 gals.
Weight	29,500#	Hull Type	Modified-V
Clearance	18'0"	Deadrise Aft	16°

See Page 535 For Resale Values

Carver Yachts
Pulaski, WI
www.carveryachts.com

Carver 390/400/404 Cockpit MY
1993–2003

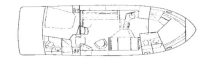

Late-model cockpit yacht (called 390 Cockpit MY in 1993–95; 400 CMY in 1996–98; 404 CMY in 1999–2003) offers market-proven mix of sturdy construction, upscale accommodations. Well-planned interior with light oak trim includes two heads, roomy galley, full dinette, double berths in both staterooms. Master suite has sliding glass door to cockpit. Note spiral cockpit stairs. Flybridge seats six around center helm. Engineroom is a tight fit. Standard gas engines cruise at 16 knots; optional 315hp Cummins diesels cruise at 20 knots.

Length	43'5"	Fuel	318 gals.
Beam	13'3"	Water	70 gals.
Draft	3'3"	Waste	36 gals.
Weight	24,300#	Hull Type	Modified-V
Clearance	NA	Deadrise Aft	11°

See Page 535 For Resale Values

Carver Yachts
Pulaski, WI
www.carveryachts.com

Motoryachts & Trawlers

www.powerboatguide.com   231-360-0827

Carver 405/406 Aft Cabin MY
1997–2001

Conservative aft-cabin motoryacht (called Carver 405 in 1997–98; 406 in 1999–2001) offers enticing blend of space, comfort, value. Expansive galley-down interior boasts huge salon with L-shaped settee, full dinette, double berths in both staterooms. Large aft deck is surrounded with weather boards; swim platform has storage compartment for fins and scuba tanks. Note wide side decks, foredeck sun pad. Standard gas inboards cruise at 16 knots; optional 330hp Cummins diesels will cruise at 20–21 knots.

Length	42'3"	Fuel	342 gals.
Beam	13'10"	Water	70 gals.
Draft	3'3"	Waste	64 Gals.
Weight	27,900#	Hull Type	Modified-V
Clearance, Arch	17'2"	Deadrise Aft	20°

See Page 535 For Resale Values

Carver Yachts
Pulaski, WI
www.carveryachts.com

---

www.powerboatguide.com   231-360-0827

Carver 41 Cockpit MY
2005–07

Graceful cockpit yacht with sweeping lines makes the cut with buyers seeking European styling with American luxury, comfort. Full-beam salon boasts excellent natural lighting, easy-on-the-eye decor. Angled double berths in both staterooms make the most of available space. Sliding door in master stateroom opens to cockpit. Aft-deck wing doors provide protection from elements. Note molded cockpit steps, extended swim platform, well-arranged engineroom. Cruise in the mid 20s with 370hp Volvo diesels (26–27 knots top).

Length	42'11"	Fuel	360 gals.
Beam	13.5"	Water	70 gals.
Draft	2.7"	Waste	50 gals.
Weight	26,000#	Hull Type	Modified-V
Clearance	15'1"	Deadrise Aft	15°

See Page 535 For Resale Values

Carver Yachts
Pulaski, WI
www.carveryachts.com

---

www.powerboatguide.com   231-360-0827

Carver 42 Cockpit MY
1986–88

Sturdy flybridge sedan was largest boat in Carver's fleet when she was introduced in 1986. While a two-stateroom floorplan was available, most were sold with dinette interior with single stateroom. Lower helm was a popular option. Cockpit is big enough for fishing; flybridge has a raised command console with overhead electronics box built into radar arch. Standard 350hp gas engines cruise at a sluggish 13–14 knots (low 20s top); optional Cat 375hp diesels cruise at 20 knots (23–24 knots wide open).

Length	42'0"	Fuel	400 gals.
Beam	15'0"	Water	170 gals.
Draft	3'6"	Headroom	6.5"
Weight	23,150#	Hull Type	Modified-V
Clearance	16'6"	Deadrise Aft	12°

Prices Not Provided for Pre-1995 Models

Carver Yachts
Pulaski, WI
www.carveryachts.com

www.powerboatguide.com   231-360-0827

Carver 42 Mariner
2004–06

Super-spacious cruiser with large cockpit, extended swim platform delivers condo-size accommodations in a midsize yacht. Expansive two-stateroom interior features cavernous full-beam salon with raised dinette, large step-down galley, island queen berth in forward stateroom. (Note big storage locker under galley sole.) Filler converts single berths in guest cabin into double. Huge flybridge has three helm chairs, wet bar, circular aft lounge. Volvo 370hp diesels cruise at 20 knots (24–25 knots top).

Length	44'5"	Fuel	400 gals.
Beam	13'11"	Water	95 gals.
Draft	32"	Waste	35 gals.
Weight	31,280#	Hull Type	Modified-V
Clearance, Arch	19'2"	Deadrise Aft	17°

See Page 535 For Resale Values

Carver Yachts
Pulaski, WI
www.carveryachts.com

---

www.powerboatguide.com   231-360-0827

Carver 42 Motor Yacht
1985–91

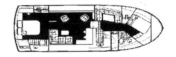

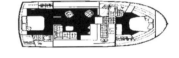

Durable aft-cabin motoryacht set class standards for popularity, value in the late 1980s. Space-efficient interior—available with or without dinette—features large owner's stateroom, expansive salon with serving counter, U-shaped galley down, stall showers in both heads. Most were sold with optional lower helm and hardtop. Big salon windows provide panoramic outside views. Flybridge seats six around centerline helm. Cruise at 13–14 knots with 300hp gas engine (20+ knots top). Cat 375hp diesels cruise at 20 knots (mid 20s top).

Length	42'0"	Fuel	400 gals.
Beam	15'0"	Water	170 gals.
Draft	3'6"	Headroom	6'4"
Weight	23,600#	Hull Type	Modified-V
Clearance	20'0"	Deadrise Aft	12°

Prices Not Provided for Pre-1995 Models

Carver Yachts
Pulaski, WI
www.carveryachts.com

---

www.powerboatguide.com   231-360-0827

Carver 430 Cockpit MY
1991–97

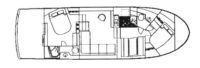

Sturdy construction, luxury-class accommodations made this contemporary cockpit yacht a popular model in 1990s. Roomy galley-down interior has angled double berths in both staterooms, full dinette, wide-open salon with L-shaped sofa. Sliding door in master suite opens directly on cockpit. Additional features include wide side decks, bow pulpit, radar arch, transom door, extended swim platform. Standard gas engines cruise at a modest 14–15 knots; Cummins 330hp diesels cruise at 20 knots (22–23 knots top).

Length	47'10"	Fuel	390 gals.
Beam	14'0"	Water	91 gals.
Draft	3'4"	Waste	75 gals.
Weight	28,700#	Hull Type	Modified-V
Clearance	15'4"	Deadrise Aft	11°

See Page 535 For Resale Values

Carver Yachts
Pulaski, WI
www.carveryachts.com

231-360-0827

Carver 43/47 Motor Yacht
2006–Current

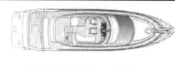

Gold-plated cockpit yacht (called the Carver 43 MY in 2006–07) gets high marks for deluxe accommodations, quality construction. Enormous full-beam salon with high-gloss cabinetry rivals many 50-footers for living space, luxury. Compact master stateroom features desk, washer/dryer, cockpit door. Note full-size refrigerator, faux-granite galley counters. Wing doors, bench seating are standard on aft deck. Cockpit opens to extended swim platform capable of stowing PWC. Yanmar 480hp diesels cruise at 20–22 knots.

Length w/Platform	49'2"	Fuel, Diesel	580 gals.
Beam	14'2"	Water	90 gals.
Draft	3'6"	Waste	75 gals.
Weight	35,811#	Hull Type	Modified-V
Fuel, Gas	400 gals.	Deadrise Aft	NA

See Page 535 For Resale Values

Carver Yachts
Pulaski, WI
www.carveryachts.com

231-360-0827

Carver 440/445 Aft Cabin
1993–99

440 Layout

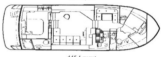

445 Layout

Conservative, broad-shouldered motoryacht from the late 1990s combines roomy interior with efficient space utilization, sturdy construction. Open-plan interior with expansive salon has galley and dinette down, double berths in both staterooms, built-in entertainment center. Relatively small aft deck for a 44-footer. Updated 445 model introduced in 1997 has integrated transom with molded steps. Among several gas or diesel engine options, twin 330hp Cummins diesels cruise at 17–18 knots (about 22 knots top).

Length	47'8"	Fuel	476 gals.
Beam	15'0"	Water	165 gals.
Draft	4'3"	Waste	80 gals.
Weight	32,000#	Hull Type	Modified-V
Clearance, Arch	18'9"	Deadrise Aft	14°

See Page 535 For Resale Values

Carver Yachts
Pulaski, WI
www.carveryachts.com

231-360-0827

Carver 444 Cockpit MY
2001–04

Lengthened version of Carver 396 MY gets extra fuel with added versatility of 60-square-foot cockpit. Spacious galley-down interior is arranged with double berths fore and aft, stall showers in both heads. Immense full-beam salon with curved Ultraleather sofa boasts nearly seven feet of headroom. Note absence of dinette. Huge bridge features center helm, wraparound seating, wet bar. Twin 370hp gas engines cruise at a modest 14–15 knots (mid 20s top); 370hp Cummins diesels cruise at 20 knots (22–23 knots top).

Length	46'6"	Fuel	404 gals.
Beam	13'11"	Water	90 gals.
Draft	3'6"	Waste	72 gals.
Weight	33,860#	Hull Type	Modified-V
Clearance, Arch	18'0"	Deadrise Aft	16°

See Page 536 For Resale Values

Carver Yachts
Pulaski, WI
www.carveryachts.com

---

www.powerboatguide.com 231-360-0827

Carver 450 Voyager
1999–2004

Salon/Pilothouse

Salon/Lower Level

Luxury pilothouse cruiser with innovative two-stateroom interior gets high marks for distinctive styling, state-of-the-art amenities. Open-plan salon with cherry trim, facing leather settees features elevated, helm-level dinette—a unique design that keeps guests close to the helmsman. Both double staterooms have full, en-suite heads. Note limited galley storage. Sliding glass doors open to partially shaded cockpit with engineroom access hatch. Cummins 480hp diesels will cruise at 19–20 knots (low 20s top).

Length w/Platform	46'11"	Fuel	560 gals.
Beam	14'11"	Water	150 gals.
Draft	3'7"	Waste	80 gals.
Weight	39,600#	Hull Type	Modified-V
Clearance	16'8"	Deadrise Aft	15°

See Page 536 For Resale Values

Carver Yachts
Pulaski, WI
www.carveryachts.com

---

www.powerboatguide.com 231-360-0827

Carver 455/456 Aft Cabin MY
1996–2000

Three-Stateroom Plan

Two-Stateroom Plan

Rakish aft-cabin yacht (called Carver 455 in 1996–98, Carver 456 in 1999–2000) led the way in late 1990s for motoryacht value. Original three-stateroom layout is unusual—galley is aft in salon permitting enormous bow stateroom, concealed guest cabin. Conventional two-stateroom floorplan with salon dinette became available in 1998. Highlights include large engineroom, transom staircase, side exhausts. Note tub/shower in forward head. Twin 315hp Cummins diesels cruise at 16 knots; 340hp Cats cruise at 18 knots.

Length	45'9"	Fuel	464 gals.
Beam	15'4"	Water	132 gals.
Draft	4'7"	Waste	80 gals.
Weight	35,000#	Hull Type	Modified-V
Clearance	18'9"	Deadrise Aft	14°

See Page 536 For Resale Values

Carver Yachts
Pulaski, WI
www.carveryachts.com

---

www.powerboatguide.com 231-360-0827

Carver 46 Motor Yacht
2001–07

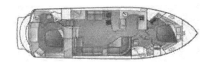

Spacious, well-bred cruising yacht with high-impact styling targets upscale buyers in search of world-class comforts. Enormous full-width salon rivals many 55-footers in size. Two-and-a-half-stateroom floorplan (note tiny berth under salon settee) is arranged with mid-level galley, breakfast bar, walkaround island beds in each stateroom, two full heads. Hardtop, wing doors enclose spacious aft deck. Roomy flybridge can seat eight. Excellent fit and finish. Twin 480hp Volvo diesels cruise at 20 knots and reach a top speed of 22–23 knots.

Length	46'11"	Fuel	480 gals.
Beam	14'11"	Water	130 gals.
Draft	3'7"	Waste	80 gals.
Weight	37,000#	Hull Type	Modified-V
Clearance	19'5"	Deadrise Aft	14°

See Page 536 For Resale Values

Carver Yachts
Pulaski, WI
www.carveryachts.com

231-360-0827

Carver 46 Voyager
2005–Current

Revised version of popular 450 Voyager (1999–2004) replaced 450's inventive two-stateroom, lower-helm interior with three-stateroom layout with no lower helm. Highlights include cherrywood furnishings and cabinetry, spacious salon with premium leather sofas, gourmet galley with generous storage, well-appointed staterooms. Stylish bridge offers plenty of guest seating. Sliding glass doors open to partially shaded cockpit with engineroom access hatch. Cummins 480hp diesels will cruise at 19–20 knots (low 20s top).

Length w/Platform	46'11"	Fuel	560 gals.
Beam	14'11"	Water	150 gals.
Draft	3'7"	Waste	80 gals.
Weight	39,600#	Hull Type	Modified-V
Clearance	16'8"	Deadrise Aft	15°

See Page 536 For Resale Values

Carver Yachts
Pulaski, WI
www.carveryachts.com

231-360-0827

Carver 500/504 Cockpit MY
1996–2000

3-Stateroom Plan

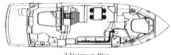

2-Stateroom Plan

Contemporary 50-foot motoryacht (called the 504 Cockpit MY in 1999–2000) was flagship of Carver's fleet in mid 1990s. Spacious interior offered with two or three staterooms has the galley positioned aft in the salon—an unusual layout in a yacht of this type. Note aft-facing bed, cockpit access door in master stateroom. Large cockpit serves anglers and bathers alike. Additional features include tub in forward head, large engineroom, molded cockpit steps, washer/dryer space, integral swim platform. Cummins 420hp diesels cruise at 20 knots.

Length	49'7"	Fuel	688 gals.
Beam	15'4"	Water	200/350 gals.
Draft	4'7"	Waste	80 gals.
Weight	43,100#	Hull Type	Modified-V
Clearance, Arch	18'9"	Deadrise Aft	14°

See Page 536 For Resale Values

Carver Yachts
Pulaski, WI
www.carveryachts.com

231-360-0827

Carver 506 Motor Yacht
2000–04

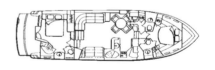

Garish floating condo with enormous, maxi-volume interior elevates tastless styling to previously unimagined heights. Cavernous full-width salon with seven-foot headroom is made possible by raising the side decks to eye level. Three-stateroom, galley-down floorplan features formal dining area, three heads, salon seating for a small crowd. Note tiered salon windows, rich cherry woodwok, generous galley storage. Enclosed flybridge is rare in a yacht this size. Cummins 450hp diesels cruise at 17 knots (20+ top).

Length	51'7"	Fuel	510 gals.
Beam	15'4"	Water	158 gals.
Draft	4'6"	Waste	95 gals.
Weight	47,900#	Hull Type	Modified-V
Clearance	20'1"	Deadrise Aft	13°

See Page 536 For Resale Values

Carver Yachts
Pulaski, WI
www.carveryachts.com

Carver 52 Voyager
2007–Current

Executive-class flybridge yacht meets cruiser's needs for elegant entertaining, comfortable cruising. Spacious three-stateroom floorplan has combined salon/galley separated from pilothouse by galley bulkhead. (Most pilothouse yachts have salon/galley area open to lower helm.) Huge deckhouse windows, vertical ports in master suite provide good natural lighting. Pilothouse door is a plus, but engineroom is tight. No rear visibility from lower helm. Bow, stern thrusters are standard. Volvo 575hp diesels cruise at 20–22 knots (high 20s top).

Length	53'9"	Fuel	800 gals.
Beam	15'4"	Water	200 gals.
Draft	4'9"	Waste	100 gals.
Weight	48,500#	Hull Type	Modified-V
Clearance, Arch	19'0"	Deadrise Aft	13°

Insufficient Resale Data To Assign Values

Carver Yachts
Pulaski, WI
www.carveryachts.com

Carver 530 Voyager Pilothouse
1998–2005

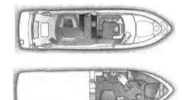

Top-selling pilothouse yacht took Carver styling, versatility to the next level. Opulent three-stateroom cherry interior features spacious salon with wraparound lounge, aircraft-style pilothouse with helm seat surrounded by guest seating, lavish full-beam owner's stateroom, luxurious VIP cabin. Note near-7-foot salon headroom, gourmet galley with hardwood flooring, inside bridge access. Extended flybridge with lounge seating can entertain a small crowd. Cruise at 16–17 knots (about 20 top) with Cummins 450hp diesels.

Length w/Platform	53'9"	Fuel	800 gals.
Beam	15'4"	Water	200 gals.
Draft	4'9"	Waste	100 gals.
Weight	48,500	Hull Type	Modified-V
Clearance, Arch	19'0"	Deadrise Aft	13°

See Page 536 For Resale Values

Carver Yachts
Pulaski, WI
www.carveryachts.com

Carver 564 Cockpit MY
2002–06

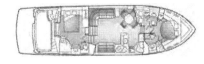

Cockpit version of Carver's slab-sided 506 MY (2000–04) offers owners added versatility, additional range, slightly better profile. Cavernous full-width salon with nearly seven feet of headroom is made possible by raising the side decks to eye level. Three-stateroom, galley-down floorplan includes formal dining area, three heads, salon seating for a crowd. Wing doors, hardtop with retractable sunroof are standard. Cummins 450hp diesels will cruise at 17 knots; Volvo 675hp diesels cruise at 22 knots.

Length	59'2"	Fuel	646 gals.
Beam	15'4"	Water	158 gals.
Draft	4'6"	Waste	95 gals.
Weight	54,167#	Hull Type	Modified-V
Clearance, Arch	20'11"	Deadrise Aft	13°

See Page 536 For Resale Values

Carver Yachts
Pulaski, WI
www.carveryachts.com

Motoryachts & Trawlers

Carver 570 Voyager PH; 56 Voyager Sedan
2001–Current

Enlarged version of best-selling 530 Voyager PH made an exceptional yacht even better. Luxurious three-stateroom interior features spacious salon with Ultra-leather seating, raised pilothouse with helm seat surrounded by guest seating, lavish full-beam owner's stateroom. Note near-7-foot salon headroom, inside bridge access. Extended flybridge provides a lavish entertainment platform for a large group. Cruise at 17–18 knots with Volvo 4800hp diesels; 24 knots with 675hp Volvos. (Called the 570 Voyager Pilothouse in 2001–04; 56 Voyager Sedan since 2005.)

Length	59'2"	Fuel	800 gals.
Beam	15'4"	Water	200 gals.
Draft	4'9"	Waste	100 gals.
Weight	52,500#	Hull Type	Modified-V
Clearance, Arch	19'0"	Deadrise Aft	13°

See Page 536 For Resale Values

Carver Yachts
Pulaski, WI
www.carveryachts.com

CHB 34 Double Cabin
1972–85

Classic family trawler enjoyed huge popularity in 1970s, 1980s thanks to low price, economical operation, rich teak interior. Compact-but-efficient layout with parquet flooring is comfortable for two, crowded for four. Storage space is at a premium, especially in galley. Built with plywood house before 1975. Decks were teak-planked until 1985 (a constant source of leaks); teak-over-fiberglass thereafter. Teak window frames eliminated in 1992. Over 1,600 built. Single 120hp or 135hp diesel cruises at 6-7 knots burning just 3 gallons per hour.

Length Overall	33'6"	Clearance	NA
Length WL	30'3"	Fuel	300 gals.
Beam	11'9"	Water	85 gals.
Draft	3'6"	Waste	40 gals.
Weight	27,000#	Hull Type	Semi-Disp.

Prices Not Provided for Pre-1995 Models

Chung Hwa Boatbuilders
Taipei, Taiwan

CHB 38 Trawler
1978–86

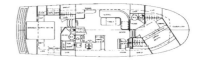

Vintage double-cabin trawler from well-regarded Taiwan builder delivers appealing mix of timeless style, economical operation. Several two-stateroom, galley-up teak interiors were offered over the years, all with parquet flooring, port/starboard deck doors, tub/shower in aft head. Teak decks, window frames and handrails were standard. Note fold-down mast, simulated lapstrake hull lines. Deep keel protects running gear. Above-average finish. Cruise at 7–8 knots with single 120hp Lehman diesel; 10+ knots with twin 120s.

Length Overall	37'10"	Clearance	NA
Length WL	35'4"	Fuel	400 gals.
Beam	13'2"	Water	200 gals.
Draft	3'9"	Waste	40 gals.
Weight	21,000#	Hull Type	Semi-Disp.

Prices Not Provided for Pre-1995 Models

Chung Hwa Boatbuilders
Taipei, Taiwan

CHB 42 Sundeck
1984–89

Appealing 1980s sundeck yacht with contemporary styling, traditional teak interior continues to enjoy strong buyer appeal. Standard twin-stateroom layout with galley and dinette down boasts roomy master suite with space for washer/dryer, teak parquet floors, standard lower helm. Topside highlights include covered aft deck with wet bar, wide side decks, flybridge seating for six. Also marketed as Present or Ponderosa 42. Among several engine options, twin 255 Lehman diesels cruise at 10-12 knots (about 14 knots top).

Length Overall	41'10"	Clearance	16'4"
Length WL	38'0"	Fuel	450 gals.
Beam	13'8"	Water	200 gals.
Draft	3'6"	Waste	30 gals.
Weight	26,000#	Hull Type	Semi-Disp.

Prices Not Provided for Pre-1995 Models

Chung Hwa Boatbuilders
Taipei, Taiwan

CHB 45 Pilothouse
1979–85

All-weather pilothouse trawler couples cruising comfort with liveaboard amenities. Spacious teak interior with split-level floorplan boasts expansive salon with U-shaped galley, parquet flooring, pilothouse watch berth, full-size head with tub/shower. Note spacious engineroom, teak-over-fiberglass decks, cabintop and flybridge. Transom door make boarding easy. Deep keel protects running gear. Also marketed as Puget 45 Pilothouse. Standard 120hp Lehman diesels cruise at 8 knots; optional 235hp Volvos cruise at 10–12 knots.

Length Overall	44'10"	Headroom	6'8"
Length WL	40'6"	Fuel	600 gals.
Beam	14'6"	Water	250 gals.
Draft	4'2"	Waste	40 gals.
Weight	30,000#	Hull Type	Semi-Disp.

Prices Not Provided for Pre-1995 Models

Chung Hwa Boatbuilders
Taipei, Taiwan

CHB 48 Seamaster MY
1983–89

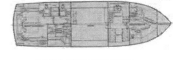

Heavily-built motoryacht with conservative lines, spacious three-stateroom interior offered 1980s buyers big-boat luxury at an unbeatable price. Highlights include full teak interior, expansive salon, booth-style dinette, luxurious owner stateroom, washer/dryer space in aft guest cabin. Both aft heads share common shower stall. Note huge aft deck with wing doors, wet bar. Basically a Taiwan knock-off of the Hatteras 48 MY (1981–84). Also marketed as Ponderosa 48. Cat 375hp diesels cruise at 12–14 knots (18 knots top).

Length Overall	47'8"	Clearance	16'10"
Length WL	43'6"	Fuel	590 gals.
Beam	15'0"	Water	200 gals.
Draft	3'10"	Waste	75 gals.
Weight	39,000#	Hull Type	Semi-Disp.

Prices Not Provided for Pre-1995 Models

Chung Hwa Boatbuilders
Taipei, Taiwan

www.powerboatguide.com   231-360-0827

Cheoy Lee 35 Sedan
1979–86

Heavily-built small trawler offers long-range coastal cruising for couples on a budget. Traditional teak interior boasts large salon with convertible L-shaped settee, roomy head with separate stall shower, large forward stateroom with double berth, lots of storage. Deckhouse galley is next to aft salon door where it's convenient to cockpit and flybridge. Note very wide side decks, folding mast, huge fuel capacity. Extended hardtop shelters cockpit. Deep keel protects running gear. Cruise at 7–8 knots with single 120hp Lehman diesel.

Length Overall	34'11"	Clearance	NA
Length WL	32'6"	Fuel	650 gals.
Beam	12'0"	Water	210 gals.
Draft	3'7"	Waste	30 gals.
Weight	21,000#	Hull Type	Semi-Disp.

Prices Not Provided for Pre-1995 Models

Cheoy Lee of North America
Ft. Lauderdale, FL
www.cheoyleena.com

---

www.powerboatguide.com   231-360-0827

Cheoy Lee 40 Trawler
1973–86

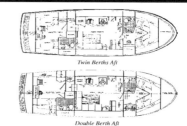

Twin Berths Aft

Double Berth Aft

Vintage Asian-built trawler with traditional trunk-cabin profile is seaworthy, economical, built to last. Generic teak interior originally had twin berths in aft stateroom; later models have doubleberth aft. Note convenient cockpit access door in aft stateroom. Well-finished engineroom offers good service access. Mast and boom assembly, teak decks were standard. Full-length keel protects props and running gear from grounding. Cruising range exceeds 1,000 nautical miles. Twin 120hp Lehman disels cruise efficiently at 7–8 knots.

Length Overall	40'0"	Clearance	NA
Length WL	35'8"	Fuel	650 gals.
Beam	14'6"	Water	250 gals.
Draft	4'8"	Waste	40 gals.
Weight	38,000#	Hull Type	Semi-Disp.

Prices Not Provided for Pre-1995 Models

Cheoy Lee of North America
Ft. Lauderdale, FL
www.cheoyleena.com

---

www.powerboatguide.com   231-360-0827

Cheoy Lee 46 Trawler
1978–81

Deckhouse Plan

Lower Level Plan

Graceful Cheoy Lee trawler with handsome Europa styling is the smallest double-deck production yacht ever built. Three-stateroom interior with combined salon/galley includes private wheelhouse with flybridge access, aft master stateroom with private salon staircase, full-beam VIP guest cabin, walk-in engineroom. Note protected side decks, cushioned bow seating. Teak-over-fiberglass decks were standard. Displacement hull is easy on the fuel. Twin 120hp Lehman diesels cruise at 8 knots with range of 800–850 miles.

Length Overall	45'11"	Clearance	NA
Length WL	42'0"	Fuel	820 gals.
Beam	14'8"	Water	510 gals.
Draft	4'8"	Waste	70 gals.
Weight	49,200#	Hull Type	Displacement

Prices Not Provided for Pre-1995 Models

Cheoy Lee of North America
Ft. Lauderdale, FL
www.cheoyleena.com

Cheoy Lee 48 Motor Yacht
1981–86

Rakish double-cabin cruiser with fully cored hull took 1980s motoryacht styling to the next level. Spacious teak interior boasts two staterooms of almost equal size, large deckhouse salon with choice of semicircular settee or dining table. Curved forward passageway completely isolates galley from salon. Topside features include teak-laid aft deck, foredeck sun lounge, full-size bridge with huge sun pad aft. Bow pulpit, radar arch were standard. GM 550hp diesels cruise at 22–24 knots and top out in the mid-to-high 20s. Total of six were built.

Length Overall	48'0"	Clearance	NA
Length WL	43'0"	Fuel	800 gal.
Beam	15'0"	Water	200 gal.
Draft	4'0"	Hull Type	Modified-V
Weight	37,000#	Deadrise Aft	NA

Prices Not Provided for Pre-1995 Models

Cheoy Lee of North America
Ft. Lauderdale, FL
www.cheoyleena.com

Cheoy Lee 55 Long Range MY
1977–86

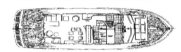

Standard Plan

Wide Body Plan

Heavy displacement cruising yacht with transatlantic range travels the world in comfort, confidence. Highlights include expansive four-stateroom teak interior with deckhouse galley, three full heads, stand-up engineroom, protected side decks, aft-deck wing doors, washer/dryer, teak-over-fiberglass decks. Note inside flybridge access, pilothouse watch berth, teak parquet flooring. Many of these yachts have been stabilized. Widebody model with extended, full-beam salon also available. Cruise at 8–9 knots with 210hp Cat diesels.

Length Overall	55'0"	Clearance	NA
Length WL	50'0"	Fuel, Std.	2,700 gals.
Beam	17'2"	Water	450 gals.
Draft	5'4"	Waste	125 gals.
Weight	80,000#	Hull Type	Displacement

Prices Not Provided for Pre-1995 Models

Cheoy Lee of North America
Ft. Lauderdale, FL
www.cheoyleena.com

Cheoy Lee 61 Long Range Cockpit MY
1983–2000

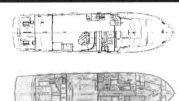

Cockpit version of Cheoy Lee 55 Long Range MY boasts revised four-stateroom interior, enhanced cruising versatility. Twin-deck layout has extended salon with home-size galley forward, private pilothouse with watchberth, opulent full-beam master suite with Jaquzzi tub and salon access, three full heads. Flybridge can be reached from pilothouse or aft-deck ladder. Note protected side decks, wing doors, teak decks. Also offered in Widebody version and unique aft-engineroom model. Cruise at 8–9 knots with 210hp Cat diesels.

Length Overall	60'11"	Clearance	NA
Length WL	55'0"	Fuel, Std.	2,700 gals.
Beam	17'2"	Water	450 gals.
Draft	5'8"	Waste	125 gals.
Weight	90,000#	Hull Type	Displacement

Insufficient Resale Data To Assign Values

Cheoy Lee of North America
Ft. Lauderdale, FL
www.cheoyleena.com

Motoryachts & Trawlers

www.powerboatguide.com   231-360-0827

Chris Craft 350 Catalina
1974–87

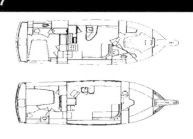

Iconic double-cabin cruiser was among best-selling Chris Craft models of her era. Expansive interior was offered in several configurations over the years, all with main-deck galley, large aft stateroom. Combined helm/aft deck area keeps skipper close to guests. Wide side decks make getting around easy. Additional features include molded foredeck seating, bow pulpit, swim platform, large engineroom. Twin 235hp gas engines cruise at 14–15 knots and top out in the low 20s. Note fuel increase to 250 gallons in 1983.

Length Overall	35'1"	Clearance	10'8"
Beam	13'1"	Fuel	180/250 gals.
Draft	2'10"	Water	55/100 gals.
Weight	17,229#	Hull Type	Modified-V
Headroom	6'4"	Deadrise Aft	NA

Prices Not Provided for Pre-1995 Models

Chris Craft
Sarasota, FL
www.chriscraft.com

---

www.powerboatguide.com   231-360-0827

Chris Craft 362 Catalina
1986–87

Roomy aft-cabin cruiser (originally built by Uniflite) combined contemporary 1980s styling with sturdy construction, comfortable ride. Practical galley-down floorplan features two double staterooms, U-shaped galley with upright refrigerator, convertible dinette, spacious salon. Lower helm was a popular option. Teak interior trim, bow pulpit, swim platform were standard. Modified-V hull can handle a chop with ease. Twin 270hp gas inboards cruise at 17–18 knots and reach a top speed of 25–26 knots.

Length	36'0"	Fuel	250 gals.
Beam	12'4"	Water	100 gals.
Draft	2'7"	Headroom	6'4"
Weight	15,500#	Hull Type	Modified-V
Clearance	12'2"	Deadrise Aft	NA

Prices Not Provided for Pre-1995 Models

Chris Craft
Sarasota, FL
www.chriscraft.com

---

www.powerboatguide.com   231-360-0827

Chris Craft 372 Catalina
1988–90

Contemporary aft-cabin cruising yacht appealed to entry-level buyers seeking liveaboard amenities at an affordable price. Beamy hull allows for unusually spacious accommodations for a 37-footer with full dinette, large U-shaped galley, wide-open salon. Both staterooms are on small side with angled berths to save space. Topside features include wide side decks, bow pulpit, swim platform, aft-deck wet bar. Hardtop was a popular option. Twin 270hp gas engines cruise at 16–17 knots (about 25 knots top).

Length w/Pulpit	42'9"	Fuel	250 gals.
Hull Length	37'5"	Water	100 gals.
Beam	13'10"	Waste	18 gals.
Draft	2'9"	Hull Type	Modified-V
Weight	17,200#	Deadrise Aft	NA

Prices Not Provided for Pre-1995 Models

Chris Craft
Sarasota, FL
www.chriscraft.com

231-360-0827

Chris Craft 380 Corinthian
1978–86

Standard Floorplan, 1978–82

Standard Floorplan, 1983–85

Popular double-cabin cruiser with houseboat profile repays in versatility what she lacks in eye appeal. Very sociable topside seating has bridge just two steps up from afterdeck. Several two-stateroom floorplans were offered, all with salon, cockpit entry doors. Lower helm was a popular option. Wide side decks make getting around easy. Note thoughtful afterdeck safety railings. Cockpit transom door, bow pulpit, swim platform were standard. A stiff ride in a chop, twin gas inboards cruise at 15–16 knots (mid 20s top).

Length Overall	38'0"	Clearance	12'2"
Length WL	33'6"	Fuel	400 gals.
Beam	14'0"	Water	65 gals.
Draft	3'0"	Hull Type	Modified-V
Weight	22,500#	Deadrise Aft	NA

Prices Not Provided for Pre-1995 Models

Chris Craft
Sarasota, FL
www.chriscraft.com

231-360-0827

Chris Craft 381 Catalina
1980–89

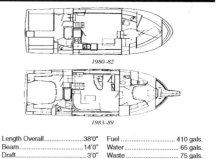

1980–82

1983–89

Enlarged version of best-selling Chris 350 Catalina has the interior space of many 45-footers. Innovative floorplan boasts huge salon with open galley, deck access door, two large staterooms, plenty of storage. Wide side decks provide secure access to cushioned bow seating. Express-style bridge/afterdeck area keeps skipper close to guests. Modified-V hull can be a stiff ride in a chop. Not the prettiest boat at the dock. Twin 330hp gas inboards cruise at 16-17 knots (low-to-mid 20s top).

Length Overall	38'0"	Fuel	410 gals.
Beam	14'0"	Water	65 gals.
Draft	3'0"	Waste	75 gals.
Weight	21,600#	Hull Type	Modified-V
Clearance	11'7"	Deadrise Aft	NA

Prices Not Provided for Pre-1995 Models

Chris Craft
Sarasota, FL
www.chriscraft.com

231-360-0827

Chris Craft 410 Motor Yacht
1972–86

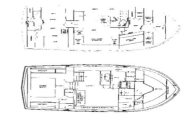

Classic flush-deck yacht introduced in 1972 became one of the best-selling motoryachts of her era. Highlights include spacious main salon, protected helm/aft-deck area, full walkaround decks, large engineroom with good service access. Early models were mostly hardtops; later models have standard flybridge. Offered with many floorplans over the years; queen berth became standard in master stateroom in 1981. Note small fuel capacity. Cruise at 14–15 knots with gas engines; optional diesels deliver 18- to 20-knot cruising speed.

Length	41'0"	Fuel	350 gals.
Beam	14'0"	Water	100 gals.
Draft	3'3"	Waste	40 gals.
Weight	26,565#	Hull Type	Modified-V
Clearance	15'10"	Deadrise Aft	NA

Prices Not Provided for Pre-1995 Models

Chris Craft
Sarasota, FL
www.chriscraft.com

231-360-0827

Chris Craft 425/426/427 Catalina
1985–90

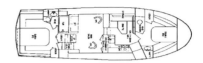

Updated version of earlier Uniflite 42 (1971–84) gave 1980s Chris Craft enthusiasts something to cheer about. Spacious galley-down interior includes double berths fore and aft, full dinette, large galley with upright refrigerator. Big aft deck is a plus. Called Chris Craft 425 Catalina in 1985; 426 Catalina in 1986; 427 Catalina in 1987–90. One of the better-riding small motoryachts of her era. Standard gas engines cruise at 17–18 knots (mid 20s top); optional Cat 375hp diesels cruise at 21-22 knots (24-25 top).

Length Overall	42'0"	Fuel	400 gals.
Beam	14'9"	Water	160 gals.
Draft	3'6"	Waste	60 gals.
Weight	33,000#	Hull Type	Modified-V
Clearance	12'10"	Deadrise Aft	13°

Prices Not Provided for Pre-1995 Models

Chris Craft
Sarasota, FL
www.chriscraft.com

231-360-0827

Chris Craft 480 Catalina
1985–89

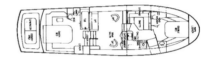

Popular double-cabin yacht from 1980s is basically a Chris 427 Catalina (1985–90) with six-foot cockpit extension. Spacious galley-down interior includes double berths fore and aft, full dinette, large galley with upright refrigerator. Note the tub in aft head. Cockpit is large enough for serious fishing. Flybridge was restyled in 1986. Modified-V hull is known for excellent seakeeping qualities, smooth ride. Standard gas engines cruise at 18 knots; optional 375hp Cat diesels cruise at 20 knots with a top speed in the mid 20s.

Length	48'0"	Fuel	590 gals.
Beam	14'9"	Water	160 gals.
Draft	3'6"	Headroom	6'4"
Weight	34,000#	Hull Type	Modified-V
Clearance	12'10"	Deadrise Aft	13°

Prices Not Provided for Pre-1995 Models

Chris Craft
Sarasota, FL
www.chriscraft.com

231-360-0827

Chris Craft 500 Constellation MY
1985–90

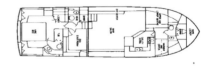

Handsome 50-footer originally built by Uniflite is basically a stretched version of the popular Pacemaker 46 Motor Yacht from the 1970s. Expansive three-stateroom interior in notable for wide-open salon, standard washer/dryer, unusual forepeak head compartment. Fully enclosed and paneled aft deck serves as second salon. Aft guest cabin doubles as den/office. Extended flybridge can seat a dozen guests. Note wide walkways. GM 550hp 6V92 diesels cruise at 16–17 knots and top out at close to 20 knots.

Length	50'6"	Fuel	600 gals.
Beam	15'3"	Water	160 gals.
Draft	4'4"	Headroom	6'6"
Weight	54,000#	Hull Type	Modified-V
Clearance	17'1"	Deadrise Aft	4°

Prices Not Provided for Pre-1995 Models

Chris Craft
Sarasota, FL
www.chriscraft.com

Chris Craft 501 Motor Yacht
1987–90

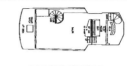

Contemporary twin-deck motoryacht with extended deckhouse salon offered Hatteras-style accommodations at a Chris Craft price. Spacious three-stateroom, three-head interior with home-sized galley, full-beam salon is huge for a 50-footer. Spiral salon staircase provides private entry to well-appointed master suite with king bed, full-size tub. Note inside bridge access, stand-up engineroom, small aft deck for line handling. GM 550hp 6V92TA diesels cruise at 16 knots and reach a top speed of 18–19 knots.

Length	50'8"	Fuel	778 gals.
Beam	15'5"	Water	260 gals.
Draft	4'6"	Cockpit	NA
Weight	49,000#	Hull Type	Modified-V
Clearance	NA	Deadrise Aft	4°

Prices Not Provided for Pre-1995 Models

Chris Craft
Sarasota, FL
www.chriscraft.com

Cruisers 3650 Motor Yacht; 375 MY
1995–2005

Popular aft-cabin cruiser (called 3650 Aft Cabin in 1995–99; 375 in 2000–05) delivered impressive mix of sportyacht styling, balanced accommodations. Spacious salon with cherry joinery is wide open to galley and dinette. Compact staterooms have athwartships double berths to preserve space. Note tall salon headroom, tub in master head. Updates in 1999 included wing doors, aft-deck weather enclosure, molded bridge steps instead of ladder. Standard 370hp gas engines cruise at 18 knots (about 25 knots top).

Length	40'10"	Fuel	300 gals.
Beam	13'8"	Water	68 gals.
Draft	3'2"	Waste	55 gals.
Weight, Gas	20,000#	Hull Type	Modified-V
Weight, Diesel	21,500#	Deadrise Aft	11°

See Page 539 For Resale Values

Cruisers Yachts
Oconto, WI
www.cruisersyachts.com

Cruisers 3850/3950 Aft Cabin MY
1991–97

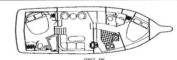

1991–96

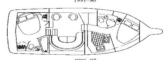

1996–97

Well-equipped flybridge yacht (called 3850 Aft Cabin in 1991–94; 3950 Aft Cabin in 1995–97) offered savvy 1990s owners good value for the money. Highlights include comfortable salon with leather seating, big U-shaped galley, built-in washer/dryer, roomy aft deck with wet bar. Rear master stateroom window provides panoramic outside view. Fully cored hull has prop pockets to reduce draft, improve efficiency. Standard gas engines cruise at a lackluster 15–16 knots; optional 350hp Cat diesels cruise at 20 knots (mid 20s top).

Length	41'6"	Fuel	400 gals.
Beam	14'0"	Water	100 gals.
Draft	3'4"	Waste	54 gals.
Weight, Gas	21,000#	Hull Type	Modified-V
Weight, Diesel	22,400#	Deadrise Aft	16°

See Page 539 For Resale Values

Cruisers Yachts
Oconto, WI
www.cruisersyachts.com

---

www.powerboatguide.com   231-360-0827

Cruisers 385/395 Motor Yacht
2006–08

Standard Layout

Optional Layout

Slightly overstyled flybridge yacht (called Cruisers 385 MY in 2006) makes good on promise of spacious accommodations, brisk performance. Elegant twin-stateroom interior is offered with choice of facing or crescent-shaped dinette. Overlapping elliptical windows provide excellent outside visibility. Topside highlights include acrylic wing doors, U-shaped bridge seating, extended swim platform with boarding steps. Note narrow side decks, good fit and finish. Standard 375hp gas inboards cruise at 25 knots (about 30 knots top).

Length	42'2"	Fuel	300 gals.
Beam	13'8"	Water	68 gals.
Draft	3'3"	Waste	51 gals.
Weight, Gas	23,500#	Hull Type	Modified-V
Weight, Diesel	25,000#	Deadrise Aft	16°

See Page 539 For Resale Values

Cruisers Yachts
Oconto, WI
www.cruisersyachts.com

---

www.powerboatguide.com   231-360-0827

Cruisers 405/415 Express Motor Yacht
2003–Current

Versatile hardtop cruiser with tall-freeboard profile blends express-boat deck layout, motor-yacht accommodations. Well-furnished interior with combined salon/galley/dinette includes two large staterooms, generous storage. Hatch in salon floor provides access to spacious engineroom. Note washer/dryer in master stateroom. Forward head is split with shower, toilet in separate compartments. Roomy aft deck features hardtop, wet bar, molded steps to swim platform. Cat 420hp diesels cruise in the low 20s (27–28 knots top).

Length	42'6"	Fuel	380 gals.
Beam	13'8"	Water	100 gals.
Draft	3'6"	Waste	70 gals.
Weight	31,000#	Hull Type	Modified-V
Clearance, Arch	14'0"	Deadrise Aft	16°

See Page 539 For Resale Values

Cruisers Yachts
Oconto, WI
www.cruisersyachts.com

---

www.powerboatguide.com   231-360-0827

Cruisers 4450 Express MY
2000–03

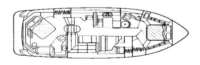

Innovative aft-cabin cruiser with open-deck layout combines express-boat styling, condo-style accommodations. Three-stateroom interior has salon, galley, slightly raised dinette on same level. Forward guest cabin with walk-in closet is nearly as large as owner's stateroom. Aft head includes whirlpool in addition to stall shower. Tiered helm and cockpit area keeps captain, passengers in close proximity. Extended swim platform can support PWC. Cruise at 18 knots with 420hp Cat diesels (23–24 knots top).

Length	45'6"	Fuel	500 gals.
Beam	15'4"	Water	140 gals.
Draft	3'3"	Waste	100 gals.
Weight	38,000#	Hull Type	Modified-V
Clearance, Arch	14'6"	Deadrise Aft	18°

See Page 539 For Resale Values

Cruisers Yachts
Oconto, WI
www.cruisersyachts.com

Cruisers 447 Sport Sedan
2007–Current

Feature-rich flybridge yacht meets cruiser's needs for on-the-water style, comfort, versatility. Expansive two-stateroom interior with two heads has split-level salon with galley and dinette forward, facing lounge seats aft. Storage compartment under salon is big enough for inflatables, bikes. Guest stateroom has space for washer/dryer. Big engineroom is a plus. Note wraparound bridge windshield, aft sun lounge, fiberglass hardtop. Yanmar 480hp V-drive diesels cruise at 25–26 knots (about 30 knots top).

Length	45'2"	Fuel	375 gals.
Beam	14'6"	Water	100 gals.
Draft	3'10"	Waste	50 gals.
Weight	29,500	Hull Type	Modified-V
Clearance	16'0"	Deadrise Aft	18°

See Page 539 For Resale Values

Cruisers Yachts
Oconto, WI
www.cruisersyachts.com

Cruisers 455 Express Motor Yacht
2004–Current

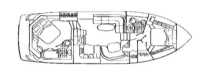

Updated version of Cruiser's 4450 Express MY (1998–2003) offers enticing mix of luxury accommodations, spirited performance. Posh three-stateroom interior has salon, galley, slightly raised dinette on same level. Forward guest cabin with walk-in closet is nearly as large as owner's stateroom; aft head includes whirlpool in addition to stall shower. Combined helm, cockpit area keeps captain, passengers in close proximity. Extended swim platform can support PWC. Cruise at 22 knots with 480hp Volvo diesels (28–29 knots top).

Length	45'6"	Fuel	500 gals.
Beam	15'4"	Water	140 gals.
Draft	3'3"	Waste	100 gals.
Weight	36,000#	Hull Type	Modified-V
Clearance, Hardtop	15'4"	Deadrise Aft	16°

See Page 539 For Resale Values

Cruisers Yachts
Oconto, WI
www.cruisersyachts.com

Cruisers 497 Sport Sedan
2006–07

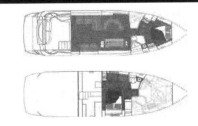

Rakish flybridge sedan (called 477 Sport Sedan in 2006) with semi-protected bridge took sportyacht comfort, styling to the next level. Luxurious midcabin interior with split-level salon, cherry cabinetry features two large staterooms, facing salon settees, huge galley with acres of counter space. Innovative bridge with hardtop, wet bar, full glass windshield offers good weather protection. Note spacious cockpit with molded bridge steps, extended swim platform. Volvo 575hp V-drive diesels cruise at 24–25 knots (30+ knots wide open).

Length	50'2"	Fuel	526 gals.
Beam	15'0"	Water	150 gals.
Draft	4'1"	Waste	75 gals.
Weight	39,500#	Hull Type	Modified-V
Headroom	6'6"	Deadrise Aft	18.5°

See Page 539 For Resale Values

Cruisers Yachts
Oconto, WI
www.cruisersyachts.com

Motoryachts & Trawlers

231-360-0827

Cruisers 5000 Sedan Sport
1998–2003

Well-mannered flybridge yacht with sleek profile, vast interior is ideal for liveaboards and cruisers alike. Wide-open salon is open to huge starboard-side galley, raised helm/dinette area forward. Inside bridge access is rare in a boat this size. Two of three staterooms have double berths; both heads have separate stall showers. Note rich cherrywood cabinetry, good engineroom access. Fully cored hull has prop pockets to reduce draft and shaft angles. Volvo 480hp V-drive diesels cruise at 18 knots; 660hp Cats cruise 24–25 knots.

Length	49'6"	Fuel	600 gals.
Beam	15'6"	Water	150 gals.
Draft	3.5'	Waste	100 gals.
Weight	42,000#	Hull Type	Modified-V
Clearance, Arch	16.5'	Deadrise Aft	11°

See Page 539 For Resale Values

Cruisers Yachts
Oconto, WI
www.cruisersyachts.com

---

www.powerboatguide.com

231-360-0827

CT 35 Trawler
1977–86

Traditional Floorplan

Sundeck Floorplan

Well-built Taiwan trawler with traditional teak interior is easy on the eye, light on the wallet, inexpensive to run. Principal highlights include roomy master stateroom with cockpit access door, large salon with efficient galley area, very spacious engineroom. Teak window frames—replaced with aluminum frames in later models—are prone to leaks. With plenty of exterior brightwork, this boat requires a fair amount of maintenance. Cruise at 7–8 knots with single 120hp diesel; 10 knots with twin 85hp diesels.

Length Overall	34'11"	Clearance	NA
Length WL	30.5'	Fuel	300 gals.
Beam	12'0"	Water	200 gals.
Draft	3.5'	Waste	60 gals.
Weight	19,800#	Hull Type	Semi-Disp.

Prices Not Provided for Pre-1995 Models

No longer in production

---

www.powerboatguide.com

231-360-0827

DeFever 40 Passagemaker
1973–84

Popular U.S.-built trawler combines all-fiberglass construction with timeless styling, practical accommodations. Highlights include twin-stateroom, galley-up teak interior, port/starboard sliding deck doors, two heads, walkaround teak decks, folding mast & boom. Note convenient deck access door in aft stateroom. Unusually large cockpit for a trawler this size. Deep forefoot, long keel provides good headsea performance. Marketed after 1980 as the Downeast 40. Cruise at 8 knots with twin 120hp (or 135hp) Lehman diesels.

Length	39'8"	Headroom	6'4"
Beam	13'8"	Fuel	450 gals.
Draft	4'0"	Water	200 gals.
Weight	28,000#	Waste	40 gals.
Clearance w/Mast	24'0"	Hull Type	Semi-Disp.

Prices Not Provided for Pre-1995 Models

DeFever designs have been built
by several manufacturers.

DeFever 41 Trawler
1980–89

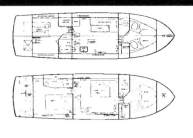

Classic DeFever trawler popular in the 1980s combines traditional trunk-cabin styling with time-tested layout, economical operation. Highlights include roomy galley-up interior with teak woodwork, post/starboard salon doors, full walkaround decks, mast and boom assembly. Cabintop can stow small dinghy. Note teak decks, tub/shower in aft head, aft stateroom deck door, simulated lapstrake hull lines. Solid fiberglass hull has prop-protecting keel. Quality boat from a good Taiwan yard. Cruise at 7–8 knots with 135hp Lehman diesels.

Length Overall	40'7"	Clearance	NA
Length WL	34'7"	Fuel	400 gals.
Beam	14'2"	Water	250 gals.
Draft	4'0"	Waste	60 gals.
Weight	23,000#	Hull Type	Semi-Disp.

Prices Not Provided for Pre-1995 Models

DeFever designs have been built
by several manufacturers.

DeFever 43 Trawler
1978–81

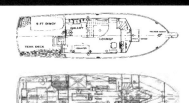

Deepwater trawler with full-displacement hull, large fuel capacity was designed for serious long-range cruising. Unusual flush-deck design results in large afterdeck suitable for entertaining or dinghy storage. Two-stateroom floorplan with U-shaped galley aft in salon differs from most trawler layouts. Large engineroom is a plus. Copious cabin storage. Teak decks, fold-down mast, bow pulpit were standard. Note fake flybridge exhaust stack. Among the heaviest boats in her class. Twin 120hp diesels cruise at 7–8 knots with 1,500-mile range.

Length Overall	42'2"	Clearance	NA
Length WL	36'7"	Fuel	1,072 gals.
Beam	14'0"	Water	500 gals.
Draft	4'5"	Waste	50 gals.
Weight	40,836#	Hull	Displacement

Prices Not Provided for Pre-1995 Models

DeFever designs have been built
by several manufacturers.

DeFever 44 Trawler
1981–2004

Heavily-built displacement trawler with covered aft deck remains among most popular DeFever designs ever produced. Expansive two-stateroom interior has galley aft in the salon—most galley-up trawlers have the galley forward. Master stateroom is huge with copious storage, space for washer/dryer. Walk-in engineroom has near-standing headroom, built-in workbench. Note generous fuel, water capacities. Full-length keel protects running gear. Twin 135hp diesels cruise at 8 knots with range of 1,500+ miles.

Length Overall	43'9"	Clearance	NA
Length WL	38'6"	Fuel	900 gals.
Beam	14'9"	Water	350 gals.
Draft	4'7"	Waste	60 gals.
Weight	44,000#	Hull Type	Displacement

See Page 540 For Resale Values

DeFever designs have been built
by several manufacturers.

Motoryachts & Trawlers

231-360-0827

DeFever 45 Pilothouse
2002–Current

Well-crafted pilothouse trawler pairs signature De-Fever styling with efficient deck layout, luxury-class amenities. Deluxe split-level interior boasts large master stateroom with desk/vanity, guest stateroom with engineroom access, U-shaped galley with Corian counters, raised pilothouse with pilot berth. Note Portuguese bridge, wide, protected side decks. Washer/dryer space is provided in portside stateroom. Most boats this size have two heads. Twin John Deere 150hp diesels cruise efficiently at 8–10 knots (12 knots top).

Length Overall	45'0"	Fuel, Std.	500 gals.
Length WL	40'6"	Fuel, Opt.	700 gals.
Beam	15'0"	Water	250 gals.
Draft	3'10"	Waste	50 gals.
Weight	38,000#	Hull Type	Semi-Disp.

Insufficient Resale Data To Assign Values

DeFever designs have been built
by several manufacturers.

231-360-0827

DeFever 47 POC Motor Yacht
1986–92

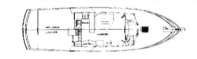

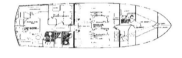

Conservative DeFever motoryacht with hard-enclosed aft deck provides extra space for cruising and liveaboard comfort. Standard galley-up interior includes three staterooms, three heads, walk-in engineroom, salon/lounge with centerline helm. Second guest stateroom (aft of engineroom) doubles as office/study. Main salon opens to small aft deck suitable for line handling. Combined double head aft shares common tub/shower. Semi-displacement hull is fully cored. Cat 210hp diesels cruise at 8 knots; 375hp Cats cruise at 12–14 knots.

Length	46'10"	Headroom	6'5"
Beam	16'0"	Fuel	600 gals.
Draft	4'8"	Water	275 gals.
Weight	43,200#	Waste	60 gals.
Clearance	15'6"	Hull Type	Semi-Disp.

Prices Not Provided for Pre-1995 Models

DeFever designs have been built
by several manufacturers.

231-360-0827

DeFever 48 Trawler
1978–92

Long-range trawler yacht with Europa styling, near bullet-proof construction ranks among the best-selling DeFever designs ever produced. Comfortable three-stateroom interior features expansive salon with U-shaped galley aft, two full heads, spacious master suite. Salon has three deck doors—very unusual. Cavernous walk-in engineroom includes sea chest, work bench. Note protected side decks. Popular model (over 200 built) is always in demand. Cruise at 8 knots with 135hp Lehman diesels, 14–15 knots with 375hp Cats.

Length Overall	47'3"	Headroom	6'5"
Length WL	40'10"	Fuel	950 gals.
Beam	15'4"	Water	500 gals.
Draft	4'9"	Waste	100 gals.
Weight	50,000#	Hull Type	Semi-Disp.

Prices Not Provided for Pre-1995 Models

DeFever designs have been built
by several manufacturers.

DeFever 49 Cockpit MY
1994–2007

Main Deck Plan

Lower Deck Plan

Cockpit version of popular DeFever 44 Trawler makes a good boat even better. Expansive two-stateroom interior is arranged with U-shaped galley aft in the salon—most galley-up trawlers have the galley forward. Master stateroom is huge with copious storage, space for washer/dryer. Walk-in engineroom has near-standing headroom, built-in workbench. Cockpit with transom door serves anglers and cruisers alike. Full-length keel protects props and running gear. Twin 150hp John Deere diesels cruise at 8 knots with range of 1,500+ miles.

Length Overall	48'10"	Headroom	6'6"
Length WL	43'6"	Fuel	1,100 gals.
Beam	15'0"	Water	370 gals.
Draft	4'7"	Waste	90 gals.
Weight	53,900#	Hull Type	Displacement

See Page 541 For Resale Values

DeFever designs have been built by several manufacturers.

DeFever 49 Pilothouse (Hard-Chine)
1978–90

Popular pilothouse yacht with hard-chined, semi-displacement hull is intended for long-range cruising in comfort, security. Split-level interior with combined salon/galley includes amidships master stateroom with queen bed, guest stateroom with upper/lower bunds, raised pilothouse with dinette and watch berth. Topside features include covered side decks, wave-breaking Portuguese bridge. Note that alternate DeFever 49 model with soft chines (built by CTF Marine) was also available. Cruise at 8 knots with 135hp diesels.

Length Overall	49'9"	Clearance	17'0"
Length WL	42'0"	Fuel	800 gals.
Beam	15'0"	Water	400 gals.
Draft	4'6"	Waste	70 gals.
Weight	50,000#	Hull Type	Semi-Disp.

Prices Not Provided for Pre-1995 Models

DeFever designs have been built by several manufacturers.

DeFever 49 Pilothouse (Soft-Chine)
1977–2004

Classic DeFever design built with ship-like profile is intended for long-range cruising in comfort, security. Split-level interior with combined salon/galley includes amidships master stateroom with queen bed, guest stateroom with upper/lower bunks, raised pilothouse with dinette and watch berth. Note wave-breaking Portuguese bridge. Semi-displacement hull with rounded chines is easily driven, economical to operate. Alternate DeFever 49 model with hard chines (built by Sen Koh Marine) was also available. Cruise at 8 knots with 135hp diesels.

Length Overall	49'9"	Clearance	NA
Length WL	43'9"	Fuel	1,000 gals.
Beam	15'0"	Water	450 gals.
Draft	4'9"	Waste	70 gals.
Weight	50,000#	Hull Type	Semi-Disp.

Prices Not Provided for Pre-1995 Models

DeFever designs have been built by several manufacturers.

231-360-0827

DeFever 52 Offshore Cruiser
1980–91

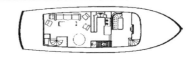

Heavy-weather displacement trawler with wide 16'8" beam couples beefy construction with spacious accommodations, long-range capability. Main deck level with U-shaped galley, extended salon with day head, is open from wheelhouse to cockpit. Pilothouse includes watch berth, deck doors, direct bridge access. Two of the three staterooms below are huge. Short foredeck adds to interior living space. Wide body version with full-width salon was also available. Cat 210hp diesels cruise at 8 knots with up to 2,000-mile range.

Length Overall	51 7"	Clearance	NA
Length WL	45 5"	Fuel	1,500 gals.
Beam	16'8"	Water	500 gals.
Draft	4'9"	Waste	70 gals.
Weight	77,000#	Hull	Displacement

Prices Not Provided for Pre-1995 Models

DeFever designs have been built
by several manufacturers.

231-360-0827

DeFever 53 POC
1986–89

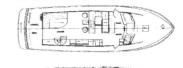

Spacious twin-deck motoryacht made good on De-Fever promise of liveaboard comfort, cruising elegance. Three-stateroom floorplan boasts spacious master with private salon access, huge VIP cabin, three full heads, walk-in engineroom. Expansive salon with home-size galley, separate dining area features inside bridge access—a convenience not always found in a yacht this size. Side decks are sheltered by bridge overhangs. Hull is fully cored to reduce weight. Twin 375hp Cat diesels cruise at 12 knots (15–16 top).

Length	52 7"	Clearance	18 5"
Beam	16'6"	Fuel	1,000 gals.
Draft	4'8"	Water	400 gals.
Weight	55,000#	Waste	80 gals.
Headroom	6'6"	Hull Type	Semi-Disp.

Prices Not Provided for Pre-1995 Models

DeFever designs have been built
by several manufacturers.

231-360-0827

DeFever 57 Yachtfish
1986–89

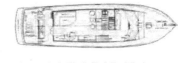

Cockpit version of popular DeFever 53 POC is ideally suited for extended coastal cruising in comfort, security. Three-stateroom floorplan boasts spacious master with private salon access, huge VIP cabin, three full heads, walk-in engineroom. Expansive salon with home-size galley, separate dining area features inside bridge access—a convenience not always found in a yacht this size. Side decks are sheltered by bridge overhangs. Hull is fully cored to reduce weight. Twin 375hp Cat diesels cruise at 12 knots (15–16 top).

Length	56 7"	Clearance	18 5"
Beam	16'6"	Fuel	1,200 gals.
Draft	4'8"	Water	400 gals.
Weight	60,000#	Waste	80 gals.
Headroom	6'6"	Hull Type	Semi-Disp.

Prices Not Provided for Pre-1995 Models

DeFever designs have been built
by several manufacturers.

231-360-0827

Eagle 32 Pilothouse Trawler
1985–93

Salty displacement cruiser with tug-like profile offers impressive mix of personality, comfort, economy. Space-efficient teak interior boasts surprisingly roomy salon considering the wide side decks. Good helm visibility from raised pilothouse. Stateroom is small, but head has separate stall shower. Optional upper helm is concealed within false smokestack. Deep keel protects prop. Tremendous eye appeal. Used Eagle 32s are always in demand. Cruise at 7–8 knots with 600-mile range with single 135hp diesel.

Length Overall	32'0"	Headroom	6'4"
Length WL	28'0"	Fuel	168 gals.
Beam	11'6"	Water	125 gals.
Draft	3'4"	Waste	25 gals.
Weight	17,000#	Hull Type	Displacement

Prices Not Provided for Pre-1995 Models

Transpacific Marine
Ningbo, China
www.transpacificmarine.com

231-360-0827

Eagle 40 Pilothouse Trawler
1994–Current

Twin-Stateroom Plan

Single-Stateroom Plan

Seaworthy single-diesel trawler with full displacement hull targets seasoned buyers with an eye for quality. Handsome teak interior—available with one or two staterooms—features combined salon/galley with convertible settee, raised pilothouse with settee/watch berth, teak-planked flooring throughout. Note spacious engineroom, wide side decks, functional mast and boom. Upper helm is concealed in false stack. Deep keel protects running gear. Excellent joinerwork, first-rate finish. Cruise at 8 knots with single Cummins diesel.

Length Overall	40'6"	Clearance	NA
Length WL	36'10"	Fuel	400 gals.
Beam	14'6"	Water	240 gals.
Draft	4'5"	Waste	40 gals.
Weight	28,000#	Hull Type	Displacement

See Page 540 For Resale Values

Transpacific Marine
Ningbo, China
www.transpacificmarine.com

231-360-0827

Eagle 53 Pilothouse Trawler
2002–Current

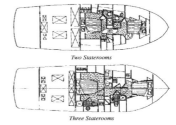

Two Staterooms

Three Staterooms

Quality-built pilothouse yacht with classic lines is designed for extended coastal cruising in comfort, security. Available with two- or three-stateroom layouts (den/office can replace third stateroom) with teak-planked flooring throughout. Bridge overhangs protect side decks and cockpit. Large engineroom is a plus. Note watertight pilothouse doors, wave-breaking Portuguese bridge. Semi-displacement hull has long, prop-protecting keel. Cruise at 14–15 knots with 450hp Cummins diesels (about 18 knots top).

Length Overall	53'3"	Headroom	6'6"
Length WL	44'9"	Fuel	830 gals.
Beam	15'9"	Water	250 gals.
Draft	4'0"	Waste	48 gals.
Weight	43,000#	Hull Type	Semi-Disp.

Insufficient Resale Data To Assign Values

Transpacific Marine
Ningbo, China
www.transpacificmarine.com

Motoryachts & Trawlers

---

www.powerboatguide.com   231-360-0827

Egg Harbor 40 Motor Yacht
1982–86

Vintage flush-deck yacht appeals to boaters with an eye for classic motoryacht lines. Built on reworked hull of earlier Pacemaker 40 MY (whose molds and tooling Egg Harbor acquired in 1980). Interior features include enormous master stateroom with walk-in closet, spacious galley, furniture-quality woodwork. Note washer/dryer tucked under salon entertainment center. Semi-enclosed lower helm/aft deck seats a small crowd. Flybridge is small by modern standards. GM 410hp 6-71TIs cruise at 20 knots (low 20s top).

Length	40'0"	Fuel	300 gals.
Beam	14'1"	Water	100 gals.
Draft	2'11"	Headroom	6'4"
Weight	30,000#	Hull Type	Modified-V
Clearance	16'2"	Deadrise Aft	8°

Prices Not Provided for Pre-1995 Models

Egg Harbor Yachts
Egg Harbor, NJ
www.eggharboryachts.com

---

www.powerboatguide.com   231-360-0827

Endeavour TrawlerCat 36
1998–Current

Original Layout

Updated Layout

Midsize catamaran trawler sold factory-direct is stable, comfortable, affordable. Highlights include roomy cockpit with standard hardtop, Original three-stateroom interior with double bed aft replaced in 2004 (2005?) with new floorplan with double forward. Comfortable salon overlooks expansive gourmet galley with copious storage in port hull. Teak-and-holly flooring is a nice touch. Note full-beam foredeck, opening front windshield. Wide side decks make getting around easy. Twin 150hp diesels cruise efficiently at 10–12 knots.

Length Overall	36'0"	Clearance	14'0"
Length WL	34'6"	Fuel	300 gals.
Beam	15'0"	Water	90 gals.
Draft	2'10"	Waste	30 gals.
Weight	16,000#	Hull Type	Catamaran

Insufficient Resale Data To Assign Values

Endeavour Catamarans, Clearwater, FL
Phone 727-573-5377
www.endeavourcats.com

---

www.powerboatguide.com   231-360-0827

Endeavour TrawlerCat 44
2001–Current

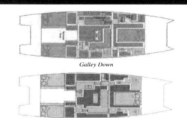

Galley Down

Galley Up

Roomy catamaran trawler appeals to cruisers attracted to multihull's seakindly handling, impressive economy. Available with galley-down or galley-up layout, both with twin aft staterooms, spacious salon, two full heads. Topside features include full-beam foredeck, semi-enclosed lower helm, wide side decks, roomy cockpit with lazarette storage. Engines are located under aft-cabin berths; running gear is recessed for grounding protection. Yanmar 240hp diesels cruise at 14–15 knots at better than 1 mpg.

Length Overall	43.5"	Clearance	NA
Length WL	41'0"	Fuel	500 gals.
Beam	18'8"	Water	115 gals.
Draft	3'0"	Waste	50 gals.
Weight	22,800#	Hull Type	Catamaran

Insufficient Resale Data To Assign Values

Endeavour Catamarans, Clearwater, FL
Phone 727-573-5377
www.endeavourcats.com

Fairline 43 Phantom
2000-04

Executive-class flybridge yacht blends seductive styling with lush accommodations, nimble performance. Elegant two-stateroom interior with two full heads boasts facing salon settees, step-down galley with generous storage, high-gloss cherry woodwork. Twin-seat lower helm provides excellent fore, aft visibility. Roomy bridge offers three helm seats, wide sun pad. Note teak-laid cockpit, extended swim platform, electric cabin windows. Engineroom is a tight fit. A good performer, 480hp Volvo diesels cruise at 27 knots (31–32 knots top).

Length Overall	44'6"	Fuel	410 gals.
Hull Length	43'1"	Water	209 gals.
Beam	13'7"	Clearance	6'4"
Draft	3'6"	Hull Type	Deep-V
Weight	29,000#	Deadrise Aft	17°

See Page 541 For Resale Values

Fairline Boats, Ltd.
Oundle, England
www.fairline.com

Fairline 46 Phantom
1999-2005

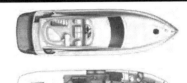

Med-inspired flybridge cruiser offers compelling blend of aggressive styling, spacious accommodations. Three-stateroom floorplan with comfortable salon is rare in a 46-footer; optional crew quarters brings total to four staterooms. Galley is on salon level rather than sunken as it is in many European yachts. Note high-gloss cherry joinery, teak cockpit sole, extended swim platform. Deep-V hull is noted as a good heavy weather performer. Popular model is always in demand. Volvo 480hp diesels cruise at 24 knots (28–29 knots top).

Length Overall	47'10"	Fuel	416 gals.
Hull Length	46'0"	Water	187 gals.
Beam	14'2"	Clearance	16'6"
Draft	3'8"	Hull	Deep-V
Weight	29,000#	Deadrise Aft	19°

See Page 541 For Resale Values

Fairline Boats, Ltd.
Oundle, England
www.fairline.com

Fairline 50 Phantom
2002-06

Sleek U.K. flybridge yacht blends world-class engineering with lavish accommodations, sportboat handling. Opulent three-stateroom, two-head interior boasts twin-seat lower helm, full-feature galley, high-gloss cherry woodwork, unique peninsular bar unit in salon. Hatch in cockpit sole opens to reveal cavernous storage area (or optional crew cabin). Note electric cabin windows, standard washer/dryer, pump room for air-conditioning units. Engineroom is tight; galley storage is minimal. Volvo 675hp diesels cruise at 25–26 knots (low 30s top).

Length	51'10"	Headroom	6'6"
Beam	14'9"	Fuel	523 gals.
Draft	3'11"	Water	148 gals.
Weight	34,000#	Hull Type	Deep-V
Clearance	17'0"	Deadrise Aft	18°

See Page 541 For Resale Values

Fairline Boats, Ltd.
Oundle, England
www.fairline.com

Motoryachts & Trawlers

231-360-0827

Fairline 52 Squadron
1998–2002

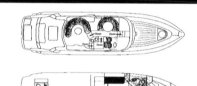

High-end European import with mini-megayacht styling, innovative layout was a bold departure from previous Fairline designs. Standard two-stateroom floorplan —most 52-footers have three staterooms—has rare cabin berth option located off galley. Highlights include spacious, open-plan salon with raised dinette forward, state-of-the-art lower helm, gourmet galley, extravagant master suite with laundry room. Oval flybridge design is completely unusual. Engineroom is a tight fit. Cat 600hp diesels cruise at 25 knots (30 knots top).

Length Overall	53'3"	Fuel	576 gals.
Hull Length	52'6"	Water	151 gals.
Beam	15'4"	Clearance	17 5"
Draft	3'8"	Hull	Deep-V
Weight	37,000#	Deadrise Aft	18°

See Page 541 For Resale Values

Fairline Boats, Ltd.
Oundle, England
www.fairline.com

www.powerboatguide.com 231-360-0827

Fairline 55 Squadron
1996–2004

Acclaimed U.K. flybridge yacht matched signature Fairline reputation for big-boat luxury, performance, quality. Remarkably open interior features salon with semi-circular settee, sunken galley, elevated dinette, and lower helm. Note open-tread bridge stairs, large utility room behind galley door. Additional features include extended swim platform, curved salon doors, aft crew quarters, super-large flybridge. Engineroom is a tight fit. Volvo 600hp—or Cat 660hp—diesels cruise at 25–26 knots (30 knots top). Over 160 were built.

Length Overall	55'11"	Fuel	576 gals.
Hull Length	54'3"	Water	150 gals.
Beam	15'3"	Clearance	17'3"
Draft	3'8"	Hull	Deep-V
Weight	48,000#	Deadrise Aft	18.5°

See Page 541 For Resale Values

Fairline Boats, Ltd.
Oundle, England
www.fairline.com

www.powerboatguide.com 231-360-0827

Fairline 58 Squadron
2002–08

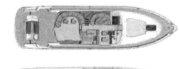

World-class motoryacht is a successful blend of modern European styling, sumptuous accomodations, impressive performance. Three-stateroom floorplan with unusually large heads is identical to earlier Squadron 55 (1999–2004) with opulent salon, sunken galley, elevated dining area forward, crew quarters aft. Note open-tread bridge stairs, large utility room behind galley door. Truly extraordinary bridge layout. Topside features include twin-pillar mast, teak decks, extended swim platform. Cruise at 28 knots with 800hp Cat diesels (low 30s top).

Length Overall	58'10"	Headroom	6'6"
Beam	16'0"	Fuel	721 gals.
Draft	4'4"	Water	247 gals.
Weight	44,000#	Hull Type	Deep-V
Clearance	19'9"	Deadrise Aft	18°

See Page 541 For Resale Values

Fairline Boats, Ltd.
Oundle, England
www.fairline.com

231-360-0827

Fairline 59 Squadron
1996–99

U.K. luxury yacht (called 56 Squadron until 1996 when extended swim platform was added) set 1990's standards for modern motoryacht styling, luxury-class accommodations. Well-appointed interior features split-level salon with open-plan galley, three double cabins forward, optional crew cabin aft. Note inside bridge access, huge storage room beneath galley floor. Large bridge with centerline helm seats ten. Cat or Volvo 600hp diesels cruise at 24 knots (26–27 knots top); optional 680hp MANs cruise at 26 knots (29 knots top).

Length Overall	59'9"	Fuel	720 gals.
Hull Length	57'10"	Water	160 gals.
Beam	15'6"	Clearance	18.5"
Draft	3'10"	Hull	Deep-V
Weight	49,200#	Deadrise Aft	18.5°

See Page 541 For Resale Values

Fairline Boats, Ltd.
Oundle, England
www.fairline.com

231-360-0827

Fairline 62 Squadron
1999–2002

Bold Med-style cruising yacht (based on previous Fairline 52 Squadron) combined then-futuristic styling with avant-garde interior, premium build quality. Classy three-stateroom interior features spacious salon with facing curved sofas, ergonomically perfect lower helm, unique circular owner's stateroom, crew cabin aft. Oval-shaped flybridge with circular lounge, sun pad forward of helm, seats a small crowd. Note twin-pillar mast, teak-laid decks. Galley and engineroom are small. Cat 800hp engines deliver top speed of nearly 30 knots.

Length Overall	64.5"	Fuel	991 gals.
Hull Length	63'1"	Water	265 gals.
Beam	16.5"	Clearance	18'10"
Draft	4'6"	Hull	Deep-V
Weight	62,700#	Deadrise Aft	18°

See Page 541 For Resale Values

Fairline Boats, Ltd.
Oundle, England
www.fairline.com

231-360-0827

Fairline 65 Squadron
1995–2003

Seductive Euroyacht with striking profile made good on Fairline promise of cutting-edge design, deluxe accommodations. Extravagant four-stateroom, three-head interior includes well-appointed salon with leather seating, full-beam master suite with king bed, enormous master bath, polished cherry woodwork. Galley has pass-through to helm, washer/dryer closet. Note fore and aft crew cabins. Restyled in 1998 for a more streamlined profile. Popular model. Cruise at 25 knots with MAN 1,100hp engines (about 30 knots top).

Length Overall	66'10"	Clearance	NA
Hull Length	65'0"	Fuel	1,105 gals.
Beam	17'4"	Water	336 gals.
Draft	4'9"	Hull	Deep-V
Weight	71,680#	Deadrise Aft	19°

See Page 541 For Resale Values

Fairline Boats, Ltd.
Oundle, England
www.fairline.com

---

www.powerboatguide.com   231-360-0827

Fleming 55 Pilothouse
1986–Current

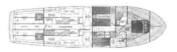

World-class pilothouse yacht built to exceptional standards makes the grade with owners demanding uncompromising quality. Highlights include full teak interior, three large staterooms, wave-breaking Portuguese bridge, protected side decks, spacious cockpit. Easily driven hull has long, prop-protecting keel. Excellent visibility from raised pilothouse. Note inside bridge access, flybridge pass-thru to galley, teak decks, large storage lazarette. A classic yacht with over 200 built. Cat 435hp—or Cummins 450hp—diesels cruise at 15–16 knots.

Length Overall	55'9"	Clearance, Arch	16'0"
Length WL	50'10"	Fuel	1,000 gals.
Beam	16'0"	Water	300 gals.
Draft	5'0"	Waste	100 gals.
Weight	66,000#	Hull Type	Semi-Disp.

See Page 542 For Resale Values

Fleming Yachts
Costa Mesa, CA
www.flemingyachts.com

---

www.powerboatguide.com   231-360-0827

Fleming 65 Pilothouse
2006–Current

Highly regarded pilothouse yacht blends exceptional beauty with luxurious accommodations, unsurpassed build quality. Maxi-volume interior boasts spacious salon with integrated galley and dining area, raised pilothouse with day head and dinette, opulent master suite, two VIP guest cabins. Note protective Portuguese bridge, stand-up engineroom, spacious cockit, feature-packed flybridge with extended hartop. This is as good as it gets in a luxury cruising yacht. Cruise comfortably at 12–14 knots with 700hp Cat diesels.

Length Overall	65'0"	Clearance, Arch	22'11"
Length WL	59'2"	Fuel	1,800 gals.
Beam	18'8"	Water	400 gals.
Draft	5'0"	Waste	100 gals.
Weight	108,177#	Hull Type	Semi-Disp.

Insufficient Resale Data To Assign Values

Fleming Yachts, Costa Mesa, CA
Phone 949-645-1024
www.flemingyachts.com

---

www.powerboatguide.com   231-360-0827

Grand Banks 32 Sedan
1965–95

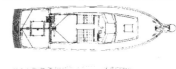

Polished sedan cruiser still commands admiration for her classic trawler profile, top-notch construction, great resale values. Single-stateroom interior with convertible salon settees, fully equipped galley is perfect for the cruising couple. Large engineroom provides good service access. Cockpit is large enough for fishing. Superb fit and finish throughout. Wood construction until 1973. Long keel protects prop and rudder. Total of 861 were built. Cruise at 6–8 knots with single 120hp or 135hp Lehman diesel.

Length Overall	31'11"	Headroom	6'4"
Length WL	30'9"	Fuel	225/250 gals.
Beam	11'6"	Water	110 gals.
Draft	3'9"	Waste	30 gals.
Weight	17,000#	Hull Type	Semi-Disp.

See Page 545 For Resale Values

Grand Banks Yachts
Seattle, WA
www.grandbanks.com

231-360-0827

Grand Banks 36 Classic
1965–2004

Highly regarded aft-cabin trawler enjoys lofty reputation for beauty, comfort, quality and seaworthiness. Several twin-stateroom interiors were offered over the years, all with solid teak woodwork, premium hardware, superb finish. Large aft stateroom has direct cockpit access. Keel protects prop and rudder. Updated in 1988 when 4 inches were added to beam. Wood construction until mid-1973. No production in 1997–99. Over 1,200 built. Cruise efficiently at 7–8 knots with single 135hp Lehman diesel; 10 knots with twins.

Length Overall	36'10"	Clearance, Mast	22'4"
Length WL	35'2"	Fuel	400 gals.
Beam	12'8"	Water	154 gals.
Draft	4'0"	Waste	40 gals.
Weight	26,000#	Hull Type	Semi-Disp.

See Page 545 For Resale Values

Grand Banks Yachts
Seattle, WA
www.grandbanks.com

231-360-0827

Grand Banks 36 Europa
1988–98

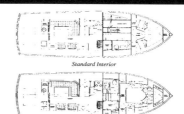

Standard Interior

Alternate Interior

Handsome sedan trawler with classic Europa styling appeals to upscale cruisers who value nautical beauty, boat-building excellence. Highlights include elegant two-stateroom teak interior, protected side decks, extended hardtop, mast and boom, teak decks, bow pulpit, deep, prop-protecting keel. Single-stateroom layout with divided head was optional. The standard by which other sedan trawlers her size are measured. Single 135hp Lehman diesel will cruise at 7–8 knots; twin 210hp Cummins diesels cruise at 10–12 knots.

Length Overall	36'10"	Headroom	6'4"
Length WL	35'2"	Fuel	400 gals.
Beam	12'8"	Water	170/205 gals.
Draft	4'0"	Waste	40 gals.
Weight	27,000#	Hull Type	Semi-Disp.

See Page 545 For Resale Values

Grand Banks Yachts
Seattle, WA
www.grandbanks.com

231-360-0827

Grand Banks 36 Sedan
1986–96

Standard Floorplan

Alternate Floorplan

Elegant sedan cruiser with extended salon, spacious flybridge sets class standard for engineering, comfort, seakeeping qualities. Standard two-stateroom layout is a model of space utilization. Highlights include full teak interior, large U-shaped galley, lower helm deck door, head with separate stall shower, roomy engine compartment, wide side decks. Front windshield opens for ventilation. Long keel protects prop and rudder from damage. Single 135hp diesel will cruise at 8 knots; twin 210hp Cummins cruise at 12 knots.

Length Overall	36'10"	Headroom	6'4"
Length WL	35'2"	Fuel	400 gal.
Beam	12'8"	Water	205 gal.
Draft	4'0"	Waste	40 gals.
Weight	26,000#	Hull Type	Semi-Disp.

See Page 545 For Resale Values

Grand Banks Yachts
Seattle, WA
www.grandbanks.com

231-360-0827

Grand Banks 41 Heritage EU
2009–Current

Handsome "fast trawler" with refined Europa profile, new hull form is the first Grand Banks model designed for Zeus pod drives. Well-appointed galley-up, two-stateroom interior features expansive salon with facing settees, lower helm with deck access door, huge head, teak-planked flooring throughout. Full-beam utility room beneath salon sole accommodates optional washer/dryer, workbench. Note cockpit engineroom access. Keel protects pods from grounding. Cummins 425hp diesels cruise at 15–16 knots (20+ knots wide open).

Length Overall	41'4"	Clearance, Mast	19'4"
Length WL	37'11"	Fuel	500 gals.
Beam	15'8"	Water	195 gals.
Draft	3'9"	Waste	50 gals.
Weight	40,200#	Hull Type	Semi-Disp.

Insufficient Resale Data To Assign Values

Grand Banks Yachts
Seattle, WA
www.grandbanks.com

231-360-0827

Grand Banks 42 Classic
1975–2004

Iconic double-cabin trawler (over 1,500 were built) is easily the most successful trawler design ever produced. Several two-stateroom floorplans were offered over the years. Highlights include full teak interior, port/starboard salon doors, wide side decks, roomy flybridge, protected prop. Mahogany construction prior to 1973. Hull was widened, lengthened in 1992 for larger galley, bigger forward stateroom. Fine bow delivers superb head sea performance. Twin 210hp Cats cruise at 10 knots; 375hp Cats cruise at 14-15 knots.

Length Overall	42'7"/43'3"	Clearance, Mast	22'6"
Length WL	41'1"	Fuel	600 gals.
Beam	13'7"/14'1"	Water	271 gals.
Draft	4'2"	Waste	50 gals.
Weight	37,400#	Hull Type	Semi-Disp.

See Page 545 For Resale Values

Grand Banks Yachts
Seattle, WA
www.grandbanks.com

231-360-0827

Grand Banks 42 Europa
1979–90; 1996–2004

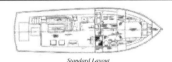

Standard Layout

Optional Layout

Elegant sedan trawler blends Europa styling with top-quality construction, time-tested layout. Standard two-stateroom teak interior boasts big U-shaped galley galley, queen berth forward, stall showers in both heads. Cockpit and side decks are protected by bridge overhangs. Note teak decks, large cockpit lazarette, prop-protecting keel. Production discontinued in 1990, resumed in 1996 when hull was redesigned with wider beam. Among several engine choices, 210hp Cats cruise at 10 knots; 375hp Cats cruise at 14–15 knots.

Length Overall	43'3"	Clearance, Mast	22'9"
Beam (1979–90)	13'7"	Fuel	600 gals.
Beam (1996–2004)	14'1"	Water	278 gals.
Draft	4'2"	Waste	50 gals.
Weight	39,000#	Hull Type	Semi-Disp.

See Page 545 For Resale Values

Grand Banks Yachts
Seattle, WA
www.grandbanks.com

Section I: Motoryachts & Trawlers

231-360-0827

Grand Banks 42 Motor Yacht
1987–2004

Standard Floorplan

Optional Floorplan

Motoryacht version of GB 42 Classic combines enlarged master stateroom layout with full-beam afterdeck, standard three-stateroom floorplan. Highlights include full teak interior, port/starboard salon doors, wide side decks, fold-down mast, roomy flybridge, bow pulpit, protected prop. Note simulated lapstrake hull lines. Two-stateroom, galley down interior was optional. Note that hull redesign in 1992 increased width, length by 6 inches. Exemplary fit and finish. Twin 210hp Cats cruise at 10 knots; 375 Cats cruise at 14–15 knots.

Length Overall	42'7"/43'3"	Clearance, Mast	25'6"
Length WL	41'1"	Fuel	600 gals.
Beam	13'7"/14'1"	Water	237 gals.
Draft	4'2"	Waste	50 gals.
Weight	40,700#	Hull Type	Semi-Disp.

See Page 545 For Resale Values

Grand Banks Yachts
Seattle, WA
www.grandbanks.com

231-360-0827

Grand Banks 46 Classic
1987–2007

Standard Layout

Optional Layout

Acclaimed long-range trawler introduced in 1987 makes good on promise of luxury-class accommodations, exceptional owner satisfaction. Three-stateroom interior was standard, two-stateroom layout was optional. Highlights include hand-crafted teak cabinetry, parquet flooring, large engineroom, teak walkaround decks, fold-down mast, bow pulpit, simulated lapstrake hull. Tooling updated in 1988 (hull #43) to provide slightly wider side decks aft. The perfect cruising yacht. Twin Cat or Cummins diesels cruise at 12–14 knots.

Length Overall	47'1"	Clearance, Mast	23'7"
Length WL	44'10"	Fuel	630 gals.
Beam	14'9"	Water	300 gals.
Draft	4'5"	Waste	80 gals.
Weight	42,960#	Hull Type	Semi-Disp.

See Page 545 For Resale Values

Grand Banks Yachts
Seattle, WA
www.grandbanks.com

231-360-0827

Grand Banks 46 Europa
1993–2008

Standard Floorplan

Optional Floorplan

Gold-plated cruising yacht combines sporty Europa styling with luxury-class amenities, unsurpassed quality. Well-appointed interior includes two comfortable staterooms, lower helm with deck door, generous storage, teak parquet flooring. Salon opens to covered cockpit with stairway to flybridge. Additional features include teak decks, extended hardtop, covered side decks, cockpit engineroom access, protected running gear. Exemplary fit and finish. Cummins 210hp diesels cruise at 10 knots; 435hp Cats cruise at 12–14 knots.

Length Overall	47'1"	Clearance, Mast	21'5"
Length WL	44'10"	Fuel	630 gals.
Beam	14'9"	Water	276 gals.
Draft	4'5"	Waste	80 gals.
Weight	43,000#	Hull Type	Semi-Disp.

See Page 545 For Resale Values

Grand Banks Yachts
Seattle, WA
www.grandbanks.com

2011 PowerBoat Guide   55

www.powerboatguide.com   231-360-0827

Grand Banks 46 Motor Yacht
1990–2001

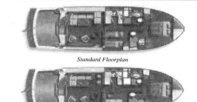

Standard Floorplan

Optional Layout

Distinctive trawler-style motoryacht from 1990s offers luxury, comfort on a grand scale. Standard three-cabin interior has deckhouse galley; optional twin-cabin layout with galley down has expanded salon, optional washer/dryer forward. Note salon deck doors, huge full-beam master stateroom, solid teak woodwork. Large aft deck is enclosed by safety rails. Large engineroom is a plus. Outstanding craftsmanship throughout. Twin 135hp Lehman diesels cruise at 8 knots; 375hp Cats cruise at 12–13 knots (about 16 knots top).

Length Overall	47'1"	Clearance, Mast	23'7"
Length WL	44'9"	Fuel	600 gals.
Beam	14'9"	Water	290 gals.
Draft	4'4"	Headroom	6'4"
Weight	39,000#	Hull Type	Semi-Disp.

See Page 545 For Resale Values

Grand Banks Yachts
Seattle, WA
www.grandbanks.com

---

www.powerboatguide.com   231-360-0827

Grand Banks 47 Eastbay Flybridge
2005–Current

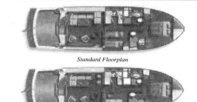

Standard Floorplan

Optional Layout

Elegant Downeast flybridge yacht boasts top-drawer build quality with spacious accommodations, luxury amenities. Available with standard two-cabin layout or optional single-cabin floorplan with two heads, open-plan "office" with sofa bed in place of second stateroom. Highlights include Burmese teak interior, wide side decks, unique spiral bridge staircase, large cockpit with built-in seating. Note teak cockpit sole, fold-down radar mast, spacious engineroom. Cruise at 25 knots (about 30 knots top) with 700hp Caterpillar diesels.

Length Overall	52'4"	Fuel	700 gals.
Length WL	43'3"	Water	206 gals.
Beam	15'0"	Waste	75 gals.
Draft	3'10"	Hull Type	Deep-V
Weight	47,900#	Deadrise Aft	18°

See Page 545 For Resale Values

Grand Banks Yachts
Seattle, WA
www.grandbanks.com

---

www.powerboatguide.com   231-360-0827

Grand Banks 47 Heritage Classic
2007–Current

Standard Layout

Optional Layout

Updated version of classic Grand Banks tri-cabin blends new high-performance hull with traditional trawler profile. Standard twin-stateroom interior features chart table/entertainment center with pop-up TV, step-down galley with granite counters, teak plank flooring. Roomy flybridge offers lounge seating around beautiful teak table. Note teak side decks, frameless windows, aft salon entry, spacious engineroom, expanded lazarette. Three-stateroom interior is optional. Cat 567hp diesels cruise at 16–17 knots (20 knots top).

Length Overall	46'10"	Fuel	600 gals.
Length WL	44'1"	Water	260 gals.
Beam	15'9"	Waste	77 gals.
Draft	3'10"	Hull Type	Modified-V
Weight	52,333#	Deadrise Aft	18°

Insufficient Resale Data To Assign Values

Grand Banks Yachts
Seattle, WA
www.grandbanks.com

231-360-0827

Grand Banks 47 Heritage Europa
2007–Current

Standard Layout

Optional Layout

Next-generation Europa built on modified-V hull combines planing-speed performance with graceful styling, signature Grand Bank's quality. Highlights include elegant teak interior with granite counters, teak-plank flooring throughout, extended aft-deck overhang, teak decks, protected side decks, frameless windows, flybridge stairway, meticulous engineroom. Guest cabin can be configured as office. Space in second head for washer/dryer. Hull extends under swim platform. Cat 567hp diesels cruise at 16–17 knots (over 20 knots top).

Length Overall	46'10"
Length WL	44'1"
Beam	15'9"
Draft	3'10"
Weight	51,233#
Fuel	600 gals.
Water	260 gals.
Waste	77 gals.
Hull Type	Modified-V
Deadrise Aft	18°

Insufficient Resale Data To Assign Values

Grand Banks Yachts
Seattle, WA
www.grandbanks.com

231-360-0827

Grand Banks 49 Classic
1980–97

Standard Floorplan

Optional Layout

Sought-after Grand Banks cruising yacht set class standards in her era for graceful trawler styling, world-class construction. Standard three-stateroom interior boasts spacious master with cockpit access door, teak parquet flooring, twin salon deck doors. Teak walkaround decks are broad, secure; standup engine room is spacious and carefully detailed. Note space in galley for washer/dryer. Popular model—about 125 were built. Early models with 120hp Lehman diesels cruise at 8 knots; later models with 210hp Cats cruise at 10–12 knots.

Length Overall	50'6"
Length WL	48'9"
Beam	15'5"
Draft	5'1"
Weight	60,000#
Clearance, Mast	26'5"
Fuel	1,000 gals.
Water	500 gals.
Waste	60 gals.
Hull Type	Semi-Disp.

See Page 545 For Resale Values

Grand Banks Yachts
Seattle, WA
www.grandbanks.com

231-360-0827

Grand Banks 49 Motor Yacht
1986–99

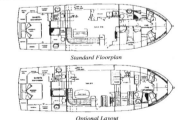

Standard Floorplan

Optional Layout

Quintessential Grand Banks trawler yacht introduced in 1986 took motoryacht elegance, sophistication to the next level. Three-stateroom, galley-up interior was standard; optional twin-cabin layout with galley down has expanded salon. Highlights include spacious, full-beam master stateroom, expansive salon with parquet flooring, stand-up engineroom. Large aft deck—enclosed by safety rail—has room for a small party. Wide side decks with high protective bulwarks are a plus. Cruise at 14 knots (18 top) with 375hp Cat diesels.

Length Overall	50'6"
Length WL	48'9"
Beam	15'5"
Draft	5'2"
Weight	60,000#
Clearance	NA
Fuel	1,000 gals.
Water	500 gals.
Waste	60 gals.
Hull Type	Semi-Disp.

Insufficient Resale Data To Assign Values

Grand Banks Yachts
Seattle, WA
www.grandbanks.com

Motoryachts & Trawlers

231-360-0827

Grand Banks 52 Europa
1998–2008

Luxury-class motoryacht was an evolutionary step up in size, comfort, for Grand Banks when introduced in 1998. Deluxe accommdations include home-size gourmet galley, open dinette, entertainment center, slide-away pilothouse privacy door, full-beam master suite. Expansive salon affords clear view from helm to aft deck. Optional lower-level layout has engineroom forward, master stateroom aft. Note protected side decks, spacious flybridge. A graceful, gold-plated cruising yacht. Cat 660hp diesels cruise at 15 knots (18–19 knots top).

Length Overall	54'1"	Clearance, Mast	29'0"
Length WL	51'9"	Fuel	1,200 gals.
Beam	15.5"	Water	500 gals.
Draft	4'10"	Waste	56 gals.
Weight	58,000#	Hull Type	Semi-Disp.

See Page 545 For Resale Values

Grand Banks Yachts
Seattle, WA
www.grandbanks.com

231-360-0827

Grand Banks 58 Eastbay Flybridge
2004–07

Standard Layout

Optional Layout

Prestigious flybridge yacht with gorgeous Downeast styling sets class standards for beauty, cruising elegance. Opulent three-stateroom, galley-down interior boasts wide-open salon; optional galley-up layout provides fourth cabin that may also serve as an office. Highlights include lower-helm deck door, holding-plate refrigeration, stand-up engineroom, wide side decks. Note curved bridge staircase, teak cockpit sole. Stidd helm seats, cockpit wet bar, bow thruster are standard. Cat 1,400hp diesels deliver a top speed of over 30 knots.

Length w/Platform	63.5"	Clearance	18'9"
Hull Length	58'8"	Fuel	1,175 gals.
Beam	17'8"	Water	280 gals.
Draft	5'4"	Hull Type	Deep-V
Weight	91,000#	Deadrise Aft	21°

Insufficient Resale Data To Assign Values

Grand Banks Yachts
Seattle, WA
www.grandbanks.com

231-360-0827

Grand Banks 58 Motor Yacht
1990–2002

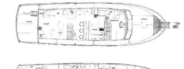

Stoutly built offshore yacht designed for extended cruising offers top-shelf construction, spacious interior, unsurpassed comforts. Lavish three-stateroom floorplan features full-beam master suite with private entry, wide-open salon, country-kitchen galley, enclosed pilothouse with centerline helm. Bridge overhangs shelter side decks and cockpit from weather. Note stand-up engineroom, huge flybridge with dinghy storage, utility room with washer/dryer. At a 9-knot cruising speed, 375hp Cat diesels deliver a range of some 1,400 miles.

Length Overall	58'11"	Clearance	17'6"
Length WL	54'4"	Fuel	1,400 gals.
Beam	17'6"	Water	450 gals.
Draft	5'6"	Waste	80 gals.
Weight	100,000#	Hull Type	Semi-Disp.

Insufficient Resale Data To Assign Values

Grand Banks Yachts
Seattle, WA
www.grandbanks.com

231-360-0827

Grand Banks 59 Aleutian RP
2007–Current

Sumptuous long-range cruiser delivers impressive mix of timeless style, aggressive performance, top-quality construction. Lavish teak interior with raised pilothouse sleeps six in two large double staterooms—including full-beam master—and one twin cabin. Topside features include hardtop, spacious flybridge with twin teak tables, protected side decks, Portuguese bridge, teak decks, curved cockpit staircase. Note convenient pass-thru between galley and flybridge. Cat C18 (1,000hp) diesels cruise at 20–22 knots (about 25 knots top).

Length Overall	58'7"	Fuel	1,400 gals.
Length WL	55'4"	Water	385 gals.
Beam	18'0"	Waste	110 gals.
Draft	5'4"	Hull Type	Modified-V
Weight	90,000#	Deadrise Aft	16°

Insufficient Resale Data To Assign Values

Grand Banks Yachts
Seattle, WA
www.grandbanks.com

231-360-0827

Grand Banks 64 Aleutian RP
2002–07

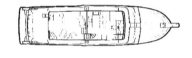

Original Grand Banks Aleutian model pairs impressive accommodations with graceful styling, luxury-class amenities. Raised pilothouse interior includes expansive main salon with entertainment center, huge U-shaped galley with Corian counters, opulent master stateroom with engineroom access. Lazarette can house optional crew quarters. Note Portuguese bridge, watertight engine room bulkheads. A stately yacht built to very high standards. Modified-V hull with prop pockets will cruise at 18 knots with 800hp Cat diesels.

Length Overall	64'4"	Fuel	2,200 gals.
Length WL	59'4"	Water	440 gals.
Beam	19'10"	Waste	150 gals.
Draft	5'6"	Hull Type	Modified-V
Weight	105,000#	Deadrise Aft	14°

Insufficient Resale Data To Assign Values

Grand Banks Yachts
Seattle, WA
www.grandbanks.com

231-360-0827

Great Harbour 37
1998–Current

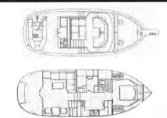

Maxi-volume liveaboard with ship-like profile targets coastal cruisers seeking true condo-style accommodations. Beamy, high-sided hull conceals tremendous interior volume with full-beam salon, home-size galley, two staterooms, covered aft cockpit, raised pilothouse with convertible settee and pilot berth. Note standard washer/dryer. Portuguese bridge surrounds pilothouse. Beachable! More small ship than boat. Designed for nearshore and coastal cruising. Cruise at an economical 7–8 knots with twin 56hp Yanmar diesels.

Length Overll	36'10"	Clearance	14'8"
Length WL	36'1"	Fuel	500 gals.
Beam	15'10"	Water	300 gals.
Draft	2'10"	Waste	100 gals.
Weight	48,000#	Hull Type	Displacement

Insufficient Resale Data To Assign Values

Mirage Manufacturing
Gainesville, FL
www.mirage-mfg.com

Motoryachts & Trawlers

Section I: Motoryachts & Trawlers

www.powerboatguide.com 231-360-0827

Hampton 560 Sedan
2005–Current

Handsome sedan yacht gets high marks for classic styling, meticulous workmanship, first-class accommodations. Spacious three-stateroom/two-head interior boasts expansive salon with day head, six-person dinette, condo-size galley. Lower helm is optional. Bridge overhangs shade cockpit and side walkways; electric hatch in cockpit sole provides access to engineroom. Hardtop, bow thruster, stabilizer, washer/dryer are standard. Cummins 670hp diesels cruise at 18 knots (low 20s knots top).

Length	58'5"	Fuel	800 gals.
Beam	16'4"	Water	250 gals.
Draft	4'0"	Waste	80 gals.
Weight	56,000#	Hull Type	Modified-V
Clearance	18'3"	Deadrise Aft	11°

Insufficient Resale Data To Assign Values

Hampton Yachts Int'l.
Newport Beach, CA
www.hamptonyachts.com

---

www.powerboatguide.com 231-360-0827

Hampton 558 Pilothouse
2004–Current

Luxurious all-weather cruiser delivers custom-yacht amenities at production-boat price. Standard cherrywood interior features two en suite staterooms with queen beds, salon entertainment center, built-in washer/dryer. Three-stateroom layout is optional. Visibility from raised pilothouse is excellent. Hatch in the cockpit sole provides good engineroom access. Large flybridge has dinghy platform aft. Note twin transom doors, wide side decks, standard hardtop. Cummins 540hp diesels cruise at 17–18 knots (20+ knots top).

Length	57'8"	Fuel	800 gals.
Beam	16'4"	Water	230 gals.
Draft	4'6	Waste	80 gals.
Weight	48,000#	Hull Type	Modified-V
Clearance	18'3"	Deadrise Aft	11°

Insufficient Resale Data To Assign Values

Hampton Yachts Int'l.
Newport Beach, CA
www.hamptonyachts.com

---

www.powerboatguide.com 231-360-0827

Hampton 580 Pilothouse
2008–Current

Full-bodied cruiser with modern pilothouse styling matches top-shelf construction with posh accommodations, impressive standard feature list. Highlights include expansive three-stateroom layout with open-galley design, deluxe master suite with lots of stowage, standup engineroom with transom entry. Wheelhouse deck doors are a plus. Wesmar stabilizer, bow thruster, cockpit controls are standard. Note bow anchor chute. Cummins 715hp diesels cruise at 16 knots (20–21 knots top).

Length	59'10"	Fuel	1,000 gals.
Beam	17'3"	Water	280 gals.
Draft	4'8"	Waste	100 gals.
Weight	66,000#	Hull Type	Modified-V
Clearance	20'0"	Deadrise Aft	12°

Insufficient Resale Data To Assign Values

Hampton Yachts Int'l.
Newport Beach, CA
www.hamptonyachts.com

---

www.powerboatguide.com   231-360-0827

Hampton 600 Motor Yacht
2006–Current

Stylish Asian-built flybridge yacht makes good on promise of space, luxury at an affordable price. Highlights include elegant four-stateroom interior, semi-enclosed bridge, extended swim platform, protected aft deck. Starboard guest cabin can be configured as office. Note private salon access to master suite, spacious walk-in engineroom. Long list of standard features include stabilizers, bow/stern thrusters, windlass, engineroom air-conditioning, rear docking controls. Cruise at 18–20 knots with Cat 800hp diesels (low 20s top).

Length	61'10"	Fuel	950 gals.
Beam	17'4"	Water	350 gals.
Draft	4'6"	Waste	100 gals.
Weight	72,500#	Hull Type	Modified-V
Clearance	20'8"	Deadrise Aft	13°

Insufficient Resale Data To Assign Values

Hampton Yachts Int'l.
Newport Beach, CA
www.hamptonyachts.com

---

www.powerboatguide.com   231-360-0827

Hampton 630 Pilothouse
2007–Current

Impeccably finished luxury yacht targets sophisticated buyers with an eye for quality, long-term value. Wide 18-foot beam results in spacious accommodations with choice of two- or three-stateroom layouts. Standard features include high-gloss cherry woodwork, raised pilothouse with home-size galley, standup engineroom, covered aft deck, huge flybridge. Note frameless pilothouse windows. Stabilizer, bow thruster, cockpit controls, hardtop are standard. Cat 850hp diesels cruise at 18 knots (21–22 knots top).

Length	63'8"	Fuel	1,200 gals.
Beam	18'0"	Water	300 gals.
Draft	4'10"	Waste	100 gals.
Weight	75,000#	Hull Type	Modified-V
Clearance	20'7"	Deadrise Aft	12°

Insufficient Resale Data To Assign Values

Hampton Yachts Int'l.
Newport Beach, CA
www.hamptonyachts.com

---

www.powerboatguide.com   231-360-0827

Hatteras 40 Motor Yacht
1986–97

1986–90

1989–97

Good-selling pocket motoryacht gets high marks for classic styling, comfortable accommodations, solid construction. Surprising amount of interior space for a 40-footer. Highlights include full-beam master stateroom, well-appointed salon, large aft deck. Excellent fit and finish. Flybridge redesigned in 1990 when helm was moved forward. Last of the "small" Hatteras motoryachts. Very popular model—over 120 were built. Cruise at 18 knots with Cat 340hp diesels (low 20s top).

Length	40'10"	Fuel	359 gals.
Beam	13'7"	Water	110 gals.
Draft	4'9"	Waste	60 gals.
Weight	38,000#	Hull Type	Modified-V
Clearance	15'9"	Deadrise Aft	14°

See Page 546 For Resale Values

Hatteras Yachts
New Bern, NC
www.hatterasyachts.com

Hatteras 42 Cockpit MY
1993–97

Standard Layout

Dinette Layout

Enduring 1990s cockpit yacht gets high marks for sporty styling, spacious interior, quality construction. Offered with choice of interior plans—standard layout boasts wide-open salon; alternate floorplan has deckhouse dinette. Topside features include large aft deck, cockpit transom door, integrated swim platform. Hardtop, radar arch were popular options. Flybridge redesigned in 1990 when helm was moved forward. Engineroom is a tight fit. Cat 375hp diesels cruise at 18 knots (22–23 knots top).

Length	42'10"	Fuel	375 gals.
Beam	13'7"	Water	115 gals.
Draft	4'9"	Hull Type	Modified-V
Weight	41,000#	Headroom	6'5"
Clearance	15'9"	Deadrise Aft	NA

See Page 546 For Resale Values

Hatteras Yachts
New Bern, NC
www.hatterasyachts.com

Hatteras 42 Long Range Cruiser
1976–85

1976–80

1981–85

Heavy-weather Hatteras cruiser with full-displacement hull ranks among the best trawlers her size ever produced. Original model with walkaround decks, single beds in aft stateroom, was replaced in 1980 with new sundeck (Mark II) model with full-beam afterdeck, queen bed in master. Highlights include teak interior woodwork, port/starboard salon deck doors, two full heads, big engineroom, fold-down mast, bow pulpit. Total of 29 were built—used models are always in demand. Cruise efficiently at 8 knots with 140hp GM diesels.

Length Overall	42'6"	Clearance	13'6"
Length WL	38'0"	Fuel	700 gals.
Beam	14'6"	Water	220 gals.
Draft	3'10"	Waste	50 gals.
Weight	36,000#	Hull Type	Displacement

Prices Not Provided for Pre-1995 Models

Hatteras Yachts
New Bern, NC
www.hatterasyachts.com

Hatteras 43 Double Cabin
1971–84

Standard Floorplan, 1971–78

Standard Floorplan, 1979–84

Classic flush-deck motoryacht from 1970s remains one of the best-selling yachts of her type ever produced. Several floorplans were offered over the years; double berth in master stateroom became available in 1979. Semi-enclosed aft deck/lower helm keeps skipper close to passengers. Note wide side decks, molded foredeck seating. Flybridge is tiny. A wet ride in steep seas. GM 285hp diesels—standard in later years—cruise at 12–14 knots (16 knots top); GM 390hp diesels cruise at 16–17 knots (20 knots wide open).

Length	43'1"	Fuel	375 gals.
Beam	14'0"	Water	130 gals.
Draft	3'5"	Headroom	6'6"
Weight	34,000#	Hull Type	Modified-V
Clearance	17'10"	Deadrise Aft	8°

Prices Not Provided for Pre-1995 Models

Hatteras Yachts
New Bern, NC
www.hatterasyachts.com

231-360-0827

Hatteras 43 Motor Yacht
1985–87

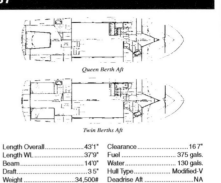

Queen Berth Aft

Twin Berths Aft

Sporty 1980s motoryacht ranks among the smallest double-cabin designs ever produced by Hatteras. Highlights include comfortable—if not spacious—salon with wraparound windows, teak interior joinery, full-beam master stateroom with space for washer/dryer, large aft deck with wing doors. Hardtop and radar arch were standard. Note wide 12" side decks, teak handrails. First-rate fit and finish throughout. Standard 375hp Cat diesels cruise at 16 knots (20–21 knots top); optional GM 465hp 6-71s cruise at 17–18 knots (20+ knots top).

Length Overall	43'1"	Clearance	16 7"
Length WL	37'9"	Fuel	375 gals.
Beam	14'0"	Water	130 gals.
Draft	3 5"	Hull Type	Modified-V
Weight	34,500#	Deadrise Aft	NA

Prices Not Provided for Pre-1995 Models

Hatteras Yachts
New Bern, NC
www.hatterasyachts.com

231-360-0827

Hatteras 48 Cockpit Motor Yacht
1981–84

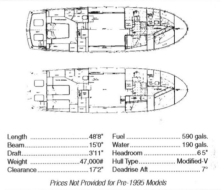

Well-built 1980s motoryacht combined upscale accommodations with traditional Hatteras luxury, genuine owner satisfaction. Standard three-stateroom, three-head layout is configured with second guest stateroom aft rather than forward. Stall shower is shared by both aft heads. Spacious aft deck with hardtop, wing doors has space for a small party. Cockpit (with transom door) makes boarding easy. Standard 285hp GM diesels cruise at 8 knots (10–11 knots top); optional 425hp GMs cruise at 15 knots (18–19 knots top).

Length	48'8"	Fuel	590 gals.
Beam	15'0"	Water	190 gals.
Draft	3'11"	Headroom	6 5"
Weight	47,000#	Hull Type	Modified-V
Clearance	17'2"	Deadrise Aft	7°

Prices Not Provided for Pre-1995 Models

Hatteras Yachts
New Bern, NC
www.hatterasyachts.com

231-360-0827

Hatteras 48 Cockpit Motor Yacht
1993–96

Standard Layout

Optional Arrangement

Deluxe cruising yacht introduced in 1993 was class leader in styling, space, comfort. Wide 16-foot beam permits expansive floorplan with two double staterooms, expansive salon, choice of dinette or optional third stateroom. Large aft deck can accommodate a small crowd. Note roomy flybridge. Additional features include spacious engineroom, standard washer/dryer, wide side decks, aft-deck hardtop. No transom door in cockpit. Twin 535hp GM diesels cruise at 18 knots (20+ knots wide open).

Length	48'11"	Fuel	667 gals.
Beam	16'0"	Water	170 gals.
Draft	5'6"	Waste	100 gals.
Weight	59,000#	Hull Type	Modified-V
Clearance	16'9"	Deadrise Aft	16°

See Page 546 For Resale Values

Hatteras Yachts
New Bern, NC
www.hatterasyachts.com

Motoryachts & Trawlers

231-360-0827

Hatteras 48 Long Range Cruiser
1976–81

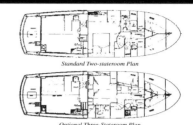

Standard Two-stateroom Plan

Optional Three-Stateroom Plan

Long-range pilothouse trawler with full displacement hull delivers signature Hatteras blend of handsome styling, bulletproof construction, luxury-class amenities. Two-stateroom teak interior boasts full-beam salon with galley forward, two full heads, full-width owner's suite. Raised pilothouse has watch berth, U-shaped dinette, sliding deck doors. Three-stateroom layout with smaller master was optional. Small cockpit has boarding gate. Note weatherdeck dinghy davit. Cruise at 8 knots with 112hp GM (or 120hp Lehman) diesels.

Length	48'10"	Clearance	16'11"
LWL	43'4"	Fuel	1,390 gals.
Beam	16'6"	Water	430 gals.
Draft	4'6"	Waste	80 gals.
Weight	54,000#	Hull Type	Displacement

Prices Not Provided for Pre-1995 Models

Hatteras Yachts
New Bern, NC
www.hatterasyachts.com

231-360-0827

Hatteras 48 Motor Yacht
1981–84

Standard Layout

Optional Arrangement

Executive-class motoryacht from early 1980s combined spacious interior with top-notch construction, modern styling. Standard three-stateroom, three-head layout is configured with second guest stateroom aft rather than forward. Single stall shower is shared by both aft heads. Very spacious aft deck with hardtop came standard with wing doors, wet bar. Note roomy flybridge, wide side decks. Standard 285hp GM diesels cruise at just 8 knots (10–11 knots top); optional 425hp GMs cruise at 15 knots (18–19 knots top).

Length	48'8"	Fuel	590 gals.
Beam	15'0"	Water	190 gals.
Draft	3'11"	Headroom	6'4"
Weight	45,000#	Hull Type	Modified-V
Clearance	17'2"	Deadrise Aft	7°

Prices Not Provided for Pre-1995 Models

Hatteras Yachts
New Bern, NC
www.hatterasyachts.com

231-360-0827

Hatteras 48 Motor Yacht
1990–96

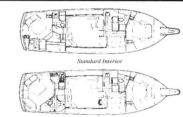

Standard Interior

Alternate Layout

Conservative styling, luxurious accommodations made this heavily built motoryacht a popular model for Hatteras in early 1990s. Offered with several floorplans over the years—most were delivered with three-stateroom layout with dinette, galley down. Wraparound salon widows provide panoramic outside views. Notable features include large aft deck, roomy bridge, wide side decks. Hardtop, radar arch, bow pulpit were standard. GM 535hp diesels cruise at 16 knots (19 knots top); 720hp 8V92s cruise at 18–20 knots (low 20s top).

Length	48'9"	Fuel	764 gals.
Beam	16'0"	Water	170 gals.
Draft	5'3"	Headroom	6'6"
Weight	63,000#	Hull Type	Modified-V
Clearance	16'8"	Deadrise Aft	14°

See Page 546 For Resale Values

Hatteras Yachts
New Bern, NC
www.hatterasyachts.com

Hatteras 50 Sport Deck MY
1996–98

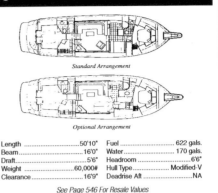

Standard Arrangement

Optional Arrangement

Quality-built motoryacht from one of America's premier builders suffered from conservative styling, expensive price. Lavish interior with expansive salon boasts large galley with home-sized appliances, spacious master stateroom with walk-in closet, optional third stateroom in lieu of dinette. Note tub in aft head. Topside highlights include huge aft deck, wide side decks, reverse transom with curved staircase, roomy flybridge. Poor aft helm visibility. Standard 535hp diesels cruise at 17 knots (low 20s top).

Length	50'10"	Fuel	622 gals.
Beam	16'0"	Water	170 gals.
Draft	5'6"	Headroom	6'6"
Weight	60,000#	Hull Type	Modified-V
Clearance	16'9"	Deadrise Aft	NA

See Page 546 For Resale Values

Hatteras Yachts
New Bern, NC
www.hatterasyachts.com

Hatteras 52 Cockpit MY
1990–99

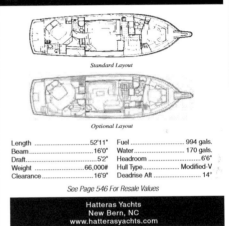

Standard Layout

Optional Layout

Shapely 1990s cruising yacht provides still-impressive balance of motoryacht luxury, quality, comfort. Offered with several interiors over the years—standard three-stateroom layout boasts expansive salon with galley, dinette down; alternate floorplan offered enlarged master stateroom by moving second guest cabin forward. Spacious aft deck with hardtop, wing doors can entertain a small crowd. Note cockpit transom door, spacious engineroom. Standard GM 720hp diesels cruise at 19–20 knots (about 23 knots top).

Length	52'11"	Fuel	994 gals.
Beam	16'0"	Water	170 gals.
Draft	5'2"	Headroom	6'6"
Weight	66,000#	Hull Type	Modified-V
Clearance	16'9"	Deadrise Aft	14°

See Page 546 For Resale Values

Hatteras Yachts
New Bern, NC
www.hatterasyachts.com

Hatteras 52 Motor Yacht
1993–96

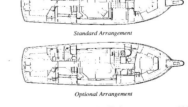

Standard Arrangement

Optional Arrangement

Handsome 1990s motoryacht courted upscale buyers with a taste for luxury-class accommodations, signature Hatteras quality. Posh three-stateroom, three-head interior features queen berths fore and aft, tub in master stateroom, home-sized galley, standard washer/dryer. Huge aft deck could be fully enclosed and air-conditioned. Additional features include stand-up engineroom (accessed via galley stairs), wide side decks, spacious flybridge. Standard 735hp GM diesels cruise at 18–19 knots (20+ knots wide open).

Length	52'9"	Fuel	994 gals.
Beam	16'0"	Water	170 gals.
Draft	5'2"	Headroom	6'6"
Weight	66,000#	Hull Type	Modified-V
Clearance	16'9"	Deadrise Aft	16°

See Page 546 For Resale Values

Hatteras Yachts
New Bern, NC
www.hatterasyachts.com

231-360-0827

Hatteras 53 Motor Yacht
1969–88

Acclaimed Hatteras cruising yacht with near 20-year production run left a sales, popularity legacy unsurpassed in motoryacht design. Spacious three-stateroom, three-head interior was long considered ideal in a yacht this size. Split-engineroom design became standard in many Hatteras motoryachts of her era. Flybridge updated in 1978; queen in master became standard in 1978. Total of 350 were built. Early models with GM 350hp diesels cruise at 12–13 knots. Later models with 435hp (or 450hp) GMs cruise at 16 knots.

Length Overall	53'1"	Clearance	18'6"
Length WL	47'3"	Fuel	550/600/700 gals.
Beam	15'10"	Water	245 gals.
Draft	4'0"	Hull Type	Modified-V
Weight	55,000#	Deadrise Aft	NA

Prices Not Provided for Pre-1995 Models

Hatteras Yachts
New Bern, NC
www.hatterasyachts.com

231-360-0827

Hatteras 53 Extended Deckhouse MY
1983–88

Deckhouse Layout

Lower Deck Arrangement

Handsome big-water motoryacht with classic Hatteras profile, executive-class amenities offered 1980's luxury on a grand scale. Spacious three-stateroom layout boasts huge full-beam salon, three full heads, home-sized galley with dinette opposite. Galley pass-through to salon is a nice touch. Split enginerooms provide easy access to motors, pumps. Small aft deck is perfect for line-handling. Many have been fitted with aftermarket stabilizers. Standard GM 465hp diesels cruise at 15 knots (18-19 knots top).

Length	53'1"	Fuel	700 gals.
Beam	15'10"	Water	287 gals.
Draft	4'0"	Waste	150 gals.
Weight	57,000#	Hull Type	Modified-V
Clearance	17'2"	Deadrise Aft	NA

Prices Not Provided for Pre-1995 Models

Hatteras Yachts
New Bern, NC
www.hatterasyachts.com

231-360-0827

Hatteras 53 Yacht Fisherman
1978–81; 1986–87

Standard Layout

Optional Arrangement

Iconic cockpit motoryacht introduced in 1978 proved extremely popular with cruisers and anglers alike. Master suite in standard two-stateroom interior is huge; optional three-stateroom layout includes three heads. Note separate enginerooms, small aft deck overlooking cockpit. Withdrawn from production in 1981, reintroduced in 1986 with enlarged flybridge, updated interior decor. Early models with GM 425hp diesels—and later models with 465hp GMs—cruise at 16–17 knots (nearly 20 knots top). Note fuel increase in 1980.

Length	52'11"	Fuel	825/1,015 gals.
Beam	15'10"	Water	235 gals.
Draft	4'0"	Headroom	6 5"
Weight	55,000#	Hull Type	Modified-V
Clearance	18'6"	Deadrise Aft	NA

Prices Not Provided for Pre-1995 Models

Hatteras Yachts
New Bern, NC
www.hatterasyachts.com

231-360-0827

Hatteras 54 Extended Deckhouse MY
1989–92

Deckhouse Arrangement

Lower Deck Floorplan

Rakish twin-deck motoryacht introduced in 1989 combined bold styling with truly spacious accommodations. Innovative galley-up floorplan features enclosed wheelhouse, full-beam salon, three full heads. Remarkably, three of the 54's four staterooms boast walkaround queen beds. Note private salon access to master suite, tub in aft head. Additional features include foredeck sun lounge, small aft deck for line-handling, large flybridge, bow pulpit. GM 720hp engines cruise at 16 knots (about 20 knots top).

Length	54'9"	Fuel	1,014 gals.
Beam	17'6"	Water	250 gals.
Draft	4'9"	Headroom	6'6"
Weight	76,000#	Hull Type	Modified-V
Clearance	20'11"	Deadrise Aft	NA

Prices Not Provided for Pre-1995 Models

Hatteras Yachts
New Bern, NC
www.hatterasyachts.com

231-360-0827

Hatteras 54 Motor Yacht
1985–88

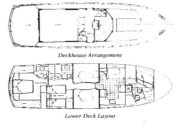

Deckhouse Arrangement

Lower Deck Layout

Stately 1980s motoryacht with "new look" Hatteras styling, wide 17'6" beam delivered big-boat luxury, comfort on a grand scale. Expansive galley-down, three-stateroom interior boasts three full heads. Lower helm (with deck access door) is open to salon. Split enginerooms provide easy access to motors. Semi-enclosed aft deck is huge for a yacht this size. Inside flybridge access is a plus. Fit and finish is as good as it gets in a production yacht. GM 650hp diesels cruise at 15 knots; 720hp GMs cruise at 16–17 knots (20+ top).

Length	54'9"	Fuel	800 gals.
Beam	17'6"	Water	250 gals.
Draft	4'2"	Headroom	6'4"
Weight	62,500#	Hull Type	Modified-V
Clearance	21'3"	Deadrise Aft	NA

Prices Not Provided for Pre-1995 Models

Hatteras Yachts
New Bern, NC
www.hatterasyachts.com

231-360-0827

Hatteras 56 Motor Yacht
1980–85

Maxi-volume 1980s motoryacht combines spacious twin-deck layout with comfortable ride, traditional Hatteras styling. Three-stateroom, three-head floorplan with galley, dinette down rivals bigger boats for space and comfort. Wheelhouse is open to salon providing near 360-degree helm visibility. Semi-enclosed aft deck is large enough for serious entertaining activities. Split enginerooms provide excellent service access. Cruise at 15-16 knots with 650hp Detroit diesels (about 18 knots top).

Length	56'3"	Fuel	1,020 gals.
Beam	18'2"	Water	350 gals.
Draft	4'11"	Waste	NA
Weight	74,000#	Hull Type	Modified-V
Clearance	18'10"	Deadrise Aft	NA

Prices Not Provided for Pre-1995 Models

Hatteras Yachts
New Bern, NC
www.hatterasyachts.com

Motoryachts & Trawlers

231-360-0827

Hatteras 58 Cockpit MY
1978–81

Standard Layout

Alternate Layout

Versatile cockpit yacht with spacious full-beam salon is often confused with more popular Hatteras 58 YF (1970–82). Standard three-stateroom interior with galley down proved more popular than alternate four-stateroom plan with galley up. Privacy door separates wheelhouse from salon. Note large master stateroom with walk-in closets, separate walk-in enginerooms, inside bridge access. Protected aft deck platform overlooks large cockpit with transom door. Standard 550hp GM diesels cruise at 16 knots (about 18 knots top).

Length	58'2"	Fuel	1,085 gals.
Beam	15'10"	Water	300 gals.
Draft	4'9"	Headroom	6'4"
Weight	73,000#	Hull Type	Modified-V
Clearance	21'2"	Deadrise Aft	NA

Prices Not Provided for Pre-1995 Models

Hatteras Yachts
New Bern, NC
www.hatterasyachts.com

231-360-0827

Hatteras 58 Long Range Cruiser
1975–81

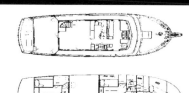

Heavyweight yacht with transatlantic range was designed for extended passages in luxury, security. Luxury-class interior includes two guest staterooms forward (each with ensuite head), crew cabin with berth and head, aft master with private entry, walk-in engineroom. Queen berth in master was optional. Pilothouse has settee, direct bridge access. Note Portuguese bridge, small boarding cockpit. Many were sold with fully enclosed aft deck. Total of 55 were built. Cruise at 8 knots with GM 4-71 (or 6-71) Detroit diesels.

Length Overall	58'2"	Clearance	18'9"
Length WL	52'0"	Fuel	2,390 gals.
Beam	17'11"	Water	440 gals.
Draft	5'10"	Waste	200 gals.
Weight	90,000#	Hull Type	Displacement

Prices Not Provided for Pre-1995 Models

Hatteras Yachts
New Bern, NC
www.hatterasyachts.com

231-360-0827

Hatteras 58 Motor Yacht
1985–87

Heavily built motoryacht with signature Hatteras styling made good on promise of executive-class accommodations, world-class quality. Wide 18'2" beam results in cavernous three-stateroom, galley-down interior with three full heads, laundry center. Expansive salon is open to helm; master suite is lavish in size, luxuries. Separate enginerooms was a Hatteras trademark in the 1980s. Huge flybridge seats a crowd. Bridge overhangs shelter side decks. GM 650hp diesels cruise at 16–17 knots (about 20 knots top).

Length	58'9"	Fuel	1,030 gals.
Beam	18'2"	Water	350 gals.
Draft	4'11"	Headroom	6'5"
Weight	79,000#	Hull Type	Modified-V
Clearance	18'10"	Deadrise Aft	NA

Prices Not Provided for Pre-1995 Models

Hatteras Yachts
New Bern, NC
www.hatterasyachts.com

Hatteras 58 Yacht Fisherman
1970–82

Versatile, always-popular cruising yacht is essentially a Hatteras 53 MY with 5-foot cockpit extension. Three-stateroom, three-head floorplan was offered with twin beds or queen berth in master stateroom. Salon is completely open to helm. Roomy cockpit with transom door is big enough for fishing. Updates include redesigned flybridge in 1978, fuel increase in 1980. Early models with GM 350hp diesels cruise at 12–14 knots (16 knots top). Twin 435hp GM engines—or 450hp GMs—cruise at 16 knots (18–20 knots wide open).

Length	58'4"	Fuel	825/1,015 gals.
Beam	15'10"	Water	250/300 gals.
Draft	4'9"	Cockpit	60 sq. ft.
Weight	62,500#	Hull Type	Modified-V
Clearance	18'6"	Deadrise Aft	NA

Prices Not Provided for Pre-1995 Models

Hatteras Yachts
New Bern, NC
www.hatterasyachts.com

Hatteras 60 Motor Yacht
1988–90

Updated version of earlier Hatteras 58 MY (1985–87) with improved styling, inside bridge access made a good yacht even better. Wide 18'2" beam results in cavernous three-stateroom, galley-down interior with three full heads, laundry center. Expansive salon is open to helm; master suite is lavish in size, luxuries. Separate walk-in enginerooms were a Hatteras trademark in the 1980s. Flybridge is huge. Large aft deck can be fully enclosed. Standard 720hp 8V92s cruise at 17–18 knots and reach a top speed of 20+ knots.

Length	60'9"	Fuel	1,033 gals.
Beam	18'2"	Water	335 gals.
Draft	5'0"	Headroom	6 5"
Weight	86,000#	Hull Type	Modified-V
Clearance	20'9"	Deadrise Aft	6°

Prices Not Provided for Pre-1995 Models

Hatteras Yachts
New Bern, NC
www.hatterasyachts.com

Hatteras 60 Extended Deckhouse MY
1991–97

Feature-rich cruising yacht with walkaround decks offered signature Hatteras luxury, quality on a grand scale. Four-stateroom floorplan with extended 200-sq.-ft salon boasts two VIP cabins with walkaround queen berths, lavish master suite with salon access, full-beam engineroom, enclosed wheelhouse. Note tub in aft head. One of the first galley-up Hatteras motoryachts. Small aft deck is designed for line-handling. Standard GM 720hp diesels cruise at 16 knots (18 knots top); 870hp GMs cruise at 18 knots (20+ wide open).

Length	60'9"	Fuel	1,033 gals.
Beam	18'2"	Water	335 gals.
Draft	5'2"	Headroom	6 5"
Weight	87,000#	Hull Type	Modified-V
Clearance	21'2"	Deadrise Aft	NA

See Page 546 For Resale Values

Hatteras Yachts
New Bern, NC
www.hatterasyachts.com

Motoryachts & Trawlers

---

www.powerboatguide.com   231-360-0827

Hatteras 61 Cockpit MY
1981–85

Stretched version of Hatteras 56 MY (1980–85) combines cockpit versatility with motoryacht comfort. Three-stateroom, three-head floorplan with galley, dinette down rivals bigger boats for space and comfort. Wheelhouse is open to salon providing good helm visibility. Semi-enclosed aft deck is large enough for serious entertaining; cockpit makes boarding easy. Split enginerooms—a Hatteras trademark—provide easy access to motors and pumps. Cruise at 15-16 knots with 650hp Detroit diesels (about 18 knots top).

Length Overall	61'3"	Clearance	18'10"
Length WL	55'9"	Fuel	1,150 gals.
Beam	18'2"	Water	350 gals.
Draft	4'11"	Hull Type	Modified-V
Weight	85,000#	Deadrise Aft	NA

Prices Not Provided for Pre-1995 Models

Hatteras Yachts
New Bern, NC
www.hatterasyachts.com

---

www.powerboatguide.com   231-360-0827

Hatteras 61 Motor Yacht
1981–85

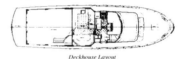
Deckhouse Layout

Queen Bed in Master

Classic twin-deck Hatteras motoryacht with full-beam salon combines spacious interior with top-shelf construction, seakindly hull. Galley-up, four-stateroom interior with enclosed pilothouse is tough to beat in a yacht this size. Extended salon rivals larger yachts for comfort, space. Highlights include second dinette on lower level, lavish master suite, separate enginerooms, huge flybridge. Note tub in aft head. Small aft deck is useful for linehandling. GM 650hp diesels cruise at 16–17 knots (about 20 knots top).

Length Overall	61'3"	Clearance	18'10"
Length WL	55'9"	Fuel	1,150 gals.
Beam	18'2"	Water	350 gals.
Draft	4'11"	Hull Type	Modified-V
Weight	82,000#	Deadrise Aft	NA

Prices Not Provided for Pre-1995 Models

Hatteras Yachts
New Bern, NC
www.hatterasyachts.com

---

www.powerboatguide.com   231-360-0827

Hatteras 63 Cockpit MY
1985–87

Deckhouse Layout

Queen Bed in Master

Quality-built cockpit yacht is basically a Hatteras 58 MY (1985–87) with 5-foot cockpit addition. Wide 18'2" beam results in cavernous interior with three staterooms and heads, roomy aft deck, full walkaround decks. Expansive salon is completely open to helm. Master suite is lavish in size, luxury. Note laundry center, home-size galley appliances, separate walk-in enginerooms. GM 840hp diesels cruise at 18 knots and reach a top speed of 20+ knots. Only a few of these yachts were built.

Length	63'8"	Fuel	1,170 gals.
Beam	18'2"	Water	375 gals.
Draft	4'11"	Headroom	6'4"
Weight	79,000#	Hull Type	Modified-V
Clearance	18'10"	Deadrise Aft	NA

Prices Not Provided for Pre-1995 Models

Hatteras Yachts
New Bern, NC
www.hatterasyachts.com

231-360-0827

Hatteras 63 Motor Yacht
1986–87

Luxury four-stateroom motoryacht with enormous full-beam salon rivals most condos for space, comfort. Expansive interior features separate galley/dinette forward of salon, private wheelhouse, lavish master suite with dressing area, walk-in closets, full-size tub in aft head. Note second lower-level dinette, separate enginerooms, formal dining area in salon. Flybridge is huge. Small aft deck provides adequate space for line-handling. Cruise at 16–17 knots with standard 650hp GM diesels (about 20 knots top).

Length	63'10"	Fuel	1,170 gals.
Beam	18'2"	Water	350 gals.
Draft	5'0"	Headroom	6'4"
Weight	92,000#	Hull Type	Modified-V
Clearance	21'3"	Deadrise Aft	NA

Prices Not Provided for Pre-1995 Models

Hatteras Yachts
New Bern, NC
www.hatterasyachts.com

231-360-0827

Hatteras 6300 Raised Pilothouse
2000–03

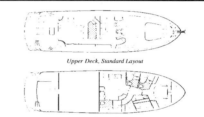

Upper Deck, Standard Layout

Lower Deck, Standard Layout

Modern pilothouse yacht introduced in 2000 took Hatteras styling in a whole new direction. Plush three-stateroom, three-head interior features huge galley open to salon, inside bridge access, raised pilothouse with centerline helm. With no obstructing bulkheads, visibility from lower helm is excellent in all directions. Topside features include massive flybridge with tender stowage, huge cockpit lazarette, walkaround decks, integral swim platform. No outside bridge access. Cat 1,400hp engines cruise at 25 knots (28–30 knots top).

Length	63'0"	Fuel	1,290 gals.
Beam	18'3"	Water	280 gals.
Draft	4'11"	Waste	100 gals.
Weight	115,000#	Hull Type	Modified-V
Clearance	18'10"	Deadrise Aft	1.5°

See Page 546 For Resale Values

Hatteras Yachts
New Bern, NC
www.hatterasyachts.com

231-360-0827

Hatteras 64 Motor Yacht
2006–Current

Refined version of earlier Hatteras 6300 MY (2000–02) with all-new interior combines European styling, extravagant comfort. Three-stateroom layout is standard; four-stateroom interior with crew quarters is optional. Spacious full-beam salon with posh seating, high-gloss cherry woodwork offers tremendous entertaining space. Note pilothouse deck door, roomy cockpit, wide side decks. Huge bridge has space for 14-foot tender. Prop pockets reduce draft, improve efficiency. Cat 1,400hp engines cruise at 24–25 knots (28 knots top).

Length	64'10"	Fuel	1,515 gals.
Beam	18'3"	Water	265 gals.
Draft	4'8"	Waste	95 gals.
Weight	116,700#	Hull Type	Modified-V
Clearance, Arch	18'10"	Deadrise Aft	2°

Insufficient Resale Data To Assign Values

Hatteras Yachts
New Bern, NC
www.hatterasyachts.com

---

www.powerboatguide.com　　　　　　　　　　　　　　231-360-0827

Hatteras 65 Long Range Cruiser
1981–86

Standard Deckhouse Layout

Standard Lower-Deck Floorplan

Heavily built displacement cruiser from 1980s took comfort, security to new levels. Spacious four-stateroom interior features fully enclosed pilothouse, extravagant owner's suite with private salon access, full-beam engineroom. Portuguese bridge protects against oncoming seas. Note deckhouse day head, home-size galley, wide side decks. Enclosed aft deck overlooks small cockpit with transom door. GM 6-71N diesels cruise at 8–10 knots with range of 2,000–2,500 nautical miles. Total of 13 were built.

Length Overall	65'0"	Clearance	18'9"
Length WL	58'8"	Fuel	2,625 gals.
Beam	17'11"	Water	455 gals.
Draft	4'10"	Waste	200 gals.
Weight	114,000#	Hull Type	Displacement

Prices Not Provided for Pre-1995 Models

Hatteras Yachts
New Bern, NC
www.hatterasyachts.com

---

www.powerboatguide.com　　　　　　　　　　　　　　231-360-0827

Hatteras 65 Motor Yacht
1988–96

Classic Hatteras motoryacht proved popular with sophisticated owners seeking maxi-volume luxury, world-class accommodations. Original four-stateroom interior with separate enginerooms was joined in 1989 with revised four-stateroom layout with full-beam engineroom, amidships VIP stateroom. Highlights include enclosed wheelhouse, lavish master suite, full-width salon, enormous flybridge, covered aft deck. Twin 870hp GM engines cruise at 17 knots (20 knots top); 1,075hp GMs cruise at 18–19 knots (low 20s top).

Length	65'10"	Fuel	1,170 gals.
Beam	18'2"	Water	350 gals.
Draft	5.5"	Headroom	6'6"
Weight	99,000#	Hull Type	Modified-V
Clearance	21.5"	Deadrise Aft	NA

See Page 546 For Resale Values

Hatteras Yachts
New Bern, NC
www.hatterasyachts.com

---

www.powerboatguide.com　　　　　　　　　　　　　　231-360-0827

Heritage East 36 Sundeck
1985–Current

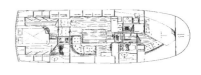

Popular import appeals to value-conscious buyers looking for big-boat comfort, small-boat economy. Traditional teak interior boasts roomy salon with full lower helm, double berths in both staterooms, generous storage, teak-and-holly cabin sole, good engineroom access. Overhead salon grabrails are a thoughtful touch. Aft deck hardtop is a popular option. Large cabin windows let in plenty of natural lighting. Very space-efficient layout. Cruise efficiently at 8-10 knots with single 220hp Cummins diesel.

Length Overall	35'9"	Clearance	15'7"
Length WL	32'1"	Fuel	420 gals.
Beam	12.7"	Water	180 gals.
Draft	3'8"	Waste	60 gals.
Weight	23,000#	Hull Type	Semi-Disp.

See Page 546 For Resale Values

Yacht Registry (Importer)
Dunedin, FL
www.yachtregistry.net

Heritage East 42 Sundeck
2003–Current

Well-built Asian import with common-sense layout appeals to liveaboards, cruisers alike. Standard galley-down floorplan features full dinette opposite galley; optional galley-up layout offers separate stall shower in forward head, queen berth in guest stateroom. Both floorplans have full teak interior, sliding helm door, space for washer/dryer. Additional features include bow pulpit, teak-and-holly cabin sole, hinged radar arch, wide side decks, large engineroom. Twin 220hp Cummins diesels cruise efficiently at 9 knots (about 12 knots top).

Length Overall	42'0"	Clearance	19'3"
Length WL	37'6"	Fuel	560 gals.
Beam	14'6"	Water	250 gals.
Draft	4'6"	Waste	NA
Weight	41,000#	Hull Type	Semi-Disp.

Insufficient Resale Data To Assign Values

Yacht Registry (Importer)
Dunedin, FL
www.yachtregistry.net

Horizon 62 Motor Yacht
2003–Current

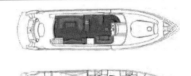

Handsome flybridge yacht is notable for graceful styling, quality construction, very competitive price. Beautifully finished interior offers luxurious accommodations for six in three staterooms including lavish full-beam master. Spacious salon is dominated by 11-foot sofa, full entertainment center. Transom—with twin lighted staircases, crew-cabin door—resembles that of a 90-footer. Note large cockpit with curved bridge steps, roomy engine compartment. Cat 1,000hp diesels cruise at 20 knots (22–23 knots top).

Length	64'3"	Fuel	1,000 gals.
Beam	17'4"	Water	350 gals.
Draft	5'7"	Waste	150 gals.
Weight	74,960#	Hull Type	Semi-Disp.
Clearance	18.5'	Deadrise Aft	12°

Insufficient Resale Data To Assign Values

Gilman Yachts
Palm Beach, FL
www.horizonyacht.com

Hyundai 49 Motor Yacht
1988–94

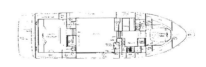

Korean-built motoryacht from 1980s (also called Elegant 49; Sonata 5300) was a lot of boat for the money. Roomy galley-down interior features two large staterooms, solid teak cabinetry, lower helm with deck access door. Wing doors, enclosure panels, wet bar were standard on the aft deck. Many of these boats were fitted with Jacuzzi in aft head. Large salon windows provide panoramic outside views. Note fully cored hull, wide side decks. Cruise at 16–18 knots with 375hp Cat diesels (20+ knots wide open).

Length w/Pulpit	53'0"	Headroom	6'4"
Hull Length	48'6"	Fuel	700 gal.
Beam	15'8"	Water	300 gal.
Draft	3'6"	Hull Type	Modified-V
Weight	34,000#	Deadrise Aft	14°

Prices Not Provided for Pre-1995 Models

Hyundai no longer builds boats.

www.powerboatguide.com   231-360-0827

Independence 45 Trawler
1985–2000

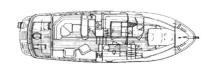

Sturdy pilothouse trawler combines handsome lines with seakindly hull, single-screw economy. Highlights include well-appointed interior with full-beam salon, roomy pilothouse, weather-tight doors, comfortable cockpit, large boat deck with room for dinghy stowage. Deep keel protects running gear from grounding. Imported from Taiwan by Hans Christian through 1995, production shifted to U.S.-based Cherubini starting with hull #19 in 1996. Cruise at 7–8 knots with single135hp Lugger diesel; 10 knots with 355hp Cummins.

Length Overall	48'8"	Clearance	13'6"
Length WL	40'9"	Fuel	630 gals.
Beam	14'6"	Water	300 gals.
Draft	4'6"	Waste	40 gals.
Weight	38,000#	Hull	Semi-Disp.

Insufficient Resale Data To Assign Values

No longer in production

---

www.powerboatguide.com   231-360-0827

Island Gypsy 30 Sedan
1975–85

Pocket sedan trawler appeals to low-budget couples drawn to sporty styling, practical accommodations, fuel-efficient operation. Traditional teak interior with V-berths forward, convertible dinette and settee can sleep up to six. Highlights include lower helm station with sliding deck door, teak parquet flooring, teak bow pulpit, teak handrails, teak swim platform. Note wide side decks, simulated lapstrake hull. Fun to drive, easy to maintain, inexpensive to own. Cruise at 6–7 knots (burning just 2–3 gph) with standard 120hp Lehman diesel.

Length Overall	30'0"	Clearance	12'0"
Length WL	27'9"	Fuel	250 gals.
Beam	11'6"	Water	120 gals.
Draft	3'8"	Waste	25 gals.
Weight	14,400#	Hull Type	Semi-Disp.

Prices Not Provided for Pre-1995 Models

**Island Gypsy/Halvorsen Marine
Kowloon, Hong Kong
www.yardway.com.hk/marine**

---

www.powerboatguide.com   231-360-0827

Island Gypsy 32 Europa
1989–2003

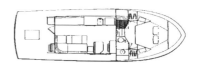

Handsome Europa-style trawler ranks among the most popular models ever built by Island Gypsy over the years. Highlights include well-crafted teak interior with open salon, lower helm with deck access door, split head with separate stall shower, covered aft deck, protected side decks. Surprisingly roomy flybridge with facing settees seats several guests. Full-length keel protects running gear from grounding. Note small holding tank capacity. Cruise at 6–7 knots with single 135hp diesel; 8-9 knots with 210hp Cummins.

Length Overall	32'0"	Clearance	12'4"
Length WL	29.7'	Fuel	250 gals.
Beam	12'0"	Water	120 gals.
Draft	3'8"	Waste	15 gals.
Weight	16,400#	Hull Type	Semi-Disp.

See Page 547 For Resale Values

**Island Gypsy/Halvorsen Marine
Kowloon, Hong Kong
www.yardway.com.hk/marine**

231-360-0827

Island Gypsy 32 Sedan
1981–94

Salty sedan trawler with handsome profile, versatile layout appeals to cruising couples on a budget. Space-efficient teak interior boasts comfortable salon with facing settees, lower helm with deck access door, teak parquet flooring, complete galley with stove/oven. Teak-over-fiberglass decks, mast and boom assembly, teak hand rails were standard. Full-length keel protects running gear from grounding. Good lower helm visibility. Small holding tank capacity. Cruise at 7–8 knots with single 250hp Cummins diesel.

Length Overall	32'0"	Clearance	12'4"
Length WL	29'7"	Fuel	250 gals.
Beam	12'0"	Water	120 gals.
Draft	3'8"	Waste	15 gals.
Weight	16,400#	Hull Type	Semi-Disp.

Prices Not Provided for Pre-1995 Models

Island Gypsy/Halvorsen Marine
Kowloon, Hong Kong
www.yardway.com.hk/marine

231-360-0827

Island Gypsy 36 Classic
1981–2002

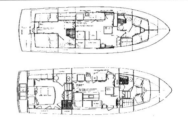

Popular double cabin trawler with signature Island Gypsy profile is is built for coastal cruising in comfort, security. Several twin-stateroom floorplans were offered over the years. Highlights include teak interior joinerwork, parquet flooring, standard lower helm, fully-equipped galley with stove/oven, port and starboard salon deck doors, full-size head with stall shower, teak-over-fiberglass decks, roomy flybridge with seating for six. Note simulated lapstrake hull lines. Cruise at 8 knots with single Cummins diesel; 10–12 knots with twins.

Length Overall	36'0"	Clearance	12'6"
Length WL	32'10"	Fuel	400 gals.
Beam	13'0"	Water	200 gals.
Draft	3'6"	Waste	50 gals.
Weight	27,000#	Hull Type	Semi-Disp.

See Page 547 For Resale Values

Island Gypsy/Halvorsen Marine
Kowloon, Hong Kong
www.yardway.com.hk/marine

231-360-0827

Island Gypsy 36 Europa
1982–98

Sought-after Eurosedan combines classic trawler styling with top-shelf construction, fuel-efficient operation. Highlights include elegant teak interior with lower helm and two staterooms, covered aft deck, protected walkways, teak-over-fiberglass decks, semi-displacement hull with prop-protecting keel. Note large engineroom, cockpit storage lazarette, simulated lapstrake hull lines. Excellent range with 450-gallon fuel capacity. Cruise at 8 knots with twin 135hp diesels; 10–12 knots with twin 210hp Cummins.

Length Overall	36'0"	Clearance	16'0"
Length WL	32'10"	Fuel	450 gals.
Beam	13'0"	Water	200 gals.
Draft	3'11"	Waste	40 gals.
Weight	25,520#	Hull Type	Semi-Disp.

See Page 547 For Resale Values

Island Gypsy/Halvorsen Marine
Kowloon, Hong Kong
www.yardway.com.hk/marine

Motoryachts & Trawlers

Motoryachts & Trawlers

231-360-0827

Island Gypsy 36 Motor Yacht
1992–2002

Standard Floorplan

Optional Three-Stateroom Interior

Stylish sundeck trawler makes good on Island Gypsy promise of solid construction, common-sense layout, proven owner satisfaction. Traditional teak interior features surprisingly spacious salon with facing settees, port/starboard deck doors, two full heads, choice of two or three staterooms. Large engineroom provides good service access. Radar mast, bow pulpit, swim platform were standard. Salon dimensions rival many 40-footers. Cruise at 8 knots with twin 135hp Lehman diesels; 10–12 knots with 210hp Cummins.

Length Overall	36'0"	Clearance	12'6"
Length WL	32'10"	Fuel	400 gals.
Beam	13'0"	Water	200 gals.
Draft	3'11"	Headroom	6'4"
Weight	28,000#	Hull Type	Semi-Disp.

See Page 547 For Resale Values

Island Gypsy/Halvorsen Marine
Kowloon, Hong Kong
www.yardway.com.hk/marine

231-360-0827

Island Gypsy 40 Flush Aft Deck
1986–94

Durable sundeck cruiser offers an inviting mix of agile handling, quality construction, practical layout. Galley-up interior boasts full-beam master stateroom aft, large salon with dinette and lower helm, queen bed in forward stateroom, two full heads. Galley is positioned aft in salon, convenient to aft deck and bridge. Note well-crafted teak woodwork. Helm-aft flybridge layout is unusual—most motoryachts have the helm forward, guest seating aft. Twin 135hp diesels cruise at 8 knots. Cat 375hp diesels cruise at 18 knots.

Length Overall	40'0"	Clearance	13'3"
Length WL	35'3"	Fuel	400 gals.
Beam	14'3"	Water	200 gals.
Draft	3'6"	Waste	60 gals.
Weight	33,500#	Hull Type	Semi-Disp.

Prices Not Provided for Pre-1995 Models

Island Gypsy/Halvorsen Marine
Kowloon, Hong Kong
www.yardway.com.hk/marine

231-360-0827

Island Gypsy 44 Flush Aft Deck
1979–96

No-nonsense sundeck yacht combines a seaworthy hull design with tank-like construction, excellent range, and a very comfortable layout. Standard three-stateroom floorplan (most 44-footers have two) boasts expansive salon with convertible dinette and lower helm, full-beam master stateroom, two small guest cabins forward. Galley is aft in salon, convenient to aft deck and flybridge. Both heads have stall showers. Super-nice interior joinerwork. Cruise at 12 knots with twin 275hp diesels (15 top); 16-17 knots with 375hp Cats (20 knots top).

Length Overall	44'3"	Clearance	13'7"
Length WL	38'9"	Fuel	800 gals.
Beam	15'4"	Water	400 gals.
Draft	4'3"	Waste	60 gals.
Weight	38,500#	Hull Type	Semi-Disp.

See Page 547 For Resale Values

Island Gypsy/Halvorsen Marine
Kowloon, Hong Kong
www.yardway.com.hk/marine

Island Gypsy 49 Classic
1988–94

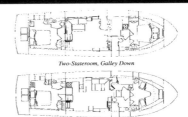

Two-Stateroom, Galley Down

Three-Stateroom, Galley Up

Heavily-built motoryacht with classic trawler lines strikes a balance between cruising comfort, economical operation. Offered with choice or two- or three-stateroom interior plans, both with beautifully crafted Burmese teak joinery, port/starboard salon deck doors, teak-planked flooring, copious storage. Good lower-helm visibility. Topside features include teak walkaround deck, mast & boom assembly, teak railings. Spacious flybridge can seat a small crowd. Excellent range at lower speeds. Cruise at 12–14 knots with twin 375hp Cats.

Length Overall	49'0"	Clearance	13 7"
Length WL	43'6"	Fuel	800 gals.
Beam	15'4"	Water	400 gals.
Draft	4 5"	Waste	80 gals.
Weight	38,000#	Hull Type	Semi-Disp.

Prices Not Provided for Pre-1995 Models

Island Gypsy/Halvorsen Marine
Kowloon, Hong Kong
www.yardway.com.hk/marine

Jefferson 42 Viscount
1990–94

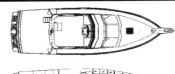

Popular 1990s Jefferson import delivered traditional motoryacht accommodations at a remarkably affordable price. Comfortable two-stateroom, galley-down teak interior boasts expansive salon with built-in settee, full lower helm, convertible dinette, U-shaped galley with generous storage. Note tub/shower in aft head, separate shower compartment forward. Roomy aft deck includes wet bar. Integral bow pulpit, swim platform, hardtop, radar arch were standard. Cruise at 20 knots with Cat 375hp diesels (low 20s top).

Length Overall	41'8"	Clearance	15 7"
Length WL	37'8"	Fuel	350 gals.
Beam	14 5"	Water	100 gals.
Draft	3'0"	Hull Type	Modified-V
Weight	28,000#	Deadrise Aft	NA

Prices Not Provided for Pre-1995 Models

Jefferson Yachts
Jeffersonville, IN
www.jeffersonyachts.com

Jefferson 43 Marlago Sundeck
1990–2001

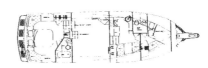

Appealing double-cabin cruiser offers enduring blend of traditional styling, practical accommodations, affordable cost. Spacious two-stateroom, galley-down layout includes tub/shower in aft head, full dinette, standard lower helm. Expansive aft deck can entertain a small crowd. Note wide side decks, roomy bridge, large cabin windows. Most were sold with optional hardtop and radar arch. Low-deadrise hull with moderate beam, shallow keel delivers comfortable ride. Cruise at 20 knots with Cat 425hp diesels (low 20s top).

Length Overall	42'10"	Clearance	16 7"
Length WL	NA	Fuel	420 gals.
Beam	15'0"	Water	200 gals.
Draft	3'10"	Hull Type	Modified-V
Weight	31,000#	Deadrise Aft	NA

See Page 548 For Resale Values

Jefferson Yachts
Jeffersonville, IN
www.jeffersonyachts.com

Motoryachts & Trawlers

Motoryachts & Trawlers

231-360-0827

Jefferson 45 Motor Yacht
1984–88

Generic Taiwan import popular from 1990s hit the sweet spot with buyers seeking low-cost motoryacht luxury. Expansive teak interior features spacious, open-plan salon with full lower helm, galley down with dinette opposite, large master staterooms. Note port, starboard deck access doors in salon. Roomy aft deck is large enough to entertain several guests. Radar arch, hardtop, swim platform, bow pulpit were standard. Perkins 200hp diesels cruise at 10–11 knots (14 knots top); 320hp Cats cruise at 16 knots and top out at close to 20 knots.

Length Overall	45'3"	Clearance	17'10"
Length WL	41'0"	Fuel	600 gals.
Beam	15'2"	Water	300 gals.
Draft	4'5"	Hull Type	Modified-V
Weight	41,000#	Deadrise Aft	NA

Prices Not Provided for Pre-1995 Models

Jefferson Yachts
Jeffersonville, IN
www.jeffersonyachts.com

231-360-0827

Jefferson 45 Rivanna SE
2007–Current

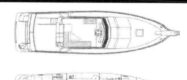

Value-priced cruising yacht couples versatile deck layout with comfortable accommodations, respectable performance. Practical two-stateroom interior boasts home-style dinette, large galley, huge master stateroom with tub in private head. Wraparound cabin windows admit plenty of natural lighting in salon. Topside features include aft-deck wing doors, molded swim platform, large bridge with seating for six. Wide side decks are a plus. Note deep draft. Cruise at 16–17 knots with Cummins 350hp diesels.

Length	44'7"	Fuel	420 gals.
Beam	14'5"	Water	200 gals.
Draft	4'6"	Waste	45 gals.
Weight	32,000#	Hull Type	Modified-V
Clearance, Bridge	12'9"	Deadrise Aft	11°

Insufficient Resale Data To Assign Values

Jefferson Yachts
Jeffersonville, IN
www.jeffersonyachts.com

231-360-0827

Jefferson 46 Marlago Sundeck
1990–2001

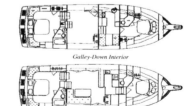

Galley-Down Interior

Galley-Up Interior

Contemporary aft-cabin motoryacht adhered to Jefferson tradition of offering good value for the money. Standard galley-down interior has dinette opposite galley; alternate mid-galley layout has expanded salon with space forward for washer/dryer. Highlights include well-crafted teak cabinets, lower helm station, full-beam owner stateroom with settee seating, aft-deck wet bar, hardtop, radar arch. Cummins 315hp diesels cruise 15–16 knots (about 18 top); optional 430hp Volvo diesels cruise in the low 20s (mid 20s knots top).

Length Overall	45'10"	Clearance	11'7"
Length WL	NA	Fuel	420 gals.
Beam	15'0"	Water	200 gals.
Draft	3'10"	Hull Type	Modified-V
Weight	34,700#	Deadrise Aft	NA

See Page 548 For Resale Values

Jefferson Yachts
Jeffersonville, IN
www.jeffersonyachts.com

231-360-0827

Jefferson 50 Rivanna SE
2004–Current

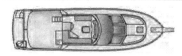

Sporty aft-cabin cruising yacht with integral swim platform gets high marks for styling, comfort, affordability. Standard two-stateroom, galley-down interior features spacious salon with wraparound windows, large master stateroom, generous storage. Teak cabinetry is expertly finished. Lower helm position is optional. Expansive aft deck with wet bar, wing doors can entertain small crowd. Note wide side decks, molded swim platform steps, bow pulpit. Cummins 480hp diesels cruise at 18 knots (low 20s knots top).

Length Overall	50'0"	Fuel	420 gals.
Beam	15'0"	Water	200 gals.
Draft	4'0"	Waste	60 gals.
Weight	37,700#	Hull Type	Modified-V
Clearance	12'10"	Deadrise Aft	12°

See Page 548 For Resale Values

Jefferson Yachts
Jeffersonville, IN
www.jeffersonyachts.com

231-360-0827

Jefferson 52 Marquessa
1989–2001

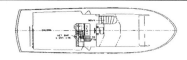

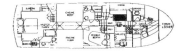

Twin-deck Jefferson motoryacht—similar in design to the Chris Craft 501 MY—combined bold styling with spacious accommodations, versatile deck plan. Three-stateroom, three-head interior with galley and dinette down boasts separate, walk-in enginerooms, large master with generous storage, deluxe owner's suite. Teak entertainment center separates lower helm from vast, full-beam salon. Small aft deck is useful for line-handling. Note wheelhouse deck doors, tub in aft head. GM 550hp diesels cruise at 15–16 knots (about 20 knots top).

Length Overall	52 5"	Fuel	700 gals.
Length WL	NA	Water	200 gals.
Beam	16'0"	Waste	45 gals.
Draft	4'0"	Hull Type	Modified-V
Weight	55,800#	Deadrise Aft	6°

See Page 548 For Resale Values

Jefferson Yachts
Jeffersonville, IN
www.jeffersonyachts.com

231-360-0827

Jefferson 52 Rivanna Cockpit MY
1994–1999

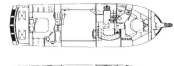

Handsome 1990s cockpit yacht with seductive teak interior paired traditional Jefferson value with sporty styling, practical accommodations. Available with two or three staterooms, both with expansive salon, standard lower helm, home-size galley. Impressive list of standard equipment included hardtop, radar arch, bow pulpit, aft-deck wing doors, swim platform. Spacious engineroom offers good outboard access to motors. Swim, dive, or fish from small cockpit. Cummins 450hp diesels cruise at 16 knots (around 20 knots top).

Length	52'4"	Headroom	6 5"
Beam	16'0"	Fuel	600 gals.
Draft	4'0"	Water	200 gals.
Weight	44,500#	Hull Type	Modified-V
Clearance, Arch	13'4"	Deadrise Aft	8°

See Page 548 For Resale Values

Jefferson Yachts
Jeffersonville, IN
www.jeffersonyachts.com

Motoryachts & Trawlers

www.powerboatguide.com

231-360-0827

Jefferson 56 Marquessa Cockpit MY
1991–2001

Roomy twin-deck cockpit yacht with full-beam salon took signature Jefferson value to the next level. Several three-stateroom, galley-down floorplans were available, all with lower helm open to salon and aft deck. Master suite is reached via corridor between separate walk-in enginerooms. Note port/starboard sliding deck doors, washer/dryer space in amidships head. Huge flybridge is accessed from salon only. Cockpit transom door makes boarding easy, convenient. GM 550hp diesels cruise at 14–15 knots (about 18 knots wide open).

Length	56'4"	Fuel	700 gals.
Beam	16'0"	Water	200 gals.
Draft	4'0"	Waste	45 gals.
Weight	57,500#	Hull Type	Modified-V
Clearance	19'6"	Deadrise Aft	6°

See Page 548 For Resale Values

Jefferson Yachts
Jeffersonville, IN
www.jeffersonyachts.com

---

www.powerboatguide.com

231-360-0827

Jefferson 56 Rivanna Cockpit MY
1994–2009

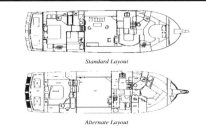

Standard Layout

Alternate Layout

Appealing cockpit motoryacht introduced in 1994 enhanced Jefferson reputation for graceful styling, versatile accommodations, exceptional value. Offered with several two- and three-stateroom interiors over the years, all with full-beam master suite, well-appointed salon with standard lower helm. Notable features include traditional teak interior, roomy aft deck with wet bar, good-size cockpit with transom door. Large engineroom is a plus. Cat 600hp—or 635hp Cummins—diesels cruise at 18 knots and reach just over 20 knots top.

Length Overall	56'4"	Fuel	600 gals.
Beam	16'0"	Water	200 gals.
Draft	4'0"	Waste	45 gals.
Weight	47,000#	Hull Type	Modified-V
Clearance	16 5"	Deadrise Aft	6°

See Page 548 For Resale Values

Jefferson Yachts
Jeffersonville, IN
www.jeffersonyachts.com

---

www.powerboatguide.com

231-360-0827

Jefferson 57 Pilothouse
2001–09

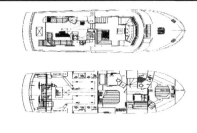

Heavily built pilothouse yacht was built for comfortable cruising in a wide range of conditions. Three-stateroom interior boasts expansive pilothouse with centerline helm, amidships master suite, VIP stateroom forward, home-sized galley. Note high-gloss teak joinery, protected decks, massive bridge, spacious engineroom. Semi-displacement hull with hard aft chines has deep prop-protecting keel. Widebody version with full-beam salon also available. Cruise at 18–20 knots with 625hp Cummins diesels (low 20s top).

Length	57 5"	Headroom	6'6"
Beam	16'0"	Fuel	800 gals.
Draft	4'6"	Water	200 gals.
Weight	57,500#	Waste	75 gals.
Clearance	19'0"	Hull Type	Semi-Disp.

See Page 548 For Resale Values

Jefferson Yachts
Jeffersonville, IN
www.jeffersonyachts.com

231-360-0827

Jefferson 60 Marquessa Cockpit MY
1999–2009

Full-body cockpit yacht offered upscale Jefferson buyers yacht-style luxury, comfort at a reasonable price. Spacious teak interior (offered with three or four staterooms) features extended, full-beam salon with galley and dinette forward, extravagant master suite with tremendous storage, built-in washer/dryer, separate walk-in enginerooms. Note salon staircase to flybridge, port/starboard deck access doors. Excellent pilothouse visibility. Small afterdeck with wet bar overlooks cockpit. Cat 800hp diesels cruise at 18 knots (20+ top).

Length	60'4"	Fuel	835 gals.
Beam	16'0"	Water	200 gals.
Draft	4'6"	Waste	45 gals.
Weight	65,000#	Hull Type	Modified-V
Clearance, Arch	19'6"	Deadrise Aft	11°

See Page 548 For Resale Values

Jefferson Yachts
Jeffersonville, IN
www.jeffersonyachts.com

231-360-0827

Jefferson 60 Marquessa MY
1987–89

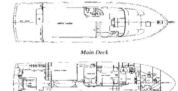

Main Deck

Lower Deck

Taiwan-built motoryacht from late 1980s combined affordable price with spacious, total-teak interior, solid fiberglass construction. Several galley-down floorplans were offered, most with four staterooms, four heads. Extended salon with day head, staircase to flybridge, is completely open to lower helm. Note separate, walk-in enginerooms, tub in aft head. Topside features include enclosed aft deck with wing doors, protected side decks, large flybridge. GM 735hp diesels cruise at 15–16 knots (about 18 knots top).

Length	59'10"	Fuel	1,000 gals.
Beam	17'6"	Water	400 gals.
Draft	4'7"	Waste	45 gals.
Weight	88,000#	Hull Type	Semi-Disp.
Clearance, Arch	21'2"	Deadrise Aft	6°

Prices Not Provided for Pre-1995 Models

Jefferson Yachts
Jeffersonville, IN
www.jeffersonyachts.com

231-360-0827

Kha Shing 40 Sundeck
1980–86

Two-Stateroom Layout

Alternate Three-Stateroom Layout

Popular Taiwan cruiser with conservative lines gets high marks for traditional teak interior, spacious accommodations, good build quality. Most were delivered with two-stateroom/dinette floorplan with lower helm. Highlights include well-crafted teak cabinetry, expansive salon with deck door, generous storage, big engineroom. Hardtop was a popular option. Called Spindrift 40 on the West Coast; Vista or Southern Star 40 on East Coast. Over 120 sold. Cruise at 10-12 knots (around 15 knots top) with Volvo 165hp diesels.

Length Overall	39'6"	Clearance	15'1"
Length WL	34'0"	Fuel	300/340 gals.
Beam	14'0"	Water	200 gals.
Draft	3'7"	Waste	60 gals.
Weight	22,800#	Hull Type	Semi-Disp.

Prices Not Provided for Pre-1995 Models

Kha Shing Yachts
Kaohsiung, Taiwan
www.khashing.com/

Motoryachts & Trawlers

231-360-0827

Krogen 39 Trawler
1998—Current

Muscular, quality-built pilothouse trawler—based on classic Krogen 42 hull—is built for big-watercruising in comfort, security. Beautifully finished interior features huge master stateroom forward, well-appointed salon, big U-shaped galley, raised pilothouse with fold-out berth. Walk-in engineroom has built-in workbench. Good visibility from both helm positions. Extended hardtop can stow 10-foot dinghy; bridge overhangs shelter side decks and cockpit. Cruise at 7-8 knots with 121hp John Deere diesel. Range exceeds 2,500 miles.

Length Overall	43'8"	Ballast	2,000#
Length WL	36'8"	Fuel	700 gals.
Beam	14'3"	Water	300 gals.
Draft	4'3"	Waste	35 gals.
Weight	33,470#	Hull Type	Displacement

See Page 548 For Resale Values

Kadey-Krogen Yachts
Stuart, FL
www.kadeykrogen.com

231-360-0827

Krogen 42 Trawler
1977—97

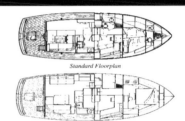

Standard Floorplan

Widebody Layout

Classic Krogen trawler with full-displacement hull is widely praised for excellent seakeeping ability, efficient operation. Highlights include very tall freeboard, roomy cockpit, wide sidedecks, superb pilothouse visibility. Glass-over-plywood decks, superstructure upgraded to fiberglass in 1985 (hull #65); cored hull became solid fiberglass in 1995. Offered with one head or two. Widebody version with full-beam salon came out in 1989. Generator doubles as get-home engine. Range exceeds 2,000 miles. Total of 206 were built including five with twin engines.

Length Overall	42'4"	Ballast	2,500#
Length WL	39'2"	Fuel	700 gals.
Beam	15'0"	Water	360 gals.
Draft	4 7"	Waste	40 gals.
Weight	39,500#	Hull Type	Displacement

See Page 548 For Resale Values

Kadey-Krogen Yachts
Stuart, FL
www.kadeykrogen.com

231-360-0827

Krogen 44 Trawler
2004—Current

Quality full-displacement cruising yacht based on classic Krogen 42 is rugged, salty, comfortable. Twin-stateroom interior is similar to the old 42, but pilothouse is larger with space for fixed helm chair. Aft deck is larger as well with more entertaining space. Additional highlights include varnished teak (or cherry) joinery, watertight aluminum doors and windows, protected walkways, well-finished engineroom. Note desk in guest cabin. Offered in widebody or walkaround versions. Cruise at 7–8 knots with single 156hp John Deere diesel.

Length Overall	49'0"	Ballast	2,500#
Length WL	40'11"	Fuel	850 gals.
Beam	15'6"	Water	350 gals.
Draft	4'6"	Waste	52 gals.
Weight	43,140#	Hull Type	Displacement

Insufficient Resale Data To Assign Values

Kadey-Krogen Yachts
Stuart, FL
www.kadeykrogen.com

Krogen 48 Whaleback
1992–2003

Sturdy full-displacement trawler with true liveaboard comforts is ready to take on the world. With wide 16'8" beam and no side decks, interior dimensions are extravagant for a boat this size. Single-level floorplan has three staterooms (one doubling as den), two full heads, expansive salon, large galley. Raised pilothouse with reverse windshield boasts 360-degree visibility, wet bar. Note protected walkway surrounding pilothouse. Cruising range with Cat 210hp engine is about 2,000 miles. Total of 30 were built.

Length Overall	48 5"	Clearance	NA
Length WL	45.5"	Fuel	1,020 gals.
Beam	16'8"	Water	540 gals.
Draft	5'0"	Waste	100 gals.
Weight	56,200#	Hull Type	Displacement

See Page 548 For Resale Values

Kadey-Krogen Yachts
Stuart, FL
www.kadeykrogen.com

Krogen 58 Trawler
2001–Current

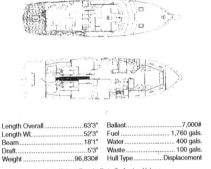

Feature-rich trawler with long-range capability travels the world in comfort, security. Built on full-displacement hull with long keel, twin prop-protecting skegs. Elegant cherrywood interior has master suite forward, guest staterooms aft with portside cabin doubling as office. Note engineroom workbench, watertight doors. Reverse pilothouse windshield reduces glare. Asymmetric layout lacks port side deck. Portuguese bridge protects against breaking seas. Single 154hp diesel delivers impressive 2,000-mile range at 8 knots.

Length Overall	63'3"	Ballast	7,000#
Length WL	52'3"	Fuel	1,760 gals.
Beam	18'1"	Water	400 gals.
Draft	5'3"	Waste	100 gals.
Weight	96,830#	Hull Type	Displacement

Insufficient Resale Data To Assign Values

Kadey-Krogen Yachts
Stuart, FL
www.kadeykrogen.com

Krogen Express 49
1995–2002

Distinctive pilothouse cruiser offers remarkable blend of seaworthiness, comfort, elegance. Efficient semi-displacement hull with plumb bow, slender beam is stable and quick. Traditional pilothouse floorplan features expansive salon with home-sized galley, two large staterooms, copious storage. Guest stateroom can serve as office. Excellent visibility from both helms. Note beautiful teak joinery, walk-in engineroom. Cat 350hp diesels cruise at 16–17 knots; 420hp Yanmars cruise at 19–20 knots. Total of 16 built.

Length Overall	49'6"	Clearance, Mast	21 7"
Length WL	47'11"	Fuel	600 gals.
Beam	14'9"	Water	300 gals.
Draft	4'0"	Waste	75 gals.
Weight	42,000#	Hull Type	Semi-Disp.

Insufficient Resale Data To Assign Values

Kadey-Krogen Yachts
Stuart, FL
www.kadeykrogen.com

Motoryachts & Trawlers

---

www.powerboatguide.com   231-360-0827

Krogen Express 52
2003–Current

Longer, wider version of Krogen Express 49 (1995–2002) boasts enlarged cockpit, more expansive salon. Easily driven hull with slender beam is stable, efficient, quick. Upscale interior features two large staterooms, two heads, combined salon/galley, quality teak woodwork. Guest stateroom can serve as office. Pilothouse seating converts to double berth. Note inside bridge access, walk-in engineroom, protected aft deck. Meticulous fit and finish throughout. Yanmar 440hp diesels cruise at 16–18 knots (about 20 knots top).

Length Overall	57'6"	Clearance, Mast	21'8"
Length WL	51'4"	Fuel	700 gals.
Beam	15'11"	Water	370 gals.
Draft	4'0"	Waste	100 gals.
Weight	43,000#	Hull Type	Semi-Disp.

Insufficient Resale Data To Assign Values

Kadey-Krogen Yachts
Stuart, FL
www.kadeykrogen.com

---

www.powerboatguide.com   231-360-0827

LaBelle 40 Motor Yacht
1983–88

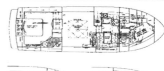

Popular Taiwan trawler with handsome teak interior offers good value to savvy used-boat buyers. Practical two-stateroom floorplan with galley/dinette down was available in several forward-stateroom configurations. Compact salon limits indoor entertaining options, but aft deck and master stateroom are big for a 40-footer. Deck access door at lower helm is a plus. Topside features include teak decks, teak swim platform, radar arch, hardtop. Standard Volvo 165hp diesels cruise efficiently at 10 knots (12–13 knots top).

Length	40'0"	Fuel	400 gals.
Beam	13'6"	Water	250 gals.
Draft	3'6"	Waste	35 gals.
Weight	25,000#	Hull Type	Modified-V
Clearance	NA	Deadrise Aft	NA

Prices Not Provided for Pre-1995 Models

No longer in production

---

www.powerboatguide.com   231-360-0827

LaBelle 43 Motor Yacht
1983–88

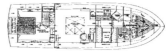

Graceful 1980s sundeck yacht with distinctive lines, roomy accommodations appealed to cruisers, liveaboards alike. Highlights include full teak interior, teak decks and cabintop, traditional two-stateroom layout with galley and dinette down. Lower helm with deck door was standard; salon sofa and dinette both convert to double beds. Party-time aft deck is huge for a boat this size. Note spacious engineroom, wide side decks, teak swim platform. Volvo 165hp diesels cruise economically at 10 knots (13–14 knots top).

Length Overall	43'0"	Clearance	NA
Length WL	NA	Fuel	450 gals.
Beam	14'2"	Water	250 gals.
Draft	4'2"	Hull Type	Semi-Disp.
Weight	26,850#	Deadrise Aft	NA

Prices Not Provided for Pre-1995 Models

No longer in production

231-360-0827

Lien Hwa 47 Cockpit MY
1990–99

Popular Taiwan import from 1990s (also marketed under Tradewinds, Vitesse nameplates) offered solid construction, comfortable accommodations. All-teak interior features roomy salon with lower helm position, U-shaped galley and dinette down. Note compact bow stateroom, absence of shower stall in forward head. Additional features include wide side decks, teak cockpit sole, hardtop, folding radar arch. Optional 375hp Cat (or 330hp Cummins) diesels cruise at 19–20 knots and reach a top speed of around 23 knots.

Length	45'11"	Fuel, Std.	540 gals.
Beam	14'11"	Fuel, Opt.	700 gals.
Draft	3'10"	Water	300 gals.
Weight	29,700#	Headroom	6'4"
Clearance	NA	Hull Type	Modified-V

Prices Not Provided for Pre-1995 Models

Lien Hwa is no longer in business.

231-360-0827

Litton 36 Trawler
1977–83

Generic 1970–80s import made the cut with buyers looking for classic styling, solid construction, low cost. Total-teak interior includes roomy master stateroom with double bed, cozy salon with convertible dinette, port/starboard salon deck doors, portside galley with double sink, V-berths forward. Note cockpit access door in aft cabin. Teak-over-fiberglass decks, teak window frames were standard. Solid fiberglass hull has deep, prop-protecting skeg. Excellent range. Cruise at 7–8 knots with twin 120hp Lehman diesels.

Length Overall	35'8"	Clearance	NA
Length WL	30'6"	Fuel	400 gals.
Beam	12'8"	Water	250 gals.
Draft	3'10"	Waste	30 gals.
Weight	19,000#	Hull Type	Semi-Disp.

Prices Not Provided for Pre-1995 Models

Litton is no longer in business.

231-360-0827

Litton 41 Cockpit Trawler
1979–85

Distinctive sundeck trawler with rakish, reverse-slanted windows took 1970s-era styling in a different direction. Highlights include two-stateroom teak interior with parquet flooring, spacious full-beam master with direct cockpit access, simulated planked hull lines, teak-over-fiberglass decks. Flybridge is large enough for a small crowd. Cockpit transom door makes boarding easy. Solid fiberglass hull has deep, prop-protecting skeg. Excellent range. Also sold as the Stuart 41. Cruise at 7–8 knots with twin 120hp Lehman diesels.

Length Overall	41'0"	Clearance	NA
Length WL	36'6"	Fuel	450 gals.
Beam	13'8"	Water	250 gals.
Draft	4'0"	Waste	40 gals.
Weight	23,000#	Hull Type	Semi-Disp.

Prices Not Provided for Pre-1995 Models

Litton is no longer in business.

Lord Nelson 37 Victory Tug
1982–89

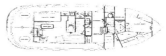

Popular coastal cruiser with bold workboat profile, ballasted keel is distinctive, secure, built to last. Single-stateroom interior boasts spacious salon with U-shaped galley forward, convertible settee aft. Raised pilothouse with Dutch doors gives helmsman superb outside views. Engineroom is accessed via walk-in galley door or pilothouse hatches. Full teak interior is finished to high standards. Total of 76 were built. Cruise at 7 knots with 800- to 900-mile range with single 150hp Cummins diesel. Burns just 2 gph at 7 knots.

Length Overall	36'11"	Clearance	12'6"
Length WL	33'4"	Fuel	250 gals.
Beam	13'2"	Water	185 gals.
Draft	3'6"	Waste	40 gals.
Weight	20,500#	Hull Type	Displacement

Prices Not Provided for Pre-1995 Models

Lord Nelson is no longer in business.

Mainship 34 Diesel Cruiser
1978–82

Iconic sedan with trawler-style profile—Mainship's original model—became one of the most popular small cruisers ever built. Practical single-stateroom interior is well suited to the needs of a cruising couple. Highlights include efficient galley with salon pass-thru, standard lower helm, enclosed head with separate stall shower, large cockpit. Easily driven hull has long, prop-protecting keel. Simple construction left a few rough edges but the price was right. Cruise at 10 knots with single 160hp Perkins diesel burning just 6 gallons per hour.

Length Overall	34'0"	Clearance	13'6"
Length WL	30'2"	Fuel	220 gals.
Beam	11'11"	Water	50 gals.
Draft	2'10"	Waste	30 gals.
Weight	14,000#	Hull Type	Semi-Disp.

Prices Not Provided for Pre-1995 Models

Mainship Corporation
Midway, GA.
www.mainship.com

Mainship 34 Motor Yacht
1996–98

Tall-freeboard miniyacht with with wide 13'8" beam packs big-boat accommodations in a midsize hull. Full-beam interior includes double berths in both staterooms, two full heads, cozy salon with convertible settee/dinette, mid-level galley with hardwood floor. Flybridge has bow walk-thru gate for deck access. Small aft deck has wet bar, hardtop. Note convenient port/starboard boarding gates, integral swim platform. Very popular model for Mainship. Twin 320hp gas inboards cruise at 15 knots (26–27 knots top).

Length w/Pulpit	36'5"	Fuel	300 gals.
Hull Length	34'6"	Water	70 gals.
Beam	13'8"	Waste	30 gals.
Draft	3'2"	Hull Type	Modified-V
Weight	18,500#	Deadrise Aft	16°

See Page 550 For Resale Values

Mainship Corporation
Midway, GA
www.mainship.com

231-360-0827

Mainship 34 Trawler
2005–09

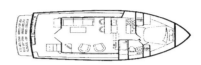

Stylish coastal cruiser with trawler profile is an impressive blend of looks, comfort, practicality. Roomy single-stateroom interior with expansive salon, large head features attractive cherry joinery, huge salon windows. Side door opening to deck is a plus; wide side decks make getting around easy. Note engineroom access hatch beneath bridge steps. Lower helm is optional. Cruise at 8 knots with single 240hp Yanmar diesel (12–13 knots top). Twin 315hp Yanmars reach 16–18 knots top, but range is limited.

Length w/Pulpit	38'10"	Headroom	6'4"
Beam	14'3"	Fuel	250 gals.
Draft	3'4"	Water	70 gals.
Weight	20,000#	Waste	34 gals.
Clearance	15'0"	Hull Type	Semi-Disp.

See Page 550 For Resale Values

Mainship Corporation
Midway, GA
www.mainship.com

231-360-0827

Mainship 350/390 Trawler
1996–2005

Popular sedan trawler (called Mainship 350 Trawler in 1996–98; 390 in 1999–2005) offered classic lines with well-planned layout, good turn of speed. Traditional teak interior features roomy salon with dinette/settee, lower helm door, opening salon windows, classy teak-and-holly sole. Molded bridge steps intrude into already-small cockpit. Transom door, radar mast, swim platform were standard; bow thruster was standard on single-engine boats. Cruise at 10–11 knots with single 300hp Cat; 14–15 knots with twin 230hp Yanmar diesels.

Length Overall	39'9"	Clearance	18'8"
Hull Length	34'9"	Fuel	300 gals.
Beam	14'2"	Water	130 gals.
Draft	3'8"	Waste	30 gals.
Weight	22,000#	Hull Type	Semi-Disp.

See Page 550 For Resale Values

Mainship Corporation
Midway, GA
www.mainship.com

231-360-0827

Mainship 36 Double Cabin
1984–89

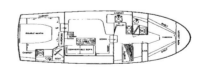

Conservative double-cabin cruiser from 1980s gave entry-level Mainship buyers a lot of boat for the money. Roomy interior with convertible salon sofa, convertible dinette can sleep as many as eight. Original teak interior was replaced with light oak joinery in 1985. Topside features include large aft deck platform, radar mast, swim platform. Easily driven hull designed for efficient low-speed operation runs well at higher speeds. Relatively small 270hp gas engines cruise at 14–15 knots (low 20s top).

Length Overall	36'2"	Clearance	11'3"
Length WL	NA	Fuel	240 gals.
Beam	13'0"	Water	100 gals.
Draft	2'2"	Headroom	6'4"
Weight	20,000#	Hull Type	Semi-Disp.

Prices Not Provided for Pre-1995 Models

Mainship Corporation
Midway, GA
www.mainship.com

www.powerboatguide.com · 231-360-0827

Mainship 37 Motor Yacht
1995–98

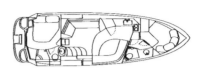

Portly aft-cabin cruising yacht from the late 1990s appealed to Mainship buyers seeking condo-size accommodations in a midsize boat. Truly expansive salon with built-in dinette, extraordinary headroom rivals many 45-footers for space, comfort. Oversized salon dimensions result in two very small staterooms. Gate in forward bridge coaming provides easy foredeck access. Note molded boarding steps on either side of aft deck. A heavy boat with lots of freeboard, twin 370hp gas inboards cruise at 14–15 knots (low 20s top).

Length w/Pulpit	39'6"	Fuel	300 gals.
Hull Length	37'9"	Water	100 gals.
Beam	13 5"	Clearance	13'6"
Draft	3 7"	Hull Type	Modified-V
Weight	21,000#	Deadrise Aft	17°

See Page 550 For Resale Values

Mainship Corporation
Midway, GA
www.mainship.com

---

www.powerboatguide.com · 231-360-0827

Mainship 40 Double Cabin
1984–88

Roomy 1980s cruiser (often called Nantucket 40) offered motoryacht space, comfort at a budget-friendly price. Roomy salon boasts lower helm position, port and starboard deck doors, convertible sofa. Full-width aft stateroom includes double berth, excellent storage, tub/shower in adjoining head. Note that light oak woodwork replaced original teak joinery in 1985. Factory hardtop was never available. Bow pulpit, hinged radar mast, swim platform were standard. Cruise at 18 knots (high 20s top) with 350hp gas inboards.

Length	40'0"	Fuel	300 gals.
Beam	14'0"	Water	140 gals.
Draft	3'4"	Headroom	6'4"
Weight	24,000#	Hull Type	Modified-V
Clearance	17'6"	Deadrise Aft	NA

Prices Not Provided for Pre-1995 Models

Mainship Corporation
Midway, GA
www.mainship.com

---

www.powerboatguide.com · 231-360-0827

Mainship 40 Trawler; 41 Expedition
2003–Current

2003–09 Layout

Current Floorplan

Handsome sedan trawler (called the 40 Trawler until 2009) made good on promise of liveaboard comfort, cruising efficiency. Expansive interior with combined salon/galley/dinette features roomy master stateroom, compact guest cabin with single berths, large head with stall shower. Large flybridge has space for huge barbecue area with wet bar, and dinette. Additional features include washer/dryer, lower helm deck door, wide side decks, deep cockpit lazarette. Cruise efficiently at 10–12 knots with single 385hp Cat—or 370hp Cummins—diesel.

Length w/Pulpit	41'4"	Clearance	19'2"
Hull Length	38'4"	Fuel	300 gals.
Beam	14'2"	Water	130 gals.
Draft	3'8"	Waste	47 gals.
Weight	24,000#	Hull Type	Semi-Disp.

See Page 550 For Resale Values

Mainship Corporation
Midway, GA
www.mainship.com

Mainship 41 Grand Salon
1989–90

Double Cabin Floorplan

Grand Salon Layout

Gaudy, slab-sided motoryacht with rectangular salon windows, maxi-volume interior may be the perfect floating condo. Two versions of the Mainship 41 were offered: Double Cabin model has master stateroom aft; Grand Salon features enormous, full-length salon stretching back to transom. Tiny cockpit is useful for line-handling; spacious bridge can accommodate several guests. Stiff ride in a chop. Standard 350hp gas engines cruise at 15 knots; optional Cat 375hp diesels cruise at 22 knots (mid 20s top). Note brief production run.

Length	40'11"	Fuel	375 gals.
Beam	14 5"	Water	130 gals.
Draft	3'6"	Headroom	6 5"
Weight	23,000#	Hull Type	Modified-V
Clearance	15'0"	Deadrise Aft	12°

Prices Not Provided for Pre-1995 Models

Mainship Corporation
Midway, GA
www.mainship.com

Mainship 430 Aft Cabin Trawler
1999–2006

2-Stateroom Layout

3-Stateroom Floorplan

Affordably priced aft-cabin cruiser combined spacious accommodations with traditional trawler styling, good turn of speed. Offered with several two- or three-stateroom interiors, all with two heads, athwartships double in aft cabin. Note teak interior joinery, cockpit door in aft cabin. Deep side decks provide secure fore-and-aft access; roomy bridge seats six to eight guests. Lower helm visibility is not great. Radar mast, transom door, bow pulpit were standard. Cruise at 14–16 knots with 370hp Cat diesels (about 20 knots top).

Length w/Pulpit	47'9"	Clearance	18'8"
Hull Length	43'0"	Fuel	500 gals.
Beam	15'6"	Water	250 gals.
Draft	3'8"	Waste	50 gals.
Weight	36,000#	Hull Type	Semi-Disp.

See Page 550 For Resale Values

Mainship Corporation
Midway, GA
www.mainship.com

Mainship 43/45 Trawler
2006–Current

Blue-chip performance trawler (called Mainship 43 Trawler in 2006–07) with well-finished interior, user-friendly layout is a lot of boat for the money. Broad 15'6" beam provides spacious interior with two roomy staterooms, fully equipped galley, lower helm with deck door, cherrywood trim. Note tub/shower in head, two-section hanging locker in bow stateroom. Plenty of lounge/entertaining space on large bridge. Big fuel capacity provides excellent range. Cruise at 18 knots (low 20s top) with Yanmar 440hp V-drive diesels.

Length Overall	47'9"	Headroom	6'3"
Hull Length	43'0"	Fuel	777 gals.
Beam	15'6"	Water	200 gals.
Draft	3'8"	Waste	56 gals.
Weight	40,000#	Hull Type	Semi-Disp.

See Page 550 For Resale Values

Mainship Corporation
Midway, GA
www.mainship.com

Motoryachts & Trawlers

Mainship 47 Motor Yacht
1990–99

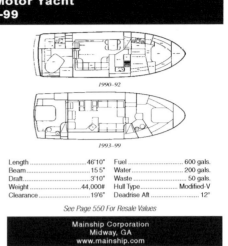

1990–92

1993–99

Rakish 1990s motoryacht matched Mainship promise of space, comfort at an affordable price. Originally offered with three staterooms; alternate floorplan introduced in 1993 has two staterooms with galley, dining area aft in salon, small office/den forward. Salon is very spacious and so is the forward stateroom, but aft cabin is small for a boat this size. Utility room with washer/dryer, workbench is forward of engineroom. Note foredeck sun lounge, underwater exhaust. Twin 485hp GM 6-71s cruise at 20 knots (23–25 knots top).

Length	46'10"	Fuel	600 gals.
Beam	15'5"	Water	200 gals.
Draft	3'10"	Waste	50 gals.
Weight	44,000#	Hull Type	Modified-V
Clearance	19'6"	Deadrise Aft	12°

See Page 550 For Resale Values

Mainship Corporation
Midway, GA
www.mainship.com

Manatee 36 Trawler
1984–92

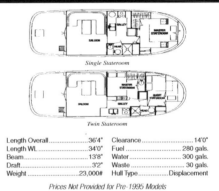

Single Stateroom

Twin Stateroom

Unorthodox coastal cruiser from 1980s has more interior space, versatility than many 40-footers. Highlights include expansive full-beam salon, semi-enclosed flybridge, dinghy platform (rare on a 36-foot boat), weather-protected cockpit. Roomy single-stateroom floorplan proved far more popular than confining twin-cabin layout. Displacement hull with rounded transom, prop-protecting keel is fully cored. Range can exceed 1,000 miles. Cruise at 6–7 knots with 100hp Volvo diesel. Very popular boat—total of 99 were built.

Length Overall	36'4"	Clearance	14'0"
Length WL	34'0"	Fuel	280 gals.
Beam	13'8"	Water	300 gals.
Draft	3'2"	Waste	30 gals.
Weight	23,000#	Hull Type	Displacement

Prices Not Provided for Pre-1995 Models

Kadey-Krogen Yachts
Stuart, FL
www.kadeykrogen.com

Marine Trader 34 Double Cabin
1972–2001

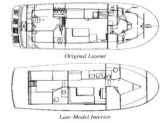

Original Layout

Late-Model Interior

Best-selling small trawler enjoyed great popularity in 1970s, 1980s thanks to low price, appealing teak interior, economical operation. Several floorplans were offered over the years, all with two heads, lower helm with deck door, compact galley. Built with plywood house prior to 1975, solid fiberglass thereafter. Decks were teak-planked until 1985-a constant source of leaks. Teak window frames were eliminated in 1992. Single 135hp diesel cruises at 6-7 knots (burning just 3 gph).

Length Overall	33'6"	Headroom	NA6'4"
Length WL	30'3"	Fuel	300 gals.
Beam	11'9"	Water	150 gals.
Draft	3'6"	Waste	40 gals.
Weight	17,000#	Hull Type	Semi-Disp.

See Page 551 For Resale Values

Marine Trading, Int'l.
Toms River, NJ
(No web site)

Marine Trader 34 Sedan
1973–2001

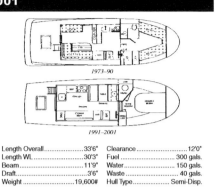

1973–90

1991–2001

Economical sedan cruiser with salty lines makes the grade with entry-level buyers on a budget. Highlights include full teak interior, lower helm station with sliding deck door, protected side decks, extended flybridge, spacious engineroom, teak bow pulpit, teak cockpit sole, swim platform, mast and boom assembly. Early models were built with glass-over-plywood construction. Teak window frames (eliminated in 1995) often leak. So-so fit and finish. Cruise efficiently at 7 knots with single 120/135hp Lehman diesel; 10 knots with 210hp Cummins.

Length Overall	33'6"	Clearance	12'0"
Length WL	30'3"	Fuel	300 gals.
Beam	11'9"	Water	150 gals.
Draft	3'6"	Waste	40 gals.
Weight	19,600#	Hull Type	Semi-Disp.

See Page 551 For Resale Values

Marine Trading, Int'l.
Toms River, NJ
(No web site)

Marine Trader 36 Double Cabin
1975–93

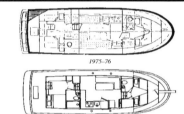

1975–76

1977–79

Value-priced Taiwan import with classic trawler profile, traditional teak interior is ideally suited for the cruising couple. Originally designed with twin berths in aft stateroom; floorplan was rearranged in 1977 with double berth aft. Lower helm with teak deck door was standard. Note tub in aft head. Cockpit access door in aft stateroom is a plus. Additional features include folding mast, teak swim platform, teak decks. Teak window frames often leak. Called the 37 DC in 1978–79. Cruise at 6–7 knots with single Lehman diesel.

Length Overall	36'0"	Clearance	NA
Length WL	32'0"	Fuel	400 gals.
Beam	12'2"	Water	150 gals.
Draft	3'6"	Waste	40 gals.
Weight	21,000#	Hull Type	Semi-Disp.

Prices Not Provided for Pre-1995 Models

Marine Trading, Int'l.
Toms River, NJ
(No web site)

Marine Trader 36 Sedan
1975–93

Durable sedan with classic trawler profile offers versatile layout with affordable price, low-cost operation. Galley-up teak interior with standard lower helm, convertible salon settee includes master stateroom with double berth to port, head with tub/shower, V-berths forward. Bridge overhangs protect decks and cockpit. Extended flybridge can stow a dinghy. Teak window frames are prone to leaks. Not-so-good workmanship and finish. Cruise at 7–8 knots with 120/135hp Lehman diesels.

Length Overall	36'0"	Clearance	NA
Length WL	32'0"	Fuel	350 gals.
Beam	12'2"	Water	150 gals.
Draft	3'6"	Waste	50 gals.
Weight	21,000#	Hull Type	Semi-Disp.

Prices Not Provided for Pre-1995 Models

Marine Trading, Int'l.
Toms River, NJ
(No web site)

www.powerboatguide.com 231-360-0827

Marine Trader 36 Sundeck
1985–94

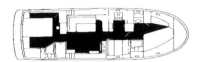

Popular sundeck trawler combines economical operation with family-friendly layout, traditional teak interior. Galley-down floorplan with booth-style dinette, convertible salon settee includes double berths in both staterooms, lower helm with deck access door, generous storage. Aft-deck hardtop, radar arch, teak swim platform, bow pulpit were standard. Good engineroom access, wide walkways are a plus. Unimpressive fit and finish. Twin 135hp Lehman diesels (or single 210hp Cummins diesel) will cruise efficiently at 8 knots.

Length Overall	36'0"	Clearance	NA
Length WL	32'0"	Fuel	350 gals.
Beam	12'2"	Water	150 gals.
Draft	3'6"	Waste	50 gals.
Weight	19,000#	Hull Type	Semi-Disp.

Prices Not Provided for Pre-1995 Models

Marine Trading, Int'l.
Toms River, NJ
(No web site)

---

www.powerboatguide.com 231-360-0827

Marine Trader 38 Double Cabin
1980–2000

Galley Up

Galley Down

Generic double-cabin trawler offers timeless blend of traditional styling, common-sense accommodations, solid construction. Two-stateroom teak interior with lower helm, port/starboard salon doors was offered with galley down or up. Large master stateroom has cockpit access door—very useful. Topside features include teak decks, bow pulpit, teak handrails, folding mast. Note tub/shower in aft head, simulated lapstrake hull lines. Cruise at 7–8 knots with twin 135hp Lehman diesels or single 210hp Cummins.

Length Overall	38'0"	Clearance	NA
Length WL	34'8"	Fuel	300 gals.
Beam	12'10"	Water	250 gals.
Draft	4'0"	Waste	50 gals.
Weight	22,000#	Hull Type	Semi-Disp.

See Page 551 For Resale Values

Marine Trading, Int'l.
Toms River, NJ
(No web site)

---

www.powerboatguide.com 231-360-0827

Marine Trader 40 Double Cabin
1974–85

Traditional double-cabin trawler with total teak interior set class standards in her day for affordability, value. Twin-stateroom layout with salon galley includes lower helm, two salon deck doors, roomy master cabin with direct cockpit access door. Note tub/shower in aft head. Topside features include teak decks, folding mast, teak bow pulpit, teak swim platform. Plenty of exterior teak will keep owners busy. Note simulated lapstrake hull lines. Unimpressive fit and finish. Cruise efficiently at 7–8 knots with twin 120hp Lehman diesels.

Length Overall	40'0"	Clearance	NA
Length WL	36'7"	Fuel	400 gals.
Beam	13'8"	Water	250 gals.
Draft	4'0"	Waste	50 gals.
Weight	30,000#	Hull Type	Semi-Disp.

Prices Not Provided for Pre-1995 Models

Marine Trading, Int'l.
Toms River, NJ
(No web site)

Marine Trader 40 Sundeck
1983–2000

Appealing sundeck cruiser blends comfortable accommodations with conservative styling, fuel-efficient operation. Standard two-stateroom interior with galley down features convertible salon settee, breakfast bar, lower helm with deck door, walkaround queen in master, tub/shower in aft head. Full-width sundeck is big for a boat this size. Hardtop, radar arch, swim platform, bow pulpit were standard. Always a popular model. Note simulated lapstrake hull lines. Twin 135hp Lehman diesels cruise economically 7–8 knots.

Length Overall	39'4"	Clearance	NA
Length WL	36.5'	Fuel	350 gals.
Beam	12'11"	Water	250 gals.
Draft	4'0"	Waste	50 gals.
Weight	25,000#	Hull Type	Semi-Disp.

See Page 551 For Resale Values

Marine Trading, Int'l.
Toms River, NJ
(No web site)

Marine Trader 44 Tri Cabin
1977–88

Two-Stateroom Floorplan

Three-Stateroom Layout

Ageing Taiwan import offered with two or three staterooms offers roomy indoor, outdoor accommodations for liveaboards or cruisers. Highlights include port/starboard salon deck doors, large aft cabin with cockpit access door, generous storage, tub/shower in aft head, large engineroom. Copious exterior teak makes this boat a maintenance nightmare. Not the last word in quality, but her salty appearance and beefy construction won over many detractors. Twin 120hp Lehman diesels cruise economically at 8–9 knots.

Length Overall	43'6"	Clearance	NA
Length WL	38'8"	Fuel	500 gals.
Beam	14'4"	Water	250 gals.
Draft	4'2"	Waste	70 gals.
Weight	33,000#	Hull Type	Semi-Disp.

Prices Not Provided for Pre-1995 Models

Marine Trading, Int'l.
Toms River, NJ
(No web site)

Marine Trader 49 Pilothouse
1979–93

Standard Upper Deck

Standard Lower Deck

Long-range pilothouse trawler introduced in 1979 delivered big-boat comfort, amenities at a super-competitive price. Spacious two-stateroom, two head floorplan offers U-shaped galley forward in salon, amidships master suite with tub/shower, pilothouse watch berth, inside bridge access. Note protected side decks, abundant outside teak. Prominent bow, wave-breaking Portuguese bridge can push through heavy seas. Fit and finish leaves a lot to be desired. Cruise at 8 knots with 135hp Lehman diesels; 10 knots with 165hp Perkins diesels.

Length	48'6"	Headroom	6 5"
Beam	15'0"	Fuel	700 gals.
Draft	4'6"	Water	375 gals.
Weight	46,000#	Waste	70 gals.
Clearance	NA	Hull Type	Semi-Disp.

Prices Not Provided for Pre-1995 Models

Marine Trading, Int'l.
Toms River, NJ
(No web site)

Motoryachts & Trawlers

www.powerboatguide.com | 231-360-0827

Marine Trader 50 Motor Yacht
1979–93

Main Deck, Standard Floorplan

Lower Deck, Standard Floorplan

Twin-deck motoryacht with classic trawler profile earned praise for solid construction, good seakeeping abilities, low price. Standard model has walkaround decks, covered aft deck. Widebody model introduced in 1985 has huge full-beam salon. Both versions share same three-stateroom floorplan with teak cabinetry and flooring, deckhouse galley with serving counter, wheelhouse deck doors. Separate walk-in enginerooms provide easy access to engines, pumps, etc. Cruise efficiently at 8-9 knots with standard 135hp Lehman diesels.

Length Overall	50'0"	Clearance	16'6"
Length WL	44'0"	Fuel	750 gals.
Beam	15.5"	Water	380 gals.
Draft	4'8"	Waste	80 gals.
Weight	46,000#	Hull	Displacement

Prices Not Provided for Pre-1995 Models

Marine Trading, Int'l.
Toms River, NJ
(No web site)

---

www.powerboatguide.com | 231-360-0827

Marlow 53 Explorer
2005–Current

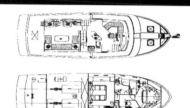

Beautifully finished pilothouse yacht with full teak interior targets buyers with an eye for timeless styling, unabashed quality. Expansive three-stateroom layout with crew quarters aft includes spacious pilothouse with home-size galley, full-beam master suite, comfortable salon with indirect lighting. Portuguese bridge adds big-water security; standup engineroom makes service easy. Note Burmese teak decks, cockpit controls, unusual twin-keel hull. Update in 2009 enlarged cockpit. Cat 700hp diesels cruise at 16 knots (20+ top).

Length	54'3"	Fuel	1,200 gals.
Beam	18'2"	Water	350 gals.
Draft	4'2"	Waste	120 gals.
Weight	59,000#	Hull Type	Semi-Disp.
Clearance	NA	Deadrise Aft	14°

Insufficient Resale Data To Assign Values

Marlow Yachts, Palmetto, FL
Phone 941-729-3370
www.marlowmarine.com

---

www.powerboatguide.com | 231-360-0827

Marlow 57 Explorer
2005–Current

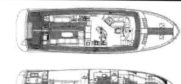

Striking pilothouse yacht with meticulous finish, Kevlar-reinforced hull takes cruising luxury to the next level. All-teak interior features expansive salon with panoramic windows, galley/dinette area forward, three private staterooms. Overhead grabrail in salon is a nice touch. Flybridge has space for dinghy aft of pilothouse. Note Portuguese bridge, protected side decks, extended swim platform. Engineroom is very spacious. Distinctive twin-keel bottom allows this beamy yacht to reach 22 knots top with 700-hp Cat engines.

Length Overall	62'2"	Fuel	1,200 gals.
Beam	18'2"	Water	300 gals.
Draft	4'2"	Waste	120 gals.
Weight	61,000#	Hull Type	Semi-Disp.
Clearance	NA	Deadrise Aft	14°

Insufficient Resale Data To Assign Values

Marlow Yachts, Palmetto, FL
Phone 941-729-3370
www.marlowmarine.com

231-360-0827

Marlow 61 Explorer
2005–Current

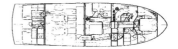

Handsome pilothouse cruiser with traditional styling makes good on promise of space, comfort, amenities. Highlights include gorgeous hardwood interior, aft crew quarters, Portuguese bridge, protected side decks. Space-efficient floorplan features expansive salon with built-in entertainment center, two roomy staterooms, private den/office. Engineroom—reached from crew cabin—provides excellent service access. Lightweight Kevlar hull with twin-keel bottom will cruise at 12–14 knots (about 20 knots top) with 700hp Cat engines.

Length	61'5"	Fuel	1,400 gals.
Beam	18'2"	Water	300 gals.
Draft	4'2"	Waste	150 gals.
Weight	77,000#	Hull Type	Semi-Disp.
Clearance	NA	Deadrise Aft	14°

Insufficient Resale Data To Assign Values

Marlow Yachts, Palmetto, FL
Phone 941-729-3370
www.marlowmarine.com

231-360-0827

Marlow 65 Explorer
2001–Current

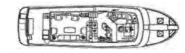

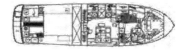

Compelling long-range cruiser introduced in 2001 established Marlow's reputation for elegant design, practical accommodations. Traditional three-stateroom interior boasts varnished cherry (or teak) cabinetry, roomy salon with hardwood floor, country kitchen/pilothouse. Portuguese bridge fronts pilothouse; wide side decks are sheltered by bridge overhangs. Note fuel increase to 1,800 gallons in 2006. Unusual twin-keel hull protects running gear. Lugger 700hp diesels cruise at 12–14 knots (around 20 knots top).

Length	65'10"	Fuel	1,400/1,800 gals.
Beam	18'4"	Water	400 gals.
Draft	4'5"	Waste	150 gals.
Weight	83,000#	Hull Type	Semi-Disp.
Clearance	18'0"	Deadrise Aft	14°

Insufficient Resale Data To Assign Values

Marlow Yachts
Palmetto, FL
www.marlowmarine.com

231-360-0827

Marquis 50 LS
2007–Current

Quality-built flybridge yacht (called the Marquis 520 since 2009) delivers impressive mix of European styling, home-like accommodations. Luxurious two-stateroom interior with galley, dinette forward boasts full-beam master with vanity/desk, roomy guest cabin, copius storage. Salon dimensions are modest for a 50-footer; lower helm is optional. Spacious flybridge gets high marks for sporty helm (with retractible electronics panel), wraparound aft seating. Good engineroom access. No racehorse, Volvo 715hp diesels max out at just over 20 knots.

Length	51'6"	Fuel	600 gals.
Beam	15'0"	Water	150 gals.
Draft	4'9"	Waste	80 gals.
Weight	56,227#	Hull Type	Modified-V
Clearance	20'0"	Deadrise Aft	14°

Insufficient Resale Data To Assign Values

Marquis Yachts, Pulaski, WI
Phone 920-822-1575
www.marquisyachts.com

www.powerboatguide.com   231-360-0827

Marquis 55 Pilothouse
2007–Current

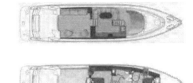

Head-turning pilothouse yacht (called the Marquis 560 since 2009) makes good on promise of luxury, style, performance. Stylish interior with split-level salon features elegant master suite with two walk-in wardrobes, third stateroom/office. Open galley and salon permit good aft visibility from lower helm. Watertight door in transom opens to spacious lazarette and engineroom. Side decks are on the narrow side. Note roomy flybridge with pop-up helm display, distinctive hullside windows. Volvo 775hp diesels cruise in the low 20s (27–28 knots top).

Length	57'4"	Fuel	836 gals.
Beam	16'0"	Water	200 gals.
Draft	4'11"	Waste	100 gals.
Weight	62,000#	Hull Type	Modified-V
Clearance	18.5'	Deadrise Aft	14°

Insufficient Resale Data To Assign Values

Marquis Yachts
Pulaski, WI
www.marquisyachts.com

---

www.powerboatguide.com   231-360-0827

Marquis 59 Pilothouse; 600 Pilothouse
2003–Current

Main Deck Plan

Lower Level Plan

Elegant pilothouse motoryacht (called Marquis 600 since 2009) combines seductive European looks with American practicality. Opulent split-level salon stretches unbroken from sliding entryway doors to pilothouse windshield. Highlights include centerline lower helm with wraparound seating, huge galley with granite countertops, full-beam master stateroom with king bed. Curved staircase leads to huge flybridge with lounge seating, wet bar, davit. Note stand-up engineroom. MAN 825hp diesels cruise in the low 20s (about 30 top).

w/Platform	59'6"	Fuel	800 gals.
Beam	16'6"	Water	200 gals.
Draft	5.5'	Waste	80 gals.
Weight	58,500#	Hull Type	Modified-V
Clearance, Arch	16'3"	Deadrise Aft	14°

See Page 551 For Resale Values

Marquis Yachts
Pulaski, WI
www.marquisyachts.com

---

www.powerboatguide.com   231-360-0827

Marquis 65 Pilothouse; 690 Pilothouse
2006–Current

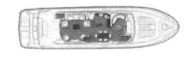

World-class pilothouse yacht (called the Marquis 690 since 2009) blends flashy Italian styling with posh accommodations, impressive performance. Interior highlights include near-perfect cherry joinery, opulent master suite with his-and-her bath, glass bridge staircase, formal dining area. Two-person crew quarters are aft of engineroom with direct transom access. Extended hardtop ensures year-round entertaining. Hydraulic swim platform makes launching a tender easy. MTU 1,350hp V-drive diesels cruise at 24–26 knots (30+ top).

Length	69'11"	Fuel, Std/Opt	1,200 gals.
Beam	17'11"	Water	200 gals.
Draft	6'0"	Waste	153 gals.
Weight	94,000#	Hull Type	Modified-V
Clearance	24.5'	Deadrise Aft	13°

Insufficient Resale Data To Assign Values

Marquis Yachts, Pulaski, WI
Phone 920-822-1575
www.marquisyachts.com

Maxum 4100 SCA
1997–2001

Low-cost motoryacht with with rakish styling matched Maxum promise of big-boat luxury, comfort at an affordable price. Spacious two-stateroom, twin-head interior—dominated by simple, plain-Jane decor—provides lots of entertaining space. Note large forward cabin, full-size galley with Corian counter. Topside features include wide side decks, twin foredeck sun pads, aft-deck wet bar, molded transom steps. Most were sold with optional hardtop. Cruise at 15 knots with standard gas engines; 20 knots with optional 370hp Cummins diesels.

Length	41'8"	Fuel	300 gals.
Beam	13'10"	Water	90 gals.
Draft	3'9"	Waste	76 gals.
Weight	30,000#	Hull Type	Modified-V
Clearance	18'2"	Deadrise Aft	10°

See Page 552 For Resale Values

Maxum discontinued operations in 2009.

Maxum 4100 SCB
1997–2001

Value-priced flybridge yacht with generous 13'11" beam combined sexy European styling with liveaboard comfort, motoryacht versatility. Expansive wood-trimmed salon with wraparound windows features booth-style dinette, large galley, full entertainment center. Both staterooms share single double-entry head with separate stall shower. Note cockpit wet locker, flybridge wet bar, extended swim platform. Engineroom is tight. Standard gas engines cruise at 15 knots; optional 370hp Cummins diesels cruise at 20 knots.

Length	42'2"	Fuel	380 gals.
Beam	13'11"	Water	100 gals.
Draft	3'9"	Waste	75 gals.
Weight	28,770#	Hull Type	Modified-V
Clearance	18'0"	Deadrise Aft	13°

See Page 552 For Resale Values

Maxum discontinued operations in 2009.

Maxum 4600 SCB
1997–2001

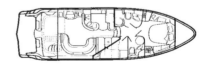

Handsome sedan yacht introduced in 1997 offered motoryacht space, luxury at budget-friendly price. Wide-open salon with cherry (or maple) cabinetry features large galley with conventional oven, raised dinette, huge U-shaped settee. Note roomy forward stateroom, large heads with stall showers. Extended flybridge includes wet bar, aft sun lounge. Wide swim platform can stow small inflatable or PWC. Cummins 370hp diesels cruise at 18 knots (20+ top); Cummins 450hp diesels cruise at 20 knots and reach a top speed of 23–24 knots.

Length	45'11"	Fuel	418 gals.
Beam	14'4"	Water	100 gals.
Draft	4'0"	Waste	75 gals.
Weight	30,400#	Hull Type	Modified-V
Clearance, Arch	14'2"	Deadrise Aft	9°

See Page 552 For Resale Values

Maxum discontinued operations in 2009.

Motoryachts & Trawlers

Motoryachts & Trawlers

McKinna 48 Pilothouse
1996–2000

Heavily-built pilothouse yacht (built in Taiwan by Lien Hwa) blurs the line between full-feature cruising yacht, blue-chip liveaboard. Standard three-stateroom interior boasts amidships master suite, spacious full-beam salon, gourmet galley. Sliding glass doors open to roomy cockpit with transom door. Note exquisite teak interior joinery, teak parquet floors. Raised pilothouse has chart table, L-shaped settee, twin deck access doors. Flybridge can stow small dinghy. Cat 375hp diesels cruise at 17-18 knots (about 20 knots top).

Length w/Pulpit	54'3"	Fuel	825 gals.
Hull Length	47'10"	Water	250 gals.
Beam	15 5"	Headroom	6'4"
Draft	4'2"	Hull Type	Modified-V
Weight	44,500#	Deadrise Aft	18°

See Page 552 For Resale Values

McKinna Yachts
Newport Beach, CA
www.mckinnayachts.com

McKinna 57 Pilothouse
1997–2006

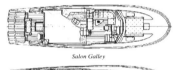
Salon Galley

Pilothouse Galley

Luxury-class pilothouse yacht (built by Lien Hwa in Taiwan) with spacious three-stateroom interior couples quality construction with tasteful accommodations, excellent range. Highlights include sociable full-beam salon with galley forward, raised pilothouse with dinette and deck door, inside flybridge access, three heads with walk-in showers, extended swim platform with dual transom doors. Large cockpit has wet bar, barbecue, docking station, insole engineroom entry. MAN 600hp diesels cruise in the low 20s (26-27 knots top).

Length Overall	62'0"	Fuel	850 gals.
Beam	15 5"	Water	270 gals.
Draft	4'2"	Headroom	6 5"
Weight	52,500#	Hull Type	Modified-V
Clearance	NA	Deadrise Aft	18°

See Page 552 For Resale Values

McKinna Yachts
Newport Beach, CA
www.mckinnayachts.com

McKinna 65 Pilothouse
2000–05

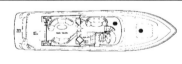

Executive-class pilothouse yacht matches sleek styling with top-shelf accommodations, world-class construction. Luxury-class interior is impressive display of furniture-quality woodwork, designer furnishings. Lower helm, galley and dinette share space on pilothouse level. Expansive salon comes with leather upholstery, full entertainment center. Note inside-only bridge access. Additional features include teak-planked decks, extended swim platform, secure side decks. Engineroom is a tight fit. Cruise at 20 knots with Cat 800hp diesels.

Length Overall	67'6"	Fuel	1,100 gals.
Beam	17'3"	Water	280 gals.
Draft	3 7"	Headroom	6'8"
Weight	70,000#	Hull Type	Modified-V
Clearance	NA	Deadrise Aft	NA

Insufficient Resale Data To Assign Values

McKinna Yachts
Newport Beach, CA
www.mckinnayachts.com

231-360-0827

Meridian 368 Motor Yacht
2005–08

Entry-level motoryacht with maxi-volume interior blurs the line between home-size liveaboard, deluxe coastal cruiser. Interior highlights include full-beam salon with facing settees, large galley with cherry cabinetry, two double staterooms with en suite heads. Tiered cabin windows provide panoramic outside views; picture window in master stateroom overlooks swim platform. Bow and stern thrusters, opening salon windows are standard. Twin 370hp gas engines cruise at 18–19 knots; 330hp Cummins diesels cruise in the mid 20s.

Length	37'8"	Fuel	250 gals.
Beam	13'7"	Water	90 gals.
Draft	3'6"	Waste	50 gals.
Weight	24,250#	Hull Type	Modified-V
Clearance	13'6"	Deadrise Aft	13°

See Page 552 For Resale Values

Meridian Yachts
Arlington, WA
www.meridian-yachts.com

231-360-0827

Meridian 408 Motor Yacht
2003–08

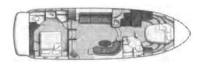

Maxi-volume motoryacht delivers the goods when it comes to amenities, comfort, versatility. Condo-style interior with huge salon, roomy staterooms rivals that of a small apartment. Tiered windows provide near 360-degree visibility. Split forward head saves space, adds convenience. Note classy cherrywood cabinets, hardwood galley sole. Topside features include molded swim-platform steps, large flybridge with wet bar. Fuel capacity is modest for a 40-footer. Cruise at 20 knots (mid 20s top) with Cummins 370hp diesels.

Length	42'2"	Fuel	330 gals.
Beam	14'4"	Water	90 gals.
Draft	3'10"	Waste	55 gals.
Weight	29,000#	Hull Type	Modified-V
Clearance	14'4"	Deadrise Aft	10°

See Page 552 For Resale Values

Meridian Yachts
Arlington, WA
www.meridian-yachts.com

231-360-0827

Meridian 459 Cockpit MY
2004–08

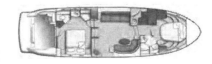

Stretched version of the Meridian 408 MY adds cockpit versatility to a proven motoryacht design. Huge interior with wide-open salon, tiered windows rivals larger yachts for living space, comfort. Highlights include cherry interior cabinetry, full-beam master suite with direct cockpit access, roomy guest stateroom with walkaround queen, space for washer/dryer. Aft deck is on the small side, but the cockpit (with extended swim platform) is large. Note modest fuel capacity. Cruise at 18 knots (low 20s top) with Cummins 370hp diesels.

Length	47'8"	Fuel	330 gals.
Beam	14'4"	Water	90 gals.
Draft	3'10"	Waste	55 gals.
Weight	30,700#	Hull Type	Modified-V
Clearance	14'4"	Deadrise Aft	10°

See Page 552 For Resale Values

Meridian Yachts
Arlington, WA
www.meridian-yachts.com

Motoryachts & Trawlers

Motoryachts & Trawlers

231-360-0827

Meridian 490 Pilothouse
2004–08

Rebranded version of popular Bayliner 4788 Pilothouse (1994–2002) offers big-boat value in a handsome, well-appointed package. Versatile three-stateroom floorplan with cherry cabinets features roomy full-beam salon with full-service galley forward, raised pilothouse with flybridge access, two full heads. Third stateroom, accessed from master stateroom, has settee with hinged upper/lower berths allowing it to double as a dressing room. Engineroom is a little tight. Cruise efficiently at 20 knots with standard Cummins 330hp diesels.

Length w/Pulpit	54'0"	Fuel	444 gals.
Beam	15'1"	Water	200 gals.
Draft	3'4"	Waste	48 gals.
Weight	29,990#	Hull Type	Modified-V
Clearance	18'2"	Deadrise Aft	NA

See Page 552 For Resale Values

Meridian Yachts
Arlington, WA
www.meridian-yachts.com

231-360-0827

Meridian 540 Pilothouse
2003–06

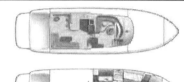

Well-bred pilothouse yacht offers levels of comfort, luxury usually associated with more expensive yachts. Luxury class interior with three private staterooms includes full-beam salon with entertainment center, U-shaped galley with hardwood floor, bathtub in master head, raised pilothouse with wraparound dinette. Engineroom is accessed from cockpit door. Note underwater exhaust system, foredeck sun pad. Graceful lines incorporate the best in modern pilothouse styling. Cruise at 22–23 knots (mid 20s top) with 635hp Cummins diesels.

Length	56'9"	Fuel	700 gals.
Beam	16'3"	Water	200 gals.
Draft	4'10"	Waste	76 gals.
Weight	50,554#	Hull Type	Modified-V
Clearance	19'3"	Deadrise Aft	12°

Insufficient Resale Data To Assign Values

Meridian Yachts
Arlington, WA
www.meridian-yachts.com

231-360-0827

Meridian 580 Pilothouse
2003–Current

Restyled version of earlier Bayliner 5788 (1997–2002) offers appealing blend of modern pilothouse styling, deluxe amenities, luxury class accommodations. Appealing three-stateroom interior boasts home-size galley with faux granite counters, built-in dinette, salon entertainment center, well-appointed pilothouse, standard washer/dryer, tub in master head. Note stand-up engineroom (with cockpit access), underwater exhaust system, foredeck sun lounge. Cummins 635hp diesels cruise at 18 knots (low 20s top).

Length	59'5"	Fuel	800 gals.
Beam	17'4"	Water	218 gals.
Draft	4'11"	Waste	74 gals.
Weight	59,920#	Hull Type	Modified-V
Clearance	19'7"	Deadrise Aft	10°

Insufficient Resale Data To Assign Values

Meridian Yachts
Arlington, WA
www.meridian-yachts.com

www.powerboatguide.com   231-360-0827

Monk 36 Trawler
1982–2006

Graceful aft-cabin trawler offers solid mix of simplicity, comfort, seaworthiness. Comfortable galley-up interior with teak cabinetry, spacious master stateroom is mostly unchanged from original, although post-1992 models eliminated tub in aft head. Room for small dinghy on aft cabintop. Wide side decks are a plus. Built in Taiwan until 1991 when production was shifted to Canada. Over 250 built. Early models have lots of exterior teak trim. Single 120hp diesel will cruise at 7 knots; single 220hp will cruise at 9-10 knots.

Length Overall	36'0"	Clearance, Mast	17'11"
Length WL	33'0"	Fuel	320 gals.
Beam	13'0"	Water	120 gals.
Draft	4'0"	Waste	42 gals.
Weight	18,000#	Hull Type	Semi-Disp.

See Page 553 For Resale Values

Uncertain whether this boat is still in production

---

www.powerboatguide.com   231-360-0827

Navigator 48 Classic
1997–2007

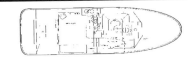

Smooth-running pilothouse cruiser combines seakindly hull with comfortable accommodations, all-weather versatility. Expansive twin-stateroom interior features well-appointed salon with U-shaped galley, raised pilothouse with wraparound dinette aft of centerline helm. Note bar seating in salon, stall showers in both heads. Cockpit hatch provides good access to engineroom. Additional features include large bridge with dinghy/davit storage, radar arch, pilothouse deck door. Cruise at 16–17 knots with Volvo 318hp diesels (20+ top).

Length Overall	52'8"	Fuel	500 gals.
Beam	15'0"	Water	130 gals.
Draft	4'5"	Waste	70 gals.
Weight	37,000#	Hull Type	Modified-V
Clearance	NA	Deadrise Aft	15°

See Page 553 For Resale Values

**Navigator Yachts
Perris, CA
www.navigatoryachts.com**

---

www.powerboatguide.com   231-360-0827

Navigator 50 Classic
1993–2000

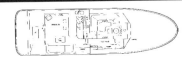

Versatile flybridge yacht combines affordable long-range cruising with efficient layout, tasteful styling. Expansive twin-stateroom interior features well-appointed salon with U-shaped galley, raised pilothouse with wraparound dinette aft of centerline helm. Note bar seating in salon, stall showers in both heads. Cockpit hatch provides good access to engineroom. Additional features include large bridge with dinghy/davit storage, radar arch, pilothouse deck door. Cruise at 16–18 knots with Volvo 340hp diesels (20+ top).

Length Overall	50'0"	Fuel	600 gals.
Beam	15'0"	Water	170 gals.
Draft	4'3"	Waste	70 gals.
Weight	38,000#	Hull Type	Modified-V
Headroom	6'6"	Deadrise Aft	15°

See Page 553 For Resale Values

**Navigator Yachts
Perris, CA
www.navigatoryachts.com**

Motoryachts & Trawlers

www.powerboatguide.com   231-360-0827

Navigator 53 Classic
1995–2006

Popular pilothouse yacht with handsome lines strikes a balance between affordable cost, appealing layout. Wide-open interior features spacious full-beam salon with U-shaped galley forward, inside bridge access, three well-appointed staterooms, two full heads. Note attractive hardwood cabinets, pilothouse deck door. Huge cockpit is a plus, but lack of bridge ladder (or steps) is notable. Easily driven hull with modest 15-foot beam is comfortable, fuel efficient. Cruise at 16 knots with Volvo 370hp diesels (about 20 knots top).

Length Overall	53'0"	Fuel	600 gals.
Beam	15'0"	Water	170 gals.
Draft	4'6"	Waste	70 gals.
Weight	42,500#	Hull Type	Modified-V
Headroom	6'6"	Deadrise Aft	15°

See Page 553 For Resale Values

Navigator Yachts
Perris, CA
www.navigatoryachts.com

---

www.powerboatguide.com   231-360-0827

Navigator 56 Classic
2000–05

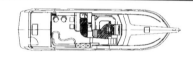

Well-bred pilothouse yacht with graceful profile makes good on promise of comfortable accommodations, all-weather cruisability. Roomy interior features expansive full-beam salon with galley forward, raised pilothouse with wraparound dinette and centerline helm. Note attractive maple and cherry woodwork, Corian galley counters, large cockpit. Engineroom is reached via hatch in galley sole. Easily driven hull with modest 15-foot beam delivers stable open-water ride. Volvo 430hp diesels cruise at 16–17 knots (around 20s knots top).

Length Overall	56'0"	Fuel	600 gals.
Beam	15'0"	Water	170 gals.
Draft	4'6"	Waste	40 gals.
Weight	45,500	Hull Type	Modified-V
Clearance	NA	Deadrise Aft	15°

See Page 553 For Resale Values

Navigator Yachts
Perris, CA
www.navigatoryachts.com

---

www.powerboatguide.com   231-360-0827

Navigator 5600 Pilothouse
1994–2002

Stretched version of popular Navigator 5300 Pilothouse (1993–99) offers more living space, improved profile. Expansive three-stateroom interior features full-beam salon with entertainment center, wet bar, large windows. Raised pilothouse includes L-shaped galley area, dinette, sliding deck door. Note private salon access to master suite, large forward cabin with island berth. No cockpit bridge access. Volvo 380hp diesels cruise at 17–18 knots and reach a top speed of around 20 knots.

Length Overall	56'0"	Fuel	600 gals.
Beam	15'0"	Water	200 gals.
Draft	5'6"	Waste	70 gals.
Weight	50,000#	Hull Type	Modified-V
Clearance	NA	Deadrise Aft	15°

Insufficient Resale Data To Assign Values

Navigator Yachts
Perris, CA
www.navigatoryachts.com

Navigator 58 Classic
1999–2001

Value-priced pilothouse cruiser with broad 17'4" beam combines stylish exterior with upscale accommodations, efficient operation. Expansive floorplan has galley on pilothouse level rather than in salon (as it is in many pilothouse boats) resulting in smallish salon. Master stateroom is separate from guest cabins with private salon access. Additional features include spacious engineroom, washer/dryer, large swim platform, maple interior woodwork. GM 485hp diesels cruise at 18 knots and reach a top speed of 20+ knots.

Length Overall	58'0"	Fuel	800 gals.
Beam	17'4"	Water	200 gals.
Draft	4'9"	Waste	70 gals.
Weight	64,000#	Hull Type	Modified-V
Headroom	6'6"	Deadrise Aft	NA

Insufficient Resale Data To Assign Values

Navigator Yachts
Perris, CA
www.navigatoryachts.com

---

www.powerboatguide.com   231-360-0827

Navigator 61 Classic
1999–2007

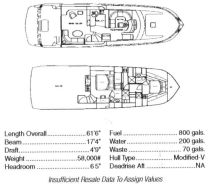

Appealing pilothouse yacht provides impressive blend of space, comfort, affordability. Expansive three-stateroom floorplan has huge gourmet galley on pilothouse level rather than in salon (as it is in many pilothouse boats) resulting in seemingly small salon. Private master suite is accessed from salon staircase. Very good lower helm visibility. Additional features include high-gloss cherry joinery, inside/outside bridge access, twin transom doors, stand-up engineroom. Cruise at 18 knots with 675hp Volvo diesels (low 20s top).

Length Overall	61'6"	Fuel	800 gals.
Beam	17'4"	Water	200 gals.
Draft	4'9"	Waste	70 gals.
Weight	58,000#	Hull Type	Modified-V
Headroom	6'5"	Deadrise Aft	NA

Insufficient Resale Data To Assign Values

Navigator Yachts
Perris, CA
www.navigatoryachts.com

---

www.powerboatguide.com   231-360-0827

Navigator 63 Classic
1998–2007

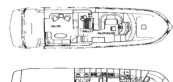

Practical long-range cruising yacht with exceptionally spacious layout offers luxury-class amenities at production-yacht cost. Highlights include lavish master suite with king-size bed, country kitchen galley, full-beam salon with built-in entertainment center. Double sliding doors open salon to large cockpit with twin transom doors, molded bridge steps. Very good lower-helm visibility. Note large stand-up engineroom, roomy flybridge. Cat 660hp diesels cruise at a 19–20 knots (low 20s top).

Length Overall	63'0"	Fuel	1,000 gals.
Beam	17'4"	Water	200 gals.
Draft	4'9"	Waste	140 gals.
Weight	68,000#	Hull Type	Modified-V
Headroom	6'6"	Deadrise Aft	NA

Insufficient Resale Data To Assign Values

Navigator Yachts
Perris, CA
www.navigatoryachts.com

Motoryachts & Trawlers

Motoryachts & Trawlers

Nordhavn 35 Coastal Pilot
2001–05

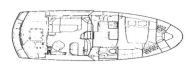

Heavily built coastal trawler with feature-packed layout is ideally suited for the cruising couple. Single-stateroom, galley-down interior boasts well-appointed pilothouse with convertible settee, large master suite with copious storage, teak-planked flooring throughout. Note commercial-grade doors and windows, huge cockpit lazarette. Early models were overbuilt, heavy and slow; later models were built with prop pocket and lighter layup schedule. Total of 35 were built. Cruise at 10-12 knots with single 370hp Yanmar diesel.

|---|---|
Length Overall	35'4"
Length WL	33'4"
Beam	13'2"
Draft	3'6"
Weight	25,000#
Clearance	NA
Fuel	590 gals.
Water	165 gals.
Waste	40 gals.
Hull Type	Semi-Disp.

Insufficient Resale Data To Assign Values

Pacific Asian Enterprises
Dana Point, CA
www.nordhavn.com

Nordhavn 40
1999–Current

Seaworthy displacement trawler offers long-range cruising credentials second to none. Spacious interior with full-beam salon features raised pilothouse with fold-down helm seat, varnished teak cabinets, commercial-quality doors and windows, beautifully finished engineroom. Raised foredeck with Portuguese bridge protects against heavy seas. Dry-stack exhaust, keel cooling system are standard. Auxiliary get-home engine is optional. Single 140hp diesel will cruise at 7 knots with a range of around 2,500 miles.

|---|---|
Length Overall	39'9"
Length WL	35'5"
Beam	14'6"
Draft	4'9"
Weight	50,000#
Ballast	2,500#
Fuel	920 gals.
Water	250 gals.
Waste	70 gals.
Hull Type	Displacement

See Page 553 For Resale Values

Pacific Asian Enterprises
Dana Point, CA
www.nordhavn.com

Nordhavn 43
2004–Current

Ship-like trawler with towering profile appeals to oceangoing cruisers demanding world-class engineering, unrivaled build quality. Twin-stateroom interior has salon offset to port leaving single, starboard-side walkway from cockpit to bow. Full-beam master stateroom is amidships, guest stateroom has head forward, berth aft for maximum comfort. Note dry-stack exhaust system, pilothouse Dutch doors, 30hp back-up wing engine. Engineroom is a work of art. Lugger 165hp diesel offers 2,500-mile cruising range at 7–8 knots.

|---|---|
Length Overall	43'0"
Length WL	38'4"
Beam	14'10"
Draft	4'11"
Weight	54,540#
Clearance, Mast	30'4"
Fuel	1,200 gals.
Water	300 gals.
Waste	50 gals.
Hull Type	Displacement

Insufficient Resale Data To Assign Values

Pacific Asian Enterprises
Dana Point, CA
www.nordhavn.com

231-360-0827

Nordhavn 46
1989–2005

Standard Floorplan

Alternate Floorplan

Compelling full-displacement trawler with classic pilothouse profile established Nordhavn reputation for engineering excellence, obsessive attention to detail. Standard interior features full-beam amidships master with private salon access; alternate floorplan has master stateroom forward. Salon is offset to port leaving single starboard walkway from cockpit to bow. Note wave-breaking Portuguese bridge, unique dry-stack exhaust system. Single 140hp diesel will cruise at 8 knots with a range of 1,800–2,000 miles. Over 80 were built.

Length Overall	45'9"	Ballast	4,800#
Length WL	38'4"	Fuel	1,000 gals.
Beam	15'5"	Waree	280 gals.
Draft	5'0"	Waste	50 gals.
Weight	60,000#	Hull Type	Displacement

See Page 553 For Resale Values

Pacific Asian Enterprises
Dana Point, CA
www.nordhavn.com

231-360-0827

Nordhavn 47
2003–Current

Heavy-weather trawler with ballasted hull carries owners in safety, comfort anywhere in the world. Deluxe interior has salon offset to port leaving a single, starboard-side walkway from cockpit to bow. Master stateroom is amidships; guest stateroom has head forward, berth aft for maximum comfort. Note Portuguese bridge, office/nav station, auxiliary diesel, dry stack exhaust, keel cooler (to dissipate engine heat). Tall bow can punch through very heavy seas. Single Lugger diesel will cruise at 8 knots for nearly 3,000 miles.

Length Overall	51'0"	Ballast	6,000#
Length WL	43'4"	Fuel	1,450 gals.
Beam	16'1"	Water	400 gals.
Draft	5'6"	Waste	120 gals.
Weight	85,000#	Hull Type	Displacement

See Page 553 For Resale Values

Pacific Asian Enterprises
Dana Point, CA
www.nordhavn.com

231-360-0827

Nordhavn 50
1997–2006

Oceangoing trawler with wide-body hull was built for heavy-weather cruising. Several layouts available—most have wide-body salon with single, starboard-side walkway. Two-stateroom interior boasts lavish amidships master (with engineroom access), raised pilothouse with nav station, roomy guest cabin with head forward, opulent salon with well-equipped galley. Bulbous bow extension beneath waterline improves fuel efficiency, hull speed. Single 300hp Lugger diesel will cruise at 7–8 knots with 2,500-mile range.

Length Overall	51'2"	Ballast	6,600#
Length WL	44'2"	Fuel	1,320 gals.
Beam	16'0"	Water	260 gals.
Draft	5'2"	Waste	50 gals.
Weight	80,000#	Hull Type	Displacement

See Page 553 For Resale Values

Pacific Asian Enterprises
Dana Point, CA
www.nordhavn.com

Motoryachts & Trawlers

Motoryachts & Trawlers

www.powerboatguide.com
231-360-0827

Nordhavn 55
2005–Current

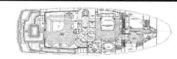

Stately ocean trawler with towering profile appeals to hardcore cruisers obsessed with quality, security. Maxi-volume interior boasts opulent master stateroom amidships, spacious guest cabin forward with office, spacious salon with breakfast bar, commercial-like pilothouse with private stateroom and head. Note quality teak woodwork, home-size galley appliances, bathtub in master head. High bow punches through heavy seas; dry exhaust eliminates need for through-hull. Range is nearly 3,000 miles at 8 knots with single 330hp diesel.

Length Overall	59'0"	Clearance, Mast	27'8"
Length WL	50'1"	Fuel	2,250 gals.
Beam	18'0"	Water	600 gals.
Draft	6'4"	Waste	120 gals.
Weight	124,500#	Hull Type	Displacement

See Page 553 For Resale Values

**Pacific Asian Enterprises
Dana Point, CA
www.nordhavn.com**

---

www.powerboatguide.com
231-360-0827

Nordhavn 57
1999–2007

Big-water passagemaker with genuine ocean-crossing potential delivers top-shelf build quality, uncompromised cruising security. Luxurious three-stateroom interior boasts spacious salon with serving bar, professional-level pilothouse, stand-up engineroom. Galley deck door is a plus. Wide keel allows for stand-up engine room. Note Portuguese bridge, high protective bulwarks, dry exhaust. Wide sidedeck to starboard, narrow walkway to port. Single Lugger 340hp diesel delivers 3,000-mile-plus range at 8 knots.

Length Overall	57'6"	Clearance	21'0"
Length WL	52'8"	Fuel	2,000 gals.
Beam	17'7"	Water	300 gals.
Draft	6'8"	Waste	60 gals.
Weight	120,000#	Hull Type	Displacement

See Page 553 For Resale Values

**Pacific Asian Enterprises
Dana Point, CA
www.nordhavn.com**

---

www.powerboatguide.com
231-360-0827

Nordhavn 62
1995–Current

Gold-plated trawler yacht with ship-like appearance is designed for transoceanic voyages in style, safety, comfort. Maxi-beam interior has three double staterooms, home-size galley appliances, crew quarters forward. Enclosed pilothouse includes head, bunk beds. Note stand-up engineroom, keel cooler, workshop, auxiliary back-up diesel, Portuguese bridge. Bulbous bow extension beneath waterline improves fuel efficiency, hull speed. Single 340hp Luggar diesel will cruise at 8–9 knots with 3,000-mile-plus range.

Length Overall	62'8"	Ballast	10,000#
Length WL	55'6"	Fuel	2,652 gals.
Beam	19'4"	Water	525 gals.
Draft	6'10"	Waste	100 gals.
Weight	150,000#	Hull Type	Displacement

Insufficient Resale Data To Assign Values

**Pacific Asian Enterprises
Dana Point, CA
www.nordhavn.com**

Nordic 32 Tug
1986–Current

Popular pilothouse cruiser with workboat lines delivers impressive blend of superior quality, deluxe accommodations, lasting value. Several cabin layouts offered over the years, all featuring full-beam salon with convertible dinette, teak cabinetry and flooring, raised pilothouse with 360-degree visibility. Updated 32+ model in 2002 has island berth forward, enlarged head, new integral swim platform. New prop-pocket hull introduced in 2008. Cruise at 12 knots with single 220hp Cummins diesel; 14 knots with 270hp Cummins.

Length Overall	34'2"	Headroom	6'4"
Beam	11'0"	Fuel	200 gals.
Draft	3'6"	Water	100 gals.
Weight	16,000#	Waste	30 gals.
Clearance	10'4"	Hull Type	Semi-Disp.

See Page 553 For Resale Values

Nordic Tugs
Burlington, WA
www.nordictugs.com

Nordic 37 Tug
1998–Current

Two Staterooms

Single Stateroom

Legendary Nordic cruiser with classic workboat lines gets high marks for craftsmanship, comfort, seaworthiness. Stylish full-beam salon with solid teak cabinetry, convertible dinette, is open to wheelhouse and aft deck. Original two-stateroom interior was joined in 2003 with alternate single-stateroom layout with enlarged master stateroom and head. Note spacious engineroom, integral swim platform. Flybridge has been a popular option in recent years. Cruise efficiently at 12–14 knots with single 330hp Cummins diesel.

Length Overall	39'2"	Clearance	12'4"
Length WL	37'4"	Fuel	320 gals.
Beam	12'11"	Water	144 gals.
Draft	4'4"	Waste	32 gals.
Weight	22,600#	Hull Type	Semi-Disp.

See Page 553 For Resale Values

Nordic Tugs
Burlington, WA
www.nordictugs.com

Nordic 42 Tug
1996–Current

Stately pilothouse yacht with rugged tugboat styling is ideally suited for coastal cruising in comfort, security. Well-appointed teak interior features large salon with U-shaped galley, two roomy staterooms, laundry center under pilothouse steps. Forward stateroom is accessed from wheelhouse in early models, salon in later models. Note wide side decks, roomy cockpit, spacious engineroom. Flybridge has been a popular option in recent years. Single 540hp Cummins diesel will cruise at 12 knots (15–16 knots top).

Length Overall	46'3"	Headroom	6'6"
Length WL	40'2"	Fuel	600 gals.
Beam	13'10"	Water	200 gals.
Draft	4'7"	Waste	50 gals.
Weight	31,400#	Hull Type	Semi-Disp.

See Page 553 For Resale Values

Nordic Tugs
Burlington, WA
www.nordictugs.com

231-360-0827

Nordic 52/54 Tug
2004–Current

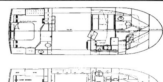

Two-Stateroom Interior

Three-Stateroom Interior

Heavily built coastal trawler with signature Nordic Tug profile combines luxury-class accommodations with fuel-miserly operation. Elegant pilothouse interior is offered with two- and three-staterrom floorplans. Highlights include spacious pilothouse, enormous engine-room, standard washer/dryer. Early hulls had twin engines; redesigned single-screw power became standard starting with hull #3. Marketed since 2009 as the Nordic 54. Cruise at 9–10 knots with single 670hp Cummins engine (about 15 knots top).

Length Overall	56'10"	Clearance, Mast	21'9"
Length WL	52'6"	Fuel	1,300 gals.
Beam	16'10"	Water	300 gals.
Draft	5'3"	Waste	130 gals.
Weight	60,000#	Hull Type	Semi-Disp.

Insufficient Resale Data To Assign Values

Nordic Tugs
Burlington, WA
www.nordictugs.com

231-360-0827

Novatec 42 Sundeck
1983–89

Iconic Taiwan import achieved great success in her era thanks to handsome styling, versatile layout, very appealing price. Well-appointed galley down, two-stateroom interior boasts spacious salon, standard lower helm station, convertible dinette (opposite galley), teak cabinets and trim. Note direct salon access to sundeck—very convenient. Teak decks, sundeck wet bar, hardtop were popular options. A modern classic by many. Cruise at 8–10 knots with twin 135hp Perkins diesels; 12–13 knots with 165hp Perkins.

Length Overall	41'9"	Clearance	NA
Hull Length	36'10"	Fuel	500 gals.
Beam	13'8"	Water	300 gals.
Draft	3'8"	Waste	50 gals.
Weight	26,000#	Hull Type	Semi-Disp.

Prices Not Provided for Pre-1995 Models

Nova Marine, Taiwan
www.nova-marine.com

231-360-0827

Ocean 42 Sunliner
1981–85

Double-cabin version of Oceans 42 Sportfisherman (1980–83) delivered comfort, performance at an affordable price. Generic galley-down interior with teak cabinets boasts spacious salon with L-shaped settee, full dinette, separate stall showers in both heads. Strong list of standard equipment included generator, garbage disposal, washer/dryer, vacuum system, instant hot water, microwave oven. Note compact engineroom. Among several engine choices, GM 450hp 6-71 diesels cruise at 24–25 knots (high 20s top).

Length Overall	42'0"	Clearance	12'0"
Length WL	38'0"	Fuel	480 gals.
Beam	14'4"	Water	100 gals.
Draft	3'6"	Hull Type	Modified-V
Weight	28,000#	Deadrise Aft	1.5°

Prices Not Provided for Pre-1995 Models

Ocean Yachts
Egg Harbor City, NJ
www.oceanyachtsinc.com

www.powerboatguide.com   231-360-0827

Ocean 44 Motor Yacht
1992–99

Rakish 1990s motoryacht set class standards in her day for sleek styling, leading-edge performance. Innovative three-stateroom floorplan boasts combined salon/galley/dinette, stall showers in both heads, guest stateroom under salon sole. Note teak interior joinerwork, designer-style decor. Protected aft deck with wet bar, wing doors can entertain several guests. Washer/dryer, central vacuum system, radar arch were standard. Engineroom is a tight fit. Detroit 485hp 6-71 diesels cruise at 24 knots (27–28 knots top).

Length	44'0"	Max Headroom	6'6"
Beam	15'0"	Fuel	466 gals.
Draft	3'7"	Water	100 gals.
Weight	40,000#	Hull Type	Modified-V
Clearance	12'0"	Deadrise Aft	5°

See Page 555 For Resale Values

Ocean Yachts
Egg Harbor City, NJ
www.oceanyachtsinc.com

---

www.powerboatguide.com   231-360-0827

Ocean 46 Sunliner
1983–86

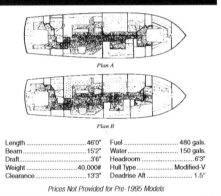

Plan A

Plan B

Aft-cabin version of Ocean 46 SF (1983–85) made the cut with Ocean owners looking for convertible performance, motoryacht amenities. Originally offered with twin-stateroom, galley-down interior, alternate three-stateroom layout became available in 1985. Notable features include teak interior cabinets, protected aft deck with wing doors, central vacuum system, washer/dryer, garbage disposal. A fast ride compared with most 1980s-era motoryachts, she'll cruise in the low 20s with standard GM 450hp 6-71 diesels (26–27 knots top).

Length	46'0"	Fuel	480 gals.
Beam	15'2"	Water	150 gals.
Draft	3'6"	Headroom	6'3"
Weight	40,000#	Hull Type	Modified-V
Clearance	13'3"	Deadrise Aft	1.5°

Prices Not Provided for Pre-1995 Models

Ocean Yachts
Egg Harbor City, NJ
www.oceanyachtsinc.com

---

www.powerboatguide.com   231-360-0827

Ocean 48 Cockpit Motor Yacht
1993–99

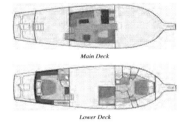

Main Deck

Lower Deck

Cockpit version of popular Ocean 44 MY (1992–99) combined rakish styling with roomy layout, sporty performance. Innovative three-stateroom floorplan boasts combined salon/galley/dinette, stall showers in both heads, guest stateroom under salon sole. Note teak interior joinerwork, designer-style decor. Protected aft deck with wet bar, wing doors can entertain several guests. Washer/dryer, central vacuum system, radar arch were standard. Engineroom is a tight fit. Detroit 485hp 6-71 diesels cruise at 24 knots (27–28 knots top).

Length	48'0"	Max Headroom	6'6"
Beam	15'0"	Fuel	466 gals.
Draft	3'7"	Water	100 gals.
Weight	42,500#	Hull Type	Modified-V
Clearance	12'0"	Deadrise Aft	5°

See Page 555 For Resale Values

Ocean Yachts
Egg Harbor City, NJ
www.oceanyachtsinc.com

Motoryachts & Trawlers

Ocean 48 Motor Yacht
1989–94

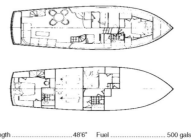

231-360-0827

Spacious twin-deck motoryacht introduced in 1989 gets high marks for maxi-volume interior space, good performance, signature Ocean value. Highlights include extended full-beam salon, gourmet galley with deck access door, inside bridge access, three double staterooms, three full heads. Large stand-up engineroom is a plus. Note inside bridge access ladder, small aft deck (for line-handling). Central vacuum system, radar arch, bow pulpit were standard. Standard 485hp GM diesels cruise at 23–24 knots and top out in the high 20s.

Length	48'6"	Fuel	500 gals.
Beam	16'4"	Water	150 gals.
Draft	4'0"	Headroom	6'4"
Weight	51,000#	Hull Type	Modified-V
Clearance	14'10"	Deadrise Aft	7°

Prices Not Provided for Pre-1995 Models

Ocean Yachts
Egg Harbor City, NJ
www.oceanyachtsinc.com

Ocean 53 Motor Yacht
1988–91

231-360-0827

Deckhouse, Layout A

Lower Deck, Layout A

Maxi-volume motoryacht with twin-deck floorplan offered luxury accommodations, good performance at reasonable price. Expansive four-stateroom interior—rare in a 53-footer—was offered with full-beam salon or shortened salon with semi-enclosed aft deck. Master stateroom has big king-size bed. Extended, full-beam flybridge has room for a small crowd. Note wheelhouse deck doors, inside flybridge access, spacious stand-up engineroom. Twin 735hp Detroit diesels cruise at 24 knots (about 30 knots top).

Length	53'0"	Headroom	6'6"
Beam	17'2"	Fuel	750 gals.
Draft	4'6"	Water	300 gals.
Weight	64,000#	Hull Type	Modified-V
Clearance	16'0"	Deadrise Aft	8°

Prices Not Provided for Pre-1995 Models

Ocean Yachts
Egg Harbor City, NJ
www.oceanyachtsinc.com

Ocean 55 Sunliner
1983–86

231-360-0827

Well-appointed 1980's cruising yacht is basically an aft-cabin version of Ocean's hugely popular 55 SS (1981–90). Comfortable three-stateroom interior boasts large galley with home-size refrigerator, big U-shaped dinette, spacious master suite forward with built-in washer/dryer and unique forepeak head. Note aft-deck wing doors, enclosure panels. Hardtop can support weight of a small dinghy. Standard 600hp GM 8V92s cruise at 22 knots (about 25 knots top); optional 675hp 8V92s are a couple of knots faster.

Length	55'8"	Fuel	750 gals.
Beam	16'4"	Water	200 gals.
Draft	4'4"	Headroom	6'4"
Weight	60,000#	Hull Type	Modified-V
Clearance	14'6"	Deadrise Aft	4°

Prices Not Provided for Pre-1995 Models

Ocean Yachts
Egg Harbor City, NJ
www.oceanyachtsinc.com

231-360-0827

Ocean 56 Cockpit MY
1990–91

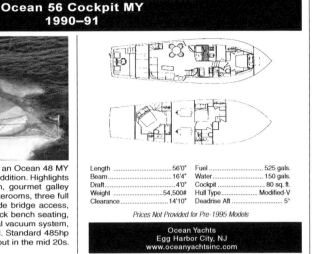

Versatile cruising yacht is basically an Ocean 48 MY (1989–94) with an 8-foot cockpit addition. Highlights include extended full-beam salon, gourmet galley with deck access door, three double staterooms, three full heads, stand-up engineroom. Note inside bridge access, small aft deck (for line-handling), foredeck bench seating, private master stateroom access. Central vacuum system, radar arch, transom door were standard. Standard 485hp 6-71 diesels cruise at 22 knots and top out in the mid 20s. Only two years in production.

Length	56'0"	Fuel	525 gals.
Beam	16'4"	Water	150 gals.
Draft	4'0"	Cockpit	80 sq. ft.
Weight	54,500#	Hull Type	Modified-V
Clearance	14'10"	Deadrise Aft	5°

Prices Not Provided for Pre-1995 Models

Ocean Yachts
Egg Harbor City, NJ
www.oceanyachtsinc.com

231-360-0827

Ocean 57 Odyssey
2004–Current

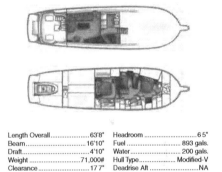

Luxurious cruising yacht is basically a repurposed Ocean 57 Super Sport with enclosed bridge, guest-friendly cockpit, transom garage. Lavish three-stateroom, three-head interior features elegant salon with direct bridge access, step-up galley and dinette, washer/dryer under companionway steps. Enclosed bridge includes custom helm chairs, refrigerator, TV/DVD. Note large engineroom with cockpit access, flybridge afterdeck with full controls, cockpit boarding gates. Cat 1,015hp engines cruise in the mid 20s (30+ knots top).

Length Overall	63'8"	Headroom	6 5"
Beam	16'10"	Fuel	893 gals.
Draft	4'0"	Water	200 gals.
Weight	71,000#	Hull Type	Modified-V
Clearance	17 7"	Deadrise Aft	NA

Insufficient Resale Data To Assign Values

Ocean Yachts
Egg Harbor City, NJ
www.oceanyachtsinc.com

231-360-0827

Ocean 65 Odyssey
2003–Current

3 Staterooms

4 Staterooms

Feature-rich cruising yacht is basically a reworked Ocean 62 Super Sport with enclosed bridge, roomy cockpit, storage garage for hard-bottom inflatable. Beautifully appointed teak interior boasts spacious salon, abundant storage, choice of three or four staterooms. Note side-by-side galley refrigeration, laundry room in three-stateroom layout. Spiral salon staircase provides access to enclosed bridge with entertainment center, aft sundeck with steering station. Cruise in the mid 20s with Cat 1,015hp diesels (33–35 knots top).

Length Overall	67'6"	Headroom	6 5"
Beam	17 5"	Fuel	1,100#
Draft	5'0"	Water	350 gals.
Weight	87,000#	Hull Type	Modified-V
Clearance, Hardtop	18'1"	Deadrise Aft	12°

Insufficient Resale Data To Assign Values

Ocean Yachts
Egg Harbor City, NJ
www.oceanyachtsinc.com

www.powerboatguide.com
231-360-0827

Ocean Alexander 38 Double Cabin
1984–87

Handsome 1980s cruiser with traditional teak interior combined classic trawler styling with solid construction, economical operation. Well-finished interior boasts roomy salon with lower helm, two salon deck doors, generous storage. Aft stateroom boasts cockpit access door, divided head compartment with shower to port. Aft cabintop can stow small dinghy. Raised bulwarks enhance side deck security; flybridge has seating for four. Twin 135hp Lehman diesels cruise efficiently at 7-8 knots.

Length Overall	38'4"	Headroom	6'4"
Beam	13'4"	Fuel	300 gals.
Draft	3'2"	Water	200 gals.
Weight	21,500#	Waste	30 gals.
Clearance	NA	Hull Type	Semi-Disp.

Prices Not Provided for Pre-1995 Models

Ocean Alexander Marine
Seattle, WA
www.oceanalexander.com

---

www.powerboatguide.com
231-360-0827

Ocean Alexander 390 Sundeck
1986–99

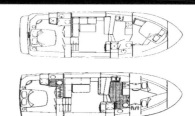

Popular Ed Monk design combined rakish styling with versatile layout, fuel-efficient operation. Well-appointed teak (or light ash) interior features expansive salon with serving counter, lower helm station, two double staterooms, separate stall showers in both heads. Note full-beam aft deck, wide side decks, standard swim platform. Most were sold with radar arch and hardtop. Offered with several diesel options over the years—cruising speeds range from 15–17 knots, top speeds are in the neighborhood of 20 knots.

Length	39'3"	Fuel	300 gals.
Beam	13'11"	Water	150 gals.
Draft	3'2"	Waste	18 gals.
Weight	24,800#	Hull Type	Modified-V
Clearance	14'0"	Deadrise Aft	12°

See Page 554 For Resale Values

Ocean Alexander Marine
Seattle, WA
www.oceanalexander.com

---

www.powerboatguide.com
231-360-0827

Ocean Alexander 40 Double Cabin
1980–89

Standard Floorplan

Alternate Floorplan

Graceful double-cabin trawler with full teak interior gets high marks for quality construction, practical layout, fuel-efficient operation. Tasteful two-stateroom interior—offered with galley up or down—features roomy salon with lower helm station, deck access door, teak parquet flooring. Cockpit access door in aft stateroom is a big plus. Note large engineroom, wide side decks, roomy flybridge with L-shaped settee. Better gelcoat finish than most Asian imports of her era. Twin 120hp Lehman diesels will cruise efficiently at 7-8 knots.

Length Overall	40'10"	Fuel	400 gals.
Length WL	36'0"	Water	240 gals.
Beam	13'4"	Waste	35 gals.
Draft	3'6"	Waste	50 gals.
Weight	22,500#	Hull Type	Semi-Disp.

Prices Not Provided for Pre-1995 Models

Ocean Alexander Marine
Seattle, WA
www.oceanalexander.com

Ocean Alexander 40 Sedan
1983–89

Versatile 1980s sedan combines classic trawler styling with solid construction, economical operation. Sedan-style layout with extended salon, small cockpit offers easy access to the water. Highlights include teak interior woodwork, home-sized galley, lower helm with sliding deck door, large forward stateroom with vanity. Expansive flybridge can seat several guests. Transom door, teak decks, teak swim platform were standard. Twin 135hp Lehman diesels will cruise at 8 knots (11–12 knots top). GM 260hp diesels cruise at 14 knots.

Length	39'8"	Fuel	400 gals.
Beam	13'4"	Water	200 gals.
Draft	3'2"	Headroom	6 5"
Weight	22,500#	Hull Type	Semi-Disp.
Clearance	NA	Deadrise Aft	NA

Prices Not Provided for Pre-1995 Models

Ocean Alexander Marine
Seattle, WA
www.oceanalexander.com

Ocean Alexander 420 Sundeck
1987–99

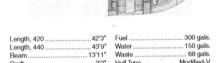

Classy cockpit yacht with sleek lines, quality construction became one of Alexander's more popular models. Features include well-appointed interior with large master stateroom, lower helm with deck door, roomy aft deck, commanding bridge with good helm visibility. Note wide side decks, large engineroom. GM or Cummins 250hp diesels cruise at 15 knots (about 18 knots top); 350hp or 375hp Cats cruise at 20 knots (23–24 knots top). Note that Alexander 440 or 460 Sundeck are the same boats with extended cockpits.

Length, 420	42'3"	Fuel	300 gals.
Length, 440	43'9"	Water	150 gals.
Beam	13'11"	Waste	68 gals.
Draft	3'2"	Hull Type	Modified-V
Weight	27,000#	Deadrise Aft	NA

See Page 554 For Resale Values

Ocean Alexander Marine
Seattle, WA
www.oceanalexander.com

Ocean Alexander 423 Classico
1993–2002

Handsome aft-cabin cruiser with walkaround decks offers comfort, performance in a timeless design. House is set well forward on foredeck to maximize salon and galley dimensions. Two-stateroom interior is arranged with V-berths forward, walkaround queen bed aft, spacious salon open to mid-level galley. Note twin salon deck doors, handcrafted teak joinerwork, roomy head with stall shower. Twin 220hp Cummins diesels cruise 11–12 knots (16 knots top); 420hp Cats cruise at 18 knot and reach a top speed of 22–23 knots.

Length	42'3"	Fuel	550 gals.
Beam	14'8"	Water	160 gals.
Draft	3'10"	Waste	60 gals.
Weight	34,200#	Hull Type	Modified-V
Clearance	NA	Deadrise Aft	10°

See Page 554 For Resale Values

Ocean Alexander Marine
Seattle, WA
www.oceanalexander.com

Ocean Alexander 426 Classico
1994–2002

Graceful sedan-style cruiser enjoyed wide popularity in recent years thanks to spacious accommodations, exceptional build quality. Standard galley-up interior with expansive teak joinery features two comfortable staterooms, roomy head with stall shower, lower helm with deck access door. Extended flybridge can accommodate an 11-foot inflatable. Heavily built hull incorporates shallow, prop-protecting keel, prop pockets to reduce draft. Cummins 220hp diesels cruise at 10–12 knots; 350hp Cats cruise at 16–17 knots.

Length	42'3"	Fuel	600 gals.
Beam	14'8"	Water	200 gals.
Draft	4'0"	Waste	60 gals.
Weight	35,000#	Hull Type	Modified-V
Clearance	12'8"	Deadrise Aft	10°

See Page 554 For Resale Values

Ocean Alexander Marine
Seattle, WA
www.oceanalexander.com

Ocean Alexander 43 Flush Aft Deck
1980–85

Polished double-cabin cruiser was instrumental in establishing Alexander's reputation for quality, durability in the early 1980s. All-teak interior includes full-size galley, two heads, large master stateroom with cockpit access, lower helm with deck door. Note wide side decks, aft-deck companionway door. Efficient semi-displacement hull with prop-protecting keel delivers comfortable open-water ride. Standard 120hp Lehman diesels cruise at 7–8 knots; optional 255hp Lehmans cruise at 13 knots and reach a top speed of 16–17 knots.

Length Overall	42'6"	Clearance	NA
Length WL	38'2"	Fuel	500 gals.
Beam	14'6"	Water	200 gals.
Draft	3'6"	Hull Type	Semi-Disp.
Weight	29,000#	Deadrise Aft	NA

Prices Not Provided for Pre-1995 Models

Ocean Alexander Marine
Seattle, WA
www.oceanalexander.com

Ocean Alexander 430/460 Classico MKI
2000–06

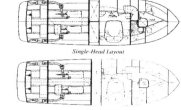

Single-Head Layout

Two-Head Layout

Sturdy pilothouse trawler projects the ship-like image of a serious cruiser. Luxurious two-stateroom interior features impeccable teak cabinetry, full-beam salon with galley forward, raised pilothouse with excellent visibility. Gate in Portuguese bridge provides access to bow; steps on port side of pilothouse lead to cabintop where a dinghy can be stored. Flybridge is optional. Prop pockets in hull reduce draft. Cruise at 10 knots with 220hp Cummins diesels (13–14 top). Note that 460 Classico is same boat with larger cockpit.

Length, 460	45'8"	Weight, 460	42,500#
Length, 430	43'6"	Fuel	600 gals.
Beam	14'8"	Water	200 gals.
Draft	4'2"	Waste	60 gals.
Weight, 430	38,900#	Hull Type	Semi-Disp.

See Page 554 For Resale Values

Ocean Alexander Marine
Seattle, WA
www.oceanalexander.com

www.powerboatguide.com   231-360-0827

Ocean Alexander 45 Sedan
2005–Current

Well-appointed sedan cruiser successfully blends traditional styling with brisk performance, luxury-class amenities. Appealing galley-up interior boasts extensive teak cabinetry, two large staterooms, generous storage. Wraparound salon windows provide panoramic views, but lower-helm visibility gets mixed reviews. Traditional flybridge ladder (instead of molded steps) will disappoint some. Prop pockets reduce draft, improve hull efficiency. Good finish for an affordably priced boat. Yanmar 480hp diesels cruise at 22 knots (mid 20s top).

Length	46'6"	Fuel	500 gals.
Beam	14'4"	Water	150 gals.
Draft	4'2"	Waste	40 gals.
Weight	33,100#	Hull Type	Modified-V
Clearance	NA	Deadrise Aft	10°

See Page 554 For Resale Values

Ocean Alexander Marine
Seattle, WA
www.oceanalexander.com

www.powerboatguide.com   231-360-0827

Ocean Alexander 450 Classico Sedan
2001–04

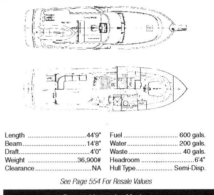

Sporty sedan yacht gets high marks for handsome styling, seakindly hull, tasteful accommodations. Practical two-stateroom interior boasts spacious master stateroom, large head compartment, teak-paneled salon with galley forward. Roomy cockpit, wide walkaround decks are valuable assets in any cruising yacht. Extended bridge can stow a small tender. Transom door, bow pulpit, hinged radar mast are standard. Twin 220hp Cummins diesels cruise at 8–10 knots and reach a top speed of about 13 knots.

Length	44'9"	Fuel	600 gals.
Beam	14'8"	Water	200 gals.
Draft	4'0"	Waste	40 gals.
Weight	36,900#	Headroom	6'4"
Clearance	NA	Hull Type	Semi-Disp.

See Page 554 For Resale Values

Ocean Alexander Marine
Seattle, WA
www.oceanalexander.com

www.powerboatguide.com   231-360-0827

Ocean Alexander 456 Classico
1992–2002

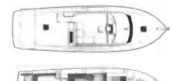

Traditional double-cabin cruising yacht with full walkaround decks delivers impressive blend of feature-rich accommodations, fuel-efficient operation. Comfortable galley-down floorplan boasts surprisingly spacious salon with serving counter, lower helm with deck access door, roomy master stateroom with vanity, two full heads. Teak joinery is finished to high standards. Note well-arranged engineroom, step-down cockpit, hinged radar mast. No lightweight, 220hp Cummins diesels cruise at 10 knots (12–15 knots top).

Length	45'6"	Fuel	550 gals.
Beam	15'8"	Water	250 gals.
Draft	4'0"	Waste	40 gals.
Weight	40,000#	Headroom	6'3"
Clearance	12'9"	Hull Type	Semi-Disp.

See Page X554 For Resale Values

Ocean Alexander Marine
Seattle, WA
www.oceanalexander.com

Motoryachts & Trawlers

Motoryachts & Trawlers

Ocean Alexander 48 Classico
2006–Current

Stout sedan trawler sets class standards for handsome trawler styling, luxury-class amenities, top-shelf construction. Premium two-stateroom interior features comfortable salon with leather salon, galley pass-thru, teak-and-holly flooring, lower helm with sliding deck door. Both heads share common stall shower. Close-fitting engineroom is accessed from salon. Note wide, well-secured side decks, cockpit flybridge stairs, hullside boarding gates, frameless windows. Yanmar 370hp diesels cruise at 15 knots (about 18 knots top).

Length	47'2"	Fuel	600 gals.
Beam	14'8"	Water	200 gals.
Draft	3'10"	Waste	60 gals.
Weight	36,900#	Hull Type	Semi-Disp.
Clearance	NA	Deadrise Aft	NA

Insufficient Resale Data To Assign Values

Ocean Alexander Marine
Seattle, WA
www.oceanalexander.com

Ocean Alexander 48 Yachtsman
1985–91

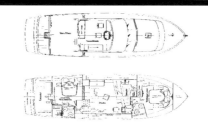

Versatile 1980s cockpit yacht combined comfort, performance in a well-styled package. Standard floorplan is unusual in that master stateroom with island berth is forward, guest stateroom with space-saving athwartships berth is aft. Teak interior joinery is exquisitely finished; large salon windows offer panoramic outside views. Topside features roomy aft deck with hardtop, cockpit transom door, radar arch. Cummins 320hp diesels cruise in the 15-knot range with a top speed of around 20 knots.

Length	48'7"	Fuel	500 gal.
Beam	15'6"	Water	210 gal.
Draft	3'10"	Headroom	6'3"
Weight	41,500#	Hull Type	Modified-V
Clearance	NA	Deadrise Aft	NA

Prices Not Provided for Pre-1995 Models

Ocean Alexander Marine
Seattle, WA
www.oceanalexander.com

Ocean Alexander 480 Sport Sedan
1993–2001

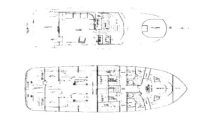

Rakish Mediterranean styling, classy accommodations set this 1990s cruiser apart from the competition. Richly paneled three-stateroom, two-head floorplan is arranged with galley and helm forward, one step up from spacious main salon. Sliding doors open salon to expansive cockpit with transom door. Note full teak interior, sunken foredeck sun pad, well-arranged engineroom. Prop pockets reduce draft requirements. Twin 420hp Cat diesels—small engines indeed for a 48-footer—cruise at 22 knots (mid 20s top).

Length	48'6"	Water	180 gals.
Beam	15'6"	Waste	40 gals.
Draft	2'9"	Clearance	NA
Weight	36,000#	Headroom	6'4"
Fuel	500 gals.	Hull Type	Modified-V

See Page 554 For Resale Values

Ocean Alexander Marine
Seattle, WA
www.oceanalexander.com

Ocean Alexander 486 Classico
1993–2002

Luxury-class pilothouse yacht with wide beam, prop-protecting keel targets serious, quality-focused cruisers. Expansive interior features two large staterooms, both with walkaround queen beds. Salon is open to roomy U-shaped galley; visibility from raised pilothouse is excellent. Both heads have separate stall showers. Note protected side decks, washer/dryer in forward stateroom. Cat 420hp diesels cruise at 14–15 knots (18 knots top). Alexander 510 Classico (1999–2002) is the same boat with slightly enlarged cockpit.

Length, 486	48'0"	Clearance	NA
Length, 510	50'6"	Fuel	700 gals.
Beam	15'8"	Water	260 gals.
Draft	4'0"	Hull Type	Semi-Disp.
Weight	48,000#	Deadrise Aft	NA

See Page 554 For Resale Values

Ocean Alexander Marine
Seattle, WA
www.oceanalexander.com

Ocean Alexander 50 Classico
2006–Current

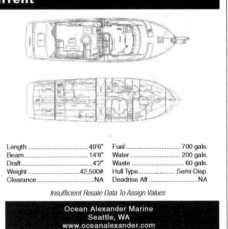

Handsome pilothouse cruising yacht splits the difference between liveaboard comforts, long-range versatility. Spacious two-stateroom design gets high marks for expansive salon, well-planned galley, generous storage space, meticulous teak woodwork. Pilothouse is fitted with burlwood dinette, pilot berth, watertight sliding doors. Note protected Portuguese bridge, portside access to flybridge. Boat deck has room for dinghy and davit. Cruise efficiently at 8 knots with a single John Deere 300hp diesel engine.

Length	49'6"	Fuel	700 gals.
Beam	14'8"	Water	200 gals.
Draft	4'2"	Waste	60 gals.
Weight	42,500#	Hull Type	Semi-Disp.
Clearance	NA	Deadrise Aft	NA

Insufficient Resale Data To Assign Values

Ocean Alexander Marine
Seattle, WA
www.oceanalexander.com

Ocean Alexander 50 Pilothouse MK I
1978–84

Two-Stateroom Layout

Three-Stateroom Layout

Classic pilothouse yacht was first Ocean Alexander design to be imported into U.S. market. Offered with two or three staterooms, both with deckhouse galley, raised pilothouse with dinette. Exterior features include protective Portuguese bridge, raised bulwarks, teak decks, transom door. Note that upper helm station is set well aft of pilothouse. Engineroom is a tight fit. Seakindly hull delivers comfortable big-water ride. Cruise at 11–12 knots with 320hp Cat—or 270hp Cummins—diesels. Total of 92 were built.

Length Overall	50'3"	Clearance	19'0"
Length WL	45'8"	Fuel	1000 gals.
Beam	15'6"	Water	420 gals.
Draft	4'6"	Headroom	6'4"
Weight	46,500#	Hull Type	Semi-Disp.

Prices Not Provided for Pre-1995 Models

Ocean Alexander Marine
Seattle, WA
www.oceanalexander.com

Motoryachts & Trawlers

Motoryachts & Trawlers

231-360-0827

Ocean Alexander 50 Pilothouse MK II
1985–90

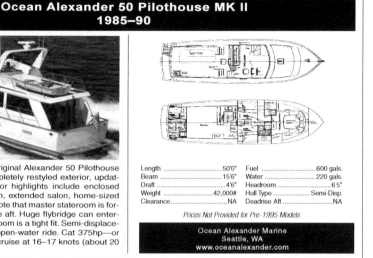

Updated version of original Alexander 50 Pilothouse (1978–85) has completely restyled exterior, updated floorplans. Interior highlights include enclosed pilothouse with watch berth, extended salon, home-sized galley, generous storage. Note that master stateroom is forward, guest staterooms are aft. Huge flybridge can entertain a small crowd. Engineroom is a tight fit. Semi-displacement hull delivers secure open-water ride. Cat 375hp—or GM 400hp 6V53—diesels cruise at 16–17 knots (about 20 knots top).

Length	50'0"	Fuel	600 gals.
Beam	15'6"	Water	220 gals.
Draft	4'6"	Headroom	6'5"
Weight	42,000#	Hull Type	Semi-Disp.
Clearance	NA	Deadrise Aft	NA

Prices Not Provided for Pre-1995 Models

Ocean Alexander Marine
Seattle, WA
www.oceanalexander.com

231-360-0827

Ocean Alexander 51/53 Sedan
1989–98

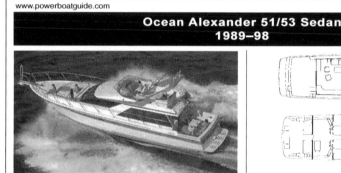

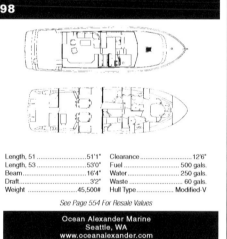

Rakish Eurostyle sedan gave 1990s Alexander buyers a compelling blend of style, comfort, amenities. Offered in two versions, the 51 Sedan (pictured above) has standard transom; 53 Sedan has a reverse transom that adds two extra feet to her length. Modern floorplan with master stateroom forward has galley, dinette on pilothouse level allowing expansive main salon. Note quality woodwork, excellent fit and finish. Early models with 400hp 6V53s cruise at 15 knots (18 top). Optional 735hp 8V92s cruise in the mid 20s (about 28 knots top).

Length, 51	51'1"	Clearance	12'6"
Length, 53	53'0"	Fuel	500 gals.
Beam	16'4"	Water	250 gals.
Draft	3'2"	Waste	60 gals.
Weight	45,500#	Hull Type	Modified-V

See Page 554 For Resale Values

Ocean Alexander Marine
Seattle, WA
www.oceanalexander.com

231-360-0827

Ocean Alexander 52 Motoryacht
2006–Current

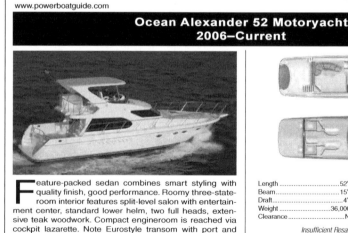

Feature-packed sedan combines smart styling with quality finish, good performance. Roomy three-stateroom interior features split-level salon with entertainment center, standard lower helm, two full heads, extensive teak woodwork. Compact engineroom is reached via cockpit lazarette. Note Eurostyle transom with port and starboard steps. Wide side decks are a plus; molded steps lead from cockpit to bridge. Prop pockets reduce draft, improve hull efficiency. Yanmar 480hp diesels cruise at 20 knots (low 20s top).

Length	52'0"	Fuel	600 gals.
Beam	15'6"	Water	180 gals.
Draft	4'0"	Waste	40 gals.
Weight	36,000#	Hull Type	Modified-V
Clearance	NA	Deadrise Aft	10°

Insufficient Resale Data To Assign Values

Ocean Alexander Marine
Seattle, WA
www.oceanalexander.com

231-360-0827

Ocean Alexander 520/540 Pilothouse
1990–2002

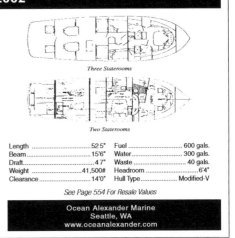

Three Staterooms

Two Staterooms

Taiwan-built pilothouse yacht from 1990s is classy, spacious, easy on the eye. (Note that Alexander 520 has standard transom; 540—pictured above—has Eurostyle transom.) Original three-stateroom interior with solid teak joinery has master suite forward; alternate two-stateroom layout (available in more recent models) has master stateroom amidships. Note very spacious engine-room, wide side decks, large flybridge with dinghy platform. Cruise at 15–16 knots with 425hp Cat—or 440hp Yanmar—diesels (18 knots top).

Length	52'5"	Fuel	600 gals.
Beam	15'6"	Water	300 gals.
Draft	4'7"	Waste	40 gals.
Weight	41,500#	Headroom	6'4"
Clearance	14'0"	Hull Type	Modified-V

See Page 554 For Resale Values

Ocean Alexander Marine
Seattle, WA
www.oceanalexander.com

231-360-0827

Ocean Alexander 546 Yachtfisher
1995–98

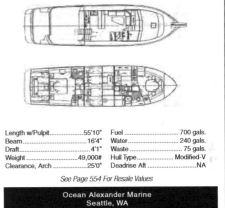

Stylish 1990s cockpit yacht made good on Alexander promise of cruising comfort, top-shelf construction. Standard three-stateroom layout with open aft deck is dominated by expansive pilothouse with U-shaped galley aft, curved dinette forward, starboard-side helm with deck access door. Covered aft deck with wing doors, built-in wet bar can entertain a large group with ease. Note cavernous cockpit lazarette, standup engineroom, wide side decks. Detroit 625hp (or Cat 660hp) diesels cruise at 14–15 knots (around 18 knots top).

Length w/Pulpit	55'10"	Fuel	700 gals.
Beam	16'4"	Water	240 gals.
Draft	4'1"	Waste	75 gals.
Weight	49,000#	Hull Type	Modified-V
Clearance, Arch	25'0"	Deadrise Aft	NA

See Page 554 For Resale Values

Ocean Alexander Marine
Seattle, WA
www.oceanalexander.com

231-360-0827

Ocean Alexander 548 Pilothouse
1996–2002

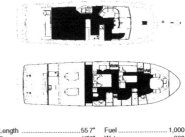

Striking 1990s pilothouse motoryacht combined sleek styling with spacious accommodations, first-rate workmanship. Good-running modified-V hull with prop pockets boasts unusually wide 17'6" beam. Highlights include three large staterooms, expansive raised pilot-house with galley and dinette, elegant salon, exceptionally large walk-in engineroom. Two-stateroom layout was optional. Note exquisite interior woodwork. Flybridge can stow a 15-foot dinghy. Cruise at 18 knots with GM 485hp diesels; 20 knots with 660hp Cats.

Length	55'7"	Fuel	1,000 gals.
Beam	17'6"	Water	260 gals.
Draft	4'0"	Waste	80 gals.
Weight	52,000#	Headroom	6'5"
Clearance	NA	Hull Type	Modified-V

See Page 554 For Resale Values

Ocean Alexander Marine
Seattle, WA
www.oceanalexander.com

Motoryachts & Trawlers

www.powerboatguide.com   231-360-0827

Ocean Alexander 58 Motor Yacht
2004–Current

Classy pilothouse cruiser combines timeless Pacific Northwest styling with seakindly hull, elegant accommodations. Varnished teak interior includes full-beam master suite, expansive salon with full entertainment center, raised pilothouse with wraparound dinette and full-size galley. Pilothouse doors provide easy access to decks; teak-laid cockpit is large enough for swimming, diving, fishing. Note large cockpit lazarette. Semi-V hull has prop pockets, underwater exhausts. Cruise at 15 knots (18–20 top) with 700hp Cat diesels.

Length w/Pulpit	64'3"	Fuel	1,000 gals.
Beam	17'6"	Water	260 gals.
Draft	4'0"	Waste	100 gals.
Weight	69,500#	Hull Type	Modified-V
Clearance	NA	Deadrise Aft	NA

Insufficient Resale Data To Assign Values

Ocean Alexander Marine
Seattle, WA
www.oceanalexander.com

---

www.powerboatguide.com   231-360-0827

Ocean Alexander 60 Pilothouse
1983–87

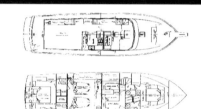

Sturdy long-range passagemaker from the 1980s combined classic pilothouse styling with top-shelf construction, executive-class accommodations. Twin-deck floorplan features three guest staterooms forward, full-beam master suite aft, combined salon/galley, raised pilothouse with centerline helm. Note convenient day head opposite galley. Bridge overhangs protect wide side decks. Transom staircase provides easy access to swim platform. GM 735hp 8V92s cruise at 15–16 knots (about 20 knots top).

Length Overall	60'0"	Clearance	17'0"
Length WL	NA	Water	365 gals.
Beam	18'0"	Fuel	1,200 gals.
Draft	4'10"	Hull Type	Semi-Disp.
Weight	65,000#	Deadrise Aft	12°

Prices Not Provided for Pre-1995 Models

Ocean Alexander Marine
Seattle, WA
www.oceanalexander.com

---

www.powerboatguide.com   231-360-0827

Ocean Alexander 600 Classico MK I
2001–03

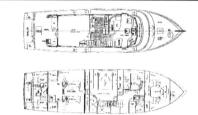

Broad-shouldered pilothouse yacht with distinctive Portuguese bridge, reverse front windshield targets serious offshore cruisers. Three-stateroom teak interior has step-up galley overlooking main salon, raised pilothouse with settee. Cockpit lazarette provides access to big stand-up engineroom (also reached from master stateroom). Huge flybridge has inside, outside access. Note protected side decks, teak swim platform, hinged radar mast. Cat 660hp diesels cruise at 15–16 knots (about 20 knots top).

Length	59'9"	Headroom	6'6"
Beam	17'9"	Fuel	1,000 gals.
Draft	4'6"	Water	360 gals.
Weight	84,122#	Waste	100 gals.
Clearance	NA	Hull Type	Semi-Disp.

Insufficient Resale Data To Assign Values

Ocean Alexander Marine
Seattle, WA
www.oceanalexander.com

231-360-0827

Ocean Alexander 610 Pilothouse
1997–2003

Sure-footed pilothouse yacht with with handsome lines took Alexander luxury, quality to the next level. Spacious twin-deck floorplan includes opulent main salon, raised pilothouse with home-size galley and dinette, two double staterooms, two full heads. Second guest stateroom can be configured as office. Large engineroom is accessed via cockpit stairs. Extended flybridge can seat a small crowd. Note large cockpit, underwater exhaust system. GM 735hp—or 660hp Cat—diesels cruise at 20 knots (22–23 knots top).

Length	61'0"	Fuel	1,000 gals.
Beam	17'6"	Water	300 gals.
Draft	4'0"	Headroom	6'9"
Weight	69,300#	Hull Type	Modified-V
Clearance	NA	Deadrise Aft	NA

Insufficient Resale Data To Assign Values

Ocean Alexander Marine
Seattle, WA
www.oceanalexander.com

231-360-0827

Ocean Alexander 630 Motor Yacht
1992–2002

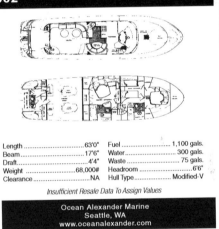

Sophisticated blend of rakish styling, leading-edge luxury made this quality pilothouse yacht a winner with 1990s buyers. Posh semicustom interior was offered in several variations over the years. Standard three-stateroom layout with galley and dinette forward is notable for spacious main salon, huge engineroom, well-appointed crew quarters aft. Seakindly hull with prop pockets delivers impressive rough-water handling. Cat 660hp diesels—or 735hp GMs—cruise at 20 knots. Called the Alexander 600 MY in 1992–93.

Length	63'0"	Fuel	1,100 gals.
Beam	17'6"	Water	300 gals.
Draft	4'4"	Waste	75 gals.
Weight	68,000#	Headroom	6'6"
Clearance	NA	Hull Type	Modified-V

Insufficient Resale Data To Assign Values

Ocean Alexander Marine
Seattle, WA
www.oceanalexander.com

231-360-0827

Ocean Alexander 64 Motor Yacht
2002–Current

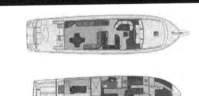

All-weather pilothouse yacht is loaded with luxury appointments experienced cruisers will appreciate. Lavish three-stateroom interior is an impressive blend of high-gloss woodwork, top-quality furnishings. Huge salon with sculpted ceiling, formal dining area rivals larger yachts for space, comfort. Gourmet galley includes dishwasher, granite counters. Additional features include stand-up engineroom, extended bridge with dinghy storage, twin transom staircases. Cruise at 20 knots with 825hp MTU diesels (22–23 knots top).

Length	69'8"	Headroom	6 5"
Beam	17'6"	Fuel	1,500 gals.
Draft	4'0"	Water	300 gals.
Weight	73,500#	Waste	100 gals.
Clearance	NA	Hull Type	Modified-V

Insufficient Resale Data To Assign Values

Ocean Alexander Marine
Seattle, WA
www.oceanalexander.com

Motoryachts & Trawlers

Offshore 48 Cockpit Motor Yacht
1985–99

231-360-0827

Sought-after cockpit yacht popular in late 1980s, 1990s delivered the right mix of style, comfort, price. Two-stateroom, galley-down floorplan with standard lower helm was available with or without dinette. Wide-open salon is big for a boat this size. Additional features include full teak interior, salon deck doors, cockpit door in aft cabin. Note wide side decks, washer/dryer in master stateroom. Swim, dive, fish from large cockpit. Cat 375hp diesels cruise at 16 knots (about 20 knots top); later models with 435hp Cats cruise at 18 knots.

Length	48'3"	Fuel	600 gals.
Beam	15'6"	Water	300 gals.
Draft	3'6"	Headroom	6'4"
Weight	41,000#	Hull Type	Modified-V
Clearance	15'2"	Deadrise Aft	11°

See Page 555 For Resale Values

Offshore Yachts
San Diego, CA
www.offshoreyachts.net

Offshore 48 Pilothouse
1999–2001

231-360-0827

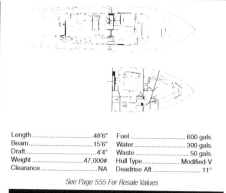

Handsome cruising yacht with conservative lines, well-planned layout offered exceptional value for the money. Spacious teak interior with raised pilothouse, main-deck galley features two large staterooms, each with en suite head. Topside highlights include roomy flybridge with tender platform, full walkaround decks, bow pulpit. Note lazarette storage locker, above-average fit and finish. Low-deadrise hull with shallow keel delivers comfortable big-water ride. Cat 420hp diesels cruise at 16 knots and reach 19–20 knots top.

Length	48'6"	Fuel	600 gals.
Beam	15'6"	Water	300 gals.
Draft	4'4"	Waste	50 gals.
Weight	47,000#	Hull Type	Modified-V
Clearance	NA	Deadrise Aft	11°

See Page 555 For Resale Values

Offshore Yachts
San Diego, CA
www.offshoreyachts.net

Offshore 48 Sedan
1987–2001

231-360-0827

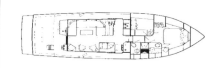

Well-bred sedan yacht introduced in 1987 delivered on Offshore promise of modern styling, comfortable accommodations. Upscale teak interior boasts roomy salon with U-shaped galley, standard lower helm, two large staterooms. Inside bridge access is rare in a boat this size. Note that both heads share common stall shower. Exterior highlights include big flybridge with tender platform, spacious cockpit, wide walkaround decks. Cat 375hp diesels cruise at 15–16 knots; later models with 420hp Cats cruise at 18–20 knots.

Length	48'6"	Fuel	600 gals.
Beam	15'6"	Water	300 gals.
Draft	3'6"	Waste	50 gals.
Weight	41,500#	Hull Type	Modified-V
Clearance	15'2"	Deadrise Aft	11°

See Page 555 For Resale Values

Offshore Yachts
San Diego, CA
www.offshoreyachts.net

Section I: Motoryachts & Trawlers

---

www.powerboatguide.com   231-360-0827

Offshore 52 Sedan
1991–99

Standard 3-Stateroom Layout

Optional 2-Stateroom Layout

Classy 1990s sedan combines spacious interior with excellent finish, seakindly hull. Teak interior was available with two- or three-stateroom layouts, both with U-shaped galley forward in salon, elevated pilothouse with centerline helm. Inside bridge access is rare in a 52-footer. Exterior features include large cockpit with transom door, protected side decks, spacious bridge with dinghy storage. Detroit 485hp diesels cruise 15 knots (about 18 knots top). Later models with 450hp Cummins— or 435hp Cats—cruise at similar speeds.

Length	52'0"	Fuel	700 gals.
Beam	16'10"	Water	400 gals.
Draft	3'10"	Waste	50 gals.
Weight	52,000#	Hull Type	Modified-V
Clearance	NA	Deadrise Aft	12°

See Page 555 For Resale Values

Offshore Yachts
San Diego, CA
www.offshoreyachts.net

---

www.powerboatguide.com   231-360-0827

Offshore 52/54 Pilothouse
1998–Current

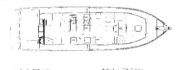

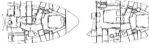

Popular pilothouse cruiser makes good on promise of upscale accommodations, meticulous finish. Teak interior is offered with choice of two- or three-stateroom layouts, both with U-shaped galley forward in salon, raised pilothouse with stairway to bridge. Topside features include covered side decks, cockpit engineroom access, large flybridge with dinghy storage. Note that Offshore 54 (pictured above) has integrated transom; 52 model has swim platform. Cummins 450hp diesels cruise at 14–15 knots; 660hp Cats cruise at 18 knots.

Length, 52	52'0"	Fuel	1,000 gals.
Length, 54	55'6"	Water	300 gals.
Beam	15'10"	Waste	70 gals.
Draft	4'6"	Hull Type	Modified-V
Weight	52,000#	Deadrise Aft	12°

See Page 555 For Resale Values

Offshore Yachts
San Diego, CA
www.offshoreyachts.net

---

www.powerboatguide.com   231-360-0827

Offshore 55/60 Pilothouse
1990–2004

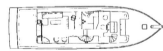

55 Pilothouse

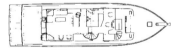

60 Pilothouse with Sport Deck

Versatile cruising yacht introduced in 1990 has well-earned reputation for quality, comfort, long-term value. Spacious three-stateroom interior boasts elegant amidships master suite, expansive salon, raised pilothouse with centerline helm, inside bridge access. Note solid teak cabinetry, concealed washer/dryer, protected side decks. Note that 55 Pilothouse (pictured above) has swim platform; 60 has integrated transom deck. Early models with 485hp Detroit 6-71s cruise at 16–17 knots; newer models with 660hp Cats cruise at 20 knots.

Length, 55	55'0'	Weight, 60	63,000#
Length, 60	59'6'	Fuel, 55	700 gals.
Beam	16'10"	Fuel, 60	1,000 gals.
Draft	5'0"	Water	400 gals.
Weight, 55	61,500#	Hull Type	Modified-V

See Page 555 For Resale Values

Offshore Yachts
San Diego, CA
www.offshoreyachts.net

Motoryachts & Trawlers

2011 PowerBoat Guide   123

www.powerboatguide.com 231-360-0827

Offshore 58/62 Pilothouse
1994–Current

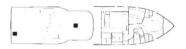

Handsome pilothouse yacht offers the space, comfort required for extended cruising. Expansive three-stateroom interior is arranged with galley forward of salon, raised pilothouse with centerline helm, twin deck doors. Luxurious full-beam master suite—with salon access—features king-size bed. Engineroom is reached via cockpit hatch. Note protected side decks, huge bridge. Beamy, low-deadrise hull delivers stable open-water ride. Detroit 550hp diesels cruise at a modest 15 knots; later models with 800hp Cats cruise at 18 knots.

Length, 58	58'0"	Fuel	1,000 gals.
Length, 62	62'6"	Water	400 gals.
Beam	16'10"	Waste	85 gals.
Draft	4'8"	Hull Type	Modified-V
Weight	65,000#	Deadrise Aft	12°

See Page 555 For Resale Values

Offshore Yachts
San Diego, CA
www.offshoreyachts.net

---

www.powerboatguide.com 231-360-0827

Pacific Mariner 65 Motor Yacht
1997–Current

Feature-rich pilothouse yacht built in Washington State is one of the better big-boat values available. Sold as fully equipped, turnkey yacht with few options. Well-appointed interior features spacious salon with panoramic views, opulent full-beam master with king bed, extended pilothouse with centerline helm. Note galley deck door, aft crew quarters, tub in master head. Upgraded "SE" version introduced in 2003 incorporates many subtle design revisions. Cat 800hp—or MTU 825hp—diesels cruise at 20 knots (25–26 knots top). Over 50 built to date.

Length	64'11"	Water	285 gals.
Beam	17'3"	Waste	110 gals.
Draft	4'9"	Headroom	6'6"
Weight	69,000#	Hull Type	Modified-V
Fuel	1,100 gals.	Deadrise Aft	10°

See Page 556 For Resale Values

Pacific Mariner
LaConner, WA
www.pacificmariner.com

---

www.powerboatguide.com 231-360-0827

Pacific Seacraft 38T Fast Trawler
1999–2002

Top-quality performance trawler with handsome styling, superb finish is loaded with personality. Luxurious two-stateroom interior with teak trim features lower helm, salon deck doors, large cabin windows, roomy aft stateroom with cockpit door. Flybridge seats six to eight on facing settees. Space for dinghy storage on cabintop. Note deep bulwarks around side decks, fold-down radar mast, boarding gates in both gunwales. Exemplary fit and finish. Twin 350hp Cats cruise at 15–16 knots and reach a top speed of about 20 knots.

Length Overall	37'6"	Fuel	320 gals.
Length WL	33'6"	Water	240 gals.
Beam	13'2"	Waste	55 gals.
Draft	3'11"	Hull Type	Modified-V
Weight	27,000#	Deadrise Aft	14°

Insufficient Resale Data To Assign Values

Pacific Seacraft Corp.
Fullerton, CA
www.pacificseacraft.com

231-360-0827

Pacific Trawler 40
2000–03

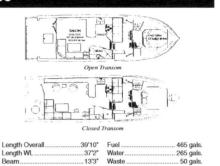

Open Transom

Closed Transom

Sturdy coastal trawler with tug-like profile combines liveaboard comfort, economical operation. First twelve were built with unique open transom with cockpit extending to end of swim platform; closed-transom model introduced in 2002 has conventional transom, slightly lengthened salon. Roomy aft-galley floorplan has head opposite galley rather than forward. Note excellent helm visibility, protected cockpit, mahogany cabin joinery, bow thruster. Single 330hp Cummins diesel will cruise at 10 knots (14–15 knots top).

Length Overall	39'10"	Fuel	465 gals.
Length WL	37'2"	Water	265 gals.
Beam	13'3"	Waste	50 gals.
Draft	4'2"	Clearance	12'6"
Weight	26,000#	Hull Type	Semi-Disp.

See Page 556 For Resale Values

No longer in business.

231-360-0827

PDQ 34 Catamaran
2000–Current

Strong-selling catamaran trawler from Canada matches great styling with outstanding economy, stable rough-water handling. Two-stateroom layout boasts huge salon with U-shaped lounge, lower helm. Galley is in portside hull; head is forward in starboard hull. Additional features include large windows, very wide side decks, roomy flybridge. Called the PDQ 32 until hulls were lengthened in 2003. Skeg protects props and rudders. Twin 75hp Yanmar diesels cruise at 13-14 knots burning 4 gallons per hour.

Length Overall	34'6"	Clearance	12'3"
Length WL	33'11"	Fuel	184 gals.
Beam	16'10"	Water	80 gals.
Draft	2'4"	Waste	38 gals.
Weight	12,000#	Hull Type	Catamaran

See Page 556 For Resale Values

PDQ Yachts
Ontario, Canada
www.pdqyachts.com

231-360-0827

Pearson 38 Double Cabin
1988–91

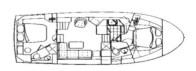

Deep-V cruiser introduced in 1988 received high marks for quality construction, exemplary fit and finish. Two-stateroom, galley-down interior is accented with satin-finished oak trim, high-end fabrics, premium furnishings. Both staterooms include walkaround double berths; both heads have separate stall showers. Additional features include well-arranged engineroom, bow pulpit, wide side decks, swim platform. Standard 320hp gas engines cruise at 16 knots cruise; optional Cat 320hp diesels cruise at 20 knots.

Length	37'9"	Fuel	300 gals.
Beam	13'10"	Water	100 gals.
Draft	3'9"	Headroom	6'4"
Weight	25,000#	Hull Type	Deep-V
Clearance	13'0"	Deadrise Aft	19°

Prices Not Provided for Pre-1995 Models

The original Pearson Yacht Company
ended operations in 1991.

Motoryachts & Trawlers

Pilgrim 40
1983–89

231-360-0827

Tug-like coastal cruiser with turn-of-the-century persona blends distinctive styling with liveaboard accommodations, efficient operation. Roomy salon with trolley-car windows boasts mahogany furnishings, big galley with in-floor storage, raised pilothouse with good visibility. Raised bulwarks provide good side deck security; extended bridge with fake stack has space for dinghy. Bow thruster was standard. Displacement hull will cruise at 8 knots (at 3 gph) with single 100hp Westerbeke diesel.

Length Overall	40'0"	Clearance	22'0"
Length WL	NA	Fuel	142 gals.
Beam	14'0"	Water	240 gals.
Draft	3'6"	Headroom	6'4"
Weight	25,000#	Hull Type	Displacement

Prices Not Provided for Pre-1995 Models

No longer in business.

Present 35 Sundeck
1982–86

231-360-0827

Popular double-cabin import combines timeless trawler profile with traditional teak interior, economical operation. Several floorplans were available, all with roomy aft cabin, port/starboard salon deck doors, parquet flooring, lower helm with deck door. Surprisingly roomy aft deck with hardtop; flybridge seating for four. Bow pulpit, swim platform, radar arch were standard. Keel protects running gear. Built by Chien Hwa in Taiwan. Cruise at 7 knots with single 135hp diesel; 8-10 knots with twin 85hp diesels.

Length Overall	34'5"	Clearance	NA
Length WL	31'6"	Fuel	300 gals.
Beam	12'0"	Water	200 gals.
Draft	4'2"	Waste	30 gals.
Weight	18,700#	Hull Type	Semi-Disp.

Prices Not Provided for Pre-1995 Models

Chung Hwa Boatbuilders
Taipei, Taiwan

Present 38 Sundeck
1981–87

231-360-0827

Sporty sundeck motoryacht (built by Nautique Marine in Taiwan) combines time-tested layout with solid construction, low-cost operation. Standard galley-down teak interior includes two double staterooms, each with en-suite head with separate stall shower. Salon with U-shaped settee is big for a 38-footer, but aft deck is smaller than most. Note serving counter overlooking galley. Big engineroom is a plus. Above-average workmanship throughout. Cruise efficiently at 12–14 knots with twin 225hp Lehman diesels (about 16 knots top).

Length Overall	38'2"	Clearance	17'6
Beam	13'3"	Fuel	300 gals.
Draft	3'4"	Water	150 gals.
Weight	21,000#	Waste	35 gals.
Headroom	6'4"	Hull Type	Semi-Disp.

Prices Not Provided for Pre-1995 Models

Chung Hwa Boatbuilders
Taipei, Taiwan

231-360-0827

Present 42 Sundeck
1984–89

Appealing 1980s sundeck yacht with contemporary styling, traditional teak interior continues to enjoy strong buyer appeal. Standard twin-stateroom layout with galley and dinette down boasts roomy master suite with space for washer/dryer, teak parquet floors, standard lower helm. Topside highlights include covered aft deck with wet bar, wide side decks, flybridge seating for six. Also marketed as CHB or Ponderosa 42. Among several engine options, twin 255 Lehman diesels cruise at 10-12 knots (about 14 knots top).

Length Overall	41'10"	Clearance	16'4"
Length WL	38'0"	Fuel	450 gals.
Beam	13'8"	Water	200 gals.
Draft	3'6"	Waste	30 gals.
Weight	26,000#	Hull Type	Semi-Disp.

Prices Not Provided for Pre-1995 Models

Chung Hwa Boatbuilders
Taipei, Taiwan

231-360-0827

Present (CHB) 46 Cockpit Motor Yacht
1984–88

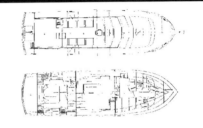

Handsome cockpit yacht (built by CHB, designed by Ed Monk) makes good on promise of cruising luxury, economical operation. Twin-stateroom layout with galley, dinette down, lower helm with sliding deck door, boasts well-appointed master suite with space for washer/dryer. Covered aft deck came standard with wing doors, wet bar. Roomy flybridge seats eight in comfort. Long keel protects running gear. Better range than most motoryachts her size. Cuise at 10 knots with Perkins 200hp diesels; 12 knots with 250hp Perkins.

Length Overall	46'3"	Headroom	6'4"
Beam	14'6"	Fuel	600 gals.
Draft	3'10"	Water	265 gals.
Weight	26,000#	Waste	50 gals.
Clearance	NA	Hull Type	Semi-Disp.

Prices Not Provided for Pre-1995 Models

Chung Hwa Boatbuilders
Taipei, Taiwan

231-360-0827

President 41 Double Cabin
1982–87

Twin Beds in Master

Double Berth in Master

Popular Taiwan import with full teak interior, modest price became one of the best-selling boats of her type during the 1980s. Offered with two- or three-stateroom layouts, all with large forward staterooms, booth-style dinette, standard lower helm. Good cabin storage. One of the more efficient boats of her type. Over 120 were built making this President's best-selling model during the 1980s. Twin 120/135hp Lehman diesels provide 8-knot cruising speed. Larger 225hp Lehmans cruise at 12 knots (15-16 knots top).

Length Overall	40'6"	Clearance	NA
Length WL	35'10"	Fuel	420 gals.
Beam	13'5"	Water	120 gals.
Draft	2'10"	Hull Type	Modified-V
Weight	22,500#	Deadrise Aft	14°

Prices Not Provided for Pre-1995 Models

President Yachts, Taiwan
www.presidentyachts.com

Motoryachts & Trawlers

---

www.powerboatguide.com   231-360-0827

President 43 Double Cabin
1984–90

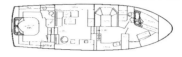

Value-priced motoryacht imported during late 1980s combined lavish teak interior with pleasing lines, economical operation. Twin-stateroom floorplan with galley/dinette down is notable for expansive salon, generous storage. Lower helm was optional. Teak-laid aft deck came standard with hardtop, wet bar. Additional features include large engineroom, wide side decks, radar arch, bow pulpit, teak swim platform. Twin 275hp Lehmans cruise at 15 knots and reach a top speed of 17–18 knots. A total of 42 were built.

Length Overall	42'6"	Clearance	12'4"
Length WL	37'10"	Water	120 gals.
Beam	13'10"	Fuel	420 gals.
Draft	3'2"	Hull Type	Modified-V
Weight	28,000#	Deadrise Aft	NA

Prices Not Provided for Pre-1995 Models

President Yachts, Taiwan
www.presidentyachts.com

---

www.powerboatguide.com   231-360-0827

PT 35 Sundeck
1984–90

Galley Up Layout

Galley Down Layout

Generic 1980s Taiwan cruiser made good on promise of solid construction, affordable price. Available with two floorplans: galley-up layout features huge forward stateroom; galley-down arrangement opens up salon with increased seating possibilities. Standard features included teak interior joinery, lower helm, salon deck doors. Note roomy full-beam afterdeck. Solid fiberglass hull has shallow keel for directional stability. Single 200hp Perkins will cruise efficiently at 8–9 knots. Twin-diesel models can reach 18–20 knots top.

Length Overall	35'4"	Weight	20,000#
Length WL	31'10"	Fuel	300 gals.
Beam	12'6"	Water	100 gals.
Draft	3'0"	Hull Type	Modified-V
Clearance	NA	Deadrise Aft	NA

Prices Not Provided for Pre-1995 Models

No longer in business.

---

www.powerboatguide.com   231-360-0827

PT 38 Double Cabin
1980–85

Traditional 1980s trawler with roomy accommodations gave budget-minded owners good value for the money. Full teak interior with deckhouse galley features two roomy staterooms, standard lower helm, generous storage. Large cabin windows offer panoramic views. Note spacious engine compartment. Lots of exterior teak means lots of maintenance. Semi-displacement hull features shallow keel for directional stability. Single 120hp diesel will cruise at 7–8 knots; twin 120hp Lehmans (or 135hp Perkins) diesels cruise at 10 knots.

Length Overall	37'6"	Clearance	NA
Length WL	31.5'	Fuel	300 gals.
Beam	13'6"	Water	150 gals.
Draft	3'6"	Waste	50 gals.
Weight (Approx.)	25,000#	Hull Type	Semi-Disp.

Prices Not Provided for Pre-1995 Models

No longer in business.

www.powerboatguide.com   231-360-0827

PT 38 Sedan
1980–85

Handsome 1980s sedan combined classic Europa styling with versatile interior, rugged construction. Full teak interior with big U-shaped galley features two roomy staterooms, standard lower helm, generous storage. Large cabin windows offer panoramic views. Note spacious engine compartment. Lots of exterior teak means lots of maintenance. Semi-displacement hull features shallow keel for directional stability. Single 120hp diesel will cruise at 7–8 knots; twin 120hp Lehmans (or 135hp Perkins) diesels cruise at 10 knots.

Length Overall	37'6"	Clearance	NA
Length WL	31'5"	Fuel	300 gals.
Beam	13'6"	Water	150 gals.
Draft	3'6"	Waste	50 gals.
Weight (Approx.)	25,000#	Hull Type	Semi-Disp.

Prices Not Provided for Pre-1995 Models

No longer in business.

---

www.powerboatguide.com   231-360-0827

PT 41 Double Cabin
1978–85

Sturdy trawler (built by CHB in Taiwan) with total-teak interior is designed for economical coastal cruising in comfort, security. Several two-stateroom interiors were offered—most have U-shaped galley aft in salon. Notable features include port/starboard salon deck doors, teak parquet flooring, tub/shower in aft head, fold-down mast. Teak-over-fiberglass decks, flybridge and cabintop. Teak interior is too dark for some. Built by CHB Marine in Taiwan. Twin 120hp Lehman diesels cruise at 7–8 knots (about 10 knots top).

Length Overall	41'0"	Clearance	NA
Length WL	34'0"	Fuel	300 gals.
Beam	13'6"	Water	150 gals.
Draft	3'6"	Waste	40 gals.
Weight (Approx.)	30,000#	Hull Type	Semi-Disp.

Prices Not Provided for Pre-1995 Models

No longer in business.

---

www.powerboatguide.com   231-360-0827

PT 42 Cockpit MY
1984–90

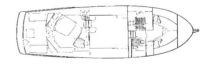

Versatile 1980s cockpit yacht with contemporary lines, traditional teak interior combined roomy accommodations with low-maintenance ownership. Conventional two-stateroom floorplan with galley down features expansive salon with built-in dinette, lower helm, twin deck doors. Galley is on the small side, but storage is excellent. Cockpit makes boarding easy; full-width aft deck is a good entertainment platform. Transom door was standard. Twin 225hp diesels cruise at 14–15 knots (about 17 knots top).

Length Overall	42'0"	Clearance	NA
Length WL	38'3"	Fuel	300 gals.
Beam	13'6"	Water	150 gals.
Draft	3'6"	Hull Type	Modified-V
Weight	25,000#	Deadrise Aft	NA

Prices Not Provided for Pre-1995 Models

No longer in business.

Motoryachts & Trawlers

231-360-0827

PT 46 Sundeck
1985–90

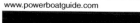
Three-Stateroom Interior

Two-Stateroom Interior

Good-looking 1980s import meets cruiser's need for comfortable accommodations, versatile layout, economical operation. Offered with several two- and three-stateroom interiors over the years, all with quality teak cabinets, generous storage, tasteful furnishings. Highlights include roomy salon with standard lower helm, spacious fore and aft staterooms, two full heads. Wide side decks are a plus. Radar arch, hardtop, bow pulpit, swim platform were standard. Cummins 270hp diesels cruise at 16 knots (18–20 knots top).

Length	46'4"	Fuel	600 gals.
Beam	15'9"	Water	200 gals.
Draft	3'8"	Waste	40 gals.
Weight	31,500#	Hull Type	Modified-V
Clearance	NA	Deadrise Aft	NA

Prices Not Provided for Pre-1995 Models

No longer in business.

231-360-0827

PT 52 Cockpit MY
1986–90

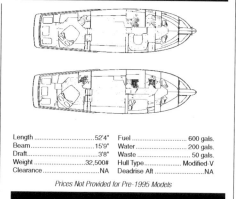

Cockpit version of PT 46 Sundeck combines clean-cut profile with versatile layout, durable construction. Offered with several two- and three-stateroom interiors over the years, all with generous cabin storage, classy teak-and-holly salon sole, sliding deck access door. Topside features include roomy aft deck, radar arch, transom door, swim platform. Fish, swim, or dive from large cockpit. No exterior teak means less maintenance. Cummins 270hp diesels cruise at 16 knots and top out at 19–20 knots.

Length	52'4"	Fuel	600 gals.
Beam	15'9"	Water	200 gals.
Draft	3'8"	Waste	50 gals.
Weight	32,500#	Hull Type	Modified-V
Clearance	NA	Deadrise Aft	NA

Prices Not Provided for Pre-1995 Models

No longer in business.

231-360-0827

Ranger R-29 Tug
2009–Current

Sturdy coastal cruiser with classic tugboat lines is salty, roomy, easy on the fuel. Highlights include nicely-appointed interior with two staterooms, roomy cockpit with transom door, bow and stern thrusters, seaworthy semi-displacement hull. Midship berth, beneath raised dinette, has privacy door. Note large cabin windows, opening hatches over helm and companion seats. Slender sidedecks aren't for use under way—foredeck is best accessed via sliding pilothouse door. Cruise at 15 knots (20+ top) with single 260hp Yanmar diesel.

Length	29'0"	Fuel	150 gals.
Beam	10'0"	Water	70 gals.
Draft	2'4"	Waste	40 gals.
Weight	9,250#	Hull Type	Seemi-Disp.
Clearance	NA	Deadrise Aft	NA

Insufficient Resale Data To Assign Values

Ranger Tugs
Kent, WA
www.rangertugs.com

www.powerboatguide.com   231-360-0827

Roughwater 41
1973–85

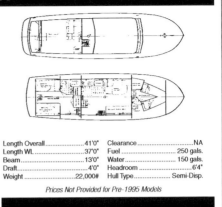

Taiwan-built cruiser with vintage lines enjoys enduring appeal with many yachting enthusiasts. Flush-deck layout features semi-enclosed pilothouse, roomy salon with large windows, fully equipped galley, convertible settee. Aft stateroom has twin beds, cockpit door. Note cavernous storage area under galley sole. Originally built with teak decks and plywood superstructure, construction became all fiberglass in 1982. Deep keel protects props in event of grounding. Perkins 185hp diesels cruise at 8–9 knots (about 12 knots top).

Length Overall	41'0"	Clearance	NA
Length WL	37'0"	Fuel	250 gals.
Beam	13'0"	Water	150 gals.
Draft	4'0"	Headroom	6'4"
Weight	22,000#	Hull Type	Semi-Disp.

Prices Not Provided for Pre-1995 Models

No longer in business.

---

www.powerboatguide.com   231-360-0827

Roughwater 42
1986–89

Updated version of the Roughwater 41 (1973–85) features improved styling, increased power. Efficient semi-displacement hull with slender beam has long, prop-protecting keel. Roomy salon with large windows houses fully equipped galley, dinette, convertible settee. Aft stateroom has queen bed, cockpit access door. Note cavernous storage area under galley sole. Excellent visibility from semi-enclosed pilothouse. Cruise at 12 knots with twin 220hp GM diesels (15–16 knots top). Last Roughwater model before company ceased business in 1989.

Length Overall	42'0"	Clearance	NA
Length WL	38'0"	Fuel	300 gals.
Beam	13'6"	Water	150 gals.
Draft	3'11"	Headroom	6'5"
Weight	24,500#	Hull Type	Semi-Disp.

Prices Not Provided for Pre-1995 Models

No longer in business.

---

www.powerboatguide.com   231-360-0827

Sabre 34 Sedan
1991–2002

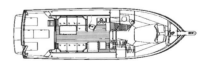

Luxury-class performance trawler with many quality features gets high marks for impressive build quality, strong resale value. Traditional teak (or cherry) interior with U-shaped galley, lower helm offers near ideal accommodations for the cruising couple. Highlights include large cabin windows, convertible dinette, separate stall shower, teak-and-holly cabin sole. Wide side decks make getting around easy. Transom door, radar mast were standard. Twin Cummins 220hp diesels cruise at 15–16 knots (about 20 knots top).

Length w/Pulpit	37'6"	Fuel	250 gals.
Hull Length	34'0"	Water	160 gals.
Beam	12'6"	Waste	25 gals.
Draft	3'3"	Hull Type	Modified-V
Weight	17,800#	Deadrise Aft	14°

See Page 561 For Resale Values

**Sabre Yachts
South Casco, ME
www.sabreyachts.com**

Motoryachts & Trawlers

231-360-0827

Sabre 36 Aft Cabin
1989–98

Quality double-cabin cruiser combines traditional trawler styling with luxury-class accommodations, spirited performance. Deluxe interior with teak or cherry joinery features expansive galley, twin salon deck doors, large cabin windows, teak-and-holly salon sole. Aft stateroom offered choice of twin berths (one double, one single) or optional double berth. Wide side decks, well-placed handrails make getting around easy. Underwater exhaust is a plus. Cat 255hp diesels cruise at 16 knots (20 top); 300hp Cats cruise at 18 knots (23-24 top).

Length w/Pulpit	40'1"	Fuel	300 gals.
Hull Length	36'0"	Water	225 gals.
Beam	12'6"	Waste	40 gals.
Draft	4'3"	Hull Type	Modified-V
Weight	20,000#	Deadrise Aft	14°

See Page 561 For Resale Values

Sabre Yachts
South Casco, ME
www.sabreyachts.com

231-360-0827

Sabre 36 Sedan
2002–07

Quality-built flybridge cruiser set class standards in her day for comfort, craftsmanship, performance. Spacious single-stateroom interior with cherry-wood joinery, expansive salon is finely finished, tastefully appointed. Highlights include spacious stateroom, sliding salon deck door, teak-and-holly cabin sole, large salon windows. Cockpit wet bar, transom door, radar mast, swim platform are standard. Wide side deck, large engineroom are a plus. Expect a cruising speed of 25–26 knots with optional 370hp Yanmar diesels (about 30 knots top).

Length	36'0"	Fuel	300 gals.
Beam	12'6"	Water	100 gals.
Draft	3'4"	Waste	30 gals.
Weight	19,500#	Hull Type	Modified-V
Clearance, Mast	19'0"	Deadrise Aft	18°

See Page 561 For Resale Values

Sabre Yachts
South Casco, ME
www.sabreyachts.com

231-360-0827

Sabre 42 Sedan
2001–Current

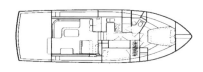

Stately Downeast sedan with beautifully appointed interior defines cruising elegance, traditional Maine craftsmanship. Lavish cherrywood interior with wide-open salon features standard lower helm, teak-and-holly cabin sole, two large staterooms, generous storage. Note that guest cabin is fitted with double French doors. Additional features include cockpit wet bar, radar mast, Sub-zero galley refrigeration, spacious engineroom, wide side decks, swim platform. Yanmar 465hp diesels cruise at 24 knots (28–29 knots top).

Length	42'3"	Fuel	450 gals.
Beam	14'4"	Water	160 gals.
Draft	3'9"	Waste	60 gals.
Weight	30,000#	Hull Type	Modified-V
Headroom	6'6"	Deadrise Aft	16°

See Page 561 For Resale Values

Sabre Yachts
South Casco, ME
www.sabreyachts.com

231-360-0827

Sabre 43 Aft Cabin
1996–2005

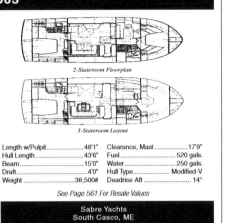

2-Stateroom Floorplan

3-Stateroom Layout

Spacious double-cabin cruising yacht courted affluent buyers with classic styling, lavish accommodations, excellent performance. Offered with two- or three-stateroom interiors, both with lower helm, salon deck doors, large master cabin, two full heads. Features include teak interior cabinetry, full walkaround decks, foredeck storage lockers, radar mast, roomy flybridge. Note convenient cockpit access door in master stateroom. Twin 370hp Yanmar diesels cruise at 15–16 knots (about 20 knots top).

Length w/Pulpit	48'1"	Clearance, Mast	17'9"
Hull Length	43'6"	Fuel	520 gals.
Beam	15'0"	Water	250 gals.
Draft	4'0"	Hull Type	Modified-V
Weight	38,500#	Deadrise Aft	14°

See Page 561 For Resale Values

Sabre Yachts
South Casco, ME
www.sabreyachts.com

231-360-0827

Sabre 47 Aft Cabin
1997–2007

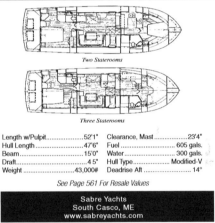

Two Staterooms

Three Staterooms

Lengthened version of popular Sabreline 43 Aft Cabin (previous entry) boasts enlarged aft stateroom, bigger cockpit. Offered with two- or three-stateroom floorplans, both with lower helm, home-size galley, two full heads. Teak interior cabinetry is beautifully finished. Topside features include full walkaround decks, folding radar mast, spacious bridge with L-shaped dinette aft. Note side exhausts, cockpit door in master stateroom. Cabintop can stow a dinghy. Yanmar 500hp diesels cruise at 18 knots (about 22 top).

Length w/Pulpit	52'1"	Clearance, Mast	23'4"
Hull Length	47'6"	Fuel	605 gals.
Beam	15'0"	Water	300 gals.
Draft	4'5"	Hull Type	Modified-V
Weight	43,000#	Deadrise Aft	14°

See Page 561 For Resale Values

Sabre Yachts
South Casco, ME
www.sabreyachts.com

231-360-0827

Sea Ranger 36 Sundeck
1979–86

Generic Taiwan sundeck cruiser (built by C&L Marine) appealed to 1980s buyers with an eye for value. Highlights include full teak interior, large owner's cabin, excellent storage, wide side decks. Note split aft head with shower to starboard, toilet to port. Galley-up layout results in roomy salon with convertible settee, teak-and-holly sole. Good lower helm visibility. Forward head is very small. Bow pulpit, swim platform, radar mast were standard. Note large aft deck. Twin 120hp Ford Lehman diesels cruise economically at 8–10 knots.

Length Overall	35'8"	Clearance	NA
Length WL	30'10"	Fuel	300 gals.
Beam	13'4"	Water	150 gals.
Draft	3'3"	Headroom	6'4"
Weight	19,000#	Hull Type	Semi-Disp.

Prices Not Provided for Pre-1995 Models

Sea Ranger yachts are no longer produced.

Motoryachts & Trawlers

231-360-0827

Sea Ranger 39 Sundeck
1980–89

Sturdy 1980s aft-cabin trawler combined heavy construction with practical accommodations, efficient operation. Two-stateroom interior with deckhouse galley boasts huge owner's cabin with built-in desk, tremendous storage. Lower helm position was standard; L-shaped dinette in salon converts to large double berth. Note bathtub in aft head. Teak window frames are prone to leaks. Full-length keel offers prop protection in event of grounding. Lehman 120hp diesels—or 124hp Volvos—cruise at 7–8 knots.

Length Overall	38'3"	Clearance	NA
Length WL	33'4"	Fuel	600 gals.
Beam	13'8"	Water	150 gals.
Draft	3'3"	Headroom	6'4"
Weight	23,000#	Hull Type	Semi-Disp.

Prices Not Provided for Pre-1995 Models

Sea Ranger yachts are no longer produced.

231-360-0827

Sea Ranger 45 Aft Cabin
1982–89

Galley Up, Three Staterooms

Galley Down, Two Staterooms

Contemporary 1980s sundeck yacht (also sold as the C&L 45) pairs heavy construction with seakindly hull, roomy accommodations. While galley-down floorplan was available, most were delivered with three-stateroom layout - rare in a 45-foot boat. Highlights include full teak interior, large engineroom, stall showers in both heads. Afterdeck is among largest in her class. Cruise at 12–14 knots with 255hp Volvo diesels (16 top); 16–18 knots with 375hp Cats (20+ top).

Length	45'0"	Headroom	6.5"
Beam	15'3"	Fuel	850 gals.
Draft	4'0"	Water	350 gals.
Weight	37,400#	Waste	60 gals.
Clearance	NA	Hull Type	Semi-Disp.

Prices Not Provided for Pre-1995 Models

Sea Ranger yachts are no longer produced.

231-360-0827

Sea Ranger 46 Sundeck
1985–89

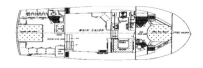

Heavily built Taiwan import from late 1980s offered compelling mix of space, comfort, affordability. Standard two-stateroom, galley-down interior includes fore, aft double berths, roomy salon with entertainment center, large aft deck with wing doors, party-sized flybridge. Note split forward head with shower stall to port. Additional features include generous storage, large engineroom, lower helm deck door, wide side decks. Volvo 255hp engines cruise efficiently at 12–14 knots (around 18 knots top).

Length	46'0"	Fuel	850 gals.
Beam	15'4"	Water	350 gals.
Draft	4'0"	Waste	45 gals.
Weight	40,000#	Headroom	6.5"
Clearance	NA	Hull Type	Semi-Disp.

Prices Not Provided for Pre-1995 Models

Sea Ranger yachts are no longer produced.

231-360-0827

Sea Ranger 47 Pilothouse
1980–87

Appealing pilothouse yacht (built by C&L in Taiwan) blurs the line between sturdy coastal cruiser, feature-packed liveaboard. Roomy interior with three staterooms, two full heads boasts roomy salon with galley forward, raised pilothouse with watchberth. Note spacious walk-in engineroom. Topside highlights include protected side decks, teak swim platform, cabintop dinghy platform. Salon day head was optional. Solid fiberglass hull has long, prop-protecting keel. Lehman 135hp—or GM 175hp—diesels cruise cruise at 7–8 knots.

Length Overall	47'3"	Clearance	20'7"
Length WL	43'0"	Fuel	720 gals.
Beam	15'2"	Water	360 gals.
Draft	4'4"	Waste	50 gals.
Weight	43,000#	Hull Type	Semi-Disp.

Prices Not Provided for Pre-1995 Models

Sea Ranger yachts are no longer produced.

231-360-0827

Sea Ranger 51 Motor Yacht
1983–89

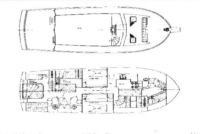

Asian-built motoryacht from late 1980s offered affordable alternative to more expensive choices from Hatteras, Viking, Ocean, etc. Highlights include full teak interior, walk-through engineroom, walkaround side decks, commanding flybridge. Lower helm is open to salon for good aft visibility. Side decks are sheltered with bridge overhangs. Teak decks are a plus. Note molded bow seating. Cat 260hp diesels cruise at 12 knots (14 knots top); GM 650hp 8V92s cruise at 15–16 knots (18+ knots top).

Length Overall	51'0"	Clearance	NA
Length WL	45'0"	Fuel	1,000 gals.
Beam	16'8"	Water	420 gals.
Draft	4'3"	Headroom	6'6"
Weight	55,000#	Hull Type	Semi-Disp.

Prices Not Provided for Pre-1995 Models

Sea Ranger yachts are no longer produced.

231-360-0827

Sea Ranger 52 Cockpit Motor Yacht
1985–89

Versatile 1980s cockpit yacht (built by C&L in Taiwan) made good on Sea Ranger promise of versatility, comfort, owner satisfaction. Standard two-stateroom interior boasts huge owner's suite (with cockpit door), booth-style dinette, home-sized galley. Note good lower-helm visibility, handcrafted teak woodwork. Full-width aft deck, roomy bridge can entertain a small crowd. Most were delivered with optional wing doors, hardtop. Among several engine options, Volvo 255hp diesels cruise at 13–14 knots (16–18 top).

Length	52'0"	Fuel	850 gals.
Beam	15'4"	Water	350 gals.
Draft	4'0"	Waste	50 gals.
Weight	44,000#	Headroom	6'5"
Clearance	NA	Hull Type	Semi-Disp.

Prices Not Provided for Pre-1995 Models

Sea Ranger yachts are no longer produced.

Motoryachts & Trawlers

231-360-0827

Sea Ray 360 Aft Cabin
1983–87

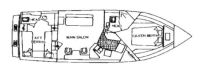

Shapely aft-cabin cruiser with innovative cabin layout offered rakish styling, comfortable accommodations at an affordable price. Teak-trimmed interior is uniquely arranged with master stateroom forward, guest cabin with single berths aft—very unusual indeed. Large galley boasts upright refrigerator, teak parquet floor. Lower helm was a popular option. Aft head is tiny; forward head has separate stall shower. Good lower helm visibility. Standard 260hp gas engines (or optional 200hp Perkins diesels) cruise at 15-16 knots.

Length	36'3"	Fuel	270 gals.
Beam	12'6"	Water	120 gals.
Draft	2'11"	Waste	40 gals.
Weight	15,100#	Hull Type	Modified-V
Clearance	NA	Deadrise Aft	9°

Prices Not Provided for Pre-1995 Models

Sea Ray Boats
Knoxville, TN
www.searay.com

231-360-0827

Sea Ray 370/380 Aft Cabin
1997–2001

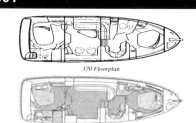

370 Floorplan

380 Layout

Beamy aft-cabin cruiser made the cut with late 1990s Sea Ray buyers seeking condo-style accommodations in a sporty package. Well-appointed interior boasts expansive salon with L-shaped sofa, two roomy staterooms, generous storage. Mini-stateroom opposite galley can be configured as utility room. Aft deck has wet bar and wing doors. Engineroom is a tight fit. Hull is fully cored. MerCruiser 380hp gas inboards cruise at 20 knots (about 30 knots top); 340hp Cat diesels cruise at 20 knots (22–23 knots top).

Length	38'2"	Fuel	300 gals.
Beam	14'3"	Water	100 gals.
Draft	3'1"	Waste	55 gals.
Weight	23,800#	Hull Type	Deep-V
Clearance, Arch	16'4"	Deadrise Aft	19.5°

See Page 563 For Resale Values

Sea Ray Boats
Knoxville, TN
www.searay.com

231-360-0827

Sea Ray 380 Aft Cabin
1989–91

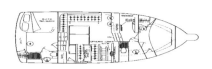

Tasteful double-cabin cruiser paired contemporary styling with feature-packed accommodations, secure handling characteristics. Comfortable galley-down interior includes open salon with dinette, breakfast bar, vanities in both staterooms, home-size refrigerator. Wide side decks afford secure bow access. Radar arch, hardtop were standard. Lower helm station was optional. Standard 340hp gas inboards cruise at 16 knots (mid 20s top); optional 330hp Cummins diesels cruise at 20 knots.

Length w/Pulpit	42'7"	Fuel	300 gals.
Hull Length	37'9"	Water	100 gals.
Beam	13'11"	Waste	40 gals.
Draft	2'7"	Hull Type	Deep-V
Weight	20,000#	Deadrise Aft	19°

Prices Not Provided for Pre-1995 Models

Sea Ray Boats
Knoxville, TN
www.searay.com

231-360-0827

Sea Ray 390 Motoryacht; 40 MY
2003–07

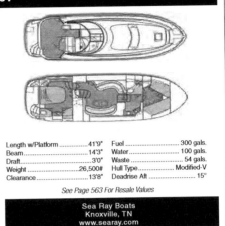

Distinctive hardtop motoryacht (called Sea Ray 390 MY in 2003–05; 40 MY in 2006–07) blends traditional flushdeck design with sleek styling, maxi-volume interior. Upscale interior with cherry cabinets boasts expansive salon with facing settees, well-appointed staterooms, space for optional washer/dryer. Galley enjoys good natural lighting from window above. Flushdeck layout keeps the skipper with guests rather than isolated on the flybridge. Gas 370hp engines cruise at 18 knots; Cummins 446hp diesels cruise at 20 knots.

Length w/Platform	41'9"	Fuel	300 gals.
Beam	14'3"	Water	100 gals.
Draft	3'0"	Waste	54 gals.
Weight	26,500#	Hull Type	Modified-V
Clearance	13'8"	Deadrise Aft	15°

See Page 563 For Resale Values

Sea Ray Boats
Knoxville, TN
www.searay.com

231-360-0827

Sea Ray 410/415/440 Aft Cabin
1986–91

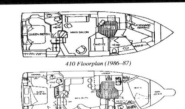

410 Floorplan (1986–87)

415/440 Floorplan (1988–89)

Good-selling aft cabin yacht (called the 410 Aft Cabin in 1986-87; 415 AC in 1988; 440 in 1989-91) offered good blend of style, comfort, performance at a reasonable price. Space-efficient interior boasts open salon with breakfast bar and dinette, large galley with upright refrigerator, comfortable staterooms, optional lower helm. Rakish Sea Ray styling kept this boat popular with buyers for many years. Standard 330hp gas engines cruise at 15 knots; 364hp Cat diesels cruise at 20 knots.

Length w/Pulpit	45'11"	Fuel	400 gals.
Hull Length	43'6"	Water	130 gals.
Beam	13'11"	Waste	40 gals.
Draft	3'2"	Hull Type	Modified-V
Weight	23,000#	Deadrise Aft	17°

Prices Not Provided for Pre-1995 Models

Sea Ray Boats
Knoxville, TN
www.searay.com

231-360-0827

Sea Ray 420 Aft Cabin
1996–2002

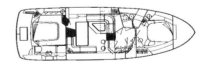

Sporty styling, spirited performance, innovative interior set this stylish aft-cabin yacht a step ahead of her late 1990s competitors. Upscale interior with large staterooms, home-size galley includes mini-stateroom—or optional laundry room—extending under salon sole. Topside features include aft-deck wing doors, transom storage locker, extended swim platform. Wide walkways provide good bow access. Hull is fully cored. Twin 420hp Cat (or 430hp Cummins) diesels cruise in the mid 20s (27–28 knots top).

Length	45'5"	Fuel	350 gals.
Beam	14'3"	Water	120 gals.
Draft	3'1"	Waste	55 gals.
Weight	27,000#	Hull Type	Deep-V
Clearance	15'6"	Deadrise Aft	18.5°

See Page 563 For Resale Values

Sea Ray Boats
Knoxville, TN
www.searay.com

Motoryachts & Trawlers

Motoryachts & Trawlers

Sea Ray 420/44 Sedan Bridge
2004–09

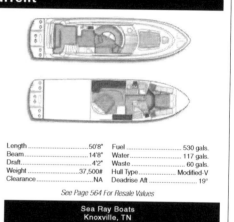

Handsome flybridge yacht with best-in-class styling gets high marks for deluxe accommodations, top-quality construction. Posh two-stateroom interior with cherry cabinets includes raised salon dinette with panoramic outside views, large master stateroom, guest cabin with twin berths, two full heads. Large flybridge with excellent helm position. Washer/dryer is under galley steps. Called 420 Sedan Bridge in 2004–05; 44 SB in 2006–09. Cummins 478hp diesels cruise in the mid 20s (about 30 knots top).

Length Overall	45'5"	Fuel	350 gals.
Beam	14'3"	Water	120 gals.
Draft	3'6"	Waste	42 gals.
Weight	28,500#	Hull Type	Modified-V
Clearance	NA	Deadrise Aft	18°

See Page 563 For Resale Values

Sea Ray Boats
Knoxville, TN
www.searay.com

Sea Ray 47 Sedan Bridge
2008–Current

Luxurious sport yacht with sweeping lines, executive-class amenities is more than just a pretty face. Innovative floorplan with split-level salon has the galley aft, raised dinette and settee forward. Flip-up window in salon bulkhead provides easy pass-thru to cockpit. Party-time flybridge,—accessed via wide bridge steps—includes wet bar, lounge seating. Premium decor with cherry woodwork, leather seating is state of the art. Hardtop is standard. Standard Cummins 600hp V-drive diesels cruise at 25 knots (about 28–30 top).

Length	50'8"	Fuel	530 gals.
Beam	14'8"	Water	117 gals.
Draft	4'2"	Waste	60 gals.
Weight	37,500#	Hull Type	Modified-V
Clearance	NA	Deadrise Aft	19°

See Page 564 For Resale Values

Sea Ray Boats
Knoxville, TN
www.searay.com

Sea Ray 480 Motor Yacht
2002–05

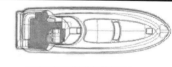

Versatile hardtop yacht with rare flushdeck layout is rich in thoughtful features, luxurious amenities. Combined helm/aft-deck platform allows owner and guests lots of room to move around. Wide-open salon with cherry cabinets features posh U-shaped lounge, full dinette, step-down galley. Small mid-cabin beneath salon sole has twin berths. Note washer/dryer combo under galley steps. Engineroom is a tight fit. Cummins 535hp diesels cruise in the low 20s; optional 640hp Cats cruise in the mid 20s.

Length w/Platform	50'5"	Fuel	500 gals.
Beam	15'3"	Water	120 gals.
Draft	3'11"	Waste	60 gals.
Weight	38,500#	Hull Type	Modified-V
Clearance	15'0"	Deadrise Aft	15°

See Page 564 For Resale Values

Sea Ray Boats
Knoxville, TN
www.searay.com

231-360-0827

Sea Ray 480 Sedan Bridge
1998–2004

Popular flybridge yacht with expansive three-stateroom interior enjoys continued appeal with buyers. Highlights include well-arranged salon with raised dinette, spacious master stateroom with entertainment center, stall showers in both heads, roomy flybridge with centerline helm, extended swim platform. Washer/dryer is located in starboard guest stateroom. Wide side decks are a plus. Power salon sofa converts to double bed. Detroit 535hp diesels cruise in the low 20s; 640hp Cats will cruise in the high 20s.

Length w/Platform	51'2"	Fuel	500 gals.
Beam	15'3"	Water	140 gals.
Draft	3'9"	Waste	68 gals.
Weight	40,400#	Hull Type	Modified-V
Clearance	NA	Deadrise Aft	15°

See Page 564 For Resale Values

Sea Ray Boats
Knoxville, TN
www.searay.com

231-360-0827

Sea Ray 500 Sedan Bridge
1990–95

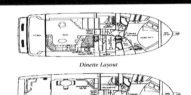

Dinette Layout

Lower Helm Layout

Onetime Sea Ray flagship combines enduring styling with spacious interior, deluxe amenities, good open-water performance. Appealing three-stateroom layout with wide-open salon boasts large owner's stateroom, full dinette, breakfast bar, concealed washer/dryer (beneath salon floor). Party-time flybridge can entertain a dozen guests. Transom door, radar arch, bow pulpit were standard. Large salon results in a fairly small cockpit. GM 550hp diesels cruise at 20 knots; 735hp GMs cruise in the high 20s (low 30s top).

Length w/Platform	55'4"	Fuel	600 gals.
Hull length	49'11	Water	200 gals.
Beam	15'0"	Waste	40 gals.
Draft	4'2"	Hull Type	Modified-V
Weight	40,000#	Deadrise Aft	17°

See Page 564 For Resale Values

Sea Ray Boats
Knoxville, TN
www.searay.com

231-360-0827

Sea Ray 500/52 Sedan Bridge
2005–Current

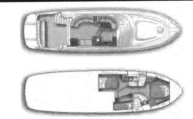

Elegant sport sedan (called the 500 Sedan Bridge in 2005; 52 Sedan Bridge thereafter) appeals to upscale buyers with an eye for classy styling, roomy accommodations, spirited performance. Three-stateroom, two-head interior with cherry cabinets boasts large salon with dinette forward, gourmet galley, two double staterooms. Utility room under galley sole houses washer/dryer. Flybridge with fridge seats a small crowd. Extended swim platform can support a small tender. Cruise at 24–26 knots with 660hp Cummins diesels.

Length w/Platform	57'1"	Fuel	500 gals.
Beam	15'3"	Water	140 gals.
Draft	4'2"	Waste	68 gals.
Weight	40,267#	Hull Type	Modified-V
Clearance	15'8"	Deadrise Aft	15°

Insufficient Resale Data To Assign Values

Sea Ray Boats
Knoxville, TN
www.searay.com

Motoryachts & Trawlers

www.powerboatguide.com   231-360-0827

Sea Ray 540 Cockpit MY
2001–02

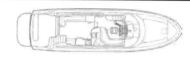

Limited production flybridge yacht with enormous bridge, well-appointed interior offered executive-class luxury, comfort, versatility. Spacious bi-level salon features wraparound dinette (or optional lower helm) forward, galley with under-counter refrigeration, posh leather seating. Note inside bridge access ladder; washer/dryer in master stateroom. Flybridge dinette converts electrically into double sun pad. Extended swim platform was optional. Standard 640hp Cat diesels cruise at 20 knots (around 25 knots top).

Length w/Platform	54'0"	Fuel	800 gals.
Hull Length	50'6"	Water	200 gals.
Beam	15'6"	Waste	68 gals.
Draft	4'9"	Hull Type	Modified-V
Weight	49,000#	Deadrise Aft	18°

See Page 564 For Resale Values

Sea Ray Boats
Knoxville, TN
www.searay.com

---

www.powerboatguide.com   231-360-0827

Sea Ray 550 Sedan Bridge
1992–98

Dinette Floorplan

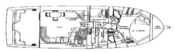

Lower Helm Floorplan

Stretched version of Sea Ray 500 Sedan Bridge (1989–95) adds much-needed cockpit space to an otherwise well-rounded yacht. Standard three-stateroom layout includes large owner's stateroom, dinette, breakfast bar, under-counter refrigeration, washer/dryer. Huge flybridge seats a small crowd. Transom door, radar arch, bow pulpit were standard. One of Sea Ray's most popular models. Portside lower helm was optional. Hull is fully cored. Twin 635hp Detroits cruise in the mid 20s; 776hp Cats cruise in the high 20s.

Length Overall	57'10"	Fuel	700 gals.
Hull Length	54'10"	Water	200 gals.
Beam	15'0"	Waste	40 gals.
Draft	4'2"	Hull Type	Modified-V
Weight	45,000#	Deadrise Aft	17°

See Page 564 For Resale Values

Sea Ray Boats
Knoxville, TN
www.searay.com

---

www.powerboatguide.com   231-360-0827

Sea Ray 560 Sedan Bridge
1998–2005

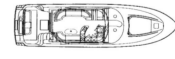

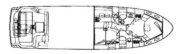

Handsome sedan yacht with seemingly endless list of amenities matched the best European imports for luxury, comfort, performance. Highlights include spacious three-stateroom, two-head cherry interior, large cockpit with foldaway seating, party-time flybridge with wraparound helm and hardtop. Extended swim platform can hold PWC or dinghy. Cockpit has livewell, fish box. Marketed as the 550 Sedan Bridge in 2006. Hull is fully cored. Cat 640hp diesels cruise at 22–23 knots; 1,050hp MANs cruise at 28–30 knots.

Length	58'6"	Fuel	800 gals.
Beam	16'0"	Water	200 gals.
Draft	4'6"	Waste	68 gals.
Weight	50,000#	Hull Type	Modified-V
Clearance	NA	Deadrise Aft	15°

See Page 564 For Resale Values

Sea Ray Boats
Knoxville, TN
www.searay.com

---

www.powerboatguide.com · 231-360-0827

Sea Ray 58 Sedan Bridge
2005–Current

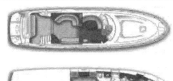

Beautifully styled flybridge yacht showcases Sea Ray's considerable design, engineering skills. Elegant three-stateroom interior with cherry cabinetry, salon sofa with pull-out bed features elevated galley and dinette, full-beam master stateroom with flat-screen TV. Flybridge comes standard with refrigerator, air-conditioning. Bow thruster is standard. Extended swim platform can be fitted with optional launching davit. Cruise at 25–26 knots with 900hp MAN diesels (30+ knots top). A classy yacht at a premium price.

Length w/Platform	58'7"	Fuel	700 gals.
Beam	16'0"	Water	150 gals.
Draft	4'3"	Waste	68 gals.
Weight	51,500#	Hull Type	Modified-V
Clearance	18'8"	Deadrise Aft	17°

See Page 564 For Resale Values

Sea Ray Boats
Knoxville, TN
www.searay.com

---

www.powerboatguide.com · 231-360-0827

Sea Ray 650 Cockpit Motor Yacht
1992–96

Deckhouse Layout

Lower Level Floorplan

Maxi-volume cockpit motoryacht with wide 18-foot beam was flagship of Sea Ray's 1990s-era fleet. Spacious four-stateroom interior features enormous salon with U-lounge seating and full entertainment center, raised pilothouse with centerline helm and watch berth, full-beam owner's suite with king bed. Note utility room with washer/dryer. Aft engineroom is unusual in a motoryacht. Hull was fully cored. Total of 12 were built. GM 1,040hp V-drive diesels cruise at 20 knots (24–26 knots top).

Length	64'6"	Fuel	1,000 gals.
Beam	18'1"	Water	275 gals.
Draft	4'10"	Waste	264 gals.
Weight	76,000#	Hull Type	Modified-V
Clearance	25'3"	Deadrise Aft	18°

Insufficient Resale Data To Assign Values

Sea Ray Boats
Knoxville, TN
www.searay.com

---

www.powerboatguide.com · 231-360-0827

Selene 36/38 Trawler
2003–Current

Seaworthy displacement cruiser with walkaround deck combines timeless design with solid construction, all-weather capability. Well-appointed interior with deckhouse galley features two large staterooms, comfortable salon with twin deck doors, teak-planked flooring, Corian counters. Note engineroom access door in aft stateroom. Reverse front windows reduce glare. Note folding mast, transom door, hullside boarding gates. Bow thruster is standard. Single 220hp Cummins diesel delivers 7-8 knot cruising speed (about 10 knots top).

Length Overall	41'9"	Clearance, Mast	21'2"
Length WL	36'6"	Fuel	500 gals.
Beam	14'6"	Water	180 gals.
Draft	4'8"	Waste	55 gals.
Weight	35,700#	Hull Type	Displacement

See Page 565 For Resale Values

Jet-Tern Marine, Canton, China
www.selenetrawlers.com

Motoryachts & Trawlers

Selene 43/45 Pilothouse
2001–Current

Heavy-weather displacement trawler hull pairs handsome lines with top-shelf accommodations, long-range versatility. Traditional interior with teak-planked flooring (offered in several configurations) includes two large staterooms, expansive salon, U-shaped galley with serving counter, washer/dryer, raised pilothouse with settee. Note hullside boarding gates, huge "commissary" area between engineroom and lazarette. Sold as the Selene 45 since 2010. Cruise at 8 knots with 2,000-mile range with Cummins 210hp diesel.

Length Overall	48'5"	Ballast	3,000#
Length WL	43'11"	Fuel	1,000 gals.
Beam	15'8"	Water	230 gals.
Draft	5'0"	Waste	60 gals.
Weight	58,000#	Hull Type	Displacement

Insufficient Resale Data To Assign Values

Jet-Tern Marine, Canton, China
www.selenetrawlers.com

Selene 47 Pilothouse
1999–Current

Stretched version of Selene 43/45 with enlarged salon, expanded aft deck delivers compelling mix of comfort, security. Spacious teak interior includes two large staterooms, two full heads, well-appointed salon with galley forward, washer/dryer, raised pilothouse with settee. Hardtop covers entire flybridge. Note protected side decks, hullside boarding gates, standard bow thruster, huge lazarette storage area. Wraparound Portuguese bridge protects against breaking waves. Cruise efficiently at 8–10 knots with 330hp Cummins diesel.

Length Overall	50'1"	Ballast	4,000#
Length WL	46'1"	Fuel	1,000 gals.
Beam	15'8"	Water	210 gals.
Draft	5'1"	Waste	60 gals.
Weight	64,200#	Hull Type	Displacement

See Page 565 For Resale Values

Jet-Tern Marine, Canton, China
www.selenetrawlers.com

Selene 48/49 Pilothouse
2006–Current

Long-range passagemaker with ballasted, full-displacement hull takes cruising comfort to the next level. Opulent pilothouse interior with traditional teak joinery, spacious salon with galley forward, boasts two large staterooms, each with ensuite head. Cockpit lazarette is huge. Note wraparound Portuguese bridge, fiberglass hardtop, protected side decks, integral swim platform. Reverse pilothouse windshield reduces glare. Marketed as the Selene 49 since 2010. Single Cummins 330hp diesel will cruise at 9–10 knots (about 12 knots top).

Length Overall	53'11"	Ballast	4,500#
Length WL	46'10"	Fuel	1,200 gals.
Beam	15'8"	Water	300 gals.
Draft	5'5"	Waste	60 gals.
Weight	68,800 gals.	Hull Type	Displacement

Insufficient Resale Data To Assign Values

Jet-Tern Marine, Canton, China
www.selenetrawlers.com

231-360-0827

Selene 53/54 Pilothouse
2002–Current

Luxury-class pilothouse yacht—Selene's most popular model—combines liveaboard comfort with solid construction, fuel-efficient operation. Versatile three-stateroom interior includes two en-suite heads, expansive salon with galley forward, walk-in engineroom (with standing headroom), large pilothouse with L-shaped settee. Note protected side decks, bow and stern thrusters, copious lazarette storage. Note inside/outside flybridge access. Called the Selene 54 since 2010. Single 430hp Cummins diesel will cruise efficiently at 9–10 knots.

Length Overall	59'10"	Ballast	6,000#
Length WL	50'10"	Fuel	1,3000 gals.
Beam	16'8"	Water	400 gals.
Draft	5'10"	Waste	120 gals.
Weight	95,000#	Hull Type	Displacement

Insufficient Resale Data To Assign Values

Jet-Tern Marine, Canton, China
www.selenetrawlers.com

231-360-0827

Senator 35 Sundeck
1983–87

Sturdy double-cabin import from 1980s combines classic trawler profile with traditional teak interior, economical operation. Several floorplans were available, all with full-beam aft cabin, port/starboard salon deck doors, lower helm with deck door. Surprisingly roomy aft deck with hardtop; flybridge seating for four. Bow pulpit, swim platform, radar arch were standard. Long keel protects running gear from grounding. Cruise at 7 knots with single 135hp diesel; 8-10 knots with twin 85hp diesels.

Length Overall	34'4"	Clearance	NA
Length WL	31'6"	Fuel	300 gals.
Beam	12'0"	Water	200 gals.
Draft	4'2"	Waste	30 gals.
Weight	18,700#	Hull Type	Semi-Disp.

Prices Not Provided for Pre-1995 Models

Senator yachts are no longer produced.

231-360-0827

Silhouette 42
1987–91

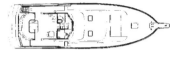

Truly unique coastal trawler makes up in comfort, practicality whatever she lacks in sex appeal. Boxy profile conceals surprisingly spacious interior with fore and aft staterooms, large salon with breakfast bar, home-sized galley, two full heads. Cockpit with hydraulic foldout platform is accessed from full-beam master stateroom. Semi-enclosed pilothouse is reached from salon or foredeck. Volvo 100hp diesels cruise efficiently at 7–8 knots. Marketed by Kady-Krogen Marine, a total of twelve were built.

Length Overall	41'10"	Clearance	NA
Length WL	37'6"	Fuel	400 gals.
Beam	14'6"	Water	150 gals.
Draft	3'2"	Cockpit	NA
Weight	28,000#	Hull Type	Modified-V

Prices Not Provided for Pre-1995 Models

Silhouette yachts are no longer produced.

Motoryachts & Trawlers

231-360-0827

Silverton 322 Motor Yacht
1989–2001

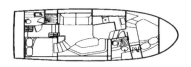

Best-selling mini-motoryacht with home-sized interior meets family needs for living, storage space. Top-heavy profile conceals truly impressive interior featuring large salon with convertible dinette, full-service galley, two double staterooms, two full heads. Silverton's signature "SideWalk" deck layout permits cavernous full-beam salon. Note very small aft deck. Curved swim platform staircase makes boarding easy. Definitely not meant for offshore use. MerCruiser gas engines cruise at 16–17 knots (mid-to-high 20s top).

Length Overall	37'0"	Fuel	200 gals.
Beam	12'4"	Water	72 gals.
Draft	2'11"	Waste	49 gals.
Weight	19,716#	Hull Type	Modified-V
Clearance	13'6"	Deadrise Aft	16°

See Page 565 For Resale Values

Silverton Marine
Millville, NJ
www.silverton.com

231-360-0827

Silverton 34 Motor Yacht
1993–96

Durable aft-cabin yacht meets cruiser's need for solid construction, roomy accommodations, enduring styling. Well-appointed interior with open front windshield, light oak trim interior consists of open-plan salon with galley and dinette down, two double staterooms, two full heads. Small aft deck has space for a couple of deck chairs. Compact flybridge has guest seating forward of helm. Hardtop, radar arch, bow pulpit, swim platform were standard. Crusader 320hp gas engines cruise at 17–18 knots (about 28 knots top).

Length w/Pulpit	39'10"	Fuel	260 gals.
Hull Length	34'6"	Water	74 gals.
Beam	12'10"	Waste	45 gals.
Draft	3'0"	Hull Type	Modified-V
Weight	16,368#	Deadrise Aft	17°

See Page 565 For Resale Values

Silverton Marine
Millville, NJ
www.silverton.com

231-360-0827

Silverton 35 Motor Yacht
2003–Current

Deluxe mini-motoryacht with edgy Silverton styling delivers vast accommodations at a budget price. Wide-open interior is dominated by lavish, full-beam salon with convertible settee, four-person dinette. Small staterooms have berths positioned athwartships to save space. Note split forward head, hardwood galley sole, raised side decks. Hardtop, bow pulpit, underwater exhausts are standard. Prop pockets reduce hull draft. Not the prettiest boat at the dock. Crusader 385hp gas engines cruise in the low 20s (26–27 knots top).

Length Overall	40'2"	Fuel	286 gals.
Beam	13'4"	Water	94 gals.
Draft	2'11"	Waste	55 gals.
Weight	22,618#	Hull Type	Modified-V
Clearance	16'0"	Deadrise Aft	12.5°

See Page 565 For Resale Values

Silverton Marine
Millville, NJ
www.silverton.com

www.powerboatguide.com   231-360-0827

Silverton 352 Motor Yacht
1997–2002

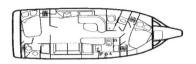

High-sided motoryacht with signature Silverton styling provides the interior space of many 40-footers. Highlights include expansive full-beam salon with dinette forward, full-service galley with upright refrigerator, two double staterooms, two full heads. Compact staterooms have berths positioned athwartships to save space. Curved staircase from swim platform to aft deck makes boarding easy. Standard 385hp gas engines cruise at 16 knots (26–27 knots top); optional 315hp Cummins diesels cruise at 18–19 knots.

Length Overall	41'4"	Fuel	286 gals.
Beam	13'0"	Water	100 gals.
Draft	3'3"	Waste	68 gals.
Weight	20,809#	Hull Type	Modified-V
Clearance	16'2"	Deadrise Aft	16°

See Page 565 For Resale Values

Silverton Marine
Millville, NJ
www.silverton.com

---

www.powerboatguide.com   231-360-0827

Silverton 37 Motor Yacht
1988–89

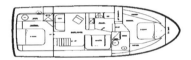

Maxi-volume cruising yacht with enormous bridge, portly profile is long on interior space, short on eye appeal. Aft-cabin floorplan features surprisingly spacious forward stateroom, U-shaped dinette, large galley. Note light oak interior woodwork, stall showers in both heads. Lack of cockpit or small afterdeck makes docking—especially shorthanded—a tedious process. Additional features include radar arch, swim platform, bow pulpit. Standard 350hp Crusaders cruise at 15 knots (23–24 knots top). Lasted just two years in production.

Length	37'6"	Fuel	300 gals.
Beam	13'9"	Water	100 gals.
Draft	3'8"	Headroom	6'4"
Weight	22,000#	Hull Type	Modified-V
Clearance	16'0"	Deadrise Aft	NA

Prices Not Provided for Pre-1995 Models

Silverton Marine
Millville, NJ
www.silverton.com

---

www.powerboatguide.com   231-360-0827

Silverton 372/392 Motor Yacht
1996–2001

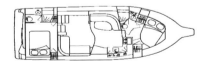

Innovative aft-cabin cruising yacht (called Silverton 372 MY in 1996–98; 392 in 1999–2001) took midsize motoryacht design to the next level. Enormous full-beam salon rivals most 45-footers in size, comfort. Highlights include stall showers in both heads, fully equipped galley with hardwood floor, extended swim platform (optional), foredeck sun pad. Huge bridge can seat a small crowd. Low-deadrise hull isn't too fond of a chop. Gas 320hp inboards cruise at 14 knots (low 20s top). A huge success, over 600 were sold.

Length	43'9"	Fuel	286 gals.
Beam	14'1"	Water	100 gals.
Draft	3'3"	Waste	60 gals.
Weight	23,577#	Hull Type	Modified-V
Clearance	16'5"	Deadrise Aft	15°

See Page 566 For Resale Values

Silverton Marine
Millville, NJ
www.silverton.com

---

www.powerboatguide.com   231-360-0827

Silverton 39 Motor Yacht
2002–Current

Maxi-volume motoryacht with portly profile favors interior volume, comfort over styling elegance. Raised walkways from bow to bridge permit expansive, full-beam deckhouse with truly expansive dimensions, generous headroom. Both staterooms are fitted with queen beds; both heads have separate stall showers. Highlights include cherry interior woodwork, extended swim platform, aft-deck hardtop, bridge seating for eight. Cruise at a modest 15–16 knots with standard 385hp gas engines (low 20s top); 20 knots with 355hp diesels.

Length w/Pulpit	43'7"	Fuel	334 gals.
Hull Length	41'5"	Water	100 gals.
Beam	14'0"	Waste	60 gals.
Draft	3'11"	Hull Type	Modified-V
Weight	24,900#	Deadrise Aft	17°

See Page 566 For Resale Values

Silverton Marine
Millville, NJ
www.silverton.com

---

www.powerboatguide.com   231-360-0827

Silverton 40 Aft Cabin
1982–90

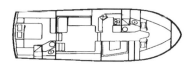

Practical double-cabin motoryacht from the 1980s meets cruiser's need for space, comfort, versatility. Standard two-stateroom interior with convertible salon settee, convertible dinette can sleep up to eight. Note separate stall showers in both heads, generous galley storage. Light oak interior trim replaced original teak cabinets in 1985. Well-proportioned flybridge and aft deck can seat several guests. Awkward two-piece entryway door from aft deck into cabin is a tight fit. Cruise at 16–17 knots with 350hp gas inboards (mid 20s top).

Length	40'0"	Fuel	300 gals.
Beam	14'0"	Water	100 gals.
Draft	3'0"	Headroom	6'4"
Weight	24,000#	Hull Type	Modified-V
Clearance	13'6"	Deadrise Aft	14°

Prices Not Provided for Pre-1995 Models

Silverton Marine
Millville, NJ
www.silverton.com

---

www.powerboatguide.com   231-360-0827

Silverton 402/422 Motor Yacht
1996–2000

402 Floorplan, 1996–98

422 Floorplan, 1999–2001

Conventional aft-cabin yacht (called 402 Motor Yacht in 1996–98; 422 MY in 1999–2000) is roomy, versatile, built to last. Two-stateroom floorplan with full dinette, big U-shaped galley (with lots of counter space), roomy salon is a model of space efficiency. Master stateroom was rearranged in 1999 with unusual aft-facing bed. Note roomy flybridge, wide side decks, aft-deck wet bar. Extended swim platform was a popular option. Engineroom is a tight fit. Standard 320hp gas engines cruise at 14 knots (low 20s top).

Length Overall	45'11	Fuel	375 gals.
Beam	14'2"	Water	132 gals.
Draft	3'6"	Waste	58 gals.
Weight	23,826#	Hull Type	Modified-V
Clearance	17'11"	Deadrise Aft	12°

See Page 566 For Resale Values

Silverton Marine
Millville, NJ
www.silverton.com

Silverton 41 Motor Yacht
1991–95

Traditional double-cabin motoryacht from early 1990s made good on Silverton promise of space, comfort at a competitive price. Well-appointed interior with roomy salon, booth-style dinette, two large staterooms sleeps six. Both heads have separate stall showers; full-service galley has plenty of storage. Roomy aft deck with hardtop, wet bar can entertatain several guests. Note side-dumping exhausts, wide side decks, integral bow pulpit. Cruise at 15 knots with big-block gas engines; 20 knots with optional 375hp Cat diesels.

Length w/Pulpit	46'3"	Fuel	408 gals.
Hull Length	41'3"	Water	200 gals.
Beam	14'10"	Waste	68 gals.
Draft	3'7"	Hull Type	Modified-V
Weight	28,000#	Deadrise Aft	17°

See Page 566 For Resale Values

Silverton Marine
Millville, NJ
www.silverton.com

Silverton 43 Motor Yacht
2001–07

Feature-rich motoryacht with huge interior suits liveaboards and cruisers alike. Raised walkways from bow to bridge permit cavernous, full-beam salon the equal of much larger boats. Interior highlights include appealing cherry cabinetry, home-size galley, posh Ultraleather salon seating. Note divided head compartments fore and aft. Master stateroom is on the small side for a 41-footer. Curved staircase from swim platform to aft deck makes boarding easy. Volvo 480hp (or Cummins 430hp) diesels cruise at 18–19 knots (low 20s top).

Length w/Pulpit	47'7"	Fuel	386 gals.
Beam	14'11"	Water	150 gals.
Draft	3'8"	Waste	80 gals.
Weight	29,000#	Hull Type	Modified-V
Clearance, Arch	17'0"	Deadrise Aft	17°

See Page 566 For Resale Values

Silverton Marine
Millville, NJ
www.silverton.com

Silverton 442 Cockpit MY
1996–2001

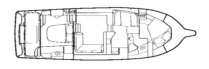

Value-priced cockpit yacht gets high marks for luxury-class comfort, built-in versatility. Expansive two-stateroom interior includes home-size galley, full dinette, stall showers in both heads. Sliding glass door provides cockpit access from master stateroom. Weatherboards, molded seating, wet bar were standard on aft deck; storage locker is built into swim platform. Note secure side decks, centerline flybridge helm. Standard gas engines cruise at 14–15 knots (low 20s top); Cummins 355hp diesels cruise at close to 20 knots.

Length	45'11"	Fuel	375 gals.
Beam	14'3"	Water	132 gals.
Draft	3'6"	Waste	58 gals.
Weight	23,826#	Hull Type	Modified-V
Clearance	18'3"	Deadrise Aft	15°

See Page 566 For Resale Values

Silverton Marine
Millville, NJ
www.silverton.com

Motoryachts & Trawlers

　　　231-360-0827

Silverton 453 Motor Yacht
1999–2003

Motoryacht Floorplan

Pilothouse Floorplan

Tall-freeboard motoryacht with Silverton's trademark "SideWalk" deck design raised the bar for space, comfort in a mid-40-foot yacht. Cavernous interior boasts vast full-beam salon with entertainment center, fully equipped galley with Corian counters, three double staterooms. Note cherry woodwork, twin recliners built into salon sofa. Topside features include molded boarding steps, foredeck sun pad, pilothouse deck door. Cummins 430hp diesels cruise at 18 knots (low 20s top). Definitely not the prettiest boat on the water.

Length	47'8"	Fuel	500 gals.
Beam	15'4"	Water	190 gals.
Draft	4'0"	Waste	66 gals.
Weight	35,530#	Hull Type	Modified-V
Clearance	19'5"	Deadrise Aft	16°

See Page 566 For Resale Values

Silverton Marine
Millville, NJ
www.silverton.com

　　　231-360-0827

Silverton 46 Motor Yacht
1990–97

Durable 1990s motoryacht balanced spacious accommodations with rugged construction, affordable price. Space-efficient interior with three private staterooms boasts large galley with full-size refrigerator, big U-shaped dinette, two full heads. Second guest cabin has foldaway berth that converts to lounge. Note trash compactor in galley, standard washer/dryer. Aft deck came with hardtop, wet bar. Large flybridge is arranged with bench seating aft of the helm. GM 485hp diesels cruise at 22 knots (mid 20s top).

Length w/Pulpit	51'6"	Fuel	580 gals.
Hull Length	46'8"	Water	200 gals.
Beam	16'2"	Waste	56 gals.
Draft	3'9"	Hull Type	Modified-V
Weight	33,874#	Deadrise Aft	17°

See Page 566 For Resale Values

Silverton Marine
Millville, NJ
www.silverton.com

　　　231-360-0827

Silverton 52 Ovation
2008–Current

Eurostyle flybridge cruiser designed for triple IPS power is spacious, comfortable, well finished. Expansive layout features raised galley and dinette forward, lavish master stateroom with flanking night stands, queen beds in both guest cabins. (Note that VIP stateroom has split head.) Well-equipped galley has plenty of storage. Cockpit can be ordered with optional hydraulic davit or hydraulic swim platform. Large engineroom, wide side decks are a plus. Triple 435hp Volvo IPS diesels cruise at 24–25 knots (about 28 top).

Length	52'0"	Fuel	610 gals.
Beam	16'4"	Water	200 gals.
Draft	4'0"	Waste	80 gals.
Weight	52,000#	Hull Type	Modified-V
Clearance	17'9"	Deadrise Aft	13°

Insufficient Resale Data To Assign Values

Silverton Marine
Millville, NJ
www.silverton.com

231-360-0827

Sundowner 30 Pilothouse Tug
1982–89

Salty pocket trawler designed for coastal cruising is affordable, stable, economical to operate. Space-efficient layout offers combined salon/galley with dining nook aft, roomy pilothouse, head-plus-V-berths forward. Excellent storage for a boat this size. Large windows, good cabin ventilation are a plus. No cockpit transom door. Lots of teak trim inside and out. Original 30-foot model ran from 1982-87; enlarged Sundowner 32 was built in 1988-89. Runs efficiently at 6-7 knots with single 85hp Perkins diesel.

Length	29'6"	Headroom	6'4"
Beam	11'1"	Fuel	100 gals.
Draft	2'10"	Water	50 gals.
Weight	9,600#	Waste	20 gals.
Clearance	NA	Hull Type	Semi-Disp.

Prices Not Provided for Pre-1995 Models

Sundowner yachts are no longer in production

231-360-0827

Sunseeker 46/48 Manhattan
1995–99

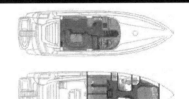

Imposing 1990s flybridge yacht (called 46 Manhattan in 1995) delivered sleek styling with top-notch construction, spirited performance. Lavish three-stateroom interior features two full heads, roomy galley, elevated lower helm, exquisite high-gloss cabinetry. Note premium galley hardware, top-shelf furnishings. Flybridge has seating for six plus sunbathing area aft. Deep swim platform can accommodate PWC, optional hydraulic davit. Typical European engineroom is a tight fit. Cat 430hp V-drive diesels cruise at 22 knots (25–26 knots top).

Length	48'0"	Fuel	378 gals.
Beam	14'5"	Water	115 gals.
Draft	2'11"	Headroom	6'6"
Weight	41,000#	Hull Type	Deep-V
Clearance	15'5"	Deadrise Aft	20°

See Page 568 For Resale Values

Sunseeker Yachts
Poole, England
www.sunseeker.com

231-360-0827

Sunseeker 50 Manhattan
2006–08

Sophisticated Euroyacht with spacious three-stateroom interior sets class standards for style, luxury, comfort. Ultra-posh interior is arranged in typical European fashion with sunken galley forward, state-of-the-art lower helm, open salon with facing settees. Huge salon windows offer panoramic outside views; full-beam owner's cabin with vertical hull ports exceeds all expectations. Note generous galley storage, surprisingly spacious engineroom. MAN 800hp diesels cruise at 26 knots (30+ knots top).

Length Overall	52'6"	Fuel	660 gals.
Beam	15'1"	Water	132 gals.
Draft	4'0"	Waste	50 gals.
Weight	50,600#	Hull Type	Deep-V
Clearance	16'2"	Deadrise Aft	19°

Insufficient Resale Data To Assign Values

Sunseeker Yachts
Poole, England
www.sunseeker.com

Motoryachts & Trawlers

---

www.powerboatguide.com   231-360-0827

Sunseeker 56 Manhattan
2001–04

Lavish med-bred flybridge yacht raised styling, luxury bars when she was introduced in 2001. Stunning three-stateroom, two-head interior features beautifully appointed split-level salon with leather seating, wrap-around dinette, sunken galley. Inside bridge access is a plus; each cabin has flat-screen TV. Topside highlights include teak decks, bow thruster, hydraulic swim platform, extended bridge with seating for ten. Note crew quarters off galley. Cat 800hp diesels cruise in the mid 20s with a top speed of just over 30 knots.

Length	61'2"	Fuel	661 gals.
Beam	15'1"	Water	198 gals.
Draft	4'3"	Headroom	6'6"
Weight	58,200#	Hull Type	Deep-V
Clearance	16'11"	Deadrise Aft	19°

See Page 568 For Resale Values

Sunseeker Yachts
Poole, England
www.sunseeker.com

---

www.powerboatguide.com   231-360-0827

Sunseeker 62 Manhattan
1997–2000

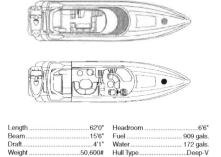

Retooled version of earlier Sunseeker 58 Manhattan (1994–96) boasts extended swim platform for tender stowage, stunning multi-level interior. Sleeping arrangements for six include dramatic master suite, side-by-side guest cabins. From spacious salon, sliding glass doors open to expansive aft deck. Note lower helm deck door, aft crew quarters, exquisite cherry joinery. Flybridge has seating for six with sunbathing space aft. Large engineroom is plus. MTU 745hp V-drive engines cruise at 25 knots (28–29 knots top).

Length	62'0"	Headroom	6'6"
Beam	15'6"	Fuel	909 gals.
Draft	4'1"	Water	172 gals.
Weight	50,600#	Hull Type	Deep-V
Clearance	14'6"	Deadrise Aft	20°

Insufficient Resale Data To Assign Values

Sunseeker Yachts
Poole, England
www.sunseeker.com

---

www.powerboatguide.com   231-360-0827

Sunseeker 64 Manhattan
2001–05

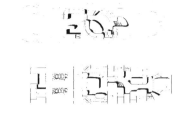

Imposing Mediterranean sportyacht combined dramatic styling (note tiered salon windows) with lavish accommodations, world-class performance. Beautifully appointed interior with split-level salon has galley aft, dining/conversation area forward—a reversal of most salon layouts. Crew quarters are aft, accessed from cockpit. Huge flybridge features wet bar, dinette, sun lounge. Note full-beam master suite, lower-helm deck door, hydraulic passerelle. MAN 800hp engines cruise at 25 knots (30 knots top).

Length Overall	71'6"	Headroom	6'5"
Beam	17'1"	Fuel	878 gals.
Draft	4'9"	Water	259 gals.
Weight	65,920#	Hull Type	Deep-V
Clearance	18'1"	Deadrise Aft	19°

Insufficient Resale Data To Assign Values

Sunseeker Yachts
Poole, England
www.sunseeker.com

---

www.powerboatguide.com   231-360-0827

Tollycraft 34 Sundeck
1986–88

Classy aft-cabin motoryacht combined roomy accommodations with top-shelf construction, leading-edge amenities. Interior highlights include well-appointed salon, expansive galley, standard lower helm. Both staterooms have private head access. Large cabin windows, generous cabin storage are a plus. Topside features include full-width aft deck, radar arch, bow pulpit, roomy bridge with seating for six. Note fuel increase to 296 gallons in 1988. Twin 350hp gas engines cruise at 18 knots (high 20s top).

Length	34'0"	Fuel	200/296 gals.
Beam	12'6"	Water	77 gals.
Draft	2'10"	Waste	35 gals.
Weight	17,000#	Hull Type	Modified-V
Clearance	12'0"	Deadrise Aft	13°

Prices Not Provided for Pre-1995 Models

Tollycraft is no longer in business.

---

www.powerboatguide.com   231-360-0827

Tollycraft 40 Sundeck
1985–94

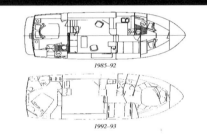

1985–92

1992–93

Premium sundeck cruising yacht made good on Tollycraft promise of quality, comfort in a good-looking package. Highlights include well-crafted interior with spacious salon, large master stateroom with generous storage, home-size galley with dinette opposite. Fuel increase in 1991. Low-deadrise hull delivers good fuel efficiency at lower speeds. Twin 350hp gas engines cruise at 17-18 knots (mid 20s top); optional 375hp Cat diesels cruise in the low 20s (25-26 knots top).

Length	40'2"	Fuel	300/398 gals.
Beam	14'8"	Water	140 gals.
Draft	3'0"	Waste	40 gals.
Weight	26,000#	Hull Type	Modified-V
Clearance	12'0"	Deadrise Aft	10°

Prices Not Provided for Pre-1995 Models

Tollycraft is no longer in business.

---

www.powerboatguide.com   231-360-0827

Tollycraft 43 Motor Yacht
1980–85

Highly regarded Northwest cruiser appeals to experienced boaters who value substance over style. Accommodations are well organized with double berths in each stateroom, and a serving bar separating the salon from the lower-level galley. Inside helm and deck access door were standard. Small cockpit with transom door makes boarding easy. Semi-displacement hull with long keel delivers superior heavy-weather performance. This boat is always—repeat, always—in demand. Cat 210hp diesels cruise efficiently at 15 knots (about 18 knots top).

Length Overall	43'4"	Clearance	13'9"
Length WL	39'5"	Fuel	400 gals.
Beam	14'2"	Water	140 gals.
Draft	3'5"	Headroom	6'4"
Weight	30,000#	Hull Type	Semi-Disp.

Prices Not Provided for Pre-1995 Models

Tollycraft is no longer in business.

Motoryachts & Trawlers

Motoryachts & Trawlers

231-360-0827

Tollycraft 44/45 Cockpit MY
1986–96

44 Interior

45 Interior

Cockpit version of Tollycraft 40 Sundeck (1985–93) is long on style and versatility, short on fluff. Twin-stateroom floorplan was updated in mid-1992 when forward stateroom, salon were enlarged at expense of smaller aft cabin. Interior highlights include solid teak joinery, sliding salon deck door, entertainment center. Note fuel increase in 1991. Twin 350hp gas engines cruise at 17–18 knots (about 25 knots top); optional 375hp Cat diesels cruise in the low 20s (25–26 knots top). Called Tollycraft 45 Cockpit MY in 1994–96.

Length, 44 CMY	44'2"	Clearance	14'9"
Length, 45 CMY	45'3"	Fuel	300/398 gals.
Beam	14'8"	Water	140 gals.
Draft	3'0"	Hull Type	Modified-V
Weight	28,000#	Deadrise Aft	10°

See Page 569 For Resale Values

Tollycraft is no longer in business.

231-360-0827

Tollycraft 48 Motor Yacht
1976–86; 1991–98

1976–94

1995–98

Classic Tollycraft cruiser enjoyed one of longest production runs of any modern motoryacht. Traditional galley-down interior—slightly updated in 1995—offers unsurpassed comfort, livability. Highlights include standard lower helm, huge aft stateroom (with space for washer/dryer), full walkaround decks, transom door. Early models with 320hp Cats cruise at 15 knots; later models with 400hp GMs cruise at 17–18 knots. Out of production in 1986, reintroduced in 1991. Total of 125 were built. Used models are always in demand.

Length w/Pulpit	52'10"	Clearance, Mast	17'0"
Hull Length	48'2"	Fuel	600 gals.
Beam	15'2"	Water	188 gals.
Draft	3'8"	Waste	98 gals.
Weight	42,000#	Hull Type	Semi-Disp.

See Page 569 For Resale Values

Tollycraft is no longer in business.

231-360-0827

Tollycraft 53 Motor Yacht
1988–94

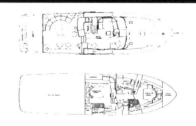

Always-desirable pilothouse yacht with wide 16'11" beam offers serious cruising comfort. Spacious interior with full-beam salon rivals many larger boats in size, amenities. Highlights include salon entertainment center, home-size galley with dishwasher, opulent master suite. Note portside wing door in salon, washer/dryer in second guest stateroom. Flybridge is huge but cockpit is on the small side. Early models with 550hp GM diesels cruise at 16–17 knots. Later models with twin 735hp GMs cruise at 22–23 knots.

Length w/Pulpit	59'6"	Fuel	800 gals.
Hull Length	52'11"	Water	280 gals.
Beam	16'11"	Waste	80 gals.
Draft	3'6"	Hull Type	Modified-V
Weight	52,000#	Deadrise Aft	11°

Prices Not Provided for Pre-1995 Models

Tollycraft is no longer in business.

Tollycraft 57 Motor Yacht
1989–98

Stretched version of popular Tollycraft 53 MY (1988–94) boasts larger cockpit, increased fuel, maximum comfort. Spacious interior has dinette, galley on pilothouse level; full-width salon has portside wing door for easy deck access. Note huge full-beam master suite, washer/dryer in second guest stateroom. Cockpit engineroom access is a plus. Walkaround model with full side decks introduced in 1996. GM 735hp, Cat 800hp, or MAN 820hp engines cruise at 20 knots (22–24 knots top). Over 30 of these quality yachts were built.

Length w/Pulpit	63'7"	Fuel	1,200 gals.
Hull Length	57'0"	Water	280 gals.
Beam	17'3"	Waste	120 gals.
Draft	3'6"	Hull Type	Modified-V
Weight	58,000#	Deadrise Aft	11°

See Page 569 For Resale Values

Tollycraft is no longer in business.

Tollycraft 61 Motor Yacht
1983–93

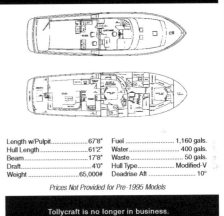

Acclaimed pilothouse yacht delivers unsurpassed blend of classic styling, luxury-class accommodations. Well-appointed interior features wide-open salon with U-shaped galley, roomy pilothouse with bridge access, full-beam master suite. Additional highlights include huge flybridge, sheltered side decks, well-organized engineroom with cockpit access, deep prop-protecting keel. Early models with GM 485hp diesels cruise at 15–16 knots. Later models with GM 735hp GM engines cruise at 20–22 knots. Total of 39 were built.

Length w/Pulpit	67'8"	Fuel	1,160 gals.
Hull Length	61'2"	Water	400 gals.
Beam	17'8"	Waste	50 gals.
Draft	4'0"	Hull Type	Modified-V
Weight	65,000#	Deadrise Aft	10°

Prices Not Provided for Pre-1995 Models

Tollycraft is no longer in business.

Tollycraft 65 Cockpit MY
1993–98

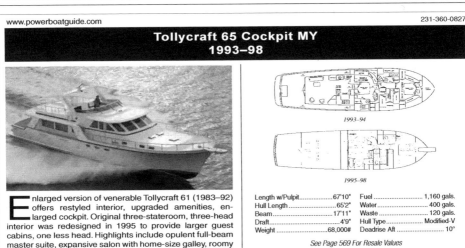

1993–94

1995–98

Enlarged version of venerable Tollycraft 61 (1983–92) offers restyled interior, upgraded amenities, enlarged cockpit. Original three-stateroom, three-head interior was redesigned in 1995 to provide larger guest cabins, one less head. Highlights include opulent full-beam master suite, expansive salon with home-size galley, roomy pilothouse with superb visibility. Note covered side decks, massive bridge, cockpit engineroom access. Twin 820hp MANs—or 800hp Cats—cruise at 22 knots (23–24 knots top). Total of 13 were built.

Length w/Pulpit	67'10"	Fuel	1,160 gals.
Hull Length	65'2"	Water	400 gals.
Beam	17'11"	Waste	120 gals.
Draft	4'9"	Hull Type	Modified-V
Weight	68,000#	Deadrise Aft	10°

See Page 569 For Resale Values

Tollycraft is no longer in business.

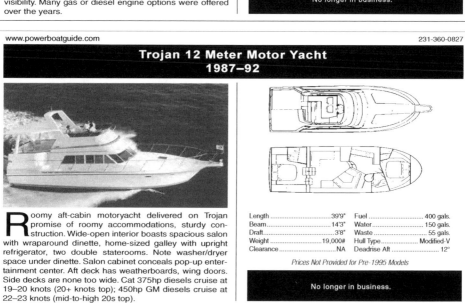

231-360-0827

Trojan 36 Tri-Cabin
1970–87

Classic aft-cabin cruiser from 1970s, 1980s set class standards in her day for interior comfort, versatility. Offered with several layouts over the years, most with double bed in aft stateroom and galley aft in the salon. Design highlights include walkaround decks, combined helm/aft-deck area, molded bow seating, bow pulpit. Early models (called the 36 Sea Raider) had teak decks and cockpit. Note tall bridge windshield, good helm visibility. Many gas or diesel engine options were offered over the years.

Length	36'0"	Fuel	150/220/300 gals.
Beam	13'0"	Water	65/85
Draft	2'11"	Waste	40 gals.
Weight	17,500#	Hull Type	Modified-V
Clearance	12'3"	Deadrise Aft	9°

Prices Not Provided for Pre-1995 Models

No longer in business.

231-360-0827

Trojan 12 Meter Motor Yacht
1987–92

Roomy aft-cabin motoryacht delivered on Trojan promise of roomy accommodations, sturdy construction. Wide-open interior boasts spacious salon with wraparound dinette, home-sized galley with upright refrigerator, two double staterooms. Note washer/dryer space under dinette. Salon cabinet conceals pop-up entertainment center. Aft deck has weatherboards, wing doors. Side decks are none too wide. Cat 375hp diesels cruise at 19–20 knots (20+ knots top); 450hp GM diesels cruise at 22–23 knots (mid-to-high 20s top).

Length	39'9"	Fuel	400 gals.
Beam	14'3"	Water	150 gals.
Draft	3'8"	Waste	55 gals.
Weight	19,000#	Hull Type	Modified-V
Clearance	NA	Deadrise Aft	12°

Prices Not Provided for Pre-1995 Models

No longer in business.

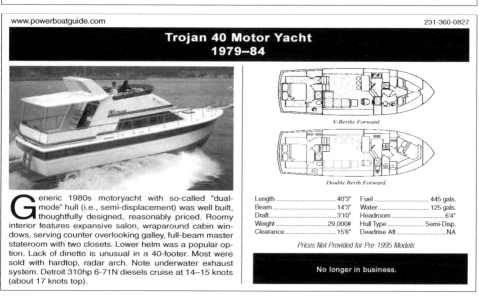

231-360-0827

Trojan 40 Motor Yacht
1979–84

V-Berths Forward

Double Berth Forward

Generic 1980s motoryacht with so-called "dual-mode" hull (i.e., semi-displacement) was well built, thoughtfully designed, reasonably priced. Roomy interior features expansive salon, wraparound cabin windows, serving counter overlooking galley, full-beam master stateroom with two closets. Lower helm was a popular option. Lack of dinette is unusual in a 40-footer. Most were sold with hardtop, radar arch. Note underwater exhaust system. Detroit 310hp 6-71N diesels cruise at 14–15 knots (about 17 knots top).

Length	40'3"	Fuel	445 gals.
Beam	14'3"	Water	125 gals.
Draft	3'10"	Headroom	6'4"
Weight	29,000#	Hull Type	Semi-Disp.
Clearance	15'6"	Deadrise Aft	NA

Prices Not Provided for Pre-1995 Models

No longer in business.

Trojan 44 Motor Yacht
1974–84

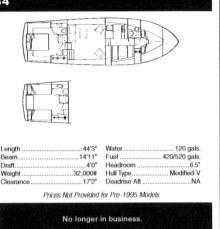

Traditional flush-deck yacht introduced in 1974 was a breakthrough boat for Trojan, a latecomer to all-fiberglass construction. Extensive redesign in 1978 included all-new superstructure, aft deck wing doors, updated flybridge. Two-stateroom, galley-down interior features teak paneling and cabinetry, full dinette, roomy galley, choice of twin beds or walkaround queen in master stateroom. Note small flybridge, wide side decks. Twin 310hp 6-71N Detroit diesels cruise at 15 knots and reach a top speed of around 18 knots.

Length	44'3"	Water	120 gals.
Beam	14'11"	Fuel	420/520 gals.
Draft	4'0"	Headroom	6'5"
Weight	32,000#	Hull Type	Modified-V
Clearance	17'2"	Deadrise Aft	NA

Prices Not Provided for Pre-1995 Models

No longer in business.

Vantare 64 Cockpit Motor Yacht
1987–92

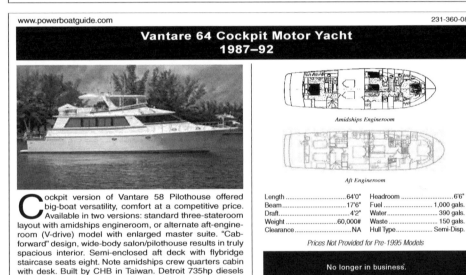

Amidships Engineroom

Aft Engineroom

Cockpit version of Vantare 58 Pilothouse offered big-boat versatility, comfort at a competitive price. Available in two versions: standard three-stateroom layout with amidships engineroom, or alternate aft-engineroom (V-drive) model with enlarged master suite. "Cab-forward" design, wide-body salon/pilothouse results in truly spacious interior. Semi-enclosed aft deck with flybridge staircase seats eight. Note amidships crew quarters cabin with desk. Built by CHB in Taiwan. Detroit 735hp diesels cruise at 16–18 knots (about 20 knots top).

Length	64'0"	Headroom	6'6"
Beam	17'6"	Fuel	1,000 gals.
Draft	4'2"	Water	390 gals.
Weight	60,000#	Waste	150 gals.
Clearance	NA	Hull Type	Semi-Disp.

Prices Not Provided for Pre-1995 Models

No longer in business.

Viking 43 Double Cabin
1975–82

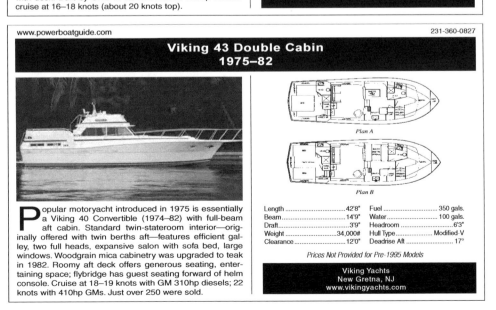

Plan A

Plan B

Popular motoryacht introduced in 1975 is essentially a Viking 40 Convertible (1974–82) with full-beam aft cabin. Standard twin-stateroom interior—originally offered with twin berths aft—features efficient galley, two full heads, expansive salon with sofa bed, large windows. Woodgrain mica cabinetry was upgraded to teak in 1982. Roomy aft deck offers generous seating, entertaining space; flybridge has guest seating forward of helm console. Cruise at 18–19 knots with GM 310hp diesels; 22 knots with 410hp GMs. Just over 250 were sold.

Length	42'8"	Fuel	350 gals.
Beam	14'9"	Water	100 gals.
Draft	3'9"	Headroom	6'3"
Weight	34,000#	Hull Type	Modified-V
Clearance	12'0"	Deadrise Aft	17°

Prices Not Provided for Pre-1995 Models

Viking Yachts
New Gretna, NJ
www.vikingyachts.com

Motoryachts & Trawlers

231-360-0827

Viking 44 Motor Yacht
1982–90

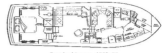
Standard Layout, 1982–88

Standard Layout, 1989–90

Quality-built 1980s motoryacht gets high marks for enduring styling, luxury accommodations, excellent performance. Well-appointed teak interior boasts salon entertainment center, home-sized galley, two large staterooms. Open aft deck with wet bar seats several guests. Engineroom is on the small side. Front salon windows were eliminated in 1987; flybridge was updated in 1989. Popular model is always in demand. Cruise at 23-24 knots with GM 485hp diesels (high 20s top). Cockpit version, the Viking 50 CMY, was built in 1983–87.

Length	44'0"	Fuel	460 gals.
Beam	15'0"	Water	180 gals.
Draft	4'0"	Headroom	6'4"
Weight	40,000#	Hull Type	Modified-V
Clearance	14'6"	Deadrise Aft	15.5°

Prices Not Provided for Pre-1995 Models

Viking Yachts
New Gretna, NJ
www.vikingyachts.com

231-360-0827

Viking 48 Motor Yacht
1986–88

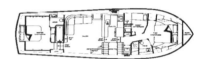

Motoryacht version of Viking 48 Convertible (1985–90) with fully enclosed aft deck was luxurious and agile, but not a great seller. Well-appointed interior features three large staterooms, home-sized galley, booth-style dinette, spacious salon with L-shaped settee, built-in entertainment center. Enclosed aft deck—complete with wing doors, wet bar—serves as second salon. Note solid teak joinery, full tub in master head, washer/dryer center, generous storage. GM 735hp diesels cruise at 24–25 knots and reach 28 knots top.

Length w/Pulpit	52'7"	Clearance	12'5"
Hull Length	48'7"	Fuel	645 gals.
Beam	16'0"	Water	200 gals.
Draft	4'7"	Hull Type	Modified-V
Weight	48,500#	Deadrise Aft	15.5°

Prices Not Provided for Pre-1995 Models

Viking Yachts
New Gretna, NJ
www.vikingyachts.com

231-360-0827

Viking 50 Cockpit MY
1983–89

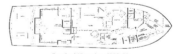
Standard Floorplan, 1983–88

Standard Floorplan, 1989

Cockpit version of Viking 44 MY (1982–90) proved popular with 1980s buyers looking for versatility, luxury, performance. Classy teak-trimmed interior boasts spacious salon, home-sized galley, full-beam master stateroom. Open aft deck with wet bar seats several guests. Flybridge—updated in 1989—has guest seating forward of helm. Note wide side decks, bow pulpit, cockpit transom door. Engineroom is on the small side. Front salon windows were eliminated in 1987. Cruise at 23–24 knots with optional GM 485hp diesels (high 20s top).

Length w/Pulpit	54'2"	Fuel	680 gals.
Hull Length	50'0"	Water	180 gals.
Beam	15'0"	Clearance w/Arch	14'6"
Draft	4'0"	Hull Type	Modified-V
Weight	43,000#	Deadrise Aft	15.5°

Prices Not Provided for Pre-1995 Models

Viking Yachts
New Gretna, NJ
www.vikingyachts.com

231-360-0827

Viking 50 Motor Yacht
1990–92

Portly twin-deck motoryacht introduced in 1990 is long on interior volume, short on eye appeal. Expansive floorplan with full-beam salon, country-kitchen galley includes private master suite with salon entry, two large guest staterooms forward, three full heads. Curved steps ascend from covered aft deck to huge, full-length bridge with dinghy platform. Lower helm was optional. Note standup engineroom, sliding galley deck doors, cushioned foredeck seating. GM 735hp diesels cruise at 18–20 knots, top out in the low 20s.

Length	50'6"	Fuel, Std.	600 gals.
Beam	16'4"	Fuel, Opt.	770 gals.
Draft	4'3"	Water	250 gals.
Weight	54,000#	Hull Type	Modified-V
Clearance	20'0"	Deadrise Aft	14°

Prices Not Provided for Pre-1995 Models

Viking Yachts
New Gretna, NJ
www.vikingyachts.com

231-360-0827

Viking 54 Sports Yacht
1992–2001

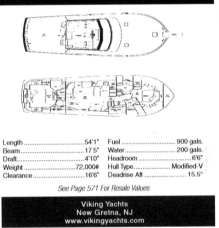

Classy aft-cabin motoryacht introduced in 1992 is stylish, roomy, built to last. Three-stateroom floorplan is dominated by spacious salon/galley/dinette with teak paneling, quality fabrics and furnishings. Palatial master suite has centerline king bed, walk-in closet. Additional features include large, semi-enclosed aft deck, standard washer/dryer, walk-in engineroom. Enclosed bridge became standard in 1998. MAN 820hp diesels cruise at 24 knots (28 knots top); 1,050 MANs cruise at 26 knots (about 30 knots top).

Length	54'1"	Fuel	900 gals.
Beam	17'5"	Water	200 gals.
Draft	4'10"	Headroom	6'6"
Weight	72,000#	Hull Type	Modified-V
Clearance	16'6"	Deadrise Aft	15.5°

See Page 571 For Resale Values

Viking Yachts
New Gretna, NJ
www.vikingyachts.com

231-360-0827

Viking 55 Motor Yacht
1987–90

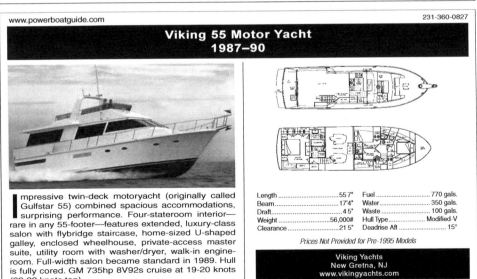

Impressive twin-deck motoryacht (originally called Gulfstar 55) combined spacious accommodations, surprising performance. Four-stateroom interior—rare in any 55-footer—features extended, luxury-class salon with flybridge staircase, home-sized U-shaped galley, enclosed wheelhouse, private-access master suite, utility room with washer/dryer, walk-in engineroom. Full-width salon became standard in 1989. Hull is fully cored. GM 735hp 8V92s cruise at 19-20 knots (22-23 knots top).

Length	55'7"	Fuel	770 gals.
Beam	17'4"	Water	350 gals.
Draft	4'5"	Waste	100 gals.
Weight	56,000#	Hull Type	Modified-V
Clearance	21'5"	Deadrise Aft	15°

Prices Not Provided for Pre-1995 Models

Viking Yachts
New Gretna, NJ
www.vikingyachts.com

Viking 57 Motor Yacht
1991–95

Lengthened version of original Gulfstar/Viking 55 MY (1987–91) raised the bar for 1990s engineering excellence, construction quality. Expansive four-stateroom interior features full-beam salon, separate eat-in galley, enclosed wheelhouse, private-entry master suite, walk-in engineroom. Extended bridge offers seating for a small crowd. Note all-glass salon bulkhead, utility room with washer/dryer, inside flybridge stairs. Hull is fully cored to reduce weight. Twin 820hp MAN engines cruise at 19–20 knots (23 knots top).

Length	57'7"	Fuel	750 gals.
Beam	17'4"	Water	350 gals.
Draft	4'5"	Headroom	6'6"
Weight	78,000#	Hull Type	Modified-V
Clearance	21'2"	Deadrise Aft	15°

See Page 571 For Resale Values

Viking Yachts
New Gretna, NJ
www.vikingyachts.com

Viking 60 Cockpit Sport Yacht
1994–2001

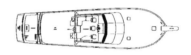

Stretched version of popular Viking 54 MY (1992–2001) added 6-foot cockpit extension for swimming, diving, fishing. Three-stateroom layout boasts fully enclosed aft deck, spacious salon/galley/dinette with teak paneling, three full heads, posh master suite with king bed, walk-in closet. Additional highlights include big walk-in engineroom, wide side decks, cockpit transom door. Bridge enclosure became standard in 1998. MAN 1,050hp diesels cruise at 25 knots (30 knots top); optional 1,200hp MANs cruise at 28 knots (32 knots top).

Length Overall	60'1"	Fuel	1,300 gals.
Beam	17'5"	Water	200 gals.
Draft	4'10"	Headroom	6'5"
Weight	78,000#	Hull Type	Modified-V
Clearance	16'6"	Deadrise Aft	15.5°

See Page 571 For Resale Values

Viking Yachts
New Gretna, NJ
www.vikingyachts.com

Viking 63 Widebody MY
1987–91

Stately widebody motoryacht defined cruising luxury, sophistication in the late 1980s. Extravagant four-stateroom interior features cavernous salon with formal dining area forward, opulent master suite with walk-in closet, gourmet galley with salon pass-thru, utility room with washer/dryer and workbench. Note spacious stand-up engineroom, enormous flybridge with wraparound seating. Extended Aft Deck model with walkaround decks, smaller salon was also available. GM 900hp diesels cruise at 20 knots (22–23 knots top).

Length	62'6"	Fuel	1,080 gals.
Beam	17'4"	Water	350 gals.
Draft	4'9"	Headroom	6'5"
Weight	61,500#	Hull Type	Modified-V
Clearance	21'5"	Deadrise Aft	15°

Prices Not Provided for Pre-1995 Models

Viking Yachts
New Gretna, NJ
www.vikingyachts.com

231-360-0827

Viking 65 Cockpit MY
1991–94

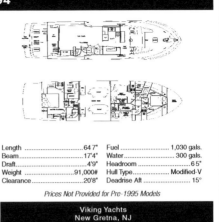

Bold 1990s cockpit yacht combined bold styling with executive-class accommodations, state-of-the-art construction. Spacious four-stateroom interior features massive full-beam salon with day head, country-kitchen galley with dinette, utility room with washer/dryer, walk-in engineroom. Note crew cabin (opposite second guest stateroom), aft deck enclosure, pass-through window from galley to salon. Large cockpit with storage lockers, transom door makes boarding easy. Hull is fully cored. Standard 1,050hp MANs cruise at 20 knots.

Length	64'7"	Fuel	1,030 gals.
Beam	17'4"	Water	300 gals.
Draft	4'9"	Headroom	6'5"
Weight	91,000#	Hull Type	Modified-V
Clearance	20'8"	Deadrise Aft	15°

Prices Not Provided for Pre-1995 Models

Viking Yachts
New Gretna, NJ
www.vikingyachts.com

231-360-0827

Viking 65 Motor Yacht
1991–95

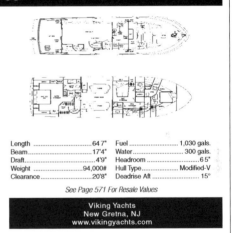

Spacious 1990s motoryacht made good on Viking promise of condo-size accommodations, top-shelf amenities. Highlights include sprawling salon with spiral bridge staircase, main deck day head, eat-in galley, opulent master suite with home-size head, enclosed aft deck with sliding—not hinged—wing doors. Note galley pass-throughs to dining area and wheelhouse, full walkaround decks. Extended flybridge has seating for a dozen guests. MAN 1,050hp engines cruise at 20 knots (22–23 knots wide open).

Length	64'7"	Fuel	1,030 gals.
Beam	17'4"	Water	300 gals.
Draft	4'9"	Headroom	6'5"
Weight	94,000#	Hull Type	Modified-V
Clearance	20'8"	Deadrise Aft	15°

See Page 571 For Resale Values

Viking Yachts
New Gretna, NJ
www.vikingyachts.com

231-360-0827

Viking Sport Cruisers 43 Flybridge
1995–99

Stylish UK import (called Viking 42 Flybridge until swim platform was stretched in 1997) made the cut with U.S. buyers looking for rakish Med styling, spirited performance. Interior highlights include wide-open salon with facing settees, elevated lower helm position, beautifully crafted woodwork. Roomy cockpit—protected by bridge overhang—has L-shaped seating with storage under, engineroom access hatch. Note curved bridge steps, wide side decks. Cat 420hp (or 370hp Volvo) diesels cruise at 23 knots (high 20s knots).

Length Overall	43'6"	Water	128 gals.
Beam	13'11"	Waste	42 gals.
Draft	3'3"	Clearance	11'6"
Weight	23,520#	Hull Type	Deep-V
Fuel	360 gals.	Deadrise Aft	19°

See Page 570 For Resale Values

Viking Yachts
New Gretna, NJ
www.vikingyachts.com

www.powerboatguide.com   231-360-0827

Viking Sport Cruisers 45 Flybridge
1999–2004

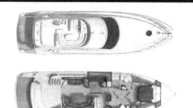

Sought-after flybridge yacht raised styling, performance bar for midsize cruisers of her era. Upscale interior with lacquered cherry cabinetry features spacious salon, twin-seat lower helm, large galley with generous counter space, two roomy staterooms. Note companionway washer/dryer, stall shower in owner's head. Hatches in cockpit sole access lazarette and small engineroom; molded steps lead to bridge with U-lounge, aft sun pad. Volvo 480hp diesels cruise at 25 knots (about 30 knots top).

Length Overall	45'0"	Water	152 gals.
Beam	14'3"	Waste	42 gals.
Draft	3'7"	Clearance	13'7"
Weight	28,000#	Hull Type	Deep-V
Fuel	383 gals.	Deadrise Aft	19°

See Page 570 For Resale Values

Viking Yachts
New Gretna, NJ
www.vikingyachts.com

---

www.powerboatguide.com   231-360-0827

Viking Sport Cruisers 45/46 Flybridge
1995–2000

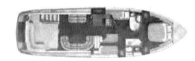

Feature-rich Med cruising yacht (called Viking 45 Flybridge until 1998 when swim platform was extended) delivered world-class mix of luxury, performance. Three-stateroom interior—rare in a boat this size—includes well-appointed salon with U-shaped dinette, fully equipped galley, raised lower helm, two heads. Cockpit with built-in seating, molded bridge steps is sheltered by bridge overhang. Note compact engineroom, wide side decks, spacious bridge with aft sun pad. Cruise at 24–25 knots (30 knots top) with Volvo 430hp diesels.

Length Overall	46'9"	Water	128 gals.
Beam	13'10"	Clearance	12'1"
Draft	3'4"	Headroom	6'5"
Weight	28,000#	Hull Type	Deep-V
Fuel	370 gals.	Deadrise Aft	19°

See Page 570 For Resale Values

Viking Yachts
New Gretna, NJ
www.vikingyachts.com

---

www.powerboatguide.com   231-360-0827

Viking Sport Cruisers 48/50 Flybridge
1994–99

Standard Two-Stateroom Layout

Optional Three-Stateroom Layout

Sleek European cruising yacht (called Viking 48 Flybridge until swim platform was extended in 1998) delivered impressive mix of style, luxury, performance. Standard twin-stateroom interior displays British craftsmanship at its best. Highlights include sliding cabin windows, generous galley storage, L-shaped lower-level dinette. Cockpit features molded bridge steps, built-in seating, transom door. Note so-so lower helm visibility, small engineroom. Volvo 380hp diesels cruise at 22 knots; Volvo 430s cruise in the mid 20s.

Length Overall	51'0"	Water	187 gals.
Beam	14'2"	Clearance	12'6"
Draft	3'9"	Headroom	6'4"
Weight	33,600#	Hull Type	Deep-V
Fuel	428 gals.	Deadrise Aft	19°

See Page 570 For Resale Values

Viking Yachts
New Gretna, NJ
www.vikingyachts.com

Viking Sport Cruisers 50 Flybridge
2001–Current

Compelling Med cruiser combines leading-edge styling with polished accommodations, sporty performance. Richly furnished interior features wide-open salon with facing settees, compact galley, two roomy staterooms, each with private head access. Additional highlights include teak-laid cockpit, extended swim platform, excellent lower helm/dash layout, washer/dryer. Note huge full-beam lazarette forward of crew cabin. Volvo 480hp diesels cruise at 22 knots (26–27 knots top); 675hp Volvos cruise at 26 knots (31–32 knots top).

Length Overall	50'3"	Water	160 gals.
Beam	14'8"	Clearance	13'1"
Draft	3'8"	Headroom	6'4"
Weight	33,600#	Hull Type	Deep-V
Fuel	540 gals.	Deadrise Aft	19°

See Page 570 For Resale Values

Viking Yachts
New Gretna, NJ
www.vikingyachts.com

Viking Sport Cruisers 52 Flybridge
1997–2002

Polished sportcruiser from late 1990s delivered high-powered blend of European styling, leading-edge luxury. Offered with several two- and three-stateroom layouts, all with step-down galley, full lower helm, aft crew quarters. Notable features include high-gloss cherry woodwork, teak-laid cockpit, extended swim platform, roomy bridge with sun pad aft. Prop pockets reduce draft, improve efficiency. Bow thruster was standard. Volvo 480hp diesels cruise at 24 knots (28–29 knots top); 610hp Volvos cruise at 27 knots (30+ knots top).

Length Overall	51'8"	Fuel	504 gals.
Beam	15'0"	Water	187 gals.
Draft	3'8"	Headroom	6'3"
Weight	44,800#	Hull Type	Deep-V
Clearance, Arch	12'8"	Deadrise Aft	19°

See Page 571 For Resale Values

Viking Yachts
New Gretna, NJ
www.vikingyachts.com

Viking Sport Cruisers 56 Flybridge
1997–2002

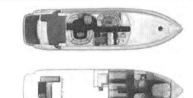

Striking U.K. import offered American buyers a high-octane mix of European styling, luxury, performance. Expansive three-stateroom interior boasts large salon with U-shaped settee, sunken galley (with attached laundry center), twin-seat lower helm, identical guest cabins, aft crew quarters. Teak-laid cockpit combines roomy storage lazarette, engineroom entryway. Note internal bridge stairs, extended swim platform, wide side decks, spacious bridge. Volvo 610hp diesels cruise at 25 knots and reach about 28 knots top.

Length Overall	55'7"	Fuel	576 gals.
Beam	15'6"	Water	199 gals.
Draft	3'9"	Headroom	6'6"
Weight	47,040#	Hull Type	Deep-V
Clearance	12'10"	Deadrise Aft	19°

See Page 571 For Resale Values

Viking Yachts
New Gretna, NJ
www.vikingyachts.com

Motoryachts & Trawlers

www.powerboatguide.com   231-360-0827

Viking Sport Cruisers 57 Flybridge
2005–08

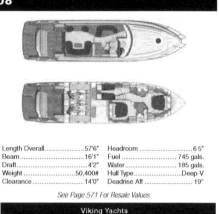

Feature-rich cruising yacht combines aggressive Mediterannean styling with posh accommodations, exceptional quality. Lush three-stateroom interior has sunken galley forward of spacious salon, twin-seat lower helm, full dinette. Large salon windows offer panoramic outside views; utility room off galley has freezer, washer/dryer. Note interior bridge steps, storage lazarette under cockpit sole, electric side windows. Extended swim platform can stow PWC or dinghy. Volvo 715hp diesels cruise at 25 knots (30 knots top).

Length Overall	57'6"	Headroom	6'5"
Beam	16'1"	Fuel	745 gals.
Draft	4'2"	Water	185 gals.
Weight	50,400#	Hull Type	Deep-V
Clearance	14'0"	Deadrise Aft	19°

See Page 571 For Resale Values

Viking Yachts
New Gretna, NJ
www.vikingyachts.com

---

www.powerboatguide.com   231-360-0827

Viking Sport Cruisers 60 Flybridge
1996–2001

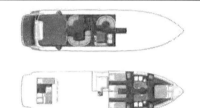

Bold UK-built luxury yacht combines sleek styling with luxury appointments, world-class performance. Posh interior with spacious salon, sunken galley features raised dinette opposite helm, three large staterooms, two full heads. Note utility room off galley, interior bridge stairs, high-gloss cherry joinery. Large hatch in cockpit sole provides access to crew quarters. Swim platform can stow tender, PWC. Engineroom is a tight fit. Volvo 610hp diesels cruise at 26 knots (29–30 knots top); optional 800 MANs cruise at 28 knots (30+ top).

Length Overall	59'11"	Fuel	756 gals.
Beam	16'1"	Water	199 gals.
Draft	3'11"	Headroom	6'5"
Weight	50,400#	Hull Type	Deep-V
Clearance	13'7"	Deadrise Aft	19°

See Page 571 For Resale Values

Viking Yachts
New Gretna, NJ
www.vikingyachts.com

---

www.powerboatguide.com   231-360-0827

Viking Sport Cruisers 61 Flybridge
2003–05

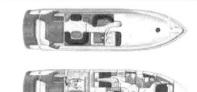

Gold-plated sportyacht provides appealing blend of European styling, American luxury, Mediteranean performance. Beautifully appointed three-stateroom interior with spacious salon features sunken galley, amidships owner's suite, three full heads. Note apartment-size galley, utility room with washer/dryer, high-gloss cherry joinery. Extended flybridge can be reached via cockpit or salon stairs; teak swim platform can stow PWC. Engineroom is a tight fit. MAN 6800hp engines cruise at 25–26 knots (about 30 knots top).

Length Overall	61'7"	Fuel	790 gals.
Beam	16'0"	Water	185 gals.
Draft	4'4"	Headroom	6'6"
Weight	58,240#	Hull Type	Deep-V
Clearance	NA	Deadrise Aft	19°

Insufficient Resale Data To Assign Values

Viking Yachts
New Gretna, NJ
www.vikingyachts.com

231-360-0827

Viking Sport Cruisers 65 Motoryacht
1999–2004

Acclaimed Euroyacht combines world-class styling with unsurpassed luxury, spirited performance. Highlights include extravagant cherrywood interior, roomy cockpit with twin transom doors, extended flybridge with radar mast, hideaway electronics console. Concealed davit disappears into transom; swim platform can support tender or PWC. Note power lower-helm deck door, inside/outside bridge access, wide side decks. Engineroom is a tight fit. MAN 1,050hp engines cruise at 30 knots (33–34 knots wide open).

Length Overall	64'10"	Fuel	959 gals.
Beam	16'9"	Water	198 gals.
Draft	4'6"	Headroom	6'6"
Weight	66,774#	Hull Type	Deep-V
Clearance	13'6"	Deadrise Aft	19°

Insufficient Resale Data To Assign Values

Viking Yachts
New Gretna, NJ
www.vikingyachts.com

231-360-0827

Vista 43 Motoryacht
1987–94

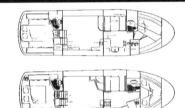

Well-regarded Taiwan motoryacht gets high marks for solid construction, comfortable layout, seakindly hull. Wide 15-foot beam allows for spacious interior with convertible dinette, light oak cabinetry, two large staterooms. Many were fitted with washer/dryer in aft cabin. Wing doors enclose large afterdeck; side decks are wide enough for easy bow access. Note aft-stateroom engineroom access. Additional features include roomy bridge, radar arch, bow pulpit. Cat 375hp diesels cruise at 18 knots (20+ knots top).

Length Overall	42'10"	Fuel	465 gals.
Hull Length	35.7"	Water	200 gals.
Beam	15'0"	Headroom	6'5"
Draft	3'6"	Hull Type	Modified-V
Weight	32,000#	Deadrise Aft	14°

Prices Not Provided for Pre-1995 Models

Vista yachts are no longer in production.

231-360-0827

Wellcraft 43 San Remo
1988–90

Standard Interioir

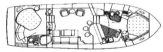

Alternate Layout

Sporty double-cabin cruiser paired aggressive styling with spacious accommodations, durable construction. Offered with choice of standard "Eurostyle" interior with curved salon sofas, or more conventional (toned-down) floorplan with L-shaped sofa. Highlights include breakfast bar with storage cabinet, spacious galley with generous storage, two large staterooms with queen beds. Note transom picture window, large flybridge with seating for eight, integral bow pulpit. Cat 375hp diesels cruise at 20 knots (low 20s top).

Length	42'10"	Fuel, Gas	300 gals.
Beam	14'6"	Fuel, Diesel	400 gals.
Draft	3'2"	Water	100 gals.
Weight	26,100#	Hull Type	Modified-V
Clearance	12'6"	Deadrise Aft	14°

Prices Not Provided for Pre-1995 Models

Wellcraft Boats
Sarasota, FL
www.wellcraft.com

Motoryachts & Trawlers

231-360-0827

Wellcraft 46 Cockpit MY
1990–95

Cockpit version of Wellcraft 43 San Remo (1988–90) combined aggressive styling with versatile layout, spacious accommodations. Offered with choice of standard "Eurostyle" interior with curved salon sofas, or more conventional (toned-down) floorplan with L-shaped sofa. Note aft picture window, cockpit access door in aft stateroom. Topside highlights include roomy flybridge with seating for six, cockpit transom door, aft deck hardtop. Big engineroom is a plus. Cruise at 18–20 knots (low 20s top) with Cat 375hp diesels.

Length	46'3"	Fuel	400 gals.
Beam	14'6"	Water	120 gals.
Draft	3'2"	Cockpit	46 sq. ft.
Weight	27,000#	Hull Type	Modified-V
Clearance	14'0"	Deadrise Aft	14°

See Page 572 For Resale Values

Wellcraft Boats
Sarasota, FL
www.wellcraft.com

231-360-0827I

Willard 30/4 Trawler
1976–2002

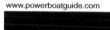

Mini flybridge trawler with rounded transom and ballasted, full-displacement hull is salty, stable, seaworthy. Cozy single-stateroom interior boasts surprisingly open salon with large windows, convertible settee, small galley aft, teak-planked flooring, lower helm station. Sailboat-like canoe stern provides good down-sea stability. Note built-in cockpit seating, slender side decks. Direct-drive engine replaced V-drive installations in 1988. About 35 were built. Single Perkins diesel delivers close to 900-mile range at 6-knot hull speed.

Length Overall	30'0"	Ballast	4,300#
Length WL	27'6"	Fuel	150 gals.
Beam	10'6"	Water	100 gals.
Draft	3'6"	Waste	25 gals.
Weight	17,000#	Hull Type	Displacement

Insufficient Resale Data To Assign Values

No longer in business.

231-360-0827

Willard 40 Trawler
1977–2003

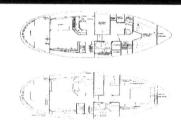

Heavy-weather trawler with ballasted, full-displacement hull combines timeless style with seakindly hull, excellent range. Two-stateroom interior includes roomy salon with convertible settee, well-equipped galley with serving counter, large head with stall shower. Hardtop shelters small cockpit. Drop-down steps open from flybridge to foredeck. No lower helm deck door. Note hullside boarding gate, staysail mast assembly. Pilothouse version was also available. About 20 were built. Cruise at 8 knots with single 120hp diesel.

Length Overall	39'9"	Ballast	7,000#
Length WL	36'1"	Fuel	600 gals.
Beam	13'8"	Water	260 gals.
Draft	4'3"	Waste	75 gals.
Weight	33,000#	Hull Type	Displacement

Insufficient Resale Data To Assign Values

No longer in business.

Section II: Sportfishing Boats

See index for complete list of models.

www.powerboatguide.com   231-360-0827

Albemarle 27/280 Express
1984–2007

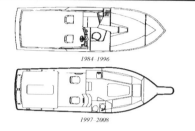

1984–1996

1997–2008

Best-selling fisherman with classic styling (called 27 Express in 1984–96; 280 Express in 1997–2007) makes the cut with anglers and cruisers alike. Spacious cockpit includes transom and in-floor fishboxes, double companion seat with livewell. Teak cabin with full galley, enclosed head sleeps two. Bridgedeck lifts for engine access. Face-lift in 1997 included redesigned helm, improved cabin headroom. Jackshaft power became available in 1986. Over 650 sold. Cruise at 24 knots with twin 280hp gas inboards; 26 knots top with twin 270 I/Os.

Length w/Pulpit	29'1"	Fuel, Twin I/B	260 gals.
Hull Length	27'1"	Fuel, Single JS	172 gals.
Beam	9'6"	Water	14 gals.
Draft	3'0"	Hull Type	Deep-V
Weight	9,500#	Deadrise Aft	24°

See Page 529 For Resale Values

Albemarle Sportfishing Boats
Edenton, NC
www.albemarleboats.com

---

www.powerboatguide.com   231-360-0827

Albemarle 290 Express
2008–Current

Heavily-built express meets tough Albemarle standards for construction, seaworthiness, fishability. Elevated helmdeck with seating for four overlooks expansive cockpit with in-floor fishbox, transom fishbox, 21-gallon livewell, tackle drawers. Transom door is optional. Forward deck section lifts for engine access. Note pop-up electronics pod at helm. Classy interior with small galley, convertible dinette, fold-down single berth sleeps four. Good range with 265-gallon fuel capacity. Yanmar 315hp diesels cruise efficiently at 25 knots (about 30 top).

Length w/Pulpit	30'6"	Fuel	265 gals.
Hull Length	28'6"	Water	28 gals.
Beam	10'9"	Clearance	8'2"
Draft	2'8"	Hull Type	Deep-V
Weight	12,500#	Deadrise Aft	21°

See Page 529 For Resale Values

Albemarle Sportfishing Boats
Edenton, NC
www.albemarleboats.com

---

www.powerboatguide.com   231-360-0827

Albemarle 305/310 Express
1995–Current

1995–2003

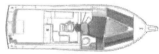

2004–Current

Hard-charging fishing machine with wide beam (called the 305 Express in 1995–2003; 310 Express since 2004) is stylish, versatile, built to last. Best-in-class layout with centerline helm includes deluxe rigging station with 30-gallon livewell, transom fishbox, dual washdowns. Roomy interior with teak trim, galley with microwave sleeps four. Bridgedeck lifts for engine access. Fuel increased, cabin & bridgedeck updated in 2004. A heavy boat for her size. Cat 350hp diesels cruise in the high 20s (about 30 knots top).

Length w/Pulpit	32'2"	Fuel	300/325 gals.
Hull Length	30'6"	Water	30 gals.
Beam	11'0"	Waste	15 gals.
Draft	2'10"	Hull Type	Deep-V
Weight	15,500#	Deadrise Aft	18°

See Page 529 For Resale Values

Albemarle Sportfishing Boats
Edenton, NC
www.albemarleboats.com

Albemarle 320 Express
1990–2006

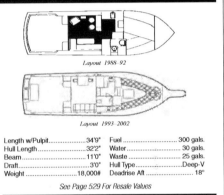

1990–98

1998–2006

Performance-driven express delivers tournament-level fishing experience with express-boat comforts, amenities. Cockpit with in-deck fishboxes, rigging station is big for a boat this size. Upscale interior has berths for four, full galley, classy teak-and-holly sole, stand-up head with shower. Updates in 2000 included raised deck for more cabin headroom, transom fishbox, improved engineroom, cockpit transom door. Excellent fit and finish. Yanmar 370hp diesels cruise at 27-28 knots and top out at 30 knots.

Length w/Pulpit	34'9"	Fuel	300 gals.
Hull Length	32'2"	Water	30 gals.
Beam	11'0"	Waste	NA
Draft	3'0"	Hull Type	Deep-V
Weight	17,000#	Deadrise Aft	18°

See Page 529 For Resale Values

Albemarle Sportfishing Boats
Edenton, NC
www.albemarleboats.com

Albemarle 325 Convertible
1988–2003

Layout 1988–92

Layout 1993–2002

Handsome small convertible with big fishing cockpit, well-appointed interior is spacious, versatile, easy on the eye. Classy galley-down interior boasts surprisingly comfortable layout (for a 32-footer) with convertible salon settee, full galley, roomy head with separate stall shower. Big engineroom, large flybridge. Major redesign in 1999 moved engines forward 10", increased cabin headroom, added cockpit transom door and lift-out fishbox. Volvo 330hp gas engines cruise at 20–22 knots; 350hp Cat 3116 diesels cruise in mid/high 20s.

Length w/Pulpit	34'9"	Fuel	300 gals.
Hull Length	32'2"	Water	30 gals.
Beam	11'0"	Waste	25 gals.
Draft	3'0"	Hull Type	Deep-V
Weight	18,000#	Deadrise Aft	18°

See Page 529 For Resale Values

Albemarle Sportfishing Boats
Edenton, NC
www.albemarleboats.com

Albemarle 360 Express
2006–Current

Hardcore fishing machine with wide beam measures up to Albemarle reputation for top-shelf engineering, premium build quality. Spacious cockpit boasts bait-prep station with sink, 25-gallon livewell, transom fishbox, in-deck fishbox. Centerline helm with flanking settees provides excellent visibility. Upscale interior with leather settee, split head, sleeps three. Hull running surface redesigned in 2010 for pod drives. Note generous fuel capacity. Cat 575hp diesels cruise at 30 knots; 435hp IPS Volvos cruise efficiently at 30 knots.

Length w/Pulpit	38'6"	Clearance	9'2"
Hull Length	36'3"	Fuel	535 gals.
Beam	13'11"	Water	95 gals.
Draft	4'0"	Hull Type	Modified-V
Weight	25,000#	Deadrise Aft	16°

See Page 529 For Resale Values

Albemarle Sportfishing Boats
Edenton, NC
www.albemarleboats.com

231-360-0827

Albemarle 410 Convertible
2005–Current

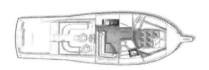

Extended-range tournament machine with wide beam, sweet styling hits all the right buttons. Upscale interior with cherry trim, quality appointments boasts surprisingly spacious salon with facing L-shaped settees, large galley with Sub-Zero refrigeration, comfortable staterooms. Cockpit comes standard with 30-gallon livewell/cooler, bait-prep center, beefy tuna door. Note spacious bridge with pod-style centerline helm, meticulous engineroom. No lightweight, 710hp Cat diesels cruise at 30 knots (about 34 knots top).

Length w/Pulpit	43'6"	Fuel	600 gals.
Hull Length	41'0"	Water	100 gals.
Beam	15'9"	Clearance	13'4"
Draft	4'0"	Hull Type	Modified-V
Weight	36,000#	Deadrise Aft	15°

See Page 530 For Resale Values

Albemarle Sportfishing Boats
Edenton, NC
www.albemarleboats.com

---

www.powerboatguide.com

231-360-0827

Albemarle 410 Express
2002–Current

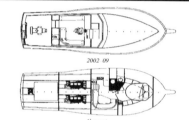

2002 09

Current

Performance-driven fishing machine delivers on promise of striking styling, first-rate amenities, quality construction. Big cockpit with in-deck fishbox, 36-gallon livewell, transom fishbox accommodates several anglers. Centerline helm with single-lever controls provides outstanding visibility. Bridgedeck with facing settees lifts on hydraulic rams for engine access. Single-stateroom interior with planked cabin sole, premium galley appliances has been updated several times. Note flared bow, tall windshield. Cat 710hp diesels cruise at a fast 30 knots.

Length w/Pulpit	43'6"	Clearance	8'4"
Hull Length	41'0"	Fuel	600 gals.
Beam	15'9"	Water	100 gals.
Draft	4'0"	Hull Type	Modified-V
Weight	32,000#	Deadrise Aft	15°

See Page 530 For Resale Values

Albemarle Sportfishing Boats
Edenton, NC
www.albemarleboats.com

---

www.powerboatguide.com

231-360-0827

Albin 28 Tournament Express
1993–2007

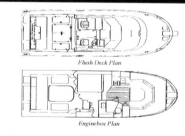

Flush Deck Plan

Enginebox Plan

Versatile fishboat/family cruiser with Downeast styling made good on Albin promise of rugged construction, seakindly hull design. Features include extended hardtop, swim platform, transom door, livewell, fishboxes, tackle storage, bow thruster. Well-appointed interior with teak-and-holly sole, quarter berth sleeps three. Flush-deck option (no engine box) in 2003 moved engine forward resulting in larger cockpit. Cruise at 18 knots with single 315hp Yanmar diesel. Cummins 380hp engine (low 20s cruise) available only with enginebox version.

Length	29'11"	Fuel	132 gals.
Beam	10'0"	Water	36 gals.
Draft	3'2"	Waste	20 gals.
Weight	7,500#	Hull Type	Modified-V
Clearance	7'9"	Deadrise Aft	16°

See Page 530 For Resale Values

Albin is no longer in business.

231-360-0827

Albin 31 Tournament Express
1995–2007

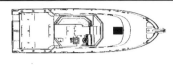

Rugged hardtop fisherman with spacious cockpit delivered on Albin promise of rock-solid construction, hardcore fishability, family-friendly layout. Very roomy cabin sleeps four with athwartships double berth aft, convertible dinette forward. Separate stall shower is a plus. Bow thruster, full-length keel are standard on single-engine models. Wide side decks, tall railings make bow access safe and secure. Over 200 built. Cruise at 18 knots with single 450hp Cummins diesel; 22 knots with twin 315hp Yanmar diesels.

Length w/Pulpit	33'0"	Fuel	300 gals.
Hull Length	31'8"	Water	73 gals.
Beam	12'4"	Waste	40 gals.
Draft	3'10"	Hull Type	Modified-V
Weight	12,500#	Deadrise Aft	14°

See Page 530 For Resale Values

Albin is no longer in business.

231-360-0827

Albin 32+2 Command Bridge
1989–2003

Versatile sportfisher with space-efficient deck layout combines sturdy construction with comfortable cabin accommodations, economical operation. Cockpit amenities include in-floor fish/storage boxes (3), transom door, livewell, sink, tackle storage. Original interior has convertible dinette forward, private stateroom aft; tri-cabin layout became available in 1996. Full-length keel protects running gear. Very wide side decks. Bow thruster was standard in later models. Cruise at 16 knots (low 20s top) with single 370hp Yanmar diesel.

Length Overall	36'9"	Fuel	260 gals.
Hull Length	34'11"	Water	117 gals.
Beam	12'2"	Waste	20 gals.
Draft	3'10"	Hull Type	Modified-V
Weight	15,000#	Deadrise Aft	13°

See Page 530 For Resale Values

Albin is no longer in business.

231-360-0827

Albin 35 Command Bridge
2004–07

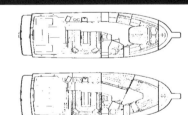

Stretched version of Albin 32+2 (1989–2003) boasts enlarged cockpit, minor cabin updates. Popular model receives high marks for surprisingly spacious interior, efficient bridge layout, solid construction. Choice of single- or twin-stateroom interiors, both with stall shower in the head. Good engine access is a plus. Note wide side decks, transom door, integral swim platform. Livewell, bow thruster were standard. Long keel protects prop in event of grounding. Cruise in the low 20s with single 370hp Cummins diesel.

Length w/Pulpit	36'9"	Fuel	260 gals.
Beam	12'4"	Water	117 gals.
Draft	3'10"	Headroom	6'4"
Weight	18,000#	Hull Type	Modified-V
Clearance	8'10"	Deadrise Aft	13°

See Page 530 For Resale Values

Albin is no longer in business.

231-360-0827

Albin 35 Tournament Express
1995–2007

Single Stateroom Layout

Two Stateroom Floorplan

Sturdy hardtop fisherman with enclosed pilothouse, protective skeg keel combines cruise-friendly interior with roomy cockpit, all-weather versatility. Highlights include spacious salon with opening windows, good helm visibility, generous galley storage, wide side decks. Offered with galley-up or galley-down floorplans, single or twin engine options. Cockpit fender storage is a nice touch. Flybridge, bow thruster were optional. Twin 370hp Cummins diesels will cruise in the mid 20s (about 30 knots top).

Length w/Pulpit	36'11"	Fuel	370 gals.
Hull Length	34'11"	Water	160 gals.
Beam	12'4"	Waste	27 gals.
Draft	3'0"	Hull Type	Modified-V
Weight	18,000#	Deadrise Aft	13°

See Page 530 For Resale Values

Albin is no longer in business.

231-360-0827

Albin 45 Command Bridge
2003–07

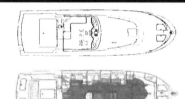

Multipurpose yacht meets the needs of hardcore anglers and family cruisers alike. Well-appointed interior includes huge master stateroom forward, complete galley, copious storage. Guest stateroom may be configured as office or utility area. Space for optional washer/dryer. Both heads share common shower stall. Salon is on the small side for a 45-footer. Note centerline bridgedeck helm position, wide side decks, integral swim platform. Cruise at 22 knots (mid 20s top) with 480hp diesels.

Length w/Pulpit	48'2"	Fuel, Std.	600 gals.
Hull Length	44'4"	Fuel, Opt.	800 gals.
Beam	16'0"	Water	200 gals.
Draft	3'11"	Hull Type	Modified-V
Weight	36,000#	Deadrise Aft	14°

See Page 530 For Resale Values

Albin is no longer in business.

231-360-0827

Angler 2700 Center Console
2003–09

Floorplan Not Available

Scaled-down version of Angler's popular 2900 Center Console is roomy, well equipped, priced right. Highlights include standard 50-gallon transom livewell, forward fishbox with overboard drain, console seat with cooler, twin pedestal seats, folding aft bench seat, console head compartment, raw-water washdown, cockpit bolsters, rod holders (4). Removable filler converts bow seating to casting platform. Recessed bow rail won't snag lines. Good finish for an inexpensive boat. About 45 knots top with twin 225s.

Length	27'6"	Fuel	200 gals.
Beam	9'6"	Water	10 gals.
Hull Draft	24"	Max HP	450
Dry Weight	5,300#	Hull Type	Deep-V
Clearance, Top	7'4"	Deadrise Aft	21°

See Page 530 For Resale Values

Angler Boats
Miami, Florida
www.anglerboats.com

www.powerboatguide.com   231-360-0827

Angler 2900 Center Console
2000–09

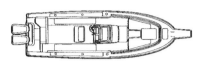

Sturdy center console from popular South Florida builder is well designed, built tough, priced right. Highlights include big 50-gallon lighted livewell, leaning post with tackle center, lockable rod storage, folding aft bench seat, four in-deck fishboxes. Large console contains stand-up head with shower. Generous beam provides cockpit space for several anglers. Deeper cockpit than many center consoles her size. No ventilation port in head compartment. Good overall finish for a price boat. Max 45 knots top with Yamaha 225s.

Length	29'6"	Fuel, Std.	200 gals.
Beam	10'0"	Fuel, Opt.	250 gals.
Draft, Up	1'6"	Max HP	600
Draft, Down	2'8"	Hull Type	Deep-V
Dry Weight	5,500#	Deadrise Aft	19°

See Page 530 For Resale Values

Angler Boats, Miami, FL
Phone 305-691-9975
www.anglerboats.com

---

www.powerboatguide.com   231-360-0827

Aquasport 275 Explorer
1999–2005

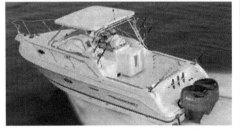

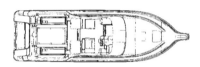

Maxi-beam express with roomy midcabin interior combines family-size accommodations with sporty styling, lots of cockpit fishing space. Fishing amenities include two large in-deck fishboxes, cockpit bolsters, lighted livewell, transom door, bait-prep center, in-deck storage locker. Foldaway transom seat frees up cockpit space. Spacious cabin with galley cabinet, quarter berth, enclosed head with shower boasts near-standing headroom. Hardtop was a popular option. Walk-thru windshield is rare in a fishing boat. About 45 knots top with twin 225s.

Length w/Pulpit	28'3"	Water	27 gals.
Beam	9'8"	Clearance, Hardtop	9'3"
Draft, Drives Down	2'10"	Max HP	500
Weight	7,000#	Hull Type	Deep-V
Fuel	188 gals.	Deadrise Aft	21°

See Page 530 For Resale Values

Aquasport ended production in 2005.

---

www.powerboatguide.com   231-360-0827

Aquasport 286/290 Express Fisherman
1982–90

Big-water express (called the 286 Express in 1982–83; 290 thereafter) ranked among the more popular 29-footers of her era. Fishing amenities include in-deck fish box, livewell, tackle center, transom door, rod holders, fresh and saltwater washdowns. Wide side decks provide secure bow access. Teak-trimmed interior with full galley, enclosed head with shower sleeps four. Excellent range. Tournament Master package included tackle station, tower. Twin 270hp gas inboards cruise at 18 knots (26–28 knots wide open).

Length w/Pulpit	31'0"	Clearance	8'0"
Hull Length	28'6"	Fuel	300 gals.
Beam	11'0"	Water	32 gals.
Draft	2'6"	Hull Type	Modified-V
Weight	9,500#	Deadrise Aft	15°

Prices Not Provided for Pre-1995 Models

Aquasport ended production in 2005.

Sportfishing Boats

231-360-0827

Atlantic 34 Express
1988–92

Midsize express fisherman was a surprise hit for company better known for trawlers and motoryachts. Large bi-level cockpit was offered in several configurations. Centerline bridgedeck hatch provides trouble-free access to motors. Roomy cabin is arranged with V-berths forward, enclosed head with shower, small galley, full dinette. Standard 350hp gas engines cruise at 25 knots (30+ knots top); optional 300hp GM 8.2 diesels cruise around 27 knots. Total of 77 were built during 5-year production run.

Length	34'0"	Fuel	300 gals.
Beam	12'0"	Water	40 gals.
Draft	3'0"	Waste	15 gals.
Weight	13,500#	Hull Type	Modified-V
Clearance	8'0"	Deadrise Aft	16°

Prices Not Provided for Pre-1995 Models

No longer in business.

231-360-0827

Bertram 28 Bahia Mar
1985–92

Classy 1980s express with wide 11-foot beam is spacious above, comfortable below. Spacious cockpit came standard with raw-water washdown rod storage lockers. Well-appointed cabin boasts convertible dinette, full galley, head with shower. Visibility through curved windshield is poor. Engine boxes eliminated in 1986 in favor of flush cockpit floor with more fishing space. Note that fiberglass fuel tanks are a problem with today's ethanol-blend gas. MerCruiser 260hp gas engines cruise at 20 knots (about 30 knots top).

Length	28'6"	Fuel	185/240 gals.
Beam	11'0"	Water	48 gals.
Draft	2'11"	Waste	40 gals.
Weight	11,700#	Hull Type	Deep-V
Clearance	7'10"	Deadrise Aft	23°

Prices Not Provided for Pre-1995 Models

Bertram Yacht
Miami, FL
www.bertram.com

231-360-0827

Bertram 28 Flybridge Cruiser
1971–94

Original Floorplan 1971-83

28 II Floorplan 1983-89

Versatile flybridge cruiser with mega-wide beam, legendary deep-V hull remains the best 28-footer ever built. Huge bi-level cockpit is great for fishing, diving or socializing. Step-down interior with convertible dinette, enclosed head with shower sleeps four adults. Cabin bulkhead extended into cockpit in 1982; fuel capacity increased in 1995; flybridge updated in 1990. Fiberglass fuel tanks are a problem with ethanol-blend gas. Excellent engine access. Twin 230hp gas inboards cruise at 18 knots; 260hp MerCruisers cruise at 20 knots.

Length	28'6"	Fuel	185/240 gals.
Beam	11'0"	Water	54 gals.
Draft	2'8"	Waste	40 gals.
Weight	12,060#	Hull Type	Deep-V
Clearance	9'4"	Deadrise Aft	23°

Prices Not Provided for Pre-1995 Models

Bertram Yacht
Miami, FL
www.bertram.com

231-360-0827

Bertram 28 Moppie
1987–94

Beamy deep-V express set high standards in her day for engineering excellence, efficient deck layout, outstanding build quality. Huge cockpit for a 28-footer has concealed on-deck galley, convenient engine access. Roomy cabin includes marine head with foldaway cover, sink, V-berth, storage. Excellent rough-water ride. Fit and finish is well above average. Fiberglass fuel tanks are a problem with ethanol-blend gas. MerCruiser 260hp gas engines cruise at 24 knots (30+ knots top).

Length	28'6"	Fuel	234 gals.
Beam	11'0"	Water	27 gals.
Draft	2'7"	Cockpit	85 sq. ft.
Weight	10,400#	Hull Type	Deep-V
Clearance	7'1"	Deadrise Aft	23°

Prices Not Provided for Pre-1995 Models

Bertram Yacht
Miami, FL
www.bertram.com

231-360-0827

Bertram 28 Sport Fisherman
1971–83

Open-cockpit version of Bertram 28 Flybridge Cruiser scored with serious anglers seeking a no-compromise fishing machine. Galley and dinette were optional; marine head is fitted between V-berths in lockable cabin. Lower helm was a popular option. Wide 11-foot beam permits a huge fishing cockpit. Notable features include excellent engine access, wide side decks, cockpit grabrails, vented windshield. Deep-V hull delivers outstanding rough-water performance. MerCruiser 230hp engines cruise at 19 knots (27–28 knots top).

Length	28'6"	Fuel	185 gals.
Beam	11'0"	Water	27 gals.
Draft	2'8"	Cockpit	85 sq. ft.
Weight	11,320#	Hull Type	Deep-V
Clearance	9'4"	Deadrise Aft	23°

Prices Not Provided for Pre-1995 Models

Bertram Yacht
Miami, FL
www.bertram.com

231-360-0827

Bertram 30 Flybridge Cruiser
1984–85

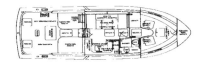

Short-lived cruiser designed to replace the classic Bertram 31 failed to catch on with buyers. Same length as the Bertram 31 but with slightly smaller cockpit dimensions, less transom deadrise (18.5° vs. 23°), improved trolling stability, and a drier ride. Well-appointed cabin offered luxuries undreamed of in the old Bertram 31. Cockpit motor boxes provide convenient seating. Too glitzy for most hardcore anglers; too expensive for others. MerCruiser 340hp gas engines cruise at 22 knots (about 30 knots top).

Length	30'7"	Fuel	220 gals.
Beam	11'4"	Water	61 gals.
Draft	3'0"	Cockpit	101 sq. ft.
Weight	16,500#	Hull Type	Deep-V
Clearance	8'5"	Deadrise Aft	18.5°

Prices Not Provided for Pre-1995 Models

Bertram Yacht
Miami, FL
www.bertram.com

Sportfishing Boats

www.powerboatguide.com   231-360-0827

Bertram 30 Moppie
1994–97

Standard Deck Layout

Sportfish Layout

Top-quality 1990s express met the needs of weekend cruisers, hardcore anglers. Clean lines exude sex appeal even without benefit of integrated swim platform. Three deck plans offered for fishing, cruising, daytime activities. Interior has double berth forward, small galley, convertible dinette, stand-up head. Note good engine access. Transom door and in-deck fishbox were standard. MerCruiser 310hp gas engines cruise at 22 knots (30+ knots top); 300hp Cummins (or Cat) diesels cruise at 26–27 knots.

Length	30'6"	Fuel	275 gals.
Beam	11'3"	Water	30 gals.
Draft	3'1"	Cockpit	64 sq. ft.
Weight	13,200#	Hull Type	Deep-V
Clearance	7'3"	Deadrise Aft	18.5°

See Page 532 For Resale Values

Bertram Yacht
Miami, FL
www.bertram.com

---

www.powerboatguide.com   231-360-0827

Bertram 31 Flybridge Cruiser
1961–83

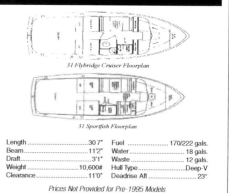

31 Flybridge Cruiser Floorplan

31 Sportfish Floorplan

Classic deep-V fishing boat with big-water DNA has never been equaled in popularity with dedicated offshore anglers. Principal features include spacious fishing cockpit, cushioned engine boxes, efficient cabin layout with enclosed head, top-quality construction. Legendary deep-V hull delivers unsurpassed seakeeping ability. Definitely a wet ride. Out of production in 1983, twenty "Silver Anniversary" models were built in 1986. Twin 330hp MerCruiser gas engines cruise at 22–23 knots (30+ top). Sportfisherman model has open cockpit, no cabin bulkhead.

Length	30'7"	Fuel	170/222 gals.
Beam	11'2"	Water	18 gals.
Draft	3'1"	Waste	12 gals.
Weight	10,600#	Hull Type	Deep-V
Clearance	11'0"	Deadrise Aft	23°

Prices Not Provided for Pre-1995 Models

Bertram Yacht
Miami, FL
www.bertram.com

---

www.powerboatguide.com   231-360-0827

Bertram 33 Flybridge Cruiser
1977–92

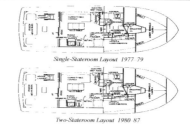

Single-Stateroom Layout 1977-79

Two-Stateroom Layout 1980-87

Premium flybridge cruiser with classic Bertram profile took small-convertible comfort to the next level. Enormous interior for a 33-foot boat. Several floorplans were offered over the years—two-stateroom layout became standard in 1980. Teak cabinetry replaced mica in 1984. Small cockpit is okay for light-tackle anglers. Lower helm was optional. Bertram 33 II, introduced in 1988, has restyled flybridge, light oak interior. Standard 340hp gas engines cruise at 18 knots; 260hp Cat diesels cruise at 22 knots.

Length	33'0"	Fuel, Gas	250/315 gals.
Beam	12'6"	Fuel, Diesel	255 gals.
Draft	3'1"	Water	70 gals.
Weight	22,800#	Hull Type	Deep-V
Clearance	12'6"	Deadrise Aft	17°

Prices Not Provided for Pre-1995 Models

Bertram Yacht
Miami, FL
www.bertram.com

231-360-0827

Bertram 33 Sport Fisherman
1979–92

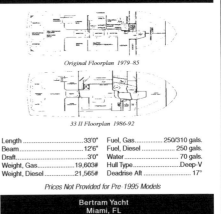

Original Floorplan 1979–85

33 II Floorplan 1986–92

Popular deep-V sportfisherman combined legendary Bertram construction with big fishing cockpit, well-appointed interior. Highlights include large cockpit with engine boxes, compact flybridge with bench seating forward of helm, roomy interior with teak trim, convertible dinette, optional lower helm. Original floorplan modified in 1986 when salon bulkhead was moved aft several inches to increase cabin space. About 350 were built. Standard 350hp gas engines cruise at 20 knots; 260hp Cat diesels cruise at 23 knots.

Length	33'0"	Fuel, Gas	250/310 gals.
Beam	12'6"	Fuel, Diesel	250 gals.
Draft	3'0"	Water	70 gals.
Weight, Gas	19,603#	Hull Type	Deep-V
Weight, Diesel	21,565#	Deadrise Aft	17°

Prices Not Provided for Pre-1995 Models

Bertram Yacht
Miami, FL
www.bertram.com

231-360-0827

Bertram 35 Convertible
1970–86

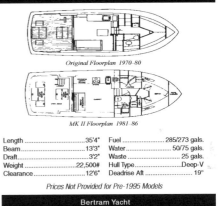

Original Floorplan 1970–80

MK II Floorplan 1981–86

Classic Bertram convertible with distinctive profile ranks among the best 35-footers ever produced. Large cockpit has space for two anglers and their gear. Single-stateroom/galley-up interior boasts comfortable salon with convertible sofa, head with stall shower, lower-level day berth, copious storage. Teak interior replaced original mica decor in 1984. Original vinyl-over-plywood cockpit sole updated in 1982 with fiberglass sole. Cruise at 20 knots with standard gas engines; 22 knots with optional 320hp Cat diesels.

Length	35'4"	Fuel	285/273 gals.
Beam	13'3"	Water	50/75 gals.
Draft	3'2"	Waste	25 gals.
Weight	22,500#	Hull Type	Deep-V
Clearance	12'6"	Deadrise Aft	19°

Prices Not Provided for Pre-1995 Models

Bertram Yacht
Miami, FL
www.bertram.com

231-360-0827

Bertram 36 Moppie
1996–2000

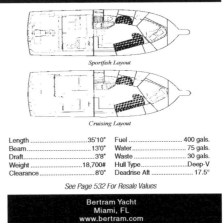

Sportfish Layout

Cruising Layout

Quality-built luxury express with many premium features came with separate cockpit layouts, one for fishing, another for cruising. Upscale interior with maple trim benefits from wide 13-foot beam. Sofa converts to upper and lower berths; head contains separate stall shower. Expansive cockpit with transom door is large enough for several anglers. Aft section of bridgedeck lifts for engine access. Excellent rough-water ride. A truly versatile yacht for serious fishing or cruising. Cruise at 25 knots with 450hp Cummins diesels.

Length	35'10"	Fuel	400 gals.
Beam	13'0"	Water	75 gals.
Draft	3'8"	Waste	30 gals.
Weight	18,700#	Hull Type	Deep-V
Clearance	8'0"	Deadrise Aft	17.5°

See Page 532 For Resale Values

Bertram Yacht
Miami, FL
www.bertram.com

Sportfishing Boats

231-360-0827

Bertram 37 Convertible
1986–93

Feature-rich tournament fisherman is widely viewed as one of the best midsize convertibles of her era. Upscale interior with oak woodwork boasts roomy salon with galley to port, built-in entertainment center, overhead rod storage. Guest cabin has over/under bunks; master stateroom has island berth. Cockpit is fitted with in-sole baitwell, tackle center, freezer. Big flybridge has guest seating forward of helm. Exceptional quality, outstanding handling. Cruise at 22 knots with 375hp Cat diesels; 27 knots with 450hp Detroits.

Length	37'9"	Fuel	473 gals.
Beam	13'3"	Water	100 gals.
Draft	3'9"	Waste	50 gals.
Weight	32,410#	Hull Type	Deep-V
Clearance	12'11"	Deadrise Aft	18°

Prices Not Provided for Pre-1995 Models

Bertram Yacht
Miami, FL
www.bertram.com

231-360-0827

Bertram 38 III Convertible
1978–86

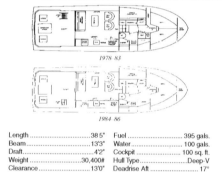

1978-83

1984-86

Good-selling convertible introduced in 1978 delivered impressive blend of comfort, performance. Large cockpit, tournament-style bridge made her well suited for serious sportfishing events. Original floorplan had toilet in forward stateroom. Lower helm was optional. Teak interior became standard in 1982, same year that original Nautilex cockpit sole was replaced with fiberglass sole. Wet ride in heavy seas. Cruise at 23 knots with 355hp Cat or 380hp Cummins diesels. Very popular model—331 were sold.

Length	38'5"	Fuel	395 gals.
Beam	13'3"	Water	100 gals.
Draft	4'2"	Cockpit	100 sq. ft.
Weight	30,400#	Hull Type	Deep-V
Clearance	13'0"	Deadrise Aft	17°

Prices Not Provided for Pre-1995 Models

Bertram Yacht
Miami, FL
www.bertram.com

231-360-0827

Bertram 38 Special
1986–87

Fast-action sportfisherman with huge cockpit, upscale accommodations enjoyed limited success due to very high price. Topside features include large bridgedeck with L-shaped seating, well-planned cockpit with bait-prep center, beefy transom door with gate. Cozy interior came complete with convertible dinette, compact galley, head with stall shower. Bridgedeck lifts for engine access. Excellent range. Cat 375hp diesels cruise at 23 knots (27–28 knots top); 435hp Detroits cruise at 25 knots (around 30 knots top).

Length	38'5"	Fuel	395 gals.
Beam	13'3"	Water	100 gals.
Draft	4'2"	Cockpit	97 sq. ft.
Weight	27,000#	Hull Type	Deep-V
Clearance	9'11"	Deadrise Aft	17°

Prices Not Provided for Pre-1995 Models

Bertram Yacht
Miami, FL
www.bertram.com

Sportfishing Boats

231-360-0827

Bertram 390 Convertible
2000–07

Leading-edge convertible with "new-look" Bertram styling set class standards for performance, luxury. Spacious two-stateroom interior with salon dinette, cherrywood cabinets compares well with many larger boats. Highlights include large head compartment, built-in entertainment center, roomy guest cabin with twin berths, overhead rod storage in salon. Engineroom—with cockpit access—is on the small side thanks to large forward fuel tank. Volvo 480hp V-drive diesels cruise at 24–25 knots (about 30 knots top).

Length w/Pulpit	41'8"	Fuel	459 gals.
Hull Length	39'0"	Water	106 gals.
Beam	13'4"	Waste	37 gals.
Draft	4'0"	Hull Type	Deep-V
Weight	34,398#	Deadrise Aft	18°

See Page 532 For Resale Values

Bertram Yacht
Miami, FL
www.bertram.com

231-360-0827

Bertram 410 Convertible
2008–Current

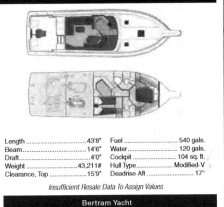

Graceful twin-stateroom convertible splits the difference between luxury cruising yacht, hardcore fishing machine. Italian-style interior features spacious salon/galley area with cherrywood furnishings, large master stateroom, guest cabin with twin berths. Note overhead rod storage in salon. Huge aft salon window overlooks cockpit. Flybridge—with raft storage locker—is big for a 40-footer. Separate machinery compartment aft of engineroom houses generator, AC units, pumps. Cummins 600hp diesels cruise at 25 knots (30 top).

Length	43'8"	Fuel	540 gals.
Beam	14'6"	Water	120 gals.
Draft	4'0"	Cockpit	104 sq. ft.
Weight	43,211#	Hull Type	Modified-V
Clearance, Top	15'9"	Deadrise Aft	17°

Insufficient Resale Data To Assign Values

Bertram Yacht
Miami, FL
www.bertram.com

231-360-0827

Bertram 42 Convertible
1976–87

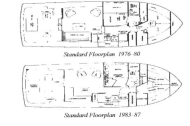

Standard Floorplan 1976-80

Standard Floorplan 1983-87

Proven tournament fishing machine with large cockpit, spacious interior needs no introduction to experienced anglers. Two-stateroom floorplan went through several updates over the years—sliding salon doors were replaced with single door in 1981; teak replaced original mica trim in 1982; queen berth became standard in master stateroom in 1983. Note that flybridge was redesigned in 1986. Deep-V hull is noted for exceptional seakeeping abilities. Cruise at 22 knots with 420hp Cummins (or 435hp GM) diesels. Total of 329 were built.

Length	42'6"	Fuel	488 gals.
Beam	14'10"	Water	150 gals.
Draft	4'0"	Cockpit	108 sq. ft.
Weight	39,400#	Hull Type	Deep-V
Clearance	14'11"	Deadrise Aft	17°

Prices Not Provided for Pre-1995 Models

Bertram Yacht
Miami, FL
www.bertram.com

Sportfishing Boats

231-360-0827

Bertram 43 Convertible
1988–96

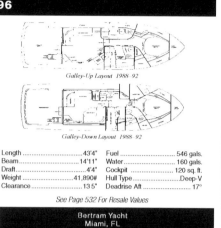

Galley-Up Layout 1988–92

Galley-Down Layout 1988–92

Strong-selling convertible earned solid reputation for top-shelf construction, superb fishability. Offered with several floorplans over the years—two-stateroom, galley-up configurations proved most popular. Huge cockpit, reinforced for fighting chair, features transom door, tackle centers, direct engineroom access. Genset was relocated to engineroom, cabin windows were slightly restyled in 1994. GM 535hp 6V92s cruise at 23–24 knots (28 knots top); 655hp MTUs (1995–96) will cruise at 26 knots (30+ knots top).

Length	43'4"	Fuel	546 gals.
Beam	14'11"	Water	160 gals.
Draft	4'4"	Cockpit	120 sq. ft.
Weight	41,890#	Hull Type	Deep-V
Clearance	13.5'	Deadrise Aft	17°

See Page 532 For Resale Values

Bertram Yacht
Miami, FL
www.bertram.com

231-360-0827

Bertram 450 Convertible
2000–Current

2-Stateroom Floorplan

3-Stateroom Floorplan

Quality-built convertible combines graceful styling, luxury accommodations, excellent performance. Standard two-stateroom interior features space-saving under-counter galley refrigeration, side-by-side berths (rather than over/under bunks) in guest cabin. Three-stateroom, galley-up floorplan became available in 2005. Salon is large for a 45-footer, but cockpit is smaller than competitors. U-shaped settee forward of helm converts to huge sun pad. Cruise at 26 knots with 660hp Cats (30 knots top); 28 knots (32 top) with 800hp MANs.

Length w/Pulpit	48'3"	Clearance	13.5"
Hull Length	45'3"	Fuel	618 gals.
Beam	14'11"	Water	159 gals.
Draft	4'4"	Hull Type	Deep-V
Weight	46,305#	Deadrise Aft	18°

See Page 532 For Resale Values

Bertram Yacht
Miami, FL
www.bertram.com

231-360-0827

Bertram 46 Convertible
1971–87

Original Two-Stateroom Layout 1971–82

46 II Galley-Down Layout 1983–85

Legendary fishing machine—dominant in 1970s, early 1980s—is one of the most popular convertible designs ever produced. Principal features include huge fishing cockpit, roomy interior, large bridge, seakindly deep-V hull. Sliding salon door replaced double doors in 1981. Fiberglass cockpit sole replaced original Nautilex liner in 1982, same year that teak interior became standard. The 46 III model (1986–87) featured a restyled interior with queen berth forward. GM 435hp engines cruise at 20 knots; 600hp GMs cruise at 25 knots.

Length	46'6"	Fuel	620/720 gals.
Beam	16'0"	Water	230/246 gals.
Draft	4'6"	Cockpit	117/130 sq. ft.
Weight	44,900#	Hull Type	Deep-V
Clearance	15'6"	Deadrise Aft	19°

Prices Not Provided for Pre-1995 Models

Bertram Yacht
Miami, FL
www.bertram.com

Bertram 46 Convertible
1995–97

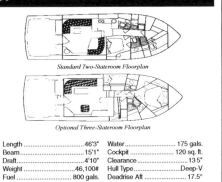

Standard Two-Stateroom Floorplan

Optional Three-Stateroom Floorplan

Powerful big-game sportfisherman is sleek, luxurious, fast across the water. Drier ride than original Bertram 46 thanks to altered keel, widened chine flats. Standard two-stateroom floorplan features mid-level galley, salon dinette, amidships owner's suite, stall showers in both heads. Three-stateroom layout was optional. Additional features include light oak interior, spacious cockpit with bait-prep center, huge flybridge. Note compact engineroom. Cruise at 26 knots (30+ knots top) with GM 735hp engines.

Length	46'3"	Water	175 gals.
Beam	15'1"	Cockpit	120 sq. ft.
Draft	4'10"	Clearance	13.5'
Weight	46,100#	Hull Type	Deep-V
Fuel	800 gals.	Deadrise Aft	17.5°

See Page 532 For Resale Values

Bertram Yacht
Miami, FL
www.bertram.com

Bertram 50 Convertible
1987–97

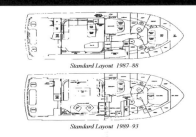

Standard Layout 1987–88

Standard Layout 1989–93

Legendary tournament machine combined muscular styling with state-of-the-art construction, executive-class accommodations. Several two- and three-stateroom floorplans were offered over the years, each with lavish salon, amidships master with queen berth. Cockpit is among the largest in her class. Updated in 1994 with larger salon windows, restyled flybridge. Considered among the best big-game sportfishing yachts ever built. Cruise at 24 knots with 735hp 8V92s; 26-27 knots with MAN 820hp diesels.

Length	50'0"	Fuel	1,046 gals.
Beam	16'2"	Water	175 gals.
Draft	5'0"	Waste	60 gals.
Weight	56,531#	Hull Type	Deep-V
Clearance	15'9"	Deadrise Aft	17°

See Page 532 For Resale Values

Bertram Yacht
Miami, FL
www.bertram.com

Bertram 510 Convertible
2000–Current

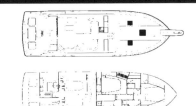

Premium sportfishing machine combines Bertram quality with sleek styling, luxurious accommodations. Three-stateroom interior is an impressive display of high-gloss cabinetry, top-shelf furnishings. Large cockpit can accommodate several anglers. Helm is well aft on the bridge to permit inclusion of U-shaped settee/dinette forward. Note control room aft of engineroom (for generator, washer/dryer), rod storage locker in salon overhead. MAN 1,050hp diesels cruise at 30 knots (33 knots top); 1,300 MANs top out at nearly 40 knots.

Length w/Pulpit	54'10"	Clearance	15'6"
Hull Length	51'5"	Fuel	1,040 gals.
Beam	16'2"	Water	185 gals.
Draft	5'0"	Hull Type	Deep-V
Weight	65,489#	Deadrise Aft	18°

See Page 532 For Resale Values

Bertram Yacht
Miami, FL
www.bertram.com

231-360-0827

Bertram 54 Convertible
1981–92

P roven tournament winner is widely regarded as one of the best sportfishing yachts of her era. Near perfect blend of design and construction—few production (or custom) boats her size compare when it comes to heavy-weather handling. Deckhouse windshield eliminated in 1986; flybridge restyled and fuel capacity increased in 1987. Several floorplans to choose from. Huge cockpit for a 54-foot yacht. Total of 177 were built. Cruise at 24 knots with 800hp 12V71s; 29-30 knots with 1,100hp 12V92s.

Length	54'0"	Fuel	1,200/1,450 gals.
Beam	16'11"	Water	250 gals.
Draft	5'2"	Waste	40 gals.
Weight	74,500#	Hull Type	Deep-V
Clearance	16'8"	Deadrise Aft	17°

Prices Not Provided for Pre-1995 Models

Bertram Yacht
Miami, FL
www.bertram.com

231-360-0827

Bertram 54 Convertible
1995–2003

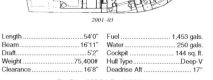

1995–2000

2001–03

U pdated version of original Bertram 54 Convertible is faster, sleeker, far more luxurious. Three-stateroom interior (updated in 2001) is an impressive display of design and workmanship. Galley and dinette are forward in huge salon; all three heads have separate stall showers. Note that single fuel tank replaced saddle tanks found in original Bertram 54. Full-featured cockpit is ready for tournament-level anglers. Superb open-water performer. GM 1,100hp—or 1,250hp Cat—diesels cruise at 28 knots (32–33 knots top).

Length	54'0"	Fuel	1,453 gals.
Beam	16'11"	Water	250 gals.
Draft	5'2"	Cockpit	144 sq. ft.
Weight	75,400#	Hull Type	Deep-V
Clearance	16'8"	Deadrise Aft	17°

See Page 532 For Resale Values

Bertram Yacht
Miami, FL
www.bertram.com

231-360-0827

Bertram 570 Convertible
2002–Current

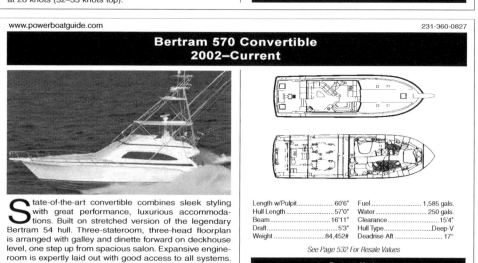

S tate-of-the-art convertible combines sleek styling with great performance, luxurious accommodations. Built on stretched version of the legendary Bertram 54 hull. Three-stateroom, three-head floorplan is arranged with galley and dinette forward on deckhouse level, one step up from spacious salon. Expansive engineroom is expertly laid out with good access to all systems. Salon rod locker, washer/dryer are standard. Note huge flybridge with U-shaped lounge seating. Cruise at 30 knots with 1,300hp MANs.

Length w/Pulpit	60'6"	Fuel	1,585 gals.
Hull Length	57'0"	Water	250 gals.
Beam	16'11"	Clearance	15'4"
Draft	5'3"	Hull Type	Deep-V
Weight	84,452#	Deadrise Aft	17°

See Page 532 For Resale Values

Bertram Yacht
Miami, FL
www.bertram.com

Sportfishing Boats

Bertram 58 Convertible
1977–83

Muscular sportfishing machine was one of the largest production convertibles of her era. Unusual construction combined fiberglass hull with aluminum decks and superstructure. Three-stateroom, three-head interior features huge salon with extravagant entertaining potential. Flybridge is arranged with second helm aft to view cockpit action. Super-size cockpit can accommodate two mounted chairs. Note big engineroom, wide side decks. No lightweight, GM 675hp 12V71 diesels cruise 18 knots and top out at 20–21 knots.

Length	58'3"	Fuel, Std.	1,300 gals.
Beam	17'11"	Fuel, Opt.	2,020 gals.
Draft	5'6"	Water	300 gals.
Weight	90,000#	Hull Type	Modified-V
Clearance	19'5"	Deadrise Aft	15°

Prices Not Provided for Pre-1995 Models

Bertram Yacht
Miami, FL
www.bertram.com

Bertram 60 Convertible
1990–2005

Standard Floorplan 1990–94

1999–2005

Powerful tournament fisherman blends classic Bertram styling with luxury interior, blistering performance. Offered with several floorplans over the years—later models reflect European styling influence of Ferretti Group, Bertram's corporate owner since 1998. Note state-of-the-art helm console, wide-open salon/galley/dinette area, spacious engineroom. GM 1,400hp 16V92 diesels cruise at 31 knots; 1,400hp Cats cruise at fast 32 knots (about 36 knots top). Enclosed Bridge model introduced in late 1995.

Length	60'0"	Fuel	1,630 gals.
Beam	16'11"	Water	250 gals.
Draft	5'6"	Cockpit	148 sq. ft.
Weight	93,500#	Hull Type	Modified-V
Clearance	16'8"	Deadrise Aft	17°

See Page 532 For Resale Values

Bertram Yacht
Miami, FL
www.bertram.com

Bertram 630 Convertible
2004–Current

3 Staterooms

4 Staterooms

Fast-action sportfisherman with open or enclosed bridge stays true to Bertram tradition for product excellence. Choice of three or four staterooms and two distinct salon layouts, both with galley, dinette forward. Circular stairway in cockpit is easier to navigate than traditional bridge ladder. (Note inside bridge access in Enclosed Bridge model.) Huge flybridge has state-of-the-art helm, seating for a small crowd. Cockpit is massive; engineroom is meticulous. MTU 2,000hp engines cruise at 35 knots (40 knots top).

Length w/Pulpit	66'9"	Fuel	1,849 gals.
Beam	18'1"	Water	251 gals.
Draft	5'3"	Cockpit	160 sq. ft.
Weight	95,609#	Hull Type	Modified-V
Clearance	NA	Deadrise Aft	16°

See Page 532 For Resale Values

Bertram Yacht
Miami, FL
www.bertram.com

Sportfishing Boats

www.powerboatguide.com   231-360-0827

Black Watch 30 Flybridge
1989–96

Solid construction, good seakeeping abilities made this compact convertible popular with many East Coast anglers. Cabin is surprisingly roomy for a 30-footer with V-berths forward, convertible dinette, small galley, generous storage. Note well-crafted teak interior trim, teak-and-holly cabin sole. Unique roll-back motor-boxes provide good access to engines. Big cockpit lacks transom door. Standard gas engines cruise in the low 20s (30+ knots top); optional 300hp Cummins diesels cruise at 27 knots.

Length	30'1"	Fuel	270 gals.
Beam	10'11"	Water	40 gals.
Draft	3'0"	Cockpit	80 sq. ft.
Weight	12,000#	Hull Type	Deep-V
Clearance	9'6"	Deadrise Aft	18°

See Page 532 For Resale Values

No longer in business.

---

www.powerboatguide.com   231-360-0827

Black Watch 30 Sportfisherman
1986–95

Sporty deep-V fisherman with wide beam gets high marks for solid construction, efficient deck layout. Cockpit is big for a 30-footer with room for a full-size fighting chair. Engine boxes provide easy access to engines while serving as convenient bait-watching seats. Compact cabin contains basic galley with sink and storage, enclosed head with shower, classy teak-and-holly cabin sole, berths for four. Above-average fit and finish. Optional 250hp Cummins (or GM) diesels cruise at 20–22 knots (mid 20s top).

Length	30'1"	Fuel	240 gals.
Beam	10'11"	Water	50 gals.
Draft	2'10"	Waste	20 gals.
Weight	9,000#	Hull Type	Deep-V
Clearance	7'0"	Deadrise Aft	18°

See Page 532 For Resale Values

No longer in business.

---

www.powerboatguide.com   231-360-0827

Blackfin 27 Combi
1985–92

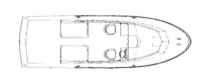

Fast-action fishing machine made good on Blackfin promise of bulletproof construction, unsurpassed rough-water performance. Cockpit in outboard models is fitted with raised fish box on starboard side, livewell and small fish box on port side —both with seat cushions. Inboard models have cushioned engine boxes. Well-appointed cuddy with teak trim has marine head with holding tank, sink, V-berth. Most 27 Combis were outboard powered. Twin 270hp gas inboards cruise at 25 knots; 225hp outboards max out at 40 knots.

Length	27'8"	Fuel	230 gals.
Beam	10'0"	Water	30 gals.
Draft	2.5"	Cockpit	61 sq. ft.
Weight	8,780#	Hull Type	Deep-V
Clearance	7'10"	Deadrise Aft	24°

Prices Not Provided for Pre-1995 Models

Blackfin is no longer in business.

Blackfin 27 Fisherman
1985–91

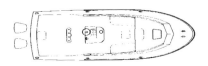

Fast-action center console with wide 10-foot beam is stable, fast, built to last. Room at the helm for two pedestal seats or wide leaning post; enough cockpit space for a full-size fishing chair. Large 230-gallon fuel capacity provides true offshore capability. Cuddy cabin features adult-size V-berth, sink, storage shelves, marine toilet. Note twin seats forward of helm console. Deep-V hull delivers one of the best small-boat rides in the business. Twin 200hp Yamahas cruise at 25 knots (about 35 knots top).

Length	27'9"	Weight, OutboardB	7,840#
Beam	10'0"	Fuel	230 gals.
Draft, Inboard	2'5"	Water	30 gals.
Draft, Outboard	2'10"	Hull Type	Deep-V
Weight, Inboard	8,780#	Deadrise Aft	24°

Prices Not Provided for Pre-1995 Models

Blackfin is no longer in business.

Blackfin 27 Sportsman
1995–98

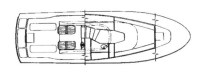

Handsome deep-V center console from late 1990s has the look, feel of a custom boat. Spacious bi-level cockpit came standard with large in-deck fishboxes, 35-gallon livewell, centerline transom fishbox. Space at the helm for an array of flush-mounted electronics. No transom door. Originally introduced as outboard-only model, Blackfin offered inboard power beginning in 1996. Yamaha 250hp outboards cruise at 26 knots (36–38 knots top); optional Yanmar 230hp diesel inboards cruise 26–27 knots.

Length	27'9"	Weight, Diesel	10,980#
Beam	10'0"	Fuel	240 gals.
Draft, Outboard	1'11"	Water	30 gals.
Draft, Inboard	2'10"	Hull Type	Deep-V
Weight, Gas	9,850#	Deadrise Aft	24°

See Page 532 For Resale Values

Blackfin is no longer in business.

Blackfin 29 Combi
1983–98

Classic fishing machine combines muscular profile with efficient deck plan, legendary rough-water ride. Teak-trimmed cabin with enclosed head, full galley is perfect for overnighting. Cushioned motorboxes double as bait-watching seats. Cabin hatch is offset to port leaving room at the helm for electronics. Low center of gravity makes for a stable trolling platform. Updated in 1995 with restyled bridgedeck, curved windshield, integral bow pulpit. Twin 320hp gas inboards—or 230hp Volvo diesels—cruise at 24–25 knots.

Length w/Pulpit	32'6"	Fuel	250 gals.
Beam	10'6"	Water	30 gals.
Draft	2'10"	Waste	20 gals.
Weight, Dsl.	12,120#	Hull Type	Deep-V
Weight, Gas	10,025#	Deadrise Aft	22°

See Page 533 For Resale Values

Blackfin is no longer in business.

www.powerboatguide.com   231-360-0827

Blackfin 29 Flybridge
1986–99

1986-98

1999

Versatile cruiser is among the smallest flybridge models built in recent years. Spacious cockpit has plenty of room for two anglers and their gear. Motorboxes provide excellent engine access, also double as bait-watching seats. Step-down cabin with convertible dinette, enclosed head with shower is surprisingly spacious, well-finished and comfortable. Deep-V hull can take on very rough water. Flybridge updated in 1995 with new seating. Twin 320hp gas inboards cruise at 22 knots; 315hp Cummins diesels cruise at 25 knots.

Length w/Pulpit	32'6"	Weight, Diesel	13,604#
Hull Length	29'4"	Fuel	250/263 gals.
Beam	10'6"	Water	50 gals.
Draft	2'6"	Hull Type	Deep-V
Weight, Gas	11,109#	Deadrise Aft	22°

See Page 533 For Resale Values

Blackfin is no longer in business.

---

www.powerboatguide.com   231-360-0827

BLACKFIN 31 Combi
1993–97

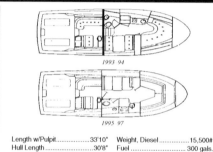

1993-94

1995-97

Proven fishing machine based on popular North Coast 31 (1988–90) meets anglers expectations for stability, fishability, dependability. Roomy cockpit includes lift-out fish/storage boxes, transom door, tackle cabinet, fresh/saltwater washdowns. Entire bridgedeck rises electrically for engine access. Well-appointed ash interior with convertible dinette, full galley, is surprisingly spacious for a 31-footer. Note wide side decks. Standard 320hp gas engines cruise at 20–21 knots (30 knots top); optional 300hp Cat diesels cruise at 23–25 knots.

Length w/Pulpit	33'10"	Weight, Diesel	15,500#
Hull Length	30'8"	Fuel	300 gals.
Beam	11'10"	Water	70 gals.
Draft	2'11"	Hull Type	Deep-V
Weight, Gas	13,300#	Deadrise Aft	21°

See Page 533 For Resale Values

Blackfin is no longer in business.

---

www.powerboatguide.com   231-360-0827

BLACKFIN 32 Combi
1988–92

Hard-hitting express with sleek profile is still regarded among the best open sportfishermen of her era. Fishing features include in-deck fishboxes, tackle station with livewell (located behind helm), rod holders, large tuna door. Cockpit is big enough for full-size chair. Upscale cabin with teak trim, convertible dinette includes roomy head, full galley, rod storage. Sportscar-like handling led one observer to call the Combi the "Porsche 911 of fishing boats." Standard 320hp gas engines cruise at 22 knots; 300hp Cat diesels cruise at 25 knots.

Length	32'0"	Fuel	304 gals.
Beam	11'11"	Water	50 gals.
Draft	2'8"	Waste	15 gals.
Weight, Gas	15,081#	Hull Type	Deep-V
Weight, Diesel	17,788#	Deadrise Aft	21°

Prices Not Provided for Pre-1995 Models

Blackfin is no longer in business.

231-360-0827

Blackfin 32 Sportfisherman
1980–91

Tournament-grade sportfisherman appeals to hard-core anglers with an eye for quality, fishability. Expansive cockpit with engine boxes can accommodate a full-size chair. Surprisingly roomy bridge has bench seat forward of helm. Step-down cabin with standing headroom, convertible dinette, teak trim sleeps four. Trim tabs, bow pulpit were standard. Low center of gravity, wide beam provide excellent stability. Deep-V hull can handle rough seas. Cruise at 18 knots with 320hp gas engines; mid 20s with optional 375hp Cat diesels.

Length	32'0"	Fuel	304 gals.
Beam	11'11"	Water	60 gals.
Draft, Diesel	2'8"	Waste	15 gals.
Weight	17,800#	Hull Type	Deep-V
Clearance	NA	Deadrise Aft	21°

Prices Not Provided for Pre-1995 Models

Blackfin is no longer in business.

231-360-0827

Blackfin 33 Combi
1993–98

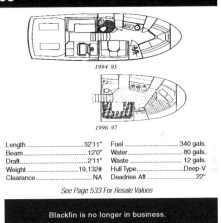

1994–95

1996–97

Handsome 1990s express with versatile deck plan led the pack in her day among midsize open fisherman. Transom door with gate, insulated in-floor fish/storage boxes, raw-water washdown, power-lift bridgedeck, tackle centers, deluxe L-shaped companion seat, two-person helm seat with icemaker under under. Upscale interior with convertible dinette, full galley, head with shower, sleeps four. Note tall windshield, wide side decks. Good engine access. Most were diesel-powered. Volvo 430hp diesels cruise at 28 knots (30+ knots top).

Length	32'11"	Fuel	340 gals.
Beam	12'0"	Water	80 gals.
Draft	2'11"	Waste	12 gals.
Weight	19,132#	Hull Type	Deep-V
Clearance	NA	Deadrise Aft	22°

See Page 533 For Resale Values

Blackfin is no longer in business.

231-360-0827

Blackfin 33 Convertible
1990–99

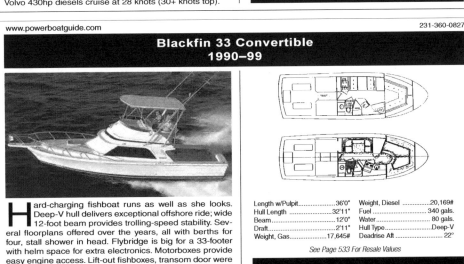

Hard-charging fishboat runs as well as she looks. Deep-V hull delivers exceptional offshore ride; wide 12-foot beam provides trolling-speed stability. Several floorplans offered over the years, all with berths for four, stall shower in head. Flybridge is big for a 33-footer with helm space for extra electronics. Motorboxes provide easy engine access. Lift-out fishboxes, transom door were standard. Crusader 320hp gas engines cruise at 22 knots (30+ knots top); 375hp Cat diesels cruise at 26–27 knots (about 30 top).

Length w/Pulpit	36'0"	Weight, Diesel	20,169#
Hull Length	32'11"	Fuel	340 gals.
Beam	12'0"	Water	80 gals.
Draft	2'11"	Hull Type	Deep-V
Weight, Gas	17,645#	Deadrise Aft	22°

See Page 533 For Resale Values

Blackfin is no longer in business.

Sportfishing Boats

231-360-0827

Blackfin 38 Combi
1989–98

Smooth-running fisherman with wide 14'5" beam offers superior offshore fishability, impressive big-water performance. Bi-level deck layout includes L-shaped lounge on bridgedeck, wide-open cockpit with lift-out fishbox, bait-prep center with sink, livewell, transom door with gate. Comfy, well-finished interior with convertible dinette, stand-up head with shower sleeps four. Most were sold with hardtop. Roomy engine compartment, good range. Detroit 485hp diesels cruise at 25 knots; 550hp Detroits cruise at 26–27 knots.

Length	38'3"	Fuel	514 gals.
Beam	14'5"	Water	100 gals.
Draft	3'9"	Waste	25 gals.
Weight	34,170#	Hull Type	Deep-V
Clearance	8'9"	Deadrise Aft	18°

See Page 533 For Resale Values

Blackfin is no longer in business.

231-360-0827

Blackfin 38 Convertible
1989–98

Two-Stateroom Floorplan

Single Stateroom w/Dinette

Heavy-duty convertible made the cut with hardcore anglers willing to pay for Blackfin quality, durability. Big fishing cockpit came standard with in-deck fishbox, bait-rigging center, dual washdowns, tackle drawers, transom door. Offered with two floorplans; standard two-stateroom layout, or alternate single-stateroom plan with full-size dinette in lieu of guest cabin. Wide side decks are a plus. Big engine compartment for a boat this size. Performance: Detroit 550hp (or 565hp) diesels cruise at 25 knots (30+ knots top).

Length w/o Pulpit	38'3"	Fuel	514 gals.
Beam	14'5"	Water	135 gals.
Draft	4'0"	Waste	40 gals.
Weight	35,970#	Hull Type	Deep-V
Clearance	13'0"	Deadrise Aft	18°

See Page 533 For Resale Values

Blackfin is no longer in business.

231-360-0827

Boston Whaler 27 Full Cabin
1984–90

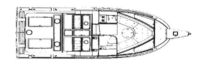

Popular 1980s express with extra-wide beam combines space, fishability in a seaworthy hull. Roomy cockpit came standard with in-deck fishboxes, rod storage, 30-gallon transom livewell. Well-finished cabin with removable dinette, compact galley, full-size head sleeps two. Unusual cathedral-sponson hull design insures outstanding stability at trolling speeds. Side decks are somewhat narrow. Note unsinkable hull construction. Offered with choice of OMC Sea Drives, various gas inboards or bracket-mounted outboards.

Length	26'7"	Fuel	170 gals.
Beam	10'0"	Water	30 gals.
Hull Draft	1'9"	Max HP	600
Dry Weight	7,640#	Hull Type	Modified-V
Clearance	NA	Deadrise Aft	18°

Prices Not Provided for Pre-1995 Models

Boston Whaler
Edgewater, FL
www.whaler.com

Boston Whaler 27 Offshore
1991–98

Floorplan Not Available

Hard-nosed fishboat with workboat profile is tough, roomy, built to last. Highlights include hardtop, in-deck fish/storage boxes, prep-station with cutting boards, tackle storage, livewell, lockable rod lockers. Roomy walk-around cabin houses a full array of galley amenities, two berths, marine head. Additional features include bow pulpit, cockpit bolsters, opening cabin ports, bow seating for three. Note wide walkways, well-placed grabrails, fold-down splashwell, unsinkable construction. Excellent helm visability. Over 40 knots top with twin 225s.

Length	26'7"	Fuel	243 gals.
Beam	10'0"	Water	30 gals.
Draft	1'9"	Max HP	500
Weight	5,800#	Hull Type	Modified-V
Clearance	NA	Deadrise Aft	20°

See Page 533 For Resale Values

Boston Whaler
Edgewater, FL
www.whaler.com

Boston Whaler 270 Outrage
2003–08

Top-notch fishing machine is unsinkable, trailerable, offshore capable. Standard features include leaning post with cooler, three in-deck storage/fishboxes, lockable head compartment with sink, lighted 23-gallon livewell, bait-prep station with cutting board. Versatile seating includes two bow bench seats, console seat, fold-away transom seat. More rod holders than a 40-footer. Big 200-gallon fuel capacity allows for long cruises. Note flawless finish, unsinkable construction. Twin 225hp Mercury outboards deliver a top speed of about 45 knots.

Length	27'0"	Fuel	200 gals.
Beam	8'6"	Water	20 gals.
Hull Draft	1'8"	Max HP	450
Dry Weight	5,160#	Hull Type	Deep-V
Clearance, Top	8'9"	Deadrise Aft	22°

See Page 533 For Resale Values

Boston Whaler
Edgewater, FL
www.whaler.com

Boston Whaler 275 Conquest
2001–05

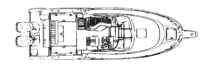

Good-looking Whaler express blurs the line between capable fishing boat, comfortable family cruiser. Lighted livewell, transom door, two in-deck fishboxes, tackle station, removable cooler, folding stern seat, fresh/salt washdowns, cockpit bolsters, transom shower, opening cabin ports, bow pulpit. Well-appointed cabin with midcabin berth, convertible dinette sleeps four. Most were sold with hardtop. Unsinkable hull construction. An expensive boat during her production years. About 40 knots max with 225 Mercs.

Length w/Pulpit	28'8"	Fuel	192 gals.
Beam	9'7"	Water	30 gals.
Hull Draft	1'6"	Max HP	500
Dry Weight	6,200#	Hull Type	Deep-V
Clearance w/Hardtop	8'9"	Deadrise Aft	20°

See Page 533 For Resale Values

Boston Whaler
Edgewater, FL
www.whaler.com

231-360-0827

Boston Whaler 28/290 Outrage
1999–2003

Quality walkaround fisherman combines efficient deck layout with roomy interior, top-notch finish. Fishing amenities include 30-gallon livewell, two in-deck fishboxes, bait-prep station with two sinks, under-seat storage/tackle drawers, fresh/salt washdowns, transom door. Well-finished interior with enclosed head, refrigerator sleeps three. Called the 28 Outrage in 1998–2001; 290 Outrage in 2002–03. Unsinkable hull construction. Outstanding range with 296-gallon fuel capacity. About 40 knots top with 225 Mercs.

Length w/Pulpit	30'8"	Fuel	296 gals.
Beam	10'4"	Water	40 gals.
Draft, Up	1'8"	Max HP	500
Draft, Down	3'0"	Hull Type	Deep-V
Weight	7,000#	Deadrise Aft	20°

See Page 533 For Resale Values

Boston Whaler
Edgewater, FL
www.whaler.com

231-360-0827

Boston Whaler 28/295 Conquest
1999–2003

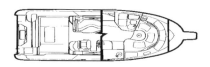

Sturdy offshore express introduced in 1999 pairs durable construction with best-in-class amenities, legendary Whaler quality. Fishing features include 30-gallon livewell, rod racks, coaming bolsters, two in-deck fishboxes, rod holders, built-in tackle drawers. Stern seat folds into transom to free up cockpit space. Well-appointed cabin with dinette/V-berth, teak-and-holly sole, midcabin berth sleeps four. Called 28 Conquest in 1998–2001; 290 Conquest in 2002–03. Excellent range. Unsinkable. Nearly 40 knots top with 225 Mercs.

Length w/Pulpit	30'8"	Fuel	296 gals.
Hull Length	28'5"	Water	40 gals.
Beam	10'4"	Max HP	500
Hull Draft	1'8"	Hull Type	Deep-V
Dry Weight	8,500#	Deadrise Aft	20°

See Page 533 For Resale Values

Boston Whaler
Edgewater, FL
www.whaler.com

231-360-0827

Boston Whaler 280 Outrage
2009–Current

Hardcore center console with integrated hardtop/windshield targets demanding anglers with big checkbooks. Highlights include foldaway transom seat, foldaway, aft-facing amidships seats, lockable rod storage, 40-gallon livewell, two mascerated fishboxes, power windshield vent, 20 rodholders. Note through-stem anchor system and recessed windlass. Slide-out cooler doubles as sunpad filler. Steep transom deadrise makes this the deepest-V Whaler yet. Foam-filled hull is unsinkable. Twin 300hp Mercs top out at close to 50 knots.

Length	27'7"	Fuel	200 gals.
Beam	9'4"	Water	28 gals.
Hull Draft	1'8"	Max HP	600
Dry Weight	6,100#	Hull Type	Deep-V
Clearance w/Hardtop	8'10"	Deadrise Aft	23°

See Page 533 For Resale Values

Boston Whaler
Edgewater, FL
www.whaler.com

Boston Whaler 285 Conquest
2006–Current

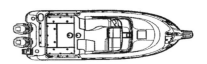

Top-shelf cruiser with graceful lines outclasses most competitors for versatility, comfort, performance. Features include hardtop with rod holders, in-deck fishboxes, dual washdowns, 20-gallon lighted livewell, foldaway stern seat, coaming bolsters, transom shower, bait-prep station with sink, tackle storage. Room at helm for mounting big-screen electronics. Roomy cabin with midcabin aft, enclosed head with shower, convertible dinette sleeps four in comfort. Foam-filled hull is unsinkable. About 40 knots max with 225 Mercs.

Length w/Pulpit	30'2"	Fuel	207 gals.
Beam	9'8"	Water	30 gals.
Draft, Drives Up	1'8"	Max HP	450
Draft, Drives Down	3'2"	Hull Type	Deep-V
Hull Weight	6,200#	Deadrise Aft	20°

See Page 533 For Resale Values

Boston Whaler
Edgewater, FL
www.whaler.com

Boston Whaler 305 Conquest
2004–Current

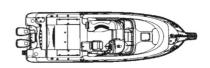

Heavily-built cruiser with executive-class amenities takes express-boat comfort, versatility to the next level. Standard features include hardtop with rod holders, 24-gallon livewell, foldaway stern seat, in-deck fishboxes with pump-outs, bait-prep center, cockpit shower, raw-water washdown, coaming bolsters, flip-up helm seat. Upscale interior with midcabin berth, cherry trim boasts surprisingly large galley, full head with VacuFlush toilet, Corian countertop. Unsinkable hull construction. Popular model. Low 30s top with 225 Mercs.

Length w/Pulpit	32'1"	Fuel	300 gals.
Hull Length	30'1"	Water	40 gals.
Beam	10'7"	Max HP	600
Hull Draft	1'8"	Hull Type	Deep-V
Dry Weight	8,500#	Deadrise Aft	20°

See Page 533 For Resale Values

Boston Whaler
Edgewater, FL
www.whaler.com

Boston Whaler 31 Sportfisherman
1988–91

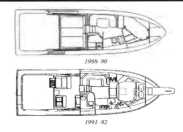

1988–90

1991–92

Popular diesel express introduced in 1988 was a rare departure from Boston Whaler's history of building outboard-only products. Fishing amenities include large insulated fishbox, transom door, livewell, fresh and saltwater washdowns. Cockpit is large enough for full-size chair. Modified-V hull with wide sponsons is stable at trolling speeds, dry in a chop. Cockpit and interior were redesigned in 1991. Bridge lifts electrically for engine access. Cummins 250hp diesels cruise at 20 knots; Cummins 300hp engines cruise at 25 knots.

Length	31'9"	Fuel	313 gals.
Beam	11'10"	Water	40 gals.
Draft	2'8"	Waste	15 gals.
Weight	13,000#	Hull Type	Modified-V
Clearance	7'6"	Deadrise Aft	20°

Prices Not Provided for Pre-1995 Models

Boston Whaler
Edgewater, FL
www.whaler.com

Boston Whaler 320 Outrage
2003–Current

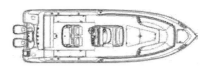

Big-water fishing machine makes the cut with serious anglers demanding the best in quality, fishability. Features include T-top with electronics box, foldaway stern seat, in-deck fishboxes, deluxe helm/passenger seats with flip-up bolsters, anchor windlass. Deluxe bait-prep station includes sink, tackle boxes, cutting board, 45-gallon livewell. Console head has standing headroom, sink, pull-out shower, vertical rod storage. Optional deck suspension system softens the ride in rough seas. Keel pad improves low-speed lift. Over 40 knots top with 250hp Mercs.

Length	32'2"	Fuel	300 gals.
Beam	10'2"	Water	40 gals.
Hull Draft	1'10"	Max HP	600
Dry Weight	8,500#	Hull Type	Deep-V
Clearance, Top	9'11"	Deadrise Aft	23°

See Page 533 For Resale Values

Boston Whaler
Edgewater, FL
www.whaler.com

Boston Whaler 320 Outrage Cuddy
2006–Current

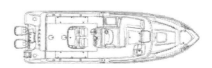

Classy fish-fighter combines efficient deck layout with forward guest seating, twin-berth cuddy. Highlights include standard hardtop with electronics box, bait-prep station with 45-gallon livewell, in-floor fishboxes, lockable rod storage. Console head compartment boasts standing headroom, vertical rod storage. Well-finished cuddy with rod racks, teak flooring sleeps two. Foam-filled hull is unsinkable. Optional deck suspension system softens the ride in rough seas. Keel pad improves low-speed lift. Over 40 knots top with 250hp Mercs.

Length	32'2"	Fuel	300 gals.
Beam	10'2"	Water	40 gals.
Hull Draft	1'10"	Max HP	600
Dry Weight	9,000#	Hull Type	Deep-V
Clearance, Top	9'10"	Deadrise Aft	20°

See Page 533 For Resale Values

Boston Whaler
Edgewater, FL
www.whaler.com

Boston Whaler 34 Defiance
1999–2002

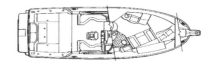

Smooth-running inboard express looks good, runs well, sold poorly. Standard features include transom livewell, bait-prep station with sink, tackle drawers, transom door, insulated in-deck fishboxes, centerline helm with flanking settees, underwater exhaust. Well-appointed interior with Corian counters, leather seating sleeps four. Traditional stringer-type hull construction differed from Whaler's signature foam-sandwich construction process. Called the 350 Defiance in 2002. Cat 350 diesels cruise at 24 knots; 420hp Yanmars cruise at 25–26 knots.

Length w/Pulpit	37'6"	Clearance, Top	8'2"
Hull Length	34'6"	Fuel	384 gals.
Beam	13'3"	Water	72 gals.
Draft	2'11"	Hull Type	Deep-V
Weight	19,000#	Deadrise Aft	20°

See Page 533 For Resale Values

Boston Whaler
Edgewater, FL
www.whaler.com

Sportfishing Boats

231-360-0827

Boston Whaler 345 Conquest
2007–Current

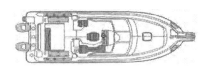

Biggest Whaler yet is packed with top-of-the-line fishing amenities, luxury-class cabin accommodations. Highlights include stylish integrated windshield/hardtop with floodlights, uncluttered cockpit with 40-gallon livewell, bait-prep station, deluxe interior with superb galley, berths for six. Air conditioning, bow thruster, 8kw genset are standard. Note foldaway stern bench seat, macerated in-sole fishboxes. Huge center hatch provides access to tanks, pumps, etc. Triple 250hp Mercury Verados deliver 40+ knots wide open. Unsinkable construction.

Length w/Pulpit	35'11"	Fuel	421 gals.
Beam	11'8"	Water	64 gals.
Hull Draft	1'10"	Max HP	750
Hull Weight	14,200#	Hull Type	Modified-V
Weight w/Engines	20,000#	Deadrise Aft	15°

See Page 533 For Resale Values

Boston Whaler
Edgewater, FL
www.whaler.com

231-360-0827

Cabo 31 Express
1995–2004

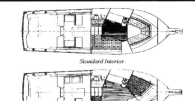

Standard Interior

Offset Double Berth

Premium West Coast express with top-level amenities blends cutting-edge quality with handsome design, unsurpassed fishability. Well-appointed cabin is spacious for a 31-footer with berths for four, full galley, teak-and-holly sole, enclosed head with shower. Cockpit amenities include bait-prep center, transom fishbox, dual washdowns, transom door with gate. Bridgedeck lifts hydraulically for engine access. Attention to detail is as good as it gets. Cat 350hp diesels cruise at 26–27 knots; 420hp Cats cruise at 29–30 knots.

Length w/Pulpit	33'2"	Fuel	350 gals.
Hull Length	31'0"	Water	50 gals.
Beam	12 5"	Headroom	6 5"
Draft	3'2"	Hull Type	Modified-V
Weight	15,000#	Deadrise Aft	17.5°

See Page 533 For Resale Values

Cabo Yachts
Adelanto, CA
www.caboyachts.com

231-360-0827

Cabo 32 Express
2005–Current

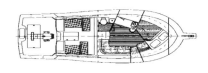

Fast-action battlewagon meets legendary Cabo standards for bold design, premium construction, unsurpassed fishability. Highlights include bait-prep center with tackle storage, 45-gallon transom livewell, transom door with gate, dual washdowns, deluxe helm/passenger seats, large-capacity in-deck fishbox. Bridgedeck lifts for access to meticulous engineroom. Upscale interior with offset double berth, convertible lounge sleeps four. Exemplary fit and finish. Cruise at 28 knots with 460 Cat diesels (low-to-mid 30s wide open).

Length w/Pulpit	35'0"	Fuel	350 gals.
Hull Length	32'10"	Water	50 gals.
Beam	13'3"	Waste	12 gals.
Draft	2'8"	Hull Type	Modified-V
Weight	19,100#	Deadrise Aft	17.5°

See Page 533 For Resale Values

Cabo Yachts
Adelanto, CA
www.caboyachts.com

Sportfishing Boats

231-360-0827

Cabo 35 Express
1994–Current

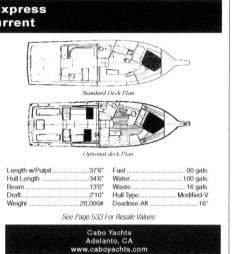

Standard Deck Plan

Optional deck Plan

Superior construction, intelligent deck layout, meticulous finish have made this muscular express a modern sportfishing classic. Uncluttered cockpit includes bait-prep center, transom door, two in-deck fish boxes, dual washdowns. Bridgedeck lifts hydraulically for excellent engine access. Single-stateroom floorplan has seen several updates over the years. Hull bottom updated in 2000 with finer entry for softer ride, improved head-sea performance. Cat 375hp diesels cruise in the high 20s; 461hp Cats cruise at 28 knots.

Length w/Pulpit	37'6"	Fuel	00 gals.
Hull Length	34'6"	Water	100 gals.
Beam	13'0"	Waste	16 gals.
Draft	2'10"	Hull Type	Modified-V
Weight	20,000#	Deadrise Aft	16°

See Page 533 For Resale Values

Cabo Yachts
Adelanto, CA
www.caboyachts.com

231-360-0827

Cabo 35 Flybridge
1992–Current

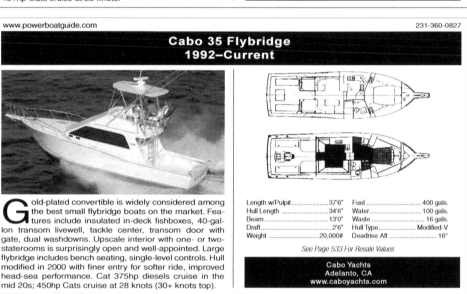

Gold-plated convertible is widely considered among the best small flybridge boats on the market. Features include insulated in-deck fishboxes, 40-gallon transom livewell, tackle center, transom door with gate, dual washdowns. Upscale interior with one- or two-staterooms is surprisingly open and well-appointed. Large flybridge includes bench seating, single-level controls. Hull modified in 2000 with finer entry for softer ride, improved head-sea performance. Cat 375hp diesels cruise in the mid 20s; 450hp Cats cruise at 28 knots (30+ knots top).

Length w/Pulpit	37'6"	Fuel	400 gals.
Hull Length	34'6"	Water	100 gals.
Beam	13'0"	Waste	16 gals.
Draft	2'6"	Hull Type	Modified-V
Weight	20,000#	Deadrise Aft	16°

See Page 533 For Resale Values

Cabo Yachts
Adelanto, CA
www.caboyachts.com

231-360-0827

Cabo 38 Express
2008–Current

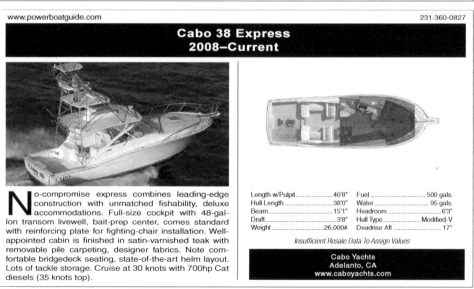

No-compromise express combines leading-edge construction with unmatched fishability, deluxe accommodations. Full-size cockpit with 48-gallon transom livewell, bait-prep center, comes standard with reinforcing plate for fighting-chair installation. Well-appointed cabin is finished in satin-varnished teak with removable pile carpeting, designer fabrics. Note comfortable bridgedeck seating, state-of-the-art helm layout. Lots of tackle storage. Cruise at 30 knots with 700hp Cat diesels (35 knots top).

Length w/Pulpit	40'8"	Fuel	500 gals.
Hull Length	38'0"	Water	95 gals.
Beam	15'1"	Headroom	6'3"
Draft	3'8"	Hull Type	Modified-V
Weight	26,000#	Deadrise Aft	17°

Insufficient Resale Data To Assign Values

Cabo Yachts
Adelanto, CA
www.caboyachts.com

231-360-0827

Cabo 40 Express
2003–Current

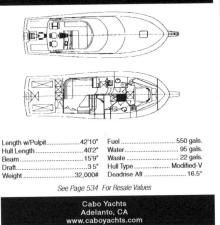

Gold-plated sportfishing machine with impressive feature list is second to none with serious anglers. Best-in-class layout includes spacious bridgedeck with centerline helm, huge cockpit with 45-gallon transom livewell, maxi-volume interior with very large stateroom, premium hardware and furnishings. Note single-lever helm controls, large-capacity fishboxes, tremendous rod storage. Engineroom is a work of art. Cruise at 28–30 knots with 715hp Cats; low to mid 30s with 788hp MANs. Newer models come with Zeus pod drives.

Length w/Pulpit	42'10"	Headroom	6'3"
Beam	15'9"	Fuel	550 gals.
Draft	3.5"	Water	95 gals.
Weight	28,000#	Hull Type	Modified-V
Clearance	14'2"	Deadrise Aft	16.5°

See Page 534 For Resale Values

Cabo Yachts
Adelanto, CA
www.caboyachts.com

231-360-0827

Cabo 40 Flybridge
2004–Current

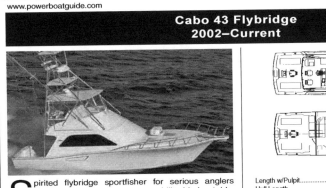

Premium midsize convertible scores with deep-pocket anglers willing to pay for Cabo quality, performance. Cockpit amenities include bait-prep center with sink, 48-gallon transom livewell, large-capacity in-deck fishboxes, transom door with gate. Handsome two-stateroom interior with teak cabinets, leather seating strikes a balance between cruising comfort, sportfish practicality. Good sightlines from centerline helm. Meticulous engineroom layout. Cruise at 28–30 knots with 715hp Cats; low to mid 30s with 800hp MANs.

Length w/Pulpit	42'10"	Fuel	550 gals.
Hull Length	40'2"	Water	95 gals.
Beam	15'9"	Waste	22 gals.
Draft	3.5"	Hull Type	Modified-V
Weight	32,000#	Deadrise Aft	16.5°

See Page 534 For Resale Values

Cabo Yachts
Adelanto, CA
www.caboyachts.com

231-360-0827

Cabo 43 Flybridge
2002–Current

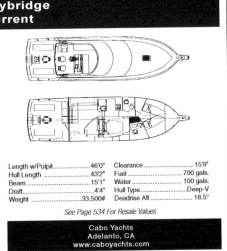

Spirited flybridge sportfisher for serious anglers combines small-boat maneuverability, big-boat ride. Large cockpit has all the features expected in a pocket battlewagon. Rich two-stateroom, two-head interior with Corian counters, teak-and-holly sole includes washer/dryer space. Bridge is fitted with large instrument console for big-screen electronics. Note single-lever helm controls, meticulous engineroom, near perfect fit and finish. Deep-V hull delivers super-soft ride. Cruise at 30 knots with 800hp MANs (35 knots top).

Length w/Pulpit	46'0"	Clearance	15'9"
Hull Length	43'2"	Fuel	700 gals.
Beam	15'1"	Water	100 gals.
Draft	4'4"	Hull Type	Deep-V
Weight	33,500#	Deadrise Aft	18.5°

See Page 534 For Resale Values

Cabo Yachts
Adelanto, CA
www.caboyachts.com

Sportfishing Boats

231-360-0827

Cabo 45 Express
1997–Current

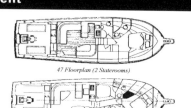

Single Stateroom

Twin Staterooms

Powerful open fishing machine is expensive, fast, loaded with features. Highlights include huge bridge-deck with centerline helm, spacious fish-equipped cockpit, elegant two-stateroom interior with U-shaped salon seating. Note massive, well-finished engineroom. Notable features include storage for over 20 rods, electric windshield vent, teak-and-holly cabin sole. Cat 660hp diesels cruise at 25 knots (about 30 knots top); 800hp Cats cruise at 28 knots (32–33 top). Popular boat—over 100 built to date.

Length w/Pulpit	48'1"	Fuel	800 gals.
Hull Length	45'1"	Water	100 gals.
Beam	15'8"	Headroom	6'6"
Draft	4'0"	Hull Type	Modified-V
Weight	33,000#	Deadrise Aft	11.5°

See Page 534 For Resale Values

Cabo Yachts
Adelanto, CA
www.caboyachts.com

231-360-0827

Cabo 47/48 Flybridge
2000–Current

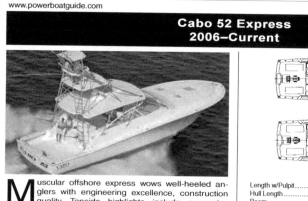

47 Floorplan (2 Staterooms)

48 Floorplan (3 Staterooms)

World-class flybridge fisherman (called Cabo 47 until 2003) is impressive blend of modern design, quality construction, leading-edge performance. Two-stateroom interior of original Cabo 47 left space for a huge cockpit; three-stateroom, two-head layout of Cabo 48 has slightly smaller-but still massive-cockpit. State-of-the-art helm, teak-and-holly salon sole, meticulous engineroom. Fit and finish is as good as it gets. Cruise at 28 knots with 800hp MAN engines; 32-33 knots with 1,050hp MANs.

Length w/Pulpit	50'7"	Clearance	16'0"
Hull Length	47'7"	Fuel	1,020 gals.
Beam	15'8"	Water	100 gals.
Draft	4'0"	Hull Type	Modified-V
Weight	45,000#	Deadrise Aft	11.5°

See Page 534 For Resale Values

Cabo Yachts
Adelanto, CA
www.caboyachts.com

231-360-0827

Cabo 52 Express
2006–Current

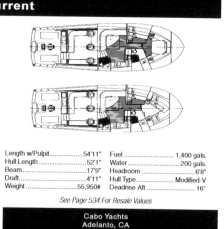

Muscular offshore express wows well-heeled anglers with engineering excellence, construction quality. Topside highlights include expansive 110-square-foot cockpit, big 75-gallon transom livewell, deluxe bait-prep center, centerline helm position. Cavernous twin-cabin interior features home-size galley, day head, bulkhead-mounted plasma TV. Walk-in engineroom boasts full 6'8" headroom. Note premium Stidd helm chairs. Cat 1,550hp MAN engines cruise at 33–35 knots (about 40 knots wide open).

Length w/Pulpit	54'11"	Fuel	1,400 gals.
Hull Length	52'1"	Water	200 gals.
Beam	17'9"	Headroom	6'8"
Draft	4'11"	Hull Type	Modified-V
Weight	55,950#	Deadrise Aft	16°

See Page 534 For Resale Values

Cabo Yachts
Adelanto, CA
www.caboyachts.com

Cape Dory 28 Flybridge
1985–94

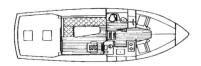

Salty Downeast cruiser with full keel is easily driven, inexpensive to operate, loaded with eye appeal. Space-efficient interior with classy teak-and-holly flooring, teak cabinets includes convertible salon dinette, standard lower helm. Tall flybridge provides great 360-degree visibility. Wide side decks allow secure bow access. Deep keel protects prop from grounding. Excellent engine access. Very popular model. Good fit and finish. Single Volvo 200hp diesel cruises economically at 14 knots (16–17 knots top).

Length	27'11"	Headroom	6'3"
Beam	9'11"	Fuel	120 gals.
Draft	2'9"	Water	71 gals.
Weight	9,500#	Waste	25 gals.
Clearance	11'2"	Hull Type	Semi-Disp.

Prices Not Provided for Pre-1995 Models

Cape Dory is no longer in business.

Cape Dory 28 Open
1985–94

Classic Downeast bass fisherman with full-keel hull combines simple elegance with spacious cockpit, comfortable cabin accommodations. Uncluttered cockpit with flush engine hatch offers lots of room for tackle boxes and rods. Very roomy interior for a 28-foot boat with quality teak joiner work, full galley, generous storage. Note good helm visibility, wide side decks, unusually tall windshield. Truly excellent fit and finish throughout. Cruise at 12–14 knots with single 200hp Volvo diesel (about 16 knots top).

Length	27'11"	Headroom	6'0"
Beam	9'11"	Fuel	120 gals.
Draft	2'9"	Water	31 gals.
Weight	8,000#	Cockpit	93 sq. ft.
Clearance	8'0"	Hull Type	Semi-Disp.

Prices Not Provided for Pre-1995 Models

Cape Dory is no longer in business.

Cape Dory 33 Flybridge
1988–94

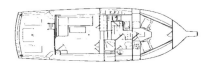

Downeast-style flybridge cruiser gets high marks for construction, thoughtful layout, planing-speed performance. Appealing galley-down teak interior with planked cabin sole features roomy salon with lower helm, large cabin windows, stall shower in head. Excellent natural lighting and ventilation. Wide side decks, lockable in-floor cockpit storage are a plus. Good visibility from both helms. Long keel protects running gear in event of grounding. Twin 200hp Volvo diesels cruise at 15 knots (18–20 knots top).

Length	32'10"	Fuel	260 gals.
Beam	12'2"	Water	90 gals.
Draft	2'11"	Waste	40 gals.
Weight	13,500#	Hull Type	Modified-V
Clearance	12'8"	Deadrise Aft	12°

Prices Not Provided for Pre-1995 Models

Cape Dory is no longer in business.

Sportfishing Boats

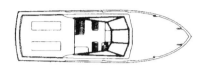

www.powerboatguide.com   231-360-0827

Carolina Classic 28
1994–Current

Hard-charging inboard express with wide 10'6" beam is roomy, stable, loaded with big-boat features. Well-appointed cabin with teak trim includes compact galley, large V-berths, enclosed head with shower. Spacious cockpit is fitted with full tackle center, in-deck fishboxes, dual washdowns, transom livewell. Bridgedeck lifts for engine access. Wide side decks are a plus. Terrific rough-water ride. Offered with inboard or jackshaft power. Yanmar 315hp diesels cruise at 28 knots. Volvo 260hp diesels cruise at 25 knots.

Length	28 5"	Fuel, Dsl.	220 gals.
Beam	10'6"	Water	55 gals.
Draft	2'6"	Waste	15 gals.
Weight	15,000#	Hull Type	Deep-V
Fuel, Gas	260 gals.	Deadrise Aft	24°

See Page 534 For Resale Values

Carolina Classic Boats
Edenton, NC
www.carolinaclassicboats.com

www.powerboatguide.com   231-360-0827

Carolina Classic 32
2004–Current

Fast-action fishing machine with big 80-sq.-ft. cockpit competes with the big boys in offshore fishing wars. Fishing features include in-deck fishboxes, full-beam tackle station, secure rod storage, transom door, icebox. Bridgedeck—with seating for six—rises electrically for full access to large engine compartment. Roomy cabin with teak-and-holly sole features stand up head and shower, double berth, seven foot bunk. Outstanding range. Impressive boat. Cruise in the high 20s (30+ knots top) with Yanmar 440hp diesels.

Length	32'0"	Fuel	355 gals.
Beam	13'0"	Water	50 gals.
Draft	3'6"	Cockpit	80 sq. ft.
Weight	26,000#	Hull Type	Deep-V
Clearance	NA	Deadrise Aft	20°

See Page 534 For Resale Values

Carolina Classic Boats
Edenton, NC
www.carolinaclassicboats.com

www.powerboatguide.com   231-360-0827

Carolina Classic 35
1998–Current

Tournament-grade express with spacious cockpit, upscale cabin appeals to experienced anglers able to afford a top-shelf fishboat. Topside highlights include full-beam rigging center, bait station with sink and icebox, cockpit toerail, in-deck fishboxes. Well-appointed interior—upscale accommodations indeed for a dedicated fishing boat—sleeps four adults. Bridgedeck lifts electrically for engine access. Truly outstanding rough-water ride. Cruise in the mid 20s with 480hp Cummins or Volvo diesels (30+ knots wide open).

Length	34'9"	Water	55 gals.
Beam	13'6"	Headroom	6'4"
Draft	3'0"	Clearance	NA
Weight	25,000#	Hull Type	Deep-V
Fuel	435 gals.	Deadrise Aft	18°

See Page 534 For Resale Values

Carolina Classic Boats
Edenton, NC
www.carolinaclassicboats.com

Sportfishing Boats

231-360-0827

Century 2900 Walkaround
2001–04

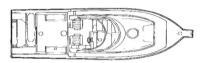

Brawny walkaround fisherman with trailerable 8'6" beam combines efficient deck layout with family-friendly cabin, sturdy construction. Roomy midberth interior with fully-equipped galley, convertible dinette, enclosed head with shower sleeps four. Cockpit amenities include two in-deck fishboxes, 45-gallon transom livewell, rigging station with sink, coaming bolsters, foldaway rear seat, transom door. Cockpit dimensions are on the small side compared with many other 29-footers. Over 40 knots top with Yamaha 250s.

Length w/Pulpit	29'4"	Fuel	250 gals.
Beam	9'6"	Water	20 gals.
Draft, Down	2'7"	Max HP	500
Dry Weight	5,300#	Hull Type	Deep-V
Clearance	6'10"	Deadrise Aft	23°

See Page 536 For Resale Values

Century Boats
Panama City, FL
www.centuryboats.com

231-360-0827

Century 2900/2901 Center Console
2000–08

2900 Deck Plan

2901 Deck Plan

Well-rigged offshore fishing machine (called 2900 in 2000-06; 2901 in 2007–08) is roomy, fast, built to last. Moderate beam combines generous cockpit space with good stability. Pressure water system, deluxe leaning post, lockable electronics box, insulated fishboxes are standard. Rear seat conceals transom sink with cutting board. Enclosed head has bunk, sink, electric head. Super range with 300-gallon fuel capacity. Twin Yamaha 250hp outboards top out at over 40 knots.

Length	29'4"	Water	22 gals.
Beam	9'6"	Waste	7 gals.
Hull Drfat	1'10"	Max HP	600
Hull Weight	7,000#	Hull Type	Deep-V
Fuel	300 gals.	Deadrise Aft	23°

See Page 536 For Resale Values

Century Boats
Panama City, FL
www.centuryboats.com

231-360-0827

Century 3000 Center Console
1994–99

Weight-efficient center console with integrated transom meets angler's need for speed, range, durability. Highlights include 32-gallon transom livewell, transom sink with cutting board, bow casting platform, three in-deck fishboxes, pressure water system with shower. Tall windshield offers good protection from wind and spray. Lockable head compartment includes sleeping berth, sink, and shower. Cockpit floor isn't flush—watch the step while going forward. Light boat for her size. Twin 250 Yamahas reach 40+ knots.

Length w/Pulpit	30'11"	Fuel	270 gals.
Hull Length	29'2"	Water	20 gals.
Beam	9'8"	Max HP	500
Draft	2'11"	Hull Type	Deep-V
Dry Weight	5,500#	Deadrise Aft	20°

See Page 536 For Resale Values

Century Boats
Panama City, FL
www.centuryboats.com

Sportfishing Boats

Century 3000 Sport Cabin
1987-2002

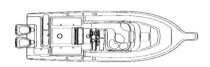

Innovative offshore cruiser blends center-console fishability with express-boat amenities, dayboat versatility. Guest-friendly deck layout has L-shaped settee, table and wet bar forward of helm console. Rod lockers, fishboxes, transom sink with cutting board, bow pulpit were standard. Cabin contains dinette/V-berth forward, small galley, enclosed head with shower, amidships double berth aft. Generous fuel capacity affords excellent range. Not much fishing space aft of leaning post. Yamaha 240s deliver 40+ knots max.

Length w/Pulpit	30'11"	Fuel	270 gals.
Hull Length	29'2"	Water	20 gals.
Beam	9'10"	Max HP	500
Draft	2'11"	Hull Type	Deep-V
Dry Weight	6,800#	Deadrise Aft	20°

See Page 536 For Resale Values

Century Boats
Panama City, FL
www.centuryboats.com

Century 3100/3200 Center Console
1999-2009

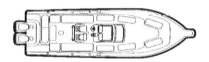

Big center console combines agile handling with excellent range, impressive rough-water performance. Cockpit is among the largest in class. Forward seating converts to optional dinette. Standard features include huge 62-gallon baitwell, in-floor fishboxes (4), lockable electronics box, leaning post with backrest & cooler, lockable rod storage, sink with cutting board. Head compartment has bunk, sink, storage. Marketed as 3100 Center Console in 1999–2000. Biggest center console ever built by Century. Tops 40 knots with 250hp Yamahas.

Length w/Pulpit	32'6"	Fuel	300 gals.
Beam	10'6"	Water	30 gals.
Draft, Up	1'8"	Max HP	700
Dry Weight	8,500#	Hull Type	Deep-V
Clearance, Top	9'6"	Deadrise Aft	23°

See Page 536 For Resale Values

Century Boats
Panama City, FL
www.centuryboats.com

Century 3200 Walkaround
2001-07

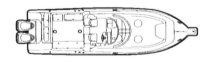

Multipurpose walkaround with deluxe cabin accommodations is ideal for extended fishing trips. Roomy midcabin interior features full galley with pullout pantry and microwave, enclosed stand-up head with shower, convertible dinette. Transom sink with cutting board, cockpit bolsters, fresh/saltwater washdowns, tilt steering were standard. Rear seat conceals 62-gallon aerated livewell. Note slick lift-out tackle box, port/starboard fuel fills, bow seating. A seriously versatile boat. Over 40 knots top with Yamaha 250s.

Length w/Pulpit	32'6"	Water	30 gals.
Beam	10'6"	Waste	8 gals.
Draft, Engines Down	3'4"	Max HP	600
Dry Weight	9,400#	Hull Type	Deep-V
Fuel	300 gals.	Deadrise Aft	23°

See Page 536 For Resale Values

Century Boats
Panama City, FL
www.centuryboats.com

231-360-0827

Cheoy Lee 48 Sport Yacht
1980–86

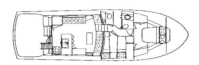

Distinctive sport sedan with fully cored hull, sporty lines took 1980s convertible styling in new direction. Roomy interior with deckhouse galley features unique curved passageway connecting staterooms with salon. Fully equipped galley is located in aft corner of salon where it's convenient to cockpit and bridge. Early models with European decor (painted walls) were quickly replaced with traditional teak interior. Note huge fishing cockpit, foredeck sun pad, wide side decks. GM 550hp diesels cruise at 22–24 knots (mid-to-high 20s top).

Length Overall	48'0"	Clearance	16'6"
Length WL	43'0"	Fuel	1,000 gals.
Beam	15'0"	Water	200 gals.
Draft	4'0"	Cockpit	140 sq. ft.
Weight	37,000#	Hull Type	Modified-V

Prices Not Provided for Pre-1995 Models

Cheoy Lee of North America
Ft. Lauderdale, FL
www.cheoyleena.com

231-360-0827

Cheoy Lee 50 Sportfisherman
1987–90

Replacement model for Cheoy Lee 48 Sport Yacht (1980–86) features greater beam, a third stateroom, much improved styling. Teak-paneled interior boasts well-planned galley area, two large heads, comfortable (if Spartan) salon with fixed table. Large fishing cockpit came standard with tackle center, freezer. Airex cored hull results in a surprisingly weight-efficient boat. Flybridge is large for a 50-footer with seating for eight. Twin 735hp 8V92 diesels cruise at 25–26 knots; later models with twin 800hp Cats cruise at 26–28 knots.

Length	50'8"	Fuel	1,000 gals.
Beam	16'1"	Water	200 gals.
Draft	3'2"	Cockpit	115 sq. ft.
Weight	36,000#	Hull Type	Modified-V
Clearance	14'0"	Deadrise Aft	NA

Prices Not Provided for Pre-1995 Models

Cheoy Lee of North America
Ft. Lauderdale, FL
www.cheoyleena.com

231-360-0827

Cheoy Lee 58 Sportfisherman
1986–91

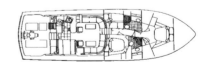

Luxury-class convertible with fully cored hull lured 1980s anglers with an eye for cutting-edge styling. Wide beam allows for very expansive interior with three double staterooms, two large heads. Innovative salon layout has wraparound seating forward, galley and dinette aft. Additional features include well-equipped fishing cockpit, roomy bridge with circular lounge seating forward of helm, side-dumping exhausts. Offered with choice of teak or ash interior woodwork. GM 900hp 12V71 diesels cruise at 25 knots (about 28 knots top).

Length	58'5"	Fuel	1,000 gals.
Beam	17'10"	Water	150 gals.
Draft	4'3"	Cockpit	138 sq. ft.
Weight	58,500#	Hull Type	Modified-V
Clearance	15'10"	Deadrise Aft	NA

Prices Not Provided for Pre-1995 Models

Cheoy Lee of North America
Ft. Lauderdale, FL
www.cheoyleena.com

Chris Craft 315 Commander
1983—90

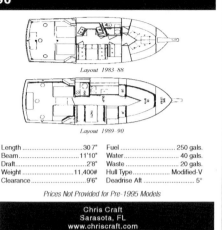

Layout 1983-88

Layout 1989-90

Practical flybridge fisherman combines spacious cockpit with all-purpose interior, rugged construction. Wide 11'10" beam allows for roomy interior with convertible dinette, complete galley, overhead rod storage, two hanging lockers. Update in 1988 replaced bi-level cockpit with engine boxes to allow full-height cabin door. Forward windows were eliminated in late models. Note wide side decks, roomy flybridge. Twin 330hp gas engines cruise at 20 knots (about 28 knots top). Low-deadrise hull can be a stiff ride in a chop.

Length	30'7"	Fuel	250 gals.
Beam	11'10"	Water	40 gals.
Draft	2'8"	Waste	20 gals.
Weight	11,400#	Hull Type	Modified-V
Clearance	9'6"	Deadrise Aft	5°

Prices Not Provided for Pre-1995 Models

Chris Craft
Sarasota, FL
www.chriscraft.com

Chris Craft 360 Commander
1973—86

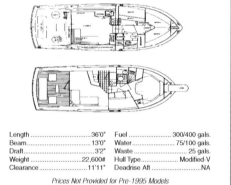

Best-selling convertible matched Chris Craft promise of solid construction, comfortable accommodations, big-water fishability. Several two-stateroom interiors were offered over the years; lower helm was a popular option. Flush cockpit came with in-deck fishbox, rod storage, but no transom door. Increased fuel capacity in 1983, restyled deckhouse in 1985. Low-deadrise hull can be a stiff ride in a chop. Cruise at 16 knots with 330hp gas engines; 20+ with 300 Cat (or 320 Cummins) diesels.

Length	36'0"	Fuel	300/400 gals.
Beam	13'0"	Water	75/100 gals.
Draft	3'2"	Waste	25 gals.
Weight	22,600#	Hull Type	Modified-V
Clearance	11'11"	Deadrise Aft	NA

Prices Not Provided for Pre-1995 Models

Chris Craft
Sarasota, FL
www.chriscraft.com

Chris Craft 382/392 Convertible
1985—90

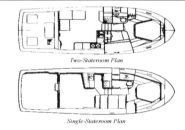

Two-Stateroom Plan

Single-Stateroom Plan

Sporty 1980s convertible is an updated version of the old Uniflite 38 Convertible (1977—84) with subtle styling, decor updates. Offered with single-stateroom/dinette floorplan or two-stateroom layout, both with teak trim, large head with stall shower, island bed in master stateroom. Lower helm was a popular option. Cockpit includes tackle centers, transom door, rod storage. Big flybridge for a 38-footer. A popular model for Chris Craft. Cruise at 17—18 knots with 340hp gas engines; 23—24 knots with 375hp Cat diesels.

Length Overall	38'0"	Fuel	350 gals.
Length WL	33'0"	Water	100 gals.
Beam	13'11"	Waste	40 gals.
Draft	3'9"	Hull Type	Modified-V
Weight	28,000#	Deadrise Aft	12°

Prices Not Provided for Pre-1995 Models

Chris Craft
Sarasota, FL
www.chriscraft.com

Sportfishing Boats

Chris Craft 422 Commander
1973–90

Classic Chris Craft convertible introduced in mid-1970s hit the right buttons with cruisers and anglers alike. Numerous updates over the years including complete exterior redesign in 1985. Principal features include large fishing cockpit with transom door, roomy cabin accommodations, stable modified-V hull. Noted for speed (back when 25 knots was fast) and toughness. Offered with several interior floorplans. GM 425 8V71s—or later models with 485hp 6-71s—cruise in the mid 20s (26–27 knots top).

Length	42'4"	Fuel	400/525 gals.
Beam	14'0"	Water	125 gals.
Draft	3'11"	Cockpit	110 sq. ft.
Weight	34,000#	Hull Type	Modified-V
Clearance	13'7"	Deadrise Aft	8°

Prices Not Provided for Pre-1995 Models

Chris Craft
Sarasota, FL
www.chriscraft.com

Chris Craft 482 Convertible
1985–88

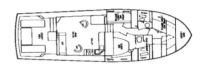

Revised version of earlier Uniflite 48 Convertible (1980–84) offered numerous exterior styling changes, interior decor upgrades. Spacious three-stateroom, two-head layout features built-in salon entertainment center, rich teak joinery, large master suite with walkaround queen bed. Most were sold with solid front windshield. Washer/dryer can be fitted in bow stateroom. Note wide side decks, uncluttered cockpit, spacious flybridge. Considered a fast boat in her day, standard 600hp GM diesels cruise at 25 knots (about 28 knots top).

Length	48'10"	Fuel	780 gals.
Beam	15'9"	Water	200 gals.
Draft	4'9"	Cockpit	133 sq. ft.
Weight	48,000#	Hull Type	Modified-V
Clearance	13'9"	Deadrise Aft	14°

Prices Not Provided for Pre-1995 Models

Chris Craft
Sarasota, FL
www.chriscraft.com

Cobia 250/260/270 Walkaround
1997–2007

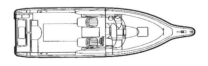

Affordably priced trailerable fisherman with efficient deck layout, compact cabin was a Cobia best-seller for several years. Roomy cockpit came standard with 25-gallon livewell, insulated fishbox, aft cutting boards, rod storage. Generic cabin with near standing headroom includes V-berth, dinette table, mini-galley, rod storage, head with portable toilet. Called Cobia 250 Walkaround in 1997; 260 Walkaround in 1998–2000; 270 Walkaround in 2001–07. Twin 150hp Yamaha outboards top out at close to 40 knots.

Length w/Pulpit	27'6"	Fuel	175 gals.
Beam	8'6"	Water	12 gals.
Hull Draft	1'8"	Max HP	400
Dry Weight	5,000#	Hull Type	Deep-V
Clearance	8'8"	Deadrise Aft	20°

See Page 537 For Resale Values

Cobia Boat Company
Ft. Pierce, FL
www.cobiaboats.com

231-360-0827

Cobia 254/264/274 Center Console
1997–2002

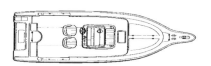

Well-mannered center console with trailerable 8'6" beam gave savvy anglers good value for the money. Highlights include single-level cockpit with transom livewell, four insulated fishboxes, cockpit bolsters, console head compartment, lockable electronics box, bow pulpit, anchor locker. Compact helm has limited space for electronics. Marketed as Cobia 254 in 1997; 264 in 1998–2000; 274 in 2001–02. Note that all-new Cobia 274 model was introduced in 2003. Over 40 knots top with Yamaha 200s.

Length w/Pulpit	27'6"	Fuel	175 gals.
Beam	8'6"	Water	7 gals.
Hull Draft	1'3"	Max HP	450
Dry Weight	3,900#	Hull Type	Deep-V
Clearance, T-Top	8'10"	Deadrise Aft	20°

See Page 538 For Resale Values

Cobia Boat Company
Ft. Pierce, FL
www.cobiaboats.com

231-360-0827

Cobia 274 Center Console
2003–07

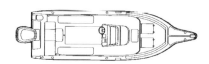

Updated version of earlier Cobia 274 Center Console (2001–02) offers improved deck layout, better range, redesigned helm. Standard fishing amenities include oval 42-gallon transom livewell, in-deck fishboxes (2), leaning post, rear cutting boards (2), cockpit bolsters, raw-water washdown, transom door, bow casting deck. Console head compartment has opening port for ventilation. Cockpit toerail is a plus. Rear seat must be removed to use livewell. Tops out around 40 knots with 200hp outboards.

Length w/Pulpit	27'6"	Fuel	200 gals.
Beam	8'6"	Water	7 gals.
Hull Draft	1'6"	Max HP	500
Dry Weight	4,500#	Hull Type	Deep-V
Load Capacity	3,900#	Deadrise Aft	20°

See Page 538 For Resale Values

Cobia Boat Company
Ft. Pierce, FL
www.cobiaboats.com

231-360-0827

Cobia 312 Sport Cabin
2003–07

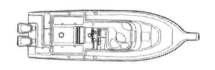

Dual-purpose family fisherman combines center-console versatility with express-boat comfort, walkaround practicality. Wide-open deck layout has lounge seating forward of helm, bench seating aft. Highlights include console head compartment with shower, 28-gallon transom livewell, in-deck fish/storage boxes, leaning post with cooler, transom sink with cutting board, raw-water washdown. Compact cabin has lounge seating forward, sink, refrigerator. Limited fishing space aft of helm seat. Over 40 knots top with Yamaha 225s.

Length w/Pulpit	30'11"	Fuel	270 gals.
Beam	9'10"	Water	20 gals.
Hull Draft	17"	Max HP	600
Dry Weight	7,300#	Hull Type	Deep-V
Clearance, Top	8'5"	Deadrise Aft	20°

See Page 538 For Resale Values

Cobia Boat Company
Ft. Pierce, FL
www.cobiaboats.com

231-360-0827

Cobia 314 Center Console
2003-07

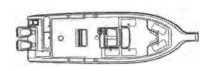

Muscular sportfishing machine—Cobia's largest boat ever—delivers enticing mix of brawny construction, big-water fishability. Features include leaning post with rod holders, cockpit bolsters, forward console seat, bow storage lockers, tackle storage, transom shower. Rear seat lifts to reveal 32-gallon livewell, bait-prep station with sink & cutting board. Walk-in console has marine head, sink, sleeping berth, opening port. Hull was modified in 2006 to carry heavier 4-stroke outboards. Yamaha 250s top out at 45 knots.

Length w/Pulpit	30'11"	Fuel	270 gals.
Beam	9'10"	Water	20 gals.
Draft, Engnes Up	1'5"	Max HP	600
Draft, Engines Down	2'10"	Hull Type	Deep-V
Dry Weight	7,300#	Deadrise Aft	20°

See Page 538 For Resale Values

Cobia Boat Company
Ft. Pierce, FL
www.cobiaboats.com

231-360-0827

Conch 27
1991-2004

Semicustom center console built by New England–based Edey & Duff appeals to sportfishing purists. Wide 9-foot beam provides roomy cockpit with in-floor livewell aft, huge insulated fishbox forward. Typical features include T-top with electronics box, deluxe leaning post, dual washdowns, pop-up cleats, forward console seat. Fiberglass engine cowling/work surface is distinctive touch. Hull is fully cored. Meticulous finish. Single Yamaha 250 four-stroke delivers a top speed of just over 35 knots.

Length	27'0"	Fuel	225 gals.
Beam	9'0"	Water	50 gals.
Hull Draft	1'4"	Max HP	400
Dry Weight	4,400#	Hull Type	Deep-V
Clearance	NA	Deadrise Aft	22.5°

Insufficient Resale Data To Assign Values

Edey & Duff, Ltd.
Mattapoisett, MA
www.edeyandduff.com

231-360-0827

Contender 27 Open
1995-2007

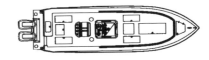

Semicustom fishing machine outguns most competitors for quality, performance, resale values. Highlights include 50-gallon round livewell, 140-gal. forward fish box, 76-gal. aft fish box, in-floor rod lockers, center storage locker, lockable electronics box, walk-in head compartment, transom door. Recessed bow rail prevents snagged lines. Slender deep-V hull delivers legendary big-water ride. Exemplary finish. Expensive. Twin 200hp Yamaha outboards reach a top speed of around 45 knots.

Length Overall	30'0"	Fuel	210 gals.
Beam	8'10"	Water	15 gals.
Hull Draft	18"	MaxHP	500
Dry Weight	4,950#	Hull Type	Deep-V
Clearance	NA	Deadrise Aft	24.5°

See Page 531 For Resale Values

Contender Boats
Homestead, FL
www.contender.com

Sportfishing Boats

Contender 31 Fish Around
1998–Current

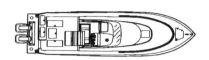

Compelling center console/walkaround hybrid combines 360-degree fishability with well-appointed cabin, top-shelf amenities. Features include insulated in-deck fishboxes, 40-gallon transom livewell, bait-prep station, forward in-deck rod lockers (port & stbd), bow seat, transom door, foldaway rear seat, recessed bow rail, integral dive platform, anchor locker. Wide walkways make getting around easy. Exemplary finish, near flawless gelcoat. Outstanding open-water performance. About 50 knots top with twin 250s.

Length	32'6"	Fuel	245 gals.
Beam	9'4"	Water	40 gals.
Hull Draft	1'6"	Max HP	600
Dry Weight	6,000#	Hull Type	Deep-V
Clearance	NA	Deadrise Aft	24.5°

Insufficient Resale Data To Assign Values

Contender Boats
Homestead, FL
www.contender.com

Contender 31 Open
1995–2007

Semicustom fishing machine with high-performance hull, best-in-class construction puts upscale anglers in the winner's circle. Standard fishing features include raised livewell, walk-thru transom, leaning post with tackle center, two large-capacity forward fishboxes, two aft fishboxes. Single-level cockpit is easier to navigate than competitive boats with bow casting platforms. Slender deep-V hull delivers a legendary rough-water ride. As good as it gets in a 31-foot center console. Over 50 knots top with 250hp Yamahas.

Length	31'3"	Fuel	240 gals.
Beam	9'4"	Water	NA
Hull Draft	1'6"	Max HP	500
Dry Weight	3,500#	Hull Type	Deep-V
Weight w/Engines	5,500#	Deadrise Aft	24.5°

See Page 538 For Resale Values

Contender Boats
Homestead, FL
www.contender.com

Contender 31T
2008–Current

Hard-hitting thoroughbred couples premium construction with cutting-edge, full-bore performance. Design highlights include single-level deck, beefy console with walk-in head, in-deck fishboxes fore and aft, twin 40-gallon transom livewells, lockable rod storage, lockable electronics storage, removable rear bench seat, K-plane trim tabs. More storage than many boats her size. Note cushioned console seat, overbuilt T-top, mirror-glass gelcoat. About 50 knots max with twin Yamaha 250s.

Length	32'7"	Fuel	310 gals.
Beam	9'8"	Water	NA
Hull Draft	23"	Max HP	700
Dry Weight	5,850#	Hull Type	Deep-V
Weight, Loaded	11,560#	Deadrise Aft	24.5°

Insufficient Resale Data To Assign Values

Contender Boats
Homestead, FL
www.contender.com

231-360-0827

Contender 33T
2006–Current

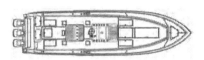

Deluxe tournament fisherman capable of handling triple 350s is slim, sleek, built for speed. High-performance hull with walk-in console boasts spacious, single-level deck layout with twin transom livewells. Tremendous storage capacity including 208-gallon insulated fishbox forward, 115-gallon box aft. Note clever lift-up console seat, stylish helm pod. Optional below-deck livewells make it possible to house a total of four wells. More freeboard than previous Contender models. Triple 250s deliver 50+ knots wide open.

Length	34'5"	Fuel	400 gals.
Beam	9'8"	Water	NA
Hull Draft	24"	Max HP	1,050
Dry Weight	6,600#	Hull Type	Deep-V
Weight, Loaded	13,500#	Deadrise Aft	24.5°

Insufficient Resale Data To Assign Values

Contender Boats
Homestead, FL
www.contender.com

231-360-0827

Contender 35 Side Console
1993–Current

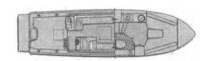

Sleek tournament winner with offset console, raised cuddy combines signature Contender quality with spirited performance, proven fishability. Notable features include 38-gallon transom livewell, fully integrated transom, lift-out fishbox, lounge seating opposite helm, forward console seat. Well-appointed cabin with full galley, enclosed head and shower, sleeps four. With full-width bridgedeck, bow access is a matter of climbing over the windshield—not so easy. Twin Yamaha 250s top out around 45 knots.

Length	35'2"	Fuel	340 gals.
Beam	10'0"	Water	40 gals.
Hull Draft	24"	Max HP	750
Dry Weight	7,500#	Hull Type	Deep-V
Clearance	NA	Deadrise Aft	24.5°

Insufficient Resale Data To Assign Values

Contender Boats
Homestead, FL
www.contender.com

231-360-0827

Contender 35 Express
1989–Current

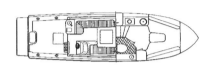

Fast-action express with integrated transom, side-console deck layout combines hardcore fishability with signature Contender ride. Raised 38 gallon livewell, spacious cockpit with lift-out in-deck fishbox, lockable electronics storage, aft-facing jump seats, L-shaped settee with bait and tackle station, transom door. Well-appointed cabin full galley, stand-up head with shower, teak and holly sole, sleeps four. Note cavernous storage area below helm and guest seating area. Outstanding finish. Over 50 knots top with triple 250s.

Length	35'0'	Fuel	340 gals.
Beam	10'0"	Water	45 gals.
Hull Draft	2'0"	Max HP	750
Dry Weight	5,500#	Hull Type	Deep-V
Clearance	NA	Deadrise Aft	24.5°

Insufficient Resale Data To Assign Values

Contender Boats
Homestead, FL
www.contender.com

Sportfishing Boats

Contender 36 Cuddy
2003–Current

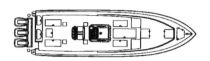

Leading-edge fishing machine with triple-outboard power takes Contender performance to the next level. Essentially a custom boat—no two are alike. Standard features include dual 50-gallon livewells, generous fishbox capacity, transom livewell, generous rod storage. Cabin has oversized V-berth, storage locker. Additional features include Kiekhaefer trim tabs, dual hydraulic steering, recessed bow rail. Superb finish, near-flawless gelcoat. Triple Yamaha 250 outboards deliver a top speed in the neighborhood of 50 knots.

Length Overall	36'3"	Fuel, Opt	600 gals.
Beam	10'0"	Water	45 gals.
Hull Draft	24"	Max HP	1,050
Dry Weight	7,050#	Hull Type	Deep-V
Fuel, Std	410 gals.	Deadrise Aft	24.5

Insufficient Resale Data To Assign Values

Contender Boats
Homestead, FL
www.contender.com

Contender 36 Open
2001–Current

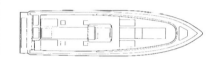

Feature-rich center console designed for triple-engine power delivers high-octane performance, no-excuses fishability. Notable features include dual 50-gallon transom livewells, transom door, step-down storage/head compartment, belowdecks rod lockers, four insulated fishboxes. Optional coffin box forward can be raised electrically for access to huge storage area beneath. Exemplary finish, flawless gelcoat. Deep-V can endure serious offshore punishment. Triple 250hp Yamaha outboards top out at close to 50 knots.

Length	36'2'	Fuel, Opt	600 gals.
Beam	10'0"	Water	45 gals.
Hull Draft	1'6"	Max HP	1050
Dry Weight	6,000#	Hull Type	Deep-V
Fuel, Std	420 gals.	Deadrise Aft	24.5

Insufficient Resale Data To Assign Values

Contender Boats
Homestead, FL
www.contender.com

Davis 47 Flybridge SF
1986–91

Polished Carolina convertible made good on promise of semicustom quality, tournament-class performance, big-water capability. Offered with several two- and three-stateroom floorplans, all with handcrafted teak cabinetry, premium furnishings, exceptional fit and finish. Notable features include roomy cockpit with engineroom access, single-lever helm controls, wide side decks. GM 735hp diesels cruise at 24 knots; 820hp MANs cruise at 27–28 knots. Note 1990 fuel increase. Total of 88 built, the first 6 with fully cored hulls.

Length	47'0"	Fuel	750/840 gals.
Beam	16'0"	Water	150 gals.
Draft	4'0"	Waste	50 gals.
Weight	45,000#	Hull Type	Modified-V
Clearance	12'10"	Deadrise Aft	14°

Prices Not Provided for Pre-1995 Models

Davis Yachts, Egg Harbor, NJ
www.buddydavis.com

Davis 61 Flybridge SF
1985–93

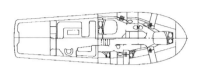

Proven big-water sportfisherman boasts world-class reputation for quality construction, exceptional head-sea performance. Standard four-stateroom interior with combined salon/galley/dinette features amidships owner's suite, premium furnishings, handcrafted teak joinery. Massive 185-square-foot fishing cockpit with teak sole is among the largest in her class. Note huge bridge with Panish controls, pop-up electronics display. Cruise at 25 knots with GM 1,040hp engines; 30 knots with GM 1,400hp diesels. Total of 35 were built.

Length	61'4"	Fuel	1,500 gals.
Beam	17'6"	Water	250 gals.
Draft	5'8"	Cockpit	185 sq. ft.
Weight	80,000#	Hull Type	Modified-V
Clearance	18'0"	Deadrise Aft	16°

Prices Not Provided for Pre-1995 Models

Davis Yachts, Egg Harbor, NJ
www.buddydavis.com

Dawson 38 Convertible
1987–94

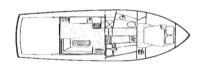

Midsize convertible with big fishing cockpit, roomy interior blurs the line between hardcore fisherman, comfortable family cruiser. Generous beam permits spacious two-stateroom, galley-up interior with extensive teak cabinetry, large head with stall shower, expansive salon with entertainment center. Flush cockpit with lift-out fishbox lacks transom door. Note well-arranged engineroom, large flybridge. Deep-V hull can be a wet ride. Standard 375hp Cats cruise at 25 knots; GM 485hp engines cruise at a fast 30 knots.

Length	38'0"	Fuel	400 gals.
Beam	13'8"	Water	90 gals.
Draft	3'6"	Waste	18 gals.
Weight	28,000#	Hull Type	Deep-V
Clearance	NA	Deadrise Aft	24°

Pricing Unavailable for Pre-1995 Models

No longer in production

Deep Impact 36 Cabin
2003–08

Floorplan Not Available

Custom sportfishing machine with double-stepped hull set market standards for sophisticated design, eye-popping craftsmanship. Highlights include deluxe 3-person helm with tackle station, custom T-top, dual sliding transom doors, livewell, three fishboxes. Upscale cabin includes full galley, adult-size V-berth, large head. Great helm layout with Gaffrig controls. Flawless gelcoat, near perfect finish. Very expensive—each was built to customer specs. Triple 225hp Mercury outboards top out at close to 55 knots.

Length	36'0"	Fuel	320 gals.
Beam	10'0"	Water	55 gals.
Draft, Up	1'10"	Max HP	900
Draft, Down	2'10"	Hull Type	Deep-V
Dry Weight	9,500#	Deadrise Aft	24°

Insufficient Resale Data To Assign Values

Deep Impact
Tavenier, FL
www.deepimpactpowerboats.com

---

www.powerboatguide.com   231-360-0827

Donzi 26/28 ZF
1999–2003

Floorplan Not Available

Go-fast kingfish boat (called the 28 ZF in 1999–2000) with double-stepped, deep-V hull rivals bigger boats for offshore fishability, seaworthy performance. Features include insulated in-deck fishbox, 35-gallon stand-up livewell, leaning post with rod holders, 4-drawer tackle center, K-plane trim tabs, console seat with cooler under, rod storage, walk-in head compartment, transom door, raw-water washdown. New 26ZF model with 8'11" beam introduced in 2007. Very well finished boat. Over 50 knots top with 225 Mercs.

Length	27'8"	Fuel	180 gals.
Beam	8'6"	Water	7 gals.
Draft, Up	19"	Max HP	500
Draft, Down	30"	Hull Type	Deep-V
Dry Weight	4,500#	Deadrise Aft	22°

See Page 540 For Resale Values

Donzi Marine
Tallevast, FL
www.donzimarine.com

---

www.powerboatguide.com   231-360-0827

Donzi 29 ZF Open
2003–Current

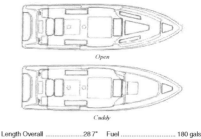

Open

Cuddy

High-performance sportfishing machine with light-weight (stepped) hull is easy to trailer, quick to ac-celerate, fast across the water. Highlights include ready-to-fish cockpit with big 50-gallon transom livewell, deluxe leaning post, console tackle box, in-deck fishbox-es, lockable electronics box, console head compartment, raw-water washdown, transom door. Slender 9-foot beam results in modest cockpit dimensions compared with most 29-footers. Also offered in Cuddy version. Yamaha 225s reach 45+ knots top.

Length Overall	28'7"	Fuel	180 gals.
Beam	9'0"	Water	7 gals.
Hull Draft	1'9"	Max HP	550
Draft, Engines Down	3'1"	Hull Type	Deep-V
Dry Weight	6,200#	Deadrise Aft	22°

See Page 540 For Resale Values

Donzi Marine
Tallevast, FL
www.donzimarine.com

---

www.powerboatguide.com   231-360-0827

Donzi 32 ZF Open
2000–07

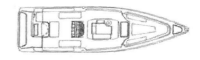

Race-bred speedster with lightweight twin-step hull, slender beam outguns most everything in her class. Standard features include insulated fishboxes, tran-som bait-prep station with sink, 50-gallon livewell, walk-in head compartment, recessed bow rails, console cooler, leaning post with drop-down bolsters, K-Planes, console tackle box, pop-up cleats, transom rod holders (5). Stor-age for 8 rods. Hull is fully cored. Good fit and finish. Twin 250hp outboards cruise at 35 knots and reach a top speed in excess of 50 knots.

Length Overall	32'1"	Fuel	290 gals.
Beam	9'2"	Water	20 gals.
Hull Draft	2'4"	Max HP	600
Dry Weight	7,600#	Hull Type	Deep-V
Clearance, T-Top	8'8"	Deadrise Aft	22°

See Page 540 For Resale Values

Donzi Marine
Tallevast, FL
www.donzimarine.com

231-360-0827

Donzi 35 ZF Open
1998–Current

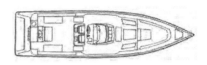

Open

Cuddy

High-performance center console with stepped hull gets anglers to fishing grounds ahead of the pack. Standard features include 28-gallon transom livewell and sink, leaning post with rod holders, cockpit shower, removable cooler, console tackle box, deluxe helm seats with flip-up bolsters, console head compartment with sink & shower, transom door. Cuddy version also available. Narrow beam means less cockpit space than many 35-footers. Twin 225hp outboards deliver 40+ knots top; triple 225hps reach close to 55 knots top.

Length Overall	33'4"	Fuel	269 gals.
Beam	9'2"	Water	15 gals.
Hull Draft	2'6"	Max HP	750
Weight	7,950#	Hull Type	Deep-V
Clearance, T-Top	8'10"	Deadrise Aft	22°

See Page 540 For Resale Values

Donzi Marine
Tallevast, FL
www.donzimarine.com

231-360-0827

Donzi 38 ZF Cuddy
2005–Current

Hardcore fishing machine with triple-outboard power takes big center console performance, excitement to the next level. Standard features include fiberglass T-top, bait-prep station w/lighted baitwell, two removable coolers, lockable tackle storage, insulated fishboxes, K-Planes, locking electronics box, console tackle box, casting deck storage, console head with sink & shower. Cuddy has large V-berth, storage beneath. Stepped hull is very quick to accelerate. Max 55 knots w/ triple 275 outboards.

Length	38'6"	Fuel	318 gals.
Beam	9.5"	Water	28 gals.
Hull Draft	3'0"	Max HP	900
Hull Weight	9,800#	Hull Type	Deep-V
Clearance, Hardtop	5 5"	Deadrise Aft	22°

See Page 540 For Resale Values

Donzi Marine
Tallevast, FL
www.donzimarine.com

231-360-0827

Donzi 38 ZFX
2006–Current

High-impact sportster built on Donzi's signature high-performance stepped hull combines hardcore fishing cockpit with comfortable wraparound seating forward. Fishing amenities include transom bait-prep center, 28-gallon livewell, raw-water washdown, in-deck fishboxes, bolster pads, transom rod holders (5), dropdown helm seat, transom door. Hardtop with electronics locker, folding rear seat, K-planes, forward wet bar, removable bow table are standard. Fast, versatile and innovative. About 60 knots top with triple 250s.

Length	38'6"	Fuel	318 gals.
Beam	9 5"	Water	28 gals.
Hull Draft	2'1"	Max HP	900
Dry Weight	10,200#	Hull Type	Deep-V
Clearance, Hardtop	5 5"	Deadrise Aft	22°

See Page 540 For Resale Values

Donzi Marine
Tallevast, FL
www.donzimarine.com

Sportfishing Boats

Sportfishing Boats

Donzi 38 ZSF
2004–Current

Feature-rich sportfisherman with double-stepped hull, well-appointed interior appeals to the dayboat crowd set as well as serious anglers. Expansive cockpit boasts 40-gallon livewell under rear bench seat, in-deck fishboxes, rod storage racks, facing lounge seats (with coolers under) forward, wet bar with sink. Comfortable interior with full galley, head with shower, twin settees, sleeps two. Note wide side decks, bow sun pad with headrest and drink holders. Fast, agile, very well finished. About 55 knots top with triple 250s.

Length	38'6"	Fuel	420 gals.
Beam	10'6"	Water	55 gals.
Hull Draft	2'0"	Max HP	900
Dry Weight	15,000#	Hull Type	Deep-V
Clearance, Hardtop	6'6"	Deadrise Aft	22°

See Page 540 For Resale Values

Donzi Marine
Tallevast, FL
www.donzimarine.com

Donzi 54 Convertible
1989–97

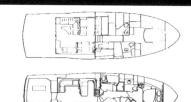

Polished 1990s convertible (built by Lauderdale-based Roscioli Yachts) combines bold styling, semicustom accommodations. Spacious interior with combined salon/galley/dinette is highlighted by high-gloss cabinetry, premium furnishings, designer-style fabrics. Tournament-size cockpit includes full array of high-end fishing amenities. Note roomy bridge, wide side decks, beefy transom door. Engineroom is reached by lifting steps at salon door. Superb open-water ride. Cruise at 25 knots (30 top) with GM 1,150hp engines.

Length	54'0"	Fuel	1,000 gals.
Beam	17'4"	Water	240 gals.
Draft	4'4"	Headroom	6'5"
Weight	51,000#	Hull Type	Modified-V
Clearance	13'3"	Deadrise Aft	14°

See Page 540 For Resale Values

Roscioli International
Ft. Lauderdale, FL
www.donziyachts.com

Donzi 65 Convertible
1987–Current

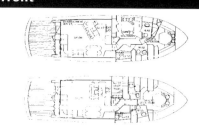

Tournament-tested convertible from Lauderdale-based Roscioli Yachts gets high marks for handsome styling, luxury accommodations, semi-custom amenities. Opulent interior with three en suite staterooms boasts exquisite teak woodwork, premium fabrics and furnishings. Note spacious engineroom, massive cockpit, huge bridge with seating for eight. Outstanding finish from bow to stern. Enclosed bridge is optional. One of the best heavy-weather rides in the business. Cat 1,350hp engines cruise at 24–26 knots (about 30 knots top).

Length	65'0"	Fuel	2,100 gals.
Beam	18'7"	Water	350 gals.
Draft	5'9"	Waste	50 gals.
Weight	72,000#	Hull Type	Modified-V
Clearance	14'4"	Deadrise Aft	12°

See Page 540 For Resale Values

Roscioli International
Ft. Lauderdale, FL
www.donziyachts.com

Dorado 30 Center Console
1992–2006

Floorplan Not Available

Distinctive, well-built offshore fishing boat with jackshaft power offers superior I/O performance without the need of an engine box. Features include insulated fishboxes, transom livewell, canvas spray hood, anchor locker, hinged console/engine box, coaming pads, raw-water washdown, forward seating, cuddy with V-berth. Trailerable—only 5,000 lbs. with engine. Low-deadrise hull is fuel efficient but a hard ride in heavy seas. Outboard model also available. Single 230hp Volvo diesel will cruise efficiently at 25 knots burning just 6 gph.

Length	30'0"	Fuel	85/180 gals.
Beam	8'8"	Water	23 gals.
Hull Draft	18"	Max HP	300
Dry Weight	4,900#	Hull Type	Modified-V
Clearance, T-top	6'5"	Deadrise Aft	4°

See Page 540 For Resale Values

Dorado Boats
www.doradomarine.com

Edgewater 318 Center Console
2006–Current

Premium fishing machine sets class standards for sophisticated engineering, leading-edge construction, unsurpassed performance. Spacious layout includes large in-deck fishbox forward, bow seating with electric high/low table, lockable rod storage, deluxe leaning post with tackle storage, transom sink with pull-out shower. Two livewells—28-gallon unit at the transom and a 66-gallon well next to it. Walk-in console houses marine head with sink, shower. Foam-filled hull is unsinkable. Superb finish. Max 45 knots with Yamaha 250s.

Length	31'10"	Fuel	300 gals.
Beam	10'2"	Water	31 gals.
Draft, Up	1'10"	Max H	600
Draft, Down	2'10"	Hull Type	Deep-V
Hull Weight	6,500#	Deadrise Aft	24°

See Page 540 For Resale Values

Edgewater Boats
Edgewater, FL
www.ewboats.com

Edgewater 335 Express
2010–Current

Brawny, blue-chip fishing boat with wide beam delivers comfort without compromising fishabilty. Tournament-grade cockpit includes dual 28-gallon and 45-gallon livewells, transom fishbox, bait-prep station, in-deck fishbox, foldaway transom seat, double helm/companion seats with flip-up bolsters. Deluxe interior with with marble counters, leather upholstery sleeps four. Note standard hardtop, lockable rod storage in cabin midberth. Keel pad boosts performance. Twin Yamaha 350s max out at over 40 knots.

Length	34'6"	Fuel	300 gals.
Beam	11'2"	Water	38 gals.
Draft, Up	27"	Max HP	700
Draft, Down	36"	Hull Type	Deep-V
Hull Weight	12,900#	Deadrise Aft	21°

Insufficient Resale Data To Assign Values

Edgewater Boats
Edgewater, FL
www.ewboats.com

Sportfishing Boats

Egg Harbor 33 Sedan
1971–81

Vintage Egg Harbor Sedan introduced in 1971 took convertible styling, comfort, versatility to the next level. Offered with several two-stateroom mahogany interiors over the years. Some models have separate stall shower in head. Big interior, but small cockpit. Built with mahogany deck and superstructure until 1978 when switch was made to all-fiberglass construction. Replaced in 1982 with all-new Egg Harbor 33 Sedan. A stiff ride in a chop. Twin 270hp gas engines cruise at a 15–16 knots; 210hp Cat diesel cruise at 16 knots.

Length	33'0"	Fuel	216 gals.
Beam	13'2"	Water	50 gals.
Draft	2'9"	Waste	20 gals.
Weight	15,000#	Hull Type	Modified-V
Clearance	NA	Deadrise Aft	8°

Prices Not Provided for Pre-1995 Models

Egg Harbor Yachts
Egg Harbor, NJ
www.eggharboryachts.com

Egg Harbor 33 Sedan
1982–89

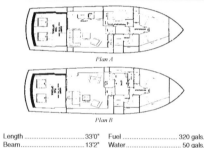

Plan A

Plan B

Updated version of classic Egg Harbor 33 (1971–80) boasts restyled deckhouse, increased fuel capacity, updated interior plans. Choice of single- or twin-stateroom floorplans. Teak cockpit sole was a popular option. Low-deadrise hull is quick to accelerate but a stiff ride in a chop. Narrow side decks, small cockpit. Large bridge for an older 33-foot boat. Originally marketed as the Pacemaker 33 SF before Pacemaker went bankrupt in 1980. Twin 340hp gas engines cruise at 18 knots; Cat 320hp diesels cruise in the low 20s.

Length	33'0"	Fuel	320 gals.
Beam	13'2"	Water	50 gals.
Draft	2.5"	Waste	20 gals.
Weight	16,500#	Hull Type	Modified-V
Clearance	NA	Deadrise Aft	8°

Prices Not Provided for Pre-1995 Models

Egg Harbor Yachts
Egg Harbor, NJ
www.eggharboryachts.com

Egg Harbor 34 Convertible
1993–96

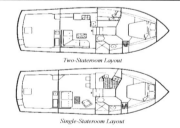

Two-Stateroom Layout

Single-Stateroom Layout

Classy mid-size convertible with rich teak interior couples luxury-class accommodations with handsome lines, secure performance. Full teak interior was offered with single or twin staterooms. Large cockpit includes bulkhead tackle center, in-deck fishbox, transom door. Front windshield was eliminated in order to provide space for salon entertainment center. Restyled—and re-branded as the Egg Harbor 35—in 1997. Performance: Cruise at 18 knots with 380hp gas engines; low 20s with 350hp Cat diesels.

Length w/Pulpit	37'8"	Fuel	400 gals.
Hull Length	34'6"	Water	70 gals.
Beam	13'2"	Waste	28 gals.
Draft	3'2"	Hull Type	Modified-V
Weight	17,500#	Deadrise Aft	8°

See Page 541 For Resale Values

Egg Harbor Yachts
Egg Harbor, NJ
www.eggharboryachts.com

231-360-0827

Egg Harbor 35 Convertible
1997–98

Two-Stateroom Layout

Single-Stateroom Layout

Sure-footed convertible—an updated version of the popular Egg Harbor 34 (1993–96)—ranked among class leaders for quality construction, leading-edge styling. Full teak interior was offered with single or twin staterooms. Large cockpit includes bulkhead tackle center, in-deck fishbox, transom door. Front windshield was eliminated in favor of salon entertainment center. Note well-arranged engineroom, roomy bridge with bench seating forward. Cruise at 18 knots with 380hp gas engines; low 20s with 350hp Cat diesels.

Length w/Pulpit	37'8"	Fuel	406 gals.
Hull Length	34'6"	Water	75 gals.
Beam	13'2"	Waste	28 gals.
Draft	3'2"	Hull Type	Modified-V
Weight	20,925#	Deadrise Aft	8°

See Page 541 For Resale Values

Egg Harbor Yachts
Egg Harbor, NJ
www.eggharboryachts.com

231-360-0827

Egg Harbor 35 Predator
2000–Current

High-tech express fisherman was originally built by Predator Yachts in Sarasota, Florida. Egg Harbor acquired the tooling in 2002, reduced costs by replacing Kevlar construction with fiberglass, but upgraded previously basic interior with high-gloss teak joinery, Ultra-leather upholstery. Centerline helm with flanking lounge seats provides excellent 360-degree visibility; large cockpit has transom livewell, rigging station, tackle lockers. Sea chest is unusual on a boat this size. Cruise at 30+ knots with 440hp Yanmar diesels.

Length	35'0"	Fuel	350 gals.
Beam	12'0"	Water	60 gals.
Draft	3'1"	Waste	15 gals.
Weight	16,000#	Hull Type	Deep-V
Clearance	6'11"	Deadrise Aft	20°

See Page 541 For Resale Values

Egg Harbor Yachts
Egg Harbor, NJ
www.eggharboryachts.com

231-360-0827

Egg Harbor 35 Sport Fisherman
1987–89

Lengthened version of popular Egg Harbor 33 Convertible (1982–89) used the extra length to create larger fishing cockpit. Well-appointed interior with quality teak joinery, open front windshield was offered with one or two staterooms. Large cockpit came standard with transom door, tackle center, bait-prep center, fish box, raw-water washdown. Teak covering boards were a popular option. Still a handsome, well-styled boat. Standard 350hp gas engines cruise at 18 knots; 320hp Cat diesels cruise in the low 20s.

Length w/Pulpit	38'2"	Fuel	400 gals.
Hull Length	35'0"	Water	50 gals.
Beam	13'2"	Waste	25 gals.
Draft	3'2"	Hull Type	Modified-V
Weight	17,000#	Deadrise Aft	8°

Prices Not Provided for Pre-1995 Models

Egg Harbor Yachts
Egg Harbor, NJ
www.eggharboryachts.com

Sportfishing Boats

www.powerboatguide.com 231-360-0827

Egg Harbor 36 Sedan
1976–85

Classic flybridge convertible introduced in 1976 made the grade with boaters impressed with graceful Egg Harbor styling, seductive teak interior, large fishing cockpit. Offered with several one- or two-stateroom floorplans, all with quality teak or mahogany woodwork. Open front windshield makes salon seem larger than modern convertibles with closed windshield. Early models have mahogany deckhouse; construction became all-fiberglass in 1978. Standard 350hp gas engines cruise at 18–20 knots (high 20s top).

Length	36'0"	Fuel	260/320 gals.
Beam	13'3"	Water	75 gals.
Draft	2'9"	Waste	25 gals.
Weight	17,000#	Hull Type	Modified-V
Clearance	NA	Deadrise Aft	6°

Prices Not Provided for Pre-1995 Models

Egg Harbor Yachts
Egg Harbor, NJ
www.eggharboryachts.com

www.powerboatguide.com 231-360-0827

Egg Harbor 37 Convertible
1985–89

Slimmed-down version of Egg Harbor 41 SF (1984–89) is more cruiser than serious fishing machine. Wide 14'5" beam provides interior space of a larger boat. Two-stateroom interior was offered with galley up or down, choice of mahogany or teak joinery. Lower helm was optional. Wide side decks, roomy flybridge. Bigger engine room than many 37-footers. Small cockpit lacks fishing space. Fuel was increased in 1986 to 400 gallons. Cruise at 18 knots with 340hp gas inboards; low 20s with 375hp Cat diesels.

Length	37'5"	Fuel	340/400 gals.
Beam	14.5"	Water	80 gals.
Draft	3'0"	Waste	30 gals.
Weight	24,000#	Hull Type	Modified-V
Clearance	NA	Deadrise Aft	9°

Prices Not Provided for Pre-1995 Models

Egg Harbor Yachts
Egg Harbor, NJ
www.eggharboryachts.com

www.powerboatguide.com 231-360-0827

Egg Harbor 37 Sport Yacht
2001–Current

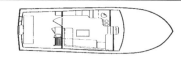

Handsome convertible with signature Egg Harbor styling impresses anglers, cruisers alike with luxury interior, top-shelf workmanship. Luxurious two-stateroom layout is an impressive display of varnished teak woodwork, designer fabrics, top-shelf furnishings. Big cockpit is fitted with transom door, tackle center, direct engineroom access, transom livewell. Flybridge is large for a 37-footer with room to walk behind both helm chairs. Standard Cat 420hp diesels cruise at 27–28 knots (30+ knots top).

Length w/Pulpit	40'8"	Fuel	400 gals.
Hull Length	37'6"	Water	80 gals.
Beam	13'6"	Waste	40 gals.
Draft	3'4"	Hull Type	Modified-V
Weight	25,800#	Deadrise Aft	12°

See Page 541 For Resale Values

Egg Harbor Yachts
Egg Harbor, NJ
www.eggharboryachts.com

231-360-0827

Egg Harbor 38 Convertible
1990–94

Two-Stateroom Layout

Dinette Floorplan

Broad-shouldered 1990s convertible delivers big-boat accommodations on the inside, too-small cockpit dimensions topside. Maxi-volume interior with varnished teak cabinets, built-in salon entertainment center came with choice of two-stateroom floorplan or (less popular) single-stateroom plan with dinette. Cockpit features include tackle center, livewell, transom door, fishbox. Standard gas engines cruise at 15–16 knots; Cat 375hp—or GM 400hp—diesels cruise in the low 20s. Replaced in 1995 with updated model.

Length w/Pulpit	41'8"	Fuel, Gas	436 gals.
Hull Length	38'6"	Fuel, Diesel	506 gals.
Beam	15'0"	Water	120 gals.
Draft	3'10"	Hull Type	Modified-V
Weight	30,900#	Deadrise Aft	8°

Pricing Unavailable for Pre-1995 Models

Egg Harbor Yachts
Egg Harbor, NJ
www.eggharboryachts.com

231-360-0827

Egg Harbor 38 Convertible
1995–97

Restyled version of previous Egg Harbor 38 (1990–94) combined all-new profile, improved bridge layout, increased cockpit dimensions. Spacious interior with varnished teak joinery was offered with two-stateroom layout or less popular single-stateroom plan with dinette. Cockpit came standard with tackle center, livewell, transom door, fishbox. Eliminating front windshield provides space for salon entertainment center. Gas engines cruise at 15 knots, top out in the mid 20s. Cat 400hp diesels cruise at 25 knots (27–28 knots top).

Length w/Pulpit	41'8"	Fuel, Diesel	506 gals.
Hull Length	38'6"	Fuel, Gas	406 gals.
Beam	15'0"	Water	115 gals.
Draft	3'10"	Hull Type	Modified-V
Weight	30,600#	Deadrise Aft	8°

See Page 541 For Resale Values

Egg Harbor Yachts
Egg Harbor, NJ
www.eggharboryachts.com

231-360-0827

Egg Harbor 40 Sedan
1975–86

Graceful 40-footer with large cockpit, upscale accommodations delivered strong sales for Egg Harbor in the late 70s, early '80s. Offered with several two-stateroom interiors over the years. Mahogany woodwork replaced with teak in 1982. Big cockpit came standard with teak sole, teak covering boards. Original wooden superstructure became all-fiberglass in 1978. Bridge was redesigned in 1978 for improved cockpit visibility. Standard 350hp gas engines cruise at 18 knots; 450hp GM diesels cruise at 24 knots.

Length	40'0"	Fuel	340 gals.
Beam	14'0"	Water	100 gals.
Draft	2'9"	Waste	30 gals.
Weight	28,000#	Hull Type	Modified-V
Clearance	NA	Deadrise Aft	6°

Prices Not Provided for Pre-1995 Models

Egg Harbor Yachts
Egg Harbor, NJ
www.eggharboryachts.com

Sportfishing Boats

231-360-0827

Egg Harbor 41 Convertible
1984–89

Luxury-class convertible is an updated version of original Pacemaker 38 whose molds were acquired by Egg Harbor in 1980. Introduced in 1984 in both Sport Fisherman and Convertible Sedan versions, the difference being the larger salon, smaller cockpit of Convertible. Several floorplans were offered, all with quality teak joinery, upscale decor package. This boat has always been noted for her graceful styling, good seakeeping qualities. Cat 375hp cruise at 22 knots (26 knots top); 6-71 Detroits cruise at 26 knots (about 30 knots top).

Length	40'10"	Water	80 gals.
Beam	14.5"	Fuel	500 gals.
Draft	3'0"	Headroom	6'4"
Weight	28,000#	Hull Type	Modified-V
Clearance	13'0"	Deadrise Aft	8°

Prices Not Provided for Pre-1995 Models

Egg Harbor Yachts
Egg Harbor, NJ
www.eggharboryachts.com

231-360-0827

Egg Harbor 42 Convertible
1990–94

Feature-rich fishing machine from early 1990s offered style, fishability, performance at a reasonable price. Large cockpit with tackle center, in-deck fishbox, livewell, transom door can accommodate full-size fighting chair with room to spare. Well-appointed interior was available with or without dinette. Tournament flybridge has good fore, aft sightlines. Note big engineroom, teak trim and cover boards. Cat 375hp cruise in the low 20s (about 25 top); later models with twin 485hp 6-71 Detroits cruise at 25 knots (high 20s top).

Length w/Pulpit	45'4"	Cockpit	100 sq. ft.
Hull Length	42'2"	Fuel	600 gals.
Beam	15'0"	Water	120 gals.
Draft	3'10"	Hull Type	Modified-V
Weight	36,300#	Deadrise Aft	8°

Prices Not Provided for Pre-1995 Models

Egg Harbor Yachts
Egg Harbor, NJ
www.eggharboryachts.com

231-360-0827

Egg Harbor 42 Convertible
1995–97

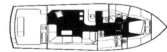

Restyled version of Egg Harbor 42 Convertible (1990–94) with redesigned bridge, revised interior compared well with best midsize convertibles of her day. Large cockpit with tackle center, in-deck fishbox can accommodate full-size fighting chair with room to spare. Well-appointed teak interior with roomy salon, comfortable staterooms was available with or without dinette. Engineroom—accessed from salon—is on the small side. Good overall finish. GM 550hp 6V92 diesels cruise at 26 knots and reach 30+ knots wide open.

Length w/Pulpit	45'4"	Fuel	600 gals.
Hull Length	42'2"	Water	115 gals.
Beam	15'0"	Waste	40 gals.
Draft	3'10"	Hull Type	Modified-V
Weight	36,300#	Deadrise Aft	8°

See Page 541 For Resale Values

Egg Harbor Yachts
Egg Harbor, NJ
www.eggharboryachts.com

Egg Harbor 42 Sport Yacht
2001–03

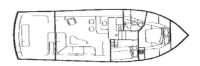

Sporty Jersey-built convertible is spacious, quick, loaded with quality features. Upscale interior with sectional salon sofa, designer decor offers two well-appointed staterooms. Satin-varnished teak cabinetry is furniture quality throughout. Note granite sole in galley, head. Spacious cockpit is equipped with tackle center, transom door, fishbox, engineroom door. Underwater exhaust system was standard. Low-deadrise hull can be stiff ride in a chop. Cat 660hp diesels cruise in the high 20s (30+ knots top).

Length w/Pulpit	45'4"	Clearance	13'0"
Hull Length	42'2"	Fuel	600 gals.
Beam	15'0"	Water	115 gals.
Draft	3'10"	Waste	25 gals.
Weight	36,300#	Hull Type	Modified-V

See Page 541 For Resale Values

Egg Harbor Yachts
Egg Harbor, NJ
www.eggharboryachts.com

Egg Harbor 43 Sport Fisherman
1986–89

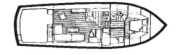

Muscular offshore fishing machine is basically a stretched version of Egg Harbor 41 Convertible (1984–89) with enlarged salon, increased fuel capacity. Two interior options were available, both with two staterooms. Eliminating front windshield allows for built-in entertainment center forward in salon. Large 120-square-foot cockpit features sink, freezer, transom door. Note teak cockpit sole, teak covering boards. Cat 375hp engines cruise in the low 20s (25 top); 485hp Detroits cruise in the mid 20s and reach 27–28 knots top.

Length	43'0"	Fuel	600 gals.
Beam	14.5'	Water	80 gals.
Draft	3'0"	Headroom	6'4"
Weight	32,000#	Hull Type	Modified-V
Cockpit	120 sq. ft.	Deadrise Aft	8°

Prices Not Provided for Pre-1995 Models

Egg Harbor Yachts
Egg Harbor, NJ
www.eggharboryachts.com

Egg Harbor 43 Sport Yacht
2004–Current

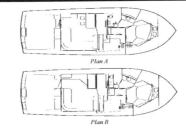

Plan A

Plan B

Updated version of Egg Harbor 42 Sport Yacht (2001–03) boasts redesigned hull with greater deadrise, prop pockets for improved performance. Several two-stateroom floorplans available, all with high-gloss cherry woodwork, designer decor package. Centerline helm with retractable electronics console offers good sightlines fore and aft. Note large cockpit with tackle center and livewell, engineroom sea chest. Above-average fit and finish. Cat 700hp diesels cruise in the mid 20s (30+ knots top).

Length w/Pulpit	45'8"	Fuel	650 gals.
Hull Length	42'6"	Water	115 gals.
Beam	15'0"	Waste	40 gals.
Draft	3'6"	Hull Type	Modified-V
Weight	38,500#	Deadrise Aft	16°

See Page 541 For Resale Values

Egg Harbor Yachts
Egg Harbor, NJ
www.eggharboryachts.com

231-360-0827

Egg Harbor 48 Golden Egg
1978–86

Muscular tournament sportfisherman was considered the last word in convertible style, performance in her era. Offered with several two- and three-stateroom floorplans over the years, all with rich hand-rubbed mahogany woodwork, wraparound salon windows. Teak cockpit with transom door, side lockers accommodates several anglers. Note large flybridge, wide side decks, big engineroom. Late-model 48s have solid front windshield. A fast boat in her day, GM 550hp 8V92s cruise at 24–25 knots (high 20s top).

Length	48'2"	Fuel	788 gals.
Beam	15'0"	Water	110/210 gals.
Draft	4'4"	Cockpit	NA
Weight	44,000#	Hull Type	Modified-V
Clearance	13'1"	Deadrise Aft	2°

Prices Not Provided for Pre-1995 Models

Egg Harbor Yachts
Egg Harbor, NJ
www.eggharboryachts.com

231-360-0827

Egg Harbor 50 Sport Yacht
2006–Current

Handsome Jersey-style convertible with tons of eye appeal delivers top-shelf luxury, spirited performance. Posh three-stateroom, two head interior is highlighted by roomy salon with furniture-quality joinerwork, leather seating, designer fabrics. Note standard washer/dryer. Cockpit has it all—tackle center, tuna door, bait freezer, in-sole fishbox. Pop-up electronics console protects equipment from weather and theft. Prop pockets reduce draft, improve efficiency. Cat 1,000hp C-18 diesels cruise at 28–30 knots (mid 30s top).

Length w/Pulpit	53'0"	Fuel	1,050 gals.
Hull Length	50'0"	Water	250 gals.
Beam	16'11"	Waste	40 gals.
Draft	4'6"	Hull Type	Modified-V
Weight	52,000#	Deadrise Aft	16°

Insufficient Resale Data To Assign Values

Egg Harbor Yachts
Egg Harbor, NJ
www.eggharboryachts.com

231-360-0827

Egg Harbor 52 Sport Yacht
1997–2005

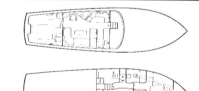

Hard-charging sportfishing machine delivers signature blend of classic Egg Harbor styling, quality, performance. Tapered hull has more bow flare than previous Egg Harbor models. Lush galley-up floorplan with high-gloss woodwork, designer decor has owner's stateroom amidships, VIP stateroom forward, third cabin tucked under salon sole. Cockpit is one of the largest to be found in a boat this size; same is true of the flybridge—it's massive. Above-average finish throughout. Cruise at 25 knots (30+ top) with 800hp Cat diesels.

Length w/Pulpit	54'9"	Fuel	900 gals.
Beam	16'4"	Water	175 gals.
Draft	4'0"	Waste	60 gals.
Weight	52,000#	Hull Type	Modified-V
Clearance	13'7"	Deadrise Aft	7°

See Page 541 For Resale Values

Egg Harbor Yachts
Egg Harbor, NJ
www.eggharboryachts.com

    231-360-0827

Egg Harbor 54 Convertible
1988–89

Scaled-down version of Egg Harbor 60 Convertible (1986-89) offered big-boat luxury, tournament-level fishability. Spacious 120-square-foot cockpit came loaded with standard fishing features. Huge bridge was considered state-of-the-art in her day. Elegant three-stateroom interior boasts expansive salon, amidships owner's stateroom (with unique step-down dressing room aft), large VIP guest cabin forward. Engineroom is on the small side. Cruise at 25 knots (27-28 top) with standard 735hp Detroit 8V92s.

Length w/Pulpit	57'8"	Clearance	15'10"
Hull Length	54'6"	Fuel	1,000 gals.
Beam	17'6"	Water	220 gals.
Draft	5'3"	Hull Type	Modified-V
Weight	72,600#	Deadrise Aft	7°

Prices Not Provided for Pre-1995 Models

Egg Harbor Yachts
Egg Harbor, NJ
www.eggharboryachts.com

    231-360-0827

Egg Harbor 58 Convertible
1990–97

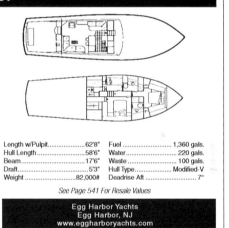

Bold tournament fishing machine set class standards in her day for leading-edge styling, luxury-class amenities. Built on low-deadrise hull with a wide beam, cored hullsides, solid fiberglass bottom. Lavish three-stateroom interior includes amidships master with step-down dressing area, washer/dryer, furniture-quality woodwork. Note home-size galley, massive cockpit. Cruise at 26 knots with 1,100hp GM diesels (30+ knots top). Later models with 1,335hp MTUs cruise at 34 knots (40+ knots wide open).

Length w/Pulpit	62'8"	Fuel	1,360 gals.
Hull Length	58'6"	Water	220 gals.
Beam	17'6"	Waste	100 gals.
Draft	5'3"	Hull Type	Modified-V
Weight	82,000#	Deadrise Aft	7°

See Page 541 For Resale Values

Egg Harbor Yachts
Egg Harbor, NJ
www.eggharboryachts.com

    231-360-0827

Egg Harbor 60 Convertible
1986–89

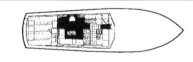

Hard-hitting tournament sportfisherman was considered state of the art in construction, size, performance in the late 1980s. Opulent three-stateroom, three-head interior features unique step-down dressing area aft of master suite, small utility room opposite. Vast salon can entertain a small crowd; apartment-sized galley will satisfy a gourmet cook. Roomy cockpit includes full array of fishing amenities. Note compact engineroom, spacious bridge with extra rod storage. GM 1,080hp 12V92 diesels cruise at 27 knots (30 knots top).

Length	59'6"	Fuel	1,200/1,500 gals.
Beam	17'6"	Water	300 gals.
Draft	5'3"	Cockpit	111 sq. ft.
Weight	72,000#	Hull Type	Modified-V
Clearance	18 5"	Deadrise Aft	8°

Prices Not Provided for Pre-1995 Models

Egg Harbor Yachts
Egg Harbor, NJ
www.eggharboryachts.com

Sportfishing Boats

231-360-0827

Everglades 260/270 Center Console
2006–Current

Top-shelf center console with semi-enclosed helm is distinctive, versatile, built to last. Combined T-top/console with wraparound windshield offers outstanding helm protection. Standard features include leaning post/bolster seat with 55-gallon livewell, bait rigging station, lockable rod storage, fold-down transom seat, docking lights, deluxe forward seating, powder-coated railings. Foam-filled hull is unsinkable. Slide-out cooler is a neat touch. Called the 260 CC in 2006–07. About 45 knots with Yamaha 250s.

Length	26'7"	Fuel	200 gals.
Beam	9'9"	Water	25 gals.
Draft, Up	1'8"	Max HP	500
Draft, Down	3'0"	Hull Type	Deep-V
Hull Weight	6,000#	Deadrise Aft	21°

See Page 541 For Resale Values

Everglades Boats
Edgewater, FL
www.evergladesboats.com

231-360-0827

Everglades 290 Center Console
2005–Current

Versatile center console with integrated hardtop/windshield combines all-weather versatility with executive-class amenities, state-of-the-art construction. Highlights include standard leaning post/helm seat with 66-gallon livewell, console head with sink & shower, lockable rod storage, foldaway transom seat, slide-out cooler, tackle lockers (2), deluxe bow seating, 120-gallon fish box, foldaway transom seat. Exceptional fit & finish. Power-coated railings are a classy touch. Foam-filled hull is unsinkable. About 45 knots with Yamaha 250s.

Length	28'7"	Fuel	200 gals.
Beam	9'9"	Water	25 gals.
Hull Draft	1'8"	Max HP	700
Hull Weight	6,300#	Hull Type	Deep-V
Clearance	7'8"	Deadrise Aft	21°

See Page 541 For Resale Values

Everglades Boats
Edgewater, FL
www.evergladesboats.com

231-360-0827

Everglades 350 Center Console
2007–Current

Floorplan Not Available

Premium center console designed for triple 350hp engines is innovative, fast, loaded with high-end amenities. Combined T-top/console module with wraparound windshield offers superb helm protection. Standard features include triple helm seats with flip-up bolsters, electric high-low bow table, foldaway stern seating, two livewells, enclosed head with berth. Unique foldaway seat on rear of baitwell doubles as fighting chair. Awesome helm layout. Foam-filled hull is unsinkable. This kind of quality doesn't come cheap. Triple 300hp Suzukis top out at over 40 knots.

Length	35'4"	Fuel	411 gals.
Beam	10'8"	Water	35 gals.
Draft, Up	2'0"	Max HP	1050
Draft, Down	3'2"	Hull Type	Deep-V
Hull Weight	9,260#	Deadrise Aft	25°

See Page 541 For Resale Values

Everglades Boats
Edgewater, FL
www.evergladesboats.com

Sportfishing Boats

231-360-0827

Everglades 350 LX
2008–Current

Floorplan Not Available

Luxury-class express makes good on promise of unsurpassed passenger comfort, state-of-the-art innovations. Expensive boat comes with lots of standards: hardtop with tinted skylights, generator, air-conditioning, windlass, flat-screen TV, electric grill, power helm seats with flip-up bolsters. Upscale cabin sleeps four; electric helm deck table coverts to additional berth. Note foldaway stern seats, thru-stem anchor system. Fit and finish is the best in the business. Triple 300hp Suzukis top out at over 40 knots.

Length	35'4"	Fuel	356 gals.
Beam	10'8"	Water	35 gals.
Draft, Up	2'0"	Max HP	1050
Draft, Down	3 5"	Hull Type	Deep-V
Hull Weight	10,800#	Deadrise Aft	25°

Insufficient Resale Data To Assign Values

Everglades Boats
Edgewater, FL
www.evergladesboats.com

231-360-0827

Fountain 29 Center Console
1996–2004

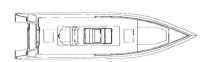

Fast-action fishing machine targets anglers who place a premium on open-water performance. Features include leaning post with integrated 50-gallon livewell, T-top with rod holders, insulated ice chest (under forward console seat), bow storage lockers, rear storage boxes, K-plane trim tabs, raw-water washdown, large fishbox. Deep-V hull is quick to accelerate. Slender 8'4" beam aids high-rpm performance but results in a smaller cockpit than most 29-footers. No console head compartment. Over 55 knots max with 225 Mercs.

Length	29'0"	Fuel	207 gals.
Beam	8'4"	Water	5 gals.
Hull Draft	1'6"	Max HP	500
Weight w/Motors	5,200#	Hull Type	Deep-V
Clearance	NA	Deadrise Aft	22°

See Page 543 For Resale Values

Fountain Powerboats
Washington, NC
www.fountainpowerboats.com

231-360-0827

Fountain 31 Tournament Edition
1997–Current

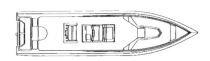

Big-water fishing machine with high-performance hull is agile, fast, loaded with eye appeal. Large-capacity fishbox, 50-gallon transom livewell, leaning post with flip-up bolsters, T-top with rod holders, lockable electronics storage, forward console seat with backrest, raw-water washdown. Lockable cuddy contains V-berth, rod storage, Porta Potti. Fully cored hull with keel-pad bottom is quick to accelerate, fast across the water. Cockpit is narrow compared with most other 31-footers. Close to 60 knots top with twin 300s.

Length	31'0"	Fuel	204 gals.
Beam	8'4"	Water	NA
Hull Draft	16"	Max HP	600
Weight	4,800#	Hull Type	Deep-V
Clearance	NA	Deadrise Aft	22.5°

See Page 543 For Resale Values

Fountain Powerboats
Washington, NC
www.fountainpowerboats.com

Sportfishing Boats

231-360-0827

Fountain 32 Center Console
2006–Current

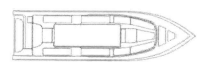

Bold tournament-grade speedster with race-proven stepped hull gets anglers to the fishing grounds well ahead of the crowd. Highlights include T-top with electronics box, 50-gallon transom livewell, in-deck fishboxes (4), walk-in head with sink and shower, pop-up cleats, forward console seat with cooler under, deluxe helm seat with rod holders, U-shaped bow seating, recessed bow rail, rear seat with backrest. Generous 9'6" beam provides good low-speed trolling stability. Impressive fit and finish. About 55 knots max with 275 Mercs.

Length	32'0"	Fuel, Opt	370 gals.
Beam	9'6"	Water	20 gals.
Hull Draft	2'0"	Max HP	550
Dry Weight	8,800#	Hull Type	Deep-V
Fuel, Std.	300 gals.	Deadrise Aft	22.5°

See Page 543 For Resale Values

Fountain Powerboats
Washington, NC
www.fountainpowerboats.com

231-360-0827

Fountain 34 Center Console
2003–Current

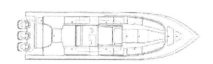

High-performance sportfishing machine makes good on Fountain promise of speed, agility, fishability. Features include circular 50-gallon transom livewell, in-deck fishboxes (4), T-top with electronics box, pop-up cleats, raw-water washdown, recessed bow rail, rear seat, console head compartment with sink and shower. Sporty helm layout with Kiekhaefer controls, Gaffrig instruments. Stepped hull is fully cored. Muscular boat has loads of eye appeal. About 55 knots max with twin 275 Mercs; over 60 knots with triple 225s.

Length	34'0"	Fuel, Std.	300 gals.
Beam	9'6"	Fuel, Opt.	461 gals.
Hull Draft	2'0"	Max HP	825
Dry Weight	10,000#	Hull Type	Deep-V
Clearance	8'4"	Deadrise Aft	23°

See Page 543 For Resale Values

Fountain Powerboats
Washington, NC
www.fountainpowerboats.com

231-360-0827

Fountain 38 Center Console
2001–Current

Open

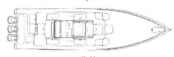

Cuddy

Notched-bottom speedster with triple-outboard power, stepped deep-V hull puts performance-driven anglers in the driver's seat. Features include 50-gallon transom livewell, in-deck macerated fishboxes (7), T-top with electronics box, leaning post with rod holders, pop-up cleats, raw-water washdown, recessed bow rail, rear seat, console head compartment with sink and shower, anchor locker. Look-alike sistership, the 38 Tournament Edition, has small cuddy cabin. About 60 knots top with triple 275s.

Length	38'0"	Fuel, Opt.	461 gals.
Beam	10'6"	Water	30 gals.
Draft, Engines Up	2'0"	Max HP	900
Dry Weight	10,300#	Hull Type	Deep-V
Fuel, Std.	300 gals.	Deadrise Aft	22°

See Page 544 For Resale Values

Fountain Powerboats
Washington, NC
www.fountainpowerboats.com

231-360-0827

Grady-White 263/273 Chase
1994–Current

Trailerable center console in production since 1994 ranks high with anglers for quality, dependability. Standard features include 32-gallon lighted livewell, lockable rod storage, aft fishbox, deluxe leaning post, transom door, pop-up electronics enclosure, foldaway transom seat, cushioned forward seating, low-profile bow rails. Fiberglass insert fits between forward fish boxes to create raised casting deck. Marketed as Grady-White 263 Chase until 2002 when console was redesigned. Max 45+ knots with Yamaha 225s.

Length	26'11"	Fuel	205 gals.
Beam	8'6"	Water	10 gals.
Hull Draft	1'3"	Max HP	500
Dry Weight	4,843#	Hull Type	Modified-V
Clearance, Top	8'3"	Deadrise Aft	18.5°

See Page 544 For Resale Values

Grady-White Boats
Greensville, NC
www.gradywhite.com

231-360-0827

Grady-White 270 Islander
2003–05

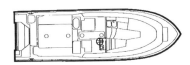

Big trailerable walkaround with roomy cockpit combines top-shelf construction with premium amenities, agile handling. Foldaway rear seat, 34-gallon livewell, transom door, insulated fishbox, deluxe helm and companion seats, lockable electronics box, bow pulpit. Well-finished cabin has galley (with slide-away butane stove), enclosed head with shower, removable dinette table, rod holders. Excellent visibility from raised helm position. Walkways around cabin are narrow. Over 40 knots max with twin 225s.

Length w/Pulpit	29'4"	Fuel	150 gals.
Hull Length	26'11"	Water	32 gals.
Beam	8'6"	Max HP	500
Hull Draft	1'5"	Hull Type	Modified-V
Dry Weight	5,594#	Deadrise Aft	18°

See Page 544 For Resale Values

Grady-White Boats
Greensville, NC
www.gradywhite.com

231-360-0827

Grady-White 272 Sailfish
1994–2000

Updated version of popular Grady-White 25 Sailfish (1978–1993) with integrated transom, redesigned bottom, ranks with the best walkarounds ever produced. Standard features include 20-gallon livewell, aft bench seat, insulated fishboxes, cockpit bolsters, deluxe helm and companion seats, raw-water washdown, cockpit shower. Roomy cabin with fully equipped galley, enclosed head with shower, athwartships aft berth, V-berth. Most were sold with factory hardtop. Became 282 Sailfish in 2001. About 45 knots with Yamaha 250s.

Length w/Pulpit	27'10"	Fuel	202 gals.
Beam	9'6"	Water	32 gals.
Hull Draft	1'6"	Max HP	500
Dry Weight	5,500#	Hull Type	Deep-V
Clearance, Hardtop	9'4"	Deadrise Aft	20°

See Page 544 For Resale Values

Grady-White Boats
Greensville, NC
www.gradywhite.com

Sportfishing Boats

Sportfishing Boats

Grady-White 275 Tournament
2007–Current

Top-level fishing boat/family runabout takes dual-console versatility to the next level. Notable features include 22-gallon and 46-gallon insulated transom fish boxes, cutting board, freshwater shower, padded coaming, cockpit toe rails. Note deluxe bow seating with removable table. Port console head compartment contains clever full-length rod storage—very cool. Foldaway transom seat, 32-gallon livewell are popular options. One of the largest dual console designs available. About 40 knots max with Yamaha 150s.

Length	26'11"	Fuel	200 gals.
Beam	8'6"	Water	20 gals.
Hull Draft	20"	Max HP	500
Dry Weight	4,972#	Hull Type	Deep-V
Clearance, Hardtop	8'6"	Deadrise Aft	19°

See Page 544 For Resale Values

Grady-White Boats
Greensville, NC
www.gradywhite.com

Grady-White 280 Marlin
1989–94

Broad-beam fishing machine with large cockpit, spacious cabin is among the biggest 28-foot walkarounds in the business. Insulated fishbox, 40-gallon livewell, tackle drawers, bait station with sink, raw-water washdown, lockable electronics box, bow pulpit. Well-finished cabin has large V-berth, quarter berth, enclosed head with shower, fully equipped galley. Cockpit can handle full-size fighting chair. Became Grady-White 300 Marline in 1995. Most were sold with optional hardtop. About 40 knots max with twin 225s.

Length w/Pulpit	32'7"	Fuel	306 gals.
Hull Length	28'0"	Water	35 gals.
Beam	10'7"	Max HP	600
Hull Draft	17"	Hull Type	Deep-V
Dry Weight	7,000#	Deadrise Aft	20°

Prices Not Provided for Pre-1995 Models

Grady-White Boats
Greensville, NC
www.gradywhite.com

Grady-White 282 Sailfish
2001–Current

2001–04

2005–Current

Updated version of best-selling 272 Sailfish (1994–2000) boasts restyled cabin windows, minor helm and cockpit revisions. Originally designed with aft bench seat and transom rigging station, cockpit was redesigned in 2005 with aft fishbox, foldaway rear bench seat. Large 40-gallon lighted livewell, cushioned fishboxes are standard. Upscale cabin with enclosed head, full galley, midcabin berth sleeps three. Note heavy-duty transom door, wide walkways. Unsurpassed fit and finish. About 40 knots max with twin 250s.

Length w/Pulpit	30'2"	Fuel	207 gals.
Hull Length	28'0"	Water	32 gals.
Beam	9'6"	Max HP	600
Hull Draft	1'6"	Hull Type	Deep-V
Dry Weight	6,781#	Deadrise Aft	20°

See Page 544 For Resale Values

Grady-White Boats
Greensville, NC
www.gradywhite.com

Grady-White 283 Release
2002–Current

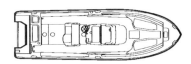

High-end center console provides the leading-edge quality, long-term satisfaction anglers expect in a Grady product. Standard features include combined leaning bar/rigging station with 45-gallon lighted livewell & tackle storage, lockable rod storage, electric pop-up electronics enclosure, sink with pull-out shower, two insulated bow fish boxes, transom fish box, lockable head enclosure. Fold-away transom seat frees up cockpit space. Superior fit and finish throughout. About 40 knots with Yamaha 225s.

Length	28'0"	Fuel, Std.	205 gals.
Beam	9'6"	Water	20 gals.
Hull Draft	1'6"	Max HP	600
Dry Weight	5,864#	Hull Type	Deep-V
Clearance, Top	8.5'	Deadrise Aft	20°

See Page 544 For Resale Values

Grady-White Boats
Greensville, NC
www.gradywhite.com

Grady-White 290 Chesapeake
2009–Current

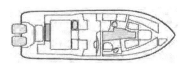

Sure-footed walkaround cabin blends signature Grady-White quality with proven deck layout, roomy cabin accommodations. Standard features include hardtop with radio box, 35-gallon livewell, foldaway transom seat, tackle storage, transom fishbox, cushioned cockpit storage boxes, cockpit bolsters. Dash space for flush-mounting twin 10" video displays. Well-appointed cabin with mini-galley, enclosed head with shower, teak and holly sole sleeps two. No lightweight, Yamaha 250s reach close to 40 knots wide open.

Length	28'6"	Fuel	206 gals.
Beam	9'11"	Water	32 gals.
Hull Draft	24"	Max HP	600
Dry Weight	7,650#	Hull Type	Deep-V
Clearance, Hardtop	9'9"	Deadrise Aft	20°

Insufficient Resale Data To Assign Values

Grady-White Boats
Greensville, NC
www.gradywhite.com

Grady-White 300 Marlin
1995–Current

Updated version of popular Grady-White 280 Marlin (1989-94) boasts revised hull bottom, reworked cockpit. Stand-up 32-gallon livewell, tackle station, insulated fishbox, aft-facing jump seat, transom door, cockpit bolsters, bow pulpit. Well-appointed cabin has small galley with fridge, stand-up head, crawl-in aft berth. Teardrop cabin windows replaced rectangular windows in 1999. Transom redesign in 2004 added larger fishbox, folding bench seat. Yamaha 225hp outboards top out around 40 knots.

Length w/Pulpit	32'7"	Fuel	306 gals.
Hull Length	30'6"	Water	35 gals.
Beam	10'7"	Max HP	700
Hull Draft	1'7"	Hull Type	Deep-V
Dry Weight	8,221#	Deadrise Aft	19.5°

See Page 544 For Resale Values

Grady-White Boats
Greensville, NC
www.gradywhite.com

Grady-White 305 Express
2007–Current

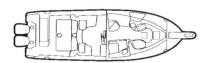

Premium big-water express combines spacious deck layout with comfortable ride, unsurpassed build quality. Fishing amenities include 32-gallon livewell, transom fishbox, fresh/saltwater washdowns, tackle trays, rocket launchers on each hardtop leg. Well-appointed cabin with midship berth, full galley, stand-up head, entertainment center sleeps four. Note centerline helm position, foldaway transom seat, power electronics box, twin cockpit showers. Bow thruster is a nice touch. Nearly 40 knots top with twin 225s.

Length w/Pulpit	32'7"	Fuel	290 gals.
Hull Length	30'6"	Water	32 gals.
Beam	10'7"	Max HP	700
Hull Draft	1'7"	Hull Type	Modified-V
Dry Weight	8,850#	Deadrise Aft	17°

See Page 544 For Resale Values

Grady-White Boats
Greensville, NC
www.gradywhite.com

Grady-White 306 Bimini
1998–Current

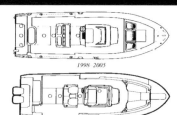

1998-2005

2006-Current

Premium 30-footer makes the cut with anglers willing to pay Grady quality. Highlights include 40-gallon transom livewell, console head with shower, three forward fishboxes, transom door, lockable rod storage. Leaning bar has rigging station with lockable storage. Helm came with electric pop-up electronics enclosure. Excellent cockpit nonskid. Updates in 2006 included twin fishboxes forward (replacing casting platform), combined helm seat/livewell, new transom with folding rear seat. About 40 knots top with twin 250s.

Length	30'6"	Fuel	290 gals.
Beam	10'7"	Water	20 gals.
Hull Draft	21"	Max HP	700
Dry Weight	6,500#	Hull Type	Deep-V
Clearance	9'4"	Deadrise Aft	19.5°

See Page 544 For Resale Values

Grady-White Boats
Greensville, NC
www.gradywhite.com

Grady-White 307 Tournament
2009–Current

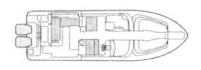

King-size dual console with luxury-class features is tough enough for anglers, roomy enough for families. Huge cockpit with deluxe wet bar (refrigerator/grill optional) includes power 2-man helm seat, double companion seat, foldaway rear seat, two fishboxes. Electric extendable portside lounge seat is a nice touch. Large head compartment in port console extends under bow seating, features lockable rod storage, fold-out 5-foot child berth. Note plush seating, top-quality hardware. Twin Yamaha 250s max out at nearly 40 knots.

Length	30'5"	Fuel	206 gals.
Beam	10'7"	Water	32 gals.
Hull Draft	22"	Max HP	700
Dry Weight	7,850#	Hull Type	Deep-V
Clearance, Hardtop	8'10"	Deadrise Aft	20°

Insufficient Resale Data To Assign Values

Grady-White Boats
Greensville, NC
www.gradywhite.com

Grady-White 330 Express
2001—Current

Gold-plated express with signature Grady-White quality is a sold performer in all conditions. Fishing features include large-capacity transom fishbox, 45-gallon livewell, rigging station with sink. Note aft-facing cockpit seats, pop-up electronics console. Spacious mid-cabin interior boasts classy teak-and-holly sole, built-in entertainment center, luxury-class amenities. Air-conditioning, hardtop, generator are standard. Yamaha 250s reach 35+ knots top. Transom was beefed up in 2009 to handle bigger Yamaha 350s (40+ knots max).

Length w/Pulpit	35'10"	Fuel	350 gals.
Hull Length	33'6"	Water	50 gals.
Beam	11'7"	Max HP	700
Hull Draft	1'9"	Hull Type	Deep-V
Dry Weight	10,840#	Deadrise Aft	20.5°

See Page 545 For Resale Values

Grady-White Boats
Greensville, NC
www.gradywhite.com

Grady-White 336 Canyon
2008—Current

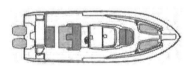

Leading-edge 33-footer with huge cockpit, leading edge components ups the ante on center-console innovation, performance. Deluxe leaning post/tackle center with 45-gallon livewell, foldaway rear seat, large-capacity transom fishbox, forward fish/storage boxes, transom door. Centerline helm with pop-up electronics module accommodates several large displays. Console interior sports full marine head, shower and sink, rod storage, twin berths forward. Big, powerful, sure to impress. About 40 knots top with twin 350s.

Length	33'6"	Fuel	350 gals.
Beam	11'7"	Water	44 gals.
Hull Draft	2'1"	Max HP	700
Dry Weight	9,200#	Hull Type	Deep-V
Clearance, Top	9'0"	Deadrise Aft	21°

See Page 545 For Resale Values

Grady-White Boats
Greensville, NC
www.gradywhite.com

Grady-White 360 Express
2005—Current

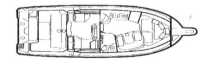

Premium (expensive) triple-outboard express takes Grady-White luxury, fishability to the next level. Standard features include transom fishbox with re-frigerator/freezer, 48-gallon livewell, refrigerator/freezer (in cockpit module), foldaway rear seat. State-of-the-art center helm has electronic controls, innovative slide-out table. Upscale cabin with teak-and-holly sole, entertainment center, aft berth sleeps four adults, two kids. Bow thruster, air-conditioning, generator are standard. The ultimate outboard express. Over 35 knots with triple 250s.

Length w/Pulpit	39'3"	Fuel	370 gals.
Hull Length	36'7"	Water	65 gals.
Beam	10'6"	Max HP	1050
Hull Draft	2'5"	Hull Type	Deep-V
Dry Weight	14,919#	Deadrise Aft	21°

See Page 545 For Resale Values

Grady-White Boats
Greensville, NC
www.gradywhite.com

Sportfishing Boats

Hatteras 32 Flybridge Fisherman
1982–88

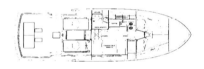

Conservative 1980s convertible combines large cockpit with comfortable cabin layout, roomy bridge. Step-down interior with galley to port, booth-style dinette, roomy head/shower sleeps four. Deck area between engine boxes is below cockpit level to allow standing headroom when entering cabin. Wide 12-foot beam provides cockpit space for a fighting chair. Prop pockets reduce draft, improve hull efficiency. Good engine access. Cruise at 18 knots with 300hp gas engines; 20 knots with 320hp Cat diesels.

Length	32'8"	Fuel	265 gals.
Beam	12'0"	Water	50 gals.
Draft	3'0"	Waste	30 gals.
Weight	18,000#	Hull Type	Modified-V
Clearance	10'6"	Deadrise Aft	18°

Prices Not Provided for Pre-1995 Models

Hatteras Yachts
New Bern, NC
www.hatterasyachts.com

Hatteras 32 Sport Fisherman
1982–86

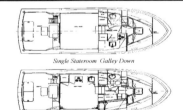

Well-built 1980s express fisherman combined efficient deck layout with upscale cabin accommodations, legendary Hatteras engineering and construction. Classy teak-trimmed interior with compact galley, convertible dinette, stand-up head with shower sleeps four. Uncluttered cockpit—big enough for 6 anglers—lacks transom door. Good helm visibility, but not much space for extra electronics. Prop pockets reduce draft, improve efficiency. Cruise at 18 knots with 300hp gas engines; 20 knots with 320hp Cat diesels.

Length	32'8"	Fuel	265 gals.
Beam	12'0"	Water	50 gals.
Draft	3'2"	Cockpit	95 sq. ft.
Weight	17,200#	Hull Type	Modified-V
Clearance, Windshield	8'8"	Deadrise Aft	18°

Prices Not Provided for Pre-1995 Models

Hatteras Yachts
New Bern, NC
www.hatterasyachts.com

Hatteras 36 Convertible
1983–87

Single Stateroom Galley Down

Twin Staterooms Galley Up

Polished 1980s convertible with wide 13'7" beam, efficient prop-pocket hull is more family cruiser than hard-nosed fishboat. Deluxe interior with spacious salon, solid teak cabinets was available with one or two staterooms. Highlights include wraparound salon windows, wide side decks, transom door, molded bow pulpit, roomy flybridge with seating for five. Hatches in cockpit sole provide access to generator. Well-appointed boat has aged well. Standard gas engines cruise at 14–16 knots; 390hp GM diesels cruise at 20 knots.

Length	36'6"	Fuel	355 gals.
Beam	13'7"	Water	115 gals.
Draft	3'9"	Waste	40 gals.
Weight	26,500#	Hull Type	Modified-V
Clearance	12'6"	Deadrise Aft	18°

Prices Not Provided for Pre-1995 Models

Hatteras Yachts
New Bern, NC
www.hatterasyachts.com

231-360-0827

Hatteras 37 Convertible
1977–83

Standard Floorplan

Alternate Floorplan (1982–83)

Versatile Hatteras convertible introduced in 1977 bridged the gap between tournament-grade sportfishing boat, luxurious family cruiser. Two-stateroom interior with salon galley boasts solid teak paneling, quality hardware and furnishings. Lower helm was optional. Cockpit is large enough for full-size fighting chair. Bow pulpit, transom door were standard. Double berth became available in bow stateroom beginning in 1982. GM 310hp diesels cruise at 16–18 knots; 390hp GMs cruise at 20 knots.

Length	37'0"	Fuel	330 gals.
Beam	14'0"	Water	135 gals.
Draft	3'3"	Waste	60 gals.
Weight	29,000#	Hull Type	Modified-V
Clearance	13.5'	Deadrise Aft	NA

Prices Not Provided for Pre-1995 Models

Hatteras Yachts
New Bern, NC
www.hatterasyachts.com

231-360-0827

Hatteras 38 Convertible
1988–93

Handsome styling, executive-class accommodations, quality construction set this high-end convertible apart from competitive models. Deluxe two-stateroom interior with teak trim includes big owner's stateroom and large head, but deckhouse galley is too small with little counter, storage space. Roomy cockpit came standard with molded tackle center, in-deck fishbox, transom door. Note wide side decks, engineroom air intakes under cockpit coaming. Modest performance, too-small galley. GM 485hp diesels cruise at 22 knots.

Length	38'10"	Fuel	490 gals.
Beam	13.5"	Water	117 gals.
Draft	4'8"	Waste	60 gals.
Weight	28,800#	Hull Type	Modified-V
Clearance	12'6"	Deadrise Aft	9°

Prices Not Provided for Pre-1995 Models

Hatteras Yachts
New Bern, NC
www.hatterasyachts.com

231-360-0827

Hatteras 39 Convertible
1994–98

Updated version of Hatteras 38 Convertible (1988–93) offered "new-look" 1990s styling, improved floor plan. Spacious, teak-trimmed interior features convenient salon serving counter overlooking galley. Guest cabin doubles as open day lounge or private sleeping area with lower berth, fold-down upper berth. Large flybridge overlooks cockpit with standard tackle centers, removable fishbox, transom door. Avoid models with small 314hp diesels. Optional Detroit 465hp 6-71 diesels cruise at 22–24 knots; 26+ knots wide open.

Length	39'0"	Fuel	490 gals.
Beam	13'7"	Water	120 gals.
Draft	4'8"	Waste	50 gals.
Weight	32,000#	Hull Type	Modified-V
Clearance	12'6"	Deadrise Aft	9°

See Page 545 For Resale Values

Hatteras Yachts
New Bern, NC
www.hatterasyachts.com

Hatteras 39 Sport Express
1995–98

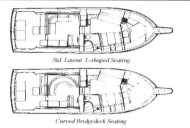

Std. Layout L-shaped Seating

Curved Bridgedeck Seating

Graceful big-water express delivers quality Hatteras construction, versatile layout, solid performance. Spacious cockpit came standard with in-deck fishbox, bait-prep station with sink, livewell, transom door, direct engineroom access. Small-but-elegant interior boasts full galley, convertible dinette, head with stall shower, teak or oak woodwork. Spacious bridgedeck came with several seating options. Offered in Cruiser or Sportfish versions. Twin 435hp Cats cruise at 22 knots; 465hp Detroit 6-71s cruise in the mid 20s.

Length	39'0"	Fuel	458 gals.
Beam	13'7"	Water	120 gals.
Draft	4'8"	Waste	50 gals.
Weight	30,500#	Hull Type	Modified-V
Clearance	8'10"	Deadrise Aft	9°

See Page 546 For Resale Values

Hatteras Yachts
New Bern, NC
www.hatterasyachts.com

Hatteras 41 Convertible
1986–91

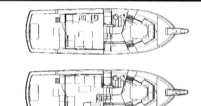

Rock-solid convertible with "new-look" Hatteras styling (note stepped sheer, rakish bridge) was forerunner of company's late-1990s convertible lineup. Offered with several interior plans, all with roomy bow stateroom, top-shelf fixtures and furnishings. Light ash woodwork became available in 1987. Spacious 120-square-foot cockpit is among largest in class. Hull was fully cored in early models. Note fuel increase in 1987. Standard 465hp 6-71 diesels cruise at 22–23 knots; optional 535hp 6V92s cruise at 25 knots (27–28 knots top).

Length	41'9"	Fuel	400/500 gals.
Beam	14'3"	Water	150 gals.
Draft	4'4"	Cockpit	120 sq. ft.
Weight	35,400#	Hull Type	Modified-V
Clearance	13'9"	Deadrise Aft	NA

Prices Not Provided for Pre-1995 Models

Hatteras Yachts
New Bern, NC
www.hatterasyachts.com

Hatteras 43 Convertible
1979–84

Standard Floorplan 1979-84

Queen Berth in Master 1982-84

Classic convertible sportfisherman introduced in 1979 incorporated all-new double-chine hull for drier ride than previous Hatteras models. Twin-stateroom interior with single head, amidships master features roomy salon with convertible lounge, galley with full-size refrigerator. Cockpit is small for a 43-footer, but flybridge is big. Note engineroom air intakes under cockpit coaming. Early models with 450hp GM diesels cruise at a modest 19–20 knots. GM 500hp engines—introduced in 1981—cruise at 21–22 knots (about 25 knots top).

Length	43'8"	Fuel	470 gals.
Beam	14'6"	Water	165 gals.
Draft	4'2"	Cockpit	110 sq. ft.
Weight	41,000#	Hull Type	Modified-V
Clearance	14'3"	Deadrise Aft	11°

Prices Not Provided for Pre-1995 Models

Hatteras Yachts
New Bern, NC
www.hatterasyachts.com

Sportfishing Boats

231-360-0827

Hatteras 43 Convertible
1991—98

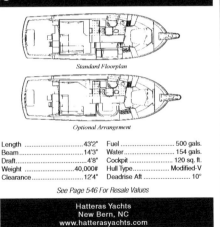

Standard Floorplan

Optional Arrangement

Rakish 43-footer with "new-look" Hatteras styling set quality, performance standards for midsize convertibles of her era. Large 120-square-foot cockpit boasts direct engineroom access, wide transom door, removable fishbox, bait and tackle center. Offered with choice of two-stateroom or dinette interior, both with large master stateroom but compact salon. Note light ash woodwork, washer/dryer space in forward passageway. Cockpit engineroom access is a plus. Twin 535hp 6V92 GM diesels cruise at 24 knots (27–28 knots top).

Length	43'2"	Fuel	500 gals.
Beam	14'3"	Water	154 gals.
Draft	4'8"	Cockpit	120 sq. ft.
Weight	40,000#	Hull Type	Modified-V
Clearance	12'4"	Deadrise Aft	10°

See Page 546 For Resale Values

Hatteras Yachts
New Bern, NC
www.hatterasyachts.com

231-360-0827

Hatteras 43 Sport Express
1996—98

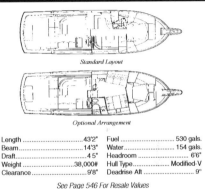

Standard Layout

Optional Arrangement

Powerful offshore express—among largest in her class in late 1990s—was stylish, fast, expensive. Standard interior with U-shaped galley, stall shower in head sleeps four; alternate layout with smaller head and galley sleeps six. Rigging station, lift-out fishboxes, livewell were standard. Aft-facing bench seat in cockpit lifts for engineroom access. Additional features include light oak interior woodwork, radar arch, side exhausts, bow pulpit. First-rate finish throughout. Twin 535hp GM diesels cruise at 27 knots (30+ knots top).

Length	43'2"	Fuel	530 gals.
Beam	14'3"	Water	154 gals.
Draft	4'5"	Headroom	6'6"
Weight	38,000#	Hull Type	Modified-V
Clearance	9'8"	Deadrise Aft	9°

See Page 546 For Resale Values

Hatteras Yachts
New Bern, NC
www.hatterasyachts.com

231-360-0827

Hatteras 45 Convertible
1984—88

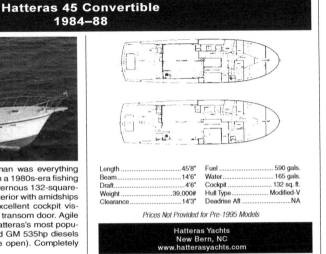

Venerable Hatteras sportfisherman was everything many anglers were looking for in a 1980s-era fishing machine. Highlights include cavernous 132-square-foot cockpit, upscale two-stateroom interior with amidships owner's cabin, large flybridge with excellent cockpit visibility. Note teak interior joinery, beefy transom door. Agile performance for a big boat. One of Hatteras's most popular models for several years. Standard GM 535hp diesels cruise at 23 knots (26–27 knots wide open). Completely restyled in 1989—see next entry.

Length	45'8"	Fuel	590 gals.
Beam	14'6"	Water	165 gals.
Draft	4'6"	Cockpit	132 sq. ft.
Weight	39,000#	Hull Type	Modified-V
Clearance	14'3"	Deadrise Aft	NA

Prices Not Provided for Pre-1995 Models

Hatteras Yachts
New Bern, NC
www.hatterasyachts.com

Sportfishing Boats

www.powerboatguide.com   231-360-0827

Hatteras 45 Convertible
1989–91

Restyled version of one of Hatteras's most popular models made a good boat even more desirable. Major updates included rearranged helm console with electronics enclosure, new bait-and-tackle center, re-designed interior with increased salon seating, walkaround queen bed in owner's stateroom. Huge 132-square-foot cockpit with transom door, coaming gate, molded tackle center is among largest in class. Engineroom is accessed from rear of salon. Standard GM 535hp diesels cruise at 23 knots (26–27 knots wide open).

Length	45'8"	Headroom	6'7"
Beam	14'6"	Fuel	590 gals.
Draft	4'7"	Water	165 gals.
Weight	43,800#	Hull Type	Modified-V
Clearance	14'3"	Deadrise Aft	NA

Prices Not Provided for Pre-1995 Models

Hatteras Yachts
New Bern, NC
www.hatterasyachts.com

---

www.powerboatguide.com   231-360-0827

Hatteras 46 Convertible
1974–85

Galley Down 1974-1981

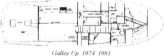

Galley Up 1974-1981

Classic Hatteras convertible with bold 1970s styling delivered lasting blend of upscale accommodations, tournament-grade fishability. Several two-stateroom floorplans were available over the years, all with handcrafted teak woodwork. Cockpit, flybridge were considered state-of-the-art in her era. Sliding door replaced original hinged salon door in 1982. One of last Hatteras convertibles with front windshield. Updated 46 model introduced in 1986. GM 425hp diesels cruise at 19–20 knots; 650hp GMs (1982–85) cruise at 25 knots.

Length	46'2"	Fuel	650/710 gals.
Beam	14'9"	Water	180 gals.
Draft	4'2"	Cockpit	125 sq. ft.
Weight	41,000#	Hull Type	Modified-V
Clearance	13'8"	Deadrise Aft	NA

Prices Not Provided for Pre-1995 Models

Hatteras Yachts
New Bern, NC
www.hatterasyachts.com

---

www.powerboatguide.com   231-360-0827

Hatteras 46 Convertible
1992–95

Standard Floorplan

Optional Arrangement

Leading-edge mix of hardcore fishability, cruising elegance set class standards in early 1990s. Luxurious two-stateroom interior with full dinette was available with one or two heads. Spacious cockpit came with tackle centers, in-deck fishbox, transom door, direct access to stand-up engineroom. Note standard washer/dryer, underwater exhaust system. A good-running boat, 735hp 8V92s cruise at 24–25 knots and reach 28 knots wide open. Optional 780hp MANs reach an honest 30 knots.

Length	46'10"	Fuel	775 gals.
Beam	15'7"	Water	188 gals.
Draft	4'6"	Cockpit	121 sq. ft.
Weight	52,000#	Hull Type	Modified-V
Clearance	13'9"	Deadrise Aft	7°

See Page 546 For Resale Values

Hatteras Yachts
New Bern, NC
www.hatterasyachts.com

Hatteras 48 Convertible
1987–91

Muscular sportfishing machine impressed 1980s buyers with huge cockpit, luxury accommodations, near 30-knot performance. Two-stateroom teak interior features expansive salon with entertainment center, wet bar. Serving counter overlooks mid-level galley, but layout lacks built-in dinette found in most 48-footers. Cockpit features molded tackle center, beefy transom door, engineroom access door. Note solid front windshield panels. Standard 720hp GM diesels cruise at 24 knots (27–28 knots top).

Length	48'8"	Fuel	812 gals.
Beam	16'0"	Water	184 gals.
Draft	5'5"	Cockpit	135 sq. ft.
Weight	51,500#	Hull Type	Modified-V
Clearance	14'0"	Deadrise Aft	8°

Prices Not Provided for Pre-1995 Models

Hatteras Yachts
New Bern, NC
www.hatterasyachts.com

Hatteras 50 Convertible
1980–83

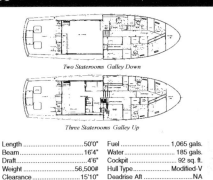

Two Staterooms Galley Down

Three Staterooms Galley Up

Beefy flybridge convertible with classic Hatteras styling was big enough, tough enough, but suffered from small cockpit. Wide beam provides generous accommodations for a boat this size. Offered with two- and three-stateroom interiors, both with amidships owner's suite. Flybridge is huge for a 50-footer of this era. Early models with 550hp GM diesels cruise at 19 knots (21–22 top); 650hp versions (introduced in 1982) cruise at 21 knots (mid 20s top). Note that Hatteras 52 Convertible (1984–91) is same boat with a bigger cockpit.

Length	50'0"	Fuel	1,065 gals.
Beam	16'4"	Water	185 gals.
Draft	4'6"	Cockpit	92 sq. ft.
Weight	56,500#	Hull Type	Modified-V
Clearance	15'10"	Deadrise Aft	NA

Prices Not Provided for Pre-1995 Models

Hatteras Yachts
New Bern, NC
www.hatterasyachts.com

Hatteras 50 Convertible
1991–98

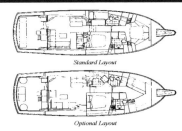

Standard Layout

Optional Layout

Heavyweight sportfishing machine hit the sweet spot with deep-pocket anglers looking for leading-edge comfort, exhilarating performance. Lavish three-stateroom, two-head interior with deckhouse galley was standard; optional two-stateroom, galley-down floorplan boasts huge salon with seating for a crowd. Posh designer decor set convertible standards in the 1990s. Massive cockpit for a 50-footer. Restyled Hatteras 50 was introduced in 1999. GM 870hp 12-cylinder diesels cruise at 26 knots (about 30 knots top).

Length	50'10"	Fuel	890 gals.
Beam	16'1"	Water	184 gals.
Draft	5'4"	Waste	85 gals.
Weight	60,000#	Hull Type	Modified-V
Clearance	13'8"	Deadrise Aft	8°

See Page 546 For Resale Values

Hatteras Yachts
New Bern, NC
www.hatterasyachts.com

Sportfishing Boats

Hatteras 50 Convertible
1999–2006

Standard Layout

Optional Layout

R estyled version of previous Hatteras 50 provides the right mix of comfort, fishability, performance. Three-stateroom interior with deckhouse galley is standard; optional two-stateroom, galley-down floorplan boasts huge salon with seating for a crowd. Note washer/dryer in bow stateroom. Oversized bridge with single-lever controls, recessed electronics box seats captain and six guests. Huge cockpit comes standard with large bait freezer, bait and tackle center. Note fuel increase in 2001. Cat 1,400hp engines cruise at a fast 35 knots.

Length	50'10"	Fuel	890/1,060 gals.
Beam	16'1"	Water	184 gals.
Draft	5'4"	Waste	85 gals.
Weight	60,000#	Hull Type	Modified-V
Clearance	13'8"	Deadrise Aft	8°

See Page 546 For Resale Values

Hatteras Yachts
New Bern, NC
www.hatterasyachts.com

Hatteras 52 Convertible
1984–87

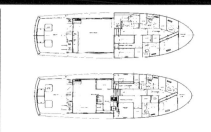

S tretched version of Hatteras 50 Convertible (1980–83) used the extra length to provide massive fishing cockpit—something her predecessor sorely lacked. Standard two-stateroom, galley-down and optional three-stateroom, galley-up floorplans are identical to 50 Convertible. Deep cockpit features molded bait and tackle center, transom door with gate, direct engineroom access. A good seaboat, GM 675hp diesels cruise at 22 knots (about 26 knots top). Popular model was completely restyled for 1988—see next entry.

Length	52'0"	Fuel	1,065 gals.
Beam	16'4"	Water	185 gals.
Draft	5'0"	Cockpit	153 sq. ft.
Weight	56,000#	Hull Type	Modified-V
Clearance	15'10"	Deadrise Aft	NA

Prices Not Provided for Pre-1995 Models

Hatteras Yachts
New Bern, NC
www.hatterasyachts.com

Hatteras 52 Convertible
1988–91

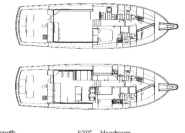

U pdated version of good-selling Hatteras 52 Convertible (1984–87) boasts restyled exterior, redesigned accommodations, increased power. Available with two-stateroom, galley-down interior, or more popular three-stateroom layout with galley and dinette up. Big 153-square-foot cockpit includes bait and tackle center, removable fishbox, in-sole baitwell, direct access to engineroom. Note wide side decks, 30" transom gate, massive flybridge. GM 720-hp diesels cruise in the low-to-mid 20s (26–27 knots wide open).

Length	52'0"	Headroom	6'6"
Beam	16'4"	Fuel	1,068 gals.
Draft	5'0"	Water	188 gals.
Weight	55,400#	Hull Type	Modified-V
Clearance	15'10	Deadrise Aft	NA

Prices Not Provided for Pre-1995 Models

Hatteras Yachts
New Bern, NC
www.hatterasyachts.com

Hatteras 54 Convertible
1991–98

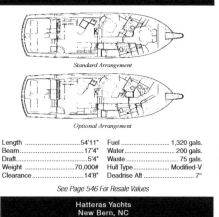

Standard Arrangement

Optional Arrangement

ompelling 1990s tournament yacht met Hatteras standards for world-class construction, exceptional open-water performance. Spacious three-stateroom interior with ash cabinetry boasts huge salon with galley and dinette area, lavish master suite, standard washer/dryer in companionway. Huge flybridge included state-of-the-art helm console. Walk-in engineroom is a mechanic's dream. Optional 1,040hp Detroit (or 1,020hp MAN) diesels cruise at 25 knots; later models with 1,300hp Cats cruise at 28 knots (32–33 knots top).

Length	54'11"	Fuel	1,320 gals.
Beam	17'4"	Water	200 gals.
Draft	5'4"	Waste	75 gals.
Weight	70,000#	Hull Type	Modified-V
Clearance	14'8"	Deadrise Aft	7°

See Page 546 For Resale Values

Hatteras Yachts
New Bern, NC
www.hatterasyachts.com

Hatteras 54 Convertible
2002–Current

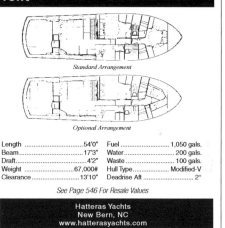

Standard Arrangement

Optional Arrangement

igh-impact convertible combines "new-look" Hatteras styling with lavish accommodations, excellent performance. Spacious salon/galley provides 195 square feet of living space with custom L-shaped sofa, full entertainment center. Topside features include state-of-the-art cockpit layout, huge flybridge with Murray chairs, pop-up helm console. Note meticulous stand-up engineroom. Prop tunnels permit shallow-water operation. Cruise at 30 knots with 1,400hp Cats (35 knots top); 1,550hp Cats top out at close to 40 knots.

Length	54'0"	Fuel	1,050 gals.
Beam	17'3"	Water	200 gals.
Draft	4'2"	Waste	100 gals.
Weight	67,000#	Hull Type	Modified-V
Clearance	13'10"	Deadrise Aft	2°

See Page 546 For Resale Values

Hatteras Yachts
New Bern, NC
www.hatterasyachts.com

Hatteras 55 Convertible
1980–86

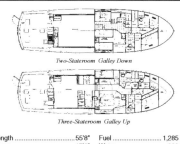

Two-Stateroom Galley Down

Three-Stateroom Galley Up

uscular, good-selling sportfishing yacht replaced iconic Hatteras 53 Convertible in 1980. Most were delivered with three-stateroom, galley-up interior with three full heads. Huge cockpit came with molded tackle center, transom door, direct access to stand-up engineroom. Flybridge is huge with efficient helm layout, plenty of guest seating. No lightweight, standard 650hp GM diesels cruise at 19–20 knots (23 knots top); 870hp GMs—available from 1982—cruise at 23 knots (about 26 knots top). Updated in 1987—see following entry.

Length	55'8"	Fuel	1,285 gals.
Beam	17'6"	Water	380 gals.
Draft	4'10"	Cockpit	158 sq. ft.
Weight	70,000#	Hull Type	Modified-V
Clearance	16'8"	Deadrise Aft	NA

Prices Not Provided for Pre-1995 Models

Hatteras Yachts
New Bern, NC
www.hatterasyachts.com

Sportfishing Boats

www.powerboatguide.com 231-360-0827

Hatteras 55 Convertible
1987–89

Three-Stateroom Layout

Two-Stateroom Layout

Updated version of popular Hatteras 55 Convertible (1980–86) features restyled windows, more aggressive flybridge profile, minor interior upgrades. Most were delivered with three-stateroom, galley-up interior with amidships owner's suite, three full heads. Huge cockpit came with molded tackle center, transom door, direct access to stand-up engineroom. Flybridge is huge. A heavy boat, GM 870hp diesels cruise at 23 knots (about 26 knots top); optional 1,040 GMs cruise at 25 knots (high 20s top). Note that all-new Hatteras 55 came out in 1999.

Length	55'8"	Headroom	6'6"
Beam	17'6"	Fuel	1,287 gals.
Draft	4'10"	Water	381 gals.
Weight	70,000#	Hull Type	Modified-V
Clearance	15'8"	Deadrise Aft	NA

Prices Not Provided for Pre-1995 Models

Hatteras Yachts
New Bern, NC
www.hatterasyachts.com

---

www.powerboatguide.com 231-360-0827

Hatteras 55 Convertible
1999–2002

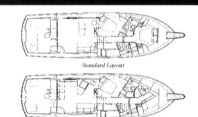

Standard Layout

Optional Floorplan

Tournament-class 55-footer is an updated version of popular Hatteras 54 Convertible (1991–98) with restyled superstructure, slightly modified cockpit, increased power. Standard three-stateroom floorplan with expansive salon is identical to older 54; huge cockpit was redesigned with transom fishbox in place of in-deck units of the 54. Note pod-style helm console, newly styled tackle center. Standard 1,450hp 12-cylinder Cat diesels deliver a cruising speed of 28–29 knots and a top speed of about 33 knots.

Length	55'2"	Fuel	1,320 gals.
Beam	17'4"	Water	200 gals.
Draft	5'4"	Waste	100 gals.
Weight	74,000#	Hull Type	Modified-V
Clearance	14'8"	Deadrise Aft	6°

See Page 546 For Resale Values

Hatteras Yachts
New Bern, NC
www.hatterasyachts.com

---

www.powerboatguide.com 231-360-0827

Hatteras 58 Convertible
1990–94

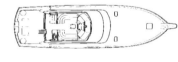

Hard-charging tournament machine from early 1990s provided motoryacht luxury with sportfishing performance. Massive 175-square-foot cockpit with oversize transom door can accommodate several anglers; two-station flybridge allows helmsman to coordinate with cockpit activity. (Fully enclosed, air-conditioned bridge was optional.) Note huge walk-in engineroom. No lightweight, standard 1,040hp GMs cruise at 22 knots (25–26 knots top). Popular GM 1,350hp engines cruise at 27–28 knots (30+ knots top).

Length	58'10"	Fuel	1,660 gals.
Beam	17'9"	Water	250 gals.
Draft	5'11"	Cockpit	175 sq. ft.
Weight	92,000#	Hull Type	Modified-V
Clearance	22'4"	Deadrise Aft	10°

Prices Not Provided for Pre-1995 Models

Hatteras Yachts
New Bern, NC
www.hatterasyachts.com

231-360-0827

Hatteras 60 Convertible
1977–86

Hard-nosed tournament fisherman ranks among best-selling big convertibles ever produced. Highlights include three-stateroom, three-head interior with combined salon/galley/dinette, separate utility room forward of engineroom, massive 175-square-foot cockpit, optional enclosed flybridge. Early models with GM 650hp engines cruise at 17–18 knots (20 knots top). High-performance 825hp model introduced in 1986 (with beefed-up stringers, cored hullsides) will cruise at 20 knots (low 20s top). Over 125 were built.

Length	60'11"
Beam	18'0"
Draft	4'11"
Weight	82,000#
Clearance	17'1"
Fuel	1,555 gals.
Water	490 gals.
Cockpit	175 sq. ft.
Hull Type	Modified-V
Deadrise Aft	NA

Prices Not Provided for Pre-1995 Models

Hatteras Yachts
New Bern, NC
www.hatterasyachts.com

231-360-0827

Hatteras 60 Convertible
1998–2006

Standard Plan 1998–2002

Standard Plan 2003–Current

World-class convertible set class standards in late 1990s for styling, luxury, flat-out performance. Three-stateroom layout with open salon/dinette/galley offers comfort equal to a Hatteras motoryacht. Huge cockpit comes with a full array of top-quality fishing features. Enclosed flybridge is optional. Note generous fuel capacity, walk-in engineroom, state-of-the-art helm. Prop pockets reduce draft requirements. Standard 1,480hp Cat diesels cruise at 27–28 knots (30+ top). Replaced in 2007 with all-new 60 Convertible.

Length	60'2"
Beam	17'4"
Draft	5'4"
Weight	74,500#
Clearance, Windshield	14'8"
Fuel	1,622 gals.
Water	200 gals.
Waste	100 gals.
Hull Type	Modified-V
Deadrise Aft	5°

See Page 546 For Resale Values

Hatteras Yachts
New Bern, NC
www.hatterasyachts.com

231-360-0827

Hatteras 60 Convertible
2007–Current

Broad-beamed tournament convertible with serious sex appeal makes the grade with performance-driven anglers. Design features include maxed-out mezzanine cockpit, rounded "tumblehome" hull sides, curved bridge stairs, wraparound windshield look. Standard three-stateroom interior offers true motoryacht luxuries. Flybridge electronics display is hydraulically concealed. High-strength resin infused hull (with prop pockets) is a Hatteras first. Cat 1,800hp diesels cruise at a fast 35 knots (40+ knots flat out).

Length	59'10"
Beam	19'0"
Draft	4'9"
Weight	90,000#
Clearance	NA
Fuel	1,800 gals.
Water	200 gals.
Waste	100 gals.
Hull Type	Modified-V
Deadrise Aft	2°

See Page 546 For Resale Values

Hatteras Yachts
New Bern, NC
www.hatterasyachts.com

Sportfishing Boats

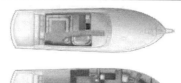

Hatteras 64 Convertible
2006–Current

Heavyweight convertible with broad 19'6" beam delivers sportfishing muscle, cruising elegance. Standard three-stateroom, three-head interior features extravagant full-beam master with king bed, huge salon with enormous U-shaped settee. Note unique opening ports in master stateroom. Small observation/lounge deck overlooks massive cockpit. Engineroom is a work of art. Enclosed bridge is optional. Prop pockets reduce draft, improve efficiency. Cat 1,800hp C-32 engines cruise at 28–30 knots (mid 30s top).

Length	63'10"	Fuel	1,950 gals.
Beam	19'6"	Water	343 gals.
Draft	4'10"	Waste	105 gals.
Weight	100,000#	Hull Type	Modified-V
Clearance	15'3"	Deadrise Aft	2°

Insufficient Resale Data To Assign Values

Hatteras Yachts
New Bern, NC
www.hatterasyachts.com

---

www.powerboatguide.com   231-360-0827

Hatteras 65 Convertible
1987–99

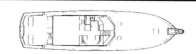

Powerful closed-bridge convertible remains one of the most successful Hatteras designs ever. Standard three-stateroom, galley-up layout is highlighted by spacious, beautifully appointed salon. Alternate floorplan with enlarged owner's stateroom, low-profile galley became available in 1996. Massive cockpit is largest to be found in any 65-footer. Prop pockets reduce draft requirements. Detroit 1,035hp engines cruise at 21 knots; 1,235hp MTUs—or 1,350hp GMs—cruise at 25 knots. Total of 120 were built.

Length	65'5"	Fuel	1,674 gals.
Beam	18'0"	Water	460 gals.
Draft	5'4"	Waste	60 gals.
Weight	102,000#	Cockpit	183 sq. ft.
Clearance	21'11"	Hull Type	Modified-V

See Page 546 For Resale Values

Hatteras Yachts
New Bern, NC
www.hatterasyachts.com

---

www.powerboatguide.com   231-360-0827

Hatteras 65 Convertible
2000–03

Standard 4-Stateroom Interior

Optional 3-Stateroom Layout

Updated version of original Hatteras 65 Convertible (1987–99) has new-look styling, retains predecessor's proven prop-pocket hull. Standard layout has four staterooms, three heads with tub in master; three-stateroom plan replaces guest cabin with larger heads, increased storage. Note leak-free frameless cabin windows, huge engineroom. Enclosed bridge model has outside control station overlooking cockpit, inside bridge access. Twin 1,400hp Cats cruise at 22–23 knots; optional 1,800hp Detroits cruise at 28 knots (30+ knots top).

Length	65'5"	Fuel	1,800 gals.
Beam	18'0"	Water	445 gals.
Draft	6'0"	Waste	90 gals.
Weight	103,000#	Cockpit	183 sq. ft.
Clearance	18'2"	Hull Type	Modified-V

See Page 546 For Resale Values

Hatteras Yachts
New Bern, NC
www.hatterasyachts.com

Sportfishing Boats

Hydra-Sports 2796/2800 CC
2000–05

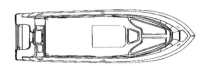

Fast-action fishing machine with big 284-gallon fuel tank allows owners to roam far offshore. Wide beam offers cockpit space for several anglers. Recessed stern seat folds away when not in use; lighted 50-gallon baitwell is built into transom. Standard features include transom door, freshwater shower, enclosed head, concealed rod storage, tackle drawers, pop-up cleats, cockpit bolsters. Well-finished boat. Called Hydra-Sports 2796 in 2000–02; 2800 Vector in 2003–05. Yamaha 225s reach 45 knots top.

Length	28'1"	Fuel	284 gals.
Beam	9'8"	Water	20 gals.
Draft, Up	1'1"	Max HP	600
Draft, Down	2'6"	Hull Type	Deep-V
Hull Weight	6,525#	Deadrise Aft	23°

See Page 546 For Resale Values

Hydra-Sports
Sarasota, FL
www.hydra-sports.com

Hydra-Sports 2800 Walkaround
2001–05

Head-turning walkaround splits the difference between hardcore fishing boat, weekend family cruiser. Features include in-deck fish boxes, transom door, 35-gallon lighted livewell, foldaway rear seat, fresh/raw-water washdowns, bait-prep center with sink, cockpit bolsters, tackle storage (under helm seats), aft-facing jump seats, in-deck storage. Cabin amenities include galley with microwave, midcabin berth, enclosed head with VacuFlush toilet, standard air-conditioning. Impressive finish. Over 40 knots top with Yamaha 225s.

Length	28'2"	Fuel	284 gals.
Beam	9'8"	Water	29 gals.
Hull Draft	18"	Max HP	500
Weight w/OBs	7,225#	Hull Type	Deep-V
Clearance, Hardtop	9'0"	Deadrise Aft	23°

See Page 546 For Resale Values

Hydra-Sports
Sarasota, FL
www.hydra-sports.com

Hydra-Sports 2800/3100 Sportfish
1992–98

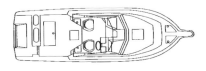

Appealing offshore express with generous beam combines roomy fishing cockpit with well-equipped cabin, smooth-running hull. Standard cockpit amenities include transom livewell, lift-out fishboxes, tackle storage, raw-water washdown, bolster pads, rod storage racks, transom door. Surprisingly roomy cabin with midberth aft, full-feature galley, enclosed head with shower, sleeps four. Wide side decks are a plus. Called 2800 SF in 1992–95; 3100 SF in 1996–98. Over 40 knots top with twin 225s.

Length w/Pulpit	30'1"	Fuel	300 gals.
Beam	10'7"	Water	31 gals.
Draft	2'3"	Max HP	550
Dry Weight	7,900#	Hull Type	Deep-V
Clearance	NA	Deadrise Aft	19°

See Page 547 For Resale Values

Hydra-Sports
Sarasota, FL
www.hydra-sports.com

231-360-0827

Hydra-Sports 2900 CC
2006–Current

Big-water center console with tournament-tested layout targets serious anglers who recognize quality. Cockpit features include transom rigging station with sink, foldaway rear seat, lighted 55-gallon livewell, three fishboxes, lockable rod storage. Helm has space for flush-mounting two 10" video screens. Standard hardtop comes with electronics box, spreader lights. Walk-in console has portable toilet, sink with hand-held shower. Excellent range. Windshield surrounds entire helm—sweet. Yamaha 250s top out at 45 knots.

Length	29'8"	Fuel	300 gals.
Beam	9'8"	Water	23 gals.
Hull Draft	1'10"	Max HP	600
Dry Weight	7,904#	Hull Type	Deep-V
Clearance	8'9"	Deadrise Aft	23°

See Page 547 For Resale Values

Hydra-Sports
Sarasota, FL
www.hydra-sports.com

231-360-0827

Hydra-Sports 2900 VX
2006–Current

Leading-edge express combines handsome styling with top-shelf amenities, no-excuses performance. Cockpit highlights include foldaway rear seat, 35-gallon livewell, insulated fishboxes, bait-prep station, padded bolsters. Portside lounge seat converts to sun pad. Well-appointed interior with midcabin berth, pilot berths is ideal for overnight trips. Note walk-thru windshield, pop-up cleats, tackle drawers. Generous 300-gallon fuel capacity delivers impressive 400-mile cruising range. Yamaha 250s reach 45+ knots top.

Length	29'8"	Fuel	300 gals.
Beam	9'8"	Water	27 gals.
Hull Draft	1'10"	Max HP	600
Dry Weight	8,396#	Hull Type	Deep-V
Clearance	8'9"	Deadrise Aft	23°

See Page 547 For Resale Values

Hydra-Sports
Sarasota, FL
www.hydra-sports.com

231-360-0827

Hydra-Sports 3000 Center Console
1997–2000

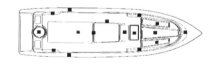

Tournament-ready fishing machine with high-performance deep-V hull combines brawn, speed, fishability. Features include walk-in console with portable head, 50-gallon transom livewell, insulated forward fishbox, pop-up cleats, rear jump seats, fresh/raw-water washdowns, lockable rod storage, leaning post, cockpit bolsters, forward console seat, bow storage lockers. Note under-gunwale tackle boxes in aft corners. One of the few trailerable 30-footers ever built. Exceptional range. Over 45 knots top with twin 225s.

Length	29'5"	Fuel	300 gals.
Beam	8'7"	Water	27 gals.
Draft, Engines Up	2'0"	Max HP	750
Draft, Engines Down	2'8"	Hull Type	Deep-V
Dry Weight	7,100#	Deadrise Aft	24°

See Page 547 For Resale Values

Hydra-Sports
Sarasota, FL
www.hydra-sports.com

www.powerboatguide.com   231-360-0827

Hydra-Sports 3300 Center Console
2003–Current

High-impact fishing machine with Kevlar-reinforced hull, triple-outboard power is strong, fast, built for the offshore tournament wars. Highlights include drop-out 3-person bolster seat with 55-gallon livewell & bait station, two forward fishboxes, lockable rod storage, foldaway rear seat, T-top with electronics box & spreader lights, pop-up cleats, washdowns, cockpit bolsters. Console head has sink, rod storage, battery access. Note cast net storage in forward floor. An impressive rough-water performer. 50+ knots with triple Yamaha 250s.

Length	33'5"	Fuel	352 gals.
Beam	10'4"	Water	29 gals.
Draft, Engines Down	2'10"	Max HP	900
Hull Weight	8,620#	Hull Type	Deep-V
Clearance	7'9"	Deadrise Aft	23°

See Page 547 For Resale Values

Hydra-Sports
Sarasota, FL
www.hydra-sports.com

---

www.powerboatguide.com   231-360-0827

Hydra-Sports 3300 Sport Fisherman
1989–92

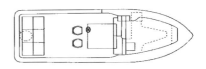

High-performance offshore fisherman from early 1990s was based on go-fast hull previously used for Donzi 33. Large 75-square-foot cockpit with padded coaming, full-height transom features aerated livewell, 6-foot-long insulated fishbox, rod storage, fold-down transom bench seat. Small cuddy with compact galley sleeps two. Additional features include enclosed head with sink and shower, double helm seat with rocket launchers, aft-facing cockpit seat, folding tower. Twin 275hp outboards deliver a top speed of 40+ knots.

Length	32'11"	Fuel	270 gals.
Beam	9'6"	Water	42 gals.
Hull Draft	1'6"	Max HP	600
Dry Weight (Approx.)	10,500#	Hull Type	Deep-V
Clearance	5'6"	Deadrise Aft	24°

Prices Not Provided for Pre-1995 Models

Hydra-Sports
Sarasota, FL
www.hydra-sports.com

---

www.powerboatguide.com   231-360-0827

Hydra-Sports 3300 VX
2004–07

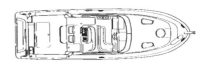

No-compromise cuddy express offers anglers tournament-grade fishability with proven big-water performance, quality construction. Roomy deck layout includes L-lounge seating forward of helm, foldaway rear seat, 55-gallon Kodiak livewell, two fishboxes, cockpit bolsters. Hardtop with sliding hatch was standard. Helm flat has room for two 10" video screens. Well-appointed cabin with enclosed head/shower, convertible dinette, midcabin berth sleeps four. Well-built boat can take a punch. About 50 knots max with triple 250s.

Length	33'5"	Fuel	352 gals.
Beam	10'4"	Water	35 gals.
Draft, Down	2'10"	Max HP	900
Hull Weight	10,500#	Hull Type	Deep-V
Clearance	9'3"	Deadrise Aft	23°

See Page 547 For Resale Values

Hydra-Sports
Sarasota, FL
www.hydra-sports.com

Sportfishing Boats

Intrepid 289 Center Console
1987–2003

Stepped-hull center console introduced in 1987 combined solid construction with efficient deck layout, good performance. Highlights include removable rear bench seat, in-deck fishbox, leaning post with livewell, transom livewells (2), dive platform, raw-water washdown, tilt-away helm, console seat/cooler, remote oil fills. Note unusual bow head compartment. Kevlar-reinforced laminates make the 289 a strong, relatively lightweight boat for her size. A good-selling model for Intrepid. Up to 45 knots with Yamaha 225s.

Length w/Bracket	28'9"	Fuel	193 gals.
Beam	9'1"	Water	20 gals.
Hull Draft	2'0"	Max HP	450
Dry Weight	3,200#	Hull Type	Deep-V
Clearance	5'2"	Deadrise Aft	22.5°

See Page 547 For Resale Values

Intrepid Powerboats
Dania, FL
www.intrepidboats.com

Intrepid 289 Walkaround
1997–2003

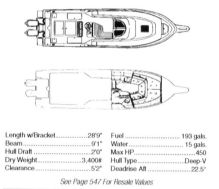

Deluxe open express with high-performance stepped hull is one part fishing boat, one part family cruiser. Guest-friendly deck layout boasts lounge seating forward of helm. Fishing amenities include insulated fishboxes, livewells, rod storage. Compact cabin has enclosed head with shower, U-shaped seating, mini-galley. Additional features include bow pulpit, anchor locker, deep walkways, small dive platform. A well-finished boat. Twin 200hp Mercury outboards cruise at 30 knots (about 45 knots top).

Length w/Bracket	28'9"	Fuel	193 gals.
Beam	9'1"	Water	15 gals.
Hull Draft	2'0"	Max HP	450
Dry Weight	3,400#	Hull Type	Deep-V
Clearance	5'2"	Deadrise Aft	22.5°

See Page 547 For Resale Values

Intrepid Powerboats
Dania, FL
www.intrepidboats.com

Intrepid 30 Console Cuddy
1984–93

Original Intrepid model with trailerable 8'6" beam is fast, agile, built to last. Highlights included double helm seat with rod holders, cushioned console seat, dive platform with ladder, rod storage, insulated fish box, livewell, raw-water washdown, removable rear bench seat, tackle cabinet. No-frills cuddy with rod storage, portable head sleeps two. Slender beam results in limited cockpit space for a 30-footer. Alternate version of this model with open layout (no cuddy) was also available. Max 50+ knots with 250hp Mercs.

Length w/Bracket	32'1"	Fuel	170 gals.
Beam	8'6"	Water	30 gals.
Draft	2'0"	Max HP	500
Weight	3,250#	Hull Type	Deep-V
Clearance	NA	Deadrise Aft	22°

Prices Not Provided for Pre-1995 Models

Intrepid Powerboats
Dania, FL
www.intrepidboats.com

Sportfishing Boats

www.powerboatguide.com   231-360-0827

Intrepid 300 Center Console
2004–Current

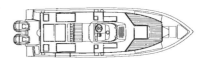

Hard-hitting 30-footer with performance-focused stepped hull can be customized for fishing, diving, entertaining. Standard features include transom door, deluxe forward seating, insulated forward fishbox, rod storage locker, lockable bow storage compartment. Forward console seat glides aside for entry into enclosed head with shower. Hullside dive door, removable rear seat, factory T-top, transom livewell, bow thruster are popular options. Quality doesn't come cheap. No bow rails. Max 50+ knots with 250hp Yamahas.

Length	30'0"	Fuel, Opt.	214 gals.
Beam	9'6"	Water	30 gals.
Draft, Up	1'10"	Max HP	500
Draft, Down	3'0"	Hull Type	Deep-V
Fuel, Std.	180 gals.	Deadrise Aft	22°

See Page 547 For Resale Values

Intrepid Powerboats
Dania, FL
www.intrepidboats.com

---

www.powerboatguide.com   231-360-0827

Intrepid 310 Walkaround
2005–Current

Sophisticated sport express with agile stepped hull, sociable deck layout takes Intrepid innovation to the next level. Bow pulpit, insulated fishbox, transom door, trim tabs are standard; everything else is optional including removable rear bench seat, Intrepid's signature hullside dive door. L-shaped lounge forward of helm seats three. Posh cabin with near standing headroom boasts full galley, wraparound seating, stand-up head with shower. More luxury cruiser than fishboat. Yamaha 250s reach 45+ knots top.

Length w/Pulpit	32'8"	Fuel	180 gals.
Hull Length	31'0"	Water	30 gals.
Beam	9'8"	Max HP	600
Hull Draft	2'0"	Hull Type	Deep-V
Weight	9,000#	Deadrise Aft	22.5°

See Page 547 For Resale Values

Intrepid Powerboats
Dania, FL
www.intrepidboats.com

---

www.powerboatguide.com   231-360-0827

Intrepid 322 Console Cuddy
1996–2003

Versatile cuddy console with notched hull is part sportfisherman, part day cruiser, full-time fun machine. Semicustom boat offered several seating options. Standard features included in-floor storage lockers, lockable electronics box, dive platforms, anchor locker. Most were sold with Intrepid's signature hullside dive door. No-frills cuddy with V-berth is great for storage, lacks ventilation. Fishing amenities—livewells, washdowns, etc.—were optional. Exemplary fit and finish. Tops 50 knots with Yamaha 250s.

Length	32'2"	Fuel, Opt.	300 gals.
Beam	9'1"	Water	22 gals.
Hull Draft	2'0"	Max HP	500
Dry Weight	3,300#	Hull Type	Deep-V
Fuel, Std.	240 gals.	Deadrise Aft	22.5°

See Page 547 For Resale Values

Intrepid Powerboats
Dania, FL
www.intrepidboats.com

Intrepid 323 Center Console
2004–Current

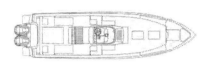

Limited-production center console with best-in-class finish targets upmarket boat buffs with an eye for yacht-class quality. Standard features include removable rear bench seat, insulated forward fishbox, deluxe double helm seat, deck storage/rod lockers forward, cockpit bolsters, transom door, dive platforms. Several custom livewell and helm console options to choose from. Power console seat slides aside for access to head with sink and shower. This kind of quality doesn't come cheap. About 50 knots top with twin 300s.

Length Overall	32'2"	Clearance	NA
Beam	9'6"	Water	20 gals.
Draft	2'6"	Max HP	600
Dry Weight	9,000#	Hull Type	Deep-V
Fuel, Std.	208 gals.	Deadrise Aft	22.5°

See Page 547 For Resale Values

Intrepid Powerboats
Dania, FL
www.intrepidboats.com

Intrepid 323 Cuddy
2004–Current

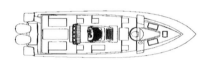

Feature-rich console cuddy combines impressive open-water performance with luxury-class comforts, state-of-the-art construction. Highlights include forward lounge seating, pop-up electronics console, transom door, cockpit bolsters, removable rear bench seat, dive platforms, fish box. Circulating livewell is a popular option. Well-appointed cuddy with V-berth, hanging locker includes space-saving head that swivels out from under the entryway step. Stepped hull is vacuum-bagged, fully cored. About 45 knots top with twin 250s.

Length Overall	32'2"	Clearance	NA
Beam	9'6"	Water	20 gals.
Draft	2'6"	Max HP	600
Dry Weight	9,000#	Hull Type	Deep-V
Fuel, Std.	208 gals.	Deadrise Aft	22.5°

See Page 547 For Resale Values

Intrepid Powerboats
Dania, FL
www.intrepidboats.com

Intrepid 339 Center Console
1996–2001

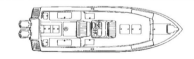

Seductive center console introduced in 1996 blends semicustom quality with quality amenities, hardcore fishability. Race-proven stepped hull reduces drag by breaking water's grip on the hull. Single-level cockpit features in-deck fish/storage boxes, lockable rod lockers; forepeak head with privacy tent is unique (if perhaps a little curious). Helm console has space for flush-mounting electronics. Forward seating folds away for fishing. Anchor locker, trim tabs, dive platform were standard. Twin 250hp outboards top out at 45+ knots.

Length w/Bracket	33'9"	Fuel, Opt	295 gals.
Beam	10'0"	Water	22 gals.
Hull Draft	2'0"	Max HP	500
Dry Weight	5,000#	Hull Type	Deep-V
Fuel, Std.	245 gals.	Deadrise Aft	20.5°

See Page 547 For Resale Values

Intrepid Powerboats
Dania, FL
www.intrepidboats.com

Sportfishing Boats

Intrepid 339 Walkaround
1995–2001

Super-quality walkaround from semicustom builder combines fishable cockpit with social deck layout, well-appointed interior. Features include factory hardtop, 35-gallon in-deck livewell, in-deck fishboxes, leaning post/rocket launcher, raw-water washdown, and recessed rod storage, wraparound seating forward of helm. Removable rear seat was a popular option. Cabin has V-berth, enclosed head with shower, mini-galley, rod storage. Note wraparound windshield. Very popular model for Intrepid. Over 40 knots top with Yamaha 250s.

Length w/Bracket	33'9"	Fuel, Opt	295 gals.
Beam	10'0"	Water	22 gals.
Hull Draft	2'0"	Max HP	500
Dry Weight	5,500#	Hull Type	Deep-V
Fuel, Std.	245 gals.	Deadrise Aft	20.5°

See Page 547 For Resale Values

Intrepid Powerboats
Dania, FL
www.intrepidboats.com

Intrepid 348 Walkaround
2002–04

Luxury dayboat/fishing machine with social deck plan offers speed, comfort, unabashed sex appeal. Highlights include factory hardtop, custom leaning post, forward L-lounge seating, cockpit bolsters, in-deck fishboxes, fresh/raw-water washdowns, transom door. Hull side dive door was a popular option. Note bow anchor chute. Sleek interior with full galley, enclosed head has V-berth that lifts electrically to access storage beneath. Lightweight stepped hull offers exceptional speed, agility. Near-flawless fit and finish. About 45 knots top with twin 250s.

Length	34'8"	Fuel	258 gals.
Beam	10'6"	Water	40 gals.
Hull Draft	2'0"	Max HP	600
Dry Weight	7,000#	Hull Type	Deep-V
Clearance w/Top	8'7"	Deadrise Aft	22.5°

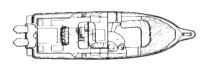

See Page 547 For Resale Values

Intrepid Powerboats
Dania, FL
www.intrepidboats.com

Intrepid 350 Walkaround
2005–Current

Re-tooled version of Intrepid 348 Walkaround (2002–04) boasts slightly lengthened cockpit, all-new reverse transom design with integral motor well and transom door. Super-quality boat (each built to owner specs) comes standard with dive platforms, macerated fishbox, anchor chute, deluxe console with L-shaped seating forward. Well-appointed cabin has convertible seating, compact galley, enclosed head with shower. Single-stepped hull offers exceptional speed, agility. Twin 250 Verados deliver 40+ knots top.

Length	35'0"	Fuel, Opt	312 gals.
Beam	10'6"	Water	40 gals.
Hull Draft	24"	Max HP	600
Dry Weight	7,500#	Hull Type	Deep-V
Fuel, Std.	258 gals.	Deadrise Aft	22.5°

Insufficient Resale Data To Assign Values

Intrepid Powerboats
Dania, FL
www.intrepidboats.com

Intrepid 356 Cuddy
1994–2001

Sporty notched-bottom speedster took 1990s engineering to the next level. Versatile deck layout with forward seating is suitable for fishing, diving, cruising. Removable rear bench seat, in-deck fish box, recirculating livewell, transom door, dive platforms, two-person helm seat were standard. Upscale cabin came with galley, dinette/V-berth, enclosed head. Cabin height slightly increased in 1998. No windscreen for front seat passengers. Intrepid 366 is the same boat with a lengthened cockpit. Max 45 knots with 250hp outboards.

Length Overall	35'6"	Fuel, Opt.	285 gals.
Beam	10'6"	Water	50 gals.
Hull Draft	2'0"	Max HP	600
Dry Weight	6,500#	Hull Type	Deep-V
Fuel, Std.	235 gals.	Deadrise Aft	22.5°

See Page 547 For Resale Values

Intrepid Powerboats
Dania, FL
www.intrepidboats.com

Intrepid 366 Cuddy
1999–2003

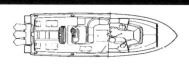

Updated version of popular Intrepid 356 Cuddy boasts enlarged cockpit, optional triple-outboard power. Versatile layout with forward seating is great for fishing, diving, cruising. Removable rear seat, in-deck fish box, recirculating livewell, transom door, dive platforms, two-person helm seat were standard. Cuddy came with galley cabinet, dinette/V-berth, enclosed head. Stepped hull is agile, fast. One of Intrepid's best-selling models. Triple 225hp Mercury outboards reach top speed of close to 50 knots.

Length Overall	36'6"	Fuel, Opt.	400 gals.
Beam	10'6"	Water	30 gals.
Hull Draft	2'0"	Max HP	675
Dry Weight	6,500#	Hull Type	Deep-V
Fuel, Std.	300 gals.	Deadrise Aft	22.5°

See Page 547 For Resale Values

Intrepid Powerboats
Dania, FL
www.intrepidboats.com

Intrepid 370 Cuddy
2003–Current

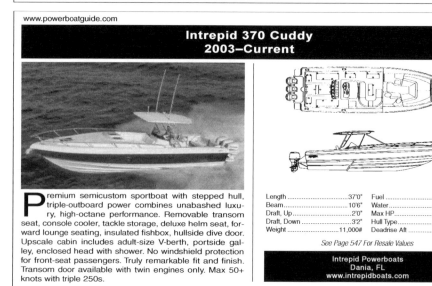

Premium semicustom sportboat with stepped hull, triple-outboard power combines unabashed luxury, high-octane performance. Removable transom seat, console cooler, tackle storage, deluxe helm seat, forward lounge seating, insulated fishbox, hullside dive door. Upscale cabin includes adult-size V-berth, portside galley, enclosed head with shower. No windshield protection for front-seat passengers. Truly remarkable fit and finish. Transom door available with twin engines only. Max 50+ knots with triple 250s.

Length	37'0"	Fuel	300 gals.
Beam	10'6"	Water	40 gals.
Draft, Up	2'0"	Max HP	600
Draft, Down	3'2"	Hull Type	Deep-V
Weight	11,000#	Deadrise Aft	22.5°

See Page 547 For Resale Values

Intrepid Powerboats
Dania, FL
www.intrepidboats.com

231-360-0827

Intrepid 377 Walkaround
2000–08

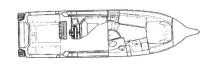

Executive-class offshore cruiser with triple-outboard power defines sportfishing luxury in the fast lane. Features include factory hardtop, in-deck fishboxes, L-lounge seating forward of helm, pop-up cleats, transom door, custom leaning post, cockpit bolsters, bow pulpit. Hull side dive door, removable rear bench seat were popular options. Well-appointed interior with galley, convertible settee, enclosed head with stall shower sleeps four. Note huge, state-of-the-art helm console. Popular, beautifully finished cruiser. Triple 275 Mercs reach 50+ knots.

Length w/o Pulpit	38'3"	Fuel	400 gals.
Beam	11'6"	Water	60 gals.
Hull Draft	2'4"	Max HP	900
Dry Weight	10,000#	Hull Type	Deep-V
Clearance	9'0"	Deadrise Aft	22.5°

See Page 547 For Resale Values

Intrepid Powerboats
Dania, FL
www.intrepidboats.com

231-360-0827

Intrepid 390 Sport Yacht
2007–Current

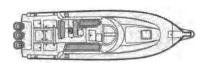

Custom-produced luxury sportyacht with triple-outboard power delivers high-octane mix of yacht-class comfort, speedboat performance. Expansive cockpit with lounge seating forward (with electric backrests) comes standard with fishboxes, livewell, removable rear bench seat. Posh interior with queen and convertible guest berths includes head with separate shower, teak-and-holly sole. Note power helm seat, distinctive shark-fin cabin windows. Hullside dive door is a popular option. Over 50 knots max with triple 300hp Verados.

Length	41'10"	Fuel	400 gals.
Beam	12'0"	Water	60 gals.
Hull Draft	24"	Max HP	1,150
Dry Weight	15,500#	Hull Type	Deep-V
Clearance	9'0"	Deadrise Aft	20°

Insufficient Resale Data To Assign Values

Intrepid Powerboats
Dania, FL
www.intrepidboats.com

231-360-0827

Jefferson 35 Marlago Cuddy
1994–Current

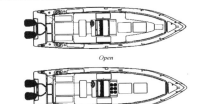

Open

Cuddy

Narrow-beam center console with high-performance hull, low-profile cuddy is agile, fast, priced right. Removable rear seat, in-deck fish boxes, console seat with cooler, flip-up helm seat, fresh- and saltwater washdowns, pop-up cleats, enclosed head with pull-out shower. Offered with two transom configurations, one with transom door, bait-prep station & livewell, or "Full Transom" option with additional sink but no transom door. Open-bow model available since 2004. Yamaha 250s deliver 45+ knots top; 300 Verados can hit 50 knots.

Length	35'0"	Fuel, Std.	245 gals.
Beam	9'2"	Water	31 gals.
Draft, Up	1'8"	Max HP	600
Draft, Down	2'3"	Hull Type	Deep-V
Dry Weight	6,000#	Deadrise Aft	24°

See Page 548 For Resale Values

Jefferson Yachts
Jeffersonville, IN
www.jeffersonyachts.com

Sportfishing Boats

Jersey 36 Dawn
1986–91

Single Stateroom

Two Staterooms

Graceful midsize convertible with signature Jersey styling remains popular with savvy East Coast boaters. Teak-paneled interior with front salon windshield was offered with single or twin staterooms. Roomy cockpit came standard with in-deck fishbox, tackle center, transom door with gate. Low-deadrise hull with moderate beam incorporates substantial bow flare. Flybridge helm was repositioned in 1991 for improved cockpit sightlines. Standard 350hp gas engines cruise at 18 knots; 375hp Cat diesels cruise in the low 20s.

Length w/Pulpit	39'4"	Clearance	11'0"
Hull Length	36'4"	Fuel	365 gals.
Beam	13'4"	Water	75 gals.
Draft	2'6"	Hull Type	Modified-V
Weight	23,500#	Deadrise Aft	10°

Prices Not Provided for Pre-1995 Models

Jersey Yachts is no longer in business.

Jersey 40 Dawn
1983–87

Dinette Floorplan

Two-Stateroom Floorplan

Well-regarded East Coast convertible is roomy, agile, built to last. Two cabin plans were offered with single-stateroom version proving more popular than twin-stateroom layout. No-frills interior with wraparound windows is finished with dark teak woodwork. Cockpit is big for a 40-footer, but absence of transom door is notable. Solid fiberglass hull incorporates shallow keel for directional stability. A popular boat for many years. Volvo 235hp diesels cruise at 14–16 knots; 320hp Cats cruise at 18 knots (low 20s top).

Length	40'0"	Fuel	400 gals.
Beam	14'6"	Water	100 gals.
Draft	3.5"	Waste	30 gals.
Weight	26,000#	Hull Type	Modified-V
Clearance	NA	Deadrise Aft	10°

Prices Not Provided for Pre-1995 Models

Jersey Yachts is no longer in business.

Jupiter 27 Open
1998–2006

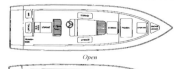

Open

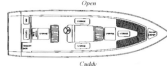

Cuddy

Top-quality center console with full array of premium fishing amenities sets class standards for performance, fishability. Features include 40-gallon livewell, 90-gallon fish box, pop-up cleats, bait-rigging station, two electronics boxes. Console head compartment has standing headroom and V-berth. Available in Open and Cuddy configurations. Running surface extended all the way aft for increased lift in 2002. Super owner satisfaction. Tops out at over 45 knots with twin Yamaha 225s.

Length	27'4"	Fuel	204 gals.
Beam	8'6"	Water	37 gals.
Draft, Up	1.7"	Max HP	450
Draft, Down	2'2"	Hull Type	Deep-V
Weight w/Engines	5,820#	Deadrise Aft	24°

See Page 548 For Resale Values

Jupiter Marine
Palmetto, FL
www.jupitermarine.com

Jupiter 29 Forward Seating
2006–Current

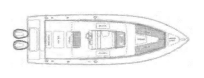

Hard-hitting canyon runner with roomy cockpit, cushioned bow seating makes the cut with hard-core anglers. Standard features include bait-prep center with 45-gallon livewell, 120-gallon macerated fishbox, leaning post, fresh/saltwater washdowns, lockable in-deck rod storage, tackle storage, low-profile bow rails. Space at the helm for twin big-screen displays. All hatches are gasketed and dogged. Plenty of fuel for a 29-footer. Yamaha 250hp outboards reach close to 45 knots wide open.

Length	29'6"	Fuel	285 gals.
Beam	9'4"	Water	35 gals.
Hull Draft	2'9"	Max HP	600
Weight w/Engines	9,200#	Hull Type	Deep-V
Clearance	8'10"	Deadrise Aft	24°

See Page 548 For Resale Values

Jupiter Marine
Palmetto, FL
www.jupitermarine.com

Jupiter 31 Open
1989–Current

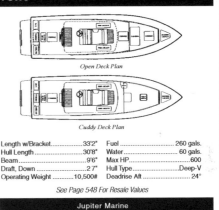

Open Deck Plan

Cuddy Deck Plan

World-class offshore performer delivers a convincing blend of quality, features, fishability. Standard fishing gear includes transom rigging station, 30-gallon stand-up livewell, rod storage lockers, dual washdowns, large-capacity fishboxes fore and aft. Oversized console permits expansive helm layout, spacious head compartment. Hull pad provides extra low-speed lift. Extraordinary finish throughout. Available in Cuddy or Forward Seating models. One of the most popular 31-footers ever. Over 45 knots with Yamaha 250s.

Length w/Bracket	33'2"	Fuel	260 gals.
Hull Length	30'8"	Water	60 gals.
Beam	9'6"	Max HP	600
Draft, Down	2'7"	Hull Type	Deep-V
Operating Weight	10,500#	Deadrise Aft	24°

See Page 548 For Resale Values

Jupiter Marine
Palmetto, FL
www.jupitermarine.com

Jupiter 34 Forward Seating
2008–Current

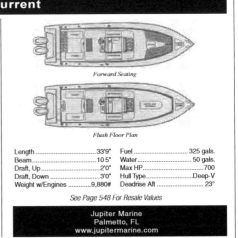

Forward Seating

Flush Floor Plan

Leading-edge center console was specifically designed to accommodate newer (heavier) Yamaha 350s. Available with standard forward seating/lounge area or optional Tournament model with flush cockpit floor and oversized coffin fish box. Standard features include deluxe leaning post/tackle center with 45-gallon livewell, fresh/saltwater washdowns, foldaway transom seat, rod storage lockers, insulated fish boxes. Walk-in head has sink and shower. Hull pad improves low-speed performance. Over 50 knots with twin 350s.

Length	33'9"	Fuel	325 gals.
Beam	10 5"	Water	50 gals.
Draft, Up	2'0"	Max HP	700
Draft, Down	3'0"	Hull Type	Deep-V
Weight w/Engines	9,880#	Deadrise Aft	23°

See Page 548 For Resale Values

Jupiter Marine
Palmetto, FL
www.jupitermarine.com

Sportfishing Boats

Jupiter 38 Forward Seating
2005–Current

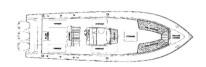

Feature-packed center console takes big-water fishability to the next level. Highlights include cushioned bow seating, leaning post with 50-gallon livewell, foldout stern seat, two macerated fish boxes, two six-foot storage boxes, two lockable rod storage boxes under forward seating area. Side lockers offer storage for life jackets. Console head includes shower, rod storage. Bow area is designed for optional concealed windlass. All hatches are gasketed, dogged. Twin Yamaha 250s top out in the low 40s; triple 250s hit 50+ knots.

Length	38'2"	Fuel, Std/Opt	320/480 gals.
Beam	10'7"	Water	60 gals.
Draft, Up	24"	Max HP	900
Draft, Down	36"	Hull Type	Deep-V
Weight w/Engines	8,970#	Deadrise Aft	24°

See Page 548 For Resale Values

Jupiter Marine
Palmetto, FL
www.jupitermarine.com

Luhrs 28 Open
2005–Current

Classy inboard express with best-in-class styling is ready to fish, equipped to cruise, fun to drive. Spacious cockpit has transom fishbox, livewell, bait-prep center with cutting board, tackle drawers, fresh/raw-water washdowns. Roomy cabin with full galley, teak-and-holly sole, overhead rod storage sleeps four. Bridgedeck lifts for engine access. Note generous fuel capacity, tall fiberglass-framed windshield. Great styling, lots of cockpit space. Twin 330hp gas engines cruise at 20 knots; Yanmar 260hp diesels cruise at 24 knots.

Length w/Pulpit	31'10"	Fuel	300 gals.
Hull Length	29'10"	Water	55 gals.
Beam	11'6"	Waste	15 gals.
Draft	2'8"	Hull Type	Modified-V
Weight	10,000#	Deadrise Aft	19°

See Page 549 For Resale Values

Luhrs Corporation
St. Augustine, FL
www.luhrs.com

Luhrs Tournament 290
1986–88

Generic inboard express satisfies anglers need for offshore fishability, cruising comfort at a reasonable price. Highlights include deep cockpit with lift-out fishboxes, raw-water washdown, coaming bolsters. Oak-trimmed interior with convertible dinette, full galley, enclosed head with shower, sleeps two. Factory marlin tower was standard. Note slender side decks. Good visibility from center helm. Replaced with new 290 Tournament model 1989. Twin 270hp gas engines cruise at 20 knots; 170hp Yanmar diesels cruise at 18 knots.

Length	29'0"	Fuel	200/260 gals.
Beam	10'9"	Water	40 gals.
Draft	2'5"	Waste	20 gals.
Weight	9,000#	Hull Type	Modified-V
Clearance	14'6"	Deadrise Aft	17°

Prices Not Provided for Pre-1995 Models

Luhrs Corporation
St. Augustine, FL
www.luhrs.com

Sportfishing Boats

     231-360-0827

Luhrs Tournament 290
1989–90

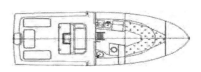

Versatile sportfisherman with distinctive lines is one part center console, one part walkaround cabin. Deep, unobstructed fishing cockpit came standard with in-deck fishboxes, transom livewell, bait-prep station, raw-water washdown. Double helm seat doubles as engine box. Teak-trimmed cabin has enclosed head with shower, full galley, convertible dinette, berths for four. Marlin tower with controls was standard. No windscreen. Not a big seller. Cruise at 20 knots with 240hp gas engines (around 28 knots wide open).

Length	29'6"	Fuel	250 gals.
Beam	10'9"	Water	40 gals.
Draft	2.5"	Waste	20 gals.
Weight	7,840#	Hull Type	Modified-V
Clearance	NA	Deadrise Aft	17°

Prices Not Provided for Pre-1995 Models

Luhrs Corporation
St. Augustine, FL
www.luhrs.com

     231-360-0827

Luhrs 290 Open
1992–2002

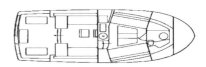

Best-selling inboard express introduced in 1992 offered great styling, proven fishability, versatile cabin accommodations. Roomy cockpit with centerline helm has two in-deck fishboxes, livewell, transom door, raw-water washdown, transom fish/storage box. Bridgedeck lifts electrically for engine access. Unique cabin layout with forward head, facing settees sleeps four. Marlin tower was standard. A great-looking boat with wide appeal. Cruise at 16-18 knots with 270hp gas engines; 20 knots with Yanmar 230hp diesels.

Length w/Pulpit	31'10"	Fuel	302 gals.
Hull Length	29'10"	Water	55 gals.
Beam	11'6"	Waste	20 gals.
Draft	2'0"	Hull Type	Modified-V
Weight	10,000#	Deadrise Aft	16°

See Page 549 For Resale Values

Luhrs Corporation
St. Augustine, FL
www.luhrs.com

     231-360-0827

Luhrs 30 Alura
1987–90

Single-inboard fishing boat with efficient semi-displacement hull is ideal for fishing, diving, cruising. Deep cockpit with high gunwales, in-deck fishboxes has over 100 square feet of space. Large bridgedeck hatches provide good engine access. Note tall windshield, wide side decks, standard swim platform. Roomy, well-appointed interior sleeps four. Keel was redesigned in 1988 to reduce vibration problems. Very fuel-efficient boat. Single 270hp gas inboard will cruise at 14–15 knots (low 20s top).

Length Overall	30'0"	Fuel	196 gals.
Length WL	28'0"	Water	38 gals.
Beam	10'3"	Waste	15 gals.
Draft	2'11"	Hull Type	Semi-Disp.
Weight	7,800#	Deadrise Aft	NA

Prices Not Provided for Pre-1995 Models

Luhrs Corporation
St. Augustine, FL
www.luhrs.com

Sportfishing Boats

231-360-0827

Luhrs 300 Tournament
1991–96

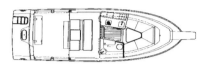

Updated version of the earlier 290 Tournament (1989–90) combines walkaround fishability with dayboat versatility. Fishing amenities include in-deck fishbox, tackle drawers, bait-prep center. Note bait-well location on transom platform—very unusual. Helm seats lift for access to tight engine compartment. Cozy cabin boasts convertible dinette, small galley, stand-up head with shower. Great for fishing, diving or overnighting. Twin 270hp gas inboards cruise at 18 knots; 170hp Yanmar diesels cruise at 18– 20 knots.

Length w/Pulpit	34'6"	Fuel	250 gals.
Hull Length	31'6"	Water	40 gals.
Beam	10'9"	Waste	20 gals.
Draft	2'6"	Hull Type	Modified-V
Weight	12,000#	Deadrise Aft	18°

See Page 549 For Resale Values

Luhrs Corporation
St. Augustine, FL
www.luhrs.com

231-360-0827

Luhrs 30/31 Open
2004–Current

Tournament-grade fishing platform (called the 30 Open in 2004–05; 31 Open since 2006) with best-in-class styling makes the cut with serious anglers. Standard features include hardtop, bait-prep center with sink, livewell, tackle drawers, washdowns, in-deck fish-boxes, transom door. Well-appointed cabin with teak trim, convertible dinette sleeps four. Bridgedeck lifts for engine access. Twin 320hp gas inboards—or 315 Yanmar die-sels—cruise at 23–24 knots. Newer models with Volvo 260hp IPS drives cruise at 22 knots.

Length Overall	34'4"	Fuel	300 gals.
Hull Length	31'5"	Water	50 gals.
Beam	11'10"	Waste	25 gals.
Draft	2'6"	Hull Type	Deep-V
Weight	13,500#	Deadrise Aft	20°

See Page 549 For Resale Values

Luhrs Corporation
St. Augustine, FL
www.luhrs.com

231-360-0827

Luhrs 320 Convertible
1988–99

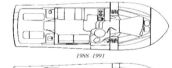

1988 1991

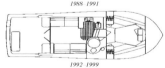

1992 1999

Popular midsize convertible hit the sweet spot with anglers looking for sporty styling, upscale accom-modations, no-excuses fishability. In-deck fishbox, transom door, fresh/raw-water washdowns, bait-prep station with sink, bow pulpit. Roomy interior with expansive salon features private stateroom with island berth, complete galley, large head with shower. Original dinette lay-out was replaced in 1992 with facing salon settees. Twin 320hp gas inboards—or optional 300hp Yanmar diesels—cruise at 20–22 knots.

Length w/Pulpit	34'8"	Fuel	272 gals.
Hull Length	31'6"	Water	60 gals.
Beam	13'0"	Waste	30 gals.
Draft	3'1"	Hull Type	Modified-V
Weight	15,000#	Deadrise Aft	18°

See Page 549 For Resale Values

Luhrs Corporation
St. Augustine, FL
www.luhrs.com

Sportfishing Boats

231-360-0827

Luhrs 32 Convertible
2001–02

Affordable small convertible with rakish styling, well-appointed interior packed a lot of features in relatively small hull. Salon is compact but offers efficient portside galley, convertible settee, attractive teak cabinetry. Note stall shower in head. Cockpit amenities include transom door, transom fishbox, bait-prep center with livewell, washdowns. Molded bridge steps are a plus. Flybridge—with standard hardtop—seats up to six. Cruise at 20 knots with 310hp gas inboards (about 30 knots top). Production for this model lasted only two years.

Length w/Pulpit	34'11"	Clearance, Hardtop	16'4"
Hull Length	32'3"	Fuel	270 gals.
Beam	11'8"	Water	60 gals.
Draft	3'4"	Hull Type	Modified-V
Weight	16,250#	Deadrise Aft	18°

See Page 549 For Resale Values

Luhrs Corporation
St. Augustine, FL
www.luhrs.com

231-360-0827

Luhrs 32 Open
1994–2008

Value-packed express combines graceful Palm Beach styling with large fishing cockpit, classy cabin accommodations. Cockpit amenities include livewell, dual washdowns, bait-prep center, fishbox, tackle drawers. Center helm position offers excellent 360-degree visibility. Teak-trimmed interior with dinette forward, slide-out settee sleeps five. Tower is standard; windshield is optional. Cruise at 20 knots with 320hp gas inboards (high 20s top). Optional 315hp Yanmar diesels cruise at 26–27 knots (30+ knots top).

Length w/Pulpit	34'8"	Fuel	340 gals.
Hull Length	31'6"	Water	60 gals.
Beam	13'0"	Waste	30 gals.
Draft	3'1"	Hull Type	Modified-V
Weight	15,000#	Deadrise Aft	18°

See Page 549 For Resale Values

Luhrs Corporation
St. Augustine, FL
www.luhrs.com

231-360-0827

Luhrs 34 Convertible
2000–03

Good-looking convertible blurs the lines between well-bred fisherman, top-shelf family cruiser. Roomy interior boasts wide-open salon with facing settees, separate head/shower compartments, large stateroom. Salon settee slides out to create double berth. Transom door, bait-prep center, transom fishbox were standard. Note molded steps to flybridge. Engineroom is a tight fit, but convenient cockpit access is rare in a boat this size. Twin 375hp gas engines cruise at 20 knots; 350hp Yanmar diesels cruise in the low 20s.

Length w/Pulpit	36'10"	Fuel	300 gals.
Beam	13'1"	Water	90 gals.
Draft	3'4"	Waste	40 gals.
Weight	18,000#	Hull Type	Modified-V
Clearance	16'5"	Deadrise Aft	18°

See Page 549 For Resale Values

Luhrs Corporation
St. Augustine, FL
www.luhrs.com

Sportfishing Boats

Luhrs 340 Sport Fisherman
1983–87

Value-priced sportfisherman from 1980s combined raised-bridgedeck styling with roomy interior, large fishing cockpit. Marketed as fully equipped fishing boat with standard marlin tower, fishboxes, washdowns, cabin rod storage. Simple interior with convertible dinette, small galley sleeps four. Note centerline helm position, roomy engine compartment, wide side decks. No transom door. Standard 340hp gas inboards cruise at 16 knots (25–26 knots top). Optional 300hp diesels cruise in the low 20s (24–25 knots top).

Length	34'0"	Fuel	260 gals.
Beam	12'6"	Water	60 gals.
Draft	3'0"	Waste	40 gals.
Weight	12,300#	Hull Type	Modified-V
Clearance	11'5"	Deadrise Aft	16°

Prices Not Provided for Pre-1995 Models

Luhrs Corporation
St. Augustine, FL
www.luhrs.com

Luhrs 342 Convertible
1986–89

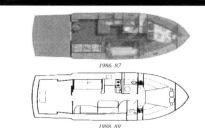

1986–87

1988–89

Appealing 1980s convertible with rakish styling offered sportfish versatility at an affordable price. Large flybridge has seating forward of helm. Cockpit is large enough for two anglers and their gear but lacks transom door. Original two-stateroom floorplan was replaced in 1988 with single-stateroom layout with more spacious salon, updated decor. Note unique cabin ventilation system with air intakes beneath forward bridge overhang. Standard 320hp gas inboards cruise at 16 knots; GM 500hp diesels cruise at 18 knots.

Length	34'0"	Fuel	300 gals.
Beam	12'6"	Water	60 gals.
Draft	3'2"	Waste	40 gals.
Weight	13,500#	Hull Type	Modified-V
Clearance	11'5"	Deadrise Aft	15°

Prices Not Provided for Pre-1995 Models

Luhrs Corporation
St. Augustine, FL
www.luhrs.com

Luhrs 350 Convertible
1990–96

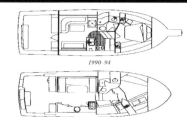

1990–94

1995–96

Muscular sportfisherman with signature Luhrs styling targets savvy anglers with an eye for value. Roomy cockpit came standard with transom door, tackle drawers, insulated fishbox, transom door, livewell. Original single-stateroom floorplan with mid-galley was replaced in 1995 with new two-stateroom, galley-up layout. Hardtop was standard. Flybridge redesigned in 1995 with improved seating. A seriously good-looking boat. Standard gas engines cruise at 17 knots; optional 350hp Cats cruise at 23–24 knots.

Length w/Pulpit	38'6"	Fuel	390 gals.
Hull Length	35'0"	Water	93 gals.
Beam	12'10"	Waste	40 gals
Draft	3'4"	Hull Type	Modified-V
Weight	20,000#	Deadrise Aft	18°

See Page 549 For Resale Values

Luhrs Corporation
St. Augustine, FL
www.luhrs.com

Sportfishing Boats

www.powerboatguide.com · 231-360-0827

Luhrs 35 Convertible
2008–Current

Handsome 35-footer with mega-wide beam provides the cockpit, cabin space of a much larger boat. Highlights include open salon with full windshield, cherry interior cabinets, oversized head with separate stall shower, two large staterooms. Lower helm is optional. Note molded bridge steps, flybridge cooler storage. Engineroom is unusually spacious for a boat this size. Hardtop, generator, bait prep center are standard. Cruise at 26–28 knots with 380hp Yanmar inboard diesels; about 28 knots with 370hp Volvo IPS drives.

Length w/Pulpit	38'10"	Fuel	400 gals.
Hull Length	35'8"	Water	100 gals.
Beam	14'6"	Waste	26 gals.
Draft	3'0"	Hull Type	Modified-V
Weight	23,500#	Deadrise Aft	15°

See Page 549 For Resale Values

Luhrs Corporation
St. Augustine, FL
www.luhrs.com

---

www.powerboatguide.com · 231-360-0827

Luhrs 36 Convertible
1998–2007

Deluxe convertible with molded flybridge steps (a new concept in 1998) is stylish, spacious, ready to cruise. Upscale two-stateroom interior with teak trim includes posh U-shaped settee/dinette in salon, big master, large head with stall shower. Engineroom is accessed via hatch in salon sole. Fishing features include transom door, fishbox, bait-prep center, tackle drawers, livewell. Half-tower was standard. Bridge steps reduce cockpit space. Yanmar 440hp diesels cruise at 22 knots (26–28 knots top).

Length w/Pulpit	38'11"	Fuel	400 gals.
Hull Length	36'2"	Water	94 gals.
Beam	13'10"	Waste	30 gals.
Draft	3'3"	Hull Type	Modified-V
Weight	22,000#	Deadrise Aft	18°

See Page 549 For Resale Values

Luhrs Corporation
St. Augustine, FL
www.luhrs.com

---

www.powerboatguide.com · 231-360-0827

Luhrs 36 Open; 36 SX
1997–2007

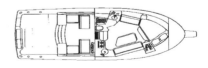

Bold tournament express with high-impact styling (called Luhrs 36 SX in 1997–2001) personifies Luhrs appeal to savvy, hardcore anglers. Wide 13'10" beam allows for spacious cockpit with transom fishbox, bait-prep center with sink, tackle drawers, wide transom door. Bridgedeck lifts electrically for engine access. Maxi-volume interior with full galley, berths for four is well suited for extended family cruising. Twin 420hp gas engines cruise in the low 20s; 420hp Cat diesels cruise at 26–27 knots.

Length w/Pulpit	38'11"	Headroom	6'4"
Hull Length	36'2"	Fuel	400 gals.
Beam	13'10"	Water	94 gals.
Draft	3'5"	Hull Type	Modified-V
Weight	22,000#	Deadrise Aft	18°

See Page 549 For Resale Values

Luhrs Corporation
St. Augustine, FL
www.luhrs.com

231-360-0827

Luhrs 37 Open (IPS)
2009–Current

Tournament-grade sportfisherman designed for IPS pod drives combines fuel-efficient operation with innovative cabin layout. Standard-feature list includes half tower with controls, 35-gallon livewell, bait-prep center with sink, washdowns, genset, removable fishbox, 20" flat-screen TV. Two-stateroom, two-head interior is unique in a boat this size. Note cavernous step-down storage room beneath helm lounge. Around 32 knots top with Volvo 370hp IPS power. Outboard version with triple Yamaha 350s delivers 40+ knots wide open.

Length	38'7"	Fuel	380 gals.
Beam	14'10"	Water	100 gals.
Draft	2'8"	Waste	30 gals.
Weight	22,500#	Hull Type	Modified-V
Clearance, Top	16'0"	Deadrise Aft	14.5°

Insufficient Resale Data To Assign Values

Luhrs Corporation
St. Augustine, FL
www.luhrs.com

231-360-0827

Luhrs 380/40/38 Convertible
1989–2008

Well-bred convertible with classic Luhrs styling delivers heavyweight canyon potential at moderate price. Offered with several two-stateroom floorplans, all with spacious salon, large head with stall shower, generous galley storage. Half-tower was standard. Tournament-size cockpit features bait-prep station, livewell, fishbox, transom door. Note large flybridge. Called Luhrs 380 in 1989–98; Luhrs 40 in 1999–2003; Luhrs 38 in 2004–08. Cruise in the low-to-mid 20s with GM 485hp, Cat 420hp, or Yanmar 440hp diesels.

Length w/Pulpit	40'10"	Fuel	423 gals.
Hull Length	37'9"	Water	94 gals.
Beam	14'11"	Waste	36 gals.
Draft	3'7"	Hull Type	Modified-V
Weight	30,000#	Deadrise Aft	18°

See Page 549 For Resale Values

Luhrs Corporation
St. Augustine, FL
www.luhrs.com

231-360-0827

Luhrs 380/40/38 Open
1991–2007

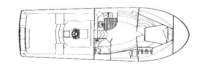

Feature-packed express with wide beam is spacious, agile, handsome. Highlights include centerline helm with flanking settees (with rod storage under), well-appointed cockpit with transom fishbox, bait-prep center, transom door. Single-stateroom interior with convertible salon settee sleeps four. Bridgedeck lifts for engine access. Note standard tuna tower. Called Luhrs 380 Open in 1991–98; 40 Open in 1999–2004; 38 Open in 2004–07. Cruise at 24–25 knots with 420hp Cat (or 440hp Yanmar) diesels.

Length w/Pulpit	40'10"	Fuel	563 gals.
Hull Length	37'9"	Water	80 gals.
Beam	14'11"	Waste	36 gals.
Draft	3'7"	Hull Type	Modified-V
Weight	30,000#	Transom Deadrise	18°

See Page 550 For Resale Values

Luhrs Corporation
St. Augustine, FL
www.luhrs.com

Luhrs Tournament 400
1987–90

Rakish 1990s flybridge cruiser mixed fishing, cruising attributes in a practical, well-priced package. Spacious twin-stateroom interior boasts expansive salon with L-shaped dinette, complete galley with microwave, large head with shower stall. Fishing accessories include dual washdowns, in-deck fishbox, transom door, rod storage. Half-tower with controls was standard. Flybridge is large for an older 40-footer. Twin 320hp gas engines cruise at 15–16 knots; optional 375hp Cats cruise around 22 knots (mid 20s top).

Length	40'0"	Fuel	400 gals.
Beam	14'0"	Water	100 gals.
Draft	3'2"	Waste	30 gals.
Weight	25,500#	Hull Type	Modified-V
Clearance	14'0"	Deadrise Aft	14°

Prices Not Provided for Pre-1995 Models

Luhrs Corporation
St. Augustine, FL
www.luhrs.com

Luhrs 41 Convertible
2004–Current

Compelling midsize convertible with flared bow is stylish, roomy, built to last. Broad 15'9" beam allows vast interior with wide-open salon, Ultraleather seating, home-size galley with under-counter refrigeration, two large staterooms. Washer/dryer can be installed in salon cabinet. Additional highlights include standard hardtop, cherrywood joinery, teak-and-holly cabin sole, electric salon sofa bed. Prop pockets reduce draft, improve efficiency. Cruise at 26–27 knots with Cummins 580hp diesels (about 30 knots top).

Length w/Pulpit	44'6"	Fuel	600 gals.
Hull Length	42'3"	Water	130 gals.
Beam	15'9"	Waste	40 gals.
Draft	3'6"	Hull Type	Modified-V
Weight	33,000#	Deadrise Aft	18°

See Page 550 For Resale Values

Luhrs Corporation
St. Augustine, FL
www.luhrs.com

Luhrs 41 Hardtop
2007–Current

Feature-rich hardtop cruiser blends all-weather versatility with family-style comforts, angler-centric cockpit. Enclosed helm deck with teak-and-holly sole, entertainment center offers panoramic outside views. Cabin layout with private bow stateroom, convertible settee sleeps four. Fishing amenities include 50-gallon transom livewell, bait prep center, in-sole fishboxes. Note that hardtop overhangs provide partial sun protection for windshield, cockpit. Cummins 540hp diesels cruise at 25 knots; 645hp Yanmars cruise at 28–29 knots.

Length w/Pulpit	44'6"	Fuel	600 gals.
Hull Length	42'3"	Water	130 gals.
Beam	15'9"	Waste	40 gals.
Draft	3'6"	Hull Type	Modified-V
Weight	32,000#	Deadrise Aft	18°

See Page 550 For Resale Values

Luhrs Corporation
St. Augustine, FL
www.luhrs.com

Sportfishing Boats

Section II: Sportfishing Boats

Sportfishing Boats

www.powerboatguide.com   231-360-0827

Luhrs 41 Open
2006–Current

Powerful deepwater express gives anglers impressive blend of hardcore fishability, luxurious accommodations. Vast cockpit with 50-gallon livewell, bait-prep station offers plenty of fish-fighting space. Note separate pump room aft of engineroom. Raised helm has watertight windshield sealed to hardtop. Upscale interior with cherry joinery, leather upholstery, uses galley counter as first step into cabin—not good. Prop pockets reduce draft, improve efficiency. Cruise at 26–27 knots with Cummins 580hp diesels (about 30 knots top).

Length w/Pulpit	44'6"	Clearance	22'0"
Hull Length	42'3"	Fuel	600 gals.
Beam	15'9"	Water	130 gals.
Draft	3'6"	Hull Type	Modified-V
Weight	33,000#	Deadrise Aft	18°

See Page 550 For Resale Values

Luhrs Corporation
St. Augustine, FL
www.luhrs.com

---

www.powerboatguide.com   231-360-0827

Luhrs 44 Convertible
2003–05

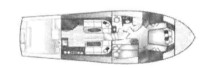

Stylish sportfisherman with innovative layout is part hardcore fishing machine, part family cruiser. Unusual salon layout has galley, entertainment center aft, seating areas forward. Long foredeck results in somewhat modest salon dimensions for boat this size; staterooms, however, are large. Note space in corridor for optional washer/dryer. Molded steps make bridge access easy, but at the expense of valuable cockpit space. Note standard hardtops. Cruise at 25 knots with 635hp Cummins diesels (28–30 knots top).

Length w/Pulpit	46'4"	Clearance	18'4"
Hull Length	43'2"	Fuel	700 gals.
Beam	16'0"	Water	125 gals.
Draft	4'6"	Hull Type	Modified-V
Weight	33,500#	Deadrise Aft	12°

See Page 550 For Resale Values

Luhrs Corporation
St. Augustine, FL
www.luhrs.com

---

www.powerboatguide.com   231-360-0827

Luhrs 50 Convertible
1999–2003

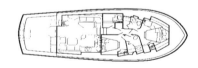

Executive-class tournament fisherman with superwide 18-foot beam delivered comfort, luxury on a grand scale. Spacious interior features three large staterooms, two heads, dinette, salon entertainment center. Huge galley puts many home kitchens to shame. Molded bridge steps are convenient, but result in slightly awkward flybridge layout. Note massive cockpit, cavernous engineroom, cherry interior joinery. Cat 800hp diesels cruise at 26–27 knots (30+ top); 1,350hp Cats cruise at 30 knots (33–34 knots wide open).

Length	50'10"	Fuel	1,000 gals.
Beam	18'0"	Water	200 gals.
Draft	5'0"	Headroom	6 5"
Weight	48,000#	Hull Type	Modified-V
Clearance	18'0"	Deadrise Aft	12°

See Page 550 For Resale Values

Luhrs Corporation
St. Augustine, FL
www.luhrs.com

Mako 282 Center Console
1998–2003

Rugged 28-footer with integrated transom, deep cockpit made the cut with anglers looking for a trailerable center console built tough. Highlights included big 42-gallon transom livewell, two in-deck fishboxes, bow casting platform, removable rear seat, recessed rod lockers, console head compartment, lockable bow storage, console seat, bow pulpit. Big fuel capacity means excellent range. Transom door, foldaway transom seat were added in 1998. Heavily built boat can take a pounding. About 45 knots with twin 225s.

Length w/Pulpit	31'1"	Fuel	235 gals.
Hull Length	28'1"	Water	10 gals.
Beam	8'6"	Max HP	450
Hull Draft	16"	Hull Type	Deep-V
Dry Weight	4,500#	Deadrise Aft	23°

See Page 550 For Resale Values

Mako Boats
Springfield, MO
www.mako-boats.com

Mako 284 Center Console
2005–Current

Maxi-volume fisherman introduced in 2005 gave seasoned anglers reason to take a fresh look at Mako boats. Wide 9'10" beam provides generous cockpit space with room for several anglers. Amenities include standard T-top with rod holders, bait station with tackle storage, big 50-gallon livewell, leaning post with sink & tackle storage, cushioned forward seating, freshwater system. Space at helm for flush-mounting electronics. Deep-V hull handles a chop without pounding; high bow freeboard insures a dry ride. About 45 knots with twin 250s.

Length	28'4"	Fuel	235 gals.
Beam	9'10"	Water	14 gals.
Draft, Up	1'9"	Max HP	600
Draft, Down	3'2"	Hull Type	Deep-V
Dry Weight	6,000#	Deadrise Aft	21°

See Page 551 For Resale Values

Mako Boats
Springfield, MO
www.mako-boats.com

Mako 293 Walkaround
1994–2003

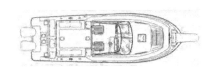

Popular 29-foot walkaround with generous 9'6" beam strikes a balance between hardcore fishing machine, family-friendly cruiser. Stand-up livewell, transom door, in-floor fishboxes, tackle center, fresh/raw-water washdowns, deluxe helm seats, rod storage, bow seating, anchor locker, bow pulpit. Roomy cabin with mid-berth aft, full galley, enclosed head with shower, convertible dinette sleeps four. Wide, deep walkarounds are a big plus. Called the 263 Walkaround in 1994. About 40 knots with 250 outboards.

Length w/Pulpit	30'10"	Fuel	240 gals.
Hull Length	28'7"	Water	40 gals.
Beam	9'6"	Max HP	500
Hull Draft	1'7"	Hull Type	Deep-V
Weight	6,100#	Deadrise Aft	23°

See Page 551 For Resale Values

Mako Boats
Springfield, MO
www.mako-boats.com

Sportfishing Boats

Mako 333 Center Console Cuddy
1997–2000

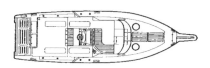

Versatile console express with comfortable interior, leading-edge styling offered something different for Mako enthusiasts. Features include foldaway rear seat, four in-deck fish/storage boxes, 60-gallon transom livewell, leaning post with rod holders, coaming bolsters, rod storage, transom door, fresh/raw-water washdowns, bow pulpit. Note L-shaped lounge seating forward of helm. Well-appointed cabin with V-berth, midcabin berth, enclosed head with shower, sleeps four. Helmdeck lifts for generator access. Over 35 knots with twin 250s.

Length w/Pulpit	36'0"	Fuel	350 gals.
Hull Length	33'9"	Water	35 gals.
Beam	10'6"	Max HP	750
Hull Draft	1'9"	Hull Type	Deep-V
Weight	11,500#	Deadrise Aft	24.5°

See Page 551 For Resale Values

Mako Boats
Springfield, MO
www.mako-boats.com

Marlin 350 Cuddy
1991–Current

Cuddy Layout

Open Bow Layout

Feature-rich cuddy built to high standards is agile, fast, ready for action. Semicustom boat can be factory-built to customer specs. Standard version features V-berth, cushioned bow seating, 50-gallon livewell, bait-prep center, deluxe two-person helm seat, in-deck fishboxes, pop-up cleats, forward console seat, walk-in console head compartment. Large dash can handle several big-screen electronics displays. Wide walkways provide excellent 360-degree fishability. Twin 250hp outboards deliver 45 knots max.

Length	35'6"	Fuel	250 gals.
Beam	9'4"	Water	40 gals.
Hull Draft	1'6"	Max HP	900
Weight w/Engines	9,000#	Hull Type	Deep-V
Clearance	8'0"	Deadrise Aft	24°

See Page 551 For Resale Values

Marlin Yacht
North Miami Beach, FL
www.marlinyacht.com

Mediterranean 38 Convertible
1985–2007

Single Stateroom

Two Staterooms

Economy-class west coast convertible sold factory-direct appealed to buyers with an eye for value. No-frills interior was available with one or two staterooms, both with queen berth in master, salon entertainment center, large head with stall shower. Uncluttered cockpit is shaded by flybridge overhang. Note molded bridge steps, wide side decks. Lower helm was optional in single-stateroom layout. So-so fit and finish. Cruise at 18 knots with 300hp gas engines; 20+ knots with 330hp Cummins diesels.

Length w/Pulpit	43'6"	Fuel	390 gals.
Hull Length	38'4"	Water	100 gals.
Beam	12'8"	Waste	25 gals.
Draft	3'4"	Hull Type	Modified-V
Weight	28,000#	Deadrise Aft	18°

See Page 552 For Resale Values

Mediterranean Yachts
Santa Ana, CA
www.mediterraneanyachts.com

231-360-0827

Midnight Express 39 Cuddy
2000–Current

Sleek triple-engine speedster delivers high-octane dose of luxury-class amenities, bold performance. Efficient deck layout is arranged with small cuddy forward, console head compartment, 45-gallon transom livewell aft, two in-deck fishboxes. Radar arch with T-top, cockpit bolsters, transom door, Kiekhaefer trim tabs, leaning post are standard. Stylish dash has space for big-screen electronics. Built on reworked Cigarette 36 racing hull with higher hullsides, slightly reduced deadrise. Over 50 knots with triple 275s.

Length	39'2"	Fuel	325 gals.
Beam	9'6"	Water	45 gals.
Hull Draft	1'10"	Max HP	900
Dry Weight	13,000#	Hull Type	Deep-V
Headroom	6'2"	Deadrise Aft	22°

See Page 552 For Resale Values

Midnight Express
Ft. Lauderdale, FL
www.midnightboats.com

231-360-0827

Mikelson 42 Sedan
1986–90

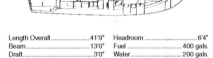

Versatile Fexas-designed sedan with distinctive styling (note long foredeck, large cabin windows) put Mikelson in the sportfish business back in 1986. Most were delivered with two-stateroom, galley-up interior with single head, standard lower helm. Interior is completely finished with handcrafted teak cabinetry. Large flybridge for a 42-footer. Cockpit came with transom door, teak sole, tackle center. Fully cored hull with rounded chines is fuel efficient, easily driven. Cruise at 16–17 knots with 260hp GM diesels (about 20 knots top).

Length Overall	41'9"	Headroom	6'4"
Beam	13'0"	Fuel	400 gals.
Draft	3'0"	Water	200 gals.
Weight	24,000#	Waste	35 gals.
Clearance	10'4"	Hull Type	Modified-V

Prices Not Provided for Pre-1995 Models

Mikelson Yachts
San Diego, CA
www.mikelsonyachts.com

231-360-0827

Mikelson 43 Sportfisher
1997–Current

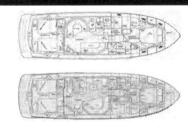

Rakish sedan fisherman with efficient, Fexas-designed hull satisfies anglers, cruisers with versatile accommodations, excellent handling, outstanding range. Original two-stateroom floorplan has galley forward in salon; aft-galley layout became available in 2006. Salon dinette is a nice touch—few boats this size have one. Engines are aft, under elevated cockpit sole. Note circular bridge settee, quality cherry interior joinery. Cummins 450hp diesels cruise in mid 20s. Newer models are offered with 480hp Zeus pod drives. Over 60 sold to date.

Length w/Pulpit	48'8"	Fuel	600 gals.
Hull Length	44'10"	Water	200 gals.
Beam	15'10"	Waste	60 gals.
Draft	3'10"	Hull Type	Modified-V
Weight	35,000#	Deadrise Aft	14.5°

See Page 552 For Resale Values

Mikelson Yachts
San Diego, CA
www.mikelsonyachts.com

Sportfishing Boats

231-360-0827

Mikelson 50 Sportfisher
1992–Current

Popular West Coast convertible with appealing profile, exceptional range blurs the line between hard-hitting fishing machine, executive-class cruising yacht. Wide 16'8" beam permits truly expansive interior with wide-open salon, large staterooms. Cockpit is big for a 50-footer. Huge flybridge boasts circular settee forward, second control station aft. Weight-efficient (fully cored) hull delivers impressive performance with relatively small engines. Cummins 540hp V-drive diesels cruise at 22 knots (26–27 knots top).

Length	50'5"	Fuel	1,000 gals.
Beam	16'8"	Water	250 gals.
Draft	3'10"	Waste	80 gals.
Weight	45,000#	Hull Type	Modified-V
Clearance	NA	Deadrise Aft	12°

See Page 553 For Resale Values

Mikelson Yachts
San Diego, CA
www.mikelsonyachts.com

231-360-0827

Mikelson 59 Nomad
2004–Current

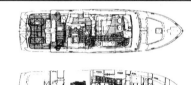

Rugged pilothouse sportfisher is spacious, efficient, completely unique. Semicustom interior boasts cavernous master suite with private access, spacious salon with breakfast bar, huge pilothouse with superb helm visibility, aft crew quarters. Small afterdeck overlooks teak-planked cockpit with twin livewells, large-capacity fishboxes. Note spacious engineroom, varnished cherry cabinets, unusual rooftop seating over pilothouse. Built on efficient hull with super-wide beam. Cruise at 12–15 knots with Cummins 635hp diesels.

Length Overall	61'4"	Fuel	2,000 gals.
Beam	18'6"	Water	350 gals.
Draft	5'6"	Waste	150 gals.
Weight	80,000#	Hull Type	Modified-V
Clearance	NA	Deadrise Aft	11°

Insufficient Resale Data To Assign Values

Mikelson Yachts
San Diego, CA
www.mikelsonyachts.com

231-360-0827

Mikelson 60 Sportfisher
1992–99

Luxury sportfisher from 1990s offers top-shelf construction, long-range fishability. Several floorplans were available—standard galley-down layout has three staterooms; alternate arrangements had two staterooms with enlarged galley. Spacious salon came with built-in settees, furniture-quality teak woodwork. Small mezzanine deck overlooks huge cockpit with direct engineroom access. Note enormous bridge with circular settee forward. Fully cored hull is efficient, easily driven. Cruise in the low 20s (26–27 top) with GM 735hp diesels.

Length	59'1"	Fuel	1,000 gals.
Beam	17'2"	Water	300 gals.
Draft	4'4"	Headroom	6'5"
Weight	55,000#	Hull Type	Modified-V
Clearance	NA	Deadrise Aft	14.5°

See Page 553 For Resale Values

Mikelson Yachts
San Diego, CA
www.mikelsonyachts.com

231-360-0827

Mikelson 61 Pilothouse Sportfisher
2000–08

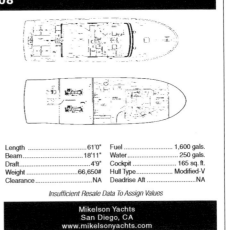

Quality-built pilothouse sportfisher with rakish profile, luxury accommodations offers space, comfort, exceptional range. Super-wide 18'11" beam provides unusually spacious interior with full-beam owner's suite, expansive salon with high-gloss joinery. Raised pilothouse hosts home-sized galley, full dinette, bridge access. Massive fishing cockpit has convenient day head—very clever. Flybridge (with aft controls) can accommodate a small crowd. Note huge engineroom, fiberglass hardtop. Cruise at 20 knots with 800hp Cat diesels.

Length	61'0"	Fuel	1,600 gals.
Beam	18'11"	Water	250 gals.
Draft	4'9"	Cockpit	165 sq. ft.
Weight	66,650#	Hull Type	Modified-V
Clearance	NA	Deadrise Aft	NA

Insufficient Resale Data To Assign Values

Mikelson Yachts
San Diego, CA
www.mikelsonyachts.com

231-360-0827

Mikelson 64 Sportfisher
1997–2001

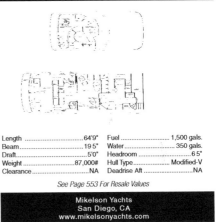

Quality-built long-range fisherman with mega-wide 19'5" beam dwarfs similar-sized boats inside and out. Broad beam translates into unusually spacious interior, massive 210-square-foot cockpit, huge flybridge with circular settee, wraparound helm, aft controls. Notable features include opulent master suite with king bed, exquisite teak cabin joinery, crew quarters, monster engineroom. Note mezzanine deck with day head overlooking cockpit. Built on fully cored hull. Cat 1,300hp diesels cruise at 25 knots (30+ top).

Length	64'9"	Fuel	1,500 gals.
Beam	19'5"	Water	350 gals.
Draft	5'0"	Headroom	6'5"
Weight	87,000#	Hull Type	Modified-V
Clearance	NA	Deadrise Aft	NA

See Page 553 For Resale Values

Mikelson Yachts
San Diego, CA
www.mikelsonyachts.com

231-360-0827

North Coast 31
1988–90

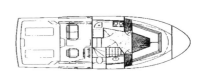

Sought-after tournament express gets high marks for sleek styling, efficient deck plan, impressive rough-water handling. Roomy cockpit came standard with in-deck fishboxes, raw-water washdown, tackle storage, rod storage. Well-finished cabin with full galley, head with stall shower, dinette/V-berth sleeps two. Terrific rough-water handling. Blackfin later acquired the molds to this model and briefly marketed her as the 31 Combi. Cruise at 24–25 knots with 350hp gas inboards; low 20s with 250hp Cummins diesels.

Length	30'8"	Fuel, Opt.	410 gals.
Beam	12'0"	Water	50 gals.
Draft	3'2"	Waste	20 gals.
Weight	11,300#	Hull Type	Deep-V
Fuel, Std.	275 gals.	Deadrise Aft	23°

Prices Not Provided for Pre-1995 Models

North Coast is no longer in business.

Sportfishing Boats

www.powerboatguide.com   231-360-0827

Ocean 29 Super Sport
1990–92

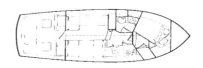

Classy 1990s convertible remains among the smallest flybridge boats ever offered by a major builder. Space-efficient teak interior boasts private bow stateroom with angled double berth, full galley, convertible salon dinette. Note unique shower enclosure in head. Central vacuum system, air-conditioning, entertainment center were standard. Athwartships bridge ladder frees up considerable cockpit space. Sleek styling still looks good today. Twin 320hp gas engines cruise at 20–22 knots; 250hp Cummins diesels cruise in the mid 20s.

Length	29'0"	Fuel	215 gals.
Beam	11'6"	Water	35 gals.
Draft	2 5"	Waste	20 gals.
Weight	13,500#	Hull Type	Modified-V
Clearance	10'6"	Deadrise Aft	14°

Prices Not Provided for Pre-1995 Models

Ocean Yachts
Egg Harbor City, NJ
www.oceanyachtsinc.com

---

www.powerboatguide.com   231-360-0827

Ocean 32 Super Sport
1989–92

Rakish 32-footer with classic Ocean styling delivered comfort, performance at an affordable price. Elegant teak interior with booth-style dinette, convertible salon settee, TV/VCR came standard with air, microwave, central vacuum system. Cockpit amenities include in-deck fishbox, bait-prep center, tackle storage, transom door, teak covering boards. Engineroom is a tight fit. Athwartships bridge ladder frees up considerable cockpit space. Cruise at 22 knots with 320 gas engines; mid 20s with 300hp Cummins diesels.

Length	32'0"	Fuel	280 gals.
Beam	12'4"	Water	60 gals.
Draft	2'6"	Waste	25 gals.
Weight	17,043#	Hull Type	Modified-V
Clearance	11'1"	Deadrise Aft	13°

Prices Not Provided for Pre-1995 Models

Ocean Yachts
Egg Harbor City, NJ
www.oceanyachtsinc.com

---

www.powerboatguide.com   231-360-0827

Ocean 35 Super Sport
1988–94

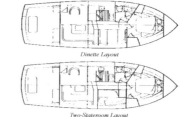

Dinette Layout

Two-Stateroom Layout

Innovative 35-footer was one of Ocean's best-selling models during her production years. Standard single-stateroom interior with teak trim is roomy, well-appointed. Cockpit is fitted with fishbox, transom door, tackle storage, cooler/freezer, teak covering boards. Impressive equipment list included generator, air-conditioning, central vacuum system. Engineroom is a tight fit. Athwartships flybridge ladder preserves cockpit space. Cruise at 20 knots with 320 gas engines; mid 20s with 300hp Cummins diesels.

Length	35'0"	Fuel	320 gals.
Beam	13'0"	Water	70 gals.
Draft	2 5"	Waste	30 gals.
Weight	19,800#	Hull Type	Modified-V
Clearance	11'9"	Deadrise Aft	13°

Prices Not Provided for Pre-1995 Models

Ocean Yachts
Egg Harbor City, NJ
www.oceanyachtsinc.com

231-360-0827

Ocean 37 Billfish
2008–Current

Nimble sportfisherman with vintage Palm Beach styling takes the retro look to the next level. Traditional fishing-boat layout has semi-enclosed helm deck with dinette, large cockpit with livewell, bait-prep center, two fishboxes. Upscale cabin with cherry cabinetry, head with stall shower sleeps three. Engineroom is surprisingly large. Compact flybridge with center helm offers good cockpit view. Prop pockets reduce draft to just 2'6". Volvo 435hp IPS pod drives cruise at 30 knots. Early models with Yanmar 480hp diesels cruise at 24–26 knots.

Length	37'8"	Fuel	400 gals.
Beam	13'10"	Water	75 gals.
Draft	2'6"	Waste	35 gals.
Weight	23,500#	Hull Type	Modified-V
Clearance	15 5"	Deadrise Aft	13°

See Page 554 For Resale Values

Ocean Yachts
Egg Harbor City, NJ
www.oceanyachtsinc.com

231-360-0827

Ocean 38 Super Sport
1984–91

Two-Stateroom Interior

Single-Stateroom Interior

Leading-edge 1980s convertible with rakish profile became one of Ocean's best-selling models ever. Inviting teak interior with spacious salon was available with one or two staterooms. Cockpit with teak sole came standard with tackle center, bait freezer, in-deck fishbox, transom door, teak covering boards. Very serviceable engineroom. Low-deadrise hull can be a stiff ride in a chop. Total of 158 built. Replaced in 1992 with new 38 SS model. Caterpillar 375hp diesels cruise at 24–24 knots (about 30 knots top).

Length	38'4"	Fuel	354 gals.
Beam	13'8"	Water	80 gals.
Draft	3'2"	Waste	35 gals.
Weight	23,000#	Hull Type	Modified-V
Clearance	13'1"	Deadrise Aft	12°

Prices Not Provided for Pre-1995 Models

Ocean Yachts
Egg Harbor City, NJ
www.oceanyachtsinc.com

231-360-0827

Ocean 38 Super Sport
1992–95

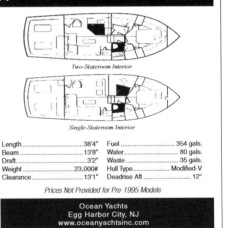
Main Deck

Lower Deck

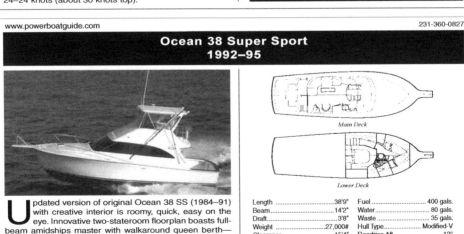

Updated version of original Ocean 38 SS (1984–91) with creative interior is roomy, quick, easy on the eye. Innovative two-stateroom floorplan boasts full-beam amidships master with walkaround queen berth—a unique layout in a boat this size. Cockpit with standard tackle center, bait freezer, fishbox, transom door is on the small side for a 38-footer. Hardtop, generator, air-conditioning were standard. Engineroom is a tight fit. Cat 425hp diesels (or Volvo 430s) cruise in the low 20s and reach 28–29 knots top.

Length	38'9"	Fuel	400 gals.
Beam	14'2"	Water	80 gals.
Draft	3'8"	Waste	35 gals.
Weight	27,000#	Hull Type	Modified-V
Clearance	15'4"	Deadrise Aft	12°

See Page XXX For Resale Values

Ocean Yachts
Egg Harbor City, NJ
www.oceanyachtsinc.com

Sportfishing Boats

231-360-0827

Ocean 40 Sport Fish
1999–2005

Innovative express with highly elevated bridgedeck blurs the lines between serious sportfisherman, capable family cruiser. Mid-stateroom layout is completely unique in an express boat this size. Transom baitwell, tackle lockers, transom door are standard; compact engineroom has near-standing headroom. Bridgedeck—6 steps up from cockpit level—boasts centerline helm, lounge seating aft. Great visibility from raised helm position. Cat 420hp Cat (or 440hp Yanmar) diesels reach 30+ knots wide open.

Length	40'4"	Fuel	390 gals.
Beam	14'2"	Water	90 gals.
Draft	3'8"	Waste	40 gals.
Weight	26,500#	Hull Type	Modified-V
Clearance	12'6"	Deadrise Aft	14°

See Page 554 For Resale Values

Ocean Yachts
Egg Harbor City, NJ
www.oceanyachtsinc.com

231-360-0827

Ocean 40 Super Sport
1997–2005

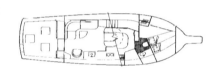

Good-selling flybridge fisherman gets high marks for sleek styling, innovative interior, excellent performance. Well-appointed two-stateroom, galley-up interior features unusual raised dinette forward in salon, amidships master stateroom with tall headroom. Cockpit features include engineroom access, tackle center, saltwater washdown, transom door. Athwartships bridge ladder preserves cockpit space. Cat 420hp—or Yanmar 440hp—diesels cruise at 24 knots and reach a top speed of 30+ knots.

Length	40'4"	Fuel	408 gals.
Beam	14'2"	Water	90 gals.
Draft	3'8"	Cockpit	80 sq. ft.
Weight	27,500#	Hull Type	Modified-V
Clearance	15'5"	Deadrise Aft	14°

See Page 554 For Resale Values

Ocean Yachts
Egg Harbor City, NJ
www.oceanyachtsinc.com

231-360-0827

Ocean 42 Super Sport
1980–83

Galley Down

Galley Up

Stretched version of Ocean 40 SS (1977–80) became one of Ocean's best-selling models. Stylish interior—considered very luxurious in her day—came as a surprise considering her comparatively low price. Versatile two-stateroom layout was available with galley up or down. Large cockpit is big enough for several anglers. Teak cockpit sole, tackle center, cockpit controls were standard. Low-deadrise hull is quick to accelerate but a stiff ride in a chop. Cruise in the mid 20s with 450hp GM 6-71 diesels (around 28 knots wide open).

Length	42'0"	Fuel	480 gals.
Beam	14'4"	Water	100 gals.
Draft	3'4"	Cockpit	100 sq. ft.
Weight	30,000#	Hull Type	Modified-V
Clearance	12'0"	Deadrise Aft	1.5°

Prices Not Provided for Pre-1995 Models

Ocean Yachts
Egg Harbor City, NJ
www.oceanyachtsinc.com

Ocean 42 Super Sport
1991–95

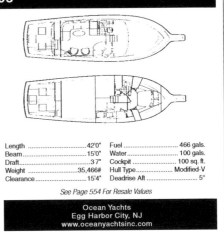

Second-generation 42 Super Sport (an earlier 42 SS model ran from 1980–83) combined leading-edge performance with iconic styling, appealing price. Well-appointed interior with L-shaped dinette features walkaround queen berth forward, double (and slide-out single) berth in guest cabin. Hatch in galley sole leads to large storage area. Expansive fishing cockpit has transom gate and door, large fishbox, tackle center, bait freezer. Cat 425hp diesels cruise at 24 knots cruise (26–27 top); GM 485hp 6-71s cruise at 26 knots (30 knots top).

Length	42'0"	Fuel	466 gals.
Beam	15'0"	Water	100 gals.
Draft	3'7"	Cockpit	100 sq. ft.
Weight	35,466#	Hull Type	Modified-V
Clearance	15'4"	Deadrise Aft	5°

See Page 554 For Resale Values

Ocean Yachts
Egg Harbor City, NJ
www.oceanyachtsinc.com

Ocean 42 Super Sport
2006–Current

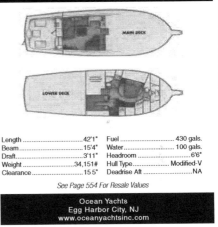

Polished sportfishing machine with handsome lines meets anglers need for space, comfort, performance. Clever two-stateroom interior boasts luxurious salon, L-shaped dinette, two full heads (most 42-footers have one), huge storage area under galley. Galley is on the small side. Note washer/dryer in guest stateroom. Roomy cockpit includes transom livewell, in-deck fishboxes, direct engineroom access. Underwater exhaust system reduces noise, cockpit fumes. Cat 510hp diesels cruise at 25–26 knots (30 knots top).

Length	42'1"	Fuel	430 gals.
Beam	15'4"	Water	100 gals.
Draft	3'11"	Headroom	6'6"
Weight	34,151#	Hull Type	Modified-V
Clearance	15'5"	Deadrise Aft	NA

See Page 554 For Resale Values

Ocean Yachts
Egg Harbor City, NJ
www.oceanyachtsinc.com

Ocean 43 Super Sport
2000–05

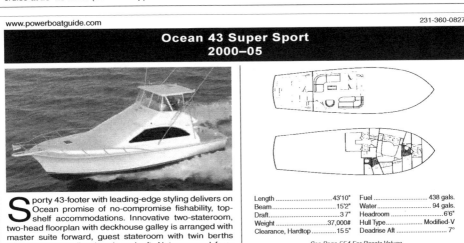

Sporty 43-footer with leading-edge styling delivers on Ocean promise of no-compromise fishability, top-shelf accommodations. Innovative two-stateroom, two-head floorplan with deckhouse galley is arranged with master suite forward, guest stateroom with twin berths (and partial standing headroom) aft. Note unusual forepeak head. Large cockpit with engineroom access comes standard with freezer, livewell, huge fishbox. Very good performer: Volvo 480hp—or 500hp Yanmar—diesels cruise at 25 knots and reach a top speed of 30+ knots.

Length	43'10"	Fuel	438 gals.
Beam	15'2"	Water	94 gals.
Draft	3'7"	Headroom	6'6"
Weight	37,000#	Hull Type	Modified-V
Clearance, Hardtop	15'5"	Deadrise Aft	7°

See Page 554 For Resale Values

Ocean Yachts
Egg Harbor City, NJ
www.oceanyachtsinc.com

Sportfishing Boats

231-360-0827

Ocean 44 Super Sport
1985–91

Fast-action convertible with classic Ocean styling raised the bar in her era for sportfishing luxury, performance, affordability. Two-stateroom interior with galley down, two full heads is ideal for a boat this size. Roomy galley is large enough for optional dishwasher and trash compactor. Note built-in clothes dryer in guest stateroom. Cockpit came standard with tackle center, teak sole, engine controls. Large engineroom offers good service access. GM 485hp 6-71 diesels cruise at 27 knots (30+ top). Total of 111 were built.

Length	44'0"	Fuel	480 gals.
Beam	15'2"	Water	100 gals.
Draft	3'6"	Cockpit	130 sq. ft.
Weight	36,000#	Hull Type	Modified-V
Clearance	13'3"	Deadrise Aft	1.5°

Prices Not Provided for Pre-1995 Models

Ocean Yachts
Egg Harbor City, NJ
www.oceanyachtsinc.com

231-360-0827

Ocean 45 Super Sport
1996–99

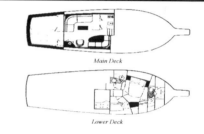

Main Deck

Lower Deck

Rakish 1990s convertible delivered high-octane blend of Ocean luxury, performance at an attractive price. Innovative two-stateroom interior with combined salon/galley/dinette features big master suite with walkaround queen berth, roomy guest cabin with double bed and slide-out single berth. Note large engineroom with cockpit access, standard washer/dryer, spacious flybridge with lounge seating, rod storage. Athwartships bridge ladder saves cockpit space. Cruise at 25 knots with GM 485hp 6-71s (30+ knots wide open).

Length	44'8"	Fuel	466 gals.
Beam	15'2"	Water	100 gals.
Draft	3'7"	Headroom	6'6"
Weight	37,000#	Hull Type	Modified-V
Clearance	15'4"	Deadrise Aft	1.5°

See Page 555 For Resale Values

Ocean Yachts
Egg Harbor City, NJ
www.oceanyachtsinc.com

231-360-0827

Ocean 46 Super Sport
1983–85

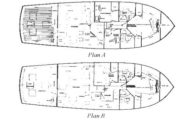

Plan A

Plan B

Best-selling 1990s canyon runner combined sleek Jersey styling with ltop-shelf amenities, exhilarating performance. Three-stateroom interior is rare in a 46-footer—most boats this size have only two. Large fishing cockpit included standard livewell, helm controls, transom gate, tackle locker, freezer. Most were delivered with optional factory hardtop. Note small engineroom. Cruise at 25 knots with GM 450hp diesels (about 28 knots top); 27–28 knots with 475hp 6V92s (30 knots top). Very popular model—total of 160 were built.

Length	46'0"	Fuel	580 gals.
Beam	15'2"	Water	150 gals.
Draft	3'6"	Cockpit	NA
Weight	40,000#	Hull Type	Modified-V
Clearance	13'3"	Deadrise Aft	1.5°

Prices Not Provided for Pre-1995 Models

Ocean Yachts
Egg Harbor City, NJ
www.oceanyachtsinc.com

231-360-0827

Ocean 46 Super Sport
2005–Current

Handsome convertible styling, deluxe accommodations, spirited performance make this luxurious 46-footer a stand-out boating value. Creative space management permits a spacious three-stateroom interior layout—rare in a 46-foot boat. Offered with full-size double berth or crossover berths in forward stateroom. Note that small aft stateroom contains only a single berth. Expansive cockpit features twin fishboxes, livewell, engineroom access. A fast ride, MTU 825hp diesels cruise at an honest 30 knots (34–35 knots top).

Length	46'6"	Fuel	620 gals.
Beam	15'10	Water	125 gals.
Draft	4'2"	Headroom	6 5"
Weight	42,561#	Hull Type	Modified-V
Clearance	16'4"	Deadrise Aft	14°

See Page 555 For Resale Values

Ocean Yachts
Egg Harbor City, NJ
www.oceanyachtsinc.com

231-360-0827

Ocean 48 Sport Fish
1997–2001

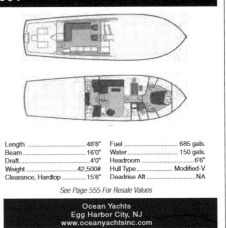

Fast-action express with rakish lines, roomy interior has the right stuff for serious offshore anglers. Unusual cabin layout offers large aft stateroom with single and double berths, compact salon, step-down galley and head, private forward stateroom with walkaround queen. Huge bridgedeck with centerline helm has seating for several guests. Stand-up engineroom provides excellent service access. Note huge fishboxes, generous rod storage, easy-to-work cockpit. Cruise in the high 20s with GM 625 diesels (34–35 knots top).

Length	48'8"	Fuel	685 gals.
Beam	16'0"	Water	150 gals.
Draft	4'0"	Headroom	6'6"
Weight	42,500#	Hull Type	Modified-V
Clearance, Hardtop	15'6"	Deadrise Aft	NA

See Page 555 For Resale Values

Ocean Yachts
Egg Harbor City, NJ
www.oceanyachtsinc.com

231-360-0827

Ocean 48 Super Sport
1986–90

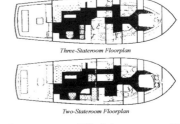

Three-Stateroom Floorplan

Two-Stateroom Floorplan

Best-selling 48-footer introduced in 1986 combined signature Ocean amenities, performance in an affordably priced package. Offered with expansive three-stateroom, mid-galley interior, or conventional (less popular) two-stateroom, galley-down floorplan with enlarged salon. Roomy cockpit has full control station, bait center with freezer, livewell, wide transom door. Note teak cockpit sole, teak covering boards. Tops out at 30 knots with relatively small GM 485hp 6-71 diesels. Total of 167 of these distinctive yachts were built.

Length	48'0"	Fuel	580 gals.
Beam	15'2"	Water	150 gals.
Draft	3'6"	Cockpit	NA
Weight	40,000#	Hull Type	Modified-V
Clearance	13'3"	Deadrise Aft	2°

Prices Not Provided for Pre-1995 Models

Ocean Yachts
Egg Harbor City, NJ
www.oceanyachtsinc.com

Ocean 48 Super Sport
1991–94

Updated version of previous Ocean 48 SS (1986–90) incorporates fresh styling, more standard features, less exterior teak. Innovative three-stateroom interior features combined salon/galley area, amidships owner's suite, two full heads. Note salon entertainment center, unusual centerline dinette. Newly configured cockpit includes recessed controls, baitwell, tackle lockers, built-in fishboxes, direct engineroom access. Teak cockpit sole was a popular option. Cruise in the mid 20s (about 30 knots top) with GM 485hp 6-71 diesels.

Length	48'0"	Fuel	580 gals.
Beam	15'2"	Water	150 gals.
Draft	3'6"	Cockpit	NA
Weight	40,000#	Hull Type	Modified-V
Clearance	13'3"	Deadrise Aft	2°

Prices Not Provided for Pre-1995 Models

Ocean Yachts
Egg Harbor City, NJ
www.oceanyachtsinc.com

Ocean 48 Super Sport
1995–2003

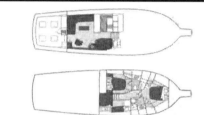

Strong-selling convertible—third in a series of Ocean 48 SS models—appealed to upscale anglers with an eye for leading-edge luxury, exceptional fishability. Well-appointed three-stateroom, two-head interior boasts combined salon/galley/dinette with entertainment center and wet bar. Two-stateroom, galley-down layout was optional. Cockpit has bait-prep station, freezer, engine controls, transom door. Angled bridge ladder saves cockpit space. GM 535hp diesels cruise at 24 knots; later models with 680hp MANs cruise at 28 knots.

Length	48'8"	Fuel	685 gals.
Beam	16'0"	Water	150 gals.
Draft	4'2"	Waste	6'6"60 gals.
Weight	45,000#	Hull Type	Modified-V
Clearance	15'6"	Deadrise Aft	2°

See Page 555 For Resale Values

Ocean Yachts
Egg Harbor City, NJ
www.oceanyachtsinc.com

Ocean 50 Super Sport
1982–85

Scaled-down version of popular Ocean 55 SS (1981–90) failed to attain the popularity of her larger sibling. Two- and three-stateroom floorplans were offered—twin-cabin version is notable for huge master stateroom dimensions. Both layouts feature expansive main salon with serving counter overlooking salon. Cockpit with freezer, tackle locker is small for a 50-footer. Note poor engineroom access. Low-deadrise hull is a stiff ride in a chop. GM 675hp 8V92s cruise at 25 knots and reach a top speed of 28–29 knots.

Length	50'0"	Fuel	750 gals.
Beam	16'0"	Water	200 gals.
Draft	4'2"	Cockpit	NA
Weight	50,000#	Hull Type	Modified-V
Clearance	14'2"	Deadrise Aft	5°

Prices Not Provided for Pre-1995 Models

Ocean Yachts
Egg Harbor City, NJ
www.oceanyachtsinc.com

Ocean 50 Super Sport
2004–Current

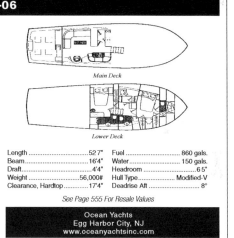

Well-styled convertible offers high-end luxury, hard-core fishability in a modern, high-performance package. Elegant three-stateroom interior is dominated by spacious salon/galley/dinette area with extended L-lounge, full entertainment center. Washer/dryer is located in companionway; forward guest stateroom is available with island berth or over/under bunks. Cockpit comes with stand-up livewell, bait-prep center, in-deck fishbox. Note spacious engineroom, large helm console. MTU 825hp diesels cruise at 28–30 knots (about 33 knots top).

Length	50'6"	Cockpit	123 sq. ft.
Beam	16'9"	Fuel	780 gals.
Draft	4'5"	Water	150 gals.
Weight	54,038#	Hull Type	Modified-V
Clearance	18'0"	Deadrise Aft	14°

See Page 555 For Resale Values

Ocean Yachts
Egg Harbor City, NJ
www.oceanyachtsinc.com

Ocean 52 Super Sport
2001–06

Main Deck

Lower Deck

Powerful tournament fisherman was smartly styled, lavishly appointed, surprisingly well priced. Spacious interior includes three staterooms and three full heads—a big floorplan for a 52-footer. Note opulent full-beam master suite beneath raised galley and dinette. Large cockpit boasts full array of fishing amenities; massive bridge features state-of-the-art helm console. Engineroom is smaller than expected. Washer/dryer, factory hardtop are standard. Twin 800hp Cats—or 825hp MTUs—cruise in the high 20s (32–33 knots top).

Length	52'7"	Fuel	860 gals.
Beam	16'4"	Water	150 gals.
Draft	4'4"	Headroom	6'5"
Weight	56,000#	Hull Type	Modified-V
Clearance, Hardtop	17'4"	Deadrise Aft	8°

See Page 555 For Resale Values

Ocean Yachts
Egg Harbor City, NJ
www.oceanyachtsinc.com

Ocean 53 Super Sport
1991–99

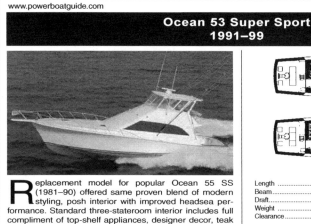

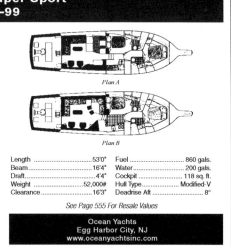

Plan A

Plan B

Replacement model for popular Ocean 55 SS (1981–90) offered same proven blend of modern styling, posh interior with improved headsea performance. Standard three-stateroom interior includes full compliment of top-shelf appliances, designer decor, teak cabinetry. Cockpit boasts full controls, tackle lockers, direct engineroom access. Twin-stateroom, galley-down layout with larger salon was optional. Factory hardtop, dishwasher were standard. GM 760hp diesels cruise at 24–26 knots; 820hp MANs cruise at a fast 30 knots.

Length	53'0"	Fuel	860 gals.
Beam	16'4"	Water	200 gals.
Draft	4'4"	Cockpit	118 sq. ft.
Weight	52,000#	Hull Type	Modified-V
Clearance	16'3"	Deadrise Aft	8°

See Page 555 For Resale Values

Ocean Yachts
Egg Harbor City, NJ
www.oceanyachtsinc.com

Sportfishing Boats

Sportfishing Boats

Ocean 54 Super Sport
2007–Current

Hard-charging convertible with sleek lines, executive-class interior makes good on Ocean promise luxury, performance at a seriously competitive price. Innovative three-stateroom floorplan boasts spacious salon, high-gloss cherry cabinetry, standard washer/dryer, three full heads. Cockpit mezzanine with lounge seating, refrigerator/freezer is unusual in a boat this size. Note roomy flybridge with center helm position. Prop pockets reduce draft, improve efficiency. MAN 10500hp engines cruise at 25 knots (about 30 knots top).

Length	54'6"	Fuel	1,000 gals.
Beam	16'10"	Water	200 gals.
Draft	4'0"	Waste	50 gals.
Weight	61,000#	Hull Type	Modified-V
Clearance	17'5"	Deadrise Aft	13.5°

See Page 555 For Resale Values

Ocean Yachts
Egg Harbor City, NJ
www.oceanyachtsinc.com

Ocean 55 Super Sport
1981–90

Plan A

Plan B

Best-selling tournament machine dominated the 1980s with her potent blend of bold styling, unsurpassed performance, appealing price. Highlights include expansive three-stateroom, three-head interior (note bow master suite), tournament-class fishing cockpit, impressive list of standard equipment. Weight-efficient hull performs well with relatively small engines. Restyled in 1986 with new flybridge, solid front windshield. Total of 170 were built. Tops out at an honest 30 knots (26–27 knots cruise) with 735hp GM diesels.

Length	55'8"	Fuel	1,000 gals.
Beam	16'4"	Water	200 gals.
Draft	4'4"	Cockpit	130 sq. ft.
Weight	58,000#	Hull Type	Modified-V
Clearance	14'6"	Deadrise Aft	4°

Prices Not Provided for Pre-1995 Models

Ocean Yachts
Egg Harbor City, NJ
www.oceanyachtsinc.com

Ocean 56 Super Sport
1999–2002

Main Deck

Lower Deck

Fast sportfisherman is a downsized version of Ocean 60 Super Sport (1996–2001) with slightly reduced cockpit dimensions. Lush three-stateroom interior—identical to the 60 SS—boasts spacious salon/galley/dinette area, posh amidships master suite, equally luxurious VIP bow stateroom with forepeak head. Washer/dryer, trash compactor were standard in galley. Easy-to-fish cockpit came with full array of premium fishing features. Note large wraparound helm console. Cruise at 30+ knots (35–36 top) with 1,050hp MAN diesels.

Length	56'0"	Fuel	900 gals.
Beam	16'10"	Water	220 gals.
Draft	4'5"	Headroom	6'5"
Weight	63,000#	Hull Type	Modified-V
Clearance, Hardtop	16'8"	Deadrise Aft	10°

See Page 555 For Resale Values

Ocean Yachts
Egg Harbor City, NJ
www.oceanyachtsinc.com

Ocean 57 Super Sport
2003–07

Main Deck

Lower Level

Updated version of Ocean 56 SS (1999–2002) with reworked running surface, additional transom deadrise, redesigned interior made a good boat even better. Elegant three-stateroom interior with open salon/galley/dinette compares well with more expensive competitors in features, amenities. Note excellent engine-room access, fully equipped cockpit, massive flybridge with hardtop and wraparound seating. (Enclosed bridge was optional.) Cat 1,015hp engines cruise at 28–30 knots; 1,300hp Cats cruise in the low 30s (35+ wide open).

Length	57'0"	Headroom	6'8"
Beam	16'10"	Fuel	1,047 gals.
Draft	4'10"	Water	200 gals.
Weight	66,269#	Hull Type	Modified-V
Clearance	17'5"	Deadrise Aft	14°

See Page 555 For Resale Values

Ocean Yachts
Egg Harbor City, NJ
www.oceanyachtsinc.com

Ocean 58 Super Sport
1990–93

Main Deck

Lower Deck

Muscular 1990s fishing machine impressed anglers with aggressive styling, luxurious accommodations, exceptional big-boat performance. Innovative three-stateroom, three-head interior with full-beam master was a giant departure from conventional convertible floorplans of her era. Tournament-sized cockpit features molded tackle centers, cockpit controls, transom door, engineroom door. Enclosed flybridge was optional. Cruise at a fast 28 knots with 1,080hp 12-cylinder GM diesels (32–33 knots top).

Length	58'0"	Fuel	1,100 gals.
Beam	17'6"	Water	250 gals.
Draft	4'10"	Cockpit	131 sq. ft.
Weight	72,215#	Hull Type	Modified-V
Clearance	14'11"	Deadrise Aft	NA

Prices Not Provided for Pre-1995 Models

Ocean Yachts
Egg Harbor City, NJ
www.oceanyachtsinc.com

Ocean 58 Super Sport
2008–Current

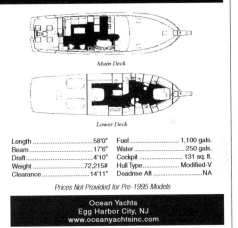
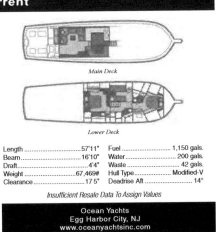

Main Deck

Lower Deck

Gold-plated sportfishing machine pairs classic Ocean styling with tournament-class fishability, leading-edge performance. Opulent three-stateroom interior features home-size U-shaped galley, huge dinette, palatial full-beam master with copious storage. Mezzanine with bait-prep center overlooks massive cockpit with transom livewell, in-sole fishboxes. Innovative flybridge has center-console-style helm station aft of giant wraparound settee. Hardtop is standard; enclosed flybridge is optional. MAN 1,550hp diesels cruise at nearly 35 knots.

Length	57'11"	Fuel	1,150 gals.
Beam	16'10"	Water	200 gals.
Draft	4'4"	Waste	42 gals.
Weight	67,469#	Hull Type	Modified-V
Clearance	17'5"	Deadrise Aft	14°

Insufficient Resale Data To Assign Values

Ocean Yachts
Egg Harbor City, NJ
www.oceanyachtsinc.com

Sportfishing Boats

231-360-0827

Ocean 60 Super Sport
1996–2001

Lower Deck Plan A

Lower Deck Plan B

Worth-class tournament machine popular in late 1990s appealed to anglers demanding big-boat comfort, performance at a moderate price. Available with three- or four-stateroom floorplans, both with top-quality amenities, full-beam master suite, home-sized galley. Spacious cockpit came with full array of top-shelf fishing features; massive flybridge with wraparound lounge seating boasts refrigerator, standard hardtop. MAN 1,350hp engines cruise at an impressive 32 knots and reach a top speed of 35+ knots.

Length	60'0"	Fuel	1,140 gals.
Beam	17'0"	Water	240 gals.
Draft	4'8"	Headroom	6'6"
Weight	72,000#	Hull Type	Modified-V
Clearance	17'0"	Deadrise Aft	10°

See Page 555 For Resale Values

Ocean Yachts
Egg Harbor City, NJ
www.oceanyachtsinc.com

231-360-0827

Ocean 62 Super Sport
2002–08

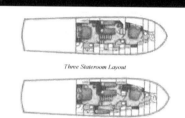

Three Stateroom Layout

Four Stateroom Layout

Handsome sportfisherman offers Ocean's signature blend of aggressive styling, eye-popping luxury, ex-hilarating performance. Opulent interior offers sev-eral high-end decor packages with choice of three or four staterooms. (Laundry room replaces starboard guest cab-in in three-stateroom layout.) Salon staircase in Enclosed Bridge model provides direct bridge access. Cockpit di-mensions are modest for a 62-footer. Cat 1,400hp diesels cruise at a fast 32 knots (about 35 knots top). Optional 1500hp MTUs will hit 38 knots wide open.

Length	62'0"	Headroom	6'5"
Beam	17'5"	Fuel	1,450 gals.
Draft	5'0"	Water	255 gals.
Weight	82,000#	Hull Type	Modified-V
Clearance	17'11"	Deadrise Aft	14°

See Page 555 For Resale Values

Ocean Yachts
Egg Harbor City, NJ
www.oceanyachtsinc.com

231-360-0827

Ocean 63 Super Sport
1986–91

Main Deck

Lower Deck

High-impact battlewagon made good on Ocean promise of speed, luxury, hardcore fishability. Opu-lent interior is arranged with four staterooms (two extending beneath the salon sole), expansive salon/galley/dinette area, amidships master, spacious VIP bow state-room. Note glass-enclosed rod locker in hallway. Cockpit is on the small side for a 63-footer, but flybridge is huge. Standard GM 900hp 12V71s cruise at 25 knots (about 28 knots top); 1,050hp GM engines cruise at 27–28 knots (30+ top). Total of 32 were built.

Length	63'0"	Fuel	1,200 gals.
Beam	17'8"	Water	300 gals.
Draft	4'8"	Cockpit	150 sq. ft.
Weight	74,000#	Hull Type	Modified-V
Clearance	14'9"	Deadrise Aft	3°

Prices Not Provided for Pre-1995 Models

Ocean Yachts
Egg Harbor City, NJ
www.oceanyachtsinc.com

231-360-0827

Ocean Master 27 Center Console
1987–Current

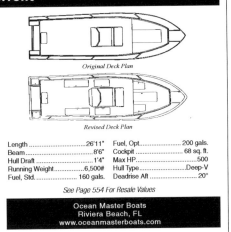

Original Deck Plan

Revised Deck Plan

Beefy 27-footer with bracket-mounted outboards gets high marks for efficient deck layout, bulletproof hull construction. Console storage compartment, huge 130-gallon forward fishbox, 50-gallon aft fishboxes, recirculating gallon livewell. Revised deck plan (with full inner liner) introduced in 2000 added more storage, increased freeboard. Excellent range with 200-gallon fuel capacity. Full-transom design results in very roomy cockpit. Terrific rough-water ride. Over 40 knots with twin 225s.

Length	26'11"	Fuel, Opt.	200 gals.
Beam	8'6"	Cockpit	68 sq. ft.
Hull Draft	1'4"	Max HP	500
Running Weight	6,500#	Hull Type	Deep-V
Fuel, Std.	160 gals.	Deadrise Aft	20°

See Page 554 For Resale Values

Ocean Master Boats
Riviera Beach, FL
www.oceanmasterboats.com

231-360-0827

Ocean Master 31 Center Console
1975–Current

Classic canyon runner launched in 1975 was among first big offshore center consoles on the market. Deck layout boasts 90 square feet of space aft of console—enough room for several anglers. Numerous updates offered over the years including reworked bottom in 1993, retooled deck in 1995, redesigned deck (with inner liner) in 1998. Note generous 310-gallon fuel capacity, step-up casting deck, deep cockpit, tremendous storage. Twin 225hp Yamahas reach about 40 knots top. Triple outboards are optional.

Length	30'7"	Fuel	310 gals.
Beam	10'3"	Cockpit	90 sq. ft.
Draft	1'4"	Max HP	750
Weight	5,500#	Hull Type	Modified-V
Water	None	Deadrise Aft	16°

Insufficient Resale Data To Assign Values

Ocean Master Boats
Riviera Beach, FL
www.oceanmasterboats.com

231-360-0827

Ocean Master 34 Center Console
1996–Current

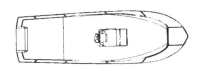

Semicustom center console with wide 11'6" beam delivers superior fishability, exceptional ride comfort. Standard deck plan is centered around large console with huge step-down storage compartment. Wide beam results in more cockpit space than many competitors. Layouts include traditional center console or Super Console with sleeping berths. Offered with gas or diesel inboard power, twin or triple outboards. Generous fuel capacity, top-quality hardware, bulletproof hull construction. About 35 knots top with twin 250s.

Length	34'0"	Fuel, Opt.	450 gals.
Beam	11'6"	Water	40 gals.
Draft	3'1"	Max HP	750
Running Weight	11,500#	Hull Type	Modified-V
Fuel, Std.	350 gals.	Deadrise Aft	16°

Insufficient Resale Data To Assign Values

Ocean Master Boats
Riviera Beach, FL
www.oceanmasterboats.com

Sportfishing Boats

Osprey 30
1999–Current

Tough pilothouse fisherman with sterndrive power offers exceptional heavy-weather performance, economical operation. Enclosed pilothouse, uncluttered cockpit will appeal to cold-weather anglers. Efficient cabin layout boasts extended galley area, convertible dinette, enclosed head with shower, but no stateroom privacy door. High freeboard results in a deep cockpit. Wide sidedecks and sturdy railings are a plus. Note heavy-duty window frames, watertight cabin door. Good engine access. Twin 188hp Volvo diesel I/Os cruise at 28 knots (low 30s top).

Length	30'4"	Water	36 gals.
Beam	10'0"	Waste	21 gals.
Draft	2'8"	Headroom	6'4"
Weight	11,000#	Cockpit	64 sq. ft.
Fuel	230/280 gals.	Hull Type	Deep-V

See Page 555 For Resale Values

Osprey Boats, Bellingham, WA
www.ospreyboats.com

Pace 40 Convertible
1988–1992

Taiwan remake of Egg Harbor 40 Sedan (1975–86) remains true to the original in all important aspects. Standard two-stateroom interior is similar to later-model Egg 40s with spacious main salon, mid-level galley, single head with separate stall shower. Extensive teak interior joinery is exceptionally well crafted. Cockpit features includes teak sole and covering boards, bait-prep center, fishbox, transom door. Still a great-looking convertible. Caterpillar 375hp diesels cruise around 22 knots; 485hp 6-71 Detroits cruise about 25 knots.

Length	40'0"	Fuel	450 gals.
Beam	14'0"	Water	100 gals.
Draft	2'9"	Cockpit	95 sq. ft.
Weight	28,000#	Hull Type	Modified-V
Clearance	NA	Deadrise Aft	NA

Prices Not Provided for Pre-1995 Models

Pace Yachts is no longer in business.

Pace 48 Convertible
1987–92

Taiwan knockoff of classic 48 Golden Egg delivered comfort, performance at an affordable price. Two-stateroom, two-head layout (similar to later-model Egg 48s) boasts wide-open salon with extensive teak cabinetry, copious storage. Tackle center, transom door, cockpit controls were standard. Roomy bridge can seat a small crowd. Note teak cockpit sole and cover boards. Narrow, low-deadrise hull with fine entry is quick to accelerate for a big boat. Standard 735hp GM diesels cruise at 25 knots (28–29 knots top).

Length	48'2"	Fuel	720 gals.
Beam	15'0"	Water	200 gals.
Draft	4'4"	Cockpit	NA
Weight	40,000#	Hull Type	Modified-V
Clearance	NA	Deadrise Aft	2°

Prices Not Provided for Pre-1995 Models

Pace Yachts is no longer in business.

231-360-0827

Pearson 38 Convertible
1987–91

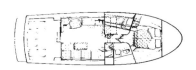

Classy flybridge cruiser introduced in 1987 was Pearson's first-ever convertible model. Rakish styling has held up well over the years. Two-stateroom interior with deckhouse galley, head with stall shower sleeps six. Note satin-finished oak trim, salon entertainment center. Additional features included bow pulpit, transom door, swim platform. Above-average fit and finish. Deep-V hull performs well in rough seas. No racehorse, Cat 375hp diesels cruise at 22–23 knots and deliver a top speed in the neighborhood of 26 knots.

Length	37'6"	Fuel	410 gals.
Beam	13'10"	Water	120 gals.
Draft	3'9"	Cockpit	NA
Weight	24,000#	Hull Type	Deep-V
Clearance	NA	Deadrise Aft	19°

Prices Not Provided for Pre-1995 Models

The original Pearson Yacht Company ended operations in 1991.

231-360-0827

Phoenix 27 Tournament
1990–99

Rugged inboard express with 90-square-foot cockpit has more fishing space than most boats her size. Topside amenities include lockable rod storage, in-deck fishbox, transom door, wide side decks. Note well-arranged helm with lockable electronics box. Commonsense cabin includes stand-up head with shower, mini-galley, convertible dinette/lounge. Deep-V hull with prop pockets delivers a good offshore ride. Cruise in the low 20s with 260hp gas inboards (28–30 knots top); Volvo 200hp diesels cruise at 22–24 knots.

Length w/Pulpit	30'3"	Clearance	7'6"
Hull Length	27'3"	Fuel	220 gals.
Beam	9'10"	Water	24 gals.
Draft	2'0"	Hull Type	Deep-V
Weight	8,200#	Deadrise Aft	20°

See Page 556 For Resale Values

Phoenix Yachts is no longer in business.

231-360-0827

Phoenix 29 Convertible
1977–87

Hugely popular convertible introduced in 1977 combined versatile layout, sturdy construction. Large bi-level cockpit, strong-running deep-V hull (with prop pockets) made this boat a favorite with offshore anglers. Modest cabin with compact galley, stand-up head with shower, convertible dinette sleeps four. Available with or without cabin bulkhead. Note small bridge, slender side decks. Volvo 124hp diesels cruise at 18 knots (22 knots top). Later models with 165hp Volvos cruise at 20–21 knots. Total of 750 were built.

Length	28'10"	Fuel	160/260 gals.
Beam	10'0"	Water	50 gals.
Draft	2'4"	Cockpit	75 sq. ft.
Weight	8,500#	Hull Type	Deep-V
Clearance	9'6"	Deadrise Aft	21°

Prices Not Provided for Pre-1995 Models

Phoenix Yachts is no longer in business.

Sportfishing Boats

231-360-0827

Phoenix 29 SFX Convertible
1988–99

Restyled version of earlier Phoenix 29 (1977–87) offered good performance, impressive quality at a reasonable price. Large fishing cockpit with transom door accommodates two anglers and their gear. Cabin sleeps four or six depending on layout. Flybridge is huge for a boat this size. Unique air duct system rids cockpit of exhaust fumes. Prop pockets reduce draft, improve fuel efficiency. Twin 270hp gas engines cruise at 22 knots (29–30 knots top). Volvo 200hp diesels cruise at 25 knots (around 30 knots top).

Length w/Pulpit	31'11"	Clearance	9'6"
Hull Length	29'0"	Fuel	180 gals.
Beam	10'0"	Water	50 gals.
Draft	2'4"	Hull Type	Deep-V
Weight	9,450#	Deadrise Aft	22°

See Page 556 For Resale Values

Phoenix Yachts is no longer in business.

231-360-0827

Phoenix 32 Tournament
1997–99

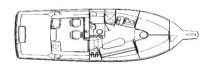

Versatile open fisherman with distinctive styling was the last Phoenix introduction before the company closed in 1999. Centerline helm puts driver in the most comfortable spot on the boat. Cockpit amenities include bait-prep center, freezer, broad transom door with gate. Comfortable cabin boasts head with stall shower, upright rod storage, full galley, berths for four. Note flared bow, small windshield. Above-average fit and finish. Optional Cat 350hp—or Volvo 370hp—diesels cruise at 25 knots (28–29 knots wide open).

Length w/Pulpit	34'8"	Weight, Diesel	19,320#
Hull Length	32'1"	Fuel	320 gals.
Beam	12'0"	Water	76 gals.
Draft	2'9"	Hull Type	Modified-V
Weight, Gas	16,360#	Deadrise Aft	17°

See Page 556 For Resale Values

Phoenix Yachts is no longer in business.

231-360-0827

Phoenix 33/34 SFX Convertible
1987–99

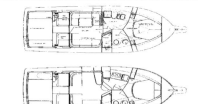

Quality convertible with appealing styling, good seakeeping ability was built to last. Large cockpit with transom door, cushioned engine boxes has room for full-size chair. Offered with several cabin layouts over the years, all with galley down, stall shower in head. Flybridge is big for a 34-footer with seating for five, lockable rod storage. Note low cockpit freeboard. Standard gas engines cruise at 19 knots (high 20s top); optional 350hp Cat diesels cruise at 22 knots and reach 30+ knots top. (Called Phoenix 33 Convertible in 1987–94.)

Length w/Pulpit	36'9"	Weight, Diesel	23,600#
Hull Length	33'9"	Fuel	300 gals.
Beam	13'0"	Water	70 gals.
Draft	2'9"	Hull Type	Modified-V
Weight, Gas	20,810#	Deadrise Aft	17°

See Page 556 For Resale Values

Phoenix Yachts is no longer in business.

231-360-0827

Phoenix 33/34 Tournament
1990–99

Sure-footed express from 1990s was designed for hardcore, tournament-minded anglers. Expansive single-level cockpit with aft-facing bait station, in-deck fishbox is ideal for stand-up fishing. Engine boxes double as bait-watching seats. Cozy cabin with U-shaped dinette, compact galley, head with shower sleeps four. Prop-pocket hull can cruise in very skinny water. Good attention to detail. Cat 375hp diesels cruise in the mid 20s (about 30 knots top); later models with 420hp Cats cruise at 28 knots and reach 30+ wide open.

Length w/Pulpit	36'9"	Weight, Diesel	23,680#
Hull Length	33'9"	Fuel	300 gals.
Beam	13'0"	Water	70 gals.
Draft	2'9"	Hull Type	Modified-V
Weight, Gas	19,600#	Deadrise Aft	17°

See Page 556 For Resale Values

Phoenix Yachts is no longer in business.

231-360-0827

Phoenix 37/38 SFX Convertible
1989–99

Premium 1990s fishing machine (called Phoenix 37 Convertible in 1989–94) delivered impressive mix of quality construction, solid performance. Wide 14-foot beam means lots of cockpit, cabin space. Fishing features include big in-deck fishboxes, transom door with gate, complete tackle center. Deluxe two-stateroom interior gets high marks for comfort and finish. Air intake vents forward of bridge channel air into cockpit to reduce fumes. No front windows. Cat 375hp diesels cruise at 22–23 knots; 485hp GMs cruise at 26–27 knots.

Length w/Pulpit	41'11"	Clearance	12'7"
Hull Length	37'10"	Fuel	440 gals.
Beam	14'0"	Water	100 gals.
Draft	3'7"	Hull Type	Deep-V
Weight	30,800#	Deadrise Aft	18°

See Page 556 For Resale Values

Phoenix Yachts is no longer in business.

231-360-0827

Phoenix 38 Convertible
1982–88

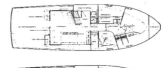
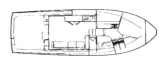

Big-water 1980s convertible proved a tournament-level fishing machine could be luxurious, tough at the same time. Wide 14-foot beam means lots of cockpit, cabin space. Original mid-galley layout with serving counter was criticized for small salon; more open layout introduced in later years moved the galley into salon. Cockpit engineroom access is rare in a 38-footer. Solid front windshield became optional in 1988. Cat 375hp diesels cruise at 18–20 knots (mid 20s top). Optional 450hp 6-71s cruise at 22 knots.

Length	38'0"	Fuel	400 gals.
Beam	14'0"	Water	100 gals.
Draft	3'7"	Cockpit	NA
Weight	25,000#	Hull Type	Deep-V
Clearance	12'1"	Deadrise Aft	18°

Prices Not Provided for Pre-1995 Models

Phoenix Yachts is no longer in business.

231-360-0827

Post 42 Sport Fisherman
1975–83

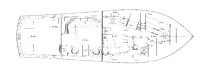

Classic Post convertible combined top-quality construction with deluxe accommodations, superior open-water handling. Mahogany galley-down interior features roomy salon, large galley, amidships master suite with double berth. Built with glass-over-wood deck and superstructure until mid-1976; fiberglass construction thereafter. Front windshield was eliminated in 1979. Considered among best mid-range sportfishermen of her era. GM 310hp diesels cruise at 18–19 knots; 410hp GMs cruise at 22–23 knots. Over 230 were built.

Length	42'0"	Fuel	460/500 gals.
Beam	15'9"	Water	120 gals.
Draft	3'0"	Cockpit	115 sq. ft.
Weight	30,000#	Hull Type	Modified-V
Clearance	12'6"	Deadrise Aft	6°

Prices Not Provided for Pre-1995 Models

Post Marine
Mays Landing, NJ
www.postyachts.com

231-360-0827

Post 42 Sport Fisherman
1997–Current

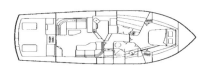

Gold-plated sportfisherman strikes near perfect balance of beauty, comfort, power. Richly appointed interior features spacious salon with L-shaped dinette, big master stateroom, guest cabin with over/under bunks. Washer/dryer installs in alcove abaft head. Extended flybridge is bigger than it looks with seating for eight, rod storage, well-arranged helm. Meticulous engineroom is accessed from under cockpit step. Cruise at 24–25 knots (28 top) with Volvo 430hp diesels. Cummins 480hp diesels cruise in high 20s (30+ knots top).

Length	42'10"	Fuel	529 gals.
Beam	15'9"	Water	114 gals.
Draft	4'0"	Waste	31 gals.
Weight	42,996#	Hull Type	Modified-V
Clearance, Hardtop	16'11"	Deadrise Aft	7°

See Page 556 For Resale Values

Post Marine
Mays Landing, NJ
www.postyachts.com

231-360-0827

Post 43 Sport Fisherman
1984–89

Updated version of classic Post 42 SF (1975–83) made a good boat even better. Second spray rail, increased transom deadrise improved head-sea performance. Spacious interior has large master stateroom forward, guest cabin with single berths to port. Note solid teak cabinetry, salon entertainment center, overhead rod storage. Post 43 III model introduced in 1989 included several standard-equipment updates. Twin GM 485hp engines cruise in the mid 20s (27–28 knots top). Optional 550hp GMs run a couple of knots faster.

Length	43'8"	Water	120 gals.
Beam	15'9"	Fuel	500/550 gals.
Draft	3'6"	Cockpit	125 sq. ft.
Weight	33,000#	Hull Type	Modified-V
Clearance	13'7"	Deadrise Aft	8°

Prices Not Provided for Pre-1995 Models

Post Marine
Mays Landing, NJ
www.postyachts.com

Post 43 Sport Fisherman
1995–96

Updated version of popular Post 44 SF (1990–94) combines hardcore fishability with plush accommodations, spirited performance. Expansive salon—much larger than earlier 44—includes built-in dinette, full entertainment center. Island berth dominates large master stateroom; solid teak cabinets, plush furnishings highlight interior. Roomy engine compartment with cockpit access is a plus. Topside helm layout was state-of-the-art in her era. GM 535hp diesels cruise in the high 20s and reach a top speed of about 30 knots.

Length	43'9"	Water	120 gals.
Beam	15'9"	Clearance	13'7"
Draft	3'6"	Cockpit	125 sq. ft.
Weight	40,000#	Hull Type	Modified-V
Fuel	543 gals.	Deadrise Aft	7°

See Page 556 For Resale Values

Post Marine
Mays Landing, NJ
www.postyachts.com

Post 44 Sport Fisherman
1990–94

Premium sportfishing yacht from early 1990s delivered successful blend of quality, luxury, performance. Two-stateroom interior includes two heads—most boats this size have just one—resulting in relatively compact salon. Rich teak woodwork, quality furnishings are typical of Post's sophisticated interiors. Note excellent helm visibility, superb helm console. Large cockpit has tackle center, in-deck fishboxes, transom door. Cockpit engineroom access became standard in 1992. Cruise at 27–28 knots (30+ top) with GM 550hp diesels.

Length	43'9"	Fuel	570 gals.
Beam	15'9"	Water	120 gals.
Draft	3'6"	Cockpit	125 sq. ft.
Weight	33,000#	Hull Type	Modified-V
Clearance	13'7"	Deadrise Aft	7°

Prices Not Provided for Pre-1995 Models

Post Marine
Mays Landing, NJ
www.postyachts.com

Post 46 Sport Fisherman
1978–96

Floorplan A 46

Floorplan A 46 II

Classic Jersey-bred convertible with graceful lines, easy-riding hull led the field in her era for beauty, workmanship, owner appeal. Several two-stateroom layouts were offered, all with handcrafted teak woodwork, top-quality appliances and furnishings. Updated 46 II model (1988–96) features cockpit engineroom door, stand-up engineroom. Early models with 410hp 6-71 Detroit diesels cruise at 20 knots. Later 46 II models with 485hp 6-71s cruise at 23–24 knots; 625hp 6V92 diesels cruise at 25–26 knots.

Length	46'9"	Fuel	620 gals.
Beam	15'9"	Water	120 gals.
Draft	3'10"	Waste	31 gals.
Weight	44,000#	Hull Type	Modified-V
Clearance, Windshield	13'7"	Deadrise Aft	3°/7°

See Page 556 For Resale Values

Post Marine
Mays Landing, NJ
www.postyachts.com

231-360-0827

Post 47 Sport Fisherman
1997–Current

Plan A

Plan B

Refined version of venerable Post 46 SF (1978–96) is beautifully styled, luxuriously appointed, competitively priced. Offered with choice of two-stateroom interiors: Plan A has master forward, Plan B has amidships master. Washer/dryer is standard. Highlights include high-gloss interior joinery, huge bridge with centerline helm, meticulous engineroom. Cockpit is among the largest in her class. Detroit 625hp diesels cruise at 25 knots (29–30 knots top); 680hp MANs cruise at 28 knots (around 32 knots top).

Length	46'9"	Fuel	635 gals.
Beam	15'9"	Water	120 gals.
Draft	4'2"	Waste	31 gals.
Weight	49,668#	Hull Type	Modified-V
Clearance, Hardtop	16'11"	Deadrise Aft	7°

See Page 556 For Resale Values

Post Marine
Mays Landing, NJ
www.postyachts.com

231-360-0827

Post 50 Convertible
1989–Current

Plan A 1989–96

Plan A 1997–Current

Muscular tournament machine with signature Post styling delivers high-octane mix of quality construction, lush accommodations, world-class performance. Wide 16'11" beam results in truly expansive interior for a 50-footer. Highlights include spacious master suite, standard washer/dryer, massive 150-sq. ft. cockpit with controls, huge flybridge. Engineroom headroom increased in 1995 when fuel tanks were moved aft. Over 100 built. GM 735hp diesels cruise 27–28 knots; later models with 860hp MANs cruise at 30+ knots.

Length	50'7"	Fuel	870 gals.
Beam	16'11"	Water	240 gals.
Draft	4'6"	Waste	42 gals.
Weight	57,122#	Hull Type	Modified-V
Clearance, Hardtop	17'2"	Deadrise Aft	7°

See Page 556 For Resale Values

Post Marine
Mays Landing, NJ
www.postyachts.com

231-360-0827

Post 53 Convertible
2005–Current

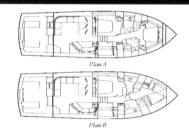

Plan A

Plan B

Premium fishing machine targets deep-poclet anglers with an eye for beauty, quality. Opulent three-stateroom interior with combined salon/galley/dinette offers unsurpassed luxury, exemplary fit and finish. Note high-gloss teak cabinetry, frameless windows, companionway washer/dryer. Additional highlights include large, tournament-ready cockpit with wide transom door, meticulous engineroom, huge flybridge with seating for a small crowd. MTU 1,200hp engines cruise at 30 knots (about 35 knots top).

Length	52'10"	Fuel	926 gals.
Beam	16'11"	Water	240 gals.
Draft	5'0"	Waste	80 gals.
Weight	59,000#	Hull Type	Modified-V
Clearance	NA	Deadrise Aft	7°

See Page 556 For Resale Values

Post Marine
Mays Landing, NJ
www.postyachts.com

Sportfishing Boats

Post 56 Convertible
2002–Current

231-360-0827

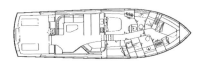

World-class convertible from one of America's premier builders is fast, luxurious, built for fishing. Lavish three-stateroom interior with lacquered teak joinery is notable for meticulous finish, top-quality furnishings. Under-counter refrigeration maximizes counter space in galley; washer/dryer is located in hallway. Tournament-ready cockpit is one of the largest of any boat this size. Flybridge boasts state-of-the-art helm, generous guest seating, rod storage. MAN 1,300hp engines cruise at 31–32 knots (35+ knots top).

Length	55'11"	Fuel	1,200 gals.
Beam	16'11"	Water	250 gals.
Draft	5'6"	Waste	80 gals.
Weight	66,830#	Hull Type	Deep-V
Clearance, Hardtop	17'6"	Deadrise Aft	7°

See Page 556 For Resale Values

Post Marine
Mays Landing, NJ
www.postyachts.com

Pro-Line 27 Express
2001–04

231-360-0827

Versatile walkaround cuddy with innovative layout blurs the line between family fisherman, weekend cruiser. Cockpit amenities include 35-gallon livewell, in-deck fishboxes, built-in tackle box, padded bolsters, cushioned rear seat, transom door. Lounge seat opposite helm seats three. Compact cabin has V-berth, portable head. Side walkways are wide with well-placed handholds, sturdy rails. Note galley cabinet forward of helm. Called Pro-Line 29 Express in 2005. About 40 knots max with twin 225s.

Length w/Pulpit	29'1"	Water	30 gals.
Beam	9'10"	Cockpit	80 sq. ft.
Hull Draft	1'9"	Max HP	500
Dry Weight	5,900#	Hull Type	Deep-V
Fuel	200 gals.	Deadrise Aft	19°

See Page 557 For Resale Values

Pro-Line Boats
Crystal River, FL
www.prolineboats.com

Pro-Line 27 Walk
1998–2004

231-360-0827

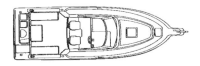

Generic walkaround cabin with generous 9'10" beam is roomy, well styled, affordable. Fishing features include 35-gallon transom livewell, two in-deck fish/storage boxes, bait-prep station, tackle storage, transom door. Roomy cabin with four opening ports includes full galley, stand-up head with shower, convertible dinette/V-berth. Tall windshield provides good wind, spray protection. Hardtop was a popular option. Note wide walkways. Called Pro-Line 2610 Walkaround in 1998–99. About 40 knots top with twin 225s.

Length	29'1"	Fuel	200 gals.
Beam	9'10"	Water	30 gals.
Hull Draft	1'9"	Max HP	500
Hull Weight	5,900#	Hull Type	Deep-V
Clearance	7'9"	Deadrise Aft	19°

See Page 557 For Resale Values

Pro-Line Boats
Crystal River, FL
www.prolineboats.com

Pro-Line 27/29 Sport
2000–06

Tough center console with wide 9'10" beam, impressive standard equipment was a lot of boat for the money. Spacious cockpit with bow casting platform offers more fishing space than most boats her size. Standard features include 35-gallon livewell, in-deck fishboxes, transom door, tackle box, pop-up cleats, leaning post with rocket launcher, console cooler. Large console houses roomy stand-up head compartment. Called the Pro-Line 27 Sport in 2000–04; 29 Sport in 2005–06. About 40 knots top with twin 225s.

Length w/Pulpit	29'1"	Fuel	200 gals.
Beam	9'10"	Water	15 gals.
Hull Draft	1'8"	Max HP	500
Dry Weight	5,200#	Hull Type	Deep-V
Clearance	NA	Deadrise Aft	19°

See Page 557 For Resale Values

Pro-Line Boats
Crystal River, FL
www.prolineboats.com

Pro-Line 2700 Sportsman
1993–99

Full-transom center console with spacious cockpit hit the right buttons with 1990s anglers looking for space, affordability. Fishing features include transom bait station with livewell, raised bow casting platform, console head compartment, leaning post with rocket launchers, rod storage racks, three in-deck fishboxes (two aft, one forward), tackle drawers, fresh/saltwater washdowns, transom door. Wide 9'10" beam is a foot wider than many 27-foot center consoles. About 40 knots top with twin 225s.

Length	27'6"	Fuel	200 gals.
Beam	9'10"	Water	15 gals.
Hull Draft	1'8"	Max HP	500
Dry Weight	4,750#	Hull Type	Deep-V
Clearance	8'4"	Deadrise Aft	19°

See Page 557 For Resale Values

Pro-Line Boats
Crystal River, FL
www.prolineboats.com

Pro-Line 2810 Walkaround
1997–2000

Popular family fisherman with center helm position delivers traditional Pro-Line mix of rugged construction, large fishing cockpit, comfortable accommodations. Amenities include large 42-gallon livewell, in-deck fishboxes, raw-water washdown, tackle storage drawers, bait-prep station, rod storage. Cozy cabin includes removable table, galley cabinet, rod storage locker, enclosed head with shower. Note large electronics box, tilt-out dash panel. Called the Pro-Line 28 Walk in 2000. About 40 knots top with 225 Mercs.

Length w/Pulpit	29'6"	Fuel	200 gals.
Beam	10'2"	Water	21 gals.
Hull Draft	2'1"	Max HP	500
Hull Weight	6,500#	Hull Type	Deep-V
Cockpit	72 sq. ft.	Deadrise Aft	21°

See Page 557 For Resale Values

Pro-Line Boats
Crystal River, FL
www.prolineboats.com

231-360-0827

Pro-Line 29 Grand Sport
2007–Current

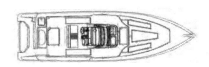

Maxi-volume 29-footer with deep cockpit, wide beam has the fishing space of many 33-footers. Standard features include leaning post with backrest, big 50-gallon livewell, two in-deck fishboxes, foldaway rear seat, fresh/saltwater washdowns, folding rear seat, transom door. Very roomy head compartment, huge electronics flat. Low-profile bow rails, pop-up cleats prevent line snags; console hinges forward for wiring access. Beamy hull is stable in rough seas. About 45 knots top with twin 225s.

Length	29'4"	Fuel	240 gals.
Beam	9'8"	Water	15 gals.
Hull Draft	1'10"	Max HP	500
Hull Weight	6,310#	Hull Type	Deep-V
Clearance	7'11"	Deadrise Aft	22°

See Page 557 For Resale Values

Pro-Line Boats
Crystal River, FL
www.prolineboats.com

231-360-0827

Pro-Line 29 Super Sport
2005–Current

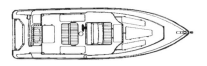

High-performance tournament machine with slender 9-foot beam targets big-water anglers who place a premium on speed, agility. Highlights include raised bow casting platform, large-capacity fishbox, leaning post with tackle station, lockable rod storage, enclosed head compartment, console cooler, fresh/saltwater washdowns, bow storage lockers. Big 45-gallon livewell is located beneath transom seat. Tall windshield offers good wind, spray protection. Deep-V hull can take a pounding. Max 45+ knots with Mercury 250s.

Length	28'7"	Fuel	192 gals.
Beam	9'0"	Water	15 gals.
Hull Draft	1'7"	Max HP	500
Hull Weight	5,300#	Hull Type	Deep-V
Cockpit	101 sq. ft.	Deadrise Aft	22°

See Page 557 For Resale Values

Pro-Line Boats
Crystal River, FL
www.prolineboats.com

231-360-0827

Pro-Line 2950 Mid Cabin
1992–2000

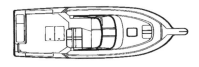

Sturdy Pro-Line express available with outboard or sterndrive power offers versatility, comfort at an attractive price. Highlights include bait station with livewell, built-in tackle box, transom door, raw-water washdown, insulated fishboxes, cockpit bolsters, rear bench seat. Mid-cabin interior with enclosed head/shower, full galley, rod storage, removable dinette sleeps three. Most were sold with optional hardtop. Very popular model for Pro-Line. Cruise at 20 knots with single 260hp MerCruiser I/O; 25 knots with twin 225 Merc outboards.

Length	30'0"	Fuel	220 gals.
Beam	10'9"	Water	42 gals.
Draft, Up	1'10"	Max HP	500
Hull Weight	7,500#	Hull Type	Deep-V
Cockpit	80 sq. ft.	Deadrise Aft	19°

See Page 557 For Resale Values

Pro-Line Boats
Crystal River, FL
www.prolineboats.com

Sportfishing Boats

231-360-0827

Pro-Line 30 Walkaround
2000—05

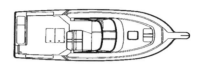

Restyled version of earlier Pro-Line 2950 (1992–2000) with integrated transom added new life to popular design. Versatile layout offers proven fishability with room for entertaining. Standard features included 45-gallon livewell, built-in tackle box, insulated fishboxes, freshwater sink, transom door. Well-appointed cabin with full galley, enclosed head with shower, mid-cabin berth sleeps three. Note deep walkways. Tops out around 40 knots with 225hp outboards. (Called Pro-Line 31 Walk in 2005.)

Length	32'6"	Fuel	300 gals.
Beam	10'10"	Water	39 gals.
Hull Draft	1'10"	Max HP	600
Hull Weight	7,600#	Hull Type	Deep-V
Cockpit	84 sq. ft.	Deadrise Aft	19°

See Page 557 For Resale Values

Pro-Line Boats
Crystal River, FL
www.prolineboats.com

www.powerboatguide.com   231-360-0827

Pro-Line 30 Express
2000—05

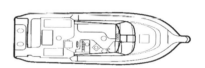

Good-looking express with innovative layout is more family dayboat than hardcore fishing boat. Expansive deck plan with open-air galey, forward lounge seating is uniquely suited for entertaining. Standard features include livewell, in-deck fishboxes, integrated tackle box, transom door, bow pulpit. Compact cabin is arranged with double berth forward, standup head with shower, storage bin aft with wine rack. Helm is well aft, reducing cockpit fishing space. Called 31 Express in 2005. About 40 knots top with twin 225s.

Length	32'6"	Fuel	312 gals.
Beam	10'10"	Water	30 gals.
Hull Draft	1'10"	Max HP	500
Hull Weight	7,700#	Hull Type	Deep-V
Cockpit	102 sq. ft.	Deadrise Aft	19°

See Page 557 For Resale Values

Pro-Line Boats
Crystal River, FL
www.prolineboats.com

www.powerboatguide.com   231-360-0827

Pro-Line 30/31 Sport
2000—06

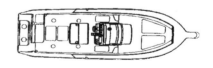

Big-water canyon runner with extra-wide beam (called Pro-Line 30 Sport in 2000–04; 31 Sport in 2005–06) meets angler's need for space, stability, comfort. Highlights include 45-gallon transom livewell, huge bow casting platform, transom door, lockable electronics storage, insulated fishboxes, rear bench seat, pop-up cleats, tackle storage. Enormous console houses enclosed head with sink and sleeping berth. More usable cockpit space than most center consoles her size. About 40 knots top with 250 Mercs.

Length	32'6"	Fuel	300 gals.
Beam	10'10"	Water	39 gals.
Hull Draft	1'10"	Max HP	600
Dry Weight	7,000#	Hull Type	Deep-V
Cockpit	145 sq. ft.	Deadrise Aft	19°

See Page 557 For Resale Values

Pro-Line Boats
Crystal River, FL
www.prolineboats.com

Sportfishing Boats

Pro-Line 32 Express
2005–Current

Versatile express combines durable Pro-Line construction with value-priced amenities, feature-rich accommodations. Standard fishing gear includes two in-deck fishboxes, 35-gallon livewell, tackle drawers, fresh/raw-water washdowns. Note aft-facing cockpit seat, foldaway stern seat. Roomy midcabin interior with full galley, enclosed head/shower sleeps four. Large lazarette can accommodate optional generator. Good range with generous 300-gallon fuel capacity. About 40 knots top with twin Mercury 250s.

Length	32'4"	Fuel	300 gals.
Beam	10'10"	Water	39 gals.
Hull Draft	1'11"	Max HP	600
Hull Weight	9,500#	Hull Type	Deep-V
Clearance, Top	10'2"	Deadrise Aft	22°

See Page 557 For Resale Values

Pro-Line Boats
Crystal River, FL
www.prolineboats.com

Pro-Line 3250/32 Express
1997–2002

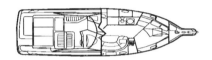

Sporty sterndrive express (called 3250 Express in 1997–99; 32 Express thereafter) combined large cockpit with no-frills interior, reasonable price. Cockpit amenities included bait station with 35-gallon livewell, cockpit bolsters, tackle drawers, lockable rod storage, transom door. Small-but-efficient cabin offers convertible U-shaped dinette forward, midberth aft, mini-galley, stand-up head with shower. Folding privacy door separates aft berth from salon. Twin 310hp MerCruiser (or Volvo) I/Os cruise in the high 20s (38–40 knots top).

Length	33'8"	Fuel	250 gals.
Beam	11'0"	Water	35 gals.
Hull Draft	2'1"	Waste	15 gals.
Weight	12,000#	Hull Type	Deep-V
Clearance	7'4"	Deadrise Aft	19°

See Page 557 For Resale Values

Pro-Line Boats
Crystal River, FL
www.prolineboats.com

Pro-Line 33 Express
1999–2006

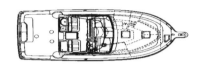

Appealing inboard fishing machine with broad beam holds her own against more expensive competitors. Cockpit came standard with bait-prep center, 35-gallon livewell, dual washdowns, transom fishbox, raw-water washdown, transom door. Teak-trimmed cabin with full galley, convertible dinette, rod storage, enclosed head/shower sleeps four. Entire bridgedeck lifts electrically for engine access. Excellent engine access. Yanmar 315hp diesels cruise at 24–26 knots (about 30 knots top); Yanmar 370 top out at 32–34 knots.

Length	33'0"	Fuel	300 gals.
Beam	12'6"	Water	40 gals.
Draft	3'5"	Waste	20 gals.
Weight	11,200#	Hull Type	Deep-V
Clearance	7'8"	Deadrise Aft	19°

See Page 557 For Resale Values

Pro-Line Boats
Crystal River, FL
www.prolineboats.com

Sportfishing Boats

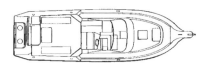

www.powerboatguide.com 231-360-0827

Pro-Line 33 Walkaround
2003–05

Well-rounded express (called Pro-Line 34 Walkaround in 2005) delivers signature Pro-Line fishability, comfort without breaking the bank account. Roomy cockpit came standard with two in-deck fishboxes, raw-water washdown, padded bolsters, lockable rod storage, transom door, tackle station with sink. Forty-gallon oval livewell resides under lift-up transom seat. No-frills cabin with convertible dinette, midcabin berth sleeps four adults, two kids. Windlass, bow pulpit were standard. Nearly 40 knots top with twin 225s.

Length	33'8"	Fuel	285 gals.
Beam	11'0"	Water	39 gals.
Hull Draft	2'1"	Max HP	600
Dry Weight	12,000#	Hull Type	Deep-V
Clearance	6'10"	Deadrise Aft	19°

See Page 557 For Resale Values

Pro-Line Boats
Crystal River, FL
www.prolineboats.com

---

www.powerboatguide.com 231-360-0827

Pro-Line 3400 Super Sport Cuddy
1998–2001

Floorplan Not Available

Full-throttle sportster with low-profile cuddy outguns most competitors for open-water speed, agility. Fishing amenities include recirculating livewell, two in-deck fishboxes, leaning post, under-gunwale rod storage, tackle station, raw-water washdown. Console houses stand-up head with sink, shower. Bow pulpit, console cooler, transom door were standard. Offered in both Cuddy and Open versions. Deep-V hull is fully cored to reduce weight. Twin 250hp Mercury outboards reach 40+ knots. Triple 200s hit 50+ knots wide open.

Length	34'10"	Fuel	300 gals.
Beam	9'2"	Water	30 gals.
Hull Draft	2'1"	Max HP	675
Dry Weight	7,500#	Hull Type	Deep-V
Cockpit	112 sq. ft	Deadrise Aft	22.5°

See Page 557 For Resale Values

Pro-Line Boats
Crystal River, FL
www.prolineboats.com

---

www.powerboatguide.com 231-360-0827

Pro-Line 35 Express
2006–Current

Hard-charging fishboat/cruiser rated for triple-outboard power blends modern styling with upmarket amenities, versatile layout. Highlights include large 45-gallon livewell, in-deck fishboxes, tackle storage center, dual washdowns, pop-up cleats, foldaway stern seat, L-shaped bridgedeck seating. Well-appointed interior with midship berth, enclosed head/shower, dinette sleeps four. Note easy access to pumps, generator. Good helm visibility. Twin 250hp outboards top out at 40 knots; triple 225s reach close to 50 knots top.

Length	35'6"	Water	60 gals.
Beam	12'6"	Waste	21 gals.
Hull Draft	2'1"	Max HP	900
Hull Weight	11,200#	Hull Type	Deep-V
Fuel	320 gals.	Deadrise Aft	19°

See Page 557 For Resale Values

Pro-Line Boats
Crystal River, FL
www.prolineboats.com

231-360-0827

Pursuit 2700 Open
1983–93

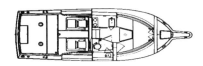

Classic inboard express—essentially a Tiara 2700 Open (1988–93) with additional fishing features—has well-earned reputation for reliability, owner satisfaction. Spacious 12-foot cockpit is large enough for a mounted chair. Upscale cabin features V-berth/dinette forward, full galley, stand-up head with shower. Motor boxes provide good engine access. Note sturdy windshield, aggressive cockpit nonskid. Deep-V hull delivers good open-water ride. Standard 270hp gas engines cruise in the low 20s (about 30 knots top).

Length w/Pulpit	29'5"	Fuel	240 gals.
Hull Length	27'0"	Water	30 gals.
Beam	10'0"	Waste	20 gals.
Hull Draft	2'2"	Hull Type	Deep-V
Dry Weight	7,500#	Deadrise Aft	22°

Prices Not Provided for Pre-1995 Models

Pursuit Boats
Ft. Pierce, FL
www.pursuitboats.com

231-360-0827

Pursuit 2800 Open
1989–92

Well-built express fishing boat introduced in 1989 appeals to anglers looking for space, quality, fishability. Wide 10-foot beam provides stability required to handle topside weight of a small tower. Uncluttered cockpit features aft-facing jump seat with livewell under, in-floor fishbox, rod holders. Classy cabin with enclosed head, complete galley, generous storage sleeps two. Note very wide side decks, sturdy windshield, integral bow pulpit. Twin 225hp outboards cruise at 25 knots (about 40 knots wide open).

Length w/Pulpit	30'4"	Clearance	6'9"
Hull Length	28'2"	Fuel	290 gals.
Beam	10'0"	Water	22 gals.
Hull Draft	1'9"	Hull Type	Deep-V
Weight	5,500#	Deadrise Aft	20°

Prices Not Provided for Pre-1995 Models

Pursuit Boats
Ft. Pierce, FL
www.pursuitboats.com

231-360-0827

Pursuit 2855 Express Fisherman
1993–95

High-end 1990s express with handsome lines gets anglers offshore in style and comfort. Topside highlights include well-designed helm with room for electronics, wide side decks, integral bow pulpit, large cockpit with bait rigging station, two large fishboxes, recirculating livewell. Upscale cabin with full galley, enclosed head sleeps four. Note center windshield vent, exemplary fit and finish. Big 300-gallon fuel capacity offers excellent range. Twin 250hp Yamahas deliver a top speed of close to 40 knots.

Length w/Pulpit	33'3"	Fuel	300 gals.
Hull Length	31'0"	Water	30 gals.
Beam	10'3"	Max HP	500
Hull Draft	1'9"	Hull Type	Deep-V
Weight	6,500#	Deadrise Aft	20°

See Page 557 For Resale Values

Pursuit Boats
Ft. Pierce, FL
www.pursuitboats.com

Sportfishing Boats

Section II: Sportfishing Boats

Sportfishing Boats

---

www.powerboatguide.com 231-360-0827

Pursuit 2870 Offshore CC
1996–2002

Innovative offshore cruiser with centerline helm splits the difference between capable fishing boat, deluxe family cruiser. Cockpit comes with large in-floor fishbox, rod holders, transom rigging station with cutting board and sink. Leaning post houses 26-gallon livewell. Aft-facing jump seat next to helm sits atop a five-drawer tackle center. Upscale cabin with removable table, mini-galley sleeps two. Huge in-deck compartment aft of console provides access to batteries, oil reservoirs. Yamaha 225s cruise at 25 knots (40+ knots wide open).

Length w/Pulpit	30'0"	Fuel	234 gals.
Hull Length	28'0"	Water	20 gals.
Beam	9'6"	Max HP	450
Hull Draft	1'8"	Hull Type	Deep-V
Hull Weight	5,950#	Deadrise Aft	22°

See Page 557 For Resale Values

Pursuit Boats
Ft. Pierce, FL
www.pursuitboats.com

---

www.powerboatguide.com 231-360-0827

Pursuit 2870 Walkaround
1996–2006

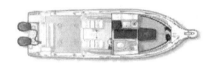

Premium fishing machine with full array of cruising comforts is rigged for tournament-level action. Topside highlights include hinged aft seat with fishbox/cooler under, hardtop with spreader lights, cockpit bolsters, aft-facing cockpit seats, tilt-away helm console. Deep cockpit, aggressive nonskid enhance safety. Well-appointed cabin—big for a 28-footer—includes convertible dinette, teak-and-holly sole, galley with sink, enclosed head. Note athwartships single berth under helmdeck. Yamaha 225hp outboards top out at 40+ knots.

Length w/Pulpit	30'0"	Fuel	234 gals.
Hull Length	28'0"	Water	20 gals.
Beam	9'6"	Max HP	500
Hull Draft	1'8"	Hull Type	Deep-V
Dry Weight	7,570#	Deadrise Aft	22°

See Page 557 For Resale Values

Pursuit Boats
Ft. Pierce, FL
www.pursuitboats.com

---

www.powerboatguide.com 231-360-0827

Pursuit OS 285
2008–Current

Stylish offshore express combines signature Pursuit quality with versatile layout. Topside features include deluxe helm and companion seats with armrests, fiberglass hardtop with PFD storage, aft-facing cockpit seats with backrests, 32-gallon livewell, hinged rear seat with macerated fish box. Tall windshield (with vents) protects helm from high-rpm wind blast. Note hot/cold shower at swim platform. Compact cabin with mini-galley, midcabin berth, enclosed head sleeps three. Twin Yamaha 250s top out at 40+ knots.

Length w/Pulpit	30'8"	Fuel	232 gals.
Beam	9'6"	Water	30 gals.
Hull Draft	1'9"	Max HP	600
Weight w/T250s	7,570#	Hull Type	Deep-V
Clearance, Top	8'4"	Deadrise Aft	22°

See Page 558 For Resale Values

Pursuit Boats
Ft. Pierce, FL
www.pursuitboats.com

231-360-0827

Pursuit 2870 CC; C 280
1997–2008

Purebred fishing machine with generous beam, top-shelf amenities (called 2870 CC in 1997–2006; C 280 in 2007–08) delivers impressive level of quality, comfort, performance. Features include leaning post with livewell, transom fishbox, in-floor fishbox, T-top, tackle rigging station, transom door, bow storage lockers, enclosed head with sink, cockpit bolsters, lockable bow storage. Tilt-away helm provides easy access to wiring. Over 40 knots top with Yamaha 225s. Note that all-new Pursuit C 280 model was introduced in 2009.

Length w/Pulpit	30'0"	Fuel	234 gals.
Hull Length	28'0"	Water	20 gals.
Beam	9'6"	Max HP	450
Hull Draft	1'9"	Hull Type	Deep-V
Weight w/T250s	7,150#	Deadrise Aft	22°

See Page 557 For Resale Values

Pursuit Boats
Ft. Pierce, FL
www.pursuitboats.com

231-360-0827

Pursuit C 280
2009–Current

Premium offshore fishing machine with classic center console lines takes legendary Pursuit quality, fishability to the next level. Single-level cockpit with forward seating comes standard with transom fishbox, large in-floor fishbox with macerator, transom bait station, custom leaning post with tackle trays and 52-gallon oval livewell. Deluxe console has space for two big-screen video displays. Bow anchor chute is a nice touch. Yamaha 250s max out around 45 knots. Note that previous C 280 model ran from 2007–08.

Length	28'0"	Fuel	220 gals.
Beam	9'6"	Water	20 gals.
Draft, Up	1'7"	Max HP	500
Draft, Down	2'10"	Hull Type	Deep-V
Weight w/250s	7,300#	Deadrise Aft	24°

See Page 558 For Resale Values

Pursuit Boats
Ft. Pierce, FL
www.pursuitboats.com

231-360-0827

Pursuit 3000 Express
1998–2003

Classy open-cockpit fisherman with semi-custom looks gets high marks for styling, finish, versatility. Cockpit came with full array of fishing amenities including centerline bait station, cushioned storage boxes, transom fishbox. Bridgedeck lifts for engine access. Super-comfortable cabin with full galley, pilot berths sleeps four. Visibility is excellent from raised helm. Twin 375hp gas inboards cruise at 25 knots (mid 30s top); 230hp Volvo diesels cruise at 23-24 knots (28-29 knots top).

Length w/Pulpit	32'8"	Fuel	210 gals.
Hull Length	30'10"	Water	30 gals.
Beam	10'6"	Waste	18 gals.
Draft	2'10"	Hull Type	Deep-V
Weight	10,600#	Deadrise Aft	21°

See Page 558 For Resale Values

Pursuit Boats
Ft. Pierce, FL
www.pursuitboats.com

Sportfishing Boats

www.powerboatguide.com   231-360-0827

Pursuit 3000 Offshore
1995–2004

Enduring inboard fisherman with classic Palm Beach styling, top-notch finish gets high marks for performance, versatility. Cockpit came with full array of fishing amenities including centerline bait station, cushioned storage boxes, transom fishbox. Bridgedeck lifts for easy engine access. Surprisingly spacious cabin with full galley, pilot berths, backlit rod storage display, sleeps four. Visibility is excellent from raised helm. Gas 375hp inboards cruise at 25 knots; 230hp Volvo diesels cruise at 23-24 knots.

Length w/Pulpit	31'2"	Fuel	250 gals.
Hull Length	29'1"	Water	40 gals.
Beam	12'0"	Waste	20 gals.
Draft	2'9"	Hull Type	Modified-V
Weight	11,500#	Deadrise Aft	19°

See Page 558 For Resale Values

Pursuit Boats
Ft. Pierce, FL
www.pursuitboats.com

---

www.powerboatguide.com   231-360-0827

Pursuit 3070 Center Console
2001–07

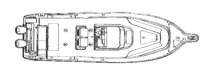

High-end fishing machine (called Pursuit C 300 in 2007) combines quality construction with first-rate amenities, agile performance. Single-level cockpit layout includes 40-gallon livewell, leaning post with rocket launchers, tackle drawers, lockable rod storage, transom rigging center with cutting board, insulated in-floor fishbox with macerator, bow storage lockers, raw-water washdown. Helm space for big-screen electronics. Big console houses marine head with sink, opening port. About 40 knots top with Yamaha 25s.

Length w/Pulpit	32'8"	Fuel	310 gals.
Hull Length	30'10"	Water	30 gals.
Beam	10'6"	Max HP	500
Draft, Down	3'3"	Hull Type	Deep-V
Dry Weight	8,945#	Deadrise Aft	21°

See Page 558 For Resale Values

Pursuit Boats
Ft. Pierce, FL
www.pursuitboats.com

---

www.powerboatguide.com   231-360-0827

Pursuit 3070 Offshore Center Console
1999–2006

Luxury-class sportfisherman combines walkaround versatility with efficient center-console deck layout, compact cabin with family-style amenities. Highlights include 44-gallon livewell, bait-prep center with sink, tackle storage, large in-floor fishbox. Electric leaning post tilts open to expose lighted storage for up to 12 rods. Well-appointed cuddy with midcabin berth, enclosed head sleeps three–four. Full wraparound windshield replaced original cut-down windscreen in 2003. Yamaha 250s deliver about 40 knots top.

Length w/Pulpit	32'8"	Fuel	310 gals.
Hull Length	30'10"	Water	30 gals.
Beam	10'6"	Max HP	500
Draft, Down	3'3"	Hull Type	Deep-V
Dry Weight	8,100#	Deadrise Aft	21°

See Page 558 For Resale Values

Pursuit Boats
Ft. Pierce, FL
www.pursuitboats.com

231-360-0827

Pursuit 3070 Offshore Express
2002–07

Deluxe offshore express (called OS 305 Offshore in 2007) appeals to serious anglers who appreciate comfort. Deck layout is highlighted by expansive bridgedeck with posh L-lounge, ladder-back helm seat. Roomy cockpit includes 30-gallon livewell, aft-facing jump seat, transom bait-prep center. Bridgedeck lifts to reveal cavernous storage compartment. Note standard hardtop. Upscale cabin with full galley, head with shower features handy aft bunk, classy teak-and-holly flooring. About 40 knots top with Yamaha 250s.

Length w/Pulpit	32'8"	Fuel	310 gals.
Hull Length	30'10"	Water	30 gals.
Beam	10'6"	Max HP	500
Hull Draft	1'6"	Hull Type	Deep-V
Dry Weight	9,640#	Deadrise Aft	21°

See Page 558 For Resale Values

Pursuit Boats
Ft. Pierce, FL
www.pursuitboats.com

231-360-0827

Pursuit 3100 Express
1993–97

Popular big-water express—essentially a Tiara 3100 Open (1979–91) with extra fishing features—meets the needs of anglers and cruisers alike. Single-level cockpit is big enough for a mounted chair. Tackle center fits behind helm seat; livewell was popular option. Roomy cabin with teak-and-holly sole, U-shaped dinette, private stateroom sleeps four. Tall windshield provides superior weather protection. Not the softest rough-water ride. Standard 300hp gas inboards cruise at 20–21 knots (around 30 knots top).

Length w/Pulpit	33'9"	Fuel, Std.	206 gals.
Hull Length	31'1"	Fuel, Opt.	276 gals.
Beam	12'0"	Water	36 gals.
Draft	2'9"	Hull Type	Modified-V
Weight	11,000#	Deadrise Aft	16°

See Page 558 For Resale Values

Pursuit Boats
Ft. Pierce, FL
www.pursuitboats.com

231-360-0827

Pursuit C 310
2007–Current

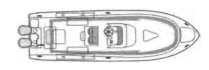

Tournament-bred center console with top-shelf amenities, superb finish makes the cut with hardcore anglers. Fishing features include big 52-gallon lighted livewell, five fishboxes (two forward, two in the deck, one at the transom), 12 rod holders, bait-prep station. Lockable rod rack under forward seat swings out for use. Deluxe helm seats with flip-up bolsters, folding transom seat, pop-up cleats, recessed bow rails are standard. Space at the helm for two 12-inch displays. Heavily-built hull can take a pounding. Yamaha 250s top out at 45 knots.

Length	31'2"	Fuel	260 gals.
Beam	9'6"	Water	20 gals.
Draft, Up	1'10"	Max HP	500
Draft, Down	2'8"	Hull Type	Deep-V
Weight w/T250s	8,500#	Deadrise Aft	24°

See Page 558 For Resale Values

Pursuit Boats
Ft. Pierce, FL
www.pursuitboats.com

Sportfishing Boats

Pursuit OS 315
2008–Current

Luxury-class express from top-tier builder delivers great mix of leading-edge styling, upscale amenities, secure handling. Versatile deck layout appeals to anglers and cruisers alike. Topside features include L-shaped bridgedeck seating, lighted 32-gallon livewell, twin in-deck fishboxes, swivel helm seat, power windshield vent, raw-water washdowns. Well-appointed midcabin interior with teak flooring, quality fabrics sleeps four. Good range with 284-gallon fuel capacity. Yamaha 250hp outboards max out at 36–38 knots.

Length w/Pulpit	32'8"	Fuel	284 gals.
Beam	10'8"	Water	30 gals.
Hull Draft	1'6"	Max HP	600
Weight w/T250s	11,000#	Hull Type	Deep-V
Clearance, Top	9'3"	Deadrise Aft	20°

See Page 558 For Resale Values

Pursuit Boats
Ft. Pierce, FL
www.pursuitboats.com

Pursuit 3100 Offshore
2004–05

Stylish inboard express combines top-shelf construction, superb performance. Single-piece windshield with epoxy frame is completely distinctive. Fishing features include removable fishbox, circulating livewell, tackle center. Aft bridgedeck raises on electronic rams for engine access. Teak-and-holly sole adds upscale tone to plush cabin with convertible dinette, enclosed head, large double berth forward. Standard 320hp gas inboards cruise in the mid 20s; optional 315hp Yanmar diesels cruise at 30 knots.

Length w/Pulpit	34'6"	Fuel	192 gals.
Hull Length	32'4"	Water	30 gals.
Beam	10'6"	Waste	18 gals.
Draft	3'3"	Hull Type	Deep-V
Weight	10,322#	Deadrise Aft	21°

See Page 558 For Resale Values

Pursuit Boats
Ft. Pierce, FL
www.pursuitboats.com

Pursuit 3250 Express
1990–92

Rugged 1990s canyon runner (called Pursuit 3300 Express in 1993) combined dependable inboard power with quality construction, upscale interior. Topside features include in-floor 20-gallon livewell, bait-rigging station, bow pulpit, transom door. Efficient cabin with full galley, convertible dinette, teak-and-holly sole sleeps four. Entire bridgedeck lifts for engine access. Note that early bow-high running angle was corrected in 1991 when bottom was redesigned. Optional 300hp Cat or Cummins diesels cruise in the mid 20s (30 knots top).

Length	33'0"	Water	50 gals.
Beam	12'6"	Fuel	305 gals.
Draft	2'8"	Cockpit	115 sq. ft.
Weight	13,500#	Hull Type	Modified-V
Clearance	8'4"	Deadrise Aft	18°

Prices Not Provided for Pre-1995 Models

Pursuit Boats
Ft. Pierce, FL
www.pursuitboats.com

231-360-0827

Pursuit 3370 Offshore; OS 335
2004–08

Handsome express (called 3370 Offshore in 2004–06; OS 335 in 2007–08) took Pursuit styling, value to the next level. Distinctive one-piece windshield, expensive vacuum-bagged construction help set this quality canyon runner apart from the competition. Notable features include fold-down transom seat, hardtop with radio box, removable in-floor fishbox, 45-gallon livewell. Richly appointed interior with leather seating, teak-and-holly sole, full-service galley sleeps four. Twin 300hp Mercs max out around 40 knots.

Length w/Pulpit	35'1"	Fuel	310 gals.
Beam	10'6"	Water	30 gals.
Draft	2'4"	Max HP	600
Weight w/T250s	10,670#	Hull Type	Deep-V
Clearance	9'7"	Deadrise Aft	21°

See Page 558 For Resale Values

Pursuit Boats
Ft. Pierce, FL
www.pursuitboats.com

231-360-0827

Pursuit 3400 Express
1997–2003

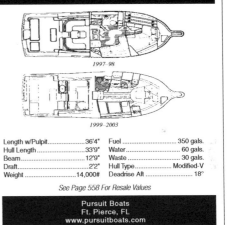

1997–98

1999–2003

Hard-hitting fishing machine targets big-water anglers with an appreciation for legendary Tiara luxury, quality. Original model with centerline helm, offset companionway was updated in 1999 with all-new deck design featuring starboard-side helm, rearranged tackle center and livewell, enlarged interior with centerline entry, full dinette, stall shower in head. Entire bridgedeck lifts for access to engines. Side exhausts keep cockpit free of fumes. Cummins 370hp diesels cruise in the mid 20s (30+ knots top).

Length w/Pulpit	36'4"	Fuel	350 gals.
Hull Length	33'9"	Water	60 gals.
Beam	12'9"	Waste	30 gals.
Draft	2'2"	Hull Type	Modified-V
Weight	14,000#	Deadrise Aft	18°

See Page 558 For Resale Values

Pursuit Boats
Ft. Pierce, FL
www.pursuitboats.com

231-360-0827

Pursuit 3480 Center Console; C 340
2005–Current

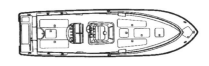

Hard core sportfishing machine (called Pursuit 3480 CC in 2006; C 340 thereafter) makes the cut with demanding, quality-focused anglers. World-class layout boasts custom leaning post with circulating 52-gallon livewell, four insulated in-floor fishboxes, cockpit bolsters, transom bait-prep station, enclosed head compartment with forward door, pop-up cleats. Transom livewell, bow seating, folding rear seat, factory T-top are popular options. Slender deep-V hull is quick to accelerate. Over 40 knots top with Yamaha 250s.

Length	34'5"	Fuel	375 gals.
Beam	9'6"	Water	30 gals.
Hull Draft	1'10"	Max HP	600
Weight w/T250s	9,300#	Hull Type	Deep-V
Clearance, Top	9'4"	Deadrise Aft	24.5°

See Page 558 For Resale Values

Pursuit Boats
Ft. Pierce, FL
www.pursuitboats.com

Sportfishing Boats

Section II: Sportfishing Boats

www.powerboatguide.com — 231-360-0827

Pursuit OS 375
2008–Current

Feature-rich fishing boat with broad 13-foot beam strikes a balance between yacht-class amenities, big-water fishability. Highlights include factory hard-top, 50-gallon livewell, tackle stowage, refrigerated fish-boxes, bow thruster, cockpit grill, windlass. Plush midcabin interior with huge galley, teak-and-maple sole features clever forward berth that allows a couple to sleep fore and aft or athwartships. Bridge air-conditioning is standard. Impressive fit and finish throughout. Triple Yamaha 350s deliver 45+ knots wide open.

Length w/Pulpit	39'2"	Fuel	370 gals.
Hull Length	36'11"	Water	65 gals.
Beam	13'0"	Max HP	1,050
Hull Draft	3'6"	Hull Type	Modified-V
Weight, 3/350	18,450#	Deadrise Aft	18°

See Page 558 For Resale Values

Pursuit Boats
Ft. Pierce, FL
www.pursuitboats.com

www.powerboatguide.com — 231-360-0827

Pursuit 3800 Express
2002–04

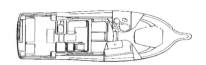

Powerful offshore express with semicustom styling stops traffic as well as she catches fish. Posh teak-trimmed interior offers luxury accommodations for four; large cockpit with foldaway transom seat is big enough for several anglers without bumping shoulders. Highlights include L-shaped bridgedeck seating, 50-gallon livewell, bait-prep station, teak-and-holly cabin sole. Note lighted rod locker, stand-up engineroom, stylish epoxy-framed windshield. Cummins 450hp—or Volvo 480hp—diesels cruise in the mid 20s (30+ knots top).

Length w/Pulpit	40'11"	Headroom	6'2"
Hull Length	38'6"	Fuel	438 gals.
Beam	14'2"	Water	110 gals.
Draft	3'11"	Waste	40 gals.
Weight	21,800#	Hull Type	Modified-V

See Page 558 For Resale Values

Pursuit Boats
Ft. Pierce, FL
www.pursuitboats.com

www.powerboatguide.com — 231-360-0827

Rampage 28 Sportsman
1986–93

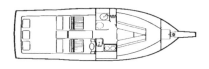

Beefy 28-footer with wide 11-foot beam offers more cockpit, cabin space than most boats her size. Top-side highlights include lockable rod storage, in-floor livewell, bow pulpit, aft-facing cockpit seats. Teak-trimmed interior with full galley, stand-up head, sleeps three. Motorboxes beneath helm, companion seats provide good access to engines. Transom door was a popular option. Note fully cored hull construction, lockable electronics storage. Twin 260hp gas inboards cruise at 22–24 knots (about 30 knots top).

Length w/Pulpit	29'6"	Fuel	240 gals.
Hull Length	28'0"	Water	25 gals.
Beam	11'0"	Cockpit	80 sq. ft.
Draft	2'6"	Hull Type	Modified-V
Weight	8,200#	Deadrise Aft	10°

Prices Not Provided for Pre-1995 Models

The original Rampage Company
ended production in 1993.

231-360-0827

Rampage 30 Express
1999–Current

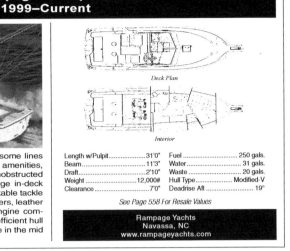

Deck Plan

Interior

Well-rigged midsize express with handsome lines delivers impressive mix of top-shelf amenities, proven big-water performance. Unobstructed cockpit includes 38-gallon lighted livewell, large in-deck fishbox, dual washdowns, bait-prep center, lockable tackle storage. Cherrywood interior with Corian counters, leather seating sleeps four. Tilt-away helm, lighted engine compartment, transom door are standard. Weight-efficient hull is fully cored. Twin 315hp Yanmar diesels cruise in the mid 20s with top speed of 30+ knots.

Length w/Pulpit	31'0"	Fuel	250 gals.
Beam	11'3"	Water	31 gals.
Draft	2'10"	Waste	20 gals.
Weight	12,000#	Hull Type	Modified-V
Clearance	7'0"	Deadrise Aft	19°

See Page 558 For Resale Values

Rampage Yachts
Navassa, NC
www.rampageyachts.com

231-360-0827

Rampage 30 Offshore
2002–06

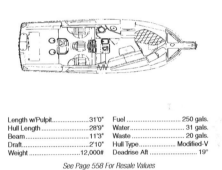

Handsome midsize express (originally called Rampage 30 Open) with appealing Palm Beach styling combines top-shelf amenities, agile performance. Spacious cockpit features 38-gallon lighted livewell, large in-deck fishbox, dual washdowns, bait-prep center with sink, lockable tackle storage. Upscale cherry-trimmed interior with convertible dinette, angled berth sleeps four. Additional features include centerline helm position, transom door and gate, fully cored hull. Twin 315hp Yanmar diesels cruise in the mid 20s (30+ top).

Length w/Pulpit	31'0"	Fuel	250 gals.
Hull Length	28'9"	Water	31 gals.
Beam	11'3"	Waste	20 gals.
Draft	2'10"	Hull Type	Modified-V
Weight	12,000#	Deadrise Aft	19°

See Page 558 For Resale Values

Rampage Yachts
Navassa, NC
www.rampageyachts.com

231-360-0827

Rampage 30 Walkaround
2005–06

Feature-rich walkaround with generous beam delivers top-quality construction, blue-chip fishability. Spacious cockpit features 38-gallon lighted livewell, large in-deck fishbox, dual washdowns, bait-prep center. Upscale cherry-trimmed interior with convertible dinette, angled double berth sleeps four. Additional features include tilt-away helm, bow pulpit, lighted engine compartment, transom door and gate. Note deep walkways, fully cored hull construction. Twin 315hp Yanmar diesels cruise in the mid 20s (30+ knots top).

Length w/Pulpit	31'0"	Fuel	250 gals.
Hull Length	28'9"	Water	31 gals.
Beam	11'3"	Waste	20 gals.
Draft	2'10"	Hull Type	Modified-V
Weight	12,000#	Deadrise Aft	19°

See Page 558 For Resale Values

Rampage Yachts
Navassa, NC
www.rampageyachts.com

Rampage 31 Sportfisherman
1985–93

Wide-beam express introduced in 1985 packed big-boat features in modest 31-foot hull. Huge cockpit dwarfs anything in her class. Highlights include huge in-floor livewell, extra-wide transom door, lockable rod storage, bow pulpit, wide side decks. Well-appointed cabin with teak trim, full galley, enclosed head with shower sleeps four. Slide-back engine hatches allow excellent engine access. Note tall windshield, fully cored hull construction. Definitely a stiff ride in a chop. Standard 330hp gas inboards cruise at 22–24 knots (30+ top).

Length w/Pulpit	31'10"	Fuel	256 gals.
Hull Length	30'10"	Water	50 gals.
Beam	11'11"	Cockpit	114 sq. ft.
Draft	2'9"	Hull Type	Modified-V
Weight	12,000#	Deadrise Aft	10°

Prices Not Provided for Pre-1995 Models

The original Rampage Company
ended production in 1993.

Rampage 33 Express
2005–08

Versatile offshore fishing boat with centerline helm matches agile handling, wide-beam accommodations. Spacious cockpit can be configured with 45-gallon livewell/bait-prep center for fishing, or wet bar and foldaway stern seating for cruising. Classy cherry-trimmed interior with Corian counters, flip-up backrests, sleeps six. Note huge engine compartment, cabin rod storage, large fishbox, wide side decks. Prop-pocket hull draws very little water. Cruise in the mid 20s with 460hp Cat C7 diesels (30+ knots top).

Length w/Pulpit	35'6"	Fuel	367 gals.
Hull Length	33'0"	Water	60 gals.
Beam	13'0"	Waste	45 gals.
Draft	2.5"	Hull Type	Modified-V
Weight	17,200#	Deadrise Aft	18°

See Page 558 For Resale Values

Rampage Yachts
Navassa, NC
www.rampageyachts.com

Rampage 33 Sportfisherman
1990–93

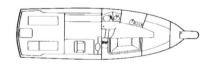

Rugged 1990s express with handsome lines made good on Rampage promise of quality construction, top-level amenities. Large cockpit with in-deck fishboxes, wide transom door, lockable rod storage is big enough for several anglers. Ergonomic helm has space for electronic add-ons. Well-finished cabin—plain but comfortable—sleeps four. Note wide side decks, excellent engine access. Fully cored hull with flared bow, generous beam is dry, stable. Cummins 300hp diesels cruise at 24–25 knots; Cat 320hp diesels run a knot or two faster.

Length w/Pulpit	34'10"	Clearance	11'2"
Hull Length	32'4"	Fuel	300 gals.
Beam	12'4"	Water	58 gals.
Draft	2'7"	Hull Type	Modified-V
Weight	14,500#	Deadrise Aft	18°

Prices Not Provided for Pre-1995 Models

The original Rampage Company
ended production in 1993.

Rampage 36 Sportfisherman
1989-93

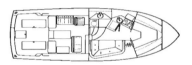

Polished 1990s canyon runner offered impressive blend of distinctive styling, agile performance. Beamy, fully cored hull provides big bi-level fishing cockpit without cutting into cabin space. Highlights include oversized transom door, large in-deck fishboxes, concealed rod storage, well-arranged helm, good engine access. Upscale interior with cherry trim sleeps four. Note tall windshield. Cummins 300hp diesels cruise at 20 knots (around 25 knots top); 425hp Cats cruise at 25 knots and deliver 29-30 knots wide open.

Length w/Pulpit	37'8"	Clearance	8'10"
Hull Length	35'6"	Fuel	435 gals.
Beam	13'9"	Water	70 gals.
Draft	2'9"	Hull Type	Modified-V
Weight	19,000#	Deadrise Aft	17°

Prices Not Provided for Pre-1995 Models

The original Rampage Company
ended production in 1993.

Rampage 45 Convertible
2002-Current

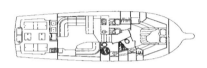

High-end tournament machine delivers impressive blend of rakish styling, state-of-the-art construction. Highlights include massive 130-square-foot cockpit, stand-up engineroom, huge bridge with lockable rod storage, luxurious two-stateroom, two-head interior with cherry cabinetry, leather upholstery. Note hidden salon rod storage, wraparound helm display, single-lever controls. Low-deadrise hull with solid fiberglass bottom has prop pockets to reduce draft, improve efficiency. Cruise at 26-28 knots (mid 30s top) with 800hp Cats.

Length w/Pulpit	48'8"	Fuel	700 gals.
Hull Length	45'10"	Water	100 gals.
Beam	16'0"	Waste	60 gals.
Draft	4'0"	Hull Type	Modified-V
Weight	36,000#	Deadrise Aft	10°

See Page 558 For Resale Values

Rampage Yachts
Navassa, NC
www.rampageyachts.com

Regulator 29 Center Console
2006-Current

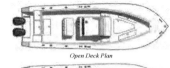

Open Deck Plan

Forward Seating Deck Plan

Top-shelf fisherman meets angler demands for superior craftsmanship, no-excuses fishability. Standard features include combined leaning post/tackle center, transom and in-floor fishboxes, 30-gallon livewell, pop-up cleats, insulated cooler, fresh/saltwater washdowns, cushioned bow seating, console head with marine toilet. Helm offers lots of space for flush-mounting electronics. Forward fishbox doubles as lockable rod locker. Excellent range. Forward Seating model available since 2006. Yamaha 250s reach 45 knots.

Length	29'0"	Fuel	285 gals.
Beam	9'6"	Water	20 gals.
Draft, Up	2'0"	Max HP	500
Draft, Down	2'7"	Hull Type	Deep-V
Hull Weight	6,900#	Deadrise Aft	24°

See Page 560 For Resale Values

Regulator Marine
Edenton, NC
www.regulatormarine.com

Regulator 32 Forward Seating
1999–Current

FS Deck Plan

Open Deck Plan

Smooth-running center console with forward seating ranks with class leaders for quality, performance, long-term owner satisfaction. Standard fishing features include deluxe leaning post/tackle center with flip-up bolsters, 50-gallon transom baitwell, transom fishbox, lockable in-deck rod storage, bait-rigging station. Console compartment houses marine toilet with sink, hand-held shower. Popular boat enjoys strong resale values. Open model (no bow seating) also available. Over 40 knots with Yamaha 200s.

Length	32'0"	Fuel	310 gals.
Beam	10.5"	Water	38 gals.
Draft, Up	2'0"	Max HP	700
Draft, Down	2'8"	Hull Type	Deep-V
Dry Weight	7,400#	Deadrise Aft	24°

See Page 560 For Resale Values

Regulator Marine
Edenton, NC
www.regulatormarine.com

Riviera 33 Convertible
1992–97

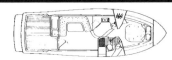

One Stateroom

Two Staterooms

Classy 1990s convertible with Bertram-like styling combined low price with solid construction, well-planned accommodations. Offered with single- and twin-stateroom floorplans, both with teak trim, convertible dinette, step-down galley, lower helm station. Large fishing cockpit came standard with transom door, fish box, tackle center. Flybridge is huge for a 33-footer. Note forward collision bulkhead. Cockpit engineroom entry is completely unique for a boat this size. Cummins 333hp diesels cruise in the low 20s (27–28 knots top).

Length	33'0"	Fuel	296 gals.
Beam	12'6"	Water	84 gals.
Draft	2'7"	Waste	25 gals.
Weight	20,500#	Hull Type	Modified-V
Cockpit	NA	Deadrise Aft	16°

See Page 560 For Resale Values

Riviera Yachts
Stuart, FL (US Office)
www.riviera.com.au

Riviera 33 Convertible
2005–Current

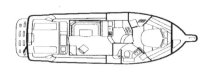

Aussie-built pocket convertible offers smart styling, roomy accommodations at a surprisingly affordable price. Single-stateroom interior with convertible dinette is available with or without lower helm. Cockpit features tackle station with freshwater sink, top-loading refrigerator cabinet to port, in-deck fishbox, bait-prep center. Cockpit engineroom entry is unique for a boat this size. Solid fiberglass hull with prop pockets, underwater exhausts boasts forward collision bulkhead. Volvo 370hp diesels cruise in the mid 20s (30+ knots top).

Length w/Pulpit	37'3"	Fuel	264 gals.
Beam	12'7"	Water	103 gals.
Draft	3'3"	Waste	18 gals.
Weight	19,800#	Hull Type	Modified-V
Clearance	14.5"	Deadrise Aft	15°

See Page 560 For Resale Values

Riviera Yachts
www.riviera.com.au

Riviera 34 Convertible
1997–2002

Affordably priced flybridge cruiser with handsome styling, rock-solid construction is part sportfishing boat, part family cruiser. No-frills interior boasts surprisingly spacious salon with U-shaped dinette, step-down galley, optional lower helm. Note in-floor galley storage compartment. Cockpit came standard with bait-prep station (with freezer), transom door, engineroom access hatch. Tournament-style bridge has bench seating forward of helm. Cummins 330hp diesels cruise in the mid 20s (28–30 knots top).

Length	34'0"	Water	84 gals.
Beam	13'4"	Clearance	NA
Draft	2'7"	Headroom	6'4"
Weight	19,400#	Hull Type	Modified-V
Fuel	296 gals.	Deadrise Aft	17°

See Page 560 For Resale Values

Riviera Yachts
www.riviera.com.au

Riviera 36 Convertible
1993–2002

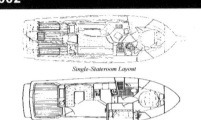

Single-Stateroom Layout

Two-Stateroom Floorplan

Popular Australian import with Bertram-like styling is handsome, sturdy, built to last. Available with choice of single- or twin-stateroom interiors, both with optional lower helm, step-down galley, separate stall shower in head. Transom door, tackle center, engineroom access hatch were standard in the cockpit. Tournament-style bridge has bench seating forward of simple helm console. Note wide side decks, forward collision bulkhead. Cummins 315hp diesels cruise at 23–24 knots; 350hp Cats cruise at 27–28 knots.

Length	36'0"	Water	119 gals.
Beam	13'5"	Clearance	NA
Draft	3'5"	Headroom	6'4"
Weight	22,800#	Hull Type	Modified-V
Fuel	324 gals.	Deadrise Aft	16°

See Page 560 For Resale Values

Riviera Yachts
www.riviera.com.au

Riviera 37 Convertible
2001–08

Australian-built convertible with rakish styling, roomy interior was designed for fishing or family cruising. Functional interior features surprisingly spacious salon, open-plan galley, two comfortable staterooms. Big cockpit with engineroom access includes transom door, insulated fishbox, molded tackle center. Cruising-style bridge has helm forward, guest seating aft. Bow pulpit, swim platform, generator, collision bulkhead are standard. Note wide side decks. Volvo 370hp diesels cruise at 25 knots (28–29 knots top).

Length w/Pulpit	42'11"	Fuel	370 gals.
Hull Length	37'11"	Water	122 gals.
Beam	13'10"	Waste	18 gals.
Draft	3'5"	Hull Type	Modified-V
Weight	24,000#	Deadrise Aft	18°

See Page 560 For Resale Values

Riviera Yachts
www.riviera.com.au

Sportfishing Boats

231-360-0827

Riviera 39 Convertible
1994—99

Spirited 1990s convertible offered clean styling, good speed, well-placed fishing amenities. Conservative twin-stateroom interior with step-down galley features spacious salon with 360-degree visibility, lower helm station, teak joinery. Unique double bed in guest cabin converts to upper/lower berths. Cockpit with tackle center, transom door, engineroom access door has room for mounted chair. Cat 350hp diesels cruise in the low 20s; 420hp Cummins diesels cruise at 25 knots and reach a top speed of 31–32 knots.

Length	39'4"	Water	100 gals.
Beam	14'6"	Clearance	NA
Draft	3'7"	Headroom	6'5"
Weight	28,400#	Hull Type	Modified-V
Fuel	400 gals.	Deadrise Aft	15°

See Page 560 For Resale Values

Riviera Yachts
www.riviera.com.au

231-360-0827

Riviera 40 Convertible
2001—06

Popular, well-priced 40-footer from Down Under ranked among the best boating vales of her era. Unpretentious two-stateroom interior includes L-shaped dinette forward in salon. Front salon windows are rare in a modern convertible. Lower helm layout is optional. Note three single berths, washer/dryer space in guest stateroom. Exterior highlights include well-equipped cockpit with engineroom access, spacious bridge, wide side decks, swim platform. Cruise in the mid 20s (28–29 knots top) with 450hp Cummins or 460hp Cat diesels.

Length w/Pulpit	46'4"	Fuel	473 gals.
Hull Length	42'11"	Water	122 gals.
Beam	14'11"	Waste	18 gals.
Draft	4'1"	Hull Type	Modified-V
Weight	29,800#	Deadrise Aft	15°

See Page 560 For Resale Values

Riviera Yachts
www.riviera.com.au

231-360-0827

Riviera 42 Convertible
2004—07

Appealing 42-foot convertible with rakish styling, solid construction was designed for serious fishing, sociable cruising. Practical two-stateroom, two-head interior features spacious salon with leather lounge, L-shaped dinette, home-size galley with slide-out dishwasher, triple-bunk guest cabin. Note salon entertainment center, high-gloss teak joinery. Bait-prep center, in-sole fishbox, cooler/freezer, trash receptacle are standard in cockpit. Engineroom is a little tight. Cruise at 22–23 knots with 480hp Cummins diesels (26–28 knots top).

Length w/Pulpit	50'10"	Fuel	476 gals.
Hull Length	42'11"	Water	122 gals.
Beam	14'11"	Waste	40 gals.
Draft	4'2"	Hull Type	Modified-V
Weight	30,900#	Deadrise Aft	15°

See Page 560 For Resale Values

Riviera Yachts
www.riviera.com.au

231-360-0827

Riviera 43 Convertible
1996–2003

Rugged Down Under convertible splits the difference between fishing machine, comfortable family cruiser. Standard two-stateroom interior (available with or without lower helm) features mid-level galley, stall showers in both heads, well-appointed salon with leather seating, teak trim. Cockpit came with freezer, storage cabinets, direct access to spacious engineroom. Flybridge is large for a 43-footer with L-lounge seating, removable table forward of helm. Twin 420hp Cats—or 430hp Cummins—cruise in the low 20s (26–28 knots top).

Length w/Pulpit	48'6"	Water	164 gals.
Beam	15'8"	Clearance	16'8"
Draft	4'2"	Headroom	6'6"
Weight	35,300#	Hull Type	Modified-V
Fuel	580/832 gals.	Deadrise Aft	16°

See Page 560 For Resale Values

Riviera Yachts
www.riviera.com.au

231-360-0827

Riviera 45 Convertible
2008–Current

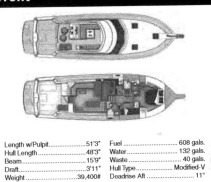

Great styling, luxury-class appointments, spirited performance make this versatile middleweight a leader in her class. Highlights include elegant two-stateroom interior with standard washer/dryer, large fishing cockpit, molded bridge steps, huge flybridge with lounge seating forward. Rod stowage in salon overhead is a plus; aft salon window swings open for ventilation. Additional features include underwater exhausts, flybridge wet bar, wide side decks, prop tunnels. Cat 715hp diesels cruise at 26–28 knots (low 30s top).

Length w/Pulpit	51'3"	Fuel	608 gals.
Hull Length	48'3"	Water	132 gals.
Beam	15'9"	Waste	40 gals.
Draft	3'11"	Hull Type	Modified-V
Weight	39,400#	Deadrise Aft	11°

Insufficient Resale Data To Assign Values

Riviera Yachts
www.riviera.com.au

231-360-0827

Riviera 47 Convertible
2003–07

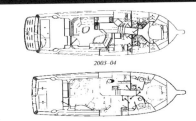

2003–04

2005–Current

Strong-selling 47-footer splits the difference between serious fishing boat, comfortable family cruiser. One of just a few boats this size to offer three private staterooms. Note that Series II model introduced in 2005 features redesigned interior with larger salon, double berth in master, underwater exhausts, prop pockets. Highlights include high-gloss cherry joinery, large 130-square-foot cockpit, forward collision bulkhead, bridge seating for eight. Engineroom is a tight fit. Cummins 660hp diesels cruise at 28 knots (30+ top).

Length w/Pulpit	53'1"	Fuel	977 gals.
Hull Length	49'10"	Water	164 gals.
Beam	16'1"	Waste	40 gals.
Draft	4'5"	Hull Type	Modified-V
Weight	43,200#	Deadrise Aft	16°

See Page 560 For Resale Values

Riviera Yachts
www.riviera.com.au

231-360-0827

Riviera 48 Convertible
1993–2002

High-end convertible from Australia delivered impressive blend of styling, comfort, performance. Offered with several three-stateroom interiors—lower helm was standard in early years; later models have dinette in place of helm. Highlights include large fishing cockpit, expansive bridge with dinette forward of helm console, well-planned bridge. (Optional enclosed bridge was introduced in 1989.) Note forward collision bulkhead, watertight engineroom bulkheads. Cat 660hp diesels cruise in the mid 20s; 800hp Cats cruise at 27–28 knots.

Length w/Pulpit	54'0"	Water	227 gals.
Beam	16'0"	Clearance	16'6"
Draft	4 7"	Headroom	6 5"
Weight	39,600#	Hull Type	Modified-V
Fuel	650/940 gals.	Deadrise Aft	18°

See Page 560 For Resale Values

Riviera Yachts
www.riviera.com.au

231-360-0827

Riviera 51 Convertible
2004–Current

Muscular Aussie convertible boasts serious eye appeal, efficient layout, solid construction. Upscale three-stateroom interior with combined salon/dinette/galley features leather settees, varnished cherry joinery, washer/dryer space, salon entertainment center. Additional highlights include spacious flybridge, teak-laid cockpit, well-finished engineroom. Note overhead rod storage in salon, forward collision bulkhead, bow thruster. Enclosed bridge version available beginning in 2007. MTU 825hp engines cruise at 26–28 knots (30+ knots top).

Length w/Pulpit	58'2"	Fuel	977 gals.
Hull Length	54'8"	Water	227 gals.
Beam	16'2"	Waste	40 gals.
Draft	4'6"	Hull Type	Modified-V
Weight	48,060#	Deadrise Aft	14°

Insufficient Resale Data To Assign Values

Riviera Yachts
www.riviera.com.au

231-360-0827

Riviera 58 Enclosed Bridge Convertible
2003–06

Powerful closed-bridge convertible delivers impressive mix of spacious accommodations, superb engineering, impressive open-water handling. Four-stateroom interior with combined salon/dinette/galley is a conservative blend of upscale furnishings, beautiful high-gloss cabinetry. Note overhead salon handholds, spacious engineroom, roomy cockpit. Cockpit is huge, but fishboxes aren't insulated and there's no rod locker. Cat 1,400hp engines cruise at a fast 30 knots, making this one of the quickest boats in her class.

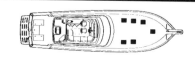
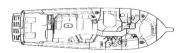

Length w/Platform	64 5"	Headroom	6'6"
Hull Length	61'0"	Fuel	1,110 gals.
Beam	17'9"	Water	215 gals.
Weight	67,200#	Hull Type	Modified-V
Draft	5'2"	Deadrise Aft	10°

Insufficient Resale Data To Assign Values

Riviera Yachts
www.riviera.com.au

Sportfishing Boats

231-360-0827

Riviera 60 Enclosed Bridge Convertible
2006–07

Bold closed-bridge convertible delivers spacious accommodations, tournament-class fishability. Highlights include four-stateroom interior with combined salon/galley/dinette, roomy cockpit with bait-prep center, expansive engineroom with excellent service access. Enclosed flybridge with seating for 10 serves as second salon. Note steering station on after bridgedeck, generous fuel capacity, wide transom door. Bridge access is via cockpit ladder only—no interior stairway. Twin 1,520hp MTUs cruise at 30+ knots (mid 30s top).

Length w/Platform	64'5"	Clearance	NA
Hull Length	61'0"	Fuel	1,506 gals.
Beam	17'9"	Water	264 gals.
Draft	5'2"	Hull Type	Modified-V
Weight	67,200#	Deadrise Aft	10°

Insufficient Resale Data To Assign Values

Riviera Yachts
www.riviera.com.au

231-360-0827

Robalo 300 Center Console
2007–Current

hardcore center console with impeccable finish takes Robalo quality to the next level. Broad 10'6" beam allows plenty of fishing space for two anglers. Single-level cockpit with wide walkways makes getting around easy. Dash has space for twin big-screen displays. Note upright rod rack in head compartment, lockable cockpit rod storage, recessed bow rails. Tilt helm access is a plus. Two livewells, both with blue LED lighting, are standard. Good range with 300-gallon fuel capacity. Yamaha 250hp outboards top out at 40+ knots.

Length	29'2"	Fuel	300 gals.
Beam	10'6"	Water	30 gals.
Draft, Up	1'8"	Max HP	600
Draft, Down	2'10"	Hull Type	Deep-V
Dry Weight	7,500#	Deadrise Aft	21°

See Page 561 For Resale Values

Robalo Boats
Nashville, GA
www.robalo.com

231-360-0827

Robalo 305 Walkaround
2007–Current

Top-quality express with serious eye appeal is proof again that you get what you pay for. Bridge deck is two steps up from cockpit for improved helm visibility. Uncluttered cockpit with bait-prep center, twin livewells. foldaway transom seat is as good as it gets in a 30-foot express. L-shaped lounge seat opposite helm has clever 3-position back rest. Freshwater washdown at bow is way cool. Upscale cabin can sleep six (in a pinch). Note pull-up cleats, standard hardtop with spreader lights. Yamaha 250hp outboards top out at close to 40 knots.

Length	29'2"	Fuel	296 gals.
Beam	10'6"	Water	40 gals.
Draft, Up	1'8"	Max HP	600
Draft, Down	2'10"	Hull Type	Deep-V
Dry Weight	9,300#	Deadrise Aft	21°

See Page 561 For Resale Values

Robalo Boats
Nashville, GA
www.robalo.com

Scout 280 Abaco
2000–05

Classy sportfisher with beamy deep-V hull (called 260 Cabrio in 2000; 260 Abaco in 2001) is easy on the eye, fast across the water. Well-placed fishing features include lighted 35-gallon livewell, two in-floor fishboxes, plenty of rod storage. Note roomy helm position, standard hardtop. Family-friendly cabin with full galley, amidships berth, enclosed head sleeps four. No cabin ventilation ports. Beefy outboard mounting system makes brackets part of the stringer system. Twin 200hp Yamahas top out at 40+ knots.

Length w/Pulpit	28'6"	Fuel	210 gals.
Beam	9'5"	Water	25 gals.
Hull Draft	20"	Max HP	600
Weight	5,100#	Hull Type	Deep-V
Clearance	10'0"	Deadrise Aft	21°

See Page 561 For Resale Values

Scout Boats
Summerville, SC
www.scoutboats.com

Scout 280 Sportfish
2001–06

Beamy center console with sleek profile gets high marks for tough construction, roomy deck layout. Standard features include factory T-top, spreader lights, 30-gallon transom livewell, leaning post with full tackle center, in-floor fishboxes, console head with opening port, cockpit bolsters, fresh/saltwater washdowns, cushioned bow seating. Lockable rod storage in cockpit sole. Unique outboard mounting system makes brackets part of stringer system. No transom door. Over 40 knots with Yamaha 200s.

Length w/Pulpit	28'6"	Fuel	210 gals.
Beam	9'5"	Water	20 gals.
Hull Draft	20"	Max HP	600
Dry Weight	4,300#	Hull Type	Deep-V
Clearance, T-Top	8'0"	Deadrise Aft	21°

See Page 561 For Resale Values

Scout Boats
Summerville, SC
www.scoutboats.com

Scout 282 Sportfish
2006–Current

Feature-rich fishboat with distinctive styling, bracket-mounted outboards takes center-console aesthetics, quality to the next level. Highlights include standard T-top with electronics box, bait-prep station with sink & tackle storage, port and starboard 35-gallon livewells, forward fishboxes, console head with sink, fresh/raw-water washdowns, cushioned bow seating. Deluxe leaning post has backrest, foldaway footrest. Recessed bow rails, pop-up cleats mean no snagged lines. Yamaha 250s reach close to 50 knots wide open.

Length	28'2"	Fuel	205 gals.
Beam	9'6"	Water	20 gals.
Draft, Up	1'6"	Max HP	600
Draft, Down	3'0"	Hull Type	Deep-V
Dry Weight	5,100#	Deadrise Aft	22°

See Page 561 For Resale Values

Scout Boats
Summerville, SC
www.scoutboats.com

Sea Ray 270 Amberjack
1986–90

Versatile 1980s express with spacious single-level cockpit is just right for fishing, cruising or diving. Highlights include walk-through transom door, swim platform with ladder, tinted windshield with side vents, back-to-back companion seat, teak bow pulpit. Big cockpit hatch provides good engine access. Cabin with full galley, enclosed head, sleeps two. Ten-foot beam is wide for a 27-footer. Great range with 200-gal. fuel capacity. MerCruiser 260hp sterndrives reach a top speed of over 30 knots.

Length w/Pulpit	29'3"	Weight	7,000#
Hull Length	27'7"	Fuel	200 gals.
Beam	10'0"	Water	28 gals.
Draft, Up	1'3"	Hull Type	Deep-V
Draft, Down	2'8"	Deadrise Aft	22°

Prices Not Provided for Pre-1995 Models

Sea Ray Boats
Knoxville, TN
www.searay.com

Sea Ray 270 Amberjack
2005–09

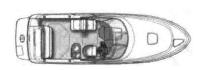

Shapely trailerable express for fishing or cruising offers the best of both worlds. Roomy single-level cockpit with foldaway rear seat can be fitted with optional fishing package with bait-prep station, livewell, raw-water washdown. Deluxe interior with cherry cabinetry, full galley, enclosed head sleeps two. Note transom storage locker, big swim platform. Easy-lift hatch provides quick engine access. Modest fuel capacity limits range. Single 320hp MerCruiser I/O delivers a top speed in excess of 30 knots.

Length	30'0"	Fuel	100 gals.
Beam	8'6"	Water	28 gals.
Draft, Up	15"	Waste	28 gals.
Draft, Down	3'8"	Hull Type	Deep-V
Weight	7,325#	Deadrise Aft	21°

See Page 561 For Resale Values

Sea Ray Boats
Knoxville, TN
www.searay.com

Sea Ray 290 Amberjack
2000–09

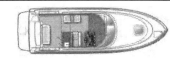

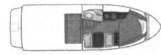

Dual-purpose express split the difference between roomy family cruiser, rugged sportfisherman. Fishing amenities include molded bait-prep station (with livewell) behind helm seat, cockpit rod storage, tiered dash with space for big-screen electronics. Well-finished interior with full galley, convertible dinette, enclosed head, sleeps six—four adults, two children. More fuel capacity than most 28-footers. Twin 260hp MerCruiser I/Os cruise at 22 knots (35 knots top); twin 300hp V-drive inboards cruise at 25 knots (40 knots wide open).

Length w/Platform	31'4"	Fuel	250 gals.
Beam	10'6"	Water	30 gals.
Draft, Up	2'5"	Waste	28 gals.
Draft, Down	2'10"	Hull Type	Deep-V
Weight	12,215#	Deadrise Aft	21°

See Page 562 For Resale Values

Sea Ray Boats
Knoxville, TN
www.searay.com

Sportfishing Boats

Sea Ray 310 Amberjack
1992–94

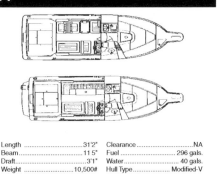

Good-looking express with versatile deck layout splits the difference between light-tackle fisherman, roomy daycruiser. Topside features include extended helmdeck with dinette, roomy cockpit with transom door, insulated fish boxes. Oak-trimmed cabin with convertible dinette, enclosed head with shower provides overnight accommodations for two. Excellent engine access. Huge fuel capacity for a boat this size. Prop pockets reduce draft. Cruise at 25 knots with 310hp MerCruiser inboards (30+ knots wide open).

Length	31'2"	Clearance	NA
Beam	11 5"	Fuel	296 gals.
Draft	3'1"	Water	40 gals.
Weight	10,500#	Hull Type	Modified-V
Cockpit	57 sq. ft.	Deadrise Aft	18°

Prices Not Provided for Pre-1995 Models

Sea Ray Boats
Knoxville, TN
www.searay.com

Sea Ray 340 Amberjack
2001–03

Repackaged version of Sea Ray 330 Express (1997–2000) has rearranged cockpit, revised floorplan. Wide 13'5" beam results in spacious interior with convertible dinette, private bow stateroom, cherry woodwork. Cockpit amenities include L-shaped transom seat, in-deck livewell and fish box, combined bait-prep station/wet bar. Bridgedeck lifts electrically for engine access. Wide side decks are a plus. Cored hull has prop pockets to reduce draft. Twin 370hp MerCruiser inboards cruise at 20 knots (about 30 knots top).

Length w/Platform & Pulpit	38'0"	Fuel	275 gals.
Hull Length	33'6"	Water	50 gals.
Beam	13 5"	Waste	28 gals.
Draft	3'0"	Hull Type	Deep-V
Weight	16,500#	Deadrise Aft	19.5°

See Page 562 For Resale Values

Sea Ray Boats
Knoxville, TN
www.searay.com

Sea Ray 340 Sport Fisherman
1984–87

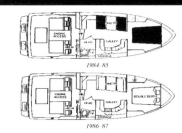

1984-85

1986 87

Good-running 1980s sedan targeted anglers seeking a mix of cruising comfort, offshore fishability. Semi-enclosed lower helm is open to large cockpit. Offered with two cabin layouts, both with convertible dinette, fully equipped galley, open bow stateroom. Topside features include double helm and companion seats, transom door, removable stern seat, swim platform, side-dumping exhausts. Modest fuel capacity for a fishing boat. Cruise at 20 knots (30+ top) with standard 340hp MerCruiser gas inboards.

Length	33 7"	Fuel	250 gals.
Beam	11'11"	Water	52 gals.
Draft	2'5"	Headroom	6'4"
Weight	10,600#	Hull Type	Deep-V
Clearance	NA	Deadrise Aft	21°

Prices Not Provided for Pre-1995 Models

Sea Ray Boats
Knoxville, TN
www.searay.com

231-360-0827

Sea Ray 360 Sedan
1980–82

Multipurpose Sea Ray sedan with wide 14-foot beam combined aggressive 1980's styling with truly expansive interior dimensions. Twin-stateroom floorplan includes mid-level galley with upright refrigerator, head with separate stall shower, space-saving slide-out berth in bow stateroom. Cockpit came with teak sole and covering boards, but no transom door. Lower helm was optional. Cockpit is too small for serious fishing. Cruise at 16–18 knots with standard 340hp gas inboards (mid 20s top).

Length w/Pulpit	38'2"	Fuel	400 gals.
Hull Length	36'6"	Water	100 gals.
Beam	13'11"	Waste	30 gals.
Draft	2'7"	Hull Type	Deep-V
Weight	18,400#	Deadrise Aft	19°

Prices Not Provided for Pre-1995 Models

Sea Ray Boats
Knoxville, TN
www.searay.com

231-360-0827

Sea Ray 390 Sedan
1983–86

Lengthened version of previous Sea Ray 360 Sedan added much-needed cockpit space. Spacious interior includes private master stateroom with slide-out double berth, guest stateroom with upper/lower berths, fully equipped galley, carpeted salon with convertible sofa. Uncluttered cockpit with transom door has room for several anglers. Lower helm was optional. Flybridge is small compared with a modern 39-footer. Standard 350hp gas inboards cruise at 17 knots; 320hp Cat diesels cruise at 20+ knots.

Length w/Pulpit	40'6"	Fuel	400 gals.
Hull Length	39'0"	Water	100 gals.
Beam	13'11"	Waste	40 gals.
Draft	2'7"	Hull Type	Deep-V
Weight	18,400#	Deadrise Aft	19°

Prices Not Provided for Pre-1995 Models

Sea Ray Boats
Knoxville, TN
www.searay.com

231-360-0827

Sea Vee 290B Open
2000–04

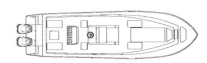

High-performance fishing machine with narrow 8'3" beam is fast, built to last. Single-level cockpit features huge fishbox forward, six in-deck storage boxes, console head compartment, 35-gallon in-floor livewell, pop-up cleats, deluxe leaning post. Space at the helm for plenty of electronics. Uncluttered deck provides full 360-degree fishability. Slender beam results in modest cockpit space compared with most other 29-footers. Replaced in 2005 with new 290B model. Nearly 50 knots top with twin 225s.

Length	29'6"	Fuel, Std.	180 gals.
Beam	8'3"	Fuel, Opt.	240 gals.
Draft, Up	1'6"	Max HP	500
Draft, Down	3'0"	Hull Type	Deep-V
Hull Weight	3,400#	Deadrise Aft	25°

See Page 564 For Resale Values

Sea Vee Boats
Miami, FL
www.seaveeboats.com

Sportfishing Boats

Sea Vee 290B Open
2005–Current

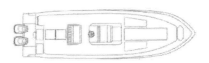

Updated version of original Sea Vee 290B (2000–04) with greater beam, increased range made a good boat even better. Expansive single-level cockpit comes standard with massive in-deck fishbox forward, 50-gallon transom livewell, transom door, freshwater washdown, pop-up cleats, walk-in head with forward entry. Tremendous rod storage. Unique cooler slides out on track from under leaning post. Deep-V hull delivers outstanding rough-water ride. Designed for today's heavy 4-stroke engines. Over 50 knots with twin 250s.

Length	29'6"	Fuel	235 gals.
Beam	9'0"	Water	40 gals.
Draft, Up	1'6"	Max HP	500
Draft, Down	3'2"	Hull Type	Deep-V
Hull Weight	4,850#	Deadrise Aft	25°

See Page 564 For Resale Values

Sea Vee Boats
Miami, FL
www.seaveeboats.com

Sea Vee 310B Open
2004–07

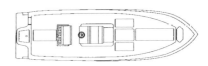

Fast-action canyon runner with serious eye appeal delivers top-shelf construction, leading-edge performance. Expansive single-level cockpit provides unsurpassed 360-degree fishability. Fishing features include big 60-gallon transom livewell, lockable rod storage, in-deck fishboxes. Unique cooler slides out on track from under leaning post and locks in place. Enclosed head compartment has electric toilet, standing headroom. Note tall windshield. Twin 250hp outboards reach 40+ knots wide open.

Length	32'6"	Fuel, Std.	250 gals.
Beam	9'4"	Fuel, Opt.	300 gals.
Draft, Up	1'8"	Max HP	500
Draft, Down	3'0"	Hull Type	Deep-V
Hull Weight	5,500#	Deadrise Aft	25°

Insufficient Resale Data To Assign Values

Sea Vee Boats
Miami, FL
www.seaveeboats.com

Sea Vee 320B Open
2007–Current

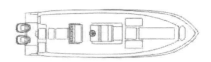

Purebred fishing machine lives up to See Vee reputation for quality construction, engineering excellence. Design highlights include 60-gallon transom livewell, transom bait station, tackle lockers, pop-up cleats, huge insulated fishbox forward, anchor locker. Front console seat lifts for access to head compartment. Lockable stowage for more than 30 rods. Unobstructed single-level cockpit provides true 360-degree fish-fighting arena. Twin 275 Mercury outboards top out at 40+ knots.

Length	32'5"	Fuel	300 gals.
Beam	9'4"	Water	46 gals.
Draft, Up	1'8"	Max HP	600
Draft, Down	3'0"	Hull Type	Deep-V
Hull Weight	6,200#	Deadrise Aft	25°

Insufficient Resale Data To Assign Values

Sea Vee Boats
Miami, FL
www.seaveeboats.com

Sportfishing Boats

Sea Vee 340B Open
2001–Current

Tournament-ready 34-footer with triple-outboard potential combines quality construction with agile performance, hardcore fishability. Single-level cockpit features huge 60-gallon transom livewell, lockable in-deck rod storage, three insulated fishboxes, pop-up cleats, tackle lockers. Roomy head compartment (with forward entry) has electric toilet, sink, shower. Plenty of space at the helm for electronics. This kind of quality isn't cheap. Cuddy and diesel inboard models also available. Yamaha 250s deliver 40+ knots top.

Length	34'9"	Fuel	350 gals.
Beam	10'0"	Water	50 gals.
Draft, Up	1'8"	Max HP	1,050
Draft, Down	3'0"	Hull Type	Deep-V
Hull Weight	6,500#	Deadrise Aft	23.5°

See Page 564 For Resale Values

Sea Vee Boats
Miami, FL
www.seaveeboats.com

Seacraft 32 Center Console
2000–08

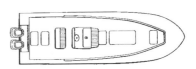

Tournament-tested fishing machine with conventional transom, full-height splashboard blends quality construction with first-rate fishing amenities. Leaning post with rocket launchers, factory T-top with rod holders, in-deck livewell, in-deck fishbox with macerator, are standard. Single-level cockpit offers unobstructed 360° fishability. Gunwales are wide enough to stand on. Optional coffin box lifts hydraulically to expose cavernous storage area. Pump room in lazarette is a nice touch. About 40 knots top with twin 250s.

Length	32'0"	Fuel	300 gals.
Beam	9'6"	Water	30 gals.
Draft, Up	1'6"	Max HP	600
Draft, Down	2'8"	Hull Type	Modified-V
Dry Weight	7,000#	Deadrise Aft	20°

See Page 564 For Resale Values

Seacraft Boats
Forest City, NC
www.seacraft-boats.com

Seaswirl 2901 Walkaround
2002–07

Popular walkaround cabin with wide beam combines angler-friendly cockpit with cruiser-ready interior. Cozy cabin with mini-galley, enclosed head with shower, V-berth with lift-up backrests sleeps four adults, two kids. Cockpit fishing amenities include 38-gallon livewell, built-in tackle boxes, in-floor fishboxes, transom door. Note folding transom seat, well-arranged helm with room for electronics, above-average finish. Generator is optional. Twin 225hp Yamahas deliver a top speed of 40+ knots. Classy boat.

Length	29'8"	Fuel	239 gals.
Beam	10'5"	Water	29 gals.
Draft, Up	1'4"	Max HP	500
Draft, Down	2'7"	Hull Type	Deep-V
Weight w/Engine	8,500#	Deadrise Aft	20°

See Page 565 For Resale Values

Seaswirl Boat
Culver, OR
www.seaswirl.com

Sportfishing Boats

231-360-0827

Seaswirl 2901 Pilothouse
2005–Current

Sterndrive Version

Outboard Model

Roomy 29-foot walkaround with enclosed pilothouse is part fishing boat, part family cruiser. Inviting cabin with full galley, enclosed head with shower, 6'5" headroom sleeps four adults, two kids. Standard fishing features include two in-deck fishboxes, 31-gallon livewell, bait station, rod holders. Rear cockpit seat lifts to provide access to sterndrive engines. Generator, air-conditioning are optional. Note sliding pilothouse windows. Volvo 260hp diesel I/Os cruise at 25 knots (38–40 knots top); 250hp Yamaha outboards top out in the low 40s.

Length	29'0"	Fuel	217 gals.
Beam	10'5"	Water	29 gals.
Draft, Up	1'10"	Max HP	500
Draft, Down	2'9"	Hull Type	Deep-V
Weight	10,350#	Deadrise Aft	20°

See Page 565 For Resale Values

Seaswirl Boat
Culver, OR
www.seaswirl.com

231-360-0827

Seaswirl 3301 Walkaround
2007–Current

Big-water express with wide 11-foot beam makes good on promise of big-water fishability, well-appointed cruiser. Roomy cockpit boasts clever foldaway seats, transom livewell, two in-deck fishboxes, baitrigging station. Walk-through windshield, wide side decks make going forward easy. Well-appointed cabin with midship berth, pipe berths forward can sleep six. Air-conditioning, hardtop, generator are standard. Not much space at the helm for electronics. Yamaha 250s max out at close to 40 knots.

Length	33'5"	Fuel	347 gals.
Beam	11'0"	Water	38 gals.
Draft, Up	1'4"	Max HP	600
Draft, Down	2'7"	Hull Type	Deep-V
Weight w/Eng.	10,700#	Deadrise Aft	20°

See Page 565 For Resale Values

Seaswirl Boat
Culver, OR
www.seaswirl.com

231-360-0827

Shamrock 270 Mackinaw
2000–Current

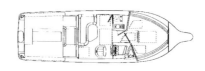

All-weather hardtop fisherman with inboard power, pocket-type hull is tough, versatile, built to last. Enclosed pilothouse contains small galley, removable table, fully equipped helm, berths for two. Head is very small with only sitting headroom. Cockpit has aft-facing bench seating, transom door, in-deck fishbox, transom livewell. Note opening cabin windows, bow pulpit. Finish is average, but construction is tough. Cruise at 18 knots with standard 320hp gas engine (high 20s top); 22–23 knots with optional Yanmar 315hp diesel.

Length w/Pulpit	30'6"	Weight	7,525#
Hull Length	28'10"	Fuel	156 gals.
Beam	9'3"	Water	20 gals.
Draft	2'5"	Hull Type	Modified-V
Clearance	8'2"	Deadrise Aft	14°

See Page 565 For Resale Values

Shamrock Boats
www.shamrockboats.com

www.powerboatguide.com 231-360-0827

Shamrock 270 Open
2000–Current

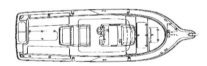

Rock-solid fisherman with inboard power combines space, versatility, economy. Highlights include large console with space for electronics, enclosed head with sink and shower, removable in-deck fishboxes, transom bait-prep center, 32-gallon livewell. Note wide transom door with gate. Relatively heavy boat delivers a good open-water ride; modified-V hull has prop pocket to reduce draft, improve efficiency. Standard 320hp gas engine will cruise at 18 knots and reach a top speed of nearly 30 knots.

Length w/Pulpit	30'6"	Weight	6,276#
Hull Length	28'10"	Fuel	160 gals.
Beam	9'3"	Water	20 gals.
Draft	2.5"	Hull Type	Modified-V
Clearance, Top	8'8"	Deadrise Aft	14°

See Page 565 For Resale Values

Shamrock Boats
www.shamrockboats.com

---

www.powerboatguide.com 231-360-0827

Shamrock 290 Walkaround
1999–2003

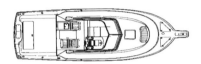

Heavily built walkaround cabin with smooth-riding deep-V hull is one part fishing boat, one part family cruiser. Standard features include 38-gallon livewell, bait-rigging station behind passenger seat, big in-deck fishbox, fresh- and saltwater washdowns, transom door. Surprisingly large cabin with galley, enclosed head with shower, sleeps four. Note tilt-away helm, deep cockpit, wide side decks. Entire bridgedeck lifts for engine access. Twin 300hp gas inboards cruise in the low 20s and top out at over 30 knots.

Length w/Pulpit	30'10"	Clearance, Top	10.5"
Hull Length	28'10"	Fuel	250 gals.
Beam	11'3"	Water	30 gals.
Draft	2'10"	Hull Type	Deep-V
Weight	10,500#	Deadrise Aft	19°

See Page 565 For Resale Values

Shamrock Boats
www.shamrockboats.com

---

www.powerboatguide.com 231-360-0827

Shamrock 31 Grand Slam
1987–94

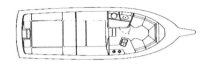

Deep-V express introduced in 1987 was a notable departure from Shamrock's signature "Keel-Drive" single-inboard hull design. Well-arranged cockpit with tackle center, 30-gallon livewell has room for full-size fighting chair. Helm seat pivots up to serve as leaning post. Cozy cabin with convertible dinette, enclosed head with shower, pipe berths sleeps four. Unique service bay houses mechanical, electrical systems. Popular boat—total of 160 built. Cummins 250hp diesels cruise at 28 knots; Cummins 300hp diesels cruise at 30 knots.

Length	31'0"	Fuel, Std.	290 gals.
Beam	11'4"	Fuel, Opt.	340 gals.
Draft	3'4"	Water	40 gals.
Weight	10,800#	Hull Type	Deep-V
Clearance	18'0"	Deadrise Aft	19°

Prices Not Provided for Pre-1995 Models

Shamrock Boats
www.shamrockboats.com

Sportfishing Boats

Sportfishing Boats

231-360-0827

Skipjack 30 Flybridge
1997–Current

Rugged California-built fisherman matches solid construction with no-frills accommodations, dependable performance. Large cockpit, sturdy rails, wide side decks appeal to experienced anglers. Efficient single-level interior with oak trim, convertible dinette, angled double berth sleeps four. Note wraparound cabin windows, generous storage. Transom fishbox, 30-gallon livewell, transom door are standard. Cockpit hatch lifts electrically for engine access. Yanmar 315hp V-drive diesels cruise at 22–24 knots (about 30 top).

Length w/Pulpit	34'10"	Fuel	300 gals.
Hull Length	30'0"	Water	75 gals.
Beam	11'2"	Waste	40 gals.
Draft	3'4"	Hull Type	Modified-V
Weight	16,000#	Deadrise Aft	16°

See Page 567 For Resale Values

Skipjack Boats
Hesperia, CA
www.skipjack-boats.com

231-360-0827

Southport 28 Center Console
2005–Current

No-nonsense fishing machine appeals to hardcore anglers with an eye for superior engineering, leading-edge quality. Leaning post with backrest, deluxe helm seat with 45-gallon livewell, fore/aft coaming pads, transom rigging station with sink, lift-out aft fishbox, console head compartment with lockable rod storage. Insulated coffin box forward doubles as lounge seating. Single-level cockpit means no stubbed toes. Very impressive finish. Deep-V hull can take a pounding. Max 40+ knots with 225hp Hondas.

Length	28'6"	Fuel	250 gals.
Beam	10'6"	Water	NA
Draft, Up	1'7"	Max HP	700
Draft, Down	2'10"	Hull Type	Deep-V
Hull Weight	5,800#	Deadrise Aft	22°

See Page 567 For Resale Values

Southport Boat Works
www.southport-boatworks.com

231-360-0827

Stamas 270 Express
1997–Current

Floorplan Not Available

Roomy 27-foot express with wide 9'7" beam is versatile, stable, quick. Standard fishing features include 18-gallon transom livewell, transom fishbox, tackle drawers, rod storage, raw-water washdown. Note aft-facing cockpit seats with insulated fish/storage boxes under. Full-featured cabin with stand-up head, midcabin berth, compact galley sleeps four. Wide side decks add extra level of security. Note excellent helm layout, generous storage capacity. Twin 200hp outboards deliver a top speed of close to 40 knots.

Length w/Pulpit	28'9"	Fuel	204 gals.
Hull Length	27'1"	Water	20 gals.
Beam	9'7"	Max HP	450
Hull Draft	1'6"	Hull Type	Modified-V
Weight w/Engine	5,800#	Deadrise Aft	18°

See Page 567 For Resale Values

Stamas Yachts
Tarpon Springs, FL
www.stamas.com

231-360-0827

Stamas 270 Tarpon
1997–Current

Conservative, time-tested fishing rig with bow casting platform hits the right note with anglers looking for solid construction, dependable operation. Standard amenities include three insulated fishboxes, abundant rod storage, tackle drawers, removable bench seats, raw-water washdown, leaning post with rod holders, pop-up cleats, transom door, walk-in head with opening port. Twin 110-gallon fuel tanks provide excellent range, but 18-gallon livewell is small for a 27-footer. About 40 knots top with Yamaha 200s.

Length w/Pulpit	28'9"	Fuel	220 gals.
Hull Length	27'1"	Water	10 gals.
Beam	9'7"	Max HP	450
Hull Draft	1'8"	Hull Type	Modified-V
Weight w/Engine	5,200#	Deadrise Aft	18°

See Page 567 For Resale Values

Stamas Yachts
Tarpon Springs, FL
www.stamas.com

231-360-0827

Stamas 288 Liberty/Family Fisherman
1987–94

Affordably priced express (called Stamas 288 Fisherman in 1993–94) with big cockpit gave anglers and cruisers a lot to like. Broad 11'2" beam made this one of the bigger 28-footers in her class. Deep, single-level cockpit came standard with two forward fishboxes, two livewells, insulated icebox. Roomy cabin with stand-up head, mini-galley, aft berth sleeps four adults. Offered with sterndrive or bracket-mounted outboard power. Twin 205hp I/Os cruise at 20 knots (30+ knots top); twin 225hp outboards reach 40 knots top.

Length w/Pulpit	30'2"	Fuel	196 gals.
Hull Length	28'4"	Water	20 gals.
Beam	11'2"	Max HP	500
Draft	1'6"	Hull Type	Modified-V
Weight	9,500#	Deadrise Aft	18°

Prices Not Provided for Pre-1995 Models

Stamas Yachts
Tarpon Springs, FL
www.stamas.com

231-360-0827

Stamas 290 Express
1992–Current

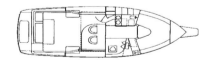

Versatile express with conservative profile is one part fishing boat, one part family cruiser. Deep cockpit comes standard with 20-gallon baitwell, transom door, insulated fishbox, tackle box. Comfortable interior with midcabin berth, full galley, enclosed head sleeps four. Original double-helm seating was replaced in 1998 with separate helm, companion seats. Tall windshield offers good wind protection. Twin 225hp Yamahas cruise at 40+ knots top. Available with sterndrive power.

Length w/Pulpit	31'7"	Fuel	250 gals.
Hull Length	29'3"	Water	27 gals.
Beam	10'4"	Max HP	500
Hull Draft	1'5"	Hull Type	Modified-V
Weight	6,550#	Deadrise Aft	18°

See Page 567 For Resale Values

Stamas Yachts
Tarpon Springs, FL
www.stamas.com

Sportfishing Boats

231-360-0827

Stamas 290 Tarpon
1995–Current

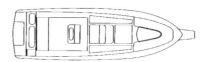

opular sportfisherman from well-regarded builder is easy on the eye, economical to operate, built to last. Uncluttered deck layout with low-freeboard gunwales boasts in-floor rod storage, transom fishbox, two forward fishboxes, built-in tackle box, transom door, removable aft storage box, raw-water washdown, lockable head compartment, electronic box. Leaning post incorporates rigging station, sink, 50-gallon livewell. Casting platform converts to dinette. Also available with sterndrive power. Yamaha 225s reach 40+ knots top.

Length w/Pulpit	31'7"	Fuel	302 gals.
Hull Length	29'3"	Water	20 gals.
Beam	10'4"	Max HP	500
Hull Draft	1.5"	Hull Type	Modified-V
Weight	6,000#	Deadrise Aft	18°

See Page 567 For Resale Values

Stamas Yachts
Tarpon Springs, FL
www.stamas.com

231-360-0827

Stamas 310 Express
1993–Current

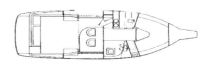

andsome midsize express gets high marks for space, construction, owner satisfaction. More fishboat than cruiser, well-appointed midcabin interior has all the amenities required for comfortable weekends away from home. Spacious cockpit comes standard with full array of fishing features including bait-prep station with sink, cutting board, tackle storage drawers, livewell, transom door. Note efficient helm layout with space for electronics. Twin 225hp Yamahas top out at close to 40 knots. Also available with inboard power.

Length w/Pulpit	32'6"	Fuel	300 gals.
Hull Length	30'9"	Water	40 gals.
Beam	11'2"	Max HP	500
Hull Draft	1'8"	Hull Type	Modified-V
Weight w/OB	9,800#	Deadrise Aft	18°

See Page 567 For Resale Values

Stamas Yachts
Tarpon Springs, FL
www.stamas.com

231-360-0827

Stamas 310 Tarpon
1999–Current

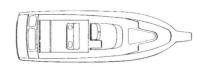

ig offshore center console appeals to savvy anglers looking for solid construction, large fishing cockpit, first-rate fishing amenities. Spacious deck layout with forward seating features standard leaning post with rigging station, 50-gallon circulating livewell, rear bench seat, transom door, forward fish boxes (2), raw-water washdown. Huge console houses roomy head with unique entry door next to helm. Excellent range. Modified-V hull delivers stable rough-water ride. Sterndrive diesel is optional. About 40 knots top with twin 250s.

Length w/Pulpit	32'6"	Fuel	400 gals.
Hull Length	30'9"	Water	20 gals.
Beam	11'2"	Max HP	500
Hull Draft	1'6"	Hull Type	Modified-V
Weight w/OB	9,250#	Deadrise Aft	18°

See Page 567 For Resale Values

Stamas Yachts
Tarpon Springs, FL
www.stamas.com

231-360-0827

Stamas 32 Sport Fisherman
1978-87

Versatile flybridge fishing boat with roomy cockpit, family-friendly interior remains a lot of boat for the money. Highlights include semi-enclosed helm deck with convertible dinette, private bow stateroom with long V-berth, enclosed head with shower, compact flybridge with bench seating. Wide side decks make getting around easy. Windshield vents are a plus. Note foredeck seating area. Cockpit is large enough for two or three anglers and their gear. No transom door. Cruise at 20 knots with 330hp gas inboards (about 28 knots top).

Length	32'3"	Fuel	250 gals.
Beam	12'0"	Water	50 gals.
Draft	2'9"	Waste	20 gals.
Weight	12,800#	Hull Type	Modified-V
Clearance	11'6"	Deadrise Aft	16°

Prices Not Provided for Pre-1995 Models

Stamas Yachts
Tarpon Springs, FL
www.stamas.com

231-360-0827

Stamas 320 Express
2004-Current

Floorplan Not Available

Competitively priced express with versatile personality lives up to promise of cruising comfort, proven fishability. Large cockpit comes standard with full array of fishing amenities including transom livewell, insulated transom fishbox, wide transom door. Engine access is via hydraulic deck hatch. Teak-trimmed interior with midcabin berth, convertible dinette, teak-and-holly sole sleeps six. Twin 320hp MerCruiser gas inboards cruise at 22 knots (30 top). Outboard version with 225hp Yamahas tops out at close to 35 knots.

Length w/Pulpit	34 5"	Fuel, IB	240 gals.
Hull Length	32'3"	Fuel, OB	316 gals.
Beam	11'2"	Water	40 gals.
Draft	2'20"	Hull Type	Modified-V
Weight	13,200#	Deadrise Aft	18°

See Page 567 For Resale Values

Stamas Yachts
Tarpon Springs, FL
www.stamas.com

231-360-0827

Stamas 340 Express
2003-Current

Floorplan Not Available

Quality midsize express splits the difference between hardcore fishboat, comfortable family cruiser. Uncluttered cockpit comes standard with full array of fishing amenities including transom livewell, insulated fishbox, wide transom door. Engine access is via hydraulic deck hatch. Well-appointed interior with midcabin berth sleeps six. Prop pockets reduce draft, improve efficiency. MerCruiser 370hp gas inboards cruise at 22 knots (30+ top); Yanmar 370hp diesels cruise at 25 knots (30 top). Outboard version also available.

Length w/Pulpit	36'2"	Clearance	7'3"
Hull Length	34'0"	Fuel	350 gals.
Beam	12'6"	Water	84 gals.
Draft	2'4"	Hull Type	Modified-V
Weight	14,000#	Deadrise Aft	18°

See Page 567 For Resale Values

Stamas Yachts
Tarpon Springs, FL
www.stamas.com

Sportfishing Boats

Stamas 360 Express

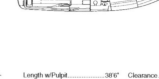

Sturdy 1990s cruiser with conservative lines, legendary Stamas construction targets family anglers with an eye for value. Fishing amenities include livewell, raw-water washdown, insulated fishboxes, rod storage. Elevated helm affords excellent visibility. Tasteful midcabin interior with convertible dinette, full galley sleeps four adults, two kids. Deep keel, prop pockets protect running gear in event of grounding. Wide side decks are a plus. Standard 310hp MerCruiser gas inboards cruise at 18

Length w/Pulpit	38'6"	Clearance	8'3"
Hull Length	36'0"	Fuel	372 gals.
Beam	13'2"	Water	90 gals.
Draft	2'4"	Hull Type	Modified-V
Weight	16,975#	Deadrise Aft	18°

See Page 567

Stamas Yachts
Tarpon Springs, FL

Stamas 370 Express
2000–Current

Updated version of Stamas 360 Express (1992–99) with many new features makes a good boat even better. Midcabin interior is rare in a dedicated fishing boat. Sizable cockpit has built-in livewell, insulated fishbox, bait-prep station, tackle drawers. Well-designed helm has space for flush-mounting electronics. Note wide side decks. Power engine hatch provides outstanding service access. Deep keel, prop pockets protect running gear in event of grounding. Yanmar 420hp diesels cruise at 24–26 knots (30+ knots wide open).

Length w/Pulpit	39'2"	Headroom	6'4"
Hull Length	36'8"	Fuel	400 gals.
Beam	13'2"	Water	84 gals.
Draft	2'4"	Hull Type	Modified-V
Weight	16,975#	Deadrise Aft	18°

See Page 567 For Resale Values

Stamas Yachts
Tarpon Springs, FL
www.stamas.com

Sunseeker 37 Sportfisher
2004–07

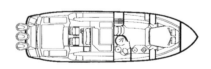

English-built fishing boat combines spirited performance with top-shelf construction, uncommon luxury. Center-console deck layout with seating forward results in relatively small aft cockpit. Beautifully finished interior features high-gloss cherry cabinetry, premium furnishings. Livewell, bait-prep center, fishboxes are standard. Side-boarding ladder keeps swimmers away from props. Note stepped hull bottom. Volvo 310hp diesel I/Os top out at 35 knots; triple 250hp Yamaha outboards reach top speed of 40+ knots.

Length w/Pulpit	39'8"	Fuel	396 gals.
Hull Length	37'1"	Water	60 gals.
Beam	11'7"	Waste	10 gals.
Draft, Drives Down	3'9"	Hull Type	Deep-V
Weight	17,420#	Deadrise Aft	19°

See Page 568 For Resale Values

Sunseeker Yachts
Poole, England
www.sunseeker.com

231-360-0827

Tiara 2700 Open
1987–93

Iconic inboard express supplies hard-to-beat mix of spacious cockpit, upscale interior, quality construction. Teak-trimmed cabin with full-service galley, stand-up head with shower, sleeps two. Single-level cockpit with back-to-back seating is large enough for mounted chair. Wide sidedecks, sturdy rails provide secure foredeck access. Note commercial-quality windshield, easy-access motorboxes, deep-V hull. Many updates/improvements over the years. Crusader 270hp gas engines cruise in the low 20s (28–30 knots wide open).

Length w/Pulpit	29'5"	Clearance	7'0"
Hull Length	27'0"	Fuel	240 gals.
Beam	10'0"	Water	20 gals.
Draft	2'0"	Hull Type	Deep-V
Weight	7,500#	Deadrise Aft	22°

Prices Not Provided for Pre-1995 Models

Tiara Yachts
Holland, MI
www.tiarayachts.com

231-360-0827

Tiara 2900 Open
1993–2006

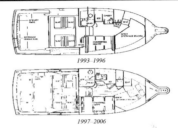

1993–1996

1997–2006

Versatile Tiara express with upscale interior, efficient deck layout delivers best-in-class engineering, construction, performance. Uncluttered cockpit features double helm and companion seats forward, twin aft-facing seats, wide transom door. Well-appointed cabin with full galley, convertible dinette sleeps four. Wide beam for a 29-footer. Entire bridgedeck lifts electrically for engine access. Used models are always in demand. Twin 320hp inboard gas engines cruise at 20 knots (close to 30 knots top).

Length w/Pulpit	30'9"	Fuel	200 gals.
Hull Length	28'9"	Water	30 gals.
Beam	11'4"	Waste	20 gals.
Draft	2'8"	Hull Type	Modified-V
Weight	10,700#	Deadrise Aft	19°

See Page 568 For Resale Values

Tiara Yachts
Holland, MI
www.tiarayachts.com

231-360-0827

Tiara 3000 Open
2007–Current

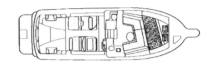

Premium hardtop express with innovative interior couples graceful styling elegance with signature Tiara quality. Wide beam creates large cockpit with jump seat, workstation/wet bar with insulated storage, sprayer, cutting board. Elegant teak cabin with hardwood sole, forward side berth features posh aft-facing lounge that converts to double berth. Note tall windshield, tilt-away helm, opening hardtop vents. Bridgedeck lifts electrically for engine access. Cruise at 22–24 knots with 385hp gas inboards (low-to-mid 30s top).

Length w/Pulpit	33'0"	Fuel	210 gals.
Hull Length	30'6"	Water	32 gals.
Beam	12'6"	Waste	20 gals.
Draft	2'8"	Hull Type	Modified-V
Weight	13,225#	Deadrise Aft	14°

See Page 568 For Resale Values

Tiara Yachts
Holland, MI
www.tiarayachts.com

Tiara 3000 Open
2007–Current

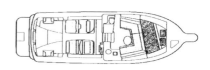

Premium hardtop express with innovative interior couples graceful styling elegance with signature Tiara quality. Wide beam creates large cockpit with jump seat, workstation/wet bar with insulated storage, sprayer, cutting board. Elegant teak cabin with hardwood sole, forward side berth features posh aft-facing lounge that converts to double berth. Note tall windshield, tilt-away helm, opening hardtop vents. Bridgedeck lifts electrically for engine access. Cruise at 22–24 knots with 385hp gas inboards (low-to-mid 30s top).

Length w/Pulpit	33'0"	Fuel	210 gals.
Hull Length	30'6"	Water	32 gals.
Beam	12'6"	Waste	20 gals.
Draft	2'8"	Hull Type	Modified-V
Weight	13,225#	Deadrise Aft	14°

See Page 568 For Resale Values

Tiara Yachts
Holland, MI
www.tiarayachts.com

Tiara 3100 Continental; 310 Convertible
1982–92

3100 Convertible

31090 Flybridge

Flybridge version of popular Tiara 3100 Open (called the 3100 Continental in 1982–86) splits the difference between polished family cruiser, practical sportfisherman. Well-finished interior has comfortable salon/pilothouse with lower helm, galley and dinette down, private bow stateroom with dinette pass-thru. Wide sidedecks, sturdy bowrails are a plus. Small cockpit lacks transom door. Note that 3100 Flybridge model (1987–92) has no salon bulkhead. Twin 340hp gas inboards cruise at 20 knots (high 20s top).

Length w/Pulpit	33'9"	Clearance	12'2"
Hull Length	31'3"	Fuel	206 gals.
Bean	12'0"	Water	36 gals.
Draft	2'11"	Hull Type	Modified-V
Weight	13,200#	Deadrise Aft	16°

Prices Not Provided for Pre-1995 Models

Tiara Yachts
Holland, MI
www.tiarayachts.com

Tiara 3100 Open
1979–91

Classic 1980s express reinforced Tiara reputation for superior engineering, top-shelf construction. Versatile layout—equally well-suited for fishing or cruising—boasts appealing teak-trimmed interior with big U-shaped dinette, large cockpit with removable bench seat, roomy engine compartment with good service acces. Note tall, commercial-quality windshield, aft-facing cockpit seats. Modified-V hull can be a wet ride. Standard 350hp gas inboards cruise in the low 20s (32–33 knots top). Replaced with all-new 3100 Open in 1992.

Length w/Pulpit	33'9"	Clearance, Arch	7'6"
Hull Length	31'3"	Fuel	196 gals.
Beam	12'0"	Water	36 gals.
Draft	2'9"	Hull Type	Modified-V
Weight	10,500#	Deadrise Aft	14°

Prices Not Provided for Pre-1995 Models

Tiara Yachts
Holland, MI
www.tiarayachts.com

Sportfishing Boats

231-360-0827

Tiara 3100 Open
1992–2004

Updated version of original 3100 Open (1979–91) made a great boat even better. Reworked hull with prop pockets, increased deadrise, delivers better head-sea ride than her predecessor; new bi-level cockpit allows installation of diesels in larger engine compartment. Luxury-class interior with U-shaped dinette, full galley sleeps four. Cockpit came with in-deck fishbox, livewell, foldaway rear seat. Transom door became standard in 1994. Cruise at 20 knots with 320hp gas engines; 22–23 knots with 330hp Cummins diesels.

Length w/Pulpit	33'10"	Fuel	246 gals.
Hull Length	31'6"	Water	38 gals.
Beam	12'0"	Waste	20 gals.
Draft	3'0"	Hull Type	Modified-V
Weight	12,300#	Deadrise Aft	18°

See Page 568 For Resale Values

Tiara Yachts
Holland, MI
www.tiarayachts.com

231-360-0827

Tiara 3200 Open
2004–Current

Graceful styling, top-shelf construction, luxury appointments make this versatile express a class leader with savvy buyers. Bi-level cockpit with in-deck fishbox, transom door is large enough for several anglers. Upscale interior with solid teak cabinetry, Ultra-leather seating sleeps four. Bridgedeck rises electrically for engine access. Optional livewell replaces standard fold-down transom seat. Hardtop is a popular option. Note prop-pocket hull bottom. Cruise at 22 knots with 385hp gas engines; mid 20ss with Volvo 310hp diesels.

Length w/Pulpit	35'1"	Fuel	256 gals.
Hull Length	32'7"	Water	38 gals.
Beam	13'0"	Waste	20 gals.
Draft	3'0"	Hull Type	Modified-V
Weight	15,950#	Deadrise Aft	18°

See Page 568 For Resale Values

Tiara Yachts
Holland, MI
www.tiarayachts.com

231-360-0827

Tiara 3300 Flybridge
1986–92

Handsome flybridge cruiser with low cabin profile is sporty, agile, sturdy. Big 100-square-foot cockpit with transom door, in-deck fishbox, livewell is among largest in her class. Easy-care cabin with offset entry, stand-up head, convertible dinette sleeps four. Low-deadrise hull is balsa-cored above waterline; side exhausts exit just forward of transom. Note good engine access, well-arranged bridge. Standard 350hp Crusaders cruise at 20–21 knots; optional 300hp GM 8.2 diesels (or 320hp Cats) cruise at 24–25 knots.

Length	32'10"	Fuel	295 gals.
Beam	12'6"	Water	46 gals.
Draft	2'8"	Waste	20 gals.
Weight	13,000#	Hull Type	Modified-V
Clearance	11'6"	Deadrise Aft	14°

Prices Not Provided for Pre-1995 Models

Tiara Yachts
Holland, MI
www.tiarayachts.com

Sportfishing Boats

231-360-0827

Tiara 3300 Open
1988–97

Feature-rich express with conservative lines, superior finish delivers exceptional cruising comfort, owner satisfaction. Elegant teak-trimmed interior with U-shaped dinette, convertible settee sleeps six in genuine comfort. Tournament-grade cockpit with transom door, fishbox is big enough for serious fishing pursuits. Wide side decks, good engine access, well-designed helm layout. Low-deadrise hull can be a stiff ride. Cruise at 20 knots with standard gas engines; 24 knots with 315hp Cummins diesels.

Length w/Pulpit	35'8"	Fuel	295 gals.
Hull Length	32'10"	Water	46 gals.
Beam	12'6"	Waste	20 gals.
Draft	2'3"	Hull Type	Modified-V
Weight	13,500#	Deadrise Aft	14°

See Page 568 For Resale Values

Tiara Yachts
Holland, MI
www.tiarayachts.com

231-360-0827

Tiara 3500 Open
1998–2004

Top-ranked express combines traditional Tiara styling with high-end construction, uncommon luxury. Spacious single-stateroom interior features solid teak joinery, leather upholstery, beautiful teak-and-holly cabin sole. Crowd-friendly cockpit with foldaway rear seat serves anglers, cruisers alike. Entire bridgedeck rises for engine access. Note wide side decks, power windshield vent, ergonomic helm layout. Standard gas inboards cruise at 16–18 knots; optional 370hp Cummins diesels cruise at 25–26 knots.

Length w/Pulpit	40'8"	Fuel	360 gals.
Hull Length	35'6"	Water	70 gals.
Beam	13'3"	Waste	30 gals.
Draft	3'3"	Hull Type	Modified-V
Weight	14,000#	Deadrise Aft	18°

See Page 569 For Resale Values

Tiara Yachts
Holland, MI
www.tiarayachts.com

231-360-0827

Tiara 3600 Convertible
1987–95

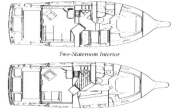

Two-Stateroom Interior

Single-Stateroom Interior

Polished flybridge sedan introduced in 1987 is one part fishing boat, two parts coastal cruiser. Offered with original two-stateroom interior or less popular single-stateroom layout with dinette in place of guest cabin. Sliding glass door leads into roomy salon whose open front windshield allowed for optional lower helm position. Modest cockpit dimensions preclude installation of tackle center. Standard 350hp gas engines cruise at 19–20 knots; optional Cat 375hp diesels cruise at 25 knots and post a top speed of 29–30 knots.

Length w/Pulpit	39'8"	Clearance	12'6"
Hull Length	36'8"	Fuel	396 gals.
Beam	13'9"	Water	85 gals.
Draft	3'0"	Hull Type	Modified-V
Weight	18,300#	Deadrise Aft	14°

See Page 569 For Resale Values

Tiara Yachts
Holland, MI
www.tiarayachts.com

231-360-0827

Tiara 3600 Open
1987–96

Standard Floorplan

Alternate Floorplan

Strong-selling express set class standards in her era for versatile mix of hard-nosed fishability, family-style accommodations. Highlights include well-appointed interior with solid teak joinery, expansive bi-level cockpit, top-quality construction. Original cabin layout with island berth forward sleeps four; alternate layout introduced in 1989 sleeps six. Entire bridgedeck lifts on hydraulic rams for engine access. Conservative lines still look good today. Standard 350hp gas engines cruise at 18 knots; 375hp Cats cruise at 24–25 knots.

Length w/Pulpit	36'8"	Headroom	6'2"
Beam	13'9"	Fuel	396 gals.
Draft	2'11"	Water	85 gals.
Weight	16,500#	Hull Type	Modified-V
Clearance	9'7"	Deadrise Aft	14°

See Page 569 For Resale Values

Tiara Yachts
Holland, MI
www.tiarayachts.com

231-360-0827

Tiara 3600 Open
2005–Current

Top-quality express appeals to anglers, cruisers alike with fish-ready cockpit, upscale cabin accommodations. Posh interior with solid teak joinery, Ultraleather dinette (with flip-up backrest) sleeps five. Professional-grade cockpit features aft-facing seats, in-deck fishboxes, transom livewell, fold-down transom seat. Bridgedeck lifts for engine access. Note aggressive nonskid, tilt-away dash, sturdy windshield. Cummins 380hp diesels cruise at 26–28 knots. Newer models with 370hp Volvo IPS drives cruise efficiently at 28 knots.

Length	36 5"	Fuel	400 gals.
Beam	13'3"	Water	70 gals.
Draft	3 5"	Waste	30 gals.
Weight	19,100#	Hull Type	Modified-V
Clearance	9'10"	Deadrise Aft	18°

See Page 569 For Resale Values

Tiara Yachts
Holland, MI
www.tiarayachts.com

231-360-0827

Tiara 3700 Open
1995–2000

Late-model open express delivers gold-plated mix of classic Tiara styling, deluxe accommodations, exceptional finish. Upscale cabin with solid teak joinery, leather upholstery features huge U-shaped dinette, surprisingly roomy galley, private bow stateroom. Topside amenities include L-shaped companion seat with aft-facing double seat, cockpit fishboxes, cooler. Radar arch, foldaway rear cockpit seat were popular options. Note wide side decks. Bridgedeck lifts for engine access. Cat 435hp diesels cruise in the mid 20s (30+ top).

Length w/Pulpit	39'8"	Fuel	411 gals.
Hull Length	37'1"	water	98 gals.
Beam	14'2"	Waste	40 gals.
Draft	3'9"	Hull Type	Modified-V
Weight	21,800#	Deadrise Aft	18°

See Page 569 For Resale Values

Tiara Yachts
Holland, MI
www.tiarayachts.com

Sportfishing Boats

---

www.powerboatguide.com   231-360-0827

Tiara 3800 Open
2000–08

Plan A

Plan B

Leading-edge express splits the difference between luxury sportcruiser, tournament-level fishing machine. Beautifully finished interior features posh seating, solid teak cabinetry, first-rate galley appliances. Note appealing teak-and-holly cabin sole, hideaway salon TV. Topside highlights include cockpit wet bar, foldaway transom seat, wide transom door. Helm layout is as good as it gets. Bridgedeck lifts for engine access. Hardtop with overhead hatches was optional. Cummins 480hp diesels cruise at 25–26 knots (about 30 knots top).

Length Overall	40'9"	Fuel	411 gals.
Beam	14'2"	Water	110 gals.
Draft	3'6"	Waste	40 gals.
Weight	22,600#	Hull Type	Modified-V
Clearance	9'7"	Deadrise Aft	18°

See Page 569 For Resale Values

Tiara Yachts
Holland, MI
www.tiarayachts.com

---

www.powerboatguide.com   231-360-0827

Tiara 3900 Convertible
2006–Current

Capable—but not hardcore—fishing boat loaded with features courts high-end buyers with an eye for beauty, quality. Elegant two-stateroom interior boasts comfortable salon with facing settees, satin-finished teak joinery, traditional teak-and-holly cabin sole. Optional front salon window will appeal to cruisers, but not anglers. Note generous galley storage, posh Ultraleather bulkheads. Hardtop is standard. Cockpit, with engineroom door, is on the small side. Cummins 540hp diesels cruise in the mid 20s (29–30 wide open).

Length w/Pulpit	41'7"	Fuel	470 gals.
Hull Length	39'0"	Water	110 gals.
Beam	14'5"	Waste	38 gals.
Draft	3'6"	Hull Type	Modified-V
Weight	30,125#	Deadrise Aft	14°

See Page 569 For Resale Values

Tiara Yachts
Holland, MI
www.tiarayachts.com

---

www.powerboatguide.com   231-360-0827

Tiara 3900 Open
2009–Current

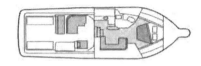

Quality dual-purpose express with broad 15-foot beam meets anglers need for fishability, cruisers need for luxury. Highlights include elegant single-stateroom interior with teak-and-holly sole, big 95-sq.ft. fishing cockpit with in-deck fishboxes, swivel L-shaped companion lounge, meticulous engine compartment. Note raised 3-person mezzanine seating aft of helm deck. Fishing package includes 55-gallon transom livewell, deluxe tackle center. Hardtop is optional. Cummins 600hp diesels cruise at 30 knots (low 30s top).

Length w/Pulpit	41'11"	Fuel	535 gals.
Beam	15'0"	Water	120 gals.
Draft	3'6"	Waste	38 gals.
Weight	24,500#	Hull Type	Modified-V
Clearance, Top	10'4"	Deadrise Aft	18°

Insufficient Resale Data To Assign Values

Tiara Yachts
Holland, MI
www.tiarayachts.com

---

www.powerboatguide.com   231-360-0827

Tiara 4100 Open
1996–2002

Muscular big-water express with spacious cockpit, upscale interior blurs the line between tournament-grade fishing machine, executive-class sportcruiser. Classy single-stateroom interior includes big U-shaped dinette, open galley with plenty of storage, very roomy head. Raised bridgedeck, three steps above cockpit, provides exceptional helm visibility. Large cockpit boasts beefy transom door, engineroom entry door. Wide side decks are always a plus. Cat 435hp diesels cruise at 22 knots (26-27 knots top).

Length w/Pulpit	43'6"	Fuel	524 gals.
Hull Length	41'3"	Water	130 gals.
Beam	14'8"	Waste	50 gals.
Draft	3'6"	Hull Type	Modified-V
Weight	27,500#	Deadrise Aft	18°

See Page 569 For Resale Values

Tiara Yachts
Holland, MI
www.tiarayachts.com

---

www.powerboatguide.com   231-360-0827

Tiara 4200 Open
2003–Current

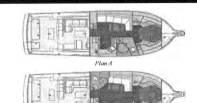

Plan A

Plan B

High-end cruising yacht capable of serious fishing raised the bar for express-boat versatility, luxury, quality. Plan A interior has portside lounge/dinette with galley and head opposite; Plan B adds starboard lounge with curtain or solid enclosure, creating second stateroom. Big 85-sq.ft. cockpit—with engineroom entry, foldaway rear seat—can be configured for fishing, diving, or cruising. Note fiberglass windshield frame, superb helm layout. Hardtop is optional. Cummins 670hp diesels cruise at 28 knots (32–33 knots top).

Length w/Pulpit	44'10"	Fuel	520 gals.
Hull Length	42'6"	Water	130 gals.
Beam	14'11"	Waste	50 gals.
Draft	4'2"	Hull Type	Modified-V
Weight	28,600#	Deadrise Aft	17.5°

See Page 469 For Resale Values

Tiara Yachts
Holland, MI
www.tiarayachts.com

---

www.powerboatguide.com   231-360-0827

Tiara 4300 Convertible
1990–2002

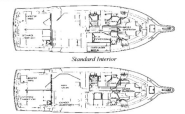

Standard Interior

Optional Dinette Floorplan

Enduring 1990s convertible coupled cruising comfort with handsome styling, hardcore fishability. Original two-stateroom interior has serving counter overlooking galley; optional single-stateroom layout replaced guest cabin with U-shaped dinette. Note overhead rod storage, built-in entertainment center in salon. Roomy cockpit features beefy transom door, bait-prep center with freezer. (Cockpit engineroom access became standard in 1994.) GM 550hp diesels cruise at 22–24 knots; Cat 660hp diesels cruise in the high 20s.

Length w/Pulpit	46'7"	Fuel	640 gals.
Hull Length	43'2"	Water	160 gals.
Beam	15'2"	Waste	60 gals.
Draft	4'0"	Hull Type	Modified-V
Weight	31,500#	Deadrise Aft	16°

See Page 569 For Resale Values

Tiara Yachts
Holland, MI
www.tiarayachts.com

Sportfishing Boats

www.powerboatguide.com   231-360-0827

Tiara 4300 Open
1991–2002

Standard

Optional

Dual-purpose express with fishboat cockpit, cruise-friendly accommodations met Tiara standards for engineering excellence, state-of-the-art construction. Standard interior with convertible L-shaped lounge, convertible dinette sleeps six; optional layout with enlarged salon sleeps four. Note hydraulic salon operated dinette, elegant teak-and-holly sole. Cockpit redesign in 1999 featured fold-down rear seat, direct access to engineroom. Cruise at 25 knots with 550hp GM 6V92s; 26-27 knots with 660hp Cats.

Length w/Pulpit	46'7"	Fuel	526 gals.
Hull Length	43'2"	Water	150 gals.
Beam	15'2"	Waste	62 gals.
Draft	4'0"	Hull Type	Modified-V
Weight	29,500#	Deadrise Aft	16°

See Page 569 For Resale Values

Tiara Yachts
Holland, MI
www.tiarayachts.com

---

www.powerboatguide.com   231-360-0827

Tiara 5000 Open
2002–03

Limited-production luxury yacht appeals to cruisers who like to fish, anglers who like to cruise. Executive-level, two-stateroom interior with SubZero refrigeration—offered with teak or cherry woodwork—is unmatched for elegance, comfort, warmth. Note washer/dryer space in guest stateroom, shared shower stall for both heads.) Expansive 90-square-foot cockpit with in-floor fishbox could be fitted with bait-prep station, 32-gallon livewell. Cat 800hp diesels cruise at 26–28 knots, low 30s top.

Length w/Pulpit	53'0"	Fuel	650 gals.
Hull Length	50'1"	Water	175 gals.
Beam	15'9"	Waste	80 gals.
Draft	5'1"	Hull Type	Modified-V
Weight	41,000#	Deadrise Aft	17°

See Page 569 For Resale Values

Tiara Yachts
Holland, MI
www.tiarayachts.com

---

www.powerboatguide.com   231-360-0827

Tollycraft 34 Convertible Sedan
1981–86

Popular West Coast cruiser from the 1980s appealed to buyers with an eye for graceful styling, rugged construction. Broad 12'6" beam permits very spacious cabin layout with comfortable salon, large galley area, generous storage. Extra-large cabin windows provide exceptional visibility from standard lower helm. Flybridge could be ordered with helm forward or aft. Deep cockpit features transom door, molded corner steps to wide side decks. Note sturdy bow rails. Twin 270hp gas engines cruise at 18 knots (26–27 knots top).

Length	34'0"	Fuel	200 gals.
Beam	12'6"	Water	100 gals.
Draft	2'10"	Cockpit	72 sq. ft.
Weight	17,000#	Hull Type	Modified-V
Clearance	12'2"	Deadrise Aft	12°

Prices Not Provided for Pre-1995 Models

Tollycraft is no longer in business.

231-360-0827

Tollycraft 34 Sport Sedan
1987-93

Feature-packed sedan hits the right buttons with Tollycraft enthusiasts focued on handsome styling, versatile accommodations. Well-appointed interior with solid teak cabinetry boasts two private staterooms—no small achievement in a 34-foot boat. Transom door, in-deck fishbox were standard in small cockpit. Flybridge was offered with helm aft for East Coast buyers, helm forward for Pacific market. Wide side decks are a plus. Note fuel increase beginning with 1988 models. Twin 340hp gas engines cruise at 20 knots (high 20s top).

Length	34'0"	Cockpit	72 sq. ft.
Beam	12'6"	Fuel	200/296 gals.
Draft	2'10"	Water	116 gals.
Weight	17,000#	Hull Type	Modified-V
Clearance	13'11"	Deadrise Aft	13°

Prices Not Provided for Pre-1995 Models

Tollycraft is no longer in business.

231-360-0827

Tollycraft 37 Convertible
1974-85

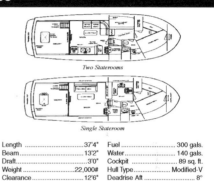

Two Staterooms

Single Stateroom

Seaworthy West Coast convertible built well-earned reputation for versatile layout, rock-solid construction. Offered with single- or twin-stateroom interiors, both featuring standard lower helm, roomy salon with convertible sofa. Original Formica interior was updated to teak in 1977. Extra-large cabin windows provide plenty of natural lighting, good helm visibility. Cockpit is large enough for serious fishing. Twin 350hp gas engines cruise at 20 knots (high 20s top); 210hp Cat diesels cruise at 16–17 knots (around 20 knots top).

Length	37'4"	Fuel	300 gals.
Beam	13'2"	Water	140 gals.
Draft	3'0"	Cockpit	89 sq. ft.
Weight	22,000#	Hull Type	Modified-V
Clearance	12'6"	Deadrise Aft	8°

Prices Not Provided for Pre-1995 Models

Tollycraft is no longer in business.

231-360-0827

Tollycraft 40 Sport Sedan
1987-95

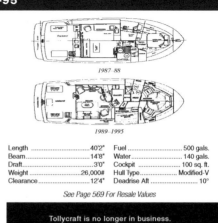

1987-88

1989-1995

Appealing sports convertible for fishing, cruising combines large cockpit with family-friendly accommodations. Two-stateroom interior—completely updated in 1989—is notable for upscale appointments, large windows, generous storage. Lower helm was optional. Cockpit amenities include two in-deck fishboxes, centerline transom door. Big fuel capacity delivers excellent range. Flybridge was offered with helm forward or aft. Cat 375hp diesels cruise at 22 knots (25 knots top); 485hp GMs cruise in the mid 20s (30 knots wide open).

Length	40'2"	Fuel	500 gals.
Beam	14'8"	Water	140 gals.
Draft	3'0"	Cockpit	100 sq. ft.
Weight	26,000#	Hull Type	Modified-V
Clearance	12'4"	Deadrise Aft	10°

See Page 569 For Resale Values

Tollycraft is no longer in business.

Sportfishing Boats

Topaz 29 Sportfisherman
1983–88

Popular 1980s sportfisherman with roomy cockpit combined rugged construction with clean lines, efficient deck layout. Roomy bi-level cockpit with in-sole fishbox offers elbow space for several anglers. Simple cabin with fully enclosed head, full galley sleeps three. Most were sold with factory tower. Low-deadrise hull can be a wet ride in a chop. Large bridgedeck hatch provides good engine access. Twin 200hp Volvo inboard diesels cruise in the mid 20s and reach a top speed of around 30 knots.

Length	29'0"	Fuel	225 gals.
Beam	10'3"	Water	30 gals.
Draft	2'6"	Cockpit	65 sq. ft.
Weight	8,100#	Hull Type	Modified-V
Clearance	NA	Deadrise Aft	NA

Prices Not Provided for Pre-1995 Models

The original Topaz Company went out of business in 1991.

Topaz 32 Sportfisherman
1986–91

Popular East Coast express from late 1980s combines classic good looks with proven fishability. Highlights include roomy fishing cockpit with in-deck storage, raised bridgedeck with centerline engine hatch, snug-but-useful interior with forward V-berth, convertible dinette. Tall windshield provides good high-rpm wind protection. Seakindly hull with generous beam is known for dry, slightly bow-high ride. Volvo 306hp diesels-or Cat 320s-cruise in the mid 20s (about 30 knots top).

Length	32'8"	Fuel	300 gals.
Beam	12'2"	Water	40 gals.
Draft	2'1"	Waste	25 gals.
Weight	16,500#	Hull Type	Modified-V
Clearance	NA	Deadrise Aft	18°

Prices Not Provided for Pre-1995 Models

The original Topaz Company went out of business in 1991.

Topaz 32/33 Express
2004–Current

Updated version of classic Topaz 32 SF (1986–91) brings a time-tested design up to current sportfish standards. Cockpit space is maximized by locating livewell, rigging station forward and placing split-lid fishbox in deck. Efficient helm console has display space for big-screen electronics. Teak-trimmed cabin with convertible dinette, full galley, stand-up head, rod storage sleeps four. Bridgedeck lifts for engine access. Cruise at 25–26 knots with 370hp Cummins diesels (about 30 knots top). Called 32 Express in 2004–06.

Length	32'8"	Headroom	6'3"
Beam	12'2"	Fuel	400 gals.
Draft	3'1"	Water	40 gals.
Weight	20,500#	Hull Type	Modified-V
Clearance	NA	Deadrise Aft	18°

See Page 569 For Resale Values

**Topaz Yachts
Egg Harbor City, NJ
www.topazboats.com**

Topaz 36 Sportfisherman
1980–85

Handsome East Coast express established the Topaz name with hardcore anglers in the early 1980s. Spacious cockpit with in-deck fishboxes has room for full-size mounted chair. Belowdecks accommodations include convertible dinette, full galley, adult-sized V-berth, large head with separate stall shower. Note tight engine access. Beamy hull is very stable, but flat after-sections make for stiff rough-water ride. Among several engine options, Cat 355hp diesels cruise in the low 20s (26–27 knots top).

Length	36'2"	Fuel	300 gals.
Beam	13'0"	Water	50 gals.
Draft	2'5"	Cockpit	NA
Weight	17,800#	Hull Type	Modified-V
Clearance	NA	Deadrise Aft	NA

Prices Not Provided for Pre-1995 Models

The original Topaz Company
went out of business in 1991.

Topaz 37 Sportfisherman
1986–91

Reworked version of best-selling Topaz 36 Sportfisherman (1980–85) boasts additional fuel, larger interior, improved engine access. Highlights include big fishing cockpit with in-deck storage, well-arranged helm with lockable electronics locker, roomy interior with U-shaped dinette, head with stall shower. Entire bridgedeck lifts for engine access. Solid fiberglass hull is heavily built, dry, stable. Handsome boat has aged well over the years. Cat 375hp diesels cruise at 25 knots (28–29 knots wide open).

Length	37'6"	Fuel	350 gals.
Beam	13'0"	Water	60 gals.
Draft	3'4"	Cockpit	81 sq. ft.
Weight	19,800#	Hull Type	Modified-V
Clearance	NA	Deadrise Aft	17°

Prices Not Provided for Pre-1995 Models

The original Topaz Company
went out of business in 1991.

Topaz 38 Flybridge
1985–87

Handsome Mid-Atlantic convertible from 1980s was long on sex appeal, short on fluff. Uncluttered cockpit with port/starboard tackle centers, in-deck fishbox, transom door has space for full-size fighting chair. Single-stateroom floorplan is spacious enough, but most 38-footers have two staterooms. Note very tight engineroom. Additional features include wide side decks, offset bridge ladder (to conserve cockpit space), teak bow pulpit. Twin 450hp GM diesels cruise in the mid 20s and deliver a top speed of about 30 knots.

Length	38'2"	Fuel	430 gals.
Beam	13'0"	Water	160 gals.
Draft	2'7"	Cockpit	125 sq. ft.
Weight	22,700#	Hull Type	Modified-V
Clearance	11'3"	Deadrise Aft	17°

Prices Not Provided for Pre-1995 Models

The original Topaz Company
went out of business in 1991.

Sportfishing Boats

www.powerboatguide.com   231-360-0827

Topaz 39 Royale
1988–91

Popular Topaz express with rakish styling combined hardcore fishability with luxury-class amenities. Well-appointed interior boasts spacious head with separate stall shower, full-featured galley, generous storage, U-shaped dinette. Raised bridgedeck features L-shaped settee; cockpit came standard with tackle center with freezer, lift-out fishbox. Note unusual portside helm position. Semi-V hull with moderate beam, generous bow flare delivers good low-speed stability. Cruise at a fast 28 knots with GM 485hp diesels (low 30s top).

Length	39'1"	Fuel	400 gals.
Beam	13'0"	Water	60 gals.
Draft	3'1"	Headroom	6'4"
Weight	21,900#	Hull Type	Modified-V
Clearance, Windshield	7'7"	Deadrise Aft	17°

Prices Not Provided for Pre-1995 Models

The original Topaz Company
went out of business in 1991.

---

www.powerboatguide.com   231-360-0827

Triton 2895 Center Console
2004–07

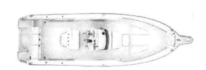

Muscular sportfishing machine with efficient deck layout makes the cut with serious anglers. Highlights include two-person helm seat with built-in 50-gallon livewell, raised casting platform, 21-gallon transom livewell, tackle locker, forward console seat, pop-up cleats, raw-water washdown, transom door, console head compartment with sink. Recessed bow rails mean no snagged lines. More storage space than many 28-footers. Deep-V hull can take a serious pounding. Over 45 knots top with Honda 225s.

Length w/Pulpit	29'10"	Fuel	204 gals.
Beam	9.5"	Water	18 gals.
Draft, Up	1'9"	Max HP	500
Draft, Down	3'0"	Hull Type	Deep-V
Hull Weight	5,300#	Deadrise Aft	20°

See Page 570 For Resale Values

Triton boats
Ashland City, TN
www.tritonboats.com

---

www.powerboatguide.com   231-360-0827

Triton 301 XD
2008–Current

Hard-charging offshore express with wide 10'10" beam lives up to Triton reputation for top-shelf construction, exceptional big-water performance. Impressive list of standard equipment includes fiberglass hardtop, electric windlass, dual helm seat with flip-up bolsters, deluxe bait-prep station, foldaway rear cockpit seat. Companion seat opposite helm has nifty drop-down jump seat. Very appealing cabin with teak-and-holly sole, 15" flat screen TV, sleeps 4–6. Mercury 300hp outboards max out at over 40 knots.

Length	30'3"	Fuel	300 gals.
Beam	10'10"	Water	35 gals.
Draft, Up	2'0"	Max HP	600
Draft, Down	3'2"	Hull Type	Deep-V
Hull Weight	8,320#	Deadrise Aft	22°

Insufficient Resale Data To Assign Values

Triton boats
Ashland City, TN
www.tritonboats.com

   231-360-0827

Triton 351 Center Console
2005–Current

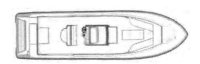

Heavily built battlewagon designed to handle triple-outboard power takes, sportfishing excitement, fishability to the next level. Highlights include triple helm seat with 50-gallon livewell, 21-gallon transom livewell, transom storage box, lockable rod lockers (2), folding rear seat, forward fender storage box, forward fishbox with macerator, walk-in head with sink. Tilt-up console has space for twin 15" displays. Cockpit hatch provides easy access to bilge. No lightweight compared with boats her size. Over 50 knots with triple 275 Mercs.

Length	34'10"	Fuel	355 gals.
Beam	10'0"	Water	20 gals.
Draft, Up	2'0"	Max HP	1,050
Draft, Down	3'0"	Hull Type	Deep-V
Hull Weight	8,352#	Deadrise Aft	24°

See Page 570 For Resale Values

Triton boats
Ashland City, TN
www.tritonboats.com

   231-360-0827

Trojan 32 Sedan
1973–91

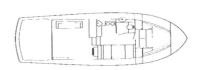

Classic flybridge sedan with large cockpit, semi-enclosed lower helm remains the most popular boat of her type ever produced. Offered with or without a flybridge, the appeal of this boat rested with her roomy accommodations, handsome lines, affordable price. Well-planned interior with convertible dinette, stand-up head, full galley sleeps four. Early models had teak decks; once-optional 220-gallon fuel capacity became standard in 1984. Cruise at 18 knots with 250hp Chrysler gas engines; 20 knots with 270hp Crusaders.

Length	32'0"	Water	40 gals.
Beam	13'0"	Fuel	120/220 gals.
Draft	2'6"	Cockpit	60 sq. ft.
Weight	12,000#	Hull Type	Modified-V
Clearance	12'6"	Deadrise Aft	8°

Prices Not Provided for Pre-1995 Models

Trojan Yachts is no longer in business.

   231-360-0827

Trojan 36 Convertible
1972–89

Well-priced, well-styled convertible introduced in 1972 turned out to be one of the most popular production boats ever designed. Several single- and twin-stateroom floorplans were available during her long production run, all with standard lower helm. Teak cockpit sole was standard through 1976—a potential source of problems. Uncluttered cockpit lacks transom door, fishbox, or livewell. Note wide side decks. Among many engine choices, twin 350hp gas engines cruise at 18 knots (24–25 knots top).

Length	36'0"	Water	80 gals.
Beam	13'0"	Fuel	250/350 gals.
Draft	2'11"	Cockpit	75 sq. ft.
Weight	16,000#	Hull Type	Modified-V
Clearance	13'0"	Deadrise Aft	9°

Prices Not Provided for Pre-1995 Models

Trojan Yachts is no longer in business.

231-360-0827

Trojan 11 Meter Sedan
1985–88

akish 1980s sedan with wide 14-foot beam combined bold styling with maxi-volume accommodations. Spacious interior with wide-open salon features large dinette, head with circular stall shower, U-shaped galley with generous stowage. Cockpit design is compromised by intrusive bridge ladder. Roomy flybridge has guest seating forward of helm. Note wide side decks, glass salon bulkhead, salon wet bar. Standard 350hp gas engines cruise at 18 knots (high 20s top); 375hp Cat diesels cruise at 22 knots (26–27 top).

Length	37'6"	Water	100 gals.
Beam	14'0"	Fuel	350 gals.
Draft	3.5"	Headroom	6.5"
Weight	18,000#	Hull Type	Modified-V
Clearance	12'6"	Deadrise Aft	14°

Prices Not Provided for Pre-1995 Models

Trojan Yachts is no longer in business.

231-360-0827

Trojan 12 Meter Convertible
1986–92

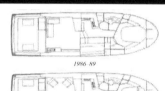

1986–89

1990–92

akish 1990s convertible combined posh accommodations with bold hull graphics, unusually wide beam. Expansive two-stateroom, galley-down layout features spacious salon with breakfast bar, home-sized galley, island berth in forward stateroom. Large 110-sq.-ft. cockpit has two in-deck fishboxes, dual washdowns, wide transom door, tackle center. Note wraparound salon windows. Flybridge is small for a 40-footer. Cat 375hp diesels cruise at 22 knots (mid 20s top); 485hp Detroits cruise at 25 knots (about 30 knots top).

Length	39'9"	Water	100 gals.
Beam	14'3"	Fuel	400 gals.
Draft	3'6"	Cockpit	110 sq. ft.
Weight	19,000#	Hull Type	Modified-V
Clearance	12'6"	Deadrise Aft	12°

Prices Not Provided for Pre-1995 Models

Trojan Yachts is no longer in business.

231-360-0827

Trojan 14 Meter Convertible
1988–92

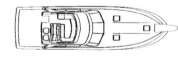

istinctive convertible introduced in 1988 combined rakish styling with mega-volume interior. Super-wide 16'3" beam affords interior dimensions of a much larger boat. Expansive two-stateroom, two-head floorplan features apartment-sized galley, L-shaped dinette, breakfast bar in salon. Guest stateroom extends under the salon sole. Huge cockpit has bait-prep center, in-deck fishboxes, wide transom door. Note oversized flybridge with lounge seating, wet bar. GM 750hp diesels cruise at 25 knots (28–30 knots top).

Length	46'3"	Water	175 gals.
Beam	16'3"	Fuel	710 gals.
Draft	3'6"	Cockpit	130 sq. ft.
Weight	34,000#	Hull Type	Modified-V
Clearance	13'7"	Deadrise Aft	12°

Prices Not Provided for Pre-1995 Models

Trojan Yachts is no longer in business.

231-360-0827

Trophy 2802 Walkaround
1997–2001

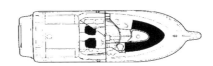

Beefy family fisherman with outboard bracket was built tough, priced right. Standard fishing amenities include 34-gallon livewell, bait-prep station, two in-deck fishboxes, fresh/saltwater washdowns, fold-down jump seats, cockpit bolsters, transom door. Wide 9'9" beam results in roomy cockpit, wide walkways. Well-arranged cabin with mini-galley, enclosed head with shower, aft midberth sleeps 3–4. Excellent helm visibility. Deep cockpit provides an extra level of passenger security. About 40 knots top with twin 200s.

Length	31'0"	Fuel	240 gals.
Beam	9'9"	Water	30 gals.
Draft, Up	1'3"	Max HP	450
Draft, Down	2'6"	Hull Type	Modified-V
Dry Weight	7,394#	Deadrise Aft	19°

See Page 570 For Resale Values

Trophy Sportfishing Boats
Everett, WA
www.trophyfishing.com

231-360-0827

Trophy 2902 Walkaround
2003–Current

Sturdy coastal fishing platform with many standard features appeals to anglers with an eye for value. Armstrong outboard bracket, 30-gallon transom livewell, aft bait-prep station, two in-deck fishboxes, fold-down jump seats, raw-water washdown, storage lockers, transom door, bow pulpit. Efficient cabin with galley cabinet, enclosed head with shower, aft midberth sleeps 3 to 4. Note sink behind helm seat. Deep cockpit, wide walkways are a plus. Good helm visibility. Trophy's largest model. Over 40 knots top with twin 225s.

Length w/Pulpit	31 5"	Fuel	218 gals.
Beam	9'9"	Water	30 gals.
Draft, Up	2'0"	Max HP	500
Draft, Down	2'10"	Hull Type	Modified-V
Weight w/OB	8,200#	Deadrise Aft	19°

See Page 570 For Resale Values

Trophy Sportfishing Boats
Everett, WA
www.trophyfishing.com

231-360-0827

True World TE288
2002–07

Floorplan Not Available

Common-sense fishing boat with super-wide side decks, semi-enclosed helm is practical, versatile, efficient. Highlights include deep cockpit with in-deck fishboxes, sturdy hardtop, leaning post with backrest, transom livewell. No-frills cabin offers cozy dinette/V-berth, mini-galley, enclosed head. Amidships engine location lowers center of gravity for improved balance, low-speed stability. Pilothouse superstructure impairs helm visibility. Yanmar 315hp diesel with jackshaft drive cruises at 22–23 knots (burning just 7 gph).

Length w/Pulpit	29'6"	Clearance	8'8"
Hull Length	28'0"	Fuel	130 gals.
Beam	9'3"	Water	15 gals.
Draft	1'8"	Hull Type	Modified-V
Weight	6,800#	Deadrise Aft	18°

See Page 570 For Resale Values

True World Marine
Beaufort, NC
www.trueworldmarine.com

231-360-0827

Venture 27 Open
2007–Current

Hard-hitting open fisherman with Kevlar reinforced hull lives up to Venture reputation for zero disappointments, maximum owner satisfaction. Generous 9-foot beam results in roomy cockpit layout for a 27-footer. Highlights include fore and aft in-floor fish boxes, 44-gallon transom livewell, bait-prep station with sink, leaning post with tackle storage. Walk-in console has 6-foot headroom. Fiberglass hardtop, pop-up deck hardware are standard. Note recessed bow rail. Twin 200hp Mercury outboards top out at close to 45 knots.

Length	27'0"	Fuel	200 gals.
Beam	9'0"	Water	20 gals.
Draft, Up	1'8"	Max HP	500
Draft, Down	2'2"	Hull Type	Deep-V
Hull Weight	5,500#	Deadrise Aft	24°

See Page 570 For Resale Values

Venture Marine
Riviera Beach, FL
www.venturemarine.com

231-360-0827

Venture 34 Open
1997–Current

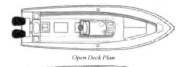

Open Deck Plan

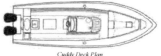

Cuddy Deck Plan

Legendary tournament fishing machine couples sleek lines with top-shelf construction, exceptional open-water performance. Notable features include factory hardtop, leaning post/tackle center, 55-gallon transom livewell, lockable electronics storage, bait-prep station with sink, three fishboxes, fresh/saltwater washdowns, in-deck storage boxes, walk-in head with sink and shower. Exemplary workmanship throughout. Also offered in Cuddy, Forward Seating models. About 45 knots top with twin 250s.

Length	34'0'	Fuel	300 gals.
Beam	10'0'	Water	55 gals.
Draft, Up	1'9"	Max HP	600
Draft, Down	2'4"	Hull Type	Deep-V
Weight	6,400#	Deadrise Aft	24°

See Page 570 For Resale Values

Venture Marine
Riviera Beach, FL
www.venturemarine.com

231-360-0827

Venture 39 Open
2005–Current

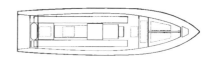

Full-throttle center console is easy on the eye, fun to fish, expensive to buy. Roomy 10'8" beam allows large cockpit with fishing space for several anglers. Highlights include vacuum-bagged construction, big 55-gallon transom livewell, walk-in console with 6-foot headroom, oversized (lighted!) anchor locker with space for hundreds of feet of line. Note tremendous dry storage, huge 550-gallon fuel capacity. Advanced technology, sophisticated engineering rank at top of her class. Tops out at over 45 knots with triple 275hp Mercury outboards.

Length	39'6"	Fuel	550 gals.
Beam	10'8"	Water	50 gals.
Draft, Up	1'8"	Max HP	900
Draft, Down	2'7"	Hull Type	Deep-V
Dry Weight	8,000#	Deadrise Aft	24°

See Page 570 For Resale Values

Venture Marine
Riviera Beach, FL
www.venturemarine.com

Sportfishing Boats

Viking 35 Convertible
1975–84

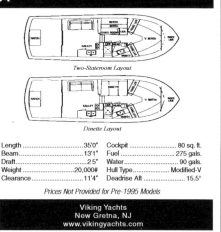

Two-Stateroom Layout

Dinette Layout

Vintage Viking convertible appealed to savvy an-glers with an eye for top-shelf quality, long-term value. Surprisingly spacious interior with dinette or two-stateroom floorplan featured roomy salon with wrap-around windows, head with separate stall shower, decent storage. Original woodgrain mica cabinetry was replaced with teak in 1980. Large cockpit has plenty of space for two anglers and their gear. Bow pulpit was standard. No transom door. Standard 350hp gas engines cruise at 18 knots and deliver a top speed of 26–27 knots.

Length	35'0"	Cockpit	80 sq. ft.
Beam	13'1"	Fuel	275 gals.
Draft	2 5"	Water	90 gals.
Weight	20,000#	Hull Type	Modified-V
Clearance	11'4"	Deadrise Aft	15.5°

Prices Not Provided for Pre-1995 Models

Viking Yachts
New Gretna, NJ
www.vikingyachts.com

Viking 35 Convertible
1985–91

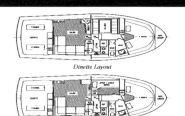

Dinette Layout

Two-Stateroom Layout

Handsome 35-footer blurs the lines between serious sportfishing boat, comfortable family cruiser. Well-appointed interior with dinette or twin-stateroom layouts features solid teak cabinetry, separate stall shower in head. Note solid front windshield, above-average finish. Flybridge is huge for a 35-footer. Cockpit has twin in-deck fishboxes, sink, bait-prep center. No transom door. Standard 350hp gas engines cruise at 18 knots; optional 375 Cat diesels cruise in the low 20s (26–28 knots top). Popular model is still in demand.

Length w/Pulpit	38'6"	Cockpit	80 sq. ft.
Hull Length	35'0"	Fuel	300 gals.
Beam	13'1"	Water	75 gals.
Draft	4'1"	Hull Type	Modified-V
Weight	20,000#	Deadrise Aft	15.5°

Prices Not Provided for Pre-1995 Models

Viking Yachts
New Gretna, NJ
www.vikingyachts.com

Viking 35 Sportfisherman
1984–86

Deluxe 1980s express with spacious cockpit, up-scale interior combined hardcore fishing attributes, family-style amenities. Topside features include large bridgedeck with tackle cabinet, deep cockpit with in-deck fishboxes, wide side decks, bow pulpit. Well-appoint-ed cabin with convertible dinette, full galley, sleeps four. Toilet is fitted in shower stall to save space. Note difficult engine access. Standard 350hp gas engines cruise at 19 knots (26–28 knots top); 355hp Cats cruise at 26 knots (30 knots wide open). Over 30 were built.

Length	35'0"	Fuel	325 gals.
Beam	13'1"	Water	70 gals.
Draft	2 5"	Headroom	6'4"
Weight	19,000#	Hull Type	Modified-V
Clearance	8'6"	Deadrise Aft	15.5°

Prices Not Provided for Pre-1995 Models

Viking Yachts
New Gretna, NJ
www.vikingyachts.com

231-360-0827

Viking 38 Convertible
1990–95

Dinette Floorplan

Two-Stateroom Interior

Polished midsized convertible from the 1990s made good on Viking promise of hardcore fishability, luxury accommodations. Expansive interior with rich teak paneling, was available with choice of dinette or twin-stateroom layouts, both with mid-level galley, wide-open salon. Large cockpit came with in-deck fishbox, transom door, tackle center with freezer. Note well-finished engineroom, roomy flybridge. Standard gas engines cruise at 15–16 knots; optional 485hp GM diesels cruise at 22 knots (25 knots wide open).

Length	39'4"	Fuel	430 gals.
Beam	14'2"	Water	110 gals.
Draft	4'1"	Cockpit	108 sq. ft.
Weight	32,890#	Hull Type	Modified-V
Clearance	11'10"	Deadrise Aft	15.5°

Prices Not Provided for Pre-1995 Models

Viking Yachts
New Gretna, NJ
www.vikingyachts.com

231-360-0827

Viking 40 Convertible
1974–82

Two-Stateroom Layout

Dinette Layout

Super-popular convertible (over 400 were sold) did much to establish Viking reputation for engineering excellence, construction quality. Several galley-down floorplans were offered. Original wood-laminate interior replaced with teak cabinetry in 1982. Steel I-beam engine beds became a Viking trademark. Note wide side decks, 100-square-foot cockpit, well-arranged bridge. Front salon windows are rare in a modern convertible. Cruise at 20 knots with GM 310hp (or 300hp Cat) diesels; low 20s with GM 410hp diesels.

Length	40'4"	Fuel	300/350 gals.
Beam	14'6"	Water	90 gals.
Draft	3'6"	Cockpit	100 sq. ft.
Weight	30,000#	Hull Type	Modified-V
Clearance	11'9"	Deadrise Aft	18°

Prices Not Provided for Pre-1995 Models

Viking Yachts
New Gretna, NJ
www.vikingyachts.com

231-360-0827

Viking 41 Convertible
1983–89

2-Stateroom Layout 1983-86

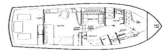

Dinette Layout 1983-88

Top-selling Viking convertible delivered winning mix of handsome styling, roomy accommodations, excellent performance. Offered with several single- or (more popular) twin-stateroom, galley-down interiors over the years, all with matched teak joinerwork, decorator fabrics, open front windshield. Uncluttered cockpit is fitted with in-deck fishboxes, tackle center with sink. Note roomy flybridge, wide side decks, sturdy bow rails. Used models are always in demand. Cruise at 25–26 knots with GM 485hp diesels (about 30 knots wide open).

Length	41'2"	Fuel	380/430 gals.
Beam	14'10"	Water	125 gals.
Draft	4'3"	Cockpit	108 sq. ft.
Weight	32,000#	Hull Type	Modified-V
Clearance	12'0"	Deadrise Aft	15.5°

Prices Not Provided for Pre-1995 Models

Viking Yachts
New Gretna, NJ
www.vikingyachts.com

Viking 43 Convertible
1990–2002

Dinette Floorplan

Two-Stateroom Layout

Gold-plated 1990s convertible with best-in-class styling enjoyed unusually long production run, tremendous owner satisfaction. Principal features include big tournament-ready cockpit with engineroom access, luxury-class interior with choice of dinette or twin-stateroom layouts, huge flybridge (extended in 1997) with seating for eight. Many updates/refinements over the years including fuel increase in 1996. Cruise at 22–23 knots with 485hp GM diesels; 25–26 knots with GM 625hp engines; 30 knots with 680 MANs (standard after 1999).

Length	43'0"	Fuel	525/600 gals.
Beam	15'3"	Water	115 gals.
Draft	4'3"	Cockpit	113 sq. ft.
Weight	38,595#	Hull Type	Modified-V
Clearance	15'10"	Deadrise Aft	15.5°

See Page 570 For Resale Values

Viking Yachts
New Gretna, NJ
www.vikingyachts.com

Viking 43 Open Sportfish
1994–2002

Single-Stateroom Floorplan

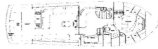
Two-Stateroom Layout

Powerful sportfishing machine with striking lines, exemplary finish delivers high-octane blast of luxury, fishability, performance. Choice of one- or two-stateroom interiors, both with large galley, exquisite teak woodwork, premium decor. Spacious helmdeck—three steps above cockpit—features wraparound lounge seating, centerline helm with best-in-class dash layout. Cockpit engineroom access is a plus. Popular model—over 70 were built. GM 550hp diesels cruise at 25 knots; later models with 680hp MANs cruise at 30 knots.

Length	43'0"	Fuel	525/600 gals.
Beam	15'3"	Water	115 gals.
Draft	4'3"	Cockpit	116 sq. ft.
Weight	34,500#	Hull Type	Modified-V
Clearance, Hardtop	9'11"	Deadrise Aft	15.5°

See Page 570 For Resale Values

Viking Yachts
New Gretna, NJ
www.vikingyachts.com

Viking 45 Convertible
1987–93

Plan A Dinette Layout

Plan B Two-Stateroom Layout

Acclaimed tournament convertible with leading-edge styling, luxury-class accommodations remains one of Viking's best-selling yachts ever. Well-crafted interior—offered with or without dinette—features open-plan salon with serving counter, two large heads, quality appliances and furnishings. Spacious cockpit came with tackle center, transom door, recessed fishboxes. Engineroom can be reached from salon or cockpit. About 250 were built. GM 485hp diesels cruise at 23–24 knots; GM 550hp diesels cruise in the high 20s.

Length	45'5"	Fuel	600 gals.
Beam	15'0"	Water	160 gals.
Draft	4'0"	Cockpit	120 sq. ft.
Weight	44,400#	Hull Type	Modified-V
Clearance	12'5"	Deadrise Aft	15.5°

Prices Not Provided for Pre-1995 Models

Viking Yachts
New Gretna, NJ
www.vikingyachts.com

Sportfishing Boats

231-360-0827

Viking 45 Convertible
2003–09

Tournament-class sportfisherman set class standards for engineering, luxury, performance. Lavish twin-stateroom interior with spacious salon features open-plan galley with under-counter refrigeration, L-shaped dinette, large master cabin. Best-in-class cockpit includes tackle storage, bait freezer, cooler under salon step. Note space-saving offset bridge ladder, rod storage under salon settee, beautifully detailed engineroom with excellent outboard access. MAN 900hp diesels cruise at an honest 30 knots (33–34 knots top).

Length	45'10"	Fuel	848 gals.
Beam	16'4"	Water	150 gals.
Draft	4'6"	Waste	50 gals.
Weight	49,750#	Hull Type	Modified-V
Clearance	16'4"	Deadrise Aft	15.5°

See Page 570 For Resale Values

Viking Yachts
New Gretna, NJ
www.vikingyachts.com

231-360-0827

Viking 45 Open Sportfish
2004–09

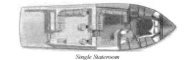

Single Stateroom

Two Staterooms

Muscular dual-purpose express blends sportfishing excellence, cruising luxury. Huge bridgedeck features centerline helm position, three Murray chairs, L-shaped lounge (with rod storage under), full wet bar. Available with one or two staterooms, both with open-plan galley, solid teak cabinetry, Ultraleather seating. Insulated fishboxes, rigging station, tackle storage are standard in large cockpit. Note well-arranged engineroom, wide side decks. Superior open-water handling. MANs 900hp diesels cruise at 30 knots (33–34 knots top).

Length	45'10"	Fuel	848 gals.
Beam	16'4"	Water	150 gals.
Draft	4'6"	Waste	50 gals.
Weight	49,760#	Hull Type	Modified-V
Clearance	NA	Deadrise Aft	15.5°

See Page 570 For Resale Values

Viking Yachts
New Gretna, NJ
www.vikingyachts.com

231-360-0827

Viking 46 Convertible
1981–85

Two-Stateroom Layout

Three-Stateroom/Dinette

Handsome sportfishing yacht delivers the speed, agility, muscle of a serious 1980s canyon runner. Well-appointed two-stateroom interior has dinette forward in salon; alternate three-stateroom layout—rare in a boat this size—has serving counter, step-down galley. Note front salon windows, solid teak joinery, standard washer/dryer. Cockpit with in-deck fishboxes, tackle locker is conservative in size, but flybridge is huge. GM 500hp engines cruise at 23–24 knots cruise (26 top); 8V92 GMs cruise at 27–28 knots (30 knots top).

Length	46'6"	Fuel	620/750 gals.
Beam	16'0"	Water	200 gals.
Draft	4'0"	Cockpit	120 sq. ft.
Weight	44,000#	Hull Type	Modified-V
Clearance	NA	Deadrise Aft	15.5°

Prices Not Provided for Pre-1995 Models

Viking Yachts
New Gretna, NJ
www.vikingyachts.com

231-360-0827

Viking 46 Convertible
2009–Current

Tournament-grade sportfishing yacht combines leading-edge design with unsurpassed luxury, exceptional performance. Lavish two-stateroom, two-head interior with spacious salon, amidships master suite boasts social walk-thru galley with island countertop and twin bar stools. Note companionway laundry center, beautiful high-gloss teak joinery. Mezzanine seat overlooking cockpit houses bait freezer, stowage compartments, engineroom access. Optional 1100hp MAN diesels cruise at a fast 35 knots.

Length	46'11"	Fuel	870 gals.
Beam	16'6"	Water	150 gals.
Draft	4'5"	Cockpit	121 Sq. Ft.
Weight	54,120#	Hull Type	Modified-V
Clearance	NA	Deadrise Aft	12°

Insufficient Resale Data To Assign Values

Viking Yachts
New Gretna, NJ
www.vikingyachts.com

231-360-0827

Viking 47 Convertible
1994–2002

Hard-charging tournament machine with classic Viking styling raised the bar in her day for yacht-class accommodations, world-class performance. Two-stateroom layout with combined salon/galley/dinette is unusually spacious, well-appointed. Note lavish teak cabinetry, premium galley appliances, standard washer/dryer. Roomy fishing cockpit with huge in-floor fishbox features direct access to meticulous engineroom. MAN 680hp diesels cruise at 26 knots (30 knots top); 800hp MANs cruise at 28–30 knots (low 30s top).

Length	47'2"	Fuel	700 gals.
Beam	15'6"	Water	160 gals.
Draft	4'5"	Cockpit	135 sq. ft.
Weight	46,300#	Hull Type	Modified-V
Clearance	16'10"	Deadrise Aft	15.5°

See Page 570 For Resale Values

Viking Yachts
New Gretna, NJ
www.vikingyachts.com

231-360-0827

Viking 48 Convertible
1985–90

Two Staterooms

Three Staterooms

Bold 1980s convertible combined bold styling with cutting-edge construction, luxury accommodations, huge fishing cockpit. Highlights include well-appointed teak interior with choice of two- or three-stateroom floorplans, massive 144-sq.-ft. fishing cockpit, state-of-the-art flybridge, spacious engineroom with cockpit access. Not the softest ride when the seas pick up. Cruise at 23–24 knots with GM 550hp engines (about 26 knots top). GM 735hp diesels cruise at 27–28 knots (30 knots wide open).

Length	48'7"	Fuel	680 gals.
Beam	16'0"	Water	200 gals.
Draft	4'7"	Cockpit	144 sq. ft.
Weight	45,500#	Hull Type	Modified-V
Clearance	12'5"	Deadrise Aft	15.5°

Prices Not Provided for Pre-1995 Models

Viking Yachts
New Gretna, NJ
www.vikingyachts.com

Sportfishing Boats

Sportfishing Boats

Viking 48 Convertible
2002–09

Two-Stateroom Layout

Three-Stateroom Layout

Purebred Viking convertible with leading-edge styling balanced executive-class luxury with muscular construction, exceptional performance. Highlights include sumptuous teak interior with choice of two or three staterooms, companionway laundry center, enormous 130-sq.-ft. fishing cockpit, state-of-the-art helm with huge electronics space, best-in-class engineroom. Note that bridge ladder is positioned over salon steps to save cockpit space. A terrific performer, 1,100hp MANs (or 1,015hp Cats) cruise at 30 knots (34–35 top).

Length	48'10"	Fuel	1,012 gals.
Beam	16'6"	Water	175 gals.
Draft	4'9"	Waste	50 gals.
Weight	56,450#	Hull Type	Modified-V
Clearance	NA	Deadrise Aft	15°

See Page 570 For Resale Values

Viking Yachts
New Gretna, NJ
www.vikingyachts.com

Viking 50 Convertible
1991–2001

Three-Stateroom Layout

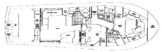
Two-Stateroom Layout

Scaled-down version of popular Viking 53 Convertible (1990–98) defined 1990s standards for sportfishing quality, luxury, performance. Spacious three-stateroom interior with amidships master boasts beautifully appointed salon/galley/dinette with entertainment center, standard washer/dryer, under-counter refrigeration. Note huge fishing cockpit, walk-in engineroom, massive flybridge. No lightweight, 820hp MANs cruise at 24–25 knots. Optional 1,200hp MANs cruise at 30+ knots (high 30s top). Over 120 were built.

Length	50'7"	Fuel	805 gals.
Beam	16'4"	Water	208 gals.
Draft	4'9"	Cockpit	144 sq. ft.
Weight	58,814#	Hull Type	Modified-V
Clearance	16'5"	Deadrise Aft	15.5°

See Page 570 For Resale Values

Viking Yachts
New Gretna, NJ
www.vikingyachts.com

Viking 50 Convertible
2009–Current

Broad-beamed convertible with graceful Viking styling takes sportfishing luxury, performance to the next level. Opulent three-stateroom, two-head interior with combined salon/dinette/galley features posh UltraLeather seating, deluxe entertainment center, standard washer/dryer. Note huge flybridge with pod-style helm console. Mezzanine seat overlooking massive cockpit houses bait freezer, stowage compartments, engineroom access. MAN 1,350hp engines cruise at a fast 35 knots. (nearly 40 knots top)

Length	50'6"	Fuel	1,000
Beam	17'0"	Water	175 gals.
Draft	4'10"	Cockpit	132 Sq. Ft.
Weight	66,500#	Hull Type	Modified-V
Clearance	NA	Deadrise Aft	12°

Insufficient Resale Data To Assign Values

Viking Yachts
New Gretna, NJ
www.vikingyachts.com

231-360-0827

Viking 50 Open
1999–2003

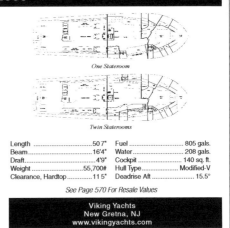

One Stateroom

Twin Staterooms

Hard-hitting sportfisherman with powerful lines, exceptional performance remains a formidable tournament contender. Wide 16'4" beam permits huge cockpit, expansive accommodations. Highlights include beautifully appointed interior with choice of layouts, huge bridgedeck with centerline helm, fully equipped cockpit with custom tackle center. Note unique salon day head, beefy transom door. Engineroom is as good as it gets. Standard 800hp MANs cruise at 30 knots (33–34 knots top); optional 1200hp MANs cruise at 35 knots (38–40 top).

Length	50'7"	Fuel	805 gals.
Beam	16'4"	Water	208 gals.
Draft	4'9"	Cockpit	140 sq. ft.
Weight	55,700#	Hull Type	Modified-V
Clearance, Hardtop	11'5"	Deadrise Aft	15.5°

See Page 570 For Resale Values

Viking Yachts
New Gretna, NJ
www.vikingyachts.com

231-360-0827

Viking 52 Convertible
2002–09

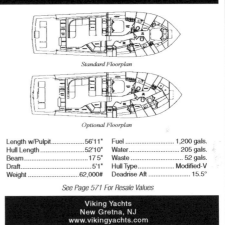

Standard Floorplan

Optional Floorplan

World-class convertible with huge fishing cockpit embodies classic Viking styling, comfort, performance. Opulent three-stateroom floorplan with combined salon/galley/dinette features amidships master suite, choice of queen or single berths forward. Note triple-entry guest head, premium Subzero galley refrigeration, washer/dryer compartment, exquisite teak joinery. Helm layout is as good as it gets; meticulous engineroom is a work of art. Optional 1,360hp MANs cruise at an honest 33 knots (36–37 knots top).

Length w/Pulpit	56'11"	Fuel	1,200 gals.
Hull Length	52'10"	Water	205 gals.
Beam	17'5"	Waste	52 gals.
Draft	5'1"	Hull Type	Modified-V
Weight	62,000#	Deadrise Aft	15.5°

See Page 571 For Resale Values

Viking Yachts
New Gretna, NJ
www.vikingyachts.com

231-360-0827

Viking 52 Open
2007–Current

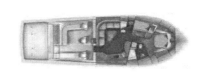

Broad-beamed express with luxury-class interior splits the difference between hardcore fishing boat, polished family cruiser. Tournament-level cockpit provides vast 145 square feet of fishing space overlooked by mezzanine deck. Lush twin-stateroom, twin-head cabin layout features walkaround queen berth forward, salon rod storage, home-size galley with Corian countertop. Visibility from center helm position is as good as it gets in a big express. Walk-in engine room is cavernous. MAN 1,360 V-12 diesels cruise at a fast 35 knots.

Length	52'10"	Fuel	1,200 gals.
Beam	17'3"	Water	200 gals.
Draft	5'0"	Waste	NA
Weight	57,040#	Hull Type	Modified-V
Cockpit	148 sq. ft.	Deadrise Aft	15°

Insufficient Resale Data To Assign Values

Viking Yachts
New Gretna, NJ
www.vikingyachts.com

Sportfishing Boats

Viking 53 Convertible
1990–98

Plan A

Plan B

Highly regarded 1990s convertible with honest 30-knot performance became one of the best-selling big sportfishing yachts ever built. Lavish three-stateroom interior with amidships master boasts combined salon/galley/dinette area, standard washer/dryer, posh furnishings. Highlights include spacious fishing cockpit, huge flybridge, well-designed engineroom. Frameless windows became standard in 1997. Over 100 built. MAN 1,000hp diesels cruise at 30 knots; 1,200hp MANs cruise at 33 knots.

Length	53'7"	Fuel	900/1,100 gals.
Beam	16'7"	Water	200 gals.
Draft	4'10"	Cockpit	150 sq. ft.
Weight	63,500#	Hull Type	Modified-V
Clearance	13'4"	Deadrise Aft	15°

See Page 571 For Resale Values

Viking Yachts
New Gretna, NJ
www.vikingyachts.com

Viking 54 Convertible
2008–Current

Handsome 54-footer with signature Viking styling takes sportfishing elegance, luxury to the next level. Roomy 160-square-foot cockpit features mezzanine deck—shaded by bridge overhang—with lounge seating, engineroom access. Posh three-stateroom, twin-head interior boasts master suite to port with walkaround queen, U-shaped galley with Sub-Zero refrigeration. Meticulous engineroom, world-class helm are reminders of Viking's production-boat excellence. MAN 1,550hp V12 engines cruise at 34–35 knots (40 top).

Length	54'8"	Fuel	1,445 gals.
Beam	17'9"	Water	225 gals.
Draft	5'2"	Waste	100 gals.
Weight	77,900#	Hull Type	Modified-V
Cockpit	160 sq. ft.	Deadrise Aft	15°

Insufficient Resale Data To Assign Values

Viking Yachts
New Gretna, NJ
www.vikingyachts.com

Viking 55 Convertible
1998–2002

Hard-charging tournament machine with elegant accommodations, remarkable performance set class standards for convertibles her size. Posh three-stateroom interior with amidships master features opulent salon/galley/dinette with high-gloss cabinetry, full entertainment center. Additional highlights include huge 153-square-foot cockpit, meticulous engineroom, massive bridge with wraparound helm. MAN 1,200hp diesels cruise at 32 knots (35–36 knots top)—impressive performance for a 55-footer. Total of 115 were built in just five years.

Length	55'10"	Fuel	1,250 gals.
Beam	17'4"	Water	250 gals.
Draft	4'10"	Cockpit	153 sq. ft.
Weight	68,800#	Hull Type	Modified-V
Clearance	17'1"	Deadrise Aft	15°

See Page 571 For Resale Values

Viking Yachts
New Gretna, NJ
www.vikingyachts.com

Viking 56 Convertible
2004–Current

Strong-selling tournament fisherman combines signature Viking styling with impressive accommodations, best-in-class performance. Lavish three-stateroom interior is an impressive display of high-gloss teak joinery, designer fabrics, top-quality furnishings. Highlights include home-size galley with under-counter refrigeration, posh owner's suite, massive fishing cockpit, walk-in engineroom, state-of-the-art helm. Prop pockets reduce hull draft, improve efficiency. MAN 1,550hp diesels cruise at a blistering 34 knots (37–38 knots top).

Length	57'6"	Fuel	1,500 gals.
Beam	18'2"	Water	240 gals.
Draft	4'10"	Cockpit	157 sq. ft.
Weight	80,800#	Hull Type	Modified-V
Clearance	20'3"	Deadrise Aft	15°

See Page 571 For Resale Values

Viking Yachts
New Gretna, NJ
www.vikingyachts.com

Viking 57 Convertible
1989–91

Sportfishing battlewagon introduced in 1989 offered anglers leading-edge blend of fishability, comfort, performance. Elegant interior with combined salon/galley/dinette includes spacious master suite forward, twin guest cabins with single berths, standard washer/dryer, three heads. Highlights include huge fishing cockpit, stand-up engineroom, wide side decks, spacious flybridge with well-designed helm. Note teak cover boards, wide transom door. Cruise at 28 knots (30+ knots top) with 1,080hp GM diesels. A total of 29 were built.

Length	57'2"	Fuel	1,500 gals.
Beam	18'0"	Water	250 gals.
Draft	5'3"	Cockpit	165 sq. ft.
Weight	69,000#	Hull Type	Modified-V
Clearance	14'6"	Deadrise Aft	15.5°

Prices Not Provided for Pre-1995 Models

Viking Yachts
New Gretna, NJ
www.vikingyachts.com

Viking 58 Convertible
1991–2000

1991–95

1996–97

Updated version of Viking 57 Convertible (1989–91) with reworked hull made a good Viking design even better. Opulent three-stateroom interior features open salon/galley/dinette with entertainment center, three full heads, amidships master suite. Spacious cockpit offers unmatched fishing space; engineroom ranks among the best to be found in a boat this size. Note huge flybridge, generous bow flare. MAN 1,100hp engines cruise at 28 knots (31–32 knots top); 1,200hp MANs cruise 30 knots (33–34 knots top). Over 110 were built.

Length	58'11"	Fuel	1,500 gals.
Beam	18'0"	Water	260 gals.
Draft	5'3"	Cockpit	168 sq. ft.
Weight	81,500#	Hull Type	Modified-V
Clearance	17'7"	Deadrise Aft	15.5°

See Page 571 For Resale Values

Viking Yachts
New Gretna, NJ
www.vikingyachts.com

231-360-0827

Viking 61 Convertible
2001–06

Standard Three-Stateroom Floorplan

Alternate Four-Stateroom Layout

World-class tournament machine introduced in 2001 set design, performance standards for other boats in her class. Offered with three- or four-stateroom interiors, both with spacious salon, home-size galley, built-in dinette. Massive cockpit is fitted with full array of fishing amenities. Flybridge features centerline helm with huge console. Note standard washer/dryer, meticulous engineroom, pump room for A/C compressors. Prop pockets added in 2003 for improved performance. Cruise at over 30 knots with 1,520hp MANs (35+ top).

Length w/Pulpit	65'11"	Clearance, Hardtop	18'3"
Hull Length	61'9"	Fuel	1,700 gals.
Beam	18'2"	Water	310 gals.
Draft	5'4"	Cockpit	170 sq. ft.
Weight	82,000#	Hull Type	Modified-V

See Page 571 For Resale Values

Viking Yachts
New Gretna, NJ
www.vikingyachts.com

231-360-0827

Viking 64 Convertible
2006–Current

Three-Stateroom Layout

Four-Stateroom Layout

Gold-plated sportfishing machine with classic Viking styling takes modern convertible design to the next level. Enormous interior (note wide 19'2" beam) with choice of three or four staterooms rivals most motoryachts for unabashed luxury, comfort. Highlights include home-size galley with serving counter, three full heads, 40" plasma TV, electric salon door. Huge 180-sq.-ft. cockpit has raised mezzanine deck with cushioned bench seat. Engineroom is a work of art. Cat 1,825hp engines cruise at 32 knots (high 30s top). Enclosed bridge model also available.

Length	63'9"	Fuel	1,930 gals.
Beam	19'2"	Water	325 gals.
Draft	5'2"	Waste	200 gals.
Weight	105,000#	Hull Type	Modified-V
Clearance	18'6"	Deadrise Aft	15°

Insufficient Resale Data To Assign Values

Viking Yachts
New Gretna, NJ
www.vikingyachts.com

231-360-0827

Viking 65 Convertible
1999–2005

Original 4-Stateroom Interior

Late-Model 4-Stateroom Interior

Graceful sportfishing yacht deliveres best-in-class mix of styling, luxury, performance. Lavish four-stateroom interior with beautifully appointed salon, huge galley, includes posh amidships master, crew quarters, hand-finished joinery. Optional closed-bridge model with aft steering station, salon access, provides genuine all-weather versatility. Massive cockpit came with full array of tournament-class fishing amenities. Prop pockets were added to hull in 2002. MAN or GM 1,800hp engines cruise at 32–33 knots (high 30s top).

Length w/Pulpit	69'10"	Fuel	2,000 gals.
Hull Length	65'10"	Water	360 gals.
Beam	18'9"	Cockpit	179 sq. ft.
Draft	6'1"	Hull Type	Modified-V
Weight	96,000#	Deadrise Aft	15.5°

See Page 571 For Resale Values

Viking Yachts
New Gretna, NJ
www.vikingyachts.com

Vista 48/50 Sportfisherman
1986–94

Rakish Fexas-designed sportfishing yacht with fully cored hull combines graceful styling with comfortable accommodations, immense cockpit. Standard two-stateroom layout features expansive salon with entertainment center, breakfast bar, two full heads, extensive teak cabinetry. Huge cockpit came equipped with livewell, fishboxes, teak cover boards, direct engineroom access. Note that Vista 50 (1988–94) has slightly larger salon than original Vista 48 (1986–87). GM 550hp diesels cruise at 20 knots (low 20s top).

Length	48'0"	Fuel	700 gals.
Beam	16'0"	Water	180 gals.
Draft	3'1"	Headroom	6'4"
Weight	36,000#	Hull Type	Modified-V
Clearance	13'10"	Deadrise Aft	3°

Prices Not Provided for Pre-1995 Models

Vista yachts are no longer in production.

Wellcraft 270 Coastal
2001–04; 2007–08

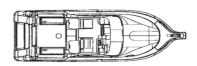

Rugged coastal express—reintroduced in 2007—splits the difference between light-tackle sportfisherman, stylish weekend cruiser. Standard fishing features include insulated fishboxes, full-height transom door, lighted livewell, raw-water washdown. Space-efficient cabin with convertible dinette, midcabin berth, enclosed head with shower, sleeps four. Hardtop became standard in 2007. Wide beam results in very roomy cockpit. Tops out at 40+ knots with Yamaha 225 outboards. Sterndrive models with 330hp Merc reach 35 knots top.

Length w/Pulpit	28'3"	Fuel	188 gals.
Beam	9'9"	Water	27 gals.
Draft, Up	1'10"	Max HP	500
Draft, Down	2'10"	Hull Type	Deep-V
Hull Weight	7,225#	Deadrise Aft	21°

See Page 571 For Resale Values

Wellcraft Boats
Sarasota, FL
www.wellcraft.com

Wellcraft 2800 Coastal
1986–94

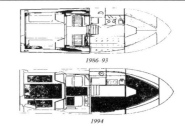

1986–93

1994

Rugged inboard fisherman with many standard features gave anglers good value for the money. Topside highlights include raised bridgedeck with swivel helm/companion seats, deep walkaround decks, big cockpit with in-floor fishboxes. Open interior with convertible settee, full galley, sleeps four. Transom door is a plus—many 28-footers don't have one. Factory hardtop was a popular option. Early models (1986–1990) had quality-control issues. Twin 260hp gas inboards cruise in the low 20s (high 20s top).

Length w/Pulpit	29'8"	Clearance	7'6"
Hull Length	27'7"	Fuel	182 gals.
Beam	9'11"	Water	20 gals.
Draft	2'4"	Hull Type	Modified-V
Weight	8,200#	Deadrise Aft	16°

Prices Not Provided for Pre-1995 Models

Wellcraft Boats
Sarasota, FL
www.wellcraft.com

231-360-0827

Wellcraft 290 Coastal
1999–2009

Appealing outboard express with sporty lines delivers solid mix of space, comfort, fishability. Well-planned cockpit comes standard with two in-deck fishboxes, fold-out rear seat, coaming bolsters, transom door. Helm seating module contains 42-gallon livewell (with Lucite window), sink with pressure water, cutting board. Midcabin interior with convertible dinette, stand-up head, sleeps four. V-berth backrests double as pilot berths. A lot of boat for the money. Twin 225hp outboards cruise in the mid 20s (35+ knots top).

Length w/Pulpit	30'2"	Fuel	225 gals.
Hull Length	27'10"	Water	42 gals.
Beam	10'5"	Max HP	600
Draft	2'9"	Hull Type	Modified-V
Weight	8,735#	Deadrise Aft	18°

See Page 571 For Resale Values

Wellcraft Boats
Sarasota, FL
www.wellcraft.com

231-360-0827

Wellcraft 29 Scarab Sport; 29 CCF
2001–04

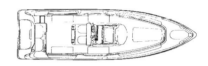

Fast-action center console with high-performance hull keeps on going when the going gets rough. Flush-level cockpit with wide walkways provides excellent 360-degree fishability. Standard features include four insulated fishboxes, 39-gallon livewell, rigging station with sink, dual washdowns, pop-up cleats, recessed bow rails, foldaway transom seat. Walk-in console houses marine head, tackle storage. Called 29 Scarab Sport in 2001–02; 29 CCF in 2003–04. Hull has keel pad for increased lift. Max 50 knots with twin 250s.

Length	28'6"	Fuel	214 gals.
Beam	8'10"	Water	8 gals.
Draft, Up	1'9"	Max HP	500
Draft, Down	2'5"	Hull Type	Deep-V
Hull Weight	6,345#	Deadrise Aft	24°

See Page 572 For Resale Values

Wellcraft Boats
Sarasota, FL
www.wellcraft.com

231-360-0827

Wellcraft 30 Scarab Sport
1979–93

Go-fast center console with narrow 8-foot beam evolved from Wellcraft's offshore racing program of the early 1970s. Standard features include under-gunnel rod racks, removable rear seat, in-deck fishbox, livewell, rod holders, forward jump seats, anchor locker, low-profile bow rails. Porta-Potti stows between V-berths in cuddy cabin. Offered with several cockpit seating options. Narrow 8-foot beam results in relatively small cockpit compared with competitive 30-footers. About 50 knots top with twin 225s.

Length	29'9"	Fuel	150 gals.
Beam	8'0"	Water	None
Draft, Up	2'0"	Max HP	500
Draft, Down	3'0"	Hull Type	Deep-V
Dry Weight	4,000#	Deadrise Aft	24°

Prices Not Provided for Pre-1995 Models

Wellcraft Boats
Sarasota, FL
www.wellcraft.com

Sportfishing Boats

www.powerboatguide.com   231-360-0827

Wellcraft 30 Scarab Tournament
2007–09

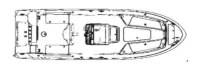

Go-fast center console has what serious anglers demand in an offshore fishing rig. Efficient deck layout features large fore and aft fish boxes, 18 rod holders, optional livewell/leaning post, transom rigging station. Fold-down transom seat frees up cockpit space when necessary. Space at the helm for flush-mounting two big-screen electronics. T-top with rocket launchers, cockpit bolsters were standard. Slender deep-V hull delivers superior rough-water ride. Yamaha 250hp outboards max out at nearly 45 knots.

Length	30'2"	Fuel	288 gals.
Beam	9'2"	Water	13 gals.
Draft, Up	1'8"	Max HP	600
Draft, Down	2'6"	Hull Type	Deep-V
Dry Weight	6,635#	Deadrise Aft	23°

See Page 572 For Resale Values

Wellcraft Boats
Sarasota, FL
www.wellcraft.com

---

www.powerboatguide.com   231-360-0827

Wellcraft 302 Scarab Sport
1995–2000

Updated version of original 30 Scarab Sport (1979–93) with bracket-mounted power targets anglers with a need for speed. Standard fishing goodies include large transom fishbox, dual leaning post with 40-gallon livewell, raw-water washdown, lockable rod storage. Compact bow cuddy contains V-berth, storage lockers, space for portable head. Helm console includes lockable electronics storage, forward-opening storage compartment. Slender beam means limited cockpit space. About 50 knots top with twin 225s.

Length	29'6"	Fuel	238 gals.
Beam	8'0"	Water	9 gals.
Draft, Up	2'0"	Max HP	600
Draft, Down	3'0"	Hull Type	Deep-V
Dry Weight	5,000#	Deadrise Aft	24°

See Page 572 For Resale Values

Wellcraft Boats
Sarasota, FL
www.wellcraft.com

---

www.powerboatguide.com   231-360-0827

Wellcraft 32 Scarab Sport; 32 CCF
2001–06

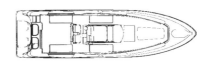

Notched-bottom speedster with roomy fishing cockpit, premium amenities is sexy, fast, built to last. Standard features included T-top with rod holders, in-deck fishboxes (4), 37-gallon lighted livewell, central rigging station with sink, leaning post with cooler, folding rear seat, pop-up cleats, glove box, dual washdowns, forward storage boxes, console head compartment with opening port. Deep-V hull is quick out of the hole. Called 32 Scarab Sport in 2001–04; 32 CCF in 2005–06. Yamaha 250s top out at 45+ knots.

Length	31'1"	Fuel	281 gals.
Beam	9'2"	Water	8 gals.
Draft, Up	1'11"	Max HP	600
Draft, Down	2'5"	Hull Type	Deep-V
Hull Weight	7,865#	Deadrise Aft	24°

See Page 572 For Resale Values

Wellcraft Boats
Sarasota, FL
www.wellcraft.com

Sportfishing Boats

231-360-0827

Wellcraft 3200 Coastal
1984–86

Heavily built express fisherman impressed 1980s anglers with practical deck layout, agile handling, roomy accommodations. Bi-level cockpit with unusual inward-opening transom door has enough space for three anglers and their gear. Teak-paneled cabin sleeps four, includes full galley, convertible dinette, stand-up head with shower. Note tall windshield, good helm visibility, wide side decks. So-so finish, but the price was right. Twin 350hp gas engines cruise at 20–22 knots with a top speed of around 30 knots.

Length	32'0"	Fuel, Std.	290 gals.
Beam	11'6"	Fuel, Opt.	350 gals.
Draft	3'0"	Water	80 gals.
Weight	13,200#	Hull Type	Modified-V
Clearance	8'3"	Deadrise Aft	14°

Prices Not Provided for Pre-1995 Models

Wellcraft Boats
Sarasota, FL
www.wellcraft.com

231-360-0827

Wellcraft 330 Coastal
1989–2009

Serious fishing platform with cruising comforts hit the sweet spot with Wellcraft buyers looking for space, comfort, value. Well-appointed interior with large galley, convertible dinette sleeps four. Roomy cockpit came standard with livewell, insulated fishboxes, tackle center, transom door. Many updates over the years—oval ports replaced original cabin windows in 1998, fuel was increased in 2005. Early models with 310hp gas inboards cruise at 18–20 knots. Later models with 375hp Volvo gas engines cruise in low 20s.

Length w/Pulpit	38.5"	Fuel	288/370 gals.
Hull Length	33'3"	Water	52 gals.
Beam	12.5"	Waste	20 gals.
Draft	3'0"	Hull Type	Modified-V
Weight	16,000#	Deadrise Aft	16°

See Page 572 For Resale Values

Wellcraft Boats
Sarasota, FL
www.wellcraft.com

231-360-0827

Wellcraft 34 Scarab Super Sport
1987–92

Fast-action center console with bracket-mounted outboards, narrow 8'4" beam gets hardcore anglers to the fishing grounds fast. Principal features include in-sole livewell, insulated transom fishboxes, rear bench seat with storage under, forward tackle center, lockable rod storage. Compact cuddy with V-berth, Porta-Potti provides generous dry storage. Far less cockpit space than other 34-footers. Deep-V hull handles rough water with ease. Slender boat is legally trailerable in all states. Over 45 knots with twin 250s.

Length	33'10"	Clearance	6'8"
Beam	8'4"	Fuel	250 gals.
Draft, Up	2'0"	Max HP	500
Draft, Down	3'6"	Hull Type	Deep-V
Dry Weight	5,100#	Deadrise Aft	23°

Prices Not Provided for Pre-1995 Models

Wellcraft Boats
Sarasota, FL
www.wellcraft.com

231-360-0827

Wellcraft 35 Scarab Sport
2007–09

Sleek console cuddy combines time-tested deck layout with deep-V performance, quality amenities. Highlights include deluxe helm seat with flip-up bolsters, aft livewell, folding rear seat, T-top with electronics box, tilt-out tackle box, cockpit bolsters, dual washdowns, forward jump seats, enclosed head with sink & shower. Helm space for big-screen electronics. Compact cuddy with V-berth sleeps two. Good-looking boat is very well finished. Twin 225hp outboards top out at 40+ knots; triple 250s reach speeds of 50+ knots.

Length	35'4"	Fuel	400 gals.
Beam	9'11"	Water	13 gals.
Draft, Up	1'11"	Max HP	900
Draft, Down	3'3"	Hull Type	Deep-V
Dry Weight	8,600#	Deadrise Aft	23°

See Page 572 For Resale Values

Wellcraft Boats
Sarasota, FL
www.wellcraft.com

231-360-0827

Wellcraft 35 Scarab Sport; 35 CCF
2001–05

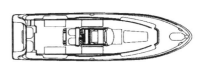

High-speed fishing rig with stepped hull was among the biggest, fastest fishing machines of her era. Highlights include T-top with electronics box, 37-gallon lighted livewell, transom bait-prep station, fold-away rear seat, dual washdowns, leaning post with tackle storage, console cooler, enclosed head with sink. Space at helm for big-screen electronics. Called 35 Scarab Sport in 2001–02; Wellcraft 35 CCF in 2003–5. Great rough-water ride. Twin 225hp outboards top out at 40+ knots; triple 250s reach speeds of 50+ knots.

Length	34'10"	Fuel	300 gals.
Beam	9'11"	Water	29 gals.
Draft, Up	1'11"	Max HP	900
Draft, Down	2'9"	Hull Type	Deep-V
Weight w/OBs	10,000#	Deadrise Aft	23°

See Page 572 For Resale Values

Wellcraft Boats
Sarasota, FL
www.wellcraft.com

231-360-0827

Wellcraft 350 Coastal
2000–03

Classy sports sedan (built for Wellcraft by Aussie-based Riviera Marine) took small-convertible styling to next level. Roomy single-stateroom interior with standard lower helm is well-suited to needs of family cruisers. Fishing amenities include large insulated fishbox, lighted baitwell (with viewing window), cockpit coaming, reinforced deck with plate for fighting chair. Engineroom access, via cockpit hatch, is a tight fit. Among several engine options, twin 370hp Volvo diesels cruise at 25 knots (about 30 knots top).

Length w/Pulpit	37'6"	Fuel	227 gals.
Hull Length	33'2"	Water	81 gals.
Beam	12'6"	Waste	20 gals.
Draft	3'4"	Hull Type	Modified-V
Weight	19,900#	Deadrise Aft	15°

See Page 572 For Resale Values

Wellcraft Boats
Sarasota, FL
www.wellcraft.com

Sportfishing Boats

Wellcraft 360 Coastal
2006–09

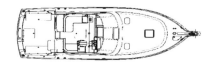

Handsome offshore express blends hardcore fishability with feature-rich interior, long-range capability. Topside highlights include huge bridgedeck with wraparound lounge seating, wide side decks, well-equipped cockpit with 37-gallon livewell, insulated fishboxes, bait-prep center. Upscale cabin with cherry trim, Corian counters, sleeps four. Note standard hardtop, single-level electronic controls. Hunt-designed hull delivers steady open-water performance. Volvo 370hp diesels cruise at 25–26 knots (about 30 knots wide open).

Length w/Pulpit	39'6"	Fuel	400 gals.
Hull Length	36'6"	Water	107 gals.
Beam	13'8"	Waste	18 gals.
Draft	3'4"	Hull Type	Deep-V
Weight	20,000#	Deadrise Aft	18°

See Page 572 For Resale Values

Wellcraft Boats
Sarasota, FL
www.wellcraft.com

Wellcraft 3700 Cozumel
1988–89

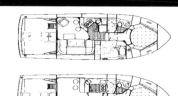

Value-priced convertible with sporty styling lasted only two years in production. Available with one or two staterooms, Eurostyle interior is a blend of cheap Formica, vinyl, chrome—too glitzy for most anglers of her era. Large cockpit came equipped with lockable rod storage, transom door, cockpit bolsters, insulated fishbox. Bridge is big for a 37-footer with guest seating forward of helm. Wide sidedecks are a plus. Unimpressive finish. Twin 340hp gas engines cruise at 18 knots; optional 375hp Cat diesels cruise at 22–24 knots.

Length	36'11"	Fuel	400 gals.
Beam	13'6"	Water	90 gals.
Draft	3'3"	Cockpit	90 sq. ft.
Weight	21,000#	Hull Type	Modified-V
Clearance	12'3"	Deadrise Aft	16.5°

Prices Not Provided for Pre-1995 Models

Wellcraft Boats
Sarasota, FL
www.wellcraft.com

Wellcraft 400 Coastal
1999–2003

Handsome sport sedan (built for Wellcraft by Riviera Marine in Australia) meets anglers need for versatile layout, solid construction. Unpretentious two-stateroom interior with leather seating, beechwood cabinetry is comfortable, simple, easy to clean. Large cockpit features 12 rod holders, rigging station with freezer, 37-gallon livewell, fishbox. Retractable sunshade extends out from bridge overhang; access to the engineroom is via hatch in cockpit sole. Note standard hardtop. Volvo 480hp diesels cruise at 26 knots (about 30 knots top).

Length w/Pulpit	44'7"	Cockpit	94 sq. ft.
Hull Length	39'1"	Fuel	469 gals.
Beam	14'4"	Water	121 gals
Draft	4'1"	Hull Type	Modified-V
Weight	23,400#	Deadrise Aft	15°

See Page 572 For Resale Values

Wellcraft Boats
Sarasota, FL
www.wellcraft.com

231-360-0827

World Cat 266/270 Sport Cabin
1998–2008

Cuddy cabin version of popular 270 TE (called 266 SC in 1998–2002) is comfortable, spacious, very fuel efficient. Uncluttered cockpit features transom fishbox, thickly padded bolsters, bait-rigging station behind helm seat, raw-water washdown. Low-headroom cabin with rod storage, athwartships double berth, marine head sleeps two. Excellent fit and finish. Semi-displacement hulls deliver superb rough-water ride. Twin 200hp Yamaha outboards cruise at 30 knots and reach a top speed of over 40 knots.

Length Overall	28'0"	Clearance	8'6"
Hull Length	26'6"	Fuel	200 gals.
Beam	8'6"	Water	32 gals.
Hull Draft	12"	Max HP	500
Hull Weight	7,000#	Hull Type	Catamaran

See Page 572 For Resale Values

World Cat
Tarboro, NC
www.worldcat.com

231-360-0827

World Cat 266 SF/270 TE
1998–Current

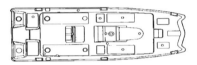

Sure-footed catamaran with wide-open cockpit combines quality construction with exceptional stability. Spacious deck layout features two 35-gallon lighted livewells, leaning post with backrest & raw-water washdown, 11 rod holders, forward fishbox, in-deck fishboxes, full-length toe rails, bow storage boxes, centerline transom door. Narrow console features tackle storage, recessed electronics box, head/storage compartment with opening port. Called 266 SF in 1998–2002; 270 TE since. About 40 knots top with Honda 225s.

Length Overall	28'0"	Clearance	8'6"
Hull Length	26'6"	Fuel	240 gals.
Beam	8'6"	Water	20 gals.
Hull Draft	12"	Max HP	450
Hull Weight	6,600#	Hull Type	Catamaran

See Page 572 For Resale Values

World Cat
Tarboro, NC
www.worldcat.com

231-360-0827

World Cat 270 Express Cabin
2003–Current

Top-quality express cat with trailerable 8'6" beam appeals to weekend cruisers and serious fishing alike. Cockpit features include 27-gallon livewell, 300-quart aft fishbox, removable tackle storage. Ladderback helm seats are mounted atop aft-facing jump seats with built-in coolers. Note sturdy low-profile bow rails, efficient helm layout with space for flush-mounting electronics. Semi-displacement hulls deliver dry, exceptionally stable ride. Twin 225hp Honda outboards deliver a top speed of 40+ knots.

Length Overall	28'0"	Clearance	8'6"
Hull Length	26'6"	Fuel	200 gals.
Beam	8'6"	Water	32 gals.
Draft	12"	Max HP	500
Weight	6,800#	Hull Type	Catamaran

See Page 572 For Resale Values

World Cat
Tarboro, NC
www.worldcat.com

Sportfishing Boats

World Cat 270 Hardtop
2004–07

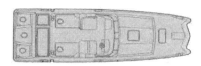

Feature-rich hardtop catamaran scores with northern anglers looking for security, comfort, economy. Semi-enclosed helm area with sliding side windows, rear drop curtain offers good protection from the elements. Cockpit features include dual captain's chairs, 27-gallon lighted livewell, aft fishbox, coaming bolsters, rod holders. Note center windshield vent, hardtop rocket launchers. Compact cabin offers queen-sized berth, marine head, rod storage. Honda 225hp outboards deliver a top speed of 40–45 knots.

Length Overall	28'0"	Fuel	200 gals.
Hull Length	26'6"	Water	32 gals.
Beam	8'6"	Headroom	6'3"
Hull Draft	12"	Max HP	500
Hull Weight	6,800#	Hull Type	Catamaran

See Page 572 For Resale Values

World Cat
Tarboro, NC
www.worldcat.com

World Cat 320 Express Cabin
2006–Current

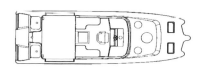

Cruise-ready catamaran with centerline helm, big fishing cockpit handles big water better than any monohull. Belowdecks accommodations include queen-size berth between hulls, head with stand-up shower, full galley, twin berth aft. Cockpit offers tackle storage, rod racks, 40-gallon livewell, bait-prep station. Bridgedeck has facing L-shaped lounges with cooler, storage under. Note fold-down cockpit seats, huge swim ladder between engines. Top-notch fit and finish. Twin 250hp outboards cruise efficiently at 28–30 knots (35+ top).

Length Overall	32'0"	Clearance	9'6"
Beam	10'6"	Fuel	260 gals.
Draft, Up	1'4"	Water	45 gals.
Draft, Down	2'4"	Max HP	600
Dry Weight	10,900#	Hull Type	Catamaran

See Page 572 For Resale Values

World Cat
Tarboro, NC
www.worldcat.com

World Cat 330 Tournament Edition
2003–08

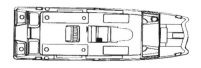

Rugged offshore fishing machine with smooth-running semi-displacement hulls offers unsurpassed stability, comfort, economy. Standard fishing features include two 45-gallon lighted livewells, two tackle centers, dual washdowns, coaming pads, three insulated fish/storage boxes. Compact cabin has room for head, berth, locking rod storage. Tall freeboard makes for a dry ride. Note huge anchor locker, generous fuel capacity. Twin 225hp outboards cruise in the mid 20s (about 35 knots top) with 300-mile cruising range.

Length Overall	34'0"	Headroom	4'11"
Beam	10'6"	Fuel	300 gals.
Hull Draft	16"	Water	20 gals.
Hull Weight	10,400#	Max HP	500
Clearance	6'2"	Hull Type	Catamaran

See Page 572 For Resale Values

World Cat
Tarboro, NC
www.worldcat.com

Sportfishing Boats

231-360-0827

Yellowfin 31
2001–07

Floorplan Not Available

Quality-built center console with stepped hull delivers cutting-edge performance, no-excuses fishability. Single-level deck layout includes leaning post with backrest, in-deck 60-gallon livewell, giant forward fishbox, enclosed head/storage compartment, pop-up cleats, fresh/saltwater washdowns, T-top with rod holders, transom door, stern seat. Space at the helm for installing plenty of electronics. Recessed bow rails means no snagged lines. Fully cored hull is fuel efficient, quick to accelerate. Over 50 knots max with twin 250s.

Length	30'11"	Fuel, Std.	225 gals.
Beam	9'6"	Fuel, Opt.	300 gals.
Draft, Up	1'6"	Max HP	600
Draft, Down	3'0"	Hull Type	Deep-V
Dry Weight	4,550#	Deadrise Aft	22°

See Page 572 For Resale Values

Yellowfin Yachts
Sarasota, FL
www.yellowfinyachts.com

231-360-0827

Yellowfin 34
2005–Current

Floorplan Not Available

Hard-nosed fishing machine matches class standards for quality, fishability, open-water performance. Highlights include 55-gallon transom livewell, cockpit coaming pads, flush-mounted cleats, leaning post with backrest, T-top, removable rear bench seat, cockpit bolsters, forward seating, recessed bow rails, dual washdowns, high-performance K-Planes. Second 70-gallon in-sole livewell is available with twin-engine models. Very well-finished boat. Twin Mercury 275s max out at 45 knots; triple 275s reach 55+ knots wide open.

Length	34'8"	Fuel, Std.	300 gals.
Beam	10'0"	Water	20 gals.
Draft, Up	1'8"	Max HP	1,050
Draft, Down	2'10"	Hull Type	Deep-V
Hull Weight	8,800#	Deadrise Aft	22°

See Page 573 For Resale Values

Yellowfin Yachts
Sarasota, FL
www.yellowfinyachts.com

231-360-0827

Yellowfin 36
2003–Current

Floorplan Not Available

Big world-class center console rated for triple-engine power runs fast, fishes hard, turns heads. Highlights include T-top with rod holders, leaning post with livewell, 50-gallon transom livewell, K-Plane trim tabs, pop-up cleats, saltwater washdown, console seat, 9-foot rod storage boxes. Optional coffin box tilts back to reveal big in-floor fishbox. High-performance stepped hull, stern lifting pad delivers exceptional high-speed handling. Twin Mercury 300 4-strokes top 45 knots; triple 300 Mercs reach 55+ wide open.

Length	36'8"	Fuel, Std.	330 gals.
Beam	10'0"	Fuel, Opt.	525 gals.
Draft, Up	1'8"	Max HP	1,400
Draft, Down	3'6"	Hull Type	Deep-V
Hull Weight	9,500#	Deadrise Aft	22°

See Page 573 For Resale Values

Yellowfin Yachts
Sarasota, FL
www.yellowfinyachts.com

Sportfishing Boats

Section III:
Cruisers & Sportboats

See index for complete list of models.

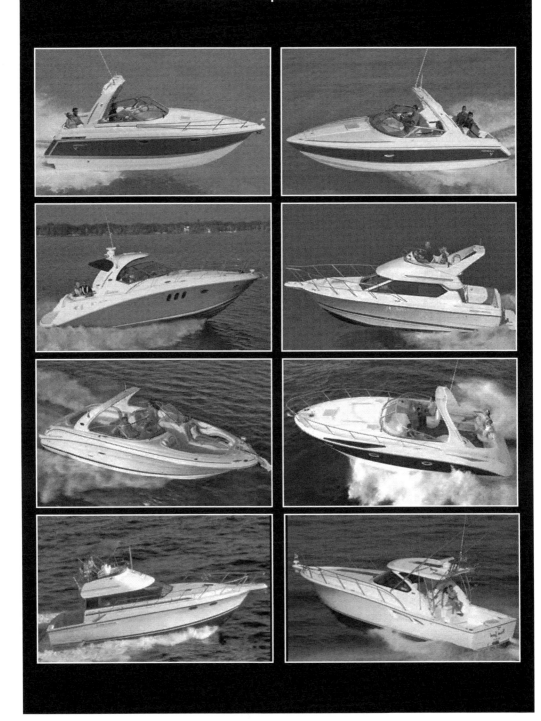

www.powerboatguide.com   231-360-0827

Sea Ray 340 Sedan Bridge
1983–87

Popular 1980s sedan hit the mark with boaters looking for comfort, versatility at a reasonable price. Single-stateroom interior—large for a 34-footer—includes convertible salon settee, convertible dinette, large stateroom with privacy door. Salon is dominated by distinctive bottle-and-glass cabinet with sliding tambour doors. Lower helm was a popular option. Transom door, swim platform were standard. Cockpit is small for a sedan this size. Twin 350hp V-drive gas inboards cruise at 20 knots (28–30 knots top).

Length	33'7"	Fuel	204 gals.
Beam	11'11"	Water	80 gals.
Draft	2'6"	Headroom	6'3"
Weight	11,400#	Hull Type	Deep-V
Clearance	NA	Deadrise Aft	21°

Prices Not Provided for Pre-1995 Models

Sea Ray Boats
Knoxville, TN
www.searay.com

---

www.powerboatguide.com   231-360-0827

Albin 30 Family Cruiser
2004–07

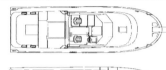

Practical family cruiser—successor to best-selling Albin 27 Family Cruiser (1983–95)—combines economical operation with easy handling, space-efficient layout. Unique aft-cabin layout sleeps five adults in two separate cabins. Visibility from semi-enclosed helm is excellent. Deep cockpit keeps kids and guests safe, secure. Solid, well-built boat requires little maintenance. Wide side decks, good engine access, ten opening ports. Good helm visibility. Cruise at 16–17 knots (about 20 top) with single 300hp diesel.

Length Overall	31'5"	Fuel	126 gals.
Length WL	26'8"	Water	26 gals.
Beam	10'0"	Waste	18 gals.
Draft	3'2"	Hull Type	Modified-V
Weight	9,800#	Deadrise Aft	19°

See Page 530 For Resale Values

Albin is no longer in business.

---

www.powerboatguide.com   231-360-0827

Back Cove 29
2004–Current

Handsome hardtop cruiser with classic lines blends leading-edge construction with practical layout, fuel-efficient operation. Warm cherry interior boasts traditional teak-and-holly sole, ash ceiling strips, adult-size berths, full galley. Semi-enclosed pilothouse has opening center windshield, sliding side windows. Bridgedeck lifts electrically for engine access. Note wide side decks, sturdy bow rails. Prop pocket reduces draft for shallow-water exploring. Single Yanmar 315hp diesel will cruise efficiently at 20 knots (26–27 knots top).

Length	29'5"	Fuel	150 gals.
Beam	10'5"	Water	30 gals.
Draft	2'6"	Waste	30 gals.
Weight	10,000#	Hull Type	Modified-V
Clearance	8'4"	Deadrise Aft	16°

See Page 531 For Resale Values

Back Cove Yachts
Rockland, ME
www.backcoveyachts.com

Back Cove 33
2007–Current

Elegant Downeast cruiser combines single-diesel efficiency with state-of-the-art construction, luxury-class accommodations. Semi-enclosed pilothouse with dinette, in-line galley offers excellent helm visibility. Surprisingly large head has separate stall shower. Stidd helm chair is a quality touch; helm deck sole lifts electrically for engine access. Upscale cabin with teak and holly sole, quality appliances, sleeps four. Prop pocket reduces draft, improves efficiency. Cruise at 20 knots with 425hp Cummins diesel (mid 20s top).

Length	34'4"	Water	60 gals.
Beam	12'0"	Waste	60 gals.
Draft	3'1"	Headroom	6 5"
Weight	16,000#	Hull Type	Modified-V
Fuel	185 gals.	Deadrise Aft	14°

See Page 531 For Resale Values

Back Cove Yachts
Rockland, ME
www.backcoveyachts.com

Bayliner 275 Cruiser
2005–07

Low-cost family cruiser boasts more cockpit, cabin space than most 27-footers. Midcabin floorplan with convertible dinette, full galley sleeps four adults and two kids. Roomy head compartment offers enough elbow room to be comfortable. Standard features include convertible lounge opposite helm, transom shower, carry-on cooler, radio/CD player, removable cockpit table. Good finish belies her low price. Small fuel capacity. Tops out in the high 30s/low 40s with optional 320hp MerCruiser power.

Length	26 7"	Fuel	77 gals.
Beam	9 5"	Water	31 gals.
Draft, Up	1'9"	Waste	20 gals.
Draft, Down	3'2"	Hull Type	Modified-V
Weight	6,485#	Deadrise Aft	15°

See Page 531 For Resale Values

Bayliner Boats
Arlington, WA
www.bayliner.com

Bayliner 2755 Ciera Sunbridge
1989–93

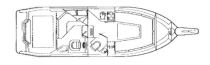

Big trailerable cruiser with lots of standard equipment offered budget-minded buyers good value for the money. Narrow midcabin interior sleeps four (two adults, two kids), includes removable dinette table, small galley, stand-up head with sink, shower. Cockpit features L-shaped lounge forward, transom seat, sink. Good helm visibility. Additional features include four opening ports, walk-through windshield, radar arch, bow pulpit. Lots of rough edges in the finish department. Cruise at 25 knots with single 300hp gas engine.

Length	27'0"	Fuel	78 gals.
Beam	8'6"	Water	28 gals.
Draft, Up	1'8"	Waste	13 gals.
Draft, Down	3'3"	Hull Type	Deep-V
Weight	5,200#	Deadrise Aft	20°

Prices Not Provided for Pre-1995 Models

Bayliner Boats
Arlington, WA
www.bayliner.com

Cruisers & Sportboats

---

www.powerboatguide.com   231-360-0827

Bayliner 2850/2855 Sunbridge
1983—89

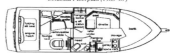

Contessa Floorplan (1983–87)

Ciera Floorplan (1988–89)

Lightweight, value-priced family cruiser became one of Bayliner's best-selling models during the 1980s. Roomy interior sleeps six with stand-up head compartment, convertible dinette, full-size galley, generous storage. Large cockpit offers seating for five. Good helm visibility. Standard features included radar arch, teak interior trim, transom platform, bow pulpit, dockside power. Called 2850 Contessa SB in 1983–87; 2855 Ciera SB in 1988–89. Floorplan revised in 1988. Single 260hp Volvo I/O will cruise at 20 knots.

Length	27'5"	Clearance	6'8"
Beam	10'0"	Fuel	120 gals.
Draft, Up	1'11"	Water	30 gals.
Draft, Down	3'3"	Hull Type	Modified-V
Weight	5,775#	Deadrise Aft	NA

Prices Not Provided for Pre-1995 Models

Bayliner Boats
Arlington, WA
www.bayliner.com

---

www.powerboatguide.com   231-360-0827

Bayliner 2850/2858 Command Bridge
1983—89

1983–85

1986–89

Affordable flybridge cruiser for coastal, inland cruising proved popular with entry-level buyers on a budget. Space-efficient interior includes amidships stateroom (with privacy curtain) under salon dinette, compact galley, enclosed head with sink and shower. Lower helm position permits all-weather operation. Swim platform, bow pulpit, teak exterior trim, and swim ladder were standard. Called 2850 Contessa CB in 1983–87; 2855 Ciera CB in 1988–89. Floorplan updated in 1986. Single 260hp Volvo sterndrive will cruise at 18 knots (mid 20s top).

Length	27'7"	Clearance	6'8"
Beam	10'0"	Fuel	120 gals.
Draft, Up	1'11"	Water	30 gals.
Draft, Down	3'3"	Hull Type	Modified-V
Weight	5,775#	Deadrise Aft	NA

Prices Not Provided for Pre-1995 Models

Bayliner Boats
Arlington, WA
www.bayliner.com

---

www.powerboatguide.com   231-360-0827

Bayliner 2855 Ciera Sunbridge
1991—93

Economy-class 1990s cruiser is clearly dated by today's styling standards. Roomy interior boasts wraparound dinette with seating for six. Midcabin berth comes with headboard storage, privacy curtain. Small galley lacks counter, storage space. Cockpit includes U-shaped lounge seating opposite helm, rear bench seat, removable table, transom shower. Modest fuel capacity, poor finish. Single 230hp MerCruiser I/O will cruise at 16–18 knots; optional 300hp I/O will cruise at 20 knots. Replaced in 1994 with all-new 2855 Sunbridge model.

Length	28'1"	Fuel	102 gals.
Beam	9'6"	Water	35 gals.
Draft, Up	1'8"	Waste	13 gals.
Draft, Down	3'3"	Hull Type	Modified-V
Weight	6,510#	Deadrise Aft	18°

Prices Not Provided for Pre-1995 Models

Bayliner Boats
Arlington, WA
www.bayliner.com

231-360-0827

Bayliner 2855 Ciera Sunbridge
1994-99

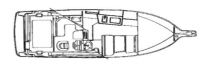

Updated version of earlier 2855 Sunbridge has improved styling, updated interior with larger galley. Midcabin layout is arranged with double berths fore and aft, convertible dinette, stand-up head with sink, shower. Privacy curtains separate sleeping areas from salon. Good engine access; well-designed helm with space for electronics. Note slide-out jump seats behind companion lounge. Bow pulpit, radar arch, and trim tabs were standard. Single 300hp sterndrive will cruise at 20 knots and reach 30+ knots wide open.

Length w/Pulpit	30'3"	Clearance	8'6"
Beam	9'7"	Fuel	109 gals.
Draft, Up	1'8"	Water	33 gals.
Draft, Down	3'4"	Hull Type	Deep-V
Weight	6,510#	Deadrise Aft	22°

See Page 531 For Resale Values

Bayliner Boats
Arlington, WA
www.bayliner.com

231-360-0827

Bayliner 2859 Ciera Express
1993-2002

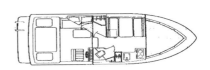

Popular hardtop cruiser (called 2859 Classic in 1993-95) is practical, affordable, exceptionally versatile. Roomy interior comes complete with galley, convertible dinette, private head, aft double berth. Excellent visibility from semi-enclosed helm position. Deep cockpit offers great security for kids and guests. Note narrow side decks. Additional features include transom door, swim platform, fold-down helm seats, swim ladder. Single 310hp MerCruiser will cruise at 22 knots and top out at close to 30 knots. Note modest fuel capacity.

Length	27'9"	Fuel	102 gals.
Beam	9'9"	Water	36 gals.
Draft, Up	1'7"	Waste	30 gals.
Draft, Down	3'0"	Hull Type	Modified-V
Weight	7,597#	Deadrise Aft	15°

See Page 531 For Resale Values

Bayliner Boats
Arlington, WA
www.bayliner.com

231-360-0827

Bayliner 285 Cruiser
2000-Current

Entry-level family cruiser (called the 2855 Ciera Sunbridge in 2000-02) makes good on promise of space, comfort at a reasonable price. Generic floorplan with convertible dinette sleeps six. Midcabin privacy door is a nice touch—most boats in this class have curtains. Cockpit with fold-down transom seat, removable cockpit table seats six. Note walk-through windshield, transom shower. Deep-V hull delivers a secure rough-water ride. Cruise economically at 20 knots (28-30 top) with single 300hp MerCruiser Bravo III power.

Length	29'6"	Fuel	102 gals.
Beam	9'10"	Water	33 gals.
Draft, Up	1'8"	Waste	20 gals.
Draft, Down	3'1"	Hull Type	Deep-V
Weight	7,185#	Deadrise Aft	21°

See Page 531 For Resale Values

Bayliner Boats
Arlington, WA
www.bayliner.com

Cruisers & Sportboats

231-360-0827

Bayliner 288 Classic Cruiser
1996–2005

Sporty flybridge cruiser (called Bayliner 2858 Ciera Command Bridge in 1996–2002) is versatile, roomy, inexpensive to operate. Impressive accommodations for a 28-footer include private midcabin berth below salon sole, convertible dinette, enclosed head with shower, full galley. Good visibility from lower helm. Note narrow side decks. Bow pulpit, radar arch, swim platform are standard. Decent finish considering her super-low price. Single 310hp MerCruiser sterndrive engine will cruise at 22 knots (32–33 knots top).

Length w/Pulpit	30'7"	Fuel	113 gals.
Beam	10'0"	Water	34 gals.
Draft, Up	1'8"	Waste	26 gals.
Draft, Down	3'2"	Hull Type	Modified-V
Weight	6,100#	Deadrise Aft	18°

See Page 531 For Resale Values

Bayliner Boats
Arlington, WA
www.bayliner.com

231-360-0827

Bayliner 2950/2958 Command Bridge
1988–90

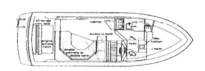

Inexpensive flybridge cruiser combined sporty styling with traditional Bayliner value. Efficient midcabin floorplan includes mini-stateroom beneath salon settee. Privacy curtain separates V-berth from galley. Visibility from lower helm—with its double seat—is very good. Note small cockpit. Lounge seating on flybridge seats several guests. Bow pulpit, radar arch, sliding cabin windows, transom door, swim platform were standard. Engine compartment is small. Twin 230hp sterndrive engines cruise at 20 knots (28–30 knots top).

Length	28'8"	Fuel	121 gals.
Beam	10'6"	Water	29 gals.
Draft, Up	2'0"	Waste	13 gals.
Draft, Down	3'6"	Hull Type	Deep-V
Weight	8,750#	Deadrise Aft	20°

Prices Not Provided for Pre-1995 Models

Bayliner Boats
Arlington, WA
www.bayliner.com

231-360-0827

Bayliner 2955 Avanti Sunbridge
1988–90

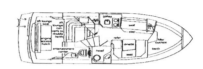

Maxi-volume express cruiser from late 1980s offered big-boat accommodations at very low price. Wide 10'6" beam permits spacious interior dimensions. Midcabin floorplan includes two private sleeping areas, stand-up head with shower, efficient galley, convertible dinette, generous storage. Unimpressive fit and finish. Engine compartment is a tight fit with twin engines. Single 340hp sterndrive will cruise at 16 knots (26–28 knots top); twin 260hp engines cruise at 22 knots (30+ knots top).

Length	28'8"	Fuel	120 gals.
Beam	10'6"	Water	30 gals.
Draft, Up	2'0"	Waste	13 gals.
Draft, Down	3'6"	Hull Type	Deep-V
Weight	7,400#	Deadrise Aft	20°

Prices Not Provided for Pre-1995 Models

Bayliner Boats
Arlington, WA
www.bayliner.com

Bayliner 300/315 Cruiser
2008–Current

Sleek twin-engine cruiser (called 315 after 2009) takes express-boat affordability, value to the next level. Roomy single-level cockpit with L-shaped lounge, small refreshment center seats six without being crowded. Note dual helm seat with flip-up bolster, optional power engine compartment hatch. Cabin, with large side windows, screened companionway door, is well lit and ventilated. Midcabin berth has fixed doorway rather than a curtain—definitely a plus. Twin 260hp MerCruiser I/Os cruise at 25 knots (around 35 knots top).

Length	30'6"	Fuel	120 gals.
Beam	10'0	Water	33 gals.
Draft, Up	2'1"	Waste	30 gals.
Draft, Down	3'4"	Hull Type	Modified-V
Weight	9,098#	Deadrise Aft	18°

See Page 531 For Resale Values

Bayliner Boats
Arlington, WA
www.bayliner.com

Bayliner 3055 Ciera Sunbridge
1991–94

Early 1990s express cruiser delivered roomy accommodations, decent performance at rock-bottom price. Midcabin floorplan features convertible dinette, full galley (refrigerator is under dinette seat), enclosed head with shower. Both staterooms have curtains for nighttime privacy. Bi-level cockpit includes lounge seating forward, wet bar, storage cabinet, transom seat. Reverse arch is a sporty touch. Low-deadrise hull is not fond of a chop. Single 300hp sterndrive will cruise at 17 knots (mid 20s knots top).

Length	30'7"	Clearance	8'9"
Beam	10'0"	Fuel	125 gals.
Draft, Up	1'6"	Water	36 gals.
Draft, Down	3'0"	Hull Type	Modified-V
Weight	8,000#	Deadrise Aft	14°

Prices Not Provided for Pre-1995 Models

Bayliner Boats
Arlington, WA
www.bayliner.com

Bayliner 305 Cruiser
1999–2007

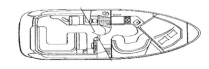

Portly family cruiser (called 3055 Ciera Sunbridge in 1999–2002) with wide 11-foot beam has much to offer in comfort, versatility. Expansive midcabin interior boasts full 6'5" headroom, two double berths, fully equipped galley, roomy head compartment. Cockpit has removable table, fill-in sun pad. Walk-through windshield provides easy bow access. Long list of standard equipment included cockpit wet bar, tilt wheel, radar arch, trim tabs, transom shower. Cruise at 25 knots (high 30s top) with twin 300hp MerCruiser I/Os.

Length Overall	31'6"	Fuel	148 gals.
Beam	11'0"	Water	35 gals.
Draft, Up	1'9"	Waste	30 gals.
Draft, Down	2'9"	Hull Type	Modified-V
Weight	11,857#	Deadrise Aft	17°

See Page 531 For Resale Values

Bayliner Boats
Arlington, WA
www.bayliner.com

Cruisers & Sportboats

231-360-0827

Bayliner 320/335 Cruiser
2008–Current

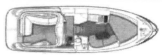

Standard Fixed Berth

Optional Open Lounge

Value-priced express (called the Bayliner 335 Cruiser since 2010) delivers the goods without causing sticker shock. Generic cabin offered with standard fixed berth or open lounge boasts private midcabin berth, fully equipped galley, good lighting, plenty of storage. Innovative cockpit design with extended portside lounge is unusual. Swivel helm seat with flip-up bolster, windlass, cockpit refreshment center, foredeck sun pads are standard. Cruise at 25 knots with twin 300hp MerCruiser I/Os (high 30s top).

Length	32'6"	Fuel	160 gals.
Beam	11'0"	Water	35 gals.
Draft, Up	2'1"	Waste	30 gals.
Draft, Down	3'2"	Hull Type	Modified-V
Weight	12,000#	Deadrise Aft	NA

See Page 531 For Resale Values

Bayliner Boats
Arlington, WA
www.bayliner.com

231-360-0827

Bayliner 325 Cruiser
2005–07

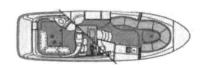

Family-friendly cruiser with spacious midcabin interior delivers plenty of bang for the buck. Wide-open cabin with generous headroom is surprisingly roomy for 32-footer. Full-featured galley includes microwave, coffeemaker; aft cabin has privacy door rather than curtain—a real plus. Swivel helm seat rotates to face the cockpit. Additional features include non-glare helm, walk-through windshield, extended swim platform, radar arch, tilt steering, windlass. Cruise at 26–28 knots (40+ top) with twin 320hp MerCruiser I/Os.

Length	35'0"	Fuel	175 gals.
Beam	11'6"	Water	31 gals.
Draft, Up	1'9"	Waste	30 gals.
Draft, Down	3'4"	Hull Type	Modified-V
Weight	11,319#	Deadrise Aft	18°

See Page 531 For Resale Values

Bayliner Boats
Arlington, WA
www.bayliner.com

231-360-0827

Bayliner 3255 Avanti Sunbridge
1995–99

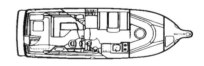

Conservative family express from late 1990s combined roomy interior with large cockpit, affordable price. Midcabin floorplan features double berths fore and aft, complete galley, enclosed head with shower, convertible dinette, large hanging locker. Pocket door—not a curtain—separates forward stateroom from salon. Cockpit wet bar, transom door, bow pulpit, swim platform, foredeck sun pad were standard. Note stylish reverse radar arch. Cruise at 20 knots (mid 30s top) with twin 310hp MerCruiser sterndrives.

Length w/Pulpit	35'0"	Fuel	180 gals.
Hull Length	32'11"	Water	35 gals.
Beam	11'0"	Waste	30 gals.
Draft	3'0"	Hull Type	Modified-V
Weight	11,000#	Deadrise Aft	16°

See Page 531 For Resale Values

Bayliner Boats
Arlington, WA
www.bayliner.com

231-360-0827

Bayliner 3258 Command Bridge
1995–2000

Good styling, spacious accommodations made this commonsense cruiser attractive to budget-minded buyers in late 1990s. Innovative two-stateroom interior is arranged with lounge, head forward in salon, U-shaped dinette, large galley aft. Stall shower in head is a useful feature. Lower helm visibility is good forward, poor to the sides. Bow pulpit, radar arch, swim platform, transom door, trim tabs were standard. Note small cockpit. Twin 250hp Merc I/Os cruise at 20 knots; 310hp Mercs cruise at 25 knots (about 35 knots top).

Length w/Platform	35'2"	Weight	10,230#
Hull Length	32'11"	Fuel	180 gals.
Beam	11'0"	Water	52 gals.
Draft, Up	2'0"	Hull Type	Modified-V
Draft, Down	3'3"	Deadrise Aft	17°

See Page 531 For Resale Values

Bayliner Boats
Arlington, WA
www.bayliner.com

231-360-0827

Bayliner 3270/3288 Motor Yacht
1981–95

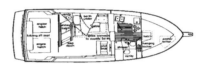

Best-selling flybridge sedan (called the 3270 MY in 1981–88; 3288 MY in 1989–95) was stylish, spacious, economical to operate. Innovative interior with teak trim boasts expansive salon with large cabin windows, raised dinette platform, full lower helm. Second stateroom beneath dinette is great for kids, okay for adults. Bow pulpit, transom door, swim platform were standard. Early models with 110hp Hino diesels cruise at 12 knots; later models with 150hp turbo Hinos cruise at 16–17 knots. Over 3,000 were sold.

Length Overall	32'1"	Fuel	200 gals.
Beam	11'6"	Water	65 gals.
Draft	2'11"	Waste	23 gals.
Weight	12,500#	Hull Type	Modified-V
Clearance	13'10"	Deadrise Aft	12°

See Page 531 For Resale Values

Bayliner Boats
Arlington, WA
www.bayliner.com

231-360-0827

Bayliner 3388 Motor Yacht
1996–2000

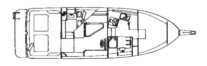

Affordable twin-diesel family cruiser was basically an updated version of previous Bayliner 3288 MY (1981–95) with fresh exterior styling, rearranged floorplan, numerous hull refinements. Midcabin floorplan with galley down includes standard lower helm, head with separate stall shower, raised salon settee, large cabin windows. Additional features include teak interior trim, radar arch, midcabin vanity and sink, swim platform, bow pulpit. Prop pockets reduce hull draft. Standard 260hp gas inboards will cruise at 16 knots (around 25 knots top).

Length	32'11"	Fuel	200 gals.
Beam	11'6"	Water	90 gals.
Draft	2'8"	Waste	30 gals.
Weight	15,500#	Hull Type	Modified-V
Clearance	13'6"	Deadrise Aft	6°

See Page 351 For Resale Values

Bayliner Boats
Arlington, WA
www.bayliner.com

Cruisers & Sportboats

www.powerboatguide.com   231-360-0827

Bayliner 340 Cruiser
2008—Current

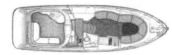
Standard Open Lounge

Optional Fixed Berth

Contemporary sterndrive express lifts the bar for sportboat styling, versatility in a low-priced cruiser. Uncluttered single-level cockpit with portside lounge, L-shaped rear seat has more space than most 34-footers. Comfortable cabin—available with fixed berth forward or wraparound lounge seat—features private midcabin berth, fully equipped galley, generous storage. Six opening ports and three deck hatches provide good cabin ventilation. Good engine access. MerCruiser 300hp Bravo III engines cruise easily at 25–26 knots (low 40s top).

Length	35'0"	Fuel	175 gals.
Beam	11'6"	Water	40 gals.
Draft, Up	2'2"	Waste	30 gals.
Draft, Down	3 5"	Hull Type	Modified-V
Weight	11,226#	Deadrise At	NA

See Page 531 For Resale Values

Bayliner Boats
Arlington, WA
www.bayliner.com

---

www.powerboatguide.com   231-360-0827

Bayliner 3488 Avanti Command Bridge
1996—99

Spacious flybridge cruiser with contemporary styling, roomy interior offered exceptional value to 1990s buyers. Interior is arranged with private midcabin below salon settee. Note separate stall shower in head compartment. L-shaped galley provides plenty of counter, storage space. Good visibility from lower helm. Additional features include bow pulpit, radar arch, transom door, swim platform. MerCruiser 310hp gas inboards (with V-drives) cruise at 18 knots (26—28 knots max). Replaced with all-new 3488 Command Bridge model in 2001.

Length Overall	36 7"	Fuel	180 gals.
Hull Length	34'4"	Water	52 gals.
Beam	11'0"	Waste	52 gals.
Draft	3 5"	Hull Type	Modified-V
Weight	12,549#	Deadrise Aft	17°

See Page 531 For Resale Values

Bayliner Boats
Arlington, WA
www.bayliner.com

---

www.powerboatguide.com   231-360-0827

Bayliner 3488 Command Bridge
2001—02

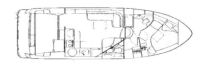

Sporty, strong-selling Bayliner cruiser was one of the most affordable 35-footers of her era. Midcabin interior includes spacious galley with plenty of counter and storage space, two private staterooms, head with separate stall shower, large cabin windows. Lower helm was a popular option. Note roomy cockpit, molded flybridge stairs. Bow pulpit, radar arch, transom door, swim platform were standard. Low-deadrise hull is a stiff ride in a chop. Standard 260hp gas inboards cruise at 14 knots (about 20 knots top).

Length	35'0"	Fuel	224 gals.
Beam	11'8"	Water	92 gals.
Draft	3'2"	Waste	30 gals.
Weight	17,000#	Hull Type	Modified-V
Clearance, Arch	13'6"	Deadrise Aft	7.5°

See Page 531 For Resale Values

Bayliner Boats
Arlington, WA
www.bayliner.com

Bayliner 3450/3485/3785 Sunbridge
1987–90

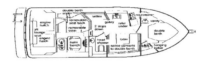

Maxi-volume express (called the 3450 Avanti SB in 1987; 3485 in 1988–89; 3785 in 1990) has little to recommend in today's market other than low price. Styling can only be described as tacky; poor finish is typical of late-1980s Bayliner boats. Generic midcabin interior includes full galley, convertible dinette, roomy master stateroom with vanity, sink, privacy door. Bow pulpit, radar arch, transom door were standard. Integral swim platform became standard in 1990. Twin 330hp V-drive gas engines cruise at 20 knots (27–28 knots top).

Length w/Pulpit	36 7"	Clearance	9'6"
Hull Length	33'9"	Fuel	205 gals.
Beam	12'10"	Water	50 gals.
Draft	3'0"	Waste	34 gals.
Weight	13,150#	Hull Type	Modified-V

Prices Not Provided for Pre-1995 Models

Bayliner Boats
Arlington, WA
www.bayliner.com

Bayliner 3555 Ciera Sunbridge
1988–94

Overstyled midcabin cruiser is long on interior volume, short on sex appeal. Generic midcabin layout includes convertible dinette, full galley, forward stateroom with privacy door and vanity. Midcabin space isn't as cramped as some. Roomy cockpit is fitted with wraparound lounge, wet bar, removable table. Bow pulpit, radar arch, transom door, extended swim platform were standard. Twin 250hp MerCruiser sterndrives cruise at 20 knots (28–29 knots wide open). Called the Bayliner 3250 Sunbridge in 1988; 3255 Sunbridge in 1989.

Length	34 7"	Fuel	205 gals.
Beam	11 5"	Water	50 gals.
Draft, Drives Up	2'4"	Waste	34 gals.
Draft, Drives Down	3'8"	Hull Type	Modified-V
Weight	10,200#	Deadrise Aft	19°

Prices Not Provided for Pre-1995 Models

Bayliner Boats
Arlington, WA
www.bayliner.com

Bayliner 3685 Avanti Sunbridge
1998–99

Value-priced inboard express with long equipment list delivered a lot of bang for the buck. Conventional midcabin floorplan has double staterooms fore and aft, full galley, convertible dinette, head with shower. Sliding doors insure real privacy in forward stateroom. Removable cocktail table stores beneath cockpit sole. Large gas-assist hatch provides good access to engine compartment. Note narrow side decks, foredeck sun pad. So-so fit and finish. Twin 310hp V-drive gas engines cruise at 18 knots (26–28 knots wide open).

Length Overall	39'4"	Fuel	244 gals.
Beam	13'0"	Water	65 gals.
Draft	3 7"	Waste	48 gals.
Weight	21,000#	Hull Type	Modified-V
Clearance, Arch	12'11"	Deadrise Aft	15°

See Page 531 For Resale Values

Bayliner Boats
Arlington, WA
www.bayliner.com

Cruisers & Sportboats

Cruisers & Sportboats

Bayliner 3688 Motor Yacht
1992–94

Rakish styling, low price, innovative interior set this early-1990s cruiser apart from the pack. Narrow staircase just inside salon door descends to private cabin with partial standing headroom, cabinet, and sink. Salon—with raised dinette, standard lower helm—is small for a 36-foot boat. Forward stateroom privacy is limited to just a curtain; absence of stall shower in head is notable. Bow pulpit, radar arch, transom door, fender rack were standard. Twin 200hp V-drive diesels cruise at 15 knots, top out at 17–18 knots.

Length	36'1"	Fuel	250 gals.
Beam	12'2"	Water	96 gals.
Draft	2'11"	Waste	23 gals.
Weight	13,700#	Hull Type	Modified-V
Clearance	13'10"	Deadrise Aft	14°

Prices Not Provided for Pre-1995 Models

Bayliner Boats
Arlington, WA
www.bayliner.com

Bayliner 3788 Motor Yacht
1996–99

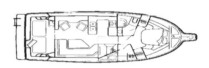

Popular 1990s flybridge cruiser offered crisp styling, family-friendly accommodations at affordable price. Spacious interior is arranged with salon-level galley, midcabin berth with hanging locker, bow stateroom with privacy door, head with tub/shower. Additional features include cockpit sink, roomy engineroom, transom door, swim platform, radar arch, bow pulpit. MerCruiser 310hp gas inboards cruise at 18 knots (27–28 knots top); 250hp Cummins diesels cruise at 20 knots and top out at 23–24 knots. Updated 3788 model came out in 2001.

Length	38'6"	Water	100 gals.
Beam	13'4"	Waste	30 gals.
Draft	2'11"	Headroom	6 5"
Weight	20,000#	Hull Type	Modified-V
Fuel	250 gals.	Deadrise Aft	10°

See Page 531 For Resale Values

Bayliner Boats
Arlington, WA
www.bayliner.com

Bayliner 3788 Motor Yacht
2001–02

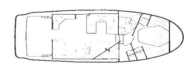

Updated version of the original Bayliner 3788 MY (above) with refined styling, updated interior made a good boat even better. Wide-open salon with dinette and galley forward offers lots of usable space, good overall finish. Both staterooms have double berths. Tub/shower is fitted in head compartment. Molded steps make bridge access easy and safe. Swim platform, transom door, radar arch were standard. MerCruiser 310hp gas inboards cruise at 17–18 knots; 330hp Cummins diesels cruise at 20 knots.

Length	39'4"	Water	125 gals.
Beam	13'7"	Waste	36 gals.
Draft	3'4"	Headroom	6 5"
Weight	22,274#	Hull Type	Modified-V
Fuel	300 gals.	Deadrise Aft	7.5°

See Page 531 For Resale Values

Bayliner Boats
Arlington, WA
www.bayliner.com

231-360-0827

Bayliner 3870/3888 Motor Yacht
1983–94

Super-popular diesel cruiser (called Bayliner 3870 MY in 1983-89) offered buyers remarkable comfort, economy at surprisingly affordable price. Boxy profile conceals expansive interior with innovative midcabin floorplan. Master stateroom is very spacious. Lower helm was standard. Fuel economy at cruise is an impressive 1 mpg. Engine room is tight. Over 1,000 were built during a decade of production. Early models with twin 135hp diesels cruise at 10 knots; later models with 210hp Hino diesels cruise at16 knots.

Length	38'2"	Fuel	304 gals.
Beam	13.5"	Water	80 gals.
Draft	3'2"	Waste	40 gals.
Weight	17,500#	Hull Type	Modified-V
Clearance	14'10"	Deadrise Aft	6°

Prices Not Provided for Pre-1995 Models

Bayliner Boats
Arlington, WA
www.bayliner.com

231-360-0827

Bayliner 4085 Avanti Sunbridge
1997–99

Maxi-volume express cruiser with roomy interior, large cockpit was stylish, practical, very affordable. Contemporary midcabin interior has pocket doors for both cabins—a real plus where privacy is concerned. Features include ash interior trim, large galley, enclosed stall shower, double-wide helm seat, radar arch, side exhausts, foredeck sun pad. Extended swim platform can store PWC. MerCruiser 310hp gas (V-drive) inboards cruise at a modest 15–16 knots (25 knots top); Cummins 315hp diesels cruise at 25 knots.

Length	42'0"	Fuel	330 gals.
Beam	13.5"	Water	77 gals.
Draft	3.5"	Waste	45 gals.
Weight	22,100#	Hull Type	Modified-V
Clearance, Arch	12'11"	Deadrise Aft	16°

See Page 532 For Resale Values

Bayliner Boats
Arlington, WA
www.bayliner.com

231-360-0827

Bayliner 4388 Motor Yacht
1991–94

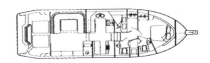

Low-priced 1990s flybridge yacht with spacious midcabin interior is well-suited to coastal cruising, dockside entertaining. Large salon offers full 360-degree visibility, extensive lounge seating, wet bar, lower helm station. Mid stateroom with partial standing headroom extends under galley. Note common shower stall between both heads. Transom door, shower, bench seat were standard in cockpit. Small fuel capacity limits cruising range. Twin Hino 250hp V-drive diesels cruise at 19 knots and (24–25 knots top).

Length	43'1"	Fuel	300 gals.
Beam	14'3"	Water	100 gals.
Draft	3'0"	Waste	46 gals.
Weight	19,000#	Hull Type	Modified-V
Clearance	13'6"	Deadrise Aft	14°

Prices Not Provided for Pre-1995 Models

Bayliner Boats
Arlington, WA
www.bayliner.com

Cruisers & Sportboats

Cruisers & Sportboats

231-360-0827

Bertram 30 Flybridge Cruiser
1984–85

Short-lived cruiser designed to replace the classic Bertram 31 failed to catch on with buyers. Same length as the Bertram 31 but with slightly smaller cockpit dimensions, less transom deadrise (18.5° vs. 23°), improved trolling stability, and a drier ride. Well-appointed cabin offered luxuries undreamed of in the old Bertram 31. Cockpit motor boxes provide convenient seating. Too glitzy for most hardcore anglers; too expensive for others. MerCruiser 340hp gas engines cruise at 22 knots (about 30 knots top).

Length	30'7"	Fuel	220 gals.
Beam	11'4"	Water	61 gals.
Draft	3'0"	Cockpit	101 sq. ft.
Weight	16,500#	Hull Type	Deep-V
Clearance	8'5"	Deadrise Aft	18.5°

Prices Not Provided for Pre-1995 Models

Bertram Yacht
Miami, FL
www.bertram.com

231-360-0827

Bertram 33 Flybridge Cruiser
1977–92

Single-Stateroom Layout, 1977–79

Two-Stateroom Layout, 1980–87

Premium flybridge cruiser with classic Bertram profile took small-convertible comfort to the next level. Enormous interior for a 33-foot boat. Several floorplans were offered over the years—two-stateroom layout became standard in 1980. Teak cabinetry replaced mica in 1984. Small cockpit is okay for light-tackle anglers. Lower helm was optional. Bertram 33 II, introduced in 1988, has restyled flybridge, light oak interior. Standard 340hp gas engines cruise at 18 knots; 260hp Cat diesels cruise at 22 knots.

Length	33'0"	Fuel, Gas	250/315 gals.
Beam	12'6"	Fuel, Diesel	255 gals.
Draft	3'0"	Water	70 gals.
Weight	22,800#	Hull Type	Deep-V
Clearance	12'6"	Deadrise Aft	17°

Prices Not Provided for Pre-1995 Models

Bertram Yacht
Miami, FL
www.bertram.com

231-360-0827

Californian 30 LRC
1978–81

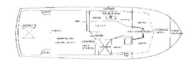

This small Californian sedan combines a versatile layout with handsome styling and very economical operation. Single-stateroom mahogany interior features a cozy salon with lower helm and convertible settee, enclosed head with shower stall, fully-equipped galley with double sink and serving counter. Note sliding window next to lower helm. Cockpit is large enough for fishing. Easy engine access is a plus. Excellent lower helm visibility. Good fit and finish. Cruise (about 12 knots top) at 8 knots with single 135hp Perkins diesel.

Length	29'6"	Fuel	120 gals.
Beam	10'3"	Water	38 gals.
Draft	1'10"	Waste	20 gals.
Weight	9,200#	Hull Type	Modified-V
Clearance	NA	Deadrise Aft	NA

Prices Not Provided for Pre-1995 Models

Californian is no longer in business.

www.powerboatguide.com   231-360-0827

Californian 35 Convertible
1985–87

Sporty flybridge convertible from 1980s doubles as family cruiser, light-tackle fisherman. Single-stateroom, galley-down interior features wide-open salon, good storage, enclosed shower in head. Roomy flybridge has bench seating forward of helm. Additional features include mahogany interior cabinetry, wide side decks, molded bow pulpit, good-sized engineroom. No cockpit transom door or tackle centers. Crusader 270hp gas engines cruise at 16 knots (22-24 knots top); 210hp Cat diesels cruise efficiently at 16 knots.

Length	34'11"	Fuel	300 gals.
Beam	12'4"	Water	75 gals.
Draft	3'2"	Waste	35 gals.
Weight	18,000#	Hull Type	Modified-V
Clearance	10'8"	Deadrise Aft	15°

Prices Not Provided for Pre-1995 Models

Californian is no longer in business.

---

www.powerboatguide.com   231-360-0827

Californian 39 SL
1999–2003

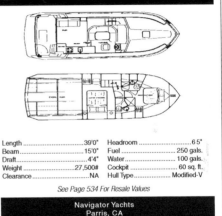

Sturdy west coast cruiser (built by Navigator Yachts) is notable for conservative styling, comfortable ride, affordable price. Innovative interior plan has dinette centered on pilothouse level, next to the helm. Bi-level galley extends into the pilothouse making it somewhat awkward to use. Both staterooms are fitted with double berths, both heads have enclosed showers. Lower helm visibility is excellent. Note flybridge dinghy stowage. Radar arch, transom door were standard. Volvo 318hp diesels cruise at 20 knots (23–24 knots wide open).

Length	39'0"	Headroom	6'5"
Beam	15'0"	Fuel	250 gals.
Draft	4'4"	Water	100 gals.
Weight	27,500#	Cockpit	60 sq. ft.
Clearance	NA	Hull Type	Modified-V

See Page 534 For Resale Values

Navigator Yachts
Parris, CA
www.navigatoryachts.com

---

www.powerboatguide.com   231-360-0827

Californian 44 Veneti
1988–89

Helmdeck/Interior Drawing

Full Interior Drawing

Rakish styling made this late 1980s express one of the more distinctive boats of her era. Unusual two-head interior resulted in compact salon dimensions. Features include big engineroom, wide side decks, radar arch, good cabin storage. Original hull was a wet ride until spray rails were added early in 1989. Slightly confusing dash layout. One of first American sportcruisers to employ integrated swim platform. Twin 375hp Cat diesels will cruise at 20–21 knots (about 24 knots top). Popular model for Californian.

Length w/Pulpit	47'10"	Clearance	10'0"
Hull Length	44'0"	Fuel	400 gals.
Beam	15'2"	Water	190 gals.
Draft	4'0"	Hull Type	Modified-V
Weight	30,000#	Deadrise Aft	15°

Prices Not Provided for Pre-1995 Models

Californian is no longer in business.

Cruisers & Sportboats

www.powerboatguide.com
231-360-0827

Cape Dory 28 Flybridge
1985–94

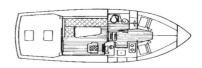

Salty Downeast cruiser with full keel is easily driven, inexpensive to operate, loaded with eye appeal. Space-efficient interior with classy teak-and-holly flooring, teak cabinets includes convertible salon dinette, standard lower helm. Tall flybridge provides great 360-degree visibility. Wide side decks allow secure bow access. Deep keel protects prop from grounding. Excellent engine access. Very popular model. Good fit and finish. Single Volvo 200hp diesel cruises economically at 14 knots (16–17 knots top).

Length	27'11"	Headroom	6'3"
Beam	9'11"	Fuel	120 gals.
Draft	2'9"	Water	71 gals.
Weight	9,500#	Waste	25 gals.
Clearance	11'2"	Hull Type	Semi-Disp.

Prices Not Provided for Pre-1995 Models

Cape Dory is no longer in business.

---

www.powerboatguide.com
231-360-0827

Cape Dory 33 Flybridge
1988–94

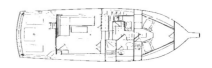

Downeast-style flybridge cruiser gets high marks for construction, thoughtful layout, planing-speed performance. Appealing galley-down teak interior with planked cabin sole features roomy salon with lower helm, large cabin windows, stall shower in head. Excellent natural lighting and ventilation. Wide side decks, lockable in-floor cockpit storage are a plus. Good visibility from both helms. Long keel protects running gear in event of grounding. Twin 200hp Volvo diesels cruise at 15 knots (18–20 knots top).

Length	32'10"	Fuel	260 gals.
Beam	12'2"	Water	90 gals.
Draft	2'11"	Waste	40 gals.
Weight	13,500#	Hull Type	Modified-V
Clearance	12'8"	Deadrise Aft	12°

Prices Not Provided for Pre-1995 Models

Cape Dory is no longer in business.

---

www.powerboatguide.com
231-360-0827

Carver 27/530 Montego
1986–93

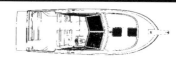

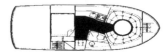

Maxi-volume cruiser packs impressive living space into modest 27-foot hull. Midcabin floorplan features unusual circular dinette/double berth forward in addition to compact galley, double-entry head compartment. Note stand-up dressing area in midcabin entryway. Swim platform was replaced in 1990 with more elaborate bolt-on unit. Unimpressive fit and finish; stiff ride in a chop. Cruise at 20 knots with 205hp sterndrive gas engines. Called Carver 27 Montego in 1986–90, 530 Montego in 1991–92, 300 Montego in 1993.

Length w/Platform	29'2"	Clearance	9'0"
Hull Length	27'3"	Fuel	120 gals.
Beam	10'0"	Water	41 gals.
Draft	2'10"	Hull Type	Modified-V
Weight	6,900#	Deadrise Aft	8°

Prices Not Provided for Pre-1995 Models

Carver Yachts
Pulaski, WI
www.carveryachts.com

Carver 27/630/300 Santego
1988–93

Good-selling family cruiser with full-beam interior (called 27 Santego in 1988–90; 630 Santego in 1991–92; 300 Santego in 1993) appealed to entry-level buyers on a budget. Spacious midcabin floorplan with V-berth, convertible dinette sleeps four adults, two kids. Hatch in cockpit sole provides good access to engines. Note foredeck sun lounge, built-in cockpit seating. Low-deadrise hull is a hard ride in a chop. Finish is less than impressive. Twin 205hp gas sterndrives cruise at 19–20 knots (around 30 knots top).

Length Overall	31'2"	Clearance	9'2"
Hull Length	27'3"	Fuel	100 gals.
Beam	10'0"	Water	41 gals.
Draft	2'8"	Hull Type	Modified-V
Weight	8,400#	Deadrise Aft	8°

Prices Not Provided for Pre-1995 Models

Carver Yachts
Pulaski, WI
www.carveryachts.com

Carver 28 Mariner/Voyager
1983–90

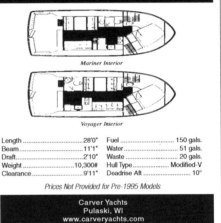

Mariner Interior

Voyager Interior

Popular 1980s flybridge sedan offered space, comfort at very competitive price. Mariner layout has galley and head forward; Voyager interior has galley and head aft with standard lower helm station. Both layouts have small private stateroom with hanging locker, vanity. Huge flybridge has seating for six with table that converts into full-width sun pad. Stiff ride when the seas pick up. Standard 220hp gas engines (with V-drives) cruise at 18 knots (26–27 knots wide open). One of just a few production 28-foot flybridge boats ever built.

Length	28'0"	Fuel	150 gals.
Beam	11'1"	Water	51 gals.
Draft	2'10"	Waste	20 gals.
Weight	10,300#	Hull Type	Modified-V
Clearance	9'11"	Deadrise Aft	10°

Prices Not Provided for Pre-1995 Models

Carver Yachts
Pulaski, WI
www.carveryachts.com

Carver 28 Riviera
1983–89

Durable family cruiser with unique aft-cabin layout makes good on promise of small-boat comfort, versatility. Open-air center cockpit with wraparound windshield, seating for six is the focal point of the boat. Forward cabin features convertible U-shaped dinette, enclosed head, compact galley. Small aft cabin with twin berths has four opening ports for ventilation. Note good engine access, wide side decks, standard bow pulpit. Low-deadrise hull is a stiff ride in a chop. Twin 220hp gas engines cruise at 18 knots (25–26 knots top).

Length	28'0"	Cockpit	NA
Beam	11'1"	Fuel	160 gals.
Draft	2'10"	Water	52 gals.
Weight	8,900#	Hull Type	Modified-V
Clearance	9'3"	Deadrise Aft	10°

Prices Not Provided for Pre-1995 Models

Carver Yachts
Pulaski, WI
www.carveryachts.com

Cruisers & Sportboats

Cruisers & Sportboats

231-360-0827

Carver 280 MidCabin Express
1988–98

25 Montego Interior, 1988–92

280 Interior, 1993–98

Lightweight express (called the Carver 25 Montego in 1988–91; 528 Montego in 1991–92) squeezed lots of living space into beamy, 28-foot hull. Original Montego interior was completely redesigned in 1993 when Carver reintroduced this model as 280 MidCabin Express. Where the original 25 Montego slept four, the 280 Mid-Cabin interior sleeps six. Notable features include double-wide helm seat, removable cockpit table, bow pulpit, swim platform. Cruise at 22 knots with standard 300hp gas sterndrive (30+ knots top).

Length	29'10"	Fuel	100 gals.
Beam	9'6"	Water	25 gals.
Draft	3'3"	Waste	18 gals.
Weight	5,900#	Hull Type	Modified-V
Clearance	NA	Deadrise Aft	19°

See Page 534 For Resale Values

Carver Yachts
Pulaski, WI
www.carveryachts.com

231-360-0827

Carver 280 Sedan
1991–98

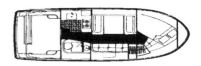

Compact coastal cruiser (called the Carver 26 Sedan in 1991–92) is among the smallest flybridge boats ever produced. Wide beam creates roomy interior with standing headroom. Cabin extends well forward on deck to maximize interior space. Layout includes convertible dinette aft, U-shaped galley, enclosed head. Lower helm was a popular option. Compact flybridge seats two guests aft of the helm. Modified-V hull isn't fond of a chop. Twin MerCruiser (or Volvo) V-6 sterndrives cruise at 18–20 knots (about 30 knots top).

Length w/Pulpit	29'11"	Fuel	112 gals.
Hull Length	27'9"	Water	45 gals.
Beam	9'6"	Waste	20 gals.
Draft	2'4"	Hull Type	Modified-V
Weight	9,778#	Deadrise Aft	15°

See Page 534 For Resale Values

Carver Yachts
Pulaski, WI
www.carveryachts.com

231-360-0827

Carver 28 Sedan; 300 Sedan
1991–93

Lower Helm Floorplan

No Lower Helm

Beamy small sedan (called the 28 Sedan in 1991–92; 300 Sedan in 1993) remains among the "biggest" 28-footers ever built. Offered with two floorplans, one with standard lower helm and small head, the other—less popular—with large forward head but no lower helm. Berths are provided for six in either layout, and a solid door (rather than a curtain) provides stateroom privacy. Flybridge is huge for a boat this size with seating that converts into a sun lounge. Very small cockpit. Crusader 260hp gas engines cruise at 18 knots (25–26 knots top).

Length Overall	32'4"	Clearance	9'1"
Length w/Platform	30'6"	Fuel	150 gals.
Beam	11'10"	Water	51 gals.
Draft	2'11"	Hull Type	Modified-V
Weight	12,500#	Deadrise Aft	16°

Prices Not Provided for Pre-1995 Models

Carver Yachts
Pulaski, WI
www.carveryachts.com

231-360-0827

Carver 29 Monterey
1985–86

Inexpensive cruiser from 1980s appealed to entry-level buyers with an eye for value. Inboard power is rare in a boat this size—most express boats feature sterndrive power. Full-beam interior with wraparound lounge seating, compact galley, convertible dinette sleeps four. Large cockpit is perfect for entertaining, big enough for fishing. Note walk-through windshield, reverse radar arch, bow pulpit. Roomy engine compartment is a plus. Cruise at 18 knots with twin 270hp gas engines (26–28 knots top).

Length w/Pulpit	32'9"	Clearance	10'8"
Hull Length	28'8"	Fuel	200 gals.
Beam	11'1"	Water	52 gals.
Draft	2'10"	Hull Type	Modified-V
Weight	10,000#	Deadrise Aft	10°

Prices Not Provided for Pre-1995 Models

Carver Yachts
Pulaski, WI
www.carveryachts.com

231-360-0827

Carver 30 Allegra
1989–90

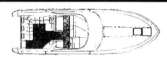

Value-priced sportcruiser designed for entry-level buyers lasted only two years in production. Highlights include color-coordinated hull graphics, reverse radar arch, bolt-on swim platform, large cockpit with seating for a small crowd. Roomy interior boasts bow stateroom with double berth and privacy door, fully equipped galley, enclosed head with sink and shower. Note transom door and foredeck sun lounge. Uneven fit and finish. Cruise at 20 knots (30 knots top) with twin 235hp gas sterndrives.

Length Overall	34'0"	Fuel	150 gals.
Hull Length	30'8"	Water	51 gals.
Beam	11'0"	Waste	37 gals.
Draft	3'1"	Hull Type	Modified-V
Weight	10,950#	Deadrise Aft	18°

Prices Not Provided for Pre-1995 Models

Carver Yachts
Pulaski, WI
www.carveryachts.com

231-360-0827

Carver 30/634/340 Santego
1988–94

Spacious party boat (called the Carver 30 Santego in 1988–90, 634 Santego in 1991–92, 340 Santego in 1993–94) has more interior volume than just about any other 30-footer on the market. Full-beam cabin is laid out on a single level with facing salon settees, complete galley. Large forward stateroom has angled double berth, bi-fold privacy doors. Flybridge was redesigned in 1991 with walk-through to foredeck. Note cheap-looking bolt-on swim platform. Available with V-drive inboards or sterndrive power.

Length	33'7"	Headroom	6'4"
Beam	11'0"	Fuel	150 gals.
Draft	3'1"	Water	48 gals.
Weight	11,150#	Hull Type	Deep-V
Clearance	14'10"	Deadrise Aft	19°

Prices Not Provided for Pre-1995 Models

Carver Yachts
Pulaski, WI
www.carveryachts.com

Cruisers & Sportboats

www.powerboatguide.com   231-360-0827

Carver 310 Mid-Cabin Express
1995–97

Standard Floorplan

Alternate Floorplan

Curvaceous 1990s express with large cockpit, roomy interior gives cruising families plenty of breathing space. Standard layout has spacious salon with L-shaped lounge aft that converts to double berth; alternate floorplan offered conventional midcabin berth at expense of smaller salon. Wraparound cockpit seating converts to sun lounge. Additional features include foredeck sun pad, walk-through windshield, bow pulpit, side exhausts, radar arch. Offered with inboard or sterndrive power.

Length	31'3"	Fuel	180 gals.
Beam	10'10"	Water	56 gals.
Draft	2'8"	Waste	28 gals.
Weight	11,400#	Hull Type	Modified-V
Clearance, Arch	10'11"	Deadrise Aft	12°

See Page 534 For Resale Values

Carver Yachts
Pulaski, WI
www.carveryachts.com

---

www.powerboatguide.com   231-360-0827

Carver 310 Santego
1994–98

Maxi-volume 1990s cruiser with amenities of small apartment had great appeal to entry-level boaters. Full-beam interior is arranged on a single level with double stateroom forward, compact galley, head with shower. U-shaped salon dinette converts to double berth; portside lounge converts to upper and lower bunk and includes privacy curtain. Center-console flybridge offers seating for five and full walkaround accessibility. Offered with inboard or sterndrive power. Note fuel increase in 1997 to 164 gallons.

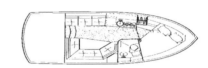

Length w/Pulpit	33 5"	Clearance	9'10"
Hull Length	31'3"	Fuel	130/164 gals.
Beam	11'0"	Water	66 gals.
Draft	2'9"	Waste	30 gals.
Weight	12,500#	Hull Type	Modified-V

See Page 534 For Resale Values

Carver Yachts
Pulaski, WI
www.carveryachts.com

---

www.powerboatguide.com   231-360-0827

Carver 32 Convertible
1984–93

Popular family convertible became one of Carver's best-selling boats in the 1980s. Innovative two-stateroom floorplan is made possible by locating engines under cockpit sole. Highlights include full-size galley refrigerator, standard lower helm, roomy cockpit with centerline transom door, stall shower in head. Cockpit is large enough for two anglers and their gear. Compact flybridge seats four. Bow pulpit and swim platform were standard. Cruise at 16 knots with Crusader 270hp V-drive gas inboards (mid 20s top).

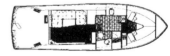

Length	32'0"	Fuel	220 gals.
Beam	11'7"	Water	84 gals.
Draft	2'10"	Waste	20 gals.
Weight	12,600#	Hull Type	Modified-V
Clearance	11'6"	Deadrise Aft	10°

Prices Not Provided for Pre-1995 Models

Carver Yachts
Pulaski, WI
www.carveryachts.com

Carver 32 Montego
1987–91

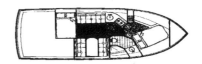

Affordable sportcruiser introduced in 1987 combined sporty styling with family friendly layout, affordable price. Full-beam interior sleeps six, boasts private forward stateroom, four-person convertible dinette, compact galley with under-counter refrigerator, double-entry head with stall shower. Roomy bi-level cockpit has generic L-shaped companion seat, numerous stowage compartments, walk-through transom. Twin 270hp V-drive gas engines will cruise at 18–20 knots (just under 30 knots top).

Length	32'3"	Fuel	192 gals.
Beam	12'4"	Water	92 gals.
Draft	2'9"	Waste	20 gals.
Weight	13,000#	Hull Type	Modified-V
Clearance	9'0"	Deadrise Aft	6°

Prices Not Provided for Pre-1995 Models

Carver Yachts
Pulaski, WI
www.carveryachts.com

Carver 320 Voyager
1994–99

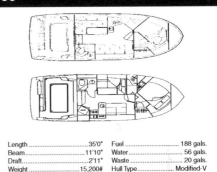

Sporty family sedan with oversized flybridge is stylish, versatile, fun to drive. Roomy interior—available with one or two staterooms—includes compact galley, head with sink and shower, private master stateroom. More cabin storage than most 32-footers. Lower helm was a popular option. Cockpit is large enough for light-tackle fishing. Note integral swim platform with fender stowage, hidden boarding ladder. Narrow side decks make bow access a bit tricky. Twin 265hp gas inboards cruise at 16 knots (27–28 knots top).

Length	35'0"	Fuel	188 gals.
Beam	11'10"	Water	56 gals.
Draft	2'11"	Waste	20 gals.
Weight	15,200#	Hull Type	Modified-V
Clearance	NA	Deadrise Aft	16°

See Page 534 For Resale Values

Carver Yachts
Pulaski, WI
www.carveryachts.com

Carver 32 Mariner; 330 Mariner
1985–96

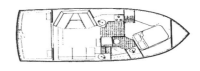

Roomy condo-boat from the late 1980s, early '90s scored with entry-level buyers for expansive accommodations, party-time bridge. Enormous full-beam, single-level interior boasts expansive salon with facing settees, full galley (with upright refrigerator), roomy head with stall shower. Unique salon ladder provides easy access to massive flybridge with walk-through gate to bow. Low-deadrise hull will knock your fillings out in choppy water. Cruise at 16 knots with 260hp gas inboards. Called Carver 330 Mariner in 1994–96.

Length w/Pulpit	35'5"	Clearance	10'10"
Hull Length	32'3"	Fuel	192 gals.
Beam	12'4"	Water	92 gals.
Draft	2'9"	Hull Type	Modified-V
Weight	12,000#	Deadrise Aft	6°

See Page 534 For Resale Values

Carver Yachts
Pulaski, WI
www.carveryachts.com

Cruisers & Sportboats

Carver 33 Mariner
1975–84

Portly 33-footer achieved popularity in late 1970s, early 1980s due to enormous interior, massive party-time bridge. Originally built with plywood superstructure (1975–76), later models are all fiberglass in construction. Single-level floorplan features facing salon settees, full galley, double-entry head with stall shower, private bow stateroom. Unique bulkhead ladder in salon offers easy bridge access. Inexpensive boat was poorly finished. Cruise at 16–18 knots (low 20s top) with 250hp gas inboards.

Length	32'6"	Fuel	145 gals.
Beam	12'0"	Water	75 gals.
Draft	2'6"	Cockpit	NA
Weight	11,620#	Hull Type	Modified-V
Clearance	NA	Deadrise Aft	NA

Prices Not Provided for Pre-1995 Models

Carver Yachts
Pulaski, WI
www.carveryachts.com

Carver 33/35/36 Super Sport
2005–08

Standard Interior

Mid-Cabin Interior

Stylish Carver cruiser (called the 33 SS in 2005–06; 35 SS in 2007; 36 SS in 2008) delivers features buyers demand in a midsize flybridge yacht. Highlights include spacious, full-beam salon, full galley with upright refrigerator, convertible dinette, private bow stateroom, head with separate stall shower. Lots of cabin storage. Wide side decks, molded bridge steps make getting around easy. Large engineroom is a plus. Midcabin layout became optional in 2007. Crusader 320hp gas engines cruise at 18 knots (26–28 knots top.)

Length	37'3"	Fuel	311 gals.
Beam	13'1"	Water	78 gals.
Draft	3'1"	Waste	37 gals.
Weight	21,753#	Hull Type	Modified-V
Clearance	14'8"	Deadrise Aft	11.5°

See Page 534 For Resale Values

Carver Yachts
Pulaski, WI
www.carveryachts.com

Carver 350 Mariner
1997–2003

Hugely popular sportcruiser combines enormous, full-beam interior with massive flybridge in what boating purists might describe as a styling train wreck. Spacious cabin floorplan boasts wide-open salon with facing settees, good-size galley, double-entry head with stall shower, private stateroom with offset double berth. Note handy bridge access ladder forward in salon. Party-time bridge seats eight. Foredeck bench seat converts into sun pad. Twin 320hp V-drive gas engines cruise at 14–15 knots (around 20 knots top).

Length	36'7"	Fuel	246 gals.
Beam	12'9"	Water	75 gals.
Draft	3'1"	Waste	20 gals.
Weight	18,800#	Headroom	6'3"
Clearance, Arch	14'2"	Hull Type	Modified-V

See Page 534 For Resale Values

Carver Yachts
Pulaski, WI
www.carveryachts.com

Cruisers & Sportboats

www.powerboatguide.com   231-360-0827

Carver 350 Voyager
1993—94

With Optional Lower Helm

Standard Floorplan

Versatile 1990s sedan is ideally suited for entry-level boaters with growing families. Super-spacious interior includes two double staterooms, head with separate stall shower, split-level salon/galley with booth dinette. Lower helm station was a popular option. Flybridge is one of the largest to be found on a 35-footer, but cockpit is very small. Note handy pass-through from galley to bridge. Bow pulpit, transom door and swim platform were standard. Standard 300hp gas engines cruise at 18—19 knots (about 28 knots top).

Length w/Pulpit	39'0"	Fuel	280 gals.
Hull Length	33'10"	Water	101 gals.
Beam	13'3"	Waste	35 gals.
Draft	2'7"	Hull Type	Modified-V
Weight	17,000#	Deadrise Aft	11°

Prices Not Provided for Pre-1995 Models

Carver Yachts
Pulaski, WI
www.carveryachts.com

---

www.powerboatguide.com   231-360-0827

Carver 36 Mariner
1984—88

Mega-volume cruiser with zero eye appeal offers big-boat accommodations in modest 36-foot hull. Enormous full-beam, single-level interior features facing salon settees, large galley with upright refrigerator, head with stall shower, private bow stateroom with double berth and sink. Massive bridge—accessed from cockpit or salon—seats a small crowd with huge sun lounge aft. Note wide side decks, foredeck sun pad, radar arch, cockpit transom door. Cruise at 16 knots with 350hp gas inboards (mid 20s top).

Length Overall	35'7"	Clearance	13'6"
Length WL	31'4"	Fuel	274 gals.
Beam	12'6"	Water	103 gals.
Draft	3'2"	Hull Type	Modified-V
Weight	19,500#	Deadrise Aft	8°

Prices Not Provided for Pre-1995 Models

Carver Yachts
Pulaski, WI
www.carveryachts.com

---

www.powerboatguide.com   231-360-0827

Carver 36 Mariner
2004—Current

Updated version of Carver's original 36 Mariner (1984—88) with spacious single-level interior is designed for entertaining on a grand scale. Full-beam salon features posh Ultraleather seating, large dinette, high-gloss cherry woodwork, full entertainment center, large galley area. Extra-large head contains separate stall shower. Party-time flybridge can accommodate a small crowd. Low-deadrise hull can be a stiff ride in a chop. Portly profile is hard on the eye. Cruise at 20 knots (28 top) with 375hp gas inboards.

Length	36'7"	Fuel	250 gals.
Beam	12'9"	Water	75 gals.
Draft	3'7"	Waste	31 gals.
Weight	19,500#	Hull Type	Modified-V
Clearance, Arch	14'2"	Deadrise Aft	4°

See Page 535 For Resale Values

Carver Yachts
Pulaski, WI
www.carveryachts.com

Cruisers & Sportboats

Carver 360 Sport Sedan
2003–06

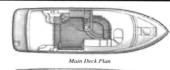

Main Deck Plan

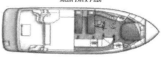

Lower Level Plan

Versatile, high-freeboard cruising yacht with condo-style accommodations is a true home away from home. Spacious two-stateroom interior includes raised dinette/lounge area forward of salon, expansive galley, large head compartment, glossy cherry trim. Tiered salon windows admit plenty of natural lighting. Hardwood floor in galley area is a nice touch. Note molded cockpit steps to bridge and side decks. Engineroom is a tight fit. Twin 320hp gas inboards cruise at 18 knots and top out in the low 20s.

Length	37'8"	Fuel	280 gals.
Beam	13'2"	Water	75 gals.
Draft	2'7"	Waste	25 gals.
Weight	24,746#	Hull Type	Modified-V
Clearance, Arch	14'6"	Deadrise Aft	14°

See Page 535 For Resale Values

Carver Yachts
Pulaski, WI
www.carveryachts.com

Carver 34/638/380 Santego
1989–2002

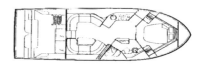

Strong buyer demand kept this maxi-volume sport-cruiser (called Carver 34 Santego in 1989–90; Carver 638 Santego in 1991–92) in production for well over a decade. Expansive full-beam salon with facing settees, large galley creates guest-friendly layout seldom encountered in a boat this size. Notable features include private bow stateroom, large head with stall shower, huge flybridge with foredeck access gate. Bolt-on swim platform looks cheap, but roomy cockpit is a plus. Twin 300hp V-drive gas inboards cruise at 18 knots.

Length w/Pulpit	41'8"	Fuel	216 gals.
Beam	13'2"	Water	90 gals.
Draft	3'4"	Waste	37 gals.
Weight	19,300#	Hull Type	Modified-V
Clearance	NA	Deadrise Aft	19°

See Page 535 For Resale Values

Carver Yachts
Pulaski, WI
www.carveryachts.com

Carver 38 Santego
1988–90

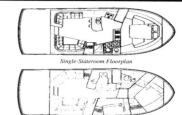

Single-Stateroom Floorplan

Optional 2-Stateroom Layout (1990 Only)

Versatile family cruiser from the late 1980s appealed to entry-level buyers with an eye for value. Full-beam interior provides far more entertaining space than most 38-footers. Highlights include large stateroom with privacy door, well-equipped galley, cavernous, full-beam salon with facing settees, built-in cockpit seating. Flybridge cutout reveals a set of molded steps leading to the foredeck. Bolt-on swim platform looks cheap. Twin 330hp gas inboards cruise at 14–15 knots (low 20s top).

Length w/Pulpit	37'6"	Fuel	265 gals.
Beam	14'0"	Water	92 gals.
Draft	3'5"	Waste	40 gals.
Weight	19,000#	Hull Type	Modified-V
Clearance	NA	Deadrise Aft	12°

Prices Not Provided for Pre-1995 Models

Carver Yachts
Pulaski, WI
www.carveryachts.com

Carver 38 Super Sport
2005–Current

Rakish sport sedan combines European styling with American-bred comfort, world-class eye appeal. Well-appointed interior with cherry trim features spacious, full-beam salon with raised dinette, expansive galley with hardwood floor, two double staterooms. Extended swim platform can carry a small dinghy. Optional sport package adds rod holders, livewell, in-deck fishboxes. Note sizeable cockpit, small foredeck, slender sidedecks. Low-deadrise hull isn't fond of a chop. MerCruiser 375hp gas engines cruise at 20 knots (28–29 knots top).

Length	39'11"	Fuel	334 gals.
Beam	13 5"	Water	86 gals.
Draft	2'4"	Waste	45 gals.
Weight	25,000#	Hull Type	Modified-V
Clearance	14'1"	Deadrise Aft	14°

See Page 535 For Resale Values

Carver Yachts
Pulaski, WI
www.carveryachts.com

Carver 410 Sport Sedan
2002–03

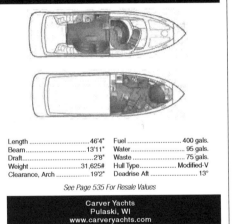

Maxi-volume sport sedan appealed to buyers seeking motoryacht-style comforts without breaking the bank. Wide-open salon is made possible by raising side decks to flybridge level. Guest quarters are positioned under dinette without sacrificing headroom or storage. Note split head/shower forward, Ultraleather seating, copious storage. Molded cockpit steps lead to bridge and portside side deck. Volvo 375hp gas engines cruise at 15 knots; 370hp Volvo diesels cruise at 18 knots (24–25 knots top). Only two years in production.

Length	46'4"	Fuel	400 gals.
Beam	13'11"	Water	95 gals.
Draft	2'8"	Waste	75 gals.
Weight	31,625#	Hull Type	Modified-V
Clearance, Arch	19'2"	Deadrise Aft	13°

See Page 535 For Resale Values

Carver Yachts
Pulaski, WI
www.carveryachts.com

Carver 42 Cockpit MY
1986–88

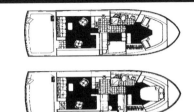

Sturdy flybridge sedan was largest boat in Carver's fleet when she was introduced in 1986. While a two-stateroom floorplan was available, most were sold with dinette interior with single stateroom. Lower helm was a popular option. Cockpit is big enough for fishing; flybridge has a raised command console with overhead electronics box built into radar arch. Standard 350hp gas engines cruise at a sluggish 13–14 knots (low 20s top); optional Cat 375hp diesels cruise at 20 knots (23–24 knots wide open).

Length	42'0"	Fuel	400 gals.
Beam	15'0"	Water	170 gals.
Draft	3'6"	Headroom	6 5"
Weight	23,150#	Hull Type	Modified-V
Clearance	16'6"	Deadrise Aft	12°

Prices Not Provided for Pre-1995 Models

Carver Yachts
Pulaski, WI
www.carveryachts.com

Cruisers & Sportboats

231-360-0827

Carver 42/43 Super Sport
2006–Current

Upper Level

Lower Level

Feature-rich sport sedan with expansive, full-beam interior couples big-boat luxury with traditional Carver quality, value. Combined salon/galley/dinette with cherry paneling offers spacious accommodations with room for nonstop entertaining. Both staterooms feature queen berths—unusual in a boat this size. Note washer/dryer beneath galley sole, low galley counters. Party-time bridge can seat a small crowd. Bridge overhang shades large cockpit. Optional Volvo 370hp diesels with IPS drives cruise at 24 knots (about 28 knots top).

Length	43'7"	Fuel	400 gals.
Beam	13'11"	Water	90 gals.
Draft	3'10"	Waste	50 gals.
Weight	33,650#	Hull Type	Modified-V
Clearance, Arch	19'7"	Deadrise Aft	NA

See Page 535 For Resale Values

Carver Yachts
Pulaski, WI
www.carveryachts.com

231-360-0827

Chaparral 26/27/270 Signature
1992–2000

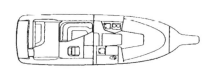

Good-running 1990s sportcruiser (called Signature 26 in 1992; Signature 27 in 1993–99; Signature 270 in 2000) delivered impressive mix of modern styling, roomy accommodations, excellent open-water performance. Highlights include well-appointed interior with sliding windows, woodgrain dash, flip-up helm seat, cockpit dinette with removable table, transom door, molded bow pulpit. Above-average fit and finish. Single 300hp 7.4L MerCruiser I/O will cruise in the mid 20s and reach a top speed of 34–35 knots.

Length w/Pulpit	28'5"	Fuel	105 Gals.
Beam	9'0"	Water	25 gals.
Draft, Drive Up	2'1"	Waste	25 gals.
Draft, Drive Down	2'9"	Hull Type	Modified-V
Weight	6,249#	Deadrise Aft	20°

See Page 536 For Resale Values

Chaparral Boats
Nashville, TN
www.chaparralboats.com

231-360-0827

Chaparral 270 Signature
2007–Current

Sporty 27-footer with traditional midcabin interior couples signature Chaparral quality with aggressive styling, first-rate amenities. Cockpit features include full-length rear sun pad, portside lounge seat, double helm seat with flip-up bolsters, wet bar with portable ice chest. Cabin accommodations are complete but—thanks to a slender beam—a bit claustrophobic. Note power engine compartment hatch, transom storage bin under sun pad. Single 320hp MerCruiser I/O tops out at close to 40 knots.

Length	28'11"	Fuel	87 gals.
Beam	8'6"	Water	29 gals.
Draft, Up	1'5"	Waste	28 gals.
Draft, Down	2'9"	Hull Type	Modified-V
Weight	7,450#	Deadrise Aft	18°

See Page 537 For Resale Values

Chaparral Boats
Nashville, TN
www.chaparralboats.com

Chaparral 275 SSi
2006–Current

Feature-packed sportster blurs the line between fast-action runabout, luxury-class day cruiser. Roomy cockpit with wraparound seating for six boasts portside refreshment center, convertible aft sun lounge/bench seat, double helm seat with individual flip-up bolsters. Nicely-finished cabin includes compact galley, enclosed head with sink. Sunpad lifts to expose big storage locker beneath. Note quality upholstery, power engine hatch. Tops out at 42–43 knots with single 280hp Volvo gas sterndrive engine.

Length	28'10"	Fuel	105 gals.
Beam	9'0"	Water	13.5 gals.
Draft, Up	1'10"	Waste	3.5 gals.
Draft, Down	3'0"	Hull Type	Deep-V
Weight	7,300#	Deadrise Aft	22°

See Page 537 For Resale Values

Chaparral Boats
Nashville, TN
www.chaparralboats.com

Chaparral 276 SSX
2006–Current

Spirited open-bow runabout combines rakish styling with deckboat utility, sportboat performance. Uncluttered cockpit with wraparound seating for six features portside refreshment center, convertible aft sun lounge/bench seat, lockable console head compartment with sink. Double helm seat with individual flip-up bolsters is a nice touch; sun pad lifts to expose big storage locker beneath. Note quality upholstery, power engine hatch. Tops out at 42–43 knots with single 280hp Volvo gas sterndrive engine.

Length	28'10"	Fuel	105 gals.
Beam	9'0"	Water	13.5 gals.
Draft, Up	1'10"	Waste	6.5 gals.
Draft, Down	3'0"	Hull Type	Deep-V
Weight	6,80000#	Deadrise Aft	22°

See Page 537 For Resale Values

Chaparral Boats
Nashville, TN
www.chaparralboats.com

Chaparral 278 XLC; Signature 27
1984–91

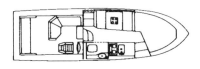

Slender 1980s express (called 278 XLC in 1984–88; Signature 27 in 1989–91) matched Chaparral claim of high-end quality, performance at a competitive price. Compact cabin provides berths for six with double berths fore and aft, convertible dinette, stand-up head with shower. Bi-level cockpit with bench seat opposite helm was updated in 1988 with L-shaped lounge seating. Hatch in cockpit sole provides easy engine access. Note narrow side decks, colorful hull graphics. Cruise at 22 knots with single 330hp MerCruiser I/O.

Length	26'6"	Fuel	140 gals.
Beam	8'2"	Water	22 gals.
Draft	2'8"	Headroom	6'2"
Weight	5,100#	Hull Type	Modified-V
Clearance	NA	Deadrise Aft	20°

Prices Not Provided for Pre-1995 Models

Chaparral Boats
Nashville, TN
www.chaparralboats.com

Cruisers & Sportboats

Cruisers & Sportboats

231-360-0827

Chaparral 270/280 Signature
2003–Current

Stylish family cruiser (called Signature 270 in 2003–05; 280 since 2006) offers proven mix of quality construction, practical accommodations. Well-appointed cabin features fixed dinette, full-size galley, premium hardware and fabrics. Guest-friendly cockpit includes wet bar, dual helm seat with flip-up cushions, removable table, portable ice chest. Walk-through windshield make bow access easy. Note transom storage locker, extended swim platform. Cruise at 26–28 knots with 225hp Volvo sterndrives (around 40 knots top).

Length w/Platform	29'3"	Fuel	100 gals.
Beam	9'6"	Water	29 gals.
Draft, Up	1 5"	Waste	28 gals.
Draft, Down	2'9"	Hull Type	Modified-V
Weight	9,100#	Deadrise Aft	20°

See Page 537 For Resale Values

Chaparral Boats
Nashville, TN
www.chaparralboats.com

231-360-0827

Chaparral 280 SSi
1999–2006

Broad-beamed bowrider earns high marks for first-rate construction, comfortable layout, good all-around performance. Highlights include wraparound cockpit seating, full-featured galley with refrigerator, enclosed head compartment with a sink and opening port. Note bi-fold wind doors, hinged in-floor ski storage, stylish dash layout. Excellent finish. Volvo 300hp sterndrive engines cruise at 30 knots and reach a top speed in excess of 50 knots.

Length w/Platform	29'6"	Fuel	143 gals.
Hull Length	27'6"	Water	30 gals.
Beam	9'3"	Waste	9.5 gals.
Draft	2'11"	Hull Type	Deep-V
Weight	6,800#	Deadrise Aft	22°

See Page 537 For Resale Values

Chaparral Boats
Nashville, TN
www.chaparralboats.com

231-360-0827

Chaparral 285 SSi
1999–2006

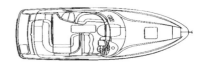

Full-size cuddy sportboat designed for big water delivers spirited performance, luxury-class amenities, strong owner satisfaction. Highlights include cockpit galley with sink, woodgrain dash, transom shower, walk-through transom, facing cockpit lounges, electric engine hatch, anchor locker. Well-appointed cabin offers convertible dinette, mini-galley, enclosed head. Deep-V hull handles the rough stuff with confidence. Volvo 300hp sterndrive engines cruise at 30 knots and reach a top speed in excess of 50 knots.

Length w/Platform	29'6"	Fuel	143 gals.
Hull Length	27'6"	Water	30 gals.
Beam	9'3"	Waste	9.5 gals.
Draft	2'11"	Hull Type	Deep-V
Weight	7,200#	Deadrise Aft	22°

See Page 537 For Resale Values

Chaparral Boats
Nashville, TN
www.chaparralboats.com

231-360-0827

Chaparral 28/29 Signature
1991–2000

Popular family cruiser (called Signature 28 in 1991–92; 29 Signature in 1993–2000) hit the sweet spot with savvy buyers focused on quality, durability. Carpeted cabin boasts wraparound sofa, full galley, convertible dinette, spacious aft cabin with privacy door. Superpractical cockpit design has settee/dinette opposite helm. Note narrow side decks, foldaway stern seat. Good engine access. Bow pulpit, radar arch, cockpit wet bar were standard. Twin 190hp MerCruiser I/Os cruise in the mid 20s (about 35 knots top).

Length w/Pulpit	31'11"	Weight	8,200#
Hull Length	29'3"	Fuel	121 gals.
Beam	9'9"	Water	30 gals.
Draft, Up	1'11"	Hull Type	Modified-V
Draft, Down	2'9"	Deadrise Aft	20°

See Page 537 For Resale Values

Chaparral Boats
Nashville, TN
www.chaparralboats.com

231-360-0827

Chaparral 280/290 Signature
2001–Current

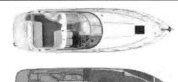

Popular sportcruiser (marketed as Signature 280 in 2001–03; Signature 290 since 2004) combines customary Chaparral quality with posh accommodations, impressive open-water performance. Highlights include well-appointed interior with cherry cabinets, well-planned cockpit with wraparound lounge seating, cockpit wet bar, extended swim platform. Note roomy engine compartment, walk-through windshield. Transom storage trunk can stow dive tank and fenders. Twin 270hp Volvo I/Os top out around 42–44 knots.

Length w/Platform	30'8"	Fuel	115 gals.
Beam	10'0"	Water	25 gals.
Draft, Up	2'1"	Waste	28 gals.
Draft, Down	2'9"	Hull Type	Modified-V
Weight	9,700#	Deadrise Aft	18°

See Page 537 For Resale Values

Chaparral Boats
Nashville, TN
www.chaparralboats.com

231-360-0827

Chaparral 300 Signature
1998–2003

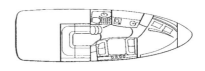

Smooth-running express with graceful styling matched Chaparral promise of leading-edge design, upscale accommodations. Open-plan interior with teak trim boasts full-size galley with generous storage, roomy midcabin with U-shaped settee, Corian counters. Cockpit seats six with double-wide helm seat, companion lounge, U-shaped settee aft. Note foldaway stern seat, walk-through windshield. Gas-assist hatch provides easy access to engine compartment. Volvo 250hp sterndrives cruise in the mid-to-high 20s (around 40 knots top).

Length w/Platform	31'3"	Clearance, Arch	11'0"
Beam	10'3"	Fuel	153 gals.
Draft, Up	2'1"	Water	30 gals.
Draft, Down	2'9"	Hull Type	Modified-V
Weight	9,800#	Deadrise Aft	20°

See Page 537 For Resale Values

Chaparral Boats
Nashville, TN
www.chaparralboats.com

Cruisers & Sportboats

Section III: Cruisers & Sportboats

Cruisers & Sportboats *(sidebar)*

Chaparral 30/31 Signature
1990–97

Full-bodied sportcruiser (called 30 Signature in 1990–92; 31 Signature in 1993–97)) set high standards for expressboat design, comfort. Well-finished midcabin interior sleeps six, includes roomy aft cabin, wraparound salon sofa/dinette. Curtains separate fore and aft double berths from main cabin. Galley is on the small side with modest storage and counter space. Single-level cockpit features lounge seating forward, foldaway bench seating aft. Helm console updated in 1993. Cruise at 18 knots (30+ knots top) with 230hp sterndrive power.

Length w/Pulpit	33'2"	Weight	9,750#
Hull Length	30'6"	Fuel	150 gals.
Beam	10'9"	Water	40 gals.
Draft, Up	1'11"	Hull Type	Modified-V
Draft, Down	2'9"	Deadrise Aft	17°

See Page 537 For Resale Values

Chaparral Boats
Nashville, TN
www.chaparralboats.com

Chaparral 310 Signature
2004–09

Luxurious family cruiser introduced in 2004 took Chaparral reputation for quality, owner satisfaction to the next level. Posh interior with high-gloss cherry cabinets, hardwood flooring, designer furnishings sleeps six. Cockpit highlights include sun lounge opposite helm, mini-galley with sink, well-designed helm, U-shaped aft seating. Electric hatch offers good access to engine compartment. Note walk-through windshield, transom storage locker. Cruise at 25–26 knots (high 30s top) with twin 270hp Volvo gas sterndrives.

Length w/Platform	33'4"	Fuel	147 gals.
Beam	10'7"	Water	29 gals.
Draft, Up	2'1"	waste	28 gals.
Draft, Down	2'9"	Hull Type	Modified-V
Weight	11,375#	Deadrise Aft	17°

See Page 537 For Resale Values

Chaparral Boats
Nashville, TN
www.chaparralboats.com

Chaparral 330 Signature
2003–Current

Polished big-water cruiser with innovative interior, thoughtful cockpit design offers something different in modern express-boat design. Unique cabin layout with circular seating forward, dual dinettes, private aft cabin is versatile, comfortable, luxurious. Partial standing headroom in midcabin entryway is a plus. Centerline transom door provides easy access to integral swim platform. Note twin transom storage lockers, walk-through windshield. Excellent finish. Twin 300hp sterndrives deliver top speed in the range of 40 knots.

Length w/Platform	35'0"	Fuel	170 gals.
Beam	11'3"	Water	45 gals.
Draft, Up	2'1"	Waste	28 gals.
Draft, Down	3'2"	Hull Type	Modified-V
Weight	13,400#	Deadrise Aft	19°

See Page 537 For Resale Values

Chaparral Boats
Nashville, TN
www.chaparralboats.com

231-360-0827

Chaparral 350 Signature
2001–Current

Quality construction, luxurious accommodations, solid performance make this midsize express a tough act to follow. Highlights include spacious cabin with cherry cabinetry and large aft cabin, ergonomic helm layout with tiered gauges, cockpit galley, transom storage trunk, generous fuel capacity. Pocket door offers privacy for forward stateroom. Electric hatch provides easy access to engines. Exceptionally well-finished boat isn't inexpensive. Twin 315hp Volvo sterndrives cruise in the low 20s (35+ knots wide open).

Length w/Platform	37'0"	Fuel	240 gals.
Beam	11'10"	Water	40 gals.
Draft, Up	2'1"	Waste	28 gals.
Draft, Down	2'9"	Hull Type	Modified-V
Weight	15,000#	Deadrise Aft	18°

See Page 537 For Resale Values

Chaparral Boats
Nashville, TN
www.chaparralboats.com

231-360-0827

Chris Craft 258/268/27 Concept
1992–96

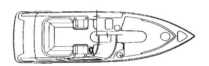

Roomy 1990s sportboat (called 258 Concept in 1992; 268 Concept in 1993–94; 27 Concept in 1995-96) offered sporty profile, good performance at very attractive price. Roomy interior with full galley, enclosed head sleeps two. Unique slide-away ladder provides unique access to walk-through windshield. Note fuel increase in 1995. Overwide permit required for trailering. Disappointing fit and finish reflects her low price. Cruise at 25 mph with single 310hp Volvo engine and reach a top speed in the high 30s.

Length	27'0"	Fuel	80/97 gals.
Beam	9'0"	Water	20 gals.
Draft	3'0"	Waste	20 gals.
Weight	5,000#	Hull Type	Deep-V
Clearance	NA	Deadrise Aft	20°

See Page 537 For Resale Values

Chris Craft
Sarasota, FL
www.chriscraft.com

231-360-0827

Chris Craft 272/282/30 Crowne
1991–97

Economy-class express (called 272 Crowne in 1991–92; 282 Crowne in 1993–94; 30 Crowne in 1995–97) targets entry-level buyers with an eye for value. Generic midcabin interior with full galley, enclosed head with shower, sleeps four. Aft stateroom privacy door is a nice touch. Roomy cockpit features companion lounge, double-wide helm seat, foldaway rear bench, sink with stowage under. Note walk-through windshield, bow pulpit, radar arch. Twin 190hp sterndrives top out in the 30- to 35-knot range.

Length w/Pulpit	31'6"	Weight	8,400#
Hull Length	29 5"	Fuel	100 gals.
Beam	10'0"	Water	25 gals.
Draft, Up	1'10"	Hull Type	Modified-V
Draft, Down	3'2"	Deadrise Aft	16°

See Page 537 For Resale Values

Chris Craft
Sarasota, FL
www.chriscraft.com

Cruisers & Sportboats

Chris Craft 28 Corsair
2003–Current

Classic Chris Craft runabout combines retro styling with quality construction, top-shelf materials. Highlights include ultra-plush cockpit seating, old-world dash layout, custom windshield, flawless gelcoat. Curved foredeck conceals useful cuddy cabin with V-berth, portable head. Electric hatch provides easy access to engine compartment. Meticulous fit and finish. Volvo 280hp sterndrives cruise in the mid 20s; optional 240hp Yanmar diesels cruise at a fast 35 knots. Premium price gives new meaning to "sticker shock."

Length	28'0"	Clearance		5 5"
Beam	10'0"	Fuel		150 gals.
Draft, Up	1'11"	Water		35 gals.
Draft, Down	3'6"	Hull Type		Deep-V
Weight	7,500#	Deadrise Aft		20°

See Page 537 For Resale Values

Chris Craft
Sarasota, FL
www.chriscraft.com

Chris Craft 28 Launch
2003–Current

Retro-style bowrider with wide 10-foot beam delivers compelling mix of quality, elegance seldom seen in a production boat. Highlights include ultra-plush cockpit seating, old-world dash layout, custom windshield, flawless gelcoat. Electric hatch provides easy access to engine compartment. Cockpit cooler, transom shower, flip-up bucket seats are standard. Roomy head compartment; large fuel capacity. Premium price may induce a heart attack. Single 385hp gas MerCruiser tops out at 40 knots; twin 300hp Mercs reach 45+ knots.

Length	28'0"	Clearance		5 5"
Beam	10'0"	Fuel		150 gals.
Draft, Up	1'11"	Water		35 gals.
Draft, Down	3'6"	Hull Type		Deep-V
Weight	7,500#	Deadrise Aft		20°

See Page 537 For Resale Values

Chris Craft
Sarasota, FL
www.chriscraft.com

Chris Craft 280/284 Amerosport
1987–90

Gaudy express cruiser with overdone graphics, cheap bolt-on swim platform is a good example of why Chris Craft lost serious market share in the late 1980s, early 1990s. Tall freeboard conceals roomy midcabin interior with stand-up head compartment, full galley, convertible dinette. Topside features include double-wide helm seat, stern cockpit seats, bow pulpit, good engine access. Note high bow rail, so-so fit and finish. Twin Volvo 271hp Duoprop sterndrives cruise at 25–26 knots and deliver a top speed of over 35 knots.

Length w/Pulpit	31'3"	Clearance		9'0"
Hull Length	27'9"	Fuel		150 gals.
Beam	10'2"	Water		25 gals.
Draft	2'9"	Hull Type		Deep-V
Weight	8,214#	Deadrise Aft		NA

Prices Not Provided for Pre-1995 Models

Chris Craft
Sarasota, FL
www.chriscraft.com

Chris Craft 280/281 Catalina
1977–86

Classic Chris Craft express achieved great popularity throughout the 1980s for practical cabin and cockpit design, rugged construction. Surprisingly open interior with convertible dinette, convertible settee sleeps six. Simple, uncluttered cockpit has plenty of room for anglers. Additional features include wide side decks, wraparound cabin windows, cockpit railings, good engine access. Single 230hp gas inboard will cruise at 15–16 knots; twin gas engines cruise at 20 knots. (Note that 280 model has single engine, 281 has twins.)

Length	28'11"	Fuel, Single	100 gals.
Beam	10'9"	Fuel, Twin	125 gals.
Draft	2'5"	Water	25 gals.
Weight	7,000#	Hull Type	Modified-V
Clearance	8'6"	Deadrise Aft	15°

Prices Not Provided for Pre-1995 Models

Chris Craft
Sarasota, FL
www.chriscraft.com

Chris Craft 292 Sunbridge
1986–89

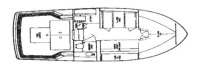

Sporty family sedan paired solid construction with common-sense layout, modest price. Wide-open interior with wraparound cabin windows, convertible settee sleeps four adults, two kids. Roomy, uncluttered cockpit is well suited for fishing, swimming, lounging. Twin cockpit hatches provide good access to the engines. Additional features include wide side decks, bridge seating for five, bow pulpit, swim platform. So-so fit and finish. Twin 220hp gas inboards cruise at 18 knots and top out in the high 20s.

Length	28'11"	Fuel	125 gals.
Beam	10'9"	Water	25 gals.
Draft	2'3"	Cockpit	NA
Weight	7,800#	Hull Type	Modified-V
Clearance	9'4"	Deadrise Aft	NA

Prices Not Provided for Pre-1995 Models

Chris Craft
Sarasota, FL
www.chriscraft.com

Chris Craft 300/308 Express Cruiser
1999–2003

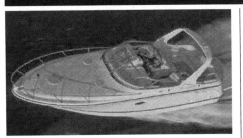

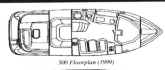

300 Floorplan (1999)

308 Layout (2000–03)

Generic family cruiser with smooth-running deep-V hull delivers mediocre blend of styling, comfort, performance. Original interior of the 300 Express—a poorly designed layout with refrigerator under forward berth—was updated in 2000 (eliminating side decks in favor of larger cabin dimensions) when she was reintroduced as the Chris 308 Express. Standard features included radar arch, doublewide helm seat, cockpit wet bar. Note walk-through windshield in 308 model. Twin 250hp sterndrive engines cruise at 25 knots (high 30s top).

Length	32'10"	Fuel	150 gals.
Beam	10'6"	Water	41 gals.
Draft	2'6"	Waste	35 gals.
Weight	10,000#	Hull Type	Deep-V
Clearance	7'3"	Deadrise Aft	21°

See Page 537 For Resale Values

See Page 537 For Resale Values

Chris Craft
Sarasota, FL
www.chriscraft.com

Cruisers & Sportboats

231-360-0827

Chris Craft 320 Amerosport Sedan
1987–90

Plain-Jane sdean offered comfortable accommodations, good turn of speed at a low price. Midcabin floorplan is arranged with second stateroom under elevated dinette. Wide beam, wraparound cabin windows create spacious, wide-open interior. Original teak interior joinery was updated in 1990 to light oak. Cockpit includes bench seating at the transom; flybridge is arranged with helm forward, guest seating aft. Bolt-on swim platform looks cheap. Twin 270hp gas inboards cruise at 18 knots (25–26 knots wide open).

Length	31'11"	Fuel	200 gals.
Beam	11'11"	Water	50 gals.
Draft	2'8"	Waste	18 gals.
Weight	12,000#	Hull Type	Modified-V
Clearance	10'9"	Deadrise Aft	NA

Prices Not Provided for Pre-1995 Models

Chris Craft
Sarasota, FL
www.chriscraft.com

231-360-0827

Chris Craft 320/322 Amerosport Express
1987–90

Poorly styled express introduced in 1987 reflected the problems Chris Craft was having in this era. Wide 11'11" beam permits large interior with convertible dinette, full galley, stand-up head with sink, shower. Single-level cockpit features double-wide helm and companion seats, bench seating aft. Radar arch, cockpit lighting, bow pulpit were standard. Note disappointing fit and finish. Twin 270hp inboard gas engines cruise at 18 knots (high 20s top); optional 350hp engines cruise at 22 knots (33–34 knots wide open).

Length w/Pulpit	34'7"	Fuel	200 gals.
Hull Length	31'11"	Water	50 gals.
Beam	11'11"	Waste	30 gals.
Draft	2'7"	Hull Type	Deep-V
Weight	12,000#	Deadrise Aft	NA

Prices Not Provided for Pre-1995 Models

Chris Craft
Sarasota, FL
www.chriscraft.com

231-360-0827

Chris Craft 320/328 Express Cruiser
1997–2003

Good-selling express with contemporary midcabin interior appealed to entry-level buyers on a budget. Expansive layout is typical of most modern cruisers with double berths fore and aft, small galley, head with shower. Large cockpit includes wraparound lounge seating, triple helm seat, transom door. Note power engineroom hatch, unusual centerline helm position. Trim tabs, transom shower, sport arch, cockpit lights were standard. Twin Volvo 280hp sterndrives cruise at 30 knots (40+ knots wide open).

Length	32'0"	Fuel	210 gals.
Beam	11'10"	Water	41 gals.
Draft	3'2"	Waste	35 gals.
Weight	12,000#	Hull Type	Deep-V
Clearance	9'7"	Deadrise Aft	21°

See Page 537 For Resale Values

Chris Craft
Sarasota, FL
www.chriscraft.com

Chris Craft 33 Corsair
2006–Current

Head-turning speedster blends classic sportboat lines, express-cruiser amenities. Roomy cockpit features double-wide helm/companion seats with flip-up bolsters, U-shaped lounge seating, hot/cold shower. Stowaway top storage is a nice touch. Note classic retro-style helm. Upscale cabin with generous galley, aft berth, cherry cabinetry, sleeps two adults, two kids. Near-flawless gelcoat, trademark Chris Craft tumblehome. Twin 320hp MerCruiser I/Os max out at close to 40 knots. Expensive.

Length	34'11"	Fuel	207 gals.
Beam	12'3"	Water	37 gals.
Draft	3'0"	Waste	20 gals.
Weight	13,200#	Hull Type	Deep-V
Clearance	NA	Deadrise Aft	20°

See Page 537 For Resale Values

Chris Craft
Sarasota, FL
www.chriscraft.com

Chris Craft 332 Express
1981–86

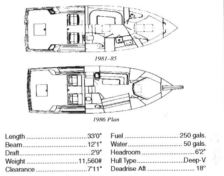

1981–85

1986 Plan

Popular inboard express from 1980s combined comfortable accommodations with expansive, wide-open cockpit. Generous 12'1" beam permits spacious interior—updated in 1986—with convertible dinette, full-size galley, double berth forward. Single-level cockpit is suitable for fishing. Note wide side decks, windshield vents, good engine access. Bolt-on swim platform became standard in 1986. Deep-V hull can handle a pretty good chop. Twin 350hp gas inboards will cruise at 20 knots (close to 30 knots top).

Length	33'0"	Fuel	250 gals.
Beam	12'1"	Water	50 gals.
Draft	2'9"	Headroom	6'2"
Weight	11,560#	Hull Type	Deep-V
Clearance	7'11"	Deadrise Aft	18°

Prices Not Provided for Pre-1995 Models

Chris Craft
Sarasota, FL
www.chriscraft.com

Chris Craft 333 Sedan
1981–87

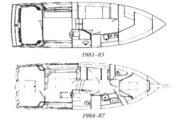

1981–83

1984–87

Good-selling 1980s sedan offered buyers impressive blend of family-friendly accommodations, good open-water performance. Roomy interior with wraparound windows (slightly updated in 1984) features private bow stateroom, convertible dinette, compact salon with lower helm. Cockpit is too small for any serious fishing pursuits. New flybridge design in 1986 located helm aft with bench seating forward of console. Standard 350hp gas engines cruise at 20 knots and deliver a top speed of close to 30 knots.

Length	33'0"	Fuel	250 gals.
Beam	12'1"	Water	50 gals.
Draft	2'9"	Headroom	6'4"
Weight, Gas	13,000#	Hull Type	Deep-V
Weight, Diesel	14,940#	Deadrise Aft	18°

Prices Not Provided for Pre-1995 Models

Chris Craft
Sarasota, FL
www.chriscraft.com

Cruisers & Sportboats

Cruisers & Sportboats

231-360-0827

Chris Craft 336 Mid-Cabin Express
1983—87

Sporty 1980s express offered contemporary styling, dependable inboard power at an affordable price. Conventional midcabin interior came with full galley, convertible dinette, private bow stateroom. Roomy cockpit can accommodate several guests. Additional features include wide side decks, bow pulpit, large head with sink and shower. Deep-V hull provides good offshore performance. Twin 340hp gas engines cruise at 20 knots and reach a top speed of 28 knots. Note that she was called the 336 Amerosport in 1987.

Length	33'0"	Cockpit	NA
Beam	12'1"	Fuel	250 gals.
Draft	2'9"	Water	50 gals.
Weight	12,360#	Hull Type	Deep-V
Clearance	7'11"	Deadrise Aft	18°

Prices Not Provided for Pre-1995 Models

Chris Craft
Sarasota, FL
www.chriscraft.com

231-360-0827

Chris Craft 33/34 Crowne
1993—97

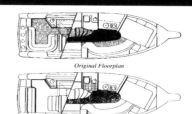

Original Floorplan

Updated Layout

Popular 1990s express—available with sterndrive or inboard power—made good on promise of affordability, performance. Extended settee dominates main cabin; both sleeping areas have privacy curtains. Cockpit redesign in 1996 replaced U-shaped aft lounge with bench seat. Standard features included wet bar, radar arch, transom door, power engine hatch. Twin 235hp I/Os cruise in the low 20s; twin 300hp V-drive inboards cruise at 25 knots. (Note that 33 Crowne has sterndrive power, 34 Crowne is inboard-powered.)

Length w/Pulpit	34'10"	Weight	10,000#
Hull Length	32'8"	Fuel	180 gals.
Beam	11'0"	Water	35 gals.
Draft, 34	2'11"	Hull Type	Deep-V
Draft, 33	3'2"	Deadrise Aft	18°

See Page 537 For Resale Values

Chris Craft
Sarasota, FL
www.chriscraft.com

231-360-0827

Chris Craft 36 Roamer
2003—05

Deck Plan

Interior Plan

Distinctive styling, posh amenities, top-quality construction personify this retro express yacht. Elegant interior is a blend of cherry cabinetry, Ultraleather upholstery, maple flooring. Head includes a separate shower stall; galley with hidden appliances occupies entire port side of salon. Innovative cockpit has unique centerline helm, L-shaped lounge aft, teak cockpit sole. Aft cockpit rises electrically for engine access. Note mahogany deck accents. Yanmar 370hp diesels cruise in the mid 20s (about 30 knots top). Expensive.

Length	36'3"	Fuel	286 gals.
Beam	12'6"	Water	54 gals.
Draft	3'1"	Waste	30 gals.
Weight	17,220#	Hull Type	Modified-V
Clearance	12'10"	Deadrise Aft	17°

See Page 537 For Resale Values

Chris Craft
Sarasota, FL
www.chriscraft.com

Chris Craft 370 Amerosport; 360 Express
1988–92

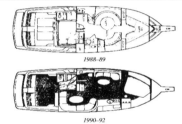

1988–89

1990–92

Widebody express cruiser (called 370 Amerosport in 1988–89) embodied bold 1980s styling with spacious floorplan, wide-open cockpit. Two floorplans were used in this boat—the first lasted just a year before being replaced in 1989 by a new layout where the midcabin lounge extends right into the salon. Bi-level cockpit with transom door, double-wide helm seat, wet bar seats six in comfort. Radar arch, bow pulpit were standard. Note cheap materials, poor finish. Twin 300hp gas inboards cruise at 18 knots with a top speed of 25+ knots.

Length	38'7"	Fuel	300 gals.
Beam	13'0"	Water	50 gals.
Draft	3'0"	Cockpit	NA
Weight	15,000#	Hull Type	Deep-V
Clearance	NA	Deadrise Aft	18°

Prices Not Provided for Pre-1995 Models

Chris Craft
Sarasota, FL
www.chriscraft.com

Chris Craft 380 Continental
1993–97

Poor-selling Chris Craft express took 1990s styling, design to unacceptable lengths. Unorthodox floorplan boasts roomy bow stateroom, circular dinette, double-entry head, full galley with generous storage. Circular cockpit is arranged with facing settees aft, centerline helm, centerline transom door. Note walk-through windshield, sunken bow area. Wraparound swim platform has storage lockers, hot/cold shower. A heavy boat, standard 330hp V-drive gas inboards cruise at 15 knots and reach a top speed in the mid 20s.

Length Overall	39'7"	Fuel	300 gals.
Hull Length	35'5"	Water	77 gals.
Beam	12'6"	Waste	20 gals.
Draft	3'1"	Hull Type	Modified-V
Weight	15,000#	Deadrise Aft	15°

See Page 537 For Resale Values

Chris Craft
Sarasota, FL
www.chriscraft.com

Chris Craft 40 Roamer
2003–08

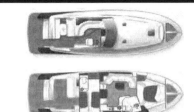

High-end express (called 43 Roamer in 2003-04) delivers unabashed blast of gorgeous styling, luxury amenities, top-tier quality. Upscale interior with wraparound dinette, full-size galley boasts two private staterooms, two heads. Salon is very roomy. Topside highlights include posh cockpit seating, wide side decks, extended swim platform, foredeck seating. Engineroom is a tight fit. Seriously expensive. Cruise at 25 knots with Volvo 480hp diesels (mid 30s top). Volvo IPS gas or diesel engines (with joystick control) available since 2006.

Length	43'6"	Water	95 gals.
Beam	14'0"	Waste	35 gals.
Draft	3'2"	Headroom	6'4"
Weight	25,200#	Hull Type	Deep-V
Fuel	400 gals.	Deadrise Aft	20°

See Page 537 For Resale Values

Chris Craft
Sarasota, FL
www.chriscraft.com

Cruisers & Sportboats

www.powerboatguide.com 231-360-0827

Chris Craft 412 Amerosport Express
1987–90

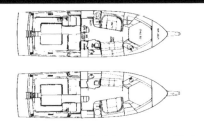

Sporty 1990s express made the cut with Chris Craft buyers looking for eye-catching styling, family-friendly accommodations. Cheap decor, so-so finish compared poorly with other boats of her era. Privacy curtains separate fore, aft sleeping areas from salon; large head stands in contrast to compact galley. Roomy cockpit with wraparound lounge seating, double-wide helm seat can entertain a small crowd. Standard 350hp gas engines cruise at 17–18 knots and top out in the high 20s. Called the Chris Craft 400 Express in 1990.

Length	38'9"	Fuel	380 gals.
Beam	14'0"	Water	100 gals.
Draft	3'2"	Cockpit	80 sq. ft.
Weight	15,000#	Hull Type	Modified-V
Clearance	9'5"	Deadrise Aft	NA

Prices Not Provided for Pre-1995 Models

Chris Craft
Sarasota, FL
www.chriscraft.com

---

www.powerboatguide.com 231-360-0827

Chris Craft 421 Continental
1993–94

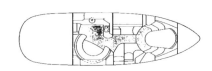

Short-lived cruiser with unorthodox (some might say ridiculous) styling was—surprise!—a serious sales disappointment. Two-stateroom floorplan is arranged on single level with excellent headroom. Lots of overhead lighting compensates for absence of cabin windows. Oversize galley consumes cabin space better used for seating. Circular cockpit is small for a 41-footer; engine compartment (beneath cockpit sole) is a tight fit. Standard V-drive gas inboards cruise at 14-15 knots; optional 320hp Volvo diesels cruise at 20 knots.

Length	43'3"	Fuel	350 gals.
Beam	13'6"	Water	108 gals.
Draft	3'2"	Headroom	6'4"
Weight	18,700#	Hull Type	Modified-V
Clearance	13'11"	Deadrise Aft	17°

Prices Not Provided for Pre-1995 Models

Chris Craft
Sarasota, FL
www.chriscraft.com

---

www.powerboatguide.com 231-360-0827

Crownline 268 CR
1998–2000

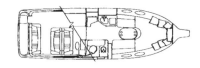

Hefty late-1990s cruiser offered sportboat comfort, performance at a reasonable price. Midcabin interior includes dinette/V-berth forward, compact galley with dorm-size refrigerator, enclosed head with shower, four opening ports. Walk-thru windshield with molded steps provides easy bow access. Note flip-up helm seat, tilt steering, windshield vents. Good engine access is a plus; swim ladder recesses neatly under small hatch. Single 5.7-liter MerCruiser gas I/O tops out at 30–32 knots; optional 7.4-liter Merc reaches 35–36 knots top.

Length	26'8"	Clearance	6'11"
Beam	8'6"	Fuel	80 gals.
Draft, Up	2'0"	Water	20 gals.
Draft, Down	3'0"	Waste	17 gals.
Weight	7,100#	Hull Type	Deep-V

See Page 538 For Resale Values

Crownline Boats
West Frankfort, IL
www.crownline.com

www.powerboatguide.com   231-360-0827

Crownline 270 Bowrider
2004–Current

Full-size bowrider with extended swim platform is big enough, tough enough for offshore use. Deep cockpit has wraparound rear seat with removable center section for access to swim platform. Twin flip-up bucket seats are forward; enclosed head compartment (with sink, exhaust fan, opening port) is built into passenger-side console. Helm boasts large storage compartment, quality Faria instruments. Note transom storage boxes, modest fuel capacity. Single 320hp MerCruiser I/O tops out at close to 40 knots.

Length w/Platform	28'3"	Clearance	5'8"
Beam	8'6"	Fuel	88 gals.
Draft, Up	1'7"	Water	12 gals.
Draft, Down	3'2"	Hull Type	Deep-V
Weight	5,500#	Deadrise Aft	23°

See Page 538 For Resale Values

Crownline Boats
West Frankfort, IL
www.crownline.com

---

www.powerboatguide.com   231-360-0827

Crownline 270 CR
2004–Current

Bold trailerable cruiser with sleek styling, leading-edge amenities offers big-boat comfort, performance at a reasonable price. Traditional midcabin interior with cherry cabinets includes convertible dinette forward, galley with ceramic cooktop, stand-up head with shower. Flip-up double pilot's seat provides good visibility for docking or close maneuvering. Stern lounge seat—which lifts electrically for engine access—converts to large sun pad. Single 300hp Volvo sterndrive tops out around 35 knots.

Length w/Platform	28'8"	Fuel	75 gals.
Beam	8'6"	Water	25 gals.
Draft, Up	1'9"	Waste	25 gals.
Draft, Down	34"	Hull Type	Modified-V
Weight	7,400#	Deadrise Aft	18°

See Page 538 For Resale Values

Crownline Boats
West Frankfort, IL
www.crownline.com

---

www.powerboatguide.com   231-360-0827

Crownline 275 CCR
2005–09

Feature-rich sportcruiser with trailerable 8'6" beam is fun to drive, easy on the wallet. Notched-bottom hull with keel pad delivers quick acceleration, agile open-water performance. Cabin accommodations seem big for a trailerable boat—complete galley, convertible dinette are standard; enclosed head comes with sink and shower. Flip-up helm seats, anchor pulpit, woodgrain dash, electric toilet are standard. Good finish for inexpensive boat. Single MerCruiser I/Os will cruise at 30 knots (40+ top).

Length w/Platform	28'8"	Headroom	5'6"
Beam	8'6"	Fuel	75 gals.
Draft, Up	24"	Water	15 gals.
Draft, Down	39"	Hull Type	Modified-V
Weight	6,500#	Deadrise Aft	20°

See Page 538 For Resale Values

Crownline Boats
West Frankfort, IL
www.crownline.com

Cruisers & Sportboats

www.powerboatguide.com   231-360-0827

Crownline 288 Bowrider
2001–04

Full-size bowrider combines modern sportboat styling with luxury-class amenities, versatile layout. Wide 9'8" beam provides plenty of deck space with built-in galley unit, generous dry storage, seating for eight. Mini-cabin concealed within driver-side console (accessed from bow seating area) houses cushioned berth. Flip-up helm seats swivel to face guests. Walk-through transom reduces sun pad length. Note extended swim platform, woodgrain dash, windshield vents, tilt wheel. Twin 280hp Volvo gas I/Os reach 40+ knots top.

Length	28'8"	Clearance	6'2"
Beam	9'8"	Fuel	129 gals.
Draft, Up	1'9"	Water	20 gals.
Draft, Down	3'2"	Hull Type	Deep-V
Weight	8,000#	Deadrise Aft	24°

See Page 538 For Resale Values

Crownline Boats
West Frankfort, IL
www.crownline.com

---

www.powerboatguide.com   231-360-0827

Crownline 290 CR
1999–2004

1999–2000

2001–04

Value-priced 29-footer offered compelling mix of practical accommodations, spirited performance, attractive price. Original midcabin floorplan had canted forward berth coupled with L-shaped dinette/lounge, spacious head. Updated interior in 2001 has U-shaped dinette/double berth forward, smaller head. Four opening ports, three deck hatches allow excellent cabin ventilation. Note flip-up helm seat, windshield vents, removable rear bench seat. Among several engine choices, twin 250hp MerCruisers top out at 35+ knots.

Length w/Pulpit	31'2"	Clearance	8'6"
Hull Length	28'11"	Fuel	146 gals.
Beam	10'4"	Water	20 gals.
Draft, Down	2'11"	Hull Type	Modified-V
Weight	9,000#	Deadrise Aft	16°

See Page 538 For Resale Values

Crownline Boats
West Frankfort, IL
www.crownline.com

---

www.powerboatguide.com   231-360-0827

Crownline 315 SCR
2007–Current

Sexy sportcruiser gets high marks for stylish lines, sporty interior, reasonable price. Spacious cockpit features full wet bar, stereo with transom remote, removable table, underseat storage. Aft bench seat converts to 6-foot sun pad; twin transom gates make boarding easy. Well-finished interior boasts split galley modules, cherrywood cabinets, enclosed head with shower. Note efficient helm layout, power engine hatch, extended swim platform. Cruise at 35 knots with twin 300hp MerCruiser I/Os (high 40s top).

Length	32'5"	Clearance	7'3"
Beam	9'8"	Fuel	139 gals.
Draft, Up	2'4"	Water	25 gals.
Draft, Down	3'2"	Hull Type	Deep-V
Weight	10,300#	Deadrise Aft	23°

See Page 538 For Resale Values

Crownline Boats
West Frankfort, IL
www.crownline.com

231-360-0827

Crownline 320 LS
2006–Current

King-size bowrider makes good on promise of guest-friendly layout, sporty performance, competitive price. Spacious cockpit features full wet bar, stereo with transom remote, removable table, under-seat storage. Enclosed head and berth provides added versatility, comfort. Aft bench seat converts to huge 6-foot sun pad; twin transom gates make boarding easy. Note ergonomic helm, power engine hatch, extended swim platform. Cruise at 35 knots with twin 300hp MerCruiser I/Os (high 40s top).

Length	32 5"	Clearance	6'0"
Beam	9'8"	Fuel	139 gals.
Draft, Up	2'2"	Water	25 gals.
Draft, Down	3'2"	Hull Type	Deep-V
Weight	9,100#	Deadrise Aft	23°

See Page 538 For Resale Values

Crownline Boats
West Frankfort, IL
www.crownline.com

231-360-0827

Crownline 330 CR
1996–2000

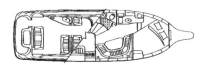

Stylish family express from late 1990s combined comfort, performance at a very competitive price. Spacious midcabin interior benefits from wide 11'7" beam. Privacy curtains separate both sleeping areas from salon; large U-shaped dinette, extended galley offer added comfort and convenience. Cockpit with built-in wet bar, removable dinette seats seven. Note power engine hatch, walk-through windshield, bolt-on swim platform, transom storage locker. Cruise at 18 knots (30 top) with 310hp MerCruiser sterndrive engines.

Length w/Pulpit	33 7"	Fuel	225 gals.
Beam	11 7"	Water	51 gals.
Draft, Up	1 5"	Waste	30 gals.
Draft, Down	2'11"	Hull Type	Modified-V
Weight	13,800#	Deadrise Aft	16°

See Page 538 For Resale Values

Crownline Boats
West Frankfort, IL
www.crownline.com

231-360-0827

Crownline 340 CR
2007–Current

Floorplan Not Available

Polished sterndrive cruiser delivers signature Crownline value in a sporty, well-equipped package. Standard features include hardtop with hatch, deluxe cockpit wetbar with refrigerator, genset, entertainment center with flatscreen TV, anchor windlass. Spacious interior with mahogany flooring, high-gloss cherry cabinets includes large hanging locker, plenty of overhead storage. Teak inlaid swim platform is a nice touch. No lightweight, twin 300hp MerCruiser I/Os cruise at 25 knots (around 35 knots wide open).

Length w/Pulpit	36'0"	Fuel	193 gals.
Beam	11'11"	Water	38 gals.
Draft, Up	2 7"	Waste	30 gals.
Draft, Down	3 5"	Hull Type	Modified-V
Weight	16,300#	Deadrise Aft	18°

See Page 538 For Resale Values

Crownline Boats
West Frankfort, IL
www.crownline.com

Cruisers 2870 Express; 280 CXi
1998–2007

231-360-0827

Polished midcabin express (called 2870 Express in 1998–2003) makes good on promise of comfort, performance. Open-plan interior with crescent-shaped dinette/sofa, full-featured galley has double berths fore and aft, each with privacy curtain. Double-wide helm seat, facing cockpit settees seat six. Helm has space for electronic add-ons. Note full-width extended swim platform, walk-through windshield. Single 375hp MerCruiser sterndrive will cruise at 22–23 knots (30+ top); twin 225hp Volvo I/Os cruise in the mid 20s (35+ top).

Length w/Platform	31'0"	Fuel	100 gals.
Hull Length	28'6"	Water	25 gals.
Beam	10'0"	Waste	20 gals.
Draft, Down	2'11"	Hull Type	Modified-V
Weight	10,000#	Deadrise Aft	16°

See Page 538 For Resale Values

Cruisers Yachts
Oconto, WI
www.cruisersyachts.com

Cruisers 2870 Rogue
1990–95

231-360-0827

Maxi-volume cruiser (called Cruisers 2870 Holiday in 1990; 2870 Rogue in 1991–94; 2970 Rogue in 1995) put emphasis on comfort, performance. Wide 9'6" beam allows for roomy interior with wraparound V-berth/dinette forward, fully equipped galley, stand-up head with shower, midcabin berth. Well-planned cockpit with double-wide helm seat features integrated ice chest, drink holders, transom door. Note narrow side decks, roomy engine compartment. Twin 235hp gas sterndrives top out at over 35 knots.

Length w/Pulpit	28'8"	Clearance	8'8"
Hull Length	26'0"	Fuel	120 gals.
Beam	9'6"	Water	30 gals.
Draft	3'2"	Hull Type	Modified-V
Weight	7,800#	Deadrise Aft	NA

See Page 538 For Resale Values

Cruisers Yachts
Oconto, WI
www.cruisersyachts.com

Cruisers 288/298 Villa Vee; 2980 Esprit
1978–90

Original Floorplan

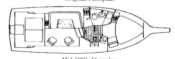

Mid-1980s Floorplan

231-360-0827

Compact flybridge cruiser (called 288 Villa Vee in 1978–83; 298 Villa Vee in 1984–87; 2980 Esprit in 1988–90) enjoyed lasting popularity with loyal owners. Wide 10'8" beam allows for surprisingly spacious interior. Several single-stateroom floorplans were offered, all with fully equipped galley, convertible dinette, roomy head with shower. Lower helm was optional. Note slender side decks. Small bridge seats for four. Twin 230hp gas inboards cruise at 18 knots (25 knots top); 260hp engines cruise at 20 knots (28–29 knots top).

Length Overall	28'8"	Clearance	9'5"
Length WL	24'11"	Fuel	150/180 gals.
Beam	10'8"	Water	45 gals.
Draft	2'9"	Hull Type	Modified-V
Weight	9,500#	Deadrise Aft	17°

Prices Not Provided for Pre-1995 Models

Cruisers Yachts
Oconto, WI
www.cruisersyachts.com

231-360-0827

Cruisers 286/2860/3000 Rogue
1987–89

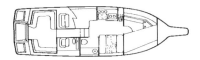

ortly family express (called 286 Rogue in 1987; 2860 Rogue in 1988; 3000 Rouge in 1989) fails to impress. Fairly stylish boat in her day with dramatic hull graphics, integrated swim platform, elongated bow pulpit. Midcabin floorplan with private forward stateroom, convertible dinette sleeps six. Note narrow side decks, modest cabin headroom. Bold hull graphics tend to fade after time. Radar arch was standard on 286 and 2860 models. Among several engine options, twin 260hp I/Os cruise at 23 knots (33–34 knots top).

Length w/Pulpit	32'11"	Headroom	6'1"
Hull Length	27'4"	Fuel	120 gals.
Beam	10'0"	Water	31 gals.
Draft, Drives Down	3'0"	Hull Type	Modified-V
Weight	7,900#	Deadrise Aft	17°

Prices Not Provided for Pre-1995 Models

Cruisers Yachts
Oconto, WI
www.cruisersyachts.com

231-360-0827

Cruisers 296 Avanti Vee
1984–87

eamy family express—obviously dated by today's sportboat standards—offered mid-1980s buyers good value for the money. Built on solid fiberglass hull with positive flotation, prop pockets to reduce draft. Roomy midcabin interior differs from most in that dinette is positioned well aft in salon. Privacy curtains separate sleeping areas from main cabin. Raised helm position offers good visibility. Note good engine access. Twin 260hp gas engines cruise at 19–20 knots and reach a top speed of around 30 knots.

Length Overall	28'8"	Clearance	7 5"
Length WL	24'11"	Fuel	200/250 gals.
Beam	10'8"	Water	45 gals.
Draft	2'9"	Hull Type	Modified-V
Weight	9,000#	Deadrise Aft	17°

Prices Not Provided for Pre-1995 Models

Cruisers Yachts
Oconto, WI
www.cruisersyachts.com

231-360-0827

Cruisers 2970 Esprit
1986–91

urable family cruiser introduced in 1986 combined interior comfort with sporty handling, affordable price. Generic midcabin floorplan boasts exceptional headroom, good-quality fixtures and furnishings. Prop-pocket hull is filled with foam flotation—a safety feature seldom found in boats this size. Good visibility from raised helm position. Radar arch, bow pulpit, swim platform were standard. Note that hull graphics tend to fade over time. Twin 260/270hp gas engines cruise at 20 knots (29–30 knots top).

Length Overall	28'8"	Clearance	7 5"
Length WL	24'11"	Fuel	200/250 gals.
Beam	10'8"	Water	45 gals.
Draft	2'9"	Hull Type	Deep-V
Weight	9,000#	Deadrise Aft	17°

Prices Not Provided for Pre-1995 Models

Cruisers Yachts
Oconto, WI
www.cruisersyachts.com

Cruisers & Sportboats

www.powerboatguide.com   231-360-0827

Cruisers 300 CXi/300 Express
2007–Current

No-frills weekend cruiser (called 300 CXi in 2007–08) delivers all the essentials without breaking the bank. Efficient cockpit layout with double helm seat, wet bar with cooler, companion lounge, rear seating is as good as it gets in a boat this size. Generic interior with aft settee, crescent-shaped dinette, roomy head, boasts 6'3" headroom throughout salon. Easy engine access is plus. Note walk-through windshield, extended swim platform. Twin 225hp Volvo gas I/Os cruise at 18–20 knots (30 knots top).

Length	31'3"	Fuel	125 gals.
Beam	10'0"	Water	30 gals.
Draft, Up	2'0"	Waste	23 gals.
Draft, Down	3'0"	Hull Type	Modified-V
Weight	10,300#	Deadrise Aft	16°

See Page 538 For Resale Values

Cruisers Yachts
Oconto, WI
www.cruisersyachts.com

---

www.powerboatguide.com   231-360-0827

Cruisers 300/310 Express
2005–07

Original Floorplan

2007 Floorplan

Stylish 30-footer with forward-facing arch, extended swim platform blends cruising comfort with agile handling. Original cabin layout with booth-style dinette, double berth aft replaced in 2007 with more open floorplan. Highlights include cherrywood cabinets, walk-through windshield, cockpit wet bar, standard windlass. Molded steps to opening windshield are quite narrow. Screen cabin door inside main door is a nice touch. Optional 320hp Volvo gas I/Os cruise at 30 knots (about 40 knots top). Marketed as Cruisers 310 Express in 2007.

Length	32'3"	Fuel	150 gals.
Beam	10'6"	Water	30 gals.
Draft, Drives Up	21"	Waste	25 gals.
Draft, Drives Down	36"	Hull Type	Modified-V
Weight	11,500#	Deadrise Aft	18°

See Page 538 For Resale Values

Cruisers Yachts
Oconto, WI
www.cruisersyachts.com

---

www.powerboatguide.com   231-360-0827

Cruisers 3070 Rogue
1990–94

Appealing 1990s express combined practical layout with solid performance, good build quality. Wide-open interior with convertible dinette, fully equipped galley, sleeps six in comfort. Note compact head compartment. Cabin ventilation is excellent thanks to six opening ports, three deck hatches. Topside features include radar arch, bow pulpit, circular foredeck sun pad, fore and aft fender wells. Standard 230hp gas I/Os cruise at 20 knots (32–33 knots top); optional 300hp engines cruise at 24 knots (40+ knots wide open).

Length w/Pulpit	30'8"	Weight	9,800#
Hull Length	28'8"	Fuel	170 gals.
Beam	10'6"	Water	35 gals.
Draft, Drives Down	3'0"	Hull Type	Deep-V
Draft, Drives Up	2'1"	Deadrise Aft	20°

Prices Not Provided for Pre-1995 Models

Cruisers Yachts
Oconto, WI
www.cruisersyachts.com

Cruisers 3075 Express
1997–2003

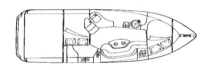

Shapely family express delivered style, performance at budget-friendly price. Well-finished interior with midberth aft, small galley, convertible dinette sleeps six. Head compartment—next to companionway steps—is easily accessed from cockpit. U-shaped cockpit settee converts to large sun pad. Note clever integrated anchor platform, good engine access, walk-through windshield. MerCruiser 260hp sterndrives cruise at 25 knots and reach 35+ knots wide open. Inboard power was optional.

Length w/Pulpit	33'4"	Fuel	150 gals.
Hull Length	32'1"	Water	30 gals.
Beam	10'4"	Headroom	6'3"
Draft, Down	2'9"	Hull Type	Modified-V
Weight	9,500#	Deadrise Aft	16°

See Page 538 For Resale Values

Cruisers Yachts
Oconto, WI
www.cruisersyachts.com

Cruisers 3020/3120 Aria
1992–97

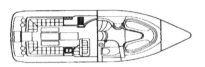

Feature-rich express (called 3020 Aria in 1992–94; 3120 Aria in 1995–97) trades cabin volume for expansive cockpit. Clever rear seat folds out to create sun lounge, or folds into transom pocket to leave cockpit open. Compact cabin has dinette/V-berth forward, minigalley, enclosed head with sit-down shower. Midcabin berth was optional; otherwise that space is used for storage. Note cockpit wet bar, big in-floor storage bin. Twin 250hp I/Os cruise at 20 knots (35 top); optional 330hp engines cruise at 25 knots (about 40 knots top).

Length w/Pulpit	30'8"	Weight	8,800#
Hull Length	28'8"	Fuel	200 gals.
Beam	10'6"	Water	32 gals.
Draft, Down	3'0"	Hull Type	Deep-V
Draft, Up	2'1"	Deadrise Aft	20°

See Page 538 For Resale Values

Cruisers Yachts
Oconto, WI
www.cruisersyachts.com

Cruisers 3175 Rogue
1995–98

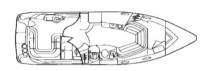

Generic 1990s sterndrive cruiser with rakish styling, midcabin interior, gave entry-level buyers a lot of boat for the money. Wide-open cabin with compact galley, wraparound dinette, features unique raised forepeak berth for kids. Note large head with stall shower, three overhead hatches. Helm has space for flush-mounted electrics. Additional highlights include cockpit wet bar, foredeck sun pad, trim tabs, walk-through windshield. Hull is fully cored to reduce weight. Twin 250hp gas I/Os cruise at 22–23 knots (high 30s top).

Length w/Pulpit	32'8"	Weight	9,300#
Hull Length	30'8"	Fuel	163 gals.
Beam	10'6"	Water	32 gals.
Draft, Up	2'1"	Hull Type	Deep-V
Draft, Down	3'0"	Deadrise Aft	20°

See Page 539 For Resale Values

Cruisers Yachts
Oconto, WI
www.cruisersyachts.com

Cruisers & Sportboats

www.powerboatguide.com   231-360-0827

Cruisers 320 Express
2002–06

Well-bred midrange cruiser (called 3275 Express in 2002–03) offers leading-edge comfort, performance, in a sporty package. Wide-open interior with aft sofa/sleeper, crescent-shaped dinette, cherry woodwork is unusually spacious for a boat this size. Topside features include radar arch, walk-through windshield, double foredeck sun pad (with headrest), anchor chute. Extended swim platform is a popular option. Cockpit sole lifts for engine access. Twin 320hp MerCruiser I/Os cruise at 20 knots and top out in the mid 30s.

Length w/Platform	35'9"	Fuel	200 gals.
Beam	11'3"	Water	40 gals.
Draft, Up	2'0"	Waste	30 gals.
Draft, Down	2'11"	Hull Type	Modified-V
Weight	13,500#	Deadrise Aft	16°

See Page 539 For Resale Values

Cruisers Yachts
Oconto, WI
www.cruisersyachts.com

---

www.powerboatguide.com   231-360-0827

Cruisers 3270 Esprit
1988–94

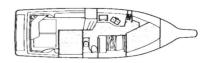

Contemporary family express introduced in 1988 offered bold styling, top-shelf accommodations. Wide 10'10" hull allows spacious midcabin interior with large galley, head with shower, generous storage, berths for six. Well-arranged cockpit features elevated helm position, L-shaped companion lounge, rear bench seat. Hatches in cockpit sole provide good engine access. Hull graphics tend to fade over time. Radar arch, bow pulpit were standard. Twin 250hp V-drive gas inboards cruise at 18–20 knots (high 20s top).

Length	30'10"	Fuel	200 gals.
Beam	10'10"	Water	45 gals.
Draft	2'10"	Waste	20 gals.
Weight	10,500#	Hull Type	Modified-V
Clearance	7'0"	Deadrise Aft	18°

Prices Not Provided for Pre-1995 Models

Cruisers Yachts
Oconto, WI
www.cruisersyachts.com

---

www.powerboatguide.com   231-360-0827

Cruisers 330 Express
2008–Current

Good-looking family express with wide beam sets high standards for comfort, livability. No side decks means interior makes full use of the beam. Roomy cockpit includes large double-wide helm seat, portside chaise lounge, aft U-shaped settee that converts into sun pad. Busy-but-comfortable cabin with vertical hull ports, cherry cabinetry is big for a 33-footer. Note cushioned master berth headboard, space-saving rectangular dinette. Volvo 375hp V-drive gas inboards cruise at 25 knots (low 30s top).

Length	35'6"	Fuel	232 gals.
Beam	11'8"	Water	40 gals.
Draft, Up	2'10"	Waste	30 gals.
Draft, Down	3'8"	Hull Type	Modified-V
Clearance	10'1"	Deadrise Aft	16°

See Page 539 For Resale Values

Cruisers Yachts
Oconto, WI
www.cruisersyachts.com

231-360-0827

Cruisers 336 Ultra Vee
1983–88

Well-rounded 1980s cruiser combined unique interior with sturdy construction, comfortable ride. Aft cabin—with partial standing headroom, privacy door—serves as master stateroom rather than guest quarters. Double-entry head offers access from both salon and aft stateroom. Hatches in cockpit sole provide good engine access. Visibility from raised helm seat is excellent. Note fuel increase in 1985. Prop-pocket hull delivers good turn of speed: 20 knots cruise, about 30 knots top with 350hp inboard gas engines.

Length	32'10"	Fuel	250/300 gals.
Beam	11'10"	Water	70 gals.
Draft	2'9"	Headroom	6'3"
Weight	11,500#	Hull Type	Modified-V
Clearance	8'6"	Deadrise Aft	18°

Prices Not Provided for Pre-1995 Models

Cruisers Yachts
Oconto, WI
www.cruisersyachts.com

231-360-0827

Cruisers 3370 Esprit
1986–94

Tall-freeboard express introduced in 1986 combined rakish styling, roomy accommodations. Well-appointed interior is surprisingly spacious. Aft sleeper/sofa (with privacy curtain) is open to salon; forward stateroom has bi-fold privacy door. Full-feature galley has generous counter, storage space. Single-level cockpit features double-wide helm seat, aft bench seats, engine-room access hatches. Prop-pocket hull delivers good turn of speed: 20 knots cruise, about 30 knots top with 350hp inboard gas engines.

Length	32'10"	Fuel	300 gals.
Beam	11'10"	Water	70 gals.
Draft	2'9"	Headroom	6'3"
Weight	11,500#	Hull Type	Modified-V
Clearance	8'6"	Deadrise Aft	18°

Prices Not Provided for Pre-1995 Models

Cruisers Yachts
Oconto, WI
www.cruisersyachts.com

231-360-0827

Cruisers 3380 Esprit
1985–94

Popular flybridge cruiser (called 338 Chateau Vee in 1985–87) with rakish lines, innovative interior enjoyed decade-long production run. Twin-stateroom floorplan features private midcabin berth beneath salon dinette, generous storage, head with stall shower, step-down galley with upright refrigerator. Hatches in cockpit sole provide good access to engines; oversized bridge has helm forward, wraparound seating aft. Note prop-pocket hull bottom. Crusader 340hp gas inboards cruise at 20 knots (about 30 knots wide open).

Length	32'10"	Fuel	300 gals.
Beam	11'10"	Water	70 gals.
Draft	2'10"	Headroom	6'4"
Weight	13,000#	Hull Type	Modified-V
Clearance	11'6"	Deadrise Aft	18°

Prices Not Provided for Pre-1995 Models

Cruisers Yachts
Oconto, WI
www.cruisersyachts.com

Cruisers & Sportboats

---

www.powerboatguide.com   231-360-0827

Cruisers 340 Express
2001–07

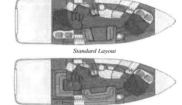

Standard Layout

Alternate Layout

Quality-built midcabin express combined unusually spacious layout with choice of inboard, sterndrive power. Standard interior has fixed midcabin berth, dinette with facing seats; alternate floorplan has aft sleeper/sofa open to salon, U-shaped dinette. Privacy curtains separate sleeping areas from salon. Note stall shower in head. Topside features include cockpit wet bar, transom door, forward-facing arch, foredeck sun pad. Twin 370hp V-drive inboards top out at 30 knots; 375hp MerCruiser sterndrives top out in the high 30s.

Length	36'6"	Fuel	232 gals.
Beam	11'8"	Water	40 gals.
Draft	3'0"	Waste	30 gals.
Weight, Gas	15,500#	Hull Type	Modified-V
Weight, Diesel	16,500#	Deadrise Aft	16°

See Page 539 For Resale Values

Cruisers Yachts
Oconto, WI
www.cruisersyachts.com

---

www.powerboatguide.com   231-360-0827

Cruisers 3570/3575 Esprit; 3572 Express
1995–2002

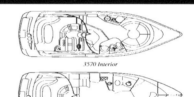

3570 Interior

3575 Interior

Innovative 1990s cruiser offered two very different floorplans in same express-boat package. Original 3570 layout features private amidships master stateroom with queen berth. Alternate interior—introduced in 1996—has traditional midcabin floorplan similar to most express cruisers. Unique cockpit layout has double-wide helm and companion seats leading aft into cockpit. Note fully cored hull with prop pockets. Twin 310hp V-drive gas engines reach 28–30 knots top. (Called 3572 Express in 2001–02.)

Length	39'3"	Fuel	300 gals.
Beam	13'0"	Water	70 gals.
Draft	3.5"	Waste	50 gals.
Weight	16,000#	Hull Type	Modified-V
Clearance, Arch	10'10"	Deadrise Aft	17°

See Page 539 For Resale Values

Cruisers Yachts
Oconto, WI
www.cruisersyachts.com

---

www.powerboatguide.com   231-360-0827

Cruisers 3580/3585 Flybridge
1996–99

3580 Floorplan

3585 Floorplan

Appealing 1990s flybridge cruiser offered choice of two very different interiors. Original 3580 floorplan has galley down with optional lower helm (with poor outside visibility); newer 3585 floorplan introduced in 1998 has elevated lower helm, galley forward in salon. Both layouts have small midcabin under salon, separate stall shower in head. Note molded bridge steps, narrow side decks, compact engineroom, prop-pocket hull bottom. Standard 320hp V-drive gas inboards cruise at 18 knots (26–27 knots wide open).

Length Overall	39'3"	Fuel	300 gals.
Hull Length	37'4"	Water	70 gals.
Beam	13'0"	Waste	40 gals.
Draft	3.5"	Hull Type	Modified-V
Weight	18,200#	Deadrise Aft	16°

See Page 539 For Resale Values

Cruisers Yachts
Oconto, WI
www.cruisersyachts.com

231-360-0827

Cruisers 360 Express
2008–Current

Contemporary express gets thumbs-up for luxury-class accommodations, very competitive price. No side decks permits the interior to make full use of the beam. Guest-friendly cockpit includes double-wide helm seat, portside chaise lounge, rear U-shaped settee that converts into sun pad. Well-appointed cabin with cherry cabinetry is big for a 36-footer. Note cushioned master berth headboard, space-saving rectangular dinette. Fiberglass hardtop is standard. Volvo 375hp V-drive gas inboards cruise at 24 knots (30+ top).

Length	38'0"	Fuel	300 gals.
Beam	12'6"	Water	64 gals.
Draft, V-Drive	3'0"	Waste	40 gals.
Draft, I/O	3.5'	Hull Type	Modified-V
Clearance, Hardtop	11'0"	Deadrise Aft	16°

See Page 539 For Resale Values

Cruisers Yachts
Oconto, WI
www.cruisersyachts.com

231-360-0827

Cruisers 3670 Esprit
1989–92

Maxi-volume cruiser introduced in 1989 delivered express-boat style, comfort at a competitive price. Well-appointed interior with 6'5" headroom features convertible U-shaped dinette, fully equipped galley, double berths fore and aft. Roomy cockpit has elevated double helm seat forward, aft bench seating, wet bar. Hatches in cockpit sole provide good engine access. Note stainless-steel arch, fender storage, cockpit shower, foredeck sun pad. Twin 310hp V-drive gas engines cruise at 18 knots (high 20s top).

Length Overall	39.5"	Clearance	9.7"
Hull Length	35'3"	Fuel	300 gals.
Beam	13'0"	Water	110 gals.
Draft	3.5"	Hull Type	Modified-V
Weight	16,400#	Deadrise Aft	17°

Prices Not Provided for Pre-1995 Models

Cruisers Yachts
Oconto, WI
www.cruisersyachts.com

231-360-0827

Cruisers 3670/3675/3775 Esprit
1991–96

Handsome inboard express (called Cruisers 3670 in 1991–92; 3675 in 1993–94; 3775 in 1997–96) offered buyers luxury, performance at a reasonable price. Spacious interior with overhead skylights features open galley with full-size refrigerator, head with separate stall shower. Aft seating area with privacy enclosure converts to sleeping berth. Large cockpit includes wraparound aft seating, transom door, wet bar. Note spacious helm, bow pulpit, foredeck sun pad. Twin 310hp V-drive gas engines cruise at 18 knots (26–28 knots top).

Length Overall	39.5"	Weight, Diesel	17,500#
Hull Length	35'3"	Fuel	300 gals.
Beam	13'0"	Water	93 gals.
Draft	3.5"	Hull Type	Modified-V
Weight, Gas	16,400#	Deadrise Aft	17°

See Page 539 For Resale Values

Cruisers Yachts
Oconto, WI
www.cruisersyachts.com

231-360-0827

Cruisers 3672/3772/370 Express
2000–07

Single Stateroom Layout

Twin Stateroom Floorplan

Stylish inboard cruiser (called 3672 Express in 2000–02; 3772 Express in 2003; 370 in 2004–07) blends upscale accommodations with quality construction, posh amenities. Offered with choice of floorplans: expansive single-stateroom layout has aft sleeper/sofa open to salon; alternate midcabin interior has private aft stateroom. Note high-gloss cherry woodwork, walk-through windshield, extended swim platform. Standard 370hp V-drive gas engines cruise at 16 knots; optional 370hp Cummins diesels cruise in the low 20s.

Length	40'2"	Fuel	300 gals.
Beam	13'0"	Water	70 gals.
Draft	3'0"	Waste	55 gals.
Weight, Gas	18,000#	Hull Type	Modified-V
Weight, Diesel	19,000#	Deadrise Aft	16°

See Page 539 For Resale Values

Cruisers Yachts
Oconto, WI
www.cruisersyachts.com

---

www.powerboatguide.com
231-360-0827

Cruisers 3870 Express
1998–2003

Good-looking express introduced in 1997 offered upmarket mix of style, luxury, performance. Spacious interior with two heads, full-service galley features unique amidships stateroom with stand-up dressing area, built-in TV, private head with shower. Cockpit has L-lounge opposite helm, wet bar, U-shaped seating aft. Note walk-through windshield, easy-access engine compartment. Extended swim platform supports dinghy, PWC. Twin 370hp gas V-drive inboards cruise at 20 knots (about 30 knots top).

Length Overall	43'3"	Fuel	300 gals.
Hull Length	40'8"	Water	75 gals.
Beam	13'6"	Waste	50 gals.
Draft	3'0"	Hull Type	Modified-V
Weight	19,500#	Deadrise Aft	16°

See Page 539 For Resale Values

Cruisers Yachts
Oconto, WI
www.cruisersyachts.com

---

www.powerboatguide.com
231-360-0827

Cruisers 390 Sports Coupe
2007–Current

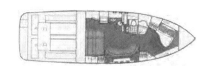

Feature-rich express with semi-enclosed bridgedeck offers passengers maximum protection from the elements. Roomy open-plan salon with single stateroom forward boasts aft sofa that converts to midcabin berth, cherry-veneer cabinetry, large head with separate stall shower. Note limited galley storage. Unique companion seat converts to dinette. Cockpit floor lifts electrically for engine access. Available with V-drive inboard or Volvo IPS Drive System. Cruise at 28 knots with Yanmar 380hp V-drive diesel inboards (30+ top).

Length	40'2"	Fuel	300 gals.
Beam	13'0"	Water	75 gals.
Draft	3'9"	Waste	55 gals.
Weight	22,000#	Hull Type	Modified-V
Clearance	11'3"	Deadrise Aft	16°

See Page 539 For Resale Values

Cruisers Yachts
Oconto, WI
www.cruisersyachts.com

231-360-0827

Cruisers 3970/400/420 Express
2003–Current

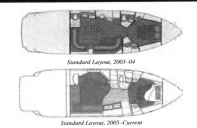

Standard Layout, 2003–04

Standard Layout, 2005–Current

Upscale sportcruiser (called 3970 Exp. in 2003; 400 Exp. in 2004–05; 420 Exp. since 2006) combines smart styling with brisk performance, quality amenities. Original midcabin interior updated in 2005 with more spacious single-stateroom layout with vertical hull ports. Cockpit—also redesigned in 2005—replaced original centerline companionway with portside entry, pod-style helm/companion seats. Twin 420hp V-drive gas engines cruise at 20 knots; Yanmar 370hp diesels cruise in the low 20s. Recent models with 370hp IPS drives cruise at 26 knots.

Length	43'0"	Fuel	300 gals.
Beam	13'6"	Water	70 gals.
Draft	3'8"	Waste	50 gals.
Weight, Gas	22,000#	Hull Type	Modified-V
Weight, Diesel	23,500#	Deadrise Aft	16°

See Page 539 For Resale Values

Cruisers Yachts
Oconto, WI
www.cruisersyachts.com

231-360-0827

Cruisers 420 Sports Coupe
2009–Current

Shapely hardtop express with seductive profile takes cruising comfort to the next level. Elegant two-stateroom, cherrywood interior with near 7-foot headroom includes nifty salon liquor cabinet, 26" flatscreen TV, Corion counters, vertical hull ports. Cockpit amenities include U-shaped lounge seating with storage under, power engineroom hatch, deluxe wetbar. Note sunroof, foredeck chaise lounge, walk-through windshield, extended swim platform. Cruise at 24–25 knots with Volvo 370hp IPS diesels.

Length w/Platform	43'0"	Fuel	300 gals.
Beam	13'6"	Water	80 gals.
Draft	38"	Waste	50 gals.
Weight, Gas	23,000#	Hull Type	Modified-V
Weight, Diesel	23,500#	Deadrise Aft	16°

Insufficient Resale Data To Assign Values

Cruisers Yachts
Oconto, WI
www.cruisersyachts.com

231-360-0827

Cruisers 4270 Express
1997–2003

Full-bodied express with extended swim platform, forward-facing arch gets high marks for aggressive styling, spirited performance. Upscale interior features wide-open salon with contoured settee, huge U-shaped galley, unique midcabin suite with twin berths, private head, stand-up dressing area. Cockpit includes removable aft seats—very practical. Note walk-through windshield, transom storage locker, concealed windlass. Space at helm for extra electronics. Cat 420hp V-drive diesels cruise at 26–28 knots (30+ knots top).

Length	46'6"	Fuel	400 gals.
Beam	14'0"	Water	100 gals.
Draft	3'6"	Waste	50 gals.
Weight, Gas	22,000#	Hull Type	Modified-V
Weight, Diesel	23,500#	Deadrise Aft	16°

See Page 539 For Resale Values

Cruisers Yachts
Oconto, WI
www.cruisersyachts.com

www.powerboatguide.com   231-360-0827

Cruisers 4280 Express Bridge
1988–94

1988–91

1992–94

Maxi-volume cruiser with party-time accommodations delivers impressive comfort, versatility. Single-level interior (updated in 1992) features full-beam salon, two staterooms, open galley with serving counter. Massive flybridge can seat a small crowd. Bridge steps in cockpit are a nice touch. Fully cored hull has prop pockets to reduce draft and shaft angles. Cat 375hp diesels cruise at 20 knots (around 24 knots top). Note that Cruisers 4285 Express Bridge is same boat with more expansive single-stateroom interior.

Length	46'6"	Fuel	400 gals.
Beam	14'6"	Water	160 gals.
Draft	3'6"	Headroom	6 5"
Weight, Gas	23,700#	Hull Type	Modified-V
Weight, Diesel	25,200#	Deadrise Aft	16°

Prices Not Provided for Pre-1995 Models

Cruisers Yachts
Oconto, WI
www.cruisersyachts.com

---

www.powerboatguide.com   231-360-0827

Cruisers 4285 Express Bridge
1990–95

Spacious family cruiser with party-time accommodations delivers impressive comfort, versatility. Single-stateroom interior features huge full-beam salon with entertainment center, open galley with serving counter, large master cabin. Massive flybridge can seat a small crowd. Bridge steps in cockpit are a nice touch. Fully cored hull has prop pockets to reduce shaft angles. Cat 375hp diesels cruise at 20 knots (around 24 knots top). Note that Cruisers 4280 Express Bridge is same boat with two-stateroom interior.

Length	46'6"	Headroom	6 5"
Beam	14'6"	Fuel	400 gals.
Draft	3'6"	Water	160 gals.
Weight, Gas	23,700#	Hull Type	Modified-V
Weight, Diesel	25,200#	Deadrise Aft	16°

See Page 539 For Resale Values

Cruisers Yachts
Oconto, WI
www.cruisersyachts.com

---

www.powerboatguide.com   231-360-0827

Cruisers 440 Express
2003–05

Standard Layout

Optional Layout

Luxury sportcruiser with maxi-volume interior offers express-boat versatility, motoryacht comforts. Opulent cabin accommodations include full-size master stateroom (with private head, shower), vast salon with crescent-shaped dinette/sofa, open-plan galley with Corian counters, generous storage. Note high-gloss cherry cabinetry, posh upholstery. Extended swim platform can support PWC. Bi-level cockpit seats 8–10 guests in comfort. Fiberglass hardtop was optional. Yanmar 440hp V-drive diesels cruise at 25 knots (high 20s top).

Length	46'9"	Fuel	400 gals.
Beam	14'0"	Water	95 gals.
Draft	42"	Waste	50 gals.
Weight, Gas	24,300#	Hull Type	Modified-V
Weight, Diesel	25,900#	Deadrise Aft	16°

See Page 539 For Resale Values

Cruisers Yachts
Oconto, WI
www.cruisersyachts.com

Cruisers 520 Express
2006–Current

Standard Layout

Optional Layout

Posh accommodations, aggressive styling, impressive performance make this maxi-volume cruiser a standout entry in today's premium sportyacht market. Enormous twin-stateroom interior boasts full-beam master with en suite head, huge galley, opulent main salon with 12-foot Ultraleather sectional. Feature-rich cockpit seats a small crowd in comfort. Note walk-through windshield, cherry interior cabinetry, optional hardtop. Volvo 715hp V-drive diesels deliver a top speed in excess of 30 knots.

Length	52'3"	Fuel	500 gals.
Beam	15'6"	Water	150 gals.
Draft	3'8"	Waste	75 gals.
Weight	42,000#	Hull Type	Modified-V
Headroom	6'6"	Deadrise Aft	15°

See Page 540 For Resale Values

Cruisers Yachts
Oconto, WI
www.cruisersyachts.com

Cruisers 540/560 Express
2001–Current

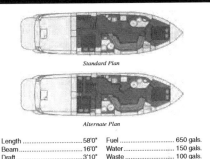

Standard Plan

Alternate Plan

Head-turning sportyacht (called 5370 Express in 2001-02; 540 Express in 2003-06) with bold styling, deluxe accommodations defines luxury in the nautical fast lane. Spacious interior with two (or three) staterooms features two full heads, enormous salon with leather sofa, home-size galley. Circular cockpit lounge converts electrically into huge sun pad. Retractable dinette table in salon is way cool. Hardtop is optional. Hull is fully cored. Volvo 715hp V-drive diesels top out at 30+ knots.

Length	58'0"	Fuel	650 gals.
Beam	16'0"	Water	150 gals.
Draft	3'10"	Waste	100 gals.
Weight	46,000#	Hull Type	Modified-V
Clearance	12'7"	Deadrise Aft	15°

See Page 540 For Resale Values

Cruisers Yachts
Oconto, WI
www.cruisersyachts.com

Donzi 275 Express
1995–2000

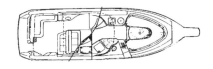

Entry-level family cruiser with plenty of standard features gave 1990s buyers good value for the money. Generic midcabin interior includes full galley, enclosed head with shower, dinette/V-berth forward. Cockpit layout with aft bench seat (convertible to sun lounge) is comfortable for six adults. Cockpit wet bar, integrated swim platform, Dino steering wheel, radar arch, integral bow pulpit were all standard. Good cabin headroom; so-so fit and finish. Single 310hp MerCruiser sterndrive will cruise at 25 knots (35+ knots wide open.)

Length Overall	29'3"	Clearance	7'0"
Beam	8'6"	Fuel	103 gals.
Draft, Drives Up	1'9"	Water	20 gals.
Draft, Drives Down	3'5"	Hull Type	Modified-V
Weight	6,500#	Deadrise Aft	19°

See Page 540 For Resale Values

Donzi Marine
Tallevast, FL
www.donzimarine.com

Cruisers & Sportboats

www.powerboatguide.com   231-360-0827

Donzi 3250 Express
1996–2000

Sporty sterndrive express combined signature Donzi performance with bold styling, practical cabin accommodations. Maxi-volume interior with berths for six includes private forward stateroom, circular salon dinette, fully-equipped galley. Flashy 1990s cabin decor may not be for everyone. Innovative cockpit design with centerline transom door, doublewide helm seat boasts lounge seating for a small crowd. Note wide sidedecks. Faster than many so-called sportboats, twin 310hp I/Os cruise at close to 30 knots (40+ top).

Length Overall	33'8"	Clearance	NA
Beam	11'0"	Fuel	198 gals.
Draft, Drives Up	2'4"	Water	35 gals.
Draft, Drives Down	3'1"	Hull Type	Modified-V
Weight	11,500#	Deadrise Aft	19°

See Page 540 For Resale Values

Donzi Marine
Tallevast, FL
www.donzimarine.com

---

www.powerboatguide.com   231-360-0827

Fairline 40 Targa
2000–07

Spirited sportcruiser with transom garage built an impressive sales record during her production years. Impeccably detailed cockpit has food-prep center with barbecue across from U-lounge. Midcabin interior with private staterooms boasts posh furnishings, stunning cherry woodwork. Aft sun pad rises hydraulically for access to tender; engineroom, beneath garage, can only be accessed if dinghy is removed. Bow thruster is standard. Note narrow side decks. Volvo 285hp diesel I/Os cruise at 27–28 knots (low 30s top).

Length Overall	41'10"	Water	79 gals.
Beam	12'1"	Clearance	13'2"
Draft, Down	3'0"	Headroom	6'4"
Weight	16,000#	Hull	Deep-V
Fuel	197 gals.	Deadrise Aft	17°

See Page 541 For Resale Values

Fairline Boats, Ltd.
Oundle, England
www.fairline.com

---

www.powerboatguide.com   231-360-0827

Fairline 43 Targa
1998–2004

Best-selling U.K. express yacht with rakish lines was designed as much for socialising as she was for speed. Highlights include lavish two-stateroom, two-head interior with lacquered cherry cabinets, teak-and-holly cabin sole, luxury-class cockpit with wraparound seating, deluxe wet bar, teak-laid swim platform, flip-up helm seat, fore and aft sunpads. Deep-V hull delivers exceptional open-water performance. Transom garage is a convenient big-boat touch. Twin 480hp Volvo diesels cruise at 28 knots (mid 30s top).

Length Overall	45'1"	Fuel	280 gals.
Beam	12'6"	Water	74 gals.
Draft	3'3	Waste	NA
Weight	20,723#	Hull Type	Deep-V
Clearance	13'3"	Deadrise Aft	18°

See Page 541 For Resale Values

Fairline Boats, Ltd.
Oundle, England
www.fairline.com

231-360-0827

Fairline 48 Targa
1998–2002

Best-selling U.K. express with eye-catching ellipti-cal windshield raised the bar in her era for sport-boat styling, nautical sex appeal. Three-stateroom interior has matching guest cabins aft, posh salon, top-shelf galley appliances. Forward head is small; doors to aft cabins are narrow. Cockpit is divided into three areas: command bridge forward, settee and wet bar in the middle, tender garage aft. Engineroom is shoehorn tight. Volvo 430hp diesels top out at 30+ knots; low 30s with Volvo 480s.

Length	49'10"	Fuel	360 gals.
Beam	12'11"	Water	120 gals.
Draft	3'3"	Waste	40 gals.
Weight	24,600#	Hull Type	Deep-V
Clearance	NA	Deadrise Aft	19°

See Page 541 For Resale Values

Fairline Boats, Ltd.
Oundle, England
www.fairline.com

231-360-0827

Fairline 52 Targa
2003–Current

Muscular, big-water express introduced in 2003 took sportyacht styling, performance to the next level. Luxury-class interior with high-gloss cabi-nets boasts three private staterooms, two full heads, opu-lent salon with home-size galley. Note king bed in mas-ter stateroom. Optional den/office can replace port guest cabin. Transom garage is big enough to handle a 12-foot tender. Additional features include impressive stowage, easy engineroom access, teak cockpit sole. Cruise in the high 20s with 715hp Volvo diesels (about 35 knots top).

Length Overall	52.5"	Headroom	6'6"
Beam	14'0"	Fuel	480 gals.
Draft	3'7"	Water	120 gals.
Weight	35,200#	Hull Type	Deep-V
Clearance	15'10"	Deadrise Aft	19°

See Page 541 For Resale Values

Fairline Boats, Ltd.
Oundle, England
www.fairline.com

231-360-0827

Formula 27 PC
1994–Current

Wide-beam sportcruiser produced since 1994 is a proven blend of solid construction, versatile ac-commodations. Upscale interior with wraparound dinette forward includes full galley with Corian counter, aft private berth with privacy enclosure. Roomy cockpit comes with double-wide helm seat, wet bar, foldaway aft lounge, sun pad insert. Note power engine compartment hatch, walk-through windshield. Single 310hp MerCruiser will cruise at 22 knots (34–35 knots top); twin 310hp Mer-Cruisers cruise at 26–28 knots (mid 40s knots top).

Length Overall	29.5"	Fuel	107 gals.
Hull Length	27'0"	Water	26 gals.
Beam	9'7"	Waste	30 gals.
Draft	3'1"	Hull Type	Modified-V
Weight	9,500#	Deadrise Aft	18°

See Page 542 For Resale Values

Formula Boats
Decatur, IN
www.formulaboats.com

Cruisers & Sportboats

Cruisers & Sportboats

231-360-0827

Formula 28 PC
1985–87

Quality-built 1980s express is roomy, quick, agile. Considered an upscale boat during her production years—rugged construction, stylish hull graphics allowed her to age gracefully well into the 1990s. Conventional midcabin interior has sliding panel forward for stateroom privacy, large settee, stand-up head with sink and shower. Open cockpit features L-shaped lounge next to helm, wet bar, foldaway stern seat. Note bow pulpit, spacious engine compartment. Twin 260hp sterndrives cruise at 23–25 knots (mid 30s top).

Length Overall	30'6"	Clearance	8'4"
Hull Length	28'0"	Fuel	160 gals.
Beam	10'0"	Water	39 gals.
Draft	2'10"	Hull Type	Deep-V
Weight	7,850#	Deadrise Aft	24°

Prices Not Provided for Pre-1995 Models

Formula Boats
Decatur, IN
www.formulaboats.com

231-360-0827

Formula 280 Bowrider
1998–2008

Versatile family cruiser with wide 9'2" beam is small enough for exploring lakes and rivers, big enough to handle an offshore chop. Well-appointed cockpit with wraparound seating, double (flip-up) helm seat, deluxe galley can accommodate a small crowd. Filler cushions turn bow seats into huge sun pad. Enclosed head compartment is among the largest in her class. Excellent helm layout with tiered dash, tilt wheel. Power engine hatch is a useful touch. Twin 260hp MerCruiser sterndrives top out at close to 45 knots.

Length Overall	29'6"	Fuel	120 gals.
Beam	9'2"	Water	120 gals.
Draft	3'0"	Waste	2.6 gals.
Weight, Single	7,300#	Hull Type	Deep-V
Weight, Twins	8,200#	Deadrise Aft	21°

See Page 542 For Resale Values

Formula Boats
Decatur, IN
www.formulaboats.com

231-360-0827

Formula 280 Sun Sport
1994–2008

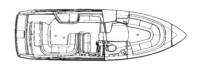

Rakish sportcruiser set class standards in her era for sleek styling, top-notch amenities, impressive owner satisfaction. Spacious cockpit boasts huge wraparound lounge aft (convertible into giant sun pad), double-wide helm with flip-up bolsters, refreshment center, passenger-side lounger. Well-appointed cabin with dinette/V-berth features enclosed head, storage lockers. Note walk-through windshield, power engine hatch. Single 310hp MerCruiser will hit 35 knots top; twin 320hp MerCruisers top out in the high 40s.

Length Overall	29'6"	Fuel	120 gals.
Beam	9'2"	Water	20 gals.
Draft	3'0"	Waste	26 gal.
Weight	8,200#	Hull Type	Deep-V
Clearance	8'6"	Deadrise Aft	21°

See Page 542 For Resale Values

Formula Boats
Decatur, IN
www.formulaboats.com

　231-360-0827

Formula 29 PC
1988–92

Maxi-volume family cruiser introduced in 1988 targeted upscale boaters focused on sporty performance, top-shelf accommodations. Tastefully furnished interior with full-featured galley, stand-up head with shower sleeps six. Cabin entry is wide, headroom is generous. Wraparound seating opposite helm keeps skipper close to guests. Note large engine compartment, swivel helm seat, foldaway stern seat. Excellent high-speed handling, above-average finish. Twin MerCruiser 5.7-liter sterndrives cruise at 20 knots (low 30s top).

Length Overall	33'9"	Clearance	8'9"
Hull Length	29'0"	Fuel	165 gals.
Beam	10'7"	Water	50 gals.
Draft	2'6"	Hull Type	Deep-V
Weight	9,700#	Deadrise Aft	20°

Prices Not Provided for Pre-1995 Models

Formula Boats
Decatur, IN
www.formulaboats.com

　231-360-0827

Formula 31 SC Express
1981–85

Roomy inboard express popular in 1980s was notable for wide 12-foot beam, quality fit and finish. Enormous single-level cockpit with removable stern seats offers plenty of room for fishing, diving, entertaining. Well-appointed interior with private stateroom, 6'5" headroom was available with berths for four or six. Note spacious engine compartment. Standard features included teak cover boards, radar arch, teak swim platform. Modified-V hull performs well in a chop. Cruise at 20 knots with twin 255hp gas engines (around 30 knots top).

Length	31'4"	Fuel	200 gals.
Beam	12'0"	Water	45 gals.
Draft	2'6"	Headroom	6'1"
Weight	10,500#	Hull Type	Modified-V
Clearance	8'4"	Deadrise Aft	18°

Prices Not Provided for Pre-1995 Models

Formula Boats
Decatur, IN
www.formulaboats.com

　231-360-0827

Formula 31 PC
1993–2004

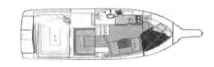

Best-selling express hit the right buttons with Formula buyers for over a decade. Topside amenities include roomy cockpit with wraparound lounge seating, wet bar, portside lounger, well-designed helm with double-wide seat. Entire aft lounge becomes large sun pad when tables are lowered. Wide-open cabin with U-shaped dinette, full-featured galley sleeps six. Hardware, furnishings, appliances are first rate. MerCruiser 320hp engines cruise at 25 knots (high 30s top). Note that all-new Formula 31 PC was introduced in 2005.

Length Overall	34'0"	Fuel	180 gals.
Hull Length	31'0"	Water	50 gals.
Beam	11'0"	Waste	40 gals.
Draft	3'2"	Hull Type	Modified-V
Weight	11,730#	Deadrise Aft	18°

See Page 542 For Resale Values

Formula Boats
Decatur, IN
www.formulaboats.com

231-360-0827

Formula 31 PC
2005–Current

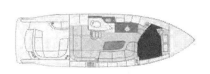

Updated version of original Formula 31 PC (1993–2004) adds stylish sport arch, extended swim platform, revised interior with Ultraleather upholstery. Cabin highlights include Corian galley and head counters, cherrywood dinette table, top-quality galley appliances. Foredeck sun pads are reached via opening windshield with molded steps, hand railing. Standard features include windlass, transom shower, flat-screen TV/DVD, power engine hatch. Not inexpensive, twin 320hp MerCruiser sterndrives top out at 35+ knots.

Length Overall	33'1"	Fuel	180 gals.
Beam	11'0"	Water	50 gals.
Draft, Up	2'6"	Waste	40 gals.
Draft, Down	3'4"	Hull Type	Modified-V
Weight	14,100#	Deadrise Aft	18°

See Page 542 For Resale Values

Formula Boats
Decatur, IN
www.formulaboats.com

www.powerboatguide.com
231-360-0827

Formula 310 Sun Sport
2007–Current

Fast-action sportster delivers appealing mix of aggressive styling, open-air comfort, impressive performance. Expansive cockpit has seating for ten including clever aft-facing transom lounge that converts to sun pad. Power hatch lifts entire aft cockpit for engine access. Well finished cabin with sitting headroom features mini galley, enclosed head, V-berth with privacy curtain. Note classy burled dash, LED lighting for swim platform. Transom storage trunk is a plus. Twin MerCruiser 320hp I/Os deliver 40+ knots wide open.

Length	31'0"	Fuel	130 gals.
Beam	9'6"	Water	30 gals.
Draft	3'1"	Waste	36 gals.
Weight	9,750#	Hull Type	Deep-V
Clearance	8'8"	Deadrise Aft	22°

See Page 542 For Resale Values

Formula Boats
Decatur, IN
www.formulaboats.com

www.powerboatguide.com
231-360-0827

Formula 310 Bowrider
2008–Current

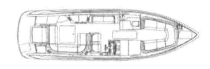

Super-size bowrider with every possible comfort takes open-bow boating to the next level. Spacious cockpit with U-shaped seating includes Corian-topped wet bar with refrigerator, doublewide helm seat with flip-up bolsters, lockable head with sit-down shower. Swimstep chaise lounge converts to sun pad with bolsters on both sides. Note cavernous in-deck storage compartment, concealed windlass. Bow seats convert to forward-facing seats for better ride. Fit and finish is excellent. Twin 320hp MerCruiser I/Os reach 40+ knots flat out.

Length	31'0"	Fuel	130 gals.
Beam	9'6"	Water	30 gals.
Draft, Up	1'6"	Waste	36 gals.
draft, Down	3'1"	Hull Type	Deep-V
Weight	9,875#	Deadrise Aft	22°

See Page 542 For Resale Values

Formula Boats
Decatur, IN
www.formulaboats.com

231-360-0827

Formula 330 Sun Sport
1996–2006

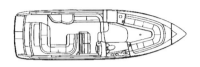

High-end sportboat with wide beam combines aggressive styling with upscale interior, exciting performance. Cockpit seating is generous and versatile; U-shaped aft lounge converts to sun pad, portside bench functions as aft-facing recliner, double-wide helm seat has flip-up bolsters for stand-up driving. On-deck galley has removable cooler. Well-finished cabin boasts convertible dinette, enclosed head with shower. Note power engine hatch, tilt wheel. Cruise at 28 knots with twin 320hp sterndrives (mid 40s top).

Length	33'0"	Fuel	160 gals.
Beam	10'2"	Water	20 gals.
Draft	2'11"	Waste	26 gals.
Weight	9,700#	Hull Type	Deep-V
Clearance	6'0"	Deadrise Aft	20°

See Page 542 For Resale Values

Formula Boats
Decatur, IN
www.formulaboats.com

231-360-0827

Formula 34 PC
1991–2002

Polished midcabin express racked up impressive sales numbers for Formula throughout the 1990s. Cockpit amenities include U-shaped aft lounge with removable table, double-wide companion seat, flip-up helm seat, wet bar. Portside floor compartment holds small cooler. Smartly appointed cabin with Ultraleather settee, large galley, contoured aft lounge sleeps six. Bow pulpit, radar arch, transom shower, foredeck sun pads were standard. Twin MerCruiser 310hp sterndrives cruise at 23–24 knots (mid 30s top).

Length Overall	37'0"	Clearance w/Arch	10'0"
Hull Length	34'0"	Fuel	222 gals.
Beam	12'0"	Water	60 gals.
Draft	2'6"	Hull Type	Modified-V
Weight	13,500#	Deadrise Aft	18°

See Page 542 For Resale Values

Formula Boats
Decatur, IN
www.formulaboats.com

231-360-0827

Formula 34 PC
2004–Current

Restyled version of previous Formula 34 PC (1991–2002) inherits best features of her predecessor in restyled, updated package. Topside amenities include wraparound cockpit seating with removable table, double-wide helm seat with flip-up bolsters, twin foredeck sun pads, extended swim platform, transom storage. Spacious cabin with Ultraleather seating, Corian counters, cherry woodwork is as good as it gets in a family cruiser. Note walk-through windshield, power engine compartment hatch. MerCruiser 320hp I/Os top out at 35+ knots.

Length Overall	35'7"	Fuel	206 gals.
Beam	11'6"	Water	55 gals.
Draft	3'0"	Waste	40 gals.
Weight	15,710#	Hull Type	Modified-V
Clearance	11'4"	Deadrise Aft	18°

See Page 542 For Resale Values

Formula Boats
Decatur, IN
www.formulaboats.com

Cruisers & Sportboats

231-360-0827

Formula 35 PC
1986–89

Late 1980s inboard express delivered bold styling, classy accommodations, good open-water performance at a competitive price. Common-sense interior boasts large U-shaped galley, full dinette, facing aft settees. Cabin fabrics, furnishings, and appliances were considered first rate in their day. Cockpit seating includes L-shaped companion lounge, foldaway stern seat. Note windshield vents, side-dumping exhausts, roomy dash, power engine hatch. Twin 340hp V-drive engines cruise at 20 knots and top out at 28–30 knots.

Length Overall	40'0"	Clearance	10'2"
Hull Length	35'0"	Fuel	275 gals.
Beam	12'0"	Water	50 gals.
Draft	2'8"	Hull Type	Deep-V
Weight	13,750#	Deadrise Aft	20°

Prices Not Provided for Pre-1995 Models

Formula Boats
Decatur, IN
www.formulaboats.com

231-360-0827

Formula 350 Sun Sport
2008–Current

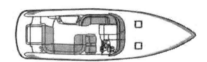

High-style runabout bridges the gap between high-performance dayboat, luxury-class cruiser. Topside features include U-shaped lounge seating for eight, adjustable aft-facing lounge with stowage under, double helm seat with individual bolsters. Well-designed helm has plenty of space for electronics. Cozy midcabin interior with UltraLeather salon sofa, top-shelf appliances sleeps four. Imron hull graphics are a plus; fit and finish is exemplary. Twin 320hp MerCruiser sterndrives reach close to 50 knots wide open. Expensive.

Length	35'0"	Fuel	172 gals.
Beam	10'9"	Water	30 gals.
Draft, Up	1'10"	Waste	37 gals.
Draft, Down	3'3"	Hull Type	Deep-V
Weight	13,470#	Deadrise Aft	21°

See Page 542 For Resale Values

Formula Boats
Decatur, IN
www.formulaboats.com

231-360-0827

Formula 36 PC
1990–95

Well-crafted family cruiser with straight inboard power set high standards in early 1990s for style, quality, performance. Roomy midcabin interior with private forward stateroom gets high marks for quality materials, excellent workmanship. Entertainment center on aft bulkhead is an innovative touch. Cockpit seating includes L-shaped companion lounge, foldaway stern seat. Note windshield vents, side exhausts, power engine hatch, generous fuel capacity. Standard 340hp gas engines cruise at 17 knots (26–27 knots top).

Length Overall	38'3"	Clearance	10'9"
Hull Length	36'0"	Fuel	300 gals.
Beam	13'3"	Water	60 gals.
Draft	2'8"	Hull Type	Modified-V
Weight	17,600#	Deadrise Aft	18°

See Page 542 For Resale Values

Formula Boats
Decatur, IN
www.formulaboats.com

Formula 37 PC
2000–Current

Leading-edge sportcruiser is well built, beautifully finished, easy on the eye. Luxurious interior with Ultraleather seating, furniture-quality woodwork should satisfy the most demanding buyers. Note large head compartment, standard central vacuum system. Topside features include wraparound cockpit seating, double-wide helm seat, walk-through windshield (with handrail), foredeck sun pads, transom storage locker. Power cockpit seat provides good engineroom access. Volvo 375hp sterndrives top out at just over 40 knots.

Length Overall	38'5"	Fuel	236 gals.
Beam	11'11"	Water	55 gals.
Draft	2'6"	Waste	57 gals.
Weight	16,500#	Hull Type	Modified-V
Clearance	14'4"	Deadrise Aft	18°

See Page 542 For Resale Values

Formula Boats
Decatur, IN
www.formulaboats.com

Formula 370 Super Sport
2001–Current

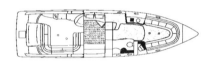

Sleek, passenger-friendly sportcruiser is built with comfort and speed in mind. Basically a Eurostyle sportboat design with more cockpit space, less interior volume than traditional midcabin cruisers. Roomy cockpit provides seating for a small crowd. Opulent cabin has convertible dinette, athwartships midberth, compact galley. Note walk-through windshield, transom shower, tilt steering, flip-up helm seat. High-speed stepped hull delivers a fast ride. MerCruiser 420hp I/O cruise at 30 knots and reach a top speed of about 45 knots.

Length	38'6"	Fuel	238 gals.
Beam	10'6"	Water	43 gals.
Draft	3'0"	Waste	50 gals.
Weight	15,100#	Hull Type	Deep-V
Clearance	10'0"	Deadrise Aft	21°

See Page 542 For Resale Values

Formula Boats
Decatur, IN
www.formulaboats.com

Formula 40 PC
2003–Current

Smooth-riding express competes with the best in luxury amenities, upscale accommodations, long-term owner satisfaction. Posh midcabin interior with private bow stateroom is a tasteful blend of high-gloss cherry cabinetry, Ultraleather upholstery, designer fabrics and furnishings. Topside features include walk-through windshield, flip-up helm seat, transom storage locker, foredeck sun pads. Outstanding finish, near flawless gelcoat. Yanmar 420hp V-drive diesels cruise at 24 knots. Volvo IPS power optional in late models.

Length	42'7"	Fuel	250 gals.
Beam	12'8"	Water	55 gals.
Draft	2'11"	Waste	57 gals.
Weight	21,550#	Hull Type	Modified-V
Clearance	16'8"	Deadrise Aft	18°

See Page 542 For Resale Values

Formula Boats
Decatur, IN
www.formulaboats.com

Cruisers & Sportboats

www.powerboatguide.com   231-360-0827

Formula 400 Super Sport
1999–Current

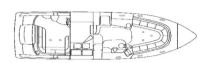

Feature-packed sportyacht with enormous cockpit blends luxury amenities with good performance, enduring sex appeal. Open-plan interior with aft owner's cabin, wraparound lounge seating forward offers remarkably upscale amenities for a purebred sportboat. Wide-open cockpit seats a small crowd. Double-stepped deep-V hull with slender beam delivers superb open-water ride. Many updates/refinements over the years. MerCruiser 425hp gas I/Os reach close to 45 knots top; Volvo 370hp diesels top out at 40+ knots.

Length	41'6"	Fuel	250 gals.
Beam	11'0"	Water	50 gals.
Draft	3'0"	Waste	50 gals.
Weight, Gas	16,100#	Hull Type	Deep-V
Weight, Diesel	17,100#	Deadrise Aft	22°

See Page 543 For Resale Values

Formula Boats
Decatur, IN
www.formulaboats.com

---

www.powerboatguide.com   231-360-0827

Formula 41 PC
1996–2004

Luxury sportyacht introduced in 1996 met Formula standards for quality, performance, nautical sex appeal. Elegant interior with private forward stateroom, home-sized galley boasts comforts of a small motoryacht. Deep cockpit has huge U-lounge aft, full wet bar, double helm seat, portside lounger. Note walk-through windshield. Entire cockpit sole lifts for engine access. Beamy deep-V hull has prop pockets to reduce draft. Standard gas engines cruise at 16–17 knots; 450hp Cummins diesels cruise at 24–25 knots (about 30 knots top).

Length Overall	43'1"	Fuel, Gas	300 gals.
Hull Length	41'0"	Fuel, Diesel	350 gals.
Beam	13'6"	Water	81 gals.
Draft	2'9"	Hull Type	Modified-V
Weight	18,520#	Deadrise Aft	18°

See Page 543 For Resale Values

Formula Boats
Decatur, IN
www.formulaboats.com

---

www.powerboatguide.com   231-360-0827

Formula 45 Yacht
2007–Current

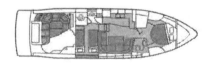

High-end luxury yacht combines signature Formula styling with spirited performance, executive-class amenities. Highlights include enclosed bridgedeck with excellent visibility, outdoor galley/wet bar, luxurious two-stateroom, two-head interior, convenient walk-through windshield. Optional hydraulic swim platform can stow PWC. Entire aft cockpit rises for engine access. Note power sunroof. Side decks are narrow. Slender beam delivers good heavy-weather handling. Volvo 575hp V-drive diesels cruise at 25–26 knots (about 30 knots top).

Length Overall	48'2"	Fuel	350 gals.
Beam	13'11"	Water	100 gals.
Draft	3'5"	Waste	75 gals.
Weight	33,500#	Hull Type	Modified-V
Clearance	15'5"	Deadrise Aft	18°

See Page 543 For Resale Values

Formula Boats
Decatur, IN
www.formulaboats.com

231-360-0827

Formula 48 Yacht
2004–07

Performance, luxury, engineering are combined in this powerful, state-of-the-art cruising yacht. Lavish interior with home-sized galley, high-gloss woodwork boasts second head compartment in aft stateroom. Elegant cockpit seats ten with room to spare. Note superb helm layout, walk-through windshield, spacious engineroom with power hatch. Extended swim platform supports PWC. Twin 660hp Cummins diesels cruise in the mid 20s (32–33 knots top). Called the Formula 47 Yacht in 2004. Impressive and expensive.

Length	51'0"	Fuel	400 gals.
Beam	14'0"	Water	100 gals.
Draft	3'8"	Waste	75 gals.
Weight	35,750#	Hull Type	Modified-V
Clearance	14'0"	Deadrise Aft	18°

See Page 543 For Resale Values

Formula Boats
Decatur, IN
www.formulaboats.com

231-360-0827

Four Winns 278 Vista
1994–98

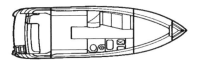

Maxi-cube 1990s cruiser combines widebody comforts with versatile layout, spirited performance. Generic midcabin interior with full galley, enclosed head, convertible dinette sleeps four adults, two kids. Note generous galley storage. Topside highlights include stylish helm layout, walk-through windshield, foldaway stern seat, double-wide helm seat. Oval cabin ports replaced original sliding cabin windows in 1996. Permit required for trailering. Single 310hp I/O tops out at 30 knots; twin 190hp I/Os reach a top speed of 32–34 knots.

Length	27'2"	Fuel	110 gals.
Beam	9'4"	Water	38 gals.
Draft	3'3"	Waste	30 gals.
Weight	6,650#	Hull	Modified-V
Clearance, Arch	8'6"	Deadrise Aft	17°

See Page 543 For Resale Values

Four Winns
Cadillac, MI
www.fourwinns.com

231-360-0827

Four Winns 278/285 Vista
2006–Current

Graceful sport express (called 278 Vista in 2006–09; V285 since 2010) delivers compelling blend of top-shelf construction, feature-rich accommodations. Topside highlights include deluxe cockpit seating, double-wide helm seat with flip-up bolsters, refreshment center with removable cooler. Luxury-class interior with cherry cabinets, top-shelf amenities is as good as it gets in a boat of this type. Note transom storage locker, sporty dash. Radar arch is a popular option. Single 375hp Volvo sterndrive tops out at 30+ knots.

Length	28'4"	Fuel	85 gals.
Beam	8'6"	Water	21 gals.
Draft, Up	1'8"	Waste	21 gals.
Draft, Down	3'3"	Hull Type	Modified-V
Weight	7,100#	Deadrise Aft	17°

See Page 543 For Resale Values

Four Winns
Cadillac, MI
www.fourwinns.com

Cruisers & Sportboats

231-360-0827

Four Winns 280 Horizon
2000–05

Family-size bowrider with generous 9'4" beam, top-of-the-line amenities combines sleek styling with sports-car handling. Highlights include roomy head compartment, wraparound rear seating, wet bar with Corian countertop, woodgrain dash, extended swim platform. Lots of standard equipment; impressive attention to detail. Engine compartment is a tight fit with twin engines. A fun boat to drive—deep-V hull can handles choppy water with ease. Twin 315hp Volvo I/Os deliver a top speed of 50+ mph.

Length w/Platform	27'9"	Fuel	130 gals.
Beam	9'4"	Water	12 gals.
Draft, Up	1'6"	Waste	12 gals.
Draft, Down	3'1"	Hull Type	Deep-V
Weight	7,140#	Deadrise Aft	21°

See Page 543 For Resale Values

Four Winns
Cadillac, MI
www.fourwinns.com

231-360-0827

Four Winns 285 Express
1991–93

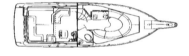

Affordable 1990s express made good on Four Winns promise of solid construction, common-sense cabin accommodations. Offered with choice of two mid-cabin layouts—standard (more popular) interior has wraparound dinette/V-berth with seating for six; alternate layout had separate dinette, double berth forward. Companion seat opposite helm rotates to face cockpit. Additional features include foldaway stern seat, good engine access, bow pulpit, swim ladder with handrail. Twin 230hp OMC I/Os top out at over 35 knots.

Length	28'11"	Headroom	6'2"
Beam	10'2"	Fuel	140 gals.
Draft	3'3"	Water	35 gals.
Weight	9,060#	Hull	Modified-V
Clearance	8'6"	Deadrise Aft	19°

Prices Not Provided for Pre-1995 Models

Four Winns
Cadillac, MI
www.fourwinns.com

231-360-0827

Four Winns 285 Sundowner
2000–05

Well-appointed sportcruiser with rakish styling offered impressive dayboat luxury, spirited open-water performance. Aft cockpit seating converts to sun pad; portside mini-galley includes refrigerator, sink, trash bin. Ergonomic helm with flip-up seat provides extra legroom for stand-up driving. Compact cuddy features enclosed head to port, microwave cabinet opposite, V-berth forward. Engine compartment is a tight fit. Note extended swim platform, power motor hatch. Twin 270hp Volvo I/Os top out at 50+ knots.

Length w/Platform	27'9"	Headroom	5'0"
Beam	9'4"	Max Headroom	4'7"
Draft, Up	1'6"	Fuel	130 gals.
Draft, Down	3'1"	Water	12 gals.
Weight	6,380#	Hull Type	Modified-V

See Page 543 For Resale Values

Four Winns
Cadillac, MI
www.fourwinns.com

231-360-0827

Four Winns 285 Vista
1988–90

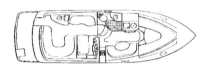

Standard 285 Floorplan

285 SE Floorplan

Vintage 1980s express paired sporty styling with versatile layout, sturdy construction. Relatively wide beam results in roomy interior with stand-up head, full galley, berths for four adults, two kids. Cockpit is arranged with an L-shaped lounge to port (that pivots fore and aft), bench seating aft. Circular foredeck hatches provide good cabin ventilation. Note that 285 SE model (introduced in 1990) has slightly revised interior, lower cost. Single 340hp sterndrive will cruise at 20 knots (about 30 knots top); twin 260hp I/Os run a few knots faster.

Length w/Pulpit	28'11"	Fuel	150 gals.
Hull Length	27'5"	Water	35 gals.
Beam	10'0"	Clearance	NA
Draft	2'9"	Hull Type	Modified-V
Weight	9,670#	Deadrise Aft	19°

Prices Not Provided for Pre-1995 Models

Four Winns
Cadillac, MI
www.fourwinns.com

231-360-0827

Four Winns 288 Vista
2004–09

Good-looking Four Winns cruiser strikes the right balance of comfort, price, performance. Expansive interior features upscale decor package with vinyl overheads, Ultraleather seating, high-gloss cherry cabinetry. Midcabin area is a tight fit, but head is large. Note that refrigerator is above galley counter for easy access. Topside highlights include power motor hatch, extended swim platform, cockpit refreshment center, freshwater shower, double helm seat with flip-up bolsters. Volvo 270hp I/Os top out at close to 40 knots.

Length w/Platform	30'0"	Fuel	120 gals.
Beam	9'8"	Water	25 gals.
Draft, Down	3'3"	Waste	25 gals.
Weight	10,380#	Hull Type	Modified-V
Clearance, Arch	9'0"	Deadrise Aft	18°

See Page 543 For Resale Values

Four Winns
Cadillac, MI
www.fourwinns.com

231-360-0827

Four Winns 298 Vista
1999–2005

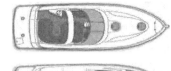

Feature-rich express paired signature Four Winns quality with deluxe accommodations, no-excuses performance. Roomy cockpit with U-shaped seating, double helm seat, refreshment center seats six to eight. Surprisingly spacious interior boasts comfortable salon, plenty of galley storage, top-quality furnishings. Good visibility from raised helm position. Transom locker provides storage for fenders, shore power connections. Note walkthrough windshield, bolt-on platform, flip-up helm seat. Volvo 270hp I/Os top out at close to 40 knots.

Length w/Platform	30'11"	Clearance, Arch	9'2"
Hull Length	28'0"	Fuel	140 gals.
Beam	10'6"	Water	31 gals.
Draft	3'3"	Hull Type	Modified-V
Weight	10,650#	Deadrise Aft	19°

See Page 543 For Resale Values

Four Winns
Cadillac, MI
www.fourwinns.com

Cruisers & Sportboats

231-360-0827

Four Winns 310 Horizon
2007–Current

Big-water dayboat with seating raised the bar for open-bow size, comfort, versatility. Spacious cockpit offers several seating options: aft sun pads convert into twin lounges; center walk-through passage can be filled with cushion and backrest. Enclosed head is fitted under starboard console; single berth is beneath portside console. Additional features include cockpit refreshment center, pop-up cleats, in-floor bow lockers, extended swim platform, flip-up helm seat. Twin MerCruiser 320hp I/Os (optional) top out at 40–42 knots.

Length	31'4"	Clearance	5'2"
Beam	9'8"	Fuel	130 gals.
Draft, Up	2'0"	Water	20 gals.
Draft, Down	2'11"	Hull Type	Deep-V
Weight	8,360#	Deadrise Aft	21°

See Page 543 For Resale Values

Four Winns
Cadillac, MI
www.fourwinns.com

231-360-0827

Four Winns 318/335 Vista
2006–Current

Spirited high-end express (called 318 Vista in 2006–09; V335 since 2010) is graceful, luxurious, built to last. Ergonomic helm is surrounded by spacious cockpit with U-shaped seating, portside lounger, refreshment center with sink, ice-maker. Expansive interior features roomy midcabin layout with table, pullout galley storage, cherrywood cabinetry, large head with shower. Screened companionway door is a plus, but steps are steep. Note transom locker for fenders, shore cord. Twin Volvo 280hp I/Os deliver a top speed of 38–40 knots.

Length w/Platform	33'0"	Clearance	11'2"
Beam	10'9"	Fuel	170 gals.
Draft, Up	1'6"	Water	35 gals.
Draft, Down	3'2"	Hull Type	Modified-V
Weight	11,200#	Deadrise Aft	19°

See Page 543 For Resale Values

Four Winns
Cadillac, MI
www.fourwinns.com

231-360-0827

Four Winns 315/325 Express
1988–93

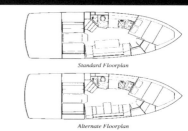

Standard Floorplan

Alternate Floorplan

Versatile express introduced in 1988 with sterndrive power (315 Express) was joined in 1991 with inboard-powered sibling, the 325 Express. Both shared identical midcabin interiors with double berths fore and aft, convertible dinette, full galley, compact head with shower. (Note that two dinette configurations were available.) Roomy cockpit seats six in comfort. Note fuel increase in 1991. Twin 260hp I/Os cruise 315 Express at 23 knots (about 35 knots top); 270hp inboards cruise the 325 at 18 knots (26–28 top).

Length w/Pulpit	30'6"	Max Headroom	6'3"
Beam	11'0"	Fuel	150/180 gals.
Draft	3'4"	Water	35 gals.
Weight	10,600#	Hull	Modified-V
Clearance	9'0"	Deadrise Aft	19°

Prices Not Provided for Pre-1995 Models

Four Winns
Cadillac, MI
www.fourwinns.com

231-360-0827

Four Winns 328 Vista
1999–2006

Rakish Four Winns cruiser struck an ideal balance between sleek styling, spacious cabin, versatile deck layout. Wide 11'9" beam affords plenty of cabin, cockpit space. Well-finished interior with tasteful decor, high-gloss cherry woodwork features home-size galley, convertible dinette, roomy head compartment. U-shaped cockpit lounge converts to big sun pad; refreshment center comes with ice-maker, sink. Note walk-through windshield, power engine compartment hatch. Volvo 280hp I/Os deliver a top speed of about 35 knots.

Length w/Platform	35'7"	Fuel	220 gals.
Hull Length	33'5"	Water	45 gals.
Beam	11'9"	Waste	30 gals.
Draft	3'2"	Hull Type	Modified-V
Weight	12,600#	Deadrise Aft	19°

See Page 543 For Resale Values

Four Winns
Cadillac, MI
www.fourwinns.com

231-360-0827

Four Winns 338/358 Vista
2007–Current

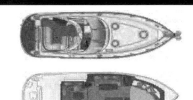

Sleek sportcruiser available with sterndrive (338 Vista) or inboard (358 Vista) power offers tough-to-beat mix of modern styling, swanky decor, good performance. Interior highlights include high-gloss cherry cabinets, 20" flat-screen TV, teak-and-holly galley sole, faux granite counters, leather upholstery. Bow access is via both side decks—which are very narrow—or walk-through windshield. Note hinged sport arch, power engineroom hatch. MerCruiser 300hp gas I/Os reach nearly 40 knots top. Twin 320hp inboards run a few knots slower.

Length	35'0"	Fuel	200 gals.
Beam	11'6"	Water	45 gals.
Draft, Up	2'6"	Waste	30 gals.
Draft, Down	3'4"	Hull Type	Modified-V
Weight	12,090#	Deadrise Aft	19°

See Page 543 For Resale Values

Four Winns
Cadillac, MI
www.fourwinns.com

231-360-0827

Four Winns 348 Vista
2001–04

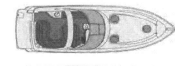

Top-level express (called 338 Vista in 2001) combines inboard dependability with appealing styling, upscale amenities. Well-finished interior with tasteful decor, high-gloss cherry woodwork features home-size galley, midcabin dinette, roomy head compartment. U-shaped cockpit lounge converts to sun pad. Note walk-through windshield, power engine hatch, transom locker, companionway screen door. Above-average fit and finish. MerCruiser 320hp inboards top out at close to 30 knots. Replaced in 2005 with all-new 348 Vista.

Length w/Platform	35'7"	Fuel	220 gals.
Beam	11'9"	Water	44 gals.
Draft	2'11"	Waste	30 gals.
Weight	13,100#	Hull Type	Modified-V
Clearance, Arch	9'2"	Deadrise Aft	19°

See Page 543 For Resale Values

Four Winns
Cadillac, MI
www.fourwinns.com

Four Winns 348/358/375 Vista
2005–Current

Updated version of earlier 348 Vista (2001–04) appeals to savvy buyers with an eye for quality. Posh midcabin interior offered with open floorplan or with stateroom bulkhead door for privacy. Topside highlights include sporty helm layout with space for electronics, double helm seat with flip-up bolsters, extended swim platform, transom storage locker, power engine hatch, wet bar with ice-maker. Inboard 320hp engines top out at 30 knots; 320hp I/Os reach about 35 knots. Called 348 Vista in 2005–07; V358 in 2008–09; V375 in 2010

Length w/Platform	37'0"	Fuel	230 gals.
Beam	12'0"	Water	51 gals.
Draft	3'4"	Waste	30 gals.
Weight	14,600#	Hull Type	Modified-V
Clearance	11'2"	Deadrise Aft	19°

See Page 544 For Resale Values

Four Winns
Cadillac, MI
www.fourwinns.com

---

www.powerboatguide.com   231-360-0827

Four Winns 365 Express
1991–94

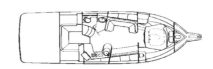

Maxi-volume express was queen of the Four Winns fleet in early 1990s. Spacious midcabin interior with U-shaped galley, convertible dinette offered waterjet spa beneath forward queen berth—a truly outrageous option. Note accordion privacy door between salon and forward stateroom. Standard features included foredeck storage lockers, tilt steering, side exhausts, cockpit wet bar, radar arch. Twin 350hp gas V-drive inboards cruise at 18–19 knots (about 28 knots top); optional 300hp Cummins diesels cruise at 20 knots (26 knots top).

Length w/Pulpit	36'0"	Fuel	315 gals.
Beam	13'2"	Water	98 gals.
Draft	3'2"	Headroom	6'4"
Weight	18,600#	Hull Type	Modified-V
Clearance	10'4"	Deadrise Aft	16°

Prices Not Provided for Pre-1995 Models

Four Winns
Cadillac, MI
www.fourwinns.com

---

www.powerboatguide.com   231-360-0827

Four Winns 378 Vista
2002–09

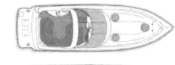

Luxury-class sportcruiser with roomy salon, huge cockpit is as good as it gets in a modern family express. Wide-open interior features expansive salon with two convertible sofas, well-appointed galley, elegant high-gloss cherry cabinetry. Bow-stateroom privacy door is optional. Cockpit—with huge wraparound settee and wet bar—is one of the largest offered in a boat this size. Bow anchor chute is better than a pulpit. Finish is well above average. Twin 375hp gas inboards cruise in the low 20s (30+ knots top).

Length w/Platform	41'3"	Fuel	300 gals.
Hull Length	37'9"	Water	66 gals.
Beam	12'9"	Waste	42 gals.
Draft	3'6"	Hull Type	Modified-V
Weight	21,300#	Deadrise Aft	19°

See Page 544 For Resale Values

Four Winns
Cadillac, MI
www.fourwinns.com

www.powerboatguide.com   231-360-0827

Four Winns V458
2008–Current

All-weather express with IPS drives couples spirited performance with sporty styling, executive-level comforts. Topside highlights include hardtop with triple skylights, wide-open cockpit layout with seating for ten, huge extended swim platform. Well-finished interior boasts two private staterooms, two heads, big home-size galley. Aft deck rises for engine access. Cockpit AC is standard. Note narrow side decks. Joystick control system makes handling easy. Cruise efficiently at 25 knots (low 30s top) with 435hp Volvo IPS diesel inboards.

Length w/Platform	49'4"	Fuel	380 gals.
Hull Length	44'6"	Water	101 gals.
Beam	14'0"	Waste	57 gals.
Draft	3'7"	Hull Type	Modified Deep-V
Weight	30,000#	Deadrise Aft	19°

See Page 544 For Resale Values

Four Winns
Cadillac, MI
www.fourwinns.com

---

www.powerboatguide.com   231-360-0827

Grand Banks 38 Eastbay Express
1994–2004

Standard Floorplan

Optional Layout

Original Eastbay model introduced in 1994 combined traditional Downeast styling with deep-V performance, meticulous finish. Expansive teak interior with top-quality furnishings is elegant, ultimately practical for a small family. Helm visibility is excellent. Large cockpit has built-in seating. Teak swim platform, radar mast, foredeck storage lockers were standard. Hardtop model became available in 2002. Note excellent engine access. Cat 300hp diesels cruise at 20 knots (mid 20s top); 375hp Cats cruise at 23 knots (high 20s top). Over 130 built.

Length Overall	38'0"	Fuel	344 gals.
Length WL	34'5"	Water	95 gals.
Beam	13'2"	Clearance	9'3"
Draft	3'4"	Hull Type	Deep-V
Weight	28,500#	Deadrise Aft	18°

See Page 545 For Resale Values

Grand Banks Yachts
Seattle, WA
www.grandbanks.com

---

www.powerboatguide.com   231-360-0827

Grand Banks 39 Eastbay SX/HX
2006–Current

SX Layout

HX Layout

Graceful hardtop cruiser—successor to the original 38 Express that launched the Eastbay series—blends classic Downeast beauty with exceptional performance, unsurpassed luxury. Deluxe single-stateroom interior is perfect for the cruising couple. Expansive, teak-laid cockpit has built-in seating, large lazarette. Note frameless windows, immaculate engineroom, wide side decks. SX model has fully-enclosed salon; HX version has semi-enclosed helmdeck. Yanmar 480hp diesels cruise at 24–26 knots (about 30 knots top).

Length w/Platform	42'4"	Fuel	352 gals.
Hull Length	39'2"	Water	100 gals.
Beam	13'3"	Waste	28 gals.
Draft	3'4"	Hull Type	Deep-V
Weight	28,494#	Deadrise Aft	18°

See Page 545 For Resale Values

Grand Banks Yachts
Seattle, WA
www.grandbanks.com

Cruisers & Sportboats

www.powerboatguide.com

231-360-0827

Grand Banks 43 Eastbay Flybridge
1998–2004

Standard Floorplan

Optional Layout

Gold-plated flybridge yacht (called Eastbay 40 until 1998 when cockpit was lengthened) with timeless Downeast styling delivers impressive blend of luxury, craftsmanship, performance. Elegant two-stateroom interior with lower helm, deluxe galley, features hand-crafted teak cabinetry, top-quality hardware and furnishings. Spacious cockpit with transom door can entertain a small crowd. Note wide side decks. Twin 300hp Cat diesels cruise at 18–20 knots (about 22 knots top); 375hp Cats cruise at 22–24 knots (high 20s top).

Length	43'0"	Fuel	450 gals.
Beam	13'4"	Water	110 gals.
Draft	3'8"	Headroom	6'6"
Weight	31,970#	Hull Type	Deep-V
Clearance	16'6"	Deadrise Aft	18°

See Page 545 For Resale Values

Grand Banks Yachts
Seattle, WA
www.grandbanks.com

---

www.powerboatguide.com

231-360-0827

Grand Banks 43 Eastbay Express
2000–04

Standard Layout

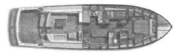

Optional Layout

Classic open express delivers sophisticated blend of style, comfort, performance. Lavish two-stateroom interior with hand-rubbed teak woodwork, leather seating is impressive display of old-world nautical elegance. Highlights include spacious helmdeck with facing settees, large cockpit, teak decking, Corian galley counters. Modified-V hull has prop pockets to reduce draft, shaft angles. Hardtop model became available in 2002. Standard 435hp Cats cruise at 24 knots with a top speed of 27–28 knots. Not cheap, but quality never is.

Length	43'0"	Fuel	450 gals.
Beam	13"2"	Water	110 gals.
Draft	3'8"	Headroom	6'4"
Weight	33,000#	Hull Type	Modified-V
Clearance	16'6"	Deadrise Aft	14°

See Page 545 For Resale Values

Grand Banks Yachts
Seattle, WA
www.grandbanks.com

---

www.powerboatguide.com

231-360-0827

Grand Banks 43 Eastbay SX/HX
2002–2007

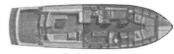

Standard HX Layout

Alternate HX Layout

Hardtop cruising yacht with semi-enclosed helm combines classic Downeast styling, meticulous finish, seakindly hull. Two-stateroom interior with hand-rubbed teak woodwork, leather seating is an impressive display of boatbuilding excellence. Highlights include spacious helmdeck with facing settees, teak-laid cockpit, wide side decks, roomy engine compartment. SX model has fully enclosed helm. Prop pockets to reduce draft, shaft angles. Twin 440hp Yanmar diesels cruise at 25 knots (28–29 knots top).

Length Overall	43'0"	Clearance, Mast	14'0"
Length WL	39.5"	Fuel	450 gals.
Beam	13'2"	Water	110 gals.
Draft	3'7"	Hull Type	Modified-V
Weight	29,760#	Deadrise Aft	14°

See Page 545 For Resale Values

Grand Banks Yachts
Seattle, WA
www.grandbanks.com

231-360-0827

Grand Banks 49 Eastbay SX/HX
1999–Current

SX Layout

HX Layout

Versatile hardtop express combines comfort, style with traditional Grand Banks quality. Rich two-stateroom, two-head interior with home-size galley, huge master stateroom is long on luxury, short on salon space. SX model has fully-enclosed salon; HX version has semi-enclosed helm. Note wide side decks, power-assisted center windshield panel, spacious engineroom. Exemplary fit and finish. Deep-V hull delivers superb big-water performance. Cruise at 25–26 knots (30 top) with 670hp Cat diesels.

Length Overall	54'7"	Clearance	NA
Length WL	45'8"	Fuel	775 gals.
Beam	16'0"	Water	176 gals.
Draft	4'4"	Hull Type	Deep-V
Weight	48,000#	Deadrise Aft	18°

Insufficient Resale Data To Assign Values

Grand Banks Yachts
Seattle, WA
www.grandbanks.com

231-360-0827

Grand Banks 54 Eastbay SX
2003–06

Standard 2-Stateroom Plan

Optional 3-Stateroom Plan

Exquisitely detailed hardtop cruiser with enclosed helm/salon combines classic Downeast styling with sumptuous accommodations, agile performance. Standard galley-down, two-stateroom floorplan is notable for spacious staterooms, huge galley; optional three-cabin layout has deckhouse galley. Office area with desk, washer/dryer is standard in either layout. Cockpit has built-in seating, teak sole, engineroom access. Outstanding finish, near perfect gelcoat. Cat 800hp diesels cruise in the mid 20s (28–29 knots top).

Length Overall	53'9"	Clearance	16'3"
Length WL	49'6"	Fuel	935 gals.
Beam	16'0"	Water	200 gals.
Draft	4'4"	Hull Type	Deep-V
Weight	56,500#	Deadrise Aft	18°

Insufficient Resale Data To Assign Values

Grand Banks Yachts
Seattle, WA
www.grandbanks.com

231-360-0827

Hatteras 36 Convertible
1983–87

Single Stateroom, Galley Down

Twin Staterooms, Galley Up

Polished 1980s convertible with wide 13'7" beam, efficient prop-pocket hull is more family cruiser than hard-nosed fishboat. Deluxe interior with spacious salon, solid teak cabinets was available with one or two staterooms. Highlights include wraparound salon windows, wide side decks, transom door, molded bow pulpit, roomy flybridge with seating for five. Hatches in cockpit sole provide access to generator. Well-appointed boat has aged well. Standard gas engines cruise at 14–16 knots; 390hp GM diesels cruise at 20 knots.

Length	36'6"	Fuel	355 gals.
Beam	13'7"	Water	115 gals.
Draft	3'9"	Waste	40 gals.
Weight	26,500#	Hull Type	Modified-V
Clearance	12'6"	Deadrise Aft	18°

Prices Not Provided for Pre-1995 Models

Hatteras Yachts
New Bern, NC
www.hatterasyachts.com

Cruisers & Sportboats

Hatteras 36 Sedan
1986–87

www.powerboatguide.com 231-360-0827

Classy sport sedan with very expansive interior but too-small cockpit is more family cruiser than hard-core fishing machine. Very well-appointed interior (by 1980s standards) with wide-open salon was offered with choice of dinette or second stateroom. Features include large head compartment with separate stall shower, teak interior cabinetry, large cabin windows, bow pulpit, wide side decks. Tiny cockpit is practically useless for serious fishing activities. Prop pockets reduce draft. Twin gas engines cruise at 15 knots (mid 20s top).

Single-Stateroom Floorplan

Twin-Stateroom Floorplan

Length	36'6"	Fuel	355 gals.
Beam	13'7"	Water	115 gals.
Draft	3'9"	Cockpit	72 sq. ft.
Weight	25,500#	Hull Type	Modified-V
Clearance	12'6"	Deadrise Aft	18°

Prices Not Provided for Pre-1995 Models

Hatteras Yachts
New Bern, NC
www.hatterasyachts.com

Hatteras 39 Sport Express
1995–98

www.powerboatguide.com 231-360-0827

Graceful big-water express delivers quality Hatteras construction, versatile layout, solid performance. Spacious cockpit came standard with in-deck fishbox, bait-prep station with sink, livewell, transom door, direct engineroom access. Small-but-elegant interior boasts full galley, convertible dinette, head with stall shower, teak or oak woodwork. Spacious bridgedeck came with several seating options. Offered in Cruiser or Sportfish versions. Twin 435hp Cats cruise at 22 knots; 465hp Detroit 6-71s cruise in the mid 20s.

Std. Layout, L-shaped Seating

Curved Bridgedeck Seating

Length	39'0"	Fuel	458 gals.
Beam	13'7"	Water	120 gals.
Draft	4'8"	Waste	50 gals.
Weight	30,500#	Hull Type	Modified-V
Clearance	8'10"	Deadrise Aft	9°

See Page 546 For Resale Values

Hatteras Yachts
New Bern, NC
www.hatterasyachts.com

Hatteras 43 Sport Express
1996–98

www.powerboatguide.com 231-360-0827

Powerful offshore express—among largest in her class in late 1990s—was stylish, fast, expensive. Standard interior with U-shaped galley, stall shower in head sleeps four; alternate layout with smaller head and galley sleeps six. Rigging station, lift-out fishboxes, livewell were standard. Aft-facing bench seat in cockpit lifts for engineroom access. Additional features include light oak interior woodwork, radar arch, side exhausts, bow pulpit. First-rate finish throughout. Twin 535hp GM diesels cruise at 27 knots (30+ knots top).

Standard Layout

Optional Arrangement

Length	43'2"	Fuel	530 gals.
Beam	14'3"	Water	154 gals.
Draft	4'5"	Headroom	6'6"
Weight	38,000#	Hull Type	Modified-V
Clearance	9'8"	Deadrise Aft	9°

See Page 546 For Resale Values

Hatteras Yachts
New Bern, NC
www.hatterasyachts.com

231-360-0827

Hinckley T29C
2002–Current

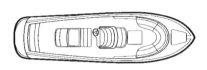

Jet-powered center console with tons of eye appeal gets high marks for versatile deck layout, flawless craftsmanship. Composite Kevlar-reinforced construction is state of the art. Highlights include cockpit seating for eight, console head compartment, power-lift engine box, joystick steering, bow thruster. Varnished teak helm is gorgeous. Note shallow draft. Lightweight hull delivers superb open-water ride. Single Yanmar 440hp diesel will cruise in the high 20s (30+ knots top). Did we say expensive?

Length Overall	29'2"	Clearance	5'3"
Length WL	26'8"	Fuel	100 gals.
Beam	9'1"	Water	20 gals.
Draft	1'6"	Hull	Modified-V
Weight	7,500#	Deadrise Aft	18°

Insufficient Resale Data To Assign Values

Hinckley Yachts
Southwest Harbor, ME
www.hinckleyyachts.com

231-360-0827

Hinckley T29R
2003–Current

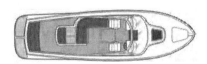

Expensive retro-runabout with jet-drive power stops traffic everywhere she goes. Composite Kevlar-reinforced construction is state of the art. Cockpit—with teak console, custom Nardi wheel—resembles a classic sports car. Engine box doubles as aft-facing passenger seat, conceals sink and cooler. Cuddy is fitted with V-berth, VacuFlush head. Additional features include power engine box, joystick steering, teak swim platform, bow thruster. Meticulous finish. Single Yanmar 440hp diesel will cruise in the high 20s (30+ knots top).

Length Overall	29'2"	Clearance	5'6"
Length WL	26'8"	Fuel	100 gals.
Beam	9'1"	Water	20 gals.
Draft	1'6"	Hull	Modified-V
Weight	7,500#	Deadrise Aft	18°

Insufficient Resale Data To Assign Values

Hinckley Yachts
Southwest Harbor, ME
www.hinckleyyachts.com

231-360-0827

Hinckley 36 Picnic Boat
1994–2007

Standard Version

Extended Pilothouse Version

Classic jet-powered weekender with Downeast profile is elegant, expensive, built to last. Comfortable cockpit layout (engine box doubles as seat or table), semi-enclosed helm, deluxe mahogany interior with compact galley, large head compartment. Truly outstanding fit and finish. Extended pilothouse model with additional seating came out in 2001. Over 360 built. Replaced in 2008 with all-new 36 Picnic Boat. Cruise at 20 knots with 350hp Yanmar diesel; 22-23 knots with 440hp Yanmar.

Length Overall	36'5"	Fuel	160 gals.
Length WL	33'7"	Water	35 gals.
Beam	10'0"	Clearance	11'4"
Draft	1'6"	Hull	Modified-V
Weight	11,850#	Deadrise Aft	15°

See Page 546 For Resale Values

Hinckley Yachts
Southwest Harbor, ME
www.hinckleyyachts.com

Cruisers & Sportboats

Hinckley Talaria 40
2002–Current

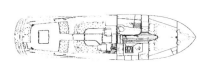

Polished jet-powered cruiser with distinctive Downeast profile bears strong resemblance to Hinckley's great-selling 36 Picnic Boat. Fully cored, shallow-draft hull is notable for high-tech construction, generous transom tumblehome. Elegant cockpit with extended hardtop features weather-protected seating and helm. Note feature-rich interior with teak-and-holly sole. Aft-facing cockpit settees lift electrically for engine access. Yanmar 440hp diesels matched to Hamilton waterjets cruise at 28 knots (32–33 knots top).

Length Overall	40'1"	Clearance	8 7"
Length WL	37'1"	Fuel	340 gals.
Beam	12'5"	Water	80 gals.
Draft	2'2"	Hull Type	Modified-V
Weight	26,000#	Deadrise Aft	16°

Insufficient Resale Data To Assign Values

Hinckley Yachts
Southwest Harbor, ME
www.hinckleyyachts.com

Hinckley Talaria 42
1990–98

Single-Stateroom Floorplan

2-Stateroom Layout

Elegant Downeast cruiser from one of America's best builders boasts meticulous workmanship, top-quality construction. Offered with single-stateroom, galley-down layout or two-stateroom interior with salon galley—both with standard lower helm. Note beautiful teak interior. Underwater exhaust system, teak cockpit sole, radar mast were standard. Deep keel protects running gear in event of grounding. Single 435hp Cat—or 520hp MAN—will cruise at 16–17 knots (20+ knots wide open). Total of 17 were built.

Length Overall	41'9"	Fuel	400 gals.
Length WL	38'7"	Water	110 gals.
Beam	13'8"	Clearance	12'6"
Draft	4'4"	Hull	Semi-Disp.
Weight	22,000#	Deadrise Aft	5°

Insufficient Resale Data To Assign Values

Hinckley Yachts
Southwest Harbor, ME
www.hinckleyyachts.com

Hinckley Talaria 44
1999–Current

Single-Stateroom Floorplan

2-Stateroom Layout

Stately jet-powered cruiser personifies Hinckley commitment to design, engineering excellence. Highlights include semi-enclosed pilothouse with facing settees, varnished teak interior with choice of one or two staterooms, wide side decks (but no bow rails). Extended hardtop protects much of the cockpit; aft-facing seats hinge forward for easy engine access. Waterjet drives can safely cruise in very shallow water. JetStick control system makes docking easy. Yanmar 440hp diesels cruise at 25–26 knots (30+ knots top).

Length Overall	44'10"	Fuel	500 gals.
Length WL	41'0"	Water	100 gals.
Beam	13'6"	Max Headroom	6'6"
Draft	2'3"	Hull	Modified-V
Weight	29,000#	Deadrise Aft	16.5°

Insufficient Resale Data To Assign Values

Hinckley Yachts
Southwest Harbor, ME
www.hinckleyyachts.com

Hinckley Talaria 44 Flybridge
2003–Current

Top-shelf flybridge yacht combines sensual Downeast styling, meticulous workmanship, jet-power propulsion. Choice of single- or twin-stateroom interiors. Visibility from enclosed lower helm is excellent in all directions. Spacious cockpit includes built-in seating for several guests, centerline transom door. Note elegant teak-and-holly cabin sole. Waterjet drives cruise safely in shallow water. JetStick control system makes docking easy. Yanmar 440hp diesels cruise at 25–26 knots (30 knots top).

Length Overall	44'10"	Fuel	500 gals.
Length WL	41'0"	Water	100 gals.
Beam	13'6"	Max Headroom	6'6"
Draft	2'4"	Hull	Modified-V
Weight	29,000#	Deadrise Aft	16.5°

Insufficient Resale Data To Assign Values

Hinckley Yachts
Southwest Harbor, ME
www.hinckleyyachts.com

Hunt 29 Surfhunter
2004–Current

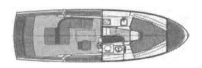

Top-quality express with deep-V hull, jackshaft power gets high marks for workmanship, comfort, performance. Basically a dayboat—large cockpit results in fairly compact interior more suitable for overnight stays than extended cruising. Tall windshield provides excellent driver protection; single-level cockpit with engine box, L-shaped lounge seats six. Upscale cabin features full galley, enclosed head, V-berth/dinette. Note classy teak-and-holly cabin sole. Single Volvo 310hp diesel I/O tops out at about 30 knots.

Length	29'6"	Fuel	150 gals.
Beam	10'6"	Water	31 gals.
Draft	3'0"	Headroom	5'8"
Weight	7,500#	Hull Type	Deep-V
Clearance	5'9"	Deadrise Aft	22°

See Page 546 For Resale Values

Hunt Yachts
South Dartmouth, MA
www.huntyachts.com

Hunt 33 Express
1999–2004

Feature-rich cruising yacht with enduring lines offers luxurious—but not glitzy—accommodations, top-shelf construction. Available in express, hardtop sedan (pictured above) versions. Features include fully cored hull with propeller tunnel, large cockpit, underwater exhaust system. Upscale interior boasts varnished mahogany trim, teak-and-holly sole. Note flawless gelcoat. Bridgedeck lifts electrically for engine access. Single 370hp Cummins diesel will cruise at 24–25 knots; Yanmar 440hp cruises at 26–28 knots.

Length	32'9"	Fuel	125 gals.
Beam	10'10"	Water	30 gals.
Draft	3'0"	Headroom	6'1"
Weight	10,000#	Hull Type	Deep-V
Clearance	15'0"	Deadrise Aft	20°

See Page 546 For Resale Values

Hunt Yachts
South Dartmouth, MA
www.huntyachts.com

Cruisers & Sportboats

www.powerboatguide.com   231-360-0827

Hunt 33 Surfhunter
2005–Current

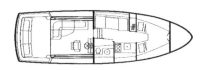

Elegant deep-V express offers extraordinary comfort for the cruising couple. Highlights include beautifully finished cabin with varnished teak joinery, roomy cockpit with removable transom seating, 7-foot-long bridgedeck with L-shaped settee. Entire bridgedeck lifts for excellent engine access. Note standard bow thruster, tall windshield with side vents, deep chain locker. Exemplary workmanship, flawless gelcoat justifies high price. Cruising speed of 22 knots (about 28 top) with single 380hp Cummins diesel is remarkable.

Length	33'0"	Headroom	6'2"
Beam	11'4"	Fuel	125 gals.
Draft	3'0"	Water	28 gals.
Weight	10,700#	Hull Type	Deep-V
Clearance	NA	Deadrise Aft	20°

See Page 546 For Resale Values

Hunt Yachts
South Dartmouth, MA
www.huntyachts.com

---

www.powerboatguide.com   231-360-0827

Hunt 36 Harrier
2003–Current

Gold-plated express delivers acclaimed blend of rich styling, superb build quality, impressive big-water performance. Elegant open-plan interior with full galley, large head boasts varnished cherry cabinetry, classy teak-and-holly sole. Bridgedeck settee extends by lowering forward passenger seat; cockpit can be left open for fishing or fitted with extra seating for cruising. Fully cored deep-V hull with slender beam is designed to handle seriously rough water. Yanmar 370hp diesels cruise at 30 knots (about 35 knots top).

Length	36'6"	Fuel	250 gals.
Beam	11'0"	Water	50 gals.
Draft	3'0"	Waste	20 gals.
Weight	13,500#	Hull Type	Deep-V
Clearance	8'0"	Deadrise Aft	22°

See Page 546 For Resale Values

Hunt Yachts
South Dartmouth, MA
www.huntyachts.com

---

www.powerboatguide.com   231-360-0827

Hylas 47 Convertible
1987–93

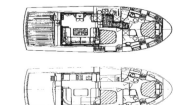

Taiwan import with a rakish lines combines very wide beam with seakindly hull, family-friendly layout. Hull was drawn by Jim Wynne, features balsa-cored hullsides, prop pockets, plenty of freeboard all around. The interior is very spacious thanks to broad beam. One of the few boats her size to have walkaround queens in both staterooms. (Three-stateroom layout was optional.) Both heads have separate stall showers. High cockpit gunwales are not well-suited to fishing. Note cockpit engine room access door. Twin 450-hp 6-71 diesels cruise in the low 20s, optional 550-hp 6V92s cruise at 24–25 knots.

Length	46'6"	Fuel	600 gals.
Beam	16'9"	Water	160 gals.
Draft	3'10"	Waste	50 gals.
Weight	38,000#	Hull Type	Modified-V
Clearance	13'4"	Deadrise Aft	14°

See Page XXX For Resale Values

Hylas models (built by Queen Long Marine) are no longer produced.

Intrepid 310 Walkaround
2005–Current

Sophisticated sport express with agile stepped hull, sociable deck layout takes Intrepid innovation to the next level. Bow pulpit, insulated fishbox, transom door, trim tabs are standard; everything else is optional including removable rear bench seat, Intrepid's signature hullside dive door. L-shaped lounge forward of helm seats three. Posh cabin with near standing headroom boasts full galley, wraparound seating, stand-up head with shower. More luxury cruiser than fishboat. Yamaha 250s reach 45+ knots top.

Length w/Pulpit	32'8"	Fuel	180 gals.
Hull Length	31'0"	Water	30 gals.
Beam	9'8"	Max HP	600
Hull Draft	2'0"	Hull Type	Deep-V
Weight	9,000#	Deadrise Aft	22.5°

See Page 547 For Resale Values

Intrepid Powerboats
Dania, FL
www.intrepidboats.com

Island Gypsy 44 Motor Cruiser
1983–96

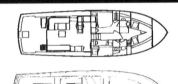

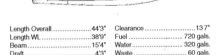

Sporty sedan cruiser delivers compelling mix of solid construction, excellent range, comfortable accommodations. Three-stateroom interior (most 44-footers have two) includes amidships master, roomy salon with galley forward, lower helm with deck access door. Unique fold-down stairwell in bridge coaming makes foredeck access easy. Flybridge layout with seating forward, helm aft is unusual. Note teak decks, cockpit transom door. Cruise at 12 knots with twin 275hp diesels; 16–17 knots with 375hp Cats.

Length Overall	44'3"	Clearance	13'7"
Length WL	38'9"	Fuel	720 gals.
Beam	15'4"	Water	320 gals.
Draft	4'3"	Waste	60 gals.
Weight	38,500#	Hull Type	Semi-Disp.

See Page 548 For Resale Values

Island Gypsy/Halvorsen Marine
Kowloon, Hong Kong
www.yardway.com.hk/marine

Legacy 28 Express
1999–2006

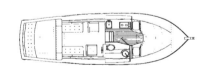

Premium New England express combines traditional styling, stem-to-stern quality, elegant practicality. Generous 9'6" beam permits roomy cabin with complete galley, enclosed head with shower, berths for two. Notable features include full-width transom seat, underwater exhaust system, well-arranged helm console, wide side decks. Tall windshield offers excellent wind, spray protection. Low-deadrise hull isn't the softest ride in rough water. Single Yanmar 315hp diesel will cruise at 22–24 knots (high 20s top).

Length	28'0"	Water	30 gals.
Beam	9'6"	Waste	25 gals.
Draft	2'2"	Headroom	6'0"
Weight	6,500	Hull Type	Modified-V
Fuel	120 gals.	Deadrise Aft	5°

See Page 548 For Resale Values

Legacy Yachts
Middletown, RI
www.legacyyachts.com

Cruisers & Sportboats

Legacy 32 Express
2007–08

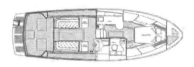

Beamy 32-footer with polished profile offers dayboat luxury, comfort at its best. Extended semi-enclosed bridge deck with large windows, facing settees can entertain several guests. (Note that helm and companion seats can be electrically lowered to extend settees.) High-gloss cherry cabin with leather seating, teak-and-holly sole has the feel of a custom yacht. Additional features include underwater exhaust system, cockpit seating, wide side decks, spacious engineroom. Cruise efficiently at 16 knots (22 top) with single 380hp Cummins diesel.

Length	32'6"	Fuel	200 gals.
Beam	12'4"	Water	60 gals.
Draft	3'10"	Waste	35 gals.
Weight	14,500#	Hull Type	Modified-V
Clearance	NA	Deadrise Aft	NA

Insufficient Resale Data To Assign Values

**Legacy Yachts
Middletown, RI
www.legacyyachts.com**

Legacy 34 Express
1996–2006

Quality Downeast cruiser delivers leading-edge comfort, elegance in a 34-foot boat. Versatile cockpit is large enough for fishing or entertaining; well-appointed interior with mahogany cabinetry, teak-and-holly sole drips luxury. Note wide side decks, excellent helm visibility. Fully cored hull has short keel for directional stability and—in single-screw version—prop, rudder protection. Engineroom is tight with twin engines. Cruise at 16–18 knots with single 440hp Cummins diesel; mid 20s with twin 440hp Cummins.

Length	34'0"	Water	94 gals.
Beam	12.5"	Waste	35 gals.
Draft	3'6"	Headroom	6.5"
Weight	15,800#	Hull Type	Modified-V
Fuel	251 gals.	Deadrise Aft	17°

See Page 549 For Resale Values

**Legacy Yachts
Middletown, RI
www.legacyyachts.com**

Legacy 34 Sedan
1997–2006

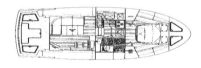

Traditional hardtop cruiser with Downeast profile sets high standards for luxury, craftsmanship. Upscale interior features spacious master stateroom, head with stall shower, varnished teak-and-holly cabin sole. Large ports, generous storage are a plus. Roomy pilothouse seats several guests in comfort. Note wide side decks, excellent helm visibility. Short keel offers prop, rudder protection in single-screw models. Cruise at 16–18 knots with single 440hp Cummins diesel; mid 20s with twin 440hp Cummins.

Length	34'0"	Fuel	251 gals.
Beam	12.5"	Water	94 gals.
Draft	3'6"	Waste	35 gals.
Weight	17,500#	Hull Type	Modified-V
Clearance	NA	Deadrise Aft	17°

See Page 549 For Resale Values

**Legacy Yachts
Middletown, RI
www.legacyyachts.com**

Legacy 40 Express
1995–2006

Seductive Downeast yacht enjoys a gold-plated reputation for quality construction, seakindly ride, luxury-class amenities. Finely crafted interior with semi-enclosed deckhouse, modest salon is well-finished, tasteful, comfortable. Stateroom is roomier than expected. Large windows provide outstanding 360° helm visibility. Wide side decks are a plus. Easily-driven hull delivers a great ride. Cruise at 16-18 knots with single 440hp Yanmar diesel; low 20s with twin 370hp Cummins diesels.

Length Overall	39'4"	Fuel	410 gals.
Length WL	36'0"	Water	120 gals.
Beam	13'7"	Waste	40 gals.
Draft	3'8"	Hull Type	Modified-V
Weight	22,000#	Deadrise Aft	17°

Insufficient Resale Data To Assign Values

Legacy Yachts
Middletown, RI
www.legacyyachts.com

Legacy 40 Sedan
1995–2006

Handsome sedan cruiser introduced in 1995 was Legacy's first-ever powerboat model. Luxurious galley-down, two-stateroom floorplan boasts comfortable pilothouse/salon area with L-shaped settee, teak-and-holly sole, deck access doors. Wide side decks make getting around easy. Note attractive teak exterior trim. Shallow keel protects running gear in single-engine installations. Single 420hp Cat diesel will cruise at 17–18 knots; twin 370hp Cummins cruise at 22–23 knots. Flybridge was optional.

Length Overall	39'4"	Fuel	410 gals.
Length WL	36'0"	Water	120 gals.
Beam	13'7"	Waste	40 gals.
Draft	3'8"	Hull Type	Modified-V
Weight	22,000#	Deadrise Aft	17°

Insufficient Resale Data To Assign Values

Legacy Yachts
Middletown, RI
www.legacyyachts.com

Luhrs 3400 Motor Yacht
1990–92

Versatile family cruiser from early-1990s was a departure from Luhr's fishing-boat tradition. Single-stateroom interior features expansive salon wide open to U-shaped dinette to port, mid-level galley opposite. Note split head/shower compartments, oak parquet galley floor, numerous storage bins. Cockpit is too small for much fishing. Huge flybridge has convenient walk-through passage to foredeck. Swim platform, bow pulpit were standard. Standard 320hp gas inboards cruise at 16 knots and reach 26–27 knots wide open.

Length	34'0"	Fuel	300 gals.
Beam	12'6"	Water	60 gals.
Draft	3'2"	Headroom	6'3"
Weight	13,500#	Hull Type	Modified-V
Clearance	22'0"	Deadrise Aft	16°

See Page XXX For Resale Values

Luhrs Corporation
St. Augustine, FL
www.luhrs.com

Luhrs 3420 Motor Yacht
1991–93

Durable flybridge sedan from early 1990s gets high marks for well-planned accommodations, roomy cockpit. Expansive single-stateroom interior includes built-in dinette, big U-shaped galley, generous storage. Note split head/shower compartments, hardwood galley floor. Uncluttered cockpit—without transom door or fishboxes—is big enough for two anglers. Baitwell is inconveniently located on swim platform. Radar arch, bow pulpit, swim platform were standard. Twin 340hp gas engines cruise at 16–17 knots (mid 20s top).

Length	34'0"	Fuel	300 gals.
Beam	12'6"	Water	60 gals.
Draft	3'2"	Headroom	6'2"
Weight	13,500#	Hull Type	Modified-V
Clearance	22'0"	Deadrise Aft	15°

Prices Not Provided for Pre-1995 Models

Luhrs Corporation
St. Augustine, FL
www.luhrs.com

Luhrs 35 Alura
1987–89

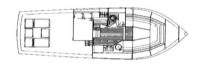

Distinctive 1980s express impressed savvy buyers with an eye for versatility, value. Spacious cockpit with bait-prep center, in-deck fishbox has room for several anglers without bumping elbows. Simple interior with standing headroom boasts private aft stateroom, stand-up shower, teak-and-holly cabin sole. Tall windshield offers good wind, spray protection. Swim platform was standard, but transom door wasn't. Note wide side decks, bow pulpit. Twin 270hp gas inboards cruise at 16–17 knots with a top speed in the mid 20s.

Length	35'5"	Fuel	260 gals.
Beam	12'2"	Water	55 gals.
Draft	2'11"	Headroom	6'2"
Weight	12,800#	Hull Type	Modified-V
Clearance	NA	Deadrise Aft	15°

Prices Not Provided for Pre-1995 Models

Luhrs Corporation
St. Augustine, FL
www.luhrs.com

Mainship 30 Pilot Express
1998–2007

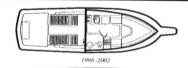

1998–2002

2003–Current

Best-selling diesel express with handsome Downeast styling makes good on promise of economical operation, common-sense accommodations. Compact cabin with U-shaped settee, full galley, stand-up head with shower sleeps two. Updated Pilot II model (introduced in 2003) boasts revised cabin layout with folding V-berth, shortened keel, prop pocket. Note good engine access, tall windshield, wide decks. Early models with 170hp Yanmar cruise at 13–14 knots; Pilot II models with 315hp Yanmar cruise at 16–18 knots.

Length w/Pulpit	33'1"	Weight	10,000#
Hull Length	30'0"	Fuel	175 gals.
Beam	10'3"	Water	40 gals.
Draft, Original Hull	2'11"	Waste	13 gals.
Draft, Series II	2'3"	Hull Type	Semi-Disp.

See Page 550 For Resale Values

Mainship Corporation
Midway, GA
www.mainship.com

231-360-0827

Mainship 30 Pilot Sedan
2000–07

1998–2002

2003–Current

Hardtop version of popular Mainship 30 Express combines semi-enclosed helm with roomy cockpit, efficient cabin layout. Well-appointed interior with U-shaped settee, full galley, stand-up head with shower sleeps two. Updated Pilot II model (introduced in 2003) boasts revised interior plan with folding V-berth, shortened keel section, hull prop pocket. Note good engine access, tall windshield, wide side decks. Early models with 170hp Yanmar cruise at 13–14 knots; Pilot II models with 315hp Yanmar cruise at 16–18 knots.

Length w/Pulpit	33'1"	Weight	11,000#
Hull Length	30'0"	Fuel	175 gals.
Beam	10'3"	Water	40 gals.
Draft, Original Hull	2'11"	Waste	13 gals.
Draft, Series II	2'3"	Hull Type	Semi-Disp.

See Page 550 For Resale Values

Mainship Corporation
Midway, GA
www.mainship.com

231-360-0827

Mainship 30 Sedan
1981–83

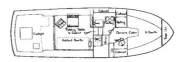

Downsized version of original Mainship 34 (1978–83) incorporated the virtues of her larger sistership in a smaller, less expensive package. Space-efficient interior with teak trim, standard lower helm includes convertible salon sofa, compact galley, enclosed head with separate stall shower. (Note that early models had foldaway "Pullman" berth that stowed inside starboard wall locker. Flybridge seats three with the helm to port. Large engineroom is a plus. Single 124hp Volvo diesel will cruise efficiently at 8–10 knots.

Length	30'0"	Headroom	6'4"
Beam	10'3"	Fuel	150 gals.
Draft	2'3"	Water	40 gals.
Weight	9,300#	Waste	25 gals.
Clearance	11'2"	Hull Type	Semi-Disp.

Prices Not Provided for Pre-1995 Models

Mainship Corporation
Midway, GA
www.mainship.com

231-360-0827

Mainship 31 Pilot
2008–Current

All-weather hardtop cruiser balances versatile cockpit design with solid construction, low-cost operation. Cherrywood interior with cherry-planked sole includes convertible sofa (expandable into full-size upper/lower berths), queen size island berth, roomy head. Semi-enclosed helm with large side windows provides good helm visibility. Transom door, bow thruster are standard. Wide side decks are a plus. Note open-air galley with electric grill. Exceptional engine access. Cruise at 14 knots (about 20 top) with single 315hp Yanmar diesel.

Length w/Platform	35'5"	Clearance	9'6"
Hull Length	33'5"	Fuel	180 gals.
Beam	10'2"	Water	40 gals.
Draft	2'6"	Waste	30 gals.
Weight	11,750#	Hull Type	Semi-Disp.

See Page 550 For Resale Values

Mainship Corporation
Midway, GA
www.mainship.com

Cruisers & Sportboats

Mainship 31 Sedan Bridge
1994–99

231-360-0827

Affordable 1990s sedan with full-beam interior took small-boat space, comfort to the next level. Highlights include spacious salon, double-entry head compartment, two private staterooms (rare in a boat this size). Small galley lacks storage, counter space. Flybridge has walk-through forward gate for bow access. Entire cockpit sole lifts for engine access. Radar arch, transom door, bow pulpit, swim platform were standard. Molded steps make bridge access easy. Cruise at 18 knots with 340hp V-drive gas engines (about 30 knots top).

Length Overall	33'3"	Clearance	14'4"
Hull Length	31'3"	Fuel	200 gals.
Beam	11'10"	Water	50 gals.
Draft	2'10"	Hull Type	Modified-V
Weight	16,000#	Deadrise Aft	13°

See Page 550 For Resale Values

Mainship Corporation
Midway, GA
www.mainship.com

Mainship 34 II
1980–82

231-360-0827

Value-priced sedan with roomy cockpit, economical single-diesel power was designed to appeal to budget-minded anglers. Well-organized interior boasts private bow stateroom, U-shaped galley, compact salon with convertible sofa, standard lower helm. Note galley pass-through window to salon, stall shower in head. Large engine compartment, wide side decks are a plus. No transom door. Very steep flybridge ladder. Not a big seller for Mainship. Cruise at 10 knots with single 160hp Perkins diesel burning just 6 gph.

Length	34'0"	Headroom	6'3"
Beam	11'11"	Fuel	220 gals.
Draft	2'10"	Water	50 gals.
Weight	14,000#	Waste	30 gals.
Clearance	13'6"	Hull Type	Semi-Disp.

Prices Not Provided for Pre-1995 Models

Mainship Corporation
Midway, GA
www.mainship.com

Mainship 34 III
1983–88

231-360-0827

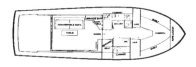

Refined version of original Mainship 34 (1978–82) boasts updated styling (note stepped sheerline), slightly revised interior, more open cockpit. Practical single-stateroom, galley-down interior is roughly similar to original Mainship 34 layout with light oak woodwork (rather than teak), larger salon windows. Salon sofa converts to double bed. Lower helm was standard. Enclosed head includes separate stall shower. Note wide side decks, large engineroom. Single 165hp or 200hp Perkins diesel will cruise efficiently at 10 knots.

Length Overall	34'0"	Clearance	13'6"
Length WL	NA	Fuel	190 gals.
Beam	11'11"	Water	40 gals.
Draft	2'10"	Waste	30 gals.
Weight	14,000#	Hull Type	Semi-Disp.

Prices Not Provided for Pre-1995 Models

Mainship Corporation
Midway, GA
www.mainship.com

231-360-0827

Mainship 34 Pilot Express
1999–2008

Popular open-water express offers conservative styling with practical cabin layout, versatile cockpit seating. Topside highlights include spacious cockpit with lounge seating, easy-access engine compartment, transom door. Comfortable interior with U-shaped dinette, bow stateroom with bi-fold door, sleeps four. Bow thruster, bow pulpit, teak-planked cabin sole were standard. Long keel protects running gear from grounding. Single 350hp Yanmar diesel will cruise 14 knots (16–17 knots top). Twin 240hp Yanmars cruise at 18 knots (20+ top).

Length w/Pulpit	36'1"	Clearance	9'0"
Hull Length	34'0"	Fuel	250 gals.
Beam	12'3"	Water	70 gals.
Draft	3'3"	Waste	20 gals.
Weight	15,000#	Hull Type	Semi-Disp.

See Page 550 For Resale Values

Mainship Corporation
Midway, GA
www.mainship.com

231-360-0827

Mainship 34 Pilot Sedan
2001–09

Downeast-style hardtop with handsome lines is classy, comfortable, built to last. Generous 12-foot beam affords plenty of cockpit, cabin space. Topside highlights include deep cockpit with lounge seating, easy-access engine compartment, efficient helm layout. Well-planned cabin with big U-shaped dinette, teak-and-holly sole sleeps four. Bow thruster, tilt-away helm, transom door were standard. Single 350hp Yanmar diesel will cruise 14 knots (16–17 knots top). Twin 240hp Yanmars cruise at 18 knots (20+ top).

Length w/Pulpit	36'1"	Clearance	9'0"
Hull Length	34'0"	Fuel	250 gals.
Beam	12'3"	Water	70 gals.
Draft	3'3"	Waste	20 gals.
Weight	16,000#	Hull Type	Semi-Disp.

See Page 550 For Resale Values

Mainship Corporation
Midway, GA
www.mainship.com

231-360-0827

Mainship 35 Convertible
1988–94

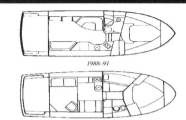

1988–91

1992–94

Value-priced sedan introduced in 1988 boasts one of the largest interiors in her class. Original single-stateroom floorplan was replaced with a two-stateroom dinette layout in 1992 when the boat was also slightly restyled. Expansive salon is wide open to L-shaped galley, booth-style dinette. Cockpit is small with transom door, engine compartment hatches. Note molded bridge steps, Eurostyle bow rails, spacious flybridge, narrow side decks. Standard 320hp Crusader gas engines cruise at 17–18 knots (mid 20s top).

Length	34'11"	Fuel	250 gals.
Beam	12'8"	Water	80 gals.
Draft	2'10"	Cockpit	80 sq. ft.
Weight	16,000#	Hull Type	Modified-V
Clearance	15'0"	Deadrise Aft	12°

Prices Not Provided for Pre-1995 Models

Mainship Corporation
Midway, GA
www.mainship.com

Cruisers & Sportboats

Mainship 35 Open Bridge
1990–92

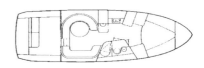

Generic family cruiser (called Mainship 36 Sedan Bridge in 1992) with spacious interior never won any beauty, quality awards. Cavernous full-beam salon with facing settees, tall headroom seats eight for cocktails; full-size galley features upright refrigerator. Small cabin windows reduce natural lighting. Note cockpit bridge steps, center bridge walk-through to foredeck. Additional features include radar arch, integrated swim platform, cockpit seating. Standard 320hp gas engines cruise at 17–18 knots (mid 20s top).

Length	36'0"	Fuel	250 gals.
Beam	12'5"	Water	85 gals.
Draft	2'8"	Headroom	6'6"
Weight	13,500#	Hull Type	Modified-V
Clearance	10'0"	Deadrise Aft	12°

Prices Not Provided for Pre-1995 Models

Mainship Corporation
Midway, GA
www.mainship.com

Mainship 35 Open; 36 Express
1990–93

Hard-riding express (called Mainship 35 Open in 1990–91; 36 Express in 1992–93) was designed for entry-level buyers more concerned with price than styling or finish. Large cockpit is a plus, but portside helm position is awkward. Generic midcabin interior is arranged with double berths in both staterooms, compact galley, head with stall shower. Interior was restyled in 1991 for brighter, more open look. Twin Crusader gas engines cruise at 19 knots and reach a top speed in the neighborhood of 27–28 knots.

Length Overall	36'5"	Clearance	10'6"
Length WL	NA	Fuel	250 gals.
Beam	12'5"	Water	75 gals.
Draft	2'8"	Hull Type	Modified-V
Weight	13,500#	Deadrise Aft	12°

Prices Not Provided for Pre-1995 Models

Mainship Corporation
Midway, GA
www.mainship.com

Mainship 36 Nantucket
1986–88

Family-oriented sedan (called Mainship 36 Sedan in 1986) combined low cost with spacious interior, economical operation. Extended salon is big for a 36-footer because bulkhead is well aft, vastly increasing interior at the expense of cockpit space. Lower helm was optional; light oak woodwork was standard. Note compact engineroom. Large flybridge seats several guests aft of helm. Transom door eases boarding. Relatively small 270hp gas engines cruise at 14–15 knots (low 20s top). About 50 were built.

Length	36'2"	Fuel	240 gals.
Beam	13'0"	Water	100 gals.
Draft	3'0"	Headroom	6'5"
Weight	20,000#	Hull Type	Semi-Disp.
Clearance	11'3"	Deadrise Aft	NA

Prices Not Provided for Pre-1995 Models

Mainship Corporation
Midway, GA
www.mainship.com

231-360-0827

Mainship 39 Express
1989–93

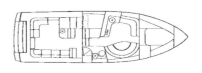

Economy-class 1990s express is clearly dated by today's sportboat standards. Wide 14-foot beam permits very spacious cockpit, expansive two-stateroom interior. Topside features include wraparound cockpit seating, transom door, foredeck sun pad, radar arch. Note unusual portside helm position. Plain-Jane interior contains two staterooms, full-size galley, large head with separate stall shower. Swim platform is tiny, side decks are narrow, finish is not great. Twin big-block Crusader gas engines cruise at 20 knots and top out at 28 knots.

Length	39'2"	Fuel	320 gals.
Beam	14'1"	Water	80 gals.
Draft	3'4"	Headroom	6'3"
Weight	15,000#	Hull Type	Modified-V
Clearance	8'0"	Deadrise Aft	12°

Prices Not Provided for Pre-1995 Models

Mainship Corporation
Midway, GA
www.mainship.com

231-360-0827

Mainship 40 Motor Cruiser
1980–84

Fuel-efficient 1980s sedan with full-beam delivered true liveaboard comfort in a midsize boat. Single-stateroom floorplan (most 40-footers have two) allows space for truly expansive salon with convenient second head compartment next to cockpit door. Large stateroom has built-in dresser, private head with shower stall. Flybridge is huge with room for a small crowd. Unusual layout is ideal for the cruising couple. Twin 165hp Perkins diesels cruise at 10–11 knots (around 15 knots top) burning only 1 gph. Total of 20 were sold.

Length	40'0"	Fuel	320 gals.
Beam	14'0"	Water	100 gals.
Draft	3'4"	Headroom	6'4"
Weight	23,500#	Hull Type	Modified-V
Clearance	17'6"	Deadrise Aft	NA

Prices Not Provided for Pre-1995 Models

Mainship Corporation
Midway, GA
www.mainship.com

231-360-0827

Mainship 40 Sedan Bridge
1993–99

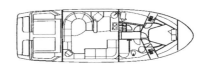

Conservative 1990s sedan with spacious interior, large flybridge was designed for casual coastal cruising. Expansive interior—one step down from cockpit level—includes two large staterooms, full-beam salon with open galley, lounge seating for eight. Small cockpit has built-in bench seating, centerline transom door, twin engine hatches. Note walk-through door in forward flybridge coaming. Unimpressive fit and finish. Standard 320hp V-drive gas engines cruise at a sedate 16 knots and deliver a top speed in the mid 20s.

Length	40'7"	Fuel	310 gals.
Beam	13'6"	Water	93 gals.
Draft	3'5"	Headroom	6'4"
Weight	20,000#	Hull Type	Modified-V
Clearance	17'0"	Deadrise Aft	18°

See Page 550 For Resale Values

Mainship Corporation
Midway, GA
www.mainship.com

Cruisers & Sportboats

231-360-0827

Mainship 41 Cockpit
1989–92

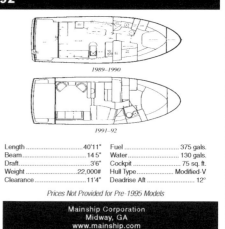

1989–1990

1991–92

Well-built sedan appealed to entry-level buyers seeking big-boat comfort on a modest budget. Chief attraction is spacious salon with generous seating, built-in entertainment center. Original two-stateroom layout was completely revised in 1991. Guest stateroom is a tight fit. Cheap furnishings, plain decor leave much to be desired. Small windows restrict natural lighting in salon. Note very roomy bridge. Standard 320hp gas engines cruise at 15–16 knots (low 20s top); 375hp Cat diesels cruise at 20 knots (24–25 knots top).

Length	40'11"	Fuel	375 gals.
Beam	14'5"	Water	130 gals.
Draft	3'6"	Cockpit	75 sq. ft.
Weight	22,000#	Hull Type	Modified-V
Clearance	11'4"	Deadrise Aft	12°

Prices Not Provided for Pre-1995 Models

Mainship Corporation
Midway, GA
www.mainship.com

231-360-0827

Mainship 45 Pilot
2008–09

Seductive coastal cruiser with generous beam is smart, practical, loaded with features. Highlights include twin-stateroom cabin with two heads, spacious cockpit with lounge seating, fantastic engine access, opening hardtop skylights. Vertical ceiling pole between helm seat and dining table is a plus; sliding side windows, opening windshield provide excellent ventilation. Hardtop overhang partially shades windshield, cockpit. Large bow locker stows windlass, anchor and chain. Yanmar 440hp diesels cruise at 17 knots (20–21 knots top).

Length w/Pulpit	47'9"	Clearance	10'7"
Hull Length	43'0"	Fuel	777 gals.
Beam	15'6"	Water	200 gals.
Draft	3'8"	Waste	56 gals.
Weight	38,000#	Hull Type	Semi-Disp.

Insufficient Resale Data To Assign Values

Mainship Corporation
Midway, GA
www.mainship.com

231-360-0827

Marquis 40 Sport Coupe
2008–Current

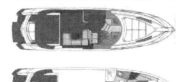

Italian-style sportcruiser (called the 420 SC since 2009) makes the grade with buyers seeking strong performance, innovative ideas. Salon/helm area is bright and airy thanks to huge sunroof, sweeping side windows. Four-section glass cockpit doors fold up for uninterrupted access to salon. Deckhouse galley means chef can socialize while preparing meals. Transom slides aft to increase cockpit space. Helm visibility could be better. Volvo 435hp IPS pod drives cruise efficiently at 25 knots (about 30 knots top).

Length	43'7"	Fuel	300 gals.
Beam	13'11"	Water	140 gals.
Draft	3'7"	Waste	45 gals.
Weight	31,000#	Hull Type	Modified-V
Clearance	13'9"	Deadrise Aft	16°

Insufficient Resale Data To Assign Values

Marquis Yachts, Pulaski, WI
Phone 920-822-1575
www.marquisyachts.com

Maxum 2700 SCR
1993–96

Durable 1990s cruiser combined leading-edge styling with wide-body interior, entry-level price tag. Roomy cockpit with triple helm seat, facing cockpit lounges has room for eight. Open-plan cabin with offset forward berth, booth-style dinette, aft double berth sleeps four adults, two kids. Good-sized head has shower, generous storage. Note walk-through windshield. Strut-supported engine hatch affords good access to engines. Twin 205hp MerCruiser I/Os cruise at 22 knots (about 35 knots top).

Length	28'9"	Fuel	102 gals.
Beam	9'8"	Water	30 gals.
Draft, Up	1'10"	Waste	16 gals.
Draft, Down	3'3"	Hull Type	Modified-V
Weight	6,450#	Deadrise Aft	18°

See Page 551 For Resale Values

Maxum discontinued operations in 2009.

Maxum 2700 SE
2001–07

Maxi-volume express with generous 9'5" beam offers more space, amenities than most 27-footers. Topside features include double helm seat, companion sun lounge, cockpit U-lounge with table, wet bar. Roomy cabin with standing headroom holds dinette/V-berth, midcabin double berth, full galley, head with shower. Note walk-through windshield, four opening ports. Good engine access. Stereo/CD, cooler, transom shower are standard. Single 320hp MerCruiser sterndrive will cruise at 20 knots and reach 30+ knots top.

Length	28'1"	Fuel	84 gals.
Beam	9'5"	Water	30 gals.
Draft, Up	1'10"	Waste	20 gals.
Draft, Down	3'3"	Hull Type	Modified-V
Weight	7,400#	Deadrise Aft	16°

See Page 551 For Resale Values

Maxum discontinued operations in 2009.

Maxum 2800/2900 SCR; 2900 SE
1993–2006

Popular midcabin cruiser (called 2800 SCR in 1997–2000; 2900 SCR in 2001–02; 2900 SE in 2003–06) delivered affordable mix of contemporary styling, versatile accommodations. Roomy cockpit with triple helm seat, wraparound lounge has room for eight. Open-plan cabin with offset forward berth, booth-style dinette, aft double berth sleeps four adults, two kids. Note walk-through windshield, molded bow pulpit. Large engine hatch affords good access to engines. Twin 220hp MerCruiser I/Os cruise at 22 knots (mid 30s top).

Length	29'10"	Fuel	102 gals.
Beam	9'9"	Water	30 gals.
Draft, Up	1'10"	Waste	16 gals.
Draft, Down	3'3"	Hull Type	Modified-V
Weight	9,100#	Deadrise Aft	18°

See Page 551 For Resale Values

Maxum discontinued operations in 2009.

Cruisers & Sportboats

Cruisers & Sportboats

Maxum 2900 SE
2008–09

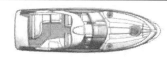

Well-rounded family express with contemporary styling took Maxum affordability, value to the next level. Practical cockpit design has bench seats forward, L-shaped lounge aft plus aft bench seat that converts to sun pad. Both forward seats rotate to face aft; dash has space for mounting big-screen video display. Generic midcabin interior with open-plan layout, teak-and-holly galley sole sleeps five. Walk-thru windshield is accessed via steps molded into cabin door. Twin 300-hp MerCruiser I/Os cruise at 25 knots (low 30s top).

Length	30'0"	Fuel	125 gals.
Beam	9'11"	Water	30 gals.
Draft, Up	2'3"	Waste	30 gals.
Draft, Down	3'3"	Hull Type	Modified-V
Weight	10,187#	Deadrise Aft	18°

See Page 551 For Resale Values

Maxum discontinued operations in 2009.

Maxum 3100 SE
2002–08

Sporty family express combines sleek styling with upscale interior, spirited performance. Topside highlights include sporty burled dash, companion L-lounge, U-shaped aft seating, wet bar with integrated cooler. Well-appointed cabin with full galley, Ultraleather dinette, faux maple cabinetry sleeps six. Note generous galley storage, roomy head. Additional features include foredeck sun pads, transom shower, large anchor locker. Twin 260hp MerCruiser sterndrives cruise in the mid 20s and reach 33–34 knots top.

Length	30'9"	Fuel	150 gals.
Beam	10'6"	Water	35 gals.
Draft, Up	2'1"	Waste	30 gals.
Draft, Down	3.5"	Hull Type	Modified-V
Weight	11,000#	Deadrise Aft	18°

See Page 551 For Resale Values

Maxum discontinued operations in 2009.

Maxum 3200 SCR
1994–98

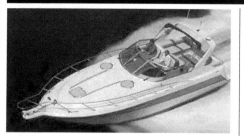

Generic 1990s midcabin express appealed to entry-level buyers looking for comfort, space at an affordable price. Wide 11-foot beam results in roomy cockpit, spacious interior. Cabin features include full 6'6" headroom, hardwood galley sole, midcabin accordion door, three overhead deck hatches. Expansive cockpit with centerline transom door has facing lounge seats aft, wet bar. Note that companion helm seat converts to sun lounge. Twin 250hp MerCruiser sterndrives cruise at 20 knots (30+ knots top).

Length	34'9"	Fuel	186 gals.
Beam	11'0"	Water	36 gals.
Draft, Up	2'3"	Waste	30 gals.
Draft, Down	3'8"	Hull Type	Modified-V
Weight	10,800#	Deadrise Aft	17°

See Page 551 For Resale Values

Maxum discontinued operations in 2009.

Maxum 3300 SE
1999–2007

Stylish sportcruiser with many standard features gets high marks for comfort, performance, affordability. Topside highlights include wide-open cockpit with facing aft settees, fold-down companion seat, sporty burled dash, wet bar, foredeck sun pad. Well-appointed interior with roomy galley, Ultraleather dinette sleeps four adults, two kids. Note relatively small head compartment, narrow side decks, huge engineroom. Twin 320hp Mer-Cruiser sterndrive engines cruise in the low-to-mid 20s and reach a top speed of 35+ knots.

Length	35'7"	Fuel	179 gals.
Beam	11'5"	Water	36 gals.
Draft	3'6"	Waste	30 gals.
Weight	11,300#	Hull Type	Modified-V
Clearance	10'6"	Deadrise Aft	17°

See Page 551 For Resale Values

Maxum discontinued operations in 2009.

Maxum 3500 SY
2001–08

Feature-rich sportcruiser with classic express-boat styling set industry standard for low-price value, affordability. Well-appointed interior includes two large staterooms with privacy curtain forward, solid door aft. Full-size head boasts VacuFlush toilet, separate stall shower. Bridgedeck hatch provides good engine access. Transom shower, walk-through windshield, wet bar are standard. Early models with 310hp V-drive inboards cruise at 20 knots (30 knots top); later models with 300hp I/Os cruise in the low 20s (mid 30s top).

Length	34'11"	Fuel	240 gals.
Beam	12'2"	Water	40 gals.
Draft, Up	2'2"	Waste	40 gals.
Draft, Down	3'1"	Hull Type	Modified-V
Weight	15,510#	Deadrise Aft	15°

See Page 551 For Resale Values

Maxum discontinued operations in 2009.

Maxum 3700 SCR
1998–2001

Roomy family cruiser introduced in 1998 paired low price with smart styling, sturdy construction. Open-plan interior with Avonite counters, earth-tone fabrics features home-sized galley with hardwood floor, large head with circular stall shower, cozy aft cabin with twin berths that quickly convert to queen bed. Note that accordion door—not a curtain—provides midcabin privacy. Twin 380hp V-drive gas inboards cruise at 18 knots (26–27 knots top); 370hp Cummins diesels cruise in the mid 20s (28–30 top).

Length	39'3"	Fuel	244 gals.
Beam	13'0"	Water	65 gals.
Draft	3'7"	Waste	50 gals.
Weight	20,700#	Hull Type	Modified-V
Clearance	12'11"	Deadrise Aft	15°

See Page 551 For Resale Values

Maxum discontinued operations in 2009.

231-360-0827

Maxum 3700 SY
2003–09

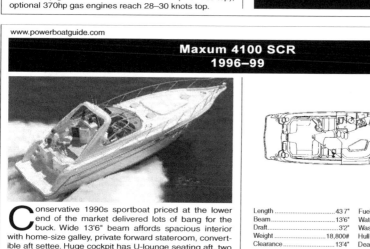

Smooth-riding sportcruiser offered Maxum's signature blend of space, comfort, value. Wide 13-foot beam allows for expansive interior as well as large cockpit area. Cabin highlights include full-size galley with plenty of storage, roomy master stateroom with island berth and privacy door, well-appointed head with stall shower. Note hardwood galley floor, generous headroom. U-shaped cockpit lounge converts to huge sun pad. Standard 320hp gas V-drives cruise at 18 knots (mid–20s top); optional 370hp gas engines reach 28–30 knots top.

Length	37'2"	Fuel	300 gals.
Beam	13'0"	Water	80 gals.
Draft, Up	2'4"	Waste	45 gals.
Draft, Down	3'6"	Hull Type	Modified-V
Weight	17,800#	Deadrise Aft	15°

See Page 551 For Resale Values

Maxum discontinued operations in 2009.

231-360-0827

Maxum 4100 SCR
1996–99

Conservative 1990s sportboat priced at the lower end of the market delivered lots of bang for the buck. Wide 13'6" beam affords spacious interior with home-size galley, private forward stateroom, convertible aft settee. Huge cockpit has U-lounge seating aft, two removable tables, centerline transom door. Unusual port/starboard transom steps access side decks. Called Maxum 3900 SCR in 1996. Twin 400hp V-drive gas inboards cruise at 20 knots (26-27 knots top); 370hp Cummins diesels cruise at 20 knots (low-20s top).

Length	43'7"	Fuel	330 gals.
Beam	13'6"	Water	77 gals.
Draft	3'2"	Waste	45 gals.
Weight	18,800#	Hull Type	Modified-V
Clearance	13'4"	Deadrise Aft	16°

See Page 552 For Resale Values

Maxum discontinued operations in 2009.

231-360-0827

Maxum 4200 SY
2002–08

Maxi-volume express with unusual "floating" hardtop, arching side windows offered luxury-class amenities at an affordable price. Expansive midcabin interior with high-gloss cherry cabinetry, Ultraleather upholstery features full-size galley with wine storage, two heads, big U-shaped settee with adjustable table. Molded steps in transom corners lead to wide side decks; aft cockpit section lifts for engine access. Lots of boat for the money. Twin 450hp Cummins V-drive diesels cruise in the low-to-mid 20s (27-28 knots top).

Length	42'9"	Fuel	480 gals.
Beam	13'10"	Water	130 gals.
Draft	3'8"	Waste	70 gals.
Weight	35,700#	Hull Type	Modified-V
Clearance, Hardtop	12'0"	Deadrise Aft	18°

See Page 552 For Resale Values

Maxum discontinued operations in 2009.

231-360-0827

McKinna 47 Sedan/481 Sedan
1999–2006

Appealing Taiwan-built sedan (called the 47 Sedan in 1999–2000; 481 Sedan in 2001–06) is stylish, roomy, built to last. Efficient galley-up floorplan with lower helm has two staterooms, both with queen-size berths and built-in vanities. Note maple cabinets, granite and marble counters, convenient pilothouse deck door. Both heads share a common shower stall. Excellent range with huge 700-gallon fuel capacity. Stout, heavily built yacht is capable of serious cruising. Cruise at 18–20 knots with 370hp Cummins diesels.

Length Overall	50'0"	Fuel	700 gals.
Beam	15'0"	Water	200 gals.
Draft	3'10"	Waste	40 gals.
Weight	29,700#	Hull Type	Modified-V
Clearance	19'6"	Deadrise Aft	18°

See Page 552 For Resale Values

McKinna Yachts
Newport Beach, CA
www.mckinnayachts.com

www.powerboatguide.com
231-360-0827

Meridian 341 Sedan
2003–04

Entry-level sedan (called Bayliner 3488 Command Bridge in 2001–02) combined rakish styling with expansive accommodations, low price. Roomy two-stateroom interior is nicely highlighted with cherry joinery, leather upholstery. Wraparound cabin windows provide plenty of natural lighting. Salon has two incliners facing full entertainment center. Note cockpit bridge steps, extended flybridge, narrow side decks. Twin 300hp gas inboards cruise at 20 knots (26–28 knots top). All-new Meridian 341 Sedan was introduced in 2005.

Length	35'3"	Fuel	224 gals.
Beam	11'8"	Water	92 gals.
Draft	3'2"	Waste	30 gals.
Weight	17,000#	Hull Type	Modified-V
Clearance	13'6"	Deadrise Aft	7.5°

See Page 552 For Resale Values

Meridian Yachts
Arlington, WA
www.meridian-yachts.com

www.powerboatguide.com
231-360-0827

Meridian 341 Sedan
2005–Current

Roomy sport sedan with rakish lines couples tasteful accommodations with spirited performance, attractive price. Expansive salon with panoramic windows, port and starboard lounge seating is wide open to large galley with cherrywood cabinets, faux-granite countertops. Forward master stateroom has island berth; guest cabin has twin single berths. Note molded bridge steps in cockpit, narrow side decks. Transom door, underwater exhaust are standard. Lower helm is optional. Cruise at 18 knots with 320hp gas inboards (26–27 knots top).

Length	35'10"	Fuel	250 gals.
Beam	12'6"	Water	90 gals.
Draft	4'0"	Waste	35 gals.
Weight	18,254#	Hull Type	Modified-V
Clearance	14'1"	Deadrise Aft	11°

See Page 552 For Resale Values

Meridian Yachts
Arlington, WA
www.meridian-yachts.com

Cruisers & Sportboats

Meridian 381 Sedan
2003–05

Updated version of Bayliner 3788 MY (2001–02) became Meridian 381 in 2003 when Bayliner got out of the big-boat business and Meridian Yachts was formed. Spacious two-stateroom interior boasts home-size galley, two full heads, faux-leather upholstery. Island berth is located in master stateroom; guest stateroom is partially tucked under salon floor. Additional features include molded bridge steps, radar arch, transom door. Twin 320hp gas inboards cruise at 15–16 knots and top out in the mid 20s.

Length	38'6"	Fuel	300 gals.
Beam	13'7"	Water	125 gals.
Draft	3'4"	Waste	37 gals.
Weight	22,275#	Hull Type	Modified-V
Clearance	14'1"	Deadrise Aft	10°

See Page 552 For Resale Values

Meridian Yachts
Arlington, WA
www.meridian-yachts.com

Meridian 391 Sedan
2006–Current

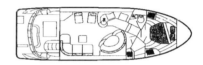

Sleek flybridge yacht delivers on promise of liveaboard comfort, feature-rich accommodations. Enormous salon/galley/dinette offers spacious living area made even larger by panoramic windows, generous headroom. Guest cabin with queen berth extends under raised dinette. Bridge steps—while convenient—consume valuable cockpit space. Huge bridge seats a small crowd. Note split head, big engineroom, narrow side decks. Standard 370hp gas engines cruise at 18 knots; optional 380hp Cummins diesels cruise at 20+ knots.

Length	40'11	Fuel	350 gals.
Beam	13'11"	Water	125 gals.
Draft	3'3"	Waste	40 gals.
Weight	25,000#	Hull Type	Modified-V
Clearance	14'0"	Deadrise Aft	10°

See Page 552 For Resale Values

Meridian Yachts
Arlington, WA
www.meridian-yachts.com

Meridian 411 Sedan
2003–07

Competitively priced sedan cruiser couples crisp styling with spacious interior, spirited performance. Split-level salon has galley and dinette forward, facing settees and entertainment center aft. Hatch in salon floor provides access to engineroom. Additional features include bridge seating for eight, extended swim platform, cherry interior cabinetry, radar arch. Single-stick control system with bow, stern thrusters makes docking easy. Lower helm was optional. Cruise at 22 knots with 370hp Cummins diesels (26–28 knots top).

Length	46'0"	Fuel	400 gals.
Beam	14'2"	Water	150 gals.
Draft	3'9"	Waste	55 gals.
Weight	25,000#	Hull Type	Modified-V
Clearance	15'0"	Deadrise Aft	7°

See Page 552 For Resale Values

Meridian Yachts
Arlington, WA
www.meridian-yachts.com

231-360-0827

Midnight Lace 44 Express
1979–89

Retro-style cruiser introduced in 1978 was based on classic commuter-style boats of the 1920s. Efficient "penetrating" hull form with narrow beam, tightly rounded bilges is fully cored to reduce weight. Offered with choice of single- or twin-stateroom floorplans, both with full-width salon. While interior volume is small for a 44-foot boat, comfort is high. Flybridge became optional in 1979. Note unique bow cockpit accessed from forward stateroom. Easily driven hull will cruise at 20 knots with small 220hp GM V-drive diesels (mid 20s top).

Length	44'0"	Fuel	250 gals.
Beam	11'0"	Water	130 gals.
Draft	2'10"	Headroom	6'4"
Weight	15,900#	Hull Type	Modified-V
Clearance	16'0"	Deadrise Aft	8°

Prices Not Provided for Pre-1995 Models

Midnight Lace is no longer in production

231-360-0827

Mikelson 42 Sedan
1986–90

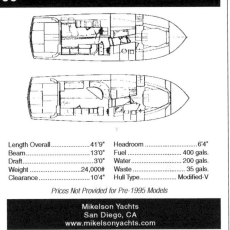

Versatile Fexas-designed sedan with distinctive styling (note long foredeck, large cabin windows) put Mikelson in the sportfish business back in 1986. Most were delivered with two-stateroom, galley-up interior with single head, standard lower helm. Interior is completely finished with handcrafted teak cabinetry. Large flybridge for a 42-footer. Cockpit came with transom door, teak sole, tackle center. Fully cored hull with rounded chines is fuel efficient, easily driven. Cruise at 16–17 knots with 260hp GM diesels (about 20 knots top).

Length Overall	41'9"	Headroom	6'4"
Beam	13'0"	Fuel	400 gals.
Draft	3'0"	Water	200 gals.
Weight	24,000#	Waste	35 gals.
Clearance	10'4"	Hull Type	Modified-V

Prices Not Provided for Pre-1995 Models

Mikelson Yachts
San Diego, CA
www.mikelsonyachts.com

231-360-0827

Navigator 57 Rival
2003–07

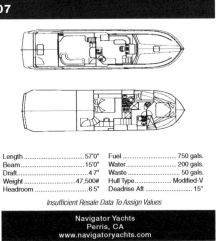

Sure-footed cruising yacht makes good on Navigator promise of sturdy construction, practical accommodations. Highlights include full-beam salon with wet bar and entertainment center, extended pilothouse with open galley, three well-appointed staterooms, large cockpit with transom door. Note inside flybridge access, private entry to master suite. Steps from salon to pilothouse open to huge storage area below. Well-arranged engineroom offers good service access. Cruise at 16 knots with Volvo 370hp diesels (about 20 knots top).

Length	57'0"	Fuel	750 gals.
Beam	15'0"	Water	200 gals.
Draft	4'7"	Waste	50 gals.
Weight	47,500#	Hull Type	Modified-V
Headroom	6'5"	Deadrise Aft	15°

Insufficient Resale Data To Assign Values

Navigator Yachts
Perris, CA
www.navigatoryachts.com

231-360-0827

Ocean Alexander 42 Sedan
1987–93

Main Deck

Lower Deck

Popular cockpit yacht with sporty lines made good on Alexander promise of top-level construction, practical accommodations. Appealing two-stateroom teak interior includes standard lower helm, step-up galley forward with serving counter, large master stateroom with walkaround queen, guest cabin with single berths. Small cabin adjacent to head can serve as storage area, laundry center. Roomy cockpit is a plus. Cummins 250hp diesels cruise at 14 knots; Cat 375hp diesels cruise at 20–21 knots. Over 140 were sold.

Length	42'0"	Fuel	500 gals.
Beam	14'4"	Water	150 gals.
Draft	3'2"	Waste	40 gals.
Weight	23,000#	Hull Type	Modified-V
Clearance	11'6"	Deadrise Aft	NA

Prices Not Provided for Pre-1995 Models

Ocean Alexander Marine
Seattle, WA
www.oceanalexander.com

231-360-0827

Ocean Alexander 420/422 Sport Sedan
1994–2001

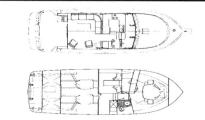

Stylish flybridge sedan (called 420 Sedan in 1994–95; 422 Sedan thereafter) offered Alexander buyers impressive blend of smart styling, tasteful accommodations. Appealing two-stateroom teak interior includes standard lower helm, step-up galley forward with serving counter, large master stateroom with walkaround queen, guest cabin with single berths. Small cabin adjacent to head can serve as storage area, laundry center. Roomy cockpit is a plus. Cat 375 diesels cruise at 22 knots (25 top); 420hp Cats run a knot or two faster.

Length	42'0"	Clearance	NA
Beam	14'4"	Water	150 gals.
Draft	3'3"	Headroom	6'4"
Weight	33,100#	Hull Type	Modified-V
Fuel	500 gals.	Deadrise Aft	NA

See Page 554 For Resale Values

Ocean Alexander Marine
Seattle, WA
www.oceanalexander.com

231-360-0827

Pearson True North 33
2004–08

Scaled-down version of popular True North 38 invokes visions of classic New England lobster boats. Galley and dinette are on pilothouse level, wide open to cockpit. Dinette seat converts electrically into forward-facing bench seat. Note glossy cherrywood trim, sliding cabin windows. Twin transom doors allow dinghy to be easily stowed in cockpit—very clever. Impressive fit and finish. Tapered hull carries beam well forward; rudder and prop are fully protected by integral skeg. Cruise at 20 knots with single 440hp Yanmar diesel (mid 20s top).

Length	36'2"	Fuel	200 gals.
Beam	12'4"	Water	80 gals.
Draft	3'4"	Waste	25 gals.
Weight	12,500#	Hull Type	Modified-V
Clearance, Mast	11'7"	Deadrise Aft	18°

See Page 556 For Resale Values

True North Yachts
Warren, RI
www.pearsonyachts.com

www.powerboatguide.com   231-360-0827

Pearson 34 Convertible
1989–91

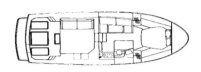

Rugged deep-V convertible with wide 13-foot beam offers spacious accommodations, impressive rough-water handling. Teak-trimmed interior boasts roomy salon with sofa/bed, convertible dinette, owner stateroom with island queen berth. Compact galley is short on storage, counter space. Large windows admit plenty of natural lighting. Additional features include well-finished engineroom, transom door, bow pulpit, swim platform. Cockpit is small for a 34-footer. Cat 320hp diesels cruise at 22-23 knots (high 20s top).

Length	33'9"	Fuel	310 gals.
Beam	13'0"	Water	70 gals.
Draft	3'4"	Headroom	6'4"
Weight	19,000#	Hull Type	Deep-V
Clearance	NA	Deadrise Aft	19°

See Page XXX For Resale Values

The original Pearson Yacht Company ended operations in 1991.

---

www.powerboatguide.com   231-360-0827

Pearson True North 38
2002–08

Distinctive hardtop express with reverse transom gets high marks for innovative design, top-shelf construction. "Sleeping loft" for kids is located above V-berth; galley is positioned aft in semi-enclosed pilothouse where it's convenient to cockpit. (Pilothouse can be fully enclosed with optional bulkhead.) Twin transom doors allow dinghy to be stowed in cockpit. Bow thruster is standard. High-tech hull boasts deep forefoot, skeg-mounted rudder. Single 440hp Yanmar diesel will cruise at 20 knots (25–26 knots top). Over 100 built to date.

Length	38'6"	Fuel	220 gals.
Beam	13'6"	Water	100 gals.
Draft	3'6"	Waste	35 gals.
Weight	15,000#	Hull Type	Modified-V
Clearance	15'5"	Deadrise Aft	12°

See Page 556 For Resale Values

True North Yachts
Warren, RI
www.pearsonyachts.com

---

www.powerboatguide.com   231-360-0827

Phoenix 27 Weekender
1979–94

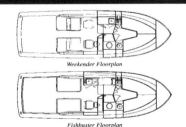

Weekender Floorplan

Fishbuster Floorplan

Versatile 27-footer with expansive single-level cockpit is great for fishing, daytime entertaining. Highlights include tackle storage locker, bait-prep center, compact cabin with V-berths, stand-up head with shower. "Fishbuster" version (1979–89) has galley forward in cockpit. Engine boxes double as back-to-back seats. Deep-V hull with prop pockets delivers good rough-water performance. Inboard 270hp gas engines cruise at 22–23 knots (about 30 knots top); optional 200hp Volvo diesels cruise around 25 knots (high 20s top).

Length Overall	27'3"	Clearance	6'9"
Length WL	23'6"	Fuel	200 gals.
Beam	9'10"	Water	24 gals.
Draft	1'10"	Hull Type	Deep-V
Weight	7,200#	Deadrise Aft	20°

Prices Not Provided for Pre-1995 Models

Phoenix Yachts is no longer in business.

Cruisers & Sportboats

Section III: Cruisers & Sportboats

Pursuit 2860/2865 Denali
1997–2004

Beautifully finished daycruiser is well adapted to fishing, swimming, occasional overnighting. Highlights include spacious bridgedeck with L-lounge seating, roomy cockpit with foldaway rear seat, upscale cabin with enclosed head, berths for two. Transom contains freshwater sink, insulated fishbox/cooler, raw-water washdown. Note stylish helm layout. Updated 2865 model introduced in 2003 features curved windshield, added cockpit seating, cabin revisions. Single Volvo 375hp gas I/O engine tops out at close to 35 knots.

Length w/Pulpit	32'10"	Fuel	148 gals.
Hull Length	28'0"	Water	30 gals.
Beam	9'6"	Waste	20 gals.
Draft, Drives Down	3'0"	Hull Type	Deep-V
Weight	7,600#	Deadrise Aft	21°

See Page 558 For Resale Values

Pursuit Boats
Ft. Pierce, FL
www.pursuitboats.com

Pursuit LS 345 Drummond Runner
2007–08

Standard Plan

Sportfish Plan

Multi-purpose express with innovative center-island galley/wet bar sets class standards for comfort, practicality, luxury. Highlights include electric helm seat, windlass, flat-screen TV, fiberglass top with canvas enclosure. Relatively small cabin with stand-up head is beautifully finished. Available in cruising and sportfish deck layouts. Deep-V hull can handle serious weather. Note sturdy single-piece windshield. Beautifully finished boat drips quality, elegance. Cruise at 30 knots with Yamaha 250s (around 40 knots top). Expensive.

Length	34'5"	Fuel	300 gals.
Beam	9'6"	Water	30 gals.
Hull Draft	1'10"	Max HP	600
Weight w/T250s	10,395#	Hull Type	Deep-V
Clearance, Top	8'0"	Deadrise Aft	24.5°

See Page 558 For Resale Values

Pursuit Boats
Ft. Pierce, FL
www.pursuitboats.com

Regal 260 Valenti; 272 Commodore
1991–96

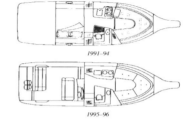

1991–94

1995–96

Portly 1990s express (called Valenti 260 in 1991–92) combines versatile layout with spirited performance, durable construction. Midcabin interior with convertible dinette, stand-up head—slightly updated in 1995—sleeps four. Topside features include double-wide helm seat, walk-through windshield, transom locker, stern seat, power engine hatch. Note fully cored hull construction. Among several sterndrive engine options, twin Volvo 180hp engines cruise at 22 knots (high 30s top); single 300hp engine will cruise at 20 knots (30+ top).

Length w/Pulpit	28'6"	Fuel	105 gals.
Beam	9'2"	Water	27 gals.
Draft, Up	1'6"	Waste	17 gals.
Draft, Down	3'6"	Hull Type	Deep-V
Weight	6,800#	Deadrise Aft	21°

See Page 559 For Resale Values

Regal Marine
Orlando, FL
www.regalboats.com

Regal 2660/2765 Commodore
1999–2005

Well-built cruiser with notched hull delivers good mix of comfort, performance at a reasonable price. Topside highlights include removable rear bench seat, refreshment center with cooler, walk-through windshield, sliding screen door, extended swim platform. Comfortable interior with upscale decor sleeps four. Called 2660 Commodore in 1999–2001. Modest fuel capacity for a 27-footer. Not many trailerable boats offer twin-engine option. Single 310hp MerCruiser I/O tops out at 35 knots; twin 220hp Mercs reach 40+ knots top.

Length	29'10"
Beam	8'6"
Draft, Down	2'9"
Weight	6,950#
Clearance	7'2"
Fuel	76 gals.
Water	28 gals.
Waste	28 gals.
Hull Type	Deep-V
Deadrise Aft	21°

See Page 559 For Resale Values

Regal Marine
Orlando, FL
www.regalboats.com

Regal 265/270/276 Commodore
1990–93

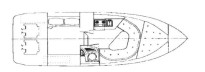

Appealing 1990s sportcruiser with mega-wide beam has more cabin/cockpit space than most boats her size. Unusual cabin layout has small double berth in forepeak, which can only be reached by climbing over U-shaped dinette. Roomy midcabin with stand-up dressing area has solid door for privacy—a real plus. Head compartment is a tight fit. Single 330hp MerCruiser sterndrive will reach 30+ knots top; twin 180hp I/Os top out in the high 30s. Called 265 Commodore in 1990, 270 Commodore in 1991–92, 276 Commodore in 1993.

Length w/Pulpit	29'6"
Hull Length	26'10"
Beam	9'6"
Draft	2'8"
Weight	6,500#
Clearance	9'8"
Fuel	110 gals.
Water	35 gals.
Hull Type	Deep-V
Deadrise Aft	19°

Prices Not Provided for Pre-1995 Models

Regal Marine
Orlando, FL
www.regalboats.com

Regal 2700 Bowrider
2007–Current

Easy-riding bowrider with extended swim platform is small enough for trailering, big enough for offshore use. Principal features include cockpit refreshment center with sink, enclosed head compartment, double helm seat, transom shower, stereo system. Walk-through transom splits rear sun pad; in-floor storage lockers stow plenty of gear. Power engine hatch opens to swim platform rather than cockpit for better service access. Notched deep-V hull can handle a nasty chop. Tops out at 45 knots with single 375hp Volvo sterndrive.

Length w/Platform	28'6"
Beam	8'6"
Draft, Up	1'7"
Draft, Down	3'0"
Weight	5,800#
Clearance	5'10"
Fuel	85 gals.
Water	11 gals.
Hull Type	Deep-V
Deadrise Aft	24°

See Page 559 For Resale Values

Regal Marine
Orlando, FL
www.regalboats.com

www.powerboatguide.com   231-360-0827

Regal 2750 Cuddy
2007–Current

Feature-rich cuddy with extended swim platform is small enough for trailering, big enough for offshore use. Deluxe cockpit layout boasts wraparound lounge seating, refreshment center, removable cooler, CD stereo system. Clever steps to walk-through windshield pivot out from bulkhead. Transom entryway splits rear sun pad. Power engine hatch opens aft to swim platform rather than cockpit for better service access. Deep-V hull can handle a stiff chop. Tops out at 45 knots with single 375hp Volvo sterndrive.

Length w/Platform	28'6"	Clearance	5'8"
Beam	8'6"	Fuel	86 gals.
Draft, Up	1'7"	Water	11 gals.
Draft, Down	3'0"	Hull Type	Deep-V
Weight	6,100#	Deadrise Aft	24°

See Page 559 For Resale Values

Regal Marine
Orlando, FL
www.regalboats.com

---

www.powerboatguide.com   231-360-0827

Regal Ventura 8.3 SC
1992–97

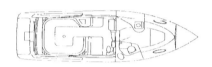

Sporty 1990s sportcruiser combines dayboat versatility with agile handling, good performance. Large cockpit includes nearly complete circle of seating. Cabin is compact but pleasant with convertible dinette forward, tiny—but adequate—toilet compartment. Note that galley (fridge and sink) is positioned in cockpit. Cockpit sole raises to reveal complete engine access. Note burlwood dash, walk-through windshield with molded steps. Single 300hp Volvo gas sterndrive will cruise in the high 20s and max out at 40+ knots.

Length	27'6"	Water	24 gals.
Beam	9'1"	Waste	12 gals.
Draft, Down	2'10"	Headroom	4'8"
Weight	5,600#	Hull Type	Deep-V
Fuel	105 gals.	Deadrise Aft	21°

See Page 559 For Resale Values

Regal Marine
Orlando, FL
www.regalboats.com

---

www.powerboatguide.com   231-360-0827

Regal Ventura 8.3 SE
1994–97

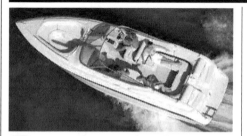

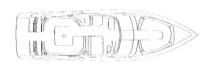

Roomy open-bow express is small enough to trailer, big enough for offshore cruising. Horseshoe-shaped cockpit lounge runs from immediately aft of the driver's seat all the way around to the portside wet bar. Deep bow seating adds extra level of safety. Cockpit sole raises to reveal complete engine access. Note burlwood dash, walk-through windshield, enclosed head/changing room. Deep-V hull delivers excellent open-water ride. Single 300hp Volvo gas sterndrive will cruise in the high 20s and max out at 40+ knots.

Length	27'6"	Fuel	105 gals.
Beam	9'1"	Water	24 gals.
Draft, Down	2'10"	Waste	12 gals.
Weight	5,600#	Hull Type	Deep-V
Clearance	5'8"	Deadrise Aft	21°

See Page 559 For Resale Values

Regal Marine
Orlando, FL
www.regalboats.com

Regal 277XL/280 Commodore
1982–89

231-360-0827

Contemporary 1980s express with family-friendly layout was one of Regal's better-selling models during her production years. Belowdecks comforts include enclosed head with shower, full galley, convertible dinette, aft cabin with double berth. Note teak cabin trim, generous headroom. Cockpit amenities include aft bench seats, double-wide helm seat, tilt steering wheel. Updated 280 model introduced in 1988 featured integrated radar arch. Twin 260hp MerCruiser I/Os cruise at 26–28 knots and reach over 40 knots wide open.

Length	27'1"	Fuel	140 gals.
Beam	10'0"	Water	35 gals.
Draft, Down	3'2"	Waste	21 gals.
Weight	8,200#	Hull Type	Modified-V
Headroom	6'3"	Deadrise Aft	16°

Prices Not Provided for Pre-1995 Models

Regal Marine
Orlando, FL
www.regalboats.com

Regal 2760/2860 Commodore
1998–2005

www.powerboatguide.com
231-360-0827

Maxi-volume express cruiser with innovative topside seating is versatile, stylish, agile. Broad 9'11" beam allows for spacious interior with large head, cherry cabinetry, berths for six. Locating refrigerator under forward berth adds storage space beneath galley counter. Pivoting helm seat, aft L-shaped lounge with removable table, foldaway aft settee maximize cockpit space. Note walk-through windshield, performance-enhancing stepped hull. Twin 220hp MerCruiser I/Os cruise at 22–23 knots and top out in the mid-to-high 30s.

Length w/Pulpit	31'0"	Fuel	103 gals.
Beam	9'11"	Water	27 gals.
Draft, Down	3'3"	Waste	17 gals.
Weight	8,350#	Hull Type	Deep-V
Clearance	8'10"	Deadrise Aft	21°

See Page 559 For Resale Values

Regal Marine
Orlando, FL
www.regalboats.com

Regal 2860 Window Express
2006–Current

www.powerboatguide.com
231-360-0827

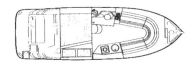

Stylish family express with unique foredeck windows packs luxury amenities into trailerable hull. Roomy midcabin interior with dinette forward, compact galley, stand-up head with shower, sleeps four. Seat backs convert dinette for sleeping. Vinyl fabrics, cherry trim presents very upscale decor. Large aft-cockpit seating area has removable table, refreshment center. Note pull-up swim-platform cleats. Modified-V hull with keel pad delivers comfortable ride. Twin 220hp MerCruiser I/Os cruise at 25 knots (38–40 knots top).

Length	29'5"	Headroom	6'3"
Beam	8'6"	Fuel	100 gals.
Draft, Down	3'3"	Water	35 gals.
Weight	9,000#	Hull Type	Modified-V
Clearance	9'1"	Deadrise Aft	18°

See Page 559 For Resale Values

Regal Marine
Orlando, FL
www.regalboats.com

Cruisers & Sportboats

Regal 2800/2900 LSR
1999–2004

231-360-0827

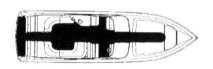

Muscular open-bow cruiser with stepped hull, curvaceous styling (called 2800 LSR in 1999–2001; 2900 LSR in 2002–04) raised the bar in her era for sportboat comfort, versatility. Guest-friendly cockpit with wraparound seating, wet bar, lockable head/change compartment accommodates a small crowd. Flip-up helm seat allows for stand-up driving. Power hatch provides good access to engine compartment. Extended swim platform was optional. Cruise in the mid 30s with single 375hp gas I/O (around 45 mph top).

Length	29'2"	Fuel	97 gals.
Beam	9'1"	Water	24 gals.
Draft, Up	1'10"	Waste	12 gals.
Draft, Down	2'10"	Hull Type	Deep-V
Weight	5,900#	Deadrise Aft	24°

See Page 559 For Resale Values

Regal Marine
Orlando, FL
www.regalboats.com

Regal 290/300 Commodore
1990–94

231-360-0827

1990–92

1993–94

Completely updated version of Regal's popular 277/280 Commodore (1982–89) paired smart styling with upscale interior, sure-footed performance. Topside highlights include big single-level cockpit with reversible helm seat, integrated swim platform with storage lockers, foredeck sun pad, wide side decks, curved windshield. Midcabin interior with convertible dinette, fully equipped galley was updated in 1993. Among several engine options, twin 260hp MerCruiser I/Os cruise at 26–28 knots (40+ knots wide open).

Length w/Pulpit	32'5"	Fuel	140 gals.
Hull length	30'0"	Water	35 gals.
Beam	10'0"	Waste	21 gals.
Draft, Down	3'2"	Hull Type	Modified-V
Weight	9,200#	Deadrise Aft	16°

Prices Not Provided for Pre-1995 Models

Regal Marine
Orlando, FL
www.regalboats.com

Regal 292/2960/3060 Commodore
1995–2003

231-360-0827

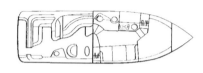

Quality-built express (called 292 Commodore in 1995–99; 2960 Commodore in 2000–01; 3060 Commodore in 2002–03) blends crisp styling, excellent performance. Plush interior with Corian counters, cherrywood trim, convertible dinette sleeps four adults, two kids. Removable settee opens up cockpit for entertaining, fishing. Transom door, wet bar were standard. Note walkthrough windshield, stylish helm. Twin 260hp MerCruiser I/Os cruise at 22 knots (high 30s top); 280hp Volvos cruise at 24 knots (about 40 knots top).

Length Overall	31'10"	Fuel	150 gals.
Beam	10'4"	Water	35 gals.
Draft, Up	1'8"	Waste	30 gals.
Draft, Down	3'2"	Hull Type	Deep-V
Weight	9,500#	Deadrise Aft	18°

See Page 559 For Resale Values

Regal Marine
Orlando, FL
www.regalboats.com

231-360-0827

Regal 3060 Window Express
2004–Current

Sporty family cruiser with foredeck windows combines distinctive Regal styling with spacious interior, exemplary finish. Upscale cabin with wraparound dining area, fully equipped galley boasts glossy cherry cabinetry, outstanding headroom. Note roomy midcabin berth, Corian galley counter. Well-designed cockpit has foldaway transom seat, swivel helm seat, walk-through windshield. Companionway screen door, extended swim platform, transom shower are standard. Twin 270hp Volvo I/Os cruise at 25–26 knots (about 42 knots wide open).

Length	30'10"	Headroom	6'2"
Beam	10'6"	Fuel	151 gals.
Draft, Up	1'8"	Water	35 gals.
Draft, Down	3'2"	Hull Type	Modified-V
Weight	10,500#	Deadrise Aft	18°

See Page 559 For Resale Values

Regal Marine
Orlando, FL
www.regalboats.com

231-360-0827

Regal 320 Commodore
1988–92

Widebody sportcruiser introduced in 1988 appealed to owners willing to pay for quality construction, top-tier amenities. Interior sports oversized double berth forward, U-shaped dinette with drop-down table, large midcabin berth. Note generous storage, good cabin lighting and headroom. Well-planned cockpit with wet bar, electric engine hatch, seats seven. Note slender side decks. Modified-V hull delivers comfortable big-water ride. Twin 260hp I/Os top out at 35 knots; twin 340hp engines reach about 40 knots top.

Length	31'10"	Clearance	9'4"
Beam	11'2"	Fuel	178 gals.
Draft, Up	1'8"	Water	50 gals.
Draft, Down	2'11"	Hull Type	Modified-V
Weight	11,000#	Deadrise Aft	19°

Prices Not Provided for Pre-1995 Models

Regal Marine
Orlando, FL
www.regalboats.com

231-360-0827

Regal Ventura 9.8; 322/3260 Commodore
1993–2004

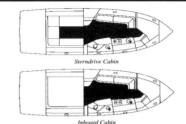

Sterndrive Cabin

Inboard Cabin

Popular express cruiser (called Ventura 9.8 in 1993–94; 322 Commodore 1995–99; 3260 Commodore in 2000–04) delivered quality, comfort at competitive price. Richly appointed interior is accented with posh Ultraleather upholstery, glossy cherry trim, Corian countertops. Cockpit table converts into sun pad; aft seating group can be removed for fishing. Note walk-through windshield, transom storage lockers. Inboard models with 300hp MerCruiser V-drives top out at 35 knots; twin 300hp I/Os reach 40+ knots top.

Hull Length	32'0"	Fuel	172 gals.
Beam	11'2"	Water	50 gals.
Draft	3'2"	Waste	30 gals.
Weight	11,800#	Hull Type	Modified-V
Clearance, Arch	10'1"	Deadrise Aft	19°

See Page 559 For Resale Values

Regal Marine
Orlando, FL
www.regalboats.com

Cruisers & Sportboats

231-360-0827

Regal 3350 Sport Cruiser
2005–Current

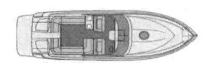

Well-styled sportboat with sleek profile is easy on the eye, fun to drive, built to last. Vast cockpit with huge U-shaped aft lounge offers more seating than just about any boat in her class. Compact cabin with Ultraleather lounge seating, enclosed head with sink, teak-and-holly sole, sleeps two in genuine comfort. Note that engine compartment is accessed from swim platform rather than cockpit. Wet bar, transom storage lockers are standard. Volvo 320hp sterndrives deliver a top speed of 40+ knots.

Length	34'8"	Headroom	5'2"
Beam	11'4"	Fuel	186 gals.
Draft, Up	1'8"	Water	30 gals.
Draft, Down	2'11"	Hull Type	Deep-V
Weight	11,400#	Deadrise Aft	19°

See Page 559 For Resale Values

Regal Marine
Orlando, FL
www.regalboats.com

231-360-0827

Regal 3360 Express
2006–Current

Classy sterndrive express with rakish lines gets high marks for comfort, quality, performance. Well-appointed salon with large foldout sleeper offers plenty of storage, lots of elbow room. Forward window inserts, side windows provide plenty of natural lighting. Note cherrywood cabinetry, posh upholstery, hardwood salon floor. Topside amenities include wet bar, transom shower, electric engine hatch. Extended swim platform, radar arch, transom storage are standard. Volvo 320hp I/Os cruise at 25 knots and reach 36–38 knots top.

Length	34'8"	Fuel	180 gals.
Beam	11'4"	Water	52 gals.
Draft, Down	2'11"	Waste	28 gals.
Weight	12,120#	Hull Type	Deep-V
Headroom	6'4"	Deadrise Aft	19°

See Page 559 For Resale Values

Regal Marine
Orlando, FL
www.regalboats.com

231-360-0827

Regal 3560/3760 Commodore
2003–Current

Luxury sportcruiser (called 3560 Commodore in 2003–06) ranks near the top of her class in quality, luxury, performance. Spacious interior with cherry cabinetry, leather upholstery offers unsurpassed comfort, elegance. Highlights include private forward stateroom, large galley with chest-level refrigerator, hardwood salon flooring. Cockpit is arranged with horseshoe lounge opposite helm, wet bar, foldaway rear seat. Volvo 420hp I/Os cruise at 28–30 knots (40+ knots top); 420hp gas inboards cruise in the low-to-mid 20s (around 35 knots top).

Length Overall	38'0"	Fuel	276 gals.
Hull Length	34'8"	Water	67 gals.
Beam	12'2"	Waste	30 gals.
Draft	3'0"	Hull Type	Deep-V
Weight	15,200#	Deadrise Aft	19°

See Page 559 For Resale Values

Regal Marine
Orlando, FL
www.regalboats.com

231-360-0827

Regal 360 Commodore
1985–90

Sporty midcabin cruiser—flagship of Regal's late-1980s fleet—was among most popular big express boats of her era. Accommodations include roomy salon with circular dining area, private forward stateroom, full galley with refrigerator/freezer, large head with stall shower. Topside features include cockpit seating for six (note foldaway transom bench), foredeck sun pad, bow pulpit. Solid fiberglass hull has prop pockets to reduce draft, increase efficiency. Twin 340hp gas inboards cruise at 18–20 knots (high 20s top).

Length	36'1"	Fuel	280 gals.
Beam	13'1"	Water	125 gals.
Draft	2'10"	Waste	65 gals.
Weight	17,000#	Hull Type	Modified-V
Clearance	9'7"	Deadrise Aft	17°

Prices Not Provided for Pre-1995 Models

Regal Marine
Orlando, FL
www.regalboats.com

231-360-0827

Regal 3860/4060 Commodore
2002–Current

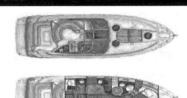

Full-bodied sportyacht (called 3860 Commodore in 2002–06) successfully blends comfort, luxury, performance. Posh interior with two private cabins boasts second head in aft stateroom—a rare luxury in boats this size. Expansive cockpit with circular bridgedeck lounge accommodates a small crowd. Rear cockpit deck lifts for walk-in access to engine compartment from swim platform. Note power windshield vent. Standard 420hp gas engines cruise at 18 knots (30+ knots top); 370hp Cummins diesels cruise at 22 knots (30 knots top).

Length w/Platform	40'1"	Fuel	277 gals.
Beam	13'0"	Water	75 gals.
Draft	3'3"	Waste	40 gals.
Weight	19,000#	Hull Type	Modified-V
Clearance, Arch	11'9"	Deadrise Aft	18°

See Page 559 For Resale Values

Regal Marine
Orlando, FL
www.regalboats.com

231-360-0827

Regal 3880/4080 Commodore
2001–Current

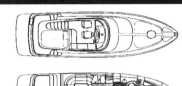

High-style flybridge yacht (called 3880 Commodore in 2001–06) delivers space, comfort on a grand scale. Luxurious two-stateroom interior offers spacious full-beam salon with oversized dinette, large galley with side-by-side refrigerator. Note storage compartments under salon sole. Topside amenities include cockpit engineroom access, foredeck sun pads, foldout cockpit seat. Note overhead cockpit storage. Gas 420hp V-drive engines cruise at 20 knots; 370hp Cummins diesels cruise at 22–23 knots. IPS pod drives available since 2010.

Length Overall	40'1"	Fuel	252 gals.
Beam	13'0"	Water	80 gals.
Draft	3'3"	Waste	40 gals.
Weight	19,300#	Hull Type	Modified-V
Clearance, Arch	16'9"	Deadrise Aft	18°

See Page 559 For Resale Values

Regal Marine
Orlando, FL
www.regalboats.com

www.powerboatguide.com   231-360-0827

Regal 380/400/402 Commodore
1991–99

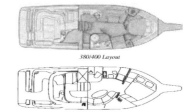

380/400 Layout

402 Layout

Popular 1990s cruiser (called Regal 380 Commodore in 1991–92; 400 Commodore in 1993–94; 402 Commodore in 1995–99) ranked among the largest express boats of her era. Roomy interior—updated in 1995—boasts privacy doors for both staterooms, fully equipped galley, rich leather seating. Note standing aft-cabin headroom. Large cockpit seats eight. Power engine hatch, bow pulpit were standard. Twin 310hp gas engines cruise at 18–19 knots (27–28 knots top); optional Cummins 330hp diesels cruise at 26 knots (30 knots top).

Length w/Pulpit	42'0"	Fuel	265 gals.
Hull Length	39'5"	Water	125 gals.
Beam	13'1"	Waste	65 gals.
Draft	3'0"	Hull Type	Modified-V
Weight	16,000#	Deadrise Aft	17°

See Page 560 For Resale Values

Regal Marine
Orlando, FL
www.regalboats.com

---

www.powerboatguide.com   231-360-0827

Regal 4160/4260/4460 Commodore
2000–Current

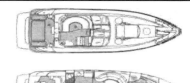

Bold American sportyacht (called 4160 Commodore in 2000-01; 4260 Commodore in 2002-05) delivers compelling mix of modern styling, posh accommodations, spirited performance. Wide-open salon with leather seating, home-sized galley with hardwood floor, two private staterooms, two heads. Huge bridgedeck boasts circular lounge seating. Transom storage locker, power engine hatch are standard. Fiberglass hardtop is a popular option. Cummins 450hp-or Volvo 480hp-diesels cruise at 28 knots (30+ knots top).

Length w/Platform	44'4"	Fuel	328 gals.
Hull Length	40'10"	Water	101 gals.
Beam	14'0"	Waste	48 gals.
Draft	2'11"	Hull Type	Deep-V
Weight	20,375#	Deadrise Aft	20°

See Page 560 For Resale Values

Regal Marine
Orlando, FL
www.regalboats.com

---

www.powerboatguide.com   231-360-0827

Riviera 3600 Sport Yacht
2007–Current

Well-bred express with fully enclosed hardtop takes cruising comfort to the next level. Unique stainless-steel–framed bulkhead swings up to expose galley/salon to cockpit with built-in settee, teak dining table. Good cabin ventilation with overhead hatches, sliding salon windows. Cherry panel conceals galley when not in use. Engineroom, reached via cockpit hatch, is very tight. Prop pockets reduce draft, improve efficiency. Note quiet underwater exhaust system. Cruise in the mid 20s with 370hp Volvo diesels (about 30 knots top).

Length w/Pulpit	38'6"	Fuel	265 gals.
Beam	12'7"	Water	103 gals.
Draft	3'3"	Waste	18 gals.
Weight	20,300#	Hull Type	Modified-V
Clearance	NA	Deadrise Aft	15°

Insufficient Resale Data To Assign Values

Riviera Yachts
Emerald Pacific Yachts - San Diego
www.riviera.com.au

231-360-0827

Riviera 4000 Offshore
1998–2003

Conservative express cruiser introduced in 1998 gave budget-minded boaters exceptional boating value for the money. Versatile layout boasts large cockpit for fishing or entertaining, roomy single-stateroom interior with convertible dinette for weekend cruising. Highlights include oak interior trim, L-shaped cockpit dinette, radar arch, swim platform, spacious engineroom, well-designed helm position. Factory hardtop was optional. Cummins 450hp—or Cat 435hp—diesels cruise in the mid 20s and reach a top speed of close to 30 knots.

Length w/Pulpit	44'7"	Fuel	394 gals.
Hull Length	41'0"	Water	119 gals.
Beam	14'4"	Headroom	6'4"
Draft	3'11"	Hull Type	Modified-V
Weight	25,353#	Deadrise Aft	15°

Insufficient Resale Data To Assign Values

Riviera Yachts
Emerald Pacific Yachts - San Diego
www.riviera.com.au

231-360-0827

Roughwater 37
1981–88

Classic diesel cruiser imported from Taiwan during 1980s combines handsome lines with versatile layout, solid fiberglass construction. Slender, easily driven hull offers better speed, economy that most modern semi-displacement designs. Step-down salon-separated from pilothouse by two-part hatch-features spacious galley, U-shaped dinette. Note very wide side decks. Engineroom is accessed via hatches in pilothouse floor. Single 200hp Perkins diesel will cruise at 8-10 knots; twin 215hp GM diesels cruise at 14-16 knots.

Length Overall	39'5"	Fuel, Single	230 gals.
Length WL	33'0"	Fuel, Twin	300 gals.
Beam	11'7"	Water	100 gals.
Draft	4'0"	Headroom	6'4"
Weight	16,000#	Hull Type	Semi-Disp.

Prices Not Provided for Pre-1995 Models

No longer in business.

231-360-0827

Sabre 34 Hardtop Express
2006–Current

Elegant express yacht blends hardtop versatility with luxury-class interior, timeless Downeast styling. Space-efficient layout is arranged with galley up (rather than down as with most boats of this type) resulting in more living space below. Posh cabin with convertible dinette, stall shower in head is perfect for the cruising couple. Note excellent helm visibility, opening side windows, wide side decks. Engine compartment is a little tight. This boat drips quality. Cruise at 25 knots (30+ top) with twin 370hp Volvo inboard diesels.

Length	34'6"	Fuel	275 gals.
Beam	13'3"	Water	80 gals.
Draft	3'0"	Waste	30 gals.
Weight	15,850#	Hull Type	Modified-V
Clearance, Mast	12'8"	Deadrise Aft	16°

See Page 561 For Resale Values

Sabre Yachts
South Casco, ME
www.sabreyachts.com

---

www.powerboatguide.com 231-360-0827

Sabre 36 Express
1996–2003

Handsome, exceptionally well-finished Downeast cruiser turns heads wherever she goes. Traditional teak interior with U-shaped galley, convertible dinette sleeps four in elegant surroundings. Deep cockpit is big enough for fishing, entertaining. Note wide side decks, radar mast. No separate stall shower in head. Cored hull was redesigned in 2000 (MKII version), increasing transom deadrise from 14 to 18 degrees, eliminating skeg. Cat 300hp engines cruise at 20 knots; MKII models with 370hp Yanmars cruise in mid 20s.

Length w/Pulpit	40'1"	Clearance, Mast	12'0"
Hull Length	36'0"	Fuel	300 gals.
Beam	12'6"	Water	100 gals.
Draft	3'4"	Hull Type	Modified-V
Weight	18,500#	Deadrise Aft	14°/18°

See Page 561 For Resale Values

Sabre Yachts
South Casco, ME
www.sabreyachts.com

---

www.powerboatguide.com 231-360-0827

Sabre 38 Express
2005–Current

Compelling hardtop express combines exceptional beauty with elegant accommodations, outstanding seakeeping abilities. Semi-enclosed pilothouse with swivel helm and companion seats, folding teak table, full wet bar provides unmatched open-air luxury. Luxurious single-stateroom interior with high-gloss cherry cabinets boasts teak-and-holly sole, posh leather settee, full-service galley, roomy head with stall shower. Note overhead hardtop hatches, wide side decks, excellent helm visibility. Yanmar 440hp diesels cruise at 25–26 knots.

Length	36'8"	Fuel	350 gals.
Beam	13'8"	Water	100 gals.
Draft	3'4"	Waste	30 gals.
Weight	21,500#	Hull Type	Modified-V
Clearance, Mast	13'5"	Deadrise Aft	18°

Insufficient Resale Data To Assign Values

Sabre Yachts
South Casco, ME
www.sabreyachts.com

---

www.powerboatguide.com 231-360-0827

Sabre 42 Express
2004–Current

Sophisticated Downeast express introduced in 2004 embodies the graceful styling, high-quality construction common to all Sabreline yachts. Semi-enclosed pilothouse with swivel helm and companion seats, well-positioned lounge seating provides extraordinary cruising luxury. Posh two-stateroom interior is highlighted with varnished cherry joinery, leather upholstery, impressive furnishings. Note hull prop pockers. Yanmar 440hp inboard diesels cruise at 22–23 knots. Newer models with 850hp Zeus pod drives cruise efficiently at 28 knots.

Length	42'3"	Fuel	450 gals.
Beam	14'4"	Water	160 gals.
Draft	3'9"	Waste	60 gals.
Weight	29,000#	Hull Type	Modified-V
Clearance, Mast	13'3"	Deadrise Aft	16°

Insufficient Resale Data To Assign Values

Sabre Yachts
South Casco, ME
www.sabreyachts.com

Sabre 52 Salon
2008–Current

Executive-class cruising yacht with timeless Downeast styling takes yachting elegance, sophistication to the next level. Roomy cherrywood interior—designed for two couples—features richly-appointed pilothouse with posh leather seating, two large staterooms, two full heads. Power sunroof, 360-degree windows bathe pilothouse/salon in natural lighting. Note built-in stand-up engineroom, built-in cockpit seating, wide side decks. Composite construction saves weight, improves efficiency. Cruise at 26–28 knots with 865hp Cat diesels.

Length	53'2"	Fuel	800 gals.
Beam	16'0"	Water	200 gals.
Draft	4'3"	Waste	80 gals.
Weight	46,000#	Hull Type	Modified-V
Clearance	11'5"	Deadrise Aft	15°

Insufficient Resale Data To Assign Values

Sabre Yachts
South Casco, ME
www.sabreyachts.com

San Juan 38
2000–Current

Top-quality "gentleman's yacht" boasts impressive mix of graceful styling, lavish accommodations, high-tech construction. Highlights include semi-enclosed pilothouse with convertible dinette, richly appointed two-stateroom interior with varnished teak cabinetry, faux granite counters, teak-and-holly sole. Large cockpit with built-in transom seat is suitable for entertaining, fishing. Note fine teak instrument console, retractable sunroof. Yanmar 350hp diesel inboards cruise in the mid 20s (about 30 knots top).

Length Overall	40'7"	Headroom	6'1"
Beam	12'2"	Fuel	300 gals.
Draft	2'2"	Water	80 gals.
Weight	15,800#	Hull Type	Modified-V
Clearance	9'11"	Deadrise Aft	14°

Insufficient Resale Data To Assign Values

San Juan Yachts
Anacortes, WA
www.sanjuanyachts.com

Sea Ray 270 Select EX
2005–Current

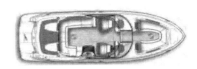

Luxury-class bowrider—trailerable with a permit—pairs top-shelf amenities with quality construction, best-in-class styling. Well-arranged deck plan includes U-shaped cockpit seating, removable cooler, wet bar, twin sun pads with filler. Enclosed head under port console has marine head and sink but no opening port. Power engine hatch, pressure fresh water system, transom shower are standard. A seriously well-designed dayboat. Single 320hp MerCruiser sterndrive tops out in the mid-to-high 30s.

Length	28'6"	Fuel	94 gals.
Beam	9'0"	Water	21 gals.
Draft, Up	1'9"	Waste	10 gals.
Draft, Down	3'1"	Hull Type	Deep-V
Weight	5,555#	Deadrise Aft	21°

See Page 561 For Resale Values

Sea Ray Boats
Knoxville, TN
www.searay.com

Cruisers & Sportboats

www.powerboatguide.com   231-360-0827

Sea Ray 270 Sundancer
1982–88

Durable 1980s-era express with 10-foot beam gave buyers a lot of boat for the money in her day. Spacious midcabin interior with full galley, enclosed head with shower, sleeps six. Roomy cockpit boasts adjustable helm seat, foldaway stern seat, transom door. Teak swim platform, bow pulpit were standard. Most were sold with optional radar arch. Narrow side decks make going forward a dicey proposition. Very popular model. Twin 260hp MerCruiser sterndrives will cruise at 25 knots (high 30s top).

Length w/Pulpit	29'2"	Fuel	120 gals.
Beam	10'0"	Water	28 gals.
Draft, Up	1'10"	Headroom	6'2"
Draft, Down	2'8"	Hull Type	Deep-V
Weight	6,700#	Deadrise Aft	22°

Prices Not Provided for Pre-1995 Models

Sea Ray Boats
Knoxville, TN
www.searay.com

---

www.powerboatguide.com   231-360-0827

Sea Ray 270 Sundancer
1992–93

Second in a series of 270 Sundancer models was among the biggest trailerable cruisers of her era. Generic midcabin floorplan is arranged with V-berth forward, removable dinette table, efficient galley, stand-up head with shower. Double berth in aft cabin is a tight fit for adults. Cockpit layout includes double-wide helm seat, pull-out jump seats, transom seat. Bow pulpit, swim platform were standard. Restyled in 2004 both inside and out. Cruise at 20 knots (mid-30s top) with single 330hp MerCruiser sterndrive.

Length w/Pulpit	28'6"	Fuel	100 gals.
Beam	8'6"	Water	24 gals.
Draft, Up	1'8"	Waste	20 gals.
Draft, Down	3'0"	Hull Type	Deep-V
Weight	5,600#	Deadrise Aft	20°

Prices Not Provided for Pre-1995 Models

Sea Ray Boats
Knoxville, TN
www.searay.com

---

www.powerboatguide.com   231-360-0827

Sea Ray 270 Sundancer
1994-97; 1999

Updated version of previous 270 Sundancer packed big-boat accommodations in a trailerable hull. Well-appointed cabin with compact galley, convertible dinette sleeps four. Surprisingly roomy cockpit features include double back-to-back helm seat, portside lounger, aft bench seat, transom door. Deep-V hull delivers stable open-water ride. Out of production in 1997; produced again in 1999 as the 270 Sundancer "Special Edition". Cruise at 22 knots with single 330hp MerCruiser I/O (about 35 knots top).

Length w/Pulpit	29'11"	Fuel	100 gals.
Beam	8'6"	Water	24 gals.
Draft, Up	1'11"	Waste	20 gals.
Draft, Down	3'0"	Hull Type	Deep-V
Weight	6,400#	Deadrise Aft	20°

See Page 561 For Resale Values

Sea Ray Boats
Knoxville, TN
www.searay.com

231-360-0827

Sea Ray 270 Sundancer
1998–2001

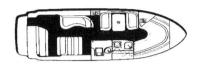

Strong-selling express with generous beam delivers traditional Sea Ray comfort, performance in a well-crafted package. Spacious interior with booth-style dinette, full galley, sleeps six. Aft stateroom has curved sliding window for ventilation. Space-efficient cockpit includes wet bar, cooler and stereo. Additional features include transom storage, cockpit shower, extended swim platform, gas-assist engine hatch. Cruise at 20 knots with single 310hp I/O (30+ top); mid 20s with twin 190hp engines (40+ knots top).

Length w/Platform	29'10"	Fuel	100 gals.
Beam	9'2"	Water	28 gals.
Draft, Up	1'11"	Waste	28 gals.
Draft, Down	3 5"	Hull Type	Deep-V
Weight	7,500#	Deadrise Aft	21°

See Page 561 For Resale Values

Sea Ray Boats
Knoxville, TN
www.searay.com

231-360-0827

Sea Ray 270 Weekender
1992–93

Good-running trailerable cruiser with very large cockpit, bare-bones interior is great for fishing, diving, daytime entertaining. Single-level cockpit with foldaway stern seat, in-floor storage can accommodate several guests or anglers. Small cabin with mini-galley, enclosed head with shower sleeps two. Big cockpit, stable deep-V hull makes this one of the more versatile boats in her class. Lasted only two years in production. Single 300hp MerCruiser sterndrive reaches a top speed of 30+ knots.

Length w/Pulpit	28'6"	Clearance	NA
Beam	8'6"	Fuel	100 gals.
Draft, Up	1'8"	Water	24 gals.
Draft, Down	3'0"	Hull Type	Deep-V
Weight	5,600#	Deadrise Aft	20°

Prices Not Provided for Pre-1995 Models

Sea Ray Boats
Knoxville, TN
www.searay.com

231-360-0827

Sea Ray 270/290 Sundancer
1990–93

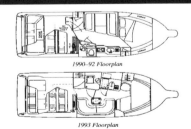

1990–92 Floorplan

1993 Floorplan

Sturdy 1990s express set class standards in her day for sporty styling, state-of-the-art amenities. Open-plan interior with full galley, convertible dinette sleeps six. Privacy curtains separate forward berth from salon—useful for cruising with friends. Cockpit came standard with foldaway stern seat, wet bar, triple-wide helm seat. Called 270 Sundancer in 1990–91; 290 Sundancer in 1992–93. Floorplan undated in 1993. Cruise at 20 knots with single 300hp Mercury I/O; mid 20s with twin 205hp Mercs.

Length w/Pulpit	30'6"	Fuel	100 gals.
Beam	9'0"	Water	24 gals.
Draft, Up	1'10"	Waste	20 gals.
Draft, Down	3'1"	Hull Type	Deep-V
Weight	5,800#	Deadrise Aft	20°

Prices Not Provided for Pre-1995 Models

Sea Ray Boats
Knoxville, TN
www.searay.com

www.powerboatguide.com   231-360-0827

Sea Ray 280 Bowrider
1996–2001

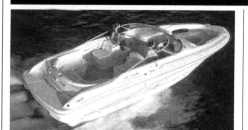

Super-popular bowrider with party-time cockpit, generous beam handles big water with ease. Big U-shaped cockpit seating accommodates a small crowd. Filler cushions turn bow area into padded sundeck. Lockable head compartment with shower is concealed in passenger-side console. Power rear seat lifts for engine access. One of the largest bowriders of her era. Twin 260hp MerCruiser I/Os reach 45+ knots top; single MerCruiser 310hp power tops out in the high 30s.

Length	27'6"	Clearance	NA
Beam	9'6"	Fuel	127 gals.
Draft, Up	2'2"	Water	24 gals.
Draft, Down	3.5"	Hull Type	Deep-V
Weight	6,400#	Deadrise Aft	21°

See Page 561 For Resale Values

Sea Ray Boats
Knoxville, TN
www.searay.com

---

www.powerboatguide.com   231-360-0827

Sea Ray 280 Cuddy
1996–99

Stylish 1990s sportcruiser pairs versatile layout with upscale amenities, above-average performance. Generous 9'6" beam results in roomy cockpit with full-width rear seat, back-to-back lounger seat, wet bar, removable table. Comfy cabin with enclosed head, portside snack bar, convertible dinette sleeps two. Flip-up helm seat, transom shower, power engine hatch were standard. Opening ports are a plus. Still a good-looking boat today. Twin 260hp MerCruiser I/Os reach 45 knots top; single 310hp Merc hits 35+ knots.

Length	27'6"	Fuel	127 gals.
Beam	9'6"	Water	24 gals.
Draft, Up	2'3"	Waste	20 gals.
Draft, Down	3'3"	Hull Type	Deep-V
Weight	6,400#	Deadrise Aft	21°

See Page 562 For Resale Values

Sea Ray Boats
Knoxville, TN
www.searay.com

---

www.powerboatguide.com   231-360-0827

Sea Ray 280 Sun Sport
1996–2001

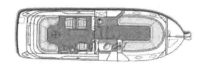

Seductive (and expensive) sport cuddy introduced in 1996 was stylish, fast, loaded with features. Well-appointed cockpit boasts back-to-back companion seat, rear U-lounge with table, wet bar with cooler. Filler cushion turns aft seating into sun pad. Upscale cabin with sitting headroom, enclosed head with shower, convertible dinette sleeps two. Aft cockpit seat rises electrically for engine access. Fit and finish is well above average. Twin 260hp MerCruiser sterndrives deliver a top speed of around 45 knots.

Length	27'6"	Fuel	127 gals.
Beam	9'6"	Water	24 gals.
Draft, Up	2'2"	Waste	20 gals.
Draft, Down	3.5"	Hull Type	Deep-V
Weight	8,200#	Deadrise Aft	21°

See Page 562 For Resale Values

Sea Ray Boats
Knoxville, TN
www.searay.com

Sea Ray 280 Sundancer
1989–91

Smooth-running express introduced in 1989 met Sea Ray promise of lasting value for the money. Generic midcabin interior with large galley, convertible dinette sleeps six. Space-efficient cockpit features double helm seat with aft-facing seat, foldaway rear seat, transom door. Bow pulpit, cockpit bolsters, ice chest, were standard. Privacy curtains separate forward berth from salon—great for cruising with friends. Twin 260hp MerCruiser sterndrives cruise in the mid 20s(about 35 knots top).

Length w/Pulpit	31'11"	Clearance	9'0"
Beam	10'6"	Fuel	120 gals.
Draft, Up	1'10"	Water	35 gals.
Draft	2'8"	Hull Type	Deep-V
Weight	8,000#	Deadrise Aft	20°

Prices Not Provided for Pre-1995 Models

Sea Ray Boats
Knoxville, TN
www.searay.com

Sea Ray 280 Sundancer
2001–09

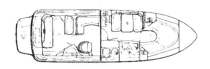

Polished Sea Ray express combines leading-edge styling with quality amenities, sporty performance. Well-appointed interior with cherry cabinetry, posh decor sleeps four adults, two kids in comfort. Cockpit has wet bar with built-in cooler, portside lounger, fold-down sun pad. Sporty helm layout includes flip-up seat, woodgrain dash, tilt wheel. Note extended swim platform, sport arch with overhead lighting. Near-flawless gelcoat, excellent finish. Cruise at 30 knots with twin 260hp MerCruiser sterndrive power (mid 40s top).

Length w/Platform	31'1"	Fuel	100 gals.
Beam	9.5"	Water	28 gals.
Draft, Up	1'10"	Waste	28 gals.
Draft, Down	3'3"	Hull Type	Deep-V
Weight	8,630#	Deadrise Aft	21°

See Page 562 For Resale Values

Sea Ray Boats
Knoxville, TN
www.searay.com

Sea Ray 290 Bowrider
2001–04

Standard Seating

Optional Seating

Sporty 29-footer with big, party-time cockpit gets high marks for quality amenities, comfortable seating, super performance. Standard deck plan has U-shaped seating aft, back-to-back companion seating, centerline transom gate; optional layout features large sun pad aft, starboard transom gate, bucket seats forward. Full wet bar, power engine compartment hatch, transom storage lockers were standard. Largest bowrider available in 2001. Twin MerCruiser 260hp I/Os cruise at 25–28 knots (around 45 knots top).

Length	29'6"	Fuel	130 gals.
Beam	9'8"	Water	24 gals.
Draft, Up	2'0"	Waste	20 gals.
Draft, Down	3'1"	Hull Type	Deep-V
Weight	7,700#	Deadrise Aft	21°

See Page 562 For Resale Values

Sea Ray Boats
Knoxville, TN
www.searay.com

Cruisers & Sportboats

Sea Ray 290 Select EX
2005–08

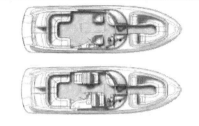

Premium version of earlier Sea Ray 290 Bowrider (2001–04) offers sports-car performance, unsurpassed passenger comfort. Highlights include wet bar with sink, cockpit table, burled helm with tilt wheel, enclosed head with sink, flip-up bolster seat. Concealed swim platform cooler is a nice touch. Deep-V hull handles rough weather without complaint. Available with three cockpit seating plans. Single 375hp MerCruiser I/O tops out at over 40 knots; twin 260hp Mercs reach 45+ knots wide open.

Length	29'6"	Fuel	130 gals.
Beam	9'8"	Water	24 gals.
Draft, Up	2'0"	Waste	20 gals.
Draft, Down	3'6"	Hull Type	Deep-V
Weight	7,700#	Deadrise Aft	21°

See Page 562 For Resale Values

Sea Ray Boats
Knoxville, TN
www.searay.com

Sea Ray 290 Sun Sport
2002–09

Standard Seating

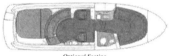

Optional Seating

Classy sportcruiser with big-time eye appeal is sexy, fast, a blast to drive. Offered with three cockpit seating plans—standard layout includes U-shaped rear seating, wet bar, woodgrain dash, in-floor storage. Surprisingly roomy cabin boasts convertible dinette, galley cabinet, enclosed head with VacuFlush toilet. Transom storage lockers, extended swim platform, power engine hatch are standard. Exemplary finish, near-perfect gelcoat. Twin 320hp MerCruiser sterndrives will hit a top speed of 45+ knots.

Length	29'6"	Fuel	130 gals.
Beam	9'8"	Water	24 gals.
Draft, Up	2'2"	Waste	20 gals.
Draft, Down	3'1"	Hull Type	Deep-V
Weight	8,300#	Deadrise Aft	21°

See Page 562 For Resale Values

Sea Ray Boats
Knoxville, TN
www.searay.com

Sea Ray 290 Sundancer
1994–97

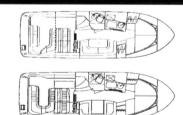

Roomy sterndrive express hit the right buttons with 1990s Sea Ray buyers. Very spacious interior with double berths fore and aft features large galley, convertible dinette, two hanging lockers. Cockpit highlights include U-shaped lounge seating, double helm seat with flip-up bolsters, very large dash with chart flat. Engine compartment is a tight fit with twin engines. No cockpit wet bar. Replaced in 1998 with all-new 290 Sundancer model. Cruise at 20 knots with single 300hp MerCruiser; 24–25 knots with twin 190hp Mercs.

Length w/Pulpit	32'1"	Fuel	130 gals.
Beam	9'8"	Water	24 gals.
Draft, Up	2'0"	Waste	24 gals.
Draft, Down	3'9"	Hull Type	Deep-V
Weight	8,500#	Deadrise Aft	21°

See Page 562 For Resale Values

Sea Ray Boats
Knoxville, TN
www.searay.com

231-360-0827

Sea Ray 290 Sundancer
1998–2001

Redesigned version of previous 290 Sundancer (1994–97) boasts enlarged cockpit, updated styling, revised interior. Topside highlights include extended swim platform, portside lounge seat (opposite helm), wet bar, flip-up helm seat. Rear bench seat can be removed to free up cockpit space. Offered with three interior layouts. Side decks are narrow. Engine compartment is a tight fit with twins. Heavy boat for her size. Cruise at 20 knots with single 310hp Merc I/O; twin 260hp Mercs cruise in the mid 20s.

Length	29'8"	Fuel	130 gals.
Beam	10'2"	Water	28 gals.
Draft, Up	2'3"	Waste	28 gals.
Draft, Down	3'1"	Hull Type	Deep-V
Weight	10,500#	Deadrise Aft	21°

See Page 562 For Resale Values

Sea Ray Boats
Knoxville, TN
www.searay.com

231-360-0827

Sea Ray 290 Sundancer
2006–08

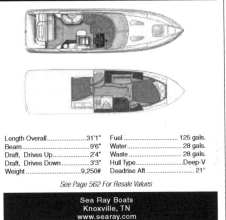

Cutting-edge express combines world-class styling with luxury amenities, no-excuses performance. Stylish interior with cherry cabinets, leather seating gets high marks for premium furnishings, excellent finish. Island berth converts to aft-facing seat with storage under. Topside features include wet bar with Corian counter, power engine hatch, transom shower, walk-through windshield. One of the best-looking boats in her class. Twin 260hp MerCruiser sterndrives cruise at 25 knots (about 40 knots wide open).

Length Overall	31'1"	Fuel	125 gals.
Beam	9'6"	Water	28 gals.
Draft, Drives Up	2'4"	Waste	28 gals.
Draft, Drives Down	3'3"	Hull Type	Deep-V
Weight	9,250#	Deadrise Aft	21°

See Page 562 For Resale Values

Sea Ray Boats
Knoxville, TN
www.searay.com

231-360-0827

Sea Ray 300 Sedan Bridge
1985–87

Well-built sedan offered 1980s buyers a blend of space, comfort, versatility in a well-styled package. Teak-trimmed interior with large galley, convertible dinette and sofa, lower helm, head with shower sleeps six. Angled berth in forward cabin preserves cabin space; compact galley is short on storage. Cockpit hatches provide good engine access. Side decks are very narrow. Side-dumping exhausts keep noxious fumes out of the cockpit. Twin 260hp MerCruiser inboards cruise at 18 knots and top out in the high 20s.

Length	29'1"	Fuel	140 gals.
Beam	11'0"	Water	40 gals.
Draft	2.5"	Cockpit	60 sq. ft.
Weight	10,500#	Hull Type	Deep-V
Clearance	NA	Deadrise Aft	21°

Prices Not Provided for Pre-1995 Models

Sea Ray Boats
Knoxville, TN
www.searay.com

Cruisers & Sportboats

www.powerboatguide.com

231-360-0827

Sea Ray 300 Select EX
2009–Current

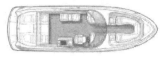

Big-water runabout delivers high-octane mix of sports-car handling, unsurpassed passenger comfort, exceptional quality. Roomy cockpit—offered with three seating plans—features wet bar with sink, removable table, enclosed head with sink. Note stylish burlwood helm with easy-to-read gauges, Eurostyle tilt wheel, flip-up bolster seat. Concealed swim platform cooler is a nice touch. Deep-V hull handles rough weather without complaint. Single 375hp MerCruiser tops out at close to 40 knots; twin 260hp Mercs reach 45+ knots wide open.

Length	29'6"	Fuel	130 gals.
Beam	9'8"	Water	24 gals.
Draft, Up	2'0"	Waste	20 gals.
Draft, Down	3'4"	Hull Type	Deep-V
Weight	7,700#	Deadrise Aft	21°

Insufficient Resale Data To Assign Values

Sea Ray Boats
Knoxville, TN
www.searay.com

---

www.powerboatguide.com

231-360-0827

Sea Ray 300 Sundancer
1985–89

Top-selling 1980s express hit the sweet spot with value-conscious families. Carpeted interior with teak trim includes fully equipped galley, stand-up head with shower, convertible dinette, double berths fore and aft. Uncluttered cockpit is arranged with elevated helm seat and companion seats, foldaway aft-facing jump seats, transom door. Radar arch, generator were popular options. One of Sea Ray's most popular models ever. Twin 260hp sterndrives will cruise at 22 knots (about 35 knots wide open).

Length w/Pulpit	31'4"	Weight	9,800#
Hull Length	29'8"	Fuel	140 gals.
Beam	11'0"	Water	40 gals.
Draft, Up	1'6"	Hull Type	Deep-V
Draft, Down	2'11"	Deadrise Aft	21°

Prices Not Provided for Pre-1995 Models

Sea Ray Boats
Knoxville, TN
www.searay.com

---

www.powerboatguide.com

231-360-0827

Sea Ray 300 Sundancer
1992–93

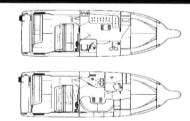

Contemporary 1990s express with integral swim platform delivered crisp styling with common-sense layout, quality construction. Generic midcabin interior with convertible dinette sleeps six. Triple-wide helm seat, aft-facing bench seat, wet bar, foldaway rear seat were standard in cockpit. Integral swim platform, vented windshield, good engine access. Small fuel capacity limits range. Replaced in 1994 with new 300 Sundancer model. Cruise at 20 knots with 230hp V-drive inboards; 22–24 knots with 230hp sterndrives.

Length w/Pulpit	31'11"	Clearance	8'8"
Hull Length	29'9"	Fuel	120 gals.
Beam	10'6"	Water	35 gals.
Draft	2'8"	Hull Type	Deep-V
Weight	8,300#	Deadrise Aft	21°

Prices Not Provided for Pre-1995 Models

Sea Ray Boats
Knoxville, TN
www.searay.com

231-360-0827

Sea Ray 300 Sundancer
1994–97

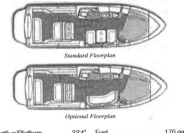

Dinette with Facing Seats

Circular Dinette

Classy midcabin express from the mid 1990s offered Sea Ray owners state-of-the-art comfort, styling at a reasonable price. Cockpit with facing bench seats, triple helm seat is larger than most 30-foot express cruisers. Traditional midcabin interior with teak trim, stand-up head, full galley, sleeps six. Chart flat in dash is a nice touch. Offered with inboard or sterndrive power. Twin 250hp V-drive inboards cruise at 20 knots (30 top); sterndrive versions of the same engines cruise in the low 20s (about 35 knots top).

Length w/Pulpit	33'1"	Fuel	200 gals.
Hull Length	30'6"	Water	35 gals.
Beam	10'6"	Waste	28 gals.
Draft	2'11"	Hull Type	Deep-V
Weight	10,200#	Deadrise Aft	21°

See Page 562 For Resale Values

Sea Ray Boats
Knoxville, TN
www.searay.com

231-360-0827

Sea Ray 300 Sundancer
2002–07

Standard Floorplan

Optional Floorplan

Sophisticated sportcruiser combined graceful styling with best-in-class accommodations, good open-water performance. Highlights include upscale interior with cherrywood cabinetry, extended swim platform, versatile cockpit with foldaway rear seat, sporty helm with flip-up bolster seat. Salon was offered with choice of dinette or curved settee. More galley stowage than many 30-footers. Cockpit sole lifts electrically for engine access. Twin 260hp MerCruiser sterndrive engines cruise at 20 knots (around 35 knots top).

Length w/Platform	33'4"	Fuel	170 gals.
Beam	10 5"	Water	35 gals.
Draft, Up	2'0"	Waste	28 gals.
Draft, Down	3'4"	Hull Type	Deep-V
Weight	12,000#	Deadrise Aft	21°

See Page 562 For Resale Values

Sea Ray Boats
Knoxville, TN
www.searay.com

231-360-0827

Sea Ray 305/300 Sedan Bridge
1988–89

Portly flybridge cruiser with slightly unorthodox styling is long on interior space, short on eye appeal. Spacious interior includes cozy mid-stateroom under salon dinette. Extended galley with double sink boasts copious storage, abundant counter space—rare luxuries in any 30-foot boat. Tiny cockpit is shaded by bridge overhang. Transom door is standard. Short production run. Called the 305 Sedan Bridge in 1988; 300 Sedan Bridge in 1999. Standard 260hp MerCruiser inboards cruise in the low 20s (28–29 knots top).

Length	29'10"	Fuel	200 gals.
Beam	12'0"	Water	60 gals.
Draft	2'6"	Cockpit	40 sq. ft.
Weight	11,500#	Hull Type	Modified-V
Clearance	NA	Deadrise Aft	18°

Prices Not Provided for Pre-1995 Models

Sea Ray Boats
Knoxville, TN
www.searay.com

www.powerboatguide.com   231-360-0827

Sea Ray 300 Weekender
1985–89

Classic family express with inboard power took 1980's styling, cruising standards to the next level. Topside features include roomy single-level cockpit with double helm and companion seats, removable rear seat, transom door, swim platform, side exhausts. Open-plan interior with convertible dinette, enclosed head with shower sleeps four. Cockpit hatches provide good engine access. Updated 300 Weekender model came out in 1991. Twin 260hp gas engines cruise at 22–24 knots with a top speed of 30+ knots.

Length w/Pulpit	31'4"	Clearance	NA
Hull Length	29'8"	Fuel	200 gals.
Beam	11'0"	Water	40 gals.
Draft	2.5"	Hull Type	Deep-V
Weight	9,500	Deadrise Aft	21°

Prices Not Provided for Pre-1995 Models

Sea Ray Boats
Knoxville, TN
www.searay.com

---

www.powerboatguide.com   231-360-0827

Sea Ray 300 Weekender
1991–95

Versatile 1990s express with large cockpit is the ideal platform for fishing, diving, daytime entertaining. Cockpit highlights include back-to-back companion seat, cockpit cooler, transom door, wet bar, folding stern seat. Efficient cabin layout with mini-galley, convertible dinette, enclosed head sleeps two. Good engine access via removable cockpit hatches. Inboard models have prop pockets. Twin 250hp MerCruiser V-drive inboards cruise in the mid 20s (30+ knots top); 250hp sterndrives reach close to 40 knots top.

Length w/Pulpit	31'11"	Fuel	200 gals.
Hull Length	29'9"	Water	28 gals.
Beam	10'6"	Waste	28 gals.
Draft	2'8"	Hull Type	Deep-V
Weight	7,800#	Deadrise Aft	21°

See Page 562 For Resale Values

Sea Ray Boats
Knoxville, TN
www.searay.com

---

www.powerboatguide.com   231-360-0827

Sea Ray 310 Sun Sport
1991–95

Rakish sportboat hit the mark with 1990 buyers looking for exciting performance, lasting eye appeal. Highlights include comfortable U-shaped cockpit seating, 2-person sun pad, electric engine hatch, integrated swim platform. Well-finished cabin with small galley, enclosed head with shower, sleeps two. Note forepeak mini-berth/storage area. Forward-facing arch represented cutting-edge styling in her era. Tight engine compartment. Cruise at a fast 30 knots with twin 350hp MerCruiser sterndrives (about 45 knots top).

Length	31'2"	Fuel	160 gals.
Beam	9'6"	Water	20 gals.
Draft, Up	2'2"	Waste	11 gals.
Draft, Down	3'1"	Hull Type	Deep-V
Weight	8,100#	Deadrise Aft	21°

See Page 562 For Resale Values

Sea Ray Boats
Knoxville, TN
www.searay.com

231-360-0827

Sea Ray 310/330 Express Cruiser
1990-95

Popular cruiser introduced in 1990 combines classic Sea Ray styling with surprisingly spacious interior, proven owner satisfaction. Versatile midcabin floorplan with U-shaped dinette sleeps six adults in comfort. Smallish cockpit has unusual triple-wide helm seat in addition to aft-facing seat, wet bar. Called 310 Sundancer in 1990–92; 330 Sundancer in 1992–94. Inboard models have prop pockets, side-dumping exhausts. Twin 310hp Merc inboards cruise at 20 knots; twin 300hp I/Os cruise in the mid 20s.

Length w/Pulpit	35'4"	Weight	10,000#
Hull Length	32'10"	Fuel	200 gals.
Beam	11 5"	Water	40 gals.
Draft, Inboard	2'3"	Hull Type	Deep-V
Draft, I/Os	3'0"	Deadrise Aft	21°

See Page 562 For Resale Values

Sea Ray Boats
Knoxville, TN
www.searay.com

231-360-0827

Sea Ray 310/330 Sundancer
1990-94

Top-selling Sea Ray cruiser from the early 1990s offered contemporary express-boat styling with spacious interior, premium amenities, quality construction. Versatile midcabin floorplan with U-shaped dinette, fully-equipped galley sleeps six adults in comfort. Cockpit includes unusual triple-wide helm seat in addition to aft-facing seat, wet bar. Called 310 Sundancer in 1990–92; 330 Sundancer in 1992–94. Twin 310hp Merc inboards cruise at 20 knots; twin 300hp I/Os cruise in the mid 20s.

Length w/Pulpit	35'4"	Weight	10,000#
Hull Length	32'10"	Fuel	180 gals.
Beam	11 5"	Water	40 gals.
Draft, Inboards	2'3"	Hull Type	Deep-V
Draft, I/Os	3'0"	Deadrise Aft	21°

Prices Not Provided for Pre-1995 Models

Sea Ray Boats
Knoxville, TN
www.searay.com

231-360-0827

Sea Ray 310 Sundancer
1981-83

Floorplan Not Available

Early-generation Sea Ray cruiser offered 1980's style, comfort, performance at a competitive price. Highlights include wide 12-foot beam, bow pulpit, aft-facing cockpit seats, windshield vents, teak exterior trim, swim platform. Original interior has bulkhead separating forward stateroom from salon; revised floorplan in 1983 eliminated the bulkhead in favor of a more open layout. Deep-V hull can handle a chop. No transom door; side decks are narrow. Twin 350hp gas inboards will cruise at 20 knots with a top speed of 30 knots.

Length w/Platform	32'4"	Clearance	NA
Hull Length	30'6"	Fuel	175 gals.
Beam	11'11"	Water	52 gals.
Draft	2 5"	Hull Type	Deep-V
Weight	10,000#	Deadrise Aft	21°

Prices Not Provided for Pre-1995 Models

Sea Ray Boats
Knoxville, TN
www.searay.com

Cruisers & Sportboats

Cruisers & Sportboats

231-360-0827

Sea Ray 310 Sundancer
1998–2002

1998 Floorplan

1999–2002

Smooth-riding express introduced in 1998 appealed to upscale cruisers willing to pay more for a quality boat. Very spacious cockpit with U-shaped rear seating, double companion seat (very unusual). Upscale interior has top-of-the-line decor and amenities. Original midcabin floorplan with horseshoe seating was replaced in 1999 with more conventional dinette layout. Twin 260hp V-drive inboards cruise at 18 knots (26-27 knots top); 260hp MerCruiser sterndrives top out in the mid 30s.

Length w/Platform	33'10"	Weight	12,000#
Hull Length	31'6"	Fuel	200 gals.
Beam	11'2"	Water	35 gals.
Draft, Drives Up	1'11"	Hull Type	Deep-V
Draft, Drives Down	3'7"	Deadrise Aft	23°

See Page 562 For Resale Values

Sea Ray Boats
Knoxville, TN
www.searay.com

231-360-0827

Sea Ray 310 Sundancer
2007–09

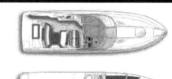

Late-model Sea Ray express combines sleek styling with luxury-class amenities, sporty performance. Classy interior with high-gloss cherry cabinets, Ultra-leather seating gets high marks for premium furnishings, hardwood flooring, generous storage. Cockpit wet bar has room for optional grill. Foldaway transom seat creates aft-facing seating on swim platform. Impressive helm with flip-up dash, burled dash. Axius drive system standard in late 2009. Twin 300hp V-drive inboards (gas) cruise at 25 knots; 320hp I/Os cruise at 28+ knots.

Length	33'4"	Fuel	200 gals.
Beam	10 5"	Water	35 gals.
Draft, Up	2 5"	Waste	28 gals.
Draft, Down	3'3"	Hull Type	Deep-V
Weight	14,000#	Deadrise Aft	21°

See Page XXX For Resale Values

Sea Ray Boats
Knoxville, TN
www.searay.com

231-360-0827

Sea Ray 320 Sundancer
2003–07

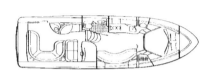

Mega-popular express introduced in 2003 set high standards for timeless styling, rich accommodations, proven owner satisfaction. Highlights include roomy, open-plan interior with lacquered cherry cabinets, expansive cockpit with U-shaped lounge seating, double helm seat with flip-up bolsters, burled dash, extended swim platform, power engineroom hatch. Side decks are narrow; engine access is a little tight. Deep-V hull can handle a stiff chop. Cruise in mid 20s with 300hp V-drive inboards (about 30 knots top).

Length w/Platform	35'6"	Fuel	200 gals.
Beam	11 5"	Water	40 gals.
Draft	2'9	Waste	28 gals.
Weight	13,200#	Hull Type	Deep-V
Clearance	10'2"	Deadrise Aft	21°

See Page 562 For Resale Values

Sea Ray Boats
Knoxville, TN
www.searay.com

231-360-0827

Sea Ray 330 Express Cruiser
1997–2000

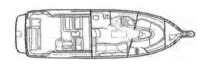

Rakish Sea Ray express with wide beam combines vast cockpit with maxi-volume cabin layout. Wide-open interior with private bow stateroom, built-in TV/VCR, convertible settee sleeps four. Cockpit amenities include foldaway transom seat, in-deck livewell and fish box, combined bait-prep station/wet bar. Entire bridgedeck lifts electrically for engine access. Power windshield vent is a useful touch. Cored hull has prop pockets to reduce draft. Twin 380hp MerCruiser inboards cruise at 20 knots (about 30 knots top).

Length w/Platform & Pulpit...38'0"		Fuel .... 275 gals.	
Hull Length ....33'6"		Water .... 50 gals.	
Beam.....................................13'5"		Waste .... 28 gals.	
Draft.......................................3'0"		Hull Type..........................Deep-V	
Weight ....16,500#		Deadrise Aft .... 19.5°	

See Page 562 For Resale Values

Sea Ray Boats
Knoxville, TN
www.searay.com

231-360-0827

Sea Ray 330 Sundancer
1995–99

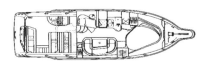

Sought-after Sea Ray sportcruiser from the late 1990s combined rakish styling with roomy accommodations, good turn of speed. Open-plan interior boasts posh seating, fully equipped galley, large head with shower. Ergonomic helm features deluxe burlwood dash, tilt steering, room for extra electronics. Transom storage locker is a plus. Slender side decks require caution. Twin 310hp MerCruiser V-drive inboards cruise at 22 knots (30+ knots top). MerCruiser 300hp I/Os run a few knots faster.

Length w/Pulpit..................35'10"		Weight ....11,200#	
Hull Length ....33'6"		Fuel .... 225 gals.	
Beam.....................................11'5"		Water .... 40 gals.	
Draft, Inboards ....2'1"		Hull Type.................... Modified-V	
Draft, I/Os ....3'0"		Deadrise Aft .... 17°	

See Page 562 For Resale Values

Sea Ray Boats
Knoxville, TN
www.searay.com

231-360-0827

Sea Ray 330 Sundancer
2008–Current

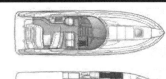

Bold sportcruiser with luxury-class amenities takes American styling, quality to European levels. Expansive cockpit boasts aft-facing transom seat, full-service wet bar with refrigerator, power engine access hatch. Luxurious interior with cherry cabinets, hardwood flooring includes built-in TV/DVD, large galley with lots of counter space, abundant storage. Excellent helm layout. Axiux 360° Control power system became standard in 2010. Twin 370hp MerCruiser gas inboards cruise at 25 knots (mid 30s top).

Length ....35'6"		Fuel .... 225 gals.	
Beam....................................11'6"		Water .... 40 gals.	
Draft, Up ....2'9"		Waste .... 28 gals.	
Draft, Down ....3'6"		Hull Type..........................Deep-V	
Weight ....15,400#		Deadrise Aft .... 21°	

See Page 562 For Resale Values

Sea Ray Boats
Knoxville, TN
www.searay.com

Cruisers & Sportboats

231-360-0827

Sea Ray 340 Express Cruiser
1984–89

Classic 1980s express sold well in her day thanks to aggressive styling, feature-rich accommodations. Roomy interior—dated by today's sportboat standards—combines large forward stateroom with full-size galley, convertible dinette, generous storage. Big single-level cockpit includes double helm and companion seats, transom door, removable stern seat. Cockpit hatches provide good engine access. Radar arch was a popular option. Cruise at 20 knots (30+ top) with standard 340hp straight-drive gas inboards.

Length w/Platform	35'11"	Clearance	NA
Hull Length	33'7"	Fuel	250 gals.
Beam	11'11"	Water	52 gals.
Draft	2'5"	Hull Type	Deep-V
Weight	12,100#	Deadrise Aft	21°

Prices Not Provided for Pre-1995 Models

Sea Ray Boats
Knoxville, TN
www.searay.com

231-360-0827

Sea Ray 340 Sedan Bridge
1983–87

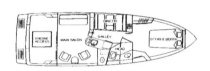

Popular 1980s sedan hit the mark with boaters looking for comfort, versatility at a reasonable price. Single-stateroom interior—large for a 34-footer—includes convertible salon settee, convertible dinette, large stateroom with privacy door. Salon is dominated by distinctive bottle-and-glass cabinet with sliding tambour doors. Lower helm was a popular option. Transom door, swim platform were standard. Cockpit is small for a sedan this size. Twin 350hp V-drive gas inboards cruise at 20 knots (28–30 knots top).

Length	33'7"	Fuel	204 gals.
Beam	11'11"	Water	80 gals.
Draft	2'6"	Headroom	6'3"
Weight	11,400#	Hull Type	Deep-V
Clearance	NA	Deadrise Aft	21°

Prices Not Provided for Pre-1995 Models

Sea Ray Boats
Knoxville, TN
www.searay.com

231-360-0827

Sea Ray 340 Sundancer
1984–89

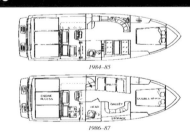

1984–85

1986–87

Maxi-volume 34-footer from the 1980s set class standards in her day for sleek styling, roomy interior, good performance. Offered with several floorplans during her production years, all with teak cabin trim, large galley, convertible dinette, double berths fore and aft. Large cockpit with double-wide helm seat, removable stern seat has more elbow space than many 34-footers. Modest 172-gallon fuel capacity limits range. Standard 340hp MerCruiser V-drive gas inboards cruise in the low 20s (30 knots top).

Length w/Platform	35'11"	Clearance	NA
Hull Length	33'7"	Fuel	172 gals.
Beam	11'11"	Water	52 gals.
Draft	2'5"	Hull Type	Deep-V
Weight	12,500#	Deadrise Aft	21°

Prices Not Provided for Pre-1995 Models

Sea Ray Boats
Knoxville, TN
www.searay.com

Sea Ray 340 Sundancer
1999–2002

Plan A

Plan B

Updated version of previous 340 Sundancer model took sportyacht comfort, styling to the next level. Highlights include roomy cockpit with facing rear seats, burlwood dash with space for electronics, double companion seat, cockpit refrigerator. Luxury-class interior with high-gloss cherry cabinetry, UltraLeather upholstery boasts built-in TV/VCR, home-size galley, choice of dinette or L-shaped settee. Replaced with restyled 340 model in 2003. Twin 320hp V-drive gas inboards cruise at 20 knots (about 30 knots wide open).

Length w/Platform	33'6"	Fuel	225 gals.
Beam	11 5"	Water	40 gals.
Draft	2 5"	Waste	28 gals.
Weight	13,000#	Hull Type	Modified-V
Clearance	NA	Deadrise Aft	17°

See Page 562 For Resale Values

Sea Ray Boats
Knoxville, TN
www.searay.com

Sea Ray 340 Sundancer
2003–08

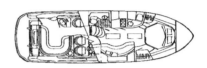

Deluxe Sea Ray express introduced in 2003 scored with savvy buyers looking for cutting-edge styling, luxury-class appointments. Polished midcabin interior with cherry cabinetry gets high marks for quality appliances, exceptional fit and finish. Topside highlights include wraparound cockpit seating, transom storage locker, extended swim platform. Twin-seat helm has dash space for flush-mounting electronics. Power hatch makes engine access easy. MerCruiser 370hp V-drive inboards cruise at 25 knots (low 30s top).

Length	37'6"	Fuel	225 gals.
Beam	12'0"	Water	45 gals.
Draft, Up	2'3"	Waste	28 gals.
Draft, Down	3'1"	Hull Type	Deep-V
Weight	15,500#	Deadrise Aft	21°

See Page 562 For Resale Values

Sea Ray Boats
Knoxville, TN
www.searay.com

Sea Ray 350 Express Bridge
1992–94

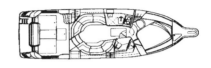

Low-profile sedan gave 1990s buyers more cabin space than most 35-footers before or since. Condo-sized interior with full-beam salon, private bow stateroom can seat a small crowd. Walk-through flybridge gate with molded steps provides convenient access to foredeck seat. Radar arch, transom door, bow pulpit were standard. No stall shower in head compartment. Hatches in cockpit sole provide good engine access. Twin 310hp V-drive gas inboards cruise in the low 20s (30+ knots wide open).

Length	35'4"	Fuel	200 gals.
Beam	11 5"	Water	60 gals.
Draft	3'1"	Headroom	6 5"
Weight	11,500#	Hull Type	Modified-V
Clearance	NA	Deadrise Aft	18°

Prices Not Provided for Pre-1995 Models

Sea Ray Boats
Knoxville, TN
www.searay.com

Cruisers & Sportboats

Sea Ray 350 Sundancer
2009–Current

Graceful hardtop express with sweeping lines takes signature Sea Ray styling, luxury to the next level. Beautifully finished interior with forward V-berth, convertible salon sofa sleeps six. Forward berth has slick push-button recliner. Large hull windows admit good natural lighting. Power engine access hatch, aft-facing transom seat, pivoting helm/companion seats are standard. Hydraulic swim platform is optional. Axius power became standard in 2010. Cruise at 24–26 knots with 375hp gas I/Os; about 20 knots with V-drive inboards.

Length	37'6"	Fuel	225 gals.
Beam	12'0"	Water	50 gals.
Draft, Up	2'3"	Waste	28 gals.
Draft, Down	3'3"	Hull Type	Deep-V
Weight	18,064#	Deadrise Aft	21°

See Page 562 For Resale Values

Sea Ray Boats
Knoxville, TN
www.searay.com

Sea Ray 355T Sedan
1982–83

Roomy 1980s sedan with tiny cockpit, large flybridge has the cabin space of many 40-footers. Unique single-stateroom interior (most boats this size have two staterooms) boasts huge salon with two sleeper-sofas, big U-shaped galley with serving counter, standard lower helm. Lots of storage space. Carpeted overheads, mica woodwork, inexpensive furnishings add up to an unimpressive decor. Not one of Sea Ray's better-selling models. Crusader 260hp gas engines cruise at 16 knots; Volvo 220hp diesels cruise at 12 knots.

Length	36'3"	Fuel	270 gals.
Beam	12'6"	Water	120 gals.
Draft	2'11"	Waste	25 gals.
Weight	13,000#	Hull Type	Modified-V
Clearance	10'3"	Deadrise Aft	9°

Prices Not Provided for Pre-1995 Models

Sea Ray Boats
Knoxville, TN
www.searay.com

Sea Ray 350/370 Express Cruiser
1990–95

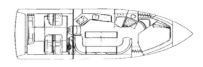

Popular 1990s express combined cutting-edge styling with comfortable interior, party-size cockpit. Roomy interior with private stateroom, king-size galley is dominated by 10-foot salon sofa, large mid-cabin area with removable dinette. Optional TV/VCR swivels out for easy viewing. Cockpit comes with double helm seat, wet bar, foldaway transom seat. Marketed as Sea Ray 350 Express Cruiser in 1990–92; 370 Express Cruiser in 1993–95. MerCruiser 310hp gas inboards cruise at 20–22 knots (about 30 knots top).

Length w/Pulpit	39'5"	Fuel	250 gals.
Hull Length	36'10"	Water	70 gals.
Beam	12'4"	Waste	20 gals.
Draft	2'5"	Hull Type	Deep-V
Weight	13,100#	Deadrise Aft	21°

See Page 562 For Resale Values

Sea Ray Boats
Knoxville, TN
www.searay.com

231-360-0827

Sea Ray 350/370 Sundancer
1990–94

1990–93

1994

Appealing styling, lush accommodations, sporty performance made this 1990s cruiser yet another sales success for Sea Ray. Spacious midcabin interior with private bow stateroom, home-size galley is dominated by huge 10-foot semicircular sofa. Triple-wide helm seat is unusual. Roomy engine compartment makes service access easy. Called Sea Ray 350 Sundancer in 1990-91; 370 Sundancer in 1992-94. Twin 310hp MerCruiser V-drive inboards cruise at 20 knots (high 20s top).

Length w/Platform	39'5"	Fuel	250 gals.
Hull Length	36'10"	Water	70 gals.
Beam	12'4"	Waste	20 gals.
Draft	2'5"	Hull Type	Deep-V
Weight	13,500#	Deadrise Aft	21°

Prices Not Provided for Pre-1995 Models

Sea Ray Boats
Knoxville, TN
www.searay.com

231-360-0827

Sea Ray 360 Express Cruiser
1979–83

Vintage Sea Ray cruiser with T-shaped hardtop took sportboat styling to the next level in the late 1970s. Obviously dated interior with mica laminates boasts a huge galley, head with separate stall shower, two private staterooms. Large cockpit has double helm and companion seats, full-width stern seat. For weather protection, slots in the T-top can be closed with clear snap-in inserts or Plexiglas panels. Prop pockets reduce draft. No transom door. Twin 340hp gas inboards cruise at 15–16 knots with a top speed in the mid 20s.

Length	36'6"	Fuel	300 gals.
Beam	13'11"	Water	100 gals.
Draft	2'7"	Waste	30 gals.
Weight	17,900#	Hull Type	Deep-V
Clearance	9'7"	Deadrise Aft	21°

Prices Not Provided for Pre-1995 Models

Sea Ray Boats
Knoxville, TN
www.searay.com

231-360-0827

Sea Ray 360 Sundancer
2002–06

Deluxe family cruiser with premium amenities combines signature Sea Ray luxury with great styling, no-excuses performance. Upscale interior with cherry cabinets, Ultraleather seating gets high marks for superior furnishings, top-shelf hardware and appliances. Cockpit floor lifts on hydraulic rams for engine access. Extended swim platform, underwater exhaust, transom locker were standard. Stateroom door is a rare luxury these days. MerCruiser 370hp V-drive gas engines cruise at 18 knots (30+ knots wide open).

Length w/Platform	39'0"	Fuel	250 gals.
Beam	12'6"	Water	55 gals.
Draft	3'1"	Waste	35 gals.
Weight	18,500#	Hull Type	Deep-V
Clearance	11'4"	Deadrise Aft	21°

See Page 562 For Resale Values

Sea Ray Boats
Knoxville, TN
www.searay.com

Cruisers & Sportboats

Sea Ray 36 Sedan Bridge
2007–09

Stylish sport sedan combined top-quality Sea Ray construction with leading-edge amenities. High-style interior with compact salon boasts roomy owner's stateroom with generous storage, small guest cabin with twin berths, divided head compartments with separate stall shower. In-floor galley compartment offers much-needed storage space. Centerline helm console has room for big-screen electronics. Engineroom is a tight fit. Gas 370hp inboards cruise at 20 knots; 380hp Cummins diesels cruise at 22+knots.

Length	38'4"	Fuel	300 gals.
Beam	13'0"	Water	75 gals.
Draft	3'4"	Waste	35 gals.
Weight	22,000#	Hull Type	Modified-V
Clearance	18'0"	Deadrise Aft	17°

See Page 563 For Resale Values

Sea Ray Boats
Knoxville, TN
www.searay.com

Sea Ray 370 Express Cruiser
1997–2000

Luxury express with huge cockpit made good on Sea Ray promise of superior build quality, unsurpassed passenger comfort. Posh interior with rare private bow stateroom sleeps four. Cockpit fishing features include in-sole rod storage, freshwater washdown, lift-out fish boxes. Entire helmdeck lifts electrically for engine access. Foldaway transom seat frees up cockpit space. Deep-V hull is fully cored. Twin 310hp gas inboards cruise at 16 knots; optional 340hp Cat diesels cruise at 25 knots.

Length w/Platform	41'4"	Fuel	350 gals.
Hull Length	37'0"	Water	70 gals.
Beam	14'2"	Waste	28 gals.
Draft	3'3"	Hull Type	Deep-V
Weight	18,000#	Deadrise Aft	19.5°

See Page 563 For Resale Values

Sea Ray Boats
Knoxville, TN
www.searay.com

Sea Ray 370 Sedan Bridge
1991–97

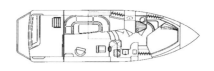

Sporty 1990s sport sedan delivered an impressive mix of rakish styling, space-efficient layout, capable open-water performance. Well-appointed interior with oak cabinets, large cabin windows includes two private staterooms, huge U-shaped salon dinette, built-in entertainment center, choice of breakfast bar or optional lower helm station. Radar arch, swim platform, transom door, bow pulpit were standard. Side decks are on the narrow side. Standard 340hp MerCruiser gas inboards cruise at 18 knots (mid 20s top).

Length w/Platform	40'10"	Fuel	250 gals.
Hull Length	36'10"	Water	70 gals.
Beam	12'4"	Waste	20 gals.
Draft	2'7"	Hull Type	Deep-V
Weight	14,600#	Deadrise Aft	21°

See Page 563 For Resale Values

Sea Ray Boats
Knoxville, TN
www.searay.com

www.powerboatguide.com   231-360-0827

Sea Ray 370 Sundancer
1995–99

Bold 1990s sportcruiser delivered a compelling blend of rakish styling, luxury-class accommodations. Lavish interior boasts spacious salon with U-shaped settee, large galley with granite bar, convertible rear dinette. Forward stateroom has privacy door—a plus for cruising with friends. Roomy cockpit with entertainment center seats a small crowd. Note stylish woodgrain helm, big transom storage locker. Underwater exhausts reduce noise, fumes. Twin 310hp gas inboards cruise at 18 knots; 292hp Cat diesels cruise in the low 20s.

Length w/Pulpit	40'1"	Fuel	275 gals.
Hull Length	37'6"	Water	70 gals.
Beam	12'7"	Waste	28 gals.
Draft	2'8"	Hull Type	Deep-V
Weight	17,000#	Deadrise Aft	20°

See Page 563 For Resale Values

Sea Ray Boats
Knoxville, TN
www.searay.com

---

www.powerboatguide.com   231-360-0827

Sea Ray 380 Sundancer
1999–2003

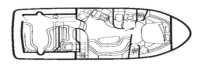

Popular express cruiser introduced in 1999 combined aggressive styling with quality construction, first-rate accommodations. Well-appointed interior with cherry cabinetry, upscale decor features private bow stateroom, built-in entertainment center, 10-foot salon sofa. Mid-stateroom lounge converts electrically to double berth. Spacious cockpit with wraparound seating has full wet bar, fender storage. New 38 Sundancer model came out in 2006. Standard 370hp inboards cruise at 18 knots; 340hp Cat diesels cruise at 25 knots.

Length w/Platform	42'0"	Fuel	275 gals.
Hull Length	38'0"	Water	70 gals.
Beam	13'0"	Waste	42 gals.
Draft	2'8"	Hull Type	Deep-V
Weight	20,000#	Deadrise Aft	19.5°

See Page 563 For Resale Values

Sea Ray Boats
Knoxville, TN
www.searay.com

---

www.powerboatguide.com   231-360-0827

Sea Ray 38 Sundancer
2006–Current

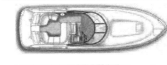

Handsome hardtop express offers potent mix of modern styling, state-of-the-art construction. Semi-enclosed helmdeck offers panoramic views. Upscale interior with cherry cabinets boasts roomy salon with leather settee, large galley, drop-down TV, private bow stateroom. Split head/shower will appeal to cruisers. Transom storage, power engineroom hatch, underwater exhausts are standard. Anchor washdown system is a nice touch. MerCruiser gas inboards cruise at 20 knots; 380hp Cummins diesels cruise at 25 knots.

Length Overall	39'0"	Fuel	250 gals.
Beam	12'6"	Water	55 gals.
Draft	3'1"	Waste	35 gals.
Weight	19,400#	Hull Type	Deep-V
Clearance	12'1"	Deadrise Aft	21°

See Page 563 For Resale Values

Sea Ray Boats
Knoxville, TN
www.searay.com

231-360-0827

Sea Ray 390 Express Cruiser
1984–91

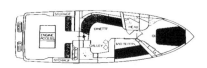

Maxi-volume express set sportboat standards in her day for contemporary styling, dockside eye appeal. Spacious interior with home-size galley, convertible dinette includes breakfast bar, head with stall shower. Guest cabin is separated from salon by retractable mirrored bulkhead. Huge cockpit can accommodate a small crowd. Cabin windows often leak. First of the big U.S. express boats when she came out in 1984. Twin 340hp gas inboards cruise at 16–18 knots; 375hp Cats cruise in the mid 20s.

Length	39'0"	Fuel	300 gals.
Beam	13'11"	Water	100 gals.
Draft	2'4"	Waste	40 gals.
Weight	16,400#	Hull Type	Deep-V
Clearance	NA	Deadrise Aft	19°

Prices Not Provided for Pre-1995 Models

Sea Ray Boats
Knoxville, TN
www.searay.com

231-360-0827

Sea Ray 390/40 Sundancer
2004–09

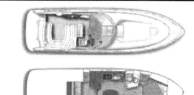

Head-turning express (called 390 Sundancer in 2004–05; 40 Sundancer in 2006–09) appeals to upscale buyers with a taste for world-class styling, premium accommodations. Lavish interior with two heads, huge galley, drop-down TV gets high marks for tasteful decor, well-placed amenities. Large cockpit with U-lounge seating, full wet bar, Euro-style helm is as good as it gets. Hardtop with full enclosure was optional. Entire cockpit sole lifts for engine access. Twin 370hp V-drive gas engines cruise in the low 20s (about 30 knots top).

Length w/Platform	41'0"	Fuel	275 gals.
Beam	13'2"	Water	70 gals.
Draft	3'4"	Waste	42 gals.
Weight	19,300#	Hull Type	Deep-V
Clearance	13'3"	Deadrise Aft	19°

See Page 563 For Resale Values

Sea Ray Boats
Knoxville, TN
www.searay.com

231-360-0827

Sea Ray 400 Express Cruiser
1992–99

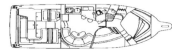

Bold 1990s sportyacht combined muscular styling with best-in-class luxury, top-shelf construction. Upscale interior with top-shelf appliances boasts home-size galley with breakfast bar, posh U-shaped dinette, private bow stateroom with TV/VCR. Pocket door converts salon sitting room into private stateroom with full-size bed, convertible upper bunk. Extended swim platform was a popular option. Big cockpit seats a small crowd. Twin 340hp gas inboards cruise at 18 knots; Cat 340hp diesels cruise in the mid 20s.

Length w/Pulpit	45'7"	Fuel	300 gals.
Hull Length	40'4"	Water	100 gals.
Beam	13'0"	Waste	30 gals.
Draft	3'3"	Hull Type	Deep-V
Weight	18,000#	Deadrise Aft	19°

See Page 563 For Resale Values

Sea Ray Boats
Knoxville, TN
www.searay.com

Sea Ray 400 Sedan Bridge
1996–2003

Plan A

Plan B

Strong-selling Sea Ray sedan introduced in 1996 combined sportyacht styling with versatile layout, leading-edge amenities. Available with three-stateroom, galley-up floorplan or two-stateroom, galley down layout with lower helm. Interior highlights include high-gloss cherry cabinetry, hardwood galley sole, leather upholstery, quality appliances. Engineroom is a tight fit. Fully cored hull has prop pockets to reduce draft. Twin 370hp gas inboards cruise at 20 knots; 340hp Cat diesels cruise at 22–23 knots.

Length w/Platform	44'0"	Fuel	350 gals.
Hull Length	41'6"	Water	120 gals.
Beam	14'3"	Waste	28 gals.
Draft	3'4"	Hull Type	Modified-V
Weight	22,000#	Deadrise Aft	18.5°

See Page 563 For Resale Values

Sea Ray Boats
Knoxville, TN
www.searay.com

Sea Ray 400 Sundancer
1997–99

Muscular 1990s express cruiser has the space, amenities owners seek in a luxury sportyacht. Sumptuous cherry interior features mid-cabin stateroom with privacy door, two heads, fully-equipped galley with generous storage. Huge cockpit with wrap-around seating can entertain a small crowd. Tiered instrument panel has room for extra electronics. Cockpit sole lifts for engine access. Twin 340hp V-drive gas inboards cruise at 16 knots (mid 20s top); Cat 340hp diesels cruise in the mid 20s (close to 30 knots top).

Length w/Platform	44'4"	Fuel	330 gals.
Hull Length	41'6"	Water	100 gals.
Beam	13'8"	Waste	28 gals.
Draft	3'4"	Hull Type	Deep-V
Weight	22,500#	Deadrise Aft	19°

See Page 563 For Resale Values

Sea Ray Boats
Knoxville, TN
www.searay.com

Sea Ray 410 Express Cruiser
2000–2003

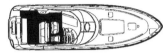

Deck Layout

Interior Floorplan

Rakish express yacht with powerful lines is as luxurious as she is handsome. Posh open-plan salon with leather seating, cherry cabinets includes semi-enclosed sitting room (opposite head) that converts into private guest stateroom. Topside features include stylish burlwood dash, transom storage locker, foredeck sun pad, extended swim platform. Aft cockpit sole lifts electrically for engine access. Hull is fully cored. Hardtop was optional. Cummins 417hp diesels cruise in the mid 20s and reach a top speed of close to 30 knots.

Length w/Platform	45'6"	Fuel	335 gals.
Hull Length	41'6"	Water	100 gals.
Beam	13'10"	Waste	42 gals.
Draft	3'4"	Hull Type	Deep-V
Weight	21,000#	Deadrise Aft	19°

See Page 563 For Resale Values

Sea Ray Boats
Knoxville, TN
www.searay.com

Cruisers & Sportboats

www.powerboatguide.com   231-360-0827

Sea Ray 410 Sundancer
2000–03

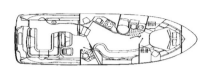

World-class express gave European sportcruisers a serious run for the money in the early 2000s. Lavish interior with high-gloss cherry cabinetry boasts two heads, electrically powered midcabin sleeper/sofa, huge galley with full-size refrigerator. Topside features include superb helm position with double companion seat, posh U-shaped cockpit seating, transom storage locker. Very good engine access. Hull with prop pockets is fully cored. Cat 420hp diesels cruise in the mid 20s and reach a top speed of 28-30 knots.

Length w/Platform	45'6"	Fuel	335 gals.
Hull Length	41'6"	Water	100 gals.
Beam	13'10"	Waste	42 gals.
Draft	3'2"	Hull Type	Deep-V
Weight	21,000#	Deadrise Aft	19°

See Page 563 For Resale Values

Sea Ray Boats
Knoxville, TN
www.searay.com

---

www.powerboatguide.com   231-360-0827

Sea Ray 420/44 Sundancer
2003–08

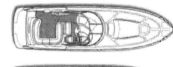

Seductive sport yacht (called 420 Sundancer in 2003–05; 44 Sundancer in 2006–08) combines bold styling with top-drawer accommodations, leading-edge design. Opulent interior with cherry cabinets boasts two private staterooms, huge galley with serving counter, two heads, abundant storage. Massive cockpit features posh U-shaped lounge seating, near-perfect helm layout. Cockpit floor lifts for engine access. Note slightly modest fuel capacity. Cummins 478hp diesels cruise in the mid 20s (about 30 knots top).

Length Overall	45'0"	Fuel	335 gals.
Beam	14'0"	Water	100 gals.
Draft	3'6"	Waste	42 gals.
Weight	22,500#	Hull Type	Deep-V
Clearance	11'3"	Deadrise Aft	19°

See Page 563 For Resale Values

Sea Ray Boats
Knoxville, TN
www.searay.com

---

www.powerboatguide.com   231-360-0827

Sea Ray 420/440 Sundancer
1990–95

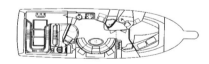

Elegant sportcruiser (called 420 Sundancer in 1990-91; 440 in 1993-95) was state-of-the-art in luxury, design in the early 1990s. Posh midcabin interior with two heads features 9-foot salon sofa, full entertainment center, large galley with upright refrigerator. Salon extends aft into midcabin with convertible sofa, sliding privacy door. Huge cockpit has triple companion seat at the helm, U-shaped aft seating. Note that 440 model has hull pockets, 420 does not. Standard gas inboards cruise at 15-16 knots; 364hp Cat diesel cruise in the low 20s.

Length w/Pulpit	47'1"	Fuel	400 gals.
Hull Length	44'0"	Water	100 gals.
Beam	13'11"	Waste	28 gals.
Draft	3'3"	Hull Type	Deep-V
Weight	20,000#	Deadrise Aft	19°

See Page 563 For Resale Values

Sea Ray Boats
Knoxville, TN
www.searay.com

231-360-0827

Sea Ray 440 Express Bridge
1993–98

Wide-beam cruising yacht with unique walk-thru bridge has the interior volume of many 50-footers. Enormous two-stateroom floorplan boasts full-beam salon with big U-shaped settee, two heads, galley with upright refrigerator. Party-time bridge with centerline helm, wet bar seats up to ten. Additional highlights include twin transom doors, built-in cockpit seat, foredeck seating, generous storage. Hull is fully cored. Prop pockets reduce draft. Cat 340hp diesels cruise at 20 knots and deliver a top speed of 23–24 knots.

Length w/Pulpit	47'1"	Fuel	400 gals.
Hull Length	44'0"	Water	100 gals.
Beam	13'11"	Waste	60 gals.
Draft	3'3"	Hull Type	Modified-V
Weight	28,000#	Deadrise Aft	19°

See Page 564 For Resale Values

Sea Ray Boats
Knoxville, TN
www.searay.com

---

www.powerboatguide.com 231-360-0827

Sea Ray 450 Express Bridge
1998–2004

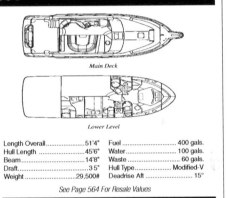

Main Deck

Lower Level

Rakish sedan yacht with walk-through bridge, huge interior offers luxury-class comforts, amenities of a larger yacht. Raised dinette in full-beam salon provides space below for second stateroom with washer/dryer combo. Spacious bridge boasts centerline helm, wet bar, lounge seating aft. Note twin transom doors, foldaway cockpit seat, molded bridge steps. Deep well creates secure foredeck area for passengers and guests. Twin 420hp V-drive Cat (or 430hp Cummins) diesels cruise at 20 knots (mid 20s top).

Length Overall	51'4"	Fuel	400 gals.
Hull Length	45'6"	Water	100 gals.
Beam	14'8"	Waste	60 gals.
Draft	3.5"	Hull Type	Modified-V
Weight	29,500#	Deadrise Aft	15°

See Page 564 For Resale Values

Sea Ray Boats
Knoxville, TN
www.searay.com

---

www.powerboatguide.com 231-360-0827

Sea Ray 450 Sundancer
1995–99

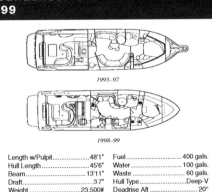

1995–97

1998–99

High-impact sportyacht introduced in 1995 showcased Sea Ray's industry-leading design, cutting-edge construction, world-class luxury. Enormous two-stateroom, two-head interior boasts home-size galley with copious storage, huge head compartment, top-shelf furnishings and hardware. Spacious cockpit with circular aft seating; superb helm position. Big transom locker is a useful touch. Hull is fully cored. Twin 340hp Cat diesels cruise in the low 20s; optional 407hp Cats cruise at 24-25 (about 30 knots top).

Length w/Pulpit	48'1"	Fuel	400 gals.
Hull Length	45'6"	Water	100 gals.
Beam	13'11"	Waste	60 gals.
Draft	3.7"	Hull Type	Deep-V
Weight	23,500#	Deadrise Aft	20°

See Page 564 For Resale Values

Sea Ray Boats
Knoxville, TN
www.searay.com

Cruisers & Sportboats

Sea Ray 460 Express Cruiser
1985–89

Plan A

Plan B

Broad-shouldered sportyacht from late 1980s combined bold styling with spacious accommodations, big-water security. Original two-stateroom interior with two heads was replaced in 1988 with more expansive single-stateroom layout boasting much larger salon. Huge bi-level cockpit with transom door has room for a crowd. Good engine access. Side-dumping exhausts were standard. Biggest U.S.-built express available in 1985. Cat 375hp diesels cruise at 20 knots; optional 550hp 6V92 Detroits cruise in the mid 20s.

Length	45'6"	Fuel	420 gals.
Beam	14'11"	Water	150 gals.
Draft	3'2"	Waste	40 gals.
Weight	27,500#	Hull Type	Modified-V
Clearance	9'9"	Deadrise Aft	17°

Prices Not Provided for Pre-1995 Models

Sea Ray Boats
Knoxville, TN
www.searay.com

Sea Ray 460 Sundancer
1999–2003

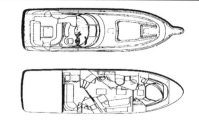

Polished sportcruiser introduced in 1999 remains an impressive blend of leading-edge styling, tasteful accommodations, quality Sea Ray construction. Expansive interior matches the finest European imports in comfort, amenities. Mid-stateroom with washer/dryer combo has complete privacy behind two sliding doors. Facing cockpit settees convert electrically to sun pad. Quiet ride thanks to underwater exhausts. Twin 430hp V-drive Volvo (or 446hp Cummins) diesels cruise in the low 20s, top out around 27-28 knots.

Length Overall	51'4"	Fuel	400 gals.
Hull Length	45'6"	Water	100 gals.
Beam	14'8"	Waste	60 gals.
Draft	3'7"	Hull Type	Modified-V
Weight	28,000#	Deadrise Aft	15°

See Page 564 For Resale Values

Sea Ray Boats
Knoxville, TN
www.searay.com

Sea Ray 48 Sundancer
2005–08

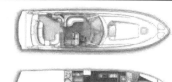

Stunning hardtop express with sweeping lines takes American sportyacht styling to the next level. Semi-enclosed helmdeck with L-lounge offers panoramic views of surrounding waters. Luxurious twin-head interior with cherry joinery, hardwood flooring features elegant salon with leather settee, spacious U-shaped galley, complete entertainment center. Extended platform can support a dinghy. Washer/dryer is optional. No power sunroof. Cruise in the low 20s with standard 526hp Cummins V-drive diesels (28–29 knots top).

Length w/Platform	50'8"	Fuel	400 gals.
Beam	14'8"	Water	110 gals.
Draft	4'0"	Waste	60 gals.
Weight	33,600#	Hull Type	Deep-V
Clearance	NA	Deadrise Aft	19°

See Page 564 For Resale Values

Sea Ray Boats
Knoxville, TN
www.searay.com

Sea Ray 480/500 Sundancer 1990-99

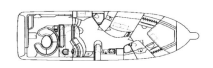

High-impact Sea Ray express from the 1990s set class standards in her day for everything that counted. Vast interior with enormous salon, up-scale furnishings rivals that of a small motoryacht for space, amenities. Highlights include huge cockpit with pit-style seating, spacious engineroom, wide side decks. Oval ports replaced sliding cabin windows in 1994. Called 480 Sundancer in 1990-91. Early models with GM 485hp diesels cruise in the low 20s; later models with 735hp GMs cruise at 28 knots.

Length w/Platform	55'8"	Fuel	500 gals.
Hull Length	50'1"	Water	150 gals.
Beam	15'0"	Waste	68 gals.
Draft	4'0"	Hull Type	Modified-V
Weight	34,500#	Deadrise Aft	17°

See Page 564 For Resale Values

Sea Ray Boats
Knoxville, TN
www.searay.com

Sea Ray 500/52 Sundancer 2003-09

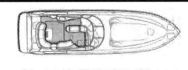

Visually stunning American sportyacht (called 500 Sundancer in 2003-05; 52 Sundancer in 2006-09) matched top-ranked European imports for sex appeal, luxury, state-of-the-art construction. Opulent cherry interior boasts expansive salon with Ultraleather lounge, gourmet galley with under-counter refrigeration, two large heads, well-appointed staterooms. Semi-sheltered cockpit offers vast entertainment potential. Good engine access; superb helm. Cummins 640hp V-drive diesels cruise at a quick 26-28 knots (30+ knots top).

Length	53'4"	Fuel	560 gals.
Beam	15'3"	water	150 gals.
Draft	4'2"	Waste	68 gals.
Weight	40,015#	Hull Type	Deep-V
Clearance	14'0"	Deadrise Aft	19°

See Page 564 For Resale Values

Sea Ray Boats
Knoxville, TN
www.searay.com

Sea Ray 510 Sundancer 2000-03

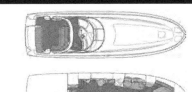

World-class Sea Ray express with wide beam delivers more cockpit, interior space than same-size European sportyachts of her era. Posh two-stateroom interior with cherry cabinets, Ultraleather seating includes two full heads, home-size galley with pull-out bar, salon entertainment center, central vacuum system, hardwood flooring. Retractable sun pad, hardtop, wraparound helm were standard. Underwater exhausts reduce cockpit fumes. Cat 660hp V-drive diesels cruise at 25 knots; 770hp Cats will cruise in the high 20s.

Length w/Platform	53'6"	Fuel	600 gals.
Hull Length	50'6"	Water	150 gals.
Beam	15'8"	Waste	68 gals.
Draft	4'3"	Hull Type	Deep-V
Weight	38,500#	Deadrise Aft	18°

See Page 564 For Resale Values

Sea Ray Boats
Knoxville, TN
www.searay.com

Sea Ray 540 Sundancer
1998–2001

O pulent express yacht outpaced late-1990s competitors for space, comfort, outright sex appeal. Posh two-stateroom interior with cherry woodwork is dominated by 10' leather sofa with electric slide-out bed. Full-service galley features copious storage, condo-size refrigerator. Cockpit settees convert electrically into huge sun pad. Hydraulic swim platform makes launching a tender easy. Washer/dryer space in bow stateroom. Cat 640hp diesels cruise in the mid 20s; 776hp Cats cruise in the high 20s.

Length w/Platform	57'8"	Fuel	600 gals.
Hull Length	54'11"	Water	150 gals.
Beam	15'11"	Waste	68 gals.
Draft	3'11"	Hull Type	Modified-V
Weight	39,000#	Deadrise Aft	17°

See Page 564 For Resale Values

Sea Ray Boats
Knoxville, TN
www.searay.com

Sea Ray 550 Sundancer
2002–04

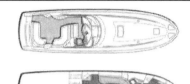

U pdated version of popular 540 Sundancer (1998–2001) boasts revised interior, redesigned hardtop. Posh two-stateroom layout with cherry woodwork includes curved salon sofa (which converts electrically into slide-out bed), gourmet galley, space for washer/dryer. Bow thruster was standard. Power cockpit settees convert into huge sun pad. Hydraulic high-low swim platform makes launching a tender easy. Engineroom is a tight fit. Twin 640hp Cat diesels cruise in the mid 20s; 765hp MANs cruise at 26–28 knots.

Length	57'8"	Fuel	600 gals.
Beam	15'11"	Water	150 gals.
Draft	4'0"	Waste	68 gals.
Weight	39,000#	Hull Type	Modified-V
Clearance	13'4"	Deadrise Aft	17°

See Page 564 For Resale Values

Sea Ray Boats
Knoxville, TN
www.searay.com

Sea Ray 55 Sundancer
2008–Current

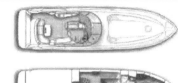
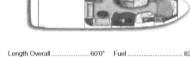

P olished sportcruiser with top-shelf amenities takes Sundancer luxury, comfort to the next level. Lavish two-stateroom interior boasts home-size galley with serving counter, full-beam owner's suite, teak salon flooring, two full heads. Twin-section cockpit lounge slides around on circular tracks—very cool. Note massive engineroom, cockpit galley with wet bar & grill, premium entertainment center. Hardtop has retractable sunroofs. Man 860hp V-drive diesels cruise at 25–26 knots (about 30 knots top).

Length Overall	60'0"	Fuel	825 gals.
Beam	15'11"	Water	200 gals.
Draft	4'6"	Waste	70 gals.
Weight	53,500#	Hull Type	Modified-V
Clearance	17'9"	Deadrise Aft	17°

Insufficient Resale Data To Assign Values

Sea Ray Boats
Knoxville, TN
www.searay.com

Sea Ray 580 Super Sun Sport
1997–2002

Standard Floorplan

Alternate Floorplan

High-powered sportcruiser with transom garage, optional hardtop epitomized Sea Ray reputation for luxury, leading-edge design. Lavish interior features two private staterooms, home-size galley with concealed appliances, electric Ultraleather salon sofa bed, premium entertainment system. Massive cockpit with wraparound seating boasts custom wet bar, sun pad atop jet-bike garage. Hull is fully cored. Foldout boarding steps are a nice touch. Cat 776hp-or 735hp GM-diesels cruise in the high 20s, top out in the low 30s.

Length w/Platform	60'10"	Fuel	700 gals.
Hull Length	58'11"	Water	200 gals.
Beam	15'9"	Waste	68 gals.
Draft	4'1"	Hull Type	Modified-V
Weight	48,000#	Deadrise Aft	17°

See Page 564 For Resale Values

Sea Ray Boats
Knoxville, TN
www.searay.com

Sea Ray 60 Sundancer; 610 Sundancer
2006–Current

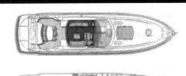

Elegant sportyacht—flagship of today's Sea Ray fleet—combines unsurpassed luxury with bold styling, top-shelf construction. Opulent three-stateroom interior includes full-beam owner's suite, enclosed pilothouse, state-of-the-art helm. Small crew cabin with transom entry is optional. Swim platform can stow tender, PWC. Bow/stern thrusters, twin sunroofs, cockpit grill are standard. Exemplary fit and finish justifies high price. MAN 1,100hp V-drive diesels cruise at a fast 28 knots (33–34 knots top). Called 610 DA in 2010.

Length	61'6"	Fuel	900 gals.
Beam	16'9"	Water	200 gals.
Draft	4'2"	Waste	70 gals.
Weight	55,700#	Hull Type	Modified-V
Clearance	NA	Deadrise Aft	17°

See Page 564 For Resale Values

Sea Ray Boats
Knoxville, TN
www.searay.com

Sea Ray 630 Super Sun Sport
1991–2000

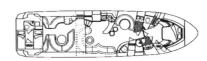

Big American-bred sportyacht set class standards in her era for deluxe accommodations, cutting-edge styling. Enormous single-stateroom, two-head interior boasts massive salon with electric sofa/bed, home-sized galley with breakfast bar, lavish master stateroom with his-and-her heads. Huge cockpit offers seating for twelve. Crew quarters aft were optional. Look-alike sibling, the Sea Ray 630 Sundancer, is powered with Arneson Surface Drives. Detroit 1,100hp diesels will cruise at 30 knots (32–33 knots top).

Length w/Platform	64'6"	Fuel	800 gals.
Hull Length	62'6"	Water	200 gals.
Beam	15'9"	Waste	70 gals.
Draft	5'0"	Hull Type	Deep-V
Weight	54,500#	Deadrise Aft	19°

Insufficient Resale Data To Assign Values

Sea Ray Boats
Knoxville, TN
www.searay.com

Cruisers & Sportboats

Silverton 271 Express
1995–97

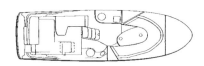

Portly 1990s express with trailerable 8'6" beam delivered interior space, cockpit versatility at an affordable price. Conventional midcabin floorplan has double berths fore and aft, full galley, removable dinette, enclosed head with sink and shower. High freeboard permits generous cabin headroom; opening ports provide modest ventilation. Cockpit seating includes wraparound companion seat, full-length stern seat. Note walk-through windshield. Cruise at 18 knots with single 300hp MerCruiser I/O (mid 20s top).

Length w/Pulpit	29'9"	Weight	7,643#
Hull Length	27'10"	Fuel	109 gals.
Beam	8'6"	Water	30 gals.
Draft, Drive Up	1'8"	Hull Type	Modified-V
Draft, Drive Down	3'1"	Deadrise Aft	14°

See Page 565 For Resale Values

Silverton Marine
Millville, NJ
www.silverton.com

Silverton 29 Sportcruiser
1985–87

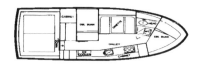

Popular 1990s cruiser with straight-inboard power combined unique floorplan arrangement with rugged construction, affordable price. Uncommon interior with two full-height private staterooms sacrifices salon dimensions (i.e., entertainment space) for sleeping comfort. Head, forward of salon, is not easily reached from the cockpit. Low-profile flybridge with tall windshield seats five. Cockpit hatches provide good engine access. Deep cockpit offers extra security for kids. Twin 195hp gas engines cruise at 15–16 knots (mid 20s top).

Length	29'2"	Fuel	150 gals.
Beam	10'10"	Water	40 gals.
Draft	1'7"	Cockpit	50 sq. ft.
Weight	7,800#	Hull Type	Modified-V
Clearance	8'2"	Deadrise Aft	NA

Prices Not Provided for Pre-1995 Models

Silverton Marine
Millville, NJ
www.silverton.com

Silverton 30X Express
1988–89

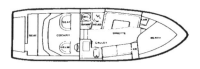

Sporty 1980s express matched appealing price with tasteful accommodations, spirited performance. Topside features include roomy bi-level cockpit with seating for six, foredeck sun pad, large helm console, radar arch with stereo speakers. No-frills interior with private bow stateroom, convertible dinette, convertible settee sleeps six. Additional features include four opening ports, integral bow pulpit, transom door. Inconsistent finish reflects low price. Standard 270hp V-drive gas engines cruise in the low 20s (about 30 knots top).

Length	30'8"	Fuel	185 gals.
Beam	10'10"	Water	37 gals.
Draft	3'0"	Headroom	6'2"
Weight	9,100#	Hull Type	Modified-V
Clearance	8'5"	Designer	NA

Prices Not Provided for Pre-1995 Models

Silverton Marine
Millville, NJ
www.silverton.com

Silverton 31 Convertible
1983–87

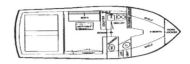

Value-priced pocket convertible appealed to entry-level boaters looking for a stable family cruiser with space, versatility. Oak-trimmed interior with private bow stateroom, convertible sofa, features surprisingly roomy salon for a boat this size. Lower helm was a popular option. Note large head compartment, small-but-well-equipped galley. Deep cockpit lacks transom door. Flybridge with helm forward seats three. Twin 220hp V-drive gas inboards will cruise at 17–18 knots (mid 20s wide open).

Length	31'0"	Fuel	220 gals.
Beam	11'11"	Water	40 gals.
Draft	2'11"	Cockpit	82 sq. ft.
Weight	11,400#	Hull Type	Modified-V
Clearance	10'8"	Deadrise Aft	NA

Prices Not Provided for Pre-1995 Models

Silverton Marine
Millville, NJ
www.silverton.com

Silverton 31 Convertible
1991–95

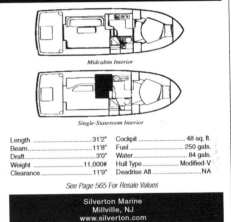

Midcabin Interior

Single-Stateroom Interior

Updated version of earlier Silverton 31 Convertible (1983–87) boasts all-new styling, redesigned hull, more standard equipment. Originally offered with midcabin interior, in 1992 Silverton offered a single-stateroom option with enlarged galley, more spacious salon. Open front windshield bathes salon in plenty of natural lighting. Cockpit is on the small side compared with most 34-foot convertibles. Swim platform, bow pulpit were standard. Twin 235hp gas engines cruise at 17–18 knots (mid 20s top).

Length	31'2"	Cockpit	48 sq. ft.
Beam	11'8"	Fuel	250 gals.
Draft	3'0"	Water	84 gals.
Weight	11,000#	Hull Type	Modified-V
Clearance	11'9"	Deadrise Aft	NA

See Page 565 For Resale Values

Silverton Marine
Millville, NJ
www.silverton.com

Silverton 31 Gulfstream
1979–86

Durable 1980s express with wide 11'11" beam built on Silverton reputation for value, affordability. Roomy, well-planned interior with convertible dinette, stand-up head with shower, full galley sleeps four. Big single-level cockpit with doublewide helm and companion seats is large enough for a small crowd. Good engine access, so-so fit and finish. Note slender side decks. Twin 270hp inboard gas engines cruise at 18–19 knots (high 20ss top); optional 350hp gas engines cruise at 24 knots (30+ top).

Length	31'0"	Fuel	250 gals.
Beam	11'11"	Water	40 gals.
Draft	2'11"	Waste	25 gals.
Weight	9,500#	Hull Type	Modified-V
Clearance	NA	Deadrise Aft	NA

Prices Not Provided for Pre-1995 Models

Silverton Marine
Millville, NJ
www.silverton.com

Cruisers & Sportboats

Silverton 310 Express
1994–2000

Value-priced 1990s sterndrive express with wide-open interior offered good value for the money. Entry steps to cabin are suspended from aluminum weldment making interior seem unusually spacious. Lounge and cocktail table in aft cabin convert to double berth. Seven opening ports, two deck hatches provide good ventilation. Removable cockpit table drops to form sun pad. Transom door, cockpit wet bar, bow pulpit, walk-through windshield were standard. Cruise at 25 knots (35+ top) with optional 300hp MerCruiser engines.

Length	32'0"	Fuel	150 gals.
Beam	11'6"	Water	54 gals.
Draft	2'2"	Waste	35 gals.
Weight	9,202#	Hull Type	Modified-V
Clearance	10'5"	Deadrise Aft	14°

See Page 565 For Resale Values

Silverton Marine
Millville, NJ
www.silverton.com

Silverton 312 Sedan Cruiser
1994–99

Popular family convertible with rakish lines is versatile, sporty, fun to drive. Space-efficient interior with raised dinette, step-down galley, includes curtained-off area opposite the head with upper/lower bunks, double berth forward with privacy curtain. Sliding glass door opens to small cockpit with transom door, molded flybridge stairs. Note extended swim platform with built-in fender racks. Very modest fuel capacity. Choice of inboard or sterndrive power. MerCruiser 235hp 5.7-liter I/Os cruise at 20 knots (about 30+ knots top).

Length Overall	32'0"	Fuel	160 gals.
Hull Length	28'0"	Water	54 gals.
Beam	11'6"	Waste	28 gals.
Draft	2'8"	Hull Type	Modified-V
Weight	9,937#	Deadrise Aft	14°

See Page 565 For Resale Values

Silverton Marine
Millville, NJ
www.silverton.com

Silverton 33 Convertible
2007–Current

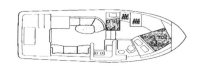

Entry-level flybridge cruiser couples family-size accommodations with good performance, very low price. Wide 12'8" beam permits expansive two-stateroom interior with open salon, small galley, decent storage—impressive accommodations for a boat this size. Sliding windows provide good ventilation. Molded steps make bridge access easy. So-so fit and finish is good enough considering the price. Additional features include radar arch, transom door, swim platform. Cruise at 20 knots with 375hp gas inboards (high 20s top).

Length	32'7"	Fuel	208 gals.
Beam	12'8"	Water	82 gals.
Draft	2'5"	Waste	30 gals.
Weight	16,800#	Hull Type	Modified-V
Clearance	15'6"	Deadrise Aft	14°

See Page 565 For Resale Values

Silverton Marine
Millville, NJ
www.silverton.com

Silverton 33 Sports Coupe
2008–Current

Beamy hardtop sedan with enclosed pilothouse/salon targets cruising couples with an eye for value. Highlights include comfortable salon with huge power-activated sunroof, large master stateroom with angled berth, guest cabin with athwartships berth, sliding glass cockpit doors. Helm visibility is excellent thanks to large salon windows. Starboard salon lounge converts to double berth. Cockpit with transom door, storage lazarette is shaded by hardtop overhang. Cruise at 20 knots (29–30 top) with twin 375hp Crusader gas engines.

Length	32'7"	Fuel	208 gals.
Beam	12'8"	Water	82 gals.
Draft	2'6"	Waste	30 gals.
Weight	16,300#	Hull Type	Modified-V
Clearance	12'1"	Deadrise Aft	14°

See Page 565 For Resale Values

Silverton Marine
Millville, NJ
www.silverton.com

Silverton 330 Sport Bridge
1999–2007

1999–2000

2001–Current

Feature-packed Silverton sedan combines spacious interior with sporty styling, solid construction. Signature "SideWalk" deck layout permits expansive full-beam salon with tremendous headroom. Floorplan was updated in 2001 with improved decor, galley design. Note opening salon windows—very unusual. Oversized flybridge with wet bar seats six in comfort. Early models with 300hp gas inboards cruise at 18 knots (25–26 knots top); later models with 385hp gas engines will cruise at 20 knots (around 30 knots top).

Length Overall	35'4"	Fuel	214 gals.
Beam	12'4"	Water	104 gals.
Draft	2'11"	Waste	30 gals.
Weight	15,685#	Hull Type	Modified-V
Clearance	11'0"	Deadrise Aft	16°

See Page 565 For Resale Values

Silverton Marine
Millville, NJ
www.silverton.com

Silverton 34 Convertible
1978–83

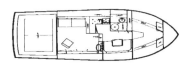

Good-selling family sedan introduced in 1978 was the first of several Silverton 34 Convertibles offered over the years. Notable features include wraparound cabin windows, standard lower helm, roomy cockpit. Single-stateroom interior sleeps six with dinette and salon sofa converted. Sporty low-profile appearance was made possible by using V-drives to locate the engines aft, under the cockpit. Low-priced boat was never known for quality furnishings or finish. Twin 270hp Crusader gas engines cruise at 18 knots (26–27 knots top).

Length	34'0"	Fuel	220 gals.
Beam	12'6"	Water	40 gals.
Draft	3'1"	Cockpit	70 sq. ft.
Weight	12,500#	Hull Type	Modified-V
Clearance	11'6"	Deadrise Aft	15°

Prices Not Provided for Pre-1995 Models

Silverton Marine
Millville, NJ
www.silverton.com

231-360-0827

Silverton 34 Convertible
1984–88

Double Berth Forward

V-Berths Forward

Restyled version of original Silverton 34 Convertible (1978–83) gave entry-level buyers exceptional value for the money. Single-stateroom, galley-down floorplan—offered with double berth or V-berth forward—sleeps six. Lower helm was optional. Topside features include deep cockpit, wide side decks, bow pulpit, roomy flybridge with good helm visibility. Modified-V hull delivers comfortable big-water ride. Note large engineroom. Twin 270hp gas engines cruise at 18–19 knots and top out in the high 20s.

Length	34'0"	Fuel	250 gals.
Beam	12'6"	Water	40 gals.
Draft	3'1"	Cockpit	70 sq. ft.
Weight	12,500#	Hull Type	Modified-V
Clearance	13'3"	Deadrise Aft	15°

Prices Not Provided for Pre-1995 Models

Silverton Marine
Millville, NJ
www.silverton.com

231-360-0827

Silverton 34 Convertible
1989–90

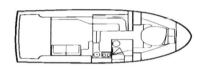

Rakish 34-footer combined affordable price with roomy interior, plenty of standard equipment. Galley-down floorplan features roomy stateroom with island berth, head with enclosed stall shower, L-shaped dinette, expansive salon with convertible sofa. Note light-oak interior woodwork, cockpit transom door, large bridge with seating for five. Tiny galley leaves a lot to be desired. Lower helm station was optional. Twin 350hp gas engines cruise at 19–20 knots (high 20s top). Only two years in production.

Length	34'6"	Fuel	300 gals.
Beam	12'7"	Water	40 gals.
Draft	3'2"	Waste	28 gals.
Weight	13,500#	Hull Type	Modified-V
Clearance	13'5"	Deadrise Aft	17°

See Page XXX For Resale Values

Silverton Marine
Millville, NJ
www.silverton.com

231-360-0827

Silverton 34 Convertible
1991–95

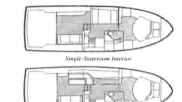

Single-Stateroom Interior

Two-Stateroom Interior

Rakish 1990s convertible combined sporty styling with tasteful accommodations, roomy cockpit. Standard single-stateroom, oak-trimmed interior features booth-style dinette opposite galley. Optional two-stateroom layout with small guest cabin fits the dinette into an already-small salon. Note full-size galley refrigerator. Topside highlights include deep cockpit, wide side decks, bow pulpit, swim platform. Flybridge was slightly restyled in 1995. Crusader 350hp gas inboards cruise at 18 knots (high 20s wide open).

Length	34'6"	Fuel	300 gals.
Beam	12'11"	Water	84 gals.
Draft	2'11"	Waste	28 gals.
Weight	18,000#	Hull Type	Modified-V
Clearance	14'11"	Deadrise Aft	17°

See Page 565 For Resale Values

Silverton Marine
Millville, NJ
www.silverton.com

www.powerboatguide.com   231-360-0827

Silverton 34 Convertible
2004–06

Good-looking convertible with graceful lines is one part coastal cruiser, one part family fisherman. Efficient two-stateroom interior boasts roomy salon with wraparound windows, huge galley with Corian counters, guest cabin with over/under berths, split head compartment. Note attractive cherry woodwork, hardwood galley floor. Transom door, in-deck fishbox were standard in the cockpit. Molded bridge steps are a plus. Standard 330hp gas inboards cruise at 16 knots; optional 385hp gas engines cruise at 20 knots (high 20s top).

Length	37'7"	Fuel	286 gals.
Beam	13'10"	Water	94 gals.
Draft	3'3"	Waste	37 gals.
Weight	18,550#	Hull Type	Modified-V
Clearance	12'7"	Deadrise Aft	12°

See Page 565 For Resale Values

Silverton Marine
Millville, NJ
www.silverton.com

---

www.powerboatguide.com   231-360-0827

Silverton 34 Express
1987–89

Generic 1980s express with inboard power offered entry-level buyers space, comfort at budget-friendly price. Midcabin floorplan with convertible dinette, double berths fore and aft sleeps four adults, two kids. Stall shower in the head is a plus; aft-cabin privacy door is a rare luxury. Topside features include standard bow pulpit, expansive cockpit with seating for six, radar arch, bolt-on swim platform. Styling is way dated by today's standards. Twin 350hp V-drive gas engines cruise at 20 knots (28–30 knots top).

Length	34'6"	Fuel	250 gals.
Beam	12'7"	Water	40 gals.
Draft	3'8"	Cockpit	62 sq. ft.
Weight	11,000#	Hull Type	Modified-V
Clearance	12'7"	Deadrise Aft	17°

Prices Not Provided for Pre-1995 Models

Silverton Marine
Millville, NJ
www.silverton.com

---

www.powerboatguide.com   231-360-0827

Silverton 34 Express
1990–94

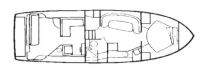

Value-priced express from early 1990s offered sporty styling, cruising amenities without breaking the bank. Expansive midcabin interior with six overhead hatches boasts big U-shaped dinette, fully equipped galley with generous storage, large head with separate stall shower. Exterior features include power engineroom hatch, foredeck sun pad, radar arch, fender storage racks, bow pulpit. So-so fit and finish. Twin 300hp gas engines (with V-drives) cruise at 20 knots and deliver a top speed of 27–28 knots.

Length	34'3"	Fuel	254 gals.
Beam	12'8"	Water	47 gals.
Draft	3'1"	Waste	28 gals.
Weight	16,500#	Hull Type	Modified-V
Clearance	9'3"	Deadrise Aft	17°

Prices Not Provided for Pre-1995 Models

Silverton Marine
Millville, NJ
www.silverton.com

Cruisers & Sportboats

231-360-0827

Silverton 351 Sedan
1997–2000

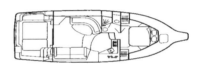

Spacious sedan cruiser with Silverton's signature "SideWalk" deck design offered more interior space than anything in her class. Expansive floorplan features full-beam salon with convertible dinette and settee, large galley with hardwood floor, roomy stateroom. Molded steps make bridge access easy and safe. V-drives allow engines to be positioned beneath cockpit sole to further increase interior volume. Prop pockets reduce hull draft, improve efficiency. No racehorse, 320hp gas engines cruise at 14–15 knots (mid 20s top).

Length	38'10"	Fuel	300 gals.
Beam	13'0"	Water	94 gals.
Draft	2'5"	Waste	37 gals.
Weight	16,094#	Hull Type	Modified-V
Clearance	12'0"	Deadrise Aft	12°

See Page 565 For Resale Values

Silverton Marine
Millville, NJ
www.silverton.com

231-360-0827

Silverton 361/360 Express
1995–2000

Bold inboard express (called Silverton 361 Express in 1995–96; 360 Express in 1997–2000) delivered comfort, performance at a low price. Roomy midcabin floorplan has double berths fore and aft, full galley, circular salon dinette. Note privacy doors for both staterooms—a convenience seldom found in modern midcabin cruisers. Walk-through windshield provides easy bow access. Solid fiberglass hull has prop pockets to reduce draft, improve efficiency. Crusader 320hp V-drive inboards cruise at 18–19 knots (high 20s top).

Length	36'1"	Water	100 gals.
Beam	12'11"	Waste	40 gals.
Draft	2'6"	Clearance	9'10"
Weight	16,032#	Hull Type	Modified-V
Fuel	286 gals.	Deadrise Aft	12°

See Page 565 For Resale Values

Silverton Marine
Millville, NJ
www.silverton.com

231-360-0827

Silverton 362 Sedan
1994–98

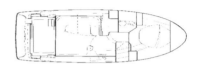

Multipurpose family convertible with large flybridge scored with 1990s buyers sold on traditional Silverton value. Well-appointed interior with expansive salon features private midcabin stateroom with twin berths, bow stateroom with island berth, well-positioned galley with generous storage. Split head/shower is especially convenient when cruising with guests. Roomy cockpit with transom door has molded steps to flybridge. Note integrated swim platform, foredeck sun pad. Cruise at 18 knots with 320hp V-drive gas engines (mid 20s top).

Length	36'1"	Fuel	300 gals.
Beam	12'11"	Water	100 gals.
Draft	3'0"	Waste	40 gals.
Weight	15,058#	Hull Type	Modified-V
Clearance	13'0"	Deadrise Aft	17°

See Page 566 For Resale Values

Silverton Marine
Millville, NJ
www.silverton.com

231-360-0827

Silverton 37 Convertible
1980–89

Smooth-running convertible enjoyed great popularity in the 1980s thanks to smart styling, user-friendly accommodations, good open-water performance. Space-efficient interior with convertible sofa and dinette, head with stall shower sleeps six. Original teak joinery was updated in 1985 to light oak. Small flybridge seats four. Deep cockpit is large enough for fishing but lacks transom door. Note that straight-drive inboards replaced V-drive power in 1981. Cruise at 18–19 knots with 350hp gas inboards (mid 20s top).

Length	37'0"	Fuel	300 gals.
Beam	14'0"	Water	100 gals.
Draft	3'7"	Cockpit	75 sq. ft.
Weight	20,000#	Hull Type	Modified-V
Clearance	12'6"	Deadrise Aft	14°

Prices Not Provided for Pre-1995 Models

Silverton Marine
Millville, NJ
www.silverton.com

231-360-0827

Silverton 37 Convertible
1990–2000

Dinette Interior, 1993–2001

Midcabin Interior, 1993–2001

Updated version of original Silverton 37 Convertible (1980–89) hit the mark with rakish styling, family-friendly accommodations, affordable price. Offered with choice of one or two staterooms, both with spacious open-plan salon, roomy head with stall shower, fully equipped galley. Fish, swim, or dive from deep cockpit with in-deck fishbox, transom door. Note side exhausts, large engineroom. Prop pockets reduce draft, improve running efficiency. Standard 320hp gas engines cruise at 15–16 knots (mid 20s wide open).

Length w/Pulpit	41'3"	Fuel	375 gals.
Hull Length	37'4"	Water	100 gals.
Beam	13'11"	Waste	40 gals.
Draft	3'7"	Hull Type	Modified-V
Weight	21,852#	Deadrise Aft	17°

See Page 566 For Resale Values

Silverton Marine
Millville, NJ
www.silverton.com

231-360-0827

Silverton 38 Convertible
2003–09

Versatile flybridge convertible delivered big-boat comfort, performance at a reasonable price. Twin-stateroom interior—highlighted by plush Ultraleather upholstery, glossy cherry cabinetry—gets high marks for tasteful decor, full-feature galley with hardwood floor, space for washer/dryer. Note split head/shower compartments forward. Relatively small cockpit has twin in-deck fishboxes, transom door, optional bait-prep center, engineroom access. Standard 385hp gas inboards cruise at 18 knots and top out in the mid 20s.

Length w/Pulpit	41'1"	Fuel	360 gals.
Beam	14'3"	Water	100 gals.
Draft	3'7"	Waste	40 gals.
Weight	26,450#	Hull Type	Modified-V
Clearance	16'8"	Deadrise Aft	17°

See Page 566 For Resale Values

Silverton Marine
Millville, NJ
www.silverton.com

www.powerboatguide.com   231-360-0827

Silverton 38 Express
1990–94

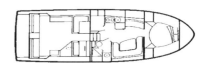

Beamy 1990s express made good on Silverton promise of family-friendly layout, economy-class price. Midcabin interior boasts double berths in both staterooms, head with stall shower, big U-shaped dinette. Note Plexiglas window/wall separating forward stateroom from salon. Cluster of six overhead skylights provide the only natural cabin lighting. Privacy door for aft stateroom is a nice touch. Bi-level cockpit can seat six. Twin 355hp V-drive gas engines cruise at 20 knots and deliver a top speed in the high 20s.

Length	37'7"	Fuel	300 gals.
Beam	13'11"	Water	110 gals.
Draft	3'2"	Cockpit	NA
Weight	21,000#	Hull Type	Modified-V
Clearance	9'9"	Deadrise Aft	17°

Prices Not Provided for Pre-1995 Models

Silverton Marine
Millville, NJ
www.silverton.com

---

www.powerboatguide.com   231-360-0827

Silverton 38 Sport Bridge
2005–Current

Top-selling family sedan with big two-stateroom floorplan gets high marks for versatility, comfort. Elevated walkways permit expansive salon whose dimensions rival those of a larger boat. Dinette is a step up from salon floor to make room for midcabin below. Note split head with toilet to starboard, shower to port. Molded bridge steps, extended swim platform, transom storage locker are standard. Engineroom is tight; flybridge is huge. Cruise in low 20s with 425hp gas engines; 24–25 knots with optional 355hp Cummins diesels.

Length	39'11"	Fuel	372 gals.
Beam	14'4"	Water	110 gals.
Draft	2'11"	Waste	40 gals.
Weight	26,900#	Hull Type	Modified-V
Clearance	14'11"	Deadrise Aft	12°

See Page 566 For Resale Values

Silverton Marine
Millville, NJ
www.silverton.com

---

www.powerboatguide.com   231-360-0827

Silverton 40 Convertible
1985–90

1985–88

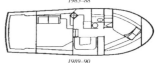

1989–90

Economy-class 40-footer with appealing lines offered 1980s convertible buyers plenty of boat for the money. Original twin-stateroom, mid-galley interior gave way to more open single-stateroom, galley-down floorplan in 1989. Most were sold with light oak interior trim. Cockpit is large enough for fishing, but this boat proved far more popular as a family cruiser. Lower helm was never offered. Note wide sidedecks, roomy flybridge, spacious engineroom. Cruise at 15–16 knots with standard 350hp gas engines (mid 20s top).

Length	40'0"	Fuel	300 gals.
Beam	14'0"	Water	100 gals.
Draft	3'0"	Cockpit	75 sq. ft.
Weight	23,000#	Hull Type	Modified-V
Clearance	13'6"	Deadrise Aft	14°

Prices Not Provided for Pre-1995 Models

Silverton Marine
Millville, NJ
www.silverton.com

Silverton 41 Convertible
1991–99

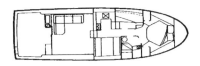

Well-built 1990s sedan with plenty of standard equipment made the cut with value-conscious buyers. Standard galley-down interior with open front windshield features wide-open salon with convertible sofa, big 6-person dinette, two comfortable staterooms. Offered with choice of oak or cherry interior trim. Deep cockpit with in-deck fishboxes, transom door is big enough for several anglers. Standard 385hp gas engines cruise at 19–20 knots (high 20s top); optional 425hp Cat diesels cruise at 24–25 knots (high 20s wide open).

Length w/Pulpit	46'3"	Fuel	524 gals.
Hull Length	41'3"	Water	200 gals.
Beam	14'10"	Waste	60 gals.
Draft	3'7"	Hull Type	Modified-V
Weight	24,975#	Deadrise Aft	17°

See Page 566 For Resale Values

Silverton Marine
Millville, NJ
www.silverton.com

Silverton 410 Sport Bridge
2001–04

Condo-style accommodations made this roomy sportcruiser popular with buyers willing to overlook her portly profile. Distinctive "SideWalk" deck configuration with elevated side decks results in cavernous—and innovative—full-beam salon with raised galley/dinette platform forward, two large staterooms, split head compartment. Huge bridge can entertain a small crowd. Note foredeck sun pad, extended swim platform. Cruise at 15 knots with standard gas engines; 20 knots with optional 420hp Cat diesels.

Length Overall	46'3"	Fuel	450 gals.
Beam	14'3"	Water	200 gals.
Draft	3'10"	Waste	40 gals.
Weight	28,495#	Hull Type	Modified-V
Clearance	15'4"	Deadrise Aft	16°

See Page 566 For Resale Values

Silverton Marine
Millville, NJ
www.silverton.com

Silverton 42 Convertible
2000–Current

Stylish family convertible with wide 14'11" beam is sporty on the outside, comfortable on the inside. Classy galley-down interior incorporates unique raised dinette forward in salon, two double staterooms, home-sized galley with generous storage. Note split head/shower arrangement, overhead rod locker in salon. Uncluttered cockpit has engineroom access door, tackle center, molded bridge steps, transom door. Fiberglass hardtop, power windows are optional. Cruise at 20 knots with 430hp Cummins diesels (mid 20s wide open).

Length Overall	44'6"	Fuel	524 gals.
Beam	14'11"	Water	200 gals.
Draft	3'7"	Waste	40 gals.
Weight	26,300#	Hull Type	Modified-V
Clearance	16'8"	Deadrise Aft	17°

See Page 566 For Resale Values

Silverton Marine
Millville, NJ
www.silverton.com

Cruisers & Sportboats

www.powerboatguide.com   231-360-0827

Silverton 43 Sport Bridge
2006–Current

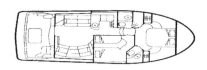

Popular sportcruiser combines leading-edge styling with vast accommodations, affordable price. Raised side decks maximize interior space, permit easy bow access from bridge. Full-beam main cabin offers comfortable seating for several guests. Interior highlights include Ultraleather upholstery, cherry cabinetry, retractable salon TV. Note split head with shower to starboard. Frameless windows eliminate leaks. Standard 425hp gas engines cruise at 16–18 knots; Volvo 370hp diesels with IPS drives cruise at 20–22 knots (about 28 top).

Length	43'5"	Fuel	430 gals.
Beam	14'4"	Water	118 gals.
Draft	3'10"	Waste	40 gals.
Weight	28,000#	Hull Type	Modified-V
Clearance	14'5"	Deadrise Aft	12°

See Page 566 For Resale Values

Silverton Marine
Millville, NJ
www.silverton.com

---

www.powerboatguide.com   231-360-0827

Silverton 45 Convertible
2006–Current

Feature-rich sports convertible signature Silverton styling is sporty, spacious, seaworthy. Space-efficient layout combines roomy three-stateroom interior (most 45-footers have two) with big 80-square-foot cockpit. Entertainment center with retractable TV is standard in salon. Washer/dryer can be fitted in second guest cabin. Additional features include standard hardtop, Ultraleather upholstery, cherry cabinets, molded bridge steps, cockpit engineroom access. Volvo 500hp diesels cruise at 22–24 knots (high 20s top).

Length	47'8"	Fuel	607 gals.
Beam	15'4"	Water	120 gals.
Draft	3'8"	Waste	72 gals.
Weight	42,048#	Hull Type	Modified-V
Clearance	16'10"	Deadrise Aft	13°

See Page 566 For Resale Values

Silverton Marine
Millville, NJ
www.silverton.com

---

www.powerboatguide.com   231-360-0827

Silverton 48/50 Convertible
2004–Current

Conservative family convertible (called Silverton 48 in 2004–06) offers style, substance at a competitive price. Upscale three-stateroom interior boasts modern blend of high-gloss cherry cabinetry, deep-pile carpeting, quality furnishings. Washer/dryer is standard; master stateroom is fitted with foldaway flat-screen TV. Cockpit is on the small side, but flybridge is among the largest to be found on a 48-footer. Prop pockets reduce hull draft, improve efficiency. Note standard hardtop. Volvo 715hp diesels cruise in the high 20s (about 30 knots top).

Length w/Pulpit	51'7"	Fuel	793 gals.
Beam	16'4"	Water	200 gals.
Draft	4'0"	Waste	80 gals.
Weight	47,600#	Hull Type	Modified-V
Clearance	17'6"	Deadrise Aft	12°

See Page 567 For Resale Values

Silverton Marine
Millville, NJ
www.silverton.com

231-360-0827

Stamas 320 Express
2004–Current

Floorplan Not Available

Competitively priced express with versatile personality lives up to promise of cruising comfort, proven fishability. Large cockpit comes standard with full array of fishing amenities including transom livewell, insulated transom fishbox, wide transom door. Engine access is via hydraulic deck hatch. Teak-trimmed interior with midcabin berth, convertible dinette, teak-and-holly sole sleeps six. Twin 320hp MerCruiser gas inboards cruise at 22 knots (30 top). Outboard version with 225hp Yamahas tops out at close to 35 knots.

Length w/Pulpit	34 5"	Fuel, IB	240 gals.
Hull Length	32'3"	Fuel, OB	316 gals.
Beam	11'2"	Water	40 gals.
Draft	2'20"	Hull Type	Modified-V
Weight	13,200#	Deadrise Aft	18°

See Page 567 For Resale Values

Stamas Yachts
Tarpon Springs, FL
www.stamas.com

231-360-0827

Stamas 340 Express
2003–Current

Floorplan Not Available

Quality midsize express splits the difference between hardcore fishboat, comfortable family cruiser. Uncluttered cockpit comes standard with full array of fishing amenities including transom livewell, insulated fishbox, wide transom door. Engine access is via hydraulic deck hatch. Well-appointed interior with midcabin berth sleeps six. Prop pockets reduce draft, improve efficiency. MerCruiser 370hp gas inboards cruise at 22 knots (30+ top); Yanmar 370hp diesels cruise at 25 knots (30 top). Outboard version also available.

Length w/Pulpit	36'2"	Clearance	7'3"
Hull Length	34'0"	Fuel	350 gals.
Beam	12'6"	Water	84 gals.
Draft	2'4"	Hull Type	Modified-V
Weight	14,000#	Deadrise Aft	18°

See Page 567 For Resale Values

Stamas Yachts
Tarpon Springs, FL
www.stamas.com

231-360-0827

Stamas 360 Express
1992–99

Sturdy 1990s cruiser with conservative lines, legendary Stamas construction targets family anglers with an eye for value. Fishing amenities include livewell, raw-water washdown, insulated fishboxes, rod storage. Elevated helm affords excellent visibility. Tasteful midcabin interior with convertible dinette, full galley sleeps four adults, two kids. Deep keel, prop pockets protect running gear in event of grounding. Wide side decks are a plus. Standard 310hp MerCruiser gas inboards cruise at 18 knots (high 20s top).

Length w/Pulpit	38'6"	Clearance	8'3"
Hull Length	36'0"	Fuel	372 gals.
Beam	13'2"	Water	90 gals.
Draft	2'4"	Hull Type	Modified-V
Weight	16,975#	Deadrise Aft	18°

See Page 567 For Resale Values

Stamas Yachts
Tarpon Springs, FL
www.stamas.com

Cruisers & Sportboats

231-360-0827

Stamas 370 Express
2000–Current

Updated version of Stamas 360 Express (1992–99) with many new features makes a good boat even better. Midcabin interior is rare in a dedicated fishing boat. Sizable cockpit has built-in livewell, insulated fishbox, bait-prep station, tackle drawers. Well-designed helm has space for flush-mounting electronics. Note wide side decks. Power engine hatch provides outstanding service access. Deep keel, prop pockets protect running gear in event of grounding. Yanmar 420hp diesels cruise at 24–26 knots (30+ knots wide open).

Length w/Pulpit	39'2"	Headroom	6'4"
Hull Length	36'8"	Fuel	400 gals.
Beam	13'2"	Water	84 gals.
Draft	2'4"	Hull Type	Modified-V
Weight	16,975#	Deadrise Aft	18°

See Page 567 For Resale Values

Stamas Yachts
Tarpon Springs, FL
www.stamas.com

231-360-0827

Sunseeker 34 Superhawk
1997–2003

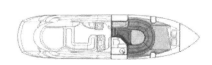

Fast-action sportcruiser combines extraordinary handling with dramatic styling, first-rate build quality. Posh cockpit seats several guests in comfort. Compact interior with double berth forward is beautifully finished but lacks headroom. Small head is nearly worthless for showers; galley is fine as long as you stick to sandwiches. Power engine hatch reveals neat (but tight) engineroom. Terrific open-water performer still outguns most competitors: 285hp Volvo diesel I/Os hit close to 45 knots wide open. Total of 160 were built.

Length	37'2"	Clearance	NA
Beam	10'2"	Fuel	185 gals.
Draft, Drives Up	2'2"	Water	18 gals.
Draft, Drives Down	3'9"	Hull Type	Deep-V
Weight	12,800#	Deadrise Aft	21°

See Page 568 For Resale Values

Sunseeker Yachts
Poole, England
www.sunseeker.com

231-360-0827

Sunseeker Portofino 400
1995–98

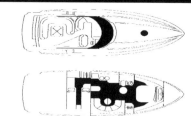

Powerful 1990s Med express delivers sportboat performance with extraordinary cruising comfort. Luxury-fitted interior with two private staterooms, posh salon sleeps four adults. Exceptionally large cockpit provides plenty of entertaining, sunbathing space. Notable features include stylish wraparound windshield, cockpit wet bar, teak swim platform, wide side decks, forward-facing radar arch. Deep-V hull delivers superb big-water performance. Engineroom is a tight fit. Cat 420hp diesels cruise at 25–26 knots (low 30s top).

Length	40'0"	Headroom	6'3"
Beam	13'5"	Fuel	260 gals.
Draft	3'3"	Water	71 gals.
Weight	18,738#	Hull Type	Deep-V
Clearance	12'2"	Deadrise Aft	19°

Insufficient Resale Data To Assign Values

Sunseeker Yachts
Poole, England
www.sunseeker.com

Sunseeker 44 Camargue
1998–2002

Good-selling U.K. import introduced in 1998 delivered best-in-class blend of luxury, finish, performance. Curvaceous cockpit includes full-size sun lounge, folding dining table with seating for eight. Uscale interior with roomy salon, two heads boasts high-gloss cherry woodwork, top-quality appliances, designer furnishings. Extended swim platform, foredeck fender storage, teak cockpit sole, bow thruster were standard. Windlass is stored inside anchor locker. Twin 420hp Cat diesels cruise in the mid 20s, top out at 30+ knots.

Length	44'0"	Fuel	265 gals.
Beam	13'6"	Water	80 gals.
Draft	3.5"	Headroom	6'4"
Weight	29,000#	Hull Type	Deep-V
Clearance	9'10"	Deadrise Aft	20°

See Page 568 For Resale Values

Sunseeker Yachts
Poole, England
www.sunseeker.com

Sunseeker 46 Portofino
2003–05

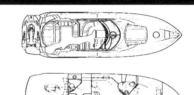

Edgy English express with seductive styling lives up to Sunseeker promise of state-of-the-art construction, luxury-class amenities. Posh interior with high-gloss cherry cabinetry, UltraLeather seating offers two private staterooms, hidden galley appliances, two heads, generous cabinet storage. Topside highlights include hydraulic swim platform, foredeck sun pad, deluxe cockpit galley with refrigerator and barbeque. Engine access is no picnic. Cruise at 28 knots (32-33 top) with 480hp Volvo diesels.

Length Overall	48.5"	Headroom	6'3"
Beam	13'9"	Fuel	346 gals.
Draft	3'10"	Water	99 gals.
Weight	32,300#	Hull Type	Deep-V
Clearance	13'1"	Deadrise Aft	19°

See Page 568 For Resale Values

Sunseeker Yachts
Poole, England
www.sunseeker.com

Sunseeker 47 Camargue
1996–99

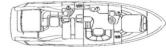

Classy sportcruiser imported in the late 1990s delivers exceptional build quality, sumptuous accommodations. Opulent midcabin interior contains two heads, large galley with hidden appliances, premium hardware and furnishings. Single-level cockpit is a full-feature entertainment center with wraparound seating, deluxe wet bar, foldaway dining table. Note chart flat with light, transom shower. Aft sun pad conceals transom garage. Cat 435hp diesel inboards cruise at 25–26 knots (30 knots top); 625hp GMs cruise at 30 knots (34–35 top).

Length	46'9"	Fuel	365 gals.
Beam	13.5"	Water	100 gals.
Draft	3'3"	Headroom	6.5"
Weight	30,644#	Hull Type	Deep-V
Clearance	9'4"	Deadrise Aft	23°

See Page 568 For Resale Values

Sunseeker Yachts
Poole, England
www.sunseeker.com

Cruisers & Sportboats

231-360-0827

Sunseeker 48 Superhawk
1996–2005

Popular high-performance express passes most anything on the water except a fuel dock. Standard topside goodies include twin racing bolsters, cockpit seating for six, sun pad, wet bar. Elegant single-stateroom interior features plush lounge seating, head with shower, small galley, built-in entertainment system. Deep-V hull has keel pad for enhanced acceleration. Note standard bow thruster. Triple 415hp gas MerCruisers (with surface drives) reach 50 knots; triple 260hp Volvo diesel I/Os hit 40+ knots. Total of 247 were built.

Length Overall	50'2"	Headroom	6'1"
Beam	10'8"	Fuel	280 gals.
Draft	2'6"	Water	58 gals.
Weight	22,100#	Hull Type	Deep-V
Clearance	10'4"	Deadrise Aft	22°

Insufficient Resale Data To Assign Values

Sunseeker Yachts
Poole, England
www.sunseeker.com

231-360-0827

Sunseeker 50 Camargue
1999–2003

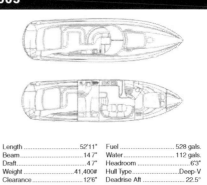

Flashy Med-inspired express became one of the more popular sportcruisers on the international market for several years. Highlights include huge cockpit seating for eight, exceptionally comfortable twin-stateroom interior with elegant salon, private en suite heads. Aft deck lifts electrically to expose large transom garage for dinghy, PWC. Hardtop was optional. Note fore and aft sun pads, excellent helm layout. Large engineroom is a plus. Twin 660hp Cats—straight inboards, not V-drives—cruise in the mid 20s (about 30 knots top).

Length	52'11"	Fuel	528 gals.
Beam	14'7"	Water	112 gals.
Draft	4'7"	Headroom	6'3"
Weight	41,400#	Hull Type	Deep-V
Clearance	12'6"	Deadrise Aft	22.5°

Insufficient Resale Data To Assign Values

Sunseeker Yachts
Poole, England
www.sunseeker.com

231-360-0827

Sunseeker 51 Camargue
1995–97

Three-Stateroom Interior

Two-Stateroom Interior

Luxury express yacht introduced to American market in 1994 impressed buyers with her sleek styling, deluxe amenities, flawless joinery. Originally offered with opulent twin-cabin interior, updated three-stateroom layout became available in 1996. Expansive cockpit with teak sole has comfortable seating for ten; aft-deck sun lounge is atop hydraulically operated storage garage with electric launch/recovery winch for PWC. Note telescoping gangway. Engineroom is a seriously tight fit. Cat 600hp (or GM 625hp) V-drive diesels top out at 30+ knots.

Length	49'0"	Fuel	465 gals.
Beam	14'5"	Water	130 gals.
Draft	3'8"	Headroom	6'2"
Weight	42,460#	Hull Type	Deep-V
Clearance	12'9"	Deadrise Aft	19°

See Page 568 For Resale Values

Sunseeker Yachts
Poole, England
www.sunseeker.com

231-360-0827

Sunseeker 53 Portofino
2004–Current

High-impact sportyacht combines elegant styling, lush interior, spirited performance buyers expect of a Sunseeker product. Opulent three-stateroom interior is an impressive display of handcrafted cherry cabinetry, leather upholstery, top-shelf hardware and appliances. Roomy cockpit with U-shaped seating, teak sole, boasts slick foldaway table. Power sun pad lifts to reveal tender garage. First-rate engine compartment, near-flawless gelcoat. Expect 30+ knots top with 715hp Cat or Volvo diesels.

Length	56'11"	Fuel	486 gals.
Beam	15'1"	Water	88 gals.
Draft	4'0"	Waste	24 gals.
Weight	42,500#	Hull Type	Deep-V
Clearance	14.5"	Deadrise Aft	19°

See Page 568 For Resale Values

Sunseeker Yachts
Poole, England
www.sunseeker.com

231-360-0827

Sunseeker 58/60 Predator
1997–2002

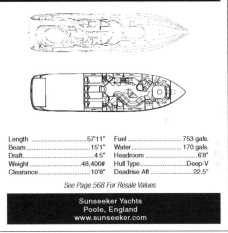

High-impact express (called Predator 58 in 1997–99) made good on Sunseeker promise of top-shelf amenities, leading-edge construction. Lush interior with warm, club-like atmosphere features spacious salon with sweeping settee, extended galley, three private cabins. Cockpit is dominated by oval sun pad over dinghy/PWC garage with a built-in launch/retrieval winch. Note excellent helm layout, wide side decks, flawless finish. Hardtop with sunroof was a popular option. Cruise at 26–27 knots with 800hp Cat diesels (30+ knots top).

Length	57'11"	Fuel	753 gals.
Beam	15'1"	Water	170 gals.
Draft	4.5"	Headroom	6'8"
Weight	48,400#	Hull Type	Deep-V
Clearance	10'8"	Deadrise Aft	22.5°

See Page 568 For Resale Values

Sunseeker Yachts
Poole, England
www.sunseeker.com

231-360-0827

Sunseeker 58/60 Predator
1997–2002

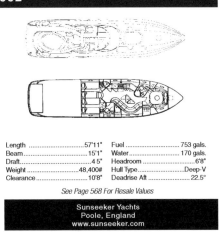

High-impact express (called Predator 58 in 1997–99) made good on Sunseeker promise of top-shelf amenities, leading-edge construction. Lush interior with warm, club-like atmosphere features spacious salon with sweeping settee, extended galley, three private cabins. Cockpit is dominated by oval sun pad over dinghy/PWC garage with a built-in launch/retrieval winch. Note excellent helm layout, wide side decks, flawless finish. Hardtop with sunroof was a popular option. Cruise at 26–27 knots with 800hp Cat diesels (30+ knots top).

Length	57'11"	Fuel	753 gals.
Beam	15'1"	Water	170 gals.
Draft	4.5"	Headroom	6'8"
Weight	48,400#	Hull Type	Deep-V
Clearance	10'8"	Deadrise Aft	22.5°

See Page 568 For Resale Values

Sunseeker Yachts
Poole, England
www.sunseeker.com

Cruisers & Sportboats

Cruisers & Sportboats

Sunseeker 61 Predator
2002–05

Deluxe hardtop cruiser with retractable sunroof combines exotic Med styling with plush accommodations, powerful performance. Beautifully crafted interior is enhanced by high-gloss cherry joinery, leather seating, hidden galley appliances. Master stateroom with en suite head is forward; twin aft cabins share day head in salon. Super-lush cockpit layout. Hydraulic swim platform makes launching/retrieving tender from aft garage simple, easy. Cruise at an honest 30 knots with MAN 1,050hp diesels (about 35 knots top).

|---|---|---|---|
Length	61'0"	Fuel	779 gals.
Beam	15'1"	Water	165 gals.
Draft	4'5"	Headroom	6'6"
Weight	57,320#	Hull Type	Deep-V
Clearance	16'1"	Deadrise Aft	19°

Insufficient Resale Data To Assign Values

Sunseeker Yachts
Poole, England
www.sunseeker.com

Sunseeker 63 Predator
1995–99

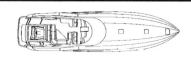
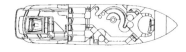

Gold-plated 63-footer imported in late 1990s was among largest production yachts of her era. Enormous cockpit has retractable soft top for weather protection. Massive aft sun lounge conceals garage capable of storing—and launching—a 13-foot jet boat. Palatial interior with wide-open salon, designer furnishings sleeps six in three staterooms. Note dual transom gates, wraparound cockpit seating, excellent helm layout. Twin 1,100hp MAN diesels (jammed into a tight engineroom) cruise at a fast 32 knots (36–38 knots top).

|---|---|---|---|
Length Overall	63'0"	Headroom	6'3"
Beam	15'6"	Fuel	798 gals.
Draft	4'1"	Water	185 gals.
Weight	48,400#	Hull Type	Deep-V
Clearance	14'5"	Deadrise Aft	21°

Insufficient Resale Data To Assign Values

Sunseeker Yachts
Poole, England
www.sunseeker.com

Tiara 2700 Continental
1982–86

Well-finished express offered 1980s buyers exceptional small-boat quality, comfort, durability. Space-efficient deck layout boasts roomy cockpit, wide side decks, well-arranged helm with tall windshield. Teak-trimmed cabin with U-shaped dinette, full galley, midcabin berth sleeps six in comfort. Swim, dive, or fish from large single-level cockpit. Note excellent nonskid, sturdy bow rails. Hatches in cockpit sole provide good access to engineroom. Twin 260hp MerCruiser sterndrives cruise at 24–26 knots (close to 40 knots top).

|---|---|---|---|
Length	27'6"	Water	24 gals.
Beam	9'10"	Clearance	7'0"
Hull Draft	2'8"	Cockpit Length	11'0"
Weight	7,400#	Hull Type	Deep-V
Fuel	137 gals.	Deadrise Aft	20°

Prices Not Provided for Pre-1995 Models

Tiara Yachts
Holland, MI
www.tiarayachts.com

231-360-0827

Tiara 2700 Open
1987—93

Iconic inboard express supplies hard-to-beat mix of spacious cockpit, upscale interior, quality construction. Teak-trimmed cabin with full-service galley, stand-up head with shower, sleeps two. Single-level cockpit with back-to-back seating is large enough for mounted chair. Wide sidedecks, sturdy rails provide secure foredeck access. Note commercial-quality windshield, easy-access motorboxes, deep-V hull. Many updates/improvements over the years. Crusader 270hp gas engines cruise in the low 20s (28–30 knots wide open).

Length w/Pulpit	29 5"	Clearance	7'0"
Hull Length	27'0"	Fuel	240 gals.
Beam	10'0"	Water	20 gals.
Draft	2'0"	Hull Type	Deep-V
Weight	7,500#	Deadrise Aft	22°

Prices Not Provided for Pre-1995 Models

Tiara Yachts
Holland, MI
www.tiarayachts.com

231-360-0827

Tiara 2900 Coronet
1997–2007

Graceful sportcruiser with inboard power delivers impressive mix of versatility, styling, performance. Single-level cockpit has double helm seat, L-lounge forward, removable bench seats aft. Entire forward section of deck lifts for engine access. Compact interior with enclosed head, mini-galley, teak-and-holly cabin sole sleeps two. Note centerline transom door, cockpit wet bar. Tall windshield has reverse-angle spray guard along top. Exemplary finish throughout. Cruise at 21–22 knots with 320hp gas inboards (30+ knots top).

Length w/Pulpit	31 7"	Fuel	200 gals.
Hull Length	28'2"	Water	30 gals.
Beam	11'4"	Waste	20 gals.
Draft	2'8"	Hull Type	Modified-V
Weight	10,000#	Deadrise Aft	19°

See Page 568 For Resale Values

Tiara Yachts
Holland, MI
www.tiarayachts.com

231-360-0827

Tiara 2900 Open
1993–2006

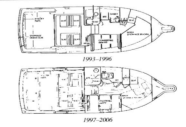

1993–1996

1997–2006

Versatile Tiara express with upscale interior, efficient deck layout delivers best-in-class engineering, construction, performance. Uncluttered cockpit features double helm and companion seats forward, twin aft-facing seats, wide transom door. Well-appointed cabin with full galley, convertible dinette sleeps four. Wide beam for a 29-footer. Entire bridgedeck lifts electrically for engine access. Used models are always in demand. Twin 320hp inboard gas engines cruise at 20 knots (close to 30 knots top).

Length w/Pulpit	30'9"	Fuel	200 gals.
Hull Length	28'9"	Water	30 gals.
Beam	11'4"	Waste	20 gals.
Draft	2'8"	Hull Type	Modified-V
Weight	10,700#	Deadrise Aft	19°

See Page 568 For Resale Values

Tiara Yachts
Holland, MI
www.tiarayachts.com

Cruisers & Sportboats

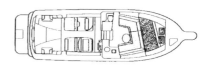

www.powerboatguide.com   231-360-0827

Tiara 3000 Open
2007–Current

Premium hardtop express with innovative interior couples graceful styling elegance with signature Tiara quality. Wide beam creates large cockpit with jump seat, workstation/wet bar with insulated storage, sprayer, cutting board. Elegant teak cabin with hardwood sole, forward side berth features posh aft-facing lounge that converts to double berth. Note tall windshield, tilt-away helm, opening hardtop vents. Bridgedeck lifts electrically for engine access. Cruise at 22–24 knots with 385hp gas inboards (low-to-mid 30s top).

Length w/Pulpit	33'0"	Fuel	210 gals.
Hull Length	30'6"	Water	32 gals.
Beam	12'6"	Waste	20 gals.
Draft	2'8"	Hull Type	Modified-V
Weight	13,225#	Deadrise Aft	14°

See Page 568 For Resale Values

Tiara Yachts
Holland, MI
www.tiarayachts.com

---

www.powerboatguide.com   231-360-0827

Tiara 3100 Open
1979–91

Classic 1980s express reinforced Tiara reputation for superior engineering, top-shelf construction. Versatile layout—equally well-suited for fishing or cruising—boasts appealing teak-trimmed interior with big U-shaped dinette, large cockpit with removable bench seat, roomy engine compartment with good service acces. Note tall, commercial-quality windshield, aft-facing cockpit seats. Modified-V hull can be a wet ride. Standard 350hp gas inboards cruise in the low 20s (32–33 knots top). Replaced with all-new 3100 Open in 1992.

Length w/Pulpit	33'9"	Clearance, Arch	7'6"
Hull Length	31'3"	Fuel	196 gals.
Beam	12'0"	Water	36 gals.
Draft	2'9"	Hull Type	Modified-V
Weight	10,500#	Deadrise Aft	14°

Prices Not Provided for Pre-1995 Models

Tiara Yachts
Holland, MI
www.tiarayachts.com

---

www.powerboatguide.com   231-360-0827

Tiara 3100 Open
1992–2004

Updated version of original 3100 Open (1979–91) made a great boat even better. Reworked hull with prop pockets, increased deadrise, delivers better head-sea ride than her predecessor; new bi-level cockpit allows installation of diesels in larger engine compartment. Luxury-class interior with U-shaped dinette, full galley sleeps four. Cockpit came with in-deck fishbox, livewell, foldaway rear seat. Transom door became standard in 1994. Cruise at 20 knots with 320hp gas engines; 22–23 knots with 330hp Cummins diesels.

Length w/Pulpit	33'10"	Fuel	246 gals.
Hull Length	31'6"	Water	38 gals.
Beam	12'0"	Waste	20 gals.
Draft	3'0"	Hull Type	Modified-V
Weight	12,300#	Deadrise Aft	18°

See Page 568 For Resale Values

Tiara Yachts
Holland, MI
www.tiarayachts.com

Tiara 3200 Open
2004–Current

Graceful styling, top-shelf construction, luxury appointments make this versatile express a class leader with savvy buyers. Bi-level cockpit with in-deck fishbox, transom door is large enough for several anglers. Upscale interior with solid teak cabinetry, Ultra-leather seating sleeps four. Bridgedeck rises electrically for engine access. Optional livewell replaces standard fold-down transom seat. Hardtop is a popular option. Note prop-pocket hull bottom. Cruise at 22 knots with 385hp gas engines; mid 20ss with Volvo 310hp diesels.

Length w/Pulpit	35'1"	Fuel	256 gals.
Hull Length	32'7"	Water	38 gals.
Beam	13'0"	Waste	20 gals.
Draft	3'0"	Hull Type	Modified-V
Weight	15,950#	Deadrise Aft	18°

See Page 568 For Resale Values

Tiara Yachts
Holland, MI
www.tiarayachts.com

Tiara 3300 Open
1988–97

Feature-rich express with conservative lines, superior finish delivers exceptional cruising comfort, owner satisfaction. Elegant teak-trimmed interior with U-shaped dinette, convertible settee sleeps six in genuine comfort. Tournament-grade cockpit with transom door, fishbox is big enough for serious fishing pursuits. Wide side decks, good engine access, well-designed helm layout. Low-deadrise hull can be a stiff ride. Cruise at 20 knots with standard gas engines; 24 knots with 315hp Cummins diesels.

Length w/Pulpit	35'8"	Fuel	295 gals.
Hull Length	32'10"	Water	46 gals.
Beam	12'6"	Waste	20 gals.
Draft	2'3"	Hull Type	Modified-V
Weight	13,500#	Deadrise Aft	14°

See Page 568 For Resale Values

Tiara Yachts
Holland, MI
www.tiarayachts.com

Tiara 3500 Express
1995–2003

Standard Floorplan

Optional Layout

Luxury-class cruiser from late 1990s gets high marks for tasteful accommodations, premium amenities, spirited performance. Interior is huge for a 35-footer thanks to wide 13'9" beam. Salon lounge converts into second stateroom at night. Huge cockpit with foldaway rear seat, twin transom doors is among largest in her class. Extended swim platform can stow inflatable or PWC. Note huge transom storage trunk. Cummins 370hp V-drive diesels top out in the high 20s; 435hp Cats reach 30 knots wide open.

Length w/Pulpit	38'10"	Weight, Diesel	21,500#
Hull Length	35'8"	Fuel	354 gals.
Beam	13'9"	Water	124 gals.
Draft	2'10"	Hull Type	Modified-V
Weight, Gas	18,600#	Deadrise Aft	18°

See Page 568 For Resale Values

Tiara Yachts
Holland, MI
www.tiarayachts.com

Cruisers & Sportboats

www.powerboatguide.com
231-360-0827

Tiara 3500 Open
1998–2004

Top-ranked express combines traditional Tiara styling with high-end construction, uncommon luxury. Spacious single-stateroom interior features solid teak joinery, leather upholstery, beautiful teak-and-holly cabin sole. Crowd-friendly cockpit with foldaway rear seat serves anglers, cruisers alike. Entire bridgedeck rises for engine access. Note wide side decks, power windshield vent, ergonomic helm layout. Standard gas inboards cruise at 16–18 knots; optional 370hp Cummins diesels cruise at 25–26 knots.

Length w/Pulpit	40'8"	Fuel	360 gals.
Hull Length	35'6"	Water	70 gals.
Beam	13'3"	Waste	30 gals.
Draft	3'3"	Hull Type	Modified-V
Weight	14,000#	Deadrise Aft	18°

See Page 568 For Resale Values

Tiara Yachts
Holland, MI
www.tiarayachts.com

---

www.powerboatguide.com
231-360-0827

Tiara 3500 Sovran
2008–Current

Beautifully finished hardtop express with efficient Volvo IPS power provides uncommon luxury for the cruising couple. Wide beam results in considerably more cockpit/cabin space than most 35-footers. Elegant open-plan interior boasts unusually spacious midcabin area with facing settees, wall-mounted flat-screen TV. Split-level cockpit seats eight in comfort. Note that hardtop lacks opening sunroof. Cockpit sole lifts electrically for access to engine compartment. Cruise at 25–26 knots (30+ top) with Volvo 300hp IPS diesels.

Length Overall	37'9"	Fuel	250 gals.
Beam	12'11"	Water	70 gals.
Draft	3'1"	Waste	30 gals.
Weight	17,600#	Hull Type	Modified-V
Clearance	9.8"	Deadrise Aft	15°

See Page 569 For Resale Values

Tiara Yachts
Holland, MI
www.tiarayachts.com

---

www.powerboatguide.com
231-360-0827

Tiara 3600 Convertible
1987–95

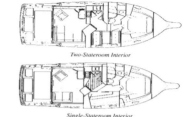

Two-Stateroom Interior

Single-Stateroom Interior

Polished flybridge sedan introduced in 1987 is one part fishing boat, two parts coastal cruiser. Offered with original two-stateroom interior or less popular single-stateroom layout with dinette in place of guest cabin. Sliding glass door leads into roomy salon whose open front windshield allowed for optional lower helm position. Modest cockpit dimensions preclude installation of tackle center. Standard 350hp gas engines cruise at 19–20 knots; optional Cat 375hp diesels cruise at 25 knots and post a top speed of 29–30 knots.

Length w/Pulpit	39'8"	Clearance	12'6"
Hull Length	36'8"	Fuel	396 gals.
Beam	13'9"	Water	85 gals.
Draft	3'0"	Hull Type	Modified-V
Weight	18,300#	Deadrise Aft	14°

See Page 569 For Resale Values

Tiara Yachts
Holland, MI
www.tiarayachts.com

Tiara 3600 Open
1987–96

Standard Floorplan

Alternate Floorplan

Strong-selling express set class standards in her era for versatile mix of hard-nosed fishability, family-style accommodations. Highlights include well-appointed interior with solid teak joinery, expansive bi-level cockpit, top-quality construction. Original cabin layout with island berth forward sleeps four; alternate layout introduced in 1989 sleeps six. Entire bridgedeck lifts on hydraulic rams for engine access. Conservative lines still look good today. Standard 350hp gas engines cruise at 18 knots; 375hp Cats cruise at 24–25 knots.

Length w/Pulpit	36'8"	Headroom	6'2"
Beam	13'9"	Fuel	396 gals.
Draft	2'11"	Water	85 gals.
Weight	16,500#	Hull Type	Modified-V
Clearance	9'7"	Deadrise Aft	14°

See Page 569 For Resale Values

Tiara Yachts
Holland, MI
www.tiarayachts.com

Tiara 3600 Open
2005–Current

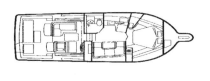

Top-quality express appeals to anglers, cruisers alike with fish-ready cockpit, upscale cabin accommodations. Posh interior with solid teak joinery, Ultraleather dinette (with flip-up backrest) sleeps five. Professional-grade cockpit features aft-facing seats, in-deck fishboxes, transom livewell, fold-down transom seat. Bridgedeck lifts for engine access. Note aggressive nonskid, tilt-away dash, sturdy windshield. Cummins 380hp diesels cruise at 26–28 knots. Newer models with 370hp Volvo IPS drives cruise efficiently at 28 knots.

Length	36 5"	Fuel	400 gals.
Beam	13'3"	Water	70 gals.
Draft	3 5"	Waste	30 gals.
Weight	19,100#	Hull Type	Modified-V
Clearance	9'10"	Deadrise Aft	18°

See Page 569 For Resale Values

Tiara Yachts
Holland, MI
www.tiarayachts.com

Tiara 3600 Sovran
2004–06

Luxury-class cruiser offers unsurpassed space, comfort, quality. Sumptuous interior with wide-open salon is highlighted by solid teak cabinetry, Corian counters, leather upholstery. Bi-level cockpit features L-lounge opposite helm, aft-facing seats, foldaway rear seat, full wet bar. Hardtop with opening hatches was standard. Bridgedeck lifts for engine access. Note large transom locker, extended swim platform. Standard 385hp V-drive gas engines cruise 22–23 knots; optional 380hp Cummins diesels cruise at 24 knots.

Length w/Pulpit	41'8"	Fuel	326 gals.
Hull Length	36'4"	Water	105 gals.
Beam	13'0"	Waste	40 gals.
Draft	3'8"	Hull Type	Modified-V
Weight	18,000#	Deadrise Aft	19°

See Page 569 For Resale Values

Tiara Yachts
Holland, MI
www.tiarayachts.com

Cruisers & Sportboats

Tiara 3700 Open
1995–2000

Late-model open express delivers gold-plated mix of classic Tiara styling, deluxe accommodations, exceptional finish. Upscale cabin with solid teak joinery, leather upholstery features huge U-shaped dinette, surprisingly roomy galley, private bow stateroom. Topside amenities include L-shaped companion seat with aft-facing double seat, cockpit fishboxes, cooler. Radar arch, foldaway rear cockpit seat were popular options. Note wide side decks. Bridgedeck lifts for engine access. Cat 435hp diesels cruise in the mid 20s (30+ top).

Length w/Pulpit	39'8"	Fuel	411 gals.
Hull Length	37'1"	water	98 gals.
Beam	14'2"	Waste	40 gals.
Draft	3'9"	Hull Type	Modified-V
Weight	21,800#	Deadrise Aft	18°

See Page 569 For Resale Values

Tiara Yachts
Holland, MI
www.tiarayachts.com

Tiara 3800 Open
2000–08

Plan A

Plan B

Leading-edge express splits the difference between luxury sportcruiser, tournament-level fishing machine. Beautifully finished interior features posh seating, solid teak cabinetry, first-rate galley appliances. Note appealing teak-and-holly cabin sole, hideaway salon TV. Topside highlights include cockpit wet bar, foldaway transom seat, wide transom door. Helm layout is as good as it gets. Bridgedeck lifts for engine access. Hardtop with overhead hatches was optional. Cummins 480hp diesels cruise at 25–26 knots (about 30 knots top).

Length Overall	40'9"	Fuel	411 gals.
Beam	14'2"	Water	110 gals.
Draft	3'6"	Waste	40 gals.
Weight	22,600#	Hull Type	Modified-V
Clearance	9'7"	Deadrise Aft	18°

See Page 569 For Resale Values

Tiara Yachts
Holland, MI
www.tiarayachts.com

Tiara 3900 Open
2009–Current

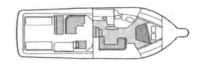

Quality dual-purpose express with broad 15-foot beam meets anglers need for fishability, cruisers need for luxury. Highlights include elegant single-stateroom interior with teak-and-holly sole, big 95-sq.ft. fishing cockpit with in-deck fishboxes, swivel L-shaped companion lounge, meticulous engine compartment. Note raised 3-person mezzanine seating aft of helm deck. Fishing package includes 55-gallon transom livewell, deluxe tackle center. Hardtop is optional. Cummins 600hp diesels cruise at 30 knots (low 30s top).

Length w/Pulpit	41'11"	Fuel	535 gals.
Beam	15'0"	Water	120 gals.
Draft	3'6"	Waste	38 gals.
Weight	24,500#	Hull Type	Modified-V
Clearance, Top	10'4"	Deadrise Aft	18°

Insufficient Resale Data To Assign Values

Tiara Yachts
Holland, MI
www.tiarayachts.com

Tiara 3900 Sovran
2007–Current

Bold hardtop express designed around Volvo's IPS drives makes good on Tiara promise of cutting-edge luxury, exceptional performance. Very spacious interior with quality teak joinery, large galley has unique lounge area aft complete with facing leather settees, flatscreen TV. Cockpit and bridgedeck seating are protected by standard hardtop. Note extended swim platform, transom storage locker. IPS joystick control provides truly precise handling. Volvo 370hp diesels cruise economically at 26 knots (30+ knots wide open).

Length	39'3"	Fuel	300 gals.
Beam	13'3"	Water	102 gals.
Draft	3 5"	Waste	38 gals.
Weight	23,000#	Hull Type	Modified-V
Clearance	10'3"	Deadrise Aft	14.5°

See Page 569 For Resale Values

Tiara Yachts
Holland, MI
www.tiarayachts.com

Tiara 4000 Express
1994–2003

Standard Floorplan

Optional Layout

Luxury-class express yacht with lush accommodations built an impressive reputation for leading-edge amenities, world-class engineering. Standard midcabin interior with two heads, open galley sleeps six; alternate floorplan offers greatly expanded salon but no aft cabin. Twin transom doors open to extended swim platform; transom trunk stows bikes, dive equipment. Center section of cockpit sole lifts for engine access. Hardtop was a popular option. Cruise at 23-34 knots with 450hp Cummins or Cat diesels (high 20s top).

Length w/Pulpit	43'6"	Fuel	444 gals.
Hull Length	40'6"	Water	160 gals.
Beam	14'6"	Waste	57 gals.
Draft	4'0"	Hull Type	Modified-V
Weight	26,500#	Deadrise Aft	18°

See Page 569 For Resale Values

Tiara Yachts
Holland, MI
www.tiarayachts.com

Tiara 4100 Open
1996–2002

Muscular big-water express with spacious cockpit, upscale interior blurs the line between tournament-grade fishing machine, executive-class sportcruiser. Classy single-stateroom interior includes big U-shaped dinette, open galley with plenty of storage, very roomy head. Raised bridgedeck, three steps above cockpit, provides exceptional helm visibility. Large cockpit boasts beefy transom door, engineroom entry door. Wide side decks are always a plus. Cat 435hp diesels cruise at 22 knots (26-27 knots top).

Length w/Pulpit	43'6"	Fuel	524 gals.
Hull Length	41'3"	Water	130 gals.
Beam	14'8"	Waste	50 gals.
Draft	3'6"	Hull Type	Modified-V
Weight	27,500#	Deadrise Aft	18°

See Page 569 For Resale Values

Tiara Yachts
Holland, MI
www.tiarayachts.com

Cruisers & Sportboats

231-360-0827

Tiara 4200 Open
2003–Current

Plan A

Plan B

High-end cruising yacht capable of serious fishing raised the bar for express-boat versatility, luxury, quality. Plan A interior has portside lounge/dinette with galley and head opposite; Plan B adds starboard lounge with curtain or solid enclosure, creating second stateroom. Big 85-sq.ft. cockpit—with engineroom entry, foldaway rear seat—can be configured for fishing, diving, or cruising. Note fiberglass windshield frame, superb helm layout. Hardtop is optional. Cummins 670hp diesels cruise at 28 knots (32–33 knots top).

Length w/Pulpit	44'10"	Fuel	520 gals.
Hull Length	42'6"	Water	130 gals.
Beam	14'11"	Waste	50 gals.
Draft	4'2"	Hull Type	Modified-V
Weight	28,600#	Deadrise Aft	17.5°

See Page 569 For Resale Values

Tiara Yachts
Holland, MI
www.tiarayachts.com

231-360-0827

Tiara 4300 Open
1991–2002

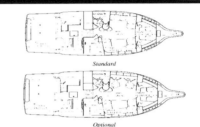

Standard

Optional

Dual-purpose express with fishboat cockpit, cruise-friendly accommodations met Tiara standards for engineering excellence, state-of-the-art construction. Standard interior with convertible L-shaped lounge, convertible dinette sleeps six; optional layout with enlarged salon sleeps four. Note hydraulic salon operated dinette, elegant teak-and-holly sole. Cockpit redesign in 1999 featured fold-down rear seat, direct access to engineroom. Cruise at 25 knots with 550hp GM 6V92s; 26-27 knots with 660hp Cats.

Length w/Pulpit	46'7"	Fuel	526 gals.
Hull Length	43'2"	Water	150 gals.
Beam	15'2"	Waste	62 gals.
Draft	4'0"	Hull Type	Modified-V
Weight	29,500#	Deadrise Aft	16°

See Page 569 For Resale Values

Tiara Yachts
Holland, MI
www.tiarayachts.com

231-360-0827

Tiara 4300 Sovran
2006–Current

Strong-selling express is the first American boat built specifically for Volvo's front-facing IPS drive system. Posh interior is big for a 40-footer—since IPS permits smaller engineroom, designers were able to include second stateroom with head. Note TV built into salon bulkhead. Abovedeck layout features raised helmdeck seating, state-of-the-art helm, wraparound cockpit settee. Major IPS benefits include improved fuel efficiency, precise handling. Volvo 370hp diesels cruise at 22–23 knots; optional 425hp Volvos cruise in the high 20s.

Length w/Pulpit	45'3"	Fuel	375 gals.
Hull Length	40'2"	Water	110 gals.
Beam	14'9"	Waste	50 gals.
Draft	3'7"	Hull Type	Modified-V
Weight	26,800#	Deadrise Aft	17°

See Page 569 For Resale Values

Tiara Yachts
Holland, MI
www.tiarayachts.com

Tiara 4400/4700 Sovran
2003–08

World-class cruiser (called 4400 Sovran in 2003–06) boasts remarkable levels of luxury, comfort, finish. Expansive twin-stateroom interior with solid teak woodwork, Corian counters, Ultraleather seating sleeps five. Note washer/dryer concealed in aft stateroom. No salon access to either head. Semi-enclosed helmdeck offers excellent weather protection. Additional features include power helm seat, hydraulic cockpit tables. Engineroom is a tight fit. Cummins 670hp diesels cruise at 26–28 knots; 715hp Cummins cruise in the low 30s.

Length w/Pulpit	50'4"	Fuel	526 gals.
Hull Length	43'8"	Water	150 gals.
Beam	14'6"	Waste	50 gals.
Draft	4 5"	Hull Type	Modified-V
Weight	33,150#	Deadrise Aft	17°

See Page 569 For Resale Values

Tiara Yachts
Holland, MI
www.tiarayachts.com

Tiara 5000 Open
2002–03

Limited-production luxury yacht appeals to cruisers who like to fish, anglers who like to cruise. Executive-level, two-stateroom interior with SubZero refrigeration—offered with teak or cherry woodwork—is unmatched for elegance, comfort, warmth. Note washer/dryer space in guest stateroom, shared shower stall for both heads.) Expansive 90-square-foot cockpit with in-floor fishbox could be fitted with bait-prep station, 32-gallon livewell. Cat 800hp diesels cruise at 26–28 knots, low 30s top.

Length w/Pulpit	53'0"	Fuel	650 gals.
Hull Length	50'1"	Water	175 gals.
Beam	15'9"	Waste	80 gals.
Draft	5'1"	Hull Type	Modified-V
Weight	41,000#	Deadrise Aft	17°

See Page 569 For Resale Values

Tiara Yachts
Holland, MI
www.tiarayachts.com

Tiara 5000/5200 Express
1999–2003

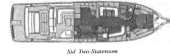
Std Two-Stateroom

Opt Three-Stateroom

Sophisticated cruiser (called 5200 Express in 2003) combines powerful styling with world-class amenities. Posh interior boasts beautifully crafted teak cabinetry, Ultraleather upholstery, top-quality furnishings. Plan A features two-stateroom layout with huge salon; Plan B has three staterooms, smaller salon. Electric cockpit tables rise for dining, lower for use as sun pad. Swim platform supports dinghy or PWC. Hardtop was optional. Note huge transom locker. Cat 800hp V-drive diesels cruise at 26–28 knots.

Length w/Pulpit	55'0"	Fuel	700 gals.
Hull Length	50'9"	Water	200 gals.
Beam	15'11"	Waste	80 gals.
Draft	5'1"	Hull Type	Modified-V
Weight	38,600#	Deadrise Aft	17°

See Page 569 For Resale Values

Tiara Yachts
Holland, MI
www.tiarayachts.com

Cruisers & Sportboats

www.powerboatguide.com | 231-360-0827

Tiara 5200 Sovran Salon
2003–06

Plan A

Plan A

Distinctly American sportcruiser with enclosed command bridge/helm is stylish, luxurious, expensive. Posh interior blends solid teak cabinetry, premium furnishings, Ultraleather upholstery. Standard two-stateroom layout boasts huge salon, aft galley; optional three-stateroom floorplan has galley forward in salon. Highlights include electric cockpit table, cockpit engineroom access, salon wet bar, power sunroof in hardtop. Exemplary finish. Swim platform is designed to carry PWC. Cat 865hp diesels cruise at 26–28 knots (30+ top).

Length w/Pulpit	58'3"	Fuel	700 gals.
Hull Length	50'9"	Water	200 gals.
Beam	15'11"	Waste	80 gals.
Draft	5'1"	Hull Type	Modified-V
Weight	49,000#	Deadrise Aft	17°

See Page 569 For Resale Values

Tiara Yachts
Holland, MI
www.tiarayachts.com

---

www.powerboatguide.com | 231-360-0827

Tollycraft 30 Sedan
1977–84

Beamy 30-foot sedan introduced in late '70s packs lots of living space in a relatively small hull. Wide-open salon with teak trim, full galley, standard lower helm boasts convertible dinette, convertible settee. Note handy pass-through window from galley to dinette. Extra-large cabin windows provide excellent natural lighting, good lower-helm visibility. Flybridge is very large, but cockpit is small. Transom door, swim platform were standard. Twin 270hp Crusader gas engines cruise at 22–23 knots and reach about 28 knots top.

Length	29'11"	Fuel	200 gals.
Beam	11'9"	Water	58 gals.
Draft	2'6"	Waste	20 gals.
Weight	13,500#	Hull Type	Modified-V
Clearance	11'8"	Deadrise Aft	10°

Prices Not Provided for Pre-1995 Models

Tollycraft is no longer in business.

---

www.powerboatguide.com | 231-360-0827

Tollycraft 30 Sport Cruiser
1985–92

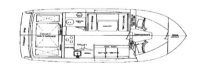

Well-built family cruiser with pleasing lines gets high marks for space, comfort, stability. Wide 11'6" beam allows for extremely roomy cabin with private V-berth, enclosed head/shower, convertible dinette, complete galley. Large cockpit with integral swim platform doubles as entertainment center or fishing platform. Flybridge—big for a 30-footer—seats six adults. Note fuel increase to 198 gallons in 1988. Transom door, radar arch, bow pulpit were standard. Twin 260hp gas engines cruise at 20 knots (around 28 knots top).

Length	30'6"	Water	42 gals.
Beam	11'6"	Fuel	150/198 gals.
Draft	2'7"	Cockpit	45 sq. ft.
Weight	11,500#	Hull Type	Modified-V
Clearance	11'8"	Deadrise Aft	10°

Prices Not Provided for Pre-1995 Models

Tollycraft is no longer in business.

231-360-0827

Tollycraft 34 Sport Sedan
1987–93

Feature-packed sedan hits the right buttons with Tollycraft enthusiasts focued on handsome styling, versatile accommodations. Well-appointed interior with solid teak cabinetry boasts two private staterooms—no small achievement in a 34-foot boat. Transom door, in-deck fishbox were standard in small cockpit. Flybridge was offered with helm aft for East Coast buyers, helm forward for Pacific market. Wide side decks are a plus. Note fuel increase beginning with 1988 models. Twin 340hp gas engines cruise at 20 knots (high 20s top).

Length	34'0"	Cockpit	72 sq. ft.
Beam	12'6"	Fuel	200/296 gals.
Draft	2'10"	Water	116 gals.
Weight	17,000#	Hull Type	Modified-V
Clearance	13'11"	Deadrise Aft	13°

Prices Not Provided for Pre-1995 Models

Tollycraft is no longer in business.

---

www.powerboatguide.com 231-360-0827

Tollycraft 40 Sport Sedan
1987–95

1987–88

1989–1995

Appealing sports convertible for fishing, cruising combines large cockpit with family-friendly accommodations. Two-stateroom interior—completely updated in 1989—is notable for upscale appointments, large windows, generous storage. Lower helm was optional. Cockpit amenities include two in-deck fishboxes, centerline transom door. Big fuel capacity delivers excellent range. Flybridge was offered with helm forward or aft. Cat 375hp diesels cruise at 22 knots (25 knots top); 485hp GMs cruise in the mid 20s (30 knots wide open).

Length	40'2"	Fuel	500 gals.
Beam	14'8"	Water	140 gals.
Draft	3'0"	Cockpit	100 sq. ft.
Weight	26,000#	Hull Type	Modified-V
Clearance	12'4"	Deadrise Aft	10°

See Page 569 For Resale Values

Tollycraft is no longer in business.

---

www.powerboatguide.com 231-360-0827

Trojan 8.6 Meter Mid-Cabin
1987–90

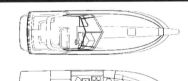

Generic midcabin express from 1980s offered space, comfort at an affordable price. Eurostyle interior features private bow stateroom, complete galley, large U-shaped dinette, compact double berth aft. Single-level cockpit has triple-wide elevated helm seat, removable bench seating at the transom, centerline transom gate. Helm was updated in 1989. Note narrow side decks, sturdy bow rails. Standard 260hp gas sterndrives cruise at 25 knots and reach a top speed in the mid 30s.

Length	28'8"	Water	40 gals.
Beam	10'6"	Fuel	140 gals.
Draft	2'2"	Cockpit	NA
Weight	9,500#	Hull Type	Modified-V
Clearance	8'7"	Deadrise Aft	14°

Prices Not Provided for Pre-1995 Models

Trojan Yachts is no longer in business.

Cruisers & Sportboats

231-360-0827

Trojan 32 Sedan
1973–91

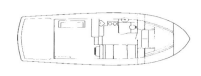

Classic flybridge sedan with large cockpit, semi-enclosed lower helm remains the most popular boat of her type ever produced. Offered with or without a flybridge, the appeal of this boat rested with her roomy accommodations, handsome lines, affordable price. Well-planned interior with convertible dinette, stand-up head, full galley sleeps four. Early models had teak decks; once-optional 220-gallon fuel capacity became standard in 1984. Cruise at 18 knots with 250hp Chrysler gas engines; 20 knots with 270hp Crusaders.

Length	32'0"	Water	40 gals.
Beam	13'0"	Fuel	120/220 gals.
Draft	2'6"	Cockpit	60 sq. ft.
Weight	12,000#	Hull Type	Modified-V
Clearance	12'6"	Deadrise Aft	8°

Prices Not Provided for Pre-1995 Models

Trojan Yachts is no longer in business.

231-360-0827

Trojan 10 Meter Express
1981–89

Bold 1980s express with mega-wide beam, Eurostyle interior was considered a breakthrough design for Trojan. Huge cockpit offers plenty of room for fishing, diving, entertaining. Wide-open interior with curved bulkheads features electrically operated doors to master stateroom and head, convertible dinette, convertible settee. Note curved companionway steps, excellent engine access, plentiful stowage. Standard 350hp gas engines cruise at 19–20 knots with a top speed in the high 20s. Over 600 were built.

Length	33'0"	Water	40 gals.
Beam	13'0"	Fuel	242 gals.
Draft	2'0"	Headroom	6'4"
Weight	11,250#	Hull Type	Modified-V
Clearance	9'4"	Deadrise Aft	9°

Prices Not Provided for Pre-1995 Models

Trojan Yachts is no longer in business.

231-360-0827

Trojan 10 Meter Mid-Cabin
1986–92

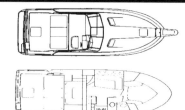

Roomy express with wide 13-foot beam offers cockpit, cabin dimensions of much larger boat. Expansive interior with private bow stateroom, home-sized galley, head with stall shower sleeps six. Big cockpit with double-wide helm seats provides plenty of entertaining, fishing space. Additional features include radar arch, bow pulpit, good engine access. Updates in 1989 included bolt-on swim platform, powder-coated deck rails. Cruise at 17–18 knots with standard 350hp gas engines (mid 20s wide open).

Length	33'0"	Water	55 gals.
Beam	13'0"	Fuel	250 gals.
Draft	2'0"	Waste	40 gals.
Weight	12,500#	Hull Type	Modified-V
Clearance	9'4"	Deadrise Aft	9°

Prices Not Provided for Pre-1995 Models

Trojan Yachts is no longer in business.

231-360-0827

Trojan 10 Meter Sedan
1982–89

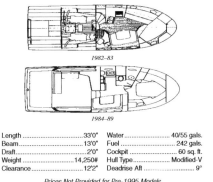

1982–83

1984–89

Rakish sedan cruiser from 1980s packs surprising living space into modest 33-foot length. Original Eurostyle interior with curved bulkheads was poorly received—an offset companionway (rare in any convertible) isolated the salon from lower-level dinette and galley. Revised layout in 1984 proved much more popular. Note that lower helm was standard in pre-1987 models. Flybridge is small for a boat this size. No cockpit transom door. Standard 350hp gas engines cruise at 18 knots (mid 20s top).

Length	33'0"	Water	40/55 gals.
Beam	13'0"	Fuel	242 gals.
Draft	2'0"	Cockpit	60 sq. ft.
Weight	14,250#	Hull Type	Modified-V
Clearance	12'2"	Deadrise Aft	9°

Prices Not Provided for Pre-1995 Models

Trojan Yachts is no longer in business.

231-360-0827

Trojan 10.8 Meter Express
1991–92

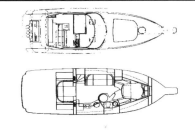

Sporty express cruiser was introduced by Trojan just before the company declared bankruptcy in 1992. Spacious midcabin interior with private bow stateroom boasts full galley, convertible dinette, head with separate stall shower. Entire deck aft of helm can be raised at the push of a button for engine access. Note twin transom gates, foredeck sun pad, sport-style dash design. Deep-V hull delivers impressive big-water ride. Twin 355hp V-drive gas engines cruise at 18 knots and reach 26–28 knots wide open.

Length w/Pulpit	39'4"	Fuel	280 gals.
Hull Length	35.5"	Water	70 gals.
Beam	13'2"	Waste	40 gals.
Draft	3'7"	Hull Type	Deep-V
Weight	19,572#	Deadrise Aft	20°

Prices Not Provided for Pre-1995 Models

Trojan Yachts is no longer in business.

231-360-0827

Trojan 10.8 Meter Sedan
1986–92

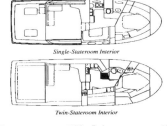

Single-Stateroom Interior

Twin-Stateroom Interior

Stretched version of Trojan's earlier 10 Meter Sedan (1982–89) boasts larger cockpit, increased fuel capacity. Standard single-stateroom interior with expansive salon was updated in 1989 to include a stall shower in the head—a modification that took some elbow space out of the bow stateroom. Two-stateroom floorplan also became available in 1989. Note compact engineroom, narrow side decks. No transom door. Standard 350hp gas engines cruise at 17–18 knots and reach a top speed in the mid 20s.

Length	35'4"	Fuel	325 gals.
Beam	13'0"	Water	55 gals.
Draft	2'4"	Cockpit	87 sq. ft.
Weight	15,000#	Hull Type	Modified-V
Clearance	12'2"	Deadrise Aft	9°

Prices Not Provided for Pre-1995 Models

Trojan Yachts is no longer in business.

Trojan 350/360 Express
1995–2002

350 Interior

360 Layout

Inboard power distinguishes this otherwise-generic express from her sterndrive competitors. Conventional midcabin interior is arranged with double berths fore and aft, convertible dinette, roomy head with sink and shower. Sliding door (instead of a curtain) provides forward stateroom privacy. Bridgedeck has triple-wide helm seat, wet bar, wraparound lounge seating. Bow pulpit, radar arch, swim platform were standard. Twin 320hp V-drive gas inboards cruise at 15–16 knots (mid 20s top). Marketed as the Trojan 350 Express in 1995–98.

Length w/Pulpit	37'8"	Fuel	220 gals.
Beam	12'0"	Water	60 gals.
Draft	2'10"	Waste	30 gals.
Weight	16,500#	Hull Type	Modified-V
Clearance	9'8"	Deadrise Aft	16.5°

See Page 570 For Resale Values

Trojan Yachts is no longer in business.

Trojan 36 Convertible
1972–89

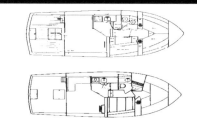

Well-priced, well-styled convertible introduced in 1972 turned out to be one of the most popular production boats ever designed. Several single- and twin-stateroom floorplans were available during her long production run, all with standard lower helm. Teak cockpit sole was standard through 1976—a potential source of problems. Uncluttered cockpit lacks transom door, fishbox, or livewell. Note wide side decks. Among many engine choices, twin 350hp gas engines cruise at 18 knots (24–25 knots top).

Length	36'0"	Water	80 gals.
Beam	13'0"	Fuel	250/350 gals.
Draft	2'11"	Cockpit	75 sq. ft.
Weight	16,000#	Hull Type	Modified-V
Clearance	13'0"	Deadrise Aft	9°

Prices Not Provided for Pre-1995 Models

Trojan Yachts is no longer in business.

Trojan 11 Meter Express
1983–89

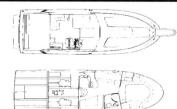

Bold 1980s express is notable for her mega-wide beam, aggressive hull graphics. So-called Eurostyle interior—completely dated by modern sportboat standards—is a blend of curved bulkheads, indirect lighting, off-white laminates. Note owner's stateroom vanity, privacy door. L-shaped galley extends well into the salon, which interrupts traffic flow. Bow pulpit, radar arch, swim platform were standard. Twin 350hp gas engines cruise at 18 knots (26–27 knots top); 375hp Cat diesels cruise at 24 knots (about 27 knots top).

Length	37'6"	Fuel	350 gals.
Beam	14'0"	Water	100 gals.
Draft	3'3"	Headroom	6'3"
Weight	16,800#	Hull Type	Modified-V
Clearance	9'4"	Deadrise Aft	14°

Prices Not Provided for Pre-1995 Models

Trojan Yachts is no longer in business.

Trojan 11 Meter Express
1990–92

Updated version of original Trojan 11 Meter Express (1983–89) received good reviews in early 1990s for appealing Med styling, luxury-class accommodations. Unusual cabin layout has portside stateroom with double berth, forward dinette area, huge head compartment. Cockpit is arranged with L-shaped lounge seating forward, wet bar, bench seating aft. Radar arch, bow pulpit, transom door were standard. Note wide side decks. Twin 360hp gas engines cruise at 18 knots; optional 425hp Cat diesels cruise at 24–25 knots.

Length w/Pulpit	39'0"	Fuel	350 gals.
Beam	14'0"	Water	100 gals.
Draft	3'3"	Headroom	6'4"
Weight	16,800#	Hull Type	Modified-V
Clearance	9'4"	Deadrise Aft	14°

Prices Not Provided for Pre-1995 Models

Trojan Yachts is no longer in business.

Trojan 11 Meter Sedan
1985–88

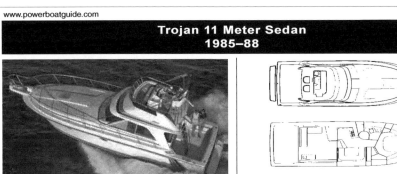

Rakish 1980s sedan with wide 14-foot beam combined bold styling with maxi-volume accommodations. Spacious interior with wide-open salon features large dinette, head with circular stall shower, U-shaped galley with generous stowage. Cockpit design is compromised by intrusive bridge ladder. Roomy flybridge has guest seating forward of helm. Note wide side decks, glass salon bulkhead, salon wet bar. Standard 350hp gas engines cruise at 18 knots (high 20s top); 375hp Cat diesels cruise at 22 knots (26–27 top).

Length	37'6"	Water	100 gals.
Beam	14'0"	Fuel	350 gals.
Draft	3'5"	Headroom	6'5"
Weight	18,000#	Hull Type	Modified-V
Clearance	12'6"	Deadrise Aft	14°

Prices Not Provided for Pre-1995 Models

Trojan Yachts is no longer in business.

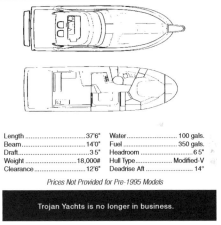

Trojan 370/390/400 Express
1993–2002

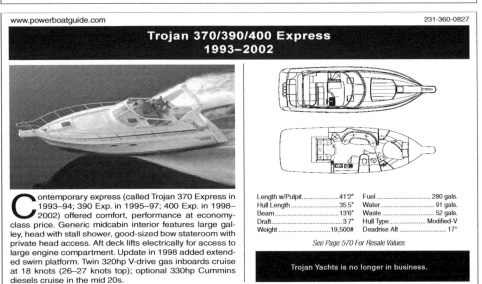

Contemporary express (called Trojan 370 Express in 1993–94; 390 Exp. in 1995–97; 400 Exp. in 1998–2002) offered comfort, performance at economy-class price. Generic midcabin interior features large galley, head with stall shower, good-sized bow stateroom with private head access. Aft deck lifts electrically for access to large engine compartment. Update in 1998 added extended swim platform. Twin 320hp V-drive gas inboards cruise at 18 knots (26–27 knots top); optional 330hp Cummins diesels cruise in the mid 20s.

Length w/Pulpit	41'2"	Fuel	280 gals.
Hull Length	35'5"	Water	91 gals.
Beam	13'6"	Waste	52 gals.
Draft	3'7"	Hull Type	Modified-V
Weight	19,500#	Deadrise Aft	17°

See Page 570 For Resale Values

Trojan Yachts is no longer in business.

Cruisers & Sportboats

Cruisers & Sportboats

www.powerboatguide.com   231-360-0827

Trojan 12 Meter Convertible
1986–92

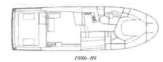

1986–89

1990–92

Rakish 1990s convertible combined posh accommodations with bold hull graphics, unusually wide beam. Expansive two-stateroom, galley-down layout features spacious salon with breakfast bar, home-sized galley, island berth in forward stateroom. Large 110-sq.-ft. cockpit has two in-deck fishboxes, dual washdowns, wide transom door, tackle center. Note wraparound salon windows. Flybridge is small for a 40-footer. Cat 375hp diesels cruise at 22 knots (mid 20s top); 485hp Detroits cruise at 25 knots (about 30 knots top).

Length	39'9"	Water	100 gals.
Beam	14'3"	Fuel	400 gals.
Draft	3'6"	Cockpit	110 sq. ft.
Weight	19,000#	Hull Type	Modified-V
Clearance	12'6"	Deadrise Aft	12°

Prices Not Provided for Pre-1995 Models

Trojan Yachts is no longer in business.

---

www.powerboatguide.com   231-360-0827

Trojan 12 Meter Express
1989–92

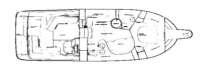

Handsome 40-foot express introduced in 1989 raised the bar in her day for bold styling, unusually spacious accommodations. Highlights include huge cockpit with fore and aft seating, full wraparound windshield, high-style helm, molded boarding steps, wide-open interior with berths for six. Hidden privacy curtain converts portside settee into a unique stateroom with over/under berths. Note wide side decks, in-deck storage well for inflatable. Optional 485hp GM diesels cruise at 26–27 knots (about 30 knots top).

Length	39'9"	Water	95 gals.
Beam	14'3"	Fuel	325 gals.
Draft	3'8"	Headroom	6'4"
Weight	18,000#	Hull Type	Modified-V
Clearance	NA	Deadrise Aft	12°

Prices Not Provided for Pre-1995 Models

Trojan Yachts is no longer in business.

---

www.powerboatguide.com   231-360-0827

Trojan 13 Meter Express
1984–90

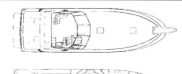

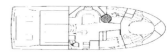

Compelling 1980s express attracted attention for her super-spacious interior, bold styling. Wide 16'3" beam blows away the competition; colorful hull graphics of early models was very distinctive. Wide-open interior features two private staterooms, huge U-shaped dinette, king-sized galley. Note push-button bow stateroom door, circular stall shower, power high/low dinette table, power windshield vent. Lack of cockpit transom door is truly puzzling. Detroit 735hp diesels cruise at a fast 30 knots (32+ knots top).

Length	43'0"	Fuel	510 gals.
Beam	16'3"	Water	175 gals.
Draft	3'2"	Waste	75 gals.
Weight	24,000#	Hull Type	Modified-V
Clearance	10'1"	Deadrise Aft	12°

Prices Not Provided for Pre-1995 Models

Trojan Yachts is no longer in business.

www.powerboatguide.com   231-360-0827

Trojan 440 Express
1995–2002

1995–97

1998–2002

Head-turning express yacht with rakish lines, luxury interior offered late 1990s buyers impressive mix of sportboat styling, competitive price. Well-finished two-stateroom interior (updated in 1998 with third stateroom) includes wraparound salon seating, home-size galley. Aft cockpit seating converts into huge sun pad. Choice of hydraulic high/low swim platform (for PWC) or standard extended platform. Good engine access. Cummins 450hp V-drive diesels cruise at 22 knots (25-26 knots top).

Length	44'7"	Fuel	432 gals.
Beam	15'0"	Water	104 gals.
Draft	4'0"	Waste	88 gals.
Weight	30,000#	Hull Type	Modified-V
Clearance	10'11"	Deadrise Aft	16.5°

Insufficient Sales Data to Predict Value

Trojan Yachts is no longer in business.

---

www.powerboatguide.com   231-360-0827

Viking Sport Cruisers V50 Express
1999–2005

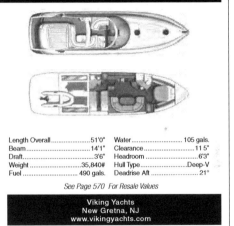

Finely crafted Eurocruiser with classic Med styling splits the difference between hard-charging sportboat, luxurious coastal cruiser. Elegant cherrywood interior features two private cabins with en suite heads, concealed galley, leather U-shaped salon sofa. Large cockpit with wet bar, contoured seating accommodates several guests. Good helm ergonomics. Transom garage is concealed under aft sun pad. Note teak cockpit sole, good engineroom access. Cruise at 28 knots (32–33 knots wide open) with Volvo 610hp inboards.

Length Overall	51'0"	Water	105 gals.
Beam	14'1"	Clearance	11'5"
Draft	3'6"	Headroom	6'3"
Weight	35,840#	Hull Type	Deep-V
Fuel	490 gals.	Deadrise Aft	21°

See Page 570 For Resale Values

Viking Yachts
New Gretna, NJ
www.vikingyachts.com

---

www.powerboatguide.com   231-360-0827

Viking Sport Cruisers V58 Express
2003–Current

High-impact Eurocruiser with folding sunroof, tender garage makes good on Viking promise of unrivaled luxury, unsurpassed performance. Teak-planked cockpit boasts U-shaped seating and dining area, wet bar with refrigerator, electric grill. Double helm seat converts to leaning post for stand-up driving. Opulent interior sleeps six in three staterooms. Note sub-floor galley storage. Additional features include spacious engineroom, hidden galley appliances, parquet salon floor. MAN 860hp engines cruise at 30 knots (34–35 knots top).

Length	58'11"	Fuel	660 gals.
Beam	15'5"	Water	125 gals.
Draft	3'6"	Waste	54 gals.
Weight	44,800#	Hull Type	Deep-V
Clearance	16'6"	Deadrise Aft	19°

See Page 571 For Resale Values

Viking Yachts
New Gretna, NJ
www.vikingyachts.com

Cruisers & Sportboats

www.powerboatguide.com   231-360-0827

Viking Sport Cruisers V65 Express
2000–04

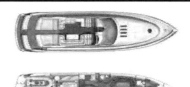

High-performance sportcruiser with aggressive styling, retractable sunroof is easy to praise, hard to fault. Standard hardtop offers security of a protected helm and—with sunroof retracted—the enjoyment of an open express. Principal features include luxurious cherrywood interior, twin transom garages (one for small tender, one for PWC), superb helm layout, large galley with serving counter and concealed appliances. Note compact engineroom, wide side decks, teak-laid cockpit. MAN 1,300hp engines top out at a fast 36–38 knots.

Length Overall	65'2"	Fuel	960 gals.
Beam	16'11"	Water	180 gals.
Draft	4 5"	Headroom	6'6"
Weight	64,752#	Hull Type	Deep-V
Clearance	14'3"	Deadrise Aft	21°

See Page 571 For Resale Values

Viking Yachts
New Gretna, NJ
www.vikingyachts.com

---

www.powerboatguide.com   231-360-0827

Wellcraft 2700 Martinique
1994–95

Generic 27-foot family express from 1990s offered rakish styling, impressive space at affordable price. Highlights include expansive cockpit with seating for six, walk-through windshield, spacious mid-cabin interior with convertible dinette, complete galley, enclosed head with shower. Note excellent cabin headroom, generous storage. Space at helm for extra electronics. Bow pulpit, transom shower were standard. Not the prettiest boat on the water. Single 300hp Volvo I/O will cruise at 22 knots (mid 30s top).

Length w/Pulpit	28'4"	Fuel	100 gals.
Hull Length	26'6"	Water	22 gals.
Beam	9'6"	Waste	15 gals.
Draft	3'0"	Hull Type	Modified-V
Weight	6,950#	Deadrise Aft	17°

See Page 571 For Resale Values

Wellcraft Boats
Sarasota, FL
www.wellcraft.com

---

www.powerboatguide.com   231-360-0827

Wellcraft 2800 Martinique
1997–99

Restyled version of earlier Wellcraft 2700 Martinique (1994–95) offered express-boat space, comfort at affordable price. Highlights include roomy cockpit with seating for six, walk-through windshield, comfortable midcabin interior with convertible dinette, full-service galley, enclosed head with shower. Note generous cabin headroom, space at helm for extra electronics. Radar arch, transom shower were standard. Single 310hp sterndrive will cruise at 22 knots (low 30s top); twin 190hp I/Os cruise at 25 knots (40 knots top).

Length w/Pulpit	28'4"	Fuel	100 gals.
Hull Length	26'6"	Water	22 gals.
Beam	9'6"	Waste	15 gals.
Draft	3'0"	Hull Type	Modified-V
Weight	7,100#	Deadrise Aft	17°

See Page 571 For Resale Values

Wellcraft Boats
Sarasota, FL
www.wellcraft.com

Wellcraft 2800 Martinique
2001–02

Generic sterndrive express with roomy midcabin interior combined durable construction with entry-level price. Cockpit amenities include double-wide helm seat with flip-up bolster, aft U-shaped lounge seating, power engine compartment hatch. Well-designed galley makes good use of limited space. Tilt wheel was standard; walk-through windshield provides easy bow access. Open-plan interior sleeps four adults, two kids. Twin 190hp MerCruiser I/Os cruise in the low 20s (35–36 knots top). Note that production lasted only two years.

Length	27'10"	Clearance w/Arch	8'6"
Beam	9'6"	Fuel	100 gals.
Draft, Up	2'0"	Water	28 gals.
Draft, Down	3'6"	Hull Type	Modified-V
Weight	6,600#	Deadrise Aft	20°

See Page 571 For Resale Values

Wellcraft Boats
Sarasota, FL
www.wellcraft.com

Wellcraft 2800 Monte Carlo
1986–89

Entry-level 1980s sportboat lived up to Wellcraft promise of comfort, performance at affordable price. Roomy single-level cockpit with fold-down jump seat, removable transom seat is great for fishing, swimming, diving. Visibility from raised helm is very good. Open-plan interior with convertible dinette, complete galley, sleeps six. Note tall windshield, good engine access, standard bow pulpit. Beamy modified-V hull delivers stable, dry ride. Twin 260hp MerCruiser sterndrives cruise at 25 knots (35+ knots top).

Length	27'7"	Clearance	NA
Beam	9'11"	Fuel	115 gals.
Draft, Up	1'9"	Water	28 gals.
Draft, Down	2'9"	Hull Type	Modified-V
Weight	7,200#	Deadrise Aft	16°

Prices Not Provided for Pre-1995 Models

Wellcraft Boats
Sarasota, FL
www.wellcraft.com

Wellcraft 2900 Express
1981–87

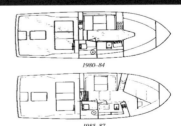

1980–84

1985–87

Traditional family cruiser (called Wellcraft 288 Suncruiser in 1981–82) gets high marks for spacious cockpit, dependable inboard power. Broad 10'8" beam makes this one of the roomiest boats in her class. Single-level cockpit with fold-out seats is great for fishing, diving, swimming. Simple interior—obviously dated by modern decor standards—offers the amenities required for comfortable cruising. Wide side decks are a plus. Note small fuel capacity. Twin 230hp MerCruiser gas engines cruise at 19–20 knots (high 20s top).

Length	28'8"	Fuel	120 gals.
Beam	10'8"	Water	28 gals.
Draft	2'6"	Cockpit	NA
Weight	9,000#	Hull Type	Modified-V
Clearance	7'4"	Deadrise Aft	16°

Prices Not Provided for Pre-1995 Models

Wellcraft Boats
Sarasota, FL
www.wellcraft.com

Cruisers & Sportboats

Cruisers & Sportboats

231-360-0827

Wellcraft 3000 Martinique
1998–2002

Stylish family cruiser delivered comfort, performance at an entry-level price. Wide 10'6" beam results in plenty of cockpit, cabin space. Roomy interior provides large salon, open midcabin area, roomy head with shower. Galley storage is increased by locating refrigerator under forward dinette seat. Well-planned cockpit with wraparound lounge, portside lounger seats eight. Note power engine compartment hatch, walk-through windshield. Twin 260hp MerCruiser I/Os cruise at 25 knots (about 40 knots top).

Length w/Pulpit	32'4"	Clearance	8 7"
Beam	10'6"	Fuel	160 gals.
Draft, Drives Up	2'3"	Water	41 gals.
Draft, Drives Down	3'1"	Hull Type	Modified-V
Weight	11,000#	Deadrise Aft	16°

See Page 572 For Resale Values

Wellcraft Boats
Sarasota, FL
www.wellcraft.com

231-360-0827

Wellcraft 3100 Express
1979–85

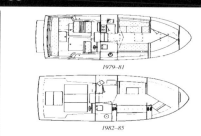

1979–81

1982–85

Entry-level sportcruiser dating back to early 1980s appealed to buyers looking for space, comfort, affordability. Highlights include smooth-riding deep-V hull, big single-level cockpit, ergonomic helm position. Space-efficient cabin layout—slightly updated in 1982—sleeps six. Removable hatches in cockpit sole access engines and V-drives. Radar arch was popular option. Dated design lacks walk-through windshield, transom door. Twin 260hp inboard gas engines cruise at 18–19 knots and reach a top speed of 26–28 knots.

Length	31'3"	Fuel	160 gals.
Beam	11'6"	Water	28 gals.
Draft	2'11"	Headroom	6'4"
Weight	10,200#	Hull Type	Deep-V
Clearance	8'1"	Deadrise Aft	19°

Prices Not Provided for Pre-1995 Models

Wellcraft Boats
Sarasota, FL
www.wellcraft.com

231-360-0827

Wellcraft 3200 Martinique
1994–2000

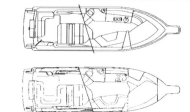

Maxi-volume express with traditional midcabin layout appealed to savvy buyers with an eye for value. Tasteful interior with U-shaped dinette boasts surprisingly large galley, spacious midcabin area, generous storage. Several cockpit seating schemes were offered over the years. Ergonomic helm layout has room for extra electronics. Note that oval hull ports replaced sliding cabin windows in 1997. Twin Volvo 310hp I/Os cruise at 25 knots (high 30s top). Inboard models with 320hp MerCruisers cruise at 22–23 knots (low 30s top).

Length w/Pulpit	34 5"	Fuel	162 gals.
Hull Length	32'0"	Water	43 gals.
Beam	11'2"	Waste	20 gals.
Draft	3'1"	Hull Type	Modified-V
Weight	10,300#	Deadrise Aft	16°

See Page 572 For Resale Values

Wellcraft Boats
Sarasota, FL
www.wellcraft.com

231-360-0827

Wellcraft 3200 St. Tropez
1985–93

Hugely popular inboard express ranks among Wellcraft's best-selling express boats ever produced. Eurostyle decor with mauve-colored fabrics, brushed aluminum accents differed from traditional teak-trimmed interiors of her era. Several updates over the years—the most significant modification came in 1988 with addition of integral swim platform. Single level cockpit is well-suited for fishing, entertaining. Engineroom is a tight fit. Standard 260hp V-drive gas engines cruise at 20 knots (high 20s top). Over 1,700 were built.

Length	31'8"	Fuel	180 gals.
Beam	11'8"	Water	40 gals.
Draft	2'10"	Waste	20 gals.
Weight	10,300#	Hull Type	Modified-V
Clearance	8'5"	Deadrise Aft	16°

Prices Not Provided for Pre-1995 Models

Wellcraft Boats
Sarasota, FL
www.wellcraft.com

231-360-0827

Wellcraft 3300 Martinique
2001–02

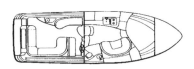

Stylish inboard cruiser with roomy accommodations, many standard features delivered the goods without breaking the bank. Generic midcabin interior with open-plan layout sleeps six. Well-planned cockpit features portside lounge forward, double helm seat, wraparound seating aft. Power hatch provides access to very well-organized engine compartment. Note walk-through windshield. Among several engine options, twin 310hp MerCruiser V-drive inboards cruise at 20 knots and reach a top speed of close to 30 knots.

Length	33'2"	Fuel	226 gals.
Beam	11'7"	Water	40 gals.
Draft	2'11"	Waste	35 gals.
Weight	11,000#	Hull Type	Deep-V
Clearance, Arch	9'0"	Deadrise Aft	22°

See Page 572 For Resale Values

Wellcraft Boats
Sarasota, FL
www.wellcraft.com

231-360-0827

Wellcraft 34 Triumph Express
1991–93

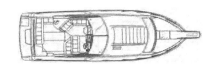

Roomy midcabin express from the early 90s offered family-size accommodations at a budget-friendly price. Elevated helm deck permits expansive, single-level interior with private owner's stateroom, double-entry head, salon/galley area with convertible dinette. Midcabin berth is a tight fit for two adults. Note large cabin windows, storage boxes under cabin sole. Bi-level cockpit boasts sun lounge, aft wet bar, L-shaped rear seat. Three cockpit hatches provide good engine access. Cruise at 18–20 knots (high 20s top) with 330hp gas inboards.

Length w/Pulpit	36'9"	Clearance	9'2"
Hull Length	34'0"	Fuel	226 gals.
Beam	12'6"	Water	46 gals.
Draft	3'0"	Hull Type	Modified-V
Weight	15,000#	Deadrise Aft	14°

Prices Not Provided for Pre-1995 Models

Wellcraft Boats
Sarasota, FL
www.wellcraft.com

Cruisers & Sportboats

Wellcraft 34 Triumph Sedan
1990–93

Maxi-volume 34-footer made good on Wellcraft promise of space, comfort, value. Single-level interior features wide-open salon with facing settees (both of which convert to double berths), huge head with separate stall shower, full-size galley, private forward stateroom. Pass-through from galley to flybridge is a nice touch. Note narrow side decks, roomy bridge, molded foredeck seating. No racehorse, Crusader 300hp V-drive gas engines cruise at a sedate 15–16 knots (about 25 knots top).

Length w/Pulpit	36'9"	Clearance	9'9"
Hull Length	34'0"	Fuel	256 gals.
Beam	12'6"	Water	60 gals.
Draft	3'0"	Hull Type	Modified-V
Weight	15,700#	Deadrise Aft	14°

Prices Not Provided for Pre-1995 Models

Wellcraft Boats
Sarasota, FL
www.wellcraft.com

Wellcraft 3400 Gran Sport
1984–92

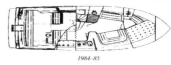

1984–85

1986–92

Beamy 1980s express with inboard power lived up to Wellcraft reputation for sporty styling, solid construction. Bulkhead-free interior allows for expansive salon with full-service galley, two-sleeper aft cabin, island double berth forward. Large single-level cockpit with wet bar can seat a small crowd without bumping elbows. Updates included new bolt-on reverse swim platform in 1988, white-on-white dash in 1990. So-so fit and finish. Standard 340hp gas engines cruise at 18 knots and reach a top speed of 26–28 knots.

Length w/Pulpit	35'5"	Clearance	9'4"
Length	33'7"	Fuel	270 gals.
Beam	12'6"	Water	75 gals.
Draft	3'0"	Hull Type	Modified-V
Weight	13,400#	Deadrise Aft	16°

Prices Not Provided for Pre-1995 Models

Wellcraft Boats
Sarasota, FL
www.wellcraft.com

Wellcraft 3500 Corsair; 3600 St. Tropez
1992–93

Contemporary 1990s cruiser with big cockpit, airy interior delivered space, comfort at a reasonable price. Considered a rakish boat by standards of her day with integrated swim platform, tall arch, sporty wraparound windshield. Cabin highlights include private forward stateroom, large head with separate stall shower, well-equipped galley, berths for six. Walk-through windshield provides easy bow access. Twin 400hp MerCruiser gas inboards (with V-drives) cruise at 18 knots (28–29 knots top). Note brief two-year production run.

Length w/Pulpit	38'7"	Fuel	270 gals.
Hull Length	33'10"	Water	76 gals.
Beam	12'6"	Clearance, Arch	9'9"
Draft	2'9"	Hull Type	Modified-V
Weight	14,400#	Deadrise Aft	16°

Prices Not Provided for Pre-1995 Models

Wellcraft Boats
Sarasota, FL
www.wellcraft.com

231-360-0827

Wellcraft 3600 Martinique
1994–2000

Popular 1990s sportcruiser delivered the space, amenities of more expensive competitors at a surprisingly affordable price. Conventional midcabin interior offers expansive salon with U-shaped dinette, well-equipped galley, separate stall shower in head. Several cockpit plans were offered over the years, all with wet bar, walk-through windshield. Additional features include radar arch, bow pulpit, well-arranged engineroom. Prop pockets reduce draft, improve hull efficiency. MerCruiser 310hp V-drive inboards cruise at 18 knots (high 20s top).

Length w/Pulpit	38'0"	Clearance, Arch	9'10"
Hull Length	35'6"	Fuel	264 gals.
Beam	12'6"	Water	47 gals.
Draft	3'0"	Hull Type	Modified-V
Weight	15,000#	Deadrise Aft	16°

See Page 572 For Resale Values

Wellcraft Boats
Sarasota, FL
www.wellcraft.com

231-360-0827

Wellcraft 3700 Corsica
1989–91

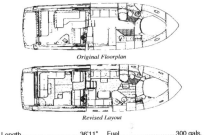

Original Floorplan

Revised Layout

Durable family express introduced in 1989 matched contemporary styling with tasteful accommodations. Original midcabin interior with diminutive dinette—judged too confining—was replaced by all-new floorplan with combined breakfast bar/galley counter after hull #15. Bi-fold privacy door for owner's stateroom (instead of just a curtain) is a plus. Expansive single-level cockpit came with double-wide helm seat, wet bar, L-shaped lounge. So-so fit and finish. MerCruiser 380hp gas inboards cruise at 20 knots (28–29 knots top).

Length	36'11"	Fuel	300 gals.
Beam	13'6"	Water	100 gals.
Draft	3'1"	Headroom	6'3"
Weight	16,800#	Hull Type	Modified-V
Clearance	9'9"	Deadrise Aft	16°

Prices Not Provided for Pre-1995 Models

Wellcraft Boats
Sarasota, FL
www.wellcraft.com

231-360-0827

Wellcraft 3700 Martinique
2001–02

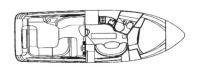

Sporty family cruiser with appealing profile, generous beam gets high marks for space, comfort. Big open-plan interior with cherry trim is arranged with double berths fore and aft, convertible dinette, private bow stateroom. Galley is on small side but storage is excellent. Inviting cockpit with double-wide helm seat, wet bar, portside lounger, seats eight. Note walk-through windshield, power engine-compartment hatch, transom shower. Twin 380hp MerCruiser V-drive gas engines cruise at 20 knots (about 30 knots top).

Length	36'11"	Fuel	288 gals.
Beam	13'0"	Water	57 gals.
Draft	3'4"	Waste	35 gals.
Weight	16,400#	Hull Type	Deep-V
Clearance	9'5"	Deadrise Aft	22°

See Page 572 For Resale Values

Wellcraft Boats
Sarasota, FL
www.wellcraft.com

Cruisers & Sportboats

Cruisers & Sportboats *(side margin)*

231-360-0827

Wellcraft 38 Excalibur
1996–2002

Sleek 38-foot sportster (built for Wellcraft by Aussie-based Riviera Marine) is part performance boat, part family cruiser. Chief attributes include smooth-riding deep-V hull, well-appointed interior, ergonomic helm, roomy cockpit with wet bar. Master stateroom has privacy door rather than curtain; helm seat can be adjusted electrically. Engine access—under aft cockpit seat—is very good, but side decks are narrow. Above-average fit and finish. MerCruiser 385hp gas sterndrives cruise at 30–32 knots and reach 40+ knots wide open.

Length	37'11"	Clearance	7 5"
Beam	10'8"	Fuel	240 gals.
Draft, Drive Up	2'3"	Water	60 gals.
Draft, Drive Down	3'2"	Hull Type	Deep-V
Weight	13,200#	Deadrise Aft	21°

See Page 572 For Resale Values

Wellcraft Boats
Sarasota, FL
www.wellcraft.com

231-360-0827

Wellcraft 43 Portofino
1987–97

1987–89

1990–97

Popular big-water express set class standards in the late 1980s for bold styling, deluxe accommodations. Originally offered with expansive single-stateroom interior; revised two-stateroom layout became standard in 1990. Huge bi-level cockpit provides seating for a dozen guests. Bridgedeck hatch provides good engine access. Helm was redesigned in 1990. Prop pockets reduce draft, improve efficiency. Standard 340hp gas engines cruise at 15 knots (24–25 knots top); optional 375hp Cat diesels cruise at 20–22 knots (mid 20s top).

Length w/Pulpit	45 7"	Fuel	436 gals.
Hull Length	42'10"	Water	100 gals.
Beam	14'6"	Waste	20 gals.
Draft	3'0"	Hull Type	Modified-V
Weight	20,000#	Deadrise Aft	14°

See Page 572 For Resale Values

Wellcraft Boats
Sarasota, FL
www.wellcraft.com

231-360-0827

Wellcraft 45 Excalibur
1995–2001

Sleek 45-footer (built by Riviera Marine in Australia) is one part performance boat, one part family cruiser. Highlights include well-appointed interior with premium furnishings, roomy cockpit with U-shaped lounge seating, excellent helm layout. Privacy doors (rather than curtains) separate both sleeping areas from main salon. Engine access—under aft cockpit seat—is very good. Side decks are quite narrow. Slender deep-V hull is agile, quick to accellerate. Big-block 415hp gas I/Os cruise at 28 knots (low 40s top).

Length	44'6"	Fuel	274 gals.
Beam	11'8"	Water	70 gals.
Draft	3'3"	Headroom	6 5"
Weight	15,000#	Hull Type	Deep-V
Clearance	8'6"	Deadrise Aft	21°

See Page 572 For Resale Values

Wellcraft Boats
Sarasota, FL
www.wellcraft.com

About These Prices

Retail high-low values are provided for boats built since 1995 except in those cases where limited resale activity makes it impossible to come up with a reliable estimate. Prices are intended to provide readers with general price estimates only and are not meant to represent precise market values. Boat depreciation depends on local and national market conditions whose fluctuations are impossible to predict. The prices are intended for use from November, 2010 until November, 2011.

The *Retail High* is the estimated selling price of a clean, well-maintained boat with average equipment. The *Retail Low* is the estimated selling price of a boat showing below-average maintenance, limited equipment, and high-hour engines.

The prices quoted in the price pages apply to boats found in the Florida, Atlantic East Coast, and Gulf Coast markets. Prices for boats located in other regions must be adjusted as follows:

Great Lakes	Add 10 to 15%
Pacific Northwest	Add 5 to 10%
California	Add 5 to 10%
Inland Rivers & Lakes	Add 5 to 10%

Note that a series of six asterisks (******) means that pricing data is unavailable.

Year	Power	Retail Low	Retail High
Albemarle 262 Center Console			
2003	320G I/O	44,000	51,000
2002	320G I/O	40,000	46,000
2001	320G I/O	36,000	42,000
2000	310G I/O	33,000	38,000
1999	310G I/O	30,000	35,000
1998	310G I/O	28,000	32,000
Albemarle 265/268 Express			
2009	375G I/O	******	******
2008	375G I/O	******	******
2007	375G I/O	67,000	78,000
2006	375G I/O	61,000	70,000
2005	375G I/O	54,000	63,000
2004	375G I/O	49,000	56,000
2003	375G I/O	44,000	51,000
2002	375G I/O	40,000	47,000
2001	310G I/O	37,000	42,000
2000	310G I/O	33,000	38,000
1999	310G I/O	30,000	35,000
1998	310G I/O	28,000	32,000
1997	310G I/O	25,000	29,000
1996	300G I/O	23,000	27,000
1995	300G I/O	21,000	25,000
Albemarle 27/280 Express (Inboard)			
2007	T280G	63,000	73,000
2007	T225D	86,000	99,000
2006	T280G	58,000	66,000
2006	T225D	78,000	90,000
2005	T280G	52,000	60,000
2005	T210D	71,000	82,000

Year	Power	Retail Low	Retail High
2003	T300G	48,000	55,000
2003	T210D	65,000	74,000
2002	T300G	43,000	50,000
2002	T210D	59,000	68,000
2001	T300G	39,000	45,000
2001	T210D	53,000	62,000
2000	T300G	36,000	41,000
2000	T210D	49,000	56,000
1999	T300G	33,000	37,000
1999	T230D	44,000	51,000
1998	T300G	30,000	34,000
1998	T230D	41,000	47,000
1997	T290G	27,000	32,000
1997	T230D	37,000	43,000
1996	T290G	25,000	29,000
1996	T230D	34,000	40,000
1995	T290G	23,000	27,000
1995	T230D	32,000	36,000
Albemarle 305/310 Express			
2009	T330D	******	******
2008	T330D	174,000	201,000
2007	T330D	159,000	182,000
2006	T330D	144,000	166,000
2005	T315D	131,000	151,000
2004	T315D	119,000	137,000
2003	T315D	109,000	125,000
2002	T300D	99,000	114,000
2001	T300D	90,000	103,000
2000	T300D	82,000	94,000
1999	T300D	75,000	86,000

Year	Power	Retail Low	Retail High
1998	T300D	69,000	80,000
1997	T300D	64,000	73,000
1996	T300D	58,000	67,000
1995	T300D	54,000	62,000
Albemarle 320 Express			
2006	T350D	158,000	182,000
2005	T350D	144,000	165,000
2004	T350D	131,000	150,000
2003	T350D	119,000	137,000
2002	T350D	108,000	124,000
2001	T350D	98,000	113,000
2000	T350D	89,000	103,000
1999	T350D	81,000	94,000
1998	T350D	75,000	86,000
1997	T350D	69,000	79,000
1996	T300D	63,000	73,000
1995	T300D	58,000	67,000
Albemarle 325 Convertible			
2003	T350D	147,000	169,000
2002	T350D	134,000	154,000
2001	T350D	122,000	140,000
2000	T350D	111,000	128,000
1999	T300D	101,000	116,000
1998	T300D	92,000	106,000
1997	T300D	83,000	96,000
1996	T300D	76,000	87,000
1995	T300D	69,000	79,000
Albemarle 360 Express			
2009	T540D	******	******

Year	Power	Retail Low	Retail High
2008	T575D	286,000	329,000
2007	T575D	263,000	302,000
2006	T575D	242,000	278,000
Albemarle 410 Convertible			
2009	T710D	******	******
2008	T725D	516,000	578,000
2007	T700D	470,000	526,000
2006	T700D	427,000	479,000
2005	T700D	389,000	436,000
Albemarle 410 Express			
2009	T710D	******	******
2008	T725D	477,000	534,000
2007	T700D	434,000	486,000
2006	T700D	395,000	442,000
2005	T700D	359,000	402,000
2004	T700D	327,000	366,000
2003	T660D	297,000	333,000
2002	T660D	271,000	303,000
Albin 27 Family Cruiser			
1995	216D	24,000	29,000
Albin 28 Tournament Express			
2007	S370D	131,000	151,000
2006	S370D	119,000	137,000
2005	S370D	108,000	125,000
2004	S370D	99,000	114,000
2003	S370D	90,000	103,000
2002	S370D	83,000	95,000
2001	S370D	76,000	87,000
2000	S370D	70,000	80,000
1999	S370D	64,000	74,000
1998	S300D	59,000	68,000
1997	S300D	54,000	62,000
1996	S300D	50,000	58,000
1995	S280D	47,000	54,000
Albin 30 Family Cruiser			
2007	S315D	106,000	122,000
2006	S315D	99,000	114,000
2005	S315D	92,000	106,000
2004	S315D	85,000	98,000
Albin 31 Tournament Express			
2007	T370D	188,000	217,000
2006	T370D	171,000	197,000
2005	T370D	156,000	179,000
2004	T370D	143,000	165,000
2003	T350D	132,000	152,000
2002	T350D	123,000	141,000
2001	T350D	114,000	131,000
2000	T350D	106,000	122,000
1999	T350D	100,000	115,000
1998	S300D	94,000	108,000
1997	T300D	88,000	101,000
1996	T300D	83,000	95,000
1995	T300D	78,000	89,000
Albin 32+2 Command Bridge			
2003	370D	108,000	124,000
2002	370D	100,000	116,000
2001	370D	93,000	107,000
2000	370D	87,000	100,000
1999	350D	81,000	93,000

Year	Power	Retail Low	Retail High
1998	300D	75,000	86,000
1997	300D	70,000	81,000
1996	300D	66,000	76,000
1995	300D	62,000	72,000
Albin 35 Command Bridge			
2007	S370D	141,000	162,000
2006	S370D	129,000	149,000
2005	S370D	119,000	137,000
2004	S370D	110,000	126,000
Albin 35 Tournament Express			
2007	T370D	175,000	201,000
2006	T370D	159,000	183,000
2005	T370D	147,000	169,000
2004	T370D	135,000	155,000
2003	T370D	125,000	144,000
2002	T370D	116,000	134,000
2001	T370D	108,000	125,000
2000	T370D	101,000	116,000
1999	T350D	94,000	108,000
1998	T350D	88,000	101,000
1997	T350D	83,000	95,000
1996	T350D	78,000	89,000
1995	T350D	73,000	84,000
Albin 36 Express Trawler			
2004	S450D	128,000	147,000
2003	S450D	119,000	137,000
2002	S450D	111,000	127,000
2001	S450D	103,000	118,000
2000	S420D	97,000	111,000
1999	S420D	91,000	105,000
Albin 40 North Sea Cutter			
2007	T315D	******	******
2006	T315D	133,000	151,000
2005	T315D	121,000	137,000
Albin 45 Command Bridge			
2007	T480D	******	******
2006	T480D	******	******
2005	T480D	261,000	294,000
2004	T450D	242,000	274,000
2003	T450D	225,000	255,000
American 34 Tug			
2009	380D	******	******
2008	380D	266,000	306,000
2007	380D	247,000	285,000
2006	380D	230,000	265,000
2005	380D	216,000	249,000
2004	380D	203,000	234,000
2003	380D	191,000	220,000
2002	370D	181,000	209,000
2001	370D	172,000	198,000
American 41 Tug			
2009	575D	******	******
2008	575D	******	******
2007	575D	401,000	482,000
2006	575D	373,000	448,000
2005	575D	347,000	416,000
Angler 2700 Center Console			
2009	T200 O/B	54,000	62,000
2008	T200 O/B	49,000	56,000

Year	Power	Retail Low	Retail High
2007	T200 O/B	44,000	51,000
2006	T200 O/B	40,000	46,000
2005	T200 O/B	37,000	43,000
2004	T200 O/B	34,000	39,000
2003	T200 O/B	31,000	36,000
Angler 2900 Center Console			
2009	T225 O/B	71,000	81,000
2008	T225 O/B	64,000	74,000
2007	T225 O/B	58,000	67,000
2006	T225 O/B	53,000	61,000
2005	T225 O/B	49,000	56,000
2004	T225 O/B	45,000	52,000
2003	T225 O/B	41,000	47,000
2002	T225 O/B	38,000	44,000
2001	T225 O/B	36,000	41,000
2000	T225 O/B	33,000	38,000
Aquasport 275 Explorer			
2005	T225 O/B	57,000	65,000
2004	T225 O/B	52,000	60,000
2003	T225 O/B	48,000	55,000
2002	T225 O/B	44,000	51,000
2001	T225 O/B	41,000	47,000
2000	T225 O/B	38,000	44,000
1999	T225 O/B	35,000	41,000
Azimut 39			
2005	T350D	234,000	270,000
2004	T350D	216,000	248,000
2003	T355D	198,000	228,000
2002	T350D	184,000	212,000
2001	T350D	171,000	197,000
2000	T325D	159,000	183,000
1999	T325D	148,000	171,000
Azimut 42			
2005	T385D	274,000	315,000
2004	T390D	252,000	290,000
2003	T390D	232,000	267,000
2002	T375D	213,000	245,000
2001	T375D	198,000	228,000
2000	T375D	184,000	212,000
1999	T375D	171,000	197,000
Azimut 43			
1998	T435D	158,000	181,000
1997	T435D	148,000	170,000
1996	T435D	139,000	160,000
1995	T435D	131,000	150,000
Azimut 46			
2004	T505D	301,000	346,000
2003	T435D	277,000	318,000
2002	T435D	255,000	293,000
2001	T435D	234,000	269,000
2000	T435D	218,000	251,000
1999	T435D	203,000	233,000
1998	T435D	188,000	217,000
1997	T435D	175,000	201,000
Azimut 50/52			
2002	T600D	345,000	397,000
2001	T600D	317,000	365,000
2000	T600D	295,000	340,000
1999	T600D	277,000	319,000

Year	Power	Retail Low	Retail High
1998	T600D	261,000	300,000
1997	T600D	245,000	282,000
1996	T600D	230,000	265,000

Azimut 54/58

Year	Power	Retail Low	Retail High
2001	T765D	417,000	480,000
2000	T765D	388,000	446,000
1999	T765D	365,000	419,000
1998	T765D	343,000	394,000
1997	T765D	322,000	370,000
1996	T765D	303,000	348,000
1995	T765D	285,000	327,000

Azimut 55

Year	Power	Retail Low	Retail High
2005	T710D	567,000	652,000
2004	T710D	527,000	606,000
2003	T660D	490,000	563,000
2002	T660D	456,000	524,000
2001	T660D	424,000	487,000

Back Cove 26

Year	Power	Retail Low	Retail High
2009	260D	******	******
2008	260D	82,000	96,000
2007	260D	75,000	89,000
2006	260D	70,000	82,000
2005	260D	65,000	76,000

Back Cove 29

Year	Power	Retail Low	Retail High
2009	260D	******	******
2008	260D	131,000	151,000
2007	260D	121,000	139,000
2006	260D	111,000	128,000
2005	260D	103,000	119,000
2004	260D	96,000	110,000

Back Cove 33

Year	Power	Retail Low	Retail High
2009	380D	******	******
2008	380D	270,000	308,000
2007	380D	249,000	283,000

Bayliner 265 Cruiser

Year	Power	Retail Low	Retail High
2008	250 I/O	36,000	43,000
2007	250 I/O	33,000	39,000
2006	220 I/O	30,000	36,000
2005	220 I/O	28,000	33,000

Bayliner 2655 Ciera SB

Year	Power	Retail Low	Retail High
1999	250 I/O	12,000	14,000
1998	250 I/O	11,000	13,000
1997	250 I/O	10,000	12,000
1996	250 I/O	9,000	11,000
1995	250 I/O	9,000	11,000

Bayliner 2655 Ciera CB/265 Cruier

Year	Power	Retail Low	Retail High
2004	220 I/O	19,000	22,000
2003	220 I/O	17,000	21,000
2002	220 I/O	16,000	19,000
2001	220 I/O	15,000	18,000
2000	220 I/O	14,000	17,000

Bayliner 275 Cruiser

Year	Power	Retail Low	Retail High
2007	250 I/O	40,000	48,000
2006	250 I/O	36,000	43,000
2005	250 I/O	33,000	40,000

Bayliner 2855 Ciera SB (1994-99)

Year	Power	Retail Low	Retail High
1999	310 I/O	18,000	22,000
1998	310 I/O	17,000	21,000
1997	310 I/O	16,000	19,000
1996	300 I/O	15,000	18,000
1995	300 I/O	14,000	17,000

Bayliner 2859 Ciera Express

Year	Power	Retail Low	Retail High
2002	300 I/O	23,000	27,000
2001	300 I/O	21,000	25,000
2000	300 I/O	20,000	23,000
1999	310 I/O	18,000	22,000
1998	310 I/O	17,000	20,000
1997	310 I/O	16,000	19,000
1996	310 I/O	15,000	18,000
1995	310 I/O	14,000	16,000

Bayliner 285 Cruiser

Year	Power	Retail Low	Retail High
2009	300 I/O	56,000	64,000
2008	300 I/O	50,000	57,000
2007	300 I/O	46,000	53,000
2006	300 I/O	42,000	49,000
2005	300 I/O	39,000	45,000
2004	320 I/O	36,000	41,000
2003	320 I/O	33,000	38,000
2002	320 I/O	31,000	35,000
2001	320 I/O	29,000	33,000
2000	320 I/O	27,000	31,000

Bayliner 288 Classic Cruiser

Year	Power	Retail Low	Retail High
2005	300 I/O	41,000	48,000
2004	300 I/O	38,000	43,000
2003	300 I/O	35,000	40,000
2002	300 I/O	32,000	37,000
2001	300 I/O	29,000	34,000
2000	300 I/O	27,000	31,000
1999	330 I/O	25,000	29,000
1998	330 I/O	23,000	27,000
1997	330 I/O	21,000	25,000
1996	330 I/O	20,000	23,000

Bayliner 300/315 Cruiser

Year	Power	Retail Low	Retail High
2009	260 I/O	73,000	84,000
2008	260 I/O	66,000	76,000

Bayliner 305 Cruiser

Year	Power	Retail Low	Retail High
2007	T260G I/O	61,000	70,000
2006	T260G I/O	56,000	64,000
2005	T260G I/O	51,000	58,000
2004	T260G I/O	46,000	54,000
2003	T260G I/O	43,000	49,000
2002	T260G I/O	39,000	45,000
2001	T260G I/O	36,000	42,000
2000	T260G I/O	34,000	39,000
1999	T260G I/O	31,000	36,000

Bayliner 320/335 Cruiser

Year	Power	Retail Low	Retail High
2009	T260 I/O	88,000	101,000
2008	T260 I/O	80,000	92,000

Bayliner 325 Cruiser

Year	Power	Retail Low	Retail High
2007	T260G I/O	72,000	83,000
2006	T260G I/O	66,000	76,000
2005	T260G I/O	60,000	69,000

Bayliner 3255 Avanti SB

Year	Power	Retail Low	Retail High
1999	T300G I/O	31,000	36,000
1998	T300G I/O	29,000	33,000
1997	T300G I/O	27,000	31,000
1996	T300G I/O	25,000	29,000
1995	T300G I/O	24,000	27,000

Bayliner 3258 Command Bridge

Year	Power	Retail Low	Retail High
2001	T300G I/O	43,000	50,000
2000	T310G I/O	40,000	46,000
1999	T310G I/O	37,000	43,000
1998	T310G I/O	35,000	40,000
1997	T300G I/O	33,000	38,000
1996	T300G I/O	31,000	35,000
1995	T300G I/O	29,000	33,000

Bayliner 3270/3288 MY

Year	Power	Retail Low	Retail High
1995	T150D	42,000	48,000

Bayliner 3388 Motor Yacht

Year	Power	Retail Low	Retail High
2000	T250D	67,000	77,000
1999	T250D	57,000	65,000
1998	T210D	53,000	61,000
1997	T210D	49,000	56,000
1996	T210D	46,000	52,000

Bayliner 340 Cruiser

Year	Power	Retail Low	Retail High
2009	T260 I/O	98,000	112,000
2008	T300 I/O	89,000	102,000

Bayliner 3488 Avanti CB (1996-99)

Year	Power	Retail Low	Retail High
1999	T310G	52,000	60,000
1998	T310G	48,000	55,000
1997	T310G	45,000	52,000
1996	T310G	42,000	48,000

Bayliner 3488 CB (2001-02)

Year	Power	Retail Low	Retail High
2002	T260G	74,000	85,000
2001	T260G	68,000	78,000

Bayliner 3587 Motor Yacht

Year	Power	Retail Low	Retail High
1999	T310G	65,000	75,000
1999	T330D	67,000	77,000
1998	T310G	60,000	70,000
1998	T330D	62,000	72,000
1997	T310G	56,000	65,000
1997	T315D	58,000	67,000
1996	T310G	52,000	61,000
1996	T315D	54,000	62,000
1995	T310G	48,000	56,000
1995	T315D	50,000	58,000

Bayliner 3685 Avanti Sunbridge

Year	Power	Retail Low	Retail High
1999	T310G	64,000	74,000
1998	T310G	58,000	67,000

Bayliner 3788 MY (1996-99)

Year	Power	Retail Low	Retail High
1999	T310G	72,000	83,000
1999	T330D	90,000	104,000
1998	T310G	68,000	78,000
1998	T330D	85,000	98,000
1997	T310G	64,000	74,000
1997	T250D	80,000	92,000
1996	T310G	60,000	69,000
1996	T250D	75,000	86,000

Bayliner 3788 MY (2001-02)

Year	Power	Retail Low	Retail High
2002	T310G	96,000	111,000
2002	T330D	117,000	135,000
2001	T310G	89,000	103,000
2001	T330D	109,000	126,000

Bayliner 3988 MY

Year	Power	Retail Low	Retail High
2002	T320G	115,000	131,000

Year	Power	Retail Low	Retail High
2002	T330D	134,000	153,000
2001	T320G	106,000	121,000
2001	T330D	125,000	142,000
2000	T320G	99,000	113,000
2000	T330D	116,000	132,000
1999	T310G	92,000	105,000
1999	T330D	108,000	123,000
1998	T310G	86,000	99,000
1998	T330D	101,000	116,000
1997	T310G	81,000	93,000
1997	T315D	95,000	109,000
1996	T310G	76,000	87,000
1996	T315D	89,000	102,000
1995	T310G	72,000	82,000
1995	T315D	84,000	96,000

Bayliner 4085 Avanti SB

Year	Power	Retail Low	Retail High
1999	T310G	72,000	82,000
1999	T330D	89,000	101,000
1998	T310G	68,000	77,000
1998	T330D	83,000	95,000
1997	T310G	63,000	72,000
1997	T-Diesel	78,000	89,000

Bayliner 4087 Cockpit MY

Year	Power	Retail Low	Retail High
2001	T320G	103,000	117,000
2001	T330D	127,000	144,000
2000	T320G	95,000	109,000
2000	T330D	118,000	134,000
1999	T310G	89,000	101,000
1999	T330D	109,000	125,000
1998	T310G	82,000	94,000
1998	T330D	102,000	116,000
1997	T310G	77,000	87,000
1997	T330D	95,000	108,000

Bayliner 4587 Cockpit MY

Year	Power	Retail Low	Retail High
1995	T300G	77,000	88,000
1995	T310D	92,000	105,000

Bayliner 4788 Pilothouse MY

Year	Power	Retail Low	Retail High
2002	T370D	216,000	248,000
2001	T370D	200,000	231,000
2000	T370D	186,000	214,000
1999	T315D	173,000	199,000
1998	T315D	163,000	187,000
1997	T315D	153,000	176,000
1996	T315D	144,000	166,000
1995	T310D	135,000	156,000

Bayliner 5288 Pilothouse MY

Year	Power	Retail Low	Retail High
2002	T610D	344,000	395,000
2001	T610D	323,000	371,000
2000	T610D	303,000	349,000
1999	T600D	285,000	328,000

Bayliner 5788 Motor Yacht

Year	Power	Retail Low	Retail High
2002	T610D	436,000	502,000
2001	T610D	406,000	467,000
2000	T610D	377,000	434,000
1999	T600D	355,000	408,000
1998	T600D	333,000	383,000
1997	T600D	313,000	360,000

Beneteau 42 Trawler

Year	Power	Retail Low	Retail High
2009	T370D	******	******

Year	Power	Retail Low	Retail High
2008	T370D	******	******
2007	T370D	247,000	284,000
2006	T370D	230,000	264,000
2005	T370D	214,000	246,000
2004	T370D	199,000	229,000

Bertram 30 Moppie

Year	Power	Retail Low	Retail High
1997	T320G	52,000	59,000
1997	T300D	66,000	75,000
1996	T320G	48,000	56,000
1996	T300D	62,000	71,000
1995	T320G	45,000	52,000
1995	T300D	58,000	67,000

Bertram 36 Moppie

Year	Power	Retail Low	Retail High
2000	T430D	168,000	193,000
1999	T430D	157,000	181,000
1998	T430D	148,000	170,000
1997	T330D	139,000	160,000
1996	T315D	131,000	150,000

Bertram 390 Convertible

Year	Power	Retail Low	Retail High
2007	460D	441,000	494,000
2006	460D	401,000	450,000
2005	480D	369,000	414,000
2004	480D	340,000	381,000
2003	480D	313,000	350,000
2002	480D	287,000	322,000
2001	480D	267,000	299,000
2000	480D	249,000	278,000

Bertram 43 Convertible

Year	Power	Retail Low	Retail High
1996	625D	204,000	231,000
1995	600D	192,000	217,000

Bertram 450 Convertible

Year	Power	Retail Low	Retail High
2009	900D	******	******
2008	900D	******	******
2007	900D	******	******
2006	900D	573,000	647,000
2005	900D	532,000	602,000
2004	660D	495,000	560,000
2003	660D	460,000	520,000
2002	660D	428,000	484,000
2001	660D	398,000	450,000
2000	660D	370,000	418,000

Bertram 46 Conv. (1995-97)

Year	Power	Retail Low	Retail High
1997	760D	304,000	347,000
1996	760D	286,000	326,000
1995	735D	269,000	307,000

Bertram 50 Convertible

Year	Power	Retail Low	Retail High
1997	900D	473,000	641,000
1996	820D	439,000	596,000
1995	735D	409,000	554,000

Bertram 510 Convertible

Year	Power	Retail Low	Retail High
2009	1000D	******	******
2008	1000D	******	******
2007	800D	******	******
2006	800D	796,000	908,000
2005	800D	740,000	844,000
2004	800D	689,000	785,000
2003	800D	640,000	730,000
2002	800D	602,000	686,000
2001	800D	566,000	645,000

Year	Power	Retail Low	Retail High
2000	800D	532,000	606,000

Bertram 54 Conv. (1995-2003)

Year	Power	Retail Low	Retail High
2003	1200D	******	******
2002	1200D	1,012,000	1,153,000
2001	1400D	941,000	1,072,000
2000	1400D	875,000	997,000
2000	1350D	814,000	927,000
1999	1350D	757,000	863,000
1998	1350D	704,000	802,000
1997	1350D	654,000	746,000
1996	1100D	608,000	694,000
1995	1100D	566,000	645,000

Bertram 570 Convertible

Year	Power	Retail Low	Retail High
2009	1300D	******	******
2008	1300D	******	******
2007	1300D	******	******
2006	1300D	1,184,000	1,350,000
2005	1300D	1,090,000	1,242,000
2004	1300D	1,002,000	1,143,000
2003	1300D	932,000	1,063,000
2002	1300D	867,000	988,000

Bertram 60 Conv. (Open Bridge)

Year	Power	Retail Low	Retail High
2005	1400D	******	******
2004	1400D	******	******
2003	1400D	******	******
2002	1400D	1,156,000	1,318,000
2001	1400D	1,075,000	1,226,000
2000	1400D	1,000,000	1,140,000
1999	1400D	930,000	1,060,000
1998	1450D	865,000	986,000
1997	1450D	804,000	917,000
1996	1400D	748,000	852,000
1995	1400D	703,000	801,000

Bertram 630 Conv. (Open Bridge)

Year	Power	Retail Low	Retail High
2009	2000D	******	******
2008	2000D	******	******
2007	2000D	******	******
2006	2000D	1,715,000	1,937,000
2005	2000D	1,612,000	1,821,000
2004	2000D	1,515,000	1,712,000

Black Watch 26 Express

Year	Power	Retail Low	Retail High
1997	T250 I/B	45,000	54,000
1996	T250 I/B	42,000	51,000
1995	T250 I/B	40,000	48,000
1994	T250 I/B	37,000	45,000
1993	T240 I/B	35,000	42,000
1992	T240 I/B	33,000	40,000
1991	T240 I/B	31,000	37,000
1990	T240 I/B	29,000	35,000

Black Watch 30 Flybridge

Year	Power	Retail Low	Retail High
1996	T250G	43,000	51,000
1996	T300D	52,000	62,000
1995	T250G	40,000	48,000
1995	T300D	48,000	58,000

Black Watch 30 SF

Year	Power	Retail Low	Retail High
1995	T250G	37,000	44,000
1995	T300D	46,000	55,000

Blackfin 27 Sportsman

Year	Power	Retail Low	Retail High
1998	T270G	35,000	42,000

See Page 529 For Price Adjustments

Year	Power	Retail Low	Retail High
1998	T230D	44,000	52,000
1997	T270G	32,000	39,000
1997	T230D	41,000	49,000
1996	T270G	30,000	37,000
1996	T230D	38,000	46,000
1995	T270G	29,000	34,000
1995	T230D	36,000	43,000
Blackfin 29 Combi			
1998	T320G	43,000	51,000
1998	T330D	54,000	64,000
1997	T320G	40,000	48,000
1997	T330D	50,000	60,000
1996	T320G	37,000	44,000
1996	T330D	46,000	56,000
1995	T320G	34,000	41,000
1995	T330D	43,000	52,000
Blackfin 29 Flybridge			
1998	T-Gas	48,000	58,000
1998	T330D	59,000	71,000
1997	T-Gas	45,000	54,000
1997	T330D	55,000	66,000
1996	T-Gas	42,000	50,000
1996	T330D	51,000	62,000
1995	T-Gas	39,000	46,000
1995	T330D	48,000	57,000
Blackfin 31 Combi			
1997	T-Gas	62,000	74,000
1997	T300D	79,000	95,000
1996	T-Gas	57,000	68,000
1996	T300D	73,000	88,000
1995	T-Gas	52,000	63,000
1995	T300D	67,000	81,000
Blackfin 33 Combi			
1998	T375D	94,000	110,000
1997	T375D	88,000	104,000
1996	T375D	83,000	98,000
1995	T375D	78,000	92,000
Blackfin 33 Convertible			
1999	T435D	104,000	122,000
1998	T375D	97,000	115,000
1997	T375D	91,000	108,000
1996	T-Gas	71,000	83,000
1996	T375D	86,000	101,000
1995	T-Gas	66,000	78,000
1995	T375D	81,000	95,000
Blackfin 38 Combi			
1998	450D	167,000	197,000
1997	450D	157,000	186,000
1996	450D	148,000	174,000
1996	450D	139,000	164,000
1995	450D	131,000	154,000
Blackfin 38 Convertible			
1998	550D	195,000	230,000
1997	550D	183,000	217,000
1996	485D	172,000	204,000
1995	485D	162,000	191,000
Boston Whaler 26 Outrage			
2002	T200 O/B	36,000	43,000
2001	T200 O/B	33,000	40,000

Year	Power	Retail Low	Retail High
2000	T200 O/B	31,000	37,000
1999	T200 O/B	29,000	34,000
1998	T200 O/B	27,000	32,000
Boston Whaler 27 Offshore			
1998	T225 O/B	30,000	36,000
1997	T225 O/B	28,000	34,000
1996	T225 O/B	27,000	33,000
1995	T225 O/B	25,000	31,000
Boston Whaler 270 Outrage			
2008	T225 O/B	83,000	100,000
2007	T225 O/B	75,000	90,000
2006	T225 O/B	68,000	82,000
2005	T225 O/B	62,000	75,000
2004	T225 O/B	57,000	69,000
2003	T225 O/B	53,000	63,000
Boston Whaler 275 Conquest			
2005	T225 O/B	78,000	93,000
2004	T225 O/B	72,000	86,000
2003	T225 O/B	66,000	80,000
2002	T225 O/B	62,000	74,000
2001	T225 O/B	57,000	69,000
Boston Whaler 28/290 Outrage			
2003	T225 O/B	75,000	90,000
2002	T225 O/B	69,000	83,000
2001	T225 O/B	64,000	77,000
2000	T225 O/B	60,000	72,000
1999	T225 O/B	56,000	67,000
Boston Whaler 28/295 Conquest			
2003	T225 O/B	82,000	98,000
2002	T225 O/B	76,000	91,000
2001	T225 O/B	71,000	85,000
2000	T225 O/B	66,000	79,000
1999	T225 O/B	61,000	73,000
Boston Whaler 285 Conquest			
2009	T225 O/B	******	******
2008	T225 O/B	92,000	110,000
2007	T225 O/B	84,000	101,000
2006	T225 O/B	77,000	93,000
Boston Whaler 305 Conquest			
2009	T225 O/B	******	******
2008	T225 O/B	126,000	152,000
2007	T225 O/B	115,000	138,000
2006	T225 O/B	106,000	127,000
2005	T225 O/B	97,000	117,000
2004	T225 O/B	89,000	107,000
Boston Whaler 320 Outrage			
2009	T250 O/B	******	******
2008	T250 O/B	124,000	149,000
2007	T250 O/B	113,000	135,000
2006	T250 O/B	103,000	123,000
2005	T250 O/B	93,000	112,000
2004	T250 O/B	85,000	102,000
2003	T250 O/B	77,000	93,000
Boston Whaler 320 Outrage Cuddy			
2009	T250 O/B	******	******
2008	T250 O/B	132,000	158,000
2007	T250 O/B	120,000	144,000
2006	T250 O/B	109,000	131,000

Year	Power	Retail Low	Retail High
Boston Whaler 34 Defiance			
2002	T355D	152,000	183,000
2001	T355D	142,000	170,000
2000	T355D	132,000	158,000
1999	T355D	123,000	147,000
Boston Whaler 345 Conquest			
2009	3/225 O/B	******	******
2008	3/225 O/B	205,000	246,000
2007	3/225 O/B	186,000	224,000
Cabo 31 Express			
2004	T385D	162,000	190,000
2003	T385D	149,000	175,000
2002	T385D	137,000	161,000
2001	T385D	126,000	148,000
2000	T385D	116,000	136,000
1999	T350D	109,000	128,000
1998	T350D	103,000	120,000
1997	T350D	96,000	113,000
1996	T350D	91,000	106,000
1995	T350D	85,000	100,000
Cabo 32 Express			
2009	T425D	******	******
2008	T425D	265,000	310,000
2007	T425D	244,000	285,000
2006	T461D	224,000	262,000
2005	T461D	208,000	244,000
Cabo 35 Express			
2009	T425D	******	******
2008	T425D	295,000	345,000
2007	T425D	268,000	314,000
2006	T461D	247,000	289,000
2005	T461D	227,000	266,000
2004	T450D	209,000	244,000
2003	T450D	192,000	225,000
2002	T435D	178,000	209,000
2001	T435D	166,000	194,000
2000	T435D	154,000	181,000
1999	T435D	143,000	168,000
1998	T435D	133,000	156,000
1997	T435D	125,000	147,000
1996	T435D	118,000	138,000
1995	T375D	111,000	130,000
Cabo 35 Flybridge			
2009	425D	******	******
2008	425D	******	******
2007	425D	340,000	398,000
2006	461D	309,000	362,000
2005	461D	284,000	333,000
2004	450D	262,000	306,000
2003	450D	241,000	282,000
2002	435D	221,000	259,000
2001	435D	204,000	238,000
2000	435D	189,000	222,000
1999	435D	176,000	206,000
1998	435D	165,000	194,000
1997	435D	155,000	182,000
1996	435D	146,000	171,000
1995	375D	137,000	161,000

Year	Power	Retail Low	Retail High
Cabo 40 Express			
2009	720D	******	******
2008	720D	526,000	605,000
2007	710D	484,000	556,000
2006	710D	450,000	517,000
2005	710D	418,000	481,000
2004	700D	389,000	447,000
2003	700D	362,000	416,000
Cabo 40 Flybridge			
2009	710D	******	******
2008	710D	******	******
2007	710D	543,000	625,000
2006	710D	500,000	575,000
2005	710D	465,000	534,000
2004	700D	432,000	497,000
Cabo 43 Flybridge			
2009	720D	******	******
2008	720D	649,000	747,000
2007	710D	597,000	687,000
2006	710D	549,000	632,000
2005	710D	505,000	581,000
2004	680D	465,000	535,000
2003	680D	432,000	497,000
2002	680D	402,000	463,000
Cabo 45 Express			
2009	800D	******	******
2008	800D	******	******
2007	800D	688,000	784,000
2006	800D	633,000	722,000
2005	800D	589,000	671,000
2004	800D	547,000	624,000
2003	800D	509,000	580,000
2002	800D	473,000	540,000
2001	800D	440,000	502,000
2000	800D	414,000	472,000
1999	800D	389,000	443,000
1998	800D	366,000	417,000
1997	800D	344,000	392,000
Cabo 47/48 Flybridge			
2009	800D	******	******
2008	800D	******	******
2007	800D	607,000	692,000
2006	800D	558,000	637,000
2005	800D	514,000	586,000
2004	800D	473,000	539,000
2003	800D	435,000	496,000
2002	800D	404,000	461,000
2001	800D	376,000	429,000
2000	800D	350,000	399,000
Cabo 52 Express			
2009	1550D	******	******
2008	1550D	1,107,000	1,261,000
2007	1550D	1,029,000	1,173,000
2006	1550D	957,000	1,091,000
Californian 39 SL			
2003	T318D	182,000	212,000
2002	T318D	169,000	198,000
2001	T318D	157,000	184,000
2000	T318D	146,000	171,000

Year	Power	Retail Low	Retail High
1999	T318D	136,000	159,000
Camano 28/31			
2009	S-Diesel	******	******
2008	S-Diesel	152,000	183,000
2007	S-Diesel	142,000	170,000
2006	S-Diesel	132,000	158,000
2005	S-Diesel	123,000	147,000
2004	S-Diesel	115,000	138,000
2003	S-Diesel	108,000	130,000
2002	S-Diesel	102,000	122,000
2001	S-Diesel	96,000	115,000
2000	S-Diesel	90,000	108,000
1999	S-Diesel	84,000	101,000
1998	S-Diesel	80,000	96,000
1997	S-Diesel	76,000	91,000
1996	S-Diesel	72,000	87,000
1995	S-Diesel	69,000	82,000
Carolina Classic 28			
2009	T375G	101,000	117,000
2009	T315D	146,000	169,000
2008	T375G	91,000	106,000
2008	T315D	133,000	154,000
2007	T375G	84,000	98,000
2007	T315D	122,000	142,000
2006	T375G	77,000	90,000
2006	T315D	112,000	130,000
2005	T375G	71,000	83,000
2005	T300D	103,000	120,000
2004	T375G	65,000	76,000
2004	T300D	95,000	110,000
2003	T375G	61,000	71,000
2003	T300D	88,000	103,000
2002	T375G	56,000	66,000
2002	T250D	82,000	95,000
2001	T375G	52,000	61,000
2001	T250D	76,000	89,000
2000	T300G	49,000	57,000
2000	T250D	71,000	82,000
1999	T300G	45,000	53,000
1999	T250D	66,000	77,000
1998	T300G	43,000	49,000
1998	T230D	62,000	72,000
1997	T300G	40,000	46,000
1997	T230D	58,000	68,000
1996	T300G	38,000	44,000
1996	T230D	55,000	64,000
1995	T300G	35,000	41,000
1995	T230D	51,000	60,000
Carolina Classic 32			
2009	T480D	229,000	266,000
2008	T425D	209,000	242,000
2007	T425D	190,000	220,000
2006	T500D	175,000	203,000
2005	T500D	161,000	186,000
2004	T440D	149,000	173,000
Carolina Classic 35			
2009	T600D	302,000	350,000
2008	T540D	278,000	322,000
2007	T540D	256,000	297,000
2006	T500D	235,000	273,000

Year	Power	Retail Low	Retail High
2005	T480D	219,000	254,000
2004	T480D	203,000	236,000
2003	T480D	189,000	219,000
2002	T480D	176,000	204,000
2001	T450D	163,000	190,000
2000	T450D	154,000	178,000
1999	T450D	144,000	167,000
1998	T450D	136,000	157,000
Carver 280 Mid Cabin Exp.			
1998	T205G	19,000	23,000
1997	T205G	18,000	21,000
1996	T205G	16,000	20,000
1995	T205G	15,000	18,000
Carver 280 Sedan			
1998	T205G	19,000	23,000
1997	T205G	18,000	21,000
1996	T205G	16,000	20,000
1995	T205G	15,000	18,000
Carver 310 Mid-Cabin Express			
1997	T220 I/O	27,000	32,000
1996	T220 I/O	25,000	30,000
1995	T220 I/O	24,000	29,000
Carver 310 Santego			
1998	T220 I/O	30,000	36,000
1997	T220 I/O	28,000	34,000
1996	T220 I/O	27,000	32,000
1995	T220 I/O	25,000	30,000
Carver 320 Voyager			
1999	T300G	38,000	46,000
1998	T300G	36,000	43,000
1997	T260G	34,000	41,000
1996	T260G	32,000	38,000
1995	T260G	30,000	36,000
Carver 325/326 Aft Cabin			
2001	T300G	51,000	62,000
2000	T300G	47,000	57,000
1999	T300G	44,000	53,000
1998	T260G	41,000	49,000
1997	T260G	38,000	46,000
1996	T260G	35,000	42,000
1995	T260G	33,000	39,000
Carver 32/330 Mariner			
1996	T260G	42,000	50,000
1995	T260G	39,000	47,000
Carver 33/35/36 Super Sport			
2008	T330G	176,000	211,000
2007	T320G	160,000	192,000
2006	T320G	145,000	174,000
2005	T320G	134,000	160,000
Carver 350 Mariner			
2003	T300G	85,000	102,000
2002	T300G	78,000	93,000
2001	T300G	71,000	86,000
2000	T300G	66,000	79,000
1999	T260G	61,000	73,000
1998	T260G	57,000	68,000
1997	T260G	53,000	63,000

See Page 529 For Price Adjustments

Year	Power	Retail Low	Retail High
Carver 355/356 Motor Yacht			
2003	T320G	102,000	123,000
2002	T320G	93,000	112,000
2001	T320G	85,000	102,000
2000	T310G	77,000	93,000
1999	T310G	70,000	84,000
1998	T310G	64,000	77,000
1997	T310G	59,000	71,000
1996	T320G	54,000	65,000
1995	T320G	50,000	59,000
Carver 36 Mariner			
2009	T320G	******	******
2008	T320G	177,000	189,000
2007	T320G	161,000	172,000
2006	T320G	148,000	158,000
2005	T320G	136,000	146,000
2004	T320G	126,000	134,000
Carver 36 Motor Yacht			
2007	T375G	199,000	239,000
2007	T315D	223,000	268,000
2006	T320G	181,000	217,000
2006	T315D	203,000	244,000
2006	T320G	164,000	197,000
2006	T315D	187,000	224,000
2005	T320G	151,000	182,000
2005	T280D	172,000	206,000
2004	T320G	139,000	167,000
2004	T280D	158,000	190,000
2003	T320G	128,000	154,000
2003	T280D	145,000	174,000
2002	T320G	118,000	141,000
2002	T280D	134,000	160,000
Carver 360 Sport Sedan			
2006	T375G	150,000	180,000
2005	T375G	138,000	165,000
2004	T375G	127,000	152,000
2003	T320G	117,000	140,000
Carver 36/370 Aft Cabin MY			
1996	T300G	69,000	83,000
1996	T300D	91,000	109,000
1995	T300G	64,000	77,000
1995	T300D	84,000	101,000
Carver 370/374 Voyager			
2002	T320G	94,000	113,000
2002	T330D	110,000	132,000
2001	T320G	86,000	104,000
2001	T330D	101,000	121,000
2000	T320G	79,000	95,000
2000	T330D	93,000	111,000
1999	T320G	74,000	89,000
1999	T315D	86,000	104,000
1998	T300G	69,000	82,000
1998	T315D	80,000	96,000
1997	T300G	64,000	77,000
1997	T315D	74,000	89,000
1996	T300G	59,000	71,000
1996	T315D	69,000	83,000
1995	T300G	55,000	66,000
1995	T315D	64,000	77,000
Carver 34/638/380 Santego			
2002	T320G	88,000	106,000
2001	T320G	82,000	98,000
2000	T310G	76,000	91,000
1999	T310G	71,000	85,000
1998	T300G	66,000	79,000
1997	T320G	61,000	73,000
1996	T320G	57,000	69,000
1995	T320G	54,000	65,000
Carver 38 Super Sport			
2008	T375G	197,000	228,000
2007	T375G	177,000	205,000
2006	T375G	159,000	185,000
2005	T375G	143,000	166,000
Carver 38/390 Aft Cabin			
1995	T330G	74,000	89,000
1995	T-Diesel	95,000	114,000
Carver 396/39 Motor Yacht			
2007	T385G	224,000	269,000
2007	T370D	258,000	310,000
2006	T385G	206,000	248,000
2006	T370D	238,000	285,000
2005	T385G	188,000	225,000
2005	T370D	216,000	259,000
2004	T385G	171,000	205,000
2004	T370D	197,000	236,000
2003	T370G	157,000	189,000
2003	T370D	181,000	217,000
2002	T370G	146,000	175,000
2002	T370D	168,000	202,000
2001	T370G	136,000	163,000
2001	T330D	156,000	188,000
2000	T380G	126,000	152,000
2000	T330D	145,000	175,000
Carver 390/400/404 Cockpit MY			
2003	T320G	132,000	159,000
2003	T370D	161,000	193,000
2002	T320G	122,000	146,000
2002	T370D	148,000	178,000
2001	T320G	112,000	135,000
2001	T370D	136,000	163,000
2000	T310G	103,000	124,000
2000	T370D	125,000	150,000
1999	T310G	96,000	115,000
1999	T370D	116,000	140,000
1998	T310G	89,000	107,000
1998	T370D	108,000	130,000
1997	T310G	83,000	99,000
1997	T370D	101,000	121,000
1996	T310G	77,000	92,000
1996	T370D	94,000	112,000
1995	T310G	72,000	87,000
1995	T315D	88,000	106,000
Carver 405/406 Aft Cabin MY			
2002	T320G	133,000	160,000
2002	T330D	159,000	191,000
2001	T320G	124,000	148,000
2001	T330D	148,000	178,000
2000	T320G	115,000	138,000
2000	T330D	137,000	165,000
Carver 34/638/380 Santego (cont.)			
1999	T310G	107,000	128,000
1999	T330D	128,000	153,000
1998	T310G	99,000	119,000
1998	T330D	119,000	143,000
1997	T310G	92,000	111,000
1997	T315D	110,000	133,000
Carver 41 Cockpit MY			
2007	T375G	211,000	253,000
2007	T370D	235,000	282,000
2006	T375G	192,000	230,000
2006	T370D	214,000	257,000
2005	T385G	176,000	212,000
2005	T370D	197,000	236,000
Carver 410 Sport Sedan			
2003	T375G	149,000	179,000
2003	T370D	173,000	208,000
2002	T375G	139,000	167,000
2002	T370D	161,000	194,000
Carver 42 Mariner			
2006	T385G	182,000	219,000
2006	T370D	212,000	255,000
2005	T385G	168,000	201,000
2005	T370D	195,000	234,000
2004	T385G	154,000	185,000
2004	T330D	180,000	216,000
Carver 42/43 Super Sport			
2009	T385G	******	******
2009	T370D	******	******
2008	T375G	255,000	306,000
2008	T370D	289,000	347,000
2007	T375G	232,000	278,000
2007	T370D	263,000	315,000
2006	T375G	211,000	253,000
2006	T370D	239,000	287,000
Carver 430 Cockpit MY			
1997	T380G	114,000	137,000
1997	T315D	133,000	160,000
1996	T380G	107,000	129,000
1996	T315D	125,000	150,000
1995	T380G	101,000	121,000
1995	T315D	117,000	141,000
Carver 43/47 Motor Yacht			
2009	T385G	******	******
2009	T370D	******	******
2008	T375G	292,000	351,000
2008	T370D	334,000	401,000
2007	T375G	266,000	319,000
2007	T370D	304,000	365,000
2006	T375G	242,000	291,000
2006	T370D	277,000	332,000
Carver 440/445 Aft Cabin			
1999	T450D	164,000	196,000
1998	T320G	147,000	176,000
1998	T420D	152,000	183,000
1997	T320G	135,000	162,000
1997	T420D	141,000	170,000
1996	T320G	124,000	149,000
1996	T420D	132,000	158,000
1995	T320G	114,000	137,000

Year	Power	Retail Low	Retail High
1995	T420D	122,000	147,000
Carver 444 Cockpit MY			
2004	T370 D	210,000	252,000
2003	T370 D	195,000	234,000
2002	T370 D	181,000	218,000
2001	T370 D	169,000	202,000
Carver 450 Voyager			
2004	T450D	299,000	359,000
2003	T450D	278,000	334,000
2002	T450D	259,000	310,000
2001	T450D	240,000	289,000
2000	T450D	224,000	268,000
1999	T450D	208,000	249,000
Carver 455/456 Aft Cabin MY			
2000	T430D	211,000	254,000
1999	T340D	199,000	238,000
1998	T340D	187,000	224,000
1997	T340D	175,000	211,000
1996	T340D	165,000	198,000
Carver 46 Motor Yacht			
2007	T480D	401,000	482,000
2006	T480D	365,000	438,000
2005	T480D	336,000	403,000
2004	T480D	309,000	371,000
2003	T480D	284,000	341,000
2002	T480D	264,000	317,000
2001	T480D	246,000	295,000
Carver 46 Voyager			
2009	T370D	******	******
2008	T370D	******	******
2007	T370D	377,000	433,000
2006	T370D	350,000	403,000
2005	T370D	326,000	374,000
Carver 500/504 Cockpit MY			
2000	T480D	212,000	254,000
1999	T450D	199,000	239,000
1998	T420D	187,000	225,000
1997	T420D	176,000	211,000
1996	T420D	165,000	198,000
Carver 506 MY			
2004	T480D	325,000	390,000
2003	T480D	302,000	363,000
2002	T480D	281,000	337,000
2001	T480D	261,000	314,000
2000	T480D	243,000	292,000
Carver 530 Voyager			
2005	T480D	299,000	359,000
2004	T480D	275,000	330,000
2003	T480D	256,000	307,000
2002	T480D	238,000	285,000
2001	T480D	221,000	265,000
2000	T480D	206,000	247,000
1999	T480D	191,000	229,000
1998	T480D	178,000	213,000
Carver 564 Cockpit MY			
2006	T480D	567,000	680,000
2005	T480D	521,000	626,000
2004	T480D	485,000	582,000
2003	T480D	451,000	541,000

Year	Power	Retail Low	Retail High
2002	T480D	419,000	503,000
Carver 570/56 Voyager Sedan			
2009	T500D	******	******
2008	T500D	******	******
2007	T500D	******	******
2006	T675D	664,000	797,000
2005	T675D	617,000	741,000
2004	T660D	574,000	689,000
2003	T635D	534,000	641,000
2002	T635D	496,000	596,000
2001	T635D	462,000	554,000
Century 2600 Center Console			
2009	T150 O/B	60,000	72,000
2008	T150 O/B	54,000	65,000
2007	T150 O/B	49,000	59,000
2006	T150 O/B	45,000	54,000
2005	T150 O/B	42,000	50,000
2004	T150 O/B	38,000	46,000
2003	T150 O/B	35,000	42,000
2002	T150 O/B	32,000	39,000
2001	T150 O/B	30,000	36,000
2000	T150 O/B	28,000	33,000
1999	T150 O/B	26,000	31,000
1998	T150 O/B	24,000	29,000
1997	T150 O/B	22,000	27,000
1996	T150 U/B	20,000	25,000
Century 2600 Walkaround			
2009	T150 O/B	64,000	76,000
2008	T150 O/B	58,000	69,000
2007	T150 O/B	52,000	63,000
2006	T150 O/B	48,000	58,000
2005	T150 O/B	44,000	53,000
2004	T150 O/B	41,000	49,000
2003	T150 O/B	37,000	45,000
2002	T150 O/B	34,000	41,000
2001	T150 O/B	32,000	38,000
2000	T150 O/B	29,000	35,000
1999	T150 O/B	27,000	33,000
1998	T150 O/B	25,000	31,000
1997	T150 O/B	24,000	28,000
1996	T150 O/B	22,000	26,000
Century 2900 Walkaround			
2004	T250 O/B	52,000	63,000
2003	T250 O/B	49,000	58,000
2002	T250 O/B	45,000	54,000
2001	T250 O/B	42,000	50,000
Century 2900/2901 Center Console			
2008	T250 O/B	75,000	90,000
2007	T250 O/B	68,000	82,000
2006	T250 O/B	62,000	74,000
2005	T250 O/B	57,000	68,000
2004	T250 O/B	52,000	63,000
2003	T250 O/B	48,000	58,000
2002	T250 O/B	44,000	53,000
2001	T250 O/B	41,000	49,000
2000	T250 O/B	37,000	45,000
Century 3000 Center Console			
1999	T250 O/B	30,000	36,000
1998	T250 O/B	28,000	34,000
1997	T250 O/B	26,000	31,000

Year	Power	Retail Low	Retail High
1996	T250 O/B	24,000	29,000
1995	T250 O/B	22,000	27,000
1994	T250 O/B	21,000	25,000
Century 3000 Sport Cabin			
2002	T250 O/B	31,000	38,000
2001	T250 O/B	29,000	35,000
2000	T250 O/B	27,000	33,000
1999	T250 O/B	25,000	30,000
1998	T250 O/B	23,000	28,000
1997	T250 O/B	22,000	26,000
Century 3200 Center Console			
2009	T250 O/B	118,000	141,000
2008	T250 O/B	108,000	130,000
2007	T250 O/B	99,000	119,000
2006	T250 O/B	91,000	110,000
2005	T250 O/B	84,000	101,000
2004	T250 O/B	77,000	93,000
2003	T250 O/B	72,000	86,000
2002	T250 O/B	67,000	80,000
2001	T250 O/B	62,000	75,000
2000	T250 O/B	58,000	69,000
1999	T250 O/B	54,000	64,000
Century 3200 Walkaround			
2007	T250 O/B	104,000	125,000
2006	T250 O/B	95,000	114,000
2005	T250 O/B	87,000	104,000
2004	T250 O/B	80,000	96,000
2003	T250 O/B	74,000	88,000
2002	T250 O/B	68,000	81,000
2001	T250 O/B	62,000	75,000
2000	T250 O/B	57,000	69,000
Chaparral 260 SSi			
2006	320 I/O	30,000	36,000
2005	320 I/O	27,000	33,000
2004	320 I/O	25,000	30,000
2003	320 I/O	23,000	28,000
2002	320 I/O	21,000	26,000
2001	320 I/O	20,000	24,000
Chaparral Signature 260			
2005	260G I/O	27,000	33,000
2004	260G I/O	25,000	30,000
2003	250G I/O	23,000	28,000
2002	250G I/O	21,000	26,000
2001	250G I/O	19,000	23,000
2000	250G I/O	18,000	22,000
1999	250G I/O	17,000	20,000
1998	250G I/O	16,000	19,000
1997	250G I/O	14,000	17,000
1996	250G I/O	13,000	16,000
Chaparral 265 SSi			
2006	300 I/O	27,000	32,000
2005	300 I/O	24,000	29,000
2004	300 I/O	22,000	26,000
2003	300 I/O	20,000	24,000
2002	300 I/O	18,000	22,000
2001	300 I/O	17,000	20,000
Chaparral Signature 26/27/270			
2000	310 I/O	23,000	28,000
1999	310 I/O	21,000	26,000

Year	Power	Retail Low	Retail High
1998	310 I/O	20,000	24,000
1997	310 I/O	19,000	22,000
1996	310 I/O	17,000	21,000
1995	310 I/O	16,000	19,000
1994	310 I/O	15,000	18,000
1993	310 I/O	14,000	17,000
1992	310 I/O	13,000	15,000
Charappal Signature 270			
2009	320 I/O	63,000	75,000
2008	320 I/O	57,000	69,000
2007	320 I/O	53,000	63,000
Chaparral 275 SSi			
2009	375 I/O	59,000	70,000
2008	300 I/O	54,000	65,000
2007	300 I/O	49,000	59,000
2006	300 I/O	46,000	55,000
Chaparral 276 SSX			
2009	375 I/O	52,000	62,000
2008	300 I/O	47,000	56,000
2007	300 I/O	43,000	51,000
2006	300 I/O	39,000	47,000
Chaparral Signature 270/280			
2009	T270 I/O	81,000	97,000
2008	T270 I/O	73,000	88,000
2007	T270 I/O	67,000	80,000
2006	T270 I/O	61,000	74,000
2005	T260 I/O	56,000	68,000
2004	T260 I/O	52,000	62,000
2003	T260 I/O	48,000	57,000
Chaparral 280 SSi			
2006	T260	44,000	53,000
2006	S375	40,000	49,000
2005	T260	40,000	48,000
2005	S375	37,000	44,000
2004	T260	37,000	44,000
2004	S375	34,000	41,000
2003	T260	34,000	41,000
2003	S375	31,000	37,000
2002	T260	31,000	37,000
2002	S320	28,000	34,000
2001	T260	28,000	34,000
2001	S320	26,000	31,000
2000	T260	26,000	32,000
2000	S320	24,000	29,000
1999	T260	25,000	30,000
1999	S320	23,000	27,000
Chaparral 285 SSi			
2006	T260	49,000	59,000
2005	T260	45,000	54,000
2004	T260	41,000	49,000
2003	T260	38,000	45,000
2002	T260	35,000	42,000
2001	T260	32,000	38,000
2000	T280	30,000	36,000
1999	T280	27,000	33,000
Chaparral 280/290 Signature			
2009	T220	94,000	112,000
2008	T220	85,000	102,000
2007	T220	77,000	93,000
2006	T220	70,000	85,000
2005	T220	64,000	77,000
2004	T220	58,000	70,000
2003	T220	53,000	64,000
2002	T190	48,000	58,000
2001	T190	44,000	53,000
Charappal 28/29 Signature			
2000	T190	36,000	43,000
1999	T190	34,000	41,000
1998	T190	32,000	38,000
1997	T190	29,000	35,000
1996	T190	27,000	33,000
1995	T190	25,000	30,000
Chaparral Signature 300			
2003	T260	47,000	56,000
2002	T260	44,000	52,000
2001	T260	41,000	49,000
2000	T260	38,000	45,000
1999	T260	35,000	42,000
1998	T260	32,000	39,000
Chaparral Signature 30/31			
1997	T260	32,000	38,000
1996	T260	29,000	35,000
1995	T260	27,000	32,000
Chaparral Signarure 310			
2009	T300	119,000	142,000
2008	T300	108,000	129,000
2007	T300	98,000	118,000
2006	T300	89,000	107,000
2005	T300	81,000	97,000
2004	T280	74,000	89,000
Chaparral Signature 330			
2009	T300	144,000	172,000
2008	T320	131,000	157,000
2007	T320	119,000	143,000
2006	T320	108,000	130,000
2005	T300	99,000	119,000
2004	T300	91,000	110,000
2003	T300	84,000	101,000
Chaparral Signature 350			
2009	T320	181,000	217,000
2008	T320	164,000	197,000
2007	T320	149,000	179,000
2006	T320	136,000	163,000
2005	T300	124,000	148,000
2004	T300	114,000	137,000
2003	T300	105,000	126,000
2002	T300	96,000	115,000
2001	T300	88,000	106,000
Chris Craft 258/268/27 Concept			
1996	310 I/O	10,000	12,000
1995	310 I/O	9,000	11,000
Chris Craft 272/282/30 Crowne			
1997	T215	21,000	26,000
1996	T215	20,000	24,000
1995	T215	18,000	22,000
Chris Craft 28 Corsair			
2009	T280	******	******
2008	T280	95,000	114,000
2007	T320	88,000	105,000
2006	T320	81,000	97,000
2005	T320	74,000	89,000
2004	T375	68,000	82,000
2003	T375	63,000	75,000
Chris Craft 28 Launch			
2009	T320	******	******
2008	T320	66,000	79,000
2007	T320	60,000	72,000
2006	T320	55,000	67,000
2005	T320	51,000	61,000
2004	T375	47,000	56,000
2003	T375	43,000	52,000
Chris Craft 300/308 EC			
2003	T270G	48,000	57,000
2002	T270G	43,000	52,000
2001	T250G	39,000	47,000
2000	T250G	36,000	43,000
1999	T250G	32,000	39,000
Chris Craft 320/328 EC			
2003	T270G	53,000	63,000
2002	T270G	48,000	58,000
2001	T280G	44,000	52,000
2000	T280G	40,000	48,000
1999	T280G	36,000	43,000
1998	T280G	33,000	40,000
1997	T280G	30,000	37,000
Chris Craft 33 Corsair			
2009	T420G	******	******
2008	T420G	195,000	234,000
2007	T420G	179,000	215,000
2006	T420G	165,000	198,000
Chris Craft 33 Crowne			
1997	T250G I/O	23,000	27,000
1996	T250G I/O	21,000	25,000
1995	T250G I/O	19,000	23,000
Chris Craft 34 Crowne			
1997	T320G I/B	23,000	28,000
1996	T320G I/B	21,000	25,000
1995	T300G I/B	19,000	23,000
Chris Craft 36 Roamer			
2005	T375G	122,000	146,000
2004	T375G	112,000	134,000
2003	T375G	103,000	124,000
Chris Craft 380 Continental			
1997	T380G	57,000	68,000
1996	T330G	52,000	63,000
1995	T330G	48,000	58,000
Chris Craft 40 Roamer			
2008	T370D	******	******
2007	T370D	******	******
2006	T370D	244,000	293,000
2005	480D	224,000	269,000
2004	480D	206,000	248,000
2003	480D	190,000	228,000
Cobia 250/260/270 Walkaround			
2007	T200 O/B	45,000	55,000
2006	T200 O/B	41,000	49,000

Year	Power	Retail Low	Retail High
2005	T200 O/B	37,000	44,000
2004	T200 O/B	33,000	40,000
2003	T200 O/B	30,000	36,000
2002	T200 O/B	27,000	32,000
2001	T200 O/B	24,000	29,000
2000	T200 O/B	22,000	27,000
1999	T200 O/B	20,000	24,000
1998	T200 O/B	18,000	22,000
1997	T200 O/B	17,000	20,000

Cobia 254/264/274 CC

Year	Power	Retail Low	Retail High
2002	T200 O/B	23,000	28,000
2001	T200 O/B	21,000	25,000
2000	T200 O/B	19,000	23,000
1999	T200 O/B	17,000	21,000
1998	T200 O/B	16,000	19,000
1997	T200 O/B	14,000	17,000

Cobia 274 Center Console

Year	Power	Retail Low	Retail High
2007	T200 O/B	39,000	47,000
2006	T200 O/B	35,000	42,000
2005	T200 O/B	31,000	38,000
2004	T200 O/B	28,000	34,000
2003	T200 O/B	25,000	31,000

Cobia 312 Sport Cabin

Year	Power	Retail Low	Retail High
2007	T250 O/B	67,000	80,000
2006	T250 O/B	61,000	73,000
2005	T250 O/B	55,000	67,000
2004	T250 O/B	50,000	60,000
2003	T250 O/B	46,000	55,000

Cobia 314 Center Console

Year	Power	Retail Low	Retail High
2007	T250 O/B	64,000	77,000
2006	T250 O/B	58,000	70,000
2005	T250 O/B	52,000	63,000
2004	T250 O/B	47,000	56,000
2004	T250 O/B	42,000	51,000
2003	T250 O/B	38,000	45,000

Contender 27 Open

Year	Power	Retail Low	Retail High
2007	T200 O/B	******	******
2006	T200 O/B	******	******
2005	T200 O/B	******	******
2004	T200 O/B	64,000	77,000
2003	T200 O/B	59,000	71,000
2002	T200 O/B	55,000	66,000
2001	T200 O/B	51,000	61,000
2000	T200 O/B	47,000	57,000
1999	T200 O/B	44,000	53,000
1998	T200 O/B	41,000	49,000
1997	T200 O/B	38,000	46,000
1996	T200 O/B	35,000	42,000
1995	T200 O/B	33,000	39,000

Contender 31 Open

Year	Power	Retail Low	Retail High
2007	T225 O/B	100,000	120,000
2006	T225 O/B	91,000	109,000
2005	T225 O/B	83,000	99,000
2004	T225 O/B	75,000	90,000
2003	T225 O/B	68,000	82,000
2002	T225 O/B	62,000	75,000
2001	T225 O/B	57,000	68,000
2000	T225 O/B	52,000	63,000
1999	T225 O/B	48,000	57,000
1998	T225 O/B	44,000	53,000
1997	T225 O/B	40,000	49,000
1996	T225 O/B	37,000	45,000
1995	T225 O/B	34,000	41,000

Crownline 262 CR

Year	Power	Retail Low	Retail High
2003	320G I/O	23,000	27,000
2002	320G I/O	21,000	25,000
2001	320G I/O	19,000	23,000

Crownline 266 Bowrider

Year	Power	Retail Low	Retail High
2002	320 I/O	21,000	25,000
2001	320 I/O	19,000	23,000
2000	310 I/O	17,000	21,000
1999	310 I/O	16,000	19,000
1998	310 I/O	14,000	17,000
1997	300 I/O	13,000	16,000
1996	300 I/O	12,000	15,000
1995	300 I/O	11,000	13,000
1994	300 I/O	10,000	12,000

Crownline 266 CCR

Year	Power	Retail Low	Retail High
2002	320G I/O	22,000	26,000
2001	320G I/O	20,000	24,000
2000	310G I/O	18,000	21,000
1999	310G I/O	16,000	19,000
1998	310G I/O	15,000	18,000
1997	300G I/O	13,000	16,000

Crownline 268 CR

Year	Power	Retail Low	Retail High
2000	310 I/O	17,000	21,000
1999	310 I/O	16,000	19,000
1998	310 I/O	14,000	17,000

Crownline 270 Bowrider

Year	Power	Retail Low	Retail High
2009	320 I/O	49,000	58,000
2008	320 I/O	44,000	53,000
2007	320 I/O	40,000	48,000
2006	320 I/O	36,000	44,000
2005	310 I/O	33,000	40,000
2004	310 I/O	31,000	37,000

Crownline 270 CR

Year	Power	Retail Low	Retail High
2009	300 I/O	56,000	67,000
2008	300 I/O	50,000	61,000
2007	300 I/O	46,000	55,000
2006	300 I/O	42,000	50,000
2005	300 I/O	38,000	46,000
2004	300 I/O	35,000	42,000

Crownline 275 CCR

Year	Power	Retail Low	Retail High
2009	320 I/O	53,000	63,000
2008	320 I/O	48,000	57,000
2007	320 I/O	43,000	52,000
2006	320 I/O	40,000	48,000
2005	320 I/O	37,000	44,000

Crownline 288 Bowrider

Year	Power	Retail Low	Retail High
2004	T250G	31,000	37,000
2003	T250G	28,000	34,000
2002	T250G	26,000	31,000
2001	T250G	23,000	28,000

Crownline 290 CR

Year	Power	Retail Low	Retail High
2004	T250G	37,000	45,000
2003	T250G	34,000	41,000
2002	T250G	31,000	37,000
2001	T250G	28,000	34,000
2000	T250G	25,000	31,000
1999	T250G	23,000	28,000

Crownline 315 SCR

Year	Power	Retail Low	Retail High
2009	T300G	107,000	128,000
2008	T300G	97,000	116,000
2007	T300G	88,000	106,000

Crownline 320 LS

Year	Power	Retail Low	Retail High
2009	T300G	88,000	105,000
2008	T300G	80,000	96,000
2007	T300G	72,000	87,000
2006	T300G	66,000	79,000

Crownline 330 CR

Year	Power	Retail Low	Retail High
2000	T310G	55,000	66,000
1999	T310G	50,000	60,000
1998	T310G	46,000	55,000
1997	T310G	42,000	50,000
1996	T310G	38,000	45,000

Crownline 340 CR

Year	Power	Retail Low	Retail High
2009	T300G	183,000	219,000
2008	T300G	166,000	199,000
2007	T300G	151,000	181,000

Cruisers 2670 Rogue

Year	Power	Retail Low	Retail High
1997	T205G	16,000	19,000
1996	T205G	15,000	18,000
1995	T180G	13,000	16,000
1994	T180G	12,000	15,000
1993	T180G	12,000	14,000
1992	T180G	11,000	13,000

Cruisers 2870 Exp; 280 CXi

Year	Power	Retail Low	Retail High
2007	T220G	51,000	61,000
2006	T220G	46,000	56,000
2005	T220G	42,000	50,000
2004	T220G	38,000	46,000
2003	T220G	35,000	42,000
2002	T220G	32,000	38,000
2001	T220G	29,000	34,000
2000	T220G	26,000	32,000
1999	T220G	24,000	29,000
1998	T220G	22,000	27,000

Cruisers 300 Cxi/300 Express

Year	Power	Retail Low	Retail High
2009	T225 I/O	84,000	100,000
2008	T225 I/O	76,000	91,000
2007	T225 I/O	69,000	83,000
2006	T225 I/O	63,000	75,000
2005	T220G	57,000	69,000

Cruisers 300/310 Express

Year	Power	Retail Low	Retail High
2007	T270G	84,000	101,000
2006	T270G	76,000	92,000
2005	T270G	70,000	84,000

Cruisers 3075 Express

Year	Power	Retail Low	Retail High
2003	T260G	49,000	59,000
2002	T260G	44,000	53,000
2001	T260G	40,000	49,000
2000	T260G	37,000	44,000
1999	T260G	33,000	40,000
1998	T260G	30,000	36,000
1997	T260G	28,000	33,000

Cruisers 3020/3120 Aria

Year	Power	Retail Low	Retail High
1997	T230G	29,000	35,000

Year	Power	Retail Low	Retail High
1996	T230G	27,000	32,000
1995	T230G	25,000	30,000

Cruisers 3175 Rogue

Year	Power	Retail Low	Retail High
1998	T260G	35,000	42,000
1997	T260G	32,000	39,000
1996	T260G	30,000	36,000
1995	T260G	27,000	33,000

Cruisers 320 Express

Year	Power	Retail Low	Retail High
2006	T320G	73,000	87,000
2005	T320G	66,000	79,000
2004	T320G	60,000	72,000
2003	T320G	55,000	66,000
2002	T320G	50,000	60,000

Cruisers 330 Express

Year	Power	Retail Low	Retail High
2009	T320G	162,000	187,000
2008	T375G	147,000	171,000

Cruisers 3375 Esprit

Year	Power	Retail Low	Retail High
2000	T300G	62,000	74,000
1999	T300G	56,000	67,000
1998	T300G	51,000	61,000
1997	T300G	46,000	56,000
1996	T300G	42,000	51,000

Cruisers 340 Express

Year	Power	Retail Low	Retail High
2007	T370G VD	123,000	145,000
2007	T375G I/O	131,000	155,000
2006	T370G VD	112,000	132,000
2006	T320G I/O	119,000	141,000
2005	T320G VD	102,000	120,000
2005	T320G I/O	109,000	128,000
2004	T320G VD	93,000	109,000
2004	T320G I/O	99,000	117,000
2003	T320G VD	84,000	100,000
2003	T320G I/O	90,000	106,000
2002	T320G VD	77,000	91,000
2002	T320G I/O	82,000	96,000
2001	T320G VD	70,000	82,000
2001	T320G I/O	74,000	88,000

Cruisers 3570/3575 Esprit; 3572

Year	Power	Retail Low	Retail High
2002	T370G	106,000	126,000
2001	T310G	97,000	115,000
2000	T310G	88,000	104,000
1999	T310G	79,000	93,000
1998	T310G	71,000	84,000
1997	T310G	64,000	75,000
1996	T310G	58,000	69,000
1995	T310G	53,000	62,000

Cruisers 3580/3585 Flybridge

Year	Power	Retail Low	Retail High
1999	T320G	69,000	81,000
1998	T320G	63,000	74,000
1997	T320G	57,000	67,000
1996	T320G	52,000	61,000

Cruisers 360 Express

Year	Power	Retail Low	Retail High
2009	T375G	211,000	246,000
2008	T375G	192,000	224,000

Cruisers 3670/3675/3775 Esprit

Year	Power	Retail Low	Retail High
1996	T310G	60,000	72,000
1995	T310G	55,000	66,000

Cruisers 370 Express

Year	Power	Retail Low	Retail High
2007	T375G	183,000	215,000
2006	T375G	167,000	195,000
2005	T370G	152,000	178,000
2004	T370G	138,000	162,000
2003	T370G	126,000	147,000
2002	T370G	114,000	134,000
2001	T370G	104,000	122,000
2000	T370G	95,000	111,000

Cruisers 3650/375 Motor Yacht

Year	Power	Retail Low	Retail High
2005	T-Gas	163,000	191,000
2005	T370D	203,000	237,000
2004	T-Gas	148,000	174,000
2004	T370D	185,000	216,000
2003	T-Gas	135,000	158,000
2003	T370D	168,000	196,000
2002	T-Gas	123,000	144,000
2002	T370D	153,000	179,000
2001	T-Gas	112,000	131,000
2001	T370D	139,000	163,000
2000	T-Gas	103,000	120,000
2000	T370D	128,000	150,000
1999	T-Gas	95,000	111,000
1999	T370D	117,000	138,000
1998	T-Gas	87,000	102,000
1998	T-Diesel	108,000	127,000
1997	T-Gas	80,000	94,000
1997	T-Diesel	99,000	116,000
1996	T-Gas	73,000	86,000
1996	T-Diesel	91,000	107,000
1995	T-Gas	68,000	79,000
1995	T-Diesel	84,000	98,000

Cruisers 3870 Express

Year	Power	Retail Low	Retail High
2003	T370G	141,000	165,000
2002	T370G	128,000	150,000
2001	T370G	117,000	137,000
2000	T370G	106,000	124,000
1999	T380G	97,000	113,000
1998	T380G	88,000	103,000
1997	T380G	80,000	94,000

Cruisers 3850/3950 Aft Cabin MY

Year	Power	Retail Low	Retail High
1997	T310G	104,000	122,000
1997	T300D	130,000	152,000
1996	T310G	96,000	112,000
1996	T300D	120,000	140,000
1995	T310G	88,000	103,000
1995	T300D	110,000	129,000

Cruisers 390 Sports Coupe

Year	Power	Retail Low	Retail High
2009	T375G	******	******
2008	T375G	280,000	327,000
2007	T375G	254,000	298,000

Cruisers 385/395 Motor Yacht

Year	Power	Retail Low	Retail High
2008	T375G	289,000	338,000
2007	T370G	265,000	311,000
2006	T370G	244,000	286,000

Cruisers 3970/400/420 Express

Year	Power	Retail Low	Retail High
2009	T370G	******	******
2009	T435D	******	******
2008	T375G	******	******
2008	T435D	******	******

Year	Power	Retail Low	Retail High
2007	T375G	236,000	271,000
2007	T435D	274,000	315,000
2006	T375G	214,000	247,000
2006	T370D	249,000	287,000
2005	T375G	195,000	224,000
2005	T370D	227,000	261,000
2004	T375G	179,000	206,000
2004	T370D	209,000	240,000
2003	T375G	165,000	190,000
2003	T370D	192,000	221,000

Cruisers 405/415 Express MY

Year	Power	Retail Low	Retail High
2009	T435D	******	******
2008	T435D	******	******
2007	T435D	288,000	331,000
2006	T370D	264,000	304,000
2005	T370D	243,000	280,000
2004	T370D	224,000	257,000
2003	T370D	206,000	237,000

Cruisers 4270 Express

Year	Power	Retail Low	Retail High
2003	T440D	213,000	245,000
2002	T440D	194,000	223,000
2001	T420D	176,000	203,000
2000	T420D	160,000	184,000
1999	T420D	146,000	168,000
1998	T420D	133,000	153,000
1997	T420D	121,000	139,000

Cruisers 4285 Express Bridge

Year	Power	Retail Low	Retail High
1995	T375D	88,000	102,000

Cruisers 440 Express

Year	Power	Retail Low	Retail High
2005	T440D	262,000	301,000
2004	T440D	241,000	277,000
2003	T440D	222,000	255,000

Cruisers 4450 Express MY

Year	Power	Retail Low	Retail High
2003	T480D	269,000	309,000
2002	T480D	245,000	282,000
2001	T480D	223,000	256,000
2000	T480D	203,000	233,000

Cruisers 447 Sport Sedan

Year	Power	Retail Low	Retail High
2009	T435D	******	******
2008	T435D	372,000	428,000
2008	T440D	338,000	389,000

Cruisers 455 Express MY

Year	Power	Retail Low	Retail High
2009	T480D	******	******
2008	T480D	479,000	551,000
2007	T480D	436,000	501,000
2006	T480D	396,000	456,000
2005	T480D	361,000	415,000
2004	T480D	328,000	377,000

Cruisers 497 Sport Sedan

Year	Power	Retail Low	Retail High
2007	T575D	493,000	567,000
2006	T575D	448,000	515,000

Cruisers 5000 Sedan Sport

Year	Power	Retail Low	Retail High
2003	T710D	356,000	409,000
2002	T660D	324,000	372,000
2001	T660D	295,000	339,000
2000	T660D	268,000	308,000
1999	T660D	244,000	280,000
1998	T625D	222,000	255,000

See Page 529 For Price Adjustments

Year	Power	Retail Low	Retail High
Cruisers 520 Express			
2009	T715D	******	******
2008	T715D	604,000	695,000
2007	T715D	550,000	632,000
2006	T715D	500,000	575,000
Cruisers 540/560 Express			
2009	T715D	******	******
2008	T715D	751,000	864,000
2007	T715D	683,000	786,000
2006	T715D	622,000	715,000
2005	T715D	566,000	651,000
2004	T715D	515,000	592,000
2003	T800D	468,000	539,000
2002	T800D	426,000	490,000
2001	T800D	388,000	446,000
DeFever 44 Trawler			
2004	T-Diesel	256,000	294,000
2003	T-Diesel	238,000	273,000
2002	T-Diesel	221,000	254,000
2001	T-Diesel	205,000	236,000
2000	T135D	195,000	225,000
1999	T135D	185,000	213,000
1998	T135D	176,000	203,000
1997	T135D	167,000	192,000
1996	T135D	159,000	183,000
1995	T135D	153,000	175,000
DeFever 49 Cockpit MY			
2007	T150D	376,000	432,000
2006	T150D	350,000	402,000
2005	T150D	325,000	374,000
2004	T150D	302,000	348,000
2003	T150D	281,000	323,000
2002	T150D	261,000	301,000
2001	T150D	246,000	283,000
2000	T150D	231,000	266,000
1999	T150D	217,000	250,000
1998	T135D	204,000	235,000
1997	T135D	194,000	223,000
1996	T135D	184,000	212,000
1995	T135D	175,000	201,000
1994	T135D	166,000	191,000
DeFever 49 PH (1977-2004)			
2004	T135D	******	******
2003	T135D	******	******
2002	T135D	310,000	356,000
2001	T135D	291,000	335,000
2000	T135D	274,000	315,000
1999	T135D	257,000	296,000
1998	T135D	242,000	278,000
1997	T135D	230,000	264,000
1996	T135D	218,000	251,000
1995	T135D	207,000	238,000
Donzi 26/28 ZF Open			
2003	T200 O/B	32,000	38,000
2002	T200 O/B	28,000	34,000
2001	T200 O/B	26,000	31,000
2000	T200 O/B	23,000	28,000
1999	T200 O/B	21,000	25,000

Year	Power	Retail Low	Retail High
Donzi 275 Express			
2000	310 I/O	20,000	24,000
1999	310 I/O	18,000	21,000
1998	310 I/O	16,000	19,000
1997	310 I/O	14,000	17,000
1996	300 I/O	13,000	15,000
1995	300 I/O	11,000	14,000
Donzi 29 ZF Open			
2009	T225 O/B	******	******
2008	T225 O/B	67,000	80,000
2007	T225 O/B	60,000	72,000
2006	T225 O/B	54,000	65,000
2005	T225 O/B	49,000	58,000
2004	T225 O/B	44,000	53,000
2003	T225 O/B	39,000	47,000
Donzi 32 ZF			
2007	T250 O/B	79,000	95,000
2006	T250 O/B	71,000	86,000
2005	T250 O/B	64,000	77,000
2004	T250 O/B	58,000	69,000
2003	T250 O/B	52,000	62,000
2002	T250 O/B	47,000	56,000
2001	T250 O/B	42,000	51,000
2000	T250 O/B	39,000	46,000
Donzi 3250 Express			
2000	T310 I/O	53,000	63,000
1999	T310 I/O	48,000	57,000
1998	T300 I/O	43,000	52,000
1997	T300 I/O	39,000	47,000
1996	T300 I/O	36,000	43,000
Donzi 35 ZF Open			
2009	T275 O/B	******	******
2008	T275 O/B	******	******
2007	T275 O/B	92,000	110,000
2006	T275 O/B	83,000	99,000
2005	T275 O/B	74,000	89,000
2004	T275 O/B	67,000	80,000
2003	T275 O/B	60,000	72,000
2002	T225 O/B	54,000	65,000
2001	T225 O/B	49,000	59,000
2000	T225 O/B	45,000	54,000
1999	T225 O/B	41,000	49,000
1998	T225 O/B	37,000	44,000
Donzi 38 ZF Cuddy			
2009	3/250	******	******
2008	3/250	140,000	168,000
2007	3/250	127,000	153,000
2006	3/250	116,000	139,000
2005	3/250	105,000	126,000
Donzi 38 ZFX			
2009	3/250	******	******
2008	3/250	143,000	171,000
2007	3/250	128,000	154,000
2006	3/250	116,000	139,000
Donzi 38 ZSF			
2009	3/250	******	******
2008	3/250	168,000	201,000
2007	3/250	151,000	181,000
2006	3/250	136,000	163,000

Year	Power	Retail Low	Retail High
2005	3/250	122,000	147,000
2004	3/250	110,000	132,000
Dorado 30 Center Console			
2006	S-Diesel	61,000	73,000
2005	S-Diesel	55,000	66,000
2004	S-Diesel	50,000	60,000
2004	S-Diesel	46,000	55,000
2002	S-Diesel	41,000	50,000
2001	S-Diesel	38,000	45,000
2000	S-Diesel	35,000	42,000
1999	S-Diesel	32,000	38,000
1998	S-Diesel	29,000	35,000
1997	S-Diesel	27,000	32,000
1996	S-Diesel	25,000	30,000
1995	S-Diesel	23,000	27,000
Eagle 40 PH Trawler			
2008	S/Diesel	223,000	257,000
2007	S/Diesel	210,000	241,000
2006	S/Diesel	197,000	227,000
2005	S/Diesel	185,000	213,000
2004	S/Diesel	174,000	200,000
2003	S/Diesel	164,000	188,000
2002	S/Diesel	154,000	177,000
2001	S/Diesel	145,000	166,000
2000	S/Diesel	137,000	158,000
1999	S/Diesel	130,000	150,000
1998	S/Diesel	124,000	143,000
1997	S/Diesel	118,000	135,000
1996	S/Diesel	112,000	129,000
1995	S/Diesel	106,000	122,000
Edgewater 260 Center Console			
2001	T150 O/B	29,000	35,000
2000	T150 O/B	26,000	32,000
1999	T150 O/B	24,000	29,000
1998	T150 O/B	22,000	26,000
1997	T150 O/B	20,000	24,000
1996	T150 O/B	18,000	21,000
Edgewater 265 Express			
2009	T225 O/B	105,000	126,000
2008	T225 O/B	95,000	114,000
2007	T225 O/B	86,000	104,000
2006	T225 O/B	79,000	94,000
2005	T225 O/B	72,000	87,000
2004	T225 O/B	66,000	80,000
2003	T225 O/B	61,000	73,000
2002	T225 O/B	56,000	68,000
Edgewater 265/268 Center Console			
2009	T225 O/B	95,000	114,000
2008	T225 O/B	86,000	103,000
2007	T225 O/B	78,000	94,000
2006	T225 O/B	71,000	85,000
2005	T225 O/B	65,000	78,000
2004	T225 O/B	59,000	71,000
2003	T225 O/B	55,000	66,000
2002	T225 O/B	50,000	60,000
Edgewater 318 Center Console			
2009	T250 O/B	124,000	148,000
2008	T250 O/B	114,000	136,000
2007	T250 O/B	104,000	125,000
2006	T250 O/B	96,000	115,000

Year	Power	Retail Low	Retail High
Egg Harbor 34 Convertible			
1996	T320G	74,000	89,000
1996	T350D	93,000	111,000
1995	T320G	68,000	82,000
1995	T350D	85,000	102,000
Egg Harbor 35 Convertible			
1998	T320G	89,000	107,000
1998	T350D	112,000	134,000
1997	T320G	81,000	97,000
1997	T350D	102,000	122,000
Egg Harbor 35 Predator			
2009	T450D	******	******
2008	T450D	******	******
2007	T440D	******	******
2006	T440D	230,000	277,000
2005	T440D	210,000	252,000
2004	T440D	191,000	229,000
2003	T440D	173,000	208,000
2002	T440D	******	******
2001	T440D	******	******
2000	T440D	******	******
Egg Harbor 37 Sport Yacht			
2009	T440D	******	******
2008	T440D	******	******
2007	T440D	******	******
2006	T440D	271,000	317,000
2005	T440D	246,000	288,000
2004	T440D	224,000	262,000
2003	T440D	204,000	239,000
2002	T420D	186,000	217,000
2001	T420D	169,000	198,000
Egg Harbor 38 Conv.			
1997	T-Gas	119,000	140,000
1997	T420D	151,000	177,000
1996	T-Gas	108,000	127,000
1996	T420D	138,000	161,000
1995	T-Gas	99,000	115,000
1995	T420D	125,000	147,000
Egg Harbor 42 Conv.			
1997	420D	175,000	203,000
1996	420D	161,000	186,000
1995	420D	148,000	171,000
Egg Harbor 42 Sport Yacht			
2003	660D	358,000	415,000
2002	660D	325,000	378,000
2001	660D	296,000	344,000
Egg Harbor 43 Sport Yacht			
2009	715D	******	******
2008	715D	******	******
2007	715D	******	******
2006	715D	438,000	504,000
2005	700D	399,000	459,000
2004	700D	363,000	418,000
Egg Harbor 52 Sport Yacht			
2005	800D	******	******
2004	800D	******	******
2003	800D	528,000	607,000
2002	760D	485,000	558,000
2001	760D	446,000	513,000
2000	760D	411,000	472,000
1999	760D	378,000	435,000
1998	760D	348,000	400,000
1997	760D	320,000	368,000
Egg Harbor 58 Convertible			
1997	900D	519,000	597,000
1996	900D	477,000	549,000
1995	900D	439,000	505,000
Everglades 260/270 Center Console			
2009	T250 O/B	84,000	100,000
2008	T250 O/B	76,000	91,000
2007	T250 O/B	69,000	83,000
2006	T250 O/B	63,000	75,000
Everglades 290 Center Console			
2009	T250 O/B	92,000	110,000
2008	T250 O/B	83,000	100,000
2007	T250 O/B	76,000	91,000
2006	T250 O/B	69,000	83,000
2005	T250 O/B	63,000	75,000
Everglades 350 Center Console			
2009	3/250 O/B	******	******
2008	3/250 O/B	142,000	166,000
2007	3/250 O/B	129,000	151,000
Fairline 40 Targa			
2007	310D	220,000	253,000
2006	310D	202,000	233,000
2005	310D	186,000	214,000
2004	310D	171,000	197,000
2003	310D	157,000	181,000
2002	310D	145,000	167,000
2001	260D	133,000	153,000
2000	260D	122,000	141,000
Fairline 43 Phantom			
2004	480D	357,000	410,000
2003	480D	328,000	377,000
2002	480D	302,000	347,000
2001	480D	278,000	319,000
2000	480D	255,000	294,000
Fairline 43 Targa			
2004	480D	230,000	264,000
2003	480D	211,000	243,000
2002	480D	194,000	223,000
2001	480D	179,000	205,000
2000	480D	164,000	189,000
1999	480D	151,000	174,000
1998	480D	139,000	160,000
Fairline 46 Phantom			
2005	500D	399,000	458,000
2004	480D	367,000	422,000
2003	480D	337,000	388,000
2002	480D	310,000	357,000
2001	480D	285,000	328,000
2000	480D	262,000	302,000
1999	480D	241,000	278,000
Fairline 48 Targa			
2002	430D	273,000	314,000
2001	430D	254,000	292,000
2000	420D	236,000	272,000
1999	420D	220,000	253,000
1998	420D	215,000	247,000
Fairline 50 Phantom			
2006	T675D	******	******
2005	T675D	******	******
2004	T675D	488,000	561,000
2003	T675D	453,000	521,000
2002	T675D	422,000	485,000
Fairline 52 Squadron			
2002	T700D	339,000	389,000
2001	T600D	315,000	362,000
2000	T600D	293,000	337,000
1999	T600D	272,000	313,000
1998	T600D	253,000	291,000
Fairline 52 Targa			
2009	T800D	******	******
2008	T800D	******	******
2007	T800D	******	******
2006	T715D	552,000	634,000
2005	T715D	507,000	584,000
2004	T715D	467,000	537,000
2003	T715D	429,000	494,000
Fairline 55 Squadron			
2004	T715D	579,000	666,000
2003	T715D	538,000	619,000
2002	T700D	501,000	576,000
2001	T660D	466,000	536,000
2000	T660D	438,000	503,000
1999	T660D	411,000	473,000
1998	T660D	387,000	445,000
1997	T660D	363,000	418,000
1996	T660D	342,000	393,000
Fairline 58 Squadron			
2008	T715D	******	******
2007	T715D	******	******
2006	T800D	******	******
2005	T800D	717,000	825,000
2004	T800D	667,000	767,000
2003	T800D	620,000	713,000
2002	T700D	577,000	663,000
2001	T660D	536,000	617,000
Fairline 59 Squadron			
1999	T650D	375,000	431,000
1998	T650D	348,000	401,000
1997	T650D	324,000	372,000
1996	T650D	301,000	346,000
Fairline 62 Squadron			
2002	T1050D	650,000	748,000
2001	T1050D	611,000	703,000
2000	T1050D	575,000	661,000
1999	T1050D	540,000	621,000
Fairline 65 Squadron			
2003	T1400D	******	******
2002	T1400D	916,000	1,054,000
2001	T1400D	852,000	980,000
2000	T1400D	792,000	911,000
1999	T1000D	745,000	857,000
1998	T1000D	700,000	805,000
1997	T1000D	658,000	757,000
1996	T1000D	619,000	711,000

Year	Power	Retail Low	Retail High
1995	T1000D	581,000	669,000
Fleming 55 Pilothouse			
2009	T450D	******	******
2008	T450D	******	******
2007	T450D	******	******
2006	T450D	******	******
2005	T450D	1,092,000	1,245,000
2004	T450D	1,026,000	1,170,000
2003	T450D	965,000	1,100,000
2002	T450D	907,000	1,034,000
2001	T450D	852,000	972,000
2000	T435D	801,000	914,000
1999	T435D	753,000	859,000
1998	T435D	715,000	816,000
1997	T435D	680,000	775,000
1996	T435D	646,000	736,000
1995	T-Diesel	613,000	699,000
Formula 260 Bowrider			
2009	300 I/O	52,000	62,000
2006	300 I/O	47,000	56,000
2007	300 I/O	43,000	51,000
2006	300 I/O	39,000	47,000
2005	300 I/O	36,000	43,000
2004	300 I/O	33,000	40,000
2003	300 I/O	30,000	37,000
2002	300 I/O	28,000	34,000
2001	300 I/O	26,000	32,000
2000	300 I/O	24,000	29,000
1999	300 I/O	23,000	27,000
Formula 260 Sun Sport			
2009	300 I/O	49,000	58,000
2008	300 I/O	44,000	53,000
2007	300 I/O	40,000	48,000
2006	300 I/O	37,000	44,000
2005	300 I/O	34,000	41,000
2004	300 I/O	31,000	37,000
2003	300 I/O	29,000	34,000
2002	300 I/O	27,000	32,000
2001	300 I/O	25,000	30,000
2000	300 I/O	23,000	28,000
1999	300 I/O	21,000	26,000
Formula 27 PC			
2009	T320G	98,000	117,000
2008	T280G	89,000	107,000
2007	T280G	81,000	97,000
2006	T280G	74,000	89,000
2005	T280G	68,000	82,000
2004	T260G	63,000	75,000
2003	T260G	58,000	69,000
2002	T260G	53,000	64,000
2001	T260G	49,000	59,000
2000	T260G	45,000	54,000
1999	T260G	41,000	49,000
1998	T260G	38,000	46,000
1997	T250G	36,000	43,000
1996	T250G	33,000	40,000
1995	T250G	31,000	37,000
Formula 280 Bowrider			
2008	T260	67,000	81,000
2008	S375	62,000	75,000

Year	Power	Retail Low	Retail High
2007	T260	61,000	73,000
2007	S375	56,000	67,000
2006	T260	55,000	66,000
2006	S375	50,000	60,000
2005	T260	49,000	59,000
2005	S375	45,000	54,000
2004	T260	44,000	53,000
2004	S375	41,000	49,000
2003	T260	40,000	48,000
2003	S375	37,000	44,000
2002	T260	36,000	43,000
2002	S310	33,000	40,000
2001	T260	33,000	39,000
2001	S310	30,000	36,000
2000	T260	30,000	36,000
2000	S310	27,000	33,000
1999	T260	27,000	33,000
1999	S310	25,000	30,000
1998	T260	25,000	30,000
1998	S310	23,000	27,000
Formula 280 Sun Sport			
2008	T260G	77,000	93,000
2007	T260G	70,000	85,000
2006	T260G	64,000	77,000
2005	T260G	58,000	70,000
2004	T260G	53,000	64,000
2003	T260G	48,000	58,000
2002	T260G	44,000	53,000
2001	T260G	40,000	48,000
2000	T260G	37,000	44,000
1999	T260G	34,000	40,000
1998	T260G	31,000	37,000
1997	T250G	28,000	34,000
1996	T250G	26,000	31,000
1995	T250G	24,000	29,000
Formula 31 PC			
2009	T320G	137,000	164,000
2008	T320G	124,000	149,000
2007	T320G	113,000	136,000
2006	T320G	104,000	125,000
2005	T320G	96,000	115,000
2004	T320G	88,000	106,000
2004	T320G	81,000	97,000
2002	T320G	74,000	89,000
2001	T320G	68,000	82,000
2000	T320G	63,000	76,000
1999	T310G	59,000	71,000
1998	T310G	55,000	66,000
1997	T310G	51,000	61,000
1996	T330G	47,000	57,000
1995	T330G	44,000	53,000
Formula 310 Sun Sport			
2009	T320G	98,000	117,000
2008	T320G	89,000	107,000
2007	T320G	81,000	97,000
Formula 310 Bowrider			
2009	T320G	95,000	114,000
2008	T320G	86,000	103,000
Formula 330 Sun Sport			
2006	T320G	83,000	99,000

Year	Power	Retail Low	Retail High
2005	T320G	75,000	90,000
2004	T320G	69,000	83,000
2004	T320G	64,000	76,000
2002	T320G	58,000	70,000
2001	T320G	54,000	65,000
2000	T320G	50,000	60,000
1999	T310G	46,000	56,000
1998	T310G	43,000	52,000
1997	T310G	40,000	48,000
1996	T330G	37,000	45,000
Formula 34 PC (1991-2002)			
2002	T375G	97,000	116,000
2001	T375G	86,000	104,000
2000	T375G	79,000	95,000
1999	T375G	73,000	88,000
1998	T310G	67,000	81,000
1997	T300G	62,000	74,000
1996	T300G	57,000	68,000
1995	T300G	52,000	63,000
Formula 34 PC (Current)			
2009	T375G	172,000	206,000
2008	T375G	156,000	187,000
2007	T375G	142,000	170,000
2006	T375G	129,000	155,000
2005	T370G	117,000	141,000
2004	T370G	107,000	128,000
Formula 350 Sun Sport			
2009	T320G	141,000	169,000
2008	T320G	97,000	117,000
Formula 36 PC			
1995	T300G	41,000	49,000
Formula 37 PC			
2009	T375G	118,000	141,000
2008	T375G	107,000	128,000
2007	T375G	97,000	117,000
2006	T375G	88,000	106,000
2005	T375G	81,000	98,000
2004	T375G	75,000	90,000
2003	T375G	69,000	83,000
2002	T375G	63,000	76,000
2001	T400G	58,000	70,000
2000	T400G	54,000	65,000
1999	T400G	50,000	60,000
Formula 370 Super Sport			
2009	T375G	222,000	266,000
2008	T375G	202,000	242,000
2007	T375G	183,000	220,000
2006	T375G	167,000	200,000
2005	T375G	152,000	182,000
2004	T375G	140,000	168,000
2003	T375G	128,000	154,000
2002	T375G	118,000	142,000
2001	T375G	109,000	130,000
Formula 40 PC			
2009	T425G	******	******
2009	T440D	******	******
2008	T425G	251,000	301,000
2008	T440D	284,000	340,000
2007	T425G	228,000	274,000

Year	Power	Retail Low	Retail High
2007	T440D	258,000	310,000
2006	T425G	208,000	249,000
2006	T440D	235,000	282,000
2005	T425G	189,000	227,000
2005	T440D	214,000	256,000
2004	T420G	174,000	209,000
2004	T440D	196,000	236,000
2003	T420G	160,000	192,000
2003	T440D	181,000	217,000

Formula 400 Super Sport

Year	Power	Retail Low	Retail High
2009	T425G	******	******
2009	T370D	******	******
2008	T425G	233,000	280,000
2008	T370D	265,000	318,000
2007	T425G	212,000	255,000
2007	T350D	241,000	289,000
2006	T425G	193,000	232,000
2006	T350D	219,000	263,000
2005	T425G	176,000	211,000
2005	T350D	199,000	239,000
2004	T425G	160,000	192,000
2004	T350D	181,000	218,000
2003	T425G	147,000	176,000
2003	T350D	167,000	200,000
2002	T425G	135,000	162,000
2002	T350D	153,000	184,000
2001	T425G	124,000	149,000
2001	T470D	******	******
2000	T415G	114,000	137,000
2000	T470D	******	******
1999	T415G	105,000	126,000
1999	T470D	******	******

Formula 41 PC

Year	Power	Retail Low	Retail High
2004	T480D	215,000	254,000
2003	T480D	196,000	231,000
2002	T450D	178,000	210,000
2001	T450D	162,000	191,000
2000	T450D	149,000	176,000
1999	T450D	137,000	162,000
1998	T420D	126,000	149,000
1997	T420D	116,000	137,000
1996	T420D	107,000	126,000

Formula 45 Yacht

Year	Power	Retail Low	Retail High
2009	T435D	******	******
2008	T435D	418,000	481,000
2007	T435D	385,000	443,000

Formula 48 Yacht

Year	Power	Retail Low	Retail High
2007	T660D	484,000	556,000
2006	T660D	440,000	506,000
2005	T660D	400,000	461,000
2004	T660D	364,000	419,000

Fountain 29 Center Console

Year	Power	Retail Low	Retail High
2004	T200 O/B	47,000	57,000
2003	T200 O/B	42,000	51,000
2002	T200 O/B	38,000	46,000
2001	T200 O/B	34,000	41,000
2000	T200 O/B	31,000	37,000
1999	T200 O/B	28,000	34,000
1998	T200 O/B	26,000	31,000
1997	T200 O/B	23,000	28,000
1996	T200 O/B	21,000	26,000
1995	T200 O/B	19,000	23,000

Fountain 31 Tournament Edition

Year	Power	Retail Low	Retail High
2009	T225 O/B	******	******
2008	T225 O/B	******	******
2007	T225 O/B	******	******
2006	T225 O/B	64,000	77,000
2005	T225 O/B	58,000	69,000
2004	T225 O/B	52,000	62,000
2003	T225 O/B	47,000	56,000
2002	T225 O/B	42,000	51,000
2001	T225 O/B	38,000	46,000
2000	T225 O/B	35,000	42,000
1999	T225 O/B	32,000	38,000
1998	T225 O/B	29,000	34,000
1997	T225 O/B	26,000	31,000

Fountain 32 Center Console

Year	Power	Retail Low	Retail High
2009	T250	******	******
2008	T250	88,000	105,000
2007	T250 O/B	79,000	95,000
2006	T250 O/B	71,000	85,000

Fountain 34 Center Console

Year	Power	Retail Low	Retail High
2009	3/225 O/B	******	******
2008	3/225 O/B	136,000	164,000
2007	3/225 O/B	124,000	149,000
2006	3/225 O/B	113,000	135,000
2005	3/225 O/B	103,000	123,000
2004	3/225 O/B	93,000	112,000
2003	3/225 O/B	85,000	102,000

Fountain 38 Center Console

Year	Power	Retail Low	Retail High
2009	3/225 O/B	******	******
2008	3/225 O/B	173,000	208,000
2007	3/225 O/B	158,000	189,000
2006	3/225 O/B	143,000	172,000
2005	3/225 O/B	130,000	157,000
2004	3/225 O/B	119,000	142,000
2003	3/225 O/B	108,000	130,000
2002	3/225 O/B	98,000	118,000
2001	3/225 O/B	89,000	107,000

Four Winns 268 Vista

Year	Power	Retail Low	Retail High
2005	280 I/O	34,000	41,000
2004	280 I/O	31,000	37,000
2003	280 I/O	28,000	33,000
2002	280 I/O	25,000	30,000
2001	280 I/O	23,000	28,000
2000	280 I/O	21,000	25,000
1999	280 I/O	19,000	23,000

Four Winns 278 Vista (1994-98)

Year	Power	Retail Low	Retail High
1998	T205 I/O	17,000	20,000
1997	T205 I/O	15,000	18,000
1996	T205 I/O	14,000	17,000
1995	T190 I/O	13,000	15,000

Four Winns 278 Vista (Current)

Year	Power	Retail Low	Retail High
2009	300 I/O	53,000	63,000
2008	300 I/O	48,000	57,000
2007	300 I/O	43,000	52,000
2006	280 I/O	39,000	47,000

Four Winns 280 Horizon

Year	Power	Retail Low	Retail High
2005	T270	44,000	53,000
2005	S375	40,000	48,000
2004	T270	40,000	48,000
2004	S375	36,000	43,000
2003	T270	36,000	43,000
2003	S375	32,000	39,000
2002	T270	32,000	39,000
2002	S375	29,000	35,000
2001	T270	29,000	35,000
2001	S375	26,000	32,000
2000	T270	26,000	31,000
2000	S375	24,000	28,000

Four Winns 285 Sundowner

Year	Power	Retail Low	Retail High
2005	T270G	43,000	52,000
2004	T270G	39,000	47,000
2003	T270G	36,000	43,000
2002	T260G	32,000	39,000
2001	T260G	29,000	35,000
2000	T260G	27,000	32,000

Four Winns 288 Vista

Year	Power	Retail Low	Retail High
2009	T270G	87,000	104,000
2008	T270G	79,000	95,000
2007	T270G	72,000	86,000
2006	T270G	65,000	78,000
2005	T270G	60,000	72,000
2004	T270G	55,000	66,000

Four Winns 298 Vista

Year	Power	Retail Low	Retail High
2005	T280G	66,000	79,000
2004	T280G	60,000	72,000
2003	T280G	54,000	65,000
2002	T280G	49,000	59,000
2001	T280G	45,000	54,000
2000	T280G	41,000	49,000
1999	T280G	37,000	45,000

Four Winns 310 Horizon

Year	Power	Retail Low	Retail High
2009	T270G	83,000	99,000
2008	T270G	75,000	90,000
2007	T270G	68,000	82,000

Four Winns 318/335 Vista

Year	Power	Retail Low	Retail High
2009	T270G	127,000	152,000
2008	T270G	115,000	138,000
2007	T270G	105,000	126,000
2006	T270G	95,000	114,000

Four Winns 328 Vista

Year	Power	Retail Low	Retail High
2006	T280G	100,000	120,000
2005	T280G	91,000	109,000
2004	T280G	83,000	99,000
2003	T280G	75,000	90,000
2002	T280G	68,000	82,000
2001	T280G	63,000	75,000
2000	T280G	58,000	69,000
1999	T280G	53,000	64,000

Four Winns 338/358 Vista

Year	Power	Retail Low	Retail High
2009	T300G	132,000	158,000
2008	T320G	120,000	144,000
2007	T320G	109,000	131,000

Four Winns 348 Vista

Year	Power	Retail Low	Retail High
2004	T320 I/B	119,000	143,000
2004	T320 I/O	115,000	138,000
2003	T320 I/B	109,000	130,000

See Page 529 For Price Adjustments

Year	Power	Retail Low	Retail High
2003	T320 I/O	105,000	126,000
2002	T320 I/B	99,000	119,000
2002	T320 I/O	95,000	115,000
2001	T320 I/B	90,000	108,000
2001	T320 I/O	87,000	104,000

Four Winns 348/358/375 Vista

Year	Power	Retail Low	Retail High
2009	T320 I/B	******	******
2009	T320 I/O	******	******
2008	T320 I/B	151,000	181,000
2008	T320 I/O	144,000	173,000
2007	T320 I/B	137,000	165,000
2007	T320 I/O	131,000	158,000
2006	T320 I/B	125,000	150,000
2006	T320 I/O	119,000	143,000
2005	T320 I/B	113,000	136,000
2005	T320 I/O	109,000	131,000

Four Winns 378 Vista

Year	Power	Retail Low	Retail High
2009	T400G IPS	******	******
2008	T375G	211,000	247,000
2007	T375G	192,000	225,000
2006	T370G	175,000	204,000
2005	T420G	159,000	186,000
2004	T420G	146,000	171,000
2003	T420G	134,000	157,000
2002	T420G	124,000	145,000

Four Winns V458

Year	Power	Retail Low	Retail High
2009	T435D IPS	******	******
2008	T435D IPS	369,000	424,000

Glacier Bay 260/2665 Canyon Runner

Year	Power	Retail Low	Retail High
2008	T150 O/B	57,000	68,000
2007	T150 O/B	52,000	62,000
2006	T150 O/B	47,000	57,000
2005	T150 O/B	43,000	51,000
2004	T150 O/B	39,000	47,000
2003	T150 O/B	35,000	42,000
2002	T150 O/B	32,000	39,000
2001	T150 O/B	29,000	35,000
2000	T150 O/B	27,000	33,000
1999	T150 O/B	25,000	30,000
1998	T150 O/B	23,000	28,000
1997	T150 O/B	21,000	25,000
1996	T150 O/B	19,000	23,000

Glacier Bay 2640 Renegade

Year	Power	Retail Low	Retail High
2008	T150 O/B	71,000	85,000
2007	T150 O/B	64,000	77,000
2006	T150 O/B	59,000	70,000
2005	T150 O/B	53,000	64,000
2004	T150 O/B	48,000	58,000
2003	T150 O/B	44,000	53,000
2002	T150 O/B	41,000	49,000
2001	T150 O/B	38,000	45,000

Glacier Bay 2670 Island Runner

Year	Power	Retail Low	Retail High
2008	T150 O/B	74,000	88,000
2007	T150 O/B	67,000	80,000
2006	T150 O/B	61,000	73,000
2005	T150 O/B	55,000	67,000
2004	T150 O/B	51,000	61,000
2003	T150 O/B	47,000	56,000
2002	T150 O/B	43,000	52,000
2001	T150 O/B	40,000	48,000

Year	Power	Retail Low	Retail High
2000	T150 O/B	36,000	44,000
1999	T150 O/B	33,000	40,000
1998	T150 O/B	31,000	37,000

Glacier Bay 2680 Coastal Runner

Year	Power	Retail Low	Retail High
2008	T150 O/B	77,000	93,000
2007	T150 O/B	70,000	85,000
2006	T150 O/B	64,000	77,000
2005	T150 O/B	58,000	70,000
2004	T150 O/B	53,000	64,000
2003	T150 O/B	49,000	58,000
2002	T150 O/B	45,000	54,000
2001	T150 O/B	41,000	49,000
2000	T150 O/B	38,000	45,000
1999	T150 O/B	35,000	42,000

Glacier Bay 2690 Coastal Runner

Year	Power	Retail Low	Retail High
2008	T150 O/B	86,000	103,000
2007	T150 O/B	78,000	94,000
2006	T150 O/B	71,000	85,000
2005	T150 O/B	65,000	78,000
2004	T150 O/B	59,000	71,000
2003	T150 O/B	53,000	64,000
2002	T150 O/B	49,000	59,000
2001	T150 O/B	45,000	54,000
2000	T150 O/B	42,000	50,000

Grady-White 265 Express

Year	Power	Retail Low	Retail High
2005	T225 O/B	63,000	75,000
2004	T225 O/B	57,000	69,000
2003	T225 O/B	53,000	63,000
2002	T225 O/B	49,000	58,000
2001	T225 O/B	45,000	54,000
2000	T225 O/B	41,000	49,000

Grady-White 263/273 Chase

Year	Power	Retail Low	Retail High
2009	T200 O/B	75,000	90,000
2008	T200 O/B	67,000	81,000
2007	T200 O/B	60,000	73,000
2006	T200 O/B	54,000	65,000
2005	T200 O/B	49,000	59,000
2004	T200 O/B	44,000	53,000
2003	T200 O/B	40,000	49,000
2002	T200 O/B	37,000	44,000
2001	T200 O/B	33,000	40,000
2000	T200 O/B	30,000	36,000
1999	T200 O/B	28,000	33,000
1998	T200 O/B	25,000	30,000
1997	T200 O/B	23,000	27,000
1996	T200 O/B	21,000	25,000
1995	T200 O/B	19,000	23,000

Grady-White 268 Islander

Year	Power	Retail Low	Retail High
2001	T225 O/B	35,000	42,000
2000	T225 O/B	32,000	38,000
1999	T225 O/B	29,000	35,000
1998	T225 O/B	26,000	32,000
1997	T225 O/B	24,000	29,000
1996	T225 O/B	22,000	26,000
1995	T225 O/B	20,000	24,000

Grady-White 270 Islander

Year	Power	Retail Low	Retail High
2005	T225 O/B	52,000	62,000
2004	T225 O/B	46,000	56,000
2003	T225 O/B	42,000	50,000

Grady-White 272 Sailfish

Year	Power	Retail Low	Retail High
2000	T225 O/B	42,000	50,000
1999	T225 O/B	38,000	45,000
1998	T225 O/B	34,000	41,000
1997	T225 O/B	31,000	37,000
1996	T225 O/B	28,000	34,000
1995	T225 O/B	26,000	31,000
1994	T225 O/B	23,000	28,000

Grady-White 275 Tournament

Year	Power	Retail Low	Retail High
2009	T150 O/B	88,000	105,000
2008	T150 O/B	80,000	96,000
2007	T150 O/B	72,000	87,000

Grady-White 282 Sailfish

Year	Power	Retail Low	Retail High
2009	T225 O/B	95,000	114,000
2008	T225 O/B	86,000	103,000
2007	T225 O/B	78,000	94,000
2006	T225 O/B	71,000	85,000
2005	T225 O/B	65,000	78,000
2004	T225 O/B	59,000	71,000
2003	T225 O/B	55,000	66,000
2002	T225 O/B	50,000	60,000
2001	T225 O/B	46,000	56,000

Grady-White 283 Release

Year	Power	Retail Low	Retail High
2009	T225 O/B	84,000	100,000
2008	T225 O/B	76,000	91,000
2007	T225 O/B	69,000	83,000
2006	T225 O/B	63,000	75,000
2005	T225 O/B	58,000	69,000
2004	T225 O/B	53,000	64,000
2003	T225 O/B	49,000	59,000
2002	T225 O/B	45,000	54,000

Grady White 300 Marlin

Year	Power	Retail Low	Retail High
2009	T225 O/B	140,000	168,000
2008	T225 O/B	127,000	152,000
2007	T225 O/B	115,000	139,000
2006	T225 O/B	105,000	126,000
2005	T225 O/B	97,000	116,000
2004	T225 O/B	89,000	107,000
2003	T225 O/B	82,000	98,000
2002	T225 O/B	75,000	90,000
2001	T225 O/B	69,000	83,000
2000	T225 O/B	63,000	76,000
1999	T225 O/B	58,000	70,000
1998	T225 O/B	54,000	65,000
1997	T225 O/B	50,000	61,000
1996	T225 O/B	47,000	56,000
1995	T225 O/B	44,000	52,000

Grady-White 305 Express

Year	Power	Retail Low	Retail High
2009	T250 O/B	152,000	182,000
2008	T250 O/B	138,000	165,000
2007	T250 O/B	125,000	151,000

Grady-White 306 Bimini

Year	Power	Retail Low	Retail High
2009	T250 I/O	125,000	150,000
2008	T250 I/O	113,000	136,000
2007	T250 I/O	103,000	124,000
2006	T250 I/O	95,000	114,000
2005	T250 I/O	87,000	105,000
2004	T250 I/O	80,000	96,000
2003	T250 I/O	74,000	88,000
2002	T250 I/O	68,000	81,000

See Page 529 For Price Adjustments

Year	Power	Retail Low	Retail High
2001	T250 I/O	63,000	76,000
2000	T250 I/O	59,000	70,000
1999	T250 I/O	54,000	65,000
1998	T250 I/O	51,000	61,000

Grady-White 330 Express

Year	Power	Retail Low	Retail High
2009	T250 O/B	235,000	282,000
2008	T250 O/B	213,000	256,000
2007	T250 O/B	194,000	233,000
2006	T250 O/B	177,000	212,000
2005	T250 O/B	162,000	195,000
2004	T250 O/B	149,000	179,000
2003	T250 O/B	137,000	165,000
2002	T250 O/B	126,000	152,000
2001	T250 O/B	116,000	140,000

Grady-White 336 Canyon

Year	Power	Retail Low	Retail High
2009	T250 O/B	160,000	192,000
2008	T250 O/B	145,000	174,000

Grady-White 360 Express

Year	Power	Retail Low	Retail High
2009	3/250 O/B	******	******
2008	3/250 O/B	278,000	333,000
2007	3/250 O/B	252,000	303,000
2006	3/250 O/B	230,000	276,000
2005	3/250 O/B	209,000	251,000

Grand Banks 32 Sedan

Year	Power	Retail Low	Retail High
1995	135D	80,000	94,000

Grand Banks 36 Classic

Year	Power	Retail Low	Retail High
2004	T210D	176,000	206,000
2003	T210D	165,000	193,000
2002	T210D	155,000	182,000
2001	T210D	146,000	171,000
2000	T210D	137,000	161,000
1999	No Prod.	******	******
1998	No Prod.	******	******
1997	No Prod.	******	******
1996	210D	104,000	123,000
1996	T210D	115,000	136,000
1995	210D	99,000	117,000
1995	T210D	110,000	129,000

Grand Banks 36 Europa

Year	Power	Retail Low	Retail High
1998	210D	******	******
1997	210D	******	******
1996	210D	110,000	130,000
1996	T210D	116,000	137,000
1995	210D	104,000	123,000
1995	T210D	111,000	130,000

Grand Banks 36 Sedan

Year	Power	Retail Low	Retail High
1996	210D	104,000	122,000
1995	210D	99,000	116,000

Grand Banks 38 Eastbay Express

Year	Power	Retail Low	Retail High
2004	T420D	249,000	287,000
2003	T350D	232,000	267,000
2002	T375D	216,000	248,000
2001	T375D	200,000	231,000
2000	T375D	186,000	214,000
1999	T375D	173,000	199,000
1998	T375D	161,000	185,000
1997	T375D	151,000	174,000
1996	T375D	142,000	164,000
1995	T375D	134,000	154,000

Year	Power	Retail Low	Retail High
1994	T375D	126,000	145,000

Grand Banks Eastbay 39 SX

Year	Power	Retail Low	Retail High
2009	T500D	******	******
2008	T500D	413,000	475,000
2007	T445D	384,000	442,000
2006	T480D	357,000	411,000

Grand Banks 42 Classic

Year	Power	Retail Low	Retail High
2004	T450D	295,000	340,000
2003	T450D	278,000	319,000
2002	T450D	261,000	300,000
2001	T450D	245,000	282,000
2000	T375D	233,000	268,000
1999	T350D	221,000	254,000
1998	T350D	210,000	242,000
1997	T375D	200,000	230,000
1996	T375D	190,000	218,000
1995	T375D	180,000	207,000

Grand Banks 42 Europa

Year	Power	Retail Low	Retail High
2004	T450D	264,000	303,000
2003	T450D	248,000	285,000
2002	T450D	233,000	268,000
2001	T450D	219,000	252,000
2000	T375D	208,000	239,000
1999	T350D	197,000	227,000
1998	T350D	188,000	216,000
1997	T375D	178,000	205,000
1996	T375D	169,000	195,000

Grand Banks 43 Eastbay Flybride

Year	Power	Retail Low	Retail High
2004	T420D	282,000	325,000
2003	T420D	263,000	302,000
2002	T420D	244,000	281,000
2001	T420D	227,000	261,000
2000	T420D	211,000	243,000
1999	T420D	196,000	226,000
1998	T420D	183,000	210,000

Grand Banks 43 Eastbay Expres

Year	Power	Retail Low	Retail High
2004	T420D	271,000	312,000
2003	T420D	252,000	290,000
2002	T420D	234,000	270,000
2001	T420D	218,000	251,000
2000	T420D	203,000	233,000

Grand Banks 43 Eastbay HX

Year	Power	Retail Low	Retail High
2007	T455D	397,000	456,000
2006	T455D	357,000	410,000
2005	T440D	321,000	369,000
2004	T440D	289,000	332,000
2003	T440D	260,000	299,000
2002	T440D	234,000	269,000

Grand Banks 43 Eastbay SX

Year	Power	Retail Low	Retail High
2007	T455D	410,000	471,000
2006	T455D	381,000	438,000
2005	T440D	354,000	408,000
2004	T440D	330,000	379,000
2003	T440D	307,000	353,000
2002	T440D	285,000	328,000

Grand Banks 46 Classic

Year	Power	Retail Low	Retail High
2006	T465D	508,000	584,000
2005	T465D	477,000	549,000
2004	T465D	449,000	516,000

Year	Power	Retail Low	Retail High
2003	T420D	422,000	485,000
2002	T420D	396,000	456,000
2001	T420D	373,000	428,000
2000	T375D	350,000	403,000
1999	T375D	333,000	383,000
1998	T375D	316,000	363,000
1997	T375D	300,000	345,000
1996	T375D	285,000	328,000
1995	T375D	271,000	312,000

Grand Banks 46 Europa

Year	Power	Retail Low	Retail High
2008	T500D	******	******
2007	T500D	******	******
2006	T500D	489,000	562,000
2005	T500D	459,000	528,000
2004	T450D	432,000	497,000
2003	T420D	406,000	467,000
2002	T420D	381,000	439,000
2001	T420D	359,000	412,000
2000	T375D	337,000	388,000
1999	T375D	320,000	368,000
1998	T375D	304,000	350,000
1997	T375D	289,000	332,000
1996	T375D	274,000	316,000
1995	T375D	261,000	300,000

Grand Banks 46 Motor Yacht

Year	Power	Retail Low	Retail High
2001	T375D	******	******
2000	T375D	******	******
1999	T375D	******	******
1998	T375D	******	******
1997	T375D	******	******
1996	T375D	285,000	327,000
1995	T375D	270,000	311,000

Grand Banks 47 Eastbay FB

Year	Power	Retail Low	Retail High
2009	720D	******	******
2008	720D	******	******
2007	720D	******	******
2006	720D	668,000	769,000
2005	700D	622,000	715,000

Grand Banks 49 Classic

Year	Power	Retail Low	Retail High
1997	T375D	******	******
1996	T375D	******	******
1995	T375D	323,000	371,000

Grand Banks 52 Europa

Year	Power	Retail Low	Retail High
2008	T660D	1,024,000	1,167,000
2007	T660D	962,000	1,097,000
2006	T660D	904,000	1,031,000
2005	T660D	850,000	969,000
2004	T660D	799,000	911,000
2003	T375D	759,000	865,000
2002	T375D	721,000	822,000
2001	T375D	685,000	781,000
2000	T375D	651,000	742,000
1999	T375D	618,000	705,000
1998	T375D	587,000	669,000

Hatteras 39 Convertible

Year	Power	Retail Low	Retail High
1998	485D	167,000	192,000
1997	485D	153,000	176,000
1996	485D	141,000	162,000
1995	485D	130,000	149,000

Year	Power	Retail Low	Retail High
Hatteras 39 Sport Express			
1998	485D	149,000	172,000
1997	485D	137,000	158,000
1996	485D	126,000	145,000
1995	485D	116,000	134,000
Hatteras 40 Motor Yacht			
1997	T340D	157,000	181,000
1996	T340D	144,000	166,000
1995	T340D	133,000	153,000
Hatteras 42 Cockpit MY			
1997	T364D	147,000	169,000
1996	T364D	137,000	157,000
1995	T340D	127,000	146,000
Hatteras 43 Convertible			
1998	T625D	226,000	260,000
1997	T625D	208,000	239,000
1996	T535D	191,000	220,000
1995	T535D	176,000	203,000
Hatteras 43 Sport Express			
1998	T625D	207,000	239,000
1997	T600D	191,000	219,000
1996	T600D	175,000	202,000
Hatteras 46 Conv. (92-95)			
1995	720D	245,000	281,000
Hatteras 48 Cockpit MY			
1996	T535D	262,000	301,000
Hatteras 48 MY (1990-96)			
1996	T720D	283,000	326,000
1995	T720D	261,000	300,000
Hatteras 50 Convertible			
2006	1000D	778,000	895,000
2005	1000D	716,000	823,000
2004	1000D	658,000	757,000
2003	1000D	606,000	697,000
2002	800D	557,000	641,000
2001	800D	513,000	589,000
2000	800D	471,000	542,000
1999	800D	434,000	499,000
1998	900D	399,000	459,000
1997	870D	367,000	422,000
1996	870D	338,000	388,000
1995	870D	311,000	357,000
Hatteras 50 Sport Deck MY			
1998	T565D	316,000	363,000
1997	T545D	290,000	334,000
1996	T545D	267,000	307,000
Hatteras 52 Cockpit MY			
1999	800D	367,000	422,000
1998	760D	337,000	388,000
1997	735D	310,000	357,000
1996	720D	286,000	328,000
1995	720D	263,000	302,000
Hatteras 52 MY			
1996	720D	331,000	380,000
1995	720D	314,000	361,000
Hatteras 54 Conv. (1991-98)			
1998	1100D	452,000	520,000
1997	1075D	416,000	478,000

Year	Power	Retail Low	Retail High
1996	1040D	383,000	440,000
1995	1040D	352,000	405,000
Hatteras 54 Conv. (Current)			
2009	1500D	******	******
2008	1500D	******	******
2007	1400D	******	******
2006	1400D	******	******
2005	1400D	834,000	959,000
2004	1400D	767,000	882,000
2003	1400D	706,000	812,000
2002	1400D	649,000	747,000
Hatteras 55 Convertible			
2002	1450D	733,000	843,000
2001	1450D	674,000	776,000
2000	1450D	620,000	713,000
1999	1450D	571,000	656,000
Hatteras 60 Convertible			
2008	1800D	******	******
2007	1800D	******	******
2006	1800D	1,409,000	1,620,000
2005	1650D	1,305,000	1,500,000
2004	1650D	1,200,000	1,380,000
2003	1400D	1,104,000	1,270,000
2002	1400D	1,016,000	1,168,000
2001	1400D	934,000	1,075,000
2000	1400D	869,000	999,000
1999	1400D	808,000	929,000
1998	1350D	751,000	864,000
Hatteras 60 Extended Deckhouse MY			
1997	870D	495,000	570,000
1996	870D	461,000	530,000
1995	870D	428,000	493,000
Hatteras 6300 Raised Pilothouse			
2003	1500D	1,071,000	1,232,000
2002	1400D	996,000	1,146,000
2001	1400D	926,000	1,065,000
2000	1400D	861,000	991,000
Hatteras 65 Convertible			
2003	1400D	831,000	956,000
2002	1400D	773,000	889,000
2001	1400D	719,000	826,000
2000	1400D	668,000	769,000
1999	1400D	621,000	715,000
1998	1450D	578,000	665,000
1997	1400D	543,000	625,000
1996	1350D	511,000	587,000
1995	1350D	480,000	552,000
Hatteras 65 Motor Yacht			
1996	870D	521,000	599,000
1995	870D	484,000	557,000
Heritage East 36 Sundeck			
2008	230D	******	******
2007	230D	******	******
2006	230D	137,000	158,000
2005	230D	129,000	148,000
2004	230D	121,000	139,000
2003	230D	114,000	131,000
2002	230D	107,000	123,000
2001	230D	102,000	117,000

Year	Power	Retail Low	Retail High
2000	230D	97,000	111,000
1999	230D	92,000	106,000
1998	230D	87,000	100,000
1997	230D	83,000	95,000
1996	135D	79,000	90,000
1995	135D	75,000	86,000
Hinckley 36 Picnic Boat			
2007	S440 Jet	293,000	337,000
2006	S440 Jet	270,000	310,000
2005	S440 Jet	251,000	288,000
2004	S440 Jet	233,000	268,000
2003	S440 Jet	217,000	249,000
2002	S350 Jet	202,000	232,000
2001	S350 Jet	187,000	216,000
2000	S350 Jet	176,000	203,000
1999	S350 Jet	165,000	190,000
1998	S350 Jet	156,000	179,000
1997	S350 Jet	146,000	168,000
1996	S350 Jet	137,000	158,000
1995	S350 Jet	129,000	149,000
Hunt 29 Surfhunter			
2009	S315D	******	******
2008	S315D	******	******
2007	S315D	******	******
2006	S315D	110,000	127,000
2005	S315D	102,000	117,000
2004	S310D	93,000	107,000
Hunt 33 Express			
2004	S370D	154,000	177,000
2003	S370D	141,000	163,000
2002	S370D	130,000	150,000
2001	S370D	120,000	138,000
2000	S370D	110,000	127,000
1999	S370D	101,000	116,000
Hunt 33 Surfhunter			
2009	S370D	******	******
2008	S370D	******	******
2007	S370D	174,000	201,000
2006	S370D	160,000	184,000
2005	S315D	147,000	170,000
Hunt 36 Harrier			
2009	T370D	******	******
2008	T370D	******	******
2007	T370D	******	******
2006	T370D	******	******
2005	T370D	216,000	248,000
2004	T370D	198,000	228,000
2003	T370D	182,000	210,000
Hydra-Sports 2595 CC			
2002	T225 O/B	33,000	40,000
2001	T225 O/B	33,000	40,000
2000	T225 O/B	33,000	40,000
Hydra-Sports 2796/2800 CC			
2005	T225/OB	47,000	56,000
2004	T225/OB	42,000	50,000
2003	T225/OB	38,000	45,000
2002	T225/OB	34,000	41,000
2001	T225/OB	31,000	37,000
2000	T225/OB	28,000	34,000

Year	Power	Retail Low	Retail High
Hydra-Sports 2800 Walkaround			
2005	T225/OB	52,000	62,000
2004	T225/OB	47,000	57,000
2003	T225/OB	43,000	52,000
2002	T225/OB	39,000	47,000
2001	T225/OB	35,000	43,000
Hydra-Sports 2800/3100 SF			
1998	T225 O/B	32,000	38,000
1997	T225 O/B	29,000	35,000
1996	T225 O/B	26,000	32,000
1995	T225 O/B	24,000	29,000
Hydra-Sports 2900 Center Console			
2009	T250 O/B	******	******
2008	T250 O/B	83,000	100,000
2007	T250 O/B	75,000	90,000
2006	T250 O/B	68,000	82,000
Hydra-Sports 2900 VX			
2009	T250 O/B	******	******
2008	T250 O/B	98,000	117,000
2007	T250 O/B	89,000	107,000
2006	T250 O/B	81,000	97,000
Hydra-Sports 3000 CC			
2000	T225/OB	33,000	39,000
1999	T225/OB	29,000	35,000
1998	T225/OB	26,000	32,000
1997	T225/OB	24,000	29,000
Hydra-Sports 3300 Center Console			
2009	3/250 O/B	******	******
2008	3/250 O/B	120,000	144,000
2007	3/250 O/B	108,000	130,000
2006	3/250 O/B	97,000	117,000
2005	3/250 O/B	88,000	106,000
2004	3/250 O/B	80,000	97,000
2003	3/250 O/B	73,000	88,000
Hydra-Sports 3300 VX			
2007	3/250 O/B	124,000	149,000
2006	3/250 O/B	113,000	135,000
2005	3/250 O/B	103,000	123,000
2004	3/250 O/B	93,000	112,000
Intrepid 26 Center Console			
1996	T200 O/B	34,000	40,000
1995	T200 O/B	30,000	37,000
Intrepid 26 Walkaround			
1996	T200 O/B	38,000	45,000
1995	T200 O/B	34,000	41,000
Intrepid 289 Center Console			
2003	T225 O/B	******	******
2002	T225 O/B	******	******
2001	T225 O/B	******	******
2000	T225 O/B	36,000	43,000
1999	T225 O/B	32,000	39,000
1998	T225 O/B	29,000	35,000
1997	T225 O/B	27,000	32,000
Intrepid 289 Walkaround			
2003	T225 O/B	******	******
2002	T225 O/B	******	******
2001	T225 O/B	******	******
2000	T225 O/B	41,000	49,000
1999	T225 O/B	37,000	44,000
1998	T225 O/B	33,000	40,000
1997	T225 O/B	30,000	37,000
Intrepid 300 Center Console			
2009	T250 O/B	******	******
2008	T250 O/B	121,000	145,000
2007	T250 O/B	108,000	130,000
2006	T250 O/B	98,000	117,000
2005	T250 O/B	88,000	105,000
2004	T250 O/B	79,000	95,000
Intrepid 310 Walkaround			
2009	T250 O/B	******	******
2008	T250 O/B	******	******
2007	T250 O/B	128,000	153,000
2006	T250 O/B	116,000	139,000
2005	T250 O/B	105,000	127,000
Intrepid 322 Console Cuddy			
2003	T250 O/B	89,000	107,000
2002	T250 O/B	81,000	97,000
2001	T250 O/B	74,000	88,000
2000	T250 O/B	67,000	80,000
1999	T250 O/B	61,000	73,000
1998	T250 O/B	55,000	67,000
1997	T250 O/B	50,000	60,000
1996	T250 O/B	46,000	55,000
Intrepid 323 Console Cuddy			
2009	T250 O/B	******	******
2008	T250 O/B	******	******
2007	T250 O/B	******	******
2006	T250 O/B	128,000	154,000
2005	T250 O/B	116,000	140,000
2004	T250 O/B	106,000	127,000
Intrepid 323 Center Console			
2009	T250 O/B	******	******
2008	T250 O/B	******	******
2007	T250 O/B	******	******
2006	T250 O/B	124,000	124,000
2005	T250 O/B	113,000	135,000
2004	T250 O/B	103,000	123,000
Intrepid 339 Center Console			
2001	T250 O/B	99,000	118,000
2000	T250 O/B	90,000	108,000
1999	T250 O/B	81,000	98,000
1998	T250 O/B	74,000	89,000
1997	T250 O/B	67,000	81,000
1996	T250 O/B	61,000	74,000
Intrepid 339 Walkaround			
2001	T250 O/B	104,000	124,000
2000	T250 O/B	94,000	113,000
1999	T250 O/B	86,000	103,000
1998	T250 O/B	78,000	94,000
1997	T250 O/B	71,000	85,000
1996	T250 O/B	64,000	77,000
1995	T250 O/B	59,000	70,000
Intrepid 348 Walkaround			
2004	T250 O/B	107,000	128,000
2003	T250 O/B	97,000	116,000
2002	T250 O/B	88,000	106,000
Intrepid 356 Cuddy			
2001	T250 O/B	98,000	117,000
2000	T250 O/B	89,000	107,000
1999	T250 O/B	81,000	97,000
1998	T250 O/B	73,000	88,000
1997	T250 O/B	67,000	80,000
1996	T250 O/B	61,000	74,000
1995	T250 O/B	56,000	68,000
Intrepid 366 Cuddy			
2003	3/225 O/B	132,000	158,000
2002	3/225 O/B	121,000	145,000
2001	3/225 O/B	111,000	134,000
2000	3/225 O/B	102,000	123,000
1999	3/225 O/B	94,000	113,000
Intrepid 370 Cuddy			
2009	3/275 O/B	******	******
2008	3/275 O/B	235,000	282,000
2007	3/275 O/B	213,000	256,000
2006	3/250 O/B	194,000	233,000
2005	3/250 O/B	177,000	212,000
2004	3/250 O/B	161,000	193,000
2003	3/250 O/B	146,000	175,000
Intrepid 377 Walkaround			
2008	3/250 O/B	******	******
2007	3/250 O/B	******	******
2006	3/250 O/B	******	******
2005	3/250 O/B	******	******
2004	3/250 O/B	******	******
2003	3/250 O/B	******	******
2002	3/250 O/B	137,000	165,000
2001	3/250 O/B	126,000	152,000
2000	3/250 O/B	116,000	139,000
Island Gypsy 32 Europa			
2003	220D	109,000	128,000
2002	220D	103,000	120,000
2001	220D	96,000	113,000
2000	220D	91,000	106,000
1999	220D	85,000	100,000
1998	220D	80,000	94,000
1997	220D	75,000	88,000
1996	210D	71,000	83,000
1995	210D	66,000	78,000
Island Gypsy 36 Classic			
2002	220D	198,000	228,000
2001	220D	94,000	109,000
2000	220D	89,000	102,000
1999	220D	83,000	96,000
1998	220D	78,000	90,000
1997	210D	74,000	85,000
1996	210D	70,000	80,000
1995	210D	66,000	76,000
Island Gypsy 36 Europa			
1998	210D	97,000	112,000
1997	210D	92,000	105,000
1996	210D	86,000	99,000
1995	210D	81,000	93,000
Island Gypsy 36 MY			
2002	220D	237,000	272,000
2001	220D	95,000	110,000
2000	220D	89,000	103,000
1999	220D	84,000	97,000
1998	220D	79,000	91,000
1997	220D	74,000	85,000

See Page 529 For Price Adjustments

Year	Power	Retail Low	Retail High
1996	210D	70,000	80,000
1995	210D	66,000	75,000

Island Gypsy 44 Flush Aft Deck

Year	Power	Retail Low	Retail High
1996	T300D	135,000	155,000
1995	T300D	127,000	146,000

Island Gypsy 44 Motor Cruiser

Year	Power	Retail Low	Retail High
1996	T135D	133,000	153,000
1995	T135D	125,000	144,000

Jefferson 35 Marlago Cuddy

Year	Power	Retail Low	Retail High
2009	T250 O/B	******	******
2008	T250 O/B	90,000	104,000
2007	T250 O/B	81,000	93,000
2006	T250 O/B	73,000	84,000
2005	T250 O/B	65,000	75,000
2004	T250 O/B	59,000	68,000
2003	T250 O/B	53,000	61,000
2002	T250 O/B	48,000	55,000
2001	T250 O/B	43,000	50,000
2000	T250 O/B	39,000	45,000
1999	T250 O/B	36,000	41,000
1998	T250 O/B	32,000	37,000
1997	T250 O/B	29,000	34,000
1996	T250 O/B	27,000	31,000
1995	T250 O/B	24,000	28,000

Jefferson 43 Marlago SD

Year	Power	Retail Low	Retail High
2001	T3305D	176,000	202,000
2000	T3305D	161,000	186,000
1999	T3305D	150,000	173,000
1998	T315D	140,000	161,000
1997	T315D	130,000	149,000
1996	T300D	121,000	139,000
1995	T300D	112,000	129,000

Jefferson 46 Marlago SD

Year	Power	Retail Low	Retail High
2001	T450D	196,000	225,000
2000	T430D	180,000	207,000
1999	T430D	165,000	190,000
1998	T430D	152,000	175,000
1997	T375D	140,000	161,000
1996	T375D	129,000	148,000
1995	T300D	118,000	136,000

Jefferson 50 Rivanna SE

Year	Power	Retail Low	Retail High
2009	500D	******	******
2008	500D	******	******
2007	500D	344,000	395,000
2006	500D	313,000	359,000
2005	480D	284,000	327,000
2004	480D	259,000	298,000

Jefferson 52 Marquessa

Year	Power	Retail Low	Retail High
2001	T600D	318,000	368,000
2000	T600D	292,000	339,000
1999	T550D	269,000	312,000
1998	T550D	247,000	287,000
1997	T550D	227,000	264,000
1996	T550D	209,000	243,000
1995	T550D	192,000	223,000

Jefferson 52 Rivanna CMY

Year	Power	Retail Low	Retail High
1999	T450D	224,000	257,000
1998	T450D	206,000	237,000
1997	T450D	189,000	218,000
1996	T450D	174,000	200,000
1995	T435D	160,000	184,000

Jefferson 56 Marquessa CMY

Year	Power	Retail Low	Retail High
2001	T600D	296,000	340,000
2000	T600D	275,000	316,000
1999	T550D	256,000	294,000
1998	T550D	238,000	273,000
1997	T550D	221,000	254,000
1996	T550D	205,000	236,000
1995	T550D	191,000	220,000

Jefferson 56 Rivanna CMY

Year	Power	Retail Low	Retail High
2009	T700D	******	******
2008	T700D	******	******
2007	T700D	******	******
2006	T700D	******	******
2005	T635D	******	******
2004	T635D	375,000	431,000
2003	T635D	348,000	401,000
2002	T635D	324,000	372,000
2001	T635D	301,000	346,000
2000	T600D	280,000	322,000
1999	T600D	260,000	300,000
1998	T600D	245,000	282,000
1997	T550D	230,000	265,000
1996	T550D	216,000	249,000
1995	T550D	203,000	234,000

Jefferson 57 Pilothouse

Year	Power	Retail Low	Retail High
2009	T700D	******	******
2008	T700D	******	******
2007	T700D	******	******
2006	T700D	******	******
2005	T635D	551,000	633,000
2004	T635D	512,000	589,000
2003	T635D	476,000	548,000
2002	T635D	443,000	509,000
2001	T600D	412,000	474,000

Jefferson 60 Marquessa CMY

Year	Power	Retail Low	Retail High
2009	T700D	******	******
2008	T700D	******	******
2007	T700D	******	******
2006	T700D	******	******
2005	T800D	445,000	511,000
2004	T800D	413,000	475,000
2003	T800D	384,000	442,000
2002	T800D	357,000	411,000
2001	T800D	332,000	382,000
2000	T800D	309,000	356,000
1999	T800D	287,000	331,000

Jupiter 27 Open

Year	Power	Retail Low	Retail High
2006	T225 O/B	56,000	68,000
2005	T225 O/B	51,000	61,000
2004	T225 O/B	45,000	55,000
2003	T225 O/B	41,000	50,000
2002	T225 O/B	38,000	45,000
2001	T225 O/B	34,000	41,000
2000	T225 O/B	31,000	37,000
1999	T225 O/B	28,000	34,000
1998	T225 O/B	26,000	31,000

Jupiter 29 Forward Seating

Year	Power	Retail Low	Retail High
2009	T250 O/B	******	******
2008	T250 O/B	******	******
2007	T250 O/B	98,000	117,000
2006	T250 O/B	88,000	105,000

Jupiter 31 Open

Year	Power	Retail Low	Retail High
2009	T250 O/B	134,000	160,000
2008	T250 O/B	120,000	144,000
2007	T250 O/B	108,000	130,000
2006	T250 O/B	97,000	117,000
2005	T250 O/B	87,000	105,000
2004	T250 O/B	80,000	96,000
2003	T250 O/B	72,000	87,000
2002	T250 O/B	66,000	79,000
2001	T250 O/B	60,000	72,000
2000	T250 O/B	54,000	65,000
1999	T250 O/B	49,000	59,000
1998	T250 O/B	45,000	54,000
1997	T250 O/B	41,000	49,000
1996	T250 O/B	37,000	45,000
1995	T225 O/B	34,000	41,000

Jupiter 34 Forward Seating

Year	Power	Retail Low	Retail High
2009	T350 O/B	159,000	190,000
2008	T350 O/B	144,000	173,000

Jupiter 38 Forward Seating

Year	Power	Retail Low	Retail High
2009	3/300 O/B	******	******
2008	3/300 O/B	180,000	216,000
2007	3/300 O/B	162,000	194,000
2006	3/300 O/B	145,000	174,000
2005	T300 O/B	131,000	157,000

Krogen 39 Trawler

Year	Power	Retail Low	Retail High
2009	121D	******	******
2008	121D	******	******
2007	121D	******	******
2006	120D	******	******
2005	120D	******	******
2004	115D	******	******
2003	115D	******	******
2002	115D	235,000	282,000
2001	80D	220,000	265,000
2000	80D	207,000	249,000
1999	80D	195,000	234,000
1998	80D	183,000	220,000

Krogen 42 Trawler

Year	Power	Retail Low	Retail High
1997	135D	210,000	252,000
1996	135D	199,000	239,000
1995	135D	189,000	227,000

Krogen 48 Whaleback

Year	Power	Retail Low	Retail High
2003	S-Diesel	438,000	513,000
2002	S-Diesel	412,000	482,000
2001	S-Diesel	387,000	453,000
2000	S-Diesel	364,000	426,000
1999	S-Diesel	342,000	400,000
1998	S-Diesel	322,000	376,000
1997	S-Diesel	302,000	354,000
1996	S-Diesel	287,000	336,000
1995	S-Diesel	273,000	319,000

Legacy 28 Express

Year	Power	Retail Low	Retail High
2006	250D	******	******

See Page 529 For Price Adjustments

Year	Power	Retail Low	Retail High
2005	250D	******	******
2004	250D	******	******
2003	250D	69,000	82,000
2002	250D	63,000	76,000
2001	250D	58,000	70,000
2000	250D	53,000	64,000
1999	250D	49,000	59,000

Legacy 34 Express/Sedan

Year	Power	Retail Low	Retail High
2006	T380D	243,000	292,000
2005	T380D	224,000	269,000
2004	T380D	206,000	247,000
2003	T300D	189,000	227,000
2002	T300D	174,000	209,000
2001	T330D	160,000	192,000
2000	T330D	147,000	177,000
1999	T270D	137,000	164,000
1998	T270D	127,000	153,000
1997	T270D	118,000	142,000
1996	T270D	110,000	132,000

Lien Hwa 47 CPMY

Year	Power	Retail Low	Retail High
1999	S250D	******	******
1998	T375D	******	******
1997	T375D	******	******
1996	T375D	188,000	219,000
1995	T375D	174,000	204,000

Luhrs 28 Open

Year	Power	Retail Low	Retail High
2009	T330G	******	******
2009	T260D	******	******
2008	T330G	113,000	136,000
2008	T260D	140,000	168,000
2007	T320G	103,000	124,000
2007	T260D	127,000	153,000
2006	T320G	94,000	113,000
2006	T240D	116,000	139,000
2005	T320G	85,000	102,000
2005	T240D	105,000	126,000

Luhrs 290 Open

Year	Power	Retail Low	Retail High
2002	T325G	56,000	67,000
2001	T325G	51,000	61,000
2000	T325G	46,000	56,000
1999	T320G	42,000	51,000
1998	T320G	39,000	47,000
1997	T270G	36,000	43,000
1996	T270G	33,000	39,000
1995	T270G	30,000	36,000
1994	T270G	28,000	33,000
1993	T270G	25,000	30,000
1992	T270G	23,000	28,000

Luhrs 300 Tournament

Year	Power	Retail Low	Retail High
1996	T270G	30,000	36,000
1995	T270G	27,000	33,000

Luhrs 30/31 Open

Year	Power	Retail Low	Retail High
2009	T260D IPS	******	******
2008	T260D IPS	******	******
2007	T320G	112,000	135,000
2007	T315D	144,000	173,000
2006	T320G	102,000	123,000
2006	T315D	131,000	157,000
2005	T320G	93,000	112,000
2005	T315D	119,000	143,000

Year	Power	Retail Low	Retail High
2004	T320G	84,000	101,000
2004	T315D	108,000	130,000

Luhrs 320 Convertible

Year	Power	Retail Low	Retail High
1999	T325G	73,000	88,000
1999	T300D	102,000	122,000
1998	T325G	67,000	80,000
1998	T300D	92,000	111,000
1997	T340G	61,000	73,000
1997	T300D	84,000	101,000
1996	T340G	55,000	66,000
1996	T300D	76,000	92,000
1995	T340G	50,000	60,000
1995	T300D	70,000	84,000

Luhrs 32 Convertible

Year	Power	Retail Low	Retail High
2002	T325G	67,000	80,000
2002	T315D	93,000	110,000
2001	T325G	61,000	72,000
2001	T300D	85,000	100,000

Luhrs 32 Open

Year	Power	Retail Low	Retail High
2008	T375G	163,000	192,000
2008	T315D	200,000	236,000
2007	T375G	148,000	175,000
2007	T315D	182,000	215,000
2006	T375G	135,000	159,000
2006	T315D	165,000	195,000
2005	T320G	122,000	145,000
2005	T315D	151,000	178,000
2004	T320G	111,000	131,000
2004	T315D	137,000	162,000
2003	T320G	102,000	121,000
2003	T315D	126,000	149,000
2002	T320G	94,000	111,000
2002	T315D	116,000	137,000
2001	T320G	87,000	102,000
2001	T300D	107,000	126,000
2000	T320G	80,000	94,000
2000	T300D	98,000	116,000
1999	T320G	73,000	86,000
1999	T300D	90,000	106,000
1998	T320G	67,000	80,000
1998	T300D	83,000	98,000
1997	T340G	62,000	73,000
1997	T300D	76,000	90,000
1996	T340G	57,000	67,000
1996	T300D	70,000	83,000
1995	T340G	52,000	62,000
1995	T300D	64,000	76,000

Luhrs 34 Convertible

Year	Power	Retail Low	Retail High
2003	T320G	114,000	134,000
2003	T315D	138,000	163,000
2002	T375G	104,000	122,000
2002	T300D	126,000	148,000
2001	T310G	94,000	111,000
2001	T300D	114,000	135,000
2000	T310G	86,000	101,000
2000	T300D	104,000	123,000

Luhrs 35 Convertible

Year	Power	Retail Low	Retail High
2009	T480D	303,000	348,000
2008	T380D	278,000	320,000

Luhrs 350 Convertible

Year	Power	Retail Low	Retail High
1996	T-Gas	78,000	93,000
1996	T300D	96,000	114,000
1995	T-Gas	72,000	85,000
1995	T300D	89,000	105,000

Luhrs 36 Convertible

Year	Power	Retail Low	Retail High
2007	T-Gas	208,000	241,000
2007	T440D	246,000	285,000
2006	T-Gas	189,000	219,000
2006	T440D	224,000	260,000
2005	T-Gas	172,000	199,000
2005	T440D	204,000	236,000
2004	T-Gas	156,000	181,000
2004	T420D	185,000	215,000
2003	T-Gas	142,000	165,000
2003	T420D	168,000	196,000
2002	T-Gas	129,000	150,000
2002	T420D	153,000	178,000
2001	T-Gas	119,000	138,000
2001	T420D	141,000	164,000
2000	T-Gas	109,000	127,000
2000	T420D	130,000	150,000
1999	T-Gas	101,000	117,000
1999	T420D	119,000	138,000
1998	T-Gas	93,000	107,000
1998	T420D	110,000	127,000

Luhrs 36 Open; 36 SX

Year	Power	Retail Low	Retail High
2007	T425G	199,000	230,000
2007	T440D	237,000	275,000
2006	T425G	181,000	210,000
2006	T440D	216,000	250,000
2005	T420G	164,000	191,000
2005	T420D	196,000	228,000
2004	T420G	150,000	174,000
2004	T420D	178,000	207,000
2003	T420G	136,000	158,000
2003	T420D	162,000	188,000
2002	T420G	124,000	144,000
2002	T420D	148,000	171,000
2001	T420G	114,000	132,000
2001	T420D	136,000	158,000
2000	T420G	105,000	121,000
2000	T420D	125,000	145,000
1999	T420G	96,000	112,000
1999	T420D	115,000	133,000
1998	T340G	88,000	103,000
1998	T420D	106,000	123,000
1997	T340G	81,000	94,000
1997	T420D	97,000	113,000

Luhrs 380/40/38 Convertible

Year	Power	Retail Low	Retail High
2008	T440D	******	******
2007	T440D	297,000	344,000
2006	T440D	270,000	313,000
2005	T440D	245,000	285,000
2004	T420D	223,000	259,000
2003	T420D	203,000	236,000
2002	T420D	185,000	214,000
2001	T420D	168,000	195,000
2000	T420D	155,000	179,000
1999	T420D	142,000	165,000

Year	Power	Retail Low	Retail High
1998	T420D	131,000	152,000
1997	T420D	120,000	140,000
1996	T420D	111,000	128,000
1995	T420D	102,000	118,000
Luhrs 380/40/38 Open			
2008	T440D	******	******
2007	T440D	270,000	313,000
2006	T440D	245,000	285,000
2005	T440D	223,000	259,000
2004	T420D	203,000	236,000
2003	T420D	185,000	214,000
2002	T420D	168,000	195,000
2001	T420D	153,000	177,000
2000	T420D	141,000	163,000
1999	T420D	129,000	150,000
1998	T420D	119,000	138,000
1997	T420D	109,000	127,000
1996	T420D	101,000	117,000
1995	T420D	92,000	107,000
Luhrs 41 Convertible			
2009	T665D	******	******
2008	T540D	******	******
2007	T540D	373,000	429,000
2006	T540D	339,000	390,000
2005	T535D	309,000	355,000
2004	T535D	281,000	323,000
Luhrs 41 Hardtop			
2009	T665D	******	******
2008	T540D	******	******
2007	T540D	369,000	424,000
Luhrs 41 Open			
2009	T665D	******	******
2008	T540D	******	******
2007	T540D	360,000	414,000
2006	T540D	327,000	376,000
Luhrs 44 Convertible			
2005	T635D	388,000	447,000
2004	T500D	353,000	406,000
2003	T500D	321,000	370,000
Luhrs 50 Convertible			
2003	T900D	558,000	641,000
2002	T900D	513,000	590,000
2001	T900D	472,000	543,000
2000	T800D	434,000	499,000
1999	T800D	399,000	459,000
Mainship Pilot 30			
2007	S315D	85,000	97,000
2006	S315D	77,000	88,000
2005	S315D	70,000	80,000
2004	S315D	64,000	73,000
2003	S315D	58,000	67,000
2002	S230D	54,000	62,000
2001	S230D	49,000	57,000
2000	S230D	46,000	53,000
1999	S230D	43,000	49,000
1998	S230D	40,000	46,000
Mainship Pilot 30 Sedan			
2007	S315D	93,000	107,000
2006	S315D	85,000	97,000

Year	Power	Retail Low	Retail High
2005	S315D	77,000	89,000
2004	S315D	70,000	81,000
2003	S315D	64,000	74,000
2002	S230D	59,000	68,000
2001	S230D	54,000	63,000
2000	S230D	50,000	58,000
Mainship 31 Sedan Bridge			
1999	T290G	47,000	55,000
1998	T290G	44,000	50,000
1997	T270G	40,000	46,000
1996	T270G	37,000	42,000
1995	T270G	34,000	39,000
1994	T270G	31,000	36,000
Mainship 31 Pilot			
2009	S315D	138,000	158,000
2008	S315D	125,000	144,000
Mainship 34 Motor Yacht			
1998	T320G	60,000	69,000
1997	T340G	55,000	63,000
1996	T340G	50,000	58,000
Mainship 34 Pilot Express			
2008	S315D	157,000	181,000
2007	S315D	143,000	164,000
2006	S315D	130,000	149,000
2005	S315D	118,000	136,000
2004	S315D	108,000	124,000
2003	S315D	98,000	113,000
2002	S300D	90,000	103,000
2001	S300D	83,000	95,000
2000	S300D	76,000	88,000
1999	S300D	70,000	80,000
Mainship 34 Pilot Sedan			
2009	S315D	******	******
2008	S315D	164,000	189,000
2007	S315D	149,000	172,000
2006	S315D	136,000	156,000
2005	S315D	124,000	142,000
2004	S315D	112,000	129,000
2003	S315D	102,000	118,000
2002	S300D	94,000	108,000
2001	S300D	86,000	100,000
Mainship 34 Trawler			
2009	T315D	******	******
2008	S315D	175,000	201,000
2007	S240D	161,000	185,000
2006	S240D	148,000	170,000
2005	S240D	136,000	156,000
Mainship 350/390 Trawler			
2005	S370D	130,000	150,000
2005	T240D	146,000	168,000
2004	S-Diesel	120,000	138,000
2004	T370D	134,000	155,000
2003	S-Diesel	110,000	127,000
2003	T-240D	124,000	142,000
2002	S-Diesel	102,000	118,000
2002	T-240D	115,000	132,000
2001	S-Diesel	95,000	109,000
2001	T-230D	107,000	123,000
2000	S-Diesel	88,000	102,000

Year	Power	Retail Low	Retail High
2000	T-230D	99,000	114,000
1999	S-Diesel	82,000	95,000
1999	T-200D	92,000	106,000
1998	S-Diesel	76,000	88,000
1998	T-Diesel	86,000	99,000
1997	S-Diesel	71,000	82,000
1997	T-Diesel	80,000	92,000
1996	S-Diesel	66,000	76,000
1996	T-Diesel	74,000	85,000
Mainship 37 Motor Yacht			
1998	T-320G	79,000	91,000
1997	T-320G	73,000	84,000
1996	T-340G	67,000	77,000
1995	T-340G	62,000	71,000
Mainship 40 Sedan Bridge			
1999	T320G	78,000	89,000
1998	T320G	71,000	81,000
1997	T320G	64,000	74,000
1996	T320G	58,000	67,000
1995	T320G	54,000	62,000
Mainship 40 Trawler; 41 Expedition			
2009	S380D	******	******
2009	T260D	******	******
2008	S370D	209,000	241,000
2008	T260D	239,000	275,000
2007	S370D	192,000	221,000
2007	T240D	220,000	253,000
2006	S370D	177,000	204,000
2006	T240D	202,000	233,000
2005	S370D	163,000	187,000
2005	T240D	186,000	214,000
2004	S370D	150,000	172,000
2004	T240D	171,000	197,000
2003	S315D	138,000	158,000
2003	T240D	157,000	181,000
Mainship 430 Aft Cabin Trawler			
2006	T370D	257,000	296,000
2005	T370D	234,000	269,000
2004	T370D	213,000	245,000
2003	T315D	194,000	223,000
2002	T315D	176,000	203,000
2001	T300D	162,000	186,000
2000	T300D	149,000	171,000
1999	T300D	137,000	158,000
Mainship 43/45 Trawler			
2009	T440D	******	******
2008	T440D	******	******
2007	T440D	316,000	363,000
2006	T440D	287,000	330,000
Mainship 47 Motor Yacht			
1999	T485D	169,000	195,000
1998	T485D	156,000	179,000
1997	T485D	143,000	165,000
1996	T485D	132,000	151,000
1995	T485D	121,000	139,000
Mako 261 Center Console			
1995	T150 O/B	12,000	14,000
Mako 282 Center Console			
2003	T225 O/B	35,000	42,000

See Page 529 For Price Adjustments

Year	Power	Retail Low	Retail High
2002	T225 O/B	32,000	38,000
2001	T225 O/B	29,000	35,000
2000	T225 O/B	26,000	31,000
1999	T225 O/B	24,000	29,000
1998	T225 O/B	22,000	26,000
1997	T225 O/B	20,000	24,000
1996	T225 O/B	18,000	21,000
1995	T225 O/B	16,000	19,000
Mako 284 Center Console			
2009	T250 O/B	******	******
2008	T250 O/B	58,000	70,000
2007	T250 O/B	52,000	63,000
2006	T250 O/B	47,000	56,000
2005	T250 O/B	42,000	51,000
Mako 293 Walkaround			
2003	T250 O/B	40,000	49,000
2002	T250 O/B	36,000	44,000
2001	T250 O/B	33,000	39,000
2000	T250 O/B	30,000	36,000
1999	T250 O/B	27,000	32,000
1998	T250 O/B	24,000	29,000
1997	T250 O/B	22,000	27,000
1996	T250 O/B	20,000	24,000
1995	T250 O/B	18,000	22,000
Mako 333 CC Cuddy			
2000	T250 O/B	57,000	70,000
1999	T250 O/B	52,000	64,000
1998	T250 O/B	47,000	58,000
1997	T250 O/B	43,000	53,000
Marine Trader 34 DC			
2001	135D	77,000	93,000
2000	135D	73,000	87,000
1999	135D	68,000	82,000
1998	135D	64,000	77,000
1997	135D	60,000	72,000
1996	135D	57,000	68,000
1995	135D	53,000	64,000
Marine Trader 34 Sedan			
2001	135D	*****	*****
2000	135D	*****	*****
1999	135D	57,000	68,000
1998	135D	53,000	63,000
1997	135D	49,000	59,000
1996	135D	45,000	55,000
1995	135D	42,000	51,000
Marine Trader 38 Double Cabin			
2000	T135D	******	******
1999	T135D	******	******
1998	T135D	******	******
1997	T135D	******	******
1996	T135D	73,000	87,000
1995	T135D	69,000	83,000
Marine Trader 40 Sundeck			
2000	T135D	92,000	110,000
1999	T135D	87,000	105,000
1998	T135D	83,000	99,000
1997	T135D	79,000	94,000
1996	T135D	75,000	90,000
1995	T135D	72,000	86,000
Marlin 350 Cuddy			
2009	T250 O/B	******	******
2008	T250 O/B	96,000	115,000
2007	T250 O/B	86,000	103,000
2006	T250 O/B	77,000	93,000
2005	T250 O/B	70,000	85,000
2004	T250 O/B	64,000	77,000
2003	T250 O/B	58,000	70,000
2002	T250 O/B	53,000	64,000
2001	T250 O/B	48,000	58,000
2000	T250 O/B	44,000	53,000
1999	T250 O/B	40,000	48,000
1998	T250 O/B	37,000	44,000
1997	T250 O/B	34,000	40,000
1996	T250 O/B	31,000	37,000
1995	T250 O/B	28,000	34,000
Marquis 59 Pilothouse			
2009	715D	******	******
2008	715D	******	******
2007	825D	774,000	890,000
2006	825D	712,000	818,000
2005	825D	655,000	753,000
2004	825D	602,000	693,000
2003	825D	554,000	637,000
Maxum 2600/2700 SE			
2009	300 I/O	45,000	54,000
2008	320 I/O	40,000	49,000
2007	320 I/O	37,000	44,000
2006	320 I/O	33,000	40,000
Maxum 2700 SCR			
1996	T190 I/O	16,000	19,000
1995	T190 I/O	15,000	18,000
1994	T190 I/O	14,000	16,000
1993	T190 I/O	13,000	15,000
Maxum 2700 SE			
2007	320 I/O	42,000	50,000
2006	320 I/O	38,000	45,000
2005	320 I/O	34,000	41,000
2004	320 I/O	31,000	37,000
2003	320 I/O	29,000	34,000
2002	320 I/O	26,000	32,000
2001	320 I/O	24,000	29,000
Maxum 2800/2900 SCR; 2900 SE			
2006	320 I/O	46,000	56,000
2006	T190 I/O	48,000	58,000
2005	320 I/O	42,000	51,000
2005	T190 I/O	44,000	53,000
2004	320 I/O	38,000	46,000
2004	T190 I/O	40,000	48,000
2003	320 I/O	35,000	42,000
2003	T190 I/O	36,000	44,000
2002	320 I/O	32,000	38,000
2002	T190 I/O	33,000	40,000
2001	310 I/O	29,000	35,000
2001	T190 I/O	30,000	36,000
2000	310 I/O	27,000	32,000
2000	T190 I/O	28,000	33,000
1999	310 I/O	25,000	30,000
1999	T190 I/O	26,000	31,000
1998	310 I/O	23,000	27,000
1998	T190 I/O	24,000	29,000
1997	310 I/O	21,000	26,000
1997	T190 I/O	22,000	27,000
1996	310 I/O	20,000	24,000
1996	T190 I/O	20,000	25,000
1995	300 I/O	18,000	22,000
1995	T180 I/O	19,000	23,000
Maxum 2900 SE			
2009	T260 I/O	82,000	98,000
2008	T260 I/O	74,000	89,000
Maxum 3000 SCR			
2001	T260 I/O	34,000	41,000
2000	T260 I/O	31,000	37,000
1999	T260 I/O	28,000	33,000
1998	T260 I/O	25,000	30,000
1997	T260 I/O	23,000	28,000
Maxum 3100 SE			
2008	T260 I/O	97,000	116,000
2007	T260 I/O	88,000	106,000
2006	T260 I/O	80,000	96,000
2005	T260 I/O	73,000	87,000
2004	T260 I/O	66,000	79,000
2003	T260 I/O	60,000	72,000
2002	T260 I/O	55,000	66,000
Maxum 3200 SCR			
1998	T260 I/O	33,000	39,000
1997	T260 I/O	30,000	36,000
1996	T260 I/O	28,000	33,000
1995	T260 I/O	25,000	31,000
1994	T260 I/O	23,000	28,000
Maxum 3300 SE			
2007	T320 I/O	95,000	114,000
2006	T320 I/O	88,000	106,000
2005	T320 I/O	80,000	97,000
2004	T320 I/O	73,000	88,000
2003	T320 I/O	67,000	80,000
2002	T320 I/O	60,000	73,000
2001	T320 I/O	55,000	66,000
2000	T310 I/O	51,000	61,000
1999	T310 I/O	46,000	56,000
Maxum 3500 SY			
2008	T370G	136,000	163,000
2007	T370G	124,000	148,000
2006	T370G	112,000	135,000
2005	T370G	102,000	123,000
2004	T370G	94,000	113,000
2003	T370G	86,000	104,000
2002	T380G	80,000	96,000
2001	T380G	73,000	88,000
Maxum 3700 SCR			
2001	T380G	99,000	119,000
2000	T380G	90,000	108,000
1999	T380G	82,000	98,000
1998	T380G	79,000	95,000
Maxum 3700 Sport Yacht			
2009	T370G	******	******
2008	T370G	155,000	186,000
2007	T370G	141,000	169,000
2005	T370G	128,000	154,000

Year	Power	Retail Low	Retail High
2004	T370G	116,000	140,000
2003	T370G	106,000	127,000
Maxum 4100 SCR			
1999	T400G	84,000	101,000
1999	T370D	95,000	114,000
1998	T400G	77,000	93,000
1998	T370D	87,000	105,000
1997	T310G	71,000	85,000
1997	T315D	80,000	96,000
1996	T310G	65,000	79,000
1996	T315D	74,000	89,000
Maxum 4100 SCA			
2001	T400G	108,000	129,000
2001	T330D	138,000	166,000
2000	T400G	98,000	117,000
2000	T330D	126,000	151,000
1999	T400G	89,000	107,000
1999	T330D	114,000	137,000
1998	T400G	82,000	98,000
1998	T330D	105,000	126,000
1997	T400G	75,000	90,000
1997	T330D	97,000	116,000
Maxum 4100 SCB			
2001	T-Gas	103,000	124,000
2001	T330D	134,000	160,000
2000	T-Gas	94,000	113,000
2000	T330D	122,000	146,000
1999	T-Gas	85,000	102,000
1999	T330D	111,000	133,000
1998	T-Gas	78,000	94,000
1998	T330D	102,000	122,000
1997	T-Gas	72,000	87,000
1997	T330D	93,000	112,000
Maxum 4200 Sport Yacht			
2008	T425D	320,000	368,000
2007	T425D	291,000	335,000
2006	T450D	265,000	305,000
2005	T450D	241,000	277,000
2004	T450D	219,000	252,000
2003	T450D	200,000	230,000
2002	T450D	182,000	209,000
Maxum 4600 SCB			
2001	T450D	157,000	180,000
2000	T370D	144,000	166,000
1999	T370D	133,000	153,000
1998	T370D	122,000	140,000
1997	T370D	112,000	129,000
McKinna 47/481 Sedan			
2006	T370D	******	******
2005	T370D	******	******
2004	T370D	******	******
2003	T370D	216,000	252,000
2002	T370D	198,000	232,000
2001	T370D	182,000	213,000
2000	T330D	168,000	196,000
1999	T330D	154,000	181,000
McKinna 48 Pilothouse			
2000	T450D	261,000	300,000
1999	T450D	242,000	279,000

Year	Power	Retail Low	Retail High
1998	T450D	225,000	259,000
1997	T450D	210,000	241,000
1996	T450D	195,000	224,000
McKinna 57 Pilothouse			
2006	T660D	******	******
2005	T660D	******	******
2004	T635D	******	******
2003	T450D	******	******
2002	T450D	******	******
2001	T450D	365,000	420,000
2000	T450D	340,000	391,000
1999	T450D	316,000	363,000
1998	T450D	294,000	338,000
1997	T450D	273,000	314,000
Mediterranean 38 Convertible			
2007	T330D	******	******
2006	T330D	******	******
2005	T330D	******	******
2004	T330D	******	******
2003	T330D	******	******
2002	T330D	123,000	144,000
2001	T330D	113,000	133,000
2000	T330D	104,000	122,000
1999	T330D	96,000	112,000
1998	T-Diesel	88,000	103,000
1997	T-Diesel	81,000	95,000
1996	T-Diesel	75,000	87,000
1995	T-Diesel	69,000	80,000
Meridian 341 Sedan			
2009	T320G	189,000	217,000
2009	T330D	217,000	249,000
2008	T320G	160,000	184,000
2008	T330D	187,000	215,000
2007	T320G	145,000	167,000
2007	T330D	170,000	195,000
2006	T320G	132,000	152,000
2006	T250D	155,000	178,000
2005	T320G	120,000	138,000
2005	T250D	141,000	162,000
2004	T260G	109,000	126,000
2004	T250D	128,000	147,000
2003	T260D	99,000	114,000
2003	T250D	116,000	134,000
Meridian 368 MY			
2008	T370G	190,000	219,000
2008	T370D	225,000	259,000
2007	T370G	173,000	199,000
2007	T330D	205,000	236,000
2006	T370G	158,000	181,000
2006	T330D	186,000	214,000
2005	T370G	143,000	165,000
2005	T330D	170,000	195,000
Meridian 381 Sedan			
2005	T320G	128,000	148,000
2005	T330D	160,000	184,000
2004	T320G	117,000	134,000
2004	T270D	146,000	168,000
2003	T320G	106,000	122,000
2003	T270D	133,000	153,000

Year	Power	Retail Low	Retail High
Meridian 391 Sedan			
2009	T370G	******	******
2009	T370D	******	******
2008	T370G	200,000	231,000
2008	T370D	240,000	276,000
2007	T370G	182,000	210,000
2007	T330D	218,000	251,000
2006	T370G	166,000	191,000
2006	T330D	199,000	229,000
Meridian 408 MY			
2008	T380D	286,000	328,000
2007	T380D	263,000	302,000
2006	T380D	242,000	278,000
2005	T370D	222,000	256,000
2004	T370D	204,000	235,000
2003	T370D	188,000	216,000
Meridian 411 Sedan			
2007	T380D	269,000	310,000
2006	T380D	248,000	285,000
2005	T370D	228,000	262,000
2004	T370D	210,000	241,000
2003	T370D	193,000	222,000
Meridian 459 Cockpit MY			
2008	T380D	378,000	435,000
2007	T380D	348,000	400,000
2006	T380D	320,000	368,000
2005	T370D	294,000	338,000
2004	T370D	271,000	311,000
2003	T370D	249,000	286,000
Meridian 490 PH			
2008	T330D	390,000	449,000
2007	T330D	359,000	413,000
2006	T330D	330,000	380,000
2005	T330D	304,000	349,000
2004	T330D	279,000	321,000
Midnight Express 39			
2009	3/275 O/B	******	******
2008	3/275 O/B	******	******
2007	3/275 O/B	******	******
2006	3/275 O/B	******	******
2005	3/275 O/B	132,000	154,000
2004	3/275 O/B	119,000	138,000
2003	3/250 O/B	107,000	124,000
2002	3/250 O/B	96,000	112,000
2001	3/250 O/B	87,000	101,000
2000	3/250 O/B	78,000	91,000
Mikelson 43 Sportfisher			
2009	T480 Zeus	******	******
2008	T540D	******	******
2007	T540D	466,000	536,000
2006	T450D	424,000	488,000
2005	T450D	386,000	444,000
2004	T450D	351,000	404,000
2003	T450D	320,000	368,000
2002	T430D	291,000	334,000
2001	T430D	267,000	308,000
2000	T420D	246,000	283,000
1999	T420D	226,000	260,000
1998	T420D	208,000	239,000

See Page 529 For Price Adjustments

Year	Power	Retail Low	Retail High
1997	T420D	191,000	220,000

Mikelson 50 Sportfisher

Year	Power	Retail Low	Retail High
2009	T600D	******	******
2008	T600D	******	******
2007	T540D	******	******
2006	T450D	491,000	565,000
2005	T450D	447,000	514,000
2004	T450D	406,000	467,000
2003	T450D	374,000	430,000
2002	T450D	344,000	396,000
2001	T435D	316,000	364,000
2000	T435D	291,000	335,000
1999	T435D	268,000	308,000
1998	T435D	246,000	283,000
1997	T435D	227,000	261,000
1996	T435D	211,000	242,000
1995	T435D	196,000	225,000

Mikelson 60 Sportfisher

Year	Power	Retail Low	Retail High
1999	T735D	******	******
1998	T735D	******	******
1997	T735D	401,000	461,000
1996	T735D	372,000	428,000
1995	T735D	346,000	398,000
1994	T735D	322,000	370,000
1993	T735D	299,000	344,000
1992	T735D	278,000	320,000

Mikelson 64 Sportfisher

Year	Power	Retail Low	Retail High
2001	T1400D	803,000	923,000
2000	T800D	738,000	849,000
1999	T800D	679,000	781,000
1998	T800D	625,000	719,000
1997	T800D	575,000	661,000

Monk 36 Trawler

Year	Power	Retail Low	Retail High
2006	230D	******	******
2005	220D	******	******
2004	220D	******	******
2003	220D	158,000	189,000
2002	220D	148,000	178,000
2001	220D	139,000	167,000
2000	220D	132,000	159,000
1999	220D	125,000	151,000
1998	220D	119,000	143,000
1997	220D	113,000	136,000
1996	220D	108,000	129,000
1995	220D	102,000	123,000

Navigator 48 Classic

Year	Power	Retail Low	Retail High
2007	T318D	336,000	386,000
2006	T318D	309,000	355,000
2005	T318D	284,000	327,000
2004	T318D	261,000	301,000
2003	T318D	240,000	277,000
2002	T318D	221,000	254,000
2001	T318D	206,000	237,000
2000	T318D	191,000	220,000
1999	T318D	178,000	205,000
1998	T318D	165,000	190,000
1997	T318D	154,000	177,000

Navigator 50 Classic

Year	Power	Retail Low	Retail High
2000	T370D	206,000	237,000
1999	T370D	190,000	218,000

Year	Power	Retail Low	Retail High
1998	T370D	174,000	201,000
1997	T370D	160,000	184,000
1996	T370D	147,000	170,000
1995	T370D	137,000	158,000
1994	T370D	127,000	147,000
1993	T370D	119,000	136,000

Navigator 53 Classic

Year	Power	Retail Low	Retail High
2006	T370D	361,000	415,000
2005	T370D	332,000	381,000
2004	T370D	305,000	351,000
2003	T370D	281,000	323,000
2002	T370D	258,000	297,000
2001	T370D	237,000	273,000
2000	T370D	218,000	251,000
1999	T370D	203,000	234,000
1998	T370D	189,000	217,000
1997	T370D	176,000	202,000
1996	T370D	163,000	188,000
1995	T370D	152,000	175,000

Navigator 56 Classic

Year	Power	Retail Low	Retail High
2005	T370D	356,000	409,000
2004	T370D	327,000	376,000
2003	T370D	301,000	346,000
2002	T370D	277,000	319,000
2001	T370D	255,000	293,000
2000	T370D	234,000	270,000

Nordhavn 40

Year	Power	Retail Low	Retail High
2009	S/Diesel	******	******
2008	S/Diesel	******	******
2007	S/Diesel	******	******
2006	S/Diesel	380,000	456,000
2005	S/Diesel	357,000	428,000
2004	S/Diesel	335,000	402,000
2003	S/Diesel	315,000	378,000
2002	S/Diesel	296,000	356,000
2001	S/Diesel	278,000	334,000
2000	S/Diesel	262,000	314,000
1999	S/Diesel	246,000	295,000

Nordhavn 46

Year	Power	Retail Low	Retail High
2005	S/Diesel	******	******
2004	S/Diesel	******	******
2003	S/Diesel	******	******
2002	S/Diesel	460,000	552,000
2001	S/Diesel	441,000	529,000
2000	S/Diesel	423,000	508,000
1999	S/Diesel	406,000	488,000
1998	S/Diesel	390,000	468,000
1997	S/Diesel	375,000	450,000
1996	S/Diesel	360,000	432,000
1995	S/Diesel	349,000	419,000

Nordhavn 47

Year	Power	Retail Low	Retail High
2009	S/Diesel	******	******
2008	S/Diesel	******	******
2007	S/Diesel	******	******
2006	S/Diesel	777,000	932,000
2005	S/Diesel	730,000	876,000
2004	S/Diesel	686,000	823,000
2003	S/Diesel	645,000	774,000

Nordhavn 50

Year	Power	Retail Low	Retail High
2006	S/Diesel	******	******

Year	Power	Retail Low	Retail High
2005	S/Diesel	******	******
2004	S/Diesel	******	******
2003	S/Diesel	******	******
2002	S/Diesel	******	******
2001	S/Diesel	585,000	702,000
2000	S/Diesel	555,000	666,000
1999	S/Diesel	527,000	633,000
1998	S/Diesel	501,000	601,000
1997	S/Diesel	476,000	571,000

Nordhavn 55

Year	Power	Retail Low	Retail High
2009	S/Diesel	******	******
2008	S/Diesel	******	******
2007	S/Diesel	1,160,000	1,392,000
2006	S/Diesel	1,113,000	1,336,000
2005	S/Diesel	1,046,000	1,256,000

Nordhavn 57

Year	Power	Retail Low	Retail High
2007	S/Diesel	******	******
2006	S/Diesel	******	******
2005	S/Diesel	1,110,000	1,332,000
2004	S/Diesel	1,054,000	1,265,000
2003	S/Diesel	1,001,000	1,202,000
2002	S/Diesel	951,000	1,142,000
2001	S/Diesel	913,000	1,096,000
2000	S/Diesel	877,000	1,052,000
1999	S/Diesel	841,000	1,010,000

Nordic 26 Tug

Year	Power	Retail Low	Retail High
1997	S/Diesel	51,000	62,000
1996	S/Diesel	49,000	59,000
1995	S/Diesel	47,000	57,000

Nordic 32 Tug

Year	Power	Retail Low	Retail High
2009	280D	187,000	218,000
2008	280D	177,000	207,000
2007	280D	168,000	197,000
2006	270D	160,000	187,000
2005	270D	152,000	178,000
2004	270D	144,000	169,000
2003	270D	137,000	160,000
2002	220D	130,000	152,000
2001	220D	125,000	146,000
2000	220D	120,000	140,000
1999	220D	115,000	135,000
1998	220D	110,000	129,000
1997	210D	106,000	124,000
1996	210D	103,000	120,000
1995	210D	100,000	117,000

Nordic 37 Tug

Year	Power	Retail Low	Retail High
2009	380D	322,000	370,000
2008	380D	305,000	351,000
2007	380D	290,000	334,000
2006	380D	276,000	317,000
2005	330D	262,000	301,000
2004	330D	249,000	286,000
2003	330D	239,000	275,000
2002	330D	229,000	264,000
2001	330D	220,000	253,000
2000	330D	211,000	243,000
1999	330D	203,000	233,000
1998	330D	195,000	224,000

Nordic 42 Tug

Year	Power	Retail Low	Retail High
2009	T540D	******	******

Year	Power	Retail Low	Retail High
2008	T540D	345,000	397,000
2007	T540D	321,000	369,000
2006	T540D	299,000	344,000
2005	T450D	278,000	319,000
2004	T450D	258,000	297,000
2003	T450D	240,000	276,000
2002	T450D	223,000	257,000
2001	330D	210,000	241,000
2000	330D	197,000	227,000
1999	330D	185,000	213,000
1998	330D	174,000	200,000
1997	330D	164,000	188,000
1996	330D	154,000	177,000

Ocean Alexander 390 Sundeck

Year	Power	Retail Low	Retail High
1999	T220D	123,000	141,000
1998	T220D	113,000	130,000
1997	T220D	104,000	120,000
1996	T220D	96,000	110,000
1995	T220D	89,000	102,000

Ocean Alexander 422 Sport Sedan

Year	Power	Retail Low	Retail High
2001	T420D	216,000	248,000
2000	T420D	198,000	228,000
1999	T420D	182,000	210,000
1998	T420D	168,000	193,000
1997	T375D	154,000	178,000
1996	T375D	144,000	165,000
1995	T375D	133,000	154,000

Ocean Alexander 423 Classico

Year	Power	Retail Low	Retail High
2002	T220D	227,000	261,000
2001	T220D	209,000	240,000
2000	T220D	192,000	221,000
1999	T220D	177,000	203,000
1998	T220D	162,000	187,000
1997	T220D	149,000	172,000
1996	T220D	137,000	158,000
1995	T220D	128,000	147,000

Ocean Alexander 426 Classico

Year	Power	Retail Low	Retail High
2002	T220D	234,000	269,000
2001	T220D	215,000	247,000
2000	T220D	198,000	227,000
1999	T220D	182,000	209,000
1998	T220D	167,000	192,000
1997	T220D	154,000	177,000
1996	T220D	141,000	163,000
1995	T220D	131,000	151,000

Ocean Alexander 420 Sundeck

Year	Power	Retail Low	Retail High
1999	T220D	139,000	160,000
1998	T220D	128,000	147,000
1997	T220D	118,000	135,000
1996	T250D	108,000	125,000
1995	T250D	100,000	115,000

Ocean Alexander 430/460 Classico

Year	Power	Retail Low	Retail High
2006	T220D	******	******
2005	T220D	******	******
2004	T220D	******	******
2003	T220D	230,000	338,000
2002	T220D	211,000	311,000
2001	T220D	194,000	286,000
2000	T220D	179,000	263,000

Ocean Alexander 45 Sedan

Year	Power	Retail Low	Retail High
2009	T480D	******	******
2008	T480D	479,000	703,000
2007	T380D	441,000	647,000
2006	T380D	405,000	595,000
2005	T380D	******	******

Ocean Alexander 450 Classico Sedan

Year	Power	Retail Low	Retail High
2004	T220D	******	******
2003	T220D	******	******
2002	T220D	253,000	372,000
2001	T220D	233,000	342,000
2000	T210D	214,000	315,000

Ocean Alexander 456 Classico

Year	Power	Retail Low	Retail High
2002	T375D	261,000	383,000
2001	T375D	240,000	352,000
2000	T375D	221,000	324,000
1999	T375D	203,000	298,000
1998	T375D	187,000	274,000
1997	T375D	172,000	252,000
1996	T375D	160,000	235,000
1995	T375D	148,000	218,000

Ocean Alexander 480 Sport Sedan

Year	Power	Retail Low	Retail High
2001	T420D	224,000	258,000
2000	T420D	206,000	237,000
1999	T420D	190,000	218,000
1998	T420D	174,000	201,000
1997	T420D	160,000	185,000
1996	T375D	148,000	170,000
1995	T375D	136,000	156,000

Ocean Alexander 486 Classico

Year	Power	Retail Low	Retail High
2002	T420D	317,000	365,000
2001	T420D	292,000	336,000
2000	T420D	268,000	309,000
1999	T420D	247,000	284,000
1998	T420D	227,000	261,000
1997	T420D	209,000	240,000
1996	T-Diesel	192,000	221,000
1995	T-Diesel	177,000	203,000
1990	T-Diesel		

Ocean Alexander 51/53 Sedan

Year	Power	Retail Low	Retail High
1998	T550D	******	******
1997	T550D	286,000	329,000
1996	T485D	266,000	306,000
1995	T735D	247,000	284,000

Ocean Alexander 520/540 PH

Year	Power	Retail Low	Retail High
2002	T420D	308,000	355,000
2001	T420D	287,000	330,000
2000	T420D	267,000	307,000
1999	T420D	248,000	285,000
1998	T435D	230,000	265,000
1997	T435D	214,000	247,000
1996	T435D	199,000	229,000
1995	T435D	187,000	215,000

Ocean Alexander 546 Yachtfish

Year	Power	Retail Low	Retail High
1998	T660D	297,000	342,000
1997	T660D	276,000	318,000
1996	T660D	257,000	296,000
1995	T660D	239,000	275,000

Ocean Alexander 548 PH

Year	Power	Retail Low	Retail High
2002	T660D	486,000	559,000
2001	T660D	452,000	520,000
2000	T660D	420,000	483,000
1999	T660D	391,000	449,000
1998	T550D	367,000	422,000
1997	T550D	345,000	397,000
1996	T550D	324,000	373,000

Ocean Master 27 Center Console

Year	Power	Retail Low	Retail High
2009	T200 O/B	******	******
2008	T200 O/B	******	******
2007	T200 O/B	******	******
2006	T200 O/B	******	******
2005	T200 O/B	******	******
2004	T200 O/B	******	******
2003	T200 O/B	******	******
2002	T200 O/B	57,000	66,000
2001	T200 O/B	52,000	60,000
2000	T200 O/B	47,000	54,000
1999	T200 O/B	43,000	49,000
1998	T200 O/B	39,000	45,000
1997	T200 O/B	35,000	41,000
1996	T200 O/B	32,000	37,000
1995	T200 O/B	30,000	34,000

Ocean 37 Billfish

Year	Power	Retail Low	Retail High
2009	T480D	******	******
2008	T480D	297,000	342,000

Ocean 38 SS

Year	Power	Retail Low	Retail High
1995	T420D	116,000	134,000

Ocean 40 Sport Fish

Year	Power	Retail Low	Retail High
2005	T420D	215,000	247,000
2004	T420D	195,000	225,000
2003	T420D	178,000	205,000
2002	T420D	162,000	186,000
2001	T420D	147,000	169,000
2000	T420D	134,000	154,000
1999	T420D	122,000	140,000

Ocean 40 Super Sport

Year	Power	Retail Low	Retail High
2005	T420D	235,000	270,000
2004	T420D	214,000	246,000
2003	T420D	195,000	224,000
2002	T420D	177,000	204,000
2001	T420D	161,000	185,000
2000	T420D	146,000	169,000
1999	T420D	133,000	153,000
1998	T420D	121,000	139,000
1997	T420D	110,000	127,000

Ocean 42 SS (1991-95)

Year	Power	Retail Low	Retail High
1995	T485D	139,000	160,000

Ocean 42 SS (Current)

Year	Power	Retail Low	Retail High
2009	T510D	******	******
2008	T510D	440,000	506,000
2007	T510D	400,000	460,000
2006	T510D	364,000	419,000

Ocean 43 Super Sport

Year	Power	Retail Low	Retail High
2005	T480D	329,000	378,000
2004	T480D	299,000	344,000
2003	T480D	272,000	313,000
2002	T480D	248,000	285,000

See Page 529 For Price Adjustments

Year	Power	Retail Low	Retail High
2001	T480D	225,000	259,000
2000	T480D	205,000	236,000
Ocean 44 Motor Yacht			
1999	T485D	196,000	226,000
1998	T485D	180,000	207,000
1997	T485D	166,000	191,000
1996	T485D	153,000	176,000
1995	T485D	140,000	161,000
Ocean 45 Super Sport			
1999	T485D	198,000	228,000
1998	T485D	182,000	210,000
1997	T485D	168,000	193,000
1996	T485D	154,000	177,000
Ocean 46 SS			
2009	T715D	******	******
2008	T715D	547,000	629,000
2007	T715D	503,000	579,000
2006	T710D	463,000	532,000
2005	T710D	426,000	490,000
Ocean 48 Cockpit MY			
1999	T485D	212,000	244,000
1998	T485D	195,000	224,000
1997	T485D	179,000	206,000
1996	T485D	165,000	190,000
1995	T485D	152,000	175,000
Ocean 48 Sport Fish			
2001	T800D	271,000	311,000
2000	T800D	246,000	283,000
1999	T660D	224,000	258,000
1998	T625D	204,000	235,000
1997	T625D	185,000	213,000
Ocean 48 SS			
2003	T700D	334,000	385,000
2002	T660D	308,000	354,000
2001	T660D	283,000	325,000
2000	T660D	260,000	299,000
1999	T660D	239,000	275,000
1998	T625D	220,000	253,000
1997	T625D	203,000	233,000
1996	T625D	186,000	214,000
1995	T625D	173,000	199,000
Ocean 50 Super Sport			
2009	T825D	******	******
2008	T825D	******	******
2007	T825D	592,000	681,000
2006	T800D	545,000	626,000
2005	T800D	501,000	576,000
2004	T800D	461,000	530,000
Ocean 52 Super Sport			
2006	T800D	582,000	669,000
2005	T800D	535,000	616,000
2004	T800D	492,000	566,000
2003	T800D	453,000	521,000
2002	T800D	417,000	479,000
2001	T800D	383,000	441,000
Ocean 53 Super Sport			
1999	T820D	317,000	365,000
1998	T820D	292,000	336,000
1997	T820D	268,000	309,000
1996	T820D	247,000	284,000
1995	T820D	227,000	261,000
Ocean 54 Super Sport			
2009	1015D	******	******
2008	1050D	******	******
2007	1050D	756,000	869,000
Ocean 56 Super Sport			
2002	1050D	538,000	618,000
2001	1050D	495,000	569,000
2000	1050D	455,000	523,000
1999	1050D	419,000	481,000
Ocean 57 Super Sport			
2007	1015D	768,000	884,000
2006	1015D	707,000	813,000
2005	1015D	650,000	748,000
2004	1015D	598,000	688,000
2003	1015D	550,000	633,000
Ocean 60 Super Sport			
2001	1350D	******	******
2000	1350D	******	******
1999	1350D	690,000	793,000
1998	1350D	641,000	737,000
1997	1350D	596,000	686,000
1996	1350D	555,000	638,000
Ocean 62 Super Sport			
2008	1500D	******	******
2007	1500D	******	******
2006	1400D	******	******
2005	1400D	******	******
2004	1400D	******	******
2003	1350D	903,000	1,038,000
2002	1350D	839,000	965,000
Ocean 66 Super Sport			
1999	1350D	645,000	741,000
1998	1350D	599,000	689,000
1997	1350D	557,000	641,000
1996	1350D	518,000	596,000
1995	1150D	482,000	554,000
Offshore 48 Cockpit MY			
1999	T435D	223,000	256,000
1998	T435D	207,000	238,000
1997	T435D	193,000	222,000
1996	T435D	179,000	206,000
1995	T375D	166,000	192,000
Offshore 48 Pilothouse			
2001	T435D	297,000	341,000
2000	T420D	279,000	321,000
1999	T420D	262,000	301,000
Offshore 48 Sedan			
2001	T435D	267,000	307,000
2000	T435D	248,000	285,000
1999	T435D	231,000	265,000
1998	T435D	215,000	247,000
1997	T435D	199,000	229,000
1996	T435D	185,000	213,000
1995	T375D	172,000	198,000
Offshore 52 Sedan			
1999	T420D	313,000	360,000
1998	T420D	291,000	334,000
1997	T450D	270,000	311,000
1996	T450D	251,000	289,000
1995	T485D	234,000	269,000
Offshore 52/54 Pilothouse			
2009	T460D	******	******
2008	T460D	******	******
2007	T460D	******	******
2006	T450D	495,000	569,000
2005	T450D	460,000	529,000
2004	T450D	428,000	492,000
2003	T450D	398,000	457,000
2002	T450D	370,000	425,000
2001	T450D	344,000	396,000
2000	T450D	320,000	368,000
1999	T450D	297,000	342,000
1998	T420D	276,000	318,000
Offshore 55/60 Pilothouse			
2007	T800D	******	******
2006	T800D	******	******
2005	T800D	******	******
2004	T800D	******	******
2003	T800D	******	******
2002	T800D	569,000	655,000
2001	T800D	529,000	609,000
2000	T800D	492,000	566,000
1999	T660D	458,000	526,000
1998	T660D	426,000	490,000
1997	T550D	400,000	460,000
1996	T550D	376,000	433,000
1995	T-Diesel	353,000	407,000
Offshore 58/62 Pilothouse			
2009	T800D	******	******
2008	T800D	******	******
2007	T800D	******	******
2006	T800D	******	******
2005	T800D	******	******
2004	T800D	******	******
2003	T800D	******	******
2002	T800D	589,000	677,000
2001	T800D	548,000	630,000
2000	T800D	509,000	586,000
1999	T660D	474,000	545,000
1998	T660D	440,000	507,000
1997	T550D	410,000	471,000
1996	T550D	381,000	438,000
1995	T550D	354,000	407,000
1994	T550D	329,000	379,000
Osprey 30			
2009	T-Diesel I/O	******	******
2008	T-Diesel I/O	******	******
2007	T-Diesel I/O	******	******
2006	T188D I/O	******	******
2005	T188D I/O	80,000	92,000
2004	T188D I/O	73,000	84,000
2003	T188D I/O	66,000	76,000
2002	T188D I/O	60,000	70,000
2001	T188D I/O	55,000	63,000
2000	T188D I/O	50,000	58,000
1999	T188D I/O	45,000	52,000

Year	Power	Retail Low	Retail High
Pacific Mariner 65 Motor Yacht			
2009	T825D	******	******
2008	T825D	******	******
2007	T825D	******	******
2006	T825D	******	******
2005	T825D	950,000	1,092,000
2004	T825D	893,000	1,026,000
2004	T825D	839,000	965,000
2002	T800D	789,000	907,000
2001	T800D	741,000	852,000
2000	T800D	697,000	801,000
1999	T800D	662,000	761,000
1998	T800D	629,000	723,000
1997	T800D	597,000	687,000
Pacific Trawler 40			
2003	220D	168,000	201,000
2002	220D	158,000	189,000
2001	220D	148,000	178,000
2000	220D	139,000	167,000
PDQ 32/34 Powercat			
2009	T100D	******	******
2008	T100D	264,000	308,000
2007	T100D	248,000	290,000
2006	T100D	233,000	273,000
2005	T100D	219,000	256,000
2004	T100D	206,000	241,000
2003	T100D	193,000	226,000
2002	T75D	184,000	215,000
2001	T75D	174,000	204,000
2000	T75D	166,000	194,000
Pearson True North 33			
2008	440D	******	******
2007	440D	******	******
2006	440D	156,000	182,000
2005	440D	145,000	170,000
2004	440D	135,000	158,000
Pearson True North 38			
2008	440D	******	******
2007	440D	******	******
2006	440D	226,000	265,000
2005	440D	211,000	246,000
2004	440D	196,000	229,000
2003	440D	182,000	213,000
2002	440D	169,000	198,000
Phoenix 27 Tournament			
1999	T260G	40,000	48,000
1998	T260G	37,000	44,000
1997	T260G	34,000	41,000
1996	T260G	31,000	37,000
1995	T260G	29,000	34,000
Phoenix 29 SFX Convertible			
1999	T-Gas	40,000	49,000
1999	T240D	51,000	61,000
1998	T-Gas	37,000	45,000
1998	T240D	47,000	56,000
1997	T-Gas	34,000	41,000
1997	T240D	43,000	52,000
1996	T-Gas	31,000	38,000
1996	T240D	40,000	48,000

Year	Power	Retail Low	Retail High
1995	T-Gas	29,000	35,000
1995	T240D	36,000	44,000
Phoenix 32 Tournament			
1999	T350D	77,000	93,000
1998	T350D	71,000	85,000
1997	T350D	65,000	78,000
Phoenix 33/34 SFX Convertible			
1999	T-Gas	78,000	93,000
1999	T385D	100,000	120,000
1998	T-Gas	71,000	86,000
1998	T375D	92,000	110,000
1997	T-Gas	66,000	79,000
1997	T375D	84,000	101,000
1996	T-Gas	60,000	73,000
1996	T375D	78,000	93,000
1995	T-Gas	56,000	67,000
1995	T350D	71,000	86,000
Phoenix 33/34 Tournament			
1999	T-Gas	72,000	87,000
1999	T385D	95,000	114,000
1998	T-Gas	66,000	80,000
1998	T375D	88,000	105,000
1997	T-Gas	61,000	73,000
1997	T375D	80,000	97,000
1996	T-Gas	56,000	67,000
1996	T375D	74,000	89,000
1995	T-Gas	52,000	62,000
1995	T-Diesel	68,000	82,000
Phoenix 37/38 SFX Convertible			
1999	480D	154,000	185,000
1998	485D	142,000	170,000
1997	485D	130,000	156,000
1996	485D	120,000	144,000
1995	485D	110,000	132,000
Post 42 Sport Fisherman			
2009	T510D	******	******
2008	T510D	******	******
2007	T510D	399,000	458,000
2006	T510D	363,000	417,000
2005	T480D	330,000	379,000
2004	T480D	300,000	345,000
2003	T480D	273,000	314,000
2002	T480D	248,000	286,000
2001	T430D	229,000	263,000
2000	T430D	210,000	242,000
1999	T430D	193,000	222,000
1998	T430D	178,000	205,000
1997	T430D	164,000	188,000
Post 43 Sport Fisherman			
1996	T550D	167,000	192,000
1995	T550D	153,000	176,000
Post 46 Sport Fisherman			
1996	T550D	209,000	241,000
1995	T550D	193,000	222,000
Post 47 Sport Fisherman			
2009	T715D	******	******
2008	T715D	******	******
2007	T715D	******	******
2006	T715D	495,000	570,000

Year	Power	Retail Low	Retail High
2005	T680D	451,000	518,000
2004	T680D	410,000	472,000
2003	T680D	373,000	429,000
2002	T680D	343,000	395,000
2001	T680D	316,000	363,000
2000	T680D	290,000	334,000
1999	T680D	267,000	307,000
1998	T680D	246,000	283,000
1997	T550D	226,000	260,000
Post 50 Sport Fisherman			
2009	T865D	******	******
2008	T865D	******	******
2007	T865D	******	******
2006	T865D	655,000	952,000
2005	T860D	596,000	866,000
2004	T860D	542,000	788,000
2003	T860D	493,000	717,000
2002	T820D	449,000	652,000
2001	T820D	413,000	600,000
2000	T820D	380,000	552,000
1999	T820D	350,000	508,000
1998	T820D	322,000	467,000
1997	T735D	296,000	430,000
1996	T735D	272,000	395,000
1995	T735D	250,000	364,000
Post 53 Convertible			
2009	T1100D	******	******
2008	T1100D	******	******
2007	T1100D	******	******
2006	T1100D	761,000	875,000
2005	T1100D	708,000	814,000
Post 56 Convertible			
2009	T1300D	******	******
2007	T1300D	******	******
2006	T1300D	******	******
2005	T1300D	1,023,000	1,176,000
2004	T1300D	951,000	1,094,000
2003	T1300D	884,000	1,017,000
2002	T1300D	822,000	946,000
2001	T1300D	765,000	880,000
Pro-Line 26 Sport			
2005	T150 O/B	29,000	34,000
2004	T150 O/B	26,000	31,000
2003	T150 O/B	23,000	28,000
2002	T150 O/B	21,000	25,000
2001	T150 O/B	19,000	23,000
2000	T150 O/B	17,000	21,000
Pro-Line 26 Super Sport			
2009	T150 O/B	44,000	52,000
2008	T150 O/B	39,000	47,000
2007	T150 O/B	35,000	42,000
2006	T150 O/B	32,000	38,000
Pro-Line 26 Express			
2009	T200 O/B	61,000	73,000
2008	T200 O/B	55,000	66,000
Pro-Line 26 XP			
2009	T200 O/B	65,000	78,000
2008	T200 O/B	59,000	70,000

Year	Power	Retail Low	Retail High
Pro-Line 27 Express			
2004	T200 O/B	37,000	45,000
2003	T200 O/B	34,000	41,000
2002	T200 O/B	31,000	38,000
2001	T200 O/B	29,000	35,000
Pro-Line 27 Walk			
2004	T200 O/B	38,000	45,000
2003	T200 O/B	34,000	41,000
2002	T200 O/B	31,000	37,000
2001	T200 O/B	28,000	34,000
2000	T200 O/B	26,000	31,000
1999	T200 O/B	24,000	29,000
1998	T200 O/B	22,000	26,000
Pro-Line 27/29 Sport			
2006	T200 O/B	47,000	56,000
2005	T200 O/B	43,000	51,000
2004	T200 O/B	39,000	47,000
2003	T200 O/B	35,000	42,000
2001	T200 O/B	32,000	38,000
2000	T200 O/B	29,000	35,000
Pro-Line 2700 Sportsman			
1999	T200 O/B	28,000	33,000
1998	T200 O/B	25,000	31,000
1997	T200 O/B	23,000	28,000
1996	T200 O/B	21,000	26,000
1995	T200 O/B	20,000	24,000
Pro-Line 2810 Walkaround			
2000	T225 O/B	41,000	50,000
1999	T225 O/B	38,000	45,000
1998	T225 O/B	34,000	41,000
1997	T225 O/B	31,000	37,000
Pro-Line 29 Grand Sport			
2009	T225 O/B	******	******
2008	T225 O/B	70,000	85,000
2007	T225 O/B	64,000	77,000
Pro-Line 29 Super Sport			
2009	T225 O/B	76,000	91,000
2008	T225 O/B	69,000	82,000
2007	T225 O/B	62,000	75,000
2006	T225 O/B	57,000	68,000
2005	T225 O/B	52,000	62,000
Pro-Line 2950 Walkaround			
1999	T225 O/B	39,000	47,000
1999	T250 I/O	41,000	50,000
1998	T225 O/B	36,000	44,000
1998	T250 I/O	38,000	46,000
1997	T225 O/B	33,000	40,000
1997	T250 I/O	35,000	42,000
1996	T225 O/B	31,000	37,000
1996	T250 I/O	32,000	39,000
1995	T225 O/B	28,000	34,000
1995	T250 I/O	29,000	35,000
Pro-Line 30 Walk			
2005	T225 O/B	59,000	71,000
2004	T225 O/B	54,000	65,000
2003	T225 O/B	49,000	59,000
2002	T225 O/B	45,000	54,000
2001	T225 O/B	41,000	49,000
2000	T225 O/B	37,000	44,000

Year	Power	Retail Low	Retail High
Pro-Line 30 Express			
2005	T225 O/B	58,000	70,000
2004	T225 O/B	53,000	64,000
2003	T225 O/B	48,000	58,000
2002	T225 O/B	44,000	53,000
2001	T225 O/B	40,000	48,000
2000	T225 O/B	36,000	44,000
Pro-Line 30/31 Sport			
2006	T225 O/B	57,000	68,000
2005	T225 O/B	51,000	61,000
2004	T225 O/B	46,000	55,000
2003	T225 O/B	41,000	49,000
2002	T225 O/B	37,000	44,000
2001	T225 O/B	33,000	40,000
2000	T225 O/B	30,000	36,000
Pro-Line 32 Express (1997-2002)			
2002	T320G	59,000	70,000
2001	T320G	53,000	64,000
2000	T310G	48,000	58,000
1999	T310G	44,000	53,000
1998	T310G	40,000	48,000
1997	T310G	36,000	44,000
Pro-Line 32 Express (Current)			
2009	T250 O/B	127,000	152,000
2008	T250 O/B	115,000	138,000
2007	T250 O/B	105,000	126,000
2006	T250 O/B	95,000	114,000
2005	T250 O/B	87,000	104,000
Pro-Line 33 Express			
2006	T370G I/B	******	******
2006	T315D I/B	140,000	168,000
2005	T370G I/B	******	******
2005	T315D I/B	127,000	153,000
2004	T370G I/B	101,000	122,000
2004	T315D I/B	116,000	139,000
2003	T370G I/B	92,000	111,000
2003	T315D I/B	105,000	126,000
2002	T370G I/B	84,000	101,000
2002	T315D I/B	96,000	115,000
2001	T310G I/B	76,000	92,000
2001	T350D I/B	87,000	104,000
2000	T310G I/B	69,000	83,000
2000	T350D I/B	79,000	95,000
1999	T310G I/B	63,000	76,000
1999	T350D I/B	72,000	86,000
Pro-Line 33 Walk			
2005	T250 O/B	80,000	96,000
2004	T250 O/B	72,000	87,000
2003	T250 O/B	66,000	79,000
Pro-Line 3400 SS Cuddy			
2001	T250 O/B	57,000	68,000
2000	T250 O/B	51,000	62,000
1999	T250 O/B	47,000	56,000
1998	T250 O/B	42,000	51,000
Pro-Line 35 Express			
2009	3/225 O/B	173,000	207,000
2008	3/225 O/B	157,000	188,000
2007	3/225 O/B	143,000	171,000
2006	3/225 O/B	130,000	156,000

Year	Power	Retail Low	Retail High
Pursuit 2655 Center Console			
1996	T200 O/B	19,000	22,000
1995	T200 O/B	17,000	21,000
Pursuit 2670 CC; C 260			
2007	T200 O/B	62,000	74,000
2006	T200 O/B	56,000	67,000
2005	T200 O/B	51,000	61,000
Pursuit 2670 Cuddy Console			
2004	T200 O/B	41,000	49,000
2003	T200 O/B	37,000	44,000
2002	T200 O/B	33,000	40,000
Pursuit LS 2670 Denali			
2007	T200 O/B	44,000	52,000
2006	T200 O/B	40,000	48,000
2005	T200 O/B	36,000	43,000
2004	T200 O/B	33,000	39,000
2003	T200 O/B	30,000	36,000
Pursuit 2855 Express Fish			
1995	T200 O/B	24,000	28,000
Pursuit 2860/2865 Denali			
2004	375G I/O	46,000	55,000
2003	375G I/O	42,000	51,000
2002	375G I/O	39,000	47,000
2001	310G I/O	36,000	43,000
2000	310G I/O	33,000	39,000
1999	310G I/O	30,000	36,000
1998	310G I/O	28,000	33,000
1997	310G I/O	25,000	31,000
Pursuit 2870 CC; C 280			
2008	T225 O/B	86,000	103,000
2007	T225 O/B	78,000	94,000
2006	T225 O/B	71,000	85,000
2005	T225 O/B	65,000	78,000
2004	T225 O/B	59,000	71,000
2003	T225 O/B	53,000	64,000
2002	T225 O/B	49,000	59,000
2001	T225 O/B	45,000	54,000
2000	T225 O/B	42,000	50,000
1999	T225 O/B	38,000	46,000
1998	T225 O/B	35,000	42,000
1997	T225 O/B	32,000	39,000
Pursuit 2870 Offshore CC			
2002	T225 O/B	44,000	53,000
2001	T225 O/B	40,000	48,000
2000	T225 O/B	36,000	43,000
1999	T225 O/B	33,000	39,000
1998	T225 O/B	30,000	36,000
1997	T225 O/B	27,000	33,000
1996	T225 O/B	25,000	30,000
Pursuit 2870 Walkaround			
2006	T225 O/B	80,000	96,000
2005	T225 O/B	72,000	87,000
2004	T225 O/B	66,000	79,000
2003	T225 O/B	60,000	72,000
2002	T225 O/B	54,000	65,000
2001	T225 O/B	50,000	60,000
2000	T225 O/B	46,000	55,000
1999	T225 O/B	42,000	51,000
1998	T225 O/B	39,000	47,000

See Page 529 For Price Adjustments

Year	Power	Retail Low	Retail High
1997	T225 O/B	36,000	43,000
1996	T225 O/B	33,000	39,000

Pursuit C 280

Year	Power	Retail Low	Retail High
2009	T250 O/B	106,000	127,000

Pursuit OS 285

Year	Power	Retail Low	Retail High
2009	T250 O/B	111,000	133,000
2008	T250 O/B	101,000	121,000

Pursuit 3000 Express

Year	Power	Retail Low	Retail High
2003	T320G	83,000	100,000
2003	T250D	99,000	119,000
2002	T320G	76,000	91,000
2002	T250D	90,000	108,000
2001	T320G	69,000	83,000
2001	T250D	82,000	99,000
2000	T320G	62,000	75,000
2000	T250D	75,000	90,000
1999	T320G	57,000	68,000
1999	T250D	68,000	82,000
1998	T320G	52,000	62,000
1998	T225D	62,000	74,000

Pursuit 3000 Offshore

Year	Power	Retail Low	Retail High
2004	T375G	97,000	117,000
2004	T285D	121,000	145,000
2003	T375G	89,000	106,000
2003	T285D	110,000	132,000
2002	T375G	81,000	97,000
2002	T260D	100,000	120,000
2001	T320G	73,000	88,000
2001	T260D	91,000	109,000
2000	T320G	67,000	81,000
2000	T260D	84,000	101,000
1999	T320G	62,000	74,000
1999	T260D	77,000	93,000
1998	T320G	57,000	68,000
1998	T260D	71,000	85,000
1997	T320G	52,000	63,000
1997	T260D	65,000	78,000
1996	T320G	48,000	58,000
1996	T260D	60,000	72,000
1995	T320G	44,000	53,000
1995	T260D	55,000	66,000

Pursuit 3070 Center Console

Year	Power	Retail Low	Retail High
2007	T250 O/B	92,000	111,000
2006	T250 O/B	83,000	100,000
2005	T250 O/B	75,000	90,000
2004	T250 O/B	67,000	81,000
2003	T250 O/B	60,000	72,000
2002	T250 O/B	54,000	65,000
2001	T250 O/B	49,000	59,000

Pursuit 3070 Offshore CC

Year	Power	Retail Low	Retail High
2006	T250 O/B	87,000	104,000
2005	T250 O/B	79,000	95,000
2004	T250 O/B	72,000	86,000
2003	T250 O/B	65,000	78,000
2002	T250 O/B	59,000	71,000
2001	T250 O/B	54,000	65,000
2000	T250 O/B	49,000	59,000
1999	T250 O/B	45,000	54,000

Pursuit 3070 Offshore Express

Year	Power	Retail Low	Retail High
2007	T250 O/B	109,000	131,000
2006	T250 O/B	99,000	119,000
2005	T250 O/B	90,000	109,000
2004	T250 O/B	82,000	99,000
2003	T250 O/B	75,000	90,000
2002	T250 O/B	68,000	82,000
2001	T250 O/B	62,000	74,000

Pursuit 3100 Express

Year	Power	Retail Low	Retail High
1997	T300G	44,000	53,000
1996	T300G	41,000	49,000
1995	T300G	37,000	45,000
1994	T300G	34,000	41,000
1993	T300G	32,000	38,000

Pursuit C 310 Center Console

Year	Power	Retail Low	Retail High
2009	T250 O/B	119,000	142,000
2008	T250 O/B	107,000	128,000
2007	T250 O/B	97,000	116,000

Pursuit OS 315

Year	Power	Retail Low	Retail High
2009	T250 O/B	158,000	189,000
2008	T250 O/B	143,000	172,000

Pursuit 3100 Offshore

Year	Power	Retail Low	Retail High
2005	T330G	119,000	143,000
2005	T315D	136,000	163,000
2004	T330G	108,000	130,000
2004	T315D	124,000	149,000

Pursuit 3370 Offshore; OS 335

Year	Power	Retail Low	Retail High
2008	T250 O/B	153,000	184,000
2007	T250 O/B	139,000	167,000
2006	T250 O/B	127,000	152,000
2005	T250 O/B	115,000	138,000
2004	T250 O/B	105,000	126,000

Pursuit 3400 Express

Year	Power	Retail Low	Retail High
2003	T375G	104,000	125,000
2003	T370D	132,000	158,000
2002	T375G	95,000	114,000
2002	T370D	120,000	144,000
2001	T370G	86,000	104,000
2001	T370D	109,000	131,000
2000	T370D	78,000	94,000
2000	T370D	99,000	119,000
1999	T320G	71,000	86,000
1999	T370D	90,000	108,000
1998	T320G	65,000	78,000
1998	T370D	82,000	98,000
1997	T320G	59,000	71,000
1997	T370D	74,000	89,000

Pursuit 3480 CC; C 340

Year	Power	Retail Low	Retail High
2009	T250 O/B	133,000	159,000
2008	T250 O/B	119,000	143,000
2007	T250 O/B	107,000	129,000
2006	T250 O/B	96,000	116,000
2005	T250 O/B	89,000	107,000

Pursuit LS 345 Drummond Runner

Year	Power	Retail Low	Retail High
2008	T250 O/B	146,000	176,000
2007	T250 O/B	135,000	162,000

Pursuit OS 375

Year	Power	Retail Low	Retail High
2009	3/350 O/B	336,000	386,000
2008	3/350 O/B	302,000	347,000

Pursuit 3800 Express

Year	Power	Retail Low	Retail High
2004	T480D	212,000	244,000
2003	T480D	193,000	222,000
2002	T480D	175,000	202,000

Rampage 30 Express

Year	Power	Retail Low	Retail High
2009	T375G	******	******
2009	T315D	******	******
2008	T375G	131,000	157,000
2008	T315D	154,000	185,000
2007	T375G	119,000	143,000
2007	T315D	140,000	169,000
2006	T375G	108,000	130,000
2006	T315D	128,000	153,000
2005	T300G	98,000	118,000
2005	T315D	116,000	140,000
2004	T300G	89,000	107,000
2004	T315D	106,000	127,000
2003	T300G	82,000	99,000
2003	T315D	97,000	117,000
2002	T300G	76,000	91,000
2002	T315D	89,000	107,000
2001	T300G	70,000	84,000
2001	T315D	82,000	99,000
2000	T300G	64,000	77,000
2000	T315D	76,000	91,000
1999	T300G	59,000	71,000
1999	T300D	70,000	84,000

Rampage 30 Offshore

Year	Power	Retail Low	Retail High
2006	T375G	99,000	119,000
2006	T315D	117,000	141,000
2005	T375G	90,000	108,000
2005	T315D	107,000	128,000
2004	T300G	82,000	98,000
2004	T315D	97,000	117,000
2003	T300G	74,000	89,000
2003	T315D	88,000	106,000
2002	T300G	68,000	81,000
2002	T315D	80,000	97,000

Rampage 30 Walkaround

Year	Power	Retail Low	Retail High
2006	T375G	96,000	116,000
2006	T315D	115,000	138,000
2005	T375G	88,000	105,000
2005	T315D	104,000	125,000

Rampage 33 Express

Year	Power	Retail Low	Retail High
2008	T425G	169,000	203,000
2008	T460D	216,000	259,000
2007	T425G	153,000	184,000
2007	T460D	196,000	235,000
2006	T370G	140,000	168,000
2006	T425D	178,000	214,000
2005	T370G	127,000	153,000
2005	T425D	162,000	195,000

Rampage 45 Convertible

Year	Power	Retail Low	Retail High
2009	T865D		
2008	T865D	******	******
2007	T865D	******	******
2006	T865D	******	******
2005	T800D	515,000	592,000
2004	T800D	473,000	544,000
2003	T800D	435,000	501,000

See Page 529 For Price Adjustments

Year	Power	Retail Low	Retail High
2002	T800D	401,000	461,000

Regal 2600 LSR

Year	Power	Retail Low	Retail High
2006	320 I/O	26,000	31,000
2005	320 I/O	23,000	28,000
2004	320 I/O	21,000	25,000
2003	320 I/O	19,000	23,000
2002	320 I/O	17,000	21,000

Regal 2650 Cuddy

Year	Power	Retail Low	Retail High
2006	320 I/O	29,000	35,000
2005	320 I/O	26,000	31,000
2004	320 I/O	24,000	29,000
2003	320 I/O	22,000	26,000
2002	320 I/O	20,000	24,000

Regal 2665 Commodore

Year	Power	Retail Low	Retail High
2009	320 I/O	52,000	62,000
2008	320 I/O	47,000	56,000
2007	320 I/O	43,000	51,000
2006	320 I/O	39,000	47,000
2005	320 I/O	36,000	43,000
2004	320 I/O	33,000	39,000
2003	320 I/O	30,000	36,000
2002	320 I/O	28,000	33,000

Regal 260 Valenti; 272 Commodore

Year	Power	Retail Low	Retail High
1996	S300 I/O	19,000	23,000
1996	T190 I/O	21,000	25,000
1995	S300 I/O	17,000	21,000
1995	T190 I/O	19,000	23,000

Regal 2660/2765 Commodore

Year	Power	Retail Low	Retail High
2005	S375 I/O	39,000	47,000
2005	T220 I/O	44,000	53,000
2004	S375 I/O	36,000	43,000
2004	T220 I/O	40,000	48,000
2003	S375 I/O	32,000	39,000
2003	T220 I/O	36,000	44,000
2002	S320 I/O	29,000	35,000
2002	T190 I/O	33,000	40,000
2001	S310 I/O	27,000	32,000
2001	T190 I/O	30,000	37,000
2000	S310 I/O	25,000	30,000
2000	T190 I/O	28,000	34,000
1999	S310 I/O	23,000	27,000
1999	T190 I/O	26,000	31,000

Regal 2700 Bowrider

Year	Power	Retail Low	Retail High
2009	300 I/O	44,000	52,000
2008	300 I/O	40,000	48,000
2007	300 I/O	36,000	43,000

Regal 2750 Cuddy

Year	Power	Retail Low	Retail High
2009	300 I/O	47,000	56,000
2008	300 I/O	42,000	51,000
2007	300 I/O	38,000	46,000

Regal Ventura 8.3 SC

Year	Power	Retail Low	Retail High
1997	S300 I/O	21,000	25,000
1997	T190 I/O	23,000	27,000
1996	S300 I/O	19,000	23,000
1996	T190 I/O	21,000	25,000
1995	S300 I/O	18,000	21,000
1995	T190 I/O	19,000	23,000

Regal Ventura 8.3 SE

Year	Power	Retail Low	Retail High
1997	S300 I/O	20,000	24,000
1997	T190 I/O	22,000	26,000
1996	S300 I/O	18,000	22,000
1996	T190 I/O	20,000	24,000
1995	S300 I/O	17,000	20,000
1995	T190 I/O	18,000	22,000

Regal 2760/2860 Commodore

Year	Power	Retail Low	Retail High
2005	T225 I/O	50,000	60,000
2004	T220 I/O	45,000	54,000
2003	T220 I/O	41,000	49,000
2002	T220 I/O	37,000	45,000
2001	T210 I/O	34,000	41,000
2000	T210 I/O	31,000	37,000
1999	T210 I/O	29,000	34,000

Regal 2860 Windows Express

Year	Power	Retail Low	Retail High
2009	T220 I/O	80,000	96,000
2008	T220 I/O	72,000	87,000
2007	T220 I/O	66,000	79,000
2006	T220 I/O	60,000	72,000

Regal 2800/2900 LSR

Year	Power	Retail Low	Retail High
2004	375 I/O	30,000	36,000
2003	375 I/O	28,000	34,000
2002	375 I/O	26,000	31,000
2001	375 I/O	24,000	29,000
2000	375 I/O	22,000	27,000
1999	375 I/O	21,000	25,000

Regal 292/2960/3060 Commodore

Year	Power	Retail Low	Retail High
2003	T260 I/O	45,000	55,000
2002	T260 I/O	41,000	50,000
2001	T260 I/O	38,000	45,000
2000	T260 I/O	34,000	41,000
1999	T260 I/O	32,000	38,000
1998	T260 I/O	29,000	35,000
1997	T260 I/O	27,000	32,000
1996	T260 I/O	25,000	30,000
1995	T260 I/O	23,000	27,000

Regal 3060 Window Express

Year	Power	Retail Low	Retail High
2009	T260 I/O	92,000	110,000
2008	T260 I/O	82,000	99,000
2007	T260 I/O	74,000	89,000
2006	T260 I/O	67,000	81,000
2005	T260 I/O	61,000	74,000
2004	T260 I/O	56,000	67,000

Regal Ventura 9.8; 322/3260 Commodore

Year	Power	Retail Low	Retail High
2004	T320 I/B	82,000	98,000
2004	T300 I/O	76,000	91,000
2003	T320 I/B	75,000	90,000
2003	T300 I/O	69,000	83,000
2002	T320 I/B	68,000	81,000
2002	T300 I/O	62,000	75,000
2001	T310 I/B	62,000	74,000
2001	T310 I/O	57,000	68,000
2000	T310 I/B	57,000	68,000
2000	T310 I/O	52,000	63,000
1999	T310 I/B	52,000	63,000
1999	T310 I/O	48,000	58,000
1998	T310 I/B	48,000	58,000
1998	T310 I/O	44,000	53,000
1997	T310 I/B	44,000	53,000
1997	T310 I/O	41,000	49,000
1996	T310 I/B	40,000	49,000
1996	T310 I/O	37,000	45,000
1995	T310 I/B	37,000	45,000
1995	T310 I/O	34,000	41,000

Regal 3350 Sport Cruiser

Year	Power	Retail Low	Retail High
2009	T300 I/O	105,000	126,000
2008	T300 I/O	95,000	114,000
2007	T300 I/O	86,000	104,000
2006	T300 I/O	79,000	94,000
2005	T300 I/O	72,000	86,000

Regal 3360 Express

Year	Power	Retail Low	Retail High
2009	T300 I/O	129,000	154,000
2008	T300 I/O	116,000	139,000
2007	T320 I/O	104,000	125,000
2006	T320 I/O	94,000	112,000

Regal 3560/3760 Commodore

Year	Power	Retail Low	Retail High
2009	T420 V/D	******	******
2009	T375 I/O	******	******
2008	T370 V/D	155,000	186,000
2008	T320 I/O	147,000	177,000
2007	T370 V/D	141,000	170,000
2007	T320 I/O	134,000	161,000
2006	T320 V/D	128,000	154,000
2006	T320 I/O	122,000	146,000
2005	T320 V/D	117,000	140,000
2005	T320 I/O	111,000	133,000
2004	T320 V/D	106,000	128,000
2004	T375 I/O	101,000	121,000
2003	T320 V/D	97,000	116,000
2003	T375 I/O	92,000	110,000

Regal 3860/4060 Commodore

Year	Power	Retail Low	Retail High
2009	T420G	******	******
2009	T370D	******	******
2008	T420G	211,000	246,000
2008	T370D	239,000	279,000
2007	T420G	192,000	224,000
2007	T370D	217,000	254,000
2006	T420G	174,000	204,000
2006	T370D	197,000	231,000
2005	T420G	160,000	188,000
2005	T370D	182,000	213,000
2004	T420G	147,000	173,000
2004	T370D	167,000	195,000
2003	T3420G	136,000	159,000
2003	T370D	154,000	180,000
2002	T3420G	125,000	146,000
2002	T370D	141,000	165,000

Regal 3880/4080 Commodore

Year	Power	Retail Low	Retail High
2009	T420G	******	******
2009	T370D	******	******
2008	T420G	215,000	251,000
2008	T370D	249,000	291,000
2007	T420G	195,000	228,000
2007	T370D	226,000	265,000
2006	T420G	178,000	208,000
2006	T370D	206,000	241,000
2005	T420G	162,000	189,000
2005	T370D	187,000	219,000
2004	T420G	149,000	174,000
2004	T370D	172,000	201,000
2003	T420G	137,000	160,000

See Page 529 For Price Adjustments

Year	Power	Retail Low	Retail High
2003	T370D	158,000	185,000
2002	T420G	126,000	147,000
2002	T370D	146,000	170,000
2001	T420G	116,000	135,000
2001	T330D	134,000	157,000
Regal 380/400/402 Commodore			
1999	T310G	85,000	100,000
1998	T310G	78,000	92,000
1997	T310G	72,000	84,000
1996	T310G	66,000	77,000
1995	T310G	61,000	71,000
1994	T310G	56,000	66,000
1993	T310G	53,000	62,000
1992	T310G	49,000	57,000
1991	T340G	45,000	53,000
Regal 4160/4260/4460 Commodore			
2009	T435D	******	******
2009	T420G	******	******
2008	T480D	298,000	342,000
2008	T420G	263,000	303,000
2007	T480D	271,000	312,000
2007	T420G	240,000	276,000
2006	T480D	246,000	283,000
2006	T420G	218,000	251,000
2005	145UD	227,000	261,000
2005	T420G	200,000	231,000
2004	T450D	209,000	240,000
2004	T420G	184,000	212,000
2003	T450D	192,000	221,000
2003	T420G	170,000	195,000
2002	T370D	176,000	203,000
2002	T420G	156,000	179,000
2001	T370D	162,000	187,000
2001	T380G	143,000	165,000
2000	T370D	149,000	172,000
2000	T380G	132,000	152,000
Regulator 26 Center Console			
2009	T225 O/B	84,000	101,000
2008	T225 O/B	75,000	91,000
2007	T225 O/B	68,000	82,000
2006	T225 O/B	61,000	73,000
2005	T225 O/B	55,000	66,000
2004	T225 O/B	50,000	60,000
2003	T225 O/B	45,000	55,000
2002	T225 O/B	41,000	50,000
2001	T225 O/B	37,000	45,000
2000	T225 O/B	34,000	41,000
1999	T225 O/B	31,000	37,000
1998	T225 O/B	28,000	34,000
1997	T225 O/B	26,000	31,000
1996	T225 O/B	23,000	28,000
1995	T225 O/B	21,000	25,000
Regulator 26 Express			
1998	T200 O/B	32,000	38,000
1997	T200 O/B	29,000	35,000
1996	T200 O/B	27,000	33,000
1995	T200 O/B	25,000	30,000
Regulator 29 Center Console			
2009	T250 O/B	115,000	138,000
2008	T250 O/B	104,000	125,000

Year	Power	Retail Low	Retail High
2007	T250 O/B	95,000	114,000
2006	T250 O/B	86,000	103,000
Regulator 32 FS			
2009	T250 O/B	136,000	163,000
2008	T250 O/B	123,000	148,000
2007	T250 O/B	112,000	135,000
2006	T250 O/B	102,000	122,000
2005	T250 O/B	93,000	111,000
2004	T250 O/B	85,000	102,000
2003	T250 O/B	78,000	94,000
2002	T250 O/B	72,000	87,000
2001	T250 O/B	66,000	80,000
2000	T250 O/B	61,000	73,000
1999	T250 O/B	56,000	67,000
Riviera 33 Conv. (1992-97)			
1997	T210D	71,000	85,000
1996	T210D	65,000	78,000
1995	T210D	60,000	72,000
Riviera 33 Convertible			
2009	T370D	******	******
2008	T370D	******	******
2007	T370D	160,000	192,000
2006	T310D	145,000	174,000
2005	T310D	132,000	159,000
Riviera 34 Convertible			
2002	T370D	99,000	119,000
2001	T370D	90,000	108,000
2000	T350D	82,000	99,000
1999	T330D	75,000	91,000
1998	T315D	69,000	83,000
1997	T315D	64,000	77,000
Riviera 36 Convertible			
2002	T370D	114,000	136,000
2001	T370D	103,000	124,000
2000	T350D	95,000	114,000
1999	T330D	87,000	105,000
1998	T315D	80,000	96,000
1997	T315D	74,000	89,000
1996	T315D	68,000	82,000
1995	T315D	62,000	75,000
Riviera 37 Convertible			
2008	T370D	******	******
2007	T330D	212,000	248,000
2006	T330D	193,000	226,000
2005	T330D	176,000	206,000
2004	T330D	160,000	187,000
2003	T330D	145,000	170,000
2002	T330D	134,000	157,000
2001	T315D	123,000	144,000
Riviera 39 Convertible			
1999	T450D	130,000	152,000
1998	T420D	120,000	140,000
1997	T420D	110,000	129,000
1996	T375D	101,000	118,000
1995	T375D	93,000	109,000
Riviera 40 Convertible			
2006	T460D	273,000	319,000
2005	T455D	248,000	290,000
2004	T430D	226,000	264,000

Year	Power	Retail Low	Retail High
2003	T430D	205,000	240,000
2002	T470D	187,000	219,000
2001	T470D	170,000	199,000
Riviera 4000 Offshore			
2003	T450D	168,000	197,000
2002	T450D	153,000	179,000
2001	T450D	139,000	163,000
2000	T450D	127,000	148,000
1999	T450D	115,000	135,000
1998	T435D	105,000	123,000
Riviera 42 Convertible			
2007	T480D	337,000	394,000
2006	T480D	307,000	359,000
2005	T480D	279,000	327,000
2004	T480D	254,000	297,000
Riviera 43 Convertible			
2003	T430D	272,000	318,000
2002	T430D	247,000	289,000
2001	T430D	225,000	263,000
2000	T450D	205,000	239,000
1999	T450D	186,000	218,000
1998	T420D	169,000	198,000
1997	T420D	154,000	180,000
Riviera 47 Convertible			
2007	T660D	465,000	535,000
2006	T700D	428,000	492,000
2005	T700D	394,000	453,000
2004	T700D	362,000	417,000
2003	T660D	333,000	383,000
Riviera 48 Convertible			
2002	T800D	256,000	294,000
2001	T800D	235,000	271,000
2000	T660D	217,000	249,000
1999	T660D	199,000	229,000
1998	T660D	183,000	211,000
1997	T435D	169,000	194,000
1996	T435D	155,000	178,000
1995	T435D	144,000	166,000
Robalo 260 Center Console			
2009	T225 O/B	77,000	92,000
2008	T225 O/B	70,000	84,000
2007	T225 O/B	63,000	76,000
2006	T225 O/B	58,000	69,000
2005	T225 O/B	53,000	64,000
2004	T225 O/B	49,000	58,000
Robalo 2620 Center Console			
2001	T200 O/B	32,000	38,000
2000	T200 O/B	29,000	35,000
1999	T200 O/B	27,000	32,000
1998	T200 O/B	24,000	29,000
Robalo 2640 Walkaround			
2002	T200 O/B	37,000	44,000
2001	T200 O/B	33,000	40,000
2000	T200 O/B	30,000	36,000
1999	T200 O/B	27,000	33,000
1998	T200 O/B	25,000	30,000
Robalo 2660 Express			
1996	T200 O/B	21,000	25,000
1995	T200 O/B	19,000	23,000

See Page 529 For Price Adjustments

Robalo 265 Walkaround

Year	Power	Retail Low	Retail High
2009	T225 O/B	81,000	97,000
2008	T225 O/B	73,000	88,000
2007	T225 O/B	67,000	80,000
2006	T225 O/B	61,000	73,000
2005	T225 O/B	55,000	66,000
2004	T225 O/B	50,000	60,000
2003	T225 O/B	45,000	55,000

Robalo 300 Center Console

Year	Power	Retail Low	Retail High
2009	T250 O/B	121,000	145,000
2008	T250 O/B	111,000	133,000
2007	T250 O/B	102,000	122,000

Robalo 305 Walkaround

Year	Power	Retail Low	Retail High
2009	T250 O/B	134,000	160,000
2008	T250 O/B	123,000	147,000
2007	T250 O/B	113,000	136,000

Sabre 34 Sedan

Year	Power	Retail Low	Retail High
2002	T220D	122,000	147,000
2001	T220D	113,000	136,000
2000	T220D	105,000	127,000
1999	T220D	98,000	118,000
1998	T220D	91,000	109,000
1997	T220D	85,000	102,000
1996	T210D	79,000	95,000
1995	T210D	74,000	89,000

Sabre 36 Aft Cabin

Year	Power	Retail Low	Retail High
1998	T300D	87,000	87,000
1997	T300D	81,000	81,000
1996	T300D	75,000	75,000
1995	T255D	70,000	70,000

Sabre 36 Express

Year	Power	Retail Low	Retail High
2003	T315D	114,000	136,000
2002	T315D	106,000	127,000
2001	T315D	98,000	118,000
2000	T315D	91,000	110,000
1999	T300D	85,000	102,000
1998	T300D	79,000	95,000
1997	T300D	73,000	88,000
1996	T300D	68,000	82,000

Sabre 36 Sedan

Year	Power	Retail Low	Retail High
2007	T315D	******	******
2006	T315D	163,000	191,000
2005	T315D	152,000	178,000
2004	T315D	141,000	165,000
2003	T315D	131,000	154,000
2002	T315D	122,000	143,000

Sabre 42 Sedan

Year	Power	Retail Low	Retail High
2009	T440D	******	******
2008	T440D	******	******
2007	T440D	******	******
2006	T440D	******	******
2005	T440D	******	******
2004	T440D	******	******
2003	T440D	221,000	258,000
2002	T420D	205,000	240,000
2001	T420D	191,000	223,000

Sabre 43 Aft Cabin

Year	Power	Retail Low	Retail High
2005	T370D	******	******
2004	T370D	******	******
2003	T370D	******	******
2002	T370D	******	******
2001	T370D	249,000	286,000
2000	T350D	231,000	266,000
1999	T350D	218,000	250,000
1998	T350D	204,000	235,000
1997	T350D	192,000	221,000
1996	T350D	181,000	208,000

Sabre 47 Aft Cabin

Year	Power	Retail Low	Retail High
2007	T465D	******	******
2006	T465D	******	******
2005	T465D	******	******
2004	T465D	******	******
2003	T465D	310,000	356,000
2002	T420D	288,000	331,000
2001	T420D	268,000	308,000
2000	T420D	252,000	289,000
1999	T420D	236,000	272,000
1998	T420D	222,000	256,000
1997	T350D	209,000	240,000

Scout 260/262 Sportfish

Year	Power	Retail Low	Retail High
2009	T150 O/B	75,000	90,000
2008	T150 O/B	67,000	81,000
2007	T150 O/B	60,000	72,000
2006	T150 O/B	55,000	67,000

Scout 280 Abaco

Year	Power	Retail Low	Retail High
2005	T200 O/B	50,000	60,000
2004	T200 O/B	46,000	55,000
2003	T200 O/B	41,000	50,000
2002	T200 O/B	38,000	45,000
2001	T200 O/B	34,000	41,000
2000	T200 O/B	31,000	37,000

Scout 280 Sportfish

Year	Power	Retail Low	Retail High
2006	T200 O/B	52,000	62,000
2005	T200 O/B	47,000	57,000
2004	T200 O/B	43,000	52,000
2003	T200 O/B	39,000	47,000
2002	T200 O/B	35,000	43,000
2001	T200 O/B	32,000	39,000

Scout 282 SF

Year	Power	Retail Low	Retail High
2009	T250 O/B	84,000	100,000
2008	T250 O/B	75,000	90,000
2007	T250 O/B	68,000	81,000
2006	T250 O/B	62,000	75,000

Sea Ray 260 Bowrider

Year	Power	Retail Low	Retail High
2001	320 I/O	21,000	25,000
2000	320 I/O	19,000	22,000
1999	310 I/O	17,000	21,000
1998	310 I/O	16,000	19,000
1997	310 I/O	14,000	17,000
1996	310 I/O	13,000	16,000

Sea Ray 260 Bowrider Select

Year	Power	Retail Low	Retail High
2001	320 I/O	22,000	26,000
2000	320 I/O	20,000	24,000
1999	310 I/O	18,000	22,000
1998	310 I/O	17,000	20,000

Sea Ray 260 Sundancer

Year	Power	Retail Low	Retail High
2008	300 I/O	54,000	64,000
2007	300 I/O	49,000	58,000
2006	300 I/O	44,000	53,000
2005	300 I/O	40,000	48,000
2004	260 I/O	37,000	44,000
2003	260 I/O	34,000	40,000
2002	260 I/O	31,000	37,000
2001	260 I/O	28,000	34,000
2000	260 I/O	26,000	31,000
1999	260 I/O	24,000	29,000

Sea Ray 270 Amberjack

Year	Power	Retail Low	Retail High
2008	320 I/O	61,000	73,000
2007	320 I/O	55,000	66,000
2006	320 I/O	49,000	59,000
2005	320 I/O	44,000	53,000

Sea Ray 270 Select EX

Year	Power	Retail Low	Retail High
2009	320 I/O	58,000	69,000
2008	320 I/O	52,000	63,000
2007	320 I/O	48,000	57,000
2006	320 I/O	43,000	52,000
2005	320 I/O	39,000	47,000

Sea Ray 270 Amberjack (Current)

Year	Power	Retail Low	Retail High
2009	320 I/O	57,000	68,000
2008	320 I/O	52,000	62,000
2007	320 I/O	47,000	56,000
2006	320 I/O	43,000	51,000
2005	320 I/O	39,000	47,000

Sea Ray 270 Sundancer (8'6" Beam)

Year	Power	Retail Low	Retail High
1999	310 I/O	19,000	22,000
1998	No Prod.	******	******
1997	310 I/O	17,000	20,000
1996	310 I/O	16,000	19,000
1995	310 I/O	14,000	17,000
1994	300 I/O	13,000	16,000
1993	300 I/O	12,000	14,000
1992	300 I/O	11,000	13,000

Sea Ray 270 Sundancer (9'2" Beam)

Year	Power	Retail Low	Retail High
2001	310 I/O	29,000	34,000
2001	T190 I/O	31,000	37,000
2000	310 I/O	26,000	31,000
2000	T190 I/O	28,000	33,000
1999	300 I/O	24,000	28,000
1999	T190 I/O	25,000	30,000
1998	300 I/O	21,000	26,000
1998	T190 I/O	23,000	28,000

Sea Ray 270 Sundeck

Year	Power	Retail Low	Retail High
2007	320 I/O	40,000	48,000
2006	320 I/O	36,000	43,000
2005	320 I/O	33,000	39,000
2004	320 I/O	30,000	36,000
2003	320 I/O	27,000	32,000
2002	320 I/O	24,000	29,000

Sea Ray 280 Bowrider

Year	Power	Retail Low	Retail High
2001	300 I/O	31,000	37,000
2001	T260 I/O	35,000	42,000
2000	300 I/O	28,000	33,000
2000	T260 I/O	32,000	39,000
1999	300 I/O	25,000	31,000
1999	T260 I/O	30,000	36,000
1998	300 I/O	23,000	28,000
1998	T260 I/O	27,000	33,000

See Page 529 For Price Adjustments

Year	Power	Retail Low	Retail High
1997	300 I/O	21,000	26,000
1997	T260 I/O	25,000	30,000
1996	300 I/O	20,000	24,000
1996	T250 I/O	23,000	28,000
Sea Ray 280 Cuddy			
1999	300 I/O	28,000	33,000
1999	T260 I/O	32,000	38,000
1998	300 I/O	25,000	30,000
1998	T260 I/O	29,000	35,000
1997	300 I/O	23,000	28,000
1997	T250 I/O	27,000	32,000
1996	300 I/O	21,000	26,000
1996	T250 I/O	24,000	29,000
Sea Ray 280 Sun Sport			
2001	320 I/O	34,000	40,000
2001	T260 I/O	38,000	46,000
2000	320 I/O	31,000	37,000
2000	T260 I/O	35,000	42,000
1999	310 I/O	28,000	34,000
1999	T260 I/O	32,000	39,000
1998	310 I/O	26,000	31,000
1998	T260 I/O	30,000	36,000
1997	30 I/O	24,000	29,000
1997	T250 I/O	27,000	33,000
1996	300 I/O	22,000	26,000
1996	T250 I/O	25,000	30,000
Sea Ray 280 Sundancer			
2009	T260 I/O	99,000	119,000
2008	T260 I/O	90,000	108,000
2007	T260 I/O	82,000	99,000
2006	T260 I/O	75,000	90,000
2005	T260 I/O	68,000	82,000
2004	T260 I/O	62,000	75,000
2003	T260 I/O	57,000	69,000
2002	T260 I/O	53,000	63,000
2001	T260 I/O	49,000	58,000
Sea Ray 290 Amberjack			
2009	T260 I/O	118,000	141,000
2008	T260 I/O	106,000	127,000
2007	T260 I/O	95,000	114,000
2006	T260 I/O	86,000	103,000
2005	T260 I/O	77,000	92,000
2004	T260 I/O	70,000	84,000
2003	T260 I/O	64,000	76,000
2002	T240 I/O	58,000	70,000
2001	T240 I/O	53,000	63,000
2000	T240 I/O	48,000	58,000
Sea Ray 290 Bowrider			
2004	T260 I/O	50,000	60,000
2003	T260 I/O	46,000	55,000
2002	T260 I/O	42,000	50,000
2001	T260 I/O	38,000	45,000
Sea Ray 290 Select EX			
2008	T260 I/O	65,000	78,000
2007	T260 I/O	59,000	70,000
2006	T260 I/O	53,000	64,000
2005	T260 I/O	48,000	58,000
Sea Ray 290 Sun Sport			
2009	T260 I/O	68,000	82,000
2008	T260 I/O	61,000	73,000
2007	T260 I/O	55,000	66,000
2006	T260 I/O	49,000	59,000
2005	T260 I/O	45,000	54,000
2004	T260 I/O	41,000	49,000
2003	T260 I/O	37,000	45,000
2002	T260 I/O	34,000	41,000
Sea Ray 290 Sundancer (1994-2001)			
2001	T260 I/O	61,000	73,000
2000	T260 I/O	56,000	68,000
1999	T260 I/O	52,000	62,000
1998	T260 I/O	47,000	57,000
1997	T190 I/O	44,000	52,000
1996	T190 I/O	40,000	48,000
1995	T190 I/O	37,000	44,000
1994	T190 I/O	34,000	41,000
Sea Ray 290 Sundancer (2006-08)			
2008	T260 I/O	91,000	109,000
2007	T260 I/O	81,000	98,000
2006	T260 I/O	73,000	88,000
Sea Ray 300 Sundancer (1994-97)			
1997	T290 VD	46,000	55,000
1997	T300 I/O	42,000	50,000
1996	T250 VD	41,000	50,000
1996	T250 I/O	38,000	45,000
1995	T250 VD	37,000	45,000
1995	T250 I/O	34,000	41,000
Sea Ray 300 Sundancer (2002-07)			
2007	T260 I/O	86,000	103,000
2006	T260 I/O	79,000	94,000
2005	T260 I/O	72,000	87,000
2004	T260 I/O	66,000	80,000
2003	T260 I/O	61,000	73,000
2002	T260 I/O	56,000	68,000
Sea Ray 300 Weekender (1991-95)			
1995	T230 I/O	32,000	38,000
1995	T250 VD	33,000	40,000
Sea Ray 310 Sundancer (1998-02)			
2002	T260 I/O	68,000	82,000
2001	T260 I/O	62,000	75,000
2000	T260 I/O	56,000	68,000
1999	T260 I/O	51,000	62,000
1998	T260 I/O	47,000	56,000
Sea Ray 310 Sundancer (Current)			
2009	T260 I/O	118,000	141,000
2008	T260 I/O	107,000	128,000
2007	T260 I/O	98,000	118,000
Sea Ray 320 Sundancer			
2007	T300 VD	112,000	134,000
2007	T300 I/O	103,000	123,000
2006	T320 VD	102,000	122,000
2006	T260 I/O	93,000	112,000
2005	T320 VD	92,000	111,000
2005	T260 I/O	85,000	102,000
2004	T300 VD	84,000	101,000
2004	T260 I/O	77,000	93,000
2003	T300 VD	76,000	92,000
2003	T260 I/O	70,000	84,000
Sea Ray 310/330 EC (1990-95)			
1995	T300 I/O	37,000	45,000
1995	T310 I/B	40,000	48,000
Sea Ray 330 Express Cruiser			
2000	T310G	76,000	91,000
1999	T310G	69,000	83,000
1998	T310G	64,000	77,000
1997	T310G	59,000	71,000
Sea Ray 330 Sundancer (1995-99)			
1999	T300 I/O	62,000	75,000
1999	T310 VD	65,000	78,000
1998	T300 I/O	57,000	68,000
1998	T310 VD	59,000	71,000
1997	T300 I/O	51,000	62,000
1997	T310 VD	54,000	65,000
1996	T300 I/O	47,000	56,000
1996	T310 VD	49,000	59,000
1995	T300 I/O	42,000	51,000
1995	T310 VD	44,000	53,000
Sea Ray 330 Sundancer			
2009	T320G I/O	176,000	211,000
2009	T3700G VD	184,000	220,000
2008	T320G I/O	160,000	192,000
2008	T370G VD	167,000	200,000
Sea Ray 340 Amberjack			
2003	T370G	112,000	134,000
2002	T370G	102,000	122,000
2001	T370G	92,000	111,000
Sea Ray 340 Sundancer (2003-08)			
2008	T375 I/O	155,000	186,000
2008	T375 VD	153,000	184,000
2007	T375 I/O	141,000	170,000
2007	T370 VD	140,000	168,000
2006	T320 I/O	129,000	154,000
2006	T320 VD	127,000	153,000
2005	T320 I/O	117,000	140,000
2005	T320 VD	116,000	139,000
2004	T320 I/O	106,000	128,000
2004	T320 VD	105,000	126,000
2003	T320 I/O	97,000	116,000
2003	T320 VD	96,000	115,000
Sea Ray 340 Sundancer (1999-02)			
2002	T320 VD	84,000	100,000
2001	T320 VD	76,000	91,000
2000	T320 VD	69,000	83,000
1999	T320 VD	63,000	76,000
Sea Ray 350 Sundancer			
2009	T375G I/O	230,000	276,000
2009	T370G VD	223,000	267,000
Sea Ray 350/370 EC (1990-95)			
1995	T310G	52,000	62,000
Sea Ray 360 Sundancer			
2006	T370 VD	153,000	184,000
2005	T370 VD	140,000	168,000
2004	T370 VD	127,000	152,000
2003	T370 VD	115,000	139,000
2002	T370 VD	105,000	126,000

Sea Ray 36 Sedan Bridge

Year	Power	Retail Low	Retail High
2009	T370G	289,000	332,000
2008	T370G	265,000	305,000
2008	T370D	244,000	281,000
2007	T370G	225,000	258,000
2007	T380G	207,000	238,000

Sea Ray 370 Express Cruiser

Year	Power	Retail Low	Retail High
2000	T380G	100,000	120,000
2000	T340G	120,000	144,000
1999	T380G	91,000	109,000
1999	T340D	109,000	131,000
1998	T380G	83,000	99,000
1998	T340D	99,000	119,000
1997	T380G	75,000	90,000
1997	T340D	90,000	109,000

Sea Ray 370 Sedan Bridge

Year	Power	Retail Low	Retail High
1997	T340G	79,000	95,000
1997	T292D	97,000	117,000
1996	T340G	72,000	86,000
1996	T292D	88,000	106,000
1995	T310G	65,000	78,000
1995	T292D	80,000	97,000

Sea Ray 370 Sundancer (1995-99)

Year	Power	Retail Low	Retail High
1999	T310G	94,000	112,000
1999	T292D	114,000	137,000
1998	T310G	85,000	102,000
1998	T292D	104,000	125,000
1997	T310G	77,000	93,000
1997	T292D	95,000	114,000
1996	T310G	70,000	85,000
1996	T292D	86,000	103,000
1995	T310G	64,000	77,000
1995	T292D	78,000	94,000

Sea Ray 370/380 Aft Cabin

Year	Power	Retail Low	Retail High
2001	T380G	132,000	158,000
2001	T340D	157,000	188,000
2000	T380G	120,000	144,000
2000	T340D	143,000	171,000
1999	T380G	109,000	131,000
1999	T340D	130,000	156,000
1998	T-Gas	99,000	119,000
1998	T340D	118,000	142,000
1997	T-Gas	90,000	108,000
1997	T340D	107,000	129,000

Sea Ray 380 Sundancer

Year	Power	Retail Low	Retail High
2003	T370G	143,000	168,000
2003	T340D	167,000	198,000
2002	T370G	130,000	153,000
2002	T340D	152,000	180,000
2001	T370G	118,000	139,000
2001	T340D	139,000	164,000
2000	T310G	107,000	127,000
2000	T340D	126,000	149,000
1999	T310G	98,000	115,000
1999	T340D	115,000	135,000

Sea Ray 38 Sundancer

Year	Power	Retail Low	Retail High
2009	T420G	268,000	316,000
2009	T306D	292,000	344,000
2008	T420G	246,000	290,000
2008	T306D	268,000	316,000
2007	T420G	226,000	267,000
2007	T306D	247,000	291,000
2006	T420G	208,000	246,000
2006	T306D	227,000	268,000

Sea Ray 390 MY; 40 MY

Year	Power	Retail Low	Retail High
2007	T370G	274,000	315,000
2007	T407D	314,000	361,000
2006	T370G	249,000	287,000
2006	T446D	286,000	329,000
2005	T370G	227,000	261,000
2005	T446D	260,000	299,000
2004	T370G	206,000	237,000
2004	T446D	237,000	272,000
2003	T370G	188,000	216,000
2003	T446D	215,000	248,000

Sea Ray 390/40 Sundancer

Year	Power	Retail Low	Retail High
2009	T420G	320,000	368,000
2009	T407D	364,000	418,000
2008	T420G	294,000	338,000
2008	T407D	334,000	385,000
2007	T420G	270,000	311,000
2007	T407D	308,000	354,000
2006	T420G	249,000	286,000
2006	T364D	283,000	325,000
2005	T370G	229,000	263,000
2005	T340D	260,000	299,000
2004	T370G	210,000	242,000
2004	T340D	239,000	275,000

Sea Ray 400 Express Cruiser

Year	Power	Retail Low	Retail High
1999	T380G	108,000	130,000
1999	T340D	130,000	156,000
1998	T380G	99,000	119,000
1998	T340D	119,000	143,000
1997	T340G	91,000	110,000
1997	T340D	110,000	132,000
1996	T340G	84,000	101,000
1996	T292D	101,000	121,000
1995	T340G	77,000	93,000
1995	T292D	93,000	112,000

Sea Ray 400 Sedan Bridge

Year	Power	Retail Low	Retail High
2003	T370G	169,000	203,000
2003	T417D	203,000	244,000
2002	T370G	155,000	187,000
2002	T417D	187,000	224,000
2001	T380G	143,000	172,000
2001	T340D	172,000	206,000
2000	T380G	131,000	158,000
2000	T340D	158,000	190,000
1999	T380G	121,000	145,000
1999	T340D	145,000	175,000
1998	T380G	111,000	134,000
1998	T340D	134,000	161,000
1997	T380G	102,000	123,000
1997	T340D	123,000	148,000
1996	T380G	94,000	113,000
1996	T340D	113,000	136,000

Sea Ray 400 Sundancer

Year	Power	Retail Low	Retail High
1999	T380G	124,000	149,000
1999	T340D	150,000	180,000
1998	T380G	113,000	135,000
1998	T340D	136,000	163,000
1997	T340G	103,000	123,000
1997	T340D	124,000	149,000

Sea Ray 410 Express Cruiser

Year	Power	Retail Low	Retail High
2003	T370G	158,000	190,000
2003	T417D	185,000	222,000
2002	T370G	144,000	173,000
2002	T417D	168,000	202,000
2001	T380G	131,000	157,000
2001	T340D	153,000	184,000
2000	T380G	119,000	143,000
2000	T340D	139,000	167,000

Sea Ray 410 Sundancer

Year	Power	Retail Low	Retail High
2003	T370G	167,000	200,000
2003	T340D	195,000	234,000
2002	T370G	152,000	182,000
2002	T340D	177,000	213,000
2001	T380G	138,000	166,000
2001	T340D	161,000	193,000
2000	T380G	126,000	151,000
2000	T340D	147,000	176,000

Sea Ray 420 Aft Cabin

Year	Power	Retail Low	Retail High
2002	T370G	187,000	216,000
2002	T417D	217,000	250,000
2001	T370G	170,000	196,000
2001	T417D	197,000	227,000
2000	T380G	155,000	178,000
2000	T407D	180,000	207,000
1999	T380G	143,000	164,000
1999	T407D	165,000	190,000
1998	T380G	131,000	151,000
1998	T407D	152,000	175,000
1997	T380G	121,000	139,000
1997	T407D	140,000	161,000
1996	T380G	111,000	128,000
1996	T407D	129,000	148,000

Sea Ray 420/44 Sundancer

Year	Power	Retail Low	Retail High
2008	T420G	302,000	347,000
2008	T478D	349,000	401,000
2007	T420G	275,000	316,000
2007	T478D	317,000	365,000
2006	T370G	250,000	288,000
2006	T417D	289,000	332,000
2005	T370G	228,000	262,000
2005	T417D	263,000	302,000
2004	T370G	207,000	238,000
2004	T417D	239,000	275,000
2003	T370G	188,000	217,000
2003	T417D	218,000	250,000

Sea Ray 420/44 Sedan Bridge

Year	Power	Retail Low	Retail High
2009	T478D	******	******
2008	T478D	385,000	443,000
2007	T478D	347,000	399,000
2006	T478D	312,000	359,000
2005	T417D	281,000	323,000
2004	T417D	252,000	290,000

Sea Ray 420/440 Sundancer

Year	Power	Retail Low	Retail High
1995	T425D	127,000	152,000

See Page 529 For Price Adjustments

Year	Power	Retail Low	Retail High
Sea Ray 440 Express Bridge			
1998	T340D	154,000	177,000
1997	T340D	142,000	163,000
1996	T340D	130,000	150,000
1995	T350D	120,000	138,000
1994	T350D	110,000	127,000
1993	T375D	101,000	117,000
Sea Ray 450 Express Bridge			
2004	T460D	288,000	332,000
2003	T450D	262,000	302,000
2002	T430D	239,000	275,000
2001	T430D	217,000	250,000
2000	T430D	198,000	227,000
1999	T420D	180,000	207,000
1998	T420D	164,000	188,000
Sea Ray 450 Sundancer			
1999	T407D	172,000	197,000
1998	T407D	156,000	180,000
1997	T407D	142,000	163,000
1996	T375D	131,000	150,000
1995	T375D	120,000	138,000
Sea Ray 460 Sundancer			
2003	T446D	293,000	337,000
2002	T446D	270,000	310,000
2001	T430D	248,000	285,000
2000	T430D	228,000	262,000
1999	T430D	210,000	241,000
Sea Ray 47 Sedan Bridge			
2009	T574D	******	******
2008	T574D	546,000	628,000
Sea Ray 48 Sundancer			
2008	T517D	504,000	579,000
2007	T517D	453,000	521,000
2006	T517D	408,000	469,000
2005	T446D	367,000	422,000
Sea Ray 480 Motor Yacht			
2005	T660D	411,000	473,000
2004	T640D	382,000	439,000
2003	T640D	355,000	409,000
2002	T640D	330,000	380,000
Sea Ray 480 Sedan Bridge			
2004	T640D	376,000	433,000
2003	T640D	342,000	394,000
2002	T640D	311,000	358,000
2001	T640D	283,000	326,000
2000	T640D	261,000	300,000
1999	T640D	240,000	276,000
1998	T640D	221,000	254,000
Sea Ray 480/500 Sundancer			
1999	T535D	305,000	351,000
1998	T535D	278,000	319,000
1997	T535D	253,000	290,000
1996	T535D	232,000	267,000
1995	T535D	214,000	246,000
Sea Ray 500 Sedan Bridge			
1995	T735D	238,000	274,000
Sea Ray 500/52 Sundancer			
2009	T765D	******	******

Year	Power	Retail Low	Retail High
2008	T765D	******	******
2007	T640D	******	******
2006	T640D	540,000	621,000
2005	T640D	491,000	565,000
2004	T640D	447,000	514,000
2003	T640D	407,000	468,000
Sea Ray 510 Sundancer			
2003	T616D	410,000	471,000
2002	T640D	373,000	430,000
2001	T640D	339,000	391,000
2000	T640D	309,000	355,000
Sea Ray 500/52 Sedan Bridge			
2009	T640D	******	******
2008	T640D	608,000	699,000
2007	T640D	553,000	636,000
2006	T640D	503,000	579,000
2005	T640D	458,000	527,000
Sea Ray 540 Cockpit MY			
2002	T640D	437,000	503,000
2001	T640D	402,000	463,000
Sea Ray 540 Sundancer			
2001	T640D	399,000	459,000
2000	T640D	367,000	422,000
1999	T640D	337,000	388,000
1998	T640D	310,000	357,000
Sea Ray 550 Sedan Bridge			
1998	T776D	274,000	315,000
1997	T735D	252,000	290,000
1996	T635D	232,000	267,000
1995	T635D	213,000	245,000
Sea Ray 550 Sundancer			
2004	T765D	572,000	658,000
2003	T765D	532,000	612,000
2002	T765D	495,000	569,000
Sea Ray 560 Sedan Bridge			
2004	T1000D	520,000	598,000
2003	T1000D	473,000	545,000
2002	T776D	431,000	495,000
2001	T776D	392,000	451,000
2000	T776D	357,000	410,000
1999	T776D	324,000	372,000
1998	T776D	295,000	3406,000
Sea Ray 58 Sedan Bridge			
2009	T861D	******	******
2008	T861D	******	******
2007	T861D	897,000	1,032,000
2006	T861D	834,000	960,000
2005	T861D	776,000	893,000
Sea Ray 580 Super Sun Sport			
2002	T776D	559,000	643,000
2001	T776D	514,000	592,000
2000	T776D	473,000	544,000
1999	T776D	435,000	501,000
1998	T776D	400,000	460,000
1997	T776D	368,000	424,000
Sea Ray 60/610 Sundancer			
2009	T1150D	******	******
2008	T1150D	******	******

Year	Power	Retail Low	Retail High
2007	T1150D	1,071,000	1,232,000
2006	T1150D	996,000	1,146,000
Sea Vee 290B Open (Current)			
2009	T250 O/B	******	******
2008	T250 O/B	99,000	119,000
2007	T250 O/B	90,000	108,000
2006	T250 O/B	82,000	98,000
2005	T250 O/B	74,000	89,000
Sea Vee 290B (2000-04)			
2004	T250 O/B	69,000	83,000
2003	T250 O/B	62,000	74,000
2002	T250 O/B	56,000	67,000
2001	T250 O/B	50,000	60,000
2000	T250 O/B	45,000	54,000
Sea Vee 340B Open			
2009	T250 O/B	******	******
2008	T250 O/B	141,000	169,000
2007	T250 O/B	127,000	152,000
2006	T250 O/B	114,000	137,000
2005	T250 O/B	103,000	123,000
2004	T250 O/B	92,000	111,000
2003	T250 O/B	83,000	100,000
2002	T250 O/B	75,000	90,000
2001	T250 O/B	67,000	81,000
Seacraft 26 Master Angler			
2009	T200 O/B	64,000	71,000
2008	T200 O/B	57,000	64,000
Seacraft 32 Center Console			
2008	T250 O/B	68,000	76,000
2007	T250 O/B	61,000	69,000
2006	T250 O/B	56,000	63,000
2005	T250 O/B	51,000	57,000
2004	T250 O/B	46,000	52,000
2003	T250 O/B	42,000	47,000
2002	T250 O/B	38,000	43,000
2001	T250 O/B	35,000	39,000
2000	T250 O/B	32,000	35,000
Seaswirl 2600 Walkaround			
2001	225 O/B	19,000	23,000
2000	225 O/B	18,000	21,000
1999	225 O/B	16,000	19,000
1998	225 O/B	14,000	17,000
1997	225 O/B	13,000	16,000
1996	225 O/B	12,000	14,000
Seaswirl 2601 Center Console			
2008	T150 O/B	46,000	55,000
2007	T150 O/B	41,000	50,000
2006	T150 O/B	37,000	45,000
2005	T150 O/B	33,000	40,000
2004	T150 O/B	30,000	36,000
2003	T150 O/B	27,000	32,000
Seaswirl 2601 Walkaround			
2009	T150 O/B	******	******
2008	T150 O/B	44,000	53,000
2007	T150 O/B	40,000	48,000
2006	T150 O/B	36,000	43,000
2005	T150 O/B	32,000	39,000
2004	T150 O/B	28,000	34,000
2003	T150 O/B	25,000	30,000

See Page 529 For Price Adjustments

Year	Power	Retail Low	Retail High
2002	T150 O/B	22,000	27,000
Seaswirl 2901 Walkaround			
2007	T225 O/B	96,000	115,000
2007	T270 I/O	100,000	120,000
2006	T225 O/B	86,000	104,000
2006	T270 I/O	90,000	108,000
2005	T225 O/B	78,000	93,000
2005	T270 I/O	81,000	97,000
2004	T225 O/B	70,000	84,000
2004	T280 I/O	73,000	88,000
2003	T225 O/B	63,000	75,000
2002	T225 O/B	66,000	79,000
Seaswirl 2901 Pilothouse			
2009	T225 O/B	******	******
2008	T225 O/B	107,000	128,000
2007	T225 O/B	96,000	116,000
2006	T225 O/B	87,000	104,000
2005	T225 O/B	78,000	93,000
Seaswirl 3301 Walkaround			
2009	T250 O/B	******	******
2008	T250 O/B	113,000	136,000
2007	T250 O/B	103,000	123,000
Selene 36/38 Trawler			
2009	230D	******	******
2008	230D	275,000	330,000
2007	230D	255,000	306,000
2006	230D	240,000	288,000
2005	230D	225,000	271,000
2004	230D	212,000	254,000
2003	230D	199,000	239,000
Selene 47 Pilothouse			
2009	330D	******	******
2008	330D	******	******
2007	330D	******	******
2006	330D	******	******
2005	330D	506,000	607,000
2004	330D	475,000	570,000
2003	330D	447,000	536,000
2002	330D	420,000	504,000
2001	220D	399,000	479,000
2000	220D	379,000	455,000
1999	220D	360,000	432,000
Shamrock 270 Mackinaw			
2009	T-Gas	******	******
2009	T315D	******	******
2008	T-Gas	******	******
2008	T315D	******	******
2007	S330G	******	******
2007	S315D	******	******
2006	S330G	******	******
2006	S315D	76,000	91,000
2005	S330G	61,000	74,000
2005	S315D	68,000	82,000
2004	S330G	55,000	66,000
2004	S315D	62,000	74,000
2003	S330G	50,000	60,000
2003	S315D	55,000	67,000
2002	S300G	45,000	54,000
2002	S315D	50,000	60,000
2001	S300G	41,000	49,000
2001	S230D	46,000	55,000
2000	S300G	38,000	45,000
2000	S230D	42,000	51,000
Shamrock 270 Open			
2009	T-Gas	******	******
2009	T315D	******	******
2008	T-Gas	******	******
2008	T315D	******	******
2007	S330G	******	******
2007	S315D	******	******
2006	S330G	******	******
2006	S315D	68,000	82,000
2005	S330G	54,000	65,000
2005	S315D	63,000	76,000
2004	S330G	50,000	60,000
2004	S315D	58,000	70,000
2003	S330G	46,000	55,000
2003	S315D	54,000	64,000
2002	S300G	42,000	50,000
2002	S315D	49,000	59,000
2001	S300G	39,000	46,000
2001	S230D	45,000	54,000
2000	S300G	35,000	43,000
2000	S230D	42,000	50,000
Shamrock 290 Walkaround			
2003	T330G	47,000	57,000
2002	T300G	43,000	52,000
2001	T300G	39,000	47,000
2000	T300G	36,000	43,000
1999	T300G	32,000	39,000
Silverton 271 Express			
1997	250 I/O	22,000	26,000
1996	250 I/O	20,000	24,000
1995	250 I/O	18,000	22,000
Silverton 310 Express			
2000	T250 I/O	39,000	46,000
1999	T250 I/O	36,000	43,000
1998	T250 I/O	33,000	40,000
1997	T250 I/O	31,000	37,000
1996	T235 I/O	29,000	35,000
1995	T235 I/O	27,000	32,000
Silverton 312 Sedan Cruiser			
1999	T260 I/O	38,000	46,000
1998	T260 I/O	35,000	42,000
1997	T260 I/O	32,000	39,000
1996	T235 I/O	30,000	36,000
1995	T235 I/O	27,000	33,000
Silverton 322 Motor Yacht			
2001	T320G	64,000	77,000
2000	T320G	59,000	71,000
1999	T320G	54,000	65,000
1998	T320G	50,000	60,000
Silverton 33 Convertible			
2009	T275G	142,000	170,000
2008	T275G	129,000	155,000
2007	T275G	118,000	142,000
Silverton 33 Sports Coupe			
2009	T275G	159,000	190,000
2008	T275G	144,000	173,000
Silverton 330 Sport Bridge			
2007	T330G	123,000	148,000
2006	T330G	112,000	134,000
2005	T330G	102,000	122,000
2004	T320G	93,000	111,000
2003	T320G	84,000	101,000
2002	T320G	77,000	92,000
2001	T320G	70,000	85,000
2000	T320G	65,000	78,000
1999	T320G	60,000	72,000
Silverton 34 Conv. (1991-95)			
1995	T300G	46,000	56,000
Silverton 34 Conv. (2004-07)			
2006	T330G	138,000	165,000
2005	T330G	125,000	150,000
2004	T320G	114,000	137,000
Silverton 34 Motor Yacht			
1996	T320G	51,000	61,000
1995	T300G	47,000	56,000
Silverton 35 Motor Yacht			
2009	T385G	******	******
2009	T315D	******	******
2008	T385G	215,000	251,000
2008	T315D	189,000	221,000
2007	T385G	197,000	231,000
2007	T315D	173,000	203,000
2006	T385G	181,000	212,000
2006	T315D	159,000	187,000
2005	T385G	167,000	195,000
2005	T315D	147,000	172,000
2004	T385G	154,000	180,000
2004	T315D	135,000	158,000
2003	T385G	141,000	165,000
2003	T315D	124,000	145,000
Silverton 351 Sedan			
2000	T320G	74,000	89,000
1999	T320G	68,000	82,000
1998	T300G	62,000	75,000
1997	T300G	57,000	69,000
Silverton 352 Motor Yacht			
2002	T370G	93,000	111,000
2002	T250D	109,000	131,000
2001	T320G	84,000	101,000
2001	T250D	99,000	119,000
2000	T320G	77,000	92,000
2000	T250D	90,000	108,000
1999	T320G	70,000	84,000
1999	T300D	82,000	99,000
1998	T320G	63,000	76,000
1998	T300D	75,000	90,000
1997	T320G	58,000	69,000
1997	T300D	68,000	81,000
Silverton 361/360 Express			
2000	T320G	62,000	75,000
1999	T320G	57,000	69,000
1998	T320G	52,000	63,000
1997	T320G	48,000	58,000
1996	T320G	44,000	53,000
1995	T300G	41,000	49,000

See Page 529 For Price Adjustments

Silverton 362 Sedan

Year	Power	Retail Low	Retail High
1998	T320G	58,000	70,000
1997	T320G	54,000	65,000
1996	T320G	49,000	59,000
1995	T320G	45,000	55,000

Silverton 37 Convertible

Year	Power	Retail Low	Retail High
2000	T-Gas	75,000	90,000
2000	T350D	90,000	108,000
1999	T-Gas	69,000	83,000
1999	T350D	83,000	99,000
1998	T-Gas	63,000	76,000
1998	T350D	76,000	91,000
1997	T-Gas	58,000	70,000
1997	T350D	70,000	84,000
1996	T-Gas	54,000	64,000
1996	T350D	64,000	77,000
1995	T-Gas	49,000	59,000

Silverton 372/392 Motor Yacht

Year	Power	Retail Low	Retail High
2001	T385G	114,000	136,000
2001	T350D	136,000	163,000
2000	T385G	103,000	124,000
2000	T350D	124,000	149,000
1999	T385G	94,000	113,000
1999	T350D	113,000	135,000
1998	T320G	86,000	104,000
1998	T350D	104,000	124,000
1997	T320G	79,000	95,000
1997	T350D	95,000	114,000
1996	T320G	73,000	88,000
1996	T350D	88,000	105,000

Silverton 38 Convertible

Year	Power	Retail Low	Retail High
2009	T385G	242,000	278,000
2009	T370D	281,000	323,000
2008	T385G	220,000	253,000
2008	T370D	256,000	294,000
2007	T385G	200,000	230,000
2007	T370D	233,000	267,000
2006	T385G	182,000	210,000
2006	T370D	212,000	243,000
2005	T385G	166,000	191,000
2005	T370D	192,000	221,000
2004	T385G	151,000	174,000
2004	T370D	175,000	201,000
2003	T385G	179,000	206,000
2003	T370D	140,000	161,000

Silverton 38 Sport Bridge

Year	Power	Retail Low	Retail High
2009	T385G	******	******
2009	T380D	******	******
2008	T385G	227,000	261,000
2008	T380D	271,000	312,000
2007	T385G	207,000	238,000
2007	T380D	247,000	284,000
2006	T385G	188,000	216,000
2006	T380D	224,000	258,000
2005	T385G	171,000	197,000
2005	T355D	204,000	235,000

Silverton 39 Motor Yacht

Year	Power	Retail Low	Retail High
2009	T385G	******	******
2009	T380D	******	******
2008	T385D	231,000	265,000
2008	T380D	266,000	307,000
2007	T385G	210,000	241,000
2007	T380D	242,000	279,000
2006	T385G	191,000	220,000
2006	T380D	221,000	254,000
2005	T385G	174,000	200,000
2005	T380D	201,000	231,000
2004	T385G	160,000	184,000
2004	T380D	185,000	212,000
2003	T385G	147,000	169,000
2003	T380D	170,000	195,000
2002	T385G	135,000	156,000
2002	T355D	156,000	180,000

Silverton 402/422 Motor Yacht

Year	Power	Retail Low	Retail High
2000	T380G	116,000	136,000
2000	T325D	134,000	157,000
1999	T380G	107,000	125,000
1999	T370D	123,000	144,000
1998	T380G	98,000	115,000
1998	T370D	113,000	133,000
1997	T380G	90,000	106,000
1997	T370D	104,000	122,000
1996	T380G	83,000	97,000
1996	T370D	96,000	112,000

Silverton 41 Convertible

Year	Power	Retail Low	Retail High
1999	T380G	104,000	122,000
1998	T380G	96,000	112,000
1997	T380G	88,000	103,000
1996	T380G	81,000	95,000
1995	T320G	75,000	87,000

Silverton 41 Motor Yacht

Year	Power	Retail Low	Retail High
1995	T320G	102,000	122,000
1995	T375D	129,000	155,000

Silverton 410 Sport Bridge

Year	Power	Retail Low	Retail High
2004	T425G	172,000	198,000
2004	T350D	197,000	226,000
2003	T425G	159,000	183,000
2003	T350D	181,000	208,000
2002	T425G	146,000	168,000
2002	T350D	166,000	191,000
2001	T385G	134,000	154,000
2001	T350D	153,000	176,000

Silverton 42 Convertible

Year	Power	Retail Low	Retail High
2009	T425G	******	******
2009	T440D	******	******
2008	T425G	232,000	267,000
2008	T440D	268,000	309,000
2007	T425G	211,000	243,000
2007	T440D	244,000	281,000
2006	T425G	192,000	221,000
2006	T380D	222,000	255,000
2005	T425G	175,000	201,000
2005	T380D	202,000	232,000
2004	T425G	159,000	183,000
2004	T380D	184,000	211,000
2003	T425G	146,000	169,000
2003	T380D	169,000	194,000
2002	T425G	135,000	155,000
2002	T-350D	155,000	179,000
2001	T405G	124,000	143,000
2001	T-350D	143,000	165,000
2000	T405G	114,000	131,000
2000	T350D	132,000	151,000

Silverton 43 Motor Yacht

Year	Power	Retail Low	Retail High
2007	T425G	279,000	321,000
2007	T440D	306,000	352,000
2006	T425G	257,000	296,000
2006	T440D	281,000	324,000
2005	T425G	236,000	272,000
2005	T380D	259,000	298,000
2004	T425G	217,000	250,000
2004	T380D	238,000	274,000
2003	T425G	200,000	230,000
2003	T380D	219,000	252,000
2002	T425G	184,000	212,000
2002	T380D	201,000	232,000
2001	T-Gas	169,000	195,000
2001	T355D	185,000	213,000

Silverton 43 Sport Bridge

Year	Power	Retail Low	Retail High
2009	T435G IPS	******	******
2009	T370D IPS	******	******
2008	T425G	******	******
2008	T480D	******	******
2007	T425G	252,000	289,000
2007	T380D	285,000	328,000
2006	T425G	231,000	266,000
2006	T380D	262,000	302,000

Silverton 442 Cockpit MY

Year	Power	Retail Low	Retail High
2001	T-Gas	125,000	144,000
2001	T355D	146,000	168,000
2000	T-Gas	115,000	132,000
2000	T355D	135,000	155,000
1999	T-Gas	106,000	122,000
1999	T350D	124,000	143,000
1998	T-Gas	97,000	112,000
1998	T350D	114,000	131,000
1997	T-Gas	89,000	103,000
1997	T350D	105,000	121,000
1996	T-Gas	82,000	95,000
1996	T350D	96,000	111,000

Silverton 45 Convertible

Year	Power	Retail Low	Retail High
2009	T500D	******	******
2008	T500D	******	******
2007	T575D	377,000	434,000
2006	T540D	347,000	399,000

Silverton 453 Motor Yacht

Year	Power	Retail Low	Retail High
2003	T430D	226,000	260,000
2002	T350D	208,000	240,000
2001	T350D	192,000	220,000
2000	T350D	176,000	203,000
1999	T350D	162,000	186,000

Silverton 46 Motor Yacht

Year	Power	Retail Low	Retail High
1997	T485D	171,000	197,000
1996	T485D	159,000	183,000
1995	T485D	148,000	170,000

Silverton 48/50 Convertible

Year	Power	Retail Low	Retail High
2009	T715D	******	******
2008	T715D	******	******
2007	T715D	******	******

See Page 529 For Price Adjustments

Year	Power	Retail Low	Retail High
2006	T715D	503,000	578,000
2005	T715D	463,000	532,000
2004	T715D	426,000	490,000

Skipjack 262 Flybridge

Year	Power	Retail Low	Retail High
2009	T-Gas	******	******
2008	T-Gas	******	******
2007	T-Gas	******	******
2006	T-Gas	48,000	57,000
2005	T-Gas	44,000	52,000
2004	T-Gas	40,000	48,000
2003	T-Gas	37,000	44,000
2002	T-Gas	34,000	41,000
2001	T-Gas	31,000	37,000
2000	T-Gas	29,000	34,000
1999	T-Gas	27,000	32,000
1998	T-Gas	25,000	30,000
1997	T-Gas	23,000	28,000
1996	T-Gas	21,000	26,000
1995	T-Gas	20,000	24,000

Skipjack 30 Flybridge

Year	Power	Retail Low	Retail High
2009	T330D	******	******
2008	T330D	******	******
2007	T330D	******	******
2006	T330D	******	******
2005	T330D	******	******
2004	T330D	******	******
2003	T330D	79,000	95,000
2002	T315D	73,000	87,000
2001	T315D	67,000	80,000
2000	T315D	62,000	74,000
1999	T315D	57,000	68,000
1998	T315D	52,000	62,000
1997	T315D	48,000	57,000

Southport 28 Center Console

Year	Power	Retail Low	Retail High
2009	T225 O/B	******	******
2008	T225 O/B	95,000	115,000
2007	T225 O/B	84,000	101,000
2006	T225 O/B	76,000	92,000
2005	T225 O/B	69,000	83,000

Stamas 270 Express

Year	Power	Retail Low	Retail High
2009	T225 O/B	******	******
2008	T225 O/B	79,000	95,000
2007	T225 O/B	73,000	87,000
2006	T225 O/B	65,000	78,000
2005	T225 O/B	59,000	70,000
2004	T225 O/B	53,000	63,000
2003	T225 O/B	47,000	57,000
2002	T225 O/B	43,000	51,000
2001	T225 O/B	39,000	47,000
2000	T225 O/B	36,000	43,000
1999	T225 O/B	33,000	40,000
1998	T225 O/B	30,000	37,000
1997	T225 O/B	28,000	34,000

Stamas 270 Tarpon

Year	Power	Retail Low	Retail High
2009	T225 O/B	******	******
2008	T225 O/B	76,000	91,000
2007	T225 O/B	68,000	82,000
2006	T225 O/B	61,000	74,000
2005	T225 O/B	55,000	66,000
2004	T225 O/B	50,000	60,000

Year	Power	Retail Low	Retail High
2003	T225 O/B	45,000	54,000
2002	T225 O/B	41,000	49,000
2001	T225 O/B	38,000	45,000
2000	T225 O/B	35,000	42,000
1999	T225 O/B	32,000	38,000
1998	T225 O/B	29,000	35,000
1997	T225 O/B	79,000	94,000

Stamas 290 Express

Year	Power	Retail Low	Retail High
2009	T225 O/B	******	******
2008	T225 O/B	103,000	124,000
2007	T225 O/B	94,000	113,000
2006	T225 O/B	86,000	103,000
2005	T225 O/B	78,000	94,000
2004	T225 O/B	71,000	85,000
2003	T225 O/B	64,000	77,000
2002	T225 O/B	59,000	70,000
2001	T225 O/B	53,000	64,000
2000	T225 O/B	49,000	59,000
1999	T225 O/B	45,000	54,000
1998	T225 O/B	41,000	50,000
1997	T225 O/B	38,000	46,000
1996	T225 O/B	35,000	42,000
1995	T225 O/B	32,000	39,000

Stamas 290 Tarpon

Year	Power	Retail Low	Retail High
2009	T225 O/B	******	******
2008	T225 O/B	92,000	111,000
2007	T225 O/B	84,000	101,000
2006	T225 O/B	76,000	92,000
2005	T225 O/B	70,000	84,000
2004	T225 O/B	63,000	76,000
2003	T225 O/B	57,000	69,000
2002	T225 O/B	52,000	63,000
2001	T225 O/B	48,000	57,000
2000	T225 O/B	44,000	53,000
1999	T225 O/B	40,000	48,000
1998	T225 O/B	37,000	44,000
1997	T225 O/B	34,000	41,000
1996	T225 O/B	31,000	37,000
1995	T225 O/B	29,000	34,000

Stamas 310 Express

Year	Power	Retail Low	Retail High
2009	T225 O/B	******	******
2008	T225 O/B	108,000	130,000
2007	T225 O/B	98,000	118,000
2006	T225 O/B	89,000	107,000
2005	T225 O/B	81,000	98,000
2004	T225 O/B	74,000	89,000
2002	T225 O/B	67,000	81,000
2002	T225 O/B	61,000	73,000
2001	T225 O/B	56,000	68,000
2000	T225 O/B	52,000	62,000
1999	T225 O/B	48,000	57,000
1998	T225 O/B	44,000	52,000
1997	T225 O/B	40,000	48,000
1996	T225 O/B	37,000	44,000
1995	T225 O/B	34,000	41,000

Stamas 310 Tarpon

Year	Power	Retail Low	Retail High
2009	T225 O/B	******	******
2008	T225 O/B	99,000	119,000
2007	T225 O/B	89,000	107,000
2006	T225 O/B	80,000	96,000

Year	Power	Retail Low	Retail High
2005	T225 O/B	72,000	86,000
2004	T225 O/B	65,000	78,000
2003	T225 O/B	58,000	70,000
2002	T225 O/B	53,000	64,000
2001	T225 O/B	48,000	58,000
2000	T225 O/B	44,000	53,000
1999	T225 O/B	40,000	48,000

Stamas 320 Express

Year	Power	Retail Low	Retail High
2009	T330 I/B	******	******
2009	T250 O/B	******	******
2008	T330 I/B	137,000	164,000
2008	T250 O/B	123,000	148,000
2007	T320 I/B	124,000	149,000
2007	T250 O/B	112,000	135,000
2006	T320 I/B	113,000	136,000
2006	T250 O/B	102,000	123,000
2005	T320 I/B	103,000	123,000
2005	T250 O/B	93,000	111,000
2004	T320 I/B	94,000	112,000
2004	T250 O/B	84,000	101,000

Stamas 340 Express

Year	Power	Retail Low	Retail High
2009	T385G	******	******
2009	T380D	******	******
2008	T385G	175,000	210,000
2008	T380D	216,000	259,000
2007	T320G	159,000	191,000
2007	T370D	196,000	236,000
2006	T320G	145,000	174,000
2006	T370D	179,000	214,000
2005	T320G	132,000	158,000
2005	T370D	162,000	195,000
2004	T320G	120,000	144,000
2004	T370D	148,000	177,000
2003	T320G	110,000	133,000
2003	T370D	136,000	163,000
2002	T320G	101,000	122,000
2002	T370D	125,000	150,000

Stamas 360 Express

Year	Power	Retail Low	Retail High
1999	T310G	82,000	98,000
1999	T300D	101,000	121,000
1998	T310G	74,000	89,000
1998	T300D	92,000	110,000
1997	T310G	67,000	81,000
1997	T300D	84,000	100,000
1996	T310G	61,000	74,000
1996	T300D	76,000	91,000
1995	T310G	56,000	68,000
1995	T300D	70,000	84,000

Stamas 370 Express

Year	Power	Retail Low	Retail High
2008	T370G	******	******
2008	T440D	******	******
2007	T370G	******	******
2007	T440D	******	******
2006	T370G	162,000	194,000
2006	T440D	213,000	256,000
2005	T370G	147,000	177,000
2005	T440D	194,000	233,000
2004	T370G	134,000	161,000
2004	T440D	177,000	212,000
2003	T370G	122,000	146,000

See Page 529 For Price Adjustments

Year	Power	Retail Low	Retail High
2003	T440D	161,000	193,000
2002	T370G	111,000	133,000
2002	T440D	146,000	176,000
2001	T370G	101,000	121,000
2001	T440D	133,000	160,000
2000	T370G	92,000	110,000
2000	T440D	121,000	145,000
Sunseeker 34 Superhawk			
2003	T285D	133,000	159,000
2002	T285D	123,000	148,000
2001	T285D	115,000	138,000
2000	T230D	107,000	128,000
1999	T230D	99,000	119,000
1998	T230D	92,000	111,000
1997	T230D	86,000	103,000
Sunseeker 37 Sport Fish			
2007	3/250 O/B	******	******
2006	3/250 O/B	******	******
2005	3/250 O/B	200,000	240,000
2004	3/250 O/B	186,000	223,000
Sunseeker 44 Camargue			
2002	T480D	188,000	225,000
2001	T480D	172,000	207,000
2000	T435D	159,000	190,000
1999	T435D	146,000	175,000
1998	T435D	134,000	161,000
Sunseeker 46 Portifino			
2005	T460D	311,000	373,000
2004	T480D	289,000	347,000
2003	T480D	269,000	323,000
Sunseeker 47 Camargue			
1999	T435D	196,000	235,000
1998	T435D	182,000	218,000
1997	T435D	169,000	203,000
1996	T435D	157,000	189,000
Sunseeker 46/48 Manhattan			
1999	T435D	270,000	324,000
1998	T435D	253,000	304,000
1997	T435D	238,000	286,000
1996	T435D	224,000	269,000
Sunseeker 51 Camargue			
1998	T600D	252,000	302,000
1997	T600D	234,000	281,000
1996	T600D	217,000	261,000
1995	T625D	202,000	243,000
1994	T625D	188,000	226,000
Sunseeker 53 Portifino			
2009	T800D	******	******
2008	T800D	******	******
2007	T800D	******	******
2006	T705D	******	******
2005	T705D	469,000	563,000
2004	T705D	436,000	524,000
Sunseeker 55 Camargue			
1996	T760D	259,000	290,000
1995	T760D	241,000	270,000

Year	Power	Retail Low	Retail High
1994	T760D	224,000	251,000
Sunseeker 56 Manhattan			
2004	T800D	531,000	595,000
2003	T800D	494,000	553,000
2002	T800D	459,000	514,000
2001	T800D	427,000	478,000
Sunseeker 58/60 Predator			
2002	T800D	573,000	642,000
2001	T800D	533,000	597,000
2000	T800D	496,000	555,000
1999	T800D	461,000	516,000
1998	T800D	429,000	480,000
1997	T800D	399,000	447,000
Tiara 2900 Coronet			
2007	T330G	72,000	86,000
2006	T330G	65,000	78,000
2005	T330G	59,000	71,000
2004	T320G	54,000	65,000
2003	T320G	50,000	60,000
2002	T320G	46,000	55,000
2001	T320G	42,000	50,000
2000	T320G	38,000	46,000
1999	T320G	35,000	43,000
1998	T320G	33,000	39,000
1997	T320G	30,000	36,000
Tiara 2900 Open			
2006	T330G	79,000	94,000
2005	T330G	71,000	86,000
2004	T330G	65,000	78,000
2003	T330G	59,000	71,000
2002	T320G	54,000	65,000
2001	T320G	50,000	60,000
2000	T320G	46,000	55,000
1999	T320G	42,000	51,000
1998	T320G	39,000	47,000
1997	T320G	36,000	43,000
1996	T320G	33,000	39,000
1995	T260G	30,000	37,000
Tiara 3000 Open			
2009	T385G	165,000	191,000
2009	T330D	198,000	230,000
2008	T385G	150,000	174,000
2008	T330D	180,000	209,000
2007	T385G	138,000	160,000
2007	T330D	166,000	192,000
Tiara 3100 Open			
2004	T385G	87,000	103,000
2004	T330D	110,000	130,000
2003	T385G	79,000	93,000
2003	T330D	100,000	118,000
2002	T320G	72,000	85,000
2002	T330D	91,000	107,000
2001	T320G	66,000	78,000
2001	T330D	84,000	99,000
2000	T320G	61,000	72,000
2000	T230D	77,000	91,000
1999	T320G	56,000	66,000
1999	T230D	71,000	83,000
1998	T320G	51,000	61,000
1998	T230D	65,000	77,000

Year	Power	Retail Low	Retail High
1997	T320G	47,000	56,000
1997	T230D	60,000	71,000
1996	T320G	43,000	51,000
1996	T230D	55,000	65,000
1995	T320G	40,000	48,000
1995	T230D	51,000	60,000
Tiara 3200 Open			
2009	T385G	171,000	201,000
2009	T355G	215,000	251,000
2008	T385G	156,000	183,000
2008	T355G	195,000	229,000
2007	T385G	142,000	166,000
2007	T355G	178,000	208,000
2006	T330G	130,000	153,000
2006	T310D	163,000	191,000
2005	T385G	120,000	140,000
2005	T310D	150,000	176,000
2004	T385G	111,000	129,000
2004	T310D	138,000	162,000
Tiara 3300 Open			
1997	T380G	53,000	64,000
1997	T315D	70,000	84,000
1996	T380G	49,000	59,000
1996	T315D	64,000	77,000
1995	T300G	45,000	54,000
1995	T300D	60,000	72,000
Tiara 3500 Express			
2003	T385G	102,000	121,000
2003	T450D	135,000	159,000
2002	T385G	93,000	110,000
2002	T435D	122,000	145,000
2001	T385G	85,000	100,000
2001	T435D	111,000	132,000
2000	T385G	78,000	92,000
2000	T435D	102,000	121,000
1999	T320G	72,000	85,000
1999	T435D	94,000	111,000
1998	T380G	66,000	78,000
1998	T435D	87,000	102,000
1997	T380G	61,000	71,000
1997	T435D	80,000	94,000
1996	T380G	56,000	66,000
1996	T435D	73,000	87,000
1995	T380G	51,000	60,000
1995	T435D	67,000	80,000
Tiara 3500 Open			
2004	T385G	98,000	116,000
2004	T370D	123,000	145,000
2003	T385G	89,000	105,000
2003	T370D	112,000	132,000
2002	T385G	81,000	96,000
2002	T370D	102,000	120,000
2001	T320G	74,000	87,000
2001	T370D	92,000	109,000
2000	T320G	68,000	80,000
2000	T370D	85,000	100,000
1999	T320G	62,000	74,000
1999	T370D	78,000	92,000
1998	T320G	57,000	68,000

Year	Power	Retail Low	Retail High
1998	T370D	72,000	85,000

Tiara 3500 Sovran

Year	Power	Retail Low	Retail High
2009	T375G	233,000	267,000
2009	T300D	262,000	301,000
2008	T375G	212,000	243,000
2008	T300D	238,000	274,000

Tiara 3600 Convertible

Year	Power	Retail Low	Retail High
1995	T355G	80,000	92,000
1995	T375D	104,000	120,000

Tiara 3600 Open (1987-96)

Year	Power	Retail Low	Retail High
1996	T355G	81,000	93,000
1996	T375D	97,000	112,000
1995	T355G	75,000	86,000
1995	T375D	89,000	103,000

Tiara 3600 Open (Current)

Year	Power	Retail Low	Retail High
2009	T385G	210,000	242,000
2009	T380D	263,000	303,000
2008	T385G	191,000	220,000
2008	T380D	239,000	275,000
2007	T385G	174,000	200,000
2007	T380D	218,000	251,000
2006	T385G	158,000	182,000
2006	T380D	198,000	228,000
2005	T385G	146,000	167,000
2005	T380D	182,000	210,000

Tiara 3600 Sovran

Year	Power	Retail Low	Retail High
2006	T385G	151,000	174,000
2006	T490D	192,000	221,000
2005	T385G	138,000	158,000
2005	T480D	175,000	201,000
2004	T385G	125,000	144,000
2004	T380D	159,000	183,000

Tiara 3700 Open

Year	Power	Retail Low	Retail High
2000	T385G	120,000	138,000
2000	T435D	136,000	157,000
1999	T435D	110,000	127,000
1998	T435D	125,000	144,000
1997	T435D	102,000	117,000
1996	T435D	115,000	133,000
1995	T435D	93,000	107,000

Tiara 3800 Open

Year	Power	Retail Low	Retail High
2008	T490D	306,000	351,000
2007	T490D	278,000	320,000
2006	T490D	253,000	291,000
2005	T490D	230,000	265,000
2004	T480D	209,000	241,000
2003	T480D	190,000	219,000
2002	T480D	175,000	202,000
2001	T480D	161,000	185,000
2000	T480D	148,000	170,000

Tiara 3900 Convertible

Year	Power	Retail Low	Retail High
2009	T540D	******	******
2008	T540D	388,000	447,000
2007	T540D	353,000	406,000
2006	T540D	321,000	370,000

Tiara 3900 Sovran

Year	Power	Retail Low	Retail High
2009	T370D	******	******
2008	T370D	371,000	426,000
2007	T370D	337,000	388,000

Tiara 4000 Express

Year	Power	Retail Low	Retail High
2003	T450D	209,000	241,000
2002	T450D	192,000	221,000
2001	T450D	192,000	221,000
2000	T435D	177,000	204,000
1999	T435D	177,000	204,000
1998	T435D	163,000	187,000
1997	T435D	163,000	187,000
1996	T435D	151,000	174,000
1995	T435D	151,000	174,000

Tiara 4100 Open

Year	Power	Retail Low	Retail High
2002	T450D	208,000	240,000
2001	T450D	192,000	220,000
2000	T435D	176,000	203,000
1999	T435D	162,000	187,000
1998	T435D	149,000	172,000
1997	T435D	137,000	158,000
1996	T435D	126,000	145,000

Tiara 4200 Open

Year	Power	Retail Low	Retail High
2009	T670D	******	******
2008	T670D	408,000	469,000
2007	T670D	371,000	427,000
2006	T670D	338,000	389,000
2005	T670D	307,000	353,000
2004	T660D	280,000	322,000
2003	T660D	254,000	293,000

Tiara 4300 Convertible

Year	Power	Retail Low	Retail High
2002	T660D	312,000	359,000
2001	T660D	287,000	330,000
2000	T660D	264,000	304,000
1999	T570D	243,000	280,000
1998	T550D	224,000	257,000
1997	T550D	206,000	237,000
1996	T550D	189,000	218,000

Tiara 4300 Open

Year	Power	Retail Low	Retail High
2002	T660D	275,000	316,000
2001	T660D	253,000	291,000
2000	T660D	232,000	267,000
1999	T550D	214,000	246,000
1998	T550D	197,000	226,000
1997	T550D	181,000	208,000
1996	T550D	166,000	191,000
1995	T550D	155,000	178,000

Tiara 4300 Sovran

Year	Power	Retail Low	Retail High
2009	T435D	******	******
2008	T435D	398,000	457,000
2007	T435D	366,000	421,000
2006	T435D	336,000	387,000

Tiara 4400/4700 Sovran

Year	Power	Retail Low	Retail High
2008	T670D	513,000	589,000
2007	T670D	471,000	542,000
2006	T670D	434,000	499,000
2005	T670D	399,000	459,000
2004	T660D	367,000	422,000
2003	T660D	338,000	388,000

Tiara 5000 Open

Year	Power	Retail Low	Retail High
2003	T800D	423,000	486,000
2002	T800D	389,000	447,000

Tiara 5000/5200 Express

Year	Power	Retail Low	Retail High
2003	T800D	439,000	504,000
2002	T800D	403,000	464,000
2001	T800D	371,000	427,000
2000	T800D	341,000	393,000
1999	T800D	314,000	361,000

Tiara 5200 Sovran Salon

Year	Power	Retail Low	Retail High
2006	T800D	591,000	680,000
2005	T800D	544,000	625,000
2004	T800D	500,000	575,000
2003	T800D	460,000	529,000

Tollycraft 40 Sport Sedan

Year	Power	Retail Low	Retail High
1995	T-Gas	114,000	132,000
1995	T400D	132,000	152,000

Tollycraft 44/45 Cockpit MY

Year	Power	Retail Low	Retail High
1996	T-Gas	******	******
1996	T400D	136,000	161,000
1995	T-Gas	******	******
1995	T400D	127,000	150,000

Tollycraft 48 Motor Yacht

Year	Power	Retail Low	Retail High
1998	T435D	199,000	229,000
1997	T435D	185,000	213,000
1996	T435D	172,000	198,000
1995	T435D	160,000	184,000

Tollycraft 57 Motor Yacht

Year	Power	Retail Low	Retail High
1998	T760D	******	******
1997	T760D	******	******
1996	T735D	354,000	407,000
1995	T735D	329,000	378,000

Tollycraft 65 Cockpit MY

Year	Power	Retail Low	Retail High
1998	T760D	500,000	575,000
1997	T760D	465,000	534,000
1996	T665D	432,000	497,000
1995	T665D	402,000	462,000

Topaz 32/33 Express

Year	Power	Retail Low	Retail High
2009	T440D	******	******
2008	T440D	******	******
2007	T440D	218,000	250,000
2006	T440D	198,000	228,000
2005	T370D	180,000	207,000
2004	T370D	182,000	209,000

Triton 2690 Center Console

Year	Power	Retail Low	Retail High
2008	T200 O/B	52,000	62,000
2007	T200 O/B	47,000	56,000
2006	T200 O/B	43,000	51,000
2005	T200 O/B	39,000	47,000
2004	T200 O/B	35,000	42,000
2003	T200 O/B	32,000	38,000
2002	T200 O/B	29,000	35,000
2001	T200 O/B	26,000	32,000

Triton 2500/2690 Walkaround

Year	Power	Retail Low	Retail High
2009	T200 O/B	******	******
2008	T200 O/B	56,000	67,000
2007	T200 O/B	50,000	61,000
2006	T200 O/B	46,000	55,000
2005	T200 O/B	42,000	50,000
2004	T200 O/B	38,000	46,000

Year	Power	Retail Low	Retail High
2003	T200 O/B	34,000	41,000
2002	T200 O/B	31,000	38,000
2001	T200 O/B	28,000	34,000
Triton 2895 Center Console			
2007	T225 O/B	74,000	89,000
2006	T225 O/B	67,000	81,000
2005	T225 O/B	61,000	74,000
2004	T225 O/B	56,000	67,000
Triton 351 Center Console			
2009	T250 O/B	******	******
2008	T250 O/B	110,000	132,000
2007	T250 O/B	99,000	118,000
2006	T250 O/B	83,000	100,000
2005	T250 O/B	75,000	90,000
Trojan 350/360 Express			
2002	T320G	83,000	98,000
2001	T320G	76,000	90,000
2000	T320G	70,000	83,000
1999	T310G	64,000	76,000
1997	T310G	59,000	70,000
1996	T310G	54,000	64,000
1995	T310G	50,000	59,000
Trojan 370/390/400 Express			
2002	T320G	103,000	124,000
2001	T320G	94,000	113,000
2000	T320G	85,000	103,000
1999	T320G	78,000	93,000
1998	T320G	71,000	85,000
1997	T320G	64,000	77,000
1996	T320G	58,000	70,000
1995	T350G	54,000	65,000
Trophy 2802 Walkaround			
2001	T225/OB	38,000	45,000
2000	T225/OB	34,000	41,000
1999	T225/OB	31,000	37,000
1998	T225/OB	28,000	34,000
1997	T225/OB	26,000	31,000
Trophy 2902 Walkaround			
2009	T225 O/B	83,000	99,000
2008	T225 O/B	75,000	90,000
2007	T225 O/B	68,000	82,000
2006	T225 O/B	62,000	75,000
2005	T225 O/B	56,000	68,000
2004	T225 O/B	51,000	62,000
2003	T225 O/B	47,000	56,000
True World TE288			
2008	315D	85,000	100,000
2007	315D	78,000	91,000
2006	315D	71,000	83,000
2005	315D	64,000	75,000
2004	315D	58,000	68,000
2003	315D	53,000	62,000
2002	315D	48,000	57,000
Venture 27 Open			
2009	T200 O/B	83,000	99,000
2008	T200 O/B	83,000	99,000
2007	T200 O/B	83,000	99,000
Venture 34 Open			
2009	T250 O/B	******	******

Year	Power	Retail Low	Retail High
2008	T250 O/B	126,000	151,000
2007	T250 O/B	113,000	136,000
2006	T250 O/B	102,000	122,000
2005	T250 O/B	92,000	110,000
2004	T250 O/B	82,000	99,000
2003	T250 O/B	74,000	89,000
2002	T250 O/B	67,000	81,000
2001	T250 O/B	61,000	74,000
2000	T250 O/B	56,000	67,000
1999	T250 O/B	51,000	61,000
1998	T250 O/B	46,000	55,000
1997	T250 O/B	43,000	51,000
Venture 39 Open			
2009	3/275 O/B	******	******
2008	3/275 O/B	173,000	199,000
2007	3/275 O/B	156,000	179,000
2006	3/275 O/B	140,000	161,000
2005	3/275 O/B	130,000	150,000
Viking Sport Cruisers 43 FB			
1999	T420D	207,000	238,000
1998	T420D	192,000	221,000
1997	T420D	179,000	205,000
1996	T420D	166,000	191,000
1995	T420D	154,000	178,000
Viking 43 Convertible			
2002	T680D	320,000	368,000
2001	T680D	294,000	338,000
2000	T680D	270,000	311,000
1999	T680D	249,000	286,000
1998	T680D	229,000	263,000
1997	T680D	211,000	242,000
1996	T600D	194,000	223,000
1995	T600D	178,000	205,000
Viking 43 Open			
2002	T680D	287,000	331,000
2001	T680D	264,000	304,000
2000	T680D	243,000	280,000
1999	T680D	224,000	257,000
1998	T680D	206,000	237,000
1997	T680D	189,000	218,000
1996	T600D	174,000	200,000
1995	T600D	160,000	184,000
Viking 45 Conv. (Current)			
2009	T900D	******	******
2008	T900D	******	******
2007	T900D	607,000	698,000
2006	T900D	552,000	635,000
2005	T900D	502,000	577,000
2004	T800D	462,000	531,000
2003	T800D	425,000	488,000
Viking 45 Open SF			
2009	T900D	******	******
2008	T900D	******	******
2007	T900D	******	******
2006	T900D	******	******
2005	T900D	480,000	552,000
2004	T800D	441,000	508,000
Viking Sport Cruisers 45 FB			
2004	T480D	472,000	543,000

Year	Power	Retail Low	Retail High
2003	T480D	435,000	500,000
2002	T480D	400,000	460,000
2001	T480D	368,000	423,000
2000	T370D	338,000	389,000
1999	T370D	311,000	358,000
Viking Sport Cruisers 45/46 FB			
2000	T430D	246,000	283,000
1999	T430D	224,000	258,000
1998	T430D	204,000	234,000
1997	T430D	185,000	213,000
1996	T430D	169,000	194,000
1995	T430D	153,000	177,000
Viking 47 Convertible			
2002	T680D	381,000	438,000
2001	T680D	351,000	403,000
2000	T680D	322,000	371,000
1999	T680D	297,000	341,000
1998	T680D	273,000	314,000
1997	T680D	251,000	289,000
1996	T680D	233,000	268,000
1995	T680D	217,000	250,000
Viking 48 Conv. (Current)			
2009	T1100D	******	******
2008	T1100D	******	******
2007	T1100D	******	******
2006	T1100D	819,000	941,000
2005	T1050D	753,000	866,000
2004	T1050D	693,000	797,000
2003	T860D	637,000	733,000
2002	T860D	586,000	674,000
Viking Sport Cruisers 48/50 FB			
1999	T435D	290,000	334,000
1998	T435D	270,000	310,000
1997	T435D	251,000	289,000
1996	T435D	233,000	268,000
1995	T435D	219,000	252,000
Viking 50 Convertible			
2001	1050D	481,000	553,000
2000	1050D	442,000	509,000
1999	1050D	407,000	468,000
1998	1200D	374,000	431,000
1997	1200D	344,000	396,000
1995	820D	317,000	364,000
Viking 50 Open			
2003	T820D	530,000	609,000
2002	T800D	487,000	560,000
2001	T800D	448,000	515,000
2000	T800D	412,000	474,000
1999	T800D	379,000	436,000
Viking Sport Cruisers 50 FB			
2009	T660D	******	******
2008	T660D	******	******
2007	T660D	******	******
2007	T675D	******	******
2005	T675D	592,000	681,000
2004	T700	545,000	626,000
2003	T700	501,000	576,000
2002	T700	461,000	530,000
2001	T700	424,000	488,000

Year	Power	Retail Low	Retail High

Viking Sport Cruisers V50 Exp.

Year	Power	Retail Low	Retail High
2005	T715D	******	******
2004	T715D	497,000	572,000
2003	T700D	457,000	526,000
2002	T700D	421,000	484,000
2001	T700D	387,000	445,000
2000	T700D	356,000	410,000
1999	T700D	328,000	377,000

Viking 52 Convertible

2009	T1360D	******	******
2008	T1360D	******	******
2007	T1360D	******	******
2006	T1300D	1,123,000	1,292,000
2005	T1300D	1,033,000	1,189,000
2004	T1300D	951,000	1,093,000
2003	T1050D	875,000	1,006,000
2002	T1050D	805,000	925,000

Viking Sport Cruisers 52 FB

2002	T615D	472,000	543,000
2001	T615D	439,000	505,000
2000	T610D	408,000	470,000
1999	T610D	380,000	437,000
1998	T610D	353,000	406,000
1997	T610D	328,000	378,000

Viking 53 Convertible

1998	T820D	352,000	405,000
1997	T820D	324,000	372,000
1996	T820D	298,000	342,000
1995	T820D	274,000	315,000

Viking 54 Sports Yacht

2001	T820D	475,000	547,000
2000	T820D	437,000	503,000
1999	T820D	402,000	463,000
1998	T820D	370,000	426,000
1997	T820D	340,000	392,000
1996	T820D	313,000	360,000
1995	T820D	288,000	331,000

Viking 55 Convertible

2002	T1300D	880,000	1,012,000
2001	T1050D	810,000	931,000
2000	T1050D	745,000	857,000
1999	T1050D	685,000	788,000
1998	T1050D	630,000	725,000

Viking 56 Convertible

2009	T1550D	******	******
2008	T1550D	******	******
2007	T1550D	******	******
2006	T1550D	******	******
2005	T1520D	1,288,000	1,481,000
2004	T1480D	1,197,000	1,377,000

Viking Sport Cruisers 56 FB

2002	T700D	519,000	597,000
2001	T700D	483,000	555,000
2000	T700D	449,000	517,000
1999	T700D	418,000	480,000
1998	T700D	388,000	447,000
1997	T610D	361,000	415,000

Viking 57 Motor Yacht

| 1995 | T760D | 388,000 | 447,000 |

Viking Sport Cruisers 57 FB

2008	T715D	******	******
2007	T715D	******	******
2006	T715D	961,000	1,105,000
2005	T715D	884,000	1,017,000

Viking 58 Convertible

2000	T1200D	580,000	667,000
1999	T1200D	534,000	614,000
1998	T1150D	491,000	565,000
1997	T1200D	452,000	519,000
1996	T1200D	415,000	478,000
1995	T1200D	382,000	440,000
1994	T1100D	355,000	409,000
1993	T1100D	330,000	380,000
1992	T1100D	307,000	353,000
1991	T1100D	286,000	329,000

Viking Sport Cruisers V58 Exp.

2009	T1100D	******	******
2008	T1100D	******	******
2007	T1100D	******	******
2006	T1100D	******	******
2005	T900D	851,000	979,000
2004	T860D	792,000	911,000
2003	T860D	736,000	847,000

Viking 60 Cockpit Sport Yacht

2001	T820D	595,000	684,000
2000	T820D	547,000	629,000
1999	T820D	503,000	579,000
1998	T820D	463,000	533,000
1997	T820D	426,000	490,000
1996	T820D	396,000	456,000
1995	T820D	368,000	424,000

Viking Sports Cruisers 60 FB

2001	T800D	561,000	645,000
2000	T800D	516,000	593,000
1999	T800D	475,000	546,000
1998	T800D	437,000	502,000
1997	T800D	402,000	462,000
1996	T800D	369,000	425,000

Viking 61 Convertible

2006	T1520D	1,389,000	1,597,000
2005	T1520D	1,291,000	1,485,000
2004	T1480D	1,201,000	1,381,000
2003	T1480D	1,117,000	1,285,000
2002	T1480D	1,039,000	1,195,000
2001	T1300D	966,000	1,111,000

Viking 65 Convertible

2005	T2030D	1,518,000	1,745,000
2004	T2000 D	1,411,000	1,623,000
2004	T1800 D	1,312,000	1,509,000
2002	T1800 D	1,221,000	1,404,000
2001	T1800 D	1,135,000	1,305,000
2000	T1800 D	1,056,000	1,214,000
1999	T1800 D	982,000	1,129,000

Viking 65 Motor Yacht

| 1995 | T1000D | 482,000 | 554,000 |

Viking Sport Cruisers 65 MY

2004	T1050D	1,100,000	1,265,000
2003	T1050D	1,012,000	1,164,000
2002	T1050D	931,000	1,071,000
2001	T1050D	866,000	996,000
2000	T1050D	805,000	926,000
1999	T1050D	749,000	861,000

Viking Sport Cruisers V65 Exp.

2004	T1050D	1,127,000	1,297,000
2003	T1050D	1,037,000	1,193,000
2002	T1050D	954,000	1,097,000
2001	T1050D	887,000	1,021,000
2000	T1050D	825,000	949,000
1999	T1050D	767,000	883,000

Wellcraft 26 Scarab Sportster

| 1996 | 200 O/B | 7,000 | 9,000 |
| 1995 | 200 O/B | 7,000 | 9,000 |

Wellcraft 2600 Coastal

| 1995 | T150 O/B | 14,000 | 16,000 |

Wellcraft 2600 Martinique

2001	250 I/O	15,000	18,000
2000	250 I/O	13,000	16,000
1999	250 I/O	12,000	15,000
1998	250 I/O	11,000	14,000

Wellcraft 264 Coastal

1997	T150 O/B	22,000	26,000
1996	T150 O/B	20,000	24,000
1995	T150 O/B	18,000	22,000

Wellcraft 2700 Martinique

| 1995 | 330 I/O | 15,000 | 18,000 |

Wellcraft 270 Coastal

2008	T225 O/B	76,000	91,000
2007	T225 O/B	69,000	83,000
2006	No Production		
2005	No Producton		
2004	T225 O/B	51,000	62,000
2004	S375 I/O	56,000	67,000
2003	T225 O/B	47,000	56,000
2003	S375 I/O	51,000	61,000
2002	T225 O/B	42,000	51,000
2002	S330 I/O	46,000	56,000
2001	T225 O/B	39,000	46,000
2001	S330 I/O	42,000	51,000

Wellcraft 2800 Martinique (2001-02)

2002	T190 I/O	32,000	38,000
2002	S310 I/O	30,000	36,000
2001	T190 I/O	29,000	35,000
2001	T190 I/O	27,000	33,000

Wellcraft 2800 Martinique (1997-99)

1999	T190 I/O	23,000	28,000
1999	330 I/O	22,000	26,000
1998	T190 I/O	22,000	26,000
1998	330 I/O	20,000	24,000
1997	T190 I/O	20,000	24,000
1997	330 I/O	18,000	22,000

Wellcraft 290 Coastal

2009	T225 O/B	******	******
2008	T225 O/B	81,000	97,000
2007	T225 O/B	73,000	87,000
2006	T225 O/B	66,000	79,000
2005	T225 O/B	60,000	72,000

See Page 529 For Price Adjustments

Year	Power	Retail Low	Retail High
2004	T225 O/B	55,000	66,000
2003	T225 O/B	50,000	60,000
2002	T225 O/B	45,000	54,000
2001	T225 O/B	41,000	49,000
2000	T225 O/B	37,000	45,000
1999	T225 O/B	34,000	41,000

Wellcraft 29 Scarab Sport; 29 CC

2004	T225 O/B	50,000	60,000
2003	T225 O/B	45,000	54,000
2002	T225 O/B	40,000	49,000
2001	T225 O/B	36,000	44,000

Wellcraft 30 Scarab Tourn.

2009	T250 O/B	******	******
2008	T250 O/B	86,000	103,000
2007	T250 O/B	77,000	93,000

Wellcraft 3000 Martinique

2002	T260 I/O	47,000	57,000
2001	T260 I/O	44,000	52,000
2000	T260 I/O	40,000	48,000
1999	T260 I/O	37,000	44,000
1998	T260 I/O	34,000	41,000

Wellcraft 302 Scarab Sport

2000	T250 O/B	55,000	66,000
1999	T250 O/B	50,000	60,000
1998	T250 O/B	45,000	55,000
1997	T250 O/B	41,000	50,000
1996	T250 O/B	38,000	45,000
1995	T250 O/B	34,000	41,000

Wellcraft 32 Scarab Sport; 32 CC

2006	T250 O/B	65,000	79,000
2005	T250 O/B	59,000	71,000
2004	T250 O/B	53,000	64,000
2003	T250 O/B	48,000	57,000
2002	T250 O/B	43,000	51,000
2001	T250 O/B	38,000	46,000

Wellcraft 3200 Martinique

2000	T310 I/O	50,000	60,000
1999	T310 I/O	46,000	55,000
1998	T310 I/O	42,000	51,000
1997	T310 I/O	39,000	47,000
1996	T300 I/O	36,000	43,000
1995	T300 I/O	33,000	40,000
1994	T300 I/O	31,000	37,000

Wellcraft 330 Coastal

2009	T370D	******	******
2008	T370D	167,000	200,000
2007	T370D	150,000	180,000
2006	T370D	137,000	164,000
2005	T360D	124,000	149,000
2004	T360D	113,000	136,000
2003	T360D	103,000	124,000
2002	T360D	94,000	112,000
2001	T350D	85,000	102,000
2000	T350D	78,000	94,000
1999	T350D	72,000	86,000
1998	T350D	66,000	79,000
1997	T300D	61,000	73,000
1996	T300D	56,000	67,000
1995	T300D	51,000	62,000

Wellcraft 3300 Martinique

| 2002 | T310G | 41,000 | 49,000 |
| 2001 | T310G | 37,000 | 45,000 |

Wellcraft 35 Scarab Sport

2009	3/250 O/B	******	******
2008	3/250 O/B	106,000	122,000
2007	3/250 O/B	95,000	110,000

Wellcraft 35 Scarab Sport; 35 CC

2005	T250 O/B	61,000	71,000
2004	T250 O/B	55,000	64,000
2003	T250 O/B	49,000	57,000
2002	T250 O/B	44,000	51,000
2001	T250 O/B	40,000	46,000

Wellcraft 350 Coastal

2003	T375G	113,000	131,000
2003	T360D	135,000	157,000
2002	T375G	104,000	121,000
2002	T360D	124,000	144,000
2001	T375G	96,000	111,000
2001	T360D	114,000	133,000
2000	T375G	88,000	102,000
2000	T370D	105,000	122,000

Wellcraft 360 Coastal

2009	T370D	******	******
2008	T370D	200,000	230,000
2007	T370D	180,000	207,000
2006	T370D	162,000	186,000

Wellcraft 3600 Martinique

2000	T385G	56,000	67,000
1999	T385G	52,000	62,000
1998	T380G	47,000	57,000
1997	T330G	44,000	52,000
1996	T330G	40,000	48,000
1995	T330G	37,000	45,000
1994	T330G	35,000	42,000

Wellcraft 3700 Martinique

| 2002 | T370G | 98,000 | 118,000 |
| 2001 | T370G | 91,000 | 109,000 |

Wellcraft 38 Excalibur

2002	T425 I/O	93,000	112,000
2001	T425 I/O	86,000	103,000
2000	T385 I/O	79,000	95,000
1999	T385 I/O	72,000	87,000
1998	T385 I/O	67,000	80,000
1997	T385 I/O	62,000	74,000
1996	T385 I/O	57,000	69,000

Wellcraft 400 Coastal

2003	T480D	203,000	244,000
2002	T480D	187,000	225,000
2001	T430D	172,000	207,000
2000	T430D	158,000	190,000
1999	T430D	146,000	175,000

Wellcraft 43 Portifino

1997	T-Gas	103,000	124,000
1997	T420D	125,000	150,000
1996	T-Gas	95,000	114,000
1996	T420D	115,000	138,000
1995	T-Gas	87,000	105,000

Wellcraft 45 Excalibur

2001	T415G	118,000	136,000
2000	T415G	110,000	126,000
1999	T415G	102,000	117,000
1998	T415G	95,000	109,000
1997	T415G	88,000	101,000
1996	T415G	82,000	94,000
1995	T415G	76,000	88,000

Wellcraft 46 Cockpit MY

| 1995 | T435D | 125,000 | 144,000 |

World Cat 266/270 SC

2009	T225 O/B	******	******
2008	T225 O/B	******	******
2007	T225 O/B	78,000	122,000
2006	T225 O/B	71,000	111,000
2005	T225 O/B	65,000	101,000
2004	T225 O/B	59,000	92,000
2003	T225 O/B	53,000	84,000
2002	T225 O/B	49,000	76,000
2001	T225 O/B	45,000	70,000
2000	T225 O/B	41,000	64,000
1999	T225 O/B	38,000	59,000
1998	T225 O/B	34,000	54,000

World Cat 270 EC

2008	T225 O/B	******	******
2007	T225 O/B	82,000	128,000
2006	T225 O/B	73,000	114,000
2005	T225 O/B	66,000	104,000
2004	T225 O/B	60,000	94,000
2003	T225 O/B	55,000	86,000

World Cat 270 Hardtop

2006	T225 O/B	68,000	81,000
2005	T225 O/B	62,000	75,000
2004	T225 O/B	57,000	69,000

World Cat 266 SF/270 TE

2009	T225 O/B	******	******
2008	T225 O/B	******	******
2007	T225 O/B	80,000	125,000
2006	T225 O/B	73,000	114,000
2005	T225 O/B	66,000	104,000
2004	T225 O/B	60,000	94,000
2003	T225 O/B	55,000	86,000
2002	T225 O/B	50,000	78,000
2001	T225 O/B	46,000	72,000
2000	T225 O/B	42,000	66,000
1999	T225 O/B	39,000	61,000
1998	T225 O/B	35,000	55,000

World Cat 320 Express Cabin

2009	T250 O/B	******	******
2008	T250 O/B	******	******
2007	T250 O/B	137,000	214,000
2006	T250 O/B	124,000	195,000

World Cat 330 TE

2008	T250 O/B	******	******
2007	T250 O/B	112,000	175,000
2006	T250 O/B	101,000	159,000
2005	T250 O/B	92,000	145,000
2004	T250 O/B	84,000	132,000
2003	T250 O/B	76,000	120,000

See Page 529 For Price Adjustments

Year	Power	Retail Low	Retail High
Yellowfin 31			
2007	T225 O/B	83,000	100,000
2006	T225 O/B	75,000	90,000
2005	T225 O/B	67,000	81,000
2004	T225 O/B	61,000	73,000
2003	T225 O/B	55,000	66,000
2002	T225 O/B	50,000	60,000
2001	T225 O/B	45,000	55,000
Yellowfin 34			
2009	3/250 O/B	******	******
2008	3/250 O/B	103,000	123,000
2007	3/250 O/B	92,000	111,000
2006	3/250 O/B	83,000	100,000
2005	3/250 O/B	75,000	90,000
Yellowfin 36			
2009	3/275 O/B	******	******
2008	3/275 O/B	134,000	161,000
2007	3/275 O/B	121,000	145,000
2006	3/275 O/B	109,000	131,000
2005	3/275 O/B	98,000	118,000
2004	3/275 O/B	88,000	106,000
2003	3/275 O/B	79,000	95,000

Index

Index

Index

–G–

–H–

–M–

–P–

Index

–T–

Index

6851484R0

Made in the USA
Charleston, SC
16 December 2010